SOCIOLOGY

ACADEMIC REVIEWERS FOR THE FIFTH EDITION

Richard Alba
State University of New York at Albany

Robert Allegrucci
Wichita State University

Bernard Beck
Northwestern University

Jean Blocker
University of Tulsa

Wayne Brady
Middlesex County College

Michael Brown
CUNY Graduate Center

Brent Bruton
Iowa State University

Richard Campbell
Duke University

David Carpenter
University of Illinois at Chicago Circle

Al Chabot
Macomb Community College

Dan Clawson
University of Massachusetts

Peter Conrad
Brandeis University

William Fairbanks
Cuesta College

Joseph Feagin
University of Texas at Austin

Scott Feld
State University of New York at Stony Brook

Gary Fine
University of Minnesota

Joseph Ford
California State University at Northridge

Beverly Gartland
Youngstown State University

Thomas Gieryn
Indiana University

Helen Ginn
St. Mary's College of Maryland

Davita Silfen Glasberg
Southern Illinois University

Rebecca Guy
Memphis State University

Bernie Halbur
University of Alabama at Birmingham

Warren Handel
Southern Illinois University at Edwardsville

Ronald A. Hardart
Arizona State University

Christopher Hern
University of Massachusetts

Cedric Herring
Texas A & M

Randy Hodson
University of Texas at Austin

Lois Horton
George Mason University

Satoshi Ito
College of William and Mary

Benton Johnson
University of Oregon

Ronald Johnstone
Central Michigan University

Jack Kamerman
Kean College

Irwin Kantor
Middlesex County College

Paul Kelly
University of Georgia

Michael Kennedy
University of Michigan

Gary Kiger
Utah State University at Logan

Michael Kimmel
Rutgers University

Ray Kinkle
University of Missouri at Flint

Marvin Krohn
State University of New York at Albany

Anthony Margavio
University of New Orleans

Alan Marks
University of Arkansas

Peter Marsden
Harvard University

Meredith McGuire
Montclair State University

Patrick McNamara
University of New Mexico

Dennis Morton
Pierce College

Christopher O'Brian
Northern Virginia Community College

Fred Pampel
University of Iowa

Robert Perrin
University of Tennessee at Knoxville

Thomas Pilarzyk
University of Wisconsin at Milwaukee

Ollie Pocs
Illinois State University

Michael Powell
University of North Carolina at Chapel Hill

Cecelia Ridgeway
University of Iowa

Barbara Risman
North Carolina State University

Roland Robertson
University of Pittsburgh

Rachel Rosenfeld
University of North Carolina

William Roy
University of California at Los Angeles

John Saltiel
Montana State University

Paul Schervish
Boston College

Michael Schwalbe
University of California at Riverside

Joseph Scimecca
George Mason University

Charles Selengut
County College of Morris

Richard Senter
Central Michigan University

Constance Shehan
University of Florida

John Skvoretz
University of South Carolina

William Snizek
Virginia Polytech

Barbara Stanford
Cuesta College

Charles Starnes
Oregon State University

John Stratton
University of Iowa

Verta Taylor
Ohio State University

Terry Timmins
Orange Coast Community College

William Tolone
Illinois State University

Theodore Wagenaar
Miami University

Edward Walsh
Pennsylvania State University

David Willer
University of Kansas

Richard Zeller
Bowling Green State University

Paul Zelus
Idaho State University

SOCIOLOGY

FIFTH EDITION

Donald Light
University of Medicine and Dentistry of New Jersey
Rutgers University

Suzanne Keller
Princeton University

Craig Calhoun
University of North Carolina at Chapel Hill

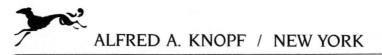

ALFRED A. KNOPF / NEW YORK

Fifth Edition
987654321
Copyright © 1975, 1979, 1982, 1985, 1989 by Alfred A. Knopf, Inc.

Library of Congress Cataloging in Publication Data
Light, Donald, 1942-
     Sociology / Donald Light, Jr., Suzanne Keller, Craig Calhoun.—
5th ed.
        p.   cm.
     Bibliography: p.
     Includes indexes.
     ISBN 0-394-37248-4
     1. Sociology.   2. United States—Social conditions.   I. Keller,
Suzanne Infeld, 1927-   . II. Calhoun, Craig J., 1952-   .
III. Title.
HM51.L52   1989
301—dc19   88-13797
                                              CIP

Manufactured in the United States of America

ACKNOWLEDGMENTS

Chapter opener credits: Chapter 1: Norman Owen Tomalin/Bruce Coleman; Chapter 2: Ron Cooper/EKM-Nepenthe; Chapter 3: Porterfield-Chickering/Photo Researchers; Chapter 4: J.C. Carton/Bruce Coleman; Chapter 5: Ivan Polunin/Bruce Coleman; Chapter 6: Uniphoto Picture Agency; Chapter 7: Peter Garfield; Chapter 8: Michael D. Sullivan; Chapter 9: Eve Arnold/Magnum; Chapter 10: David Austen/Stock, Boston; Chapter 11: Robert V. Eckert, Jr./EKM-Nepenthe; Chapter 12: Eve Arnold/Magnum; Chapter 13: Chris Morris/Black Star; Chapter 14: T. Matsumoto/Sygma; Chapter 15: Christopher Springmann/The Stock Market; Chapter 16: Christopher Springmann; Chapter 17: Ellis Herwig/The Picture Cube; Chapter 18: Craig Aurness/West Light; Chapter 19: Henley and Savage/Uniphoto Picture Agency; Chapter 20: Daily Telegraph Colour Library/International Stock Photo; Chapter 21: Michael D. Sullivan; Chapter 22: Sepp Seitz/Woodfin Camp & Associates.

Mechanical art: Peter Krempasky
Line art: Rick Del Rossi

Cover art: Sculpture by Allen Jones, 1986. Untitled (maquette).
Oil enamel on paper on aluminum.

Cover and text design by Howard Petlack.

PREFACE

Much of the excitement in writing an introductory sociology text lies in keeping abreast of a constantly changing field. Since the first edition of this book in 1975, Donald Light and Suzanne Keller have worked to include the best of modern sociology: a lively blend of important theories and new scientific research, interwoven with analysis of social topics of great current interest. For this fifth edition, our team has been expanded to include Craig Calhoun, and we have worked together on a top-to-bottom revision. As always, our goal has been to convey the excitement of sociological discovery and our love for the field. From the classical scholarship of Marx, Weber, and Durkheim to the latest research findings, we believe that sociology offers provocative insights into the contemporary world. Our goal is to encourage our readers to apply these insights to their own lives and to the major issues of their times.

MAJOR CHANGES IN THE FIFTH EDITION

As we enter the 1990s, sociology is experiencing a new wave of excitement. Major theoretical projects like those of Pierre Bourdieu, Jurgen Habermas, and Anthony Giddens are coming to fruition. Sociological research is having visible impacts on public policy issues from Sunbelt migration and job creation to arts policy and media regulation. Sociologists are in demand in business and government as well as academic careers. Enrollments are up; good students are seeking the help of sociological knowledge in understanding the world in which they live and work. To serve these students, and to reflect contemporary sociology as accurately as possible, we have extensively revised the organization and contents of the text.

1. We have reorganized the table of contents into six well-integrated sections: The Sociological Perspective, The Individual and Society, Social Groupings, Inequality and Power, Social Institutions, and The Transformation of Society.
2. We have added new chapters on science and technology and the life course to reflect key areas of current sociological research and public concern.
3. We have also expanded our treatment of politics into a full chapter with a substantial section on war; expanded our treatment of the economy into a new chapter on business, work and the economy; expanded our treatment of population and health care into a full chapter each.
4. Wherever possible, we have used vivid case studies and striking social patterns to introduce chapters and sections within chapters. Leading inductively with these examples makes the book more interesting to students and makes concepts clearer and more memorable.
5. To reflect the diversity of theoretical approaches active in sociology today, including especially the wide range of perspectives often labelled "conflict" theory, we have revised our presentation of theory. In Chapter 1, we show how

different answers to the basic question "What holds society together?" lead sociologists toward a more functional or a more power- (and therefore conflict-) oriented perspective. And we show how different answers to the question "How are individuals and society related?" lead sociologists toward a greater focus on action or on social structure. Throughout the book we show how sociological research and analysis can be seen as functional, power-oriented, action-oriented, or structural.

6. To make illustrations more useful as teaching tools, we have increased our use of graphics, chosen photographs and art works which help students grasp sociological points, and given each an expanded caption directly related to coverage in the text.

7. We have made only selective use of boxes, all of which expand upon rather than digress from the text material. These often treat sociological aspects of current issues: e.g., South Africa's Apartheid (Ch. 13), or The Demography of AIDS (Ch. 10).

8. We have introduced new In-Depth sections which explore alternative points of view or specific research studies to provide a fuller sense of how sociologists think and do research: e.g., How Children Interpret Television (Ch. 5) and Cohort Experiences of the Great Depression (Ch. 6).

9. We have developed an analysis of American society in cross-cultural context throughout the book, drawing especially on recent work in comparative and historical sociology, and encouraging students to develop skills in critical thinking.

ADDITIONAL CHANGES

Revision of *Sociology*, 5th edition, did not stop with these major changes. Nor was this revision just a matter of inserts and patches. Every chapter has been rewritten to achieve the greatest possible clarity of presentation.

We have strongly reconceptualized our treatment of culture, groups and organizations, communities and urbanization, gender roles and inequalities, and social change.

The most recent sociological research and analysis have been used on every topic. We have surveyed leading sociologists to identify important subjects to address and research to draw on. We have responded to many helpful users of previous editions who have told us what new features they want and what sociological studies really engage their students. Here are just a few of the results:

Chapter 1: Not only a new treatment of theory, but a fuller account of varying perspectives in sociology, including rational-choice theory as well as Marxian, Weberian, Durkheimian, and Interactionist approaches. And a new introduction based on Pierre Bourdieu's landmark work in the sociology of culture.

Chapter 2: Durkheim's *Suicide* is analyzed as a classic of sociological research and compared with recent state-of-the art work on the same subject by David Phillips and others.

Chapter 3: Linked examples show how various levels of sociological analysis, from the most micro to the most macro, can complement each other and sometimes be integrated. We introduce such key sociological approaches as network analysis and Peter Blau's macrosociological structuralism.

Chapter 4: Exciting new work from one of sociology's fastest-growing subfields: Wendy Griswold on literature, Howard Becker on art worlds, Michael Schudson and others on advertising, a whole new section on communications media, and an In-Depth feature on the impact of television.

Chapter 5: Gary Fine's *With the Boys* helps to show how peer socialization, as exemplified in Little League baseball, goes on alongside socialization taking place at home and in school.

Chapter 6: Major works from Glen Elder, Jill Quadagno, Bernice Neugarten, Samuel Preston, and others help us address the overall pattern of the life course, the place of cohorts like the baby boomers within it, the situation of the aged, and the changing relationship between children and older people.

Chapter 7: The case of Ivan Boesky and the broader problem of insider trading on Wall Street give a contemporary twist to the issue of deviance—and one which is relevant to today's largely business-oriented college students. Recent research helps us offer a whole new section on corporate crime.

Chapter 8: A focus on business organizations helps us integrate work on small groups, organizational structure, bureaucracy, organizational culture, and the births and deaths of organizations.

Chapter 9: New thinking about the effects of urbanization on community is combined with classic studies of urban life and smaller communities. The history of cities is told through a focus on four different cities.

Chapter 10: Improved graphics and lively examples like China's one-child family policy play a major role in making demography come alive. The chapter is placed earlier in the book so that the relationship of population to social structure can be stressed.

Chapter 11: More current work—especially from sociologists focused on the power dimension of class relations: Erik Olin Wright, Randall Collins, and others.

Chapter 12: The work of recent feminist sociologists figures prominently. Also, a special focus on the relationship of gender to economic opportunities and political participation, and use of cross-cultural comparisons.

Chapter 13: Policy issues such as the place of the urban underclass are addressed through key work like that of William J. Wilson. The contemporary situation in South Africa receives extended treatment. The coverage of minority groups in American society is updated and expanded.

Chapter 14: Beginning with a sociological look at terrorism, this chapter raises key contemporary issues and relates them to such major sociological themes as nationalism, revolutions, and the rise of the state and its transformation under capitalism and socialism. We make more use of contemporary survey data on political attitudes and political participation. And the chapter concludes with a major new section on war, including both the social organization of the military and the relationship between macrosocial change and changing patterns of warfare.

Chapter 15: The recent work of economic sociologists such as Mark Granovetter, Michael Schwartz and Beth Mintz, James O'Connor, and Immanuel Wallerstein helps us address the social dimensions of economic activity and structure. Corporations and other business institutions are analyzed and a major section addresses changes in the social organization of work, combining classic perspectives with new studies from Charles Sabel and others.

Chapter 16: We include very recent work on single fathers, grandparenting, abuse of the elderly, and couple relationships. Changing family patterns are linked more directly to contemporary policy issues. Future trends are explored as we examine the changing roles of family members and the exceptional needs of dual-career couples.

Chapter 17: We add more on higher education, more on the relation of education to class structure and economic opportunity, and more on teaching as a profession. A focus on key public issues such as the rising rate of illiteracy in America is a prominent theme.

Chapter 18: We add new perspectives from Robert Wuthnow, Rodney Stark, and William Bainbridge, among others, to discussions of the rise of the religious right, the restructuring of American religion, the foundation of new religions, the experience of conversion, and the debate over secularization.

Chapter 19: This new, full chapter analyzes the social dimensions of health and the revolution in health care. Topics include AIDS, smoking, the spiral of medical costs, and efforts to contain costs through competition and privatization.

Chapter 20: Just as the American Sociological Association has added a new Section on Science and Technology, our new chapter addresses science as a social institution, the nature of scientific discovery and discourse, the relationship of science to public debates like that over evolution, and the involvement of science and technology in massive social change.

Chapter 21: Recent work by Charles Tilly, Theda Skocpol, and others helps us focus on the contrast between functional and social psychological approaches to collective behavior and rational-choice, structural and power-oriented approaches to collective action. This edition places less stress on transient phenomena such as fads and crazes and more on social movements.

Chapter 22: Addressing the relationship of broad patterns of social change such as the rise of the modern West to the classic founding theories of the discipline and to recent sociological research helps this chapter serve as a conclusion. We also look in-depth at a contemporary case study of social change: the impact of computers.

PEDAGOGICAL AIDS

To help students more easily identify and understand important terms and concepts, we have paid close attention to how information is organized in the fifth edition. All key terms are boldfaced, clearly defined, and carefully illustrated. A glossary is located conveniently at the end of each chapter, as is a concise summary.

To supplement the pedagogical aids in the text, the fifth edition of *Sociology* is accompanied by a comprehensive package of teaching and learning aids.

Review Guide. Theodore C. Wagenaar (Miami University) and Thomas F. Gieryn (Indiana University)

have written an excellent review guide entitled *Reading and Review*. This guide contains learning objectives, chapter summaries, a clarification of key concepts, multiple-choice review questions with answers, critical thinking questions, and supplementary readings and questions that pertain to the use of sociology in careers and business.

Professional Resource Guide. To aid in the difficult task of teaching introductory sociology, a *Professional Resource Guide* is available with this edition. The manual was revised by John R. Maiolo (East Carolina University) and reflects the teaching ideas of specialists in each of sociology's subfields.

Computerized Test Bank. The *Computerized Test Bank* by Peter J. Kott (Borough of Manhattan Community College), designed for both Apple and IBM personal computers, has 125 questions per chapter: one hundred multiple-choice and twenty-five true/false questions. The questions can be selected by computer to provide an almost infinite variety of tests. These tests can also be prepared by our customized test service.

Transparencies. Approximately sixty transparencies are available to instructors. The transparencies have been selected from among the illustrations appearing in the text.

Videotapes. Finally, eight videotapes on various topics relevant to coverage in the text are available to instructors. Notes on using the videotapes are included in the *Professional Resource Guide*.

THANKS AND APPRECIATION

We are fortunate to have had the support and collaboration of superb colleagues at Alfred A. Knopf. Barry Fetterolf guided the entire project. Maggie Murray was a superlative editor, working closely with us on every chapter and every feature of the book, far above the call of duty. Mary Marshall helped us achieve the clarity of prose for which this book is known. We are also grateful to other members of the Knopf editorial staff for their many contributions: Sylvia Shepard, development editor; Roberta Meyer, special projects manager; Suzanne Thibodeau, managing editor; Martha Wiseman, project editor; and Della Mancuso, manager of production operations. The fine staff of the Visual Education Corporation is to be credited with the production of the book: Howard Petlack, cover and text design; Marcia Dobbs, layout artist; Mary Lyn Koval, production assistant; Denise LaSalle, production supervisor; Yvonne Gerin, photo researcher; David LaMotte, writer/editor; Cindy George, editor; Lisa Alzo, photo assistant; Lisa Black, permissions; Ellen Gordon, Estelle Silberman, and Gail Weiss, copy editors; and Susan Ashmore, senior project director.

We also want to thank our research assistants who spent long hours in the library and at their computers to help us gather data and resource materials for this book.

They include Bart Dredge, Kevin Everett, Rekha Mirchandani, Tim Stephens, and Victoria Velkoff.

Numerous academic reviewers (listed facing the title page) and survey respondents offered invaluable help first in the planning stage, and then in responding to chapter drafts. We thank them for their time and thoughtfulness, and for the wisdom many of them brought from their teaching experience. We also benefitted from references and suggestions provided by and discussions with our colleagues at Rutgers, Princeton, and the University of North Carolina.

Last in this case is anything but least. Thomas Gieryn has worked with us throughout this revision process. He had an active role in helping us plan the book, he served as our best critic and sounding board, and he is the main author of the chapter on science and technology. We are especially grateful to Tom.

CONTENTS

PART FOUR

INEQUALITY AND POWER   287

CHAPTER 11

Social Stratification and Social Class   289

BOXES

SOCIOLOGY

PART ONE
THE SOCIOLOGICAL PERSPECTIVE

During the next few years you are likely to confront important personal choices about such matters as continuing your education, pursuing a career, getting married, and raising children. Sociology, while it may not make those decisions any easier, does offer you a new way of seeing them. It allows you to step back and look at the social forces that shape even the seemingly most private aspects of your life—not only the "big" decisions, but everyday concerns such as your tastes, your political views, and how you spend your leisure time. Sociology invites you to place your personal experience in the context of a social world.

Chapter 1 introduces you to the sociological perspective and to the fundamental questions that sociologists ask about the dynamics of social life. The chapter also traces the development of sociological thinking and identifies core theoretical questions in sociology today. Various theoretical perspectives provide frameworks for studying the social world and help sociologists dispel common-sense myths about how people behave in social settings.

Chapter 2 describes the methodology of sociological research—the step-by-step process by which a sociologist's curiosity about social patterns gets transformed into a scientific investigation capable of producing valid, reliable data. The sociologist's investigative techniques include surveys, laboratory experiments, and systematic observations. The nature and focus of an investigation are influenced by the theoretical perspective from which the sociologist begins.

In their investigations of the social world, sociologists examine both the way people interact in social settings and the structures that influence or are built out of their actions. Chapter 3 discusses various approaches to the study of social interaction. To what extent are our actions constrained by prescribed roles we play in particular social settings? To what extent do we define our social roles through a dynamic process of negotiating expectations and interactions? These questions are examined on both the micro level of person-to-person encounters and on the macro level of institutions and social structure.

CHAPTER 1
Approaches to Sociology

"If I'd seen this pile of bricks on the side of the road I'd never have thought it was art."

"But now that you've seen it in an art gallery, do you think it's art?"

"Well, I suppose it must be if *they* think so. Somebody must think so or else they wouldn't have paid so much money for it."

"Well, it may be art to them, but it isn't to me. It's still just a pile of bricks. Why do they put this rubbish on show instead of some real art?" (adapted from Williams 1982, pp. 131–132)

Tastes. We all have them. In fact, most of us have so many different tastes we could talk about them for hours. You prefer certain styles of artwork, certain kinds of food and clothing, certain types of music, certain ways of decorating your room. The list could go on and on. *De qustibus non est disputandum* the old saying goes—there is no accounting for taste. Tastes, presumably, can't be explained by outside forces that *make* us like or dislike things. Instead, tastes just seem to spring from somewhere inside us, rather mysteriously. We can't really say why we prefer rock to Mozart, burgers to paté, jeans to neatly pressed slacks. These tastes are simply part of us, our individual selves.

Sociologists understand this individualistic perspective and how true it seems to people. But they ask you to try to discard it for a while in order to see the world through different eyes. From the sociologist's viewpoint there are identifiable reasons why one person considers the pile of bricks artwork while the other person does not. These reasons lie in social forces—forces that develop as a result of people living and interacting with one another and influencing each other's thoughts and actions.

One important social force is the social context, that is, the social situation in which an event occurs. The social context provides us with vital cues about the behaviors considered appropriate. For instance, the fact that the conversation above occurs in an art gallery makes an enormous difference to what the people present say and think. Had they seen the same pile of bricks at a construction site, no one would have given it a second glance, much less talked about it as "art." But because the pile of bricks *is* being exhibited as art, the observers feel obligated to debate its artistic merits. It is important, too, that more than one person is viewing the brick sculpture. When in the company of others we are much more concerned about voicing the "right" opinions. Thus, the person who hesitantly expresses the view that this *must* be art, might be doing so simply to keep others from thinking that he or she lacks sophistication.

Our social backgrounds also affect our attitudes toward art. For example, people from upper social classes with a higher level of education are more likely to appreciate abstract art, or at least make an effort to understand it. Because their education often includes some introduction to art, they may be more apt to grasp the "point" of a work that seems simply an interesting arrangement of shapes and colors. People from lower

What one person sees as a piece of junk or a pile of bricks another may consider fine art. Education, cultural background, and social class affect such views. So does seeing the object hung on the wall of a gallery or museum instead of dumped in a construction site. (F.B. Grunzweig/Photo Researchers, Inc.)

social backgrounds, however, are less likely to appreciate abstract art. In fact, they may consider it a sign of bad art when it is unclear what a work is all about. The last speaker in the art gallery conversation expresses this point of view. His or her dislike for the brick sculpture is not just a personal preference; it is very much the product of a certain social background. Because social background so strongly influences people's tastes in art, sociologists can predict with a fair degree of accuracy the social characteristics of those who will like one painting or the other.

But why do upper-class, better educated people prefer art that has less appeal to lower-class people? What social forces could create this pattern? According to Pierre Bourdieu (1984), a leading sociologist of culture, it is not simply a matter of exposure to and knowledge about art. It also has to do with efforts on the part of social elites to distinguish themselves from those of lower social status. To elites, the ability to appreciate abstract art is considered an indication of their higher education and breeding. So elites cultivate a taste for art that appeals more to the intellect than it does to the emotions and the senses. The same preference can be seen in elites' taste in furniture. Whereas working-class people tend to prefer furniture that is comfortable and *feels* good (a large-cushioned velour sofa, for instance), elites tend to prefer pieces that have beauty of form but may be much less pleasing to the body (such as a finely carved but straight-backed antique chair). In these ways elites

help to maintain their social distinction.

Along with reflecting social class background, tastes in art are also the product of a particular social time and place. What is proclaimed an excellent drawing in one culture may look like primitive doodling in another; what is dismissed as a pile of bricks in one era may be tomorrow's masterpiece sculpture. Figure 1.1 gives some quotes from literary reviews written at the time that the works they criticize were first published. Today all those works are considered classics, yet in their own day many people viewed them as affronts to public morals. Henry Fielding's *Tom Jones*, for example, today believed to be one of the finest eighteenth-century English novels, was considered shockingly licentious by some critics of its era. Similarly, Emily Brontë's *Wuthering Heights* is often regarded today as a work of genius, but its tragic lovers were considered rude savages when viewed from the delicate tastes of people in Victorian times. Thus, "masterpiece" and "worthless," "brilliant" and "degenerate" are very relative terms—relative, among other things, to the tastes that define particular eras and cultures.

To sum up, sociologists show that our likes and dislikes are very much social creations. A great deal of the differences in tastes that people exhibit can be explained on the basis of differences in social background, current social position, and the time and place in which someone lives. These social forces, moreover, shape tastes in matters beyond furniture and art. Prefer-

FIGURE 1.1   Excerpts from Literary Reviews Written by Contemporary Critics

HAMLET
WILLIAM SHAKESPEARE   1601

It is a vulgar and barbarous drama, which would not be tolerated by the vilest populace of France, or Italy. . .one would imagine this piece to be the work of a drunken savage.

Voltaire, (1768), in *The Works of M. de Voltaire*   1901

TOM JONES
HENRY FIELDING   1749

A book seemingly intended to sap the foundation of that morality which it is the duty of parents and all public instructors to inculcate in the minds of young people.

Sir John Hawkins, *Life of Samuel Johnson*   1787

WUTHERING HEIGHTS
EMILY BRONTË   1847

. . .wild, confused, disjointed and improbable. . .the people who make up the drama, which is tragic enough in its consequences, are savages ruder than those who lived before the days of Homer.

The Examiner

ON
EDGAR ALLAN POE

After reading some of Poe's stories one feels a kind of shock to one's modesty. We require some kind of spiritual ablution to cleanse our minds of his disgusting images.

Leslie Stephen, *Hours in A Library*   1874

ON
WALT WHITMAN

He is morally insane, and incapable of distinguishing between good and evil, virtue and crime.

Max Nordau, *Degeneration*   1895

LADY CHATTERLEY'S LOVER
D.H. LAWRENCE   1928

D.H. Lawrence has a diseased mind. He is obsessed by sex. . .we have no doubt that he will be ostracized by all except the most degenerate coteries in the literary world.

John Bull

THE CATCHER IN THE RYE
J.D. SALINGER   1951

Recent war novels have accustomed us all to ugly words and images, but from the mouths of the very young and protected they sound peculiarly offensive. . .the ear refuses to believe.

New York Herald Tribune Book Review

Source: Rotten Reviews: A Literary Comparison, ed. by Bill Henderson, Penguin, 1987.

Many books now considered great classics were greeted by bad reviews. We are unlikely to hold these negative opinions today not only because tastes have changed but because we have been taught to believe in the classic status of certain works and authors.

ences in everything from food and clothing to cars, hobbies, music, education, and much, much more are heavily influenced by social factors. Even who we consider attractive, fall in love with, and marry is not a strictly individual choice. Ideas about personal beauty are shaped by the very same social forces that shape ideas about beauty in a painting or a sculpture. At the very least, our place within society determines the kinds of people we are likely to meet. In your own case, the fact that you are attending college greatly increases the chances that you will date and marry a college educated person. Love, then, is not as mysterious a thing as poets claim it is. Like all human feelings and behaviors, it is governed partly by social forces.

Sociology, the study of human society and behavior in social settings, is a science dedicated to revealing these social forces to people. Sociologists look beyond individual psychology and idiosyncratic cases to the many recurring patterns in people's attitudes and actions, and to how these patterns vary across time, cultures, and social groups. As you learn to adopt a sociological perspective, you will come to see that you are not just a lone actor involved in your own personal drama. Instead, you are often caught up in larger social forces, acting out your part on a broader social stage. And things that you do may, in turn, influence others' actions, perhaps even encouraging a new social script to develop. A sociological perspective allows you to see these social processes at work. In the next section we will describe more fully just what this perspective entails.

THE SOCIOLOGICAL PERSPECTIVE

Social Facts and Social Causes

The idea that much of human experience is shaped by social forces not of the individual's making had an important place in the writings of Émile Durkheim, a pioneering French sociologist of the nineteenth century. Durkheim described what he called **social facts,** properties of group life that cannot be explained by the actions, feelings, or characteristics of individual persons. For example, many of the personal attributes that we deem physically attractive are defined by society, not by the individual. You have only to think about trends in women's fashions over the last two centuries (from the

pinched waists and bustled hips of the nineteenth century to the flat, curveless lines of the 1920s) to see how much ideas about beauty are socially prescribed. Falling in love is also a social fact in that how we act when in love is something we learn from our culture—its books, magazines, movies, television shows, song lyrics, and so forth. In fact, in some parts of the world the rather flighty and obsessive behavior that we call "being in love" is virtually unknown. Selecting a wife or husband is considered a much more practical matter. Romantic love, then, like any belief, attitude, or behavior that people in a society share, is a product of the social group; in short, a social fact (Luhmann 1986; Brain 1976).

Another important kind of social fact is the *rate* of some social phenomenon, that is, the number of cases of it found in a population. A crime rate is a social fact, as is a birthrate, a marriage rate, or the rate of new car sales. Although each of these involves adding up individual cases, the overall rate provides important new information. It reveals social patterns that would not be apparent from analyzing a few separate cases. Indeed, generalizing from one or two cases is a very risky way to gauge the rate of something. Suppose, for example, that you come from a poor family but have an uncle who got rich from hard work and smart business deals. If you conclude that this is the way most rich people get their money, you would be mistaken. Most rich Americans inherited a substantial part of their wealth, and the majority of those who amassed fortunes on their own started out from at least a middle-class background. These statistical rates are social facts that can be known only by studying a representative sample of the whole wealthy population, not just a few rich people.

In addition to identifying social facts, sociologists also seek to determine the social forces that give rise to them. For example, if a sociologist learns that a high crime rate exists in a particular neighborhood, he or she would search for *social* explanations, causes for a particular event that lie in aspects of community life. Such causes might include a high poverty rate, a low level of police protection, and the presence of racial or ethnic group conflict. Sociologists, in other words, seek to explain social facts in terms of other social phenomena. A crime rate, a marriage pattern, a taste in art, or whatever: if it is a fact revealed through the collective observation of people, it is assumed to have *social* causes. This assumption is an important part of the sociological perspective.

Sociology's stress on social facts and social causes helps distinguish it from other disciplines concerned

Sociology is an extremely broad discipline which can help one understand all fields of human interaction, including (top left) the office as a social environment; (top right) hunting as a sporting event; (center left) a political rally; (center right) preparing for a religious ceremony; (bottom left) learning cultural traditions; (bottom right) a community agricultural project. (Top left: Lawrence Migdale/Photo Researchers, Inc.; top right: Jean-Claude Lejeune/EKM-Nepenthe; center left: Charlie Cole/Picture Group; center right: Jill Lesser Bilderberg/The Stock Market; bottom left: Ray Ellis/Photo Researchers, Inc.; bottom right: Mathias Oppersdorff/Photo Researchers, Inc.)

People in all societies interact as social beings. Such encounters generate, shape, and maintain our attitudes and actions. (Top: Sepp Seitz/Woodfin Camp & Associates; center: Carl Frank/Photo Researchers, Inc.; bottom: Joel Gordon.)

with human behavior. Economics is primarily concerned with the production and exchange of goods and services, including the use of money and other forms of property. Psychology focuses mainly on the individual, and is concerned as much with internal influences on behavior (biological makeup, learning, emotions, motivation) as with external ones. Anthropology focuses on small traditional societies. Political science specializes in the study of government, public administration, and the exercise of power, as well as in the study of conflicts and how they are resolved. Some researchers in each of these disciplines work on topics that overlap. This is especially true of sociologists, whose discipline is broader than any of the other social sciences. The great breadth of topics that sociologists study include interpersonal relationships, families, communities, small businesses, giant corporations, schools, religions, governments, relationships among people from different cultures, sources of social inequality, and the effectiveness of public policies. This broad spectrum of themes helps to make sociology such a fascinating field.

The Sociological Imagination

The sociological stress on social facts and social causes gives people a new way of looking at themselves. Sociologists argue that in order to understand ourselves and our personal experiences, we must understand our society, both its past and its present, as well as our place within it. The distinguished American sociologist C. Wright Mills called the ability to adopt this perspective the **sociological imagination.** "The sociological imagination," Mills explained, "enables us to grasp history and biography and the relations between the two within society. This is its task and its promise . . . The first fruit of this imagination—and the first lesson of the social science that embodies it—is the idea that the individual can understand his own experience and gauge his own fate only by locating himself within his period, that he can know his own chances in life only by becoming aware of those of all individuals in his circumstances" (Mills 1970, p. 12).

A good example of the sociological imagination is the ability to understand your own chances of finding a job after graduating from college. Suppose you are a woman with a degree in science. Your job prospects depend on more than just your own personal abilities and motivation. They depend on the status of *all* women in society and the roles deemed appropriate to them. You are fortunate that in the last thirty to forty years attitudes toward women in the workplace have changed. While a woman of the 1950s was considered somewhat "odd" if she wanted a career in science, that attitude no longer prevails. There are still many obstacles that make it hard for women to reach the top in scientific fields, but most people no longer question a woman's desire to do so. This change in attitudes is a product of many social forces, including a changing economic organization, a rising rate of divorce, a growing demand for scientists and technical personnel, and the influence of a strong women's rights movement. In any case, your prospects for finding a challenging job in science are much better than they were when your mother was your age. The sociological imagination allows you to understand why. Throughout this book the sociological imagination will enable you to see yourself and your experiences in the context of social forces.

Science, Sociology, and Common Sense

Throughout history certain people have been respected for their knowledge of social customs and the ways that human relationships work. But only in the modern age has the study of society been carried out according to a carefully organized, *systematic* research method that reduces the likelihood of overlooking facts or misunderstanding causes. This means that information is collected, studied, and analyzed in accordance with the principles and procedures of modern science. The **scientific method** began to emerge in the seventeenth century, the age of Galileo and Newton. Sociology was created as part of the development and expansion of science that followed in the eighteenth and nineteenth centuries.

Fundamental to the scientific method is the careful collection of **data** (facts, statistics, study results, and other pieces of observable information). These data are recorded and made available to other researchers so that their accuracy can be verified. Data are the raw materials of science. It is from data that scientific theories are built.

A **theory** is a systematic and formal explanation of how two or more phenomena are related to each other. Scientific theories usually try to indicate cause and effect. They say which factors are causing others and which of the various causes are most important. Some sociological theories are very narrow; they focus on only one small aspect of social life, often exploring the relationship between just two factors in a fairly specific setting. These are called **local theories.** An example is the theory that intergroup prejudice is caused by intense competition for scarce and valuable rewards (land, jobs, income, prestige, and so forth). At the other extreme are

Galileo, pictured here on trial before the Inquisition, helped to usher seventeenth-century Europe into a new era of scientific understanding, with discoveries made through experimentation and observation. (The Bridgeman Art Library/Art Resource.)

sociological theories that try to explain how a number of social factors all fit together. The most comprehensive of these are called **general theories,** while those that are less comprehensive are called **middle-range theories.** All theories, however, regardless of their scope, must be systematically tested before they can be tentatively accepted. Such testing involves conducting studies and seeing if the results are consistent with the theory's predictions. In this way, unsubstantiated theories can be revised or discarded.

Because it is created using systematic, scientific procedures, sociological knowledge differs from knowledge based on common sense. Common-sense views about society and social relationships derive from people's personal experiences. As such, they are always deeply biased by the limits of that experience, for most people personally encounter only some of the social conditions and forces that actually exist. Common-sense views are also limited in the sense that they are never organized into systematic theories and so are never checked for accuracy against all the known facts. Science, in contrast, goes beyond common sense by methodically amassing a large quantity of data and rigorously testing all plausible explanations of the observed information.

This is not to say that common-sense ideas are always incorrect. Sometimes our intuitive notions about how society works turn out to be quite accurate. Other times, however, our common-sense judgments are wrong, or they contain only a measure of truth. The problem is that, without scientific methods, we cannot tell when we are right and when we are wrong. Try, for example, to gauge the accuracy of these three common-sense statements:

- TRUE OR FALSE? Most people on welfare could support themselves if they had to.

- TRUE OR FALSE? Once people become poor they remain poor.

- TRUE OR FALSE? After World War II poor blacks began to leave the South for northern cities because the welfare payments were larger there.

Although millions of Americans believe that these statements are true, scientific research shows them to be false (Rosenbaum 1977; Schiller 1980, 1981). For instance, contrary to popular belief, nearly all of those receiving welfare are either mothers with young children, the young children themselves, or elderly people.

Most of these individuals are not able to take jobs outside the home. Similarly, although many people assume that poverty is almost always a permanent condition, this is often not the case. There is indeed a category of hard-core poor, but there are also families that fall into poverty temporarily (because of a prolonged job layoff, for instance, or a serious illness). Thus, each year about 10 million families drop below the official poverty line, while another 10 million move above it. Finally, the common-sense idea that the poor are attracted to northern cities to collect larger welfare payments is also questionable. One study of six northern cities with large black populations revealed that southern blacks who had migrated there were *less* likely to be on welfare than were blacks who had been born in those cities (Rosenbaum 1977, p. 3). Today, moreover, black migration is more often from North to South, despite the lower welfare payments in southern states (Clark 1985).

Such findings clearly show the value of scientific methods for testing the validity of common-sense views and accumulating a body of reliable data. Common-sense ideas can provide valuable hunches about how society works, but those hunches must then be put to scientific scrutiny. The methods of science are therefore a vital part of sociology.

Levels of Sociological Analysis

Throughout this book we will also be seeing two major levels of sociological analysis. One is the *micro* (or small-scale) level of analysis, or **microsociology.** It focuses mainly on everyday patterns of behavior and face-to-face interactions. Studying how students and professor negotiate a set of social relationships in a college classroom is an example of microlevel research. Microsociologists explore human interaction in any of hundreds of different settings. A sociologist doing microlevel research might explore the interactions of men and women at a singles' bar, of children at a summer camp, or of workers on an assembly line. The possibilities are limitless. No aspect of social life is too small for this level of sociological inquiry. Researchers may turn their social microscopes on the most minute details of everyday life, revealing patterns never before apparent.

The second major level is the *macro* (or large-scale) level of analysis, or **macrosociology.** It focuses on overall social arrangements, how they are structured, and what long-term effects they have. Studying the functions of higher education for American society is an example of macrolevel research. So is the study of how higher education helps to maintain the social class system. Other macrolevel studies concentrate on politics, economics, business, religion, science, technology, the health-care system, and many other larger-scale aspects of social life.

Microlevel and macrolevel sociological studies often complement each other. Consider studies of the Catholic church, for example. Macrosociologists might ask how the church's policies on birth control affect Latin America, or how the church's leadership exercises its authority in remote parts of the world. Microsociologists, in contrast, might look at how belief in the church's teachings affects a person's everyday behavior, or at how a young seminary student is indoctrinated into the priesthood. Clearly, both these levels of analysis make important contributions to our overall understanding of the social world. To ignore either would give us a very lopsided picture of what sociological analysis is all about.

The Piggly Wiggly stores founded by Clarence Saunders helped to transform food retailing in America. The new "self-service" concept had wide-ranging effects on the business community and consumer behavior. (Courtesy of Piggly Wiggly Corporation.)

BASIC SOCIOLOGICAL QUESTIONS

In 1916 Clarence Saunders, a grocer from Memphis, Tennessee, opened his first Piggly Wiggly store, an innovation in retail food sales. Saunders called his new establishment a "self-service" store because customers selected their own merchandise; they were not waited on by salesclerks as in other grocery stores. But how were Saunders' customers to find the products that they wanted with no clerks to help them? To solve this problem Saunders hit upon an innovative scheme. He installed a turnstile at the store entrance which channeled shoppers into the beginning of a maze of aisles and shelves. The maze was laid out in such a way that the people had to pass by every counter and see every item on display. At the end of the maze the customers exited through another turnstile which led them to a checkout counter where a single employee rang up their purchases on a cash register. So successful was Saunders' retailing concept that within a mere six years he had built or franchised over 1,200 Piggly Wiggly stores. As anyone

who has lived or traveled in the American Southeast knows, the Piggly Wiggly chain still flourishes today. Although the original layout of the store has long since been changed, Saunders' basic idea laid the foundation for the design of the modern supermarket.

The Piggly Wigglys helped mark the start of a new era in food retailing. Not only did Saunders' "self service" concept catch on; so did the concept of a "chain" of stores owned or franchised by a parent company that centralized the wholesale buying of merchandise. Another successful retail grocery chain that started in this era was the Great Atlantic and Pacific Tea Company, better known as the A&P. It expanded from sixty-seven stores in 1876, to over 1,000 by 1915, and some 15,000 by the 1930s. The decade of the 1920s saw the creation of the first true "super" market, a mammoth establishment called the Crystal Palace in San Francisco. The building contained over an acre and a half of floor space and had a parking lot that could hold well over 4,000 cars. By the late 1930s the Crystal Palace was breaking sales records: 365 tons of apples in a single year, five freight-car loads of eggs in a single month, five tons of sugar in a single hour! The age of mass marketing in food had clearly arrived.

But this trend in retail food sales was not without resistance. The owners of small grocery stores organized to oppose both the growing power of huge food retailers and the increasing systematization in how customers and merchandise were processed. One opponent, the National Association of Retail Grocers, supported measures that would curb the power of the large chain stores. These included special taxes to reduce chain-store profits and laws to restrict the number of such stores that could be built in any given area. Most states eventually enacted some legislation favorable to the small grocer. But this was not enough to check the trends in food marketing that had already begun. Today, the large supermarket chains account for some 95 percent of retail food sales. In recent years their stores have grown bigger than ever, with greater variety in brand names and in the kinds of merchandise carried. The systematic processing of goods and people has also been enhanced by the laser scanner that reads bar codes on package labels in order to tabulate bills and keep track of inventory. Because most Americans find this food shopping system economical and efficient, the large grocery store chain remains a fixture of our society.

This brief history of the modern supermarket (based on Beniger 1986) is more than just an interesting story. It is an excellent way to introduce you to two basic sociological questions that will provide a framework for thinking about topics in this book and in your own social world. The first question is: *What holds society together?* What, in other words, is the major factor that binds individuals and groups into a social whole? The second question is: *What is the relationship between the individual and society?* Are individuals constantly engaged in creating the society they live in? Or is it more accurate to say that society shapes individual behavior and limits the choices open to people? In the following sections we'll consider answers that have emerged to each of these questions.

What Holds Society Together?

Some sociologists would say that twentieth-century changes in the retail sale of food were the result of automatic adjustments within the food market, adjustments that allowed food distribution to better meet the changing needs of Americans. From this point of view, a chain like Piggly Wiggly or the A&P, or a giant supermarket like the Crystal Palace, are one among other functional parts of a larger social/economic system. Each part serves a certain needed function within that system —growing food, processing and packaging it, bringing it to market and onto grocery store shelves, and getting it transferred to consumers' cupboards. As social conditions and consumers' needs change, these functional parts and their relationship to each other tend to adjust themselves. The result is an integrated system that holds together because its parts play complementary roles.

Similarly, the same group of sociologists argues that society as a whole is held together in the same way— through the interaction of complementary parts. Sociologists who hold this view have what is called a **functional perspective** on social integration. They see society as bound together by an automatic process of self-regulation in which many different parts (businesses, governments, families, schools, and so forth), all serving different functions, evolve so as to work together in an integrated fashion. These sociologists acknowledge that social conflicts and disruptions do arise. Conditions change and a particular part of society (such as a failing economic system) may no longer be meeting people's current needs. From a functional perspective, however, such incidents are temporary periods of readjustment. In the functional view, society has a natural tendency to evolve toward a state of **functional integration**, in which its various pieces fit together into a smoothly operating whole.

But other sociologists have a very different answer to the question of what holds society together. In analyzing the twentieth-century trends in retail food sales, they would argue that the functional perspective leaves out the important role of power. In the process of carving out their enormous share of the food market, large chains of supermarkets exercised substantial power over their smaller competitors. Practices like sharply undercutting competitors' prices in order to attract customers is something that a large business can afford much more than a small one. It is a way in which a large corporation can flex its economic muscles. From this perspective, the small grocery store and the huge supermarket chain are in natural conflict with each other, and in this conflict the large, powerful chain is likely to prevail. Despite resistance on the part of small store owners, the huge supermarket chain is in a position to guide economic outcomes in its own favor. This exercise of power on the part of those who control important resources is seen as the major factor shaping and maintaining the social order.

This emphasis on the role of power is the starting point of the **power perspective.** Sociologists who hold this view see conflict as the natural and inevitable state of affairs in society as different people, groups, and organizations struggle to gain the upper hand. In this struggle the privileged few who control the most resources are the ones who are likely to win out and shape society to their own advantage. Then, through their continued exercise of power, they persuade or force the disadvantaged to accept the established social order. From this perspective, the ideology of free enterprise, often lauded by the rich and powerful, can be seen as a convenient rationale for perpetuating their economic privileges.

Clearly, sociologists do not agree on what holds the larger society together. Given these contrasting views on the basic question of social order, it is not surprising that sociologists have different expectations when studying any element of society or social relations. For example, sociologists who take a functional perspective would expect to find that most enduring social arrangements (the family, the educational system, the economy, and so forth) make at least some contribution to social integration and stability. Power-oriented sociologists would expect to find that enduring social arrangements are the result of some group or individual, in a powerful and dominant position, exerting control over subordinate groups or individuals.

What Is the Relationship Between the Individual and Society?

In answer to our second basic sociological question, some sociologists stress the importance of **social structure.** Social structure is simply the way that people, groups, and institutions are organized with respect to one another. This structural organization is believed to influence behavior, or at the very least to limit the choices open to people. Returning to our example of trends in food markets, sociologists who emphasize social structure would search for ways that structural factors shaped store owners' decisions. For instance, the structural factor of an increasingly large American popu-

lation encouraged men like Clarence Saunders to take advantage of economies of scale (efficiencies that come from running a larger business, such as a chain of stores). From this perspective, supermarkets do not just pop out of the blue. Instead, they are the product of social structural forces that make big stores very profitable. And once self-service stores such as the Piggly Wiggly were established, they set off a chain reaction of other structurally induced changes in the selling of food. For example, when items were simply displayed on grocery shelves rather than being sold by clerks, producers were encouraged to design enticing packages geared to "sell themselves." Thus, coffee cans now proclaim their beans to be "mountain grown"; bread wrappers encase loaves that allegedly will help children "build strong bodies"; and the label on a bar of soap announces that the contents are "99 44/100 percent pure." Were it not for the development of the self-service store, it is unlikely that this advertising-on-the-shelf would have evolved.

Sociologists who focus on the structural aspects of social phenomena are said to be adopting a **structural perspective.** According to a structural perspective, peo-

In this photo, individual action is taking place in each driver or pedestrian's decision of where and when to go. But when one steps back to see the overall picture, there is a definite structure or pattern. The same is true for the social relationship of the individual and society. Social forces are organized in ways that limit individual behavior, and individuals make their own choices and behave in ways that in turn shape society. (Charles Harbutt/Archive Pictures, Inc.)

ple's choices can be explained by social forces that arise from the ways in which society is organized. These social forces are seen as being outside of individuals, as enduring longer than individuals, and as being very difficult for individuals to change. Although people are often unaware of the existence of these social forces (such as the influence of education and social background on tastes in art), our behavior is greatly constrained by them. Forces that derive from the external structure of society are constantly limiting our choices and making us think and act in predictable ways.

In contrast to a structural perspective is a view that looks at the other side of the relationship between the individual and society. Instead of dwelling on how individual behavior is the product of social forces, it stresses that individual action is constantly creating the many social arrangements that make up society. Clarence Saunders, for example, the founder of Piggly Wiggly, was not just a product of his times. He was also a very imaginative innovator who creatively solved the problem of how to process customers through a self-service store. Saunders' actions, in turn, influenced much more than his own immediate world. They helped to dramatically change the way that food was marketed in our society.

Sociologists who analyze phenomena this way are adopting what is known as an **action perspective.** Action-oriented sociologists believe it is a mistake to see society as strictly external to people. They stress that society is always shaped by the actions of individuals. Although these actions are often influenced by social forces, they do not involve succumbing to such forces in robotlike fashion. Instead, human behavior is a creative process, based on how people interpret and redirect these social forces. According to the action perspective, then, interpreting the subjective beliefs and outlooks that underlie individual action is a central task of sociology.

Summing Up

In short, two basic questions help frame sociologists' efforts to understand society and social behavior. These questions apply whether a sociologist is trying to understand an enormous social change, such as the rise of capitalism, or a more specific issue, such as the development of large supermarket chains. The first question concerns what holds society together. What is responsible for maintaining the order in social relationships? Answers to this question tend to focus on one of two factors, or on some combination of the two. One factor is *functional integration*, the natural tendency for pieces to hold together as a unit because they play complementary roles. The other factor is the exercise of social *power*, the ability of one person, group, or organization to dominate another. The second basic question concerns the relationship between the individual and society. To what extent do social forces shape individual behavior, and to what extent do individual actions shape society? Again, the answers tend to focus on one of two factors, or on some combination of the two. The first factor is *social structure*, the organization of society, which substantially limits the options open to people. The second factor is *individual action*, the tendency of people to interpret their surroundings, make their own choices, and behave in often distinctive ways that influence society.

Thus, in response to the question of what holds society or any of its parts together, some sociologists offer a functional explanation, others a power-oriented one, while most hold various positions in between. Likewise, in responding to the question regarding the individual's relationship to society, most sociologists favor explanations that fall somewhere between an action perspective and a viewpoint based on social structure. In fact, relatively few sociologists take extreme positions regarding the basic questions. Most try to analyze society and social forces in ways that take into account both power and functional integration, and both individual action and social structure.

THE ORIGINS OF SOCIOLOGY

How were present-day answers to the two basic sociological questions arrived at? To find out, we must look back to the eighteenth and nineteenth centuries, a tumultuous era when sweeping social changes such as the American Revolution, other colonial upheavals, and four separate revolutions in France jarred the minds of people who once held traditional views of society. The Industrial Revolution, too, heralded a wide range of social changes, as factories sprang up, people flocked to the cities, and worker-employer contact faded in a haze of impersonal bureaucracies. Crime rates rose, and some traditional values seemed to be eroding. It was a bewildering age to live in. Society seemed to have been turned upside-down. In these extraordinary times some gifted thinkers tried to make sense of the changes around them using the tools of science. In doing so they fashioned a new discipline—sociology. The term was coined by the pioneering French thinker Auguste Comte (1798–1857).

Four major changes in the modern era contributed to the creation of sociology. One was the transformation of political philosophies and government. Through wars, marriages, and political machinations, the kings of Europe extended their rule over larger and larger territories. They began to create bureaucracies to administer their realms, rather than ruling indirectly through local noblemen. As a result, the common people began to feel more distanced from their rulers, more apart from those who controlled their fates. With government more remote and more impersonal, popular support for monarchies began to weaken. Discontent grew as the increasing size of modern nations made them more and more difficult for a king and his court to administer. When enough people felt that the old political order was intolerable, revolutions were ignited and whole forms of government changed. Understanding these turbulent changes and where they would lead was a central aim of the first modern sociologists.

Another aim was to understand the far-reaching economic transformations occurring at the same time. European economies grew rapidly not just in total wealth, but also in productivity. Farmers, for example, were able to use technological advances to more easily plant, tend, and harvest crops. As a result, much more food was produced with a much smaller input of labor, which in turn caused the demand for agricultural workers to drop. Thousands of rural residents, no longer needed on the farms, flocked to the cities where factories were rapidly supplanting the traditional craft guilds and home-based workshops. Here human relationships were much more impersonal than they had been in small rural villages. People did not even know many of their neighbors and co-workers, much less have face-to-face dealings with their employers. The majority of factory workers also toiled long hours for meager wages, often in unhealthy surroundings. People wanted to know how this new social order had come about, and the first sociologists tried to give them answers.

The Industrial Revolution uprooted a predominantly rural social order. The chaos and misery that prevailed in overgrown cities in the nineteenth century led many social thinkers to try to make some sense of the changes. In this way the discipline of sociology began. (The Bettmann Archive.)

The first sociologists also tried to provide insights into the wide diversity of human customs and values that existed around the world. Europeans had always assumed that their own practices were natural and right. But as colonial empires grew and distant trade links were established, it became clear that the European way of life was not shared by everyone. Europeans wanted to know what to make of the other cultures they heard so much about; they wanted to understand how such an array of beliefs and customs could possibly have arisen. They also wanted to grasp the implications for their own society. Perhaps European practices were not the moral imperatives that they seemed to be. Perhaps they were merely choices about social organization that might change with time.

Finally, the first sociologists wanted to understand the new ways that people were starting to think about themselves and their world. Increasingly, humans saw themselves as rational creatures, not as slaves to superstition and emotion. As rational creatures, they could apply the systematic methods of science to ordering and comprehending their lives. Sociologists were both a product of this new rationalistic outlook and observers of it. They were part of the scientific tide that was sweeping the modern world, and they were the scholars who tried to put this tide into historical perspective.

In summary, the major social transformations that shook Europe and North America in the eighteenth and nineteenth centuries provided much of the "push" that led to the creation of sociology. These transformations were very unsettling to those who lived through them, and they created social problems of a magnitude never before encountered. People had to admit that common-sense ideas about the social world were inadequate. What was needed instead was a large body of factual information put into perspective by systematically tested theories of society. The early sociologists gathered this information and constructed these theories. Their ideas about what holds society together and about the relationship between society and the individual laid the foundation for much of current sociological thinking. In fact, some of the theories of the nineteenth and early twentieth centuries are the most influential ever developed. In the following sections we will introduce you to five classic examples of sociological thought.

Rational-Choice Theory

Before the social sciences became separate disciplines, politics, economics, and other aspects of society were studied together as related phenomena. The most important perspective that developed as a framework for these early views is called rational-choice theory. Rational-choice theory holds that, in making decisions, people weigh the gains to be made from a particular action against the costs incurred. Only when they perceive the gains to outweigh the costs do they adopt the behavior. Rational-choice theory stresses the role of individual

actions in shaping social facts. As such, it has contributed to the development of the action perspective in sociology. But rational-choice theory is more concerned with using formal models of rational decision-making to predict social behavior than it is with highlighting creativity or cultural differences in people's thought. In this way it differs from other theories that stress an action perspective.

Prominent among the founders of rational-choice theory was the eighteenth-century Scottish philosopher Adam Smith (1723–1790), a founder of classical economics as well as an influence on nineteenth- and twentieth-century sociologists. Smith (1776/1976) believed that people make economic choices (what to buy, what to manufacture, at what cost to sell) on the basis of very rational cost/benefit calculations. In doing so they consider only the consequences to themselves; they do not consider how their actions will affect others. Yet, in a free-market system, Smith maintained, economic choices motivated purely by self-interest ultimately lead to the efficient production of the goods consumers want and a corresponding rise in society's wealth. This occurs because competition works like an "invisible hand" to streamline production, maximize profits, and guide labor and investment into areas where demand is greatest. Smith's version of rational-choice theory incorporates the idea of functional integration. Smith saw society as a self-regulating system in which many different parts, all acting in their own interest, are meshed together through market forces to form a whole that operates for the common good.

A generation after Smith, the philosopher Jeremy Bentham (1748–1832) expanded on the concept of rational decision making. Bentham (1789/1970) stressed that humans everywhere are motivated to obtain pleasure and avoid pain. He argued that people try to evaluate their different experiences so as to act in ways that maximize pleasure over pain. Bentham disagreed with Smith's view that the sum of individual decisions, made on the basis of self-interest, automatically adds up to the greatest good for society as a whole. To Bentham, the public good (defined as the greatest benefit at the lowest cost for the greatest number of people) could best be achieved by scientifically planned government action —what he called a "visible hand." Bentham maintained that we cannot rely on an automatic tendency for society to function smoothly and in the public interest. Instead, we need to exercise power in order to provide the maximum benefit to as many people as possible.

Adam Smith believed that the rational choices made by individual consumers would result in a self-regulating economy geared to satisfying the common demand for goods. (Culver Pictures.)

Jeremy Bentham believed individuals left to their own decision-making would not produce a smoothly functioning society. He favored government planning and legal controls to achieve the ideal of utility: the greatest good for the greatest number of people. (The Bettmann Archive.)

The rational-choice theory that Smith and Bentham pioneered is still influential in several areas of sociology. For example, this approach has been applied to how businesses make market decisions, to how people decide to invest in more education, and even to how young people choose whom to date and marry. In the case of dating, individuals are viewed as confronting a large pool of possible romantic partners (Blau 1963; Becker 1976). They must somehow decide who to approach or whose advances to encourage. This they do only partly on the basis of physical attraction. In addition, they weigh a whole range of costs and benefits related to making a particular choice. These might include the costs of possible rejection and of disapproval from one's parents versus the benefits of feeling comfortable with a particular person and of enhancing one's social status if that person impresses one's friends. From this perspective, dating is like a market where people search for the best possible "product" given their own resources. Although this perspective sounds crass to most Americans, some research suggests that rational calculations do enter into dating choices. You will encounter other examples of rational-choice theory at various points in this book.

The Theory of Karl Marx

Fourteen years before the death of Jeremy Bentham, a man was born who would help to change the course of history. His name was Karl Marx. An economic histori-an, social theorist, political agitator, and revolutionary, Karl Marx (1818–1883) contributed much to sociological and economic thinking. He also laid the foundations of modern Communism.

Marx (1867/1976) believed that the most significant thing about the industrial societies of his time was that they were capitalistic; that the means of production were privately owned and were used to maximize profits. In Marx's view this economic system shaped all other aspects of social life and bred persistent conflict (tension, disagreements, competition) over social values and goals. The conflict arose because the **capitalists** (the owners of the land, factories, and machines), could increase their wealth only by exploiting the **proletariat** (the workers who actually produced economic goods). To Marx the interests of the capitalists and the proletariat were inherently contradictory. The competitive market compelled the capitalists to force wages down to the lowest possible level to maximize their profits. The workers, for their part, were increasingly driven to revolt and overthrow the capitalist system and to establish a classless society in which wealth would be distributed evenly (see Chapters 11 [Stratification] and 22 [Social Change]).

But before the workers could unite and rise in revolt, Marx argued, they had to develop **class consciousness,** a sense of their shared interests and plight. Until then the capitalists would use their power to shape the religious beliefs, leisure activities, and consumer preferences of the oppressed proletariat. This would foster a "false consciousness" among the workers and discourage them from realizing that they were being exploited. The interests of the capitalists would thereby be furthered and the system would endure, with the

In Karl Marx's view, capitalist society is dominated by those who control the means of production and reap profits from the labor of others. This produces a deep division between social classes, which leads to struggles over social power and eventually revolution. (The Bettmann Archive.)

Émile Durkheim believed that shared social bonds hold modern society together. Mutual trust and interdependency create a "collective conscience," or sense of belonging, and help to make society as a whole greater than and distinct from the sum of its individual members. (The Bettmann Archive.)

capitalists passing on to their descendants their property and privileged status. Thus, in answer to the question what holds society together, Marx's theory is power-oriented. It argues that a capitalist society is held together by the capitalists' ability to dominate the workers. Power, according to Marx, is the source of social advantage.

In answer to our other basic sociological question (the relationship between the individual and society), Marx's theory takes into account both structure and action. It is structural in that it sees the historical circumstances of capitalism as limiting most of the choices open to people. It is action-oriented in that it recognizes the capacity of workers to join together in class struggle and collectively change existing conditions. Marx expressed both these ideas when he wrote: "Men make their own history, but they do not make it under circumstances chosen by themselves, rather under circumstances directly encountered, given, and transmitted from the past" (1852/1979, p. 103). One of the most fundamental differences among later followers of Marx has been whether they stress the structural aspects of his theory or put more emphasis on class action as the determinant of social change (Gouldner 1980).

The Theory of Émile Durkheim

Another early sociologist with enormous influence was the Frenchman Émile Durkheim (1858–1917). In looking at the creation of modern industrial societies, he focused on how underlying social forces bind people together, a phenomenon he called **social solidarity**

(Durkheim 1893/1984). In Durkheim's view, there were two basic forms of social solidarity. One is solidarity based on a strong sharing of beliefs, values, and customs, what Durkheim called **mechanical solidarity.** Mechanical solidarity is the glue that holds together small, simple, tribal societies, where everyone views the world in much the same way and engages in the same activities. Large, complex, modern societies, in contrast, are knit together by what Durkheim called **organic solidarity,** interdependence that is based on a complex division of labor. In a modern society each person earns money from a specialized occupation and then uses that money to buy goods and services that thousands of others have specialized roles in producing. The social bonds this system creates are extremely strong. People are interconnected because differences in their skills and roles make them *need* each other to survive.

Durkheim (1895/1982) argued that the study of society is at a different level from the study of individuals, and that society forms a whole that is greater than the sum of its parts. To clarify these points he used the analogy of a living organism (this is where the term "organic" solidarity came from). Studying a living organism, such as a human being, is different from studying that organism's component parts. A whole person is more than the sum of his or her heart, lungs, brain, liver, blood, bone, and so forth. There are characteristics of the interconnected living system that transcend its collection of parts. Yet we can profitably study the parts and how each is important to the functioning of the whole body.

We can sum up Durkheim's major contributions to sociological thought in terms of his answers to our two basic sociological questions. In answer to the question of what holds society together, Durkheim's perspective was a strongly functional one. He argued that society naturally tends toward a state of functional integration. The whole, in his view, is held together through the interrelated workings of the parts. In answer to the question of the relationship between the individual and society, Durkheim took a predominantly structural perspective. He saw society as external to people, as imposing powerful limits on their behavior, and as resisting people's efforts to bring about social change. Unlike many structural theorists, however, Durkheim and his followers placed a considerable stress on culture, people's ideas and values (Durkheim 1912/1965; Alexander, ed. 1988).

Durkheim's stress on functional integration led him to believe that the origins of a social fact are in some ways less important than the role played by that fact in the social order. For example, Durkheim emphasized the social roles that crime and deviance play. He believed that in small amounts crime and deviance can actually be socially useful. They awaken people to their shared moral bonds and unite them in condemnation of those who violate social rules. High rates of crime and deviance, however, have the opposite effect. They weaken everyone's belief in the rules and lead people to question society's moral authority. In Durkheim's view, rapid social change is one cause of this serious problem. He described a state called **anomie** in which people, as a result of rapid change, lose their bearings in society and their faith in social rules and institutions. We will return to the concept of anomie at other points in this book.

The Theory of Max Weber

Max Weber (1864–1920) was one of the most important German intellectuals of his day. He believed that sociological explanations must derive from an understanding of why people choose the actions they do. This belief differed sharply from Durkheim's view that society and individuals should be studied at different levels. Weber (1904/1949) acknowledged that there are social facts that must be analyzed using scientific methods, but he argued that social facts are the cumulative result of individual actions.

This stress on individual action led Weber to look beyond objective behavior and to focus on people's subjective beliefs, attitudes, values, and motives. According to Weber, sociologists must interpret, not just observe. They must try to see actions from the point of view of the actor. This approach he called **verstehen,**

which in German means empathic understanding. Weber stressed that *verstehen* could be systematic. It did not reduce sociological knowledge simply to a matter of opinion. But explanations, in his view, had to go beyond the objective counting of who in society has which social attributes. Explanations, according to Weber, must consider the subjective thoughts and feelings that lead to particular actions.

Like Marx and Durkheim, Weber wanted to understand the rapid social changes occurring in his time. To Weber the most fundamental trend in the modern era was an increasing *rationalization* of social action and social institutions. More specifically, Weber (1922/1968) saw the history of Western society in terms of a shift from traditional orientations (in which people simply follow in their ancestors' footsteps), to more rational orientations (in which the logical assessment of effects tends to govern behavior) (Roth and Schluchter 1979; Brubaker 1984).

Weber believed that the general trend toward increased rationalization could be seen in many aspects of social life. One was the rise of science as the principal method of acquiring knowledge. By the eighteenth and nineteenth centuries people were increasingly coming to "believe in" science, to consider its rational, systematic methods superior to simple intuition and common sense. Increased rationalization could also be seen in the growth of government bureaucracies, where laws are the basis of authority. Weber believed that bureaucracies were an advance over earlier forms of government in which people either followed informal customs or obeyed the king's commands. Having written rules that were determined by representatives of the people could facilitate orderly change. A third area where the rise of rationalization could be seen was in the development of

Max Weber focused on the interplay of economic, political, and cultural factors in producing the distinctive social organization of the modern West. He stressed that this depended on individuals adopting a more rational and less traditional orientation to social action. (Courtesy of the German Information Center.)

capitalism. Capitalism requires people to analyze markets, maximize the efficiency of production, calculate returns on investment, and create financial institutions to support economic expansion, all things that demand a logical, reasoned approach to the world.

In keeping with his search for explanations in people's subjective beliefs and values, Weber (1904/1958) argued that the ideas of the Protestant Reformation played an important role in fostering capitalism during its early years. Protestantism encouraged saving and investment by teaching that indulgence in luxuries is a sin. It also encouraged hard work ("Idle hands are the devil's workshop") and a drive to become economically successful as proof of God's favor. In these ways religious ideas promoted individual actions that culminated in the emergence of a new kind of economic system. This focus on subjective beliefs and values leading to particular kinds of actions, and actions in turn producing certain broader social patterns, is typical of Weber's approach.

One tool that Weber used to analyze phenomena like the rise of capitalism is a model called an **ideal type.** An ideal type is created to examine the most important characteristics of some social entity or event. It does not necessarily describe what actually exists, nor even what *ought* to be. The ideal type of capitalism, for example, might include lack of government intervention even though there is at least some government involvement in virtually all capitalist systems. Thus, an ideal type is simply an abstraction that allows sociologists to highlight certain features of a phenomenon. Today such models are still employed to analyze many social factors.

In answer to the question of the individual's relationship to society, Weber clearly took an action perspective. He believed that society is produced by the actions of individuals. This action orientation is central to his theory. But Weber also addressed himself to the issue of what holds society together. Like Marx, he believed that people compete for power to determine the nature of social arrangements, including governments. Unlike Marx, however, he argued that people's political groupings and views do not always reflect their economic interests. To Weber, membership in a certain economic class was only one of many social identities on the basis of which people join forces. For instance, an elite group might define its members by *non*economic criteria, such as a proper accent, education at the best schools, having the right friends, or having ancestors who arrived on the *Mayflower*. Such **status groups** tend to predominate at the top of the social hierarchy, where people have an

interest in excluding others from their privileged position. In contrast, class-based groups (an organization of labor unions, for example) tend to be found at the bottom of the social hierarchy, where people find strength in numbers (Parkin 1976). But whatever their basis, social groups in Weber's view compete for power and influence. Like Marx, Weber believed that the exercise of power is fundamental to the social order.

Interactionist Theory

Another founding theory in sociology, interactionism, originated in part from a school of philosophy called **phenomenology,** which developed in Europe at the turn of the twentieth century. Phenomenological sociologists wanted to get away from a one-sided focus on large-scale generalizations about social behavior, such as those made by Marx and Durkheim. Instead, they chose to concentrate on how people subjectively experience and understand the social world, thus constructing their own social reality, a focus somewhat closer to Weber's (Schutz and Luckman 1973). At the same time, phenomenologists wanted to know how different people come to share a common definition of reality. This led to a focus on language, the major means by which humans communicate their thoughts and feelings to each other.

A focus on language and communication was one of the factors that linked phenomenology to an American school of sociology called **symbolic interactionism.** One founder of this school was George Herbert Mead (1863–1931), a philosopher at the University of Chicago who turned to sociology and social psychology in the early twentieth century. Mead believed that through social interaction we come to learn our "places" in the social world. Even a person's identity is a social creation, Mead (1934) asserted. By this he meant that we come to know ourselves largely by seeing how others react to us. For all this social learning to occur communication is essential, and human communication always involves symbols. This is because a person's thoughts and feelings are not directly accessible to others. They must first be encoded into symbols such as words, gestures, facial expressions, and nonlinguistic sounds that others then interpret. This process of symbolic communication is what the term symbolic interaction refers to.

The focus of the **interactionist perspective** is that people address and respond to others depending on how they interpret the social situation. Think about what happens when you approach your instructor after class with a question. You first assess what the instructor is doing in order to determine how best to make your approach. If the instructor is talking to another student you probably interpret this to mean that she is temporarily busy and so remain silent, waiting for a more appropriate time. When you do speak, you monitor your words and actions and your instructor's responses to them. If the instructor smiles and leans slightly toward you, you probably assume she is being encouraging and so you continue confidently. If, however, she frequently glances out the window or at her watch as you speak, you probably read this as signs of impatience and try a different tack. In this way you engage in a back-and-forth exchange of tentative cues and feedback as you go about fashioning your social behavior. The end result is the emergence of a shared understanding of what the situation means. Such shared understandings are essential to social life and of primary concern to interactionists (Blumer 1986).

Comparing the Founding Theories

Our two basic sociological questions provide a valuable framework for comparing sociology's founding theories and summarizing their contributions to social thought. Figure 1.2 shows where the founding theories stand on the questions of what holds society together and how the individual and society are related.

Regarding the first question, Marx and Weber argued that the answer is power. They maintained that competition for power is fundamental in every human society. But whereas Marx saw power as deriving from the structure of the economic system, Weber saw it as deriving from many different factors (education, ancestry, social connections, and so forth, in addition to control over economic resources). And whereas Marx saw power as played out in the relationships between social classes, Weber saw it as played out in contacts between individuals. In sharp contrast to the power perspectives of Marx and Weber, Durkheim took an exclusively functional view. He believed that modern society endures because its various parts play interdepen-

Everyday human interactions were of major interest to George Herbert Mead. He viewed words, gestures, and expressions as symbols of what we think and feel; these symbols constitute the very foundations of social life. (Courtesy of The University of Chicago, Joseph Regenstein Library.)

dent roles. One of the early rational-choice theorists, Adam Smith, also leaned toward a functional outlook. He argued that, barring government intervention, the sum of individual choices motivated by self-interest produces an efficient economic system that benefits society as a whole. Jeremy Bentham, in contrast, saw conflict arising when people and groups pursue their individual goals. He thought that the power of government is needed to ensure the broader social good. Like rational-choice theorists, interactionists also differ in the stress they give to functional integration or power. While some see their perspective as complementing Durkheim's, others emphasize conflict and the exercise of power.

Regarding the question of the individual's relationship to society, the founders of sociology again held a wide range of opinions. Max Weber, for one, took a strong action perspective. To him social arrangements are the product of the actions people choose, which in turn stem from a variety of subjective outlooks and motives. Rational-choice theory, too, follows an action perspective, but an unusual one in that it does not stress individual distinctiveness and creativity. Perhaps the most action-oriented of all the founding theories is interactionism. Its proponents see the entire social world as created out of individual action. At the other extreme of action is the strongly structural perspective of Émile Durkheim. Durkheim explained human behavior in terms of social forces and patterns that exist outside of people, and that often exert a coercive influence on them. Marx also believed in the coercive nature of social forces, but not as absolutely as Durkheim did. Although he saw capitalism as a system that limits available

FIGURE 1.2   Positions Held by the Founding Theories of Sociology

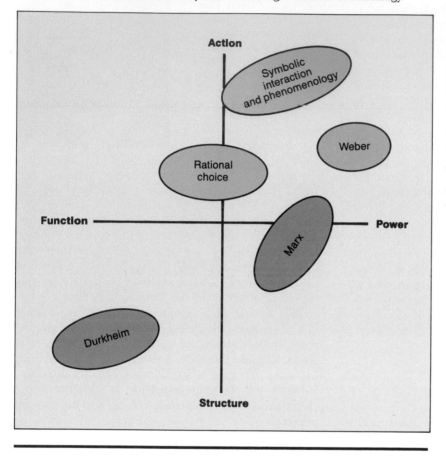

To simplify, we can place the found-ing theories on a grid formed by the dimensions of possible answers to the two basic questions of sociology. The circles indicate that some theorists offer slightly varying answers to the basic questions at different times in their work. Marx, for example, some-times stressed action (class struggle) and sometimes structure (capitalist class structure). When Marx stressed structure, his focus was somewhat less on power. There is a general tendency for more functional approaches to also be more structural, and more power-oriented approaches to also be more action-oriented.

choices, he argued that action on the part of social classes can bring about dramatic social change.

We will continue to use the two basic sociological questions and the answers that have emerged to them as analytical frameworks throughout this book. They have value not just in helping us analyze the founding theories of sociology, but also in understanding and comparing the views of contemporary sociologists on a great variety of issues. Debates over what holds society together and over the individual's relationship to society continue to influence sociological work today, and will undoubtedly continue to be of fundamental importance to sociologists in the future.

FOUNDING THEORIES AND CONTEMPORARY SOCIOLOGY

The five founding theories that we have just described helped to launch sociology as a scientific discipline. Each revealed something important about the nature of society or the process of social interaction. Today, sociologists are still influenced by the ideas of Marx, Durkheim, Weber, rational-choice theory, and inter-actionism. Granted, contemporary sociologists have ex-panded on the original versions of these theories, making them more applicable to modern-day issues. And efforts have been made to combine functional and power perspectives, as well as structural and action-oriented views (Collins 1975; Giddens 1986; Bourdieu 1977). Nevertheless, the core ideas of the founding theories are still relevant today. That is why we will refer to them at many points on the pages that follow.

One thing you will see again and again as you read this book is that the general theoretical perspective a sociologist takes greatly influences the kind of research questions he or she asks. Suppose that different sociologists are looking at the workplace in modern American society. A Marxist might ask how the social class system hinders the rise of minority-group workers to positions of status and power. A follower of Durkheim might ask how solidarity develops as workers who perform specialized tasks become interdependent. A Weberian might ask if the development of a rational, more bureaucratic way of organizing business has contributed to greater efficiency of production. A rational-choice theorist might ask how employers weigh costs and benefits in making choices about whom to hire. And an interactionist might ask how people in a workplace negotiate informal roles (workaholic, "idea" person, mediator, scapegoat) through their interactions with each other.

Thus, choosing what questions to ask about social life is like choosing where to point a camera. It all depends on what you want to highlight in the scene you see. By focusing on certain questions, of course, you may ignore others that might also be valid. That is why

Like photographers, sociologists look at their subjects from many points of view, each portraying the material in a new light. Which of the theoretical approaches described in this chapter do you find helpful or persuasive? (Charles Harbutt/Archive Pictures, Inc.)

many sociologists use a number of different theoretical perspectives depending on the particular issue they are exploring. Each theory looks at the scene from a different angle and together they provide a broader understanding than any one theory could alone.

SUMMARY

1. Sociology, the study of human society and behavior in social settings, invites us to set aside our private view of the world in order to see more clearly and objectively the social forces that shape and control our lives. The sociological perspective allows us to see how such factors as our social background, social position, and the time and place in which we live affect how we view the world, how we act, how we are perceived by others, even who we interact with.

2. Social facts are properties of group life that cannot be explained by reference to the activities, sensibilities, or characteristics of individuals. Instead, social facts emerge in the process of social interaction. Sociologists have revealed that many of our experiences are defined by

society, not by the individual. Sociologists' stress on social facts and how they develop helps to distinguish sociology from other disciplines concerned with human behavior.

3. According to C. Wright Mills, the sociological imagination refers to the ability to view our personal experiences in the context of what is happening in the world around us. Our own experiences, however, are limited, and sociologists are careful not to make generalizations based on common-sense observations and what people assume to be true. When sociologists decide to study a facet of the social world, they begin by collecting data, formulating one or more theories, and then testing these theories in accordance with the principles of the scientif-

ic method. Sociological studies might be on a micro (small-scale) level, in which researchers look at everyday patterns of behavior, or a macro (large-scale) level, in which overall social arrangements are scrutinized.

4. Two basic questions that provide a framework for talking about the social world are: "What holds society together?" and "What is the relationship between the individual and society?" In answering the first question, some sociologists favor a functional perspective (a belief that the different parts of society contribute to the whole); others favor a power perspective (a belief that those who control most of society's resources are likely to shape society to their own advantage). The second question is usually answered from a structural perspective (a belief that individual choices can be explained by forces that arise from the ways in which society is organized) or an action perspective (a belief that society is shaped by the actions of people).

5. Sociology is a relatively young discipline. It emerged during the eighteenth and nineteenth centuries, when a great deal of social change and turmoil raised many questions about the workings of society.

6. Adam Smith was a founder of rational-choice theory, which holds that in making decisions people choose the course of action that is most advantageous to them. Jeremy Bentham expanded this concept; he maintained that government intervention is needed to help society function smoothly and to allow as many people as possible to benefit from society's resources.

7. Karl Marx believed that the economic system of a society shaped all other aspects of social life and bred persistent social conflict. According to Marx, power in the capitalist system is in the hands of the capitalists who dominate the workers. The only way for workers to overcome their oppression was through planned social action and revolution.

8. Émile Durkheim focused on the social forces that bind a society together, a phenomenon he called social solidarity. Mechanical solidarity is based on a strong sharing of values, customs, and beliefs. Organic solidarity is interdependence that is based on a complex division of labor. Durkheim was both extremely functional and structural in outlook. He argued that society was external to people and imposed strong limits on their behavior.

9. Max Weber is important for introducing into sociology an awareness of the subjective nature of social life, and for balancing Marx's emphasis on economic forces with an equal stress on politics and culture. To Weber, the most fundamental trend in the modern era was an increasing rationalization of social action and social institutions. Weber also addressed himself to the question of the individual's relationship to society. He believed that society is produced by the actions of individuals and this action orientation is central to his theory.

10. George Mead and the interactionists, who focused on language and symbolic communication, maintained that people address and respond to others depending on how they interpret the social situation.

11. The theoretical perspective that a sociologist takes strongly affects the types of research questions he or she asks. For this reason, a number of theoretical perspectives are needed to obtain the broadest possible understanding of the social world.

GLOSSARY

Action perspective. A theoretical perspective that holds that society is shaped by the actions of individuals.

Anomie. Social instability and the loss of faith in social rules and institutions as a result of rapid social change.

Capitalists. The members of an industrialized society who own and control the means of production (the land, factories, machinery, and so forth).

Class consciousness. A sense of shared interests and problems among members of a social class.

Data. Facts, statistics, and other bits of observable information from which a deduction is made.

Functional integration. The condition that exists when all aspects of society fit together in a smoothly operating whole.

Functional perspective. A theoretical perspective that emphasizes how each part of a society or social institution contributes to the whole.

General theories. Comprehensive scientific theories that try to explain how a broad range of social factors fit together.

Ideal type. A pure model of a particular social pattern or process that is used as a basis for comparing social arrangements in the real world.

Interactionist perspective. A theoretical perspective that focuses on how people interact in everyday situations and how they make sense of their social relationships.

Local theory. A scientific theory that concentrates on a very specific aspect of social life.

Macrosociology. The large-scale analysis of sociological data derived from studies of the structure and effects of overall sociological arrangements.

Mechanical solidarity. Solidarity that is based on common beliefs, values, and customs.

Microsociology. The small-scale analysis of data derived from studies of everyday behavior patterns and face-to-face interactions.

Middle-range theories. Scientific theories that are more narrow in scope than general theories.

Organic solidarity. Interdependence among a group of people that is based on an intricate division of labor.

Phenomenology. A philosophy that holds that people construct their own social reality in accordance with the ways they experience and understand their social world.

Power perspective. A theoretical perspective that views power as the major factor maintaining and shaping the social order and sees conflict as the natural and inevitable result of the struggle for power among individuals and groups.

Proletariat. The members of an industrialized society who have no control over the means of production—primarily the workers.

Scientific method. The rules, principles, and methods of science that are used for the systematic pursuit of knowledge.

Social facts. Properties of social life that cannot be explained by reference to the activities, sensibilities, or characteristics of individual persons; instead, they emerge in the course of social interaction.

Social solidarity. The condition that results when underlying social forces bind people together.

Social structure. How people, groups, and organizations are arranged with respect to one another.

Sociological imagination. A way of looking at our personal experiences in the context of what is going on in the world around us.

Sociology. The systematic study of human societies and human behavior in social settings.

Status groups. People who predominate at the top of the social hierarchy and who strive to exclude others from their privileged position.

Structural perspective. A theoretical perspective that holds that individual behavior can be explained by social forces that arise from the ways in which society is organized.

Symbolic interactionism. A branch of sociology concerned with the communication between people that occurs by means of symbols—such as words, gestures, facial expressions, and sounds.

Theory. A systematic explanation of how two or more phenomena are related.

Verstehen. Weber's term for an empathic understanding of what people are thinking and feeling.

CHAPTER 2
Methods of Sociological Research

Research in sociology, as in most of the other sciences, begins with a person curious enough to ask *why*. Nearly a century ago, the French sociologist Émile Durkheim became interested in the phenomenon of suicide. *Why*, he asked, do people kill themselves? In his day, as in our own, this question was often answered in individual terms: the suicidal person is depressed or mentally ill or has suffered an unbearable loss. But Durkheim was not satisfied with this explanation. He thought it likely that forces within society influenced people's decisions to commit suicide; from this perspective, the decision to kill oneself was never simply personal.

To find out whether his ideas were correct, Durkheim considered the explanations for suicide that were common in his day and systematically assembled the evidence for each. As his sources, Durkheim used government records that listed numbers of suicides and gave information about the people involved—their age, sex, nationality, religion, marital status, and so on. Upon analyzing this material, Durkheim saw that the usual explanations for suicide were contradicted by the evidence. Suicide rates varied from one time period to another and from one country to another. If suicide were caused merely by personal problems, why was there so much variation? Why was the suicide rate higher in one country than another? If suicide were related to mental illness, Durkheim would have found relatively stable proportions of suicide and mental illness within social groups. But he found just the opposite: some groups

shared high rates of mental illness but little suicide; other groups shared high rates of both. Durkheim also noticed that women were more likely than men to be diagnosed as mentally ill, but less likely to commit suicide. Other contradictory information surfaced: Durkheim discovered that most people committed suicide during warmer, sunnier times of the year, not, as might be expected, during the cold, gloomy days of winter.

Based on the facts and statistics that he collected, Durkheim concluded that suicide, at least in part, depended on social circumstances. As Durkheim wrote in his classic study, *Suicide* (1897/1951, p. 145), suicide is based on "social causes and is itself a collective phenomenon." Characteristics of the *social group* in which people find themselves make suicide more or less likely; self-destruction is not simply a private act.

In analyzing his information, Durkheim looked for the social conditions under which suicide occurred most and least often. He found that Protestants committed suicide three times more often than Catholics and Catholics more often than Jews. Single people committed suicide more often than married people, and married people with children least often of all. Durkheim reasoned that suicide rates are higher when people feel few or weak ties to a social group or community. The Jewish community was more tightly knit than the Catholic, the Catholic more tightly knit than the Protestant. Married people, especially those with children, had stronger social attachments than single people. People with few ties to a community are likely to commit what Durk-

Durkheim proposed that there are three types of suicide, distinguished by the motivations causing them. Top left: The death of Marilyn Monroe, which captured media attention from around the world, is an example of egoistic suicide. Right: The Japanese Kamikaze pilots shown posed here in this photo before a mission, gave up their lives through altruistic suicide. Bottom left: This view of a crowded Wall Street shows the panic during the 1929 Stock Market crash which caused widespread despair and led to cases of anomic suicide. (Top left: Wide World Photos; right: U.S. Navy; bottom left: UPI/Bettmann Newsphotos.)

heim called **egoistic suicide,** or suicide related to social isolation and individualism. At the other extreme are people whose ties to their group are so strong that they commit suicide for the good of the group. Japanese soldiers who sacrificed themselves and Indian widows who threw themselves on the funeral pyres of their dead husbands had committed **altruistic suicide.**

Durkheim also saw that suicides increased when there were sharp economic reversals *or* upturns, and decreased when there was stability. He reasoned that any change that causes people stress—whether economic boom or bust—makes suicides more likely. When times are stable, people feel better integrated into the social fabric and more committed to social norms. When times are stressful and disrupted, the resulting state of **anomie** (social normlessness) leads people to commit **anomic suicide.** Durkheim's analysis of suicide marked the beginning of a revolution in our thinking about social life.

THE RESEARCH PROCESS

In pursuing his study of suicide, Durkheim shaped sociology as an *empirical* science: a discipline with the capacity to analyze data objectively. Durkheim established signposts for a clear **methodology** (the procedures that guide research) and a clearly sociological way of knowing things. His research followed seven "model" steps: defining the problem, reviewing the literature, forming a hypothesis, choosing a research design, collecting data, analyzing the data, and drawing conclusions (see Figure 2.1).

Defining a Problem

The first step in the model research process, defining the problem in a precise way, can be harder than you might think. For example, Durkheim had to define what counted as an act of suicide. If people died because they had miscalculated danger or failed to take precautions, had they committed suicide? Durkheim (1897/1951, p. 44) concluded that *suicide* referred to "all cases of death resulting directly or indirectly from a positive or negative act of the victim himself, which he knows will produce this result." By "positive act," Durkheim meant such things as jumping off a bridge or shooting oneself. By "negative act," he meant such things as not taking necessary medicine or not getting out of the way of a moving vehicle. With this definition, a soldier's sacrifice of his own life to save his comrades counted as a case of (altruistic) suicide, even though many people might not have thought of it in those terms.

In our own time, researchers have argued that many fatal single-car accidents that take place on clear roads with good visibility are really disguised (perhaps even unconscious) forms of suicide (Phillips 1974). How researchers define the behavior under study shapes the outcome of their research. If two researchers use different definitions of the same behavior, they may reach very different conclusions even though the information in both studies is accurate. When sociologists use such abstract concepts as suicide or social integration, they must define the idea in measurable terms. This procedure gives them an **operational definition.** In the operational definition of social integration, for example, Durkheim included marriage (having family ties) and being Catholic (having religious ties).

Not only must researchers define their object of study, they must also choose where to start looking for possible explanations of the defined behavior. As we noted in Chapter 1, Durkheim formulated a functional theory that the cement of society is a sense of social solidarity that derives from shared beliefs, rituals, and laws. Influenced by his theory, Durkheim wished to determine whether the lack of social bonds influences such seemingly individual acts as suicide. Sociologists since Durkheim might also look for explanations—of

FIGURE 2.1 Steps in the "Model" Research Process

1. **DEFINING THE PROBLEM**

Selecting a topic for research and defining key concepts

2. **REVIEWING THE LITERATURE**

Familiarizing oneself with the existing theory and research on a topic

3. **FORMING A HYPOTHESIS**

Defining the relationship between measurable variables so that they can be measured and the hypothesis tested

4. **CHOOSING A RESEARCH DESIGN**

Selecting a method for study: experiment, survey, field observation, or a historical approach

5. **COLLECTING THE DATA**

Collecting the information that will test the hypothesis

6. **ANALYZING THE DATA**

Working with and examining the data to shed light on the hypothesis

7. **DRAWING CONCLUSIONS**

Summarizing the outcome of the study, indicating its significance, relating the findings to existing theory and research, and identifying problems for future research suicide or any other event—in terms of the extent of people's integration into society. Thus, choosing a theoretical perspective from which to begin research is like choosing where to point a camera; it selects one particular vantage point from among the many available.

Reviewing the Literature

Sociologists decide what questions to ask in their studies largely on the basis of a *review of the literature* in the field. Good researchers look to see what is already known about the subject that they want to study. Durkheim, for example, reviewed the existing literature on the link between suicide and suggestion—that is, on the question of whether people committed suicide in imitation of others—and rejected the idea (Phillips 1974). In turn, David Phillips, a present-day sociologist, reviewed Durkheim's conclusion about imitation and decided to investigate it further. In the end, his findings differed from Durkheim's. Researchers check to see what is known about the questions they are investigating to avoid duplication of effort, to help settle conflicts and disputes within the field, and to focus as precisely as possible on the relationships among the factors being studied.

Forming a Hypothesis

Durkheim did not just set out to study suicide in general. He began by forming a **hypothesis,** a tentative statement that predicts how two or more variables affect, or are related to, one another. The term **variable** is applied to any factor that can change over time or differ in various cases. In sociology, variables usually consist of some attitude, behavior pattern, or condition. Durkheim developed several hypotheses, but his major hypothesis was that suicide varies inversely with the degree to which a person is integrated within the social life of society. He then had to specify which variables he would consider. In Durkheim's main hypothesis, the two variables were: (1) the degree to which a person is integrated into the social group, and (2) the suicide rate.

Sociologists define problems in terms of clusters of variables that they think might be related. Durkheim hypothesized that people's degree of integration into

Struck by a new phenomenon, researchers form hypotheses to determine the cause. For example, in the summer of 1987, professional baseball players hit an unusually high number of home runs. Various theories developed to explain this, attributing the change to weather conditions, differences in the balls, player nutrition and training, and so on. Not surprisingly, testing these theories and determining the cause is a subject of great interest to the teams and their fans. (George Mars Cassidy/The Picture Cube.)

social life—being married, having children, having religious ties, and the like—might be related to their likelihood of committing suicide. Many years later, David Phillips (1974) hypothesized that imitations of suicide might be related to the amount of publicity surrounding notable people's suicides. In most investigations, one or more variables are the objects of research (in Durkheim's investigation, it was suicide rates) and other variables are the possible explanations (for Durkheim, the degree of social integration). Which variables researchers examine is largely determined by what hypothesis they want to test.

Choosing a Research Design and Gathering Data

To test their hypotheses, researchers need facts, statistics, study results, and other pertinent material. The first step in gathering these bits of observable information—called data—is to decide how to look for them. This entails choosing a research design, which is the actual plan for the collection and analysis of data. Some researchers conduct surveys and ask questions of many different people. Some choose participant observation; the investigators live and work among the people being studied to learn firsthand how they think and behave. Some researchers conduct experiments, that is, they create an artificial situation in which they can observe how people respond to different stimuli. Still other researchers use historical records to gather data. For many problems, the best approach involves a combination of several research strategies: surveys plus observation plus document searches. Researchers can also draw on the results of previous research to supplement the new data that they collect. We discuss all these specific data-gathering methods in the concluding section on research methods.

Whatever research design is used, the researchers' crucial task is to gather enough information on which to base a sound understanding of the problem and to test their hypothesis. Although this may sound simple and straightforward, it can often be very difficult. Not only can a researcher encounter problems in collecting data, but a given set of data can often be interpreted in several different ways. Durkheim, for example, chose to rely on official government records that listed causes of death. But this meant that he had to accept the interpretations that government officials, physicians, and family members gave of why a person died. Because people generally base their observations about society on their interpretations of what others do, a researcher must take care to evaluate "the facts" with as much objectivity as possible.

Analyzing the Data and Drawing Conclusions

Once sociologists have collected their data, the next step is to analyze this information. Analysis is the process of looking to see which parts go together to form a pattern or whole, and how these pieces of information are related. In a sense, analysis begins with defining the research problem, for there the sociologist decides just what factors to study and how to measure them.

In analyzing his data Durkheim looked for the social conditions under which suicide occurred most and those under which it occurred least often. He found that more Protestants than Catholics and more Catholics

than Jews committed suicide. Single people committed suicide more often than married people, and married people with children least of all. Durkheim also discovered that suicide rates rose during periods of sharp economic reversals (inflations or depressions) but fell during periods of political instability. Had he undertaken his research today, Durkheim would have found computers to be of immeasurable assistance in analyzing his data and using the many sophisticated statistical procedures now available. The box on p. 32 discusses some simple but important statistical measures.

The final step in the research process is to draw conclusions based on the results of analysis. Depending on what patterns have emerged, and how these patterns are interpreted, the hypothesis may be confirmed, rejected, or left unsettled. Durkheim's analysis confirmed his hypothesis that suicide rates rise when people's attachments to significant groups are weakened and fall when they are strengthened. The stronger the ties people have to social groups, the more they depend on these groups and the more likely they are to take other people into account when making decisions. People who have few ties to their community are more likely to take their own lives than people who are deeply involved with their community.

The research process allows sociologists to evaluate one another's conclusions independently. Thus conclusions are not regarded as final, but are always open to question and reinvestigation. When research makes a significant contribution to sociological knowledge, it is usually published and made available for use by other sociologists.

Subsequent Research

Sociological knowledge grows when theory spurs research and research in turn generates new theories that produce more research, and so on. As we have seen, a contemporary sociologist, David Phillips, took one of Durkheim's conclusions—that imitation plays no significant part in the decision to commit suicide—as the starting point for his own research. For many years, sociologists accepted Durkheim's finding. But in 1974, Phillips concluded the opposite—that publicized sui-

Basic Statistical Concepts

To analyze statistics derived from research projects and experiments, sociologists use a number of measures. The most basic of these measures are averages and correlations.

Averages. Researchers distinguish three kinds of central tendencies, or averages, in the data that they collect.

The **mode** is the figure that occurs most often in a set of data. For example, a researcher studies seven families and finds their yearly incomes are:

$3,000
$3,000
$7,500
$9,000
$11,000
$15,000
$90,000

In this group, the modal income is $3,000 a year. The mode provides no information about the range of the data but is useful for discerning which statistic appears most frequently.

The **mean,** commonly referred to as the "average," is found by adding all the figures in a set of data and then dividing the sum by the number of items. The mean income of the seven families is $19,786 ($138,500/7). The mean is useful because it reflects all the available data, but it can be misleading: the $90,000 income of one of the families obscures the fact that the other six families all have incomes of $15,000 a year or less. The mean is most helpful when the range of data does not include extremes.

The **median** is the number that falls in the middle of a sequence of data. For the seven families here, the median income is $9,000. Unlike the mean, this measure doesn't allow extremes to mask the central tendency. Researchers often calculate both the mean and the median to present an accurate impression of their findings.

Sociologists may also want to find out to what extent a statistic varies from the mean (or another central point). Variation from the mean is measured by units of **standard deviation.** When taking this measurement, investigators calculate how far other recorded instances fall from the mean and then express whether each instance falls into the group closest to the mean, second closest to the mean, and so forth. The findings might be expressed as something like, "Most of the families in the study are within one standard deviation of the mean."

Correlation coefficients. A correlation, as discussed in the text, refers to a regular relationship between two variables. The strength of a correlation is usually expressed as a **correlation coefficient,** a decimal number between zero and one. When there is no correlation between variables (that is, the two have no relationship to each other), the correlation coefficient is zero. When two variables are found together all the time, there is a perfect positive correlation, expressed as $+1.0$. When two variables are inversely related (that is, the presence of one is always associated with the absence of the other), there is a perfect negative correlation. This is expressed as -1.0. Usually, in the real world, researchers do not find perfect correlations. They usually find less extreme examples of association between variables.

The most common questions in analysis concern whether two variables that are correlated have any *causal* connection to one another. It is always possible that a correlation is coincidental or the result of some third variable that is influencing the other two. Correlations therefore have to be checked for a possible independent cause. This is one way of checking validity (sometimes called statistical independence).

cides do spawn imitations—after he examined patterns of suicide following the widely publicized suicide in November 1965 of Daniel Burros, a leader of the Ku Klux Klan, a violently anti-Semitic organization. Burros killed himself after a newspaper reporter revealed that he was Jewish. Phillips (1974) found that suicides increased significantly after the press made Burros' suicide front-page news.

The question that Phillips raised was whether suicides spawned imitation, and his research led to his hypothesis that, in fact, they did. To test this hypothesis, Phillips charted the amount of front-page press coverage that a suicide received, then he compared the number of expected suicides during the following month with the actual number of suicides. He found a direct correlation between a highly publicized suicide and an increase in the suicide rate. But he wasn't finished yet. He had to test alternative hypotheses.

Perhaps all the publicity merely prompted people who were already considering suicide to take their own lives. Perhaps people who were already so bereaved or depressed as to be virtually certain to kill themselves responded to the publicity by going ahead with the act (Phillips and Carstensen 1986). If so, Phillips expected to find first a peak in suicides after the publicity and then an abnormal drop. But he found no such drop. Another hypothesis was that perhaps coroners became suggestible after so much publicity about suicide and classified more deaths as suicides and fewer as homicides or accidents. If so, Phillips expected to find a proportionate decrease in the rates of other causes of death. He didn't find that either. Maybe, then, the increase in suicides had to do with other conditions. If so, the suicides should not peak just after a front-page story, and the amount of publicity should not correlate with the increase in suicides. But the suicides did peak, and the variables did correlate. Finally, perhaps the increase was caused not by imitation but by grief. Phillips selected a sample of widely admired people whose suicides should have generated an unusual amount of grief, but he found that the suicide rate was no more affected by the stories of these deaths than it was affected by the suicides of less well-known people. (The "How to Read a Table" box includes two tables from Phillips' research.)

Phillips kept up his systematic investigation of patterns of imitation. He found that the rates of fatal motor-vehicle accidents also rise after publicized suicides (Phillips 1986). He found imitation after widely publicized stories of robberies and assaults; even heavyweight championship boxing matches were followed by a rise in murders, with victims looking more like the loser of the prizefight than one would statistically expect.

In trying to measure how violence reported in the mass media affects violence in the real world, Phillips (1986) was conducting a found experiment. Rather than investigate subjects directly, researchers who do **found experiments** generally rely on data that has already been collected, often by government agencies. Phillips concluded that three types of publicity trigger imitation: stories about suicide, murder-suicide, and championship boxing matches and prizefights. His conclusions also suggest new questions for future research: What other types of deviant behavior does publicity trigger? Does publicity trigger prosocial as well as antisocial behavior?

Thus, from Durkheim one line of systematic investigation has extended to contemporary sociologists, and from the social researchers of today new questions extend into the future.

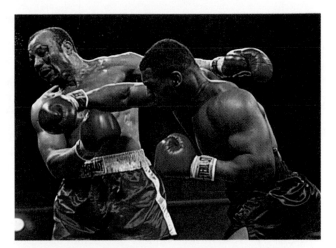

An increase in murder rates following championship boxing matches was one of the statistics found by David Phillips to support his theory of patterns of imitative behavior. (The Associated Press/AP Photo-Color.)

DIFFICULTIES IN SOCIOLOGICAL RESEARCH

Social scientists are concerned with digging for information about some observable phenomenon involving people, and interpreting the data in such a way that the findings can be tested by others and achieve widespread acceptance. However, sociology presents the would-be scientist with some formidable research problems, simply because it is necessary to deal with people.

Durkheim's study of suicide highlights some of the problems that sociologists confront when studying social behavior. Like any other scientific study, Durkheim's research must be assessed in terms of its validity and reliability. **Validity** is the degree to which a scientific study measures what it is attempting to measure—for example, the degree to which the suicide rates of different social groups measure their different levels of anomie. **Reliability** is the degree to which a study yields the same results when repeated by the original researcher or by other scientists.

Subsequent studies of suicide rates have shown Durkheim's results to be reliable, but critics have questioned whether Durkheim's data were valid (Pescolodi and Mendelsohn 1968). Might the data have been distorted? Perhaps Catholics appear to have fewer suicides than Protestants because they disguise and cover up

How to Read a Table

Social scientists frequently choose to depict their research findings in tables. These tables, which often appear in journal articles, textbooks, newspapers, and magazines, provide an overview of information and express relationships between variables. As popular as tables are, however, they raise a number of questions: How valid is the information in tables? Can tables be used to draw conclusions? What should one look for when interpreting a table? The following steps for interpreting Table 2.1 are general guides that can be applied to any table or chart.

1. Read the table title to find out what data are in the table and how this information is presented. In Table 2.1, the data are presented as numbers, but in other tables the data may appear as percentages or as some other measurement.

TABLE 2.1   Rise in the Number of Suicides after Stories on the Front Page of the *New York Times*

Name of publicized suicide	Date of suicide story	Observed no. of suicides in month after suicide story	Expected no. of suicides in month after suicide story	Rise in suicides after suicide story (observed minus expected no. of suicides)
Lockridge, author	March 8, 1948	1510	1521.5	−11.5
Landis, film star	July 6, 1948	1482	1457.5	24.5
Brooks, financier	August 28, 1948	1250	1350	−100.0
Holt, betrayed husband	March 10, 1948	1583	1521.5	61.5
Forrestal, ex-Secretary of Defense	May 22, 1949	1549	1493.5	55.5
Baker, professor	April 26, 1950	1600	1493.5	106.5
Lang, police witness	April 20, 1951	1423	1519.5	−96.5
Monroe, film star	August 6, 1962	1838	1640.5	197.5
Graham, publisher, and Ward, implicated in Profumo affair	August 4, 1963	1801	1640.5	160.5
Burros, Ku Klux Klan leader Morrison, war critic	November 1, 1965 November 3, 1965	1710	1652	58.0

Source: From Phillips (1974, p. 344). Original souce of suicide statistics: U.S. Department of Health, Education, and Welfare, Public Health Service (yearly volumes, 1947–1968).

their suicides better. A good case could be made for the hypothesis that the better integrated a person is within society, the less likely it is that his or her death will be *classified* as a suicide. For example, officials in a close-knit community might respect a family's wish to avoid embarrassment and record the suicide as a death resulting from natural causes. Or the officials might not suspect suicide because the individual was deemed a leading citizen of the community (Douglas 1967). Such concerns undermine Durkheim's argument.

Another difficult task that researchers must confront is specifying the relationship between variables. Ideally, sociologists are most interested in specifying cause-and-effect relationships, or relationships in which a change

2. To assess the quality of the data, look for headnotes and footnotes that may explain how the data were collected, why certain variables were studied, and whether data were collected differently for certain variables. The source of the data, usually given at the bottom of a table or chart, is another potential measure of quality. The sources for Table 2.1 are: (1) sociologist David Phillips' published article, "The Influence of Suggestion on Suicide," and (2) suicide statistics published by the federal government. If the source had been a group with a vested interest in the subject, such as a suicide prevention agency, you might suspect bias.

3. Read the labels for each column (i.e., up and down) and row (i.e., across) to learn exactly what data appear in the table. Table 2.1, which depicts the rise in suicides after stories of suicides appeared in the *New York Times*, lists the names of well-known people who committed suicide, the date that the story appeared in the newspaper, the numbers of expected suicides and actual suicides in the month following a publicized suicide, and whether the suicide rate was higher or lower than expected.

TABLE 2.2 Rise in the Number of Suicides after Stories on the Front Page of the *New York Daily News*

	Number of days on page 1 of the *News*[a]				
	0	1	2	3	4
Average rise in the United States suicides after each suicide story[b]	25.26	28.54	35.25	82.63	197.5

Source: From Phillips (1974, p. 345) with permission. Original source of suicide statistics: U.S. Department of Health, Education, and Welfare, Public Health Service (yearly volumes, 1947–1968).

[a]The suicide stories carried in the *New York Times* and listed in Table 2.1 fall into the following categories: 0 days—Lockridge, Baker, Lang, Graham, Morrison; 1 day—Landis, Brooks, Forrestal, Burros; 2 days—Holt; 3 days—Ward; 4 days—Monroe.

[b]Ward and Graham died on the same day, August 4, 1963. Half the rise in suicides in August 1963, has been credited to Ward, and half to Graham. A similar procedure has been followed for Burros and Morrison, who died on November 1 and November 3, 1965.

4. Look at the patterns in the data. Note that some publicized suicides were followed by rises in the overall suicide rate, while some were not. The suicide of the film star Marilyn Monroe, for example, led to almost 200 more suicides than expected the following month.

5. Draw conclusions about the information in the table, and consider what other questions the data raise. Do suicides in fact increase after highly publicized stories of suicides? Is there some imitative effect, contrary to what Durkheim concluded? If so, does the *amount* of publicity have further influence? In other words, if a suicide is publicized for more than one day, is there a correspondingly greater increase in imitative suicides? David Phillips checked this question, and the data he found appear in Table 2.2.

in one variable is caused by a change in another. (A familiar example of cause-and-effect in the natural world is the relationship between the moon and the tides.)

In many cases, however, sociologists may not be able to determine a causal relationship between variables. They may only be able to show that two variables change together—are *correlated*—in some measurable way. A **correlation** refers to a regular relationship between two variables. For example, a correlation would tell how often a high value of one variable (say the divorce rate) is found together with a high value of another variable (say the suicide rate). As previously noted, Durkheim did not have the sophisticated statistical techniques now available to measure correlation.

The task of the sciences—from physics to sociology—is to trace the causes of events as influence of variables upon one another. (Mark Godfrey/Archive Pictures, Inc.)

However, he was able to demonstrate that suicide rates vary with membership in different religious groups and with other social conditions.

The discovery of a correlation between variables, however, does not prove that they have a cause-and-effect relationship. Two variables may be correlated but have no casual link to one another. This is known as a **spurious correlation,** and it is a source of error in research. A crucial part of sociological analysis is distinguishing meaningful from spurious correlations. For example, someone might ask whether the relationship that Durkheim found between suicide rates and religious affiliation had a causal basis or if the connection was a spurious one. Perhaps both variables are the result of some third factor, such as differences in wealth or geographic region. Durkheim was aware that some third cause might explain his findings, and he tried to establish that this was not the case.

Related to the difficulties of determining causal relationships is the fact that people, unlike many objects of study in the natural sciences, are not reducible to simple cause-and-effect equations. A meteorologist knows that when air pressure and air temperature mix in a particular way, it will rain. But the social scientist who attempts to predict the effect of a factory's closing on a nearby community's suicide rate has to sort out the many conflicting emotions and motivations of the people who live and work there.

Further, social variables may not remain constant over time or from place to place. The law of gravity and the composition of water are the same everywhere, the same today as they were yesterday. But no two families, for example, are exactly alike, and ideas about what the family should be vary enormously from one culture to another. In the words of Swedish social scientist Gunnar Myrdal:

> The really important difference between [social scientists] and our natural science colleagues is that we never reach down to constants—like the speed of light or sound in a particular medium, or the specific weights of atoms or molecules. We have nothing that corresponds to the universally valid measurements of energy, voltage, ampere, etc. The regularities we find do not have the firm general validity of "laws of nature." (1973)

As we will see later in the chapter, there are limits to how far a scientist can experiment with human beings as subjects. People must be treated with dignity and respect. For example, a sociologist cannot deliberately stage a factory's closing or an accident at a nuclear power plant to determine the effect on the community.

Finally, objectivity is a major problem for all social scientists. It is difficult to study race relations or a nuclear arms race without some emotional involvement. The astronomer who studies the stars and the botanist who experiments with plants are likely to be more objective in their respective fields.

All this suggests that sociologists do not simply assume that social facts "speak for themselves." Instead, as you saw in Chapter 1, sociologists try to interpret these facts, thereby developing the most systematic and precise understanding of society and social issues that they can. This process requires the formulation of theories, which are then tested with empirical research. Indeed, facts and theories are inseparable. Without a theory we lack a framework for understanding facts. By the same token, without facts our theories are simply unproven speculations.

The methods of research allow us to arrive at facts that confirm or disprove our theories. Let us turn, therefore, to a consideration of the interplay between method and theory.

THE INTERPLAY OF METHOD AND THEORY IN SOCIOLOGY

Methods in science are not just tools lying around on the workbench, any one of which may be picked up by the researcher. The methods that researchers use to investigate a problem need to be appropriate to the theories that guide them. In science, a theory is an explanation of something. For instance, Durkheim based his research dealing with suicide on a theory that may be summarized as follows: Society is not simply a collection of people; it has an existence of its own and influences how people think and act. In other words, a person is a product of the groups to which he or she belongs. He felt his findings supported this view because it could explain variations in suicide rates.

Durkheim took a functional approach to suicide (see Chapter 1). To see how methods and theory work together, let us consider an alternative perspective regarding suicide—that associated with George Herbert Mead and symbolic interactionism. Interactionists fault Durkheim for "imposing" his interpretation on the data he analyzed. They say that Durkheim assumed that no matter which groups were being compared, the meaning of suicide was obvious: It reflected a lack of integration into society and it violated norms. Because Durkheim was influenced by this theory, his methods did not allow

for exploring the possibility that suicide has different meanings for different people. A symbolic interactionist, by contrast, would look closely at how each death occurred and what it *meant* to those involved. This perspective would complement but not replace Durkheim's approach to the subject.

Interactionists would begin with the suicides themselves. The question of why people commit suicide must be answered by a study of what suicide means to the victims and to those immediately involved. Take the example of a man who is known to feel trapped by his suburban and business life. While on vacation in the Bahamas he swims out too far and drowns, even though he was considered a strong swimmer. Did he intentionally swim out too far? Was this a suicide or an accident? A look at his life and personal relationships might enable us to answer these questions in terms of the man's own perceptions and definitions.

Interactionists examine the meanings embedded in the situation (*situated meanings*) and hence are less concerned than functionally oriented theorists with generalized data. Instead of imposing a meaning on statistical data, interactionists analyze real-world events to *draw out* their meanings. Only then can they discern patterns and work up to abstract conceptions and theory.

It is clear that this theoretical perspective calls for a methodology different from the one Durkheim chose. Interactionists would consider official statistics on suicide to be too removed from the event and too filtered of content to be of use in determining why people commit suicide. Instead, interactionists would get down to the details of cases, gradually building up comparative information across social situations. They would analyze such documents as a suicide note and coroner's report, interview people close to the suicide victim, and observe the social context in which the person lived. Interactionists would also assess the impact of a suicide on others. A person who commits suicide often uses the act as a way of communicating a message to someone else in a forceful, dramatic fashion.

Both of these theoretical positions have merit, but in different ways. Their basic claims are not at odds. Suicide occurs when people's social bonds weaken, *and* suicide is an event having symbolic meaning.

At the same time, each points to a potential weakness in the other. The symbolic interactionist approach raises doubts about the categorizations used in Durkheim's study. Conversely, a follower of Durkheim might point out how hard it would be to develop large-scale, statistically tested generalizations by way of the symbolic interactionist approach. Ideally the two approaches—and others—are complementary.

In sum, one's theoretical perspective influences but does not determine how one goes about doing research. Because Durkheim was seeking to explain differences in group rates of suicide, he analyzed large-scale data. Another investigator, more interested in examining how people construct a social reality around unnatural deaths, might instead carry out detailed interviews of the survivors to see why some deaths are labeled "suicides" and others "accidents." Some researchers use only statistical studies or other large-scale data, and others use only interviews, though this need not be so. In all cases sociological theory affects what questions are asked, and those questions in turn dictate what methods will be most effective in obtaining answers. In the section that follows, we will look more closely at the various methods available to researchers.

RESEARCH METHODS

Durkheim's analysis of suicide set sociologists on the course of systematically explaining events by establishing cause and effect relationships. No matter what the event being examined—a suicide, a race riot, an earthquake —scientists believe that some order, constancy, or regularity underlies it. Consequently, under the same set of circumstances, a given action will consistently produce the same effect. Social scientists have at their disposal a number of methods for determining cause-and-effect relationships.

Surveys

Sociologists use surveys to measure public opinion, to test assumptions about behavior, and to predict how people will act. **Surveys** are the systematic gathering of answers to standardized questions from a designated sample of respondents. Respondents may be asked to answer questionnaires by mail, over the phone, or in face-to-face interviews. Surveys are especially useful when sociologists want information about events that they cannot measure directly. For example, sociologists may want to know how many people in the United States believe that elective abortion should be illegal. Most people will never be in a position to act on such a belief, but public opinion is often consequential in bringing about political and legal change.

Surveys are common in the United States; their results turn up often on the nightly news and in popular magazines. Sociological surveys, however, involve much more than simply asking people a few questions. If the results are to be reliable and valid, sociologists have to be systematic in choosing *whom* to question and *how* to ask the questions.

Choosing a Sample

Most surveys are designed to collect information from a small number of people that can be used to make generalizations about the attitudes, behavior, or other characteristics of a much larger population. The **population** of any survey is simply the total number of people who share a characteristic that the sociologist is interested in studying. Say that a team of sociologists is interested in comparing attitudes toward abortion between younger (defined as aged twenty to thirty) and older (defined as aged fifty to sixty) American women. The survey population in this case would be all the women living in the United States between the ages of twenty and thirty, and between fifty and sixty.

Because it is usually too costly and time consuming to interview everyone in a population, sociologists canvass a **sample**—a limited but representative subset of the population being studied. The sociologists studying abortion, for example, might choose a representative sample of American women from the two age groups. If the characteristics of the sample match those of the population as a whole, then the responses of the people in the sample give a good idea of the distribution of attitudes among the population as a whole.

Many people think that a large sample gives more accurate results than a smaller one, but that is not always so. Perhaps the most famous counterexample was an attempt to predict the outcome of the 1936 presidential election. A popular magazine, *Literary Digest*, sent postcard ballots to ten million people whose names were collected from telephone directories and car registrations. From the two million postcards returned, the magazine predicted that Alfred Landon would beat Franklin D. Roosevelt by a landslide. Meanwhile, a young man named George Gallup sampled a mere 312,551 people and correctly predicted that Roosevelt would win. In this case, the smaller sample was more representative of the population at large. For one thing, in 1936, deep in the Great Depression, many voters did *not* own cars or telephones. These people—most of whom voted for Roosevelt—were excluded from the *Literary Digest* sample. Gallup used a **random sample,** in which everyone within the population had an equal chance of being selected. In sophisticated sociological surveys, each member of a population is assigned a number, and then a sample is drawn by using a table of random numbers. Sociologists may choose every tenth person in the population, or every hundredth person, depending on the size of the sample that they want to use. Random samples do not exclude, for example, all potential voters without cars or telephones.

Designing a representative sample is a real challenge. If you wanted to survey the students at your school to find out their career plans (or their views on suicide or abortion or presidential candidates), you would be making a mistake if you arbitrarily polled the first hundred students to walk out of a campus building. What about the possibly large number of students who never use that building? You would have a more genuinely representative sample if you randomly chose 100 names from the complete roster of students at your school.

Interviewing is a research technique widely used by sociologists to gather data. Because of the human element involved, however, great care must be taken to avoid biasing the outcome of the research. (Peter Simon/Stock, Boston.)

Constructing and Asking Questions

The very wording and sequence of the questions that sociologists ask in interviews or on questionnaires affect the validity and reliability of the data that they get (Schuman and Presser 1981).

Wording.   The choice of words in survey questions can and does affect the results of the research. At first glance, for instance, it would seem that questions with the words "forbid speeches" and "allow speeches" would be logical opposites. But apparently the connotations of the words are different. In 1976, some respondents were asked, "Do you think the United States should forbid public speeches against democracy?" Others were asked, "Do you think the United States should allow public speeches against democracy?" The responses did not dovetail: 21.4 percent said that they would "forbid" the speeches, but 47.8 percent said that they would not "allow" the speeches (Schuman and Presser 1981).

Sequence.   The order in which sociologists ask questions can affect the pattern of responses. Issues raised in earlier questions can affect how respondents think about later questions. Sometimes sociologists get different results just by reversing the order of two questions. For example, people were asked the following two questions: (a) "Do you think the United States should let newspaper reporters from Communist countries come here and send back to their papers the news as they see it?" and (b) "Do you think a Communist country like Russia should let American newspaper reporters come there and send back to America the news as they see it?" When people were asked question *a* first, 54.7 percent said yes to it. But when people were asked question *b* first, 74.6 percent said yes to question *a* (Schuman and Presser 1981).

Form of Response.   On surveys, people can answer questions in one of two forms. In a **closed response** question, respondents must choose from the set of answers provided by the researchers. In an **open response** question, respondents answer in their own words. For example, sociologists might want to know what people most prefer in a job. They can ask this in a closed form: "Would you please look at this card and tell me which thing on this list you would most prefer in a job?" The card then lists five choices: high income, no danger of being fired, short working hours, chances for advancement, and satisfying work that gives a feeling of accomplishment. The question can also be asked in an open form: "People look for different things in a job. What would you most prefer in a job?" When people were actually asked these questions, the answers differed with the form of presentation. For example, 17.2 percent of the respondents chose "chances for advancement" when they saw it among the responses. But only 1.8 percent volunteered this answer when they were asked the question in an open form. Sociologists have to be aware that the wording, sequence, and form of survey questions affect research results.

Interviewing

For some kinds of research, sociologists need more information than a short questionnaire allows. Then they may resort to interviewing by phone or in person. If they use open response questions, interviewers can tell when to probe for more information and when to move to the next question. Good interviewers also know that the validity and reliability of interviews depend on the

interaction between interviewer and respondent. They learn to tailor the tone or the pace of an interview to different kinds of respondents.

The sociologist Harriet Zuckerman was interested in investigating the careers of scientists who had won a Nobel Prize. She wanted to interview this ultra-elite about their family histories, education, relationships with other scientists, organizational affiliations, and the changes in their lives since winning the Nobel Prize (Zuckerman 1972). First she had to make contact with the Nobel recipients and persuade them to talk with her. This can be one of the most difficult and time-consuming stages of a study. Not everyone—especially not a busy scientist—is eager to spend an hour or two with an inquisitive sociologist. Zuckerman, however, was quite successful in making contact: she managed to interview forty-four of the fifty-five Nobel laureates living in the United States in 1963. She suggests that she overcame some resistance by presenting her professional credentials, by clearly stating the purpose of the interview, by mentioning the names of other Nobel laureates who had agreed to participate, and by persevering. She prepared thoroughly for each interview, not only constructing in advance the set of questions that she would ask, but also researching the background of each scientist. She made sure to establish rapport during the interview—avoiding sensitive topics, using scientific language, and framing questions to establish continuity within the interview ("You said earlier that . . .").

These talks with Nobel laureates were **semi-structured interviews**—that is, the general and specific issues to be covered were worked out in advance but the subjects were free to talk about each topic in the terms most meaningful to them. In contrast, **structured interviews** are ones in which the wording and sequence of questions are carefully planned in advance. In an **unstructured interview**, the questions and topics are not predetermined and the interviewer and the subject engage in free-flowing conversation.

Experiments

The **experiment** offers scientists the most effective technique for establishing a cause-and-effect relationship. In experiments, social scientists can test a hypothesis—that

Philip Zimbardo, a social psychologist, set up a mock prison in which students played the roles of prisoners and guards. The results were frightening: guards took their "jobs" so seriously that they threatened prisoners' well-being. Zimbardo's experiment shows how the roles that we play deeply influence our social behavior. (Professor Philip G. Zimbardo/Stanford University.)

one variable (X) causally influences another variable (Y). For instance, sociologists may wish to test the hypothesis that people who undergo a severe initiation to gain admission to a group (variable X) develop a strong attachment to the group (variable Y) (Aronson and Mills 1959; Aronson and Carlsmith 1968). In choosing to perform an experiment to test their hypothesis, the sociologists are thinking about the problem in these terms: If you change one variable (X) and another variable (Y) also changes, and if all the other factors have been held constant (controlled) the change in Y must have been caused by the change in X.

Thus, in order to test a hypothesis, researchers: (1) systematically manipulate one variable (X), and (2) observe the effect of the manipulation on the other variable (Y). The factor that is systematically varied is termed the **independent variable;** it is assumed to be the causal factor in the relationship being studied. The factor being studied is termed the **dependent variable;** it is the factor that is affected by the manipulation of the independent variable. In our illustration, the initiation condition would be the independent variable and the intensity of the subjects' attachment to the group would be the dependent variable.

Sociologists rely on two kinds of experiments —laboratory and field.

Laboratory Experiments

In laboratory experiments, sociologists bring subjects into artificial conditions that can be regulated carefully by the investigator. That is, the person doing the research can control for the effects of some factors while isolating the factor or factors that are of experimental importance. For example, social psychologist Bibb Latané and his associates (1979) studied the behavior called "social loafing" under laboratory conditions. Social loafing is the tendency for people to work less hard when they are in a group than when they are not. It is a concept with social significance: for instance, the researchers wondered whether it might be related to the relatively low productivity of American factory workers.

First, Latané and his associates brought volunteers into the laboratory, where they were asked to cheer and clap (the task) alone and in groups of two, four, and six people. When the researchers measured the sound of the cheering and clapping, they found that the amount of sound from each person diminished as the size of the group increased. The experiment showed that an increase in group size (the independent variable) *caused* people to participate less in the task (the dependent variable). In other words, the larger the group, the more the social loafing.

To get the data about social loafing, however, the researchers had to deceive the volunteers. The researchers said that the purpose of the experiment was to see how well people in crowds could judge sound levels. Had the volunteers been told that this was a study of social loafing, they might have acted in ways that would have invalidated the results of the experiment.

This kind of "deceptive methodology" has been common in laboratory social experiments. But in the last few decades the issue of protecting people from harm in research has raised new and sometimes disturbing questions. Do researchers have the right to deceive people or cause them anxiety or humiliation in the name of scientific inquiry? In response to these concerns, the federal government has tightened regulations on human research, and universities have set up review boards to approve experiments involving people. Current guidelines for this type of research are clear: explain the experiment or procedure to the subject; do not lie; warn the subject about any hazards; describe how the data are to be used; ensure the subjects' confidentiality; make certain that before a subject gives consent, he or she is fully informed about the experiment.

Field Experiments

Is it possible to do social experiments in real-world ("field") settings? Without the controlled conditions of a laboratory, where sociologists can measure precisely the effects and changes in independent variables, can a cause-and-effect relationship be established?

Until recently, sociologists thought it was unethical or impossible to manipulate conditions in the real world for the sake of an experiment. How could they disrupt people's lives in the name of social research? Years ago, however, Durkheim insisted that sociologists had a duty not only to investigate social problems but to try and solve them. Perhaps special research could be conducted that would actually *benefit* the participants.

If poor people were asked what would benefit them most, many would undoubtedly say "money." In the largest sociological field experiment ever undertaken, researchers carefully matched samples of poor people (in Hunt 1985). The experimental group (those who actually underwent the experimental conditions) got a guaranteed annual income. The control group got traditional welfare benefits. Interviews and monthly reports of income and expenses provided the researchers with information about whether, first, a guaranteed income was a more efficient way to distribute money than a traditional welfare system and, second, whether a guaranteed income would discourage people from finding better paying jobs. The experiment yielded some unexpected results.

People who were given a higher guaranteed annual income earned less on their own than those who received a lower guaranteed income, but the evidence did not suggest that guaranteed incomes discouraged people from trying to find better paying jobs. Surprisingly, more marital breakups occurred among the families receiving guaranteed incomes than among welfare recipients. Although income maintenance may have increased family stability among some of the participants in the study, it may also have made the poorest of the nonworking women less dependent on their partners and thus more likely to seek a divorce or separation.

These findings raise a number of ethical questions. When the experiment began, the researchers could not predict its outcome. Some of the study's effects, such as increased marital instability, might be seen as harmful. Is it fair to ask people to participate in research when they may be hurt by it? Other ethical questions focus on the issue of privacy. The researchers asked the subjects highly personal questions, such as, Have you ever committed a crime? Had an abortion? Although the sociologists were concerned with gathering as much relevant data as possible, did certain questions nonetheless constitute an invasion of privacy? Finally, some subjects in the experimental group got more financial rewards than others. Is it right for some people to have to make do with less money because they have been placed in the control group? Undoubtedly, experiments in the real world as well as in the laboratory raise serious questions about research ethics.

Ethnography

In experiments, sociologists attempt to influence or change people's behavior. In ethnographies, this is not usually the case. **Ethnographies** are studies in which researchers observe people in everyday settings, usually over a considerable period of time. The researchers' goal

Distinctive social groups, such as this group of Hare Krishna followers, are often the subject of ethnographic studies, which attempt to describe and interpret the group's social system. In participant observation, the researchers actually join an existing group to record thoughts and feelings accessible only to group members. (Robert Eckert/EKM-Nepenthe.)

is to provide detailed descriptions and interpretations of social life as it happens—among, for example, children on playgrounds, homosexual men in bathhouses, or street gangs in urban neighborhoods. Ethnographic studies provide the kind of eyewitness accounts of social life that are not possible in experimental designs.

Overt Participant Observation

In **overt participant observation,** the investigator participates in the social life of his or her subjects and the investigator's role is made known to the people under study. The sociologist William Corsaro (1985) acted as an overt participant observer of children's play. For several months, he watched and recorded how nursery school children played together. He did not try to hide his purpose. The children thought of him as a "big person" who acted more like them than other adults, and this perception gave him access to the children's culture.

In conducting the participant observation, Corsaro had to solve some problems of method. How could he enter the children's world without upsetting or changing it? He had to remain unobtrusive, but not so distant as to lose sight of how the children themselves understood their social world. Before he could even enter the playground, Corsaro had to negotiate with the "gatekeepers"—the school director, secretary, teachers, and parents. He had to convince them, for example, that he would violate no one's rights. Once he had the adults' permission, he watched the children from behind a one-way mirror. He learned the children's names (which would be important during the participant observation) and got a sense of how they routinely interacted.

Once on the playground, Corsaro played with the children but did not affect the nature or the flow of episodes between them. (He considered play episodes the central unit of behavior in his study.) He never tried to start an activity or to substantially redirect one. He never settled children's conflicts. During this time, Corsaro filled many notebooks with field notes. Later, he brought video and audio taping equipment to the playground so that he could replay episodes between children as many times as he needed for his analysis.

Like other ethnographers, Corsaro had a dual purpose: to understand the subjective meaning of events to his subjects, and to remain analytical, systematic, and *sociological* in his investigation.

Covert Participant Observation

Sociologists sometimes do not tell their subjects that they are being observed for an ethnography. In **covert participant observation,** sociologists enter social worlds without identifying themselves as researchers and try to pass as bona fide members of the groups they are studying. The research subjects usually do not learn the sociologist's true identity or purpose. Sociologists have posed as members of cults prophesying the end of the world, as practitioners of "open marriages" who exchange sex with other married couples, and in a variety of other roles. Covert participation solves the problem of intrusion (that the sociologist's presence might alter the group's behavior) and allows sociologists to observe groups that are usually closed to outsiders. But this research method, in turn, raises serious ethical questions. Is it ethical to deceive people deliberately by pretending to belong to their group when, in fact, the real intent is to study them? Is a covert operation by definition an invasion of privacy?

Nonparticipant Observation

A variation on covert participant observation is **nonparticipant observation,** in which sociologists do not join in the activities of the group under study. They simply observe the group in its everyday settings as its members go about their daily business. When nonparticipant observers are successful, the group does not notice that it is being studied. In one such ethnography, for example, sociologists who had been researching sexual behavior went to homosexual bathhouses and passively watched the behavior of the men there (Weinberg and Williams 1975). Many of the gay men themselves stood around and watched the encounters passively, so the observing sociologists did not stand out. The sociologists also blended in because the patrons at the bathhouse stayed emotionally and personally detached from one another, despite their sexual encounters. To maintain their inconspicuousness, the researchers took field notes in private areas of the bathhouse or after leaving. In interpreting what they saw, the researchers drew on several years' experience of studying sexual behavior. Clearly, they were not functioning as voyeurs, but approached the situation with a set of theoretical questions. However, observing behavior from a distance may make it difficult to perceive all of the nuances involved.

One-way mirrors are sometimes used to observe the behavior of experimental research subjects so they are not affected by the presence of the researcher. The choice of research methods depends upon the nature of the questions being studied. (Cary Wolinsky/Stock, Boston.)

Historical Studies

Sociologists can only observe in the here and now. But understanding the past is often extremely useful for understanding the present, as Durkheim demonstrated when he used historical records of deaths in his study of suicide. Because sociologists are also concerned with the changes that take place in institutions, groups, and societies, they turn to **historical materials**—data about acts, ideas, and events that have shaped human behavior in the past.

Sociologists are more likely to choose a historical approach when studying sociological phenomena that do not occur frequently. In such instances, sufficient statistical data might not be available, and interviews and surveys may be impossible to conduct. To observe the effects of a rare event, a sociologist might have to wait decades for a chance to gather fresh information. For example, it makes little sense for sociologists to postpone their research on revolutions until one occurs. And in the event of an actual revolution, the conditions surrounding it might make sociological research dangerous or impractical.

Theda Skocpol (1979) conducted a historical study of three successful revolutions: the French Revolution of the late eighteenth century and the Russian and Chinese revolutions of the twentieth century. She addressed some of the important questions about social change that had concerned early sociologists. Skocpol also examined data from several unsuccessful revolutions and looked at examples of nonrevolutionary change to see how social modifications brought about by successful revolutions differed from other types of social change. Through comparative analysis, she identified three stages in successful revolutions: the breakdown of an old regime's government, the mass mobilization of the peasantry into class-based uprisings, and the consolidation of power by a new political elite.

A second instance in which sociologists conduct historical studies is when analyzing events that unfold over extended periods of time. Most sociological research focuses on fairly brief events, like marriage and divorce, adolescence, or the creation of new businesses. Other phenomena of great importance, however, happen over longer time frames. Industrialization, immigration to the United States, the creation of the modern form of the family, and the spread of popular democracy are a few examples of developments that took many centuries to unfold. If sociologists looked only at present-day cases, they would not only be led to faulty generalizations but would miss the essential historical pattern of the events.

Finally, in doing historical and other research, sociologists may draw on documents created for other purposes. Like historians, sociologists study business records, old newspapers, diaries, church records on births and deaths, and data and statistics collected by government agencies. (For example, Durkheim and others investigating suicide have used coroners' reports.) Sociologists may also draw on the published works of historians, especially when an investigation covers a long period of time or several different countries are being

Major social upheavals such as the French Revolution against the monarchy of Louis XVI have been the subject of numerous sociological studies attempting to explain the particular course of events and identify more general patterns of social behavior. (Art Resource.)

To study the effects on the United States of numerous waves of immigrants, sociologists may draw on historical records dating from the earliest arrivals down to the present day. Such long-range historical research is useful for studying gradual changes whose impact only becomes apparent over an extended period of time. (EKM-Nepenthe.)

compared. This method, called **secondary analysis,** includes the analysis of data that was originally collected for another reason. In some cases, a sociologist might reinterpret data collected by another sociologist with different research objectives.

Content Analysis

Sociologists often employ **content analysis** to uncover relevant information in historical and contemporary materials. Content analysis may be applied to almost any type of recorded communication—letters, diaries, autobiographies, memoirs, laws, novels, song lyrics, consti-

tutions, newspapers, even paintings, all of which can reveal much about people's behavior. This research method is especially useful in historical studies, because it provides a way to systematically organize and summarize both the manifest and latent content of communication. The computer, which allows researchers to analyze content from many perspectives, has proven a powerful research tool.

As an example of how content analysis works, suppose that a group of researchers has decided to study the images of men and women in rock music videos. Because they cannot study every music video ever made, the investigators begin by collecting a representative sample of rock videos. Next, they list all the possible categories of content, such as song lyrics, clothing styles, gestures, and so forth. They then examine the sample videos, noting as many specific items of content as possible. So far, the researchers have relied heavily on **qualitative research**—research that depends on interpretations by the researcher. Once sufficient data have been collected the researchers can move to statistically-based —or **quantitative**—research methods: for example, they can count the frequency with which women appear in subordinate roles to men and they can check to see whether these instances correlate with other variables. Sociologists have actually carried out this particular content analysis and have found that music videos often portray women in subordinate roles, as sexual objects, or as targets of violence (Brown and Campbell 1986; Sherman and Dominick 1986).

Content analysis is a good example of research that combines qualitative and quantitative research. Researchers generally use quantitative analysis when a common occurrence or form of behavior is being studied. Qualitative analysis is more likely to be used when a behavior or event occurs rarely or the information needed is not easily quantifiable, that is, it exists as words, pictures, or the like.

SUMMARY

1. In his study on suicide, Émile Durkheim set an important precedent for examining a problem from a sociological point of view.

2. The first step in the research process is to define the problem. Defining a concept in measurable terms produces an operational definition.

3. Sociologists formulate questions to ask in their studies on the basis of a review of the literature in the field—a survey of the findings of other researchers who have studied a particular subject.

4. After a review of the literature, a researcher forms a hypothesis, a statement that predicts how two or more variables affect, or are related to, one another.

5. The first step in gathering data, or information, is to choose a research design. The design, in turn, depends on the questions one is asking. Among research designs are survey, participant observation, and experiment.

6. The results of a study are valid when a measure of a variable describes the phenomenon being investigated. The results of a study are reliable when repeated research produces the same findings.

7. Sociological knowledge develops as research generates additional theories and more research. One example of continuing research is David Phillips' studies of imitation as a factor in suicide; his findings contradict those of his predecessor, Durkheim.

8. Sociologists confront a number of difficult research tasks. Like any scientific investigation, studies of social behavior must be shown to be valid and reliable. Researchers must also try to specify the relationships between two variables. Because they study people, sociologists have to be particularly careful that they protect the rights of subjects. Finally, social scientists encounter greater problems with objectivity than do scientists who study the natural world.

9. The particular approaches chosen by sociologists tend to be suited to the theoretical perspectives that guide them. For instance, in researching his functional theory, Durkheim compared group patterns of suicide. A symbolic interactionist would be more interested in examining the meanings embedded in individual cases of suicide, gradually accumulating enough data to reveal general patterns.

10. A survey is a systematic gathering of answers to standardized questions from a designated sample of respondents. A sample is a representative subset of the population being studied. In a random sample, everyone within a population has an equal chance of being selected. Survey responses can be affected by the wording of questions, the sequence in which they are asked, and the form of response that is permitted.

11. The sociological interview may be structured (with the questions elaborated in advance), semistructured, or unstructured. Interviewing is a technique that depends to some extent on the skill of the interviewer.

12. In an experiment, one or more independent variables are manipulated so the researcher can examine the

effect on a dependent variable. In laboratory experiments, sociologists carefully manipulate people under artificial conditions. In field experiments, real-world conditions are manipulated. Instances of deceptive methodology have led to stricter federal and university guidelines for research.

13. Ethnographies are studies in which researchers observe groups in their everyday settings, usually for a long period of time. Overt participant observers study others' behavior openly; covert participant observers do so without revealing themselves as sociologists. In nonpartici-

pant observation, investigators simply note the behavior of others without participating in their activities.

14. In historical studies, sociologists use data about acts, ideas, and events that have shaped human behavior in the past. Historical studies are valuable for analyzing rare events, events long in the past, or events that unfold over a long period of time.

15. Content analysis provides a way to systematically organize and summarize both the manifest and latent content of communication. It is an example of research that combines qualitative and quantitative approaches.

GLOSSARY

Altruistic suicide. In Durkheim's view, suicide that results from extreme commitment to a group or community.

Anomic suicide. In Durkheim's view, suicide that results from a condition of social normlessness.

Anomie. A condition within society in which people's integration within the social fabric is weakened and their commitment to societal norms lessened.

Closed response. A form of response to survey questions in which respondents must choose from the set of answers provided by the researchers.

Content analysis. A research method that provides a way to systematically organize and summarize both the manifest and latent content of communication.

Correlation. Term for a regular relationship between two variables; also, a simple statistical measure of the extent of association between two variables.

Correlation coefficient. A decimal number between zero and one that is used to indicate the strength of a correlation.

Covert participant observation. A research technique in which people's activities are observed without their knowledge and the investigators never identify themselves as sociologists.

Data. Facts, statistics, study results, and other pieces of observable information that are collected and used to construct theories.

Dependent variable. In an experiment, the quality or factor that is affected by one or more independent variables.

Egoistic suicide. In Durkheim's view, suicide that results from social isolation and individualism.

Ethnographies. Studies in which researchers observe people in their everyday settings, usually over an extended period of time.

Experiment. A research method that exposes subjects to a specially designed situation. The most effective technique for establishing cause-and-effect relationships among variables. Experiments may be done in laboratories or field settings.

Historical materials. Data pertaining to acts, ideas, and events that shaped human behavior in the past.

Hypothesis. A tentative statement that predicts how two or more variables affect, or are related to, one another.

Independent variable. In an experiment, the quality or factor that affects one or more dependent variables.

Interview. A conversation through which an investigator seeks information from a research subject. Interviews may be more or less structured.

Mean. The average; obtained by adding all figures in a series of data and dividing the sum by the number of items.

Median. The number that falls in the middle of a sequence of figures.

Mode. The figure that occurs most often in a series of data.

Nonparticipant observation. A research technique in which the investigators observe behavior closely but do not actually participate in the activities of the group under study.

Open response. A form of response to survey questions in which respondents answer in their own words.

Operational definitions. Measurable indicators for variables in a hypothesis.

Overt participant observation. A research technique in which the investigator participates in the activities of those being observed and the investigator's role is made known.

Population. In a survey, the total number of people who share a characteristic that is being studied.

Qualitative research. Research that depends primarily on subjective interpretations by the investigator of the material or event.

Quantitative research. Research that relies on statistical analyses of data.

Random sample. In a survey, a method used to draw a sample in such a way that every member of the population being studied has an equal chance of being selected.

Reliability. The degree to which a study yields the same results when repeated by the original or other researchers.

Sample. A limited number of people selected from the population being studied who are representative of that population.

Secondary analysis. Reanalysis of data previously collected for other purposes.

Spurious correlation. A correlation between two variables that has no meaningful causal basis.

Standard deviation. A statistical measurement of how far other recorded instances fall from the mean or another central point.

Survey. A research method using questionnaires or interviews, or both, to learn how people think, feel, or act. Good surveys use random samples and pretested questions to ensure high reliability and validity.

Validity. The degree to which a scientific study measures what it attempts to measure.

Variable. Any factor that is capable of change.

CHAPTER 3
Interaction and Social Structure

I magine a recent college graduate on the way to a new social situation—his first job interview. Flushed from running, slightly damp with perspiration, he arrives fifteen minutes late for his appointment. Even before he thinks to shake hands with the interviewer, he starts to apologize. The interviewer responds with an impassive face and gestures the applicant toward a chair. The young man sits down, still talking rapidly about traffic jams and parking problems. Suddenly the interviewer interrupts him and asks to see his résumé. The applicant fumbles through his pockets, and then realizes that he has left his freshly typed résumé in the car. He has only a rough draft with him in his coat pocket. Again he apologizes profusely. Squirming in his seat, the applicant fiddles with the cord of the phone on the interviewer's desk while she skims over the piece of paper. The interviewer stares at the twisted phone cord, and then glances briefly at her watch. There is no question in either person's mind that the interview is "over" before it ever really began.

It is probably clear to you that this interview got off to a bad start and never really recovered. But why have you come to this conclusion? What makes you so sure this person will never be offered the job? The answer lies in your understanding of social interactions. The interviewer's initial flat expression conveyed an unmistakable annoyance with the young man's lateness. We assume that she interpreted the applicant's late arrival (and the forgotten résumé) as a sign of disorganization, undependability, or lack of interest in the job. The

applicant tried to change her opinion by explaining why he was late, but the interviewer's lack of responsiveness indicated her rejection of his excuses. The applicant next signaled uncertainty about how to proceed by squirming and fidgeting with the phone cord. The interviewer answered with continuing disapproval by saying nothing and staring at what he was doing to the cord. Her glance at her watch told him that he had no chance of salvaging the interview. What is fascinating is that although much of this social "conversation" occurred without any words, meanings were understood and communicated. What intrigues sociologists is how people, in the course of their daily activities, shape and give meaning to their social encounters by their mutual, interrelated behaviors (Taylor and Sniezek 1984).

But social behavior is more than just a matter of individual choices about how to react to others. Social behavior is always framed by socially defined expectations and meanings. At this job interview, we see more than two people who meet, exchange words and gestures, and fail to "hit it off." What we see in addition are individuals conforming (or failing to conform) to social expectations: an interviewer constrained by her schedule and her need to find the right candidate for the job opening, an applicant hampered by traffic problems and his own carelessness. In every interaction, individuals play social roles and occupy social statuses. A social **status** is a position in a social structure—any position that determines where a person "fits" within the social order. A **role** is a set of behaviors, attitudes, obligations,

Interviewer and interviewee play the roles considered appropriate to the situation. What meanings do their relative physical positions and their "body language" reveal to us about this simple interaction? (Doranne Jacobson/United Nations.)

recent college graduate is among the millions of unemployed people who are having trouble finding work or someone with a large number of job offers. From this perspective, our job interview is far from a unique and isolated encounter; it is the product of a certain set of structures in an intricate social order.

This chapter explores both social interaction and social structure, two aspects of the way in which people are socially linked to one another. In the earlier sections we take a more action-oriented approach, whereas in the later sections, a more structural one predominates. As we saw in Chapter 1, an action perspective emphasizes how people construct their own social worlds, whereas a structural one emphasizes the relatively stable social patterns that are imposed on us. But both social interaction and social structure can be studied from either of these perspectives. It depends on which features of social life a researcher wants to emphasize.

There is also some tendency among sociologists to approach social interaction and social structure from different levels of analysis, micro and macro (see Chapter 1). Studies of social interaction usually focus at the micro (or small-scale) level of analysis, where we can examine the many small details of person-to-person encounters. Studies of societal organization usually focus at the macro (or broad scale) level of analysis and attempt to explain how structural patterns arise and the relationships among them. But the fact that the different levels of analysis have distinctive subject matter is not to imply that a focus at one level can ignore the other. To take the opening to this chapter as a specific example, the focus on the job interview (micro level) went on against the backdrop of the economic market of unfilled jobs (macro level).

Some sociologists believe that all macro-level analyses should be built out of micro-level elements (Collins 1986). Others, however, argue that macrosociology represents a completely different approach; it is complementary to microsociology but in no way reducible to it (Blau 1977, 1986). In this chapter we will be focusing primarily on the more micro-level patterns of interaction. Several later chapters will focus on more macro-level patterns.

Distinctions drawn between interaction and social structure, micro-level and macro-level, are distinctions that must be made to achieve a greater clarity of sociological thinking. But these distinctions are hard to see in everyday life (every episode is at once social interaction *and* social structure). The distinction is made

and privileges expected of anyone who occupies a particular status. In our example, one person has the status of job-seeker and is expected to behave as such. The other status is that of interviewer, the dominant position of the two. The interviewer's role is to critically "look the candidate over" and to decide whether he is appropriate for the job. These statuses and roles transcend any particular set of people; they exist, in a sense, outside the individuals who fill them at any given time.

Such statuses and roles structure the business of the firm and allow it to exist even though particular employees come and go. The firm, in turn, is part of a broader economy in which thousands of firms compete for the dollars that consumers spend. This broader economy, moreover, is the structural backdrop against which the business of job-seeking and hiring takes place. Conditions in the economy determine, for example, whether a only to help us see better what goes on in social life. With this in mind, we turn our attention to a micro look at social interaction.

SOCIAL INTERACTION

We all engage in countless actions during our daily lives. We cough, laugh, scratch our heads, and grimace when we struggle to carry a heavy package, to name just a few of our behaviors. Other people often see our actions and alter their own behavior in response. In response to our cough, they may look in our direction; in response to our grimace, they may offer assistance; in response to our laugh, they may smile. We, in turn, being aware of the responses we have triggered in others, may adjust our behavior accordingly. When our cough gets someone's attention, we may begin to speak; when our laugh gets a smile of enjoyment, we may smile back. This process of people orienting themselves to others and acting in response to each other's behavior is what sociologists mean by **social interaction.** The word *social* denotes that more than one person is involved in the situation. The term *interaction* means that all parties to the exchange are influencing one another.

Social interaction occurs for the purpose of accomplishing some aim and is always directed toward *specific* other people. You cannot have social interactions with the telephone company or with your university, for instance. But you *can* interact socially with members of these organizations, such as the dean of students. Physical proximity is not always needed for social interaction to occur. People interact socially by letter or by personal computer without ever hearing each other's voice or seeing each other's face. By the same token, just being next to others does not always mean that social interaction will take place. You could be hurrying through a

One aspect of social interaction is the process of "reading" the subtleties of other people's facial expressions and responding appropriately. Our behavior is shaped in part by expectations about and cues from another's smiles, coughs, frowns, and our interpretation of these actions. Here, different types of smiles, as studied by Paul Ekman, convey different sorts of messages. How would you respond to the genuine smile at left and to the false smiles below? (Paul Ekman.)

crowded train station, surrounded by hundreds of people, and never even make eye contact with a single person. Thus, social interaction is a process of behaviorally *relating* to other people whom you recognize as specific partners in the relationship.

What interests sociologists most about individual social interactions are the form and meaning that people give to them. (Of course, sociologists are also interested in aggregate patterns, for example, who interacts with whom.) When it comes to interaction we are not separate players, each performing a part solely of our own making. To the contrary, what we say and do is shaped by both social expectations and cues that others provide us. This was illustrated in the job interview described at the start of this chapter. Both parties entered the situation with very clear ideas of what was expected of them. For instance, they both knew that they were to shake hands and introduce themselves. They both knew that the interviewer was to control the situation; she was the one who was to ask most of the questions and decide when the meeting was over. They both knew that certain topics had to be covered (a discussion of the candidate's background, skills, and job-related experience), whereas others were generally taboo (one doesn't discuss the details of one's sex life in a job interview). Finally, both parties had an implicit understanding of many looks and gestures that could signal how the interaction was going. If the interviewer had looked directly at the applicant, leaning forward and smiling slightly, the young man would probably have thought that she was assessing him favorably. As it turned out, the woman looked at the phone and then at her watch, gestures not of acceptance but of annoyance and dismissal.

Social interaction, then, is never free to proceed in any way it might. Rather it is always regulated to some extent by shared expectations. In the following section we look more closely at some of the factors that frame and give structure to social interaction. These include our efforts to define social situations and our implicit understandings of statuses and roles.

Frameworks for Interaction

Defining the Situation

As soon as we are thrown into contact with others we search for clues about the various people involved and how we should act toward them. Sociologist Elijah

Anderson observed this process among the men who hang out at "Jelly's," a run-down bar on Chicago's South Side (Anderson 1978). These men are cautious when they talk to strangers. A stranger, after all, might turn out to be "the law" or, at the other extreme, the "baddest cat in Chicago." So before communicating much to a stranger, the men at Jelly's try to "read" the person:

> For this they pay close attention to a variety of symbols the person displays. . . . They listen to the person's language or, as the men say, his "total conversation" and examine it for clues to his residence, associates, and line of work. They check out the way he is dressed. They watch him interact with others. . . . They may even ask someone else, either secretly or publicly, about his trustworthiness. (Anderson 1978, p. 6)

In this way the men at Jelly's seek to define the social situation.

We are so anxious to define social situations because our expectations for behavior can vary greatly from one situation to the next. You do not behave in a job interview as you do on a romantic date. You do not behave at a funeral as you do at a football game. If you have any doubts about the power of the social expectations that apply to these different situations, just try acting in one situation as you are expected to act in another. On a romantic date, for instance, give your partner a firm handshake, politely introduce yourself, and describe your work experience. Or at a football game try sitting quietly, your head slightly bowed, with a sorrowful expression on your face. There is little doubt that the people you are with will remark about the strangeness of your behavior. They may even become angry if you refuse to "cut it out." In any new social encounter we are anxious to come to a shared definition of the situation in order to avoid the tension that inappropriate behavior causes.

But defining a social situation is seldom a clear-cut task. Even when we know the general purpose of a social encounter (this is a funeral; this is a Christmas dinner), we do not know the nuances of the *particular* interaction. To take a familiar example, all Christmas dinners are not alike. Some are very jovial celebrations, others have a serious religious tone, and still others are considered a time for sadness because the participants miss

Public places, such as city streets, can be the setting for many types of social behavior, from no interaction at all to very personal interaction. Conversation, facial expression, gestures, and physical contact help to define this specific situation. (Gilles Peress/Magnum.)

those who cannot be there. So when people gather for a Christmas dinner, they must work out some agreement as to what kind of occasion it is. The same collective search for the meaning of the situation occurs in every social encounter we have.

Some sociologists stress that in defining a situation we actually construct our own social reality. If we define a Christmas dinner as a time for laughter, it becomes carefree and gay. If we define the dinner as a time for sorrow, it becomes somber and sad. Sociologist W. I. Thomas referred to this process when he developed the sociological theorem that if people "define situations as real, they are real in their consequences" (Thomas and Thomas 1928, p. 572).

The consequences of a social definition can have great importance for people. Suppose that you are a personnel representative for a corporation. It is almost noon and you are waiting at your desk for the next job applicant to arrive. A man dressed in a black leather jacket and carrying a white paper bag enters your office. You assume he is delivering your lunch from the deli so you tell him to put the bag on the table and ask him, "How much will that be?" The man looks at you quizzically and takes out a résumé from the bag. You apologize for your mistake, interview him briefly, but do

not offer him a job. In initially defining the applicant as a delivery person, you created a social reality that made him seem inappropriate for the kind of job openings you have.

A focus on how people define their social situations is an action-oriented one. Action theorists stress the dynamic way that parties to a social interaction define and redefine the situation, depending upon how their interaction develops. Action theorists see this dynamic process as essential because the situations we encounter are usually ambiguous to some extent. As a result, we must constantly "test out" actions and modify our behaviors as we strive toward a more precise definition of what the situation involves. Sociologists with an action perspective, in short, speak of people *negotiating* their interactions—that is, continually molding and "fitting" their behaviors to each other.

Sociologists with a structural perspective, in contrast, are not concerned about how people define their social situations. They take the situation as given and look instead at aspects of social structure within it. Social structural factors, they contend, constrain people's options for social interaction and tend to channel behavior in predictable ways. For instance, the proximity, or nearness, of one person to another is a social structural factor that strongly influences the likelihood of their interacting at all. In a classic study of the effects of proximity on social interaction, researchers surveyed residents in a student housing complex (Festinger, Schachter, and Back 1950). All of the residents were asked to name their three closest friends in the building. The nearer to each other that two people lived, the more likely they were to identify each other as close friends. People who lived next door to each other were much more likely to have become friends than were people who lived two doors apart. People who had quarters in a heavily trafficked area (at the head or foot of the stairs, for example) were much more likely to lead very active social lives than were those who lived in more secluded spots. In this case, how people defined their social situations did not seem to play a major part in their decisions about whom to interact with. The structural factor of proximity promoted interaction regardless of how people viewed their circumstances.

It is not necessary to decide whether an action or a structural perspective is correct. Both views offer valuable insights into the nature of social interaction. Structural accounts correctly point out that our interactions are affected by how people are organized with respect to one another. Our proximity to someone, the size of the group we are in, how that group is divided as to age, sex, and so forth, are all social structural factors that encourage us to act in certain ways. But a structural view can go too far in suggesting that people's behavior is rigidly controlled by external social forces. An action perspective, with its stress on the constant negotiation of social patterns, is a useful corrective to analyses that overstate a structural point of view.

Understanding Statuses and Roles

In addition to defining their situations, people involved in interaction must also develop some idea of one another's statuses and roles. Statuses and roles are part of the structure of society, the ways in which individuals and their behaviors are organized with respect to each other. Statuses and roles facilitate social interaction by giving people some idea of the behaviors expected of them and others in different circumstances.

Statuses

Ordinarily, we use the word *status* to mean "prestige." We speak of a person as having high or low status, or of being a status-seeker. In sociology, however, status refers more particularly to a position in the social structure—any position that determines where a person "fits" within the society. Being a job-seeker, a waiter, a student, a mother, a child, or a friend are all social statuses.

Every person occupies a number of different statuses at any given time. A certain student is not just a student but can also be a man, a son, a fiancé, a Protestant, and so on. Some statuses are assigned to people without effort on their part; they are called **ascribed statuses.** Being male or female, a Mexican-American, a Rockefeller, and a senior citizen are examples of ascribed statuses. You have almost no control over whether or not you occupy these kinds of social positions (Light 1986). You are *born* a Rockefeller, or adopted into that family, just as you are born white or black, male or female, beautiful or plain. The meanings attached to ascribed statuses do change, however. For example, the meaning attached to being an American female has changed greatly in recent years, as more and more

opportunities have become available to women (see Chapter 12).

In contrast to an ascribed status, an **achieved status** is a position a person attains largely through personal effort. Physician, politician, artist, teacher, town drunk, or Boston Strangler—each of these is an achieved status. But what people achieve is heavily shaped by the **opportunity structure** available to them. For instance, the children of a woman living on welfare in an inner-city slum have a different set of achieved statuses available to them than the sons and daughters of a successful corporate executive.

When one of a person's statuses largely determines many of the other statuses that he or she acquires, it is called a **master status.** Being the Prince of Wales, for instance, is a master status because it determines so many of the person's other social positions (ceremonial leader, military officer, even husband and father since a future king must have heirs).

Not everyone has a master status. Many people simply have a variety of ascribed and achieved statuses that take on more or less importance depending upon the social situation. For instance, when you step into a college classroom your status of student comes to the fore and is the major influence on your attitudes and behavior. It is not particularly important that you are also a friend, a son or daughter, a part-time employee, and so forth. In the classroom context your student status dominates. In contrast, when you visit your parents your status of son or daughter is the one that tends to influence your thoughts and actions. Here your student status recedes to the background and your position in the family takes the foreground. When a status dominates in a certain social context, it is called a **salient status.**

Roles

Every status carries with it a socially prescribed role—that is, a set of expected behaviors, attitudes, obligations, and privileges. For instance, we expect friends to be helpful, sharing, loyal, and concerned about our problems, because that is the role that we associate with the status of friend. The difference between a status and a role is that we *occupy* a status but *play* a role (Linton 1936). A status is a position; a role is how we think and act.

People learn how to play their roles by observing and interacting with others more experienced than themselves. This process, discussed in Chapter 5, is known as *socialization*. Socialization into the role of student is one familiar example. From the age of five, American children are taught to raise their hands in order to speak in a classroom, to do their homework, to study for tests, and to avoid cheating; all of which is part of the role that students are expected to play.

No role is cast in stone, however. Within certain limits, individuals are free to interpret the roles they play, giving them their own personal styles. You can see this in the way that different classmates play the role of student. Some study constantly, others study only when they must; some initiate class discussions, others wait to be asked a question. Despite these variations, however, most students conform to the basic behaviors that are expected of students. Those who do not usually find themselves expelled from the student status.

Sociologist Charles Powers (1981) argues that certain situations encourage more improvisation of roles than others. For instance, the longer the same people have been performing a set of interrelated roles, the more likely they are to be liberal in interpreting role-related norms. One example can be seen among people who have worked together for many years. At first they perform their jobs "by the book," each being careful to live up to the others' expectations. Gradually, however, they feel freer to relax, to give new twists to their performances, and sometimes even to stray "out of role." Part of the reason for this increased role improvisation is the fact that as people come to know each other better, they feel more familiar with one another and less concerned about keeping up a "proper" image. Greater role improvisation also occurs when a role relationship is not being observed by outsiders. A police officer, for instance, is more likely to improvise in his law enforcement tactics when he is not in view of reporters. Being among people who are equal to you in power is another situation that makes for more improvisation. A woman, for example, is more likely to improvise the role of friend when with former classmates than she is to improvise the role of employee in a meeting with her boss. Finally, periods of role improvisation seem to be encouraged when role enactment generates strong emotions. Surgical teams, for example, who are involved in life-and-death work, often have periods of informal banter following a difficult procedure. It is as if this time to relax from the roles of doctor, technician, and nurse gives everyone a chance to "unwind" from the stress of role performance.

In this one moment alone, Prince Andrew is simultaneously playing the roles of son to Queen Elizabeth and Prince Philip, Duke of York, Officer in the Royal Navy, and ham. (de Wildenberg/Sygma.)

Powers' view emphasizes an important fact about roles. Roles are both imposed by social rules that come from outside us (as a structural perspective contends) and improvised by the people who play them (as an action perspective says). In almost every situation there is some validity to each of these perspectives. However, the relative importance of each perspective can vary greatly with the circumstances. In some circumstances we follow prescribed rules very closely, although there is always *some* room for personal style. In other situations we improvise freely, following only the general outlines of social expectations. Thus, structural and action views are not mutually exclusive. They simply look at different aspects of the social world.

Another important fact about roles is that they exist in relation to each other. The role of daughter cannot be understood apart from the role of parent, the role of lawyer apart from the role of client, the role of professor apart from the role of student, the role of police officer apart from the role of lawbreaker. Furthermore, a single status typically involves several roles. A personnel manager, for instance, plays one role in relation to the company president, another in relation to a department manager, a third in relation to a sales representative, a fourth in relation to a new employee, a fifth in relation to an administrative assistant, and a sixth in relation to a product manager (see Figure 3.1). Similarly, an actor relates somewhat differently to other actors, to the director, to the stagehands, to the audience, and to the press. The cluster of different roles associated with a particular status is called a **role set** (Merton 1968).

Sometimes a person has trouble meeting the obligations of a role or role set. If this occurs because the role's obligations are too demanding for the resources that the person has, sociologists call the problem **role strain** (Goode 1960). Elliot Liebow found cases of role strain when he studied a group of black men who hung out on a Washington, D.C., street corner. Whereas most of the men had married at a young age with high hopes of being good husbands and fathers, most had failed at these roles—at first financially, then emotionally.

A personnel manager has a variety of role relations (the arrows) with people occupying related statuses. This constellation of role relations is called a role set, and it makes up an important part of an organization's social structure.

FIGURE 3.1   A Simplified Role Set of a Manager

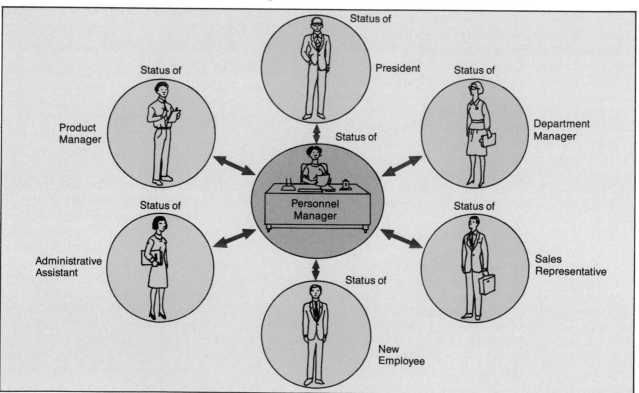

"Where the father lives with his own children, his occasional touch or other tender gesture is dwarfed by his unmet obligations. No matter how much he does, it is not enough" (Liebow 1967, p. 87). Apparently, the inability of these largely unemployed men to perform the role of "good provider" caused enough stress to lead to failure at their nurturant, loving roles as well.

Another reason why people may feel role strain is that the performance of one role is at odds with the performance of another role. This clash between two competing roles is called **role conflict.** A classic example occurs in the world of business when a manager hires a close friend. The demands of the managerial role (giving employees directives, criticizing their work when needed, not showing favoritism) can conflict with the demands of being a good friend. Another example of role conflict occurs when the demands of a high-powered job (total dedication, long hours at the office) are at odds with the demands of being an adequate spouse and parent. In such situations, people often try to separate the conflicting roles by situation (employee at the office, wife and mother at home) in an effort to minimize the friction between them. But because this separation is difficult, some role conflict usually remains.

For the most part, people reconcile themselves to a world in which they will not always be able to perform their roles as well as they want to. This situation is not entirely negative, however, for problems in fulfilling role obligations can be a source of structural change. When enough people resist being caught in roles they have trouble playing, those roles gradually may be made more realistic. Such change may now be under way regarding the role of working parent, as evidenced by the more flexible working hours that some companies are allowing their employees with children. The result is structural change in the traditional expectations associated with the role of corporate employee.

Different Views of Interaction Processes

Defining social situations and understanding statuses and roles are fundamental to the sociological perspective on social interaction. But not all sociologists explain the specific mechanisms and processes involved in exactly the same way. One of the first to develop a distinctive viewpoint on interaction was the philosopher George Herbert Mead, who founded sociology at the University of Chicago during the early part of this century (see Chapter 1). The approach that Mead helped to launch is called **symbolic interaction.**

Symbolic Interaction

George Herbert Mead (1934) provided an important insight into the nature of human interaction by pointing out the symbolic quality of our social behavior. The words, the gestures, the facial expressions, and the bodily postures we use in our dealings with others have specific meanings that we share because of our common culture. A handshake, for instance, is a symbolic expression of greeting in Western societies. As such, it conveys more than just a mutual grasping of fingers and palms. It expresses both parties' shared understanding that a social interaction is beginning.

The same symbolic gesture can have different meanings, depending on the social context. When you stare at someone who pushes in front of you as you wait to get on a bus, your look will probably be interpreted as a sign of anger. But when you stare at a member of the opposite sex across a barroom floor, your look is likely to be read as a sign of sexual interest. We easily make such adjustments in the meanings we attribute to symbols, depending upon the particular situation and the people involved in them.

Mead noted that our ability to interpret symbolic messages enables us to take the role of our partners in social interaction. This **role-taking** involves imagining ourselves in the other person's place, judging how that person is thinking and feeling, and anticipating what further actions he or she might take. For example, the young man applying for a job showed signs of having taken the perspective of the interviewer. His nervousness suggested a concern that the interviewer was viewing him negatively. In order for him to experience such a concern, he must have imagined himself in the role of the interviewer and perceived her displeasure with him. Such role-taking is an important part of fully understanding the meanings that others intend to convey.

Role-taking is also important in that it helps us to tailor our words and actions to those of other people. As Mead pointed out, we do not respond to others in an unreflective manner. Instead, we try to assess the effects that different responses may have on our audience. Suppose, for example, in a job interview you were suddenly asked a question that you had not anticipated.

A single social action can have vastly different meanings depending on the context. Dunking a member of the community in a body of water can signify (clockwise): a victory celebration after a boat race; testing a person suspected of witchcraft (floating proves witchcraft; drowning proves innocence); the religious sacrament of baptism. In these public actions, each individual, like an actor, plays a given role—and plays it to the audience of all the others involved. (Top left: Rick Friedman/The Picture Cube; above: The Bettmann Archive; lower left: David S. Strickler/The Picture Cube.)

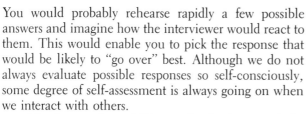

You would probably rehearse rapidly a few possible answers and imagine how the interviewer would react to them. This would enable you to pick the response that would be likely to "go over" best. Although we do not always evaluate possible responses so self-consciously, some degree of self-assessment is always going on when we interact with others.

Mead stressed our ability to role-play in our minds, to imagine ourselves saying or doing something and then to anticipate another person's response by imagining ourselves in that person's place. Other sociologists have also used the role-playing concept, but with a different slant. They emphasize not how people mentally analyze their own and others' role behaviors but rather how all of us are active role *performers*, much like actors performing roles on a stage. This view of social interaction is called the **dramaturgical approach.**

The Dramaturgical Approach

The author George Orwell once wrote about his experiences when he was a dishwasher in a Paris restaurant. Here is Orwell's description of how a maître d' is transformed as he leaves the noisy confusion of the kitchen (where his job is to keep things running smoothly) and enters the elegant dining room (where his job is to "serve" the diners):

As he passes the door a sudden change comes over him. The set of his shoulders alters; all the dirt and hurry and irritation have dropped off in an instant. He glides over the carpet, with a solemn priest-like air. I remember our assistant maître d'hotel, a fiery Italian, pausing at the dining-room door to address an apprentice who had broken a bottle of wine. Shaking his fist above his head he yelled (luckily the door was more or less soundproof):

"Tu me fais—do you call yourself a waiter, you young bastard? You a waiter! You're not fit to scrub floors in the brothel your mother came from. Marquereau!"

Then he entered the dining-room and sailed across it dish in hand, graceful as a swan. Ten seconds later he was bowing reverently to a customer. And you could not help thinking, as you saw him bow and smile, with that benign smile of the trained waiter, that the customer was put to shame by having such an aristocrat to serve him. (Orwell 1961, pp. 68–69)

It is hard not to think of this man as an actor playing two different roles. One role is that of supervisor of the restaurant staff. This role he interprets as needing a sharp tongue and critical eye. He chastises the apprentice waiter without mercy for breaking a bottle of wine. He rants and raves, struts and fumes, portraying an intense anger. Then he steps through the door to the dining room and his whole demeanor changes. He is like a performer who has stepped through a curtain onto a different stage where a new role awaits him. Now he becomes the elegant, smiling maître d' who treats his customers with refinement and elaborate courtesy.

This man's behavior is a good example of the way that all of us adapt to the different roles we play. On the field, for instance, the football player tries hard to act tough and aggressive, but he can also present himself as gentle and romantic toward a woman he is trying to impress. Similarly, a college student may try to present a very intellectual image toward her professors, but she can turn around and play the role of clown in dealing with her friends. A number of sociologists have elaborated on the analogy between playing roles in a dramatic performance and playing roles in real life. Most prominent among those who have taken this dramaturgical approach is sociologist Erving Goffman (1959; 1974).

In viewing social interaction as a kind of theatrical performance, Goffman saw different social situations as being analogous to different stages where different dramas are unfolding. Each person on a particular stage is an actor with a certain role, as well as an audience to the other actors. The actors interpret and play their roles in ways that they think appropriate and that they hope will elicit the desired responses from others. Thus, social life involves shaping the impressions of ourselves that we present to others, and trying to make those impressions as convincing as possible. In much the same way, actors try to convince their audiences that they *are* the people who they play.

But why do we have to devote so much attention to managing the social impressions we make? Goffman's answer is that people need to define social situations in order to know how to behave in them, and part of defining a situation involves understanding the roles that different individuals are playing. These roles are not immediately apparent to others unless we deliberately convey them through our words and actions, our dress and the "props" we use. A maître d', for example, wears a tuxedo, politely greets customers, consults his reservation book in an official manner, and leads diners to a table of *his* choosing. In all these ways he immediately tells new arrivals that he is the maître d', not a waiter or a busboy. This enables customers to smoothly adjust their own behaviors to suit the interaction they are in.

Goffman argues that those involved in a social interaction are motivated to support each other's presentation of self. This is because each individual's success at impression management depends on other people playing complementary roles. You cannot present yourself successfully as a maître d', for example, if waiters and customers ignore you. Nor can you successfully be a restaurant diner if the maître d' refuses to seat you and the waiter never takes your order. In an effort to maintain each other's performances in a social situation, people try to rectify any mistakes that occur. For instance, if the maître d' in an elegant restaurant accidentally burps as he greets some customers, the customers pretend not to notice (a reaction that Goffman calls "studied nonobservance"). Or if a waiter inadvertently drops some salad off a plate, the maître d' steps in. Like a good actor who observes that a fellow actor has forgotten his or her lines, the maître d' improvises and salvages the social drama. In these ways all parties to the interaction keep their roles and the elegance of the situation intact. As Goffman describes it: "Much of the activity during an encounter can be understood as an effort on everyone's part to get through the occasion and all the unanticipated and unintentional events that can cast participants in an undesirable light, without disrupting the relationships of participants" (Goffman 1967, p. 41).

But it is hard to be on stage every minute, trying to stay in role for a situation, carefully managing the impression one makes. This is why social life has both "frontstage" and "backstage" regions. In a frontstage region, people are required to play their roles with all the skill they can muster. Slipping "out of character" here is considered bad form. The dining room is a frontstage region for waiters. No matter how harried, annoyed, or

The line of a jacket, the angle of a hat, the carriage of the head are just a few of the powerful nonverbal signals by which people convey who they think they are, and how you should approach them. (Bernard Pierre Wolff/Photo Researchers.)

exhausted they feel, waiters are expected to remain polite and helpful toward their customers. Once in the kitchen, however, waiters are backstage. Here they can drop the image of perpetual geniality. They can make sarcastic comments about the table manners of a diner; they can joke about returning some dropped food to a plate. The kitchen is where waiters "let down their hair" so to speak, where they relax and prepare themselves for their next onstage performance. Virtually every role has a backstage to which one can retreat. The doctors' lounge is backstage to physicians at a hospital, as is the teachers' room to teachers at a school. Backstage in their dorms students laugh about their professors, while backstage in their offices professors joke about their students.

Goffman's dramaturgical approach has been criticized for making people seem insincere in their frontstage roles. His critics say these roles seem to be merely façades, no more real than a mask someone might put on. But Goffman answers that all people must project *some* image, even if it is the image of someone who is unconcerned about images. Presenting the self in some way is a social necessity. Moreover, as we take up a role in a particular situation and begin to play that part, the sense that we are merely acting gradually fades away. The more we are in a role the more genuine it feels to us, until eventually we are as convinced as our audience that we *are* the person we portray. As sociologist Peter Berger has explained it:

> One feels more ardent by kissing, more humble by kneeling and more angry by shaking one's fist. That is, the kiss not only expresses ardor but manufactures it. Roles carry with them both certain actions and emotions and attitudes that belong to these actions. The professor putting on an act that pretends to wisdom comes to feel wise. The preacher finds himself believing what he preaches. The soldier discovers martial stirrings in his breast as he puts on his uniform. In each case, while the emotion or attitude may have been present before the role was taken on, the latter inevitably strengthens what was there before. (Berger 1963, p. 96)

Goffman's approach is especially valuable because it combines a structural perspective with an action-oriented one. Goffman was concerned with the implicit "scripts" that order and make predictable human interactions in particular situations. In this sense he took a structural outlook, concerned with the recurrent patterns and rules that guide social behavior. But Goffman also believed that people have to "work at" interaction, particularly in unfamiliar social situations when they must negotiate the identities and roles they will play. Consider the members of a newly formed committee that has been charged with the task of raising funds. The members have a general idea of the script they are to follow, for all have been part of such committees before, but no specific positions have been assigned to each member. As a result, the members start by hinting at the roles they would like to claim, without making any definite commitment to any particular role. (Goffman called this a "deniable communication.") The members then observe how others react to their tentative self-presentations. If the reactions are positive, the members proceed more boldly to stake out a certain identity and part. If the reactions are negative, they adjust their behavior, adopting a role that better meshes with the other roles being played. In this way a negotiated cast of characters emerges, and the roles they claim proceed to shape the rest of the social drama.

Ethnomethodology

Like Goffman, sociologist Harold Garfinkel (1967) also focused on the activities of everyday social life. But unlike Goffman, who observed social interaction like an audience watching a play, Garfinkel tried to discover how people *themselves* come to grasp and reaffirm the shared understandings that order their relationships. This task is particularly difficult because we are not even aware of most of these shared understandings. They are simply tacit, taken-for-granted bits of knowledge that we somehow come to have and to obey as social rules. Garfinkel called his approach to studying interaction **ethnomethodology.** (*Ethnos* is a Greek word meaning "people" or "culture"; so the word refers to the methods or ways in which people make sense out of everyday interactions.)

Garfinkel has tried to reveal the unconsciously shared understandings that structure social life by deliberately violating social expectations. In one experiment, for instance, Garfinkel asked some of his students to act as if they were guests when they returned home to their families. For fifteen minutes to an hour, the students maintained a polite distance—talking about general topics, rather than personal ones; asking permission to use the bathroom or to get a glass of water; expressing gratitude to the "host" and "hostess" for their kind hospitality. Two of the forty-nine families thought the students were joking; one ignored the behavior; the remainder were upset and annoyed. "Family members demanded explanations: What's the matter? What's gotten into you? Did you get fired? Are you sick? What are you being superior about? Why are you mad? Are you out of your mind or just being stupid?" (pp. 47–48). In one way or another, the students' families tried to restore "normal" relations and in doing so they revealed some of their unstated assumptions about family interaction.

In other experiments, Garfinkel's students "made trouble" by attempting to bargain for items in a store (something Americans generally do not do); by breaking the rules in a game of tic-tac-toe (erasing the opponent's first move); and by closing in during a conversation so that they were nose to nose with the unsuspecting subject. Each of these violations of the rules of interaction produced confusion and often anxiety (in the students as well as in the "victim") and frequently culminated in an angry rebuke.

The purpose of Garfinkel's experiments was to bring out the tacit rules of interaction as they are intuitively structured by the people who live by them. He has argued that sociologists must get as close as possible to the actual experiences of social life, for in his view that is the only way we can perceive the details of social interaction. The anger and anxiety that Garfinkel's experiment provoked confirmed for him how much people unconsciously depend on conventional assumptions about social life to order their social encounters.

Garfinkel and his students studied the unspoken assumptions that people use to produce and sustain a sense of social order. In their view, social order is not something engineered by a society that functions as an independent entity. Instead, order arises through processes of everyday life in which people simply *assume* that social interactions will proceed in a predictable manner. From this perspective, people don't have to understand each other's thinking and motives in order to interact. They just proceed under the assumption that a given interaction will follow certain conventional patterns. In so doing, people prefer not to question what holds the social order together, for fear that too much questioning will cause that order to collapse. As sociologist Randall Collins (1985) describes this process: "[People] intuitively feel that the social world is a set of arbitrary constructions built over an abyss. These constructions remain in place because we don't question them, and we resist questioning lest the whole thing fall down" (p. 214). It is only when our conventional assumptions are ignored and social interactions go to pieces that we get some insight into the fragility by which the social order is held together.

Social Exchange

Both Goffman and Garfinkel study the taken-for-granted and invisible underpinnings of human social interaction. They seek to pull back the veil from social life and lay bare its otherwise hidden rules and mechanisms. We gain a quite different view of what holds interaction together from theorists such as Peter M. Blau (1964) and George C. Homans (1974). These sociologists analyze a wide range of social behaviors as processes of exchange. Although exchange can take many forms, it is usually guided by the norm (a value or rule) of reciprocity

(Gouldner 1974). When someone does us a favor or gives us something of worth, reciprocity requires that we repay the kindness, balance the social ledger, and keep the relationship going. The original giver then has an obligation to reciprocate in response to us, and so the social dialogue continues. The social ties created by these feelings of mutual obligation are intangible but very strong. As sociologist Georg Simmel wrote, "often the subtlest as well as the firmest bonds among [people] develop from [reciprocity]" (quoted in Nisbet and Perrin 1977, p. 58).

Social exchange theorists see this mutual reciprocation as the most basic form of human interaction. It can be observed everywhere, Peter Blau argues, "not only in market relations but also in friendship and even in love . . . as well as in many social relations between these extremes of intimacy. Neighbors exchange favors; children, toys; colleagues, assistance; acquaintances, courtesies; politicians, concessions; discussants, ideas; housewives, recipes" (Blau 1964, p. 88). To Blau and other social exchange theorists, reciprocity is a glue that helps to hold society together.

What is exchanged in the process of reciprocation need not be identical. If a straight-A student helps you to study for an exam, you would probably not reciprocate by helping *her* to study, for your help to her is not as valuable as her help is to you. Instead, you might invite her out to dinner or to a movie she has been wanting to see. Or if you cannot afford these gestures of appreciation, she would probably consider the social ledger balanced if you simply praised her generosity and admired her talents. These "gifts" repay her by raising her social status and feelings of self-worth. Whatever form the reciprocation takes, however, it strengthens a social bond and keeps the interaction alive by creating new social obligations.

Social exchange theory is a variant of rational choice thinking in which people weigh the gains their actions bring against the costs that are incurred. In social exchange, people are also weighing gains and payments, keeping track of credits and debits so to speak. Although we don't actually keep an accounting ledger for each of our relationships, we have a good sense of who "owes" whom. These calculations not only help to bind us to other people, they also affect the content of our interpersonal dealings as we strive to live up to expectations of reciprocity.

Other kinds of rational calculations likewise affect our social interactions. In fact, a key point in rational choice theory is that the costs and benefits people weigh in deciding on their actions are important in establishing patterns of social relationships. A good example is the student who is trying to decide where to sit in a large lecture hall. Sitting up front, the student calculates, means being more visible, increasing the chances of being called on to answer questions, and generally encouraging more interaction with the professor. Sitting in the back, in contrast, allows for greater anonymity and less likelihood of being drawn into class discussions. Which of these consequences the student considers costs and which the student considers benefits depends upon his or her values and personality. But when a choice is made on the basis of rationally weighing the benefits and costs, that choice will clearly affect the student's interactions with other people.

Comparing Views of Social Interaction

Having discussed various views about the nature of social interaction, it is useful to step back and make some comparisons. Each view provides a different answer to the question of what holds society together. This is one of the basic sociological questions that was introduced in Chapter 1.

George Herbert Mead, with his symbolic interactionist approach, stated that society is held together by our ability to take the role of others. Because of this ability, we can adjust our behavior to suit how we perceive others to be perceiving us. The actions of different people consequently mesh into an integrated whole. Erving Goffman also believed that people "read" one another's behavior and modify their own behavior to suit. But in Goffman's dramaturgical perspective, society is also held together by the social roles that structure people's actions. These roles provide guidelines for behavior and relate individuals to each other as if they were actors sharing the same social stage. Harold Garfinkel's view differs from that of Goffman and especially from that of Mead. According to Garfinkel, society is held together not by mutual efforts to understand the perspectives of others and to adjust behavior accordingly, but by the assumption that people will follow certain social conventions of which they are often only vaguely aware. This assumption and the social conventions related to it are what keep interactions running smoothly in Garfinkel's view. Finally, exchange theorists think

Attraction and love, say social exchange theorists, are governed like other social ties by reciprocity. Like does tend to attract like: partners do tend to pair off according to perceived similarities in attractiveness, easing potential strain. But no matter how these bonds are formed, they are sure to participate in a broad network of relationships in each partner's life. (Left: Jamie Tanaka/Bruce Coleman; right: Bohdan Hrynewych/Southern Light.)

that the rule of reciprocity is a primary factor underlying human relationships. According to this perspective, the members of a society are bound together by an ever changing network of mutual obligations.

NETWORKS: WEBS OF SOCIAL RELATIONSHIPS

The processes of social interaction are the bases for creating social relationships. A social relationship is any relatively enduring pattern of interaction between two or more people. Most people have many social relationships, from casual acquaintances to intimate friendships and close family bonds. These acquaintances, friends, and relatives, in turn, interact with others, and so an intricate set of crosscutting social ties develops. The web of relationships among a set of people who are linked together, directly and indirectly, through their various communications and dealings is called a **network.** To see how networks can be used to accomplish people's goals, let

us consider the process of using networks to find a job.

> Karl E. is an engineer just out of college. His father, also an engineer, heard from a colleague that there was a job opening in a nearby company. The colleague had heard about this opening from a salesman who had visited the company and heard of it from a secretary. The secretary had heard from her boss. Karl applied and was later accepted for the job. (Granovetter 1974, p. 57)

Karl E.'s job search started through one of the relationships in his personal network, his link to his father. But Karl's personal network also includes many other relationships—not just links to other relatives but also to friends, former teachers, and acquaintances of various kinds. All these people, whom he knows and interacts with, form Karl's network of direct social ties. Each of the people in Karl's network also has a network of his or her own. His father's network, for example, includes many colleagues at work. One of these colleagues has a network that includes a salesman, and the salesman's network includes a secretary at the company where Karl found a job. Through all these many crisscrossing, interpersonal links, a larger society is built and structured.

The Importance of Network Patterns

Sociologists have developed diagrams to show the different patterns of relationships that networks can involve. Figure 3.2 shows four such patterns. Karl E.'s case is a chain-connected network. Karl (A) knows his father (B), who knows a colleague (C), who knows a salesman (D), who in turn knows a secretary (E). So Karl is directly linked to his father and indirectly to the other four people through one or more intermediaries. This is not a very closely knit network. At most, each person has dealings with two out of the five individuals. Compare this pattern with that depicted in diagram a, in which each person has a direct tie to every other person. This is the pattern that would exist in, say, a group of friends.

Sociologists doing network analysis stress the importance of these structural patterns (Laumann and Knoke 1986). It is not the individuals and their personal characteristics that they consider important. Rather, it is the ways in which the individuals are interconnected. The nature of these interconnections has been shown to make a difference to how people think and behave.

Take the example of a community in which people have trouble organizing to achieve common goals. Are the personalities of the individuals at fault here? Or might they be inhibited by their patterns of social networks? Sociologist Mark Granovetter (1973) thinks that often the second answer is the right one. He argues that in a community where people are clustered into small, exclusive cliques, opportunities for community-wide organization are limited. This is not because the people involved are apathetic, but rather because their social networks do not provide many channels by which support for a community project can spread throughout the population. If support develops in one clique it is not likely to be transmitted to another, for people in different cliques seldom associate with one another. Thus, support would have to develop in each clique separately, and this is not a very likely possibility. Here, then, the predominant pattern of social networks makes a critical difference to what goes on in the community as a whole. The cliquish networks are constraining people's access to information, to a sense of shared objectives, and to community leadership.

Because the patterns involved in social networks are so important, sociologists have developed a number of concepts to describe them (Wellman 1983; Mitchell 1969; Burt 1987). One is the concept of **density**, the degree to which all the possible links among people in a network are in fact made. This characteristic is expressed as a percentage. For instance, in the network that includes Karl E., as described earlier, only four out of ten possible links among the five people were actually made, giving a density of 40 percent. Related to the concept of density is the concept of **reachability,** the number of steps it takes for any given person in a network to reach someone else in that network. Because Karl's job search network is not very dense, one or more intermediaries is often needed for him to contact another network member. For instance, four steps were needed for Karl to reach the secretary at the company with a job opening. Another useful concept for describing the structure of networks is the concept of range. The **range** is the number of direct contacts that any person has within a given network. In the network we have been considering Karl's range is very narrow. He has direct contact with only one person, his father. Karl's father, in contrast, has a range of 2, his direct contacts being both his son and a colleague at work.

Density, reachability, and range are aspects of networks that can be quantified. Other network characteristics are more qualitative. One of the most important of these is *content*, the meaning that people attach to their network relationships. The link between Karl and his father is that of close family, whereas the link between Karl's father and his colleague is that of two work-related friends. People can attribute many other possible meanings to their social connections depending upon the purposes around which particular links are formed. Identifying these purposes is important to understanding how different networks operate. Also important to understanding how networks operate is the directness of links—that is, the degree to which communication, influence, and so forth flows both ways or just in one direction.

Network Analysis as a Powerful Tool

Analyzing the networks that exist among people is a powerful tool for sociologists. Using just a few concepts, network analysis can define the basic building blocks of social life. A status, for instance, can be seen as a position within a social network; a role as an agreement about who does what, again within a network; and a group as a small, densely organized network in which the people interact on a regular basis and share certain values and goals. Researchers can use network concepts

FIGURE 3.2   Four Different Types of Networks

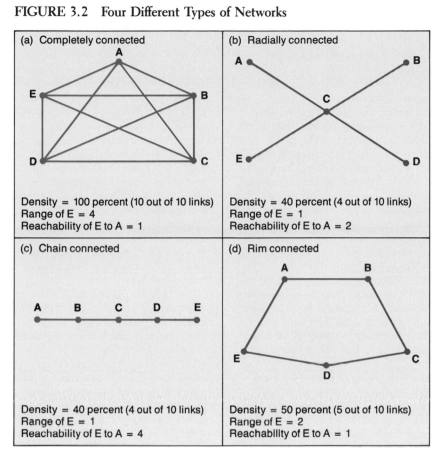

(a) Completely connected

Density = 100 percent (10 out of 10 links)
Range of E = 4
Reachability of E to A = 1

(b) Radially connected

Density = 40 percent (4 out of 10 links)
Range of E = 1
Reachability of E to A = 2

(c) Chain connected

Density = 40 percent (4 out of 10 links)
Range of E = 1
Reachability of E to A = 4

(d) Rim connected

Density = 50 percent (5 out of 10 links)
Range of E = 2
Reachablilty of E to A = 1

The group relations and communication in these four networks vary considerably. The completely connected network (a) is a tightly knit clique, in which each member is in touch with all other members. The radially connected network (b) orbits around one key person, C. In network b, members A, B, D, and E can only communicate with one another through member C. The chain connected network (c) also has member C as the central link. In c, member E must rely on three other people in order to reach member A. In the rim connected network (d), each member can be reached by any other in two links or less, and no one member has a leadership position.

to compare social organizations. For instance, they might study the social networks in a number of rural villages in order to discover any recurring patterns in how the residents form social ties. Without network concepts it might be difficult to describe these fairly large social structures in ways that made meaningful comparisons possible (Laumann and Pappi 1976; Burt 1983).

Network analysis can also show us how a variety of factors—information, influence, resources, assistance—flow from one individual to another along network links. For example, studies of very low-income neighborhoods reveal that the poor are constantly exchanging a variety of possessions and favors (from food stamps and rent money to child care or the use of a car) within their

networks of relatives and close friends (Lomnitz 1977; Stack 1975). Network analysis encourages us to see these social exchanges because it focuses on the *relationships* among individuals, not on the individuals themselves. Thus, network analysis gives us a very dynamic picture of society, one in which factors are constantly moving between people, thereby creating social ties.

Network analyses repeatedly demonstrate that the kinds of social ties we have matter in ways that people often don't expect. For example, if you were looking for an entry-level job in business management, what kind of network do you think would be most helpful to you? One that is made up mostly of people you are very close to, with whom you have strong ties? Or one that

Types of Societies

A **society** is an autonomous grouping of people who have a common territory and a common culture (a shared set of beliefs, values, customs, and so forth), and who are linked to one another through numerous social interactions and interdependent roles. Americans form a society, as do the people of Japan or the Soviet Union. In fact, in the modern world the borders of nation-states usually define the boundaries of societies. This is not necessarily the case, however. Societies existed for thousands of years before modern nation-states were created, and some separate societies still exist *within* the boundaries of nations.

One common way of classifying societies is by their means of subsistence, that is, by their means of obtaining food and other material necessities of life (Lenski and Lenski 1978, 1982). This classification scheme includes five major types: hunting and gathering societies, horticultural societies, pastoral societies, agrarian societies, and industrial societies. These types evolved not only in their means of subsistence, but in many other ways as well, such as their size, their technology, the complexity of their social structures, and the degree to which their resources are unequally distributed.

Until about 10,000 years ago all human beings lived in **hunting and gathering societies.** In some remote parts of the world, a few such societies still exist today, although they are fast disappearing. Because hunters and gatherers must usually move their settlements in search of food, their way of life cannot support large concentrations of people. The typical hunting and gathering band is consequently very small, with a maximum of fifty people, and often fewer. This means that everyone in the band knows one another; and they often know each other's relatives in other bands as well. In such societies, personal networks overlap extensively.

Hunting and gathering bands have very simple social organizations. The family is the only subgroup in the band. It assumes most of the economic, political, and educational responsibilities that large formal organizations assume in our own society. For instance, the family is the group that organizes the production of clothing, tools, and utensils; it is the group in which children learn most of their skills, and the group that cares for the sick, disabled, and elderly. Beyond the family, the entire band works together as a unit. The major division of labor is based on sex. All men hunt and make their own weapons; all women gather and do other chores close to home. There are no specialists of any kind in hunting and gathering societies, no chiefs, no artisans, no religious leaders. Although some people may be respected for their talent at certain tasks, everyone performs the same jobs and has the same responsibilities. Not surprisingly, social inequalities are minimal among hunters and gatherers. No one has the power to order others. Decisions are made jointly. Everyone's possessions are few and modest.

About 10,000 years ago some people started to become food *producers.* Instead of searching for wild plants and game, they began to cultivate their own crops and tend their own animals. At first these methods of food production were extremely simple, and in some societies such simple methods are still used today. In **horticultural societies,** for example, people cultivate small garden plots with digging sticks and hoes. Not all terrains support horticulture, however. Some are too dry, too rocky, or too mountainous for gardening to be successful. Here people often develop **pastoral societies,** in which the major foods are meat and milk derived from herds of domesticated animals. Some societies combine horticulture with herding. They tend simple gardens but also keep small flocks of sheep, chickens, or pigs. This combined approach reduces the risks of overdependence on a single subsistence method. If drought decimates the crops one year, animal products can compensate; if disease kills off most of a flock, vegetables can make up a greater proportion of the diet.

Because they are able to produce a more reliable food supply, both horticulture and pastoralism can support larger societies than hunting and gathering can. Several hundred people often live in a horticultural village, for example. Compared with hunting and gathering communities, horticultural ones are also more permanent. Those that depend on tree crops may remain indefinitely in the same location. Others move only when the soil becomes depleted, which usually takes a number of years.

In both horticultural and pastoral societies, social roles are more differentiated than they are in hunting and gathering bands. While the division of labor is still based largely on sex and age, there is also the beginning of more specialization, at least on a part-time basis. For example, most horticultural villages have a headman who coordinates certain activities, such as religious celebrations, the settlement of disputes, and the redistribution of food surpluses. These headmen do not have absolute power to make laws and issue orders. But their guidance is generally respected and they often have high prestige. A similar position

The growth in sophistication of a society is accompanied by increased social complexity. Those pictured here include: (top from left to right) hunting and gathering society, pastoral society, horticultural society, (bottom from left to right) agrarian society, industrial society, and postindustrial society. (Top: Lars Smith/Anthrophoto; David Austen/Stock Boston; R. and S. Michaud/Woodfin Camp & Associates; bottom: Bruno Barbey/Magnum; Gabe Palmer/The Stock Market; Gabe Palmer/The Stock Market.)

usually exists in pastoral societies. Other specialized roles found in both horticultural and pastoral communities include the shaman (or "medicine man") who serves as both priest and doctor. Horticultural and especially pastoral societies often develop elaborate kinship systems to govern interaction patterns. These determine not only patterns of marriage and descent, but alliances, economic cooperation, and so forth. Kinship relations are the most important factor in determining individuals' personal networks. (continued on page 70)

Types of Societies (continued)

Finally, in many such societies there are associations capable of integrating several local communities when collective action is needed. This might be an association based on kinship (a clan, for example) or a military association. In any case, we see the start of a more complex kind of social organization than exists among hunters and gatherers.

More complex still are **agrarian societies,** those that engage in farming using agricultural innovations such as the plow, irrigation, and crop rotation. With these innovations much more food can be produced on the same land year after year. In fact, these farmers can produce enough food to support a sizable number of other people. Agrarian societies, therefore, grow quite large and their populations are not spread out in widely scattered settlements. Instead, they tend to be concentrated in cities with thousands of inhabitants, cities that serve as the hubs for networks of surrounding villages. This dramatic increase in the scale of society is associated with equally dramatic changes in social networks. No longer does an individual's personal network include an entire community, as it does in a hunting and gathering band, a pastoral tribe, or a horticultural village. Rather, we see a complex web of crosscutting networks, with each person encountering only a tiny fraction of the society's members.

Agrarian societies are also marked by a tremendous increase in the number of different social roles. This is due to the fact that some people are totally freed from agricultural or other food-producing labor. They are consequently able to turn their energies full-time to a variety of specialized jobs: craftsman, blacksmith, merchant, priest, to name just a few. This

is also the first kind of society that allows people to amass substantial amounts of wealth and power. Because agrarian societies are so large and complex, elaborate political, economic, and religious systems develop to govern the social order. Those who gain control of these systems become members of elite groups who are able to distribute resources and privileges to themselves. Thus, agrarian societies are the first in which we find kings and subjects, lords and commoners, great land holders and lowly serfs. In fact, such societies usually have more social inequality than any other type. These social inequalities often become hereditary, so that people in many agrarian societies are born into a set of rigidly ascribed statuses. Agrarian states can also rule over people of different ethnic backgrounds or religions. So, in Blau's terms, heterogeneity can increase along with inequality.

Until a few hundred years ago, agrarian societies were the most complex form of human social organization. Then an industrial revolution began. Machines were invented to facilitate production and new sources of energy were harnessed. Goods became produced on a scale unheard of in earlier times. The end result was that **industrial societies** began to dominate the globe. Even the less developed countries of today's world cannot easily escape being tied into an international economy which is larger than that of any single country.

With their tremendous productivity, industrial societies support millions of people, mostly in urban settlements. Personal social networks and face-to-face relationships organize only certain parts of social life, such as family and community. The majority of workers find jobs in major corporations, and bureaucracies help coordi-

nate all parts of the social order. Information-related institutions, such as science and education, are far larger and more important than in agrarian societies. At the same time, the roles people play are more specialized than in any other kind of social system. A doctor, for instance, is not just a physician, but a neurologist, a cardiologist, or an orthopedic surgeon specializing in sports injuries. This great variety of specialized roles is often accompanied by an influx of people from other cultural backgrounds, other races, other religions, and so forth. Large, advanced industrial societies are typically marked by the highest degree of heterogeneity of any society. At the same time, they also have substantial amounts of inequality, although opportunities to rise in the social order are greater than in agrarian societies.

Some social analysts would contend that we have moved from the industrial to the postindustrial age (Bell 1973). In **postindustrial society,** the central force is the organization of theoretical knowledge. Energy production drove industrial society; information production drives the postindustrial one. The primary value of postindustrial society is on efficient systems of production. Education, science, and technology are of key importance and the narrow specialization of roles reflects the society's overall complexity (see also Chapter 22).

Industrial and postindustrial societies, with their massive size and great diversity, cannot be held together by kinship, common beliefs or daily interaction as some smaller-scale societies (such as pastoral or horticultural societies) can. The last section of this chapter explores some of the sources of large-scale social unity that sociologists have identified.

incorporates a large number of casual acquaintances, people to whom you are only weakly linked? Common sense might suggest that a network of strong ties would give the most assistance. People you are close to, after all, are strongly motivated to give your needs high priority. But although this reasoning seems to make sense, it is actually shortsighted. Research shows that, generally speaking, the people who are most useful in providing us with job leads are *not* those toward whom we feel the closest (Granovetter 1974; 1983). The fact that Karl E. found his position through his father is atypical. Usually, our more fruitful contacts are people we do not see often and with whom we have weak emotional ties. What is the reason for this pattern? The answer lies in the benefit of broadening one's sources of information. The closest ties in your social network tend to be connected to many of the same people you are, whereas the weak ties have links to many people who you do not know. The weak ties, therefore, offer a greater range of information than your close friends and family can provide.

Over a decade of research into the value of weak ties in social networks has helped sociologists refine their understanding of when and for whom such relationships are most beneficial. For example, studies show that in job searches weak ties are used more by better-educated people who are seeking managerial and professional positions (Ericksen and Yancey 1980; Langlois 1977). Such people tend to maintain a large network of colleagues who will know about possible openings in a wide variety of places (Bridges and Villmez 1986; Marsden and Hurbert 1986). In addition, the kind of job a person finds through a weak tie is strongly influenced by the prestige of that particular acquaintance. Acquaintances who are high in prestige and have links to other high-prestige people are generally more instrumental in helping a person find a good job (Lin, Ensel, and Vaughn 1981). But even seeking job leads from a high-prestige contact is no guarantee that one will find a high-quality job. The success of using network contacts also depends a great deal on the industry and firm in which one is seeking work (Hodson 1984; Marsden and Hurbert 1986; Zucker and Rosenstein 1981).

Sociological research into the process of finding a job shows that the nature of a person's social network can have important consequences for his or her career. Without network analysis, it might not be apparent why two people with equal skills and credentials can have very different degrees of success when looking for a job.

Network analysis is also very useful for showing how a person's position in a social structure can greatly influence what that person does. To reveal this kind of social force at work, researchers often compare people who hold structurally equivalent positions within different networks. If they find that these people think and act similarly, they have reason to believe that having a certain position in a network encourages a certain type of behavior.

One thing that adds to the power of network analysis is that the links in networks need not connect individual people. Instead, the connected units (or **nodes,** as they are called) can be corporations, labor unions, political parties, public agencies, or any other kind of organization or group. They can also be categories of people who share a certain attribute, such as people of a certain ethnic background or a certain social class. Considering networks that encompass organizations, groups, and categories of people greatly increases the usefulness of network analysis. For instance, a researcher might want to learn how a corporation exerts its influence in support of a particular piece of legislation. Network analysis would identify the corporation's range of contacts and their reachability, the company's relationship to each group or person whose opinions on the issue might matter, the durability and intensity of its ties to opinion leaders, among many other valuable pieces of data.

Network analysis is also valuable in that it serves as a bridge between the micro and macro levels of study. "In one way or another," Mark Granovetter explains, "it is through social networks that small-scale interaction becomes translated into large-scale patterns, and that [large-scale patterns], in turn, feed back into small groups" (1973, p. 1360). We interact, in other words, with people in our networks, and through these interactions a larger social order is built. The nature of this larger social order, and the influences it exerts, are the subjects we turn to next.

THE STRUCTURE OF SOCIETY

No analysis of human social relations is complete without a look at the largest-scale social patterns that exist, those that give structure and predictability to society as a whole. Sociologists who study these very large-scale patterns are not necessarily concerned with the factors that govern everyday interactions, nor with the ways in which networks of social relationships are constructed. They may leave these topics for others to investigate. Instead, they want to describe the ways in which society as a whole is put together, and how macro-level social forces impose constraints on people's opportunities and behavior. "The macrosociological focus," writes Peter M. Blau,

> is appropriate for the study of entire societies or other large collectivities because it is impossible to trace and dissect the interpersonal relations of many thousands of millions of people. Neither would it be meaningful if all [these interpersonal relations] *were* described. In this case, the minutiae of daily social life must be neglected and the major regularities and patterns must be abstracted from them. (1977, p. 20)

Different sociologists have different ideas about the nature of these large-scale social patterns and how they should best be studied. Those with a structural perspective see the patterns as externally imposed on people, essentially having a life of their own apart from individuals (Mayheur 1980). Those with an action perspective, in contrast, emphasize that even the largest-scale social patterns are ultimately the products of individual decisions and activities. Sociologists who take a functional perspective have yet a different view. They search for ways in which large-scale social patterns contribute to the functional integration of society and its smooth operation. Sociologists with a power perspective, in contrast, stress that many broad social patterns are outgrowths of the fact that elite groups in society dominate subordinate ones.

The Effects of Social Distributions: A Structural Perspective

Why do American whites tend to marry other whites, blacks tend to marry blacks, and Hispanics tend to marry Hispanics? Why are most of your parents' friends at roughly the same income level, and why are most of your friends approximately the same age as you? Your first answer is probably that people *prefer* these relationships. "Birds of a feather flock together" the old saying

goes, and people *like* it that way. In addition, you might argue, cultural forces tend to encourage similar people to gravitate to each other. Cultural beliefs often teach us that it is "good" and "right" to stick with one's "own kind." Although there is evidence to support both of these explanations, some sociologists have argued that this is not the whole story. Also influential, they maintain, are the external constraints and opportunities for social relationships that are created by the overall composition of a population. These external constraints and opportunities influence—even shape—all kinds of social dealings, even ones as seemingly personal as choosing a friend or a marriage partner. This view is highly structural in nature, as you may recognize. One sociologist who strongly supports it is Peter M. Blau.

According to Blau, patterns of marriage, friendship, and other social interactions are the unintended consequences of the way a population is distributed along a few key sociological dimensions, such as gender, race, religion, income, and education (Blau 1986, 1977; Blau and Schwartz 1983). Some of these dimensions (such as gender, race, and religion) divide people into categories with fairly clear-cut boundaries. A person is either male or female, black, white, or Oriental, Christian, Muslim, or Hindu, and so on. The number of such categories and the distribution of people in them, Blau maintains, determines how homogeneous or heterogeneous a society is. Sweden, for example, is relatively homogeneous because its population consists of mostly white Christians; New York City, on the other hand, has an extremely heterogeneous population.

Other dimensions (such as levels of income, education, and power) do not divide people into clear-cut categories but instead range them along a distribution from small to large amounts. Some people, for example, have almost no income, whereas others have a great deal. In between there is a gradual progression up the income scale, just as the notes of a musical scale gradually move from one to another. When people are unevenly distributed along one or another of these dimensions, *inequality* results. That uneven distribution, says Blau, is what inequality actually means. There is much inequality in the distribution of U.S. wealth, for instance. A third of all the wealth in this country is owned by only 1 percent of the population (Page 1983).

But what does a society's degree of heterogeneity and inequality have to do with individuals' decisions about friendship and marriage? Blau argues that a high degree of heterogeneity in a society promotes intergroup relations, such as intergroup marriages. Structurally, there are more opportunities for contact, for chance encounters that may develop into social relationships. Suppose, for example, that a woman lives in a society such as Japan, which has very little racial heterogeneity (which is not characteristic of most modern industrialized societies). Her chances of meeting a potential husband from a different race than her own, in this case, are obviously slim. But suppose this Japanese woman moves to San Francisco. The city's racial heterogeneity makes it more likely that she will meet and date men from other races, even if she personally prefers to date Japanese. Racial heterogeneity, a purely structural factor, has thus greatly increased the chances of an interracial marriage.

By the same logic, Blau contends that a high degree of inequality in a population promotes relations among people of different social classes. Suppose, for example, that a young woman attends a private high school where all the students come from middle-income families. In this setting with virtually no economic inequality, her chances of dating young men from other economic classes are virtually nil. But suppose that afterward she goes to a state college where there are students from all social classes. Now the chances of her meeting and dating men from different economic backgrounds have risen from almost zero to a significant percent. Structural inequality has become a determining force in her dating patterns.

Both heterogeneity and inequality encourage people to interact with others who are different from themselves. To the extent that people who come into contact with one another are socially different (say, of different races and different occupations), intergroup relations are promoted. Blau sees such crosscutting relationships among social categories as helping to bind a large complex population like our own into a more integrated and harmonious whole. Substantial amounts of both heterogeneity and inequality in our society work to promote such intergroup relations.

The major point about Blau's analysis is his emphasis on how large-scale social patterns affect people's interactions. He is not concerned with the psychological motivations that draw people together or push them apart. Rather, he focuses on how key social attributes are distributed in populations, believing that these distributions greatly influence opportunities for social contact.

Societal Integration: Functional and Power Perspectives

The question of what integrates society, what holds it together, is a central one in sociology. In Blau's view, crosscutting relations between different groups of people are important in holding the various parts of a complex society together; these relations serve to bind dissimilar elements into an integrated whole. Not all sociologists stress the same factors as Blau does, however. Some focus on the characteristics of interpersonal relations, whereas others look for different kinds of social structural patterns. In either case, there are those who favor a more functional outlook and those who favor power.

One functional point of view is to see society as composed of specialized subsystems called **institutions.** An institution consists of patterned behaviors and status/role relationships that fulfill certain basic societal needs. For example, society has a need to produce new members and to teach them the customs, beliefs, and values shared by those who live in their world. This task falls mainly upon the institution of the family. The traditional American family consists of parents and children. The parents' role is to produce the children, to nurture and provide for them until they reach adulthood, and to teach them "right from wrong." The children's role is essentially that of learner, a kind of trainee for the society's next generation.

In the functional perspective, institutions have evolved to meet several other important societal needs. One is the need to mobilize scarce resources in order to produce and distribute the goods and services that people want. This need is largely met by our economic institutions. Another societal need involves protecting people from external threats, such as military invasions, and from internal threats, such as crime. In our society this need is the province of the political institutions. Societies also have a need to teach people about certain statuses and roles, especially those that have to do with being a citizen and a worker. This is a primary function of our educational institutions. Finally, societies have a need to motivate people to perform their social roles by giving life meaning and purpose. Religious institutions are deeply involved in fulfilling this requirement. From a functional viewpoint, societal integration becomes a matter of these various institutions successfully meeting the basic needs that they evolved to serve. When institutions *are* meeting these important requirements,

FIGURE 3.3   Some Major Social Institutions

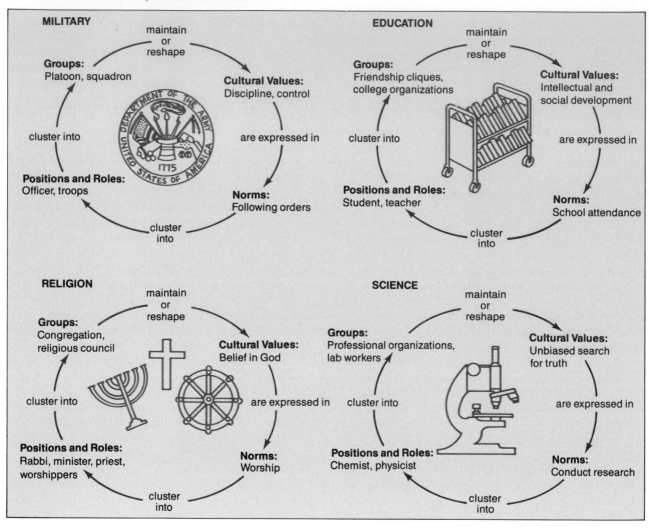

Social institutions evolve in each society as people address important needs. They organize roles, statuses, and groups around key values and norms so that basic needs are met through stable patterns of action.

society is a smoothly running, well-put-together whole. (Figure 3.3 shows some major social institutions; we look more closely at the set of social institutions in Part V.)

Other sociologists have a very different view and see power as the basis of social integration. Those who agree with the ideas of Karl Marx, for example, see society as a system of fundamentally antagonistic social classes held together by the domination of the capitalists over the working masses (Poulantzas 1975). The capitalists (or owners of the means of production, including large corporations) have the power to shape society's institutions to serve their own interests and perpetuate their own control. Thus, Marxists see capitalist society as held together by the exercise of power on the part of an elite social class for its own aggrandizement. Far from being the smoothly running system that a functional perspective describes, capitalist society, from the Marxist view,

has undercurrents of class conflict that are never far beneath the surface. (We will see more of the power perspective on societal integration in Part IV.)

Still another important way of thinking about what holds society together focuses neither on functional institutions nor on the exercise of power. Rather, it looks to the customs, values, knowledge, beliefs, and symbols that people in a society share, factors that help to bind them together into an integrated whole. These shared factors are collectively called a culture, the topic of our next chapter.

SUMMARY

1. We engage constantly in social interaction —orienting ourselves to other people and acting in response to them. Social interaction occurs for the purpose of accomplishing some aim and is always directed toward specific other people. What interests sociologists is the meaning people give to social interaction.

2. When we are in contact with others, we seek to define the social situation. We give the situation a particular meaning that allows us to behave appropriately. Action theorists hold that defining the situation is a dynamic process, in which people modify their behaviors and negotiate their interactions. In contrast, other sociologists emphasize the social structural factors that constrain our opportunities for interaction and channel behavior in particular ways.

3. Every person occupies a number of different statuses at any given time. Some statuses are ascribed (assigned to people without effort on their part) and others are achieved (attained largely by personal effort). Statuses always affect how people interact with one another.

4. Every status carries with it a socially prescribed role—a set of expected behaviors, attitudes, obligations, and privileges. Within certain limits, people are free to interpret the roles they play, giving them their own personal styles.

5. Symbolic interaction, a sociological approach founded by George Herbert Mead, focuses on the symbolic nature of aspects of social interaction. Being able to imagine ourselves in the roles of others allows us

to understand the meanings that others convey through their behavior.

6. The dramaturgical approach sees social interaction as a kind of theatrical performance in which we are all playing certain roles.

7. Ethnomethodology is a sociological viewpoint that focuses on the ways that people make sense out of everyday interactions by developing shared understandings about behavior.

8. Social exchange theorists view reciprocity as the most basic form of human interaction. Social exchange theory is a variant of rational choice theory, in which people weigh the gains their actions bring against the costs they incur.

9. The web of social relationships among a set of people who are linked together, directly and indirectly, through their various communications and dealings is called a network. Sociologists have developed a precise system of network diagrams to show the different patterns of relationships involved. Networks differ from one another in density, reachability, and range.

10. On the scale of society as a whole, social interaction is affected by large-scale social patterns. According to Peter Blau, a leading structuralist, a society's degree of inequality and heterogeneity affect how (and whether) people will interact with one another.

11. A functional view of society at large sees it as composed of specialized subsystems called institutions: the family, the government, religious establishments,

and so on. Institutions are a set of patterned behaviors and status/role relationships that fulfill basic societal needs. In contrast, a power view sees power as the basis of societal integration. The dominant class in a society has the power to shape society's institutions to serve their own interests and perpetuate their own control.

GLOSSARY

Achieved status. A status a person attains largely through personal effort.

Agrarian societies. Societies that practice large-scale farming employing agricultural innovations such as the plow, irrigation, and crop rotation.

Ascribed status. A status assigned to people without effort on their part.

Density. The degree to which all the possible links among people in a social network are made.

Dramaturgical approach. A sociological perspective in which social interaction is viewed as resembling a theatrical performance in which people "stage" their behavior in such a way as to elicit the responses they desire from other people.

Ethnomethodology. A viewpoint on social interaction developed by Harold Garfinkel that focuses on the ways people make sense out of everyday interactions.

Horticultural societies. Societies dependent upon the cultivation of garden plots for food production.

Hunting and gathering societies. Societies dependent upon hunting game and gathering wild plants to obtain food.

Industrial societies. Societies that practice large-scale mechanized production of goods.

Institutions. Patterned behaviors and status/role relationships that fulfill certain basic societal needs.

Master status. One status of a person that largely determines his or her social identity.

Network. The web of relationships among a set of people who are linked together, directly or indirectly, through their various communications and dealings.

Nodes. The connected units within a social network.

Opportunity structure. The organization of opportunities available in different parts of society, such as the quality of local schools, the availability of different types of jobs, and the wealth of the area.

Pastoral societies. Societies dependent upon herds of domesticated animals for food production.

Postindustrial societies. Advanced societies marked by extremely efficient systems of production and an emphasis on information services.

Range. The number of direct contacts that any one person has within a social network.

Reachability. The number of steps it takes for any person in a network to reach someone else in that network.

Role. A set of behaviors, attitudes, obligations, and privileges expected of anyone who occupies a particular status.

Role conflict. The clash between two competing roles.

Role set. The cluster of different roles associated with a particular status.

Role strain. Difficulty in meeting the obligations of a role because it is too demanding.

Role-taking. Imagining oneself in the role of another and using it to understand the meanings that others intend to convey.

Salient status. A status that dominates in a certain social context.

Social interaction. The process of people orienting themselves to others and acting in response to each other's behavior.

Society. An autonomous grouping of people who share a common territory and participate in a common culture.

Status. A position in a social structure that determines where a person fits within the social order.

Symbolic interaction. A sociological viewpoint founded by George Herbert Mead that focuses on the symbolic nature of social interaction.

PART TWO
THE INDIVIDUAL AND SOCIETY

Sociology focuses on the forces at work in social groups and in society at large. It also studies the complex interaction between these larger patterns and the lives of individuals. What does it mean to say that we are shaped by our society? The next four chapters examine how social forces and social structures impinge on the life of the individual and how in turn individual actions reinforce or modify societal patterns.

Chapter 4 explores the sociologist's understanding of culture: the enduring values, beliefs, customs, symbols, and artifacts that give expression to a shared way of life. From this perspective, television ads, clothing fads, and popular music are as much a part of culture as operas or art museums. Culture is not merely something imposed on us, but a sort of shared language, of things and ideas, that we both develop and use.

We begin to internalize cultural values and norms in early childhood through processes of socialization. Chapter 5 discusses socialization from several theoretical perspectives and looks at the ways in which family, peers, school, TV, and the workplace contribute to this life-long process.

Sociologists identify the life course as a series of predictable changes that take place as people move from childhood to adulthood to old age. Chapter 6 considers the stages and transitions in the life course, which vary from culture to culture and from era to era. The baby boom generation exemplifies how a particular group moving through the life course precipitates social changes that in turn shape both that group's experience and the opportunities open to others.

Although most people conform to cultural norms and expectations, deviance is nonetheless a universal phenomenon. Deviance, in sociological terms, is any behavior that members of a group perceive as violating their norms. Chapter 7 explores the social factors that give rise to deviance and considers the different types of deviant behavior as well as society's strategies for controlling them.

CHAPTER 4
Culture

In a recent television advertisement, a sleek new car surges over the crest of a hill and along an open road. A lone male driver skillfully maneuvers around a smooth bend, as wide rays of sunlight fall onto the auto, giving it a spiritual aura. A rapidly changing montage of driving scenes follows. The car rolls effortlessly past the neon lights of a city street at night; we see it easing to a graceful stop before an elegant restaurant; we glimpse it as it crosses a magnificent bridge with a powerful river below. In the end the lone driver, now in the foothills of a mountain range, steps from the car and gazes out across an expansive plain. The song that accompanies these pictures tells the viewer that the American road "belongs to Buick."

This TV advertisement obviously has something to do with Buicks, but what does it have to do with culture? To most people, the word *culture* conjures up images of people who regularly attend the opera, prefer Shakespeare to Stephen King, speak knowledgeably about fine wines, and know their way around the art museums of Europe. It is a discriminating word, applied to discriminating tastes and pastimes. A TV ad for Buicks simply doesn't qualify as "culture."

But sociologists do not restrict their idea of culture to fine arts or sophisticated styles of living. They define **culture** as *all* the learned customs, beliefs, values, knowledge, artifacts, and symbols that are constantly communicated among a set of people who share a common way of life. The sociological use of the word *culture* signifies a society's entire learned way of life. The TV ad for Buick is a part of American culture because it embodies a whole array of symbols, the meaning of which Americans share. The moving car, the open road, the lone driver, the unpopulated landscape, all symbolize to us a sense of freedom and autonomy that we, as Americans, revere. At the same time, this material object, a luxury car, is imbued with cultural messages about gender, status, privilege, affluence, and social class. The man who drives it is considered a cut above the rest. One reason why advertising is so prominent in our culture is because it is so successful in communicating these kinds of messages among Americans (Schudson 1984). It is a primary means by which information about the social meaning of material objects gets distributed throughout our population. As such, "advertising is not just a business expenditure undertaken in the hope of moving some merchandise off the store shelves, but is rather an integral part of modern culture" (Leiss et al 1985).

Our cultural communications include a multitude of things besides advertisements. Some we consider rather trivial, others quite significant. For instance, everyday patterns of American speech are part of American culture, such as the custom of saying "hello" when answering the telephone. (The British, in contrast, typically answer by stating their telephone number or name without saying hello.) Styles of American dress are part of American culture, from designer jeans, to Bermuda shorts, to disposable diapers for babies. Many gestures used in social interaction are also part of our

These boys are learning about the material and nonmaterial components of American culture. In our society, the automobile is more than just a form of transportation. This material object embodies the cultural meanings of freedom, mobility, individualism, and technological progress. Americans, too, are proud of their country's history, leaders, and moral position. This detail from a painting by Norman Rockwell shows these ideas without embedding them in physical objects. (Left: Burk Uzzle/Archive Pictures, Inc.; right: The Norman Rockwell Museum at Stockbridge.)

culture. A handshake, for instance, is a cultural custom. The things we admire or revere are part of culture too. We praise democracy, worship God, and value competition because our culture teaches us to.

Because we have little say about the culture we grow up with, there is a tendency to think of it as something external to ourselves and almost forcibly imposed. But this way of thinking ignores the active, creative side of our relation to culture. Culture is not just a set of elements that *dictates* behavior; it is also something that people themselves *develop* and *use*. Sociologist Howard Becker (1986) captures this idea in describing culture as "shared understandings that people use to coordinate their activities." By creating and expressing the elements of our culture, by living them day to day, we are constantly communicating to each other an understanding of our social world. In the process, there is also room for reshaping culture, for adapting it to meet new demands and situations. As a result, culture is never static. It is constantly changing.

Elements of culture can be divided into two basic kinds: material and nonmaterial. **Material culture** consists of all the physical objects, or artifacts, that people make and attach meaning to—books, clothing, schools, churches, and guided missiles, to name just a few. A compact disk, for instance, is part of American material culture. It is a physical object that people in our society have created, and we have a shared understanding of its purpose and meaning. To a person living in a remote village in some nonindustrialized society, this same physical object would probably mean nothing of what it does to us. Such a person has not been socialized into our knowledge, beliefs, and symbols, and does not share our cultural communications. One important source of material culture is technology, the branch of knowledge that deals with applied science and engineering. Nations such as the United States and Japan have spread the material products of their advanced technologies to far corners of the world. American airplanes and Japanese cars can be found almost everywhere.

In contrast to material culture, **nonmaterial culture** consists of human creations that are not embodied in physical objects—values, beliefs, rules, customs, systems of government, the languages we speak, and so forth. The value that Americans place on individualism, for instance, is not embodied in any tangible thing. Rather, it is an abstract idea that guides our thoughts and actions and therefore is part of our nonmaterial culture. Other examples of American nonmaterial culture are the values we place on freedom, democracy, equality, and competition, our belief that hard work is a major ingredient in success, the rules of the road we follow when driving on our highways, and the custom of celebrating a national holiday on the fourth of July.

A further way to appreciate what culture entails is to distinguish it from society. Although in the real world culture and society are never separated, sociologists differentiate them for purposes of analysis. *Culture* refers to the things (both tangible and intangible) that a given group of people have created and to which they attach similar meanings (their beliefs, values, knowledge, symbols, norms prescribing customs, and so forth), whereas *society* refers to the networks of social relationships among those who share a culture. Clearly, culture cannot exist without society, nor society without culture. While people use culture to guide and give meaning to their social relations, culture itself is the product of people interacting in a social system (Bordieu 1977; Griswold 1987). Thus, culture and society are inextricably related.

In this chapter, we are going to look at many other aspects of culture. We begin with an overview of various elements of culture, including norms and values; symbols of all kinds, including language; and knowledge. Although our own elements of culture may seem so "right" to us that it is hard to conceive of any other ones, these elements are simply learned ways of seeing and dealing with the world. We then ask how elements of culture are integrated into a coherent whole. Without some degree of cultural integration, a society is apt to experience conflict and instability. We follow this by exploring a key theme in American culture: the value we place on individualism. Next we take up the subject of how new elements of culture are created. The complementarity of the action and structure points of view will be particularly evident in our examination of this process. We then look at culture and the modern media of communication, especially television. In what ways, we ask, is modern media transforming our view of the world?

THE ELEMENTS OF CULTURE

We commonly overlook the elements of our culture, although we use them all the time. They include our knowledge, language, symbols of all kinds, values and norms. Although the particular content varies from place to place, these are basic elements of all human cultures. People use them to create, sustain, and change their way of life. Let's look more closely at each of these elements, beginning with values and norms that guide our behavior.

Values

In a popular TV show of the late 1970s, a human-looking visitor from another planet was sent to observe earth culture. This visitor, called Mork, made countless blunders in his interactions with earthlings. In one episode, Mork was told that because Americans value assertiveness he should stop complying with every request made of him. When a Girl Scout selling cookies came to the house shortly thereafter, Mork screamed "No!" and abruptly slammed the door in her face. In another episode, Mork violated social conventions by describing out loud the nonverbal reactions expected of him. When someone described a serious personal problem Mork replied: "Choke! Gasp! Look of sincere empathy!" Needless to say, the listener was very put off.

When Mork practiced assertiveness by refusing to buy Girl Scout cookies, he was working at adopting one of many American values. A **value** is a general idea that people share about what is good or bad, desirable or undesirable. Values transcend any one particular situation. If you value assertiveness, for example, you think it is appropriate in many different social contexts. Mork's problem was that he generalized values to absurd extremes. No value applies in *every* situation. There are always exceptions. Nevertheless, the values people hold tend to color their overall way of life.

Values are reflected even in seemingly trivial day-to-day behaviors. Consider the games people play. The Tangu of New Guinea, for example, play a game called *taketak*. It involves two groups of coconut stakes that look like bowling pins and a toplike object made from a dried fruit. The players divide into two teams, and the members of the first team take turns throwing the top at their group of stakes. Every stake they hit is removed. Then the members of the second team toss the top at their stakes. The object of the game, surprisingly, is not to knock over as many stakes as possible. Rather, the game continues until both teams have removed the *same* number of stakes. To Americans, who value competition so highly, such a game seems senseless. But to the Tangu, this game makes perfect sense. The Tangu value equivalence, not competition (Burridge 1957). They are bothered by the idea of one group winning and another losing, for they believe this situation causes ill will. When Europeans brought soccer to New Guinea, the Tangu changed the rules so that the object was for the two teams to score the same number of goals. Sometimes their soccer games went on for days! American games, in contrast, are highly competitive; there are always winners and losers.

There are many other American values besides competition. Sociologist Robin M. Williams, Jr. (1970) has identified fifteen basic ones. These include achievement and success, activity and work, humanitarianism, efficiency and practicality, progress, material comfort, equality, freedom, conformity, science and rationality, nationalism and patriotism, democracy, individuality, and racial and ethnic group superiority. Williams' list of values is not necessarily shared by all Americans, nor is it exhaustive of all the possibilities. In addition, because values change over time, some on Williams' list may well be disappearing. Nonetheless, his compilation is still regarded as a core set of distinctively American values.

For example, if Americans value material comfort, it makes sense that they would also value the success that can buy that comfort, as well as the hard work needed to achieve success. Other American values, however, are not so compatible. It seems contradictory to value conformity *and* individuality, equality *and* racial superiority. How do Americans manage to live with these contradictions? Often they do so by applying different values in different situations. For instance, the value we place on equality has sometimes prompted affirmative action, by which members of minority groups are hired in proportion to their numbers. Here the conflicting value of free competition is relaxed because pressure for social justice is so strong. You can probably think of instances in your own life in which you have tried to reconcile conflicting values. For example, you have undoubtedly been in situations in which telling the truth would hurt someone, while being kind meant lying.

Hinting gently at the truth is one attempt to reconcile the two conflicting values involved here.

When values are repeatedly in sharp conflict, and reconciliation is difficult, pressure for social change may build. For instance, in recent years the traditional American value of racial superiority may have begun to weaken. This is suggested by a lessening of overt racist attitudes. The 1983 annual survey of college freshmen found that, for the *first* time, a majority supported busing to achieve racial integration in schools (Astin 1983). It may be that conflict between racism and equality has led to new laws that in turn have prompted new behaviors and helped to shift values. Values also change as social events and circumstances change. For example, in 1985 nearly 70 percent of college freshmen said that being well off was very important to them, whereas in 1970 only about 50 percent voiced this opinion (Astin and Green 1986). Perhaps a change in economic conditions (greater competition in the job market, for instance) has prompted students to place more value on achievement and material success. Whatever the reason, these figures show that values are not static. Like all aspects of culture, values undergo change.

Norms

Values provide the framework within which people in a society develop norms of behavior. A **norm** is a specific guideline for action; it is a rule that says how people should behave in particular situations. Sometimes norms are made explicit, as in written laws or biblical commandments. But more often, norms are unspoken customs that people implicitly know and follow. Mork broke an unspoken norm when he voiced his nonverbal responses ("Choke! Gasp! Look of sincere empathy!"). Although people often think about their nonverbal reactions while they are performing them, it is considered a sign of insincerity to describe them out loud. Yet probably no one has ever explicitly *told* you about this social convention. It is a norm that you implicitly grasped in the process of learning your culture. Mork's violation of this norm illustrates how disruptive of smooth social interaction breaking a norm can be. The listener is startled by Mork's responses. They violate one's expectations about "proper" conversation. A person in this situation might even become flustered and not know how to proceed.

In traditional Japan, bowing is the appropriate social norm for exchanging greetings. (Rene Burri/Magnum.)

Like values, norms can vary greatly from society to society. Polite and appropriate behavior in one society may be disgraceful in another. For example:

> Among the Ila-speaking peoples of Africa, girls are given houses of their own at harvest time where they may play at being man and wife with boys of their choice. It is said that among these people virginity does not exist beyond the age of ten. [In contrast] among the Tepoztlan Indians of Mexico, from the time of a girl's first menstruation, life becomes "crabbed, cribbed, confined." No boy is to be spoken to or encouraged in the least way. To do so would be to court disgrace, to show oneself to be crazy or mad. (Ember and Ember 1977, p. 277)

Norms also vary from group to group within a single society. Just think of the difference in dating mores between teenagers and adults in our society.

Most norms are situational; that is, they apply to specific circumstances and settings. For instance, we employ the norm of shaking hands upon meeting or leaving someone, not midway through a conversation (unless perhaps we are cementing an agreement). Similarly, the norm of quietly raising a hand and waiting to be called upon to speak is appropriate in a classroom but not in a group of friends. Part of the process of acquiring a culture is learning exactly when each of the norms that are part of that culture is expected of us.

Much of the time, people follow norms more or less automatically. Alternatives never occur to them. This is particularly true of unspoken norms that seem self-evident, such as answering a person who addresses you. People conform because it seems right, because to violate the norm would damage their self-image or hurt their conscience, and because they want approval and fear ridicule, ostracism, or punishment.

It is important to understand the difference between norms and values. Consider a man at a baseball game when the national anthem is sung. He stops talking with his friends, removes his hat, and stands quietly facing the flag. He is following the norms that prescribe how one should act in this particular situation. If asked why he does these things, he will probably tell you it is "right" to

Symbols occur in all aspects of daily life. Some, like the stop sign, are univocal in that they convey one meaning specifically and clearly. Others, like the cross, are multivocal. They have several different meanings and say somewhat different things to different people. The cross thus says "this is a church" and at the same time reminds a Christian of a whole range of personal religious meanings. (Left: Philip John Bailey/Stock, Boston; right: Tony O'Brien/Stock, Boston.)

show respect for our nation; to do otherwise would be unpatriotic. Here the man is assessing his behavior according to a broad, abstract value: patriotism. Norms, then, are the rules that govern behavior in particular contexts, while values are the broad, internalized standards against which we evaluate behavior.

Folkways, Mores, and Laws

Norms vary in the importance that people assign to them and in the leeway they permit violations. **Folkways** are everyday habits and conventions people obey without giving much thought to the matter. For example, Americans eat three meals a day and call other food "snacks." We have cereal for breakfast but not for other meals; we save sweets for the end of dinner. Even though we could easily begin a meal with cherry pie, we don't. Other customs we observe are covering our mouths when we yawn, shaking hands when introduced, closing zippers on pants or skirts, and *not* wearing evening clothes to class. People who violate folkways may be labeled eccentrics or slobs, but as a rule they are tolerated.

In contrast, violations of mores provoke intense reactions. **Mores** are the norms people consider vital to their well-being and to their most cherished values. Examples are the prohibitions against incest, cannibalism, and sexual abuse of children. People who violate mores are considered unfit for society and may be ostracized, beaten, locked up in a prison or a mental hospital, exiled, or executed. (Hence, most Americans

would not condemn an individual who gave a child molester a severe beating.)

Some norms are formalized into laws. A **law** is a rule enacted by a political body and enforced by the power of the state. Whereas folkways and mores are typically enforced by the collective and spontaneous actions of the members of the community, laws are enforced by the police, the military, or some other special organization. Laws may formalize folkways (as some traffic regulations do) or back up mores (as laws against murder and treason do). Political authorities may also attempt to introduce new norms by enacting laws such as those governing the disposal of toxic wastes or the extension of civil rights to various minorities. In general, the laws that are most difficult to enforce are those that are not grounded in the folkways or mores—for example, laws against gambling or the use of marijuana.

Symbols

In addition to giving us guidelines for behavior and ideas about what is "good" and "right," culture also gives us notions about what things in our world mean. These meanings may involve **symbols**—objects, gestures, sounds, or images that represent something other than themselves. A cross, for example, is merely two intersecting lines, but for Christians a cross symbolizes pain and suffering, faith, and the hope of salvation. Similarly, an American flag is nothing more than a rectangle of tricolored fabric, but for people around the world it symbolizes a powerful nation and that nation's entire way of life. Words, too, are symbols with meanings that people share. The word *green*, for instance, is just a string of sounds with no inherent meaning, but for speakers of English these sounds symbolize a certain family of colors.

Symbols vary in the range of meanings that are assigned to them. At one extreme are **multivocal symbols** that carry a great many different meanings. An American flag, for instance, conveys any number of meanings in most people's minds (freedom, democracy, capitalism, military power, and so forth). In contrast, the word *green* is linked to a much more restricted range of meanings. Some symbols have just one meaning; they are **univocal symbols.** A univocal symbol allows very precise expression of the concept it represents. This is desirable in certain situations, such as when drafting a legal contract. But what they gain in precision, univocal symbols lose in flexibility and richness. It is no accident that most of our most emotionally charged symbols are multivocal ones (Turner 1970).

As the examples we have given illustrate, symbols do not necessarily look like, sound like, or otherwise resemble what they stand for. Granted, symbols may sometimes derive their meaning partly from qualities inherent in them (a lion symbolizing a powerful empire, for instance). But the meaning given symbols is frequently quite arbitrary, simply a matter of tradition and concensus. That is why, in different cultures, different symbols are often used to represent the same concept. In some societies, for instance, black is the color of mourning, while in others white or red suggests grief. There is nothing about these colors that dictates their meaning. The meaning is arbitrarily assigned.

When meanings are arbitrarily assigned to symbols, those meanings can more easily be changed. For example, in England the index and middle fingers held in a V with the palm facing inward is considered a rude insult. During World War II, Churchill turned this symbol around (palm facing outward) and made it stand for victory. Two decades later, students protesting the Vietnam War made this same gesture a symbol for peace.

Even when people think they assign the same meaning to a symbol, their meanings may in fact be somewhat different. For instance, in the United States a gold band worn on the third finger of someone's left hand symbolizes that he or she is married. To some, this suggests that the person has made an exclusive, lifelong commitment. To others it means that the commitment will last only as long as the relationship "works." Thus, each of us brings to the cultural meaning of symbols our own interpretations as well.

The meaning of a powerful symbol may change with its context. In front of the U.S. Capitol Building the flag stands for American patriotism and national identity. When a protestor wears the flag painted on his face, however, he challenges this sort of patriotic reverence and respect for the symbol. (Left: Art Stein/Photo Researchers, Inc.; right: Ellis Herwig/Stock, Boston.)

But the act of personally interpreting symbols should not be taken to mean that each of us defines them idiosyncratically. If people are to align their actions with one another, they must have reasonably similar understandings of the world. That is why the collective creation and use of symbols is the very heart of social life. As Clifford Geertz has written:

> Undirected by . . . organized systems of significant symbols . . . man's behavior would be virtually ungovernable, a mere chaos of pointless acts and exploding emotions, his experience virtually shapeless. Culture, the accumulated totality of such [symbols], is not just an ornament of human existence but . . . an essential condition for it. (1973, p. 46)

Language

A **language** is a system of verbal and, in many cases, written symbols with rules about how those symbols can be strung together to convey more complex meanings. It is impossible to overstate the importance of language in the development, elaboration, and transmission of culture (see Figure 4.1). Language enables people to store meanings and experiences and to pass this heritage on to new generations. Through language, we are able to learn about and from the experiences of others. In addition, language enables us to transcend the here and now, preserving the past and imagining the future. It also makes possible the formulation of complex plans and ideas. These capacities are particularly augmented by the use of writing. People could reason only on the most primitive level if they did not possess language.

The study of language has long been an area of interest to sociologists with a more structural orientation. These researchers analyze how language is put together —how it is built up from smaller speech sounds into words, and from words into meaningful phrases and sentences. Such analysis shows that the structure of language is a key factor in conveying meaning. We cannot arbitrarily rearrange the sounds in a word or the words in a sentence and create a statement that another person is necessarily likely to comprehend. Languages have rules of grammar and syntax that must be followed if we want to be understood. Of course, sociologists with a more structural view of language acknowledge that it is a highly flexible and creative form of communication. But still, its flexibility is constrained by structural rules that are formally established and externally imposed on us.

In Western society we associate black with mourning, but in Chinese culture white is the symbol of mourning. The traditions and consensus within a society give symbols their meanings. (Brian Brake/Photo Researchers.)

FIGURE 4.1   A Comparative Look at Languages

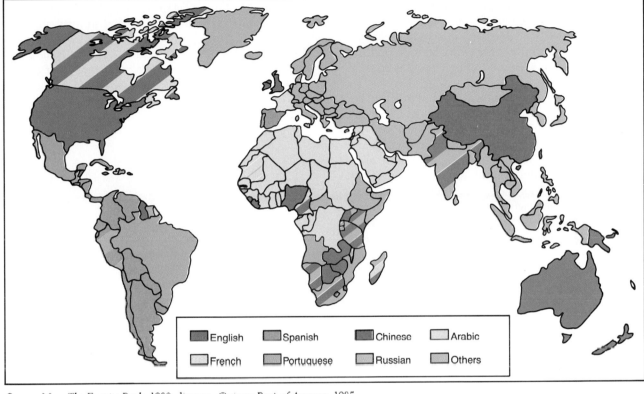

English   Spanish   Chinese   Arabic
French   Portuguese   Russian   Others

Source: Map: *The Europa Book*, 1980; diagram: *Guiness Book of Answers*, 1985.

There are hundreds of languages in the world, but only a few are spoken by the citizens of several different countries. Linguistic differences are an important bar to communication among people of different cultural backgrounds.

Using Language in Social Contexts

Action-oriented sociologists look beyond the structural aspects of language to study how language is actually used and understood in social contexts (Levinson 1983). They have discovered that people seem to change their patterns of speech as social contexts change. For instance, a woman asking her son to mow the lawn might give a direct order ("Get that lawn mowed!") but use an indirect phrasing when addressing her husband ("The lawn's getting awfully long"). Such indirect phrasing is considered more polite, and therefore more appropriate between adults of equal status. A frequent mistake that people make in learning to speak a new language is to overlook cultural conventions about how that language should be used in different social contexts. Thus, Germans sometimes sound domineering when they speak English because their native language allows more direct phrasing of requests and complaints than English does (House and Kasper 1981).

When people use aspects of language to judge the meaning of a situation, they are employing language as a kind of social marker (Sherer and Giles 1979). A **social marker** is any pattern of behavior that provides indications about who people are, what groups they belong to, and what their understanding of a situation is. Imagine, for instance, that after a week in a new job you are asked to attend a staff meeting. Having no idea what a staff meeting entails, you approach it in a cautious, exploratory manner, searching for clues about how you should act. Among these would be linguistic clues. Do the participants at the meeting use formal language? Do they follow a fairly rigid format of who speaks when and for how long, or are their interactions more loosely structured, as in casual conversations? Such clues would give you a good idea of what kind of meeting this is.

Pronunciation, word choice, tone of voice, and grammar would give you additional social insights. They would suggest the position each participant holds relative to the others, that person's place in the social class system, and perhaps his or her ethnic background. A person in authority, for example, usually conveys dominance by phrasing things in an assertive manner ("Get that information tomorrow"). A subordinate, in contrast, is apt to adopt a more tentative style of speaking, liberally sprinkled with linguistic "hedges" ("It seems to me . . .," "Maybe . . .," "You know . . .") and rising intonations at the end of declarative statements (as in answering "Thursday?" to a question about when a particular report will be ready). Often without realizing it, we categorize people on the basis of these speech patterns (Andrews 1984). Thus, to a large extent a person's social identity is established and maintained through the patterns of language he or she uses (Gumperz 1982).

Knowledge

Knowledge is the body of facts and beliefs that people accumulate over time. It consists partly of procedural information, such as how to drive a car or operate a computer. It also consists of information about places, people, and events (Where is the Rose Bowl? Who was our first president? What happens when milk is poured on Rice Krispies?). Often we have knowledge about things that we cannot verify for ourselves but which we accept as "truths." In our society, this includes knowledge that atomic energy can be harnessed and that germs cause disease. However, one person's "true" knowledge may be another person's "mere" belief. Witness the debates over the biblical story of creation and evolutionary theories of human origin. All these kinds of knowledge are part of our culture, our shared heritage.

Modern society is accumulating knowledge at a fantastically rapid pace. This is partly due to the contributions of the various branches of science, the funda-

mental goal of which is to provide new knowledge. The amount of knowledge that science could generate would be greatly limited, however, if it were not for modern methods of storing data. Modern books, microfilm, magnetic tapes, computer disks, and so forth can store vast quantities of information for long periods of time. People in widely separated locations can then have easy access to this data. Some sociologists think that control over all this accumulated knowledge is central to a modern "information society" such as ours (Bell 1980).

CULTURAL INTEGRATION AND DIVERSITY

A description of the various norms, values, symbols, knowledge, and other elements of a culture provides only a limited picture of a people's social life. This is because a culture is more than the sum of its individual elements. These elements are intricately interwoven to form a complex whole. The degree to which the parts of a culture form a consistent and interrelated pattern is termed **cultural integration**.

Cultural Integration

When their culture is well integrated, members of a society face few contradictions between the ways they think and act. Following established traditions people can carry out the business of living with minimal inner conflicts. Yet, as anthropologist Ralph Linton (1947) has emphasized, a highly integrated culture, where religious, economic, and family life are all of one piece, is extremely vulnerable. The customs, beliefs, values, and technology are *interdependent*. Changes in one area invariably affect other areas, sometimes throwing the entire system out of balance.

For example, when European missionaries succeeded in converting large numbers of Madagascans to Christianity, theft became commonplace and people no longer diligently cared for their homes and villages. The reason? Traditional sanctions against theft and in support of village upkeep lost their power in light of the newly adopted European beliefs and practices: "The fear of hell and the police are a poor substitute," Linton explains, "for the fear of ancestral ghosts who know everything and who punish an evil doer with sickness on earth and exclusion from the ancestral village in the hereafter" (Linton 1947, p. 357).

Similarly, the introduction of steel virtually destroyed the highly integrated Stone Age culture of Australian aborigines. To the Europeans who introduced them, steel axes were simply tools that were functionally superior to stone implements. But to the aborigines the ax was more than a tool: Relations between families and tribes were based on the ceremonial exchange of cherished stonework (Arensberg and Niehoff 1964). These patterns of exchange were undermined when the aborigines abandoned their stone implements for those made of steel.

Most cultures are more loosely integrated than those of the traditional Madagascans or the Australian aborigines. This is especially true in large, diverse societies like our own that include people from many different racial and ethnic backgrounds. Thus, American culture is more loosely integrated than that of Japan, which for generations has been a very closed society despite its many economic ties with the rest of the world. Intermediate in its amount of cultural integration is a society like England. England has experienced immigration from various parts of the Commonwealth, so it has more cultural diversity than Japan does. But immigration to England has been on a small scale compared with immigration to the United States, so England is less culturally diverse than America is. Cultural integration, then, is always a matter of degree. In large part it depends on how diverse or homogeneous a society has been throughout its history.

Cultures that are very heterogeneous and loosely integrated involve a certain amount of internal contradiction. "Cultures," Linton (1947, p. 358) writes, "like personalities, are perfectly capable of including conflicting elements and logical inconsistencies." We saw examples of such inconsistencies within American culture in our earlier discussion of values. Many other large, heterogeneous societies live with similarly contradictory elements of culture.

Dominant Culture and Subcultures: Functional and Power Perspectives

Unlike small, very homogeneous societies in which nearly everyone shares the same values and customs,

ours is a society in which some groups of people do not fully participate in the **dominant culture**. Our dominant culture is the culture of the white, Christian, middle and upper-middle classes that tend to impose their outlooks and traditions on society as a whole. Members of certain subordinate groups, such as ethnic and religious minorities, may reject some of the cultural elements of the dominant group. Instead they may adhere to many of their own norms, beliefs, and values, and communicate with their own sets of symbols, including their own languages. When the perspective and life-style of such people differ significantly from the dominant culture, and when they identify themselves as different, they are said to belong to a **subculture.**

Subcultures may develop not just out of ethnic and religious groups. They also form out of occupational groups, socioeconomic groups, age groups, and so on. Adolescents, for example, build a private world out of their peculiar position of being not quite adults yet no longer children. Similarly, medical students share common experiences, goals, and problems, and hence a common viewpoint. Subcultures typically arise when people in similar circumstances find themselves isolated from the mainstream world. They may be isolated physically (such as inmates in prison, soldiers on a military base, poor people in a ghetto), or isolated by what they do and think, that is, by their shared worlds of meanings.

What is the relationship of subcultural groups to the larger society? Do agents of mass socialization (public schools and the media, for example) slowly work to assimilate them into the dominant culture? Most sociologists who approach this question from a functional perspective believe that the answer is yes. They argue that the dominant culture serves to tie individuals together by means of a broadly shared set of understandings about how people should think and act. These sociologists, of course, acknowledge the existence of substantial cultural diversity in the United States. But they see the mainstream culture as a thread that weaves diverse groups together.

In contrast, sociologists who answer in terms of power sharply disagree with this functional view of dominant culture. They see the dominant culture not as a thread that ties people together but rather as a set of ideas and customs that the group in power tries to impose on subordinate groups. As a result, in their view, our society is characterized by an undercurrent of intracultural tension.

Such tension becomes more overt when counter-cultures develop. A **counterculture** is a group whose norms, attitudes, values, and life-style directly clash with or are opposed to those of the dominant or mainstream culture. The youth movement of the late 1960s and early 1970s had many components of a counterculture. Its members rejected the hard work-success ethic, the materialistic focus, the deferred gratification, and the sexually restrictive morality of the "establishment." Religious groups such as Hare Krishna and the Reverend Sun Myung Moon's Unification Church likewise have many countercultural overtones.

There is probably some truth to both the functional and the power orientations on the relationship between a dominant culture and subcultural groups. While members of subcultures in our society are constantly being drawn into the dominant culture, this process is not without tension and resistance. Both these patterns can be seen regarding the second-largest ethnic minority in the United States: Americans of Hispanic heritage, who comprise about 5 percent of our population.

The Case of the Hispanics

Although Hispanics are often lumped together in the public mind as a single people, they embrace a rich and varied set of cultures. According to the 1980 census, 59 percent of the nation's 14.6 million Spanish-speaking population are of Mexican heritage; 13.8 percent are Puerto Ricans, most of whom live in New York City; and 6.3 percent are Cubans, most of whom are concentrated in southern Florida. All groups have grown since the census was completed. These groups use various names to describe themselves. Some use the umbrella term "Hispanic"; others prefer to identify themselves by their nationality—Puerto Rican, Dominican, or Cuban. Still others prefer "Latino," and some Mexican-Americans prefer "Chicano."

Although there are many middle-income and wealthy Hispanics, this population has an especially high percentage of poor people. As a result, Hispanics, on average, earn only half to two-thirds of the average American income (Canino et al. 1980). The Spanish median income is $17,465; the national median income is $23,618 (*Statistical Abstract* 1987). Many Hispanics make up an underclass of workers who take jobs no one

else wants at wages no one else will accept. This structural and economic isolation helps to preserve the subculture from mainstream influences.

Distinctive Cultural Patterns

In 1987 Henry Cisneros, the Hispanic mayor of San Antonio, Texas, surprised many political observers by announcing that he would not be a candidate for governor in 1990, a post for which he was widely acknowledged to be the front-runner. Cisneros' reason for dropping out of the race was to devote more time to his infant son who suffered from birth defects. In a San Antonio Catholic church, a Hispanic priest praised Cisneros' decision in one of his Sunday sermons. Cisneros, he said, affirmed one of the most deeply rooted values of Hispanic culture: family.

This incident points to one of the important ways that the norms and values of Hispanics differ from those of the dominant Anglo-American culture. Hispanics emphasize the family above all else, even political ambition and a man's career. For them the family is a source of comfort, support, security, and identity (Cortés 1980). By "family," Hispanics mean the extended family that includes not just parents and children, but also grandparents, aunts, uncles, and cousins by blood or by marriage. An intense sense of family obligation, loyalty, and respect typically cements the individual members to the group. When one member relocates, others may follow, drawing the family back together again. A strong commitment to mutual assistance within the family often keeps Hispanics from turning to public agencies or social services for help in time of need. For instance, elderly Mexicans are seldom placed in nursing homes because the elderly enjoy a special status in Hispanic culture, and the traditional family assumes responsibility for them.

Hispanics also place a high value on the inner worth of the individual. They tend to be sensitive to inner dignity and the respect that is owed to others. For this reason they are often particularly sensitive to personal insults or scorn. Spiritual values often take precedence over materialistic ones. The Hispanic "tends to think in terms of transcendent qualities, such as justice, loyalty, or love, rather than in terms of practical arrangements which spell out justice or loyalty in the concrete" (Fitzpatrick 1971, pp. 91–92). Hispanic culture emphasizes one-to-one relationships more than the Anglo culture does. Impersonal systems or organizations geared to efficiency make many Hispanics feel uneasy. They are used to dealing with others in highly personal ways.

Dynamics of Subcultural Change

Subcultures such as those of Hispanics exist *within* a larger culture, not apart from it. Consequently, subcultures and the mainstream culture meet and exert influence on each other at many points. Sometimes the effects of the subculture on the dominant culture are so great that a new, and in many ways amalgamated, culture emerges. In the case of Hispanics influencing the larger American culture, however, the effects are much more selective. The Anglo-American culture has been enriched by the introduction of Hispanic food, clothing, music, architecture, and words, but it has not undergone fundamental change as a result of this subcultural contact.

In contrast, the norms and values of some Hispanic Americans have been profoundly challenged by the need to interact with the pervasive Anglo world. One example can be seen in language. Hispanics have had to make their way in a "foreign" society in which English is the language of the workplace, the marketplace, the school, and the political arena. Until recently, Hispanic children in many schools of the Southwest were punished for speaking Spanish in the classroom or on the playground. Even today, many Spanish-speaking children are handicapped in classrooms with predominantly English-speaking activities and programs. Hispanic traditions also face challenges in the realm of values. The realities of American life often force Hispanics into a highly individualistic and competitive environment that in many respects is hostile to their ideals of human interaction. Because of these pressures, some Hispanics have gradually relinquished their traditional language and values to conform to the dominant Anglo culture.

This response is far from universal, however. Compared with other groups of immigrants to the United States, Hispanics have been among the least inclined to merge into the dominant culture (Oxford Analytica 1986). Such merging is called **assimilation,** the process by which members of a subculture come to accept the cultural patterns of the larger society. Researchers have found that it has taken about three generations for members of most immigrant groups to achieve an identity as Americans rather than as Armenians, Germans, Russians, or whatever. Sociologist Milton Gordon (1964) has identified three stages of this process. The first stage is **cultural assimilation,** which allows the newcomers to function within the host society by taking on many of its lifeways without necessarily relinquishing their definitions of themselves as a distinct ethnic group. Thus, Puerto Ricans may learn English, perform their jobs satisfactorily, vote, observe laws and regulations, but still maintain a separate identity as members of a Hispanic subculture.

The next stage (if it occurs at all) is **structural assimilation,** whereby newcomers seek entrance into cliques, clubs, and institutions of the larger society

The Amish of Pennsylvania immigrated to the United States during the 19th century. Because of their religious beliefs and close-knit rural communities they have resisted assimilation into more typical American cultural patterns. They use horse drawn carriages, for example, even though they live alongside Americans with cars, trucks, and motorcycles. (Richard Reinhold/EKM-Nepenthe.)

through personal contact with dominant group members. This type of assimilation gradually erodes the structural ties binding individuals within the subculture. Eventually, it may lead to **marital assimilation,** whereby some members of the subculture intermarry with members of the larger society. Gordon believes that, at this point, the subculture has become essentially a historic entity with little influence on a person's life.

The assimilation process often brings uncertainty and pain. People may suffer severe identity shocks as they give up old, deep-rooted values for new and often conflicting ones. For instance, the Hispanic value of an individual's inner worth and goodness is not at all the same as the dominant culture's emphasis on the freedom of the individual to move upward and compete for higher status. As some young Hispanics embrace the American ideal of the autonomous individual, they find themselves cut loose from the close-knit, supportive community of their subculture, which they have come to reject as stifling. But once they have accepted the American ideal of individual freedom and opportunity, they discover that they are often educationally handicapped and the targets of prejudice. Many feel stranded, cut off from a traditional culture that offers identity and support but without a real anchor in the new culture.

Ethnocentrism and Cultural Relativism

When considering the ideas and practices of other cultures or subcultures, people often pass value judgments. Most Anglo-Americans, for instance, see the extensive family obligations of Hispanics as a burdensome arrangement that inhibits individual freedom. Hispanics, in contrast, view the isolated nuclear family of Anglo-Americans as a lonely institution that cuts people off from the love and assistance of their more distant kin. This tendency to view one's own cultural patterns as good and right and those of others as strange or even immoral is called **ethnocentrism.** As anthropologist Robin Fox (1970, p. 31) has pointed out: "Any human group is ever ready to consign another recognizably different human group to the other side of the boundary. It is not enough to possess culture to be fully human, you have to possess *our* culture."

Accounts of the first European contacts with black Africa are a study in ethnocentrism. The letters and

journals of fifteenth- and sixteenth-century explorers, merchants, and missionaries overflowed with lurid descriptions of cannibalism, incest, and "unbridled lust." Since the Africans did not practice Christianity, they were labeled "heathens"; since their laws were incomprehensible to the Europeans, they were said to be "lawless"; and since their marriage and family practices differed from those prevalent in Europe, they were judged to be "savages" and "barbarians." The Europeans viewed the Africans as objects of loathing. Ethnocentrism led them to overlook the accomplishments of great African dynasties such as that of the Sonniki in Ghana, founded in the second century A.D. Not untypical was the following account by a European:

> The majority of them . . . are entirely savage and display the nature of the wild beast . . . and are as far removed as possible from human kindness to one another; and speaking as they do with a shrill voice and cultivating none of the practices of civilized life as these are found among the rest of mankind, they present a striking contrast when considered in light of our own customs. (quoted in George 1968, p. 25)

Ironically, such accounts tell us more about the biases of the Europeans than about the behavior of the Africans.

For most people, culture operates outside awareness. Their own customs, beliefs, and values are so inculcated in them that they consider these learned elements of culture part of "human nature." Such ethnocentric attitudes promote group solidarity and loyalty, improve morale, encourage conformity, and foster nationalism and patriotism. But by the same token, ethnocentric sentiments increase hostility toward outsiders, foster conflict among groups, engender racism, and intensify resistance to change. In sum, although ethnocentrism is a source of unity and stability *within* groups, it is a source of misunderstanding and friction *between* groups.

Social scientists contend that in order to understand a culture fully, we must do more than just try to suspend our ethnocentrism. We must also strive to consider the elements of that culture on their own terms, in their own setting, and in light of the social forces that impinge on the people who have created and who use those cultural traditions. This perspective is called **cultural relativism.** Cultural relativism stresses that any element of culture is *relative* to a particular time, place, and set of circum-

Decorating the body, especially the face, is a cultural universal, a behavior pattern found in different forms in all known cultures. (Left: Jack Fields/ Photo Researchers; right: Ethan Hoffman/Archive Pictures.)

stances. If we try to analyze that element outside the cultural context in which it evolved, we will probably distort its meaning. For practical purposes of studying human behavior, social scientists try, as far as possible, to adopt cultural relativism when assessing the customs of people in societies different from their own. It is important to recognize that cultural relativism is a matter of understanding and not necessarily of approval. We can understand a tribal practice of infanticide without approving it. Unlike ethnocentrism, cultural relativism as a position encourages mutual understanding and tolerance between groups.

Cultural Universals

While all sociologists try to adopt cultural relativism in their study of the differences among societies, some are particularly concerned about finding underlying cultural characteristics common to all human societies.

Edward O. Wilson, a biologist who has been a major proponent of **sociobiology,** maintains that social groups adapt to their environment primarily through the evolution of genetic traits that shape social behavior. This view has been adopted but also criticized by a number of sociologists (see the box "Sociobiology and Its

Critics"). Wilson also believes that "there are social traits occurring through all cultures which upon close examination are as diagnostic of mankind as are distinguishing characteristics of other animal species" (1978, p. 21). Social scientists define **cultural universals** as those behavior patterns and institutions found in all known cultures. The anthropologist George Peter Murdock (1945) identified over sixty cultural universals, such as a system of social status, marriage, body adornments, dancing, myths and legends, cooking, incest taboos, inheritance rules, puberty customs, and religious rituals.

While some social scientists think these "universals" are too vague to have any analytical value, sociobiologists such as Wilson believe they show how much of culture is biologically inherited rather than learned. Wilson maintains that people raised from birth in an environment free of cultural influence would exhibit these cultural universals on their own. He quotes Robin Fox on this issue:

> If our new Adam and Eve could survive and breed—still in total isolation from any cultural influences—then eventually they would produce a society which would have laws about property, rules about incest and marriage, customs of taboo and avoidance . . . beliefs about the supernatural . . . courtship practices . . . gambling of some kind . . . dancing, adultery, and various doses of homicide, suicide, homosexuality, schizophrenia, psy-

Sociobiology and Its Critics

Sociobiology owes much to the discoveries of Charles Darwin regarding natural selection, the process whereby nature favors those best equipped to survive and to reproduce their characteristics by genetic transmission. Take the example of the giraffe, with its long neck particularly well-suited for nibbling at leaves in trees. At one time, a chance genetic mutation may have given one giraffe a slightly longer neck than others in the species. Because this genetic trait gave the animal a competitive edge in the fight to survive (in this case, reaching food), it had a better chance to live and pass on the successful trait to its offspring. By contrast, the less fit have a harder time surviving and thus have less reproductive success. Gradually, successive generations of offspring represent in increasing numbers the genetic characteristics that are adaptive. Through this process, evolutionary change in the makeup of a species comes about.

The startling claim of sociobiologists is that even human culture and social behavior have evolved largely through natural selection and genetic transmission of traits. To those who insist that our social behavior is learned, they reply that genes may *predispose* us to learn certain things. Consider the following experiment taken from the animal world (Barash 1977). The experiment requires a dog and a squirrel to move away from food in order ultimately to reach it. The dog fails miserably at the task, while the squirrel solves the problem easily. Why? Although less intelligent than the dog, the squirrel is a member of a species whose nervous system is "wired" to engage in such behavior. To reach its food, the squirrel must often jump from tree to tree, choosing a path that takes advantage of branches of adjacent trees that are close together. This approach often entails a circuitous route to the goal. In contrast, a dog must remain on the ground and typically charges straight at its food goal. In the case of the squirrel, natural selection favored the ability to conduct detours and left the squirrel predisposed to learn how to reach the type of goal presented by the experiment. In sum, sociobiologists say that genes construct a brain that is organized in such a way that information is processed more readily in one manner than in another.

The main issue posed by sociobiology is whether culture is a distinctive human creation or the product of genetic programming. Anthropologists such as Marshall Sahlins (1981) maintain that the critical feature distinguishing human beings from other species is the human use of symbols to give meaning to objects and events. More specifically, human beings fashion their behavior according to a meaningful scheme that they themselves have devised. Sahlins says that this scheme—"culture"—does not have its origins in genes, and for this reason sociobiologists have been unable to identify any specific genes for specific behavior.

The sociologist Kenneth Bock (1980) contends that the rapid pace of human history and the wide diversity

chosis and neuroses, and various practitioners to take advantage of or cure these, depending on how they are viewed. (Wilson 1978, p. 24)

Wilson cites the universal taboo against incest as an example of a cultural universal with a basis in heredity. He says that in avoiding incest, "human beings are guided by an instinct based on genes" (p. 38). Inbreeding, claims Wilson, produces offspring that are genetically less fit than their parents and less capable of producing their own offspring. Darwinian natural selection tends to weed out these individuals while favoring those possessing an inborn mechanism that discourages inbreeding. The transmission of this genetic predisposition through thousands of generations has resulted in a species that culturally proscribes incest.

INDIVIDUALISM: A KEY THEME IN AMERICAN CULTURE

Brian Palmer, a successful businessman, lives in a comfortable San Jose suburb and works as a top-level manager in a large corporation. He is justifiably proud of his rapid rise in the corporation, but he is even prouder of the profound change he has made recently in his idea of success. "Two years ago," he says, "confronted with the work load I have right now, I would stay in the office and work until midnight, until such time as it got done. Now I just kind of flip the bird and walk out. My family life is more important to me than that, and the work will wait I have learned." A new marriage and a houseful of children have become the center of Brian's life.

of human cultures demonstrate that social behavior cannot be explained by biological mechanisms. For instance, in less than two hundred years a revolution has occurred in human modes of transportation, including trains, automobiles, airplanes, and space vehicles. He points out that biology contributes little, if anything, to our understanding of the forces leading to these massive changes.

Likewise, the anthropologist Marvin Harris (1980, p. 125) argues that the human species is capable of acquiring an overwhelming number of behavioral responses through learning processes, "without the slightest exchange or mutation of genes." These social responses cannot be considered genetically determined because they can be acquired or wiped out in a single generation. For example, influenced by Christian missionaries, some Polynesian peoples gave up their relatively uninhibited sexual ways and took up premarital chastity. And the Mohawk Indians of New York State are well known for their abilities as construc-

tion workers on skyscrapers. "Walking across narrow beams eighty floors above street level, they [are] not troubled by an urge to build wigwams rather than office buildings" (p. 125). Harris insists that the major steps in human cultural evolution—the rise of agriculture, the nation-state, and industrial organizations—have all occurred too quickly for biological evolution to have played a part.

Harris concedes that certain behavior patterns became part of "human nature" because they contributed to the fitness of humans and their reproductive success. But he acknowledges fewer cultural universals than the sociobiologists do. For example, Harris believes it is doubtful that the incest taboo is genetically programmed as a universal trait. He cites practical social and economic reasons for a brother-sister incest taboo in groups that depend on intergroup marital alliances for defense and trade. Similarly, the social fact that both mother and son fear the wrath of a dominant husband and father probably accounts for the

rare occurrence of mother-son incest. In contrast, given the greater power and resources of the male, father-daughter incest is *not* rare; an estimated several hundred thousand cases occur each year in the United States alone.

Harris acknowledges that one trait is universal and has a genetic foundation, namely, the human facility for language. Natural selection favored "individuals able to transmit, receive, and store ever-more-complex messages" (p. 123). But Harris points out a paradox here. Language capabilities enhanced our learning and enabled us to acquire and modify behaviors that do not require genes to control them. The learning ability made possible by language helps to account for the enormous variation found in the social behavior of the human species. Hence, critics of sociobiology argue that human behavior is no longer rigidly tied to genes, and cultural evolution has come to be seen as the chief source of behavioral change for human beings.

Brian's reasons for changing his life seem mainly to be a shift in his notions of what makes him happy. His new goal—devotion to marriage and children—seems as arbitrary and unexamined as his earlier pursuit of material success. Both are justified as idiosyncratic preferences rather than as representing a larger sense of the purpose of life (Bellah et al. 1985, pp. 3–6).

Margaret Oldham, a composed woman in her early thirties, has a strong sense of discipline and has achieved an outstanding academic record and professional success [she is a psychotherapist]. . . . Margaret understands that human relationships require give-and-take, that you must work hard for the satisfactions you expect in life, and that you are ultimately responsible for your own life. But this clear-sighted vision of each individual's ultimate

self-reliance turns out to leave very little place for interdependence and represents a fairly grim view of the individual's place in the social world. Self-reliance is a virtue that implies being alone. "I do think it's important for you to take responsibility for yourself, I mean, nobody else is going to really do it. I mean people do take care of each other, people help each other, you know, when somebody's sick, and that's wonderful. But in the end you're really alone and you really have to answer to yourself, and in the end, if you don't get the job you want or, you know, meet the person you want, it's at least in part your responsibility. . . ." (Bellah et al. 1985, pp. 13–15)

American culture places a strong emphasis on individualism. The right of people to think, judge, and decide for themselves, to fashion their own behavior and live their own lives, is considered unquestioned. All our aspirations revolve around our sense of individual achievement and fulfillment. Even the fictional heroes we create—the Western cowboy or sheriff, the hard-boiled city detective—tend to be loners who depend only on their own abilities and instincts. Alexis de Tocqueville, a French social observer and theorist who toured the United States during the 1830s, was one of the first to write about American individualism and its consequences. Tocqueville (1835) saw this powerful American value as closely tied to a spirit of equality. The idea that people should be free to make their own choices goes hand in hand with the notion that no one is above anyone else.

Brian Palmer and Margaret Oldham, express the central American themes of self-reliance, self-responsibility, self-interest, and self-choice. Brian Palmer prides himself in having "done his own thing" by independently rejecting a workaholic life-style in favor of spending more time with his family. Margaret Oldham's commitment to individualism is stated even more explicitly. She insists that all of us are ultimately alone, necessarily dependent primarily on ourselves to obtain what we want from life.

The stress on individualism has increased in the modern era. This increase was spurred partly by the Protestant religious movement, which advocated an individual relationship with God (not one mediated by a church hierarchy). It was also spurred by the political and economic desire to gain freedom from oppressive control by monarchs and aristocracies (Abercrombie, Hill, and Turner 1986). In America, this desire gave rise to a revolution and a government dedicated to the individual's right to "life, liberty, and the pursuit of happiness." As our society became more industrialized and our population more mobile, individual freedoms broadened. Many people no longer felt that they were *born* into a particular religion, a particular occupation, a particular social status that must endure for life. These areas increasingly became open to individual initiative, effort, and choice. At the same time, marriage became more private. People began to think of it not as an alliance between families or a social obligation, but as an individual decision between two people. The nuclear family also became more private as people moved to distant areas in search of jobs and a better life. Husbands and wives increasingly sought what was best for *me, my* future, *my* children. But even these commitments to the nuclear family were not absolute. In the modern age,

divorce became increasingly common, as marriage became viewed as something to be dissolved if it failed to provide individual fulfillment.

It may seem that this greater and greater stress on individualism is at odds with the growth of large-scale social organization, which has also occurred in the modern era. The two, however, are not incompatible. In contemporary society, individuals participate *within* large organizations. Individual citizens vote and express their personal opinions within the political system; individual workers make job choices and seek their personal career goals within big corporations; individual consumers buy products according to their personal tastes within enormous economic markets. Room for individualism, then, is woven into the fabric of large-scale social organization.

Individualism is not just a value in our society; it is also a social condition, protected by law. This condition has been prompted partly by our institution of private property. Private property requires that individuals have extensive rights over the use and sale of material things, including land and capital (Macpherson 1974). The fact that such protections evolved shows that an individualistic society doesn't just happen by itself. It can grow only in an environment that supports and fosters it.

Although Americans extol their individualism, they pay a price for it. Several sociologists have argued that our highly individualistic culture neglects the basic human needs for community and dependence (Bellah et al. 1985; Reisman 1961; Slater 1976). Determined to carve our own destinies free from constraints by others, we often leave ourselves in lonely, sometimes frightening isolation. Especially vulnerable are those who are frequently moving, constantly living among strangers. Even at times when they wish to turn to others for assistance and support, they have few opportunities to do so.

But there is also evidence that Americans are recognizing the need to reconnect with others and strengthen their social bonds. For instance, more and more people are trading in the anonymity of city life for the more intimate ties offered by small communities. What's more, many of those who stay in the cities are organizing neighborhood associations to address their common needs. Many other groups are forming for the sole purpose of allowing people to exchange information and deal with shared problems (from coping with cancer, to losing weight, to investing wisely in the stock market). These trends attest to a growing effort among Americans

The drinkers in the painting by Degas are clearly lonely isolated strangers; in Renoir's painting they form lively social bonds. These two scenes portray an important point about individualism and culture: Sometimes, the accent on individualism frustrates the needs for community, engagement, and dependence. But at other times, too much emphasis on community may stifle individualism. (Left: Art Resource; right: The Phillips Collection.)

to regain a sense of community, shared responsibility, and the interdependence of people (Boyte 1986). We will return to the theme of Community in Chapter 9.

THE PRODUCTION OF CULTURE: COMBINING ACTION AND STRUCTURE

Some twenty years ago, sociologist Herbert Blumer had an opportunity to study the women's fashion industry. He was impressed by the fact that fashion trends do not simply spring forth from the drawing boards of famous fashion designers. Instead, these trends are the end result of a complex social process by which a large number of potential new "looks" are screened and selected from. As Blumer described one of the later stages in that process:

At a seasonal opening of a major Parisian fashion house there may be presented a hundred or more designs of women's evening wear before an audience of from one to two hundred buyers [representatives of retail stores that sell women's clothing]. The managerial staff of the fashion house is able to indicate a group of about thirty designs of the entire lot, inside of which will fall the small number, usually about six to eight dresses, that are chosen by the buyers. But the managerial staff is typically unable to predict this small number on which the choices converge. Now, these choices are made by the buyers—a highly competitive and secretive lot—independently of each other and without knowledge of each other's selections. Why should their choices converge on a few designs as they do? When the buyers were asked why they chose one dress in preference to another—between which my inexperienced eye could see no appreciable difference—the typical, honest, yet largely uninformative answer was that the chosen dress was "stunning." (Blumer 1969, pp. 278–279)

Blumer's descriptions of the fashion world illustrate a central assumption in an examination of the produc-

The production of culture is a social process. In film-making, for example, there is a strong sense of team-work and social organization. The film will result from a collective effort on the part of the director, writers, actors and actresses, gaffers, make-up artists, costum-ers, cinematographers, and assistants. (Peter Sorel/Sygma.)

tion of culture (Peterson 1979). The assumption is that the elements of a culture do not arise full blown, as if created by the stroke of some magical brush. Instead, those elements are shaped by a variety of decisions about what is desirable and good. Fashion designers, for instance, do not turn out the "look" of the season simply from their own imaginations. They are influenced by clothing trends of the past, by what other designers are doing, and by the views of the members of their staffs. They are also influenced by the opinions of the buyers they must sell to, who in turn are affected by their own ideas about what will appeal to the public. The public, for its part, is influenced by what designers, buyers, and fashion editors tell them is "in" for this particular year. Thus, women's fashions are the product of an elaborate social process in which many people make decisions based on a variety of factors that constrain their choices.

The women's fashion industry is just one example of how new aspects of culture are produced. Richard Peterson (1979), a proponent of the production of culture perspective, argues that in advanced industrial-ized societies like our own, new elements of culture are often deliberately created and disseminated by people who specialize in this task. The fashion designer is one

such specialist. Others are artists, scientists, and members of the legal profession, all of whom are in the business of adding new ideas to culture. Peterson and others seek to analyze how these people introduce, market, and distribute new cultural elements, from the time these elements are first conceived of to the time that others use them.

Sociologists who study the production of culture are particularly concerned about the interplay between the individual actively creating culture and the social structures that influence those creations. Rather than taking an extreme action or structural approach, they seek to bridge the gap between the individual and society. Consequently they examine the social aspects of cultural innovation just as intently as they analyze the efforts of the individual creator.

No matter how solitary the task of producing a new cultural element may seem, it is always the result of a collective effort, not the work of one individual. Consider the artist who produces a new style of painting. Is he or she solely responsible for this new aspect of culture? Sociologist Howard Becker explains why the answer is no:

> Painters depend on manufacturers for canvas, stretchers, paint, and brushes; on dealers, collectors, and museum curators for exhibition space and financial support; on critics and aestheticians for the rationale for what they do; on the state for the patronage or even the advantageous tax laws which persuade collectors to buy works and donate them to the public; on members of the public to respond to the work emotionally; and on other painters, contemporary and past, who created the tradition which makes the backdrop against which their work makes sense (Becker 1984, p. 13).

The production of culture, then, is always a social process. No matter how isolated the cultural innovator may seem, he or she is always embedded in a social context that enables the innovation to come about and guides the direction it takes.

Sociologists who study the production of culture examine these social contexts in great detail. They have found that cultural innovation is not a matter of "anything goes." Instead, there are many constraints on exactly which innovations will find social acceptance. Consider the role technology plays in new elements of culture. Without the technology of the microscope, for instance, modern medicine would never have developed. Without the technology of the computer, space exploration and all the new knowledge of the universe it has brought would never have become a part of our culture. Even in the arts, new technology has been very influential. Without the invention of the tape recorder and the synthesizer, for example, electronic music would never even have entered our imaginations, let alone our culture.

Also important in constraining what new elements enter a culture are the existing abilities of those who must execute the innovation. For instance, in the early 1900s, before people were familiar with polytonality in music (the use of more than one key at the same time), the composer Charles Ives experimented with it. But musicians told him they couldn't play his pieces, that instruments couldn't make the series of sounds he wrote. It was not until much later, after styles of music had changed and musicians had acquired new skills, that Ives' work found an audience. The work of the poet e. e. cummings was similarly resisted. The layouts of his poems were so unusual when he first tried to get them published that many printers flatly refused to take on the job (Becker 1984). The examples of Ives and cummings illustrate an important point: The task of producing a cultural innovation is much easier when that innovation is not so unorthodox that it hinders cooperation from people whose assistance is needed.

A third factor that helps determine the acceptance of a new cultural element is the conventions and traditions that have already been established. Fashion designers, for instance, could conceivably design clothing that bears no resemblance at all to what we are accustomed to wearing. But no designers who are successful depart from the norm in such a radical way. Instead, most create styles that are reasonably in line with public expectations. To do otherwise would usually mean dooming one's cultural innovations to obscurity. Similarly, many so-called formula novels, such as the Harlequin romances, involve new plots, but require that these conform to established conventions—like the guarantee of a happy ending (Griswold 1988).

The fate of a cultural innovation is also affected by those who have a hand in disseminating the new idea. Such people are often called **cultural gatekeepers** because they regulate the flow of new elements of culture into society. Gatekeepers decide which of a huge number of proposed cultural innovations will end up getting widespread exposure through traditional distribution channels. The retail buyers of new clothing designs that

Herbert Blumer wrote about are gatekeepers of the fashion world. Their decisions determine which of hundreds of would-be fashions actually get displayed on retail store racks.

When sociologist Paul Hirsch (1971) studied the creation of new products in three entertainment industries (book publishing, popular records, and movies), he likewise found that gatekeepers play an important role. Because producers in these industries are uncertain about what the ingredients of a "blockbuster" are, they hedge their bets by creating many more new releases than consumers would ever want. They certainly cannot afford to give each one of these new products a large advertising budget. So they depend on autonomous gatekeepers (book reviewers, disc jockeys, film critics, talk-show hosts) to bring the products to public attention. The fate of any given product is therefore made or lost at this strategic checkpoint. In the world of art, gallery owners and museum administrators play a similar function. They are the ones who decide what pieces will be displayed to the public and therefore which have a chance of being accepted into the mainstream culture (Becker 1984).

But what about the role of public tastes in the acceptance of new elements of culture? Aren't public tastes just as important as the exposure given to particular innovations by cultural gatekeepers? The answer is that public tastes are indeed important. Because of public tastes, *Star Wars* played in more movie theaters than any European "art" film released in the same year. Because of public tastes, Madonna gets more radio and TV airtime than the very best singers of medieval madrigals. But note that people's cultural preferences are partly a result of what they are repeatedly exposed to. When cultural gatekeepers barrage us with certain kinds of products, we are apt to decide that these are in fact the products we like best. Often, then, our role as "consumers" of culture is simply to decide among the relatively small number of new cultural items that gatekeepers preselect for our consideration (Hirsch 1971).

How new elements of culture are introduced, distributed, and accepted is quite a complex social process, as our discussion has shown. Those who study the production of culture explore this process extensively. In doing so, they remind us that culture is never a static, "finished" product. Instead, it undergoes constant change as a result of decisions made by many different people who are both consumers of culture and creators of it.

CULTURE AND THE MEDIA

Television is usually the first thing that comes to mind when we think of electronic media of communication. These media also include the radio, the telephone, the tape recorder, the motion picture, the computer, the VCR—in short, any electronic invention that enables people to collect, process, and exchange information with one another (Rogers 1986). Clearly, an enormous amount of communication today occurs with the aid of such electronic devices.

The electronic media are the latest step in a long line of inventions aimed at helping people communicate. Language was the first distinctly human medium of communication. When people developed language, they set their lives on a course distinctly different from the course followed by their nonspeaking ancestors. Language dramatically changed the nature of society. It enabled people to create complex cultures, to share a variety of beliefs, values, knowledge, and symbols, and to pass those cultural elements on to future generations. None of these changes came overnight; they occurred gradually. But in the end, the essence of human life had been transformed because of the creation of a medium of communication.

Subsequent innovations in communications media are often overshadowed by the importance of spoken language. But these innovations, in their turn, have also had a marked effect on how people live. Consider the invention of writing and later of the printing press. Writing made possible the long-term storage of information. No longer did people have to hold in their heads all the knowledge of their culture. They could turn to written records for such information, and they could study and analyze it. Then came the idea of printing words using movable type and a press. This invention is usually attributed to Johannes Gutenberg, a fifteenth-century German goldsmith. The printed word enormously increased the distribution of books. A skilled copyist, working by hand, would require six months to produce a book, whereas a printer, working on a Gutenberg press, could turn out several pages in a day (Eisenstein 1979). With books available to a wider audience, new ideas spread rapidly. It is no wonder that Francis Bacon, the English philosopher and statesman, said that printing (along with the compass and gunpowder) "changed the appearance and state of the whole world."

In our own times, the new electronic media of communication have again transformed Western cul-

Unlike mass media, storytelling involves face-to-face contact between storyteller and audience. The social contact is usually between people who are very similar to one another rather than diverse. (N.R. Farbman/ Time Inc.)

ture. The telegraph, telephone, radio, television, record player, tape recorder, movie camera, computer, and so forth have greatly extended the speed and distance over which people can "talk" to one another, as well as the size of the audiences involved in communications. For instance, millions of Hong Kong residents can hear about a sharp decline in American stock prices almost as soon as it happens, and their own responses to this event will be news to millions of Americans within a matter of hours. At the same time, the electronic media have dramatically altered how we think about the world and how we relate to other people. The famine in Ethiopia is of concern not just to Ethiopians but also to Americans and to others around the world who receive news by electronic communications. The electronic media are also changing the boundaries between public and private spheres of life. On radio and TV talk shows, for example, people discuss their sex lives while millions of strangers listen in. What was once a highly private, "backstage" subject becomes the topic in an open forum. In contrast to this, electronic devices like stereos with headphones and "Walkman" radios allow people to be in their own private worlds even when they are in public places (Meyrowitz 1985). To see more of the changes that electronic media have fostered, let us consider in depth the example of television, so ubiquitous in our society.

In Depth: The Impact of Television

The *CBS Evening News* for June 20, 1985 began with the words and image of Allyn Conwell, an American held hostage in Beirut: "I am speaking on behalf of my fellow forty hostages, who have elected me as their spokesman to make a brief press conference to advise our families, friends, and loved ones of our welfare . . ." Dan Rather then cut in to introduce the day's events:

"For the first time in a week, the first look at and word from some of the passenger hostages from TWA flight 847 in Beirut.

And in El Salvador, the bodies of six Americans gunned down by leftist rebels, a grim reminder that terrorism is not exclusive to the Middle East.

Good evening, this is the *CBS Evening News*, Dan Rather reporting.

New assurances in Beirut today, assurances from one of the American hostages that all thirty-seven of the passengers still captive from that hijacked jetliner are still safe. This is on the seventh day of the hijacking ordeal. Welcome news to the families of the hostages.

But it was news of a different, more tragic kind from El Salvador, where thirteen people, four of them U.S. Marines, two of them U.S. civilians, were killed in a guerrilla attack."

The broadcast closed with a report on the funeral of the Navy diver killed by the hijackers in Beirut, and the reactions of the families of the Americans killed in El Salvador:

VIDEO	AUDIO
Still of sailor in uniform in inset behind Rather.	"On this seventh day of the hijacking of the TWA plane, they buried the young hostage brutally beaten and then murdered by terrorists. But as the killing of Americans in El Salvador reminds us, that death proved to be preamble, the title page written in blood to a volume of terrorist violence against the United States."
Drawing of American flag at half staff in inset.	

Bugler plays taps (sound continues under narration by Bruce Morton reporting from Arlington National Cemetery).

Still of American flag.

Camera zooms out slowly to show huge flag hanging above flag-draped coffin and honor guard.

Stills of Marines in uniform, alternating with stills of Arlington funeral.

"The Marine Corps hymn says, 'We'll fight our country's battles, on the land and on the sea.' But these young men did not die fighting battles, fighting an enemy in a war they knew about. More and more American servicemen are going peacefully about their peaceful rounds and being murdered for it."
(Then a pause while video continues.)
"Bruce Morton, CBS News, Arlington."

Source: Hallin, 1986, pp. 9–10.

At first, it may not appear that listening to Dan Rather report the evening news is any different from reading about current events in a newspaper or a book. This appearance is mistaken, however. Each medium of communication—speech, print, photographs, TV—shapes the content and meaning of the messages it conveys.

Compared with print, television is an image-oriented medium; it is produced largely to be *seen*. As a result, what gets broadcast on TV is largely selected for and framed according to the visual impact it will make. If a news story has no exciting visual content to speak of, such content will be created for it. As Dan Rather spoke of U.S. servicemen being killed by terrorists, for instance, pictures of American flags and soldiers accompanied his words. Because these symbols are visual, it seems natural to choose them for their dramatic impact. This is another way in which TV messages differ from those in print. The TV messages considered most successful are action-filled and sensational, whereas successful messages conveyed in print are usually thoughtful, well structured, and well reasoned. With TV messages there is little need to worry about building a well-reasoned argument, for words on TV are almost never long, essaylike monologues. Consider the way Dan Rather began his evening news report. His statements were more like dramatic, emotionally charged headlines than full-fledged stories. This dramatic, action-filled format makes TV messages much more fragmented and discontinuous than messages in print. A few sentences and some film footage about a plane hijacking are quickly followed by pictures and some comments about a guerrilla attack in El Salvador. The goal is to keep the material constantly moving, filled with exciting glimpses into different events. On a news program such as Dan Rather's, the average length of a "story" is only 45 seconds (Postman 1986). The entire transcript of a nightly news broadcast contains only as much text as one and a half columns on the front page of the *New York Times* (Meyrowitz 1985). The result is a kaleidoscope of images. Nothing is dwelled on long enough to become boring. But at the same time, nothing is given enough attention to be analyzed in any depth. Television, in contrast to the written word, is a medium of communication for which drama, not analysis, seems most appropriate (Eisslin 1982).

Some observers are concerned that these characteristics of television are shaping the way that Americans view other aspects of the world. Ours may be a culture in which people believe that law enforcement, politics, education, and so forth should be fashioned to make them entertaining, just as we expect of TV. As a result, we may so blur the distinction between reality and entertainment that we fail to take important public matters seriously enough. Critic Neil Postman (1986, pp. 93–97) gives examples of this trend:

In Chicago, the Reverend Greg Sakowicz, a Roman Catholic priest, mixes his religious teaching with rock 'n' roll music. . . . On his radio show, "The Journey Inward," Father Sakowicz chats in soft tones about such topics as family relationships or commitment, and interposes his sermons with "the sound of *Billboard's* Top 10." He says his preaching is not done "in a churchy way," and adds, "You don't have to be boring in order to be holy." . . .

In Phoenix, Arizona, Dr. Edward Dietrich performed triple by-pass surgery on Bernard Schuler. . . . The operation was carried by at least fifty television stations in the United States, and also by the British Broadcasting Corporation. A two-man panel of narrators (a play-by-play and color man, so to speak) kept viewers informed about what they were seeing. It was not clear why this event was televised, but it resulted in transforming both Dr. Dietrich and Mr. Schuler's chest into celebrities. . . .

As reported with great enthusiasm by both WCBS-TV and WNBC-TV in 1984, the Philadelphia public schools have embarked on an experiment in which children will have their curriculum sung to them. Wearing Walkman equipment, students were shown listening to rock music whose lyrics were about the eight parts of speech. Mr. Jocko Henderson, who thought of this idea, is planning to delight students further by subjecting mathematics and history, as well as English, to the rigors of a rock music format. . . .

In New Bedford, Massachusetts, a rape trial was televised, to the delight of audiences who could barely tell the difference between the trial and their favorite mid-day soap operas. In Florida, trials of varying degrees of seriousness, including murder, are regularly televised and are considered to be more entertaining than most fictional courtroom dramas. All of this is done in the interests of "public education." . . .

Prior to the 1984 presidential elections, the two candidates confronted each other on television in what were called "debates." . . . The men were less concerned with giving arguments than with "giving off" impressions, which is what television does best. Post-debate commentary largely avoided any evaluation of the candidates' ideas, since there were none to evaluate. Instead, the debates were conceived as boxing matches, the relevant question being, Who KO'd whom? The answer was determined by the "style" of the men—how they looked, fixed their gaze, smiled, and delivered one-liners. . . .

Postman believes that ours is becoming an entertainment culture in which the line between show business and serious public affairs is becoming increasingly fuzzy. "Our priests and presidents," he writes, "our surgeons and lawyers, our educators and newscasters need worry less about satisfying the demands of their discipline than the demands of good showmanship" (p. 98). He thinks that this pervasive show-business outlook arises in large part from our constant exposure to television.

Other observers see other effects of TV on American society. J. Meyrowitz (1985) believes that TV is breaking down the former distinctions between face-to-face encounters among people and encounters that occur through communications media that distance people in time and space. Dan Rather is not actually in our living rooms every evening telling us the news of the day, but television makes us feel as if he is. We hear his words, we see his face, we watch his expressions and experience his style in much the same way that we would if he were sitting right on the living-room sofa. As a result, Meyrowitz argues, people come to feel that they "know" those they meet on television in the same way they know their friends. This helps to explain why, when a "television friend" dies, millions of people respond with a sense of loss that would normally be expected only with the death of an intimate acquaintance.

Meyrowitz also points out that TV changes the boundaries of social situations, prompting people to act in new and different ways because their audiences are different. He gives the example of the president and his wife talking in their living room with a reporter before TV cameras. How should the president and first lady behave? Should they act as if this is a private social encounter between three people, or should they act as if they are making a public appearance before the entire nation? The answer is that they must do both and, therefore, they cannot fully do either. They cannot behave as if they are totally alone with the reporter, chatting among friends, nor can they behave as if they are delivering an inaugural address. "To the extent that actions are shaped to fit particular social settings, this new setting leads to new actions and new social meanings. In this sense we have not only a different situation, but also a different President, and—in the long run—a different presidency" (Meyrowitz 1985, p. 43).

Yet another effect that TV has on American culture is to reinforce some of our stereotyped beliefs. For instance, many Americans have come to believe that racial struggle and conflict are largely a thing of the past in our society. Current shows on television bolster this outlook.

In a recent analysis of black males in four popular comedy shows ("Benson," "Webster," "Different Strokes," and "The Jeffersons"), predominant themes were upward mobility, economic success, and racial invisibility (Gray 1986). The subject of black-white relations was seldom treated, and when it was, an image of general interracial harmony prevailed. In reality, of course, this TV world is overly idealized. The affluence and lack of racial tension seen in these programs is simply not within the experience of millions of black Americans. The result is that TV reinforces a distorted view of the degree to which black Americans have "made it" in our society. This deflects attention from the persistence of racism and racial inequality in America.

Such bias on television indicates the substantial power that people who control the TV industry possess. Network managers, in particular, decide what cultural information gets distributed over the television airwaves. Even the news is not just a matter of reporting what occurred on a particular day. There are simply too many events of potential interest to viewers and too many different perspectives a reporter might take. So TV newswriters and editors are necessarily selective in determining what fragments of the day's happenings will be aired. And that selectivity inevitably reflects their own biases as well as the biases of their bosses. Thus, network staffs serve as important cultural gatekeepers. They decide which cultural ideas and innovations get exposure through a medium of communication that touches the lives of several hundred million people.

SUMMARY

1. The elements of culture can be divided into two different kinds, material and nonmaterial. Material culture consists of all the physical objects that people make and attach meaning to. Nonmaterial culture consists of human creations not embodied in physical objects. Important aspects of nonmaterial culture are values, norms, symbols, language, and knowledge.

2. Values are general ideas that people share about what is good or bad. Americans typically share a number of values, among them achievement and success, practicality, progress, material comfort, democracy, and individuality. When values are in conflict, pressure for social change may build.

3. Norms are specific guidelines for action that say how people should behave in particular situations. Norms are often unspoken customs that people implicitly know and follow. Norms vary from society to society and also from group to group within a single society.

4. Symbols are objects, gestures, sounds, or images that represent something other than themselves. The meaning given symbols is often arbitrary, and particular symbols may have slightly different meanings to different people.

5. A language is a system of verbal (and, in many cases, written) symbols with rules about how those symbols can be strung together to convey more complex meanings.

Language is extremely important in the development, elaboration, and transmission of culture. Language often offers many clues to the meaning of social interactions.

6. The degree to which the parts of a culture form a consistent and interrelated whole is termed cultural integration. In a highly integrated culture, customs, beliefs, values, and technology are interdependent. In large, diverse societies such as the United States, culture is very loosely integrated.

7. In a heterogeneous society, usually a dominant culture tends to impose its outlooks and traditions on society as a whole. In the United States, it is the culture of the white Christian middle and upper-middle classes. Members of subcultures and countercultures dissent from or reject various customs or values of the dominant culture. Sometimes subcultures merge into the dominant culture, a process known as assimilation.

8. Ethnocentrism is the tendency to see one's own cultural patterns as the good and right ones and the standard by which to judge others. Ethnocentric attitudes promote group solidarity and loyalty but increase hostility toward outsiders and foster conflict among groups.

9. Cultural relativism stresses that any element of culture is relative to a particular time, place, and set of circumstances. Cultural relativism fosters understanding of other groups and tolerance of their practices.

10. Sociobiologists maintain that social groups adapt to their environment by evolving social traits that are programmed and transmitted by genes. They cite cultural universals as evidence that social traits are hereditary, not learned. Cultural universals are those behavior patterns and institutions found in all known cultures.

11. An important theme in American culture is individualism, the idea that people should be free to make their own choices and should rely on their own efforts. Although individualism is highly valued, some have argued that a strongly individualistic culture neglects basic human needs for community and dependence.

12. The assumption behind the production of culture perspective is that the elements of culture do not arise on their own, but are shaped by a variety of decisions about what is desirable and good. The production of culture is always a social process: Cultural innovators always act within a social context. Cultural gatekeepers are people who decide which of a number of proposed cultural innovations will be accepted.

13. The electronic media have had a great impact on Western culture, dramatically increasing the speed and range of communication. The media have also made many matters that were once private into public issues. Finally, some have argued that television, with its orientation to images rather than rational speech, is changing how people view the world.

GLOSSARY

Counterculture. A group whose norms, attitudes, values, and life-style directly clash with or are opposed to those of the dominant or mainstream culture.

Cultural assimilation. The process in which newcomers take on many of the cultural patterns of the host society.

Cultural gatekeepers. People who regulate the flow of new elements of culture into society.

Cultural integration. The degree to which the parts of a culture form a consistent and interrelated whole.

Cultural relativism. The idea that any element of culture is understandable only in relation to the rest of its cultural context and to a particular time, place, and set of circumstances.

Cultural universals. The behavior patterns and institutions found in every known culture.

Culture. All the learned customs, beliefs, values, knowledge, artifacts, and symbols that are constantly communicated among a set of people who share a common way of life.

Dominant culture. The group whose values, norms, traditions, and outlooks are imposed on the society as a whole.

Ethnocentrism. The tendency to view one's own cultural patterns as good and right and to judge others by those standards.

Folkways. Everyday habits and conventions.

Knowledge. The body of facts people accumulate over time.

Language. A system of verbal (and usually also written) symbols with rules about how those symbols can be strung together to convey more complex meanings.

Laws. Rules that are enacted by a political body and enforced by the power of the state.

Marital assimilation. The intermarriage of subcultural group members with the members of the larger society.

Material culture. All the physical objects, or artifacts, that people make and attach meaning to.

Mores. Norms that people consider vital to their well-being and to their most cherished values.

Multivocal symbols. Symbols that carry a number of different meanings.

Nonmaterial culture. Human creations, such as values, beliefs, rules, customs, systems of government, language, and so on, that are not embodied in physical objects.

Norms. Specific guidelines for action that say how people should behave in particular situations.

Social marker. Any pattern of behavior that provides indications about who people are, what groups they belong to, and what their understanding of a situation is.

Sociobiology. A theoretical perspective that holds that social groups adapt to their environment primarily by the evolution of genetically determined traits.

Structural assimilation. Entrance of members into cliques, clubs, and institutions of the larger society through contact with new primary groups.

Subculture. A group of people whose perspective and life-style differ significantly from that of the dominant culture and who identify themselves as different; members share norms, values, and attitudes.

Symbol. An object, gesture, sound, image, or design that represents something other than itself.

Univocal symbols. Symbols that have only one meaning.

Values. General ideas that people share about what is good or bad, desirable or undesirable.

CHAPTER 5
Socialization

I n a primary school in China third graders are busily employed in their school workshop. The workshop is associated with a nearby factory that makes, among other things, wooden pieces for the game of Chinese chess. Squads of youngsters work diligently on a series of consecutive tasks: shaping the edges of the pieces, stamping characters on them, painting them, and finally packing them into boxes. Some children serve as monitors, making sure that everyone has the materials needed to keep the operation running smoothly. A bulletin board on the wall charts the total number of pieces produced and the number returned because of defects. The chart boasts a steadily rising rate of output and declining rate of errors. Every third grader in the school spends two class hours a week in the workshop. Older children spend more time; younger children less. The children are proud to be contributing "productive labor" to the state. They tell a team of American social scientists who have come to observe education in China that their efforts are "serving the people" (Kessen 1975).

Every society shapes its children in the image of its own culture. In ancient Sparta, young boys were taught discipline, obedience, physical prowess, and self-denial through harsh treatment and deprivation. In nearby Athens, parents raised their sons to be artistically sensitive and broadly educated as well as athletic. These practices produced quite different individuals as well as different societies (Berger and Berger 1979). In modern times, middle- and upper-class Americans encourage children to cultivate their individual abilities and com-

pete with their peers for success. The Chinese, in contrast, foster group loyalty and cooperation, and a willingness to endure self-sacrifice for the good of society. The process of instilling such fundamental elements of culture in a society's new members is called **socialization**. Through socialization people learn to participate effectively in the communities to which they belong.

A further look at childhood in China provides a good example of how socialization can be accomplished. In China, infants, from the age of about two months, often spend the day in a "feeding station" associated with the mother's place of work. Here their lives center around the routine tasks of eating, sleeping, and diaper changing. The caretakers do not think that children "do much" as infants, so they tend not to give the babies active stimulation. When Chinese children reach toddler age they are commonly placed in a state-run nursery school. Here they are discouraged from exploring freely and choosing their own activities as American toddlers do. Instead, the teachers highly structure their daily routines, so that the youngsters spend almost all of their time in organized group activities. In quiet, but persistent ways they are taught to follow instructions, control their impulses, and play cooperatively with other children. By the time Chinese youngsters reach kindergarten age, they have learned a great deal about placing the good of the group above their own interests. The stories they hear, the songs they sing, the little dramas they enact usually celebrate those who selflessly serve the people. In primary school, the message of group over self

The contrasting details of these two scenes highlight differences in socialization between China and the United States. While the American children work on their own in a loose setting that accentuates individual differences, the Chinese children work in carefully supervised groups that subordinate the individual. (Left, John Zoiner/Peter Arnold; right, Martin Parr/Achive.)

becomes even stronger by the practice of requiring children to criticize their own selfish behavior. For instance, a boy might be asked to explain to the group why it was wrong not to pick up a piece of litter he saw in the schoolyard; or a girl might be asked to describe how she overcame the temptation not to share a new toy. In these ways, Chinese youngsters are encouraged to accept the fundamental values of their culture (Kessen 1975).

This example of childhood in China illustrates two critical aspects of socialization. First, socialization creates individuals who are part of a human community. Through socialization we learn to live within a group, to be competent members of the society into which we are born. From this perspective, socialization is the process whereby individuals are made to "fit" within the social order. Second, socialization is the process whereby a society reproduces itself in a new generation. Through socialization the values and traditions of the past are carried forward and perpetuated. Thus, socialization is

what gives a society continuity over time. It is the process that ensures that the China (or United States) of today will be reflected in the China (or United States) of tomorrow.

This chapter is devoted to exploring the process of socialization. In the first section we consider how nature and nurture interact to produce individuals who are like all other human beings and like other members of their society, but also unique persons, capable of innovative actions. In the second section we look at different theories of how socialization works and what it accomplishes. Next we examine how American socialization differs by social class, and we ask if these differences help perpetuate class status across generations. Our next section explores major agents of socialization, the major groups and organizations that teach people the elements of their particular culture. The last section deals with secondary socialization and sets the stage for Chapter 6, which focuses on the human life course.

SOCIALIZATION: "NATURE" *AND* "NURTURE"

New scientific procedures have made it possible for many couples who could not have borne children in the past to become parents. If the husband is infertile, the couple can try artificial insemination. If the problem lies with the wife, the couple may choose test-tube fertilization, or have another woman carry the fetus, or adopt a child. These new options raise legal and ethical questions about matters of heredity and social environment. Are the child's "real" parents the two people who provided the egg and sperm, the child's genetic heritage? Or are the real parents the couple (or single person) who raises the child and provides him or her with a home? Custody cases over children conceived by unconventional means are forcing the courts to take a position on an age-old debate about the roles of "nature" and "nurture" in human development.

Is a child's character determined by his or her biological makeup (nature) or by the social environment in which he or she is reared (nurture)? Scientists have argued this point for decades. At one extreme were those who held that the infant is a blank slate, and that the kind of person he or she becomes is determined by experience. The most famous statement of this position comes from the American psychologist John B. Watson (1878–1958):

> Give me a dozen healthy infants, well-formed, and my own specific world to bring them up in and I'll guarantee to take any one at random and train him to become any type of specialist I might select—a doctor, lawyer, artist, merchant, chief, yes even a beggarman and thief, regardless of his talents, penchants, tendencies, abilities, vocations, and the race of his ancestors. (1925/1970, p. 104)

At the opposite extreme were those who argued that who we become is determined by heredity, and that experience cannot change what nature ordained. This position was most often invoked to explain differences between the sexes or between ethnic and racial groups, and to explain extremes of behavior (from geniuses to hardened criminals).

For decades, the debate over nature and nurture was framed in either-or, win-or-lose terms: either behavior is determined by biology or behavior is determined by experience. Today, however, scientists recognize that both are essential. The development of a human being is the result of *interaction* between biological and environmental forces. An infant is not a lump of clay that experience can mold in any shape; but neither is an infant made of unbending steel.

The Interaction of Heredity and Environment

Genes establish the basic blueprint for human development. They direct a fertilized human egg to develop into a human baby, not an oak tree. They also establish a timetable for development. All babies progress from

These Hare Krishna children underscore the powerful influence of environment regardless of their genetic makeup. Their beliefs, their view of other people, their social life, and even their haircuts and clothes are shaped by this religious sect. (Birgit Pohl.)

crawling to walking and from babbling to talking in the same order and at about the same ages. No amount of coaching can make an eight-month-old speak; by the same token, it is almost impossible to prevent a twenty-four-month-old from talking. This timetable shapes the course of socialization (Elkin and Handel 1984). A similar timetable governs physical skills. One cannot teach a child to eat with utensils, for example, until she has developed sufficient hand-to-eye coordination to grasp the utensils, spear or scoop up some food, and then bring the food to her mouth. It doesn't matter whether the utensils are a knife and fork or chopsticks; she won't be able to use them until she is biologically ready.

Researchers are discovering that the development of emotions also follows a biological timetable (summarized in Goleman 1984). Newborns have intense feelings, but their emotional repertoire is limited to pleasure and surprise, distress and disgust. Joy emerges between six and eight weeks; anger, between three and four months; fear and sadness, between eight and nine months. Feelings of shame develop around eighteen months, pride around two years, and guilt between ages three and four. The social emotions (insecurity, humility, confidence, envy, and the like) do not appear until the child is five or six years old. These psychological and social developments are tied to maturation of the central nervous system, which continues through early childhood (Kagan 1984). The nerve connections that enable an older child to experience doubt and envy are not yet functioning in the infant and toddler—a biological fact that has obvious implications for socialization. But biological plans are not immutable; experience can disrupt the emotional timetable. Abused infants as young as three months show premature expression of fear and sadness (Gaensbauer and Hiatt 1984).

Some traits are genetically fixed: genes dictate whether the baby will be male or female, blond or brunette, blue-eyed or brown-eyed, light- or dark-skinned. But the list of characteristics that are directly determined by the genes is shorter than one might think. In most cases, genes do not dictate how a child will develop, but rather establish a range of possible outcomes. How much of a child's potential is realized depends on the environment. For example, height is hereditary. As a rule, tall parents have tall children and short parents, short children. But how tall an individual actually grows depends on nutrition and health. If a boy with "tall genes" grows up in a poor rural village where protein is scarce, or is sickly as a child, he might be

five-feet-seven-inches tall as an adult. If he is healthy and well-fed as a child, he might grow to six-feet-two-inches. (This is why children of immigrants to America often tower over their parents.)

The same principle applies to other traits. As Figure 5.1 shows, a child with only average musical or athletic ability may outperform a potential superstar if the child practices and receives the right social supports.

A rich learning environment can stretch genetic potential to its limit, as shown in experiments with chimpanzees, who have been taught to communicate with sign language, play games like blindman's buff, and function to some extent as socialized members of human families (Temerlin 1975). But even so, a rich environment cannot overcome the limitations imposed by the genetic endowment. Chimps lack an inherent biological capacity to generate complex sentences and to engage in sophisticated thought. Thus, although the capabilities exhibited by chimps are clearly related to human capabilities, they are not equivalent to human capabilities.

Personality development reveals a more complex pattern of gene-environment interactions. Personality can be defined as the characteristic modes of thinking, feeling, and acting individuals develop as a result of experience. Infants, who have little experience, do not have personalities in this sense. But they do come into the world with distinctive emotional orientations, or **temperaments** (Goleman 1986). From the first days of life, infants differ in their level of activity, their responses to new experiences (approach/withdrawal), their adaptability, the intensity of their reactions, their general mood (happy-friendly to unhappy-unfriendly), and other characteristics. Alexander Thomas and Stella Chess (1979, 1980) followed 140 children from birth to adolescence. They found that temperamental qualities tend to cluster into three patterns. "Easy babies" are calm, playful, and adaptable. They approach new experiences with enthusiasm. "Difficult babies" are agitated, fearful, and easily distressed. They have high activity levels but low attention spans. "Slow-to-warm-up babies" fall between these two patterns. Their emotional responses are less pronounced, and they tend to withdraw from new situations. The fact that these differences among children are present from birth and tend to persist over time suggests that temperament is inborn or innate.

Whereas most studies of gene-environment interaction focus on how the environment affects inborn potentials, studies of temperament show how inborn traits affect social interaction (Scarr and McCartney

FIGURE 5.1 The Interaction of Inherited Potential and Social Environment

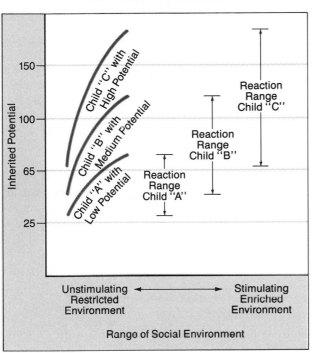

Although inherited potential establishes the range of socialization, social environment greatly affects the extent to which inherited potential can be realized. This is particularly true for child "C," who has the greatest potential range of the three children in the figure above. With an impoverished environment, a child "C" might develop less than a child "A" who has an advantageous environment.

1983). Children with different temperaments *evoke* different responses from other people. A baby who is quick to smile and likes to be picked up receives more attention than a baby who is sober and unresponsive or one who bursts into tears at the sight of a stranger. An easy baby's more outgoing nature allows for more interactions with other people and he or she experiences a friendlier environment. Even mothers find they avoid difficult babies (Maccoby, Snow, and Jacklin 1984). Furthermore, children with different temperaments *choose* different activities. At one year old, the easy baby sits with a

picture book, slowly turning the pages and pointing to things he wants his grandmother to name. At the same age, the difficult baby is crawling about the room at top speed, banging into furniture, scattering toys, and generally creating havoc. The first child is gaining social experience; the second, exercising his physical skills. Meanwhile, the slow-to-warm-up child watches her mother's every move, fearful that she might be left alone with a stranger. As a result, both her social and her physical experiences are limited. If her mother responds to her tendency to withdraw by making an extra effort to interest her in books and games and to introduce her to playmates, however, she may have experiences that other, more outgoing children miss.

In much the same way, inherited physical characteristics evoke different responses from other people and can cause children to seek or avoid certain activities. Children who meet their culture's standards of good-looking tend to have different experiences than those who do not. When adults and other children are shown pictures of attractive and not-so-attractive children they describe the former as smarter, nicer, and friendlier than the latter (Langlois and Stephan 1977). These expectations can function as a self-fulfilling prophecy: People respond positively to a good-looking child; these positive responses enhance the child's social self-esteem and sociability; and this, in turn, confirms the belief that good-looking children are nicer and smarter than their unattractive peers. In adolesence, early-maturing boys are more likely to excel in athletics, to be popular with their peers, and to be viewed as social leaders than are late-maturing boys (Jones 1965). Peers describe them as poised, relaxed, good-natured, and unaffected. These personality traits are a result of social responses to their physical characteristics. In short, the meanings of these traits are socially constructed.

In summary, biology provides the raw material for development, but that raw material is shaped by experience—experiences the child seeks on his own and the responses he evokes from other people, as well as the more general resources a particular family and society provide a growing child.

The Impact of Socialization

The nature of the human animal both allows and requires socialization (Elkin and Handel 1984, p. 18). At birth, the human infant is one of the most helpless creatures on earth. Other animals are equipped with instincts, or built-in responses that promote survival. They do not have to learn how to find food or avoid danger; they "know in their genes" how to react to events in their environment. Human beings are born with a very limited number of instincts, but a great capacity to learn from experience. The ability to learn enables us to adapt to an enormous range of environments in flexible and complex ways. Without learning, without socialization, we would not become social beings.

No social scientist would raise an infant in isolation to find out what kind of person he or she would become without socialization. Unfortunately, due to extreme neglect, some people have spent their early years almost totally alone, and these instances provide clues to the impact of socialization (Curtiss 1977). One such case is that of Anna (Davis 1949), the illegitimate and unwanted child of a farmer's daughter. After trying unsuccessfully to place her in a foster home or an institution, Anna's mother confined her to a dark room in the attic. She fed the child enough milk to keep her alive, but rarely bathed her and never cuddled or played with her. This appalling neglect continued for five years.

When social workers discovered Anna, she was so apathetic they thought she was deaf, mentally retarded, or both. She didn't walk or talk. She didn't know how to dress or feed herself, or even how to chew. She never laughed or cried. In the hospital where she was taken, she lay on her bed staring at the ceiling and clicking her tongue. When approached, she would freeze in terror or fly into a tantrum. Observers felt that there was something inhuman about her. And there was. Anna's socialization did not begin until age six, when she was placed in a foster home. With care and attention, she slowly began to talk, walk, run, and play with other children. She also began learning how to take care of herself. In other words, she began to develop human interests and abilities. However, she was never able to totally overcome her early years of neglect, and died of jaundice at age 11½.

Other evidence of the importance of socialization comes from less extreme cases of neglect. Rene Spitz (1951) studied babies who had been placed in an orphanage. The youngsters received adequate physical care—good food, regular diaper and clothing changes and baths, clean sheets, bright and airy nurseries—but little personal attention. Psychological tests given when the infants were one year old showed that most were mentally retarded. They hardly ever smiled or cried and made no effort to speak. Other studies (Bowlby 1973) report similar results. Physical care is not enough; children need socialization as much as they need food. To develop into a full-fledged human being a child must be treated like a human being.

Finally, the impact of socialization is not felt just by children, but by their parents and others involved in their socialization. Few parents emerge from the experience of raising children without some changes in character, attitude, or behavior. Children's ability to affect their parents increases as they gain language competence and encounter new experiences outside the home (Berger and Berger 1979). For example, when children of immigrant parents attend American schools, they carry back into their homes patterns of behavior that have an enormous impact in hastening the parents' "Americanization." More subtly, different children have different effects on parents. The outcome of early social encounters—on parents and children—depends on how well the child's inborn temperament meshes with his or her parents' personalities and expectations. Thomas and Chess call this *goodness of fit.* An easy baby is a perfect fit for an anxious, first-time mother: his happy moods and ability to adapt to new situations reassure her that she is a good parent. A strong-willed mother who admires independence and spunkiness might find a difficult baby a better fit. Becoming a parent is a new social role, and babies have almost as much impact on their parents' socialization to that role as parents have on their children's initiation to society. In short, socialization is a dynamic and reciprocal process.

THE DYNAMICS OF SOCIALIZATION

The year is 1973; the place China. A twelve-year-old boy named T'an Shan-li is in the fifth grade. For some time he has been pestering his parents for a new bookcase because his old one is falling apart. Then, through his school, he has a chance to talk with members of the People's Liberation Army. They praise self-sacrifice, productive labor, and people who are more than merely consumers. T'an Shan-li is deeply impressed by this experience. He applies the words of the PLA members to his own life and decides that he should repair his old bookcase rather than getting a new one. His classmates learn of his decision and commend it over the school public-address system. As a result of this incident T'an Shan-li becomes a somewhat different person. (Based on Kessen 1975)

This is clearly an instance of socialization, but how exactly should sociologists define it? Those who take a functional perspective regarding the basic question of what holds society together would focus on the ways in which T'an Shan-li is learning values that prepare him for life in modern China. These sociologists see society as composed of many different parts that evolve to work together in an integrated fashion. From a functional perspective, T'an Shan-li, like all Chinese children, is being socialized to suit the roles that his society makes available to people. Here socialization is seen as serving the beneficial function of producing the kind of people needed to maintain the social order.

But sociologists who take a power perspective would see this episode quite differently. Even in a Communist society, they would argue, certain people, groups, and organizations wield power over others. From a power perspective, the values that T'an Shan-li hears expressed by the PLA members are the end result of an ideological power struggle between different factions in Chinese society. In the late 1960s, Chairman Mao Zedung started a campaign to purge Chinese leadership of liberal "bourgeois" elements, including those in education. The result was a repudiation of "bookish" learning in favor of teaching more practical skills related to work and economic production. Thus, T'an Shan-li is being indoctrinated into the values characteristic of those who have the upper hand in an ideological battle to influence the Chinese people's thinking.

Other perspectives that sociologists might take on this incident have to do with their views on the individual's relationship to society. Those with a structural perspective would argue that T'an Shan-li's choices are greatly constrained by forces that arise from how his society is organized. For instance, China in the early 1970s had an enormous problem of rapidly growing cities and a shrinking farm population, to the point where there were not enough farm workers to feed the hundreds of millions in urban areas. The urban centers also had their own dilemmas, namely, outdated production methods and low output levels in the factories. These structural conditions set the stage for a renewal of revolutionary values. People like T'an Shan-li were simply swept along in a tide of social forces over which they had little control.

Sociologists with an action perspective, in contrast, do not deny the influence of structural forces, but they think it a mistake to see individuals as passively carried along by them. From an action perspective, T'an Shan-li is an active participant in his own socialization. He interprets what he hears from the PLA members according to his own subjective feelings and outlooks, and he creatively applies his understanding of their values to his particular situation. In his own small way, T'an Shan-li is helping to define and elaborate Chinese culture. His thoughts and actions, in turn, may influence other students, so that his particular interpretation of Communist ideology might even become widely shared. In this way Chinese culture develops and is kept alive.

Different perspectives on the process of socialization have existed since researchers first started to explore this topic. Rather than being mutually exclusive, these perspectives are complementary. Each emphasizes particular factors that the others do not, so together they provide a fuller outline of socialization. In the following sections, we are going to examine the theories of socialization proposed by three influential thinkers: Charles Horton Cooley, George Herbert Mead, and Sigmund Freud. While they may disagree about the process of socialization, or certain aspects of it, they agree on one very important point: human individuality is not purely "natural," but achieved through socialization. We begin with the ideas of Charles Horton Cooley, an American sociologist who stressed the active role developing children play in their own socialization.

Cooley: Looking-Glass Self

The **self** is the notion that each of us has that we possess a unique and distinct identity—that we are set apart from other things and people. It is the cluster of ideas that we employ in defining ourselves. Like other aspects of social life, our self-image and self-conception are not givens; infants are not born with a sense of self. Rather, we actively derive our self-conception from interactions with other people (see Figure 5.2).

Charles Horton Cooley (1864–1929) was one of the first theorists to consider the social origins of self. Observing his own children, Cooley developed the idea of the **looking-glass self:** We acquire our sense of self by seeing ourself reflected in other people's attitudes and behavior toward us and by imagining what they think of us. According to Cooley (1956, 1964), the looking-glass self has three parts: what we imagine others see in us; how we imagine they judge what they see; and how we feel about those judgments. From other people's comments and actions, a four-year-old boy thinks his parents see him as someone who runs and jumps and climbs trees, and he imagines that they are proud that he is growing big and strong. He may feel good about this image of himself, or worried that his parents see him as more independent than he really is. A fourteen-year-old boy thinks his classmates see him as a "brain" and imagines that they judge braininess as "weird." This reflected image may make him feel bad about himself and wish he were more athletic, or make him feel

As this young woman gazes in the mirror, she is participating in a worldwide effort of young people to decide how they want to look and what social identity they want to convey. (Gabe Palmer/Stock Market.)

pleased that he is different. Thus, the looking-glass self is not a direct reflection (a mechanical reproduction) of what other people see in us. It is a mixture of observation, imagination, and subjective interpretation. It is also a social construction, involving influences such as values and social class. We will discuss these influences more specifically in later sections.

Mead: Role Taking

Building on Cooley's analysis, George Herbert Mead (1863–1931) traced the development of self-awareness to early social interaction (Turner 1981). Almost from the beginning, infants realize that they are dependent on others to satisfy their needs, and that their own actions influence how others behave toward them. They learn, for example, that crying brings food and smiles bring cuddling. Over time, as they learn many different ways of arousing desired responses in others, children acquire a repertoire of gestures (looking, reaching, pointing, imitating) and, later, words that those around them understand. Mead called these signs, gestures, and language **significant symbols.** He believed that human social interaction cannot exist without symbols and that symbols gain significance only in social interaction. Through symbolic interaction, children learn to anticipate what other people expect, and to evaluate and adjust their own behavior accordingly.

Mead suggested that the self is composed of two parts: the active, spontaneous, idiosyncratic self, which he called the "I," and the social self (the internalized social expectations and demands), which he called the "me." The subjective "I" is the product of individual distinctiveness; the objective "me," the product of socialization. Without the "me," orderly social interaction could not occur; without the "I," social interaction would be mechanical and monotonous. With these two complementary parts, we are able to reflect on our own behavior and develop a sense of inner continuity, or identity.

> The self is something which has a development; it is not initially there at birth, but arises in the process of social experience and activity, that is, develops in the given individual as a result of his relations to [the social] process and to other individuals within that process. (Mead 1934, p. 135)

Mead did not resolve the problem of how we gain a sense of I, the subjective sense of self, but the sociologist Norbert Wiley (1979) has offered a solution. Initially, infants have no sense of I. They view themselves simply as part of other objects as they are fed and bathed and changed. Eventually, baby and parent exchange smiles or giggles, and the baby begins to experience a "we" relationship. And in that "we" experience the baby gets a sense of a subjectivity, or an I, from the parent. The baby begins to understand that it too has an ego, or subjective sense of I. It realizes that the parent is reacting to that I, just as the baby is reacting to the parent's I. Thus the I, like the me, is social in origin. A sense of I enables the baby to hold internal conversations with the "me" and thus extend the socialization process. "The development of conscious and moral responsibility seems to require that baby think of himself as having agency, or subject quality, in which responsibility inheres" (Wiley 1979, p. 96).

The puzzle is how children develop a me, how each child comes to perceive himself or herself as a distinct person whom others observe and judge. Mead proposed that this aspect of the self develops in early childhood as a result of playing at being others and participating in games. Children spend much of their time role-playing. For hours on end, they make believe that they are mothers and fathers, doctors, policemen, and fantasy characters like Superman. Most often they take the roles of people who figure importantly in their social world, what sociologists call **significant others** (Sullivan 1953). Young children are especially fond of playing mothers fussing over babies who have wet themselves and fathers lecturing children on their behavior. In play, children have the opportunity to see themselves from another person's point of view. What keeps it as simple play is that children have not yet learned to take on more than one role at a time.

As children gain in social experience, they can begin to move from simple play involving a single role to games involving the interaction of many roles. Games are significant in the emergence of the self because they require children to understand how different roles are coordinated. To play baseball, for example, the base runner must be able to anticipate what various other players will do when the ball is hit. Without an understanding of the different actions and responses of others, the child cannot play his or her role effectively. Similarly, "to play the game of life" a person must be able to grasp the organization of roles and see a situation from

Boys and girls play a bow-and-arrow hunting game at the seashore. This play-acting works on several levels as a form of socialization. These children are learning how the roles of each sex are coordinated. (P. Bion Griffin.)

many different but coordinated points of view. The work of later researchers based upon Mead's views of play and games is illustrated in the accompanying box.

The self finally emerges when children begin to see themselves as part of society as a whole, and to **internalize** the standards, attitudes, and beliefs of parents and others within their own personalities. Mead referred to this internalized general impression of what society believes and expects as the **generalized other** (see Figure 5.2).

Since Mead's pioneering work on the social origins of self, others have elaborated on and refined his points. Robert Leahy (1983), for example, sees Mead's theory as "optimistic functionalism," a vision of the child moving from a primitive state of isolation to a mature state of socialization in which the youngster "shares the views of others toward the self." Looking beyond childhood to adolescence, Leahy concludes that the reality is more complex (Leahy and Shirk 1985). Concern with how others regard the self peaks in early adolescence. At eleven, twelve, and thirteen, youngsters are almost obsessed with how they appear to others, and devote enormous energy to being like (and liked by) their peers. In later adolescence, however, they begin to move from other-directed reasoning to more self-directed reasoning

FIGURE 5.2   Stages and Capacities of Socialization

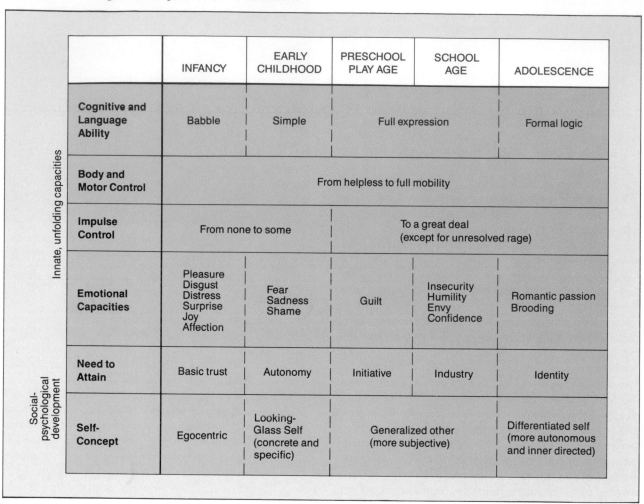

	INFANCY	EARLY CHILDHOOD	PRESCHOOL PLAY AGE	SCHOOL AGE	ADOLESCENCE
Cognitive and Language Ability	Babble	Simple	Full expression		Formal logic
Body and Motor Control	From helpless to full mobility				
Impulse Control	From none to some		To a great deal (except for unresolved rage)		
Emotional Capacities	Pleasure Disgust Distress Surprise Joy Affection	Fear Sadness Shame	Guilt	Insecurity Humility Envy Confidence	Romantic passion Brooding
Need to Attain	Basic trust	Autonomy	Initiative	Industry	Identity
Self-Concept	Egocentric	Looking-Glass Self (concrete and specific)	Generalized other (more subjective)		Differentiated self (more autonomous and inner directed)

Innate, unfolding capacities (left axis, top rows)
Social-psychological development (left axis, bottom rows)

Source: Kagan 1984; Maccoby 1984; Goleman 1984; Erikson 1950; Mead 1934; Cooley 1956, 1984; Leahy and Shirk 1985.

This chart integrates new research on the unfolding capacities of children to think, talk, move and experience complex emotions with Erikson's stages for a healthy ego and Mead's and Cooley's theories about developing a social self. All three have stressed the importance of social context and social interaction in shaping these capacities. Erickson's stages will be discussed in Chapter 6 on the life course.

and an image of themselves that is relatively independent from others' views and expectations. At this more advanced stage, young people are able to think about why their parents, peers, and others see them in this or that light, and to distinguish between their social self-image and their real self-image.

Freud: Socialization as a Power Struggle

No theory of socialization has had a greater impact on Western thought than that of Sigmund Freud (1856–1939), a giant of twentieth-century psychology. Freud (1920, 1923) saw socialization as a lifelong battle within

Learning to control our physical urges is an important part of growing up. Freud thought that the ego—the rational part of the self—develops as the child learns to adapt to society's demands. (Peeter Vilms/Jeroboam.)

a person's mind. This battle, in his view, involved three powerful forces: the **id**, a reservoir of innate biological drives aimed at obtaining physical pleasure; the **ego**, the rational part of the self, which mediates between the id and reality; and the **superego**, essentially a person's "conscience," which embodies the moral standards of society. The ego's job, as Freud saw it, was to find safe ways to satisfy the id without causing guilt or remorse to the superego. Because these three parts of the psyche all contend for control, Freud's theory can be seen as power-oriented. Freud, however, was a psychologist, not a sociologist. He was not concerned with the power struggles that shape society, but rather with the conflicts and struggles that occur inside a person when biological drives meet the reality of societal demands.

In Freud's view, people are not born with an ego or a superego. These parts of the psyche develop through interaction with the world, especially with the social world. Freud believed that at birth humans are irrational, amoral creatures, nothing more than whirlpools of pleasure-seeking id impulses. But it is not long before the baby begins to learn that biological drives cannot always be gratified immediately or harmlessly. The urge to get sensual pleasure from sucking on objects, for instance,

may cause pain if the object chosen has a sharp edge. It is through such discoveries that the ego begins to develop. The ego's role is to channel id impulses toward outlets that are realistic and safe. Freud argued that through this basic ego function the mind develops and refines all its higher intellectual capabilities: perception, learning, memory, problem solving, decision making, and planning.

The third aspect of the psyche in Freudian theory, the so-called superego, develops through the child's encounters with the demands of society as conveyed by his or her parents. Freud focused on societal demands that attempt to curb the child's natural id drives to obtain sensual pleasure. One such demand is toilet training, which occurs in the late toddler period. Another is the parents' prohibition of masturbation during the preschool years. Freud argued that how these conflicts between the id and society are resolved is what shapes an individual's personality. According to Freud, a final coalescing of the superego occurs around the fifth year, when the child finally accepts the enormous power that the parents wield. Instead of continuing to be embroiled in conflicts, the child seeks vicarious power by adopting the parents' attitudes and moral values.

Despite the liberation of women, striking differences remain between the quiet, intimate ways in which girls choose to play and the noisy, externalized games that bunches of boys play. Why do these differences persist? (Left, Donald Dietz/Stock Boston; right, Bill Stanton/Magnum Photo.)

Freud's view of socialization is radically different from Cooley's and Mead's. While Cooley and Mead saw socialization as the gradual, complementary merger of individual and society, Freud saw socialization as a perennial battle between society and a person's biological inclinations and drives. But socialization, in Freud's view, is absolutely essential if civilization is to survive. Without socialization we would all be totally egocentric, pleasure-seeking creatures, with no goals beyond the gratification of our own immediate physical needs. Freud (1930) argued that the great achievements of humankind—art, philosophy, literature, science—are the result of a rechanneling of id drives in socially productive ways.

SOCIAL CLASS AND SOCIALIZATION

All I wanted was just to grow up and get out of there [referring to her childhood home, which was poor and overcrowded]. I used to dream about how I'd grow up and get married and live in one of those big, beautiful houses like they show in the magazines—you know, magazines like *House Beautiful.* God, all the hours I spent looking at those magazines, and dreaming about how I would live in one of those houses with all that beautiful furniture, and everything just right. . . . Life turns out a lot different in the end, doesn't it? [thirty-six-year-old cannery worker, mother of three, married twenty years; quoted in Rubin 1976, p. 43]

As you can see, that dream I had about getting married and having a storybook life didn't exactly work out. . . . Here I am living in this old, dumpy house and the furniture is a grubby mess. I still have those pictures of the storybook life in my head, but I have a lot more sense now than when I was young. Now I know we're lucky just to be able to keep up with the bills. [twenty-seven-year-old sales clerk, mother of three, married ten years; quoted in Rubin 1976, p. 72]

Although in every generation there is some movement up and down the social ladder, leaps from "rags to riches" are extremely rare. Most adults, like these women, end up in the same social class into which they were born. Why does this happen? Why aren't dreams and hard work enough to win most working-class people the life to which they aspire? Does the answer have something to do with how they were socialized? Does socialization reinforce social class differences generation after generation?

Play and Games in Socialization

The theme in George Herbert Mead's work that has attracted the most attention is the role of play and games in socialization. As William Corsaro (1985) has stressed, peer play is not simple reproduction of the adult world, but reproduction *within a peer culture*. It is something children do together. In playing Mommy and Daddy, or Big Sister and Baby, children begin to understand not only how people in these roles behave, but also how they interact with others (Mommies and Daddies talk to one another as equals. Big Sisters are bossy toward Babies, Babies misbehave and must be controlled by Mommies and Daddies, and so forth). Peer play is essential to the development of social knowledge and interactive skills.

Inge Bretherton (1984) traced the development of make-believe and role-taking to infancy. The first sign of make-believe is self-representation: The child imitates his or her own everyday activities, pretending to be asleep or pretending to eat. This is followed by other-representation: The child pretends to be an adult and "reads" the newspaper or "answers" a toy phone. Around their second birthday, children begin to include dolls or stuffed animals in their play. At first the doll is a passive figure (the baby feeds the doll or combs its hair); later the doll becomes an extension of the child (the baby feeds the doll, then herself); and still later, the doll becomes a partner (the child ascribes

feelings to the doll and talks to it as she plays). True role-play emerges soon after: The child pretends the doll can act on its own. Even more significantly (from Mead's perspective), the child pretends that she herself is another person.

Small children often involve adults in their games, but adults usually play along with the child's fantasies. When children begin to play together, they are forced to negotiate. Two four-year-olds are playing Mommy and Daddy:

> FATHER: So long, I'll see ya later. It's time to go to work.
> MOTHER: Hey, wait for me! I gotta go to work too!
> FATHER: Hey, my mom don't work . . . you stay here.
> MOTHER: Well my mom works . . . lotsa womens work ya know. My mom is a professor at the unibersity.
> FATHER: O.K. then, just hurry so we won't be late. Are you sure ya wanna work? (K. H. Rubin 1980, p. 75)

Bretherton's analysis suggests why make-believe is a major source of social understanding. In their play, children move from imitating actions to awareness that others have feelings, from playing at being themselves to playing the role of others, from solitary play to social play. By the beginning of Mead's play stage, children are ready not only to try on adult

roles, but also to internalize some elements of those roles. The "mother" and "father" in the scene above have already tuned in to the adult issue of a woman's place in society!

Games-with-rules add another dimension to socialization (Bettleheim 1987). When not supervised by adults, children often spend more time arguing about what game they will play, what rules they will follow, who will be on what team, and other related issues than they do actually playing the game. From an adult's point of view, these results look ragged. From the child's point of view, these occasions provide important experience in resolving disputes, testing social skills, and learning when and why rules are useful. Children on their own often surprise adults with their generosity: displays of temper are often excused, and there are frequent calls to "let the little guy" (or in some cases the girl) have a turn.

Close analysis of child's play provides another clue to the puzzle that underlies all theories of socialization: How do norms and values that were once outside the child come to be inside the child? (Elkin and Handel 1984, p. 58). Play promotes the ability to take the role of others (first seen in make-believe) and internalization of such basic social rules as "taking turns" and "playing fair" (developed in peer play and games).

In the last twenty years, many studies have been conducted in an attempt to answer these questions. Comparing lower-, middle-, and upper-class families, researchers have found that there are indeed differences in how children are socialized. Some of these differences have to do with *language*—the various forms of communication that parents teach their children depending upon the parents' position in the social-economic hierarchy. Other important differences involve *values*—the things that parents admire and respect and try to convey to their children. Both these differences in socialization across social classes may help to channel children toward the same kinds of occupations as their parents.

The Impact of Language

At the heart of socialization is language, the system of symbols and meanings that people use to understand their world and communicate about it. Based on many carefully conducted observational studies and experiments, Basil Bernstein and his students have found significant differences in the language that predominates in working-class and middle-class homes. Bernstein (1971, 1977, 1981) argues that in Britain and America there are two distinct "speech codes," two different sets of rules regarding how people should select their words and put them together in ways appropriate to the situation. One of these codes Bernstein calls a **restricted speech code.** A restricted speech code is based on the assumption that the people we are talking to share the same knowledge, assign the same meanings, and generally have the same views. When we are with those we know very well, all of us tend to use a restricted speech code. Such a code allows us to leave a great deal unsaid. We don't have to bother elaborating on our meanings or making explicit connections between everything we say. We can use a kind of linguistic shorthand and our listeners will still understand us because they share our basic perspective on the world. Bernstein suggests that working-class parents are often limited to a restricted speech code.

Many middle-class parents, however, have had the education and occupational experience needed to develop what Bernstein calls an **elaborated speech code.** An elaborated speech code is used to convey ideas and meanings *different from* those of the other people around us. This is the speech of persuasion, differentiation, and explanation, not of everyday chitchat. Not surprisingly, it is more complex and detailed than is speech based on a restricted code. To listeners, elaborated speech sounds more embellished and more logical, more exacting and precise in its meaning, and generally more planned and "in control."

Bernstein believes that a child who has a chance to acquire an elaborated speech code will develop in a different way, intellectually and socially, from a child who is limited to a restricted speech code. Because a restricted code is based on the assumption of *shared* knowledge and understandings, it does not encourage youngsters to develop a sense of themselves as separate individuals, with ideas distinct from those of others in the groups to which they belong. An elaborated code, because it is the language for differentiating and making clear one's own ideas, gives children ample opportunity to develop a sense of individuality. Thus, children who acquire an elaborated code are encouraged to be more independent in their relationships with others, more self-sufficient and autonomous in their thinking. These traits are important to success in a professional or managerial career.

Bernstein sees speech codes as closely related to the social structure within a family. Middle-class families, he has found, are more likely to have an open role system, one in which each member's role is partly open to negotiation. In such a family, children have a good deal of discretion in the roles they play. They can choose among a range of alternatives (baby, prankster, tomboy, mother's helper) depending upon their individual inclinations. In an open-role family, the parents encourage this kind of independence. Individual qualities and personal choices become frequent topics of discussion. For talk of this nature, in which individuality and autonomy are stressed, an elaborated speech code is essential. In sharp contrast is the family with a very closed role system, common in many working-class households. Here roles are assigned to children with no chance for questioning. Youngsters are simply taught to accept their positions in the social order. There are no complex discussions exploring individual needs and outlooks. In such a family, a restricted speech code is perfectly adequate.

Bernstein argues that speech codes and family social structure are related to a third important factor: the type of control that parents favor when socializing their children. Many working-class families with closed role systems, Bernstein contends, depend a great deal on what he calls *position-oriented control.* Position-oriented control emphasizes a person's status or position within the group and the behaviors deemed appropriate to it. Thus, a working-class mother might insist that her teenage daughter baby-sit her little brother simply because she is the oldest girl in the family. Working-class mothers, as in this example, are also inclined to issue orders. They impose a rule with little explanation or opportunity for discussion. A restricted speech code is all that is needed for this kind of communication. In contrast, a middle-class mother is more apt to use what Bernstein calls *person-oriented control*. Person-oriented control involves tailoring the rules to suit both the situation and the traits of the particular child. Thus, a middle-class mother might say to her teenage daughter, "Would you please baby-sit tonight because no one else is available and you're so good with children." Here the daughter is given the chance to participate in the decision, and to understand why the request is reasonable and appropriate under the circumstances. An elaborated speech code is needed to get this kind of message across. This speech code, in turn, will encourage the daughter to be more open-minded and analytical in her thinking, thereby helping to prepare her for higher-status roles in life. In contrast, the more restricted speech codes and tendency toward position-oriented control in working-class families may limit a child's ability to reach for higher-status careers. These patterns are a possible reason why social class position tends to endure from one generation to another.

The Impact of Values

Another reason that social class distinctions seem to perpetuate themselves may lie in the values that parents pass on to their children. One researcher who has extensively studied class-based differences in values is sociologist Melvin Kohn. Kohn's work in this area spans a period of over twenty years and involves data collected from thousands of people. He and his co-workers have found very consistent differences in the values people hold for themselves and their children depending upon their social class (Kohn 1959; Kohn and Schooler et al. 1983). People in higher social classes are more likely to value traits that involve self-direction, while people in lower social classes are more likely to value traits that involve conformity to external authority. Figure 5.3 summarizes the different values that working-class and middle-class parents stress. Working-class parents place more value on manners, neatness, being a good student, honesty, and obedience. Middle-class parents, in contrast, place more value on consideration, interest in how and why things happen, responsibility, and self-control.

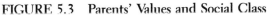

FIGURE 5.3   Parents' Values and Social Class

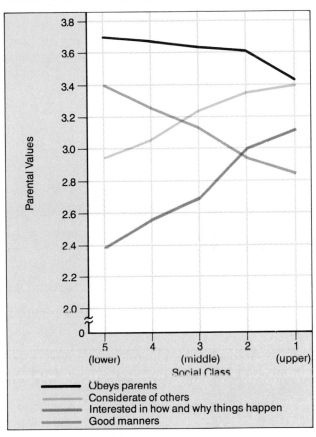

Source: Kohn and Schooler 1983.

Extensive sociological research has found that the emphasis of working-class parents on manners, obedience and neatness contributes to their children's aiming for subordinate jobs, while the emphasis of middle- and upper-class parents on curiosity, considerateness and responsibility leads their children to seek jobs that are more interesting and gives them a greater feeling of self-control.

Comparing the items on these lists makes clear the basic difference between the two value systems. Valuing manners, for example, involves caring about whether a child follows the rules of etiquette that society sets for people, whereas valuing consideration involves caring about whether a child feels empathy for others. The first

FIGURE 5.4   What People Value About Work

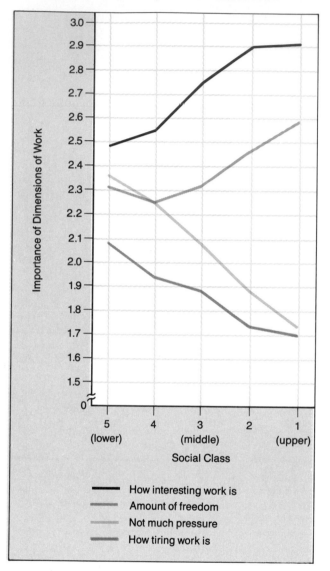

Source: Kohn and Schooler 1983.

People value different dimensions of work and pass those value judgments on to their children. Sociological research has shown these orientations toward work to be influential and long-lasting. As this figure indicates, the differences in work values between classes are striking and may help perpetuate class differences in the next generation.

value stresses conformity to an *external* authority; the second value stresses the development of one's own *internal* standards. Notice the close connection between this class-based difference in values and Bernstein's idea of a class-based difference in speech codes. Working-class families value conformity and use language that assumes people share the same perspective. Middle-class families value self-direction and use language that promotes the expression of individuality.

Working- and middle-class parents, moreover, do not just differ in what they *say* they value. Their behavior is also greatly influenced by their different ideals about how children should act. Because working-class parents value conformity to established rules and traditions, they tend to focus on the immediate consequences of a child's actions. If a child breaks a rule, he or she is likely to be punished, even if the youngster did not mean to do wrong. Middle-class parents, in contrast, are apt to be more concerned with children's motives and intentions than with their actions per se. For instance, if a little boy trips his sister and makes her cry, middle-class parents would be inclined to ask if this act was deliberate before punishing it. Middle-class parents are also more likely to reason with their children in order to make them understand *why* they should or should not do something. Working-class parents, on the other hand, are apt to punish without much discussion, and they are more likely than middle-class parents to administer physical punishments.

But where do these different sets of values and related behaviors come from? Why do working-class parents want their children to follow established conventions and obey with no questions asked, while middle-class parents are more concerned with instilling self-direction and internalized standards? Kohn's research has shown that these class-based differences are directly related to the parents' experiences at work (Kohn 1976; Kohn and Schooler 1978; Kohn 1981). Work that provides opportunities for independent thought, initiative, and judgment tends to foster middle-class values; work that restricts these opportunities tends to encourage working-class values. Certain aspects of work are especially important in this regard (Figure 5.4 summarizes the different aspects of work that working-class and middle-class people value). When a person is not closely supervised, deals with data or people instead of with things, and has work that is complex enough to allow various approaches, he or she has the job-related independence conducive to valuing self-direction. Thus, Kohn sees experiences at work as having a spillover effect into family life. Success in the blue-collar world depends on following procedures and the supervisor's orders, so working-class parents tend to value obedience and conformity in their children. Success in the middle-class world depends much more on autonomous thinking and judgment, particularly at the upper managerial level. Middle-class parents consequently tend to value self-direction, self-initiative, and self-reliance in their children.

Do these values stressed in the home really make a difference to the traits that children develop? Researchers interested in Kohn's work have tried to answer this question. For instance, Jeylan Mortimer and his co-workers (1986) focused on Kohn's finding that parents who value self-direction tend to be more supportive and encouraging toward their children than those who value conformity. In their research into father–son relationships, Mortimer and his associates discovered that a father's encouragement and support is related to a number of traits in the child that would tend to foster achievement. One is a strong sense of self-competence, another the tendency to become very involved in work. These are precisely the kinds of traits found in people who pursue high-status careers.

If the value of self-direction is so important to occupational achievement, couldn't this value be stressed in schools? In this way, working-class youngsters might also acquire the personal outlook needed for higher-level jobs. Such a program is certainly possible. The question is how much society wants to broaden the opportunities open to working-class children. We will return to this question in Chapter 17, which explores education.

AGENTS OF SOCIALIZATION

Socialization occurs in many different settings, through interaction with many different people, groups, and organizations (Elkin and Handel 1984, p. 123). Agents of socialization play different roles in children's lives, and have different goals, responsibilities, and impacts on children's development. They may reinforce one another on some issues, contradict one another on others. For example, parents may want their children to see males and females as equals, and teachers may support this aim. But situation comedies, advertisements, and rock videos on television glamorize and "humorize" the differences between the sexes, and peer groups often demand sex-stereotyped behavior (girls who play with guns are ignored, while boys who play with dolls are ridiculed).

In examining these influences, it is important to distinguish between intentional and unintentional socialization. The mother who insists that a preschooler return a toy to its owner may be concerned about teaching him to get along with others, but she is also teaching him to respect "private ownership of property." Certainly she does not intend a lesson in the basic principles of capitalism, but that is the effect of her actions. In another society that places less value on private property, mothers might be more concerned about a child who guards his possessions and resists giving things away. Parents may intend to teach a child that a person's race or religion does not matter. But their activities (the friends they invite to the house, the groups they join, the neighborhood in which they live) and their comments on other people's life-styles may convey a different message.

The key point here is that socialization does not follow a clear-cut path to a predetermined goal (Wrong 1961). There are many overlapping and unrecognized influences on the child, and many possible outcomes.

Family Life

The family is the first social world the child encounters, and family members the mirror in which children begin to see themselves. To be sure, the family does not play the all-encompassing role in socialization it once did; schools and various other social agencies have taken over many of its functions. Children used to start school at age six; now most go to kindergarten or nursery school at age four or five, and many attend day-care centers as infants and toddlers. Television is widely used as a baby-sitter. Still, the family remains the primary agent of socialization, for important reasons (Elkin and Handel 1984).

The family introduces children to intimate, personal relationships and gives them their first experience of

The family is the primary agent of socialization for children, who are in the process of developing fundamental values and learning about social relationships. For many years the family serves as the foremost agent of socialization in a child's world. (Claudia Parks/Stock Market.)

being treated as a distinct individual. The family is the child's first reference group, the first group whose norms and values the child adopts as his or her own and refers to in evaluating his or her behavior. The family also introduces children to group life. Living together in a household means learning to share household resources, including space, objects, and parental time and attention.

Fathers and mothers have different parental styles, and thus provide their offspring with different experiences (Easterbrooks and Goldberg 1984). With small children, fathers tend toward physical play and new, unfamiliar games; mothers tend toward vocal interaction and familiar games like peek-a-boo. Patterns of socialization in the home also reflect the parents' relationship with one another and the general family environment: whether "interaction in the family is characteristically relaxed and good-humored or tense and guarded, whether it emphasizes or minimizes the distance between parents and children or between males and females, whether it is

typically cooperative or competitive" (Elkin and Handel 1984, p. 132).

The birth of siblings adds new complexities to family life. Through interaction with siblings, children gain experience in cooperation and conflict, negotiation and bargaining, inequalities based on size and experience, and the limits of other people's tolerance. In addition, how a mother responds to a child depends not only on "goodness of fit" (as described earlier), but also on family position: mothers spend twice as much time with firstborn children as with later-born children (White, Kaban, and Attanucci 1979).

Most experts agree that birth order has a significant impact on socialization. Firstborn children tend to be more strictly disciplined than later-born children and to be more of a focus of parental attention. The appearance of a sibling arouses competitive responses in the firstborn. As a result, firstborns "tend to be more conscientious, achieve higher scholastically, and go to school longer than later-borns" (Forer 1976, p. 11; Blake 1986). They are also fortune's favorites, more likely than later-borns to be presidents, members of Congress, astronauts, and to appear on the cover of *Time* magazine (Goleman 1985). Second-borns must learn to work their way around an older, stronger sibling, so they often become adept at diplomacy and negotiation (Jiao, Ji, and Jing 1986). Parental discipline is usually less stringent in the case of the second-born, which encourages relaxed relationships with people (Snow et al. 1981). The "pioneering" function of older siblings frequently continues across the life span, providing their younger brothers and sisters with role models in coping with divorce, bereavement, widowhood, and retirement (Sobel 1980). Indeed, because of today's frequent divorces and remarriages, many children form stronger bonds with their brothers and sisters than they do with their parents (Cicirelli 1980).

Finally, the family introduces a child into society, locating him or her on the social map. To be born into a particular family is to acquire a social status. Whether a child's parents are wealthy or on welfare is no fault of the child; nevertheless, family status has a strong effect on how neighbors, teachers, and others see that child. Moreover, the family's values, attitudes, and life-style reflect the social class, religion, ethnic group, and region of which it is a part. Through the family the child acquires not an uncut version of the culture, but a selected one, based on family members' position and experiences in society.

Peers

INTERVIEWER: Why is Caleb your friend?
TONY: Because I like him.
INTERVIEWER: And why do you like him?
TONY: Because he is my friend.
INTERVIEWER: And why is he your friend?
TONY (with mild disgust): Because . . . I . . . choosed
. . . him . . . for . . . my friend. (Z. Rubin 1980)

Sociologists have long recognized that peers play a unique and important role in the child's initiation to society. Peer groups provide children with their first experience of egalitarian relationships. Because adults are older, stronger, "wealthier" (they control such resources as the refrigerator and the television dial), and presumably wiser than children, adult-child relationships are always asymmetrical. At home and in school, children are always subordinate to adults to some extent. But peers, on the other hand, are social equals. They "stand in the same relation to persons of authority" and "see the world through the same eyes" (Davis 1949, p. 217). Among peers, there are opportunities to learn the meaning of give-and-take that do not exist in the same sense in adult-child interactions. Children can teach their friends new skills or help them solve problems, opportunities they rarely have with adults. Adults know the rules and have the power and authority to enforce

them; among their peers, children can participate in the creation and enforcement of norms.

In peer groups children can develop close relationships of their own choosing (as Tony demonstrated forcefully in the interview above). Children cannot select their parents and siblings (or vice versa), but they can pick their own friends outside of the family. Friendships give children insight into other people's feelings and practice in developing mutual understanding. In early childhood friendships are usually based on opportunity (children who live near one another play together); in middle childhood, on shared interests and activities; in adolescence, on shared secrets and mutual trust. Children also learn from peers that social interaction can be difficult and that friendship is not always automatic (Corsaro 1985).

Peers also teach one another about subjects adults consider sensitive or taboo, such as sex. Youngsters get most of their information about, and most of their experience with, sex from age-mates; our society does not encourage an adult to initiate a child into this domain of behavior. Many parents tell their children about reproduction, but most are uncomfortable talking to youngsters about what sex entails and how it feels. Peer education, however, is not confined to taboo subjects. Iona and Peter Opie (1959) have identified a body of children's "lore and language" transmitted from one generation of children to the next in the form of

Peer groups play important roles in the adolescent's struggles to form identity and to form deeply held adult values. (Left, C. Simonpietri/Sygma; right, Chuck Nacke/Sygma.)

games, rhymes, and moral codes ("finders keepers, losers weepers").

During adolescence, the influence of peers increases and parental influence declines as peers support one another's steps toward independence. This is especially important because, as children enter their teens, they need some help in defending themselves against the ambiguities of adolescence. In our society, adolescents are neither children nor adults. Their responsibilities and their capacity and desire for new experiences increase; yet in many ways they are forced to remain dependent. By aligning themselves *with* peers and *against* adults, young people who are still financially dependent on their parents (they may remain so for years if their parents finance college and graduate education) and who are still learning instead of working, can achieve some sense of autonomy.

For most teenagers both their parents and the peer group are important anchors in their lives (Troll and Bengtson 1982). When the issues involve matters of musical tastes, personal dress, entertainment idols, drinking, marijuana use, smoking, and academic cheating, adolescents tend to be most responsive to the preferences of their peers. But when the issues have to do with future life goals and core values, they tend to be most responsive to the preferences of their parents (Davies and Kandel 1981; Krosnick and Judd 1982).

Finally, the peer group applies its own standards on socialization. We now turn to some differences between adult and peer socialization using Gary Fine's study of the Little League as a basis.

Adult and Peer Socialization: Some Contrasts

Gary Fine's (1987) observations highlight the differences between adult and peer socialization. Adults, according to Fine, see interaction with children as a "moral enterprise." They believe they have an obligation to teach children correct values, and create opportunities to do so. Little League, whose motto is "Character, Courage, and Loyalty," is one such opportunity.

Fine found that Little League coaches stress four moral themes: the importance of effort ("If it's worth doing, it's worth doing well"); sportsmanship (the "golden rules" of athletics); teamwork (as a form of social responsibility); and learning how to behave in both victory and defeat. Fine notes that adults want youngsters to think of these moral rules as absolute, as beyond negotiation. But their own behavior shows that adults invoke the rules selectively. When teams with a long-standing rivalry meet, for example, a coach may encour-

With intense concentration they rarely give their parents, these boys listen to their Little League coach. Peer socialization works alongside adult socialization as boys learn how to balance norms of sportsmanship with a burning desire to win. (Daemmrich/ Uniphoto.)

Television and computers have become major instruments of socialization and the subject of much controversy. What do you think are the similarities and differences between interacting with television and with computers? Do they make a significant difference in the child's attitude and behavior? (Left, Rick Brady/Uniphoto; right, Gabe Palmer/The Stock Market.)

age his players to "rattle" the opposition, and he may "ride" their coach himself—hardly good sportsmanship. Small children may not perceive the difference between what adults say and what they do. Preadolescent boys, however, are quick to see the chink in adult moral armor. In effect, what they learn from adults is when and how to employ moral rhetoric to defend themselves or make another person toe the line.

Meanwhile, peers have their own moral agenda, their own standards that they apply to one another with or without adult approval. First, children expect each other to display appropriate emotions. A boy who cries when his team wins (because he performed poorly himself) is labeled "strange"; one who smiles nervously after striking out is "crazy." The second standard is self-control. Boys expect other boys to control their anger, to refrain from crying, and to be stoic in the face of pain. They understand when their peers lose control, but gently (or not so gently) tell them to "shape up." Third, Little Leaguers are obliged to display a desire to win. Boys who do not hustle, who do not get involved in the game, or who do not act and dress the part of a Little League player, are scorned. Finally, peers demand loyalty. "Ratting" or "tattling" on a peer to an adult is seen as criminal. Acting as if you are superior to your peers is also against the rules. Sarcastic remarks when a youngster excels (telling a boy who hit a triple "Don't come back" or one who hit a homer "It's just a figment of your imagination") cut peers down to size.

As Fine points out, peer socialization does not work against adult socialization, but beside it. The boys he observed were working hard to achieve the ideals of the adult male sex role, but in their own way.

Mass Media

Children are exposed to a variety of mass media, the forms of communication that reach large numbers of people—television, radio, movies, videos, records, comic books, magazines, and newspapers. While all the mass media are crucial agents of socialization, the most influential is probably television. Certainly no other medium consumes more of children's time than television. At nine months many infants are watching television (although not necessarily comprehending it) for an hour-and-a-half each day (Singer 1983). By three or four years of age, they average four hours a day (Singer and Singer 1981; National Institute of Mental Health 1982). In middle childhood and adolescence, twenty to twenty-five hours a week is about average, and some youngsters manage a forty-hour week in front of the tube (Hodge and Tripp 1986). Overall, children in the United States (and other Western nations) spend more time watching television than they spend in school or, very likely, in direct communication with their parents (Winn 1985).

Parents often feel hopeless about controlling their children's television viewing. Fewer than half establish clear regulations about when and what children may watch (Robertson 1980).

Parents and others are concerned about how television is socializing children. They are unhappy with the content of many shows (especially the amount of violence); they worry about the intensity of children's involvement with television; and they believe television keeps children away from healthier activities (such as outdoor play) and learning experiences (especially reading). Underlying these specific complaints is the general feeling that television is an exceedingly powerful medium, and that children are not mature enough to protect themselves from harmful messages. One sociologist, Neal Postman (1979), has suggested that television has begun to erase the boundaries between things known to children and things known only to adults.

A report issued by the National Institute of Mental Health in 1982 suggested that parents were right to be concerned. "Television can no longer be considered as a casual part of daily life, as an electronic toy. Research findings have long since destroyed the illusion that television is merely innocuous entertainment" (p. 87). Nonetheless, a close examination of studies of the impact of television on children yields mixed results. On the positive side, experiments show that watching programs that emphasize sharing, cooperation, and self-discipline (such as "Mister Rogers' Neighborhood") encourages prosocial behavior in children (Cater and Strickland 1975; Singer and Singer 1983). And for children who live in an impoverished environment, shows like "Sesame Street" are undoubtedly a source of stimulation and instruction. On the negative side, numerous studies have shown that watching violence on television encourages aggression. One long-term study of teenagers found that a preference for violence on television was a more accurate predictor of aggressive behavior than socioeconomic background, family relationships, IQ, or any other single factor (Cater and Strickland 1975). It is difficult to say which comes first, the aggressive disposition or the preference for violent shows, but the relationship between the two stands. Other research suggests that heavy television viewing in the preschool years puts a child at risk for problem behavior in elementary school (Singer and Singer 1981, 1983). What is a parent to do? One recent study takes a different position regarding the effects of television.

In Depth: How Children Interpret Television

Robert Hodge and David Tripp (1986) argue that fears about the impact of television on children may be exaggerated. The debate about the impact of television on children suggests that children are passive viewers. It has been suggested that the impact of television on youngsters is as direct and dramatic as a bat hitting a ball. Hodge and Tripp disagree:

> Balls don't think; children do. Television sends out messages, which are interpreted and acted on by social agents responsible for their actions. Television communicates meanings. It does not pick children up and send them rampaging through the streets. If television affects behavior, it can only do so very indirectly via meanings, beliefs, values. (1986, pp. 2–3)

Hodge and Tripp approach television viewing from an action perspective. For them, the key question is: What message is television sending to children and (most significantly) how do children interpret the message?

In one recent study, the researchers showed forty-two children ages six to twelve a cartoon called "Fangface." The hero of the story is a teenage boy named Sherman Fangsworth, who just happens to be a werewolf. The cartoon is typical of children's television fare in both the high level of violence and in sex stereotypes (the heroes are all boys; the one girl, Sally, is a classic "damsel in distress"). First, the researchers showed the program to small groups of children. Then an interviewer held discussions with mixed-sex groups of five or six youngsters, and their conversations were videotaped.

Like other television shows, "Fangface" does not send a single, simple message; rather, there are many ambiguous and contradictory messages. Fangface, for example, is presented as a force for good, but he is also a werewolf and therefore associated with lightning, wolves, darkness, and forces of destruction. He speaks like a person and also howls like a wolf; he has the deep voice of an adult, but a childish obsession with food. Hodge and Tripp found that the youngsters were skilled at decoding these messages. Even the youngest children in the study were emphatic in stating that "Fangface" was a cartoon and the story, pure fantasy.

> INTERVIEWER: Er, how do we know that that was a cartoon?
> ADRIAN: Oh, you can tell by the . . . picture and . . .
> CRAIG: Pictures.
> CHRISTIE: It's colored in. Not like real people.
> ADRIAN: And they weren't that well drawn . . . .
> CHRISTIE: And you can't go out and see a cartoon walking across the road or something. It's just . . . [others laugh] a piece of paper.
> ADRIAN: And I don't think that cartoon was really true. [Other boys laugh.]
> INTERVIEWER: Don't you? Why not?
> ADRIAN: Oh, you wouldn't see the heap runnin' about in the streets and Fangface changing and changing back again.
> CHRISTIE: You don't, you don't have those sorts of things like people changing into things, really. (1986, pp. 110, 111)

The ability to distinguish fantasy from fact is important. Other studies (e.g., Feshbach 1976) have shown that television violence increases the tendency to be aggressive if, and only if, viewers believe the violence is real. Even the youngest child in Hodge and Tripp's study knew the difference.

> INTERVIEWER: What about if someone gets killed on television?
> GEORGE: Um . . . They're not really killed.
> INTERVIEWER: They're not really killed on television?
> GEORGE: They're just pretend bullets and they just pretend they're killed and they get all dead on purposely.
> INTERVIEWER: I see . . . and what happens in real life when somebody gets killed?
> GEORGE: Um . . . they die. (1986, p. 112)

The Hodge and Tripp study also touched on another controversial aspect of television programming, sex stereotypes. In real life, the ratio of males to females is 1:1; in "Fangface" (and most television programs) the ratio is 4:1 in favor of males. The researchers tested children's reactions to this bias by asking them to describe the most significant characters in the story. The boys' choices were overwhelmingly (96 percent) male; the girls' choices were more varied (64 percent male, 36 percent female),

but also skewed. The key point is that neither was an accurate or mechanical reproduction of the sex ratio in the cartoon: Both sexes imposed their own interpretations on what they saw. The boys *magnified* the importance of boys by a factor of 8, for a ratio of 32:1; the girls *resisted* this bias, halving the ratio to 2:1. Indeed, when asked which character they would like to be, 75 percent of the girls chose Sally, the only female character. Clearly the bias in the show did not affect their gender identity or liking for female characters. Hodge and Tripp take the unusual position that the sex bias on television may actually work in girls' favor: girls have many opportunities to observe and understand the "male other," but boys have few opportunities to learn about the "female other."

This in-depth analysis of how children interpret the meaning of what they see on television makes the point that children are anything but zombies when watching the tube. Youngsters *interact* with television in much the same way they interact with their toys. Television promotes internalization of social norms and values by forcing children to use and apply their knowledge of good and evil, reality and fantasy. Like fairy tales and classical myths, cartoons and other television shows explore a culture's boundaries—its limits, problems, and contradictions. The characters are often transgressors, deviants, and monsters. Children thus gain experience in working out problems. "Television is not time-out from thinking, as so many fear: it provides grist for the mills of thought, innumerable opportunities for normal cognitive growth" (1986, p. 92). As one child put it, "You sorta listen with your eyes" (p. 41).

Hodge and Tripp do not mean to suggest that all television shows are good for all children. Small children prefer (and benefit most from) cartoons, in which the line between fantasy and reality is clearly drawn. Older children prefer (and benefit most from) shows with live actors that challenge their grasp of social realities. Adolescents are ready for the news. Hodge and Tripp conclude that television is no better or worse than dollhouses and tree houses, books and museums. Like these other socialization tools, television invites interaction, experimentation, and mental and social growth—particularly if parents watch with their children and the content of shows is brought into family (and even classroom) discussions.

School

Just as preconceptions about television as a medium for entertainment can blind us to its role in socialization, preconceptions about school as a place for learning "the three Rs" (and other subjects) tend to obscure the fact that considerable socialization takes place in school. While the official purpose of school is to teach young people technical and intellectual skills, it also teaches cultural values and attitudes that prepare them for their roles as adults.

In modern societies, school is the primary agent for weaning children from home and introducing them to the larger society. Life in school is a drastic change from life at home. In the family, children are valued for who they are; at school, they are graded for what they do. Parents (ideally) adjust activities to the child's particular interests; teachers usually expect all children to follow the same curriculum. At home, discipline is mixed with love; in school, children are expected to conform because rules and regulations must be obeyed. School is a youngster's introduction to impersonal, bureaucratic organizations.

These lessons are part of what Talcott Parsons (1959) called "the hidden curriculum"; never explicitly taught, they are built into the structure of the classroom.

In most schools students do not participate in decision making about rules or curricula or other issues that affect their lives; they do not even have the right to speak up, move around, or go to the bathroom without permission. An extensive study of today's schools concluded:

> [There] is no more firmly rooted tradition than the one that holds that children must sit still at their desks without conversing at all, both during periods of waiting, when they have nothing to do, and during activities that almost demand conversation. Yet even on an assembly line, there is conversation and interaction among workers, and there are coffee breaks and work pauses as well. (Silberman 1971, p. 128)

How well children do in school depends in part on how well they learn to play the role of student. Some youngsters are better prepared for this role than others. For example, the qualities working-class parents encourage—obedience, conformity, good manners—are appropriate for grammar school; the qualities middle-class parents encourage—curiosity, independent thinking, self-direction—become important in college preparatory programs. (We will say more about the impact of schooling on students in Chapter 17.)

SECONDARY SOCIALIZATION

Up to this point, we have been describing socialization in the early stages of life, or what we might call *primary socialization*. But the process of acquiring the norms and values of one's society, learning how to function effectively in one's community, and finding ways to express individuality within this framework does not stop when young people celebrate their eighteenth birthday or graduate from school. Starting a career, living on one's own, marrying, becoming a parent, changing jobs or neighborhoods or spouses, and growing old all require learning new social roles. We will examine different roles in the life course in Chapter 6. Here we will look at additional processes of socialization that come into play as children grow up and enter the adult world.

Resocialization

As suggested above, some life transitions continue to build on existing norms, values, and roles (Bachman et al. 1978). Others require **resocialization,** or the internalization of a different set of norms and values. Resocialization is most obvious in institutional contexts, such as army boot camp, a prison, or a mental hospital. But certain professions (medicine, nursing, law, police work, and others) depend on a training program that strips individuals of the self-image and values acquired through previous socialization—a process known as **desocialization**—and replaces these with a new outlook and self-image.

Resocialization to a profession usually entails six stages (Light 1980). During the first stage, recruits are made to feel different. For example, psychiatric residents, who had learned to see themselves as competent

The Resocialization of College Athletes

Socialization does not necessarily benefit individuals or society. It can have a negative impact. Peter and Patricia Adler's study of college athletes (1985) revealed a pattern of deceit, disillusionment, and detachment that undermines the stated goals of a college education. Peter Adler spent four years as a participant observer (see Chapter 2) at a midwestern university with a "big-time" basketball team. As the "team sociologist," Adler gained the confidence of players and coaches and was able not only to track the athletes' careers, but also their attitudes toward college and themselves.

Contrary to popular belief, most athletes enter college with high educational ideals and a strong desire to graduate. Recruiters tell them their athletic skills are their ticket to academic and later occupational success; their parents and the culture at large reinforce this hope. In the words of one freshman, "If I can use my basketball ability to open up the door to get an education, hopefully I can use my degree to open up the door to get a good job . . ." (1985, p. 243). Their first semesters in college support this anticipatory socialization. Coaches arrange special preseason programs, make sure they enroll in freshman sections with instructors who are sympathetic to the university sports program, arrange tutoring, and otherwise buffer athletes from academic demands.

The college athlete's sophomore year is best characterized as a period of desocialization. The coach can no longer protect "his" athletes from regular academic standards. Rather suddenly, the athletes realize that they will not automatically get a degree and that their high school backgrounds have not prepared them for college work. They imagined that they would be as popular on campus as they had been in high school. Instead, they find that they are socially isolated. Athletes in some universities are required to live in a special dorm on a remote part of the campus. Long hours of practice, frequent trips, and other sports functions cut them off from campus social life. Because of their size and build, and their racial and socioeconomic status, other students see them as "different." The majority of the students at the university the Adlers studied were white, suburban, and middle class; most of the athletes, in contrast, were working or lower-middle class, and 70 percent were black. Further, they realize that "playing ball" isn't a game anymore, it's big business for the university. "In college the coaches be a lot more concerned on winning and the money comin' in. If they don't win, they may get the boot, and so they pass that pressure onto us athletes" (1985, p. 244).

The final stage in the athlete's "education" is resocialization. Rather than face academic embarrassment and failure, they distance themselves from the role of student. The Adlers found that three-quarters of those who chose business, engineering, or other preprofessional majors switch to easier courses; others give up on college and dream of being drafted by a professional team (only a dream for most college stars). The subculture of the athlete's dorm supports an anti-academic, anti-intellectual stance—neutralizing the importance of grades, providing excuses and justifications for academic failure, and mocking those who continue to try. Coaches, boosters (alumni who fund the athletic program), and the media do little to halt this drift. In the end, athletes embrace the stereotype of "dumb jocks" who eat, sleep, and breathe sports.

The Adlers conclude that all star athletes are subjected to this negative resocialization, regardless of their individual potential. "The structural factors [lack of preparation for college, false hopes, social isolation, pressures to perform on the court, etc.] are ultimately much stronger predictors of athletes' academic success than any of their individual characteristics" (1985, p. 248). The researchers suggest that the cycle of disillusionment and detachment could be broken if athletes were integrated into regular dormitories, given academic role models and advisers rather than athletic personnel "masquerading" as advisers, and protected from media attention. They also suggest that this negative pattern of desocialization and resocialization might apply to other students whose anticipatory socialization has not prepared them for the realities of college.

Source: Adler, Peter and Patricia A. Adler. 1985. From idealism to pragmatic detachment: The academic performance of college athletes. Sociology of Education 58: 241–250.

young doctors, are told they will go slightly "crazy." The second stage involves a discrediting process. Veteran cops tell rookies to forget everything they learned at the police academy because it will be useless on the streets. Typically, a third stage of conflict and confusion follows. Nursing students mutter that school is not what they expected (Davis 1968; Simpson 1979); rookie cops find that their ideas of absolute right and wrong are attacked. The fourth stage is characterized by despair. Some initiates consider dropping out. Others muddle through. They no longer understand or try to justify what is going on; they simply do what is expected of them. In the fifth stage, the recruits begin to see themselves as what they hoped to become. Nursing students, for example, begin to align themselves with their teachers (who conceive of nursing in broad, theoretical terms), against ward personnel (who see nursing in terms of specific tasks). The sixth stage is one of reaffirmation. The individuals internalize the world view of the career, and accept its norms and values as their own. They look back on their initiation with some amusement about how naive they were at the outset. The rookie has become a cop; the student, a nurse; the resident, a psychiatrist.

Current interest in resocialization reflects changing ideas about the nature of socialization. In the past, many (perhaps most) social scientists believed that childhood experiences determined what kind of people we become. Adult socialization was seen as mere "icing on the cake." (Freud was a leading exponent of this view.) Today, many sociologists believe that adult experiences (working, becoming a parent, divorce, becoming middle-aged, and so on) have as much impact on adult patterns of adaptation as childhood experiences.

Anticipatory Socialization

Anticipatory socialization refers to the mental rehearsals, concrete plans, and subtle changes in values and perceptions we go through when we know a significant change in social roles is about to occur. Children are engaging in anticipatory socialization when they play house or doctor. But their knowledge of adult roles is both limited and idealized. Adults are more knowledgeable and more practical. A twenty-year-old who wants to become a doctor takes premed courses in college, talks to the student adviser about applying to medical school,

and asks physicians he or she knows personally for advice. A mother-to-be talks to her own mother and to friends with new babies, reads books on prenatal development, attends childbirth classes, plans a leave of absence from her job, and decorates the nursery; a father-to-be often feels an urgent need to get family finances in order. Adults may also use anticipatory socialization to prepare themselves for an unwelcome role—such as serving a prison term. Although mental rehearsal and imagination play a major role in anticipatory socialization, consulting with significant others is also crucial. However thorough, anticipatory socialization, such as that for a first job or a first marriage or a career in sports (see the box), is rarely complete.

Occupational Socialization

Occupational socialization is the process of aligning the norms, values, and beliefs of a new worker with those of the organization or occupation.

At best, schools prepare individuals in only a very general way for positions in the workplace. All occupations require "on-the-job" training, whether in the form of formal classes and a set curriculum or informal initiation. In addition to acquiring certain knowledge and skills, socialization to a job entails learning the values and ethics of the organization or occupation, the unofficial rules, and the way people on different rungs of an organization's hierarchy are expected to relate both to clients and to colleagues. Like other forms of socialization, occupational socialization is a reciprocal process. The organization socializes employees to its core norms, values, and practices; the individual acquires the knowledge and skills needed to get along and get ahead.

Workplaces vary in how much they want to socialize their workers to new roles. At one extreme, socialization at IBM, in many fine hotels, in leading accounting firms, or in the State Department touches the most subtle and personal aspects of self. Employees are expected to personify the organization's image every minute of the day. But most companies and organizations demand much less, expecting only that workers do their jobs well.

Whether one is socialized individually or in groups makes a difference. In army boot camp or a large sales training program one goes through the experience with others. Peer relations and group norms become significant sources of sharing and sometimes of resistance to the organization. Being socialized individually makes one more dependent on the superiors who are doing the "breaking in" (Wheeler 1966; Van Maanen 1976; Mortimer and Simmons 1978).

Edgar Schein (1978), of the Sloan School of Management, has found that socialization to one's first major job involves four tasks.

The first task is to come to terms with the organization. New employees soon discover that others in the organization frequently constitute a roadblock to what they want to get done. Co-workers do not seem as bright, competent, or productive as they should be. Too often they appear to be illogical, irrational, and unmotivated. The novice must learn to accept the human organization with all its weaknesses. "Selling," "compromising," and "politicking" become essential skills.

The second task is learning to cope with resistance to change within the organization. New employees complain that their "good ideas" are undermined, sidetracked, sabotaged, or simply ignored. They discover that their recommendations, which seem so technically sound, are not implemented for one reason or another. The degree to which new employees learn to cope with resistance to change has important consequences for their future career paths.

The third task is resolving ambiguity in their jobs. Novices find that some aspects of their work are ill-defined. And they have difficulty acquiring the feedback essential for judging their own performance. Thus, carving out one's own job is a critical task in learning how to work.

The fourth task is learning how to get ahead. New employees must learn how to relate to their boss, evolving a balance between being too dependent and becoming too independent. Simultaneously, they must learn to decipher the reward system. This involves identifying what is really expected of them, what is really rewarded, and how much they can trust official formal statements.

The degree to which people internalize the values and folkways of an organization or occupation depends on their degree of involvement. The sociologists Jon Lorence and Jeylan Mortimer (1985) studied job involvement for a large sample of American workers over a number of years. They found that autonomy on the job has a strong impact on their degree of involvement in the work (much as Kohn found that job autonomy has a

For generations, apprentices have learned from experienced seamstresses—not only how to hold the cloth, but also a whole approach to their work. (Earl Dotter/Archive.)

powerful influence on child-rearing practices). In general, job involvement is intense in the early years of a worker's career, then stabilizes.

In recent years, overinvolvement in a job or "workaholism" has been attracting more and more attention. Doctors LaBier and Berglass, who studied hundreds of exceptionally successful men and women, found that intense involvement in an occupation often causes people to neglect other areas of their lives: Despite clear signs of success, such as promotions and raises, they feel empty and joyless. Those who achieve occupational success very early in life are especially prone to depression. "You cannot outdo yourself forever," says Dr. Berglass. "A spectacular early success is sure to doom you to relative failure by comparison with your past record" (New York Times, August 17, 1986, p. F1, F12).

SUMMARY

1. *Socialization* is the process by which we learn to become members of the human community and internalize the values and roles of the society into which we are born.

2. What kind of person we become depends on the interaction of biology and experience. Genes establish a basic timetable for development and for socialization. They also establish a "reaction range" for traits ranging from height to intelligence. Children with different temperaments evoke certain responses from people, and choose different activities.

3. Studies of children who have been neglected or institutionalized show that socialization is a necessary part of becoming fully human. But it is not a one-way street: children and their parents influence one another.

4. Some theories of socialization focus on the outcome of socialization. The functional perspective holds that socialization contributes to the functional integration of society. The power perspective is more concerned with the influence of powerful groups on socialization. Other theories of socialization focus on the process of relating the individual to society. The structural perspective emphasizes how children are fitted into a particular cultural mode or social structure, while the action perspective focuses on individual capacities and actions.

5. Charles Horton Cooley used the image of a looking glass to explain how other people influence the way we see ourselves. George Herbert Mead traced the development of self-awareness to early interaction between parent and child. Socialization is extended in the play stage, when children learn to take the roles of others, and the game stage, when they develop a generalized impression of what people expect from them and where they fit in the larger social picture.

6. Sigmund Freud saw socialization as working against our natural inclinations and drives. But he also considered socialization essential to the preservation of the social order.

7. Social class differences in child-rearing practices and even language styles reflect different experiences in the workplace and tend to reproduce social inequality generation after generation.

8. Socialization is the result of overlapping, sometimes contradictory forces, as well as intentional and unintentional lessons.

9. The family, which introduces the child to intimate relationships and group living, is a primary agent of socialization. The family also provides the child with a social status.

10. Among peers, children experience egalitarian relationships, make friends of their own choosing, and learn about subjects adults consider taboo. The importance of peers increases as children move toward adolescence and young adulthood. Peer socialization works alongside adult socialization, but is subject to its own standards.

11. Television has the most impact of any medium on children, and its socializing influences are strongly debated. New research shows that television does not turn children into passive observers, but invites interaction and exploration of cultural boundaries.

12. The official function of school is to teach children technical and intellectual skills; the "hidden curriculum" introduces children to impersonal, bureaucratic organizations.

13. Secondary socialization may entail anticipatory socialization, occupational socialization, and desocialization and resocialization.

GLOSSARY

Anticipatory socialization. The mental rehearsals, concrete plans, and changes in values and perceptions individuals use to prepare for a significant change in social roles.

Desocialization. The process of shedding one's self-image and values; usually followed by resocialization to a different set of values.

Ego. According to Sigmund Freud, the rational part of the self that finds socially acceptable ways of satisfying biological cravings.

Elaborated speech code. A more complex and precise language style used to convey ideas and meanings that are different from those in use around us.

Generalized other. An internalized general impression of what society as a whole expects.

Id. Freud's term for the reservoir of innate biological drives, aimed at obtaining physical pleasure.

Internalization. The process by which individuals come to incorporate the standards, attitudes, and beliefs of their society within their personalities.

Looking-glass self. Cooley's term to explain how others influence the way we see ourselves. We gain an image of ourselves by imagining what other people think about our appearance and behavior.

Occupational socialization. The process of aligning the norms, values, and beliefs of a new worker with those of the organization or occupation.

Resocialization. The internalization of a new and different set of norms and values.

Restricted speech code. A simplified language style based on assumptions of shared knowledge, views, and meanings.

Self. The notion that each of us has that we possess a unique and distinct identity—that we are set apart from other objects and people.

Significant others. People who are emotionally important in one's life.

Significant symbols. According to Mead, conventionalized gestures and words acquired in infancy and early childhood that arouse desired responses in others and make possible social interaction.

Socialization. The process by which new members of a society are instilled with the fundamental elements of their culture; means by which we become members of human society.

Superego. Freud's term for the conscience, the part of the personality that internalizes the society's views of right and wrong.

Temperament. The emotional orientation toward experience with which a child is born.

CHAPTER 6
Sociology and the Life Course: From Childhood to Old Age

For two centuries, the birthrate in the United States (and other Western nations) has declined steadily—with one major exception. In 1946, GIs returning from World War II enthusiastically embraced family life, launching the phenomenon known as the *baby boom*. This trend, which continued for almost two decades, peaked between 1954 and 1964, when close to 4 million babies were born in the United States each year.

As the so-called "baby-boom generation" moves from childhood to adolescence to adulthood, it has affected almost every aspect of American society, including the educational system, the job market, and the economy. In the process, the baby boomers were shaped by, and helped to shape, our cultural views of youth and adulthood, and ultimately they will affect how we view old age.

Individuals and age groups both reflect and affect society as they live out their lives and interact with the larger social world. The baby boom generation provides us with a useful example of this interaction, partly because of this group's sheer size, and partly because of the constant social flux that has marked its passage through life. At the same time, however, like an individual who must retain a sense of identity in the midst of change, this generation has a particular profile, expressive of the similarities in age-related individuals growing up in a particular social context.

In the baby boom, we see some essential aspects of American life in the second half of the twentieth century. Baby boomers were the first mostly suburban generation, the first to grow up with television, the first to attend high schools intent on competing scholastically with the Soviet Union (a result of the Soviets' launching of the first man-made satellite, Sputnik, in 1957). They were twice as likely as their parents to attend college, and also twice as likely to get divorced. Unique events—the assassinations of President John F. Kennedy and the civil rights leader Martin Luther King, Jr., the war in Vietnam, the Watergate scandal that toppled the presidency of Richard M. Nixon—helped to determine their relationship to history and give them their own world view.

So the baby boomers can be seen as a product of a particular time and place, and—because they heavily outnumber the generations that preceded and followed them—they can also be viewed as agents for social change. In the late 1940s and early 1950s baby boomers crowded maternity wards and kindergartens, making Dr. Spock and Dr. Seuss national figures. In the 1950s they overloaded elementary school systems. As they moved through adolescence and young adulthood, their needs and passions, foibles and vices, created instant fads and whole new industries (such as rock music). Once at college, in the 1960s and early 1970s, their great numbers fueled a "youth culture," or counterculture, with its own values, traditions, rituals, and language. They protested the war in Vietnam, demanded a voice in university administration, flouted the strict sexual codes of the past, and smoked marijuana in the open, daring adults to stop them.

Where have all the children gone? They have grown up, waited longer to have families of their own, and had fewer children. Consequently, doors have closed in recent years on many schools built in the 1950s and 1960s to accommodate the post World War II baby boom. As these "baby boomers" move through the life course, they leave dramatic changes in their wake and are themselves shaped by those very changes. (Above: Wayne Miller/ Magnum Photos; right: Charles Feli/Stock Boston.)

Although their actions and beliefs may not have changed society as much as the baby boomers hoped, this generation nevertheless left a mark on American society. Increasing numbers of unmarried couples are now openly living together, and the government, the military, and the church have lost some of their authority, widening the gap between young people and their parents. At the same time, unprecedented numbers of college educated men and women have crowded into business and the professions, placing a strain on the job market and forcing some baby boomers to settle for less prestigious jobs than they had planned for. Housing, too, has become scarce, and because the supply of available dwellings has not kept up with the demand, prices of homes and apartments have skyrocketed.

With the oldest baby boomers moving into middle age, this generation now forms the single largest group of consumers in the nation (Jones 1980, p. 275). And when the baby boomers retire, our society will have the highest percentage of elderly in recorded history—a situation that will certainly affect health care, the Social Security system, and retirement facilities. The numbers of the elderly are already beginning to climb, so we will look at this social phenomenon later in the chapter and make some predictions.

As the baby boomers have progressed from playpen to college campus, and then to careers, homes, and families, they have also altered the way Americans think about youth and adulthood. This affects our historical perspective, too. Just as an analysis of the 1960s would not be meaningful without reference to the "youth revolution" of that time, the first decades of the twenty-first century may be dominated by a bourgeoning, politically powerful older generation.

THE LIFE COURSE IN SOCIOLOGICAL PERSPECTIVE

As this brief glimpse at the baby boom illustrates, the study of a particular generation (or a much more narrowly defined age-related group, as you'll see shortly) is one way to look at social stability, social change, and social views of the life cycle. And one way sociologists approach this study is to consider the **life course,** or collective biography, of groups of people as they move through life.

The life course is a relatively new frame of reference for sociology. The term "life course" implies a meaningful flow of years (Levinson 1976). On the most basic level, the life course is the journey from birth to death. On another level, the life course is a series of more or less predictable changes. As the year is divided into seasons, so the life course is divided into stages: childhood, adolescence, adulthood, and so on. Each stage of the life course has its own particular character and its own necessary place, linking past to future. On yet another level, the life course is a series of phases in which an individual's (or generation's) life is shaped by particular experiences, such as being part of the baby boom.

How is this approach different from the psychological study of human development? Whereas psychologists look at changes in the ways individuals think, feel, and behave as they grow, sociologists analyze the changing ways of aggregates as they age against the backdrop of historic development. Thus, in both psychological and sociological terms, aging is much more than the addition of years. In distinctly sociological terms, aging involves a socially patterned sequence of changes in roles, responsibilities, and privileges. Individuals may deviate from the cultural expectations that are associated with each stage of the life course, but the sequence itself—its stages and their length and content—is socially defined.

Social Definitions of Life-Course Stages

All societies classify individuals into age groups (this is known as **age grading),** rank members according to age, and establish timetables for major life events (Elder 1978). But how many stages in the life course a society recognizes, how it defines these stages, and where it draws the boundaries between the stages vary from culture to culture and from one historical period to another. Within our own culture, for example, the meanings of infancy and childhood have changed radically in the last 150 years; and the stage known as adolescence was unheard of until fairly recently (Kett 1977). Concepts of life-course stages and the language used to describe them reflect social relationships. When these relationships change, definitions of stages also shift.

Certainly, all societies differentiate in some way between childhood and adulthood. Children enjoy opportunities and suffer restrictions that do not apply to adults, and vice versa. Generally, the older one becomes, the more power and privilege one is accorded (Foner and Kertzer 1978). (The one exception is old age: the elderly are treated with deference in some societies but devalued in others.) So age usually contributes to social status (Jones 1980), but the *degree* to which it contributes to status varies from one society to the next. In some societies, age is the basis for a formal system of social stratification. Social roles, and the rights and privileges that accompany them, are distributed primarily on the basis of age. For example, the Masai, a pastoral society in East Africa, recognize four age grades for males—boy, warrior, junior elder, and senior elder —and each age grade is assigned a distinct social role (Bernardi 1955; Ole Saitoti and Beckwith 1980). Boys have been initiated into Masai society and are responsible for herding their family's livestock on a daily basis, but are still under the authority of their parents. Warriors (called *morani*), who range in age from about fifteen to thirty, live in separate villages, supervised by a committee of elders. Junior elders (about ages thirty to forty-five) are permitted to marry, own cattle, and establish their own homesteads. Senior elders (age forty-five plus) are in charge of public affairs.

In other societies, such as our own, age is only one of many sources of social identity and social status, although the distribution of certain social opportunities and obligations is age-linked to some extent. We cannot drive until age sixteen, vote until age eighteen, drink until age twenty-one (in most states), or retire with full Social Security benefits until age sixty-five. We are required to attend school from age six to about age sixteen. Nevertheless, *boundaries* between stages in our life course are only loosely defined—very loosely in comparison with the Masai. When does an American child become an adolescent, or a young adult become middle-aged? In one recent survey, respondents were asked the ages they associated with the phrase "young man," and answers ranged from eighteen to forty! (Neugarten and Neugarten 1987, p. 32)

But, of course, even though we do not base social roles on age alone in our society, norms regarding age-appropriate behavior are woven into our social fabric (see Table 6.1). Here we are talking about much more generalized and complex activities and opportunities than drinking or voting. Generally accepted timetables and age expectations govern major transitions like completing school, establishing economic independence, marrying, having children, and retirement. Although age norms have been modified in recent years, most people still are concerned about whether they are "on schedule" or not. When asked about major events in his or her life, a person often refers directly to the social timetable: "I got off to a late start because I served in Vietnam," or "I married very young." In making a major decision, such as a change in career, people ask

themselves whether the time is "right." The "rightness" is simply a reference to social norms.

When life events occur on schedule, they are usually taken in stride because they have been anticipated and rehearsed. Unforeseen events, however, may cause some stress (Rindfuss et al. 1987). The departure of the youngest child and the beginning of the so-called "empty nest" phase of family life is not a crisis for most middle-aged parents because it is expected. But when offspring do *not* depart at the appropriate time, or move back for an extended interval (after a divorce or during a period of unemployment), both parent and child tend to be confused about what is expected of them. Even positive events may cause stress if they occur at the "wrong time." A woman who achieves enormous professional success by age thirty, for example, may slip into

TABLE 6.1   Opinions About Age-Appropriate Behavior

Activity/Event	Appropriate Age Range	Late '50s Study % Who Agree		Late '70s Study % Who Agree	
		Men	Women	Men	Women
Best age for a man to marry	20–25	80%	90%	42%	42%
Best age for a woman to marry	19–24	85	90	44	36
When most people should become grandparents	45–50	84	79	64	57
Best age for most people to finish school and go to work	20–22	86	82	36	38
When most men should be settled on a career	24–26	74	64	24	26
When most men hold their top jobs	45–50	71	58	38	31
When most people should be ready to retire	60–65	83	86	66	41
When a man has the most responsibilities	35–50	79	75	49	50
When a man accomplishes most	40–50	82	71	46	41
The prime of life for a man	35–50	86	80	59	66
When a woman has the most responsibilities	25–40	93	91	59	53
When a woman accomplishes most	30–45	94	92	57	48

Source: Rosenfeld and Stark 1987, p. 72.

Two surveys asking the same questions 20 years apart (late 1950s and late 1970s) have shown a dramatic decline in the consensus among middle-class, middle-aged people about what's the right age for various major events and achievements of adult life.

depression because she does not know what to do with the rest of her life.

Transitions and Changes in the Life Course

However the stages of the life course are defined by a society, any movement from one stage to another must involve a **transition,** a point at which the familiar role is relinquished and a new role is assumed (Foner and Kertzer 1978). Each major life event requires a transition. Coming of age, for example, requires us to give up the prerogatives of childhood and shoulder the unfamiliar responsibilities of adulthood. Marriage means we must give up sexual and domestic freedom and learn to accommodate ourselves to others. The birth of a first child, the launching of the last child, and retirement are other transitions. Traditionally, **rites of passage** have marked transitions. These rites publicize the passage from one social stage to another with socially supervised ceremonies and ritual, explain the meaning of the transition to all concerned, and involve the community in the process (Van Gennep 1960; Gluckman 1962; Turner 1970).

In societies where the stages of life are sharply outlined and closely tied to age, the transitions from stage to stage and the accompanying rites of passage are less ambiguous and more broadly meaningful than such ceremonies in more complex societies. Here again we can contrast traditional societies like the Masai, where transitions are clear-cut and rites of passage are culturally significant, with modern societies like our own. Certainly, we hold ceremonies to mark transitions: bar and bat mitzvahs and confirmations, graduations, debutante balls and coming-out parties, marriages, retirement dinners, and funerals. But these ceremonies do not necessarily constitute absolute thresholds in our life cycles. According to Jewish tradition, for example, the bar mitzvah symbolizes entry into manhood; but today, even though the ceremony is still held when a boy turns thirteen, it certainly does not signify that the boy has become a man in larger social terms.

Again, we see that the definition of stages and the meaning of transitions have become increasingly ambiguous in our contemporary society. Indeed, one of the distinguishing features of contemporary societies is that these meanings are changing and sometimes changing quite rapidly. The timing of events all along the life course has become more variable, and age norms have

Transitions are an important part of the life course, and they are celebrated in all cultures—especially the rite of passage from adolescence to adulthood. The Masai initiation rite marks significant changes in the role of the tribe's young men. In our society, such initiation rituals, like this Jewish bar mitzvah, are largely symbolic; this young man may not assume adult responsibilities for several years. (Left: Peter Arnold/ Arthus/Bertrand; right: Yoram Lehmann/Peter Arnold, Inc.)

loosened (Neugarten and Neugarten 1987). Some people enter the work force at age sixteen or seventeen; others are still in school, training for a profession, at age thirty. Some women have their first child before age fifteen, while others do not become mothers until they are thirty-five or older. Men and women may marry, divorce, remarry, and divorce again. Women, especially, enter and exit the work force, leave and reenter school, and start several new careers over the course of their adult lives. As a result of this fluidity, full-time jobs, marriage, and parenthood no longer serve as reliable markers for the transition to adulthood.

Changes in the last stages of the life course are particularly striking and will merit a more detailed consideration later in this chapter. In the past, old age was seen as a period of physical and intellectual decline, social disengagement, and often poverty. By contrast, many retirees today lead healthy, vigorous lives.

Changes in the life course are both a cause and an effect of wider social change. In today's technologically changing world, no one can expect to live as their parents did. Demands to learn new roles, and even new ways of life, are continuous, and individuals must become adept at improvised socialization and on-the-spot learning. For example, the dramatic changes in sexual attitudes and behavior over the last twenty-five years—some of these changes the results of the baby boomers' beliefs and actions—have demanded resocialization. Both men and women now freely engage in sexual activity outside of marriage, from "one-night stands" to cohabitation. The rules of the game have changed enormously, and they may very well change again: the AIDS crisis may cause a dramatic reversal of relaxed sexual behavior, making singlehood less attractive and marriage more so. Such a change would force today's young people into resocialization (discussed in Chapter 5).

In short, modern life entails a continuous process of adjustment to new developments and new demands. As we live longer and the life course is extended, the process of socialization is extended, too.

Cohorts and the Historical Context

How do sociologists take account both of rapid changes in life-course stages and of the historical contexts that influence these changes? They focus on groups of people

who were born close to the same time (usually within a year or so) and who thus age together, sharing a very similar historical experience. Such a group is known to sociologists as a **birth cohort** (Riley 1987; Rosow 1978). Studying cohorts is a way of recognizing that different historical circumstances at every stage of life separate members of a society somewhat from one another (Elder 1978, 1987). Particular economic, political, and social conditions constitute each cohort's frame of reference and foster development of a common set of attitudes and beliefs. As conditions alter, as they are bound to do, the world views, opportunities, aspirations, and beliefs of successive cohorts change too, overlapping, shifting, or moving dramatically apart.

Successive cohorts are exposed to society-wide events at different stages of the life course, and thus they age in distinctive ways. (The In Depth feature examines a study of cohorts that illustrates just this.) As the process continues, cohorts reach the same stages under different social circumstances: they grow old in a different society than the one they began in.

Over time, the number of people at each stage of the life course (the so-called **age structure**) changes. Eventually, cultural views of age-related roles will also change, which will in turn affect social conditions. Thus, the flow of successive cohorts through the life course is at once a reflection and a source of social change (Riley 1987; Elder 1978). Focusing on cohorts allows sociologists to assess and predict social change.

In Depth: Cohort Experiences of the Great Depression

G len Elder (1978, 1987) studied the impact of the Great Depression on two cohorts, those born in 1920–1921 and those born in 1928–1929. (See Table 6.2.) Members of the first of these cohorts were born in the prosperous 1920s, and thus had relatively secure childhoods. Preteens when the depression began, they were old enough to help their families stay "above water" financially. As adolescents, boys in this cohort often worked part-time to supplement their family's income; girls often took over responsibility for the household when their mothers went to work. Thus the social boundary between youth and adulthood was lowered somewhat, especially in deprived families. This cohort graduated from high school during the early stages of mobilization for World War II. Service in the military represented a clear transition, a passage from family dependence to independence and autonomy. After the war they were able to use G.I. bills that provided support for college education and home ownership.

In contrast, the cohort born in 1928–1929 experienced prolonged economic hardship, beginning in the vulnerable years of early childhood (the 1930s) and extending into their teens (the 1940s). For two decades, they were exposed to the strains of downward mobility. Fathers were often unable to fill the traditional role of breadwinner, and overburdened mothers tended to be preoccupied with maintaining family status—or, in many cases, family survival. As adolescents, those in this second cohort watched World War II from a distance, often separated from their fathers and with no opportunities to become heroes themselves.

Because of their different stages in the life course, the effects of the Great Depression on these adjacent cohorts were quite different. Elder found that those in the first cohort were more hopeful, self-directed, and confident about their futures, and in general achieved more in their adult lives than those in the second cohort. As Riley has noted, "cohort membership [does not] mark individuals at birth alone; it affects them at every age, through the groups to which they belong, the others with whom they interact, and the social and cultural conditions to which they are exposed" (1987, p. 7).

The Ages and Stages of Man

We are ready to look more carefully at our own society's definitions of life-course stages. Broadly, we divide life into childhood, adolescence, young or early adulthood, middle adulthood (or middle age), and late adulthood or old age, each with various subdivisions. This division of the life span is distinctly modern (Neugarten and Neugarten 1987, pp. 29–30), particularly the inclusion of adolescence, middle age, and the subdivisions of old age (the result of more and more people living longer).

One of the pioneers in the analysis of stages of the entire life span was Erik Erikson, who extended Freudian psychological theory beyond childhood and considered important cultural factors. In *Childhood and Society* (1950, 1963), Erikson proposed a *psychosocial* theory of lifelong development that included eight stages, which he called the "eight ages of man." At each stage, suggested Erikson, the individual faces a basic conflict between one of her or his predominant needs and society's ability to satisfy it. The conflict creates a crisis; the way the individual resolves each crisis will affect self-image, identity, social relations, productivity, satisfaction—in short, all of the rest of development, which continues through old age.

Erikson's theory has been debated and criticized. Some have argued that he represented life-course transitions as too neat and clear-cut and that his consideration of social and cultural factors is far from complete —although within psychology he has been a strong voice for giving society's role its due, as the title of his major work implies. Despite the criticisms, his theory still

TABLE 6.2   The Social Context of Cohorts

Date	Event/Social Context	Age of Cohort Members	
		Cohort 1	*Cohort 2*
1923–1929	Economic boom	1–9	Birth (1928–1929)
1932–1933	Depth of Great Depression	11–13	3–5
1941–1945	World War II and the war effort	20–25	12–17
1946–1953	Postwar period: unprecedented affluence; baby boom begins	25–33	17–25
1974–	Crisis of affluence; energy crisis; pollution	54–	46–

Source: Adapted from Elder 1978.

provides a concise and comprehensive framework for understanding development and change over the entire life course; it also helps us recognize the continuity of each individual, cohort, or generation moving from stage to stage. Erikson's descriptions of the conflicts and tasks at each stage should prove useful as you proceed through the rest of this chapter.

CHILDHOOD

The experience of being a child depends not only on levels of physical, mental, and emotional maturity, but also on historical circumstance. Ideas about who children are, what they need from adults, and which social roles they should be allowed to play have changed over time.

Historical Changes

Childhood as we know it today in the Western world did not exist in the Middle Ages (Aries 1962). Before the sixteenth century people did, of course, recognize that children were immature, but childhood was not considered a special and important stage of life. Rather, it was seen as a biologically necessary prelude to the socially important business of adulthood, which began much earlier than it does today. The role of parent, too, had a very different meaning centuries ago. The children of the well-to-do were cared for first by "wet nurses" and then by servants. No one felt it necessary to shield youngsters from the everyday realities of birth, death, or sex. As soon as they were physically able to perform useful chores, sometimes as early as age five or six, children worked alongside adults.

The idea that children should be cherished, nurtured, and protected from a separate adult world dates from the Renaissance. By the eighteenth century, most upper-class families had accepted the new view of childhood as a time to learn, explore, and play. The growing middle class, which is sometimes said to have "invented" childhood as an accepted, clearly marked-off period of life, followed suit toward the end of the nineteenth century. But life changed little for lower-

Today, we recognize childhood as a period of critical development and value it as a rich and vital stage in the life course. In contrast, this 18th century portrait conveys a sense that children were viewed as "little adults," ready to take on adult responsibilities as soon as their stature and strength would permit. Childhood was merely a time to be endured, as is reflected in the Victorian dictum that "children should be seen and not heard." (Joseph Badger, 1760/Abby Aldrich Rockefeller Folk Art Center.)

class children until the early decades of the twentieth century. Like adults, they worked from dawn to dusk in fields, mines, or factories. The child protection movement in the United States was led by middle- and upper-class adults who were alarmed at the numbers of immigrant children roaming city streets in unsupervised bands. The laws that banned child labor and made schooling compulsory were passed as much to protect society as to protect the children themselves. Not until the 1920s were these laws widely enforced, making childhood a reality for all (or almost all) American youngsters.

Childhood in Today's Society

Today, we see childhood as an extended period of learning and growth, from the total dependency of infancy to the near-independence of adolescence. It is a period in which each child must acquire many of the skills needed to function in the adult world. How does all this happen?

Just as definitions of childhood have changed from one historical period to another and from society to society, so have views of what governs development during childhood. As you saw in Chapter 5, developmentalists today focus primarily on the interaction of heredity and environment—on nature *and* nurture working together in complex ways. The important point

is that the individual cannot really be cut free of historical context, social trends, social class, and so on. The enormous amount of research done in the past fifty years on all aspects of infancy and childhood, especially on the competence of the newborn and infant, has established, first, that there is a genetically programmed timetable for physical maturation, for major steps like smiling, babbling, crawling, walking, first words, running, and so forth (see Figure 6.1). Second, researchers have found that some aspects of the child's development

The Gessell Institute in New Haven, a leading center for the study of child development, has outlined these milestones in development.

FIGURE 6.1   Childhood Achievements

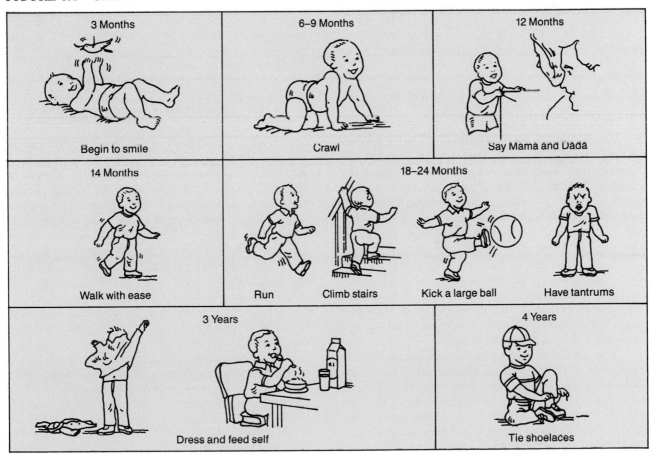

are controlled primarily by genetics, while others are less dependent on biological factors. Finally, this body of research has confirmed the significant role of the environment, of the social worlds of child and parents. All this research is important in another way: Everything that has been learned and is being learned about the child's development gets channeled into our society's definition of childhood.

Erikson, in his analysis of the conflicts children must resolve, focused primarily on environmental influences (especially parents and, later on, peers), but he acknowledged biological drives and the role of physical maturation (see Figure 6.2). According to his theory, the infant faces the issue of *basic trust vs. mistrust*. Ideally, infants learn that the world is a fairly safe place where their needs will be met. If care is erratic, however, infants come to view the world as a harsh place where they must fend for themselves. As toddlers torn between striving for independence and craving parental protection, children face a crisis of *autonomy vs. shame and doubt*. If they are allowed to "stand on their own two feet" and are at the same time protected from harm, they develop self-confidence; if they are over- or under-protected, they experience self-doubt and too great a dependency on the opinion of others.

The early childhood crisis, *initiation vs. guilt*, begins at four or five when children begin to extend their mastery over their own bodies to the world around them. If parents and others are supportive of their explorations, children develop feelings of self-worth. But if their pioneering steps are ridiculed or dismissed, they punish themselves for their failures and feel guilt. Then, when they reach school age, children face the conflict of *industry vs. inferiority* as they struggle to acquire skills and information and to relate to a larger social circle. Depending on their experiences, they may develop pride in their abilities and accomplishments and learn to pursue activity joyfully for its own sake; or they may begin to feel increasingly inferior and fear that if required to perform, they will inevitably fail.

Perhaps the most important development of early childhood is the acquisition of language. One of the most basic and complex social tools humans possess, language enables a child to communicate with other people, to think symbolically, and to become a competent member of his or her society. Language also allows children to learn *about* their society from others. To acquire language the child learns vocabulary and grammatical rules, grasps the subtleties of pronunciation and intonation, and masters polite forms of address for different people and occasions—no small achievement!

All these physical, emotional, social, and cognitive accomplishments prepare the child to move on to the next stage: adolescence.

ADOLESCENCE

Adolescence is an even more recent invention than childhood (Kett 1977). Toward the end of the nineteenth century, social commentators began to describe the period between childhood and adulthood as a particularly dangerous and vulnerable stage in development. In one of his most detailed and important works, *Adolescence: Its Psychology and Its Relation to Physiology, Anthropology, Sociology, Sex, Crime, Religion, and Education* (1904), the psychologist G. Stanley Hall described adolescence as a period of storm and stress, but also of possibility and promise. He argued that young people should be given a chance to experiment and explore before being pushed into the adult world.

Hall's ideas both reflected and projected social conditions. As twentieth-century America became increasingly industrialized and urbanized, and positions for unskilled laborers became scarce, education was no longer a luxury—it was a necessity. So instead of being rushed into the adult world, young people were urged to finish high school or even college. During the Great Depression, staying in school was encouraged for another reason: it kept young people from crowding the shrinking job market. Indeed, between 1900 and 1956, the proportion of Americans graduating from high school rose from 6.3 to 62.5 percent.

Adolescence as we know it today really took shape in the 1940s and 1950s, when the segregation of young people in schools fostered the development of an adolescent society (Coleman 1961), or subculture, with its own tastes and standards. Many of the changes that took place were the result of post–World War II affluence, which set the stage for a dizzying series of social changes and role redefinitions. For example, many teenagers now had access to cars. This meant that much teenage dating was no longer under the watchful eyes of adults, a circumstance that may, in part, account for the increase in teenage sexual activity. By the 1950s, adolescence was a

This figure shows the developmental crises that must be resolved at each stage of life and the outcome of successful resolution.

FIGURE 6.2   Erikson's Stages of Life and Developmental Issues

Stages	Developmental Tasks	Basic Strengths	Basic Antipathies
Infancy	Basic Trust vs. Basic Mistrust	Hope	Withdrawal
Early Childhood	Autonomy vs. Shame, Doubt	Will	Compulsion
Play Age	Initiative vs. Guilt	Purpose	Inhibition
School Age	Industry vs. Inferiority	Competence	Inertia
Adolescence	Identity vs. Identity Confusion	Fidelity	Repudiation
Young Adulthood	Intimacy vs. Isolation	Love	Exclusivity
Adulthood	Generativity vs. Stagnation	Care	Rejectivity
Old Age	Integrity vs. Despair	Wisdom	Disdain

Source: Reproduced from *The Life Cycle Completed: A Review*, by Erik H. Erikson, by permission of W.W. Norton & Company, Inc. Copyright © 1982 by Rikan Enterprises, Ltd.

legal as well as social classification (Kett 1977): sixteen- to eighteen-year-olds were now under the protection of the juvenile courts in virtually all states.

There are signs that the age at which children become adolescents is slowly creeping downward. The "bobby-soxers" who swooned over Frank Sinatra in the 1940s were fifteen to eighteen years old; the "teenyboppers" who mobbed the Beatles in the 1960s were twelve to fourteen years old. The age at which youngsters begin dating and using cosmetics (not to mention drugs) has dropped from fifteen to sixteen years old to eleven to twelve years old. Even younger children are knowledgeable about sex, drugs, alcoholism, suicide, and nuclear war, all taboo topics for children a generation ago (Neugarten and Neugarten 1987). Some see this as a loss of childhood innocence and attribute it to a number of converging influences, including the sexual revolution, television, the high divorce rate, and working mothers whose children may be unsupervised after school (Winn 1983).

The children of the 1980s are also much more likely to be exposed to parents' problems and even to become their parents' confidants, familiarizing themselves with adult emotions and dilemmas that they are not equipped to handle. At the same time, some events and processes that have traditionally marked the beginning of adulthood have been postponed. The percentage of young people who go to college and remain financially dependent on their parents into their twenties began increasing in the 1960s, as the baby boomers reached college age. Although the number of college students is smaller today than in the 1960s, the proportion of young

people who "delay" (according to the more traditional timetable) commitments to work and family has remained high. You can see that, taken together, pressures upward toward adulthood and pressures downward toward maintained dependence have helped to solidify adolescence as its own defined stage.

Who Am I?

The search for oneself is probably the predominant theme of adolescence. By acknowledging this period as a life-course stage, society has in effect granted many teenagers the chance to ask "Who am I?" and as G. Stanley Hall suggested, to experiment with answers. Adolescents also tend to use this period to test society's conventions and morality as a means of defining their own ideas.

Adolescence is a modern phenomenon. These spindle boys in a Georgia cotton mill in the early 1900s passed directly from childhood to the pressures and dangers of the adult world. Changes in work laws, education, and social attitudes have contributed to the recognition that adolescence is a special time for questioning the self and testing society's rules—a distinct life stage with its own set of pressures, risks, and rewards. (Below: Lewis Hines/The Bettmann Archive; right: David G. Houser/Uniphoto.)

Erikson, in his analysis of this stage, also focused on identity as the central task of adolescence. What Erikson means by **identity** is a sense of continuity about one's past, present, and future, and coordinating feelings about the way one sees oneself and is seen by others. Those who are unable to develop a sense of who they are and where they are going experience role confusion. Thus, the crisis adolescents face is *identity vs. role confusion*.

Transitions to Adulthood

Adolescence may begin in biology, with rapid and dramatic physical changes, but it ends in culture (Conger and Peterson 1984). Precisely when an adolescent becomes an adult depends on numerous cultural and social factors. In traditional societies, as you've seen, rites of passage mark the transition clearly, and there is little doubt about who is a full-fledged adult. In complex, modern societies, the transition is ambiguous, as noted in the early part of the chapter; it is a gradual process rather than a specific event (Hogan and Astone 1986, p. 112). In other words, the passage to adulthood involves multiple transitions.

The timing and significance of these transitions depend in part on race, ethnic background, and social class, so that different groups within modern society experience transitions at different times. Traditionally, sex-role socialization has also played a part: men and women are encouraged to choose different paths to adulthood. In addition, transitions to adulthood can be analyzed as *voluntary* (you choose your first job and first home-away-from-home according to your own desires); *anticipated* (you are expected to get married in your mid-twenties and become a parent several years later, and you do); *unanticipated* (the death of a parent or an unwanted pregnancy forces you to take on adult responsibilities suddenly); or, in effect, *nontransitional* (you are unable to find a job or a spouse or to have a child) (Schlossberg 1987). Obviously, "nontransitions" also affect roles, choices, and expectations.

The accompanying feature on teenage motherhood looks at various types of transitions into adulthood and ties these in with another important topic, the life course of an entire family.

Though we think of marriage as a unique rite of passage, it is just one of many important decisions that may mark the gradual transition to adulthood. Decisions about friendships, career, family, home, and lifestyle are choices that embrace some possibilities, exclude others, and bind the individual to a community beyond the self. (Spencer Grant/The Picture Cube.)

ADULTHOOD

Once considered a period of relative stability, adulthood is now recognized as a time of continuous challenge and change. Marriage, parenthood, family, and work mean different things to today's adults than they did to their parents and grandparents. And no wonder! As we approach the twenty-first century, Americans are increasingly unlikely to have the same spouse, job, or home throughout their adult lives.

Teenage Motherhood

Most people feel that unanticipated transitions and disruptions of the life course trigger stress and create problems. But how does this happen? What are the problems? And what are their long-term effects? Several recent studies of the impact of unplanned parenthood on individuals and families give some answers, shedding light on what is a very difficult, sudden, but increasingly common transition into adulthood. And because the lives of all family members are interdependent, the research also reveals how a family's life course is affected by its members' role transitions (Elder 1986).

L. M. Burton studied forty-one urban, multigenerational black families (Burton 1985; Burton and Bengtson 1985). Each family included a new mother, a grandmother, and a great-grandmother. In twenty-three of the families, the transition occurred "on time": the new mothers were young adults (ages twenty-one to twenty-six), the grandmothers middle-aged (ages forty-two to fifty-seven), and the great-grandmothers elderly

(ages sixty to seventy-three). In eighteen of the families, the transition was "early": the new mothers were teenagers (ages eleven to eighteen), the grandmothers young adults (ages twenty-five to thirty-eight), and the great-grandmothers middle-aged (ages forty-six to fifty-seven).

Burton found that on-time transitions were welcomed by all three generations; family members were prepared to move to the next step on the generational ladder. In contrast, the accelerated role transitions that resulted from teenage pregnancy—a child became a mother; a young woman, a grandmother; and a middle-aged woman, a matriarch—disrupted the expectations, relationships, and life courses of all concerned. Because the teenagers were not prepared for the responsibilities of motherhood, virtually all of them expected *their* mothers to care for the baby. More than 80 percent of the young grandmothers, however, refused to assume the role of primary caretaker.

According to Burton, becoming a grandmother so early conflicted with

the life-course plans of these relatively young women—plans that included work, education, and romance. Burton also points out that most of the young grandmothers had been teenage mothers themselves and did not want to be pushed into a *second* premature role transition. Some were still wrestling with unresolved conflicts from their own adolescence, trying to recapture the youth they had lost when they became mothers. So the teenage mothers and young grandmothers were, in a sense, attempting to come to grips with similar personal issues. Not surprisingly, with the age difference between them fairly small (an average of fifteen years), the mothers and grandmothers tended to behave more like sisters than like mothers and daughters.

In some cases, the grandmother's rejection of the role of caretaker forced the teenage mother to assume full responsibility for the baby. This early transition to adulthood meant that the young mothers had to reroute their life course, discarding plans for marriage, college, and careers—at

Ongoing Transitions: Early Adulthood Through Middle Age

Daniel Levinson (1978) was a pioneer in the systematic investigation of the adult life cycle, especially the shift from young or early adulthood to middle age. His major study, done in the late 1960s and early 1970s, has been both praised and criticized. He studied only men, aged thirty-five to forty-five, and though he chose his forty subjects from various backgrounds and walks of life (ten business executives, ten hourly workers, ten novelists, and ten university biologists), his sample cannot be considered representative of the male population as a whole. Levinson's work, however, was instrumental in

turning attention to the life course in adulthood and to altering our conception of this time of life.

In *Childhood and Society*, Erikson says that the crisis for young adults (ages twenty to forty) is *intimacy vs. isolation*. Young adults must partially fuse their identities with those of other people, forming deep friendships and starting a family. The danger is that young adults will fail to commit themselves because they fear loss of self. In middle adulthood (ages forty to sixty), the crisis is between *generativity*, the feeling that one is making a contribution to the world and guiding younger generations, and *stagnation*, feelings of boredom and resignation, as youthful dreams clash with the reality of middle age.

least for the time being—while they struggled to provide for the child and perhaps get through high school. More often, however, the teenage mothers did shift responsibility up the generational ladder—to the great-grandmothers of the new babies. Having taken care of their daughters' children, these women assumed this role again for their granddaughters. Many were responsible for aging relatives as well. One middle-aged great-grandmother exclaimed, "I ain't got no time for myself. I takes care of babies, grown children [the teenage mother was still in her household], and old people. I work too. . . . I get so tired I don't know if I'll ever do something for myself" (Elder 1986, p. 21). The great-grandmothers also feared that *their* daughters, who had abdicated first the role of mother and now that of grandmother, would never grow up and never take their responsibilities seriously.

Frank Furstenberg and colleagues, who conducted a longitudinal study of 300 women from Baltimore, found that, contrary to most predictions,

teenage parenthood did not inevitably damage the adolescent's life chances (Furstenberg 1976, 1984; Furstenberg, Brooks-Gunn, and Morgan 1987). In his research, which suggests how lives that have been thrown off schedule can be put back on track, Furstenberg identified three "escape routes" for teenage mothers. The first was education: teenage mothers who completed high school were half as likely to be on welfare in adulthood as those who did not. The second was birth control. Women who did not have a second child in the five years after their first was born were three and a half times more likely to be economically secure as adults. They were also somewhat more likely to get married. The third escape route was in fact a stable marriage, which usually meant independence from the mother's family of origin. Women who remained in their parents' household long after becoming mothers did not make other transitions to adulthood; simply put, they remained childlike and dependent throughout their lives.

What about the next generation?

Furstenberg and his colleagues found that when these youngsters became adolescents they showed more symptoms of maladjustment—acting out, social withdrawal, and so on—than did the children of more mature mothers. In general, the adolescents who fared best were those whose mothers had followed an escape route. For example, youngsters whose mothers did *not* have a second and third child soon after the birth of their first did better in school than those whose mothers had other babies while they were still teenagers.

Thus, although role transitions in our society may be more ambiguous than in more traditional societies, they are nevertheless very real. Studies of teenage motherhood reveal the consequences of marked departures from our society's timetable, and show us how important that timetable can be. Not only can unanticipated transitions throw an individual's life off course (at least temporarily); they also reverberate up and down the generational ladder, thus altering the life course of the family as a whole.

Like Erikson, Levinson sees two distinct periods within adulthood, early and middle adulthood (or middle age). But Levinson went much further. He concludes that the adult male life cycle is divided into stable (or structure-building) periods, in which a man reviews and evaluates his past choices and considers the future. Transition periods are difficult, often painful: suspended between past and future, a man struggles to bridge the gap. Levinson argues that although the age at which men enter a particular period may vary somewhat, all men progress through the same stages in the same order (see Figure 6.3).

In the young man's transition into early adulthood (roughly speaking, during the twenties), he becomes a

novice adult with a home base of his own. He begins to make choices about marriage, occupation, residence, and life-style that will define his place in the adult world. Around age thirty, these decisions take on a new seriousness: now his choices are "for real." The later thirties are a time of settling down and settling in —establishing a niche in society, anchoring his life more firmly, and advancing in his chosen occupation.

The mid-life transition, according to Levinson, usually occurs between ages forty and forty-five. In early adulthood, men are at their physical and mental peak; now they must face the signs and limitations of aging. For most of the men Levinson studied (70 to 80 percent), the mid-life transition—popularly dubbed the "mid-life

FIGURE 6.3   Levinson's Adulthood Transition Chart

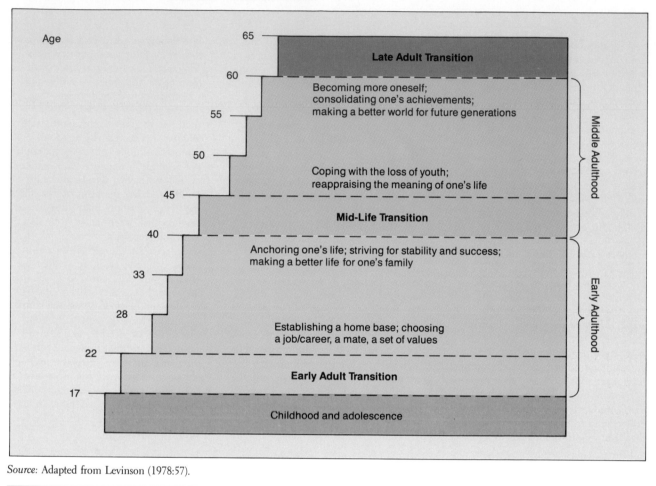

Source: Adapted from Levinson (1978:57).

crisis"—was psychologically wrenching. Suddenly the men began to question their marriage and family, and their career. "What have I done with my life? What do I really get from and give to my wife, children, friends, work, community—and self? What is it I truly want for myself and others?" (p. 60). For some, the realization that their youthful dreams might never be realized was particularly agonizing.

However, the men who negotiated this transition well found middle adulthood the most creative time of the life course. They became more attached to others and more secure in themselves. Echoing Erikson, Levinson suggests that the most successful middle-aged men de-

velop generativity. They use authority creatively, accepting paternal responsibility for younger generations.

Levinson holds that another transition begins at about age sixty. As men approach old age, they must recognize that their generation is no longer the dominant one. Their task is to sustain their vitality in new forms appropriate to late adulthood and old age.

Other research confirms some of Levinson's findings but qualifies other points. The Grant Study of Adult Development followed 270 Harvard freshmen from college into adulthood. George Vaillant (1977) interviewed ninety-four of these men at their twenty-fifth college reunion, when they were in their mid-forties, and again in their mid-fifties. (This study is of course subject to the same criticism as Levinson's—it focused only on one cohort of men.) Like Levinson, Vaillant found early adulthood to be a period of launching and consolidating families and careers, and mid-life a period of inner turmoil. Indeed, he describes mid-life as a second adolescence: "Men leave the compulsive unreflective busywork of their occupational apprenticeships, and once more explore the world within" (p. 220). Unlike Levinson, however, Vaillant found that the age at which men began questioning their life choices varied by as much as a decade. Some became introspective at thirty;

This young woman's first day at college is as challenging, exciting, and fraught with uncertainty for her parents as it is for her. Middle adulthood, when children have been reared and careers have been established, can be a time of introspection and self-appraisal as painful and promising as if it were a second adolescence. (Gabe Palmer, MUG Shots 1986/The Stock Market.)

at age forty-five, others were still struggling with unresolved issues of identity and intimacy (conflicts Erikson associates with adolescence and the early twenties). Vaillant argues that self-questioning can occur at any point in the life course, and depends more on events (for example, divorce or failure to get a promotion) than age.

What About the Women?

To date, a major in-depth analysis of women's life course has not yet appeared (though Levinson is now completing his study of adult women). The available evidence suggests that the "ages-and-stages" approach may not apply as well to women (Rosenfeld and Stark 1987, p. 69), primarily due to the timing of childbearing, which in turn affects a woman's decisions about work and career. A woman who has children in her twenties may not enter the work force until her late thirties, and so she reaches the stage of career consolidation in her mid- to late forties, ten to fifteen years "behind" men. Another woman may concentrate on her career in her twenties and postpone motherhood until her thirties. In today's world, knowing a woman's age tells you very little about her marital, parental, or occupational status. However, if you know when she had children and how many, this is still the best predictor of her occupational participation and advancement (Hanson 1983).

On the whole, it is not yet clear how the recent influx of women into the labor force and the trend for younger women to combine job and family roles will alter the female life course in adulthood—besides increasing its diversity. At this point, women still tend to be more identified with family life, more centrally defined by family commitments and priorities, than men are. A study of four groups of men and women, for example, found that at all stages, men were essentially career-oriented, while women gave their primary goals as marriage and family—whether or not they were involved in careers (Lowenthal et al. 1975). These sorts of differences, however, are more evident at some stages than at others: For instance, in the study just mentioned, sex differences were most pronounced in adolescents and middle-aged people, and least pronounced in newlyweds and those approaching retirement (Lowenthal et al. 1975). All in all, though, a woman's roles at different stages of the family's life course will tend to determine her roles as an individual to a greater degree than is true for men.

Even if women do not go through specific stages in as predictable a way as men, they seem to go through similar types of changes in adulthood. According to a longitudinal study of 132 graduates of Mills College, a woman's college in California (Helson, Mitchell, and Moane 1984), women became more committed to duties and more self-disciplined in their twenties; more confident, assertive, and achievement-oriented in their thirties; and more generative and involved in affairs outside the family in their forties. This study also found that those women who were committed neither to family nor to career changed less over their adult years than committed women.

Some researchers have chosen to focus on the life course of the contemporary family itself, as well as that of individuals (Aldous 1978; Waite 1980; Elder 1987). Trends like later marriage, delayed childbearing, births outside marriage, and single parenthood can of course affect the life pattern in adulthood. Dissolving one family and starting another can skew timetables and force both men and women into new or combined roles. Indeed, family life-course diversity has come to be a hallmark of our times.

AGING, OLD AGE, AND THE LIFE COURSE

People have always dreamed of living to a ripe old age, but it is only in the last few decades that large numbers of people have realized this dream. Americans are getting older, and as a result new stages, or substages, are being added to the life course. Although there is no firm agreement on terminology, most social scientists distinguish between *the old* or *the elderly* (about ages sixty-five to eighty-five), and *the aged* or *the "old-old"* (age eighty-five and beyond).

The aging of the American population and the expansion of the life course are the results of several converging trends. First, *survival rates* have improved steadily since the nineteenth century. Improvements in public health and nutrition have meant that more and more infants and children grow to adulthood. A second reason is *increased longevity*, due in part to medical advances. In 1900, only two in five of Americans lived to be at least sixty-five years old; today the figure is three out

of four (Statistical Abstracts of the United States 1988). Average life expectancy for those born in 1984 is 71.1 years for men and 78.3 years for women. Most of this increase has taken place in the last three decades (Horn and Meer 1987, p. 80). Between 1960 and 1980, the number of Americans age sixty-five and older more than doubled. At the same time, the number of "old-old" quadrupled, reaching 2.6 million. All told, the elderly population of the United States grew faster than the population of India (Preston 1984, p. 435).

A third reason for the aging of the American population and the lengthening of the life course has been the *declining birthrate:* the "boom" in older people has been paired with a "bust" in births (Horn and Meer 1987, p. 80). With the notable exception of the baby boom, birthrates have declined steadily since 1800. Only one in four Americans is under age sixteen today. As the baby-boom generation reaches age sixty-five (beginning in 2010), the aging of the population will accelerate. Estimates are that by 2030 the proportion of Americans age sixty-five and older will have climbed from 12 to 21 percent.

As you might guess, the aging of the population has altered the social structure. Demographers used to describe the age structure of a population as a pyramid: Newborns and infants formed a broad base for successively smaller tiers, as older people died from disease, accidents, war, and other causes. However, current trends are "squaring the pyramid." By 2030, the numbers of people in each five-year age group from birth to age seventy will be about equal, creating a near-perfect rectangle. Indeed, surviving members of the baby-boom generation will make the age structure slightly top-heavy (see Figure 6.4).

The aging of the population reflects tremendous social change. In the nineteenth and twentieth centuries, the United States, along with other Western nations, changed from an agricultural, high-fertility society to an industrial society with controlled fertility. In traditional agricultural societies, the knowledge, wisdom, and skills of older people are held in high regard. Although the elderly may not perform the same jobs they performed when they were younger, retirement is unknown. Typically, the elderly control society's most valued resource—land—and their children remain economically dependent well into middle age.

With industrialization, however, the valuation of age has been almost reversed. Advancing industrialization places a premium on education and innovation.

Rapid technological change renders the knowledge and skills of the elderly obsolete; education is geared toward the young; and generational competition for jobs leads to pressures on the elderly to retire. Typically, control of vital resources shifts to the middle-aged, and older workers are pushed into positions of economic dependency and social marginality.

Retirement gave the final stage of the life course a clear demarcation. By fixing sixty-five as the age that benefits begin, the Social Security Act, passed in 1935, effectively established a starting point for the social definition of old age and created a whole new social category. "The old became defined as a dependent group in society, a group whose members could not and should not work, and who needed economic and social assistance that the younger population was obliged to provide" (Malcolm H. Morris, in Horn and Meer 1987, p. 90).

How has the younger population responded? How do we treat our "senior citizens" in this country? How does our society today perceive the older person, and what do we look forward to in our old age? How do we define the elderly's role among us—and do we allow them to take active roles?

Social Responses to Aging: Myths and Realities

An older person thinks and moves slowly. He does not think as he used to or as creatively. He is bound to himself and to his past and can no longer change or grow. He can learn neither well nor swiftly and, even if he

The Census Bureau predicts that by the year 2030 the traditional population pyramid will have changed to an almost perfect rectangle, with about the same number of people in each five-year age group from birth to 70.

FIGURE 6.4 Changes Predicted for Population Pyramids

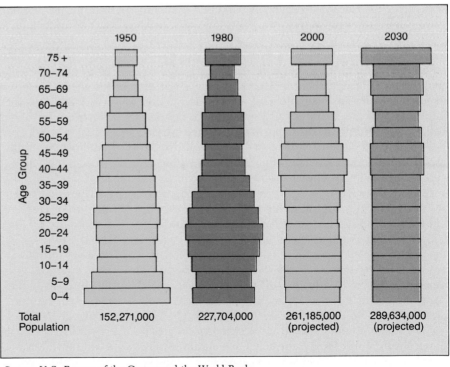

Source: U.S. Bureau of the Census and the World Bank.

could, he would not wish to. . . . He dislikes innovations and is not disposed to new ideas. Not only can he not move forward, he often moves backward. He enters a second childhood, caught up in increasing egocentricity and demanding more from his environment than he is willing to give to it. . . . He becomes irritable and cantankerous, yet shallow and enfeebled. He lives in his past; he is behind the times. He is aimless and wandering of mind, reminiscing and garrulous. . . . He is often stricken by disease. . . . He has lost his desire and capacity for sex. His body shrinks, and so too does the flow of blood to his brain. . . . Feeble, uninteresting, he awaits his death, a burden to society, to his family and to himself. (Butler 1975, pp. 6–7)

Is this what you think of old age? Taken from Robert Butler's *Why Survive?* this is a portrait based on the myths and misconceptions Americans tend to have about old people. For, as a culture, we idealize youth and reject the elderly.

In some societies—notably Japan—the elderly are revered. Despite industrialization and rapid technological advances in that country, younger people seek opinions of the elderly, expect aging parents to live with them, defer to these parents on family matters, and reserve the best of everything for the old. Their attitude grows out of longstanding, deeply felt religious and cultural traditions. By contrast, in our society, and in most industrialized, affluent societies, **ageism**—a system of negative beliefs about the elderly—is the norm. It is built into our culture and social structure. Our cultural beliefs and social practices denigrate not only the capacities, skills, and health of older people, but also their moral worth and social significance. To be sure, many people are deeply attached to aging family members or keep in close touch with a former teacher or boss who served as a mentor. But most dread the idea of growing old themselves, and few actively seek to live with older people or work alongside them. You can see why, given the portrait quoted above. And not only do polls consistently show that Americans under sixty-five hold negative stereotypes of the elderly; according to the same polls, many older Americans agree, and simply see themselves as exceptions to the rule (Harris 1981).

Let's take a closer look at some stereotypical views of the elderly. First, there is the belief that old age means inevitable physical, mental, and sexual decline. Unquestionably, the body does slow down with age. Speed, strength, stamina, perception, and sensation decline. A seventy-year-old cannot walk as fast, see or hear as well, react as quickly, or climb the same mountain as a thirty-year-old. But the differences between younger and older adults are smaller, develop more gradually, and do not affect functioning until much later than most of us realize—the eighth decade of life. Compared with the young, the old are less likely to suffer from acute or short-term diseases, such as the common cold, but more likely to suffer from chronic or long-term diseases, such as hypertension and heart disease, arthritis, or emphysema. Even these chronic ailments are not usually disabling, although they pose more serious problems for the "old-old." There is another reality that contradicts a misconception. Sexuality, given the availability of partners, can be and often is very much a part of older people's lives and adds a great deal to a sense of overall satisfaction. Some people who never really enjoyed sex in the first place may use old age as an excuse to give up sex (Horn and Meer 1987), but those who were sexually active in their youth remain so in old age—if they have the opportunity.

It is important to distinguish between *primary aging*, a biologically programmed process that begins early in life and affects all body systems, and *secondary aging*, limitations that result not from aging per se but from disease, abuse, and/or disuse (Horn and Meer 1987, p. 81). The fact that a person's heart pumps less blood at age seventy than it did at age twenty or forty is the inevitable result of primary aging; heart disease is not. It is also important to remember that most studies of the effects of aging are based on cross-sectional data —that is, comparisons of people of different ages at the same point in time. The results may tell us more about generational or cohort differences than about aging itself. For example, studies from a number of modern societies find that men ages twenty-five to twenty-nine are, on average, three inches taller than men ages seventy-five to seventy-nine. Does this mean that men shrink as they grow older, or that young men are taller because nutrition, medical care, and physical fitness have improved greatly over the past fifty years? Without longitudinal studies, in which a single cohort is monitored year by year, or decade by decade, no definitive answer is possible.

What about senility: does it strike all older people eventually? This too is a myth, the result of misinformation. Until quite recently, any older person who was forgetful, irrational, or childlike in thought patterns and behavior was labeled as senile. People who work with the

Mellowing with age. . . . Despite our culture's idealization of youth, old age can be a stage as challenging and satisfying as any other in the life course. Perhaps the goal of the transition to late adulthood is not just to be "as young as you feel," but to feel, as this couple clearly does, that you are in the right place at the right time. (Paul Fusco/ Magnum Photos, Inc.)

elderly now know that this single term masks a host of separate problems and disorders, including Alzheimer's disease (an incurable brain disorder), depression, malnutrition, alcoholism, and adverse reactions to prescribed drugs. Most of these conditions can now be diagnosed accurately, and many can be treated effectively. None is an inevitable consequence of growing old.

In fact, cognitive skills, such as verbal and reasoning ability, continue to improve from ages forty to sixty. There may be some loss of short-term memory in old age (the ability to recall a phone number or the name of someone you just met), but other skills remain intact. Even short-term memory is less likely to decline the more the mind, like a muscle, has been and continues to be consistently used. Thus, given opportunity and stimulation, people can continue to assimilate new information throughout the lifespan (Burdman 1986).

"You can't teach an old dog new tricks." This sums up the myth of inflexibility (Butler 1975). But there is no evidence to support this bit of folklore. Older people respond to innovation and change with the same mixture of acceptance and rejection found in younger people. Indeed, older people manage to cope successfully with the kinds of change (loss of job, loss of a spouse, a move to an unfamiliar community) that younger people often find devastating.

Another myth holds that older people are disengaged from the world around them (Butler 1975). According to this view, the elderly choose to retire, not only from the work force, but from society as a whole,

withdrawing into themselves, avoiding social contacts, and losing interest in the larger world. Although some people do withdraw somewhat with age, they are exceptions to the rule. Poor health, financial limitations, limited access to transportation, and the like may force an older person to cease activities he or she formerly enjoyed. But withdrawal is not a natural part of the aging process. For example, consider one seventy-eight-year-old man's description of his typical day:

I awaken about seven o'clock and put on the earphones and listen to the news. I get up before eight and take a shower and shave and dress. Then [I] come downstairs and get the paper, and get breakfast for my wife and myself. Read the news. After breakfast I clean up a little bit, then I usually come up here and putter around this desk, write letters, do a little research. I check the mail, and try to be through here around noon. Then we have lunch. In the afternoon we usually go out—might go downtown, might go to the park. Occasionally visit somebody. Do the shopping. Go home about five o'clock and make a fire. Then turn on the news about six. . . . Then get the dinner ready, and we have a nice dinner. After that, there might be a TV program, somebody might come over. Or we might go out to dinner with friends like we did last night. (Kaufman 1986, p. 107)

This sort of engagement in others' lives and in the outside world in general seems to be more typical than many believe. It should help refute another myth: that all old people are lonely. Most are not isolated, and most are not dependent, either.

On the other hand, there is also a myth that is unrealistically positive, that sees the last part of life as perfectly serene, "as a kind of adult fairyland" in which the stresses and strains of everyday life have magically disappeared (Butler 1975, p. 10). Of course, this is not the case. If anything, day-to-day problems can increase in the last stage of the life course. And as Erikson emphasized, conflicts must still be worked out and resolutions reached. In late adulthood, his eighth and last age of man (Erikson defined this period as extending from age sixty on—he did not subdivide old age as we do today), one can either work toward accepting oneself and one's past, integrating the various aspects of the lived life, or regret the past, feel hopeless about the remaining years of life, and fear death. Erikson called the central crisis in the last stage of life *integrity vs. despair.*

How do old people face and resolve such conflicts today? How do they integrate these concerns with daily life? The actual experience of aging is an eye-opening and important topic to consider. Research in the last twenty years reports high levels of life satisfaction among all older Americans (Foner 1986, p. 71). What is responsible?

The Experience of Aging

The experience of aging has changed in recent years, thanks to better medical care, improved diets, and increased interest in physical fitness. One long-term study, which followed the health history of 1,600 married couples for many years, was extended to their offspring. The researchers found that when the offspring were the same age as their parents were when the study began, they scored significantly lower on three major risk factors for heart disease—high blood pressure, high serum cholesterol, and smoking (in Foner 1986, p. 113 [fn 13]). "Our society is getting older," write Jack Horn and Jeff Meer, "but the old are getting younger" (Horn and Meer 1987, p. 77).

Self-Reliance, Social Involvement, and Life Style

At age ninety-nine, Ethel Nixon is on the run. She lives in a retirement village in California but still does her own shopping and cleaning. And she regularly drives to visit her two sons, five grandchildren, and six great-grandchildren. When Mrs. Nixon appeared on Johnny Carson's "Tonight Show," she became an overnight celebrity. Why? Because she defies the stereotype that people her age are confined to nursing homes, dependent on their middle-aged children, or neglected, abandoned, and alone. Mrs. Nixon may be unusual, but she is not unique. Actually, only about 5 percent of elderly Americans live in nursing homes; another 5 percent live in age-segregated retirement communities. The great majority maintain their own houses or apartments, despite the difficulties this entails.

Self-reliance characterizes the "old-old" as well as the "younger old." A majority (54.6 percent) of the 2.5 million Americans age eighty-five and older still maintain independent households, even though many (21.3 percent) are poor and most (96 percent) have no income other than Social Security benefits. Only 11.6 percent of the "old-old" live with their children. Like so many other myths about old age, the belief that aging parents are a drain on their children's finances is generally false. A 1987 poll by Louis Harris & Associates found that older Americans are four times more likely to *give* financial aid to their children than to receive such aid themselves. Also, less than 1 percent of older people say that they would actually want to live with their children (Horn and Meer 1987, pp. 87–89).

But this does not mean that the elderly necessarily feel cut off from their families. In fact, an older parent's financial independence prevents one source of tension between generations from opening up. And as you'll see when we discuss grandparents and the family in Chapter 16, the loving bond between grandparents and grandchildren seems to be getting stronger.

Not only family but friends are important sources of social satisfaction and social support for older Americans, just as they are for other age groups. In one study, half the older subjects said they had between eleven and forty friends they could call on for assistance in their daily lives (Quadagno 1986, p. 243 [fn 52]). These relationships were reciprocal: someone who had a car drove friends to church and the shopping mall; another made a larger cake or pot of soup than she needed and took the extras to her neighbors; still another regularly read to a friend who had trouble with her eyes.

A small minority of the elderly ensure that they have an available social circle by living in retirement communities. Of course, this type of communal life is not for everyone, but for those who choose it (and can afford it), it seems to be beneficial. Most studies show that people in these communities welcome the sociability, enjoy better health, and live longer than older people in other settings (Quadagno 1986, p. 240 [fn 41]). Note, though, that because women usually live longer than men, retirement communities tend to be predominantly female.

In short, we see again that the image of the elderly as dependent and isolated applies only to a small minority. Most older men and women are both independent and socially active, which in turn increases the satisfaction they feel with their lives.

Social Security, Work, and Retirement

Social Security has had both positive and negative consequences for the daily lives of older people. Certainly, it has provided money and thus some independence for many. At the same time, it has tended to reinforce ageism.

The Social Security Act itself was passed at the height of the Great Depression. The manifest, or official, function of the act was to provide assistance to unemployed people whose savings had been wiped out.

The latent (unofficial or unspoken) function, however, was to open up desperately needed opportunities for younger workers by encouraging older workers to retire.

Since its passage, the act has been expanded enormously to extend benefits, in particular to finance **Medicare,** a mandatory health insurance program for those sixty-five and older. Indeed, one of the primary reasons older Americans are so much better off today than in the past is because they have these extended benefits. It is clear that Medicare has distinctly improved older Americans' standard of living (Preston 1984).

Social Security gave official sanction to the relatively modern phenomenon called retirement. With this, the numbers of the working elderly have been significantly reduced. In 1900, approximately two out of three men age sixty-five and older were in the work force; today only one out of five older men (and one out of seven older women) are employed (Statistical Abstract of the United States 1988). The major reason for unemployment in this stage of the life course is mandatory retirement. About 80 percent of American workers—at least 30 percent of whom would prefer to keep working (Quadagno 1986, p. 240 [fn 41])—face mandatory retirement at age sixty-five or seventy. Ironically, the laws and regulations that now force older people out of the work force were created with the best intentions. For example, unions fought hard to protect older workers

Old age can be an especially rich time for pursuing hobbies, exploring new ideas, and sharing one's interests with others. These art students may be fulfilling a long-deferred ambition or deepening a life-long engagement; in either case, they demonstrate that old age is as much a time of growth and inquiry as any other life stage. (Jim Pickerell/Black Star.)

(especially those in their fifties) from layoffs through job security based on seniority. In exchange, they accepted mandatory retirement at age sixty-five (Horn and Meer 1987, p. 90). Congress passed a law banning mandatory retirement in 1986, but this is being phased in gradually and will not cover all workers until 1994.

In many cases, age discrimination forces people to "retire" before they have officially reached mandatory retirement age. The belief that older workers are less productive than younger workers, less motivated, unable to learn new skills, and more likely to lose time because of poor health—all false—often makes employers reluctant to hire even middle-aged workers. Although unemployment rates are lower for men age forty-five and over than for younger men, the effects of unemployment on the individual older person are devastating, as the following case illustrates.

A 50-year-old-man with a high school education lost his managerial position in an electrical machinery firm where he had been employed for 17 years. His annual earnings prior to his separation, which occurred between 1969 and 1971, were $13,000. In . . . 1971 this man reported 44 weeks of unemployment during the preceding 12 months but was then working as a sales clerk in a retail store. In 1973 he was doing clerical work for a farm machinery store, where his annual earnings were $8,500. Two years later he was unemployed and had worked only 22 weeks in the previous year, as a farm manager with earnings of $4,500. By . . . 1976 he had apparently given up; after 42 weeks of unemployment during the preceding 12 months he finally ceased looking for work. By this time his health, which had deteriorated over the preceding three years, prevented him from working entirely. (Quadagno 1986, p. 239)

There is a law that prohibits discrimination against workers ages forty-five to seventy, called the Age Discrimination in Employment Act (1967), but it is difficult to enforce. As the case illustrates, unemployment, poor health, or discouragement may lead a person to retire before he or she is compelled to do so. In 1980, 60 percent of retired workers drew Social Security benefits before age sixty-five (Quadagno 1986, p. 247 [fn 68]).

Retirement has become an important transition in the life course, and it can be very stressful, especially for men, even if it occurs at age sixty-five or seventy. Men approaching old age today are more fully engaged in the world of work and more likely to derive their key identity from their job status than are women of the same generation. A job is not only a source of income and status but also a source of pride and meaning. A job structures one's days, weeks, and years, offers social contact, and ideally provides opportunities for creativity and personal fulfillment.

However, most studies show that a majority of older Americans look forward to retirement (Quadagno 1986, p. 234 [fn 27]). Once the transition is made from a worker's role to a retiree's role, many do take to their new situation with pleasure. Many retirees express a sense of well-being as high or higher than that of younger working people. Health worries aside, they appear to lead less pressured lives and to appreciate the freedom to structure life according to their own interests and at their own pace.

Socioeconomic differences enter here, though. In general, workers in high-status occupations retire later than do workers in low-status occupations. High-status workers are also more likely to report that they enjoy retirement, probably because, in general, they are healthier and have more money than retirees from low-status jobs.

Socioeconomic Status

As the difference between high- and low-status workers makes clear, socioeconomic status is an important factor in an elderly person's—or any other individual's—quality of life. As a group, older people are economically much better off today, partly because of Social Security and Medicare. The proportion of men and women age sixty-five and older living below the poverty line has fallen from 35 percent in 1959 to 12 percent today. In 1970, the incidence of poverty among the elderly was double the national average; today it is actually below the average (Preston 1984). At the upper end of the socioeconomic scale, many of the nation's largest corporations are headed by "senior citizens." Between the extremes of poverty and wealth is a growing leisure class of older Americans "with money to spend and the time to enjoy it" (Horn and Meer 1987, p. 77). A 1982 Gallup poll found, just as other surveys have, that a majority (more than 70 percent) of people sixty-five and over said that they were highly satisfied with their standard of living—by far the highest satisfaction level reported by any age group (Gallup 1983, pp. 18–19).

Old age is a time of isolation and despair. . . . Such myths can be self-fulfilling for those living alone, on a fixed income, in a culture disinterested in their abilities and impatient with their needs. This gray-haired demonstrator has a different story to tell. Like others who have experienced discrimination, the elderly make energetic and determined activists. Through groups like the Gray Panthers, they have become increasingly effective at mobilizing political activism in their own behalf. (Left, Birgit Pohl; right, Alain Keler/Sygma.)

Even so, most people experience a reduction in income in old age, and a substantial minority still experience extreme economic hardship. Widows and members of minority groups are the most likely to suffer: because they earned less than white males during their lifetimes, they receive less in Social Security benefits (and other pensions for which they might be eligible). Fifteen percent of households headed by females age sixty-five and older have incomes below the poverty line, compared to 8 percent of households headed by males the same age. Elderly blacks and Hispanics are three times as likely to be living in poverty as elderly whites (Quadagno 1986, p. 228). Poverty also increases with age: people age eighty-five and older are twice as likely to live in poverty as those ages sixty-five to sixty-nine.

Housing is a major problem for elderly people living near or below the poverty line. Although almost 70 percent of older Americans own their own homes, mortgage-free (Butler 1975), this does not mean that retirees on a fixed income are able to keep up with the rising costs of home maintenance, utilities, and real estate taxes, much less adapt the home to current needs.

Medical expenses are another financial burden for many elderly people, not just those living at the poverty level or below. Medicare does not cover the costs of medical expenses such as prescription drugs, checkups, eyeglasses, or full-time nursing.

Again, one answer is life in a retirement community. But, of course, one has to be able to afford initial maintenance costs in the first place, so this is not an option for poorer people. In many retirement communities, residents pay an entrance fee (ranging from $10,000 to $57,000 in 1975), which gives them a lifelong lease on an apartment plus lifelong medical care. In addition, they pay a monthly maintenance charge (ranging from $240 to $595 in 1975) for meals in a central dining room, heat, electricity, laundry, and the like. Note that the entrance fee is nonrefundable. The apartment cannot be sold to another retiree or left to heirs.

Gender and Widowhood

We must recognize that, first of all, men and women experience old age very differently. Both men and women confront negative age-stereotypes, but because society values youth and beauty more highly in women than in men, women suffer a greater loss as they age. Americans attach the label "old" to a woman under age sixty far more often than they do to men (Riley and

Foner 1968). Differences in cultural perceptions are only part of the story, however.

Women in the United States live seven to eight years longer, on the average, than men do. The simple fact of longevity has numerous ramifications. Because women tend to marry older men, they are much more likely to be widowed a large portion of their old age. In 1981, only 13 percent of men age sixty-five and older, but 51 percent of women the same age, were widowed. By age seventy-five, only one in five women was living with a spouse, compared with two out of three men (Horn and Meer 1987, p. 84). (See Figure 6.5.)

The experience of widowhood itself is different for men and women. In some ways, it is more difficult for men to adjust, for they lose not only their wives but often a system of emotional and domestic support they had always taken for granted. Men now in their sixties and seventies tend to be unfamiliar with cooking and household chores and may experience physical decline due to skipped meals and poor nutrition. Widowhood also clashes with men's self-definitions as independent and resourceful. They are not accustomed to asking for help and may get less support from relatives and friends because they are not seen as "needy."

FIGURE 6.5   Sex Differences in Marital Status for the Older Population

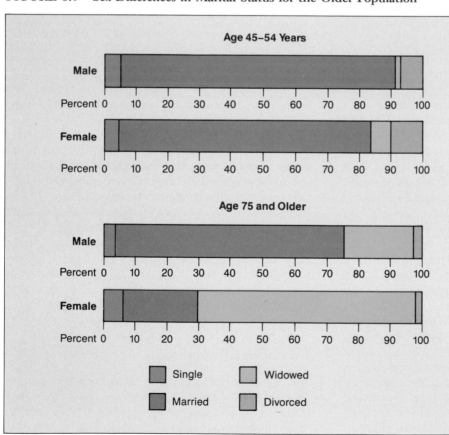

The distribution of the population according to marital status shifts considerably with increasing age. The changes are similar in broad pattern for both men and women, but they are more dramatic for women than for men.

Source: Current Population Reports, P-23, No. 138, p. 93, 1983.

At the same time, however, remarriage is almost exclusively a male prerogative, for both demographic and cultural reasons (Berardo 1980). In 1981, there were only twenty-three unmarried men age sixty-five and older for every 100 unmarried women. In addition, older men still have the option of marrying younger women, which makes their pool of eligibles even larger. As a result, men age sixty-five and older are eight times more likely to remarry than older women are (Horn and Meer 1987, p. 84). Interestingly, social status affects remarriage rates—and affects them in opposite ways for men and women. The more education a woman has and the higher her income, the less likely she is to remarry; the reverse is true for men (Hagestad 1986).

For a woman, widowhood usually brings a decline in standard of living that often compounds her personal loss. Many women now in their sixties and seventies were full-time housewives for most of their lives. Since they entered the labor force sporadically, if at all, they are unlikely to have savings and income from pension plans. In many cases, the husband's pension did not include a provision for widows, so this source of income is cut off. Even if the woman worked most of her life, the chances are that she earned much less than her husband and so receives less in Social Security benefits and pension after his death. This is one gender difference that is likely to decrease as the working and career women of the baby boom reach old age. Today, however, older women are a disadvantaged minority (see Table 6.3).

Solidarity and Political Activism

Given their many shared experiences and problems, one might expect older Americans to feel a strong "consciousness of kind" and to act together on many political issues. To some extent this is true. Recent studies have shown that "identification with older people [is] as widespread as race consciousness among blacks and more widespread than sex identification among women" (Foner 1986, p. 89). But age consciousness is not universal. On the one hand, many older Americans accept the view that after a certain age they should step aside to make room for the young. On the other hand, many people age sixty-five and older still think of themselves as middle-aged. Age consciousness is highest among the oldest old, who as a group have the lowest income and the least education. But action does not

TABLE 6.3 Social Security Retirement Benefits by Sex

	Average Monthly Benefits	Full Benefits	Reduced Benefits
Males	538	628	480
Females	412	511	372

Source: U.S. Bureau of the Census, 1987.

necessarily follow from consciousness in this case. The oldest old are the least likely, indeed the least able, to organize politically.

This is not to say that the elderly are inactive politically. The Gray Panthers, a group organized on the model of the radical political groups of the 1960s and 1970s to combat ageism, had 10,000 members in 1980. The more moderate American Association of Retired Persons (A.A.R.P.) boasts 24 million members and an annual budget of $145 million (Collins 1987). In addition to lobbying on issues that concern older Americans, A.A.R.P. runs its own group health insurance plan, its own mutual fund, a nonprofit mail order pharmacy, travel programs, and a variety of social service programs.

In terms of more conventional political participation, older Americans are among the most active groups in the nation. In the 1982 congressional elections, for example, the percentage of people age sixty-five to seventy-four who voted was double that of voters ages twenty to twenty-nine, and the absolute number of voters age sixty and older exceeded that of either young (under thirty-five) or middle-aged voters (thirty-five to forty-nine) (Preston 1984, p. 446). Polls also show that the elderly tend to be more politically knowledgeable than younger citizens. They are much more likely to be able to identify their congressional representative, for example (Gallup 1983, p. 75).

Death and Dying

Today, because of increased longevity and the growing size of the aging population, most deaths occur among the old. The meaning of death, for individuals and society, has changed as a result. In the past, death, the final transition we are all required to make, came at unpredictable times. More people today are in a position to contemplate their own deaths. Fatalism about death has given way to a greater sense of predictability and control. Yet social norms and institutions have lagged behind these social facts.

In a now-famous book, *The Denial of Death* (1973), Ernest Becker charged that failure to accept the inevitability of death and fear of dying were major sources of unperceived stress in modern societies. The denial of death inhibits preparation for dying, making the final transition in the life course even more difficult. Western societies insulate the young and healthy from the old and dying. As a result, people are deprived of the opportunity to learn about death through personal observation. Because we do not usually talk about our own deaths with our family and friends, there are no guidelines or social supports for a "good" death. The dying are left in hospital rooms and old-age homes to cope with their anxieties and fears alone.

At the time Becker wrote, most physicians felt it was unwise to inform a patient that he or she was terminally ill. Patients were required to maintain the fiction that they were going to get better, even though everyone knew the truth. Elisabeth Kübler-Ross's book *On Death and Dying* (1969) had already broken this silence. Through observation and interviews with the terminally ill, she was able to outline five stages in the process of dying: denial, bargaining for a reprieve, anger, depression, and finally acceptance of the inevitable. She argues

that preventing dying persons (and their families) from working through these stages is cruel. In effect, Kübler-Ross helped to give the dying—and their family and friends—some sense of what the final stage of life involves.

Kübler-Ross struck a responsive chord. Polls taken in the late 1970s and early 1980s showed that most people were not threatened by death, but agreed with such statements as "death is sometimes a blessing" and "death is not tragic for the person who dies, only for the survivors." Less than half agreed that "death always comes too soon"; and only one in ten felt "to die is to suffer" (Riley 1983, p. 195).

New medical technologies that prolong life have raised concerns about the autonomy of the dying, and their right to refuse treatment and to choose the manner and place of their death. "Living wills," requests *not* to be kept alive through artificial means, have gained popularity. Physicians have acknowledged patients' rights to know their condition. And support has grown for **hospices**—nonbureaucratic, homelike facilities that provide care and support for the terminally ill and their families.

Changes in the demography and meaning of death have posed challenges for individuals and for social institutions concerned with human mortality. Whether our society as a whole will become more accepting of death, more able to face it, and more willing to socialize its members for death remains a question (Riley 1983, p. 213).

SUMMARY

1. Sociologists now study social changes, social stability, and age-related social roles by considering the life course, the sequence of more or less predictable stages in the life cycle. The sociology of the life course analyzes the way growth and aging both reflect and affect social roles and social conditions.

2. The life course is socially defined. The number of stages, the roles at each stage, and how transitions are marked all vary from culture to culture and from one historical period to another.

3. Transitions, in which old roles give way to new ones, are important aspects of the life course. Transitions in our society tend to be more ambiguous than in tradition-

al societies, where rites of passage occur at fixed times and clearly mark the transition for the individual and for the whole community.

4. Focusing the study of life-course stages on birth cohorts helps sociologists to assess the effects of the changing times on people's norms and values.

5. Erik Erikson was one of the first to analyze the entire life course. He saw it as a series of eight stages, each with its own developmental task or crisis.

6. Childhood, now an extended period of learning and growth, was not always a well-defined stage. The notion that children should be nurtured and protected from the adult world dates from the Renaissance; but only in the

early part of this century, when child labor was outlawed and compulsory schooling took effect, did this notion become a reality for the lower class.

7. Adolescence, a time of questioning and experimentation, became an accepted stage of the life course during the 1940s and 1950s. Forging an identity is the primary task of adolescence.

8. Adulthood is also a period of change and challenge. Levinson divided the male adult life course into two relatively stable periods—early and middle adulthood—preceded and followed by unstable times of transition. The mid-life transition is a time of painful questioning for men. The stages of the female life course are less predictable than those of men, largely because a woman's role at any given time is heavily influenced by her childbearing decisions.

9. The U.S. population is aging due to increased survival rates, increased longevity, and declining birth rates. This trend, which has expanded the life course and altered social structure, is expected to continue.

10. The Social Security Act (1935) set a fixed age for the onset of retirement benefits, thus creating a new social category: the retired. Expanded benefits, including Medicare, are in part responsible for the improved economic condition of the average older person today.

11. However, Social Security has also helped to reinforce ageism in our culture, based on myths of senility, inflexibility, isolation, and the general decline of the elderly. In addition, employment among the elderly has sharply decreased due to mandatory retirement; sometimes people are forced to retire before the age of sixty-five. Laws against age discrimination exist but are difficult to enforce.

12. The transition from employment to retirement can be stressful, especially for men. Nevertheless, most Americans look forward to retirement and enjoy it once they've made the transition. Socioeconomic status is an important factor in retirement. The number of elderly living in poverty has decreased in the last thirty years, but a substantial number of elderly, many of them widows or members of minority groups, face extreme hardship.

13. Because women usually live longer than men, they are more likely to be widowed. Widowhood may be psychologically harder for men to adjust to, but they are more likely to remarry.

14. Aging women encounter greater prejudice than men, due to society's views of youth and beauty. Women's standard of living usually declines with widowhood, although this may change as career women of the baby-boom generation reach old age.

15. Age consciousness and feelings of solidarity among the elderly are fairly widespread but not universal. There are several prominent political action and lobbying groups for the old.

16. Today, death usually comes in old age, and increasing numbers of people can now contemplate their own ends. The failure to accept death, fear of death, and inadequate preparation for it make this transition a dreadful one for many. Elisabeth Kübler-Ross's *On Death and Dying* broke our society's silence about death and outlined five essential stages in the dying process.

GLOSSARY

Ageism. A system of negative beliefs about the capacities, skills, and health of the elderly.

Age grading. Classifying people into different social categories according to age.

Age structure. The number of people at each stage of the life course.

Birth cohort. The category of people who were born in the same year or period, and who age together.

Hospice. A homelike facility that provides care and support for the terminally ill and their families.

Identity. The sense of "who you are"; a sense of continuity of self-image in past, present, and future.

Life course. The socially defined sequence of stages in the life cycle, from birth to death. Each stage has characteristic tasks, expectations, and privileges.

Medicare. An extended benefit of the Social Security Act, which provides mandatory health insurance for people age sixty-five and older.

Rites of passage. Ceremonies that celebrate and publicize the transition from one stage of life to the next.

Transition. A point in the life course when old roles must be relinquished and new roles assumed.

CHAPTER 7
Deviance and Social Control

I van Boesky was a classic example of the great American success story. The son of a Russian immigrant, young Ivan struggled to earn a degree from the Detroit School of Law. After serving unhappy stints as a law clerk and an accountant, he landed a job on Wall Street at the age of twenty nine (Russell 1986b). His wealthy father-in-law, who was then paying Boesky's rent, nicknamed him "Ivan the Bum." By age forty nine, however, the nickname seemed misplaced. Boesky had amassed a personal fortune estimated at $200 million. A high-stakes gambler who often bet millions on risky stocks (and won), he had become known on Wall Street as "Ivan the Terrible."

Boesky rode to fortune on the wave of a new business phenomenon—the corporate takeover—that changed the very nature of American business. In the "old days," businesses grew by discovering new markets, increasing production, buying out competitors, and selling stock to finance their expansion. When one company acquired another, or when two companies merged, the deal was negotiated by officers of the companies involved. Then, in the 1960s and 1970s, corporate America was "invaded" by a new type of entrepreneur. Rather than dealing directly with the officers of a company they sought to take over, the corporate "raiders" purchased stock of the target company on the open market, often acquiring a controlling share before the target company knew what was happening. Enormous profits could be made from these takeovers, for the investors as well as the corporations involved. When news of a potential takeover became public, the price of the stock in the target company jumped as the raider and the management of the target company struggled for control.

Ivan Boesky at this time was riding high. A superstar of takeover finance, Boesky had an uncanny ability to *anticipate* takeover bids before they were announced. For example, between May 22 and 29, 1985, Boesky bought 377,000 shares of Nabisco; when Nabisco and R. J. Reynolds announced a merger on May 30, he sold out his Nabisco shares for a profit of $4 million (Russell 1986a). In April of that year Boesky's "crystal ball" told him to buy 301,800 shares of Houston Natural Gas; two weeks later, when a merger with another company was announced, he banked $4.1 million in profits. Boesky attributed his success at prediction to a combination of instinct and information. In fact, as was later revealed, his success was the result of fraud.

One of the rules of the investment business, as enforced by the Securities and Exchange Commission (SEC), prohibits insiders from profiting on information that is not available to the general public. Insider trading is against the law, and Boesky violated this prohibition on a grand scale. He had agreed to pay investment banker David Levine huge sums for advance notice of takeover bids. When Levine was charged with insider trading in August 1986, he named Ivan Boesky as an accomplice. Caught red-handed, Boesky made a deal with the SEC in which he agreed to pay $100 million in fines, to dispose of all of his stock holdings over the next year and a half, to be barred from securities trading for life, and to plead guilty to an unspecified criminal charge with a possible prison sentence of five years or less. Boesky also agreed to cooperate with the SEC in its investigation of insider trading, and allowed his conversations with other suspects to be taped for several months.

The unmasking of Ivan Boesky was only the tip of the iceberg. Over the next several months, subpoenas were issued to some of the nation's oldest and most respected investment firms. Four top executives of major financial institutions were arrested, one was led from his office in handcuffs. The investigation revealed a web of insider trading—complete with Caribbean bank accounts, midnight raids on investment bankers' desk drawers, secret passwords, and briefcases loaded with cash (Sterngold 1987). Where the arrests would stop, nobody knew. A study of 172 successful takeovers, released by the SEC in March, revealed that in every case, stock in the target company had risen sharply three weeks *before* the takeover bid was announced (*New York Times*, March 11, 1986, p. A1). By spring, all of Wall Street was reacting to the discovery of deviance within its ranks.

In preceding chapters we examined some of the patterned and orderly characteristics of social life and social interaction. But social life does not always proceed according to plan. In every society and time there are people who break rules and who are regarded as deviant; deviance as well as conformity is universal. Why this should be so is the subject of much sociological inquiry. In the first section of this chapter we look at deviance from a sociological point of view. In the second section we consider the different theoretical perspectives that contribute to our understanding of deviance. Next we look at different levels of social control, which like deviance itself, can take various forms. In the last sections, we focus on crime and the criminal justice system, returning to Wall Street at a number of points along the way.

THE NATURE OF DEVIANCE

We tend to take the nature of deviance for granted: Everybody more or less knows what is and what is not approved and respectable behavior. A truly precise notion of deviance, however, is hard to pin down. Is

wearing short skirts deviant? Is belonging to a religious cult? Is living with someone without benefit of marriage? In the not too distant past, many people described an unmarried couple who lived together as "living in sin." Many people now think that cohabitation is acceptable . . . under certain conditions. If the couple are both young, childless heterosexuals, few eyebrows are raised. But suppose the individuals are in their seventies, or the woman is twenty years older than the man, or she is a divorcée with young children, or her lover is another woman. These living arrangements have been known to strain social tolerance, sometimes to the breaking point. Deviance, as these examples suggest, is in the eyes of the beholder.

The sociological perspective seeks to untangle the complexities that surround the topic of deviance. Sociologists define **deviance** as any behavior that members of a social group *define* as violating their norms. This concept applies both to criminal acts of deviance (behavior that the entire society has formally declared illegal) and to noncriminal acts that members of a group view as unethical, immoral, peculiar, sick, or otherwise outside the bounds of respectability.

As used by sociologists, deviance is a relatively neutral term. The term is also neutral inasmuch as sociologists are not seeking to agree or disagree with socially defined standards of behavior. But the sociological perspective highlights a number of popular misconceptions about deviance. One is that certain acts are inherently deviant. Sociologists point out that whether an act is considered deviant depends on the society and on the social circumstances. Most societies have norms forbidding murder, theft, rape, and other forms of "hard core" criminal deviance. Yet these same societies recognize exceptions to these rules (Ben-Yehuda 1985). Killing in the form of murder is a crime—but killing the enemy in war is not. Thus one person may receive a life sentence and another may receive a Congressional Medal of Honor for having performed the same act. Similarly, virtually all societies condemn theft, but many guerrilla movements (which may later come to power) allow and even sanctify burglary and armed robbery as a means to revolutionary ends. To the British, the men who organized the Boston Tea Party were outlaws; to many American colonists, they were heroes. It follows that because people's norms differ from one social situation to the next and from one society to another, what they regard as deviant also varies (see Table 7.1).

Behavior considered deviant in one culture may be considered normal in another culture. While the ornaments worn by these two people are strikingly similar, the person on the left is considered deviant, while the person on the right is not. In everyday life subtle differences in dress on campus mark people as deviant or belonging to a subculture. (Left: Dennis Stock/Magnum; right: David Austen.)

The relativity of deviance to situation surfaced in a poll taken by *Business Week* magazine (December 6, 1986, p. 34) at the height of the Wall Street scandal. A majority of those polled (62 percent) said that Boesky was a criminal and deserved the punishment he got. Yet quite a large number (55 percent) said that they would buy stock on an inside tip from a friend who knew of a coming takeover bid and 34 percent of those who said they wouldn't act on inside information gave as their reason that the tip might be wrong! By implication, it is proper behavior for a small, private investor to use inside tips, but criminal for a financier to make millions the same way!

A second misconception is to consider deviance as any activity that is uncommon or atypical. Many deviant acts are characteristic of only a minority of the population, but, the uncommonness of a behavior is not sufficient to determine whether it is considered deviant. Many uncommon acts are not deviant, and some deviant acts are rather common. For example, skydiving is uncommon but not deviant, whereas exceeding the speed limit is deviant (in the sense of being illegal) but common.

Another prevalent idea is that deviance is confined to a small category of marginal people—so-called "nuts, sluts, and perverts." By implication, deviants belong to a different class of people from you and me. However,

most "normal" people commit deviant acts from time to time, even though their deviance goes largely undetected. How many people do you know who have *never* stolen a library book or pads and pens from an office? Who have never run a red light? Who never told a lie? Who never cheated on their income taxes? Clearly, people other than those whom society labels deviant violate social norms.

The Role of Social Definitions and Power

From the sociological point of view, deviance exists only in relation to the values and norms that prevail among people in a particular place at a particular time. In other words, deviance is a matter of *social definition*. Certain acts, such as murder, rape, theft, perversion, and mental pathology, would occur whether or not they were defined as deviant. But by defining them as deviant, we set in motion a series of events that would not otherwise take place.

This matter of social definition emphasizes the point that deviance is not a property that is inherent in particular behaviors. Rather it is a property that people confer on some forms of behavior by their social definitions. Moreover, social definitions may change over time as attitudes change. Shifting attitudes toward business takeovers illustrate this point (Hirsch 1986). When news of takeovers first appeared in the business pages, the financial establishment viewed takeovers as an aberration, a disreputable activity that would not affect big business. Major Wall Street firms refused to become involved in what they saw as illegitimate business practices. However, as takeovers became more common, and the profits to be made became more visible, Wall Street attitudes toward takeovers subtly began to change. By the early 1980s, Wall Street firms that had once treated corporate raiders as deviant outsiders were rushing to jump on the takeover bandwagon.

If deviance is relative to the values and norms that prevail at a particular time and place, key questions that arise are *whose* values and norms are being violated and *who* has the power to identify and punish violators. Not surprisingly, these questions are often hotly contested, frequently in the political arena. A clear instance of the first question is the debate on abortion. The voluntary termination of a pregnancy violates the moral principles of some groups who equate abortion with murder—a deviant act. However, many women's groups strongly believe that every woman should have the right to exercise control over her own body and hence should be able to choose to end an unwanted pregnancy. The issue then becomes one of whose values should prevail. In the case of takeovers, the contested issue revolves around who should be the watchdog. The financial community,

one of the most powerful lobbies in Washington, has for decades argued to Congress that it must be allowed to police itself—on the grounds that stricter regulation would handcuff the economy. In the wake of the insider trading scandal, lawmakers are insisting that stricter regulation be up to Congress.

Viewed in this way, definitions of deviance are decided by those with the power to enforce their definitions. Through the manipulation of rewards and the imposition of penalties, some individuals and groups can make their standards prevail even when others object.

EXPLANATIONS OF DEVIANCE

What drives people like Ivan Boesky to risk the fortunes they have made through legal stock trades, their country estates and limousines, their respectability, even their freedom, to commit illegal acts? Were Boesky and his cohorts "bad apples," or were they victims of changing times? (If Boesky had never broken a law, would another Boesky have come along?) Is a certain amount of deviance an inevitable part of social life? Or is it a product of particular social situations? Are deviants fundamentally different from other people, or are they simply the unlucky ones who got caught?

Table 7.1   The Cultural Relativity of Deviance

Type of Act	Percentage Who Think Act Should Be Prohibited by Law*				
	India	Iran	Italy (Sardinia)	U.S.	Yugoslavia
Homosexuality in private between consenting adults	74	90	87	18	72
Public, nonviolent political protest	33	77	35	6	46
Failure to help another person in danger	45	56	80	28	77
Air pollution caused by a factory	99	98	96	96	92

*Percentages have been rounded off.
Source: Adapted from Graeme Newman, 1976, *Comparative Deviance: Perception and Law in Six Cultures.* New York: Elsevier, p. 116, Table 4.

Studies that ask national samples of people in different cultures the same questions about the same behaviors are rare. In this major study, note that Americans are far more tolerant of protest and homosexuality than any of the other cultures, with Iran being the least tolerant. On the other hand, condemnation of air pollution is uniformly high—a global norm that did not exist a generation earlier.

The fact that an activity is uncommon does not mean that it is deviant; it must also violate a norm accepted by the society. (A) Early attempts at flying may have seemed deviant at a time when human flight was considered impossible. (B) Today, our understanding of aerodynamics has developed to such an extent that even flying without wings is not considered deviant, although it is practiced by a small number of people. (Left: The Bettmann Archive; right: F. Rickard/Photo Researchers, Inc.)

There is no simple explanation of why deviance arises at all and where the deviant individual fits within the larger society. One can look at deviance from the point of view of individual actors, or one can examine structural factors that might discourage or promote deviance. The action approach raises questions about why people come to view certain acts as deviant, as well as questions about why people violate social norms. The structural orientation directs attention to such factors as the age and sex of the individuals (see Why Women Are Outsiders to Insider Trading). One can view deviance as a political issue that is grounded in the power structure of a society, or as a universal feature of social life that must serve some function in maintaining social order. All these basic approaches contribute something to an understanding of deviance. A number of middle-range theories deal specifically with the topic of deviance and include elements of one or more of these basic orientations. No one of these theories provides a complete explanation of every incidence and every facet of deviance. The complete sociological investigation requires a multilayered approach.

Here we have divided explanations of deviance into two general categories. The first set of theories attempts to explain deviance in terms of the characteristics and experiences that distinguish deviant individuals from nondeviants. The second set of theories attempts to explain deviance in terms of social factors that make it

more likely that people will engage in deviant behavior. These are not separate, isolated explanations of deviance. The theories have relationships to one another and all contribute to the history of sociological thought on deviance.

Individual Perspectives

Individualistic theories of deviance seek to identify the "kind of person" who becomes deviant and to pinpoint the factors that led to that person's becoming deviant. Modern biological theories look for explanations in the person's heredity and physiological makeup; psychological theories look at the individual's personal history and psychological makeup. Underlying both approaches is the question, How do deviants differ from nondeviants? Rational choice theory suggests that anyone might break the rules, given the opportunity and sufficient incentive.

Biological Explanations

Biological theories of deviance are not a recent innovation. Over the years, many attempts have been made to explain deviance in terms of biological factors. In the

Conflicting beliefs about norms sometimes coexist in society. Efforts to establish a consensus highlight the divisions that separate different value systems. The ongoing debate in America about abortion, for example, has ardent supporters on both sides, such as those pictured here. (Steve Woit/Picture Group.)

nineteenth century, Cesare Lombroso, an Italian criminologist, thought an answer to the question Who is deviant? could be found in the shape of the skull. Lombroso developed his theory when he was examining the skull of Villela, a master criminal.

> At the sight of that skull, I seemed to see all of a sudden, lighted up as a vast plain under a flaming sky, the problem of the nature of the criminal—an atavistic being who reproduces in his person the ferocious instincts of primitive humanity and the inferior animals. Thus were explained in the enormous jaws, high cheekbones, prominent superciliary arches . . . found in criminals, savages, and apes. (Lombroso, in Cohen, 1966, p. 50)

Lombroso and his students set about measuring the heads of Italian prisoners. All of the measurements they made seemed to confirm Lombroso's belief that criminals were a throwback to an earlier stage of evolution, "savages" among civilized men. He concluded that criminals were *born*, not made. From a scientific point of view, however, Lombroso made one fatal error: He only examined criminals, a sample that was not representative of the entire population. When the British physician Charles Goring compared the measurements of skulls of criminals and ordinary citizens some years later, he found no difference between the two (Goring 1913). Nevertheless, the concept of "born criminals" lives on in popular, common-sense explanations of deviance. The idea that criminals are born rather than made is appealing in that it offers a simple solution to complex social problems.

A recent historical study (Hughes 1987) may settle the issue. Australia began as a penal colony. During the late eighteenth and nineteenth centuries, Britain sent 121,000 of its criminals "down under." Other Australian settlers were convicts from the British colonies of South Africa and Canada and from Ireland. Eighty percent of the criminals were thieves, and well over half had been convicted more than once. These criminals made up the majority of Australia's founding population, and a majority of present-day Australians are descended from these criminals. Nonetheless, the transportation of convicts did not, as its supporters hoped, rid Britain of its "criminal class," still less rid Britain of crime. Nor does modern Australia have a particularly high crime rate. This natural experiment offers rich evidence that a propensity to break the law is not carried in the genes.

This does not necessarily mean that biology plays no role in deviance. Recent advances in genetics, biochemistry, and neuropsychology have led to renewed scientific interest in biological explanations of deviance. Scientists have developed sophisticated methods for identifying genetic traits, neurological disorders, chemical imbalances, and the like. Evidence is mounting that certain forms of deviance, especially mental pathology, are at least partly biological in origin (Wender and Klein 1981). Research suggests that people who suffer from the mental disorder of schizophrenia inherit a vulnerability to the disorder. When under stress, the nervous systems of these individuals overreact, creating chemical imbalances that lead to disordered thinking, hallucinations, and other symptoms. A similar pattern has been found for manic depressives, who experience extreme mood swings. If genetic and biochemical abnormalities explain these deviations from normal behavior, it is logical to suspect that biology plays a role in other forms of deviance as well.

No one seriously suggests that biological research will one day explain sophisticated financial fraud, but it may help solve other puzzling patterns of crime. Why, for example, are men responsible for 90 percent of violent crimes and homicides? One prominent theory is that aggression is a key variable. Biological research points to hormonal bases of aggression that are different in men than in women (Wilson and Herrnstein 1978).

Research into the genetic and biochemical bases of behavior is still in its infancy. But new theories and research are gaining scientific as well as public attention (Kamin 1986, Wilson 1983). This does not mean a return to the old idea of born criminals (or other deviants). One result of recent research in this area is a recognition that, even in the simplest of creatures, behavior reflects the interaction of biological and environmental factors (see Chapter 5). This is particularly true of the least simple of creatures, human beings.

Psychological Explanations

Whereas some scientists have looked to the biological characteristics of people to explain deviant behavior, others have turned their attention to the psychological makeup of individuals. Psychologists following in Sigmund Freud's psychoanalytic tradition maintain that all people have deviant impulses toward sexuality and aggression. However, in the process of growing up, most of us learn to inhibit or productively channel these inclinations. Freud argued that through identification with their parents, children acquire a superego, or conscience, that forbids deviant kinds of behavior; they also acquire an ego that enables them to deal realistically with internal drives and social demands. Psychoanalytic theory suggests that acts of wanton cruelty and crimes committed without apparent motives may indicate an underdeveloped superego. Conversely, an *overdeveloped* superego may also lead to deviance. People who are repulsed by their own urges may commit deviant acts to provoke the punishment they feel they deserve for hating their parents or for having sexual fantasies.

The popularity of Freudian theory has faded in recent years, and many scientists have looked to alternate psychological explanations of deviance. Some contend that deviance, like any form of behavior, is learned from observing those around us. In a classic study, Albert Bandura and Richard H. Walters (1959) compared groups of delinquent and nondelinquent white boys from financially stable homes. They found that the most aggressive youngsters typically came from families in which the parents urged or condoned aggression. This and other research by Bandura also reveals that punishing children for aggression results in more, not less, aggressive behavior:

> Indeed, parental modeling behavior may often counteract the effects of their direct training. When a parent punishes his child physically for having aggressed toward peers, for example, the intended outcome of this training is that the child should refrain from hitting others. The child, however, is also learning from parental demonstration how to aggress physically and this imitative learning may provide the direction of the child's behavior when he is similarly frustrated in subsequent interaction. (Bandura 1967, p. 43)

Bandura (1973, 1977) contends that exposure to models of violent behavior and reinforcement for aggressive acts explains why people so often act aggressively toward one another.

Other perspectives on deviance have come from cognitive psychology, which focuses on the mental processes that underlie behavior. A cognitive analysis of deviance would be likely to consider how people think about the events and relationships in their lives and how their thinking affects their actions. For example, deviance may occur when, for one reason or another, people think that the cultural values governing the rest of society do not apply to them. A number of observers believe this kind of thinking explains the rash of deviance on Wall Street (Arenson 1986, Elliott 1986). The men who became involved in the scandal were wheeling and dealing with millions of dollars; the fate of corporations with dozens of offices and thousands of employees lay in their hands; they were among Wall Street's superstars. Power and success can lead to feelings of specialness, or what some have called the "Nixon syndrome": I am the President and above the law. In addition, the Wall Street insider traders may have felt that the demands of their jobs—100-hour workweeks, lost time with family and friends, constant pressure—entitled them to extra, illicit earnings.

Rational Choice Explanations

Some psychological explanations suggest that deviance is not based on judgment and choice: in effect, that people who deviate do not know what they are doing. Rational choice analyses reject this line of thinking. They argue that in many (if not most) cases, deviance is the result of highly rational calculation of risks and rewards. Prospective deviants weigh their chances of gain against the risks of getting caught, and thereby decide a course of action. For example, in rational choice terms, Boesky and other insiders calculated that the enormous profits to be made through insider trading outweighed the risk of getting caught. Simply put, a deviant is an opportunist.

The rational choice perspective also implies that whether or not people commit deviant acts depends on prevailing norms and standards. If the potential rewards for breaking the rules are great, the temptation to break the rules will be strong. If, on the other hand, the possibility of being caught and punished is great, the rewards will not be worth the risk. For decades, there was an unwritten rule that the press would not report on the private lives of presidential candidates, before or after the election. Presidents Roosevelt, Eisenhower, and Kennedy's extramarital affairs only came to light in biographies published after their deaths. In 1987, however, the press broke that silence: compromising photographs forced Democratic front-runner Gary Hart out of the race. Given the new threat of publicity, future candidates will probably not take the risks that Hart took.

In equating deviance with opportunism, rational choice theory creates a bridge between theories of deviance that focus on individuals and theories that focus on the social system.

Deviance and Structural Stress

Although biological, psychological, and rational choice theories of deviance provide insights into *individual* cases, they do not explain why *rates* of deviance (the number of deviant acts per unit of population) vary from group to group and from neighborhood to neighborhood. Consequently, sociologists seek answers to the question of deviance in the larger social environment. One sociological approach looks to the part that social structure plays in producing stresses that prompt people to engage in deviant behavior.

The sociologist Robert Merton (1968) used a form of stress theory to explain deviance. In his view, high rates of deviance are the result of a discrepancy between societal expectations and opportunities, between cultural goals and the means available for achieving them. Merton reasoned that to some degree all people internalize the goals that are considered worth striving for in their culture. Everyone also internalizes the norms that govern proper and legitimate ways of working toward those goals. But when legitimate opportunities for achieving culturally defined goals are limited or nonexistent, people may seek alternative ways to achieve those goals, or they may abandon the goals altogether. Merton's key point is that strains in the social structure *invite* deviance. In his words, "some social structures exert a definite pressure upon certain persons in the society to engage in nonconforming rather than conforming behavior" (Merton 1968, p. 132).

American society was Merton's prime example. Our culture places tremendous emphasis on financial success. Children are raised not only to believe that they might become President of the United States but also to dream that they might become millionaires. At the same time, legitimate opportunities to become wealthy in our society are limited. Very few adults are able to achieve these childhood dreams; hardly any become multimillionaires. What do people do when there is a wide gap between culturally defined goals and legitimate means of achieving them?

Merton identified five possibilities (see Figure 7.1).

1. **Conformity:** Despite the discrepancy between their expectations and opportunities, conformists continue to seek culturally approved goals by culturally approved means. Bankers and brokers who adhered strictly to the rules against insider trading, even though they suspected that many of their most successful colleagues were bending the rules, are an example.
2. **Innovation:** Pursuing culturally approved goals by culturally disapproved means (including illegal activities). Boesky and the others who engaged in insider trading fall into this category. They made money (a culturally approved goal) any way that they could.
3. **Ritualism:** Conforming so strictly to socially prescribed means of achieving goals that the larger goals are forgotten in the process. The deviance lies in conforming to such a degree

This figure illustrates the five patterns of coping with social expectations specified by Robert K. Merton. While conformists accept both culturally approved goals and means, deviants reject either these goals or these means, or both.

FIGURE 7.1 Merton's Five Modes of Social Adaptation

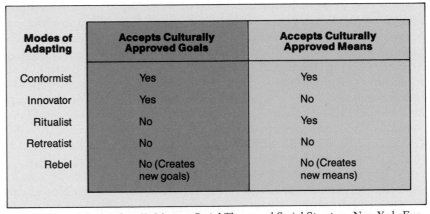

Modes of Adapting	Accepts Culturally Approved Goals	Accepts Culturally Approved Means
Conformist	Yes	Yes
Innovator	Yes	No
Ritualist	No	Yes
Retreatist	No	No
Rebel	No (Creates new goals)	No (Creates new means)

Source: Adapted from Robert K. Merton. *Social Theory and Social Structure.* New York: Free Press, 1968, p. 194.

that the negative consequences of doing so are ignored. The classic example of ritualism is the bureaucrat who rigidly adheres to rules and regulations even when they no longer contribute to the efficiency of the organization, or worse, stifle individual creativity and imagination.

4. **Retreatism:** Abandoning both the goals and the means one's culture prescribes. Retreatists are dropouts in the eyes of society—the people who give up looking for work and become skid row bums, chronic drug addicts who don't even try to kick their habits, vagrants who drift aimlessly through life.

5. **Rebellion:** Rejecting the approved goals and means of allowing them and embracing new, socially disapproved ones instead. Men such as T. Boone Pickens, who pioneered hostile corporate takeovers, can be described as rebels. These financial rebels fashioned a new goal: restructuring American business. And they invented new means of achieving their goal: the hostile corporate takeover. As this example suggests, yesterday's rebels may become tomorrow's conformists. Virtually all Wall Street firms now have divisions that handle all aspects of mergers and acquisitions.

Since its publication in 1938, Merton's theory has been highly praised for its logical tightness, but it has also been widely criticized (see Johnson and Turner 1984). One criticism is that the theory cannot explain some types of deviance, for example, alcoholism or mental disorders. A second criticism is that it does not explain how people move from alienation (perception of a gap) to adaptation (doing something about this), or why some people innovate whereas others retreat or rebel. Merton argued that people deviate when they cannot attain their goals through legitimate means, but research shows that this does not happen in all cases. Travis Hirschi (1969), for example, found little evidence to support the hypothesis that delinquency arises in response to the frustration of having one's efforts to succeed blocked. Merton assumed that people try as best they can to adopt conventional goals and means, when, in fact, acceptance of social conventions varies from person to person, situation to situation. Albert K. Cohen (1965, 1966) made an important contribution to Merton's theory when he pointed out that how people respond to social stresses depends in large part on the social groups to which they belong, the pressures for or against deviance in those groups, and opportunities to learn the "techniques" of innovation, retreatism, rebellion, and so on. The theory to which we now turn, differential association, emphasizes this point.

Differential Association

The theory of **differential association** is based on the idea that just as people must learn through socialization how to conform to their society's norms, they must also learn how to depart from those norms. In other words, deviance, like conforming behavior, is a product of socialization. This perspective on deviance grew from a research project.

In the 1920s Clifford Shaw and Henry McKay found that high crime rates had persisted in the same Chicago neighborhood for over twenty years. Yet during this time, different ethnic groups had come and gone. Obviously, ethnic cultural traditions could not explain the crime rate. In one of the classic studies of deviance, Shaw and McKay (1969) hypothesized that newcomers were continuously learning deviant ways from established residents, primarily in juvenile play groups and teenage gangs. Once the newcomers had absorbed the neighborhood norms and values, they in turn passed them on to the next wave of immigrants. More recent research (Akers et al. 1979) supports the role of learning in deviance.

In *Principles of Criminology* (1960) Edwin Sutherland and Donald Cressy expanded on this perspective by explaining how **cultural transmission**—the process by which deviance is learned through the transmission of norms within a community or group—takes place. Everyone is exposed to different and conflicting definitions of right and wrong. The standards that people eventually adopt as their own are learned through differential association with others. If individuals spend more time with deviants and have more intense relations with them, those influences will outweigh nondeviant influences on them. Through the transmission of norms within a community or group, people can be socialized to the drug subculture, the homosexual subculture, the so-called yuppie subculture that developed on Wall Street, and so on. Thus, some communities offer young people opportunities for education, role models of people who have achieved success by established means, and contacts with people who can help advance their careers through conventional channels. In contrast, other communities offer opportunities to learn how to hustle and to evade authorities, role models of people who have achieved success as gamblers and pimps, and contacts with people who control underworld career opportunities.

In his classic study of marijuana users, Howard Becker (1963) emphasized the role of associative learning and subcultures in deviance. Becker was writing at a time when marijuana was widely considered as dangerous as heroin, when use of the drug had not yet spread to the middle class, and when marijuana users constituted a deviant subculture. He found that the first time people smoked marijuana, most had either no reaction or extremely unpleasant reactions (spatial disorientation, sound distortion, severe thirst, and the like). Experienced users had to teach initiates how to smoke a joint and how to recognize its effects (if they had no reaction), or how to regulate the amount they smoked (if they had adverse reactions). Even more important, experienced users taught first-time users to redefine what was unpleasant and frightening as pleasant and desirable. One experienced marijuana user described his role as coach.

> [T]hey don't know what is happening to them. Because they think they're going to keep going up, up, up till they lose their minds or begin doing weird things or something. You have to reassure them, explain to them that they're not really flipping or anything, that they're gonna be alright. You have to just talk them out of being afraid. Keep talking to them, reassuring, telling them it's all right. And come on with your own story, you know: "The same thing happened to me. You'll get to like it after a while." Keep coming on like that; pretty soon you talk them out of being scared. And besides they see you doing it and nothing horrible is happening to you, so that gives them more confidence. (p. 55)

Deviant subcultures provide new definitions of nonconforming behavior, a vocabulary that justifies violation of norms, and, most important of all, social acceptance. Experienced marijuana users, who sometimes had "bad trips," also needed group support. Becker found that whether or not a person became an occasional or regular user depended on the extent of his or her participation in the marijuana subculture.

Subcultures serve another important role by providing members with a system of beliefs that explains and justifies their deviance. Homosexuals, for instance, believe that their persuasion is as natural for them as heterosexuality is for others (Simon and Gagnon 1970). Subcultures may even develop a public collective identity to fight against society's discriminatory ways: think of gay liberation and of the organizations dedicated to bettering the lot of ex-convicts.

Deviant behavior is transmitted through subcultures in the same way that the society's accepted norms are transmitted. For this reason, peer groups have an enormous influence on the values of young people. Graffiti to these youths is a way to put their messages and mark on the impersonal environment. To others it means defacing the buildings. (Barbara Burnes/Photo Researchers, Inc.)

In sum, differential association theory describes how deviance is learned from others and supported by a sympathetic subculture. This is unquestionably an important insight (Matsueda 1982). Yet it also has limitations. For one thing, the theory does not explain why a sizable number of people in a community in which deviant norms prevail do *not* become deviant. For instance, two persons may be exposed to criminal patterns, yet only one of them becomes a criminal. Moreover, differential association does not explain why deviance occurs in the first place. The functional approach to deviance provides an answer.

Social Functions of Deviance

The idea that deviance performs a necessary and important social function dates back to Émile Durkheim's *The Rules of Sociological Method*, published in 1895. In this working manual for students of society, Durkheim made the surprising statement that deviance is a natural part of social life, indeed "an integral part of all healthy societies" (1895/1958, p. 67). What did he mean? How can deviance be healthy for society?

Durkheim's answer had two parts. First, in defining certain kinds of behavior as deviant, a group or community also defines what behavior is acceptable. The boundaries between acceptable and unacceptable behavior are rarely hard and fast. Societies typically have a "permissive zone of variation" around even strongly supported and quite specific norms. In addition, most norms are not expressed as firm rules or official codes. Rather rules are defined in the course of people's day-to-day activities. By testing the boundaries of permissiveness, deviants force other members of society to think about what they believe is normal and proper.

Second, in uniting against the deviant, that group or community comes together and reaffirms its solidarity. Thus, when people in the Old West formed a posse, when parents unite to fight porno shops in their neighborhoods, when citizens vote for a new, more trustworthy politician, they are united by a sense of shared outrage against what brought them together—the outlaw who stole their horses, the adult bookstore owner who opened the shop, the corrupt politician who accepted bribes. The public trial of deviants not only reaffirms the norms and values that were threatened, it also allows members of a group or community to work together and to pour energy into shoring up the social order they believe in.

The sociologist Kai T. Erikson (1966) provides an illustration of the functional contributions that deviance makes to social order in his study *Wayward Puritans*. In 1630, when Anne Hutchinson began to proclaim that Boston's ministers did not have the exclusive right to interpret the Bible, she drew large audiences, angering the Puritan ministers who ruled colonial Boston. In challenging the ministers, she was challenging an entire way of life. Yet Mrs. Hutchinson was an upright, God-fearing citizen. There was no law against what she was saying; indeed, she was adept at citing passages from the Bible to support her beliefs and actions. The trial was tense, as the prosecution fumbled to establish a charge against her. Ultimately, Mrs. Hutchinson "hung herself" by stating that she communicated directly with God, a heresy for Puritans. Her punishment was expulsion from the community. "I desire to know wherefore I am banished," she said. Governor Winthrop gave her this answer: "Say no more, the court knows wherefore and is satisfied." "And that was exactly the point," writes Erikson (1966, pp. 100–101):

> The court *did* know why Mrs. Hutchinson had to be banished, but it did not know how to express that feeling in any language then known in New England. The settlers were experiencing a shift in ideological focus, a change in community boundaries, but they had no vocabulary to explain to themselves or anyone else what the nature of these changes were. The purpose of the trial was to invent that language, to find a name for the nameless offense which Mrs. Hutchinson had committed.

Anne Hutchinson, who was tried in the 1630s for challenging the nature of religious authority in colonial Boston, helped to strengthen the solidarity of the citizens who united to convict her. Thus, while her behavior was considered deviant, it actually served a purpose for the rest of the community. Are there any forms of deviant behavior in modern society that serve this purpose? (The Granger Collection.)

Thus, without realizing it, Anne Hutchinson helped the Massachusetts Bay Colony to redefine the limits of acceptable religious belief. And, somewhat ironically, she also contributed to the social solidarity of the community she left behind.

Although the times and the acts of deviance were very different, the men arrested in the insider trading scandal on Wall Street performed a similar function. The financial community had undergone rapid and profound change. Not only "rebels" such as corporate raider T. Boone Pickens and "innovators" such as Ivan Boesky, but also old, established financial houses that valued their public reputations for integrity were engaging in new activities for which few rules had been written. The scandal provided the excuse to stop and consider the boundaries of acceptable trading in stocks and bonds. As of the spring of 1987, nine bills to place stricter controls on Wall Street had been introduced in Congress (Nash 1987).

In addition to the functional aspects of helping groups and communities to define the boundaries of acceptable behavior, deviants may also serve as agents of social change. For example, the unwillingness of blacks to comply with segregation laws during the 1950s —considered criminal acts at the time—gave rise to a new legal and moral code. And during the past decade or so, efforts by women to achieve equality have also involved behavior—such as the refusal to relinquish their own last name upon marriage—that initially appeared, or may even still be thought of by some people, as deviant.

Elaborating on Durkheim's views of the functions of deviance, Nachman Ben-Yehuda (1985) showed that whether deviance leads to reaffirmation of existing social norms or serves as a catalyst for social change depends in part on the type of society in which it occurs. Simple, traditional societies—such as the Puritans of colonial Boston—tend to produce a high degree of consensus regarding acceptable behavior. In such societies, the identification and public trial of deviants usually lead to increased commitment to the status quo and conformity to existing norms. Complex, modern societies tend to be pluralistic—that is, there are many competing life-styles and moral points of view. "In such societies, values, norms, and moral boundaries are not given; they are negotiated" (Ben-Yehuda 1985, p. 15). Deviance more often leads to renegotiation of norms and social change. Thus the spreading use of marijuana as a "social drug" led to a relaxation of the laws against it, though not its complete legalization. The Wall Street scandal will probably lead to a renegotiation of regulations among members of Congress, SEC commissioners, and the heads of investment firms, but not to a set of specific laws that would drastically limit corporate takeovers. Consensus and conflict coexist in complex, modern societies. Such societies depend on education, secular rituals (such as Fourth of July celebrations), symbols, and ideas (such as "rule by law") to remind people of their common interests and identity.

Labeling Theory

Imagine two individuals who are addicted to different drugs. They cannot get going in the morning without a fix. By lunchtime their bodies are crying for more; if they do not get what they need, they become confused and irritable. During the afternoon they slip away from their desks for another hit. At the end of the workday, the only thing on their minds is another dose. They each know the drug they use is bad for them, but each feels that life is hardly worth living without it. Suppose, now, that one of these individuals is hooked on cocaine, whereas the other is hooked on nicotine, or merely caffeine. The first person will be labeled a "deviant," the second will not. And this, according to labeling theory, makes all the difference.

Labeling theory is unique among sociological theories of deviance in focusing, not on who commits deviant acts and why, but on the *process* of successfully **labeling** certain individuals and groups as deviant. This theory stresses the relativity of deviance. The same behavior may be labeled differently from one situation to another according to how the people involved respond to one another and negotiate their interaction. Labeling theory is based on action-oriented perspectives of social interaction, emphasizing that deviance is defined by people themselves in the context of a situation.

Labeling theory also helps explain the longer-term consequences of a deviant label on a person's social identity. This perspective originated in the work of sociologist Edwin M. Lemert (1951), who believed there was a crucial difference between primary and secondary deviance. Lemert defined **primary deviance** as the initial violation of a social norm, about which no inferences are made regarding motives or the character of the person who committed the act. Primary deviance occurs all the time. Nearly everyone breaks the law occasionally, but most people do not have criminal records. An exhaustive study found that nearly one in five people interviewed in a random sample had serious emotional and psychological problems, but none of those interviewed was confined to a mental hospital (Srole and Fischer 1978). However, a small number of primary deviants are singled out and labeled as "criminal," "mentally ill," "homosexual," and the like. Typically, people who have been labeled deviant are excluded from the mainstream of life. The man who has been convicted of a crime and sent to prison cannot get an honest job; the divorced woman who has been declared a lesbian is considered an unfit mother for her children; and so on.

One response to being labeled as deviant is to embrace the role (Goffman 1963b, p. 30). In **secondary deviance,** people come to define themselves as deviant and adopt a deviant life-style as a response to being labeled as deviant by others. A person can be deviant without being labeled as such, or be labeled without committing a deviant act. What matters is not the act, but the social label applied to the actor.

The sociologist William J. Chambliss (1973) found the labeling process at work at "Hannibal High School," where he identified two cliques, which Chambliss nicknamed the Saints and the Roughnecks.

The eight members of the Saints came from upper-middle-class families. They were good students and active in school affairs. On weekends and on days when they would sneak out of school, the Saints amused themselves with various forms of delinquency: heavy drinking, reckless driving, petty theft, vandalism, and games of "chicken." One of their favorite pastimes was to remove the wooden barricades and lanterns from street repair sites and watch unsuspecting drivers cruise into the hole. In spite of these hazardous activities, the people of the town considered them good boys who were sowing a few wild oats. The police did not arrest one Saint in the two years Chambliss spent at "Hannibal High" as an observer.

In contrast, the six Roughnecks were constantly in trouble with the police, and the townspeople considered them good-for-nothings. The Roughnecks came from lower-class families and were not particularly good students. Most weekends they could be found hanging around the local drugstore, drinking from concealed bottles of alcohol. About once a month they got into some sort of fight—usually among themselves. The Roughnecks also engaged in petty theft. Even so, Chambliss estimates that property damage done by the Saints cost the townspeople *more* than the Roughnecks' thefts. And although the Saints rarely fought, they endangered their own and other people's lives nearly every time they got behind the wheel of a car.

Why did the townspeople excuse the Saints but condemn the Roughnecks as delinquents? The Saints dressed well, drove expensive cars, and spoke politely to teachers, police, and other authority figures. Anyone could see that they were "good boys," tomorrow's leaders. The Roughnecks were different: "Everybody agreed that the not-so-well-dressed, not-so-well-mannered, not-so-rich boys were heading for trouble (1973, p. 27). In addition, the police knew that the Saints' upper-middle-class parents would cause trouble if their sons were arrested. The Roughnecks' parents lacked the power and influence to fight back. In short, the community's social structure protected the Saints but not the Roughnecks. Through selective perception and labeling, the visible, poor, defiant "tough kids" were identified as "delinquents," whereas the equally delinquent middle-class youth went unnoticed.

This is not the end of the story. With few exceptions, the Saints and Roughnecks lived up (or down) to the community's expectations. Several members of the Roughnecks were arrested repeatedly, not only as teenagers but also as young adults. In contrast, the Saints left adolescence behind, moved along middle-class pathways, and remembered their delinquency fondly as a youthful fling.

As this example suggests, deviant labels tend to become self-fulfilling prophecies. The labeling process pushes people toward a **deviant career,** the adoption of a deviant life-style and identity within a supporting subculture. Cut off, the addict begins to associate almost exclusively with other addicts, the prostitute with other prostitutes, and so on. Gradually they learn from more experienced offenders the various techniques for deviating. Equally important, they learn rationalizations for deviant behavior. For example, prostitutes grow to regard their work as a social service and consider those who condemn sex for money as hypocrites. The deviant subculture begins to play an increasingly central role in the person's identity and life-style. As one addict told a researcher, she realized she was addicted when she

noticed that all her friends were junkies (Becker 1963). In sum, by labeling certain people deviant and shutting them out of conventional life, society virtually *ensures* the behavior that it is trying to prevent.

While this description of the drift into deviant careers is compelling, it may overstate the facts. Labeling theorists imply that the people who fill the wards of mental hospitals, for example, are there because someone more or less arbitrarily decided to label them sick and subject them to the consequences. They tend to ignore the fact that most of the people in mental hospitals were unable to cope with their lives and their problems outside. Sociological studies have found that both families and authorities usually consider commitment to a mental hospital as a last resort (Gove 1975, 1979).

Labeling theorists also tend to pay relatively little attention to the fact that not all labeled people accept their stigma (strong negative label) passively. Mentally retarded people who have been released from institutions, for instance, go to great lengths to hide their stigma not only from others but also from themselves (Edgerton 1967). In addition to those who hide their stigma, others actively seek out their labels. The punk rockers who appeared in the late 1970s went to considerable lengths—mohawks, multiple ear piercings, dyed hair, etc.—to appear deviant.

It is also true that some labels can be shed. Many alcoholics, for example, have been able to delabel themselves by joining Alcoholics Anonymous, an organization that makes it possible for problem drinkers to replace their stigmatized deviant status with a socially acceptable "repentant role" (Trice and Roman 1970).

All this is not to say that labeling theory is "wrong," but that it only partly explains deviant careers. It does not explain why people violate rules in the first place or why some people are able to resist or overcome the stigma of deviance. The Saints were able to resist labeling because of their middle-class connections and manners. Will those implicated in the Wall Street scandal be able to return to their communities and pick up where they left off? Will Wall Street be able to fend off efforts to place tighter restrictions on financial activities by convincing Congress that it can successfully police itself? Such questions point to the social identities of deviants, and issues of social control, as part of any explanation of deviance. These are addressed by the Marxist perspective described in the next section.

Why Women Are Outsiders to Insider Trading

Lois L. Evans is chairperson of the Federal Home Loan Bank of New York. Her daughter, Heather H. Evans, is chief financial officer of a film production company. At the height of the Wall Street scandal, the Evanses wrote to the *New York Times* about "missing persons" in the insider trading scams.

Why is it that no women were among the professionals indicted in the recent Wall Street insider trading scandal? . . .

Approximately one-quarter of the Street's professionals, and a larger share of corporate lawyers, are women. Moreover, eight of the men indicted are younger than 35. Proportionately, the number of women in this age group is even higher. Simple statistical probability suggests that at least three women should have been in the indicted group. Perhaps something more than probability is at work here.

Businessmen, it seems, are still too uncomfortable with women to include them in the sort of network of trust and complicity that forms an insider trading ring . . . .

One clear example of a close male relationship that excludes women is locker room conversation. The men's locker room at New York's Vertical Club was purportedly a forum for the exchange of information among the trading ring called the "Yuppie five." . . .

Men's resistance to sharing sensitive information with women has [also] kept women out of mergers and acquisitions and arbitrage, the specialties that involve the most sensitive, confidential information. Chief executive officers already mistrust Wall Street types, but a female outsider is even worse in their view. Mergers and acquisitions are therefore the last bastion of maleness in corporate finance departments. . . .

As partial outsiders, women can more easily retain the sense of perspective that causes noninvestment bankers to wonder why Dennis Levine, who at age 33 was earning more than a million dollars a year, would be motivated to steal. Our mere presence on Wall Street is too newly and dearly won to jeopardize it.

Moreover, a Wall Street job is a significant achievement for any woman. While women [on Wall Street] are constantly made aware of their specialness by colleagues, friends and neighbors, men may feel a greater need to distinguish themselves from the pack.

The drive to be a star also encourages bravado. Mr. Levine drove an $80,000 Ferrari and boasted about his million dollar earnings. This showy materialism is representative of the rising, somewhat crass breed of younger investment bankers.

Such showiness, however, is considered particularly unattractive in women. Even if an ostentatious woman could muscle her way into acceptance among chauvinistic security bankers, she would soon recognize that swearing and flashing a wad of bills would turn off clients as well as colleagues. Modesty among women is rewarded over bravado. . . .

Although women have the opportunity and the power to be corrupted, they have not as yet succumbed.

Perhaps absolute power corrupts absolutely—only if you're male.

Source: New York Times, February 12, 1987, p. A27.

The Marxist Perspective

The various theories we have described so far imply that all members of a society have an equal chance at being defined as deviant and an equal stake in limiting deviance. Marxists disagree sharply with these presumptions. In their view, the labeling and treatment of deviants reflect the structure of power in a society. In the Marxist view, those who control the economic life of a society also control its morality, because norms serve to support the economic system. As a result, the severity of society's response to the violation of its norms depends on how much the violation threatens the economic system. For example, some Marxists would argue that drug addiction was temporarily tolerated by the ruling class because it affected mainly the disadvantaged—poor people, blacks,

These workers are removing toxic waste to a safe location. Careless disposal of toxic waste is an example of a corporate crime against society. It can threaten the health and safety of a community, and damage the environment and the economy. Marxists would say that the power wielded by corporations protects them from punishment for this form of negligence. (Dale Wittner/West Stock, Inc.)

and the like. However, once levels of drug use and drug-related problems increased among middle-class whites, the social action against drugs intensified.

Viewed from the Marxist perspective, law is "first and foremost a reflection of the interests of the governing class" (Chambliss 1974, p. 34). The criminal justice system reflects the values and interests of those who have the power to control the legislative, policing, and judi-

cial processes. This image of law sharply contrasts with the ideals of "equality before the law" and the "separation of powers." Marxists argue that such ideals obscure the underlying reality of class conflict. The legal order serves the interests of the ruling class rather than the collective will and general good of the people. The state designates acts as criminal because they run counter to the interests of those in power (Quinney 1979).

Marxists further point out that the nation's policing efforts are directed toward controlling the crimes of the disadvantaged—burglary, theft, robbery, vandalism, drug use, public intoxication, and traffic offenses. Violations against consumers or the commonwealth, such as water or air pollution, are typically handled by regulatory agencies that enjoy little power and minimal funding. The Federal Bureau of Investigation, for example, routinely records every murder, rape, assault, and auto theft reported in the nation. Law-enforcement agencies also log thefts from corporations. But no agency tracks crimes commited by the corporations themselves.

The sociologist Amitai Etzioni estimates that two-thirds of America's 500 largest corporations have broken the law, in varying degrees, during the past ten years (in Gellerman, 1986). In one case recently uncovered, the crime was described by investigative agents as a kind of murder. The Johns-Manville Corporation is one of the oldest and largest manufacturers of asbestos in the United States. Evidence that exposure to asbestos dust causes debilitating, often fatal, lung disease began appearing in medical journals in the late 1920s. Executives at Johns-Manville knew about this information, but did nothing to warn or protect its workers. To the contrary, the Johns-Manville executives suppressed research on the dangers of working with asbestos, instructed company physicians not to tell workers when their chest X-rays showed symptoms of asbestosis, and quietly settled workers' claims out of court. This deadly cover-up continued for forty years (Calhoun and Hiller 1988).

To Marxists, corporate crime is not a surprise. The capitalist system, in their view, is based on exploitation, and they consider the idea that corporations would demonstrate social responsibility and ethical conduct a delusion. From their perspective, the Wall Street scandal was little more than a scrap on the playing fields of capitalism, or capitalists trying to beat other capitalists at their own game. Moreover, the scandal illustrated cooperation between financiers and the agencies that are supposed to regulate them. When Boesky was caught, he made a deal with the SEC. To be sure, he was required to pay a huge fine ($100 million). He was also permitted to quietly unload $440 million in securities *before* the charges against him were made public, which saved him an estimated $100 million. The SEC rationalized this arrangement on the grounds that if Boesky had sold these shares after the announcement, the stock market would have plummeted and countless innocent investors would have been hurt. Marxists would see this as an example of capitalists helping their fellow capitalists.

The Marxist perspective calls attention to the element of power behind social definitions of deviance. Often, the degree to which a given act is viewed as deviant is not a measure of the amount of harm done to individuals or society, but a measure of the power of those who consider the behavior unacceptable versus the power of those who step across the line. A major criticism of the Marxist perspective is that it fails to identify the specific individuals and groups that make up what it calls the "capitalist elite" or "governing class." Related to that, it fails to recognize power conflicts within the governing class itself. In addition, it does not explain the power wielded by outside interest groups. Beginning in the 1960s, the consumer protection group headed by Ralph Nader ("Nader's Raiders"), hardly a "capitalist tool," was able to lobby the federal government to protect consumers against faulty and dangerous products, such as rear-engine automobiles. A very current example is the public pressure leading to ever-stronger rules against cigarette smoking, despite objections by the capitalists who profit from the sale of cigarettes.

SOCIAL CONTROL AND DEVIANCE

Social control refers to a group's or society's efforts to regulate itself (Janowitz 1978). It entails motivating people to behave in ways that serve their collective interest and solve their collective problems. Social control depends on voluntary (if grudging) cooperation. Ideally, it is the opposite of coercive control, which depends on the threat or use of force. In practice, however, the most effective system of social control requires an element of coercion. To be emphatic, even the most rigidly totalitarian system (the society in George Orwell's novel *1984* or a penitentiary) depends on some minimum degree of compliance.

Social controls operate on a number of different levels. Consider the warnings against smoking. Cigarettes are one of the greatest preventable health hazards known. Since the first Surgeon General's Report warning of the dangers of smoking was published in 1964, evidence of harm, to smokers as well as to the people around them, has mounted. Yet millions continue to endanger their lives by smoking. What can be done to control smoking? One possibility is to outlaw smoking in designated public places; steps have already been taken in this direction. Since the mid-1970s, smoking has been banned in department and grocery stores, theaters and churches, buses and subways, and other public places, and smokers have been segregated from nonsmokers on trains and planes and in restaurants and offices. The problem with efforts to outlaw smoking altogether is that this probably would create a black market, as Prohibition did in the 1920s. A different approach to controlling smoking relies on informal pressures. Numerous studies (Chassin et al. 1984, Hirschman et al. 1984, Krohn et al. 1985) show that teenagers are most likely to start smoking if their friends smoke, if their friends define smoking as "sexy" and "cool" (and not smoking as "chicken"), and if smoking brings the social reward of feeling closer to other people. Conversely, adolescents are less likely to smoke if their friends do not smoke, if they define smoking as harmful and stupid, and if their friends make derogatory comments if they light up. (Note the impact of differential association.) But informal pressure alone is not enough. The same studies show that youngsters are most likely to give in to peer pressure to smoke if they have a pattern of disregarding authority and of engaging in risky behavior. Ultimately, the strongest and surest control on smoking (and by implication other deviant behavior) is internal.

Internalization

On the internal level, social control rests on socialization, the process by which a society transmits its values and norms to its new members (see Chapter 5). Sociologists use the term **internalization** to describe the process by which cultural standards become part of a person's personality structure. Through internalization, people thoroughly accept certain social norms and values. They abide by these rules not because they fear punishment but because following the rules seems "natural" —deviance does not even come to mind. As members in good standing within a group, people simply do what other group members do. Further, deviating from the group's norms makes most people feel guilty and disoriented. In an important sense, internalized norms and values form the basis of social order, for people police themselves. Social control becomes self-control.

But socialization is never perfect; people may not internalize all the rules that society deems "proper" and "right." Moreover, many situations that arise are not covered by the rules, and people must improvise new behaviors. Because socialization is not adequate to ensure conformity, external constraints are required. Sociologists term these constraints **sanctions**—rewards for conforming to a social norm or penalties for violating a social norm.

Informal Social Controls

Some sanctions are applied informally. **Informal social control** involves subtle and unofficial pressure to conform to norms and values. It is effective because people want to live up to the expectations of others, even in ways they do not always consciously or explicitly recognize. Positive informal sanctions include a smile, praise, and a kiss; negative informal sanctions include ostracism, ridicule, and verbal and physical threats. Informal social controls are so tightly woven into the fabric of everyday life that it is easy to overlook their impact.

From his studies of how people interact with one another, the social anthropologist Erving Goffman (1967) concluded that people go to great lengths to keep up appearances. Most conversations, according to Goffman, are "ritual exchanges" in which the main object is to avoid awkward moments. We expect that each person will cover up conversational lulls, or at least pretend to be interested in the speaker, and end the conversation tactfully. Should someone say something rude or engage in an inappropriate emotional display, we hold in reserve a variety of techniques for repairing the breach. Ideally, the offending party offers an apology or excuse, the injured party bestows forgiveness, and the offender concludes with an expression of gratitude. Such ritual gestures allow everyone to feel that social order has somehow been restored.

Embarrassment plays a particularly powerful role in the workings of informal social control. Goffman believed that the discomfort we feel when we are embar-

rassed creates a strong motivation to avoid engaging in behavior that again will produce social disapproval.

In Goffman's view, informal social controls satisfy the basic social requirement that people be able to predict one another's behavior. The obligations and expectations associated with roles achieve this end (see Chapter 3). You are obligated to conform to the rules associated with a particular role and others expect you to conform. When rules are broken, both parties in a reciprocal role relationship are discredited. Hence, it is to everyone's advantage to obey the rules.

Nonconformity can incur informal penalties ranging from mild disapproval to differential treatment. For example, patients who conform quietly to hospital norms and procedures typically receive better care than those who interrupt well-established routines by arguing with staff members and by complaining excessively about pain and discomfort. These latter individuals acquire the label "problem patients." Consequently they may encounter deliberate neglect, early discharge, or referral to a psychiatrist. Word about "problem patients" travels quickly through hospitals, and thereafter staff members are less likely to define their complaints as legitimate (Lorber 1975).

Formal Social Controls

Formal social control involves direct and official pressures to conform to social norms and values. Some control is the product of special organizations such as police departments, legislatures, courts, prisons, juvenile facilities, drug rehabilitation centers, and settlement houses. It tends to be coercive. The medical system, especially psychiatry, also operates as an agency of social control by defining who is "sick" and then by managing "illness." Likewise, the welfare system, particularly as embodied in the activities of social workers, defines who is eligible for various benefits and polices conformity to the rules for welfare assistance. Further, viewed in Marxist terms, the entire corporate system dominates the economy, deciding which activities in the production and distribution of goods and services are legitimate and which are deviant.

Formal social control implies power—sometimes coercion—to regulate the behavior of individuals and groups. Marxists, in particular, ask who is controlling whom, by what means, under what circumstances, and for what reasons (Schur 1980).

The relationship between deviance and formal social control is a complex one. Agents and agencies of social control and the deviants they are supposed to control are not entirely opposite and separate. To the contrary, they are intertwined in significant ways. First, the police, mental health workers, and other agents of social control are themselves subject to norms and sanctions. In some cases, the line between legitimate and illegitimate control is clear (for example, reading a prisoner the Miranda rights); in others, however, it is subject to interpretation. Second, law enforcers often rely on lawbreakers to obtain information. In drug control, for example, the police routinely allow street dealers to continue to operate in the hope that small-scale dealers will lead them to major suppliers. Ivan Boesky was able to negotiate with the SEC because he agreed to have his conversations taped.

Third, the creation of new rules and laws often has the unintended consequence of creating new forms of crime and deviance. The 1986 immigration bill illustrates the last point (Reinhold 1986). The law allows immigrants who have resided in this country continuously since January 1, 1982, to become legal residents. At the same time, the law makes it a crime for employers to knowingly hire workers who do not have the necessary documents. As a result, the market for fake Social Security cards, rent receipts, income tax forms, and birth certificates is booming.

In small, traditional societies, where there is a high degree of consensus about what is and what is not acceptable, informal controls are usually sufficient to contain deviance. However, in complex, modern societies, where there are many competing ideas of right and wrong, formal social controls are necessary. As a result, behavior that might be handled through social pressure and shame in a small society is redefined as a crime and punishable by fines, imprisonment, and other formal sanctions. We now turn to an examination of crime and its activation of the criminal justice system.

CRIME AND CRIMINAL JUSTICE

A **crime** is a violation of a norm that has been entered into the law and is backed by the power and authority of the state. Although crime and deviance often coincide, they are not identical. Crimes are not necessarily viewed as deviant, and deviance is not always a crime. Here again, social definitions are important. Most people do not consider driving five to ten miles above the speed limit on the open highway deviant, for example, but it is against the law. On the other hand, most people would consider a man who withdrew all his money from the bank and walked down the street passing out $100 bills to strangers deviant, but there is nothing illegal in what he is doing. The main difference between the two activities

Buying and selling illegal drugs are classified as crimes because society finds such behavior unacceptable. Yet their illegality has fostered a complex social structure and an international subterranean society that appears beyond social control. What, then, should society do about controlling dangerous drugs? (Hugh Patrick Brown/Sygma.)

is that crimes are illegal and carry the threat of formal sanctions (fines, prison sentences, and the like).

Like other forms of deviance, crime is not absolute; what constitutes a crime changes with the times. Some crimes that were once considered serious, such as smoking marijuana, are now receiving less attention. Other illegal activities that used to be largely neglected, such as dumping industrial wastes in unauthorized areas, are now receiving greater attention. Boesky and other financiers involved in the insider trading scandal were charged with crimes that didn't exist ten years ago, before the takeover mania.

Changing definitions of crime are prompted not only by changes in norms and values; social control agencies also influence the formulation of laws. The mental health establishment, for example, has contributed to the redefinition of many former crimes as "medical problems" (Conrad and Schneider 1980). For a long time alcoholism was considered a sign of moral weakness, and behaviors that were associated with excessive drinking (disorderly conduct, public intoxication) were treated as crimes. Today, alcoholism is widely viewed as a disease, and many alcohol-related offenses have been decriminalized (made legal), and the offenders are more likely to be treated as sick persons. In less than a quarter century, the "crime" of homosexuality was redefined as a mental illness, and was then redefined again as an alternative life-style (Bayer 1981). Laws against homosexual acts are still on the books, but they are rarely enforced.

Despite highly publicized examples of decriminalization (drunkenness, homosexuality, and abortion), the overall trend in the United States has been toward more rather than fewer legal restrictions. States have passed more than 500,000 new criminal laws in this century (Calahan 1979). This raises the question of whether the United States is becoming "overcriminalized" in its attempt to deal with the growing problems of crime.

Types of Crime

There are many types of crime. Perhaps the crime with which we are most familiar is **index crime**—those crimes that the Federal Bureau of Investigation cites in its annual *Uniform Crime Reports*. Local and regional police agencies are required by law to submit data to the FBI on two types of offenses, Type I and Type II crimes. Type I crimes, those with criminal intent, include both crimes against people—murder, rape, robbery, and assault—and crimes against property—burglary, theft, auto theft, and arson (see Table 7.2 and Figure 7.2).

TABLE 7.2 National Crime Rate, 1985, and Percentage Change Since 1976

Index Crime	Number Reported	Rate per 100,000	Percent Change* Since 1976
Violent Crime			
Murder and non-negligent manslaughter	18,980	7.9	−10.2
Forcible rape	87,340	36.6	+37.6
Aggravated assault	723,250	302.9	+29.9
Robbery	497,870	208.5	+4.6
Total	1,327,440	556.0	+18.9
Property Crime			
Burglary	3,073,300	1,287.3	−11.1
Larceny-theft	6,926,400	2,901.2	−0.7
Motor vehicle theft	1,102,900	462.0	+2.7
Total	11,102,600	4,650.5	−3.5
Total Index Crime 12,430,000			

*Change in rate

Source: Uniform Crime Reports for the United States, 1985. Washington, DC: U.S. Department of Justice, Federal Bureau of Investigation, p. 41, Table 1.

FIGURE 7.2   Crime in the United States

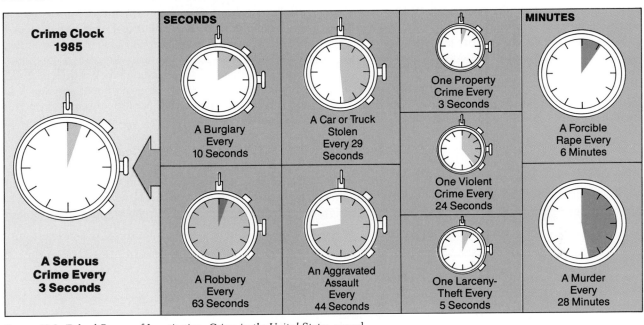

Source: U.S. Federal Bureau of Investigation, *Crime in the United States*, annual.

Type II crimes include white-collar crime, prostitution, sex offenses, gambling, vandalism, and receiving stolen property. In reporting Type I crimes to the FBI, police agencies include data on *all crimes* known to them as well as the number of arrests made, number of people charged, weapons used, and so on. For Type II crimes only *arrests* are reported (*Crime in the U.S.* 1982).

Official statistics on crime are based on reports from law enforcement agencies. Not all agencies required to report to the FBI do so, and the FBI makes estimates when it publishes its annual crime reports. Moreover, when a criminal incident involves more than one crime, such as a robbery that results in a death, only the most serious crime (murder, in this example) is counted (*Crime in the U.S.* 1982). Local politics can also have a profound impact on the reporting of crime to the FBI. If a local police department is seeking a substantial budget increase, for example, it may exaggerate either the extent of crime in its area or the number of people it has arrested, depending on which will justify the largest budget increase. However, most official statistics under-

estimate crime. Some crimes are never detected: Others are detected but not reported. Crime surveys indicate that, overall, about half of all crimes are not reported (Shogan 1984). According to estimates by the U.S. Department of Justice, only 30.7 percent of all motor vehicle thefts, 58.5 percent of all rapes, and somewhat less than half of all robberies, aggravated assaults, and burglaries are reported to the police. At 72.5 percent, larcenies and thefts are most likely to be reported (*Criminal Victimization* 1980). Victims' decisions about whether to report a crime are based on how much good they think the police can do and on how serious the crime is.

Crimes Without Victims

We think of crime as having an identifiable victim who suffers as a result of another person's criminal behavior. Some crimes, however, do not have a victim in this sense. So-called **victimless crime** includes prostitution, illegal sexual acts among consenting adults, illicit drug use, gambling, and drunkenness (see Table 7.3). These acts are designated in the society's criminal laws as crimes because the community as a whole, or powerful groups within the community, regard them as morally repugnant. The laws are intended to uphold certain moral standards of society.

Crimes without victims are highly controversial, although some people argue that these acts are not victimless. Every year tens of thousands of innocent people are killed by drunken drivers, and compulsive gamblers rob their families of needed income. Prostitutes who carry the AIDS virus can spread the disease to others, and drug users are victims of their own addiction even if they do not steal to support their habit. According to this view, *self*-destructive behavior (which may harm others, directly or indirectly) should be controlled. Other people question whether the government should be in the business of legislating morality. According to this view, no one has the right to tell consenting adults what they can or cannot do in the privacy of their homes. Still other critics take a pragmatic stance that when a significant proportion of the population desires certain goods and services, the laws prohibiting their sale are counterproductive. Not only are such laws difficult to enforce, they create black markets and opportunities for organized crime.

TABLE 7.3   Arrests for Crimes Without Victims, 1986

Crime	Estimated Number of Arrests
Prostitution and commercialized vice	97,000
Drug abuse violations (all)	692,000
Illegal gambling	26,000
Drunkenness	778,000
Curfew, loitering (juveniles)	73,000
Runaways (juvenile)	139,000

Source: Statistical Abstract of the United States, 1987, 1988. Washington, DC: U.S. Department of Commerce, Bureau of the Census.

Organized Crime

Everybody knows about **organized crime** from the mass media, but ideas about what constitutes a crime syndicate vary. The state of Oregon comes as close as any to a concise definition: "Organized crime is a self-perpetuating, continuing conspiracy operating for profit

Prostitution is often categorized as a victimless crime. But because it violates accepted moral values, it is considered illegal in most of the United States. Who is being hurt, directly or indirectly, by prostitution? What social forces perpetuate it? (Ethan Hoffman/Archive Pictures, Inc.)

or power, seeking to obtain immunity from the law through fear and corruption" (in Abadinsky 1981, p. 4). Organized crime differs from other businesses in its heavy involvement in illegal activities and in its almost routine use of bribery and violence. It differs from other types of crime in its reach and organization. But crime syndicates are not organized on the bureaucratic model of legitimate large-scale businesses; rather they are organized like traditional societies in which kinship and patron-client relationships override all other obligations (Ianni 1972).

Organized crime specializes in the provision of illegal goods and services, including selling illegal drugs; fencing stolen and illegal products (untaxed cigarettes and alcohol, illegal handguns, illegally produced tapes and records, stolen credit cards, and the like; and loan-sharking (charging interest above the legal limit). Illegal services provided by organized crime further include bookmaking (bets on horse races and sporting events), the numbers (a form of lottery), gambling, and prostitution. In addition, organized crime provides legal goods and services by illegal means. In many cities, organized crime exercises a monopoly over garbage collection, vending machines, and taxi and limousine services, monopolies achieved through the bribery of public officials and by the use or threat of violence against potential competitors. Organized crime may also use legitimate companies to "launder" money earned through illegal activities by investing it in such respectable assets as real estate and stocks and bonds.

Crime syndicates often develop among immigrants who are not sufficiently familiar with the mainstream culture to participate in its economy and who are suspicious of the police and other authorities who do not speak their language. As a result, organized crime has followed the pattern of "ethnic succession." The Irish crime syndicates in the nineteenth century were followed by European Jews. And then, in the 1920s, by Italians, whose crime families gained power during Prohibition. When alcohol was legalized again in the 1930s, the Italian syndicates had the capital, the experience, the personnel, and the overseas contacts to move into the heroin trade. In the 1960s, most heroin was made from opium grown in Turkey, processed in Marseilles, France, or Corsica, and then sold in the United States. In the 1970s, however, Turkey cracked down on opium production. Groups with contacts in other opium-producing nations—Mexico, Colombia, Paki-

stan, Iran, and Southeast Asian countries—began to move in. Today's crime syndicates have been described as "a United Nations of drug smugglers, including Chinese, Thais, Pakistanis, Indians, Iranians, Afghans, Nigerians, and Israelis" (Kerr 1987, p. 1).

White-Collar and Corporate Crime

One man robs a gas station of $250 and is sent to prison for six months; another man makes $2.5 million on illegal stock trades and is required only to return the money (plus "interest" in the form of fines). Terrorists plant a bomb in a diplomat's car; when caught, they are charged with conspiracy and criminal homicide. Ford Motor Company sold millions of Pintos, even though its own tests had shown that the rear-mounted gas tank might explode if the car were hit from the back. Over the next eight years, 500 people were burned to death in accidents involving Pintos. Ford paid millions of dollars in damages, but was found innocent of criminal charges. No one went to jail. As these examples suggest, the social response to white-collar and corporate crime is quite different from the treatment of "common criminals."

The term **white-collar crime** was first used by the sociologist Edwin Sutherland (1949, p. 9) to refer to "a crime committed by a person of respectability and high status in the course of his occupation." Embezzlement, padding expense accounts, stealing from an employer, and personal income tax evasion all fall into this category. So does the misuse of public funds by government officials (accepting bribes, padding payrolls, and the like). One difference between white-collar and "common" crime is that the former more often relies on the sophisticated manipulation of records and concealment than on physical force. A second difference is the magnitude of the crime: In general, white-collar crimes are more costly. For example, bank embezzlers steal an average of $23,000 apiece, whereas bank robbers steal only one-eighth as much ($3,000 or less). A third difference is the treatment of offenders. Ninety percent of bank robbers go to prison, but only about 17 percent of embezzlers are put behind bars (Clinard and Yeager 1980).

White-collar crimes are committed for personal gain; **corporate crimes** are illegal acts committed on behalf of a formal organization. As in the Ford Pinto case, many individuals may be involved in a corporate

Corporate crimes may harm customers, employers, owners, or the public-at-large. The demonstrators in this photograph are protesting pollution caused by a manufacturer. Environmental pollution typically constitutes a crime against the public-at-large. (Jacques Gardin/ Sygma.)

crime, directly or indirectly, knowingly or unknowingly. The primary goal of such crimes is to boost company profits (or avoid losses). Unlike other criminals, corporations are not persons and cannot be jailed. Charges against them are usually filed in the civil courts (in the form of individual or class-action lawsuits), rather than in the criminal courts. Indeed, corporate crimes are often handled outside the court system by government regulatory agencies (the SEC, Federal Trade Commission, Environmental Protection Agency, and the like). In most cases, sanctions against the lawbreakers take the form of relatively small fines in relation to earnings (see Table 7.4).

David Ermann and Michael Lundman (1982) identify four types of corporate crime. The Ford Pinto case was an example of a *crime against customers.* This category includes not only the sale of unsafe products but also false advertising and price fixing. A second type is *crime against employees.* In the previously mentioned Johns-Manville case, workers were knowingly exposed to harmful levels of asbestos dust. Unfair hiring and promotion policies and mismanagement of pension funds are also crimes against employees. The third type of corporate deviance is *crime against the public-at-large.* The case of Love Canal is one example of a corporation's blatant disregard of public welfare (Ermann and Lundman 1982). In 1947 the Hooker Chemical and Plastics Corporation purchased Love Canal to use as a dump for toxic wastes. When the site had outlived its usefulness, Hooker donated it to the local school board for $1. Innocent of the potential danger, the board built a school on part of the site and sold the rest to a housing developer. Over the years, complaints from residents of Love Canal about chemical burns, high cancer rates, and other health problems mounted, but Hooker did nothing. Finally, in 1978, the New York health commissioner took action, declaring that residents of Love Canal were in "great and immediate peril," ordering the evacuation of pregnant women and children under age two, and closing the school. Extensive press coverage of Love Canal was in part responsible for public awareness of the dangers of chemical dumps: Hooker was not alone. The fourth type of corporate deviance rarely makes newspaper headlines. If *crimes against owners* are reported at all, it is on the business page. What does this phrase mean? Most major corporations are "owned" by large numbers of small independent stockholders. In most cases, stockholders have no more information about how a company is being run than does the general public, and few of them attend the annual stockholders' meetings that are required by law. When corporate officers act in their own best interests at the expense of stockholders, they are committing crimes against the corporation's owners.

The most obvious explanation of corporate crime is profit (Ermann and Lundman 1982, p. 70). For example, in 1972 it would have cost Johns-Manville $12 million to install dust control equipment, and $5 million a year to maintain this equipment, whereas paying workmen's compensation only cost the company $1

To a person earning $15,000 a year (a decent salary in 1970), the fines levied on corporations might seem enormous. When viewed as a percentage of income, however, the same fines seem insignificant. Column 3 translates corporate fines into equivalent fines for the wage earner.

Table 7.4   **Large Nonsubsidiary Corporations Involved in 1961 and 1976 Price-Fixing Cases**

Corporation	Gross Revenues	Criminal Fine [a]	Equivalent for Individual Earning $15,000 [b]
1961 Defendants			
Allis-Chalmers	$ 502,200,000	$127,500	$ 3.75
Carrier	266,300,000	7,500	0.42
Cutler-Hammer	118,300,000	45,000	5.70
Federal Pacific	88,200,000	65,000	10.95
Foster Wheeler	197,900,000	20,000	1.50
General Electric	4,456,800,000	437,500	1.47
I-T-E	111,500,000	92,500	12.30
Ingersoll Rand	181,400,000	20,000	1.65
McGraw-Edison	329,200,000	70,000	3.15
Square D	115,300,000	75,000	9.75
Wagner Electric	65,900,000	10,000	2.25
Westinghouse	1,913,800,000	372,500	2.85
Worthington	189,000,000	20,000	1.50
1976 Defendants			
American Can	3,142,500,000	50,000	0.24
Champion International	2,910,500,000	50,000	0.26
Diamond International	887,100,000	50,000	0.84
Federal Paper	393,600,000	50,000	1.80
International Paper	3,540,000,000	50,000	0.21
Mead	1,599,300,000	50,000	0.47
Potlatch	624,100,000	50,000	1.20
St. Regis	1,642,100,000	50,000	0.45
Weyerhauser	2,868,400,000	50,000	0.26

[a] 1961 data reported in *The New York Times*, February 7, 1961, p. 26 and February 2, 1961; 1976 data reported in "Notice of Hearing on Proposed Class Action Settlements and Proposed Plan of Distribution" In Re Folding Carton Antitrust Litigation, U.S. District Court, Northern District of Illinois, Eastern Division, MDL 250, July 26, 1979.

[b] To determine equivalent for individual earning $15,000, we first divided the criminal fine by 1961 gross revenues. The resulting figure was then multiplied by $15,000. For example, Allis-Chalmers was fined $127,500 and had gross revenues of $502,200,000; $127,500 divided by $502,200,000 equals .00025 and .00025 times $15,000 equals $3.75, the equivalent for an individual earning $15,000.

Source: M. David Ermann and Richard I. Lundman, 1982. *Corporate Deviance.* New York; Holt, Rinehart and Winston.

million a year. Protecting workers was not "cost effective" for Johns-Manville. More subtly, the structure of corporations encourages these types of crime.

The complexity of organizations also makes it exceedingly difficult to discover, investigate, and prose-cute corporate crime. Figure 7.3 presents ten rationalizations of corporate crime (Clinard and Yeager 1980).

The costs of white-collar and corporate crime far exceed the costs of other crimes. Government experts estimate that violations of federal antitrust, tax, fraud,

FIGURE 7.3   Rationalizations of Corporate Crime

Legal barriers represent government interference with the free enterprise system.

Governmental regulations drink up costs, slow down progress, and cut heavily into profits.

Governmental regulations are incomprehensible and too complex to bother with.

Most corporate violations are unintentional: many of them are errors of omission rather than commission, and many are mistakes.

Our competitors are breaking the law and getting away with it. If we don't do the same, we'll lose business.

By doing this, we can save (or make) millions, and it will cost each of our customers only pennies.

If there is no increase in corporate profits a violation is not wrong.

We *have* to do this in order to: protect the value of our stock, ensure an adequate return for our stockholders, or protect the job security of our employees.

Source: Adapted from Clinard and Yeager 1980, pp. 69–72 passim.

If these rationalizations sound familiar, it is because they are not unlike ones used by kids and adults when they cheat. Most of them invoke norms of one kind or another to normalize a deviant act: it was harmless. It actually did good. The rules are unfair or oppressive anyway. I had to do it to protect myself.

bribery, and other laws cost the nation *billions* of dollars each year. Many more lives are lost through corporate "negligence" than by individual criminal homicide (Clinard and Yeager 1980, p. 9). But until quite recently, the public generally regarded "crime in the streets" as far more serious than "crime in the suites." Attitudes are changing. Recent polls show that people are more concerned about corporations polluting the water supplies than about burglaries, and regard price fixing as more serious than muggings (Wolfgang 1980). Nevertheless, most discussions of crime control focus on common or index crimes.

The Control of Crime

From an international perspective, crime in the United States appears to be out of control. The number of murders committed in Manhattan alone each year is the same as that committed in all of England and Wales, more burglaries are committed each year in Chicago than in all of Japan, there are more cases of drug addiction in Los Angeles than in all the countries of Western Europe combined (Radzinowicz and King 1977). Between 1960 and 1976 one's chances of being murdered, robbed, raped, or assaulted in the United States nearly tripled (Silberman 1980). Although some crime rates in the United States have declined somewhat from their peak in 1981, others remain very high compared to other nations or to pre-1960s rates (Currie 1985, FBI 1986) (See Figure 7.4).

One disturbing trend is that more and more violent crimes are being committed by people who are strangers to the victims. The result is that in certain high-crime neighborhoods people do not know whom to trust. A major cause of the increase in crime is that the informal controls that restrain people have broken down with the fragmentation of society (Silberman 1980).

In part, the high rate of crime among Americans may reflect Merton's argument about resorting to deviant means when desirable goals are out of reach. In a major study of crime, Charles Silberman puts it this way: "In the United States, the premium placed on winning —on success—encourages people to violate rules that get in the way, and to feel justified in doing so" (1980, p. 50). Those who are poor and those who are discriminated against have good reason to believe that they will not achieve "success" except through unlawful means. As criminal activities become an established part of the social environment of poor whites and blacks and Hispanics, children are socialized into that life-style, and crime gets culturally transmitted from one generation to the next.

How do we break this vicious cycle? Elliott Currie (1985) holds that conventional techniques, such as putting more policemen on the beat and sending more criminals to prison for longer sentences, will not work. In his view, the only answer is to attack the root causes of crime—unemployment, social and economic inequality, lack of community bonds, and family breakdown. Contrary to popular belief, Currie maintains that the government can bring about major and positive changes in social structure. Attractive jobs can be made more available to young people (especially minority youths), community life can be supported, and families can be helped to cope. Such far-reaching changes would re-

quire a major commitment on the part of the public and the government, but much of the public is convinced that the police, courts, and prisons cannot do the job. We now examine these assumptions.

Police: Key Agents of Control

Many people see building up local police forces as the answer to the crime problem. However, numerous studies have shown that in most instances increasing the

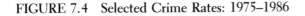

Although there are peaks and valleys, crime rates (per 100,000 population) in the United States are high and keep rising over the long term, with property crimes many times more frequent than violent crimes. Durkheim observed that social rates, whether of crime or marriage, are stable characteristics of a society. What more would you want to know to interpret what these rates tell us about our society?

FIGURE 7.4   Selected Crime Rates: 1975–1986

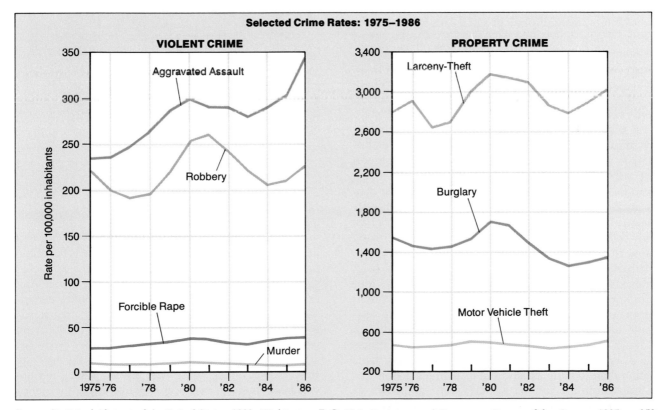

Source: Statistical Abstract of the United States, 1988. Washington, D.C.:U.S. Department of Commerce, Bureau of the Census, 1987, p. 158.

number of police, conducting random patrols, and other conventional measures have not had the anticipated effect on crime rates (Skolnick and Bayley 1986). Police seldom encounter muggings, rapes, or homicides while on patrol. Moreover, most crimes are solved not through detective work but because the victim or a witness identifies the criminal. But this does not mean that the police cannot have any impact on crime, as illustrated in the following in-depth discussion.

In Depth: A New Blue Line

In *The New Blue Line* (1986), Jerome Skolnick and David Bayley describe and analyze six innovative police forces, including one in Santa Ana, California. In the late 1960s, hostility between the police and civilians in Santa Ana was at an all-time high. In the early 1970s, Santa Ana Police Chief Raymond Davis began a series of reforms that brought the police and the community back together again. The first step was *civilianization*. In conventional police departments, officers spend more time filing reports than they do carrying out criminal investigations. Davis reasoned that civilians could do this work as well as sworn police officers. Civilian employees not only cost less than trained officers; they also come from the community and are seen as insiders rather than as an outside force. The second step was *community mobilization*: appointing block captains to serve as liaisons between the police and the community. In many cases, the block captains' activities created a community where none had existed before: Neighbors who had been strangers became friends. Third, Davis set up four *substations* within communities that function as combination police station/social service centers. Here residents can get information about how to handle all manner of personal and community problems. Officers are assigned to a substation on a semipermanent basis (rather than rotating weekly) and many more are on foot patrol than in the past. As a result, police and residents come to know one another personally. In addition, Davis appointed a Hispanic Affairs Officer, and created a special gang detail and a committee to work with

In Japan, the police are easily accessible to the public, and officers become well acquainted with local residents. As a result, the Japanese public and police enjoy a close and trusting working relationship. (© Rick Smolan/Contact.)

businessmen who wanted to clean up the city's downtown area. Underlying these varied activities was the idea that the police and the public are "co-producers of crime prevention" (Skolnick and Bayley 1986, p. 213).

Skolnick and Bayley conclude that the Santa Ana experiment offers a model for other city police departments. Crime rates in Santa Ana did not fall dramatically (in part because more Santa Ana residents are more willing to report crimes), but neither did they rise as fast as in other cities. Moreover, Santa Ana was the only city studied by Skolnick and Bayley in which they did not see, hear, or read anything negative about the police force. But the police are only part of the criminal justice system.

The Criminal Justice Funnel

A study of the criminal justice system carried out in New York City examined all 1979 felony cases—offenses punishable by more than a year in prison. In that year, approximately 829,000 felonies were committed in the city. About 104,000 people were arrested, 16,000 indicted, and 1,000 imprisoned (*New York Times*, January 4, 1981). In effect, the criminal justice system works as a funnel, and only a small percentage of criminals are sent to prison. The great majority get off "scot free" (see Figure 7.5).

What are we to make of these figures? Does the criminal justice system simply not work? Actually, there are a number of valid reasons for the dwindling numbers before prosecution and conviction. It is not simply a question of overcrowded and underfunded courts, as is commonly believed.

A study by the Vera Institute of Justice (1977) has found that many felons are never prosecuted or convicted because their victims or the complainants refuse to testify against them. When people call the police, they often do so to frighten the offender and show their anger; they cool off when it comes to giving testimony that will send the person to prison.

Another explanation for the funnel effect is that felonies may get reduced to misdemeanors (less serious offenses) through **plea bargaining**. Plea bargaining is the process in which the district attorney offers to reduce charges if the suspect will plead guilty and relinquish the right to a trial. Plea bargaining saves the state time, expense, and trouble, but it pressures some innocent people to plead guilty, and it puts some serious offenders back on the streets in less than a year.

As a result of the way the criminal justice system works, almost half of the people in jail have not been convicted of a crime; they are being held for trial (*Statistical Abstract* 1983). Malcolm Feeley (1979) contends that for many felons, these pretrial procedures constitute a punishment in itself, sometimes even more severe than an actual sentence or fine. He believes that these conditions induce the accused to waive a trial and plead guilty: they will do anything to minimize the pretrial costs to themselves.

Generally, it is poor nonwhites who get funneled into the prison system. All along the way formal controls work in discriminatory ways, intentionally or not. First, the police use their judgment in deciding whom to arrest. Public prosecutors use their judgment in deciding who will be allowed to plea bargain, that is, to plead

guilty to a lesser charge. Judges decide which individuals are a danger to the community and whether these individuals will be let out on bail during trial or sent to prison after conviction. The last stage in this process is by far the most controversial.

The Imprisoning Society

In 1969, the National Commission on the Causes and Prevention of Violence predicted that our cities would become armed camps, as the rich barricaded themselves

FIGURE 7.5 Crimes Resolved by Arrest, 1985

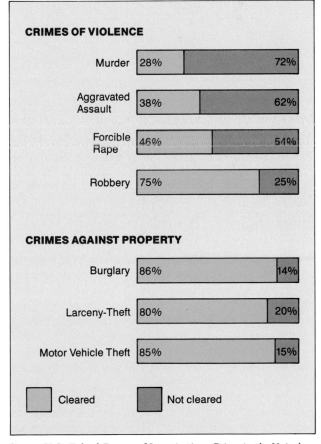

Source: U.S. Federal Bureau of Investigation, *Crime in the United States*, annual.

Public fear of crime has led to (A) an increasing rate of imprisonment for convicted criminals, and (B) a tendency for urban and suburban dwellers to barricade their homes, virtually imprisoning themselves. Controversy about the effectiveness of the prison system has caused debate concerning the best way for society to cope with criminal behavior. (Left: Alex Webb/Magnum Photos, Inc.; right: Rapho/Photo Researchers, Inc.)

against the poor. To a certain extent, this prediction has come true. City dwellers put triple locks on their doors and iron grids on their windows; they hire block guards and organize neighborhood patrols. Suburban condominiums are surrounded by high brick walls, and a guard at the entrance demands identification from anyone who wishes to enter. Fear of crime is making us prisoners in our own homes.

At the same time, public support for imprisonment is increasing. In the 1980s, certain crime rates began to level off and even decline. During the same period, however, rates of imprisonment climbed steadily. Between 1980 and 1986, the number of inmates in U.S. prisons increased by almost 60 percent, reaching a record high of 525,000. The cost of incarceration also rose to an average of $14,591 per prisoner per year. The total operating budgets for prisons in 1986 reached $9.8 billion (*Corrections Year Book* 1986). Even so, prison systems have not been able to keep pace with the flood of inmates. Cells that were built to house one inmate now house two or three, with the overflow being bedded in gyms, recreation rooms, corridors, basements, and tents. To ensure security, San Quentin, which was designed to hold 2,700 prisoners, confines its 3,900 inmates to their cells except for meals and showers (Logan 1985).

Many of the problems surrounding the prison system stem from a confusion of purposes. Are prison sentences designed to deter the criminal and others from committing crimes? To rehabilitate the criminal and return him (or less frequently her) to society a reformed person? To punish offenders? To protect the public? In recent years, the pendulum has swung from a societal emphasis on rehabilitation to demands for longer imprisonments.

Although there is little agreement on the goal of imprisonment, there is widespread agreement that the prison system is inadequate on many counts.

In the first place, prisons do not protect the public as well as people think. Most criminals are never imprisoned: arrests were made in only 16 percent of the more than 13 million crimes reported to the FBI in 1986 (FBI 1986). Only 3 percent of the people known to have committed crimes ever go to jail (only 1.5 percent if we include unreported crimes). Moreover, most prison officials estimate that only 15 to 25 percent of inmates are actually dangerous. Studies suggest that fewer than 10 percent of criminals commit nearly 30 percent of crimes (Moore 1983).

The harsh conditions found in prisons (overcrowding, lack of sanitation, neglect, and brutality by guards) combined with the humiliating conditions of living in a total institution (constant supervision and regulation, degradation, loss of personal identity and personal possessions) make the prison, in Charles Silberman's words, "a crucible of intimidation and conflict." The only way an inmate can achieve status or identity is to put someone else down "verbally, physically, financially, or sexually . . . there is exaggerated emphasis on toughness: the ability either to victimize others or to withstand victimization" (1980, p. 523). This kind of prison culture is hardly conducive to rehabilitation. After their release, at least a third of former prison inmates end up back in prison. Indeed, prisons may socialize people *to* deviance. Many observers consider them "schools for crime," where first offenders learn the tricks and rationalizations of deviant careers.

Alternatives to prison sentences are currently being tried out (Locayo 1987). Some states are experimenting with giving certain criminals a choice between a prison sentence and a combination of fines and public service. Other states are putting some criminals under house arrest in which they are allowed to live in their own homes and go to work, but must obey strict curfews and meet frequently with corrections officers. Still other states are trying work-release centers, which require criminals to live in prisonlike dormitories but also permit them to work. A few localities have even tried the "scarlet letter" approach, in which motorists convicted of drunk driving are required to display bumper stickers announcing their crime and other offenders are required to print public apologies (complete with their picture) in local newspapers. The basic rationale behind these alternatives is that some categories of offenders are better able to repay society on the outside than they are inside prison walls. Only a few alternatives to imprisonment have gotten beyond the idea stage, however, and judges seem reluctant to take chances. What if a criminal under house arrest committed another, more serious crime?

As things stand, social attitudes are not inclined toward leniency to criminal offenders, and imprisonment remains more likely than other proposed alternatives (Applebombe 1987).

SUMMARY

1. Deviance is behavior that members of a group or society see as violating their norms. In other words, deviance is a matter of social definition. Moreover, whether a particular act is considered deviant depends on the time, place, and social circumstances.

2. Explanations of deviance fall into two basic categories. Biological and psychological theories focus on the individual characteristics and experiences that distinguish deviants from nondeviants. Sociological theories deal with the social conditions that make deviance more likely.

3. *Social stress theory* holds that deviance arises when conformity to widely accepted norms fails to satisfy people's legitimate desires. *Cultural transmission theory* holds that people are socialized to deviance through immersion in a deviant subculture.

4. The *functional perspective* maintains that the identification of deviance clarifies group norms and thus contributes to social order.

5. *Labeling theory* focuses not on why some people violate the norms in the first place but on the conse-

quences of singling out certain rule breakers and labeling them as deviants, perhaps forcing them into deviant life-styles and subcultures.

6. The *Marxist perspective* argues that definitions of deviance reflect the power structure in a society and serve the interests of the ruling class.

7. Social control refers to a group or society's efforts at self-regulation. The most powerful form of social control is internalization of norms. When internalization fails, informal social controls and (especially in complex modern societies) formal sanctions are called into action.

8. Crimes are acts that have been formally defined as illegal and are subject to formal sanctions by the state.

9. There are five basic types of crime. *Index crimes* are "common" crimes against persons and property. *Crimes without victims* are violations of the so-called vice codes, which may not cause harm, but arouse indignation.

10. *Organized crime* refers to underground organizations that provide illegal goods and services and/or use violence and bribery to overcome competition. *White-collar* and *corporate crime* refer to illegal acts committed by employees of legitimate companies or by the companies themselves. The latter category includes crimes against customers, employees, the public-at-large, and stockholders.

11. Discussions of crime control usually focus on index crimes. Studies of police action suggest that the police are most effective when they collaborate with community groups. The criminal justice system is highly selective; only a small percentage of those people who commit crimes are caught, arrested, and sent to prison.

12. Although crime rates have leveled off in the United States, the rate of imprisonment is increasing, which leads to questions about the goals and purposes of the prison system.

GLOSSARY

Conformity. Seeking culturally approved goals by culturally approved means (Merton).

Corporate crime. Illegal activity committed on behalf of a formal organization.

Crime. A violation of a norm that has been entered into the law and is backed by the power and authority of the state.

Cultural transmission. The process by which deviance is learned through the transmission of norms within a community or group.

Deviance. Behavior that the members of a social group define as violating their norms.

Deviant career. The adoption of a deviant life-style and identity within a supporting subculture that provides techniques for breaking rules and rationalizations for nonconformity.

Differential association. The process by which individuals are socialized into a particular group of people, such as criminals, and come to adopt the standards of that group as their own.

Formal social controls. Official pressure to conform to social norms and values specifically enforced by organizations such as police departments, courts, and prisons.

Index crime. Those crimes that the Federal Bureau of Investigation annually cites in its *Uniform Crimes Reports.*

Informal social controls. Unofficial pressures to conform, including disapproval, ridicule, and the threat of ostracism.

Innovation. Pursuing culturally approved goals by deviant means (Merton).

Internalization. The process by which cultural standards become part of a person's personality structure.

Labeling. The assigning of a deviant status to a person, which then dominates his or her social identity.

Organized crime. Continuing conspiracy operating for profit and power, and seeking immunity from the law through fear or corruption; specializes in the provision of illegal goods and services.

Primary deviance. The initial violation of a social norm, about which no inferences are made regarding motives or the character of the person who committed the act.

Rebellion. Creating new goals and new means for pursuing them (Merton).

Retreatism. Abandoning culturally prescribed goals and means (Merton).

Ritualism. Adhering rigidly to norms, yet abandoning related goals (Merton).

Sanctions. Rewards for conforming to a social norm or penalties for violating it.

Secondary deviance. A pattern by which people come to define themselves as deviants and undertake life patterns as a reaction to their being labeled as deviants by others.

Social control. Society's efforts to regulate itself; those mechanisms by which social norms are upheld and by which their actual or potential violation is restrained.

Victimless crime. Crimes that lack victims, except perhaps the people who commit them.

White-collar crime. Crime committed by individuals of high status in the course of their occupations.

PART THREE
SOCIAL
GROUPINGS

Can you name all of the social groups of which you are a member? The list might begin, for example, with your family or with the class in which you are reading this book. Some of the groups to which you belong have formal sets of rules and objectives; others may appear to be more casual, their goals and behavioral norms implicitly understood by the group's members. The next three chapters explore the dynamics of social groups on a scale of increasing size and complexity from small groups to large organizations to entire communities and populations.

Chapter 8 discusses the defining characteristics of social groups and the ways in which sociologists classify them. The text illustrates the nature of commitment to a group, using the example of an Amish community. It also examines the structure and function of formal organizations, focusing in particular on bureaucracy as an organizational technique widely used in our society.

Chapter 9 moves from Main Street in a small Montana town to the metal-framed glass canyons of Manhattan, offering a sociological perspective of communities and cities while tracing the growth of the modern metropolis. Today more than half the world's population lives in cities, and the chapter discusses dynamics of urban growth, decay, and renewal; theoretical models for urban ecology; the special problems confronting Third-World cities; and current trends such as gentrification and rural industrialization.

The shift of population from the country to the city is an aspect of demography—the study of how births, deaths, and migrations affect populations. In Chapter 10 you will learn how sociologists gather and interpret data on the size, composition, and distribution of populations. Studying population change is a particularly useful way for sociologists to "read" the ongoing story of social stability and social change. The chapter explores the dynamics of population change both in the United States and in the world. A rapid increase in worldwide population density, with population growth centered in developing countries, raises difficult and controversial issues about how to control populations and how to protect the environment.

CHAPTER 8
Groups and Organizations

You live your life as a member of social groups and organizations. The moment you were born you became part of a group consisting of your parents, a doctor, some nurses, and other medical personnel involved in your delivery. From here you joined a group of other newborns and their caretakers in the hospital nursery room. After spending several days in the hospital, you went home to a third group, the family, which has influenced your life ever since. Over the years you have also been part of a long list of clubs, teams, classes, and circles of friends, each of which is a group that has affected your behavior. Some of these groups, like the sociology class in which you are now involved, are embedded in larger, formal organizations (in this case your college or university). Other formal organizations that touch your life are the corporations that manufacture the products you buy and the many government agencies whose forms you fill out and whose rules and regulations you abide by.

It is more than size that differentiates groups from organizations. Consider the differences between the family and the General Motors Corporation. Although the family is small and General Motors is large, there are other important differences between them. One important difference is the formality of their organizational structures. Whereas a family is *in*formally structured (it has no official job descriptions or official chains of command), General Motors is formally organized into a hierarchy of work relationships. Every employee at GM can precisely state his or her position in the organization.

In the family, in contrast, statuses, roles, and responsibilities are relatively fluid. Another critical difference between groups and organizations lies in the explicitness of their goals. A family's goals are more *im*plicit; they are not often expressly stated. Family members do not regularly discuss their joint objectives or establish five-year plans. The goals families have are loosely set and quite easily changed. General Motors, in contrast, explicitly establishes a program for itself and determines how each division of the firm will work to carry out that program. Summing up these differences, a **social group** is a set of individuals who identify with one another and interact in informally structured ways based on norms, goals, and values they implicitly share. A **formal organization,** on the other hand, is a set of individuals whose activities are consciously and precisely designed for the purpose of achieving explicitly stated goals.

In this chapter we examine both social groups and formal organizations. We begin with a look at the nature of groups—their defining characteristics, the dynamic processes within them, and the ways that sociologists classify them into types. Here we use numerous examples from the events in a well-known novel, *Lord of the Flies*. Next we consider how people become committed to groups, sometimes to the point of giving up their individual identities. In the process, we explore commitment in the Amish community, a social group with extraordinarily high degrees of loyalty and devotion. We then turn our attention to techniques of formal organization, examining their advantages in large, complex

Most of us take for granted the groups and organizations to which we belong or on which we depend. Imagine a world in which they no longer existed. This is the dramatic situation of William Golding's novel, Lord of the Flies, *about a group of schoolboys marooned on a tropical island. In this scene from the story, what details might a sociologist find noteworthy in examining the characteristics of the group and its dynamics? (Culver Pictures.)*

societies. We also discuss bureaucracy—its major features and variations, as well as its shortcomings. Finally, we look beyond bureaucracy to collectivist organizations. Do they provide a viable alternative to the problems that bureaucracies pose? Examining an unusual school, Black Mountain College, helps provide some answers.

THE NATURE OF SOCIAL GROUPS

What do you think would happen if thirty boys were marooned on an uninhabited tropical island? Some might take advantage of the freedom from adult surveillance to act out their wildest fantasies. Others might try to reestablish the rules and structures they had at home by holding meetings and delegating responsibilities. Still others might whimper for their parents and look for someone to fill the role of their older brother. Leaders

would emerge who would weld together cliques and vie for power. The group might even divide into hostile camps, each declaring "war" on the other. Eventually the boys might get carried away, find themselves swept up by group momentum, and do things they would never do alone.

This is essentially what happens in William Golding's novel *Lord of the Flies* (1954). The story opens on an uninhabited tropical island after a plane carrying a load of British schoolboys, ranging in age from six to twelve, makes a crash landing. All the adults are killed, and the boys are left alone to organize themselves and try to effect a rescue. But things do not work out as the boys had originally hoped. A rational, democratic group organized by Ralph is overcome by an irrational and violent one led by Jack. The boys become consumed by groundless fears, intense competition and hatred, and the drive to experience immediate pleasures and express primitive aggressions.

Throughout the story, Golding shows that group experiences influence us to a remarkable degree. Social groups link our private lives to the larger society. They provide us with security and support. They shape our values, attitudes, and behavior. How we act within a group is seldom how we would act if we were entirely alone. These important sociological insights are dramatically illustrated in *Lord of the Flies*.

Group Characteristics

When the boys in *Lord of the Flies* crash-landed on the tropical island, the first to emerge from the jungle are a fat, overprotected, intellectual boy nicknamed Piggy and a blond, athletic twelve-year-old named Ralph. At Piggy's suggestion, Ralph summons the other survivors by blowing into a large conch shell. Small boys, wearing tattered uniforms from an assortment of different schools, make their way out of the jungle and onto the beach. These boys do not yet constitute a social group. They are simply an **aggregate** of individuals who happen to be in the same place at the same time, much like pedestrians on the same sidewalk or passengers on the same bus. However, the boys soon become a group by repeatedly interacting with one another, by developing an informal social structure, by agreeing on norms to guide their behavior, and by establishing a feeling of unity and belonging.

A social group has four characteristics. First, group members interact on a fairly regular basis. People who do not communicate with one another, who barely acknowledge each other's existence, constitute a social aggregate, not a social group. In *Lord of the Flies*, the ragged collection of survivors started to become a group only with the blowing of the conch and the calling of the first "assembly."

A second characteristic of a social group is that the members' interactions are structured. People in a group do not deal with one another in a haphazard way. Each typically assumes a certain status and adopts a certain role. These statuses and roles are seldom established officially as they are in formal organizations. They tend to evolve informally and are always open to renegotiation. Nevertheless, relationships in a group are structured in some fashion, as can be seen in *Lord of the Flies*. For instance, at the first assembly the oldest boys quickly take control; they become the group leaders. The youngest boys are deferential and obedient; they see themselves as followers, not leaders.

A third characteristic of a social group is that members agree to some extent on norms, goals, and values. A collection of people at cross-purposes is unlikely to form a group. When Golding's assembly of young survivors initially agreed on the need for orderly procedures and the importance of being rescued, they were more of a group than when this consensus later began to dissolve. A group's norms, goals, and values need not be explicitly stated; often they are implicit. But even implicit, shared understandings can strongly bind a group together.

Finally, the members of a social group feel a sense of shared identity. They think of themselves as united and interdependent, somewhat apart from other people. This sense of collective belonging quickly emerged on Golding's tropical island, where the boys, separated from all other people, soon began to see themselves as Robinson Crusoes sharing a common adventure. "This is *our* island," proclaims Ralph to the others at their second assembly. "It's a good island. Until the grownups come to fetch us we'll have fun." The boys in Golding's novel thus form a set of individuals who identify with one another and who interact in informally structured ways based on norms, goals, and values they implicitly share—in short, a social group.

Group Dynamics

Although the boys in *Lord of the Flies* imagine a fun-filled adventure, their reality turns out very differently. From the beginning a struggle for control exists between the fair-haired, attractive Ralph, who represents civilized, rational, rule-governed society, and the tall, thin, ugly Jack, who represents the primitive, spontaneous instincts of violence and excitement. At first Ralph prevails; the boys are orderly and adopt a set of rules to help effect a rescue. But gradually Jack gains the upper hand. In the end most of the boys are persuaded to join Jack's "tribe," which then turns on the remaining "outsiders" and systematically subjugates or destroys them. Eventually Ralph is the only voice of reason and civilization left on the island, and he is hunted down like an animal. The hunt is frenzied. There appears to be no hope for Ralph until a naval cruiser happens by the island and the adult world intervenes.

Lord of the Flies provides some excellent examples of group dynamics at work. Group dynamics are the recurrent patterns of social interaction among the members of a group. These patterns are influenced by a number of factors, of which group size is one of the most important.

The Influence of Group Size

When Ralph and Piggy first emerged from the jungle, they formed a **dyad,** or two-person group. Striking differences exist between the dynamics of a dyad and those of a **triad,** or three-person group. In a dyad, both members *must* participate or the group ceases to exist. This means that a member of a dyad "is much more frequently confronted with All or Nothing than is the member of a larger group" (Simmel 1950, p. 135).

Golding shows this in *Lord of the Flies* when Piggy and Ralph first meet. Ralph is not very interested in Piggy's overtures of friendship. He does not view this fat, nearsighted, asthmatic child as a very desirable companion. So Piggy is forced to follow doggedly as Ralph heads for the beach, coaxing Ralph into interaction. Since Ralph can terminate the relationship at any time simply by ignoring Piggy, Piggy must proceed carefully lest Ralph reject him completely. This threat of withdrawal by one member, causing the end of the group, tends to make a dyad more tension-prone than a triad (Hare 1976).

Another difference between dyads and triads is that participants in a dyad cannot hide their responsibility for events that occur within the group. If, for example, one of two roommates finishes the last piece of candy, both know with certainty who did it. When three or more roommates live together, only the person who ate the

Dyads and Triads: Dyad members enjoy direct communication and immediate responsibility for one another. Triad members are able to form coalitions, share (or avoid) responsibility, and mediate disputes. In one context or another, each of us has experienced these basic units of social interaction. (Left: Cyril Toker/Photo Researchers, Inc.; right: John Launois/Black Star.)

candy knows with certainty who that person was. In groups of three or more, one member can also reconcile conflicts between other members. If members of a dyad disagree, there is no insider to act as mediator. On the other hand, dyads do not have to deal with the problem of intruders or spectators. Neither of the two needs to perform for the benefit of a third party; nor do they both have to worry about giving a third party "air time."

The possibilities of building coalitions and creating majorities also distinguish dyads from triads. A coalition and a majority are impossible in a dyad. If Ralph and Jack had been the only survivors in *Lord of the Flies*, a division into two hostile camps could never have occurred. But if only one more person is added, a whole range of new possibilities opens up, as sociologist Theodore Caplow suggests in his book *Two Against One* (1969). Suppose there is a triad in which A is more powerful than B or C, but not stronger than B and C together. Three possibilities for winning coalitions exist: A and B against C, A and C against B, and B and C against A. The power of the majority is particularly marked in a triad because the minority is always a single person who is left potentially alone and vulnerable. To preserve the group's solidarity and viability, the members of most triads tend to switch coalitions from one disagreement to another (Hare 1976).

As group size increases, so does the potential for a specialized division of labor. Early in Golding's novel, when all of the boys are united into one large group, they successfully assign tasks to different individuals. Some boys are given the role of hunters; others are asked to be water-carriers; still others are given the job of keeping a smoke signal going in case a ship happens by. But near the end of the book, when Jack has lured most of the boys to his rival tribe, Ralph is left with only a few followers and the elaborate division of labor breaks down. Now Ralph's group cannot even manage to keep the signal fire burning. The organization and structure that were possible when the group was large are no longer feasible in a tiny band.

Other patterns of interaction also differ between large and small groups. For instance, in large groups there is much more of a limit on the amount and quality of communication that can occur among members. This is evident in *Lord of the Flies*. At the first large assembly, a handful of boys dominate the proceedings, and many have no chance to speak at all. In general, rank-and-file members are more inhibited in participating during discussions as a group's size increases. Problem solving is another interaction pattern that differs with group size. A large group has within its membership a greater variety of resources for solving problems. However, the average contribution of each member tends to slacken off as a group grows larger, and it becomes increasingly difficult for the group to reach consensus on a solution (Hare 1976). Such differences in group dynamics, which occur entirely because of size, have an enormous impact on our experiences in groups with different numbers of members.

Conformity and Control

Initially the band of boys in *Lord of the Flies* formed a fairly harmonious group. They adopted the familiar norms of the school and adult world that they had so recently left behind. At an early assembly Ralph points out:

> ". . . We can't have everybody talking at once. We'll have to have 'Hands up' like at school. . . . Then I'll give him the conch."
> "Conch?"
> "That's what this shell's called. I'll give the conch to the next person to speak. He can hold it when he's speaking." . . .
> Jack was on his feet.
> "We'll have rules!" he cried excitedly. "Lots of rules!" (Golding 1954, p. 31)

The boys agree upon rules concerning where a signal fire should be built, who will keep it burning, how food and water will be gathered, and so forth. Acceptance of such shared norms helps to bind a group together. The norms define the behaviors that are needed to accomplish group goals. Then, by bringing pressure on one another to conform to the rules, members achieve concerted action and facilitate group life.

But conformity to group norms and values is seldom permanent. In *Lord of the Flies*, conformity begins to break down not long after the boys established their community. Jack, who was placed in charge of keeping the fire going, takes the fire tenders away from their task so they can help him hunt wild pigs. The boys also become lackadaisical in their efforts to build sleeping shelters and to collect drinking water. Soon their originally orderly way of life becomes aimless and haphazard. Jack, with his aggressive, bullying ways, increasingly asserts himself. Conformity based on con-sensus gives way to control by force. In a scene that marks this transition, Jack first challenges the norm that the person holding the conch can speak:

> Piggy has settled himself in a place between two rocks, and sat with the conch on his knees. . . .
>
> "I got the conch," said Piggy indignantly. "You let me speak!"
>
> "The conch doesn't count on top of the mountain," said Jack, "so you shut up."
>
> "I got the conch—"
>
> Jack turned fiercely.
>
> "You shut up!"

This threat of force works because of Jack's superior physical strength. Later Jack solidifies his control by destroying the conch and with it whatever meager authority Ralph still holds. Without the conch as a symbol of group consensus and shared rules, control is imposed by spears and stones. The threat and use of force had replaced shared values as the basis for govern-ing group activities.

Leadership

Just as the basis of conformity and control changes during the life of a group, so leadership also changes as a group faces new situations. In *Lord of the Flies*, Ralph is first chosen as leader because the boys perceive him as having **charisma**, a special quality that causes them to accept his authority. Not only is Ralph one of the older and larger boys, he is also physically attractive and takes the initiative in first calling the survivors together. His easy self-assurance earns him respect. The other boys applaud when they elect him chief, and they look to him to call meetings, establish rules, and assign tasks. But as the story unfolds, it becomes increasingly clear that the leadership role is largely forced on Ralph by circum-stances—his being a bit older and abler than most of the boys, his desire for order and eventual rescue, and his happening to be the one who finds and first blows the conch. Far from being a natural leader, Ralph is uncom-fortable with the attention and responsibility that leader-ship brings. Often he is at a loss as to what to do next. Jack soon emerges as a rival leader who appeals to the boys' needs for adventure and emotional release.

Based on his careful observation of groups in the process of formation, Harvard sociologist Robert Bales and his students concluded that groups need leaders for two basic reasons: to direct various tasks and to maintain good spirits and relations within the group (Sécord and Backman 1974). The first is known as **task leadership,** the second as **socioemotional leadership.** In most groups, one person at first performs both of these roles, just as Ralph performed both roles early in Golding's novel. But eventually, these roles are often divided between two people. The socioemotional leader is usual-ly a well-liked person. Ralph has the qualities of a good socioemotional leader. He values harmonious and dem-ocratic social relations; he protects Piggy and other underdogs; and he listens to everyone's ideas and needs. But he becomes so intent on the task of keeping a smoke signal going in hope of rescue that he begins to neglect the socioemotional needs of the group.

> "Look at us. How many are we? And yet we can't keep a fire going to make smoke. Don't you understand? Can't you see we ought to—ought to die before we let the fire out?"
>
> There was a self-conscious giggling among the hunt-ers. Ralph turned on them passionately. . . .
>
> "And another thing."
>
> Someone called out.
>
> "Too many things." . . .
>
> There was a row immediately. Boys stood up and shouted and Ralph shouted back. (Golding 1954, p. 73)

Jack, greedy for power, senses the unmet needs of the group and moves to fill the gap that Ralph has created by making a single, very tedious task assume overriding importance. While Ralph concentrates on keeping the fire going, Jack offers fun and adventure to those who will leave Ralph.

> "Bollocks to the rules! We're strong—we hunt! If there's a beast, we'll hunt it down! We'll close in and beat and beat and beat—!"
>
> He [Jack] gave a wild whoop and leapt down to the pale sand. At once the platform was full of noise and excitement, scramblings, screams and laughter. (p. 83)

Thus, the leadership roles on the island shifted over time, although task and socioemotional needs still had to be met.

Group Decision Making

The boys on Golding's island have no idea why events take the course they do. Things just happen; decisions get made. Sociologists who study group dynamics are more insightful. They have found that, whatever a group's composition or the task at hand, it typically goes through four stages in making choices (Bales and Strodtbeck 1951).

The first stage involves orientation. Members analyze the task before them, exchange information, and suggest solutions. The second stage is evaluating the possibilities, whereas the third stage is eliminating the less desirable option and selecting the one that seems best. The fourth stage is restoring equilibrium—that is, normalizing group relationships after the tension of making a decision. When the boys in *Lord of the Flies* made the decision to remain on the island and await rescue, a period of joking and informal banter restored equilibrium, drawing even those boys with misgivings into the fold.

The boys' decision to remain on the island and await rescue was the best one under the circumstances. If they had fashioned a makeshift boat and ventured out on the ocean, they would have courted disaster. Not all decisions are this sound, however. Even when a group of highly intelligent adults is analyzing reliable data, serious errors in judgment can occur. When are groups most prone to poor decision making? Social scientist

Irving Janis (1972) believes that small, highly cohesive groups with forceful and respected leaders are prone to produce decisions that have critical flaws. Such groups, according to Janis, can give rise to a process he calls *groupthink*—the tendency for members to be so intent on maintaining group unanimity that they overlook or dismiss as unimportant the problems with the choices they make. Victims of groupthink collectively rationalize their decision. They suppress their own doubts and the doubts of others in the group. They insulate themselves from the opinions of knowledgeable outsiders, while negatively stereotyping views at odds with their own. As a result, they convince themselves that their decisions are sound and that their actions will inevitably bring success. Needless to say, they are often unpleasantly surprised.

A classic example of a groupthink-induced fiasco is the Bay of Pigs invasion planned by President John F. Kennedy and his advisers in 1961. Fourteen hundred CIA-trained exiles were to land in Cuba and overthrow the Castro regime. The invasion, however, was a total failure. It embarrassed the United States and solidified the Cuban-Russian alliance. In making its decision, the group considered only two plans. It failed to reconsider the second plan when the flaws of the first became

Groupthink: *A small and tightknit group may seek to preserve unity and agreement at the expense of careful reasoning and a thorough consideration of alternatives. This was Irving Janis's analysis of the group dynamics in Kennedy's cabinet during the Bay of Pigs episode. Have group dynamics at the same high level of government continued to support Janis's argument? (UPI/Bettmann Newsphotos.)*

apparent, it did not consult with a wide range of experts, it ignored contradictory information brought to its attention, and it failed to provide adequate contingency plans. Janis argues that the major reason for this debacle was a strong compulsion among members of this group, which is common in small, closely knit groups, to maintain unity and agreement at all costs—in short, not to rock the boat.

This tendency can be seen in *Lord of the Flies* when the boys persistently ridicule and suppress any views that contradict majority opinion. For instance, in one scene a perceptive boy named Simon tries to warn the others that the "beast" they are dismissing as nonexistent may actually lie within themselves (it is a mental creation that reflects the boys' own destructive potential). The other boys immediately scoff at Simon's warning and force him to drop the subject. Simon never publicly expresses his view again. Given such strong group pressures toward conformity, it is not surprising that the boys fail to confront the problem of the "beast" until they are overwhelmed by violent impulses. But then it is too late.

Types of Groups

To the boys on Golding's tropical island, the social groups they form are both similar to and different from other groups to which they have belonged. Sociologists have analyzed the similarities and differences in groups, and have suggested ways in which groups can be classified. One fundamental classification is the distinction between in-groups and out-groups.

In-Groups and Out-Groups

An **in-group** is one with which a person identifies and in which he or she feels at home. An **out-group** is one with which a person does not identify and toward which he or she feels like an outsider. An in-group, in other words, we think of as "we"; an out-group we think of as "they."

We are all constantly positioning ourselves in terms of in-groups and out-groups. If we are drug users, the out-group is the straight world; if we do not use drugs, then users are the out-group. To the wealthy, out-groups are the middle and lower classes; to the middle class, the wealthy and the poor are out-groups. To the residents of ethnic neighborhoods, people of their own nationality are the in-group, whereas those of other ethnic backgrounds are the out-groups.

The distinction between in-groups and out-groups draws attention to group *boundaries*, the implicitly understood lines demarcating who is in and who is out. Without boundaries, there would be no way of setting groups off from one another, of distinguishing members from nonmembers. Boundaries serve two functions. First, they keep outsiders out. They prevent outsiders from entering certain spheres of interaction with insiders. At the same time, boundaries keep insiders in. They inhibit insiders from moving beyond the confines of the group. A group's boundaries "encapsulate" members, so to speak, focusing their lives within a particular social arena.

People often have to work to maintain group boundaries and make them clear to others. One way to do this is through the use of symbols. For instance, a fraternity T-shirt or a college decal placed on a car window announces one's insider status, symbolically telling the world that one "belongs." Forms of slang and specialized vocabularies serve much the same purpose. One of the most effective ways to create and maintain group boundaries is through conflict with outsiders. A common enemy helps draw people together. Through confrontation with out-groups, insiders begin to develop a sense of "we-ness." Sports contests between colleges, especially between traditional rivals, serve this purpose well.

In the concluding chapters of *Lord of the Flies*, Jack forms a tight in-group from which Ralph, Piggy, and a handful of others are excluded. The members identify themselves by dressing and acting like "savages" (wearing war paint, tying their long hair back from their foreheads, and dancing and chanting together). They also build a fortress to keep out "outsiders." Jack actively exploits Ralph and Piggy's enemy status to unify his band:

> "Tomorrow," went on the chief [Jack], "we shall hunt again."
> He pointed at this savage and that with his spear.
> "Some of you will stay here to improve the cave and defend the gate. I shall take a few hunters with me and bring back meat. The defenders of the gate will see that the others don't sneak in."
> A savage raised his hand and the chief turned a bleak, painted face toward him.
> "Why should they try to sneak in, Chief?"

The chief was vague but earnest.

"They will. They'll try to spoil things we do. So the watchers of the gate must be careful." (Golding 1954, pp. 145–146)

Primary and Secondary Groups

Although we all identify with a number of different in-groups, we do not necessarily interact often with all of these groups nor do we know the members of all these groups intimately. When a group has a close-knit nature, it is called a **primary group.** This term was introduced by Charles Horton Cooley (1909) who described a primary group as having five features:

1. Continuous face-to-face interaction.
2. Strong personal identity with the group.
3. Strong ties of affection among group members.
4. Multifaceted relationships.
5. A tendency for the group to be very enduring.

The nuclear family, in its ideal form, is the primary group *par excellence.* Members of a nuclear family engage in frequent face-to-face interaction. For them the family is an important source of identity and purpose. Love and affection bind the family members together, and they have many kinds of relationships with one another (ranging from exchange of services—"You set the table, I'll wash the dishes"—to emotional support and physical protection). Finally, the family is enduring. Even when members move away from each other, they still consider themselves part of the unit.

Cooley chose the term *primary* to describe this kind of group because these groups are the primary or "first" agents of socialization. They are the principal means by which people acquire their social selves. This is why Cooley called primary groups the "nurseries of human nature." The values and norms we learn in our primary groups tend to remain with us for life. Golding illustrates this in a scene in which Roger and Maurice (two of the older boys) kick over the sand castles that some little boys are making. In the process Maurice accidentally kicks sand in one of the "littluns'" eyes. The little child whimpers, and Maurice feels guilt even though there is no adult to chastise him. Golding explains that Maurice had once been reprimanded by his parents for doing this very thing, which is why he feels guilty about doing it

In-groups and Out-groups—tied at the half . . . *The fervor generated by college rivalries is just one example of how we embody in outward symbols our need to establish boundaries between the good guys and the bad guys, us and them. (Jeff Jacobson/Archive Pictures, Inc.)*

again. The socialization that occurred in that faraway primary group still affects the way he thinks.

This example illustrates a second reason why groups such as the family are aptly called primary groups. They are primary not just because they are where we learn many social norms, they are where social norms are often enforced. In their frequent and intimate interactions, members of primary groups have countless opportunities to scrutinize each other's behavior and to bring those who deviate from the norms back into line. They do this with a look of displeasure, some words of rebuke, or by a withdrawal of affection. Maurice's parents did one or more of these things when they saw him kicking sand in another child's face. In such ways primary groups serve as "front line" agents of social control.

Primary groups are primary in a third sense as well, that is, because relationships within them meet people's basic emotional and psychological needs. Members of primary groups give each other a sense of love and security, of recognition, companionship, and well-being. Such groups are our principal anchors in society. Without them we would feel alone and vulnerable.

Secondary groups have the opposite characteristics of primary groups:

1. Limited face-to-face interaction.
2. Modest or weak personal identity with the group.

These three generations of accordion players in one family epitomize the intimate, affectionate, and enduring qualities of a primary group, whereas relations among members of the New York State Assembly are necessarily less personal and shorter-lived. While the latter group has a legislative responsibility for the orderly function of society, primary groups, such as the nuclear family, play a direct, "front-line" role as the conveyors and enforcers of social values. (Left: Stephanie Maze/Woodfin Camp & Associates; right: Peter Vadnai/The Stock Market.)

3. Weak ties of affection among group members.
4. Limited relationships.
5. A tendency not to be very enduring.

An example of a secondary group is a faculty committee organized to study the curriculum at a large university. Members of the committee meet infrequently, for only a few hours at a time, and for an explicit purpose; their interactions are not an end in themselves. In fact, the members will probably view digressions from their stated task with a good deal of impatience. Although members may hold similar attitudes and values, their basic ties are task-oriented, not emotional ones. Sometimes secondary groups become rather informal, and the members get to know each other fairly well. But even so, their friendships are in a limited context; they are not intimately bound together in multifaceted relationships.

Like other distinctions in sociology, the one between primary and secondary groups is useful because it highlights social dimensions we might not otherwise see. The distinction is not absolute, however. Often it is more accurate to view primariness and secondariness as matters of degree, not of kind. For example, many work groups in businesses, although task-oriented, provide

their members with close and warm relationships. In these groups we see some primary group traits within a basic secondary group context. Such blending of features does not make the primary group/secondary group distinction invalid. It simply means that in actual practice, group characteristics can be quite complex and may have elements of both.

Reference Groups

In in-groups the identification with the group is a key factor creating a sense of "we-ness." Not all the groups with which we identify, however, are ones to which we actually belong. Groups to which we refer when we evaluate our behavior, but to which we may not necessarily belong, are called our **reference groups.**

Reference groups serve two functions. One is to provide us with standards against which we evaluate ourselves and our life situations. For instance, if you get a B on an exam you can feel either great or inadequate depending on whether you use as your reference group the C students or the A students. The particular reference group you choose is not just a matter of whim. The choice reflects the social groups that you come from and the expectations they have encouraged you to set for yourself. This comparison function of reference groups can be seen in *Lord of the Flies* when Piggy, Ralph, and Simon compare their own bungled efforts to those of adults.

> "Grownups know things," said Piggy. ". . . They'd meet and have tea and discuss. Then things 'ud be all right—"
> "They wouldn't set fire to the island. Or lose—"
> "They'd build a ship—"
> The three boys stood in the darkness, striving unsuccessfully to convey the majesty of adult life.
> "They wouldn't quarrel—"
> "Or break my specs—"
> "Or talk about a beast—"

In comparison to this older, more mature reference group, the boys' behavior comes up pathetically short.

Reference groups also serve a normative function—that is, they provide guidelines for appropriate thought and action. We want to be identified with our reference groups, and so we try to act like people we think typify these groups. If your reference group is the jocks on campus, you will dress, speak, and act quite differently than if your reference group consists of intellectuals. One's reference groups, in other words, help to shape one's outlook, appearance, and style.

INDIVIDUAL COMMITMENT AND GROUP SURVIVAL

It is a beautiful September morning. The sun shines brightly into the faces of the audience through large, swinging, red barn doors. . . . The rows of benches on the barn floor are almost filled—men on one side and women on the other—except for two rows in the middle. . . .

Several hymns are sung and the applicants for baptism—on this occasion six girls aged eighteen and upward—file up the barn bank and take their seats in the center section near the minister's bench. Both young and old intently watch the six young women who are ready to make their vows to God and the church, to say "no" to the world and "yes" to Jesus Christ and his *Gemein* [church] here on earth. Each sits with bowed head, as though in deep meditation and prayer for the lifelong vow about to be taken. . . . Their clothing is strictly uniform: black organdy caps, black dresses, white organdy capes, long white organdy aprons, black stockings, and black oxfords. . . .

Like other distinctions in sociology, that between primary and secondary groups helps to identify sets of characteristics that will often overlap in real situations. Although relations among these marketing specialists are limited to the workplace, their teamwork may be imbued with the "primary" traits of intimacy, affection, and loyalty. (Michael L. Abramson/Woodfin Camp & Associates.)

Sitting silently in anticipation the audience listens to two sermons. Two hours of intense waiting finally give way to the climax of the day as the bishop turns to the applicants with a personal admonition. The deacon leaves the service and returns with a small pail and tin cup. The bishop . . . requests the applicants to kneel if it is still their desire to become members of the body of Christ. All six kneel.

The bishop, a deacon, and the deacon's wife proceed with the baptism. . . . The bishop . . . instructs those just baptized to be faithful to the church and to the ministry. To illustrate the importance of obedience, he retells the story of the idolatry committed by the children of Israel while Moses was up on the mountain praying, comparing Israel to the young people who throw parties and engage in other sinful activities while parents are away from home. . . . After four hours the service ends in the usual way: everyone kneels for prayer, a short benediction is given, and a hymn is sung. (Hostetler 1980, pp. 81–83)

This is a description of baptism into one of the most conservative groups in American society—the Old Order Amish. The Old Order Amish are simultaneously a social group, a church, a community, and a spiritual union. Their way of life has survived for nearly 300 years, with almost no changes in the customs, beliefs, and values established by their founder, Jacob Amman, before 1700. Today over 100,000 Old Order Amish live in settlements in twenty states and Canada. In some areas the Amish population has been doubling every twenty-three years. This rapid growth results from a high birthrate, coupled with a low rate (only about 6 percent) of members who leave the group (Kephart 1982).

The Amish stress the need to separate themselves from the larger world, with all its vices and temptations, in order to live the truly righteous life that is necessary for eternal salvation. This doctrine stems especially from two passages in the Bible. One is: "Be not conformed to this world, but be ye transformed by the renewing of your mind, that ye may prove what is that good and acceptable and perfect will of God" (Romans, 12:2). To the Amish this means that they must cut themselves off from the values, beliefs, and material possessions of the larger society. Accordingly, they shun all "worldly" things, from modern styles of clothing, to personal adornments (jewelry, watches, makeup, haircutting or hair curling for women), to every kind of modern convenience (cars, electricity, running water, central heating, telephones, sewing machines, and so forth). The other biblical passage that strongly shapes the Amish way of life is: "Be ye not unequally yoked together with unbelievers; for what fellowship hath righteousness with unrighteousness? What communion hath light with darkness?" (2 Corinthians, 6:14). To the Amish this means that they must not enter into close relationships of any kind with "outsiders." Aside from the minimal contact with non-Amish people that is unavoidable in their daily life, the Amish spend their entire lives interacting only with the thirty or forty families who live within their local church district (Hostetler 1980).

The Amish community demands enormous commitment from its members. It is what sociologist Lewis Coser (1974) calls a "greedy" group, by which he means a group that makes exclusive, all encompassing claims for the hearts, minds, and undivided loyalty of its members. All groups must obtain some degree of commitment if they are to survive. Without a minimum amount of willingness to devote their time and energy to the group, members will drift away and gradually cease to belong to the group. A group to which there is little commitment will also have trouble attracting new recruits, for it is usually through the enthusiasm of current members that new ones are persuaded to join. Thus, commitment is central to the process of keeping a group

alive. What prompts commitment to a group to develop? Why do some groups succeed whereas others fail?

To answer these questions, Rosabeth Kanter (1972) conducted a study of nineteenth-century utopian communities, some of which were similar to the Amish. She concluded that the communities that succeeded had a number of important "commitment-building processes" arising from the ways in which those groups were structured. Six commitment-building processes were especially important: namely sacrifice, investment, renunciation, communion, mortification, and transcendence. These six processes have enabled the Amish to exist in a manner that remained unchanged for so long.

Sacrifice

Sacrifice means that group members are required to give up something of value in order to join the group, something that is readily available in the outside world. The greater that sacrifice, Kanter argues, the stronger are the members' love of and devotion to the group, for people need to justify giving up so much. Sacrifice also builds commitment by weeding out potential members who are not sure they are prepared to devote themselves totally to the group. Thus, the ambivalent back away because the personal cost of entry is too high, leaving only those who are ready to commit themselves entirely to the group.

The Amish are required to sacrifice hundreds of things. They cannot, for example, own cars, radios, television sets, telephones, stereos, musical instruments, electrically driven refrigerators, washing machines, and other household appliances. They are also not permitted to own "luxury" furnishings such as carpets, curtains, and wallpaper; no fashionable clothing; no personal adornments; not even any mirrors, for looking at oneself is considered vain. Members must also sacrifice the chance of going on to get a higher education (most Amish do not go to school beyond the eighth grade) as well as the chance of finding satisfying work in a field that involves "outsiders."

Investment

Investment requires members to contribute their resources to the group—either tangible resources such as property or money, or intangible ones such as time and

Sacrifice, investment, renunciation, communion, mortification, and transcendence —how many of these commitment-building processes are at work in the Amish custom of a barn-raising? (Blair Seitz/Photo Researchers, Inc.)

effort. The more people are required to invest in a group, the greater the stake they have in continuing to work for the group's survival. Investment also builds commitment by reminding people that the needs of the group take priority over their selfish individual desires.

Investment in Amish communities takes the form of contributions of time and labor. For instance, after a fire that destroys an Amish barn or house, all the men of the district will gather to rebuild what was lost. Or when a death occurs in an Amish family, members of the community will help out by doing the bereaved family's chores. Another example of investment occurs when Amish men are called upon to serve as ministers of the church. This job does not pay a salary, but Amish men consider it an honor. By investing their own efforts in the community in these ways, the Amish heighten their sense of group commitment.

strengthening group ties and their importance to the group's members.

Renunciation occurs in the Amish community, where members are required to remain apart from the larger society. To help enforce this cardinal rule, many symbolic boundaries are erected between insiders and outsiders. One such boundary is the strict dress code of the Amish. Amish men with their black suits, collarless shirts, and wide-brimmed hats, Amish women with their long dresses, black stockings, and traditional aprons and caps, set themselves off distinctly from other twentieth-century Americans. "Whether as a language of protest or as custom," John Hostetler writes, "Amish patterns of dress form a strong basis of identity and exclusion. Like all boundary mechanisms, dress serves to keep the insider separate from the world and to identify the outsider" (1980, p. 237).

Renunciation

Renunciation means that members of a group are required to relinquish any interpersonal relationships that could disrupt group cohesion by interfering with members' obligations or causing them to question their beliefs and values. At its most extreme, renunciation leaves members only each other to interact with, thus

Communion

Communion involves the coming together of the group for joint activities, often of a ritualized, symbolic nature. Going to church on Sunday, attending a wedding or a funeral, celebrating an event considered important in a group's history, are all instances of communion, as each requires members to act in concert. Communion builds commitment by enhancing a sense of "we," a view of the self as being intermingled with others who are part of the group. In this way communion complements renunciation. Whereas renunciation requires that people give up relationships with outsiders, communion strengthens the bonds that exist between insiders.

The Amish calendar is filled with communal occasions. Religious services are held every other Sunday, not in a church but in Amish homes. These services include every adult and child in the district, which could be as many as several hundred people. Many Amish separate their downstairs rooms with sliding partitions instead of walls in order to accommodate the congregation when it is their turn to "host" Sunday worship. Community "sings" are another communal event that occurs on a regular basis among the Amish and helps to build a sense of fellowship. Occurring less often, but extremely important for strengthening group commitment, are the baptism rituals described at the beginning of this section. Upon being baptized into the Amish church, young adults make a solemn promise to uphold the rules of the Amish community and to strive to lead a virtuous life. For all those who attend such a service, devotion to the group is renewed. Other Amish community rituals that enhance group commitment include weddings and funerals (often attended by everyone in the district) and the periodic celebration of Christian communion, which for the Amish is accompanied by the ritual washing of one another's feet (just as Jesus washed the feet of his disciples at the Last Supper).

Mortification

Kanter uses the term *mortification* to mean "death of the private self." Groups that require mortification demand that members let their private, autonomous selves perish and replace them with a self that is fulfilled only as part of the group. Mortification builds group commitment because it makes members *need* the group in order to feel whole. Without the group, the self, in a sense, can no longer exist.

The Amish encourage mortification through their practice of constantly condemning feelings of self-pride. Neither women nor men are allowed to show pride in their physical appearance. Even owning a mirror or having one's picture taken is strictly forbidden. At

school, Amish children are not to show pride in their academic achievements. To actively compete with other students and boast about good grades is considered the worst kind of self-aggrandizement. In fact, boasting is almost nonexistent in Amish society. The Amish demand intense humility from each other. Calling special attention to the self in any way is looked upon as vain and disgraceful.

Transcendence

Transcendence means that people feel a special power or virtue as a result of being part of the group. They have a sense that group membership lifts them above the ordinary, giving their lives a higher meaning than is available to other people. The group life, in other words, transcends the ordinary; it rises above it and bestows superiority. Transcendence strengthens commitment because those who experience it seek to increase their devotion to the group that gave them such an elevated sense of being.

Transcendence is built into the Amish way of life. The Amish consider their community the true Christian church. "The true church," explains John Hostetler (1980), "is to be distinguished from the 'fallen church.' Like numerous other Christian groups, the Amish hold that at some point in Christian history the established church became corrupt, ineffectual, and displeasing to God" (p. 76). As members of the true church, the Amish strive to be a "peculiar" people, in the sense of being different from the rest of the world, which they consider blind and perverted. The apostle Peter used the term in this sense when he addressed the early Christians: "Ye are a chosen generation, a royal priesthood, a holy nation, a peculiar people" (1 Peter, 2:9). The Amish believe that righteous, obedient members of the true church will enjoy eternal life in heaven.

Summing Up

Sacrifice, investment, renunciation, communion, mortification, and transcendence are commitment-building processes that can arise in many kinds of groups, not just religious ones. Marine Corps recruits in boot camp, for example, must totally relinquish the freedom to run their own lives (sacrifice). They must devote long, arduous hours to military training (investment), and temporarily cut off relationships that might diminish their devotion to the corps (renunciation). While they are in training marine recruits are constantly together and engaged in joint activities (communion). Their uniform clothing, hairstyles, and behavior submerge the private self and create a new sense of self that exists as part of the group (mortification). Finally, as the recruits succeed at their goals, they acquire a sense of being special, members of a fighting force that is far above all others (transcendence). At this point, they are truly committed to the Marine Corps.

The degree to which these six processes are present in a social group largely determines the level of commitment that that group enjoys. *Some* commitment-building processes will exist in most social groups, for without at least a few of them, a group is unlikely to survive. When all of Kantor's six commitment-building processes are woven into a group's social structure, the commitment to that group will be very strong. Such strong commitment is essential in "greedy" groups such as the Amish, which demand undivided loyalty from their members.

TECHNIQUES OF FORMAL ORGANIZATION

Since the Amish traditionally farm for a living, their families tend to be quite large. Couples have an average of seven or eight children, and those with ten to fifteen children are far from rare. Each Amish family has virtually the same structural patterns. From an early age, young boys learn to help their fathers tend the crops and livestock, while young girls learn to help their mothers cook, sew, clean, and so forth. The whole family comes together for breakfast and dinner. The father always sits at the head of the table, with his wife to his right or his left. Along the wife's side sit the daughters, from the youngest to the oldest. Along the opposite side sit the sons, also in order from youngest to oldest. In this way everyone has a "place" at the meal.

The Amish family seems highly structured to those of us who come from more typical American house-holds. But actually, a family of any kind is very informal in its organization. Even among the Amish, job descriptions are never explicitly given to each family member. Instead, tasks are often assigned on an informal basis around the breakfast table. Similarly, family rules are never formally written down. Instead, members have a tacit understanding of what is expected of them. This system works fine for a group of under twenty people. But imagine using it to run General Motors, with its several thousand employees. The task of building and marketing cars would dissolve into chaos if it were carried out in such an informal way. It takes formal organization to structure such an enormous productive enterprise. Thus, General Motors is organized into several divisions, each of which has departments assigned to explicit tasks (production, sales, marketing, accounting, personnel). Within departments, people are hierarchically structured, from top executives, to middle managers, to lower-level supervisors, to rank-and-file workers. Each person in the hierarchy has a formal job description, and each job is governed by rules that make behavior predictable. Everyone knows who is responsible for which tasks, and who reports to whom. Only with such formalized roles and procedures can General Motors operate successfully.

Formal organizations such as General Motors are a prominent feature of modern societies. We are born in big hospitals, we are taught in formal educational complexes, we are employed by huge international corporations, we are governed by bureaucratic state and federal agencies, and even buried by large mortuary firms. Indeed, most of the crucial decisions affecting our lives—especially those having to do with economic matters and issues of war and peace—are made by large organizations. Why have formal organizations become so pervasive in our world? Why can most Americans not get through a day without encountering a formal organization, or at least the products or services of one?

The answer is that formal organization is a rational and efficient response to the ever-growing scale and complexity of social structure. As groups become larger and take on more functions, organizing in a formal, hierarchical manner with explicit rules and procedures provides a competitive advantage. Large groups and institutions that have chosen to organize formally have tended to win out over their rivals. In the following sections we look at some specific techniques that formal organizations use to give them a competitive edge over informal organizations.

Given the size and complexity of modern armies, effective command depends on coordination of effort and standardization of procedures and material. Teamwork and organization take precedence over innovation and daring; the Napoleons have to survive boot camp along with everyone else. (Left: Antoine Jean Gros/Art Resource; right: R. Eckert/EKM-Nepenthe.)

Techniques for Controlling Large Numbers of People: The Case of the Military

Napoleon I was one of the greatest military leaders of all time. During a battle, this famous French emperor oversaw every detail, often catching only a few sporadic hours of sleep each night. He was in constant motion: traveling from one strategic position to another, inspecting his troops, conferring with his subordinates, extracting information from civilians and prisoners of war, even doing his own reconnaissance which sometimes brought him within firing distance of the enemy lines. At night he would pull together all the available data, formulate his plans, and compose his highly detailed orders. Sometimes he would dictate orders to four separate secretaries on four separate topics at once! (Van Creveld 1985). But even Napoleon's impressive powers of control

began to break down as his army continued to grow in size. At the battle of Austerlitz in 1805 Napoleon brilliantly controlled an army of 85,000 men, whereas at Jena a year later he lost control of a third to a half of his 150,000 troops (Van Creveld 1985). The grand army that Napoleon assembled for his disastrous invasion of Russia had over 500,000 men. Not even Napoleon, with his computerlike mind, could keep track of such a huge fighting force.

After Napoleon's defeat, Helmut von Moltke, chief of the Prussian general staff, addressed the problem of how to exercise command over a large, modern army. One important change that von Moltke made was to improve the system for training staff officers. No longer were young men given staff positions simply because they came from a military family. Instead, potential staff officers were carefully selected from each year's graduates of the prestigious *Kriegsakademie* (War College). These young men were themselves selected by competitive examinations from a much larger group that sought admittance to the school. In this way von Moltke skimmed the cream of the young officer candidates (Howard 1961). Moreover, even when he was appointed to the general staff, an officer was on probation for a period of several years, during which time he was given further training in war strategy and execution. Only if von Moltke was fully satisfied with the man's performance was the young officer made a permanent member of the staff. In this way von Moltke thoroughly trained his staff officers to think and respond as he would, much as a large corporation such as IBM trains its junior executives to think and act in the "IBM way." This unanimity of thought and action among staff members helped ensure their finely tuned coordination during warfare (Ropp 1959). No staff member was indispensable, since all were highly trained and similarly skilled. Each of his officers could do whatever von Moltke ordered him to do.

Another organizational innovation employed by von Moltke was the standardization of the Prussian army's divisions. The divisional system was first introduced during the Seven Years' War (1756–63) by the French general Duke Victor de Broglie. De Broglie combined infantry brigades and artillery brigades, which had formerly been independent, into the same unit, which he called a division. These divisions enabled much better coordination among the various kinds of troops. In 1794, the French minister of war created divisions that included three troop types: infantry, artillery, and cavalry. Within a few years this system was adopted throughout the French army, and not long thereafter the British and the Prussians also switched to a divisional system (Dupuy and Dupuy 1986). Von Moltke carried the divisional idea to its ultimate by making divisions very similar to each other in size, composition, and structure. Divisions in the Prussian army, in a sense, became interchangeable parts in a well-designed military machine.

The great efficiency of von Moltke's system largely explains Prussia's rapid victory over France in the Franco-Prussian War (1870–1871). The two sides were relatively equal in armaments and manpower, but von Moltke's organizational innovations gave the Prussians a decisive edge. Von Moltke's innovations were soon copied throughout the West. Today all armies exploit von Moltke's basic bureaucratic innovations. They train their officers in a common set of skills, tactics, and procedures, and they extensively standardize the makeup and structure of their military units. These organizational techniques are essential to permit modern armies to fight with the necessary efficiency.

Techniques for Integrating Diverse Operations: The Case of Swift and Company

The nineteenth century saw the birth not just of huge armies but also of huge industrial corporations. These companies were enormous in terms of their volume of output as well as the diversity of the operations they controlled. How were business executives to manage a sprawling enterprise that supplied its own raw materials, manufactured a large line of products, and sold those products directly to retailers rather than using middlemen? The answers to these questions, again, came through new techniques of formal organization.

Swift and Company is a good example of how organizational techniques enabled diverse operations to integrate (Chandler 1962). Gustavus Swift was a butcher from Massachusetts who moved to Chicago in the mid-1870s. He knew that there was a much greater demand for fresh meat in eastern cities such as Boston, Philadelphia, and New York than east-coast farmers could satisfy. Swift hit upon the idea of using refrigerated railway cars to transport large quantities of western-raised beef to the eastern seaboard. But selling this beef in the East was at first not an easy matter. People were wary of eating meat that was so long in transport; they had to be convinced that refrigeration would keep the meat fresh. So Swift decided to set up his own marketing operation in each of the major eastern cities. This operation consisted of a refrigerated warehouse in which the arriving shipments could temporarily be stored, as well as a network of wholesale and retail outlets to sell the meat to stores and consumers. A branch manager in each metropolitan area coordinated the various marketing activities there.

By the mid-1880s Swift was systematizing his buying of cattle, building additional meatpacking plants, and expanding his marketing efforts. In addition to marketing beef, he was marketing other meats, as well as a number of meat-related products (leather, soap, ferti-lizer, glue). Other companies in the meatpacking busi-ness had to copy Swift's organization in order to compete with him. Soon the meatpacking industry was dominat-ed by a few huge, well-organized firms, each of which integrated a variety of operations.

Techniques for Reducing Opposition: The Case of the TVA

The military and business have no monopoly on formal organization. In fact, the epitome of formal organization is often thought to be government. Government agen-cies have thrived in this century not only because their centralized administration makes sense in terms of heightened efficiency, but also through their adept use of techniques that reduce opposition to their programs and policies. One such technique is **co-optation,** the process of defusing potential opponents by making them a part of one's own organizational structure.

An excellent example of co-optation occurred in the case of the Tennessee Valley Authority (TVA), a U.S. government-owned corporation established in 1933 to integrate the development of the Tennessee River basin (Selznick 1949). The TVA was empowered to build dams to control flooding, to deepen the river channel and make it more navigable, to produce and distribute inexpensive electricity and operate some ferti-lizer plants, and to generally plan for the proper use and conservation of the region's natural resources. In an effort to involve the residents of the area in the running of the TVA, representatives of powerful local groups and organizations were given positions on its decision-making board. Many of these board members were initially opposed to the TVA, but by being co-opted into the organization their opposition was essentially elimi-nated. In this way the TVA, a New Deal agency, was able to survive in a very conservative part of the country (Blau and Meyer 1987).

Co-optation, however, is a two-way street (Hall 1982). Although an organization can defuse its opposi-tion by giving potential critics a voice in its operation, this process increases the chances that the views of co-opted parties will find their way into the organiza-tion's policies. This is what happened with the TVA, which often favored the private interests of its directors

over the public interest it was created to support. For example, land with improved soil that bordered TVA reservoirs was allowed to be privately purchased, and reforested land that was meant to be left as undisturbed watershed area was allowed to be exploited by powerful lumber companies (Scott 1981). Thus, co-optation may be a successful technique for helping an organization survive, but it can also change that organization's goals and policies.

Summing Up

This section opened with the question of why formal organization has become so widespread. The three cases we examined reveal that for certain kinds of groups in certain circumstances, formal organizational techniques have proved to be highly advantageous. When the Prussian army standardized the training of its officers and the structure of its divisions, it was better able to control large numbers of people. When Swift and Company established hierarchies of personnel, it was better able to integrate diverse operations. And when the TVA co-opted some of its local opposition, it was better able to survive in a conservative part of the country. Thus, techniques of formal organization enabled those who used them to achieve important goals and to defeat their rivals and opponents. As a result, these techniques were widely imitated and formal organization spread, so that today it can be found operating throughout modern societies.

BUREAUCRACY

Around the turn of the twentieth century, Max Weber assessed the many kinds of formal organizations that had come to dominate modern societies. He asked what all these organizations had in common, and concluded that they were all **bureaucratic** in structure. To Weber the term "**bureaucracy**" did not have negative connotations as it often does today. Although Weber recognized that bureaucracy may sometimes have dehumanizing side effects, he believed it to be a technically superior means of coordinating the activities of large numbers of people. When bureaucracy works well, Weber argued, it has three benefits: (1) It *maximizes* the *effectiveness* with which an organization's goals are accomplished; (2) it *maximizes efficiency* by getting the most done at the least cost; and (3) it *controls uncertainty* by regulating workers, supplies, and markets.

Weber's Ideal Type

In order to highlight the major features of bureaucracy, Weber constructed an ideal type, a model created to define bureaucracy's most important characteristics (see Chapter 1). Weber's ideal type did not describe all bureaucracies as they actually function. Actual bureaucracies are much too varied to fit a single model. Instead, Weber's ideal type was an analytical tool that abstracted the *general* features commonly found in bureaucracies. There were five such features:

1. *Specialization.* In bureaucracies the work to be accomplished is broken down into a clear-cut division of labor and people are trained to specialize in performing each task. It is assumed that such specialization is the most efficient way to get the job done. Gustavus Swift used specialization in his meat-marketing operation. Some employees specialized in purchasing cattle at the stockyards; others in butchering the beef; others in loading the meat onto train cars; others in running the warehouses in the East; and still others in selling the Swift and Company products to wholesale meat dealers and retail markets. This system was far more efficient than having a team of workers follow each beef shipment from the western prairies to grocery store counters in New York.
2. A *hierarchy of offices.* Once an organization's operation is divided into smaller, more manageable tasks, the various activities must be integrated—the gears of the machine must mesh. If they do not, the people in one department might design a bolt an eighth of an inch larger than the nut designed in another department (Blau and Meyer 1971). The solution is to organize workers into a hierarchy, with each person being responsible to the person directly above in the chain of com-

The modern multinational corporation is both the epitome and the end-product of bureaucratic organization —a fact often celebrated in corporate architecture. What organizational values or features are embodied in this facade? (Bohdan Hrynewych/Stock, Boston.)

mand. A hierarchy is typically pyramid-shaped, with rank and authority increasing as one moves up. Swift established such a hierarchy in his meat-marketing business. For example, employees in each metropolitan area were under the direction of a branch manager, who in turn reported to executives at company headquarters. In this way all the various parts of Swift's system were coordinated.

   Organizational hierarchies, such as Swift's, consist of positions, not specific people. Each position carries with it certain duties and privileges, and each pays a certain salary. The authority of those in higher positions resides in the offices they hold, not in the people themselves. That authority is always clearly defined and limited. A Swift and Company branch manager, for instance, might have the authority to fire a warehouse worker, but not the authority to tell that individual where to live and whom to marry.

3. *Rules.* Activities and relationships among people in a bureaucracy are governed by explicit rules. In this way, everyone knows what is required of him. Rules, then, make the workings of bureaucracy orderly and predictable, even with changes in personnel. Von Moltke

clearly used this principle in his organization of the Prussian army, in which military procedures were to be carried out in explicitly stated ways. No activities of any consequence were left to personal discretion.

4. *Impersonality.* Weber believed that because emotions impede efficiency, they have no place in a bureaucracy. Personal detachment promotes rational decision making, he argued. Impersonality toward both co-workers and those who do business with the organization encourages the equitable treatment of all individuals and the subordination of personal interests to organizational goals. Such impersonality was certainly part of von Moltke's approach to running the Prussian army. Von Moltke was himself an austere person for whom emotionally motivated decisions would have been completely out of character. This stern Prussian chief of staff was the epitome of emotional detachment and strict objectivity in bureaucratic administration.

5. *Rewards based on merit.* Positions in a bureaucracy are awarded on the basis of technical qualifications (as measured by tests, educational degrees and diplomas, and other standardized yardsticks), not on the basis of who one knows. If supervisors make a practice of giving jobs and promotions to people because they are friends or relatives, the organization will eventually suffer. Not only will less competent people fill many positions but individual effort will also be discouraged and the bureaucracy's *esprit de corps* will be reduced. People must know that their work will be properly rewarded in order for them to give their best efforts to an organization. In an organization in which hiring and promotion are based on merit, workers tend to view their employment not just as a job but as a "career." Again, the Prussian army is an excellent example of this principle put into practice. Von Moltke was a firm believer in awarding positions strictly on the basis of performance. He looked upon officers as professionals who earned their rank through training and hard work. This new professionalism in the Prussian army was one of the reasons for its success.

Sources of Bureaucratic Variation

Because Weber defined bureaucracy in terms of these five features, it is easy to assume that virtually all formal organizations have these particular traits. This, however, is not always the case. Formal organizations vary considerably in how close they are to Weber's ideal type (Hall 1963–4; Udy 1959; Zey-Ferrell 1981). They also vary in terms of other key characteristics such as *size* (from the huge federal government with its millions of employees to a business with under 100 workers), *complexity* of organization (how many different kinds of jobs there are), *centralization* of control (whether decision making is concentrated in a few hands or widely dispersed), and the *range of goals* set (many or few). Sociologists wonder why so many differences exist among formal organizations (Hannan and Freeman 1977). Why is there so much variation in the ways that bureaucracies are structured?

Although different researchers have given different answers to this question, most look for causes in the external environments of organizations. Swift and Company, for example, was greatly affected by a number of important environmental factors in its early years. These included the enormous demand for fresh beef in eastern cities, consumer hesitation about eating meat that had not been recently slaughtered, the railroads' resistance to accepting Swift's refrigerated cars, and the opposition of local butchers who feared the new competition. How large the Swift organization grew, and how it structured its operation, were undoubtedly influenced by all these factors. Similarly, the local centers of power were opposed to the organizational goals of the TVA. These pressures from outside elements helped to change the way the TVA was run.

Although there is much agreement that the external environment may help to shape an organization's structure, there are differences of opinion regarding how, exactly, this process takes place. One theory holds that an organization actively *adapts* to its external environment by structuring itself so as to increase its chances of succeeding in that particular environment. The organization of Swift and Company is a good example of this **adaptation model.** Gustavus Swift faced two key elements in his external environment: the existence of an unmet demand for beef in east-coast cities, and the fact that in the United States very large herds of cattle could be raised only on the western prairies. The way that

Swift structured his firm was a direct response to these two environmental givens. He deliberately integrated most phases of the meat-selling business (slaughtering, packing, shipping, marketing) into one large-scale operation. This enabled him to direct the supply of beef to where it was most needed. In the process, Swift not only adapted to his external environment, he actually controlled it to a significant degree. For instance, when Swift decided to build his own refrigerated railway cars, he reduced his dependence on the railroad companies that were often thwarting his efforts. Here his actions overcame a major environmental obstacle.

Another theory of the relationship between organizations and their external environments is called the **selection model** (Aldrich and Pfeffer 1976). This theory holds that there is often too much inertia in large organizations for them to adapt effectively to the environment (Hannan and Freeman 1977). This approach views the external environment as determining which organizational structures will succeed and which ones will fail. Organizations will thrive if they have chosen structures that are well suited to the external environment, and they will perish if they have chosen structures that are poorly suited.

The selection model is supported by empirical research. For example, Freeman and Hannan (1983) have predicted that in a very unstable environment (one with a great deal of change), business firms that are generalists in the products they offer will tend to have an edge over specialist firms. This is because the generalists are protected by their diversity. If one good or service that a generalist firm sells falls out of favor with the public or becomes too expensive to make, it can always rely on its other product lines for profits. Specialist firms or organizations, in contrast, are more vulnerable to market changes. Freeman and Hannan have found, as they expected, that specialist organizations tend to fail more than generalist organizations in certain kinds of unstable settings. In a study of several hundred California restaurants, the generalists (those offering diverse kinds of foods) tended to outlive the specialists when the economic climate was variable and there was much seasonal fluctuation in sales. Here survival was not the result of adaptation by the organizations, but rather of the selective power of the environment.

It is still unclear which of these two theories better explains the relationship between bureaucratic structure and the external environment. These two processes—adaptation and selection—may exert major influences at different points in the life of an organization (Blau and Meyer 1987). Selective pressures may be greatest when an organization is young, which may be the reason that so many newly established firms fail (Freeman, Carroll, and Hannan 1983). Then, after an organization has survived a number of years, it may be better able to adapt to its environment.

From the consumer's point of view, a fashionable ethnic eating place may provide yet another opportunity to identify oneself with a particular group. But from the restaurant's point of view, such specialization is risky business: a restaurant with a diversified menu is more apt to survive in a troubled economy than one catering to a particular palate. (Jeff Perkell/The Stock Market.)

The Limitations of Bureaucracy

Even the best bureaucratic organization has limitations. For one thing, bureaucracy may have side effects on its workers that reduce their overall efficiency. In addition, modern research has shown that many of Weber's assumptions about bureaucracy are not necessarily true. In the following sections we examine some of the major limitations of bureaucracies.

Formal Versus Informal Structure

In 1927 two industrial sociologists began a study at the Hawthorne plant of the Western Electric Company (Roethlisberger and Dickson 1961). In one part of the study, they observed fourteen men who worked together wiring telephone switchboards on an assembly line. Their results would surprise anyone who thinks that formal organizations are run strictly "by the rules." The men's behavior was governed as much by unofficial norms as by the official regulations of Western Electric.

For example, the workers were expected to work at a steady rate throughout the day. In reality, they set their own pace, working harder in the morning and "taking it easy" in the afternoon. Similarly, although Western Electric tried to maximize output by paying the workers on a piece rate, the workers ostracized any worker who finished more boards than the "normal" amount. This was because the workers believed that their piece rate would be lowered if the overall output was too high. The workers also relieved their monotony by trading jobs with one another, against company rules, and they sometimes dropped their own work to help someone who had fallen behind, again in violation of regulations. Even supervisors did not act in the manner that Western Electric expected them to act. Although higher management assumed that assembly-line inspectors would exercise authority and "report" on the behavior of workers, in reality, the workers strongly discouraged the inspectors (considered "one of their own") from acting in such an official way.

The Western Electric findings pointed to the existence of both a formal and an informal structure in organizations. The **formal structure** consists of the official positions, duties, rules, and regulations as set by top management. The **informal structure** is made up of the *un*official norms that workers inevitably develop among themselves. These unofficial norms are designed to solve problems not covered by regulations, to eliminate unpleasant or unnecessary labor, and to generally protect the workers' interests. Although informal structures sometimes promote official organizational goals, at other times they hinder them. In the case of Western Electric, the company's informal structure reduced output in ways that top executives were not aware of.

Ritualism

Would it be preferable for an organization to inhibit informal structures and insist that its workers follow its rules and regulations to the letter? Weber believed that rules facilitate rational decision making and maximize efficiency, but contemporary sociologists are not so certain. For example, Robert Merton (1968) concluded that when people become devoted to procedures, they may perform them simply as rituals and lose sight of why these procedures were established in the first place (see Chapter 7). The procedures become an end in themselves and are carried out in an unreflective manner. Such **ritualism** can prevent people from recognizing and dealing with new conditions and problems. As a result, organizational efficiency and goals may be undermined.

Waste Making and Parkinson's Law

Another criticism of bureaucracy is that it may encourage waste making—performing tasks just to fill time. This tendency is captured in **Parkinson's law**: "Work expands to fill the time available for its completion" (Parkinson 1957). One example is the bureaucrat who appears busy to justify his or her job. Such bureaucrats create extra tasks for themselves but soon find that they need assistance to handle all of their work. Suppose they each hire two assistants (two being safer than one since one might become a competitor). In all likelihood, the bureaucrats will reserve the power to make decisions for themselves, thereby adding supervision to their original workload. If all goes well, the assistants will need their own assistants in a year or two, and there will then be seven people to do the work that one person once did. But the rituals of holding conferences and shuffling papers back and forth will be enough to keep all of them *demonstrably* busy.

What is going on inside the monolith? We have become accustomed to revelations of impropriety, waste, or ineptitude emerging from bureaucracies in both the public and private sectors. We might ask whether the "Peter Principle" applies to the whole as well as to its individual parts: what happens when an expanding bureaucracy reaches its level of incompetence? (Seth H. Goltzer/The Stock Market.)

Peter F. Drucker (1983), an authority on management, points out that colleges and universities are no exceptions to Parkinson's law:

> A liberal arts college I know had, in 1950, a president, a dean, an assistant dean of students who handled admissions, and a chief clerk who kept the books. Enrollment has doubled, from 500 to 1,000; but administrative staff has increased six-fold, with three vice presidents, four deans, and 17 assistant deans and assistant vice presidents. . . . [In 1950] five secretaries did the same work now being done by seven or eight deans, assistant deans, and assistant vice presidents—and did it very well.

The force of Parkinson's law was seen during the recession of the early 1980s. By December 1982 there were nearly 9 percent more managers and administrators in the American economy than there were in January 1980. During the same period, however, blue-collar jobs dropped by 12 percent (Arenson 1983). As a result, many more managers were supervising many fewer workers.

Protection of the Inept

Weber believed that bureaucratic organizations encourage the optimal use of available talent, weeding out deadwood as a matter of course. But in actual fact many firms are reluctant to demote incompetent employees for fear of incurring the expense of personnel turnover and undermining company morale (Goode 1967). These firms thus adopt a benevolent approach and retain marginal workers, thereby reducing overall efficiency.

Managers also tend to promote people who display superior performance in their present jobs. This rational practice, however, can have an irrational consequence. People who prove capable of handling their new assignments are advanced again and again—until they finally reach their level of *in*competence, the point at which their responsibilities exceed their talents. Laurence Peter and Raymond Hull termed this the **Peter principle** (1969). A good teacher who becomes a good principal, for example, might be promoted to district superintendent, a job that may be beyond the person's abilities. But at this point someone with such commendable past performance is not likely to be demoted. Instead, he or she will probably be kept on as superintendent and everyone will make the best of a bad situation, including the superintendent who will try to disguise his or her ineptitude. Meanwhile, the real work is being carried out by those who have not as yet reached their own levels of incompetence.

BEYOND BUREAUCRACY: COLLECTIVIST ORGANIZATIONS

Imagine attending a college that has no president, no dean, no bursar, no director of admissions—in fact, no administrators of any kind in the traditional sense. You are not required to take any particular courses, nor to stay at the school for any specified length of time. At the beginning of each semester, you simply "shop around" for classes that appeal to you. Once enrolled in a class you will not be given any formal tests; you will not even receive a formal grade. When you think you are ready to graduate, you submit to the faculty a written statement of "what you know and what you have accomplished." If the faculty accepts your statement, they will prepare for you *personally* a set of written and oral examinations to be taken over several days. Upon your successful completion of the exams you will be considered a graduate, even though no formal ceremony marks your new status.

If this college sounds strange to you, even somewhat bizarre, it is because it departs so completely from the traditional, bureaucratic system of American education. Yet such a school actually existed in the 1930s, 1940s, and early 1950s (Duberman 1973). It was called Black Mountain College and was located in the foothills of the Blue Ridge Mountains of North Carolina. The founders of Black Mountain College deliberately rejected bureaucratic structure, which they felt stifled creativi-

ty and independent thought. Instead, they fashioned what can be called a **collectivist organization**, an organization that was intended to be an alternative to traditional bureaucracy.

A collectivist organization is the direct opposite of a bureaucracy in a number of important ways (Rothschild-Whitt 1979):

1. *Authority.* A major feature of bureaucracies is the organizational hierarchy in which those at the top have authority over those at the bottom. In collectivist organizations, in contrast, hierarchies are done away with. Collectivist organizations want to abolish formal leadership and instead vest authority in the group as a whole. This pattern existed at Black Mountain College, where the entire community had a voice in making decisions. Students, for example, shared in the responsibility of running the college. Representatives of the student body attended faculty meetings, where educational policies were discussed. There was also a student member on the Board of Fellows, which made decisions about business matters.

2. *Rules.* Bureaucracies operate according to a set of formally established rules, whereas collectivist organizations try to minimize regulations. What rules collectivist organizations have emerge from group consensus and are never coercively imposed. At Black Mountain College there were very few guidelines for behavior. One was that members of the community

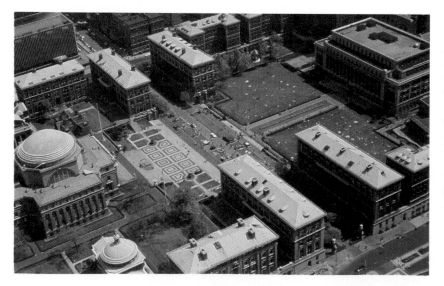

Did Black Mountain College fail because the collectivist approach is inadequate to the task of guiding and administering a large organization? Or are we so accustomed to bureaucracy that we are incapable of embracing other organizational concepts? Most educational institutions, like Columbia University pictured here, rely heavily on bureaucracy. Are there any organizations in your community that do not employ a bureaucratic structure? (Katrina Thomas/ Photo Researchers, Inc.)

should always act "intelligently." Another was that a "Do Not Disturb" sign on someone's study door should always be respected. Each year, students held a meeting at which they came to general agreements about other aspects of campus life. But no vote was ever taken on any of the issues discussed, for the idea of a majority forcing its views on others was strongly disapproved of.

3. *Social control*. In bureaucracies, rules and the authority to enforce them are powerful means of social control, both of which are absent in collectivist organizations. Collectivist organizations tend to control the behavior of members by making personal appeals to their sense of right and wrong, and by choosing as members those who share the group's values to begin with. In an incident at Black Mountain College, for example, four students (two males and two females) decided to take a trip to Florida during their spring vacation. The rest of the community felt that the trip was not "intelligent" behavior because it jeopardized the moral reputation of the school (remember that this was the 1930s). So some faculty and students talked to the four "deviants" and convinced them that such behavior should not be repeated. No other form of social control was ever needed to bring the four back into line.

4. *Social relations*. In bureaucracies social relations are impersonal, based solely on the specialized roles that people play in the organizational structure. In collectivist organizations, in contrast, social relations are not so segmented. They are in fact highly personal and multifaceted. In addition, collectivist organizations avoid the extensive division of labor that is the hallmark of bureaucracies. People perform many of the same tasks and have an egalitarian outlook. This was certainly true at Black Mountain College where faculty and students ate in the same dining hall, took turns helping to serve the tables, performed manual jobs around the campus such as gardening and cleanup, and generally shared many responsibilities.

5. *Incentives and advancement*. Whereas in bureaucracies people are always paid for their labor and promoted in accordance with formally stated criteria, in collectivist organizations remuneration and assessment of performance are much more informal. In the early years of Black Mountain College, for example, many instructors received no money at all because of the school's tight budget. Their "payment" came from the pleasure of being part of this experiment in education. Later, when salaries were issued, the amounts were set partly by "need," a criterion totally foreign to a bureaucracy.

Is a collectivist organization such as Black Mountain College a superior alternative to bureaucracy? Is it wise to abolish bureaucratic structure in favor of this model? It is difficult to draw any general conclusions. Each form of social organization is based on a different set of values. Each has its own advantages and limitations. But the fact remains that bureaucracies are far more widespread than collectivist organizations. Black Mountain College closed its doors in 1956, but thousands of bureaucratically structured schools are still in existence. This raises the question of whether bureaucratization is a necessary and inevitable part of modern life.

SUMMARY

1. A social group is a set of individuals who identify with one another and who interact in informally structured ways based on norms, goals, and values that they implicitly share.

2. The patterns of interaction that occur in social groups are greatly influenced by group size. The differences between interactions in dyads (two-person groups) and triads (three-person groups) are particularly striking. The members of triads can build coalitions, whereas those in dyads cannot. Dyads are also more prone to tension, because if one member leaves a dyad it ceases to exist. As group size increases beyond a triad, there is more potential for a specialized division of labor and more limits on the amount and quality of communication among group members.

3. Conformity to group goals may be based on group consensus or on the threat and use of force. In the course of group interactions, leaders emerge. Groups need leaders to direct various activities (task leadership) and to maintain good spirits and relations within the group (socioemotional leadership). Close-knit groups with strong, respected leaders are prone to groupthink.

4. Groups can be classified in a number of ways. An in-group is one with which a person identifies and in which he or she feels at home. An out-group is one with which a person does not identify and toward which he or she feels like an outsider. Groups to which we refer when evaluating ourselves and shaping our behavior, but to which we do not necessarily belong, are called reference groups.

5. Sociologists also distinguish between primary and secondary groups. A primary group is characterized by continuous face-to-face interaction, strong personal identity with the group, strong ties of affection among group members, multifaceted relationships, and a tendency to be very enduring. A secondary group has the opposite features: limited face-to-face interaction, modest or weak personal identity with the group, weak ties of affection among group members, limited relationships, and a tendency to be unenduring.

6. All groups must obtain some degree of commitment if they are going to survive. Rosabeth Kanter has identified six commitment-building processes: sacrifice, investment, renunciation, communion, mortification, and transcendence. The degree to which these six processes are present in a social group largely determines the level of commitment that that group enjoys.

7. A formal organization is a set of individuals whose activities are consciously and precisely designed for the purpose of achieving explicitly stated goals. Formal organization allows big groups and institutions to be more effective in controlling large numbers of people, in integrating diverse operations, and in overcoming rivals or reducing opposition. As a result, techniques of formal organization have been widely copied and have spread.

8. Virtually all formal organizations are structured bureaucratically. According to Weber's ideal type, a bu-reaucracy has five features: (1) division of labor into relatively narrow, specialized tasks, (2) a hierarchy of offices with each person responsible to the one above, (3) explicitly stated rules and regulations, (4) impersonality in decision making so as to promote rational choices, and (5) rewards and advancement based on merit.

9. In reality, formal organizations vary considerably in their closeness to Weber's ideal type. Sociologists believe that these variations are related to the fact that different organizations exist in different external environments. There are two arguments as to how the external environment actually affects organizational structure. The adaptation model holds that an organization actively adapts to its external environment by structuring itself so as to increase its chances of succeeding in that particular environment. The selection model argues that the external environment exerts selective power over which organizational structures will succeed and which ones will fail.

10. Although bureaucratic organization can be rational and efficient, it also has limitations. One is the fact that people are often guided by unofficial norms developed among themselves, rather than by official regulations. In addition, bureaucracy can promote overemphasis on regulations and give rise to ritualism. Bureaucracy may also encourage waste making, as well as the protection of inept workers.

11. An alternative to bureaucracy is the collectivist organization, which in many ways is the opposite of bureaucracy. In a collectivist organization there is no formal leadership; authority is vested in the group as a whole. Those who establish collectivist organizations believe that they overcome the dehumanizing aspects of bureaucracy. But the fact remains that bureaucracy is far more widespread.

GLOSSARY

Adaptation model. The theory that an organization actively adapts to its external environment by structuring itself so as to increase the chances of succeeding in that particular environment.

Aggregate. Individuals who happen to be in the same place at the same time.

Bureaucracy. An organizational structure characterized by specialization and division of labor, a hierarchy of offices, explicit rules and regulations, impersonality in decision making, and rewards and promotions based on merit.

Charisma. A special quality that causes others to accept a leader's authority.

Collectivist organization. An alternative to bureaucracy characterized by the absence of hierarchical structure, a minimum of rules, informal social-control mechanisms, highly personal social relationships, and the absence of standardized criteria for advancement.

Co-optation. The process of defusing potential opponents by making them part of one's organizational structure.

Dyad. A two-person group.

Formal organization. A set of individuals whose activities are consciously and precisely designed for the purpose of achieving explicitly stated goals.

Formal structure. The official positions, duties, rules, and regulations as set by the leaders of an organization.

Informal structure. The unofficial norms that develop among the members of an organization in order to solve problems not covered by the formal rules, eliminate unpleasant duties, and protect their own interests.

In-group. A group with which a person identifies and in which he or she feels at home.

Out-group. A group with which a person does not identify and toward which he or she feels like an outsider.

Parkinson's law. An explanation of why bureaucratic employees often appear busier than they should be: "Work expands to fill the time available for its completion."

Peter principle. An attempt to account for the incompetence of many bureaucratic employees by arguing that "in a hierarchy, every employee tends to rise to his [or her] level of incompetence."

Primary group. A group characterized by continuous face-to-face interaction, strong personal identity with the group, strong ties of affection among group members, multifaceted relationships among group members, and a tendency to be very enduring.

Reference group. A group to which people refer when evaluating themselves and shaping their behavior, but to which they may not necessarily belong.

Ritualism. Merton's term for following rules and regulations without regard for original goals or the consequences of one's actions.

Secondary group. A group characterized by limited face-to-face interaction, modest or weak personal identity with the group, weak ties of affection among group members, limited relationships, and a tendency not to be enduring.

Selection model. The theory that the external environment determines which organizational structures will succeed and which ones will fail. Organizations will thrive if they have chosen structures that are well suited to the external environment, and they will perish if they have chosen structures that are poorly suited to the environment.

Social group. A set of individuals who identify with one another and who interact in informally structured ways based on norms, goals, and values that they implicitly share.

Socioemotional leadership. Leadership for the purpose of maintaining good spirits and relations within a group.

Task leadership. Leadership for the purpose of directing group members to perform various tasks.

Triad. A three-person group.

CHAPTER 9
Communities and Cities

Main Street in Mineville starts to awaken at about 5:00 A.M. The cook at the restaurant arrives at this hour to start heating the stove and brewing the coffee. The postmaster makes an appearance at 5:30 to empty the one mailbox in this town of 1,400 people. All the out-of-town letters must be sorted and stamped in time to leave on the 6:30 train. Shortly before 6:30 the quiet is broken by the rumblings of the large dump truck that carries ore from the mine to the train station. Next, Reavley's cab pulls up at the depot to let off the few passengers who are taking the early train to Gold for shopping or business. By 7:00 the street is filled with miners on their way to work. They walk in groups, carrying their lunches; most of them have known each other since boyhood. At 8:30 a wave of children floods Main Street. Laughing, talking, running to catch up with friends, they head for the local school. The next big event is the arrival of the bus from Smelters, which delivers the daily papers. By 11:00 everyone is asking: "Is Julius [the bus driver] here yet?" With the papers in, attention turns to the arrival of the noontime mail train. For the rest of the day the post office is the busiest place in town. The people of Mineville go there not just to pick up their mail, but to chat with friends and neighbors and to catch up on town gossip (Blumenthal 1932).

New York City is 2,000 miles away from Mineville (a pseudonym for a town in Montana), but considering its life style the distance seems more like 200,000. On Manhattan's Upper West Side, for example, Columbus Avenue is the center of conspicuous consumption. Young urban professionals stroll through its stores on weekends, buying $400 sports jackets and $200 slacks, perfect for sitting in a fashionable café sipping Perrier at $5 a glass. On a typical Sunday thousands of people are part of this yuppie scene. One store owner reports that his new hardwood floor wore out from foot traffic in just two years! Some of these shoppers come from the suburbs, some from other sections of New York City, but a great many are Upper West Siders. They live in the same small area (five blocks wide by roughly twenty-seven blocks long), and yet while browsing through a new shop, dining in a restaurant, or drinking at a bar, they usually do not know *any* of the people around them. The Upper West Side is decidedly a "community" of strangers. Each resident is acquainted with only a tiny fraction of its 100,000 population (McKeon 1985; Morrisroe 1985).

Comparisons between Mineville and the Upper West Side of Manhattan could fill many pages. In Mineville the residents are involved in a continual round of community-centered activities, such as dances, club meetings, church programs, and projects sponsored by civic organizations. People are expected to participate, at least to some extent, in these activities. Those who do not are considered aloof and antisocial. In contrast, on the Upper West Side most people's social lives are not at all neighborhood oriented. In fact, to be extremely neighborly tends to invite suspicion. Most Upper West Siders know almost nothing about the people who share their apartment building. It is common not even to know the tenant next door except as a name beneath a doorbell. Such anonymity is unheard of in Mineville. There, people know countless details about one another's lives. Sharing gossip about fellow residents is a favorite town pastime. Such close scrutiny of everyone's activities helps to keep the people of Mineville from stepping very far out of line. Of course, sexual indiscretions, incidents of drunkenness, and occasional teenage vandalism take place. But serious crime is so rare that the town council declared the office of police chief indefinitely vacant. Upper West Side residents would be horrified at the prospect of dismissing their police force. Muggings, robberies, rapes, and murders are a daily occurrence in New York City. Fear of crime drives many residents to install two, three, even four locks on their apartment door.

How can we sum up the differences between Mineville and the Upper West Side of Manhattan? What is the essence of the contrasts between them? Those contrasts are essentially differences of *place*, differences between a small town and a large city. Granted, Albert Blumenthal wrote his sociological description of Mineville in the early 1930s, a time when the United States was in many ways different than it is today. But small towns like Mineville still exist in our society. There are still places where, despite modern technology and mass communication, the basic features of small-town life remain. According to sociologist Ernest Burgess, these features include "close acquaintanceship of everyone with everyone else, the dominance of personal relations, and subjection of the individual to continuous observation and control by the community" (Preface to Blumenthal 1932, p. xii). None of these features are found on the Upper West Side of Manhattan. In fact, the Upper West Side seems to present the opposite spectrum in all three respects. Can we therefore conclude that the Upper West Side is nothing at all like Mineville? Probably not, because, as you will see later in this chapter, some sociologists argue that vestiges of traditional communities—and sometimes entirely new kinds of communities—thrive in even the most urbanized settings.

This chapter takes a sociological look at life in towns and cities. First, we examine the question of whether urbanization has destroyed community or simply given new form to the close, enduring relationships found in places like Mineville. Second, we consider the historical process of urbanization. Where and when did

cities first appear and why did they develop? Has the basic form and function of cities changed much over the centuries? What are the differences between, say, Venice, Italy, during the Renaissance and the sprawling metropolis of Los Angeles today? Third, we look more closely at the contemporary urban environment and evaluate several theories that attempt to explain its spatial organization. We conclude the chapter by returning to the relationship between community and urbanization and by considering two recent trends: revitalization of inner-city neighborhoods and commercial districts, and the rapid growth of small towns where huge new industrial plants have been built.

THE EFFECTS OF URBANIZATION ON COMMUNITY

Urbanization is the process whereby large numbers of people leave the countryside and small towns in order to settle in cities and surrounding metropolitan areas. Thus, urbanization involves migration from sparsely populated regions to densely populated ones. The extent of this migration has been enormous in the twentieth century. In 1900, 86.4 percent of the world population lived in rural areas, whereas only 13.6 percent lived in cities. Today, only 37.5 percent of people are rural residents, whereas 62.5 are now city dwellers (Palen 1986). Densely populated urban regions have, in short, become a dominant feature of the modern landscape.

But migration statistics do not convey the scope of the social transformation that urbanization has entailed. Living in a city is profoundly different from living in the countryside. Some see this difference as a change for the better. They view cities as the epitome of human civilization: places where people of different backgrounds can mingle and exchange ideas and outlooks, places that encourage innovations in business, science, technology, and the arts. Those who praise city life also stress the tremendous specialization of products and services it allows. A large, dense population is composed of buyers and suppliers of virtually anything a person might wish. A look through the yellow pages of the New York City phone book, for example, shows a huge number of listings. The Automobile section alone has nearly a hundred subsections—from accessories, air conditioning, alarm systems, and appraisers, to vinyl

The epitome of civilization or a dehumanizing force? The question may be asked about either the microchip or the metropolis. In fact, the metropolitan area shown on the left is the microchip's home town—Silicon Valley, Sunvale, California. Does the similarity of appearance and structural organization reflect similarities of function and purpose? (Left: Jim Balog/Black Star; right: David Parker/Science Photo Library.)

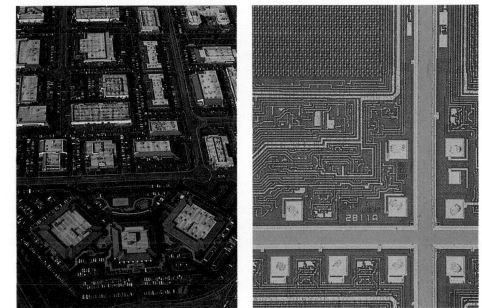

tops, washing and polishing, wheel alignment, and wreckers. But others contend that the problems of city life outweigh the benefits. Cities, they say, are polluted, crime-ridden, and so hectic that they promote stress and mental illness.

Sociologists also disagree on the consequences of urbanization. Some emphasize the positive outcomes it has had, others the negative ones. Much of their debate centers on whether urbanization has meant a loss of community. By community, sociologists mean more than a particular place inhabited by people; the term also describes a certain quality of relationships. People who form a **community** have common values and interests, as well as relatively enduring ties to one another. Because they have frequent face-to-face interactions, they feel close and tend to think of themselves as part of a group (they have a sense of "we-ness"). You may notice that this definition of community is very similar to the definition of primary groups in Chapter 8. This similarity is intentional, since the two concepts have much in common. The major difference between them is that communities tend to involve much larger numbers of people than primary groups do.

The term community certainly applies to life in a small town like Mineville, where everyone personally knows everyone else. But can community also be found in settings such as Manhattan's Upper West Side?

Sociologists suggest three different answers (Hunter 1978). One is that urbanization has destroyed all possibility of community in large, densely populated urban areas like the Upper West Side of Manhattan. A second view holds that a sense of community similar to that of Mineville persists within the neighborhoods of even the biggest, most populated cities. New York, Chicago, and Boston, it contends, have enclaves where relationships are in some ways like those in small towns. A third view is not concerned about finding traditional "villages" embedded in urban areas. Instead, it argues that urbanization has given rise to community of a different kind, one that does not depend on people living near one another. In the following sections we will explore the evidence for each of these perspectives.

Disintegration of Community

The idea that community disintegrates as urbanization occurs has deep roots in sociology. As early as 1887 the German sociologist Ferdinand Tönnies compared social relations in a small isolated village (which he called a *Gemeinschaft*) with social relations in a large urban center (which he called a *Gesellschaft*). In a **Gemeinschaft** everyone knows everyone else, and they interact on a daily basis. Each person is embedded in a close-knit network of relatives and friends. The members of the community also have many things in common. They share a common ancestry, common values, aspirations, and traditions, as well as many common roles. These shared elements and frequent face-to-face relations help to create strong social and emotional bonds. In addition, the status of each person in the community tends to be ascribed at birth. The squire's son does not become a tenant farmer, just as the tenant farmer's son does not marry a daughter of the gentry. People tend to remain what they were born to be. Geographic mobility, moreover, is as limited as social mobility. A person often lives and dies in the same small area. Thus, individual identity is closely tied to the community. People think of themselves in terms of their place within the *Gemeinschaft*.

Urban, industrial **Gesellschaft** society is dramatically different. For one thing, the dense population guarantees that many of the people who encounter each other in the course of a typical day will be strangers to each other. Those strangers with whom individuals must interact such as store clerks, waiters, and bank tellers, for example—are dealt with in very impersonal ways. In fact, relationships tend to be very superficial, even with neighbors. It is rare for urban neighbors to form a close-knit social group. Often they come from very different backgrounds, so they may not share ancestry, values, norms, or attitudes. Nor are they likely to have the same work roles, since work in urban society is highly specialized. All these differences make urban dwellers socially distanced from each other. What ties they have tend to be fragmented. Friends may live across town, co-workers miles away, and relatives virtually on the other side of the country. Moreover, unlike people in rural villages who spend their whole lives in the same location, urbanites are extremely mobile. In the United States, one out of every ten people moves each year. Urbanites also move socially, leaving old friends behind as they make new ones.

Tönnies's descriptions of life in a rural village versus life in a large city were part of his general theory of social change. He believed there was a major trend in the modern world: a shift from rural to urban, from *Gemeinschaft* to *Gesellschaft*. Tönnies regretted this development, for he thought increasing urbanization meant a growing loss of community. And he was not the only European sociologist to see urbanization as having corrosive effects on social relationships. In a classic essay, "The Metropolis and Mental Life" (1902–1903), German sociologist Georg Simmel described the constant stimulation that occurs in a noisy, crowded, ever-changing urban environment. Today this intense stimulation is often called "psychic overload" (Milgram 1970). According to Simmel, such stimulation encourages people to develop a blasé attitude toward what is going on around them. This attitude enables them to screen out much of what they see and hear, thus shielding them from emotional exhaustion. The result is that city dwellers seem to be cold and heartless, totally indifferent to the feelings and actions of others. This protective shell of reserve contrasts sharply with the mutual concern and caring typical of people in very small towns.

In the United States, Louis Wirth echoed the ideas of Tönnies and Simmel (Wirth 1938). Wirth was a member of the University of Chicago's Department of Sociology, which did a great deal to develop the field of urban sociology. In his study of Chicago during the 1920s and 1930s, Wirth argued that city populations have three characteristics: large size, high density (crowding), and great heterogeneity (many differences among people). Each of these, according to Wirth, is detrimental to close personal relationships. For instance, a large population makes it impossible for everyone to know everyone else. Because the Upper West Side of Manhattan has 100,000 residents, encounters with strangers need to be mostly superficial. Similarly, dense populations can give rise to friction and irritation, as people find it hard to obtain space and privacy. Wirth agreed with Simmel that the closer physical contacts amidst strangers, the more distant we tend to make our social relations. Finally, a heterogeneous population can undermine close personal ties. When neighbors no longer have values, norms, and attitudes in common, they tend to lose the sense of we-ness characteristic of community.

Wirth went on to link the impersonal nature of city life to the spread of serious social problems. For example, when people feel isolated and cut off from emotional support, they are more apt to suffer mental breakdowns, experience depression, or attempt suicide. Similarly, an indifferent attitude toward others, which Simmel saw in city dwellers, can permit increased rates of crime, delinquency, and corruption. Urban residents are more likely to prey upon each other because they think of their neighbors as anonymous faces, not as individuals. Deviance in cities, moreover, is difficult to control because people are so socially distanced. They do not scrutinize each other's lives and ostracize wrongdoers, as people in small towns do. Instead, city dwellers try to maintain social order through formal mechanisms of control: the law, the police, the courts. These mechanisms, however, are seldom as effective as the informal social pressures that operate in villages and towns.

Was Wirth right to claim that the fundamental features of urban life breed serious social problems? Recent empirical evidence suggests that he may have overstated his case. For instance, after reviewing a number of studies conducted by different researchers, Harvey Choldin (1978) concluded that population density is not the primary cause of crime and juvenile delinquency. Instead, these social problems are better predicted by a variety of social structural factors such as the racial mix of a population or the distribution of wealth and jobs. Thus, cities are not the cause of urban problems, but rather factors such as population mix, deprivation, and job opportunities, factors that vary considerably from one city to another.

The idea that urban life does not necessarily undermine human relationships was suggested by a number of

sociologists even before Choldin and others conducted their empirical research. Among those who held this view were some who argued that the traditional ties of community found in small towns often persist within the neighborhoods of large, modern cities.

Persistence of Community

Evidence that supports the persistence of community in urban settings was collected by sociologist Herbert Gans. In 1957 he rented an apartment in Boston's West End to observe life there firsthand. At the time, the West End of Boston was a low-income, working-class district of about 7,000 people living in three- and five-story tenement buildings. Most were second and third generation Italian Americans, although enclaves of Poles, Jews, Greeks, Ukranians, and other nationalities could be found there, too. Government officials considered the

Recent studies suggest that city dwellers establish new kinds of social networks to replace the traditional sense of community found in a small town. Still, the inhabitants of this tiny fishing village in the Faroe Islands of Denmark enjoy deeply rooted bonds of ancestry, friendship, work, and play impossible among the 8½ million residents of Tokyo. (Left: Adam Woolfitt/ Woodfin Camp; right: Ben Simmons/Stock Market.)

West End a decaying slum and planned to demolish it. But Gans found that the area was far from the depersonalized, alienating kind of place that Wirth described in his writings. In fact, he discovered that the West End was a community with the same close, enduring ties and networks of mutual support thought to exist only in very small towns. The book Gans wrote about West End residents he aptly called *The Urban Villagers* (1962).

What exactly was it about life in the West End that made it an urban village? Gans believed it was the extent to which the people there knew and interacted with one another. For instance, although all 7,000 West End residents were certainly not intimately acquainted, they did know and routinely talked with the neighbors on their own block. In fact, a very active social life took place in the hallways of buildings, in the shops, and on the streets. Neighbors would greet each other, stop to chat, and catch up on gossip. Moreover, even beyond their own block, West Enders often knew much about other members of their own ethnic group, even about people they had never personally met. They might learn, for instance, that a friend's second cousin three blocks away just gave birth to twins, or that the father-in-law of another friend's niece just lost his job. Through such intimate personal information, West Enders felt connected to hundreds of others around them. They knew each other's joys and sorrows, strengths and weaknesses, triumphs and failures. By no means were they a collection of strangers, hardly acknowledging one another's existence. They enjoyed the close social ties characteristic of a true community, even though they lived within the midst of a modern city.

The most intensive social interactions among West Enders took place among their small peer groups made up of relatives and close friends. Such groups would get together several times a week in someone's home. The men would congregate in the living room, the women around the kitchen table. For hours on end they would talk, joke, laugh, swap stories, report the latest gossip, and simply enjoy being part of the group. For the Italian West Enders on which Gans focused, group life was all-important. Peer groups started to form in early childhood and continued into adolescence and adulthood. A person would feel truly lost if cut off from his or her peer group. These groups provided companionship, emotional support, and even outlets for expressing individuality.

The West End of Boston is not unique in providing city dwellers with the sense of community found in small towns. For instance, when sociologist Gerald Suttles (1968) studied the Near West Side of Chicago, he, too, found enclaves that could be called urban villages. The Near West Side was clearly divided into ethnic neighborhoods—Italian, Mexican, black, Puerto Rican—each with its own turf. Like Boston's West End, this district of Chicago was also considered a slum, but life there was not the lonely, alienating experience that Wirth and others had described. The Near West Siders, like the West Enders, were well acquainted with neighbors from their own ethnic group. To walk along one's own block was not to pass through a sea of strangers, but to encounter people one had known all one's life.

The experience of shopping in local stores provides a good example of the small-town atmosphere that prevailed. Stores in a certain ethnic neighborhood catered to people of that ethnic group. Thus, an Italian-owned grocery store, a black-owned barber shop, or a Mexican-owned café were places where people of these ethnic backgrounds could find the products and services they preferred. At the same time, these establishments became centers of neighborhood social life. People would stop by to banter and gossip, discuss their problems, and air their views. Very often when a customer left, he or she would not have purchased anything.

It has been thought that the very basic features of urban life—overcrowding, social fragmentation and isolation, indifference, and impersonality—themselves create serious social problems. But some sociologists claim that the roots of urban crime, delinquency, and emotional breakdown are far more complex. And they note the persistence of community in many city neighborhoods, which may indeed offset other disadvantages. (Photo Researchers, Inc.)

Economic transactions were considered secondary to the real business of social give-and-take. If someone was a little tight for cash, credit would readily be extended with no embarrassment or fuss. These social patterns are very similar to those that existed in Mineville, where residents would frequent the shops of Main Street just to see and chat with their friends. They bear little relationship to the stereotyped view of cold and highly depersonalized life in a large city.

Transformation of Community

Gans, Suttles, and like-minded researchers argue that community persists *despite* urbanization. They point out that even in the largest cities, the residents of a neighborhood may develop a shared sense of belonging, intimacy, and caring. Often these urban villagers, to use Gans's term, also share a certain ethnic background. The residents may be immigrants from small rural towns in Europe or South America, or the children or grandchildren of such immigrants. They are maintaining in an urban environment the kind of community ties that their families have always thought of as natural and right.

But close-knit ethnic neighborhoods are not the only places where community survives in inner cities. Other sociologists have argued that the high concentration of people in urban settings gives rise to new forms of community attachments, which are not necessarily based on residential proximity. According to this view, city dwellers often form networks that transcend neighborhood boundaries and even city lines. These networks are based on shared interests, occupations, and activities. Thus, feminists from different parts of a city might regularly meet to share their views and undertake joint projects. Or people who have in common a love of classical music might form an amateur chamber orchestra and play together once a week. Rural villages are not conducive to these kinds of interest-based networks, for their populations are not large and diverse enough to support them. Only the city, with its huge concentration of people, allows such urban subcultures to form. Ironically, then, population size and density (the very traits that Wirth thought alienated people from each other) cause new kinds of social ties to develop and help perpetuate community.

Sociologist Claude Fischer (1982) tested this theory by interviewing over a thousand men and women who lived in places that varied greatly in their degree of urbanism. He found that urbanism did encourage people to find friends in a wider geographical area. However, physical distance between friends in no way weakened the personal bonds they formed. Friends who lived in widely separated sections of a city were just as apt to feel close to one another as friends who lived next door. Urbanism, in other words, did not destroy community. It simply broadened the geographical boundaries within which community was built up. Fischer also found that living in an urban area changed the composition of people's social networks. Relationships tended to be based less on kinship and membership in the same church and more on shared work roles and shared involvement in secular associations (such as clubs, interest groups, and civic organizations). Compared with rural residents, then, city dwellers tended to make more friends with people who enjoyed the same kinds of activities they did.

If community survives in cities, why do we get the sense that people there are aloof and uncaring? The answer, according to Fischer, is that city dwellers differ from rural residents in their general distrust of strangers. This distrust stems partly from a greater fear of crime and other forms of victimization, which tend to be more prevalent in urban areas. Thus, city dwellers' aloofness in public often acts as a kind of protective shell. But in their private lives these people have as close and caring relationships as people in more sparsely settled places.

The view that a new form of community is emerging in cities is not universally true, however. It is more accurate to say that community in cities is disintegrating, persisting, and being transformed all at the same time. Depending upon the particular urban districts we look at, we can find empirical support for each of the three theories we have outlined in this section. The task for sociologists is to identify the specific conditions under which urbanization destroys, sustains, or creates community ties. We will return to this task later in this chapter.

HISTORICAL DEVELOPMENT OF URBAN LIFE: A TALE OF FOUR CITIES

A **city** is a relatively large, densely populated, and permanent settlement of people who are socially diverse and who do not directly produce their own food. This definition includes cities through the ages, from ancient Thebes in Egypt and Athens in Greece, to modern-day New York, Tokyo, and Paris. At the dawn of human culture there were no cities, not even towns or villages. People lived in small bands, hunting, fishing, and foraging for their food. Because the bounty of nature in most parts of the world was not plentiful enough to support more than a few people in any one spot, humans were forced to be nomadic. They would settle in a place for only a short time, moving on when the food supply was depleted.

Why did people begin to live in cities? What social, cultural, and technological innovations enabled them to adopt this new form of social organization? To answer these questions, we must start by looking back to the era when people first began to domesticate plants and animals some 10,000 years ago. In certain parts of the world (probably those where the natural food supply was fairly precarious), people began attempting to tame nature for their own ends. They began weeding and watering stands of edible plants, adding organic matter to help fertilize the soil, and saving the seeds from the strongest, most desirable plants to sow the next spring. At the same time, they began protecting from predators herds of small wild animals, such as goats and sheep, moving them to more plentiful pastures during the dry months of summer, and supplementing their diets during the harshest periods of winter. These innovations, coupled with a few simple techniques for storing grain and meat, enabled people to abandon a nomadic life style in favor of settlement in small semipermanent villages. These villages, which housed only 200 to 400 people, were the basic form of human social organization for the next several thousand years (Childe 1952).

Then, sometime between 6000 and 5000 B.C., in the basins of the Nile, Tigris-Euphrates, and Indus river valleys, settlements emerged more than ten times the size of any earlier ones. Housing between 7,000 and 20,000 people, these first true cities developed largely because innovations in agriculture and transportation enabled people to take advantage of the valleys' exceptionally fertile soils. The domestication of new, higher-yield grains and the development of the ox-drawn plow, metallurgy, and irrigation resulted in a large food surplus. This surplus permitted some portion of the population to become artisans, merchants, teachers, lawmakers, soldiers, and priests rather than farmers. Such specialization of labor, in turn, required that people live in close proximity to others on whom they depended.

Densely populated areas therefore became necessities, and cities began to increase in size and number (Davis 1955).

Yet the emergence of cities cannot be explained solely in terms of an increased diversity of occupations. A centralized power structure was also needed for cities to grow and flourish (Sjoberg 1960). This centralized power structure was essential to coordinate the new diversity of social and economic activities. It was also essential to settle an increasing number of conflicts between groups with competing interests. Not accidentally, then, the development of the first true cities coincided with the emergence of powerful governments, formal lawmakers, judges, and administrators.

During most of the Middle Ages (from the fall of Rome in the fifth century A.D. until about 1350), the growth of cities in Europe came to a virtual standstill. But then the Renaissance began, and with it a rebirth of urban expansion. Cities grew not only in size but in political, technological, and artistic achievements. Fairly typical of cities during this period is Venice in northeast Italy, on the Adriatic Sea.

The Preindustrial City: Venice in Its Golden Age

Venice was built on a group of small islands nestled close together in a large lagoon. It is famous for its intricate network of 177 canals that serve as roads to move people and goods throughout the city. Ten centuries after its founding in 421, Venice had grown to the point of filling all the available land on the islands. Its population size was unstable, however, as epidemics of contagious diseases swept the city and waves of pilgrims, refugees, merchants, and seamen came and went. One estimate is that in 1422 Venice had 190,000 inhabitants (Davis 1955).

Preindustrial Venice was unquestionably a very crowded city, for the number of acres it covered was not very great. Interestingly, even if Venice had not been confined to a tiny group of islands, it would still have remained small in geographical area by today's standards. The reason is that transportation within preindustrial cities was limited to horse- and ox-drawn wagons, small river boats, or foot. In order for its interdependent residents to get fairly quickly from one point to another, a preindustrial city could be no more than a few miles

Even the earliest urban centers grew out of advances in agriculture and in the means of transporting surplus food from farm to town. Here an Egyptian pharoah oversees the harvest on his estates and makes decisions on how much and by what means the food will reach his people. (Egyptian Expedition of The Metropolitan Museum of Art, Rogers Fund, 1930.)

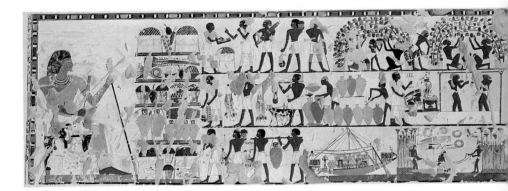

across. Urban sprawl, in other words, is a modern-day phenomenon. Before the nineteenth century, the cities of the world were small, concentrated settlements of people dotting a vast rural landscape.

Just as preindustrial cities were limited in size, they were also limited in population. Only so many people could be packed within the confines of their borders, because of the problem of transporting food for inhabitants. Food for Venice, for example, first had to be carried by wagon to the water's edge, then conveyed by barge to the islands and by gondola throughout the city. Because this system was so slow, food had to originate in the countryside very near to Venice, and farmers there produced only a limited amount. The 190,000 people who inhabited the city in 1422 were probably close to the maximum that could be adequately fed.

Without modern technology, a city with such a dense population tended to be dirty and a breeding ground for disease. Rotting garbage and raw sewage were dumped into the canals, causing foul odors to permeate the city. In 1438 a Spanish visitor to Venice described how residents tried to camouflage the stench by burning sweet-smelling spices in the streets (Chambers 1970). But spices do little to halt the spread of bacterial and viral infections. Epidemics periodically struck. The victims were banished to death houses or boarded up inside their homes in a desperate effort to stop the contagion. If this method sounds callous, remember that no medical tools were available to fight these scourges. Isolating the sick from the healthy was the only way of preventing most of the community from being wiped out.

The absence of modern lighting also made Venice dark and dangerous at night. The city's narrow alleys and shadowy canals were the scene of many murders and other acts of violence. Some of these crimes were the result of personal conflicts, while others were politically motivated. Some involved common workers and tradesmen; others, members of the aristocratic class. A special police force, the *signori di notte*, patrolled the city at night to protect law-abiding residents who ventured out of their homes. Anyone found carrying a sharp knife (even a small one) was immediately fined and imprisoned for half a month. Despite these efforts, the Venetian crime rate remained quite high throughout the preindustrial era (Chambers 1970).

Life in preindustrial Venice was not all negative, of course. Venice has always had a reputation for being a beautiful city, an architectural masterpiece. Magnificent churches, piazzas, and houses grace the major canals, many of which were built during the fifteenth and sixteenth centuries. Preindustrial Venice also excelled in the production of fine art and handicrafts. Wealthy Venetians were the patrons of some great painters, and the city's glassware and textiles were coveted throughout Europe (Davis 1973). Like many preindustrial cities, then, Venice was a center for the arts. It was also a center for the sciences and learning of all kinds (Davis 1973).

Although life in preindustrial Venice was generally harmonious, the population was sharply divided as to social class. A huge gap in wealth existed between the *tabarro* (ordinary citizens) and the *toga* (aristocrats). Most aristocratic families lived in great luxury. Their palaces had large, richly furnished rooms with glass windows; their tables were spread with excellent foods, which they ate with silver utensils; their beds had real mattresses and their gondolas were elegantly crafted (Davis 1973). A laborer would have to work for a year to earn the price paid for a single aristocrat's cloak. Still, the commoners of Venice were better off than their counterparts in most other European cities. The employment rate in preindustrial Venice usually remained high. Although the city certainly had its beggars, they were not as numerous nor as destitute as in Rome, Paris, or London. The relative well-being of the common working people is one reason that intense class conflict never erupted in Venice. Another reason was the absolute power of the ruling class. Secret "inquisitors of state" ferreted out those disloyal to the existing regime. Fear of the consequences of rebellion or treason kept most Venetians in line (Rowdon 1970).

Industrialization and Urbanization: Nineteenth-Century Boston

The explosion in urban growth that gave rise to the modern city depended on the process of industrialization. We tend to think of the Industrial Revolution as transforming the production of things like iron and steel, textiles and clothing. But the Industrial Revolution also affected farming, by changing the ways that crops and livestock were raised. The introduction of new agricultural equipment (tractors, cultivators, harvesters, milking machines) reduced the need for farm labor while greatly increasing yields. Mass-produced and mass-applied pesticides, herbicides, fertilizers, and feeds had the same effects, as did new, mechanized methods of irrigation. The result was a tremendous leap in the number of people a single farmer could supply. Whereas in 1820 one American farmer fed only four people (including himself), by 1900 one American farmer fed seven people, almost twice as many. Over the next eighty years even more impressive gains were made. Such massive food production has been capable of supporting huge urban settlements.

Just as industrialization made possible urban growth, so urban growth made possible industrialization. The two processes were interdependent. Workers forced off farms flocked to burgeoning cities, where they supplied the labor force needed to run the growing number of urban factories. In nineteenth-century Boston, for example, waves of immigrants from Europe were largely displaced farmers.

This enormous and continuous influx of people made Boston a great labor pool. Early industrialists had set up their factories in the small towns of New England not only for water power but also to tap the surplus labor

resources of the farm—young women and children. Now next to a fully developed seaport there existed a whole army of [immigrant] men and women desperately in need of work. The industrial prosperity of the Boston region dates from the 1840s when improvements in steam engines provided the power, and the flood of cheap labor provided the hands to tend factories and machines. (Warner 1962, p. 6)

Boston and other growing cities could support a huge industrial labor force for several reasons. One reason, which we already mentioned, was the great increase in agricultural productivity. Another was the development of railroad systems, which tremendously improved the speed and efficiency of transportation. Trains could deliver large amounts of food to downtown Boston, much more than could be hauled in with horses, carts, and wagons. The invention of refrigerated freight cars and warehouses further improved this system, making it possible to feed huge concentrations of city dwellers. At the same time, new building materials, such as steel and reinforced concrete, plus the invention of the elevator, enabled architects to design much taller buildings in their efforts to accommodate the increasingly dense population. Finally, improvements in public hygiene (indoor plumbing, municipal sewer systems, citywide garbage collection) cut the mortality rate caused by contagious diseases that for centuries had periodically decimated urban populations. By the late nineteenth century in Boston, for example, the public health movement had paid off. The city's dense population no longer suffered inevitable outbreaks of virulent epidemics.

Nineteenth-century Boston differed from preindustrial cities in other ways as well. There was its physical layout, for instance. While fifteenth-century Venice was a city of narrow, crooked alleys and canals, nineteenth-century Boston was increasingly developed in a gridlike pattern, with rows of parallel streets crisscrossing others at right angles. The square blocks of land thus formed were divided into uniform lots, each with a relatively narrow frontage on the street. This grid arrangement became the norm for neighborhoods of all kinds, from the tightly spaced three- and five-story tenements of the West End, to the spacious one-family houses of the outlying suburbs.

Suburbs themselves were another new feature of industrial urbanization. In nineteenth-century Boston and other cities of that era, new suburbs tended to spring up along expanding trolley lines (first horse-drawn trolleys and then electrically powered ones). From an aerial view Boston began to look like a giant bicycle wheel: the crowded industrial district lay at the center and suburbs extended out along the fixed-rail spokes. Later, manufacturing plants also started to migrate from the city's central hub to suburbs, where land was less expensive (Warner 1962). But they still remained close to train depots, for they depended upon the railroads to deliver raw materials and ship finished products.

The development of nineteenth-century suburbs also intensified residential segregation by social class. Because of the small size of preindustrial cities, the rich and poor in them never lived very far apart. A canal in preindustrial Venice, for example, might be lined with the homes of aristocratic families as well as those of working-class people. Nineteenth-century Boston, on the other hand, was developing into a divided city. By 1900 mainly lower-income families lived in the central core, within walking distance of the large factories in which they worked. Most middle- and upper-income families had moved to the suburbs, where the surroundings were less noisy, hectic, and dirty. Still, the distance between rich and poor was not very great. In the 1880s and 1890s the distance from Boston City Hall to the farthest outlying suburb was only about six miles. Beyond the outermost ring of commuter housing lay great stretches of farms and undeveloped woodland.

The Modern Metropolis: Los Angeles Today

This picture of nineteenth-century Boston bears little resemblance to the huge, contemporary **metropolis,** a major city with surrounding municipalities caught up in its economic and social orbit (Herbers 1983). Greater Los Angeles, for instance, covers some 1,500 square miles, an area about *fourteen* times larger than that of greater Boston at the turn of the century. Rather than being dominated by a single downtown district, this metropolis has many urban centers, fluidly linked by an enormous system of freeways. In sharp contrast to the settlement pattern of older industrial cities of the East, Los Angeles's settlement pattern is quite low in density (Warner 1972). The single-family unit is the most common form of housing. High-rise apartment buildings are relatively rare. But housing subdivisions, retail

shopping districts, entertainment centers, and industrial parks stretch for mile after mile.

The Bureau of the Census calls a metropolis like this one a **Consolidated Metropolitan Statistical Area (CMSA),** or an interlinked cluster of one or more cities and their surrounding suburbs that together have a population of over one million people. There are 21 CMSAs in the United States, and the Los Angeles one, with its 13 million inhabitants, is the second largest in population size. (The greater New York CMSA is first, with a total population of nearly 18 million.)

Some CMSAs have sprawled so much in geographical area that their outermost edges are starting to merge

Eighteenth-century Venice, planned for pedestrians, was a tightly confined city whose graceful Piazza San Marco provided a focal point for official or informal gatherings. Twentieth-century Los Angeles, a city with neither center nor limits, could only exist in the age of the automobile. (Top: Granger Collection; bottom: Ellis Herwig/Picture Cube.)

In the nineteenth century, the railroad and the steam engine were central symbols for man's invasion of the natural world. In Claude Monet's "Train in the Country," nature still holds the foreground, but those black, boxlike cars suggest that just over the horizon lie the first drab subdivisions. (Art Resource.)

with those of other neighboring metropolises. Such a vast urban stretch, hundreds of miles long, is called a **megalopolis** (literally meaning "great city"). The urban sprawl between Los Angeles and San Diego to the south forms one megalopolis. At its northern end this huge urban region may soon start to merge with the southern-most tip of the San Francisco metropolis. On the East Coast an enormous megalopolis extends from Kittery, Maine, to Quantico, Virginia, and includes the major urban centers of Boston, New York, Philadelphia, Balti-more, and Washington. Over 40 million people, a fifth of the nation's population, live in this sprawling 500-mile belt. Other growing megalopolises are Palm Beach–Miami, Dallas–Fort Worth, Pittsburgh–Youngstown–Canton–Akron–Cleveland, and Milwaukee–Chicago–Detroit.

Why have urban areas spread so relentlessly? Many think that the single most important reason has been the advent of the automobile. As more and more people traveled by car instead of by rail, they were much less restricted as to where they could live and still be able to commute to work. No longer did people have to build houses near trolley or train lines. They could settle in any area *between* these fixed transportation routes, or

even in districts beyond them. The same freedom applied to businesses deciding where to locate plants. With trucks delivering raw materials and shipping fin-ished products, a factory could now be far removed from railroad facilities. Relatively inexpensive roads were all that were needed to link one place with any other. The result was sprawling urban development crisscrossed with an intricate system of highways.

In southern California the devotion to private cars is such that it can almost be called a love affair. In 1915, when car ownership was still quite rare, the 750,000 residents of Los Angeles County had over 55,000 cars. Only three years later Los Angeles car registration had doubled to 110,000, by 1924 it had reached 440,000, and by 1929 there were 800,000 cars in this one California county (Brodsly 1981). Today most Los Ange-les residents (some 85 percent) have at least one car, and 96 percent of all weekday trips in the Los Angeles metropolitan region are made by car or truck. This amounts to some 5.8 million trips a day, covering some 75.2 million miles! (Brodsly 1981).

A complex system of freeways has been constructed to accommodate all this travel. The system is laid out in a grid pattern to maximize people's access to the roads. With each additional highway, people, businesses, and jobs were dispersed even farther, thus creating a need for more freeways. Today the freeway system is still insuffi-cient to handle all the traffic in greater Los Angeles. About 20 percent of all roads are classified as "congest-ed," with rush-hour travelers moving at under twenty miles an hour (Steiner 1981).

Extensive car travel and sprawling development make the life style in a modern metropolis like Los Angeles very different from that in an early industrial city like Boston. While nineteenth-century Bostonians considered ten miles a substantial round-trip commute, contemporary residents of Los Angeles often commute ten times that distance in order to get to and from work. And unlike their nineteenth-century counterparts, rela-tively few modern-day Los Angeles residents commute to the central city. The majority have jobs in outlying areas, making daily commuting an immense crisscross-ing of the entire metropolitan area. Most retail shopping, as well as entertainment, has also moved to the suburbs. Vast indoor shopping malls, usually located at the intersections of freeways, offer all the attractions of a central city—restaurants, theaters, department stores, boutiques, and gourmet food shops—without the park-ing problems. Significantly, the stores of downtown Los

Angeles account for only 3 percent of all retail sales in the metropolitan region (Brodsly 1981).

The central city embedded within the Los Angeles metropolis, like most older cities, has tended to lose population or remain static, while the outlying suburbs have grown. Nationwide, between 1970 and 1980, the number of suburbanites rose by 16 million, but the number of city dwellers stayed about the same. The social composition of central cities changed dramatically, however. Overall, their white populations declined by 6 million people, while their black populations increased by 2 million. This black/white shift occurred in Los Angeles, as it did in cities throughout the country. In addition, Los Angeles experienced an increase in its Latino population. The end result is that the segregation by race and income characteristic of nineteenth-century cities has remained and even intensified in the twentieth century.

The twentieth-century city is also marked by a distinctive occupational structure. Gone are most of the "smokestack," or heavy manufacturing, industries of the nineteenth century. The modern metropolis is dominated by service industries. Thus, downtown Los Angeles today is increasingly a center for banking, financial, and commercial enterprises, as well as for corporate headquarters. Industries like aerospace and electronics have moved their production facilities to the metropolitan periphery (Steiner 1981).

One might think that the patterns of life in the modern metropolis have been imposed on people as an unwanted byproduct of the private automobile. Perhaps it is more accurate to say that Americans have partly chosen the kind of life style that a city like Los Angeles offers. When asked where they would prefer to live if given a choice, most Americans say the suburbs or a small town (Gallup 1987). Greater Los Angeles, in a sense, answers their wishes. It is primarily one giant suburb, and some of the outermost communities are very much like small towns. As Dan Brodsly describes it in his book *L.A. Freeway*:

> Los Angeles emerged as America's first essentially middle-class metropolis. Southern California was the right place at the right time, a relatively virgin landscape waiting to be exploited by advancing technology and rising incomes. It was one of America's great experiments, an attempt to build a modern city free from the traumas of overcrowding and the gray ugliness of high-density urbanization. As such, it blazed the trail for much of the nation's future development. (1981, p. 136)

Third-World Cities: Modern Calcutta

Greater Los Angeles may be the essence of urban America in the late twentieth century, but it does not represent urban life in all parts of the world. In underdeveloped third-world nations, patterns of urbanization are unlike anything seen in the industrialized West. The city of Calcutta, India, illustrates these differences.

One dramatic difference is in rates of population growth. Whereas populations in many American cities have tended to level off, the populations of most third-world cities are growing at an explosive rate. Rapid growth is fueled by a high birthrate, coupled with a decrease in the death rate due to improved health care and hygiene. Of course, the death rate due to malnutrition and disease is far greater in Calcutta than in Los Angeles or Boston. But it is low enough *relative* to the birthrate to produce an ever-growing population. Particularly fast growing are the populations of third-world urban slums. They currently house over a billion people and are growing at an average rate of more than 15 percent a year (Werlin 1987).

Adding to rapid population growth in third-world cities is a high rate of rural-to-urban migration. Rural residents in third-world nations are constantly being pushed to the cities by changes in agriculture. These changes include the concentration of land ownership in the hands of fewer and wealthier people (thus displacing the poorer, smaller farmers) and the increased mechanization of agricultural production, which reduces the need for farm labor. At the same time, rural residents in third-world nations are also being pulled to the cities, lured by the hope that cities will provide escape from the poverty of the countryside. More often than not, this hope is unfulfilled, for conditions in the cities are bitterly poor for the masses of low-paid or unemployed workers. Still, the belief exists that conditions there *may* be better, and so rural residents are drawn by the thousands to the large urban centers.

The huge, ever-growing populations of third-world cities have made for tremendous overcrowding. Overall, Calcutta is three times as densely settled as New York City. About a third of its 10 million residents are packed into tightly cramped *bustee* (slum) quarters. The *bustee* houses are makeshift (constructed of mud, bamboo, or thatch), and most have only one room. The average living space for an entire family is only twelve square feet. These huts have no running water or sewer service. Large groups of neighbors must share an outdoor water tap and a primitive latrine (Werlin 1987). These extremely overcrowded conditions are typical of third-world city slums.

The kind of poverty that accompanies this kind of overcrowding is more severe and extensive than anything most Westerners can imagine. Calcutta is among the poorest of third-world cities. Eighty-two percent of its residents are classified as living near or below the poverty line. The net income per capita is under $50 a year. The reason for these conditions is that Calcutta is an economically crippled city. Its industrial production is dropping; its businesses are failing; its port is dying; its commerce is drying up. The economy can supply nowhere near enough jobs for the teeming population. An estimated 50 percent of the labor force has no formal employment; these people scrape together income in whatever way they can. Government cannot do much to help because it lacks the vast amounts of capital needed for the job. Among many other things, the city's roads, bridges, waterlines, sewers, and drainage systems are old and hopelessly inadequate, so it is hard to know where to begin trying to solve the problems.

And yet at first glance a Western visitor to Calcutta might not guess how dire the situation really is. Parts of the central city appear to be fairly modern, even prosperous: the government buildings, the successful businesses, and the homes of the affluent, for example. But surrounding this small, modern core are the slum districts, some 3,000 of them in all. The picture of poverty is worsened by the large number of homeless people who live and die on the streets. In Calcutta the homeless number half a million, making this city one of the world capitals of misery and despair. Thus, although we tend to think of large cities as centers of progress, many that are found in developing nations are far from progressive. The rest of this chapter will deal in more detail with cities in the modern, industrialized United States. But bear in mind that for billions of people around the world, the American style of urbanization is very much removed from their experience.

EXPLAINING PATTERNS OF URBAN LAND USE

No city ever develops at random. Affluent housing does not spring up in the middle of decaying slums, nor do smoke-belching factories suddenly get built next to elegant office towers. The shape of a city, in other words, is not haphazard. It is the product of social, economic, political, and geographical forces (see the box on Race, Poverty, and America's Suburbs). But exactly which forces are most important and what influences do they exert? In this section we consider answers from two different perspectives: the urban-ecology perspective and the political-economy view.

Urban Ecology

Ecology is a subfield of biology that studies how living organisms interact with their physical environment and with each other to affect the development of their communities. In the mid-twentieth century a number of sociologists began to borrow ecological concepts and apply them to the study of cities. Calling their approach **urban ecology,** they examined how the social uses of urban land result from an interaction between diverse groups of people and their physical/geographical environment. The urban ecology perspective has produced three major models of urban area development.

Many Third-World cities present the stark contrast of a progressive, affluent urban center surrounded by abject poverty, as in this view of a tent-city outside Bombay, India. American cities also present such contrasts, particularly with the recent growth in numbers of street people. But in the Third World, the desperate condition of the shantytown poor is intensified by high birthrates, continued migration from country to city, and severe unemployment. (Porterfield/Chickering/Photo Researchers, Inc.)

FIGURE 9.1   Models of Urban Space

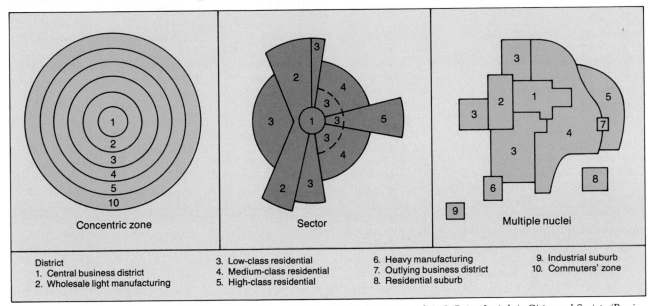

District	3. Low-class residential	6. Heavy manufacturing	9. Industrial suburb
1. Central business district	4. Medium-class residential	7. Outlying business district	10. Commuters' zone
2. Wholesale light manufacturing	5. High-class residential	8. Residential suburb	

Source: Chauncy D. Harris and Edward Ullman, "The Nature of Cities." In Paul K. Hatt and A. J. Reiss, Jr. (eds.), *Cities and Society* (Peoria, Ill.: Free Press, 1957).

Attempts to describe the structure of cities have produced the three alternative models shown here: Burgess's concentric zone model, with the business district at the center and other districts radiating out from it; Hoyt's sector model, emphasizing transportation routes; and Harris and Ullman's multiple nuclei model, organized around land uses, costs, and interests. A newer approach to the analysis of urban structure is called social area analysis. Analysts, using the census and other social indicators, attempt to explain residential patterns by correlating broad social categories, such as social rank, family structure, and ethnicity. With the advent of the computer, even more factors are being taken into account in models of urban land use and social structure.

Three Models of Urban Land Use

The earliest model of urban land use was proposed by Ernest Burgess, a leading spokesman for the Chicago school of sociology. Burgess argued that as the size of an urban population increases, people compete for the use of urban space (Park, Burgess, and McKenzie 1925). This competition tends to produce five concentric zones of development, each serving a different purpose (see Figure 9.1). The first zone, at the center of the city, is the business district, made up of stores and offices. Adjacent to and outward from this central area of commerce is a zone in transition. It is characterized by residential instability, low rents, high crime rates, and

various forms of vice, but is it slowly being invaded by business and light manufacturing. Beyond the zone in transition lie three residential zones. The first is inhabited by the working class, the second by the middle and upper classes, and the third is a zone of commuter suburbs outside the city limits. Burgess did not intend this **concentric zone model** to describe all American cities. It best describes a city like Chicago that developed very rapidly after the Industrial Revolution but before the introduction of the automobile.

In the 1930s sociologist Homer Hoyt (1943) proposed another ecological model of urban development, one that applied to some of the cities that don't fit Burgess's model. Hoyt emphasized the importance of

Race, Poverty, and America's Suburbs

On many streets in Ford Heights half the houses are empty. Their windows are shattered, their doors hang off the hinges, their driveways are littered with junk. In the downtown area, men loiter on street corners, idling away the hours with no jobs to go to and no prospects in sight. The steel mills and fertilizer plants have all shut down. So have many retail stores, their buildings boarded up or barred with steel gates. The unemployment rate in Ford Heights is over 55 percent. Per capita income in 1985 was barely over $4,500. Recently, the area changed its name from East Chicago Heights to Ford Heights, in honor of the Ford Motor Company stamping plant that still survives there (the only large employer left). "Maybe a new name will give us a fresh start," said one politically active resident. "Maybe it will urge people to try harder and not lose hope. It's easy to lose hope here." (Johnson 1987:A18)

Where is this economically blighted community? In some decaying part of downtown Chicago? Surprisingly, Ford Heights is *not* an inner-city district, but rather a small suburb—a town of only 5,300 people 25 miles south of Chicago. In a recent study of

America's 15 largest metropolitan areas, Ford Heights ranked the poorest of all the communities surveyed (see the accompanying table). Like most low-income suburbs, Ford Heights is predominantly black. The exceptions to this pattern are mainly in California where some of Los Angeles's poorest suburbs are primarily Hispanic.

Ford Heights shatters the image that most people have of the suburbs. To Americans the typical suburb has tree-lined streets, neatly painted houses, backyard barbeques, and well-cut lawns. Places like Ford Heights are so far removed from this mental picture, that the term "suburb" hardly seems to apply to them. The accompanying table shows just how large a gap in income exists between the poorest and the richest of America's suburbs. Kenilworth, which is also outside Chicago, is the wealthiest with a 1985 per capita income of $48,950. The average resident of Kenilworth, in other words, earns nearly eleven times as much as the average resident of Ford Heights (Johnson 1987).

Are places like Ford Heights the best most minority-group families can expect when striving for the dream of a house in the suburbs? Fortunately

not. There are also more prosperous American suburbs where racial and ethnic minorities have found homes. But often these are still predominantly black or Hispanic, either "spillover" ghettos adjacent to a central city, or older "fringe" towns (Muller 1981). The movement of minorities into the *white* suburbs has been slow to come. In the 1960s, blacks made some inroads by "leapfrogging" into white towns with older, less desirable residential sections where the white demand for houses had dropped. These inroads were facilitated by the civil rights movement and the changing racial attitudes of the time (Stahura 1986).

This leapfrogging pattern, however, was sharply curtailed during the 1970s, as the country in general grew more conservative, and fewer and fewer white suburbs became open to blacks. It seemed for a time as if black suburban growth would be largely confined to already black areas, at least for the near future. But then a new trend emerged. Some smaller, higher-status white suburbs began to experience sagging population growth and erosion of their tax bases. Many of these towns attempted to revitalize

transportation routes—such as railroad lines, highways, rivers, and canals—in shaping the growth of cities. His model featured an outward movement of population, just as Burgess's did, but in Hoyt's model the zones of land use took the form of pie-shaped sectors surrounding a central business district (see Figure 9.1). According to this **sector model,** the various zones of urban land use tend to be distributed along major transportation routes radiating out from the downtown area. As land use of a certain type expands, it tends to do so within its particular sector, extending outward toward the edge of the metropolis. One example is the development of the

Boston suburbs along trolley lines. Another is the recent development of Silicon Valley in California, where computer firms have settled along freeways running south out of Oakland and San Francisco.

Both the concentric zone and the sector models assume that cities expand outward from a single business district that lies at the city center. This is not true of all urban areas, however. To describe those that have followed a different pattern, Chauncy Harris and Edward Ullman (1945) proposed the **multiple nuclei model.** In this model, cities develop a series of separate centers, called nuclei, each with its own specialized themselves by promoting development of local business and industry. These efforts spurred population growth, sometimes to the point where the towns became so large and diverse that they could no longer effectively control their racial compositions. As a result, more black families began moving into these once largely white communities (Stahura 1986).

It is wrong to conclude, however, that the American suburbs are fast becoming as racially mixed as the inner cities. The most desirable suburbs, especially, have a much smaller percentage of black residents than the percentage of blacks in the entire metropolitan regions in which those suburbs are found. Moreover, racial segregation by neighborhood remains a fact of life in suburbs throughout the country. American suburbs, in short, are still a very long way from being color-blind.

20 Suburbs: Wealth and Poverty
Per Capita Income in 1985 in 10 Richest and Poorest Suburbs in the United States

Richest		Poorest	
Kenilworth, Ill. (Chicago)	$48,950	Ford Heights, Ill. (Chicago)	$4,523
Hunter's Creek, Tex. (Houston)	47,957	Cudahy, Calif. (Los Angeles)	5,040
Cherry Hills, Colo. (Denver)	46,105	Bell Gardens, Calif. (Los Angeles)	5,187
Mission Hills, Kan. (Kansas City, Mo.)	46,030	Coachella, Calif. (Los Angeles)	5,225
Piney Point, Tex. (Houston)	45,940	Kinlock, Mo. (St. Louis)	5,529
Bloomfield Hills, Mich. (Detroit)	44,456	Florida City, Fla. (Miami)	5,628
Sands Point, L.I. (New York)	43,494	Huntington Park, Calif. (Los Angeles)	6,067
Rancho Santa Fe, Calif. (San Diego)	41,756	Opa-Locka, Fla. (Miami)	6,320
Nichols Hills, Okla. (Oklahoma City)	40,772	Compton, Calif. (Los Angeles)	6,403
Ladue, Mo. (St. Louis)	40,700	Robbins, Ill. (Chicago)	6,436

Income is projected from Census Bureau figures for 1983. Richest suburbs are communities of 2,500 or more; Kenilworth is defined to include an unincorporated area on its western border. Poorest suburbs include only suburbs of 15 largest metropolitan areas.

Source: The New York Times National News, Thursday, April 30, 1987.

functions (see Figure 9.1). Four basic factors encourage this pattern. First, certain activities require specialized facilities. Heavy manufacturing, for example, requires proximity to highways or railroad lines, just as international importing requires proximity to a port. Second, certain activities (such as retail trade) benefit when those involved in it are clustered close together (because this increases the pool of shoppers in an area). Third, certain dissimilar activities can be mutually detrimental when located together. Warehousing, for example, with its high demand for truck traffic, is detrimental to pedestrian shopping, and vice versa. Fourth, certain activities (such as wholesaling, which requires a great deal of space) cannot afford to be located in high-rent districts. These four factors together give rise to various specialized districts within a city. The city grows as the specialized districts expand and proliferate.

These models of urban land use are valuable tools for comparing the different ways that urban space has been developed. The ecological perspective, however, is not limited to such descriptions of the shapes that cities take. Much attention has also been paid to the ecological processes that produce these various spatial patterns. How, for instance, do the uses of urban land gradually change as population grows? Some of the answers that urban ecologists give are nicely illustrated by the development of the Harlem section of New York City.

Ecological Processes and Neighborhood Change

Today New York's Harlem is one of America's best-known urban slums. Because of its reputation for poverty and violence, crime, drug traffic, and general urban decay, few visitors to New York are encouraged to venture into this part of town. Yet in the late nineteenth century Harlem was among the most fashionable residential districts of the city. The story of this dramatic change in urban land use begins around the turn of the twentieth century, when Harlem was at its peak of affluence (based on Osofsky 1982).

In the late 1890s construction began on a new subway line that would extend into Harlem. The news set off a wave of speculation in Harlem real estate. People were convinced that property values, which were already high, would double and triple when the subway link to the central city was completed. So developers began to build apartments on every piece of vacant land. And the dwellings that were springing up all over were not modest, middle-class homes. Harlem was the home of the genteel and wealthy. Most in demand was expensive, "high-class" housing, which would reap the greatest profits for developers. Thus, most of the new apartments were large and richly appointed, with spacious living and dining rooms, maids' quarters, a butler's pantry, dumbwaiters, and elevators. The building boom quickly led to a glut of new housing at highly inflated prices. Many units were completed years before the new subway was in operation, so the massive influx of wealthy new residents that everyone expected never materialized. Buildings stood partly or even entirely vacant. The rents began to drop precipitously. Developers risked losing huge investments. How could they salvage this nightmare of overbuilding?

One group in the city was in desperate need of more and better housing: New York's large black population. Black realtors took advantage of the now plummeting rents in Harlem and began trying to place their clients there. At first only a few black families settled in Harlem, all of them in the newly developed west section. Many white apartment owners tried to prevent more from coming by signing agreements among themselves that they would not rent to blacks. These efforts proved ineffective, however, because the whites could not create a totally unified front. Some were willing to cut their losses and open their buildings to blacks. Others engaged in panic selling (disposing of their property to whoever would buy it at whatever price they could get). The end result was a steady movement of blacks into west Harlem, and from there into other parts of the district. By World War I much of Harlem was predominantly black.

But black Harlem at first was not a slum. It was initially the most luxurious black ghetto in American history. Occupying elegant apartments intended for the rich, black families finally had a decent neighborhood to live in. The problem was that more and more blacks wanted to move to Harlem. A steady stream pushed rentals up beyond the level that most blacks at the time could afford. Families were forced to begin taking in boarders, and many smaller buildings were converted to rooming houses. Conditions became increasingly overcrowded:

> People were packed together to the point of "indecency." Some landlords, after opening houses to Negro tenants, lost interest in caring for their property and permitted it to run down—halls were left dark and dirty, broken pipes were permitted to rot, steam heat was cut off as heating apparatus wore out, dumbwaiters broke down and were boarded up, homes became vermin-infested. (Osofsky 1982, p. 192)

By the 1920s Harlem had become one of the worst slums in the country.

One ecological theory that has tried to explain neighborhood change, such as that which occurred in Harlem, is the **invasion/succession model** (Park, Burgess, and McKenzie 1925). Its two major concepts of invasion and succession are borrowed from plant and animal ecology, in which *invasion* refers to the appearance in an environment of a new species, and *succession* refers to a change in the mix of different species present until a new, stable community is formed. In urban ecology, the invasion/succession process begins when social forces, including land values, begin to attract a new kind of resident to an urban district, a resident who is socially or racially different from those who are already there. In turn-of-the-century Harlem that new kind of resident was the black family. The perceived invasion is met with resistance by established residents, who are forced to compete with outsiders for available land. Competition may give way to conflict as the groups vie for space. Sometimes an accommodation is reached and the two manage to live together. This is one form of neighborhood succession. Other times, no accommodation is possible and one or the other group abandons the area. When the established residents are the ones who leave, as occurred in New York's Harlem, another type of succession has taken place.

Complementing the invasion/succession model of neighborhood change is the **neighborhood life-cycle model** (Hoover and Vernon 1959). It sees change in urban districts as part of a larger series of invasion/succession episodes. An area may begin by undergoing extensive *development*, just as Harlem did in the late nineteenth century. Then a period of *transition* may occur in which key social forces change (the overbuilding in Harlem, for example, followed by plummeting land values and a black invasion). A *downgrading* of the area may follow, as occurred in Harlem when landlords let their property run down. Eventually stores and residences may be so decayed that a *thinning out* of population occurs. The final stage may be urban *renewal* and a new wave of development. Of course, city neighborhoods do not necessarily pass through all these stages. Sometimes a certain neighborhood will become fixed at a certain point. Research suggests that movement through the stages depends on a number of factors, including the extent to which population and new housing are expanding, the extent to which area residents have access to jobs, the extent to which resources are mobilized to resist change, and the extent to which public officials pursue redevelopment (Schwirian 1983).

The ecological perspective remains influential in urban sociology today, but some new concepts have been added to it. One is the idea of interdependence, which counterbalances the traditional stress on competition for resources (Berry and Kasarda 1977). Contemporary urban ecologists see cities as integrated wholes, each part serving functions that complement and support those being served by other parts. Thus, as one part adapts to a changing environment, adjustments are needed in other parts so that the whole remains vital. For instance, if a certain district of the city is invaded by manufacturing, nearby areas will develop working-class housing to shelter the work force the new factories need. Note that these manufacturing and residential districts are mutually beneficial and interdependent. The facto-

This chapter defines various characteristics of a city and offers various models for its development. In this Hong Kong scene, with the headquarters of the Hong Kong & Shanghai Bank in the background, what details might a sociologist point to in order to illustrate the nature of a city and the dynamics of its growth? (Allen Green/ Photo Researchers, Inc.)

ries need the workers and provide jobs for them, just as the workers need the factories and supply them with labor. Contemporary urban ecologists believe that cities constantly adapt so as to improve their chances of survival in a certain environment (Hawley 1971). In doing so, they are constantly moving toward a state of equilibrium, in which the various interdependent parts are smoothly functioning.

The Political Economy of Urban Space

Sociologists emphasizing a power perspective see things very differently than urban ecologists do. They believe the shape of cities arises not from a process of functional adaptation to the environment, but rather because powerful groups direct urban growth to their own advantage. These powerful groups control the major economic and political institutions of the city: its corporations, banks, financial markets, real estate and construction industries, local government and government programs. Through such control they are able to constrain the choices open to working people who live within the metropolis. Because of its stress on economic and political power, this perspective on urban development is called the **political-economy view.** Let us see, first, how the political-economy view explains the rise of the modern corporate city.

Rise of the Corporate City

Sociologist David Gordon (1984) argues that the modern corporate city, with its downtown corporate headquarters and production facilities in the suburbs, was not primarily created by the advent of cars, trucks, and highways, as urban ecologists contend. These changes in technology, in Gordon's view, *enabled* the corporate city to emerge, but they were not its fundamental cause. According to Gordon, the corporate city was the product of capitalist profit making carried out by huge, wealthy corporations with immense control over worldwide markets.

One change that these corporations deliberately brought about was a shift in the location of production plants from the downtown district to the periphery of the city, or even beyond the city limits. The major motivation behind this shift was a need to control labor unions and reduce worker-management conflict. In the early twentieth century, capitalists were increasingly faced with picketing, strikes, and even sabotage of their operations. The clustering of factories in central cities made the problem worse, for workers in different plants could compare conditions and foment unrest among one another. One solution was to move to the suburbs, where employees would be more isolated from incidents of labor unrest. And so corporations moved there in ever-increasing numbers. Gordon believes that this exodus of production from the central cities was made possible by the wave of corporate mergers that occurred between 1898 and 1903. Many corporations were now large and sufficiently well financed to afford the investment in new facilities. The move to the suburbs fit the growing size and wealth of American business.

The proliferation of downtown corporate headquarters lodged in towering skyscrapers was a development that also fit the tenor of twentieth-century capitalism. By the 1920s many American corporations had acquired control over vast markets. "They were now large enough to separate administrative functions from the production process, leaving plant managers to oversee the factories while corporate managers supervised the far-flung empire" (Gordon 1984, p. 43). As anyone knows who has ever stood at the foot of a huge corporate tower, this ubiquitous feature of the modern city is the very symbol of enormous, highly centralized economic power.

The City as Growth Machine

While Gordon and others have tried to explain the spatial organization of capitalist cities, other sociologists with a political-economy perspective have looked at the forces that fuel the general process of urban expansion. According to sociologist Harvey Molotch (1976), "the city is, for those who count, a growth machine" (p. 310). By this he means that the city is a giant man-made device that helps expand business and commerce, increase the labor force, and make more intensive and widespread use of land resources. Growth, in short, is the essence of cities in capitalistic nations like the United States. The reason is simple. Growth is a source of greater wealth and power for those who own the city's land resources. Through growth, an acre that once sold for a few hundred dollars becomes worth millions. Through growth, urban landowning elites multiply their profits manifold.

Molotch sees the American city as an aggregate of land-based interests: a coalition of individuals, groups, and organizations that stand to gain or lose financially from how the city's land resources are developed. More intensive use of land is the objective, for this means greater profits. Many of the property owners in New York's Harlem, for instance, turned large apartments into one-room flats in order to maximize their profits. By the 1920s space in Harlem that would normally have earned only $40 a month was earning $100 or $125 because of intensified use. Some landlords even rented out space in basements and coalbins to get the most they could from their landholdings (Osofsky 1982). Increasing the total number of people that could be packed into the district was the overriding goal of the landowning elites. This example shows how the conditions of life in a city are the direct result of the urban growth machine and the interests of those who control it.

Local government assists urban growth, for elected officials are often deeply involved with the city's land interests. Many are large landowners themselves, or they are bankers, realtors, investment brokers, and other occupations whose success and income depend on a growing community. These officeholders try to maintain a favorable "growth climate," which means sizable tax breaks for developers and investors, harmonious labor relations to attract new industry, and a police force that gives high priority to protecting private property.

Molotch stresses that growth is not good for the whole community, as those in power contend. Urban growth can bring many distressing problems such as air and water pollution, traffic congestion, and residential overcrowding. It can also increase what people must pay for public utilities, police and fire protection, and other city services. And growth does not necessarily make jobs for residents, as proponents of it usually claim. Because workers are so mobile, the entire nation can be thought of as one huge labor pool. Thus, new jobs that growth creates in a particular city may be filled by people in other communities many miles away. Urban growth, in other words, bestows the greatest benefits on those who own the resources used in the process. This means the community's economic elites.

Urban Growth and the World Economy

Sociologist Joe Feagin (1985) takes the concept of an urban growth machine one step further by viewing it within the context of a worldwide capitalist economy. Feagin claims that the expansion of many modern metropolises can be fully understood only with this broader global picture as background. The relentless growth of Houston, Texas, oil capital of the United States, provides an excellent illustration of Feagin's point of view.

By every measure, Houston has grown phenomenally. Population has increased a minimum of 29 percent in every decade from 1850 to 1980, and in one decade (the 1920s) it more than doubled. Whereas in

The corporate tower, symbol of a centralized economic power, now dominates many a city skyline. Big companies make use of this symbol to define their corporate images in their advertising. This pyramid on the skyline of San Francisco is a familiar image of the Transamerica Corporation. (F. Scianna/Magnum.)

1890 Houston ranked only 112th in population among all U.S. cities, today it ranks fourth (after New York, Los Angeles, and Chicago). This growth has been accomplished partly by migration, but it has also resulted from land annexation. Houston covered only nine square miles in 1900, but it had annexed nearly 550 additional square miles by 1980 (Feagin 1985).

Feagin explains this impressive rate of growth not just by the push of local land-based interests, but also by the pull of the worldwide demand for oil and oil products. Over the years Houston has become a global center for the export of oil technology and equipment, as well as for oil refining and the manufacture of petro-chemicals. It has a special niche, so to speak, in a global capitalist system. As such, Houston's fate is more closely tied to global economic trends (especially the price of crude oil) than to national ones. When the price of oil rises (as it did in the 1970s), Houston is a boomtown; when the price of oil falls (as it did in the 1980s) Houston experiences serious recession. This boom-and-bust cycle in Houston during the last two decades illustrates how sensitive the city's development is to changes in the global economy. Because Houston is a key component of a capitalist worldwide market system, its fortunes ebb and flow with decisions made in the boardrooms of multinational corporations.

THE FUTURE OF URBANIZATION

What is the future of urbanization in the United States? What settlement patterns will be increasingly common as we enter the twenty-first century? Two developments in recent years are likely to accelerate, at least in the near future. One is the renovation of inner-city neighbor-hoods, a process called gentrification. The other is boomtown growth in previously small communities chosen as the sites of huge new industrial plants. In the rest of this chapter we will explore each of these developments.

Gentrification: Revitalization or Displacement of Community?

Gentrification is the conversion of working-class, often run-down areas of a city into middle- and upper-middle-class urban neighborhoods. Gentrification involves white-collar professionals taking over a district and total-ly refurbishing it. Architecturally interesting buildings are restored to their original beauty, inside and out. Gardens, trees, and shrubbery are planted, giving the area the look of well-tended prosperity. At the same time that residential streets are renovated, nearby stores may also be transformed. The old mom-and-pop variety

store, lunch counter, or laundry is replaced with a trendy boutique or a gourmet food shop. Recently gentrified neighborhoods include the Adams-Morgan section of Washington, Society Hill in Philadelphia, Mount Adams in Cincinnati, Inman Park in Atlanta, Mission District in San Francisco, Reservoir Hill in Baltimore, Boerum Hill in Brooklyn, and Kitsilano in Vancouver. In fact, scarcely a major metropolitan area in the Western world has not seen its share of gentri-fication.

On the face of it, gentrification seems to contradict Americans' long-standing preference for escaping the ills of the city by choosing life in the suburbs. It flies in the face of the common assumption that once a city district has run down, the well-to-do are not likely to risk buying property there (nor are banks likely to risk granting mortgages). And yet gentrification is a fact of modern urban life. What causes underlie it?

Some researchers have probed the personal motives of the "gentrifiers," the people who are actually renovat-ing inner-city areas. Their motives are usually varied. They want to be close to work in the city and avoid a long commute; to have easier access to urban places of entertainment (restaurants, museums, concert halls, theaters); and to satisfy a taste for living in old (some-times historic) houses rather than in the monotonous modernity of most suburbs. On the other hand, institu-tional factors also encourage gentrification. Before the gentrifiers arrive, laws have often been passed that protect the district from being razed for urban renewal by designation as a landmark area. At the same time, tax laws may offer financial benefits to those willing to invest in this decaying section of the city. Real estate develop-ers may then start buying cheap, not-yet-renovated buildings, with the expectation of reselling them for a handsome profit. The area gets labeled "up and coming" and gentrifiers start to move in (Zukin 1987).

The people who gentrify an urban neighborhood often share some social characteristics. One is their former place of residence. Most gentrifiers come not from the suburbs but from other parts of the city. Gentrification, in other words, is not a *back*-to-the-city movement but a shifting of population *within* the city. Gentrifiers also have in common their age (most are in their twenties, thirties, or early forties), their race (over 90 percent are white), their income (the majority are at the middle to upper end of the income range, with earnings well above the median for the city), their occupations (mostly professional and managerial, although a few lower-status white-collar workers may be included), and their household structures (predominantly single adults, living alone or cohabiting, or married couples without children) (LeGates and Hartman 1986).

Profiling the typical gentrifier is easier than profiling those whom gentrifiers displace. The displaced population is much more heterogeneous. Its members span all age groups, from children to the elderly, although in some gentrified neighborhoods the very old and the very young make up a disproportionate number of those who move out. Some racial heterogeneity also exists. Until recently, most of those displaced have been white, but gentrification is currently spreading to black and other minority neighborhoods. Thus, in the future minority groups probably will make up a larger percentage of the displaced population. As for income, those displaced by gentrification tend to be in the lower-middle range. Overall, however, earnings vary widely from very low to very high. A wide variation also exists in occupation, from the unemployed poor and welfare recipient to the occasional professional. Most displaced residents, however, have blue-collar or low-status white-collar jobs. Finally, the displaced population is made up

of diverse household types: from singles living alone, to married couples with or without children, to cohabiting individuals and other alternative arrangements (LeGates and Hartman 1986).

Interestingly, most of those displaced by gentrification settle close to (or even within) the area being gentrified. But they then risk being displaced again as the urban renovation process spreads. Not surprisingly, most of those displaced must pay more for rent, which is a particular burden to low-income families. This fact helps explain why the lower the income of a displaced family, the more likely its members are to feel dissatisfied with their new housing (LeGates and Hartman 1986).

How can we sum up the process of gentrification? Does it represent a truly new development in American residential patterns? Sociologist Irving Allen (1986), among others, thinks not. He contends that chic row houses in an inner city may simply be a new generation's way of expressing their status and success, just as their parents expressed their achievements with large, modern houses in the suburbs. In both cases the white upper-middle class is looking for a place to live that is buffered

Just as suburban development replaces rural communities and farmland, so gentrification displaces those city dwellers who cannot afford to buy renovated homes or pay higher rents. Gentrification, coupled with cutbacks in government support for low-income housing, has contributed to an increase in the number of homeless. (Left: John M. Roberts/The Stock Market; right: Jim Pickerell/Click/Chicago.)

from social strata and life styles other than its own. Gentrifiers appear to be no different from suburbanites in shunning racial, ethnic, and social-class diversity within their neighborhoods. Gentrification gives them an exclusive residential setting, while still allowing them to be close (but not too close) to the city's entertaining diversity.

Rural Boomtowns: Community or Alienation?

If cities are being redeveloped, so are small towns, but for different reasons. Corporations are again playing a major role in shaping land development. When General Motors executives announced that they had chosen Spring Hill, Tennessee, as the site of the company's new multi-billion-dollar plant, the audience assembled in nearby Columbia stood up and sang "God Bless America." Many Tennesseans, from the governor and legislators to the real estate agents near Spring Hill, were delighted with GM's decision. The little town of 1,100, twenty-eight miles south of Nashville, was to receive an economic boost that would have repercussions throughout the state. Twenty thousand new jobs would be created: 6,000 in the new plant itself with its annual payroll of $200,000,000 and 14,000 in businesses that would supply GM with materials, equipment, and parts. Such an economic bonanza seemed sorely needed in an area where unemployment ranged from 10 to 19 percent. And yet many Spring Hill residents had mixed feelings. They welcomed an economic boost of some kind, but not one of such gigantic proportions as the new GM plant (150 acres of floor space under one roof, the biggest single industrial investment in the history of the United States). They feared that the GM invasion would ruin farming and put an end to Spring Hill's quiet, peaceful way of life. Some were openly hostile toward the "Yankees" from Detroit. Was their apprehension groundless?

Sociological research can help to answer this question, for corporate investment in rural areas is far from rare today. In the decade of the 1970s, the number of manufacturing jobs in metropolitan areas of America increased by only 4 percent, whereas the number of

manufacturing jobs in *non*metropolitan areas grew by 24 percent, or six times as much (Summers and Branch 1984). This nonmetropolitan growth, moreover, was not just in rural districts adjacent to city suburbs. It even occurred in parts of the country that were quite removed from large metropolitan areas (Fuguitt 1985). The trend gives sociologists substantial data for predicting the impact that the GM plant will have on Spring Hill, Tennessee.

Based on their review of studies investigating 728 manufacturing plants in 245 small towns, Gene Summers and Kristi Branch (1984) conclude that rural industrialization has mixed effects. On the one hand, it creates new jobs, increases the flow of money through the local economy, improves housing, raises property values, and expands community services—all of which are positive effects. On the other hand, it does not confer all of the benefits that its proponents often predict.

One disappointment, according to Summers and Branch, is in the area of reducing local unemployment. The logical assumption is that if thousands of new jobs are created, the demand for labor will be so high that almost no one who wants employment will have trouble finding it. But this assumption is flawed. The community in which the new production facility is built is not closed to outsiders. People from many miles around and even from distant parts of the country are part of the labor pool from which the new jobs will be filled. And job applicants from outside the local community may be much better qualified than longtime residents for the available work. Spring Hill, for example, is largely a farming community. Its residents know virtually nothing about building modern cars. General Motors, therefore, is much more apt to hire experienced auto workers, especially those recently laid off from its other plants. In fact, GM has an agreement with the United Auto Workers that union members will be given first chance at jobs in Spring Hill.

This common pattern helps explain why rural industrialization often does little to reduce rural unemployment. In most of the studies Summers and Branch reviewed, less than 10 percent of the new jobs were filled by disadvantaged local residents (the local poor, unemployed, and minority group members). The state of Tennessee has tried to reverse this trend by creating a training program in modern car manufacturing. But the program is open to *all* Tennesseans, not just to Spring Hill residents and not just to those most in need of work.

Rural industrialization has disappointed local residents in other ways as well. The assumption that industry will bring in new tax dollars and thereby reduce the tax burden on individuals has proved wrong in many cases. The problem is that industries are often offered tax breaks to lure them to rural locations. General Motors, for example, is not required to pay property taxes for the first ten years its Spring Hill plant is in operation. After that, it will pay taxes on only 25 percent of the factory's assessed value (Borden 1986). Consequently, GM will do relatively little to defer the cost of increased municipal services to itself, its satellite industries, and any influx of new workers. Summers and Branch found that this pattern was relatively common. In many small towns where industrial plants were built, the cost of providing additional services (such as more police and fire protection, more waterlines, sewers, garbage pickup and disposal, and schools) exceeded the increased tax revenues.

Rural industrialization may also exact a psychological price. Spring Hill residents worry that a large and sudden invasion of new people will weaken the strong sense of community they have always had. Sociological research suggests that this concern is not unwarranted, at least for some segments of the population. One study compared people in a small town that had grown rapidly after the building of a power plant with people in neighboring towns that had experienced little growth (Freudenburg 1984). It found that adolescents in the boomtown had more negative attitudes toward their communities and their own lives, and felt more alienated from other people. Adolescents, in short, seemed particularly susceptible to losing a sense of community under conditions of rapid economic growth and accompanying social change.

Rural industrialization, then, is not an unmitigated good. Although it can generate employment and a general rise in income, those benefits do not affect all local residents. The prosperity tends to bypass those who are economically disadvantaged. In addition, local government faces increased costs that the industry may not help to meet, and some longtime residents may begin to lose their former sense of community. Only through concerted efforts to avoid these problems will people in places like Spring Hill, Tennessee, enjoy a future that improves upon their past.

SUMMARY

1. In the twentieth century the world has become fully urbanized, with people leaving the countryside and small towns to settle in cities and surrounding metropolitan areas. Today a majority of the world's population (almost 63 percent) lives in cities.

2. Sociologists disagree on the consequences of urbanization. Some argue that it inevitably brings a loss of community: a loss of the common values and the close, enduring ties characteristic of small towns. But others contend that community persists within urban neighborhoods. They say that cities have enclaves where relationships are similar to those in small towns. Still others argue that urbanization has produced a different kind of community, one that does not depend on people living near one another. Research suggests that each of these views has validity, but each tends to apply under different circumstances.

3. Cities have undergone great changes since they first arose. Preindustrial cities were necessarily small because ground transportation was limited to horse, wagon, and foot. In this confined space, aristocrats and commoners lived in close proximity. Preindustrial cities were also foul-smelling and dirty, prone to outbreaks of infectious diseases.

4. The explosive urban growth that gave rise to the modern city was made possible by the Industrial Revolution, and the greatly improved agricultural technology it brought. Farmers could now grow enough food to support very large, densely populated cities. Displaced farm workers migrated to these cities, where they provided the labor to run the factories that dominated the downtown area. Beyond the central city, residential suburbs developed along rail and trolley lines. These suburbs housed mainly middle- and upper-income fami-

lies. Low-income families remained in the cities near their places of work.

5. Suburbs expanded with the development of the sprawling metropolis, traversed by an intricate network of highways. In the metropolis, manufacturing has also moved out to the suburbs, as has much of retail trade and entertainment. The downtown area, now the home of financial institutions and corporate headquarters, is surrounded by the traditional low-income residential districts.

6. Whereas populations in many American cities have tended to level off, those in most third-world cities are growing at an explosive rate. Jobs, housing, and city services are hopelessly inadequate for these burgeoning populations, and, consequently, millions suffer abject poverty.

7. According to the urban ecology approach, cities are integrated wholes, each part serving functions that complement and support those being served by other parts. Urban ecologists have proposed several models to explain the development of a city's spatial organization. They include the concentric zone model, the sector model, and the multiple nuclei model. Urban ecologists have also described the processes involved in neighborhood change. Change often begins with invasion by a new group of residents, which then leads to a shift in the population's composition and a new use for that particular area.

8. The political-economy perspective stresses the importance of powerful groups in directing urban growth to their own advantage. These groups often form a coalition of land-based interests, including landlords, real estate developers, bankers, and financial investors. Powerful corporations did much to encourage the rise of the modern metropolis. According to the political-economy view, corporations moved their manufacturing operations to the suburbs largely to avoid labor unrest in the central cities. Today huge multinational corporations continue to affect the development of cities that are part of the global capitalist system.

9. Two important developments in recent years are gentrification (the renovation of working-class, inner-city neighborhoods) and the building of large industrial plants in rural areas. Sociologists are concerned that both these trends may weaken community ties; gentrification might do so by displacing low-income families, and rural industrialization by causing small towns to grow too fast.

GLOSSARY

City. A relatively large, densely populated, and permanent settlement of people who are socially diverse and who do not directly produce their own food.

Community. A relatively large group of people who have common values and interests, relatively enduring ties, frequent face-to-face interaction, and a sense of being close to one another.

Concentric zone model. Burgess's model of urban land use in which cities develop a central business district that is surrounded by several concentric rings, each devoted to a different set of economic and social activities. The first ring, nearest the central city, is an area of instability and high crime rates, gradually invaded by business and manufacturing. The next three rings contain working-class housing, middle- and upper-class housing, and commuter suburbs.

Consolidated Metropolitan Statistical Area (CMSA). An interlinked cluster of one or more cities and their surrounding suburbs that together have a population of over one million people.

Gemeinschaft. Tönnies's term for a small traditional place in which everyone knows everyone else and people tend to remain where they were born, both socially and geographically. In a *Gemeinschaft* people share a common ancestry, common values, aspirations, and traditions, and many common roles. These factors, plus daily face-to-face interaction, tend to create strong social and emotional bonds.

Gentrification. The conversion of working-class, often run-down areas of a city into middle- and upper-middle-class urban neighborhoods.

Gesellschaft. Tönnies's term for a society characterized by a large, densely settled population in which most people are strangers to one another and interact in impersonal ways. In a *Gesellschaft* people have diverse values, work roles, and ancestries, loosely knit networks of relatives and friends, and much social and geographical mobility.

Invasion/succession model. A model of neighborhood change that focuses on invasion by a new kind of resident, followed by competition for available land, and ultimately by the emergence of a new use for the area.

Megalopolis. Two or more neighboring metropolises that have sprawled so much in geographical area that their outermost edges merge with one another.

Metropolis. A major city with surrounding municipalities caught up in its economic and social orbit.

Multiple nuclei model. Harris and Ullman's model of urban land use in which cities develop as a series of separate centers, called nuclei, each with its own specialized functions.

Neighborhood life-cycle model. A model of neighborhood change that sees this process as part of a larger series of invasion/succession episodes. The complete cycle includes the following stages: development, transition, downgrading, thinning out, and renewal.

Political-economy perspective. A sociological view of cities that sees them as the product of decisions made by powerful groups on their own behalf.

Sector model. Hoyt's model of urban land use in which cities develop a series of pie-shaped sectors surrounding a central business district. The sectors tend to be distributed along major transportation routes radiating out from the downtown area, and each is devoted to distinct purposes.

Urban ecology. A sociological approach to studying cities that examines how the social uses of urban land is the result of an interaction between various groups of people and their physical/geographical environment.

Urbanization. The process whereby large numbers of people leave the countryside and small towns in order to settle in cities and surrounding metropolitan areas.

CHAPTER 10
Population

China today is home to 1,050 million people —nearly one-quarter of the world's population. Its population is four times that of the United States but its economy produces far less. The growth of China's population is largely the result of modernization, which has brought with it more food, better medical care, less disease, and fewer epidemics and famines. The death rate in China has decreased, more children survive to become parents, and the number of births has increased. (In the 1960s China experienced a "baby boom," just as the United States did slightly earlier—see Chapter 6.) The higher survival rate in China means that more people are entering childbearing age—so many, in fact, that in the early 1980s Chinese social scientists realized that even if each married couple had fewer than two children, the country would still face rapid population growth. This population growth was threatening to destroy China's chances to become a richer country: just providing food and basic necessities for everyone would consume all of its economic gains. Similar prospects face India and other countries in the developing world.

During the years that China's revolutionary leader Mao Zedong (also sometimes spelled Mao tse-Tung) was in power, the situation in China was largely ignored. Mao subscribed to the Marxist view that so-called population "problems" were merely secondary symptoms of poor economic development or the unfair distribution of goods. The problems, he thought, were not too many mouths, but too little food; not too many

workers, but too few jobs. But after Mao died, China's new leaders paid close attention to social research, showing how ignoring population problems only made them worse. Drastic measures seemed inevitable. The sheer numbers of people somehow had to be kept down.

To tame the explosive population growth, the Chinese government in the 1970s instituted a moderate policy, which encouraged married couples to have only two children. But a moderate policy did not check the tide of population growth, and the Chinese government launched a drastic policy of allowing one child per family, in the hopes of stabilizing the population at 1.2 billion by 2001 (Kane 1987). Today, a couple who plans to conceive a child must obtain official permission, in the form of a small red certificate. Otherwise, the couple is expected to be sterilized or to use contraceptives, which can be obtained from the state at no cost. To enforce the policy, the government has a variety of incentives for those who comply and punishments for those who do not. For example, couples who have only one child get a monthly stipend until the child is fourteen, special consideration for scarce housing, free medical care, and extra pension benefits. The pressure to conform is powerful. Communities and workplaces monitor their female members to keep up with pregnancies, and quotas for pregnancies have been established. Couples who ignore the state's directive suffer social stigma and economic penalties.

The family-planning policy, instituted in China in 1979, has been remarkably effective (though considera-

Many nations of the world have adopted vigorous policies aimed at reducing birthrates. The billboard in the background is part of an extensive campaign by the Chinese government to promote one-child families. This policy includes financial benefits to couples who meet this goal and penalties to those having more than two children. (Owen Franken.)

over age 64. In 2000, 8 percent will be over age 64, and in 2050, 25 percent will be (Chen 1984). At the family level, children without siblings will each have to care for two aging parents. At the national level, the great numbers of aging people will tax the society's resources. China shares this problem—a rapidly aging population without a large enough following generation to support it—with many of the developed nations of the world.

Our look at China and its population dilemma dramatically illustrates an important way of telling a society's story: through the numbers, characteristics, and distribution of its people. Population data—information from periodic national censuses and from records of births, marriages, and deaths—are indispensable to an understanding of social life. Population size takes on added significance when we assess the adequacy of a people's environmental resources and the impact that population numbers have on an ecological setting. Similarly, a society's composition—the age, sex, education, income, occupation, marital status, race, and religion of its members—has enormous implications for the nature of relationships among its people. And the distribution of people—their location in world regions, countries, provinces, states, cities, localities, and blocks—has consequences for institutional arrangements (for instance, when many people move into an area, they are likely to increase the demands on its schools, hospitals, shopping centers, and roads; when they move out of an area these facilities may be underused). Indeed, in recent years, the study of population has emerged as one of the most important influences on business and public policy. In part, because they had the benefit of more sophisticated data (in particular, the 1982 census), Chinese policymakers were able to recognize and assess their nation's dilemma.

bly more so in cities than in the countryside). Births to women of childbearing age have fallen dramatically—to about 2.5 children for every woman (Chen 1984). Between 1968 and 1980, the fertility rate fell by an extraordinary 65 percent. But the larger goal—a stabilized population—is not yet in sight.

China may eventually succeed in stabilizing its population growth, but in doing so, it is creating a new problem. The irony is that because of the very success of China's population policy, the Chinese population is aging rapidly. In 1982, 5 percent of the population was

POPULATION AND SOCIETY

Much of our information about a society, including data from opinion and attitude surveys, cannot be usefully interpreted without reference to population data. For example, current survey data indicate that 90 percent of American men and women still profess a strong attachment to the institution of marriage (Walsh 1986). Yet Census Bureau statistics show that increasing numbers of people are postponing marriage until their late twenties and thirties, remaining single, and/or getting divorced.

Clearly, neither the population statistics nor the survey data tell the whole story. A simple interpretation—either that marriage as an institution is in deep trouble or that it is problem-free—is misleading (see Chapter 16). Sociologists, using both kinds of data, make further, more potentially useful inquiries: about why fewer people are choosing to marry or to stay married, about who they are—by age, education, income, and region—and about the economic and social correlates of these statistical patterns.

In this chapter we look first at general approaches to the study of population. Then we examine the dynamics of population change and how they have affected our society. In the last two sections of the chapter, we turn to worldwide population patterns and to the policies developed for dealing with them.

Studying Populations

Social change and in particular the shifts in size, composition, and distribution of a population are barely perceptible in the short run. It is only the long view that can show us these changes in their true light and full scope. Nevertheless, you have probably noticed this type of change yourself, over time: when you return to a city after being away for several years, for example, perhaps you are shocked either by its decline and deterioration or by its growth and development. Population change may occur slowly, but over time its effects can be striking: here a booming young city such as Phoenix, Arizona; or San Antonio, Texas; there a shrinking, boarded-up community such as Camden, New Jersey; here a housing shortage, there empty apartment buildings. **Demography** is the scientific study of how births, deaths, and migration affect the composition, size, and distribution of populations. Demography has two aspects, both of which are necessary to a full understanding of the way sociologists make use of demographic data. First, demographic information is used in a broad way, to describe social *structure*, particularly age structure. This helps to build an overview of a society and its possible future trends, just as in China, where a clear view of the age structure shows that trouble lies ahead. Nevertheless, we can never forget that *individuals and their actions* are involved, and this is demography's second aspect. Population is based on the birth of children, and the creation of children is an intensely personal issue. Whether to

have children, when, and how many to have are matters of individual choice. This is not true just of our modern affluent society, though the wide acceptance and availability of birth control technology has obviously affected choices in this area. There is evidence of the use of some form of birth control and family planning in very ancient societies. Each of the personal decisions that affects the birth of children in a family, including whether and when to marry, to have sex, to use birth control, to breastfeed, and to wean, influences a society's birthrate.

Individual choice is also involved in other aspects of the population picture: migration is a matter of choice as well as a response (both of individual and groups) to structural social pressure. Even death rates are affected by human choices, including decisions about staying in good health, eating well, maintaining life with medical technology, and so on. Thus, demography can be seen in both a structural and an action perspective. We glimpsed this dual approach—and some of the ways it can be applied—in our discussion of the life course, which described both the progress of the individual through the life cycle and the progress of groups within age structures. Numbers of people are always a significant correlate of social life; and at times—during wars, famines, and epidemics or on frontiers and in newly settled territories—they can become decisive for a society's progress or decline.

Sources of Population Data

The science of demography calls for an accurate assessment of a population's composition and distribution to provide a basis for predicting future trends and for making informed decisions based on these projections. Thus, demographers require precise and detailed information from a wide variety of sources. The most important source of demographic data is a population **census.** A census, in addition to being a "head count," is a tally of regional composition and distribution of people according to their origins, skills, and activities.

The United States conducts an elaborate census every decade. But many less-developed nations have no established program for conducting a regular and efficient census. In such cases, demographers use surveys, interviews, and ethnographic methods to arrive at indications of population patterns and a view of the personal side—the action side—of population issues. The World Fertility Survey, for instance, has provided data on childbearing patterns in areas in which censuses were

The two aspects of demography: demographic data provides an overview of social structure and future population trends, such as the need for more high rise apartment buildings like this one in Hong Kong, but behind the data are highly personal decisions about where and how people choose to live. (Top: Alain Evrard/Photo Researchers; bottom: Jeff Dunn/The Picture Cube.)

either unavailable or unreliable. Or, a field-worker living among a Third World people may, based on interviews and observation, develop a fairly accurate picture of the values these people place on their children, how they make their childbearing decisions, what kinds of indigenous birth control methods they use, how they feel about modern birth control methods, and so forth.

The U.S. Census

Article I of the U.S. Constitution requires that the population of the United States be enumerated every ten years (Table 10.1 shows the resident population of the

United States at each decennial census). Census results provide the basis for the state-by-state allocation of seats in the House of Representatives. With so much at stake in terms of political power, all censuses have been the subject of much controversy. Since funds for the federal entitlement programs are distributed on the basis of census results, the rapid expansion of these programs has led to intensified debate in recent years. In the early 1980s, for example, the allocation of an estimated $100 billion in federal funds was directly tied each year to census figures. State and local officials have a vital interest in seeing that every individual in their jurisdiction is counted, since each person who is *not* counted means the loss of hundreds of government dollars (Mitroff, Mason, and Barabba 1983).

The greatest possible accuracy is the goal of a census. How accurate are the U.S. censuses? One way to assess accuracy is to compare census figures with predictions based on other data. Between the full-census years, the Census Bureau also collects data on very specific concerns, such as employment, welfare patterns, and immigration. The censuses of 1950, 1960, and 1970 each counted 5 million *fewer* people than calculations based on this kind of data had predicted (Keyfitz 1981). In 1970, for instance, the Census Bureau used birth and death certificates and immigration, Medicare, and welfare figures to show that the population of the United States was closer to 208.5 million than the 203.2 million figure revealed by the 1970 census. And in 1980 special efforts were made to find the missing people and the census counted nearly five million *more* Americans than had been predicted. Nonetheless the Census Bureau believes that about 7 million people were overlooked (Hauser 1981; Mitroff, Mason, and Barabba 1983). How did this happen? Sociologists and demographers know that immigrants are undercounted, particularly undocumented aliens (many of whom are Hispanics). These people are reluctant to answer the census for fear that once their presence in the country is discovered, they will be deported. In addition, many undocumented aliens are poor, and undercounts are most prevalent in poor neighborhoods. Overall, the poor, the young, aliens, males, and minorities—the more mobile groups in our society—are more difficult to count than are the middle class, adults, nonaliens, females, and non-minorities.

Problems also exist with the wording of questions, especially among non-English speaking populations who need bilingual census forms and census takers. Moreover, many Americans may view the census as an intrusion of their privacy. Many wonder why the government needs so much personal information, and some doubt the information will remain confidential. All of these factors may affect the accuracy of the final census data.

Recognizing the difficulties inherent in counting the population with a system that relies heavily on voluntary cooperation, in 1980 the Census Bureau mounted the biggest advertising campaign in its history. It used actors and actresses, sports heroes, and eye-catching posters to convey two messages: (1) all information is confidential, so we do not care if you are a criminal or an illegal alien, and (2) an accurate census is vital to the nation and to the respondent's share in community resources. Finally, on March 28, 1980, 164 million questionnaires were mailed out. As each return came in, it was checked against a master checklist. Forms that were not returned were followed up by an elaborate system of procedures that were designed to find everyone. The 1980 census cost more than $1 billion.

DYNAMICS OF POPULATION CHANGE

In order to assess change in the overall numbers of a population, demographers concentrate on three variables: fertility (births); mortality (deaths); and migration (movement to or away from an area). We now consider these variables in turn.

Birthrates

The **crude birthrate** is the number of births per 1,000 people during a given year. In 1947, during the baby boom, the crude birthrate in the United States was about 27 per 1,000. In 1984, by contrast, it was about 15.6 per 1,000 (3.7 million babies). The **fertility rate** (often referred to simply as *fertility*) is the number of actual births per 1,000 women between the ages of fifteen and

TABLE 10.1   Resident Population of the United States at Each Decennial Census

Census Date	Number	Increase Over Preceding Census		Average Annual Rate of Increase
		Number	Percent	
1980	226,545,805	23,243,774	11.4	1.08
1970	203,302,031	23,978,856	13.4	1.26
1960	179,323,175	27,997,377	18.5	1.70
1950	151,325,798	19,161,229	14.5	1.39
1940	131,669,275	8,894,229	7.2	0.70
1930	122,775,046	17,064,426	16.1	1.50
1920	105,710,620	13,738,354	14.9	1.39
1910	91,972,266	15,977,691	21.0	1.91
1900	75,994,575	13,046,861	20.7	1.88
1890	62,947,714	12,791,931	25.5	2.27
1880	50,155,783	10,337,334	26.0	2.31
1870	39,818,449	8,375,128	26.6	2.36
1860	31,443,321	8,251,445	35.6	3.04
1850	23,191,876	6,122,423	35.9	3.07
1840	17,069,453	4,203,433	32.7	2.83
1830	12,866,020	3,227,567	33.5	2.89
1820	9,638,453	2,398,572	33.1	2.86
1810	7,239,881	1,931,398	36.4	3.10
1800	5,308,483	1,379,269	35.1	3.01
1790	3,929,824	. . .	. . .	. . .

Source: U.S. Bureau of the Census. *Statistical Abstract of the United States, 1982–83* (Washington, DC: U.S. Government Printing Office, 1982), Table 1.

forty-four—in other words, the number of children born to the average woman of childbearing age. Fertility is *not* the same as **fecundity,** the *theoretical* biological potential for reproduction. In 1982, the fertility rate in the United States stood at 67.8 live births.

As we saw in the life course chapter (Chapter 6), except for the baby boom, birth and fertility rates in the United States have been declining steadily for a number of years (Rindfuss, Morgan, and Swicegood 1988). The pattern of the decline has varied according to socioeconomic status. That is, birthrates declined first for upper- and middle-class families and later for poorer families. Differences are also evident in white and nonwhite patterns; the white birthrate began declining earlier than did that among blacks. The overall black birthrate is now declining, but socioeconomic stratification is at work here too: middle-class black families have fewer children than middle-class whites, but poor blacks have more children than poor whites. Hispanic and Asian birthrates are still high, although some observers have noted a small decrease. This has meant that since 1972, the U.S. birthrate has been below its replacement level of 2.1 children per woman of childbearing age. This, in turn, coupled with higher life expectancy, has altered the age structure of the U.S. population.

The long decline in fertility has been accompanied by another significant change in the U.S. population—a decrease in family size. At the turn of the century, most Americans preferred a family of three or more children. Nowadays the two-child family is the ideal (Gallup 1986). A number of influences seem to be at work here. One is the high cost of having and rearing children (feeding and clothing them, providing good child care, sending them to school, and so forth). Another is the increasing participation of women in the labor force, many of whom are pursuing careers. A third and related fact is that career-minded women are tending to marry later and to postpone starting families—natural limitations on the number of children they will have.

Figure 10.1 shows the number of births in the world population. The birthrate in industrialized countries such as the United States is relatively low in relation to the rest of the world. The most important factor influencing a nation's birthrate is whether women (or couples) want to have children, and this cultural attitude is strongly influenced by religion and economics. The number of fertile women in the population at any time also influences the birthrate. Since most babies are born to married parents, the marriage rate and age at marriage

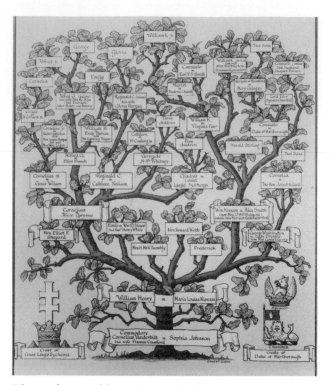

The profusion of branches in this family tree from the early 1900s reflects the fact that larger families —families of three or more children—were once the norm in the United States. How would a family tree reflecting current trends in family size appear by comparison? (EKM-Nepenthe.)

are two additional factors that influence the birthrate. Still another influence is the availability of effective contraceptives. There is a commonly held belief that before the advent of modern methods of contraception, people were not very successful at preventing pregnancies. In fact, this is not true. Most of the great decline in the birthrate during the eighteenth and nineteenth centuries was accomplished without modern methods of birth control. Nevertheless, effective contraceptive methods further separate sexual activity from conception and fundamentally change the nature of the decision involved. For a married woman in 1880 a decision not to have children was the exception; today, many women are interested in careers and are inclined to delay having children or to avoid it altogether.

The vast majority of the world's population is in the developing countries. So is an even higher percentage of the world's births.

FIGURE 10.1   World Population, Births 1986

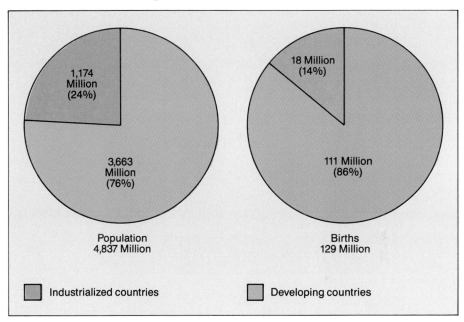

1,174 Million (24%)

3,663 Million (76%)

Population 4,837 Million

18 Million (14%)

111 Million (86%)

Births 129 Million

▦ Industrialized countries   ▦ Developing countries

Source: The State of the World's Children 1987, United Nations Population Division, UN Statistical Office and WHO estimates.

Death Rates

The **crude death rate** is the number of deaths per 1,000 people during a given year. In 1984, there were just over 2 million deaths in the United States, for a rate of 8.6 deaths per 1,000 population. A knowledge of how many people die *per se* is not particularly important—because death comes to us all at one time or another. Rather, the death rate focuses on what proportion of the population dies annually and at what ages death occurs. Death rates do not vary much in the first year of life and after age fifty. The chances of an infant's dying in the first year of life are still quite high, but after the first year the mortality rate drops sharply until the later years of life.

The **infant mortality rate** is the number of deaths among infants under one year of age per 1,000 live births in a given year. In 1984 there were 10.8 infant deaths per 1,000 live births in the United States, the lowest rate ever recorded in this country. This rate is somewhat higher than in some other developed countries. For example, Sweden, Japan, and Switzerland had the three lowest

infant mortality rates, respectively. Infant death rates in this country are much higher among blacks (18.4) than among whites (9.4); and infant mortality rates are even higher in the country's poorest neighborhoods, both rural and inner-city (Children's Defense Fund 1987).

Mortality rates are tied in closely to **life expectancy,** which is the average number of years of life remaining for an individual of a given age. Death rates, however, have little effect on **life span,** the maximum number of years a human being can possibly live. This has not changed substantially over the centuries. But because of the overall decline in the infant mortality rate, advances in modern medicine, better nutrition, and improved sanitation, life expectancy in the United States has increased dramatically in the last seventy-five years, approaching the life span. The life expectancy of people in industrialized countries now averages about seventy-four years. White females can count on living the longest lives, slightly more than seventy-eight years; nonwhite women can expect to live 74.5 years. Men have shorter life expectancies than do women: White

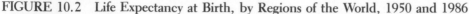

FIGURE 10.2   Life Expectancy at Birth, by Regions of the World, 1950 and 1986

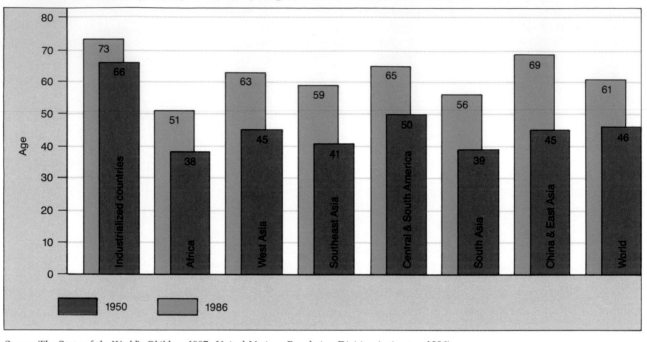

Source: The State of the World's Children 1987, United Nations Population Division (estimates, 1986).

males can expect to live 70.6 years and nonwhite males about 65.6 years. Figure 10.2 shows the differences in life expectancy at birth for various regions of the world.

One of the reasons for the decline in the overall infant mortality rate is the decline in deaths caused by infectious diseases. This means that more infants and children are surviving into adulthood, as you may remember from Chapter 6. Another trend related to increased life expectancy for Americans is changes in causes of death. Demographers have observed recently that Americans are dying increasingly of diseases and conditions that kill them *later* in life—more deaths from some types of cancers, for instance. In other words, there are lower rates for most sorts of deaths, but higher rates for others. In general, Americans are living longer, dying later, and dying of different causes than in the past (Stockwell and Groat 1984). Despite any declines in most death rates, the United States still has the highest murder rate in the industrialized world—higher even than Northern Ireland with its highly publicized violence (Oxford Analytica 1986).

Of all demographic variables, changes in mortality have had the strongest impact on the demographic history of the human population. What lies behind the present "population explosion" is not a marked rise in fertility but a spectacular drop in the death rate (Donaldson 1986). Figure 10.3 shows the crude death rate and infant mortality rates among world societies. In contrast to the industrialized nations, some parts of the world are still characterized by fairly high death rates. In the years to come, declines in mortality in these regions can be expected to be a major influence on population growth and the overall size of the world's population (Stockwell and Groat 1984).

Migration Rates

The movement of people from one country or one region to another is measured by migration rates. The **migration rate** is the difference between the number of people who leave and those who arrive each year, per 1,000 people. **Emigration** is migration *from* one's native land; **immigration** is migration *to* a new country. These terms are usually used to refer to international migration, which we first consider with an in-depth look at immigration to the United States. But **internal migration,** movement within a country, is also very important, and that we consider as well.

People migrate for several reasons, among them natural disasters, government and religious persecu-tion, the desire for adventure or improvement in life chances, and—once migration starts—group momen-tum (Petersen 1975). All of these reasons have brought people to the United States. The potato famine of the 1840s—a natural force—started a wave of Irish immigra-tion. Racism and genocide propelled Jewish immigra-tion just before and during World War II. *Pogroms* (organized massacres) prompted many Russian Jews to settle in the United States in the late nineteenth and early twentieth centuries. And many Southeast Asians

How rapidly a population grows has to do not only with how many children are born, but with how many survive. Although they have been reduced in many areas, infant mortality rates are still high in much of the world.

FIGURE 10.3   A Comparative Look at Infant Mortality

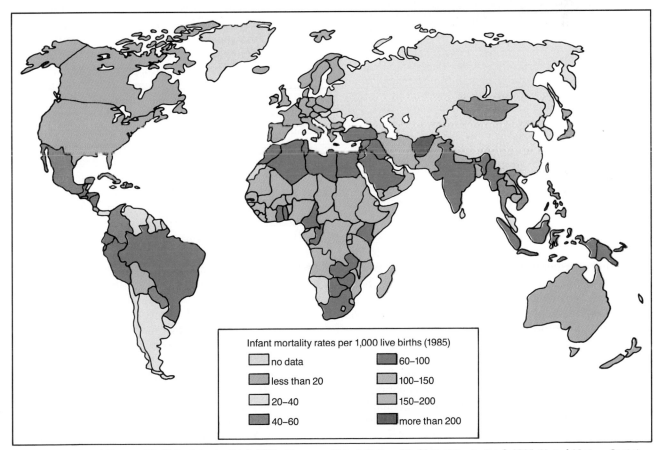

Source: Map: United Nations World Statistics in Brief, 1985. Diagrams: United Nations World Statistics in Brief, 1985; United Nations Statistics Yearbook, 1982. Data: World Bank, World Development Report, 1987.

Today, many U.S. communities, large and small, are home to one or more families of Vietnamese, Cambodians, or Laotians—a wave of immigration from Southeast Asia that began with the fall of Vietnam in the 1970s. These migrants are called "Boat People," because they risked crossing the South China Sea in crowded and often unseaworthy vessels, rather than endure political oppression in their war-torn homelands. (J. P. Laffont/Sygma.)

have fled political conditions in their part of the world since the 1970s and the war in Vietnam. The desire for economic betterment attracted immigrants from southern and eastern Europe in the 1800s. Word of their relative success filtered back to their native lands, creating a social momentum that brought an influx of 6 million of their compatriots by 1910.

With 5 percent of the world's population, the United States still takes in about 50 percent of the world's immigrants (Oxford Analytica 1986; this figure does not include refugees whose movement to another country is assumed not to be permanent). Clearly, immigration has always been a major source of growth (and, very often, intergroup tension) for this country. Since 1820 more than 50 million people came to live in the United States, including some 3 million slaves who came against their will.

In Depth: U.S. Immigration

Immigration to the United States was largely unregulated until 1882, when Congress enacted the Chinese Exclusion Act, which halted Chinese immigration. In the 1920s, new laws established a quota system of national origins for immigrants; all East Asian immigration stopped, for example. Groups from northern Europe got preference; the underlying assumption was that some ethnic groups were preferable to others. Not until the Immigration Act of 1965 was this quota system based on national origins abolished. Today, 170,000 people from the Western Hemisphere can enter the United States legally every year, and the same number can enter legally from the Eastern Hemisphere. The 1965 law favors the entrance of those immigrants with family ties to other Americans and those with essential occupational skills. Thus among its other effects, the 1965 immigration law has meant greater numbers of immigrants from Latin America and the Caribbean and has changed the social composition of Chinese immigrants from single adults to whole families who immigrate together.

Since the mid-1960s, immigration to this country has sharply increased, to levels not seen since immigration was capped in the 1920s. Three million people came in the 1960s, 4 million in the 1970s, and even more have come in the 1980s. One million Cubans and 400,000 Southeast Asians came to this country when the pro-American governments in their homelands fell (Massey 1981). Southeast Asians made up 7 percent of immigrants in the 1960s; by the 1980s, they made up 44 percent of immigrants to this country (Kelly 1986). Many of the Cubans who had been professionals, managers, landowners, and business owners in their native land were forced to take lesser jobs when they came to this country. Most of the Vietnamese immigrants also enjoyed higher status in Vietnam than they did in the United States. But both groups show evidence of upward mobility. The new law's occupational requirements have meant a "brain drain" for many countries—the emigration of highly skilled, highly educated people. The brain drain has been especially severe in Asian countries. Although there are certainly exceptions, recent immigrants to the United States are unlike earlier immigrants in that they are better educated, more highly skilled, and therefore unlikely to remain for long at the bottom of the social hierarchy. Indeed, the prospect of a higher standard of living and upward mobility has been a major force behind immigration to the wealthier nations, including our own, from poor Third World countries (Massey 1981). Some groups, as in the recent influx of Senegalese street peddlers in New York City, come to make money they can take back home with them as soon as possible.

Since 1980, many immigrants to this country have been Afghans and eastern Europeans, especially Rumanians and Poles. This has to do with the foreign policy of the United States. We accept only "political" refugees, not economic ones. This means that many people from some nations are accepted, whereas only few are accepted from others. We discriminate against Africans, for example. During the height of the famine and civil wars in Ethiopia in the mid-1980s, only 2,000 Africans a year were allowed into this country. This was a tiny fraction of the number of Europeans and Asians we accepted. Although we define as a political refugee nearly anyone who wants to leave an eastern European Communist country, including the thousands of Poles who come here every year for essentially economic reasons, we refuse as "economic" refugees most refugees from Ethiopia, as from El Salvador and other war-torn Latin American countries.

Desperate political and economic conditions in their homelands, particularly Mexico and other Central American countries, have also led many immigrants to enter the United States illegally. No one knows exactly how many illegal aliens are now living in the United States. Some estimates place the number at more than 12 million. The Census Bureau has concluded that 2.5 to 3.5 million illegal aliens were counted in the 1980 census, and that by 1987 4.7 million illegal aliens resided in the United States, with another 200,000 coming each year (Robey 1987). It has been estimated that 45 percent of the undocumented aliens who were counted in the 1980 census were Mexican; 17 percent Central American and Caribbean; 12 percent European; 12 percent Asian; 5 percent African, Australian, and Pacific Islanders; and 2 percent Canadian (Pear 1983).

For years, undocumented aliens have formed a pool of cheap labor for American businesses—many illegal immigrants work for less than the minimum wage. Hispanics, for example, provide cheap, seasonal, agricultural labor; Asians form a pool of cheap garment workers. But in 1987, the Immigration Reform and Control Act went into effect. It is an attempt by the government to deter illegal immigration—an effort that polls show Americans widely support (Robey 1987)—to legalize many of the immigrants who have entered illegally, and to deport those who remain here illegally. Employers now must see proof of legal residence before hiring an immigrant, or they must pay stiff fines and penalties. Immigrants who entered the United States illegally can get amnesty from deportation if they can prove that they have lived here continuously since January 1, 1982. Nonetheless, illegal immigration has not ended. Mexico, a close neighbor and a poor nation with a high birthrate, has been a source of many legal and illegal immigrants, many of them young. But immigration from Latin America, and especially from Mexico, is expected to remain high. As we discuss in Chapter 13, on Race and Ethnic Relations, Hispanics form an ever-increasing proportion of the U.S. population. With their high birthrate and continued immigration, Hispanics are expected to become the largest minority ethnic group in the country early in the next century. This may eventually mean that in 100 or 150 years, white, non-Hispanic Americans will be a minority in the U.S. population.

Regional Population Shifts: Country to City to Suburbs

Internal migration can affect a society as deeply as movement into and out of a country. In China, for example, internal migration is tightly controlled by the state. But even so, too many people have migrated to cities such as Shanghai, where they spill onto the sidewalks—to eat, get haircuts, buy and sell, even to sleep—and where now even the sewage system is overburdened.

Americans have always been a people on the move. Almost 17 percent of the U.S. population moves every year, with more than 6 percent moving to a new state or country (U.S. Bureau of the Census 1987). According to one observer, this translates into an average of eight moves for every adult (Gordon 1978).

Westward migration, so much a part of American mythology, is still going on. Today, the Sunbelt, Western Mountain, and Pacific states are showing the greatest gain in population (see Table 10.2). Their sunny climate, open spaces, and other resources have attracted

TABLE 10.2 Population Growth by Region, Expressed in Percents

Years	Northeast	Midwest	South	West	Total United States
1970–1980	0.15	4.02	20.00	23.92	11.43
1980–1985	1.47	0.56	8.61	10.78	5.38
Total 1970–1985	1.63	4.61	30.32	37.28	17.43

Source: U.S. Bureau of the Census, *Statistical Abstract of the United States,* 1987.

businesses and people who, in an age when many jobs are readily transportable, migrate because they *want* to live in an area with more amenities. With the shift in population has come a shift in political power: four of the last five U.S. presidents have been from the South or the West.

Like the Chinese who crowd into Shanghai from rural areas, and like the English farmers and laborers who left their rural cottages for jobs in urban centers, Americans of all groups for over a century moved from country to cities. After the Civil War in the United States, industrialization began in earnest. As farming became mechanized, farm workers left rural areas and were lured to the cities to work in factories. In 1900, 60 percent of the population lived on farms; in 1980, only 6 million people lived on farms, 25 percent fewer than in 1970. The number of people living on farms has continued to fall.

Many cities in the Northeast and Midwest are losing population to adjacent suburbs, and these are the fastest growing places of residence. Demographers first noted this trend around the turn of the century, and its pace increased in the 1940s. Because this movement seemed to coincide with the northward migration of rural southern blacks, some demographers called it "white flight." Today, 57.7 percent of American blacks live in big cities, compared to 24.9 percent of whites. In 1900, 90 percent of black Americans lived in the rural South. But by 1980, fewer blacks were migrating to the northern central cities, and more, at least those in the middle class, were migrating to the suburbs (Hauser 1981). Blacks who move into cities have tended to settle in *southern* cities, again because of the Sunbelt's economic growth.

Demographers have also noted that during the 1970s, Americans across the United States were reacting to the problems caused by urban density and moving to smaller towns and to rural areas. At the end of that decade, two-thirds of all *non*metropolitan counties were gaining population, whereas for years they had been losing it (U.S. Census Bureau 1980). For the first time in over a century, small towns and rural areas (though *not* farms) were growing faster than metropolitan areas. This marked a major turning point in the regional development of the United States (Clark 1985). Since the 1970s, there has been some indication that the population

What does demographic change look like? Actually, this suburban community in southern California is the embodiment of two demographic trends in the United States: movement from urban centers to suburbs and rural areas and continued westward migration to the sunbelt and Pacific states. This image also suggests another dilemma created by population growth: people come and go, but fertile farmland, once it has been paved over, is gone forever. (Dan McCoy/Rainbow.)

growth in small towns and rural areas is slowing down. Some analysts speculate that metropolitan areas may be reestablishing themselves as prime locations for upwardly mobile young professional people (Peterson 1986).

Age Structure and the Population Pyramid

The impact of the population dynamics we have just discussed—the birth, death, and migration rates within a given country—can be summarized in the population pyramid. As discussed in Chapter 6, the traditional pyramid shape is the result of a high birthrate, as in the U.S. baby boom, as in China in the 1960s, or as in many developing nations today (see Figure 10.4). A fairly steady death rate, particularly in the aging population, also helps maintain the triangular form of the age structure. When the birthrate declines, the age structure takes on more of a diamond shape. If the population as a whole is aging, as it is now in the United States, and more people are living through every stage of the life course and far into old age, then the pyramid begins to square off or even become top heavy. This in turn poses such problems as an overburdened Social Security system, which does not easily adapt to population trends.

A large increase in deaths or migration will also change the shape of the pyramid. Mass immigration will create a big bar of adults in the middle of the population pyramid, as in the case of the postwar population of Israel. From 1948 to 1951, the period immediately after the establishment of Israel, this new country grew in population by 24 percent a year, and 90 percent of this growth was the result of immigration. On the other hand, mass emigration or a serious war will create a short bar among young adults. For example, the Soviet Union lost 20 million people in World War II and another 15 million to Stalin's purges, leaving a gap in their population pyramid that affected Soviet life profoundly for decades. The recent war between Iran and Iraq has nearly wiped out a generation of young men, especially in Iran. This will have effects on everything from the economy to marriage chances for young women.

Population distribution by age is an example of a structural force at work. As we have seen, the effects are far from abstract, both for the population as a whole and for the individuals making up that population. One very important effect of an increasing number of very young and very old people in a population is an increased dependency: the more very young and very old there are, the more productive the midrange adults must be to take care of their society's children and elders (Preston 1984). Unfortunately, in the United States, poverty among the elderly remains a concern—though Social Security, Medicare, IRAs, and pensions have lifted the majority to a decent standard of living—and poverty among children has substantially increased. Will young and middle-aged adults be able to increase productivity enough to help? Will they, for instance, apply political pressure in an attempt to make Social Security more responsive and aid to poor families more available? The answers to these questions will depend in part on individual choice, which will in turn produce structural change in the long run. We now look at the interaction of individual action and structural forces on a worldwide scale, as the human population begins to crowd our planet.

WORLD POPULATION PATTERNS

The impact of demographic forces does not stop at a nation's boundaries—it has global implications. Overall, the world's population grew slowly until about the mid-1800s—so slowly, in fact, that several hundred thousand years were needed for the world's population to reach 1 billion (Wilford 1981). This was not, however, a pattern of slow yet continuous growth. Rather, the human population underwent dramatic ups and downs, as whole societies were cut back by famines, wars, and disease. After about 1850, as modernization began to spread throughout northern Europe, the world's population began a long period of uninterrupted growth. Advances in medicine, sanitation, and agriculture, greatly reduced the death rate. The world's population reached the second billion milestone by 1930. The third billion was added by 1960, and the fourth by 1975. Unless massive famine, epidemics, or nuclear holocaust intervene, population experts foretell a 6.2 billion world population by the year 2000 (Pear 1986). (The boxed insert [p. 274] discusses the impact of acquired immune deficiency syndrome [AIDS] in a demographic context.)

Although overall the world's population is growing more slowly than it was in the 1960s and 1970s, 146 new humans are still being born each minute, 8,790 an hour, 210,959 a day, 77 million a year. In 1987, the world's population passed the 5 billion mark (see Figure

FIGURE 10.4   Contrasting Population Structures

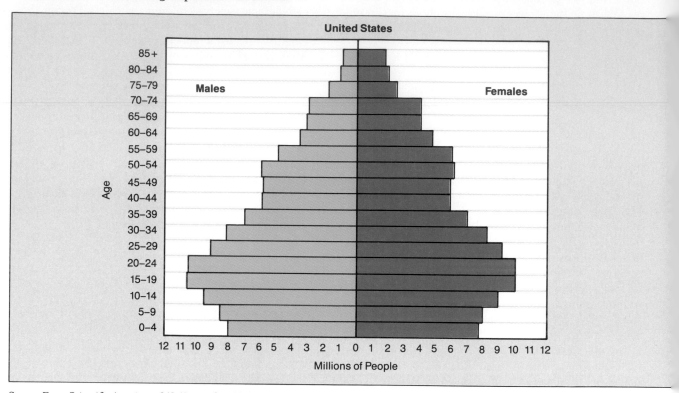

(Above) This figure represents the age structure of the United States in 1980. The longest bars in the figure signify the baby boom generation. The size of this cohort will probably diminish the chances for the advancement and prosperity of the cohort that follows. (Near right) The population pyramid depicts the somewhat square structure typical of a developed nation (the population of England and Wales in 1968). (Far right) The structure graphically represents the triangular pyramid characteristic of a developing nation (Madagascar in 1966).

10.5). Even more significant are the changes that are taking place in population distribution (Donaldson 1986). Three-quarters of these 5 billion people live in the less developed countries. Current estimates predict that from 1990 to 2000, the population of these countries will grow by 828 million, which is more than three times the *current* population of the United States. Thus more and more people will be concentrated in those areas of the world that are the least able to provide for them.

Density

Shanghai, one of China's bustling cities, is so densely populated that each person's living space amounts to about four square meters—roughly the size of a king-sized bed. The **density** of a population is the number of people who live in a given territorial area. The overall density of the United States in 1985 was 67 people for every square mile of land. But residents of New Jersey felt far more crowded (with 1,013 people per square

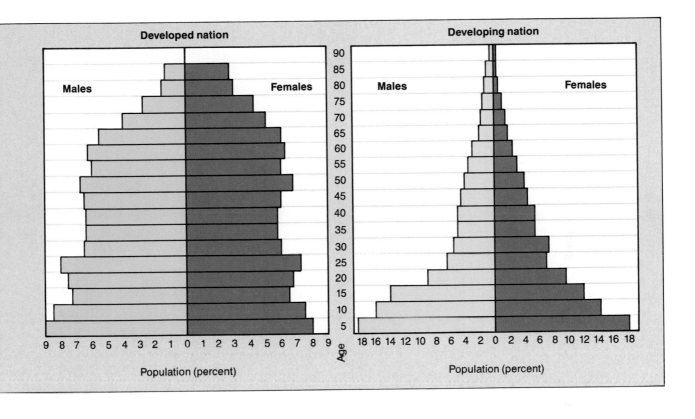

Developed nation

Males   Females

Developing nation

Males   Females

Age

9 8 7 6 5 4 3 2 1 0 1 2 3 4 5 6 7 8 9

Population (percent)

18 16 14 12 10 8 6 4 2 0 2 4 6 8 10 12 14 16 18

Population (percent)

mile) than residents of Montana (with only 6). In fact, Montana's population density in 1985 equaled that of the entire United States in 1800. By 1900, there were 25.6 people for every square mile of territory of the United States, and by 1950, the figure had risen to 50.7. Table 10.3 documents the different levels of population density (inhabitants per square mile) in the U.S.

Density can be measured numerically, but it is also a condition that people experience subjectively. One of the first things we usually notice about other places is how crowded they are compared to what we are used to. To someone from rural Montana, almost any large city will seem crowded. A native of Indianapolis may not quite agree with that, but will admit that Chicago or Los Angeles feels crowded. Even New Yorkers who are used to the hustle and bustle of city crowds are likely to be taken aback by the density of Mexico City or Shanghai.

Modern cities everywhere are able to achieve population densities that would have been unimaginable only a few generations ago (see Chapter 9). New Yorkers and Tokyoites, for example, live and work in high-rise buildings—and park their cars underground. Increases in density also depend on improvements in agricultural productivity that have allowed smaller farmland areas to supply food to ever more people. Moreover, modern transportation methods allow food and other necessities to be shipped from sparsely settled rural areas to densely packed cities. Beef from wide-open Montana is shipped to New Jersey, just as vegetables from Chinese farms are sent to Shanghai and other Chinese cities.

But when people settle densely into an area, they create enormous problems. Where is the sewage to go? How are adequate housing and transportation facilities to be provided? Where are enough "green spaces"—open

FIGURE 10.5   World Population Growth from 8000 B.C. to the Present

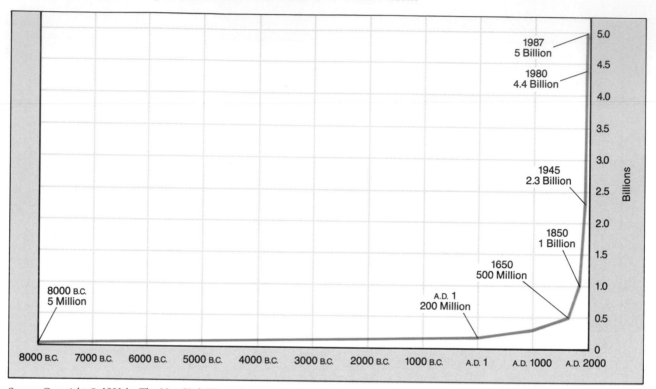

Source: Copyright © 1981 by The New York Times Company. Reprinted by permission.

This figure indicates the growth of the world's population since 8000 B.C. If stretched all the way back to the emergence of Homo sapiens, *the line would be a barely visible one starting many feet to the left of the graph.*

areas where trees and other plants generate oxygen for people to breathe—to be found? Because these challenges were poorly met by cities in the early industrial period, these cities were generally much less healthy than the surrounding countryside. "Killer fogs" hung over London for days. Life expectancy in some cities was ten years lower than in the countryside (Inglis 1972; Thompson 1968). Many of the cities of today are faced with these same challenges. The denseness and rapid growth of many Third World cities have resulted in huge squatter settlements where housing is primitive—cardboard boxes or corrugated tin roofs on flimsy walls, fetid ditches for sewage—and services are few. In Calcutta, tens of thousands of people live on the sidewalks. In Cairo, the "city of the dead," an ancient cemetery is home to thousands of people who find stone tombs far more attractive than other available housing (a few have even strung up electrical wires to the tombs in which they have set up housekeeping, and stuck television antennas on top). In Brazil, nearly every major city is surrounded by miles of slums in which recent immigrants from the countryside live in extreme poverty.

Malthus Versus Marx

The rapid increase in world population and accompanying density have raised a number of questions. How large can world population ultimately become, and,

TABLE 10.3   U.S. Population Density, by State

Division and State	Resident Population (July 1) per Square Mile, 1986	Division and State	Resident Population (July 1) per Square Mile, 1986
United States	68	Virginia	146
		West Virginia	80
New England	202	North Carolina	130
Maine	38	South Carolina	112
New Hampshire	114	Georgia	105
Vermont	58	Florida	216
Massachusetts	745	*East South Central*	85
Rhode Island	924	Kentucky	94
Connecticut	655	Tennessee	117
Middle Atlantic	374	Alabama	80
New York	375	Mississippi	56
New Jersey	1,020	*West South Central*	63
Pennsylvania	265	Arkansas	46
East North Central	171	Louisiana	101
Ohio	262	Oklahoma	48
Indiana	153	Texas	64
Illinois	208	*Mountian*	15
Michigan	161	Montana	6
Wisconsin	88	Idaho	12
West North Central	35	Wyoming	5
Minnesota	53	Colorado	32
Iowa	51	New Mexico	12
Missouri	74	Arizona	29
North Dakota	10	Utah	20
South Dakota	9	Nevada	90
Nebraska	21	*Pacific*	40
Kansas	30	Washington	67
South Atlantic	153	Oregon	28
Delaware	328	California	173
Maryland	454	Alaska	1
District of Columbia	9,936	Hawaii	165

Source: U.S. Bureau of the Census, *Statistical Abstract of the United States*, 1988 (Washington, DC: U.S. Government Printing Office, 1987).

more particularly, how many human beings can the planet feed and the environment sustain? These questions are not new. They haunted the English scholar Thomas Malthus (1766–1834) whose theories appeared in 1798 in "An Essay on the Principle of Population." Malthus took an exceedingly pessimistic view, arguing that human populations are inescapably caught in a conflict between their "need for food" and the "passion between the sexes." Population, he maintained, increases geometrically (2, 4, 8, 16, . . .), while food supplies increase only arithmetically (2, 3, 4, 5, . . .). No population can continue to grow indefinitely, because people will increase their numbers to the limit of subsistence. Since populations increase to the ultimate

point of subsistence, low standards of living must prevail. The population will always catch up, "eating" away the higher standards of living.

To Malthus, the only solution to the population problem was for people to marry later and have fewer children (he did not approve of birth control or abortion). Otherwise, population growth would inevitably be checked by drastic means: starvation, pestilence, or war.

Critics have found fault with Malthusian theory. Logically speaking, a population cannot increase more rapidly than food production. If a population is growing, the means to support it must also be growing. Otherwise, mortality would rise and the population would not grow. The world's population can no more "outrun" its food

The Demography of AIDS

As of November 1987, more than 27,000 cases of acquired immune deficiency syndrome (AIDS) had been reported in the United States; of these, there were more than 15,000 deaths. Not only is this statistic grim in human terms, it is startling in demographic terms. For one thing, given advances in medicine, the loss of tens of thousands of lives from an infectious disease is profoundly shocking—and humbling to our assumption that most microbe-caused diseases can be controlled by modern medicine (see Chapter 19). But not only is the appearance of a deadly infectious disease a surprise; even more shocking is the population most affected by it —young adults. Most cases of AIDS (47 percent) are diagnosed in persons aged 30 to 39. Another 21 percent of AIDS victims are 20–29, and 21 percent are 40–49 (AIDS Alert, 1987). The reason AIDS is concentrated in people between 20 and 50, is that this is the body of the population that is most sexually active, and AIDS is primarily a sexually transmitted disease.

One question demographers must ponder as they consider the impact of AIDS is what its implications are for population growth and for the economy. Simply put, even if a vaccine against AIDS is developed (and none is likely until at least the 1990s), many thousands more people will die. Current estimates are that about 1.5 million people are infected with the AIDS virus. No one knows how many of these people will eventually develop the deadly disease (estimates run from 10 to 20 percent to 100 percent), but all of them are capable of transmitting the disease to others through sexual contact or sharing drug paraphernalia. Women with the AIDS virus, may also infect their babies with it *in utero*, and babies who are born with the AIDS virus typically fare even worse than adult AIDS victims.

One emerging characteristic of AIDS demographics is the disproportionate number of minorities involved. About 40 percent of people with AIDS in the U.S. are black or Hispanic, although these groups constitute less than 20 percent of the population. The disease presents a different picture among whites and minorities; white AIDS victims are far more likely to be homosexual men, and minorities are predominantly intravenous drug users and their heterosexual sex partners. Blacks and Hispanics with AIDS tend to be poorer and sicker, and they die of the disease much sooner on average than whites do. Homosexual men are better informed about AIDS and its transmission than minority drug users are, and the rate the disease is spreading among homosexuals is slowing compared with the rate among minorities. This means that AIDS may eventually become a disease in which most victims are black or Hispanic—drug users, their partners, and their children. (This is already the case in some metropolitan areas, such as New York City.) Thus, the ultimate impact of the disease on population is likely to be most substantial among minorities.

Even though most Americans are primarily concerned about AIDS as it exists in the U.S., it should be remembered that it is now nearly a worldwide disease. Cases of AIDS have been reported in 71 countries. The most cases so far have been identified in the United States; other areas with substantial numbers include Western Europe, Central Africa, Brazil, and Haiti. The World Health Organization has reported that a minimum of 10,000 cases a year may now be occurring in Africa, but in Africa as in other developing areas of the world it is difficult to obtain a precise estimate of disease prevalence. Record keeping, diagnostic testing, and medical care in general are inadequate in such areas, and many people who get sick never come to the attention of medical authorities. On the world scale, therefore, demographic forecasts are even less certain. It is likely that as in the U.S., where people are informed about AIDS and its transmission, cases will drop off, and where people are not educated about taking precautions against AIDS the disease will continue to spread more rapidly.

This points to another aspect of AIDS demographics: the numbers of cases currently reported only suggest where we are now—not necessarily where we are headed. Education about AIDS can lead people to protect themselves from infection, and if enough people do this, the numbers of cases will eventually decline. For the moment, however, what we mainly know is that there will be more cases in the next five to ten years, because of the long dormancy period of the virus. How many more cases there will be depends greatly on what percentage of those infected with the AIDS virus actually develop AIDS. And that, like so much about the disease, is a question that as yet has no definite answer.

Sources: "Surgeon General's Report on Acquired Immune Deficiency Syndrome," JAMA 256 (November 1986): 2784–2789; "AIDS ALERT," Centers for Disease Control, 1987; Kathleen McAuliffe, "The Uneven Odds," *U.S. News and World Report*, August 17, 1987, pp. 31–34.

supply than the hind feet of a horse can outrun the front feet (Wrong 1977). Malthus also failed to anticipate the full possibilities of the Industrial Revolution, and he did not foresee the technological revolution in agriculture. Indeed, in the United States, farm machinery, fertilizers, pesticides, irrigation, hybrid plants, and genetically selected animals have contributed to a more rapid growth in the nation's subsistence than in its population. In fact, for the past fifty years the United States government has sponsored farm programs designed to curtail agricultural production (though U.S. agricultural surpluses have not ended hunger and starvation in other parts of the world).

One of the foremost critics of Malthus was Karl Marx (Marx 1867). Malthus had placed the blame for overpopulation and poverty on the individual members of society who succumbed to their sexual urges. But Marx saw the matter quite differently. For Marx, there was no "overpopulation" as such—the real issue was underproduction. Marx believed that the system of capitalism had the capacity to produce food and other necessities for an indefinitely expanding population. It was only capitalism's unequal distribution of social wealth that made it seem that there had to be a "natural" limit on population. Moreover, in Marx's view, the system of property relations in capitalism skewed production away from the needs of poor people, and into the hands of the capitalists. Capitalists further benefited from a surplus population which created competition for jobs, thus driving down wages and maximizing profits. The solution to the problem of overpopulation that Marx proposed was socialism. Thus, whereas Malthus focused on the individual and sought the answer to population problems in moral restraint, Marx focused on the economic structure of society and sought the solution in a new social order.

Mao Zedong was following Marx's lead when he decreed that China did not need population control —only economic expansion. However, as we saw earlier in the chapter, Mao's successors in the Chinese government disagreed and called for drastic measures to halt population growth. On the basis of a new census, they concluded that if the growth of the Chinese population was not slowed drastically, all of the benefits of economic improvement would go toward providing basic subsistence for the larger population instead of a rising standard of living.

Though Marx may have been too optimistic, many contemporary sociologists believe that Malthus was too pessimistic. In the first place, Marx was clearly right that

A scene such as this one in India reminds us that overpopulation is one of the most serious social problems in the world today. Many millions of people are beset by hunger and malnourishment, and live in conditions of extreme poverty, overcrowding, and hardship. The consequences of rapid population growth demand global recognition and participation. (Boreau/Sygma.)

technological and social factors—not just natural limits—determine how many people the earth can support. And demographers point out that economic development has generally brought reductions in the rate of population growth. This process is known as the demographic transition, a topic to which we now turn.

The Demographic Transition

Although some demographers continue to be haunted by the Malthusian specter of starvation, plague, and war, others believe that humanity may be able to avert such a disaster. Some evidence suggests that we can achieve a population with low mortality and low fertility, perhaps even zero population growth. In fact, many industrialized countries have brought their rapid rate of population growth down in a process known as the demographic transition.

The concept **demographic transition** refers to the three characteristic stages of the population dynamics for societies undergoing industrialization (see Figure 10.6). In the first stage, which is characteristic of preindustrial societies, both the birthrate and the death rate are high and relatively stable. The second stage is a transitional

FIGURE 10.6   The Demographic Transition

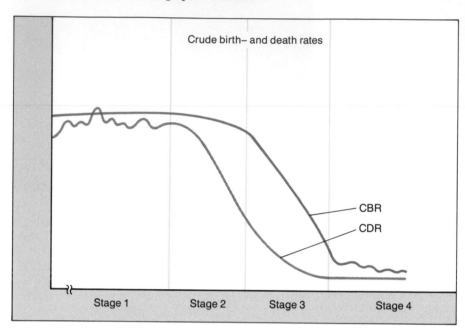

Crude birth– and death rates

CBR
CDR

Stage 1   Stage 2   Stage 3   Stage 4

This schematic graph shows the differences in behavior of birth-rates and death rates during the demographic transition in the industrialized nations. The gap between births and deaths in stages 2 and 3 produced rapid population growth. Today, the gap has narrowed, although jumps in the birthrate may produce spurts of population growth, as in our postwar baby boom. Even though its population is not growing as fast as that of the developing nations, the industrialized world still must be concerned with population growth because of the heavier demands its people place upon the environment. The United States, for example, has one-sixteenth of the world's population, but consumes over one-third of the world's resources.

one: The birthrate remains high but the death rate declines as nutrition, health, and sanitation improve. In particular, as the infant mortality rate is lowered, a larger proportion of the huge yearly crop of babies survives and in due course become parents themselves. Hence, this stage has the potential for explosive population growth. In stage three, both the birthrate and the death rate are low and in balance again. People now bear fewer children because of the dramatic increase in the chances for infant survival. Applying this model, China was in stage one of demographic transition in the 1950s, the years following its political revolution. Some African nations today are still in stage one, with high birth and death rates. India, Nigeria, and most Latin American countries are in stage two, with transitional high growth. Europe, North America, and Japan are in the third and (apparently) final phase, with a low but fluctuating birthrate and a low, steady death rate. In some cases, the number of births has fallen below the number of deaths in industrialized countries, as they have in West Germany, causing a nation's population to decline (unless immigration offsets the decline).

Demographers caution that demographic transition should not be seen as a fixed sequence that is inevitably experienced by all industrializing countries. Under some conditions, cultural and other factors have altered fertility patterns more profoundly than economic developments and socioeconomic status. The Netherlands is a historical example of a nation that did not follow the course predicted by demographic transition theory (Petersen 1960). The Dutch death rate rose continuously between 1750 and 1850. However, the fertility rate increased even more rapidly. This was partly because improving economic conditions allowed more young couples to set up their own independent households. At the present time, the Soviet Union is experiencing a decline in life expectancy and an increase in infant mortality that is partly due to high rates of alcoholism and a decline in the quality of health care.

The demographic transition that occurred in the industrialized countries of the West may not happen in exactly the same way in many currently developing nations. The death rate has dropped precipitously in India, for example, not because of indigenous reasons such as better nutrition or sanitation but because of the introduction of vaccines, pesticides, and other imported technology. The words of an elderly man in Calcutta capture the suddenness of this change:

> When I was a boy, they took away forty or fifty bodies after a cholera epidemic. It happened every five or ten years. Now they come and vaccinate our children. I have lived here almost seventy years. The biggest change in my time has been health. We've learned to keep from dying. (quoted in Thomlinson 1976, p. 29)

As this reflection suggests, the population histories of the Third World differ from Western nations in significant ways (Yaukey 1985). Changes that took place over one or two hundred years in the Western world have been compressed in the Third World into just a few decades. Although such public health measures as those introduced in India were clearly an advance, they were introduced "overnight" into a culture that had long esteemed large families. People in these societies have not yet had the time to adjust their religious and cultural values that shape the birthrate.

These cultural factors are of major concern when sociologists use demographic transition theory to try to predict what will happen in the developing world. Despite a sharp decline in the death rate, in many poor countries the birthrate has actually risen and large families are still the norm. The reason appears to be a reluctance to accept changes in cultural values, particularly those related to the economic basis of the family (Entwisle and Mason 1985; Harrison 1984). In rural village life, children are viewed as an economic asset. At a young age children can help with the housework, care for chickens and livestock, plant seed, and begin to hoe. They may also labor in small factories or at crafts. Second, in a simple, farm-based economy, parents may want many children both to help them produce food and eventually to produce food for them in their old age. In societies without Social Security, children are a form of old-age insurance. People may also choose to have large families for other than simply economic reasons. They may simply enjoy the companionship of children and be given encouragement from government and religious leaders to maintain the tradition of large families. Because of the force of tradition, age-old customs favoring high fertility are necessarily slow to change. Despite declining mortality, the longstanding experience of high infant mortality in these societies may make people feel they *need* to have many children (Eberstadt 1981). Until

Whereas mortality rates may be reduced relatively quickly through imported technology, birthrates depend on deeply rooted cultural values. In simple, farm-based economies large families are a form of security and wealth. On this family farm in Indonesia, many hands are needed to harvest the rice. (David Robert Austen/Stock Boston.)

the people in poor developing countries lose their reasons for having many children, they are unlikely to adjust their rate of fertility. As such, these societies may remain indefinitely in a stage characterized by low mortality and high fertility. As these examples suggest, demographic change does not always follow in accordance with the scenario outlined by demographic transition theory. The prospects of a global demographic transition have as yet to be determined. The more immediate picture is that of worldwide demographic polarization, a topic to which we now turn.

Population Growth Trends

Where is population growth heading? As documented in Table 10.4, the world is dividing sharply into regions where the population is growing slowly (at 1 percent annually or less) and regions where it is growing rapidly (at 2.2 percent annually or more). Expressed in percentage terms, these numbers appear small, but their long-term impact on population is enormous. The reason for this is that population growth is exponential—the increase is based on the population doubling and redoubling itself within a given amount of time. For example,

TABLE 10.4   World Population Growth by Geographic Region, 1986

Region	Population (million)	Population Growth Rate (percent)	Annual Increment (million)
Slow Growth Regions			
Western Europe	381	0.2	0.8
North America	267	0.7	1.9
Eastern Europe and Soviet Union	392	0.8	3.1
Australia and New Zealand	19	0.8	0.1
East Asia[1]	1,263	1.0	12.6
Total	2,322	0.8	18.6
Rapid Growth Regions			
Southeast Asia[2]	414	2.2	9.1
Latin America	419	2.3	9.6
Indian Subcontinent	1,027	2.4	24.6
Middle East	178	2.8	5.0
Africa	583	2.8	16.3
Total[3]	2,621	2.5	65.5

[1]Principally China and Japan.
[2]Principally Burma, Indonesia, the Philippines, Thailand, and Vietnam.
[3]Numbers may not add up to totals due to rounding.

Source: Population Reference Bureau, *1986 World Population Data Sheet* (Washington, DC: 1986).

a population growing at an annual rate of 2 percent will double in size every 35 years. At 3 percent it will double every 23 years. Even the more modest rate of 0.5 percent will cause the population to double in 140 years (Stockwell and Groat 1984). Thus the population of Sweden, which is growing at a rate of 0.1 percent, will take about 700 years to double if present rates are maintained. At the other extreme, India's population, which is growing at 2.3 percent, is expected to more than double by 2010, making it more populous even than China. These figures give some sense of the diverging prospects for countries in the slow and rapid growth categories. If these rates continue as projected (see Table 10.5), the developing countries will fall further behind the industrialized nations in their efforts to raise their standard of living. The continued rapid population growth of the developing countries accentuates existing social and economic problems. We now look at some of the consequences of the cycle of poverty and overpopulation.

Population and the Food Supply

The Malthusian nightmare is a reality for hundreds of millions of people. For example, of forty-one nations in Africa south of the Sahara, only five are managing to produce enough food to feed their growing populations (Knight 1983). Further, two billion people in the developing nations—nearly half the world's population—are undernourished to the point of low vitality and high vulnerability to disease, and many millions are near starvation (Crittenden 1981; Green and Fearey 1978). Malnutrition predisposes people to disease and death by contributing to prematurity and low birth weight and by impairing immune processes.

Ironically, the world already produces more than enough food to feed its population. About half of it, however, goes to feed animals (some of which are eventually used for food—but mostly in the developed countries). Much food is lost to rot and pests because of poor storage practices. And much of it is wasted or consumed in excess by people in the industrialized nations, who routinely throw away food and eat far more than they need. And although significant advances have been made in food production in recent years—in the so-called green revolution—these advances have solved some problems but created others. The green revolution refers to the invention of new strains of food plants that are designed to double the yield per acre. When they were first introduced in the 1950s, in countries such as India and Pakistan, these high-yielding grains were hailed as the solution to world hunger. But the new agriculture has had its social costs. First, it requires the intensive use of fertilizers, which are made from oil and thus have become expensive. This has accelerated the trend toward large commercial farms and away from small, self-supporting ones. Second, green revolution technology is risky. The usual method is to plant huge

expanses of land with a single crop, which means a possible loss of the entire crop when weather conditions destroy a harvest. If farmers planted a variety of crops, some would survive. Third, the new high-yield grains are genetically more uniform than older stocks, so when a disease attacks them, all may succumb (Enzer, Drobnick, and Alter 1978; Scrimshaw and Taylor 1980). Another cost of the green revolution is that workers lose jobs to machines that are more efficient. In the Punjab region of India, as many as half of all agricultural jobs have been eliminated and thousands of workers have been turned off the land. The irony is that there is more food, but the people it was intended for cannot afford to buy it. Some of this food is even exported rather than used to feed the indigenous hungry population.

The most practical goal for the future is to reduce population growth and to help the developing nations

TABLE 10.5   Projected Population Size at Stabilization

Country	Population in 1986 (million)	Annual Rate of Population Growth (percent)	Size of Population at Stabilization (million)	Change from 1986 (percent)
Slow Growth Countries				
China	1,050	1.0	1,571	+ 50
Soviet Union	280	0.9	377	+ 35
United States	241	0.7	289	+ 20
Japan	121	0.7	128	+ 6
United Kingdom	56	0.2	59	+ 5
West Germany	61	−0.2	52	− 15
Rapid Growth Countries				
Kenya	20	4.2	111	+455
Nigeria	105	3.0	532	+406
Ethiopia	42	2.1	204	+386
Iran	47	2.9	166	+253
Pakistan	102	2.8	330	+223
Bangladesh	104	2.7	310	+198
Egypt	46	2.6	126	+174
Mexico	82	2.6	199	+143
Turkey	48	2.5	109	+127
Indonesia	168	2.1	368	+119
India	785	2.3	1,700	+116
Brazil	143	2.3	298	+108

Source: World Bank, *World Development Report 1985* (New York: Oxford University Press, 1985).

Sacks of grain destined for Ethiopia lie rotting in a port, while another farm family in the United States is driven off the land by low prices. Over production and waste at one end of the world and undernourishment at the other suggest that we have not yet learned how to respond as a global community to the problems of population and food supply. (Left: Alexander/ Spooner/Gamma; right: Roy Roper/EKM-Nepenthe.)

become more self-reliant (Selim 1980). Agricultural self-sufficiency has not been easy for developing nations to achieve, however. The irony is that many developing countries must now buy so much food from the United States and other countries with a surplus that they have accumulated massive foreign debts, which leaves them with no funds to spend on their own agricultural development.

Population, Resources, and Living Standards

When a country has too many people for its resources, most people live in poverty, the resources needed for capital development are used up, and its unemployment is high. In addition, overcrowding occurs, public services are strained, and the environment is polluted.

The social picture in the world's poorer countries is generally bleak. Millions of people unable to find work in the countryside migrate to large cities in the hope of finding work. Unemployment and underemployment trap large segments of the population in poverty. As a result, cities such as Calcutta, Mexico City, and Cairo are becoming vast agglomerations of people surrounded by acres of miserable shantytowns in which residents live

in houses made from packing crates and other urban refuse. Living five or six in a room, these people lack clean water, sanitation, and decent food.

With such vast numbers of people cut off from even the rudiments of modern civilization it is little wonder that other urban services are also inadequate. Education and health care are virtually nonexistent in many areas, and entire families live out their lives without ever going to school or seeing a doctor.

An additional misfortune for the developing countries has been the destruction of the environment. When too many people populate an area, they begin to destroy the local forests, grasslands, croplands, and water supplies. Trees and vegetation disappear, soil erodes, the productivity of the land declines, water tables fall, and wells dry up (Brown 1987). Throughout most of the Third World, wood is the most important fuel for cooking and heating. But as populations grow, supplies of wood are quickly exhausted. People—usually women —must walk farther every day to gather wood. As the trees are cut down, and cut down ever younger, they offer less protection against erosion by wind and water. Fertile, productive land becomes desert, and populations experience massive food shortages and starvation. None of these problems is caused solely by the demographic surplus, but it aggravates existing economic, political, and social difficulties.

Conflicting Perspectives on the Environment and Growth

A sharp debate has opened in recent years over the direction of the world's population trends (Holden 1986). One appraisal is pessimistic, the other optimistic. The gloomy view is reflected in the *Global 2000 Report,* issued in 1980 by President Carter's Council on Environmental Quality. It predicted, "If present trends continue, the world in 2000 will be more crowded, more polluted, less stable ecologically and more vulnerable to disruption than the world we live in now" (quoted by Boffey 1983, p. 9). The Council called for decisive action on the part of nations to preserve natural resources, through centralized government planning and international cooperation. This assessment is shared by the Worldwatch Institute, a privately financed research organization. It finds that the world's overpopulation has changed the very chemistry of the earth, the number of living species, and the earth's temperature. It warns that we have crossed many natural thresholds in a short period of time, without clear scientific knowledge of how the affected natural systems will respond, much less how this will effect political and economic systems (Brown 1987).

In addition, Worldwatch analysts say that virtually all the world's productive land is currently under cultivation. As new cropland has become scarce and as fertile topsoil has eroded, the growth in world food output has slowed. Rising energy costs and diminishing returns from the use of chemical fertilizers have contributed to the leveling off of food production. Matters are complicated by increased emissions of environmental pollutants and the buildup of toxic chemicals in food chains. Most of the world's other biological systems—forests, grasslands, and fisheries—are also deteriorating. And essential nonrenewable resources, such as petroleum and natural gas, and nonfuel minerals, such as tungsten, tin, and platinum, are rapidly being depleted. Consequently, a smaller amount of each resource is available for each person. As world population increases, the problem grows. In sum, these investigations contend that the world is on the edge of an environmental crisis that is impairing the global economy.

The pessimistic perspective follows in the Malthusian tradition that portrays the "population problem"

resulting from a rapidly growing population pressing on limited resources. Quite a different view emerges from the highly controversial writings of the late futurist Herman Kahn and the economist Julian L. Simon (1984). They reject the idea that resources are finite. Throughout human history Simon and Kahn find that enterprising management and resourceful technicians have discovered new reserves of minerals, have made increasingly efficient use of lower-grade ore, and have found substitutes for many other minerals. Thus, not too long ago ships were dispatched to kill whales for their oil; then blankets were spread over oily pools and the petroleum extracted by wringing the blankets by hand; more recently holes were drilled in the earth to release deposits of oil. Based on historical trends, these two analysts expect the future to bring declining scarcity, falling real prices, and increased wealth.

Simon also claims that our water and air are less polluted now than in 1900. In nineteenth-century cities coal smoke, horse manure, and human excrement posed severe health hazards. When these problems were mastered, life expectancies increased. And to nail down the point, he notes that Lake Erie is again teeming with fish.

Simon contends that the key to the recurring problem associated with the depletion of resources is not a lowering of population growth. He sees the human mind as "the ultimate resource," and hence the "amount of improvement depends on the number of people available to use their minds" (1981, p. 197). Wealth is not a fixed quantity; it is produced by people. Thus the more people, the greater the wealth. The human mind gives us technological marvels, which Simon believes will continue to increase yields per acre and will afford humankind ample food. Indeed, he notes that birthrates are falling throughout the world in response to the demographic transition. Simon holds that the world will sort itself out if left to its own devices, a view that many demographers have criticized as naïve if not downright wrong. In sum, pessimistic and optimistic analysts draw on many of the *same* data sources only to arrive at startlingly different conclusions (Holden 1986).

POPULATION POLICY WORLDWIDE

What kinds of policies have been proposed to close the gap between burgeoning numbers of people and available food and employment? We have seen one extreme attempt by the Chinese government to cope with the problem there. What other goals have been considered? And who has the right to make policies, direct or indirect, that affect individuals so personally?

Many people see another and opposite type of problem facing us today; a long-declining birthrate and decreased population in the technologically advanced societies of the world. What policies have been devised to address this problem of *declining* numbers? What are the underlying moral implications? Is a worldwide policy that would embrace both types of problem—population growth in some areas, population decline in others—actually feasible?

Sociologists have long pointed out that high birthrates are more common in predominantly agricultural, nonindustrialized nations, such as those in the Third World, and that lower birthrates and smaller family size tend to be found in affluent, industrialized countries such as ours. As noted earlier, one reason this is true is that in agricultural communities, the more children there are, the more certain are the futures of the family and its land (Cain 1985). Historically, faced with high infant mortality rates, rampant infectious disease, and a shortened life expectancy, people in these societies tended to believe that the more babies they had, the greater would be their chances of having offspring survive. Even when modern medicine and public health programs have made some impact and altered mortality rates and life expectancy, the value invested in the notion of many offspring has not necessarily changed. Thus, high birthrates are maintained in less-developed, preindustrial countries. Any policy that is aimed at curbing fertility in the Third World must take these factors into account.

On the other hand, families in developed industrialized nations tend to be limited in family size, particularly in the middle and upper classes. Why? Partly because additional children mean additional expense. This may not seem to be much of a problem compared with the economic means of a Third World family, but societally, there are enormous differences in life-styles and values. The more children a middle-class American couple has, for instance, the lower are each child's chances of, say, going to a "good" university and finding a comfortable niche in the job market. Also, more and more women not only work but pursue careers—which, despite the Supermom ideal, does conflict with childbearing and child rearing and has contributed to the smaller family size.

Curbing Fertility

Some sociologists have gone so far as to say that, given the situation we have outlined, the best way to curb fertility in countries where this poses a problem is simply to concentrate on economic development; decreased population growth will follow (Lieberson 1986). However, Peter Donaldson (1986) argues that Third World countries face a more complex set of problems that may not respond to economic development alone. First, Donaldson notes that even *with* decreased infant and overall mortality rates, high birthrates and high fertility continue in the poorer nations. Thus, the population increases in two ways—at the bottom of the age structure and at the top, with more infants surviving and more old people living longer.

But perhaps more central to the problem, Donaldson suggests, is that the poorer countries cannot develop *fast* enough to keep up with the population growth; they cannot provide enough food, education, and jobs to match the growing population and its age structure. Greater numbers of children mean, in economic development terms, a greater investment in child care and education. But that takes money away from capital and industrial investment—which in turn means that even if the children are adequately educated for a more modernized society, there may very well be no jobs for them in that society when they reach adulthood, or there may not be a more modernized society at all. According to Donaldson, population size, age structure, and growth rates are tied closely to structural and overall societal change. Family planning also becomes an important factor in efforts to generate societal change.

Family planning and birth control are clearly crucial for the developing areas of the world, particularly as part of broad development plans (Donaldson 1986). Here, however, we note the intersection of the individual with society-wide demographics and economic change. For it is at the level of the individual that family planning works. Attempts to "legislate" birth control have often failed because the individual and her or his personal motivation to limit fertility and family size were not taken into account. In Kenya, for example, a family planning program has done little to curb population growth (Cordes 1985). In China, where, as we have seen, some success from a radical population control program has been reported, the program does not seem to be working as well as was expected. By 2050, the Chinese population is expected to reach some 200 to 300 million more than the government had planned (*New York Times*, November 15, 1987).

Nonetheless, there are also some noteworthy family planning successes, such as in Tunisia and Thailand. In many places, simple availability (or affordability) of birth control devices is the issue. Educational programs have had some major success in changing people's attitudes toward birth control (for example, by showing that babies spaced further apart are generally healthier).

Resistance to family planning is often based on moral or religious grounds, which are deeply embedded. Policymakers are then faced with a chicken-and-egg situation: in order to develop, population growth must be curbed, but in order to curb population growth, the culture and its values must change enough so that individuals will *choose* to practice birth control. The society must also change enough so that birth control will seem worthwhile.

There is, finally, a moral issue involved in all matters of population growth and policy. Does a government have a right to invade people's bedrooms and tell them how many children they can or cannot have? After all, as we have just discussed, traditional values may not fit with the notion of control over natural fertility. In India in the 1970s, a program of forced sterilization of men brought much protest and even rioting. Western reactions to the Chinese one-child-per-couple program have often come close to moral indignation at such control being exerted over personal life. Sometimes the moral issue is obscured, buried under other concerns. Many nations, unlike China, do not have population "policies" per se. Rather, a country's economic, industrial, and educational policies reflect policymakers' stances on population growth and/or reduction.

Women's Status and Reducing Growth

As one social scientist has so aptly observed, "Just as strong as direct teaching is the indirect effect of the status of women on fertility" (Harrison 1984, p. 232). The status of women remains low in most traditional societies —and whatever status women do have derives from marriage and mothering, particularly of sons. Traditionally, marriage in developing countries has been universal —and early. Women have been denied access to formal education and to work outside the home, and have

Public policy versus private choice . . . controlling population growth is such a difficult problem because it is both a societal and a personal issue. How far should governments be permitted to go in intervening in the life choices of their citizens? (Richard Dunoff/The Stock Market.)

usually had no alternative to the customary style of motherhood—numerous pregnancies, often with several children dying in infancy. A reduction in birthrates in such societies clearly involves a dramatic change in women's role (Cramer 1980; Stevens 1981).

As we have seen, demographers have noted that people will not change their pattern of childbearing until they are given motivations to do so. A reduction in infant mortality can be one important motivating factor. Other motivations come with the expansion of basic education, especially for girls (Rindfuss, Bumpass, and St. John 1980). As China has recognized and incorporated into its population-control policies, when girls stay in school longer, they marry later. They may also be able to obtain some kind of work, thus bettering their status. Schooling also presents both young men and women with the idea of an alternative future. And education for both sexes helps reduce suspicion of social change, making contraception a less frightening idea. Thus governments in many developing countries seek to expand educational opportunities for women as a means of slowing population growth. Government programs may also encourage women to enter the labor force so that women have other ways than motherhood to gain society's respect. Women with jobs are much less likely to have children than

In cultures that value women primarily as child-bearers and child-rearers, issues of birth control and family planning can be bewildering and threatening. Expanded opportunities for education and employment can help women achieve higher status, self-esteem, and power of choice. This hygiene class for women in a village in Bangladesh is a small but vital step in this process. (Bruce Thomas/The Stock Market.)

women not working outside the home. The lower fertility rate of employed women reflects the time constraints of coordinating motherhood and employment (U.S. Census Bureau 1986).

One indication of women's changing status worldwide is the increasing availability of contraceptives, which usually puts the ability to control the number of births into the hands of women. However, modern contraceptives are still not available to much of the world's population. In the developing countries, nearly 80 percent of couples "at risk" do not have access to (or for other reasons do not use) contraception (Green and Fearey 1978; Harrison 1984). Although some couples manage to limit their families by traditional methods (abstinence, withdrawal, rhythm), there is a clear need for the diffusion of contraceptive information and devices. When these are widely available and free, the birthrate can fall dramatically.

Promoting Fertility

What about *increasing* slow population growth, the second type of population problem? How should we deal with what Ben Wattenberg (1987) has called the "Birth Dearth"? In the United States and in much of Europe slowed population growth is the trend. As we noted earlier, after a long decline in fertility, the United States has been, since 1972, below the replacement level of 2.1 children for women of childbearing age. Birthrates in West Germany and Denmark have decreased to 1.3 children per childbearing woman. The British and French rates have also fallen, as have those of most Eastern European nations except for Poland. Wattenberg as well as others (Kelley 1986) consider all of Western Europe, Canada, the United States, Japan, New Zealand, Australia, Israel, and Iceland—all of the "free world"—to be experiencing "fertility free-fall" (Wattenberg 1987). Just as the American Social Security system may be overburdened by an aging population, so may the European welfare state be in trouble, since projections show fewer and fewer adult workers available to support the remainder of the populace.

To counteract the trend of fewer children and smaller families that seems to accompany ever-increasing affluence, pronatalist (probirth) policies have been designed and implemented in several Western and Eastern European countries. Such policies support the choice to have children (and to have more children) by providing parents with free child care, long maternity and/or paternity leave for new parents, first choice in housing, and even cash incentives. France, for example, to combat its low level of births, has introduced "salary" payments to young mothers who have had more than two children. East Germany over ten years ago began offering families extra vacation time and longer maternity leaves; in Rumania, abortion has been outlawed, and single adults and childless couples are taxed; and in the USSR, paid maternity leave was recently expanded from 12 to 18 months. To overcome the "Birth Dearth," Wattenberg has called for similar big-spending, pronatalist policies in the United States and Western Europe. But it is not clear that such programs have any long-term effects (Sullivan 1986).

The political, social, and economic implications of pronatalist policies and programs have been much debated. Wattenberg's recent predictions in particular have fueled enormous controversy. His forecasts of the long-term detrimental effects of the "Birth Dearth"—reduced military power and world influence, disruption of American and Western European business as a result of lowered demand and a shortage of young consumer-workers, the inability to adapt to the aging population—have all been called into question. Wattenberg's arguments that a lowered free-world population will increasingly endanger Western civilization and its influence over the developing world have been labeled ethnocentric and even racist. Certainly, if Westerners represent less of the world population, it will be harder to convince the Third World nations (should this prove necessary) that Western values should apply to them. But this for some is already a questionable stance in any case. What can be said of a world where pronatalist programs encourage fertility in the developed countries, and family-planning programs seek to reduce fertility in the disadvantaged, developing countries?

The controversies on each side are compelling. In addition to moral issues, there are also economic,

policy, political, and even gender-role considerations. How will funds for contraceptives, for education, for job and capital development, be provided? How can contraception and education actually be made available? How can people be motivated to accept either birth control or larger families? How should comprehensive development policies, that take everything from ecology to family size into account, be administered? What will be the status of women in the home and in the labor market? Who will bear the brunt of child care—and who will make that decision? How can worldwide population control programs be coordinated? The questions go on and on. The peace and prosperity of the entire world may eventually depend on finding answers to some of these questions and in reuniting a demographically divided world.

SUMMARY

1. Demography is the study of how births, deaths, and migration affect the composition, size, and distribution of populations. Both action and structural perspectives are needed in population studies. Demographers put their information to use in describing social structure and in understanding the effects of individuals and their choices on the population picture.

2. The main source of population data is the census, a periodic counting of the population and a collection of data about it. A full census of the U.S. population is taken every ten years. Surveys, interviews, and ethnographic methods are used along with census enumeration to get at the action side of population issues.

3. Population growth depends on the relationship between three demographic variables: births, deaths, and net migration. The rate of population growth is the extent to which births and immigration exceed deaths and emigration.

4. The United States takes 50 percent of the world's immigrants, a major source of its population growth. This policy is partly the result of a longstanding tradition of openness to certain immigrant groups and the success of these groups in ensuring that others can follow them. It is also partly the result of the high involvement of the United States in international affairs, including military

conflicts, which gives it a strong sense of commitment to certain populations.

5. Americans have always been a highly mobile population. A major population shift has been from the North and East to the South and West. Today the Sunbelt, and the Western Mountain and Pacific states are experiencing the highest growth rates.

6. There has been a substantial increase in worldwide population density during the past few generations. This increase has influenced—for better or worse—employment, food production, transportation, housing, and even life expectancy. Industrialization and modern technology have facilitated and encouraged high density in cities all over the world, but in Third World nations, overcrowding and rapid population growth have resulted in extreme poverty and poor living conditions.

7. Thomas Malthus was the first scholar to analyze population growth and to worry about its consequences for humankind. He felt that increases in food supply could never keep pace with population growth. Malthus thought that the only way to halt population growth was by voluntary abstinence from sexual relations; otherwise, population would be checked drastically by war, pestilence, or starvation.

8. Karl Marx took exception to Malthusian doctrine, believing that the problem was not one of overpopula-

tion but of underproduction and the inequitable distribution of the world's wealth. Where Malthus saw the solution to population problems in moral restraint, Marx sought the solution in socialism.

9. The basic model of population change in the West over the past two centuries is known as the *demographic transition*. In stage one, a high, steady birthrate and an equally high death rate, which shot up during epidemics and famines, moderated the rate of population growth. In the second phase, the death rate began to decline as public hygiene and sanitation improved, and better food supplies became available. Populations grew rapidly. Finally, in the third phase, as in the industrialized nations of today, the death rate is slow and steady, whereas the birthrate is low but fluctuates with social trends.

10. Demographers are careful in applying the demographic transition model to developing areas of the world to predict what will happen in the future. There the demographic transition has taken a different form as more advanced technology greatly reduced the death rate within just a few years. The birthrates in many developing countries, moreover, have remained high, despite lowered death rates and economic gains. The birthrate in these countries is not likely to fall until people are motivated to limit the number of children they have.

11. The slowing of population growth for some nations and the acceleration of growth for others has resulted in a demographically divided world. Demographic changes divide the world economically as well, causing the developing world to fall further behind in its efforts to improve living conditions for its citizens.

12. The Malthusian nightmare is a reality for millions of people. As population growth strains the available resources, hunger, unemployment, destruction of natural resources, and other social ills result.

13. Analysts are divided on the future trends of the world's population. Many experts express grave concern about policies of economic growth that disregard the pollution of the biosphere and the conservation of limited resources. Other authorities take a more optimistic view, defending technology as "the ultimate resource" in preserving our environment.

14. The low status of women in traditional societies has contributed to high birthrates and continued population growth. One significant aspect of reducing the population growth in such societies involves a change in women's roles.

15. Dire predictions of an overpopulated, starving planet are being tempered, but the problem of population growth in developing countries is very real. Policies intending to curb fertility have often not been successful, partly because of ingrained personal and cultural values, moral issues, the treacherously large gap between increasing populations and available food and funds, and the difficulty of forming comprehensive, coordinated development priorities. The developed countries face the opposite problem: a declining population. Pronatalist policies aimed at combatting this problem are controversial.

GLOSSARY

Census. A periodic counting of the population, in which facts on age, sex, occupation, and so forth, are also recorded.

Crude birthrate. The number of births per 1,000 people in a given year.

Crude death rate. The number of deaths per 1,000 people in a given year.

Demographic transition. A three-stage process in which a population shifts from a high birthrate and a high death rate to a low birthrate and a low death rate.

Demography. The scientific study of how births, deaths, and migration affect the composition, size, and distribution of populations.

Density. The number of people who live in a given territorial area.

Emigration. The movement of people out of an area.

Fecundity. The biological potential for reproduction.

Fertility rate. The number of births per 1,000 women between the ages of fifteen and forty-four.

Immigration. The movement of people into an area.

Infant mortality rate. The number of deaths to infants in their first year of life per 1,000 live births in a given year.

Internal migration. The movement of people from one place to another within the same country.

Life expectancy. The average number of years of life remaining to a person of a given age.

Life span. The maximum number of years of a human life.

Migration rate. The difference between the number of people leaving and those arriving each year, per 1,000 people.

PART FOUR
INEQUALITY
AND POWER

"America is the land of opportunity." "America is the melting pot of nations." "A woman's place is in the home." Such statements, with their appeal to the emotions, to tradition, or to "common sense," often escape rational scrutiny. But they tend to support one social group's interests against the interests of competing groups. The next four chapters go beyond "common sense" to explore how social systems distribute rewards such as wealth, power, and prestige, and why those patterns of distribution prevail.

For example, how well does our society conform to the ideal of the American Dream—that everyone has a chance to move up in the class structure? Chapter 11 examines the causes and consequences of social stratification, the effects of poverty, and social programs for the redistribution of wealth.

Where do we get our ideas about masculinity and femininity? Are they based on biological differences between the sexes or on society's expectations of how men and women should act? Chapter 12 discusses gender stereotypes, gender roles, and the changing economic and political status of women.

Chapter 13 offers a sociological perspective on critical issues pertaining to racial and ethnic relations. What makes a minority group in sociological terms? How do different societies respond to new and alien groups? How and why are some groups discriminated against? And how does society respond to institutionalized forms of discrimination?

News reports are full of politics, but rarely examine the social organization behind the democratic process and other ways of wielding power. Chapter 14 looks at politics as a social process and considers such issues as the use of power, types of authority, the rise of the modern state, and the development of modern warfare. We look at the role of money, political parties, and the media in U.S. politics and compare our democratic system to more totalitarian states.

When you hear about stock prices or the balance of trade, you probably do not think of them as social issues. Chapter 15 illustrates how economic systems are grounded in social forces by comparing the two major economic systems of capitalism and socialism. The role of multinational corporations in a global economy is among the other issues to be examined. Because the work we do is part of our identity as social beings, the text explores the meaning and organization of work in an age of increasing automation.

CHAPTER 11
Social Stratification and Social Class

Homeless people. In cities across the country, people wearing tattered clothing and carrying bags of their belongings can be seen sleeping in train stations, bus terminals, even on the sidewalk. Huddled over warm-air gratings, they live through the winter on handouts of food and money begged from passersby (Bingham, Green, and White, eds. 1987).

The increasing visibility of the homeless serves as a disturbing reminder that some people in our society are considerably worse off than others. At the very bottom of the American social ladder, even more destitute than the inhabitants of shabby slum dwellings, are these people whose wordly goods fill a few shopping bags, who lack even the most rudimentary shelter. Social workers who investigate the circumstances of homeless people, however, usually find that these people once were better off, but that some unexpected misfortune led to their losing their home. For example, an apartment building is sold to a developer for renovation and its poor tenants are evicted. A breadwinner loses his or her job because of a plant closing or a protracted illness. A woman leaves an abusive husband but cannot afford an apartment on her own. Whatever the precipitating event, the result is the same: a person, a couple, a mother and her children, or an entire family living in an encampment on the street. Having fallen from a higher rung on the social ladder, many of the homeless are unable to regain their position (Hope and Young 1986).

A lack of resources and opportunities characterizes those at the bottom level of our society; conversely, an abundance of resources and opportunities characterizes those at the top. This structured ranking of people in a hierarchy is the essence of **stratification,** which refers to the division of a society into layers (or strata) of people who have unequal amounts of scarce but desirable resources, life chances, and social influence. Stratification refers also to inequality among categories of people; for instance, people with similar levels of education, in similar occupations, or possessing similar access to power may occupy the same rung of the social ladder. These inequalities are built into the social structure and may persist from generation to generation. Social stratification does not occur by chance; it is a systematic arrangement that serves the interests of some people above the interests of others. As we will see, societies differ in their degree of social mobility—in the opportunities available for individuals to move up or down the stratification hierarchy by their own efforts.

In this chapter, we will look at several aspects of inequality in human affairs, starting with the nature of social stratification in American society. Other topics that will be addressed include why social stratification arises, social mobility in America, poverty, and programs to reduce inequality.

DIMENSIONS OF STRATIFICATION

Sociologists have taken the word stratification from geology (stratum means layer). The conventional imagery of stratification is one in which human societies are

A *plant closes, a spouse leaves or dies, an apartment building is sold to developers. Most of America's homeless are not permanent residents of the street, but men, women, and often entire families who have temporarily lost the ability to provide their own basic needs. (Roy Morsch/The Stock Market.)*

described as looking like the many layers inside rocks or the layers of a cake. Seen this way, social layers are blendings of similar statuses rather than sharply differentiated groups.

The imagery of stratification formulated by Karl Marx (and used by some contemporary sociologists) is of a very different kind. Rejecting the multilayered view of society, Marx emphasized a simple, sharp economic division between groups—or **classes**. Marx knew that in the short run many other differences between groups were significant, but in the long run he believed the essential division to be between those who own the means of production in capitalistic societies (the **bourgeoisie**) and those who must work for wages in order to survive (the working class, or **proletariat**) (1848, 1852). The sociologist Max Weber agreed with some of Marx's views, but he felt that Marx had oversimplified the terms of stratification (1922). According to Weber, social stratification is not a matter of economic status alone. Weber identified three distinct but related dimensions of social stratification: economic status or wealth, political status or power, and social status or prestige. Attainment of one of these statuses, Weber emphasized, does not necessarily imply attainment of the others. Someone who wins the lottery, for instance, has acquired wealth

but probably not great prestige or power. A member of the clergy may possess considerable prestige but usually has little power or wealth. A terrorist who hijacks an airplane may possess a great deal of power, at least for a time, but it is unrelated to either wealth or prestige. In short, social position is a far more complex phenomenon than Marx envisioned.

Although wealth, power, and prestige are distinct dimensions of social ranking, they are not mutually exclusive. Indeed, they often coincide, reinforcing and sustaining one another. Sometimes one dimension can be converted into another (Goode 1978; Bourdieu 1987). Consider the dimension of power. In Communist countries, top political officials are able to use their positions to gain privileges not enjoyed by the rest of the population such as spacious apartments, imported goods, and fancy cars. Similarly, people with great wealth often attain power and the trappings of eminence. Prestige, too, can be advantageous. Popular entertainers and celebrities frequently use their renown to acquire wealth and influence (an actor becomes president; an astronaut becomes a senator). In the United States and elsewhere, the dimensions of wealth, power, and prestige are distributed quite unequally, a matter to which we now turn.

Wealth and Income

One question of timeless interest is who gets what share of the goods and services produced by an economic system. The answer not only influences an individual's chances for material well-being and opportunities for earning and learning, but it also affects a society by shaping people's motivations to work and their willingness to support existing social arrangements.

Economic stratification is based on what people own (wealth) and what they earn (income). *Wealth* refers to what people *have;* it consists of the value of everything a person or group owns. *Income* refers to how much people *get:* it is the amount of money a person or group receives. People in their early twenties typically have steady incomes but little accumulated wealth. Conversely, retired people generally have assets (home, car, and other ownings) but their incomes are not large. Most people get income from wages or salaries; relatively few people derive revenue from property.

Economists view wages and salaries as a return on labor, and they view interest, dividends, and rent as a return on property (or *capital,* which is defined as precisely that property which can bring such a return). Interest income comes from bonds and bank accounts; dividend income, from the ownership of stock; and rental income, from payments for the use of property. The uneven distribution of wealth and income contributes to social stratification in our society. Stratification also exists and causes tension between societies.

Industrial nations tend to be wealthier than agricultural and preindustrial nations, and opportunities vary accordingly. Moreover, the gap between rich and poor nations is widening (see Figure 11.1). The United States, the world's richest nation, emerged from World War II with a decided advantage. While most of the developed nations were cleaning the rubble from their bombed-out factories and cities, the United States turned its economy from war production to consumer goods, creating a standard of living that for a time was unprecedented in

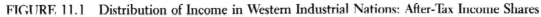

FIGURE 11.1 Distribution of Income in Western Industrial Nations: After-Tax Income Shares

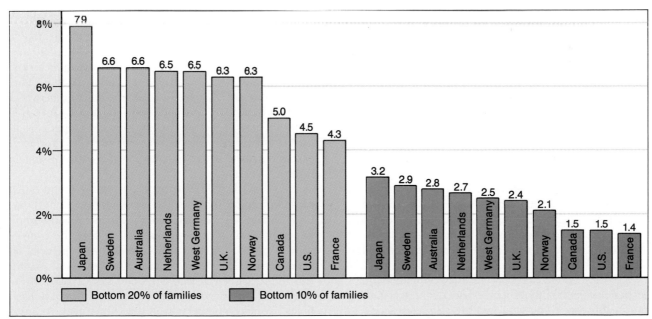

Source: Excerpted from *Minding America's Business* by Ira C. Magaziner and Robert B. Reich. Copyright © 1982 by Law & Business, Inc. Reprinted by permission.

history. But by 1979 many industrialized countries had achieved higher absolute income levels than the United States. Moreover, as revealed in Figure 11.1, the United States ranks near the bottom of Western industrial nations when egalitarianism is measured by the distribution of income. Only France and Canada provide approximately the same small share of their national income to those at the bottom of the economic scale. The lowest 10 percent of families in Japan, West Germany, and the Netherlands receive about double the share of national income received by the bottom 10 percent in the United States (Magaziner and Reich 1983).

Wealth

Information about the wealth of Americans, especially the affluent, is not readily available. It is generally agreed that information about the concentration of wealth is much harder to secure than information on earned income. Wealthy people are often reluctant to talk about the extent of their holdings, and they may not even have a clear idea of what they are "worth" at any given time. This is especially true of people whose wealth is concentrated in investments such as stocks, bonds, and real estate, the value of which fluctuates over time and may only be known for sure when they are sold. Statistics on income are more readily available; many salaries are a matter of record, and various governmental bodies (the Census Bureau, the Internal Revenue Service) compile statistics on income levels within the U.S. population. Available data suggest that most Americans have little wealth; little more than half the population own their own homes and an even smaller number own assets such as stocks and real estate. And though most people have savings, checking, and/or retirement plan accounts (IRA and KEOGH), the majority of Americans have savings worth less than $4,000 (U.S. Bureau of the Census, 1987). Great wealth is typically either inherited or obtained by capitalizing on a valued resource like land or mineral rights or a new product.

Wealth confers distinct advantages to individuals beyond the availability of such essentials as food, shelter, and health care. The very wealthy also have access to services, travel, and hobbies not available to less advantaged individuals. Moreover, substantial wealth often brings income, power, and independence.

TABLE 11.1   Percentage of Aggregate Family Income Received by Each Fifth and Highest 5 Percent, 1980 and 1985

All families	Percentage of aggregate income	
	1980	1985
Lowest fifth	5.1%	4.6%
Second fifth	11.6	10.9
Middle fifth	17.5	16.9
Fourth fifth	24.3	24.2
Highest fifth	41.6	43.5
Highest 5 percent	15.3	16.7

Source: U.S. Bureau of the Census, *Current Population Reports*, P-60 Series, No. 154. Washington, D.C.: Government Printing Office, 1986.

Income

A common way of examining the distribution of income is to divide the population into fifths and compare each segment's share of the total national income. Table 11.1 provides this information for 1980 and 1985. It shows that in 1985 the lowest fifth of American families received 4.6 percent and the highest fifth received 43.5 percent of all income. It also reveals that the top 5 percent of families received 16.7 percent of the nation's total income, three times the share they would receive if all Americans were to receive an equal income. The more significant changes in percent occurring between 1980 and 1985 are at the bottom and top ends of the scale. Income in the two lowest fifths has dropped by at least 0.5 percent, while income has risen by close to 2 percent in the highest fifth and by 1.4 percent in the highest 5 percent.

In 1985, 17,000 Americans reported to the Internal Revenue Service that they had incomes over $1 million. Only 16 percent of the income they reported came from wages or salaries; the remainder came from the ownership of property. Other data reveal that 1 percent of Americans hold 33 percent of the nation's total wealth and 62 percent of all the corporate stock (Page 1983). Table 11.2 summarizes 1983 income statistics of households, families, and persons in the United States adjusted to reflect 1986 conditions.

A few Americans earn substantial incomes. For example, in 1987, one hundred forty seven top corporate executives earned in excess of $1 million. Of these, three earned more than $5 million. In addition to their salaries, some corporate officers also receive several million dollars in gains from various stock options and other long-term financial agreements (Bronson and Morse 1983). Accordingly, with the growth of multinational corporations, we can no longer examine stratification only in terms of personal inequalities of wealth and income. We also have to look at inequalities of power.

Social Power

The word *power* has a generally negative connotation (Marger 1981). We talk about people being "power mad," "power hungry," or "only out for power." And we often associate power with tyrants, dictators, and the leaders of totalitarian regimes. Yet the notion that evil is imposed by power while good flies on its own wings is untenable. Power can also be used to combat sexism, racism, and tyranny.

Social power is a fundamental and inherent element in all interaction at every social level; it can be used for constructive as well as selfish ends. Wherever we look in human affairs, be it families, juvenile gangs, or nation-states, we find that some people get their way more often than others.

Power is exercised at both an *interpersonal* level and a *societal* level (Marger 1981). At the interpersonal level, power operates in direct face-to-face relationships such as those between husbands and wives, supervisors and subordinates, and teachers and pupils. For the most part, the use of power within these contexts has immediate consequences only for the individuals involved. But when individuals or groups bring power to bear in situations that affect many, if not all, elements of society, the power is societal. The presidency of the United States is an example of societal power. The decisions the president makes are not like those of other people: few of us think in terms of billions of dollars, of millions of people, or of triggering a nuclear war.

Although we will explore the concentration of power in America more fully in Chapter 14, the highlights of that discussion are relevant here. Like wealth and prestige, power is an important dimension of social stratification, and there is no doubt that it is unequally distributed in this country. The question sociologists debate is not *whether* the possession of power is unequal in America, but rather *how* unequal it is.

Prestige

The third dimension of stratification is prestige. **Prestige** is "the esteem, respect, or approval that is granted by an

TABLE 11.2   Summary of Americans' Income in the 1980s

	Total	Median/Income	Income in Thousands of Dollars							
			0–5	5–10	10–20	20–30	30–45	45–60	60–85	85+
Total Figures	1000	$23,450	67	113	248	209	165	103	65	30
Husband/wife couples	718	$28,300	16	48	156	168	142	96	62	30
Single women with and without dependents	179	$11,800	35	46	59	23	11	4	1	0
Single men with and without dependents	103	$15,500	16	19	33	18	12	3	2	0
Racial Summary										
Whites	836	$24,700	46	85	206	174	146	92	59	28
Blacks, Hispanics, and Others	164	$17,700	21	28	42	35	19	11	6	2

Source: U.S. Bureau of the Census, *Current Population Reports*, P-60 Series, No. 146. Washington, D.C.: Government Printing Office, 1986.

Wealth, power, and prestige reinforce one another, contributing to extremes of social stratification. In industrialized societies such stratification is ingrained, its edges softened; in developing countries, such as those in the oil-rich Middle East, the process of stratification is often more acute and its effects more glaring. (Left: Robert V. Eckert, Jr./EKM-Nepenthe; right: René Burri/Magnum.)

individual or a collectivity for performances or qualities they consider above the average" (Goode 1978, p. 7). As such, it provides people with a sense of worth and respect, a feeling that somehow they are admired and valued by others. Emphasizing their potential for conversion into economic advantage, Pierre Bourdieu has referred to such signs of prestige as "cultural capital" (1984).

Societies attach prestige to different attributes. In a society preoccupied with religion, holiness and zeal may be the most important attributes for prestige; in a military setting, physical courage is often what counts the most; people in the film or the fashion fields often equate status with talent or good looks. In America we bestow prestige according to how people earn their money (their occupation), how they spend it (their mode of consumption), who they are (their ancestry), whom they know, and how successful or well-known they are.

Being a neurosurgeon, earning several hundred thousand dollars a year, owning a large yacht, having an Anglo-Saxon surname, belonging to the "right" clubs, and having friends in positions of power are all sources of prestige in our society. However, the main general determinant of prestige appears to be one's occupation. Sociologists measure the prestige of occupations by asking representative samples of the population to assess the social standing of various types of work, and to rank the occupations on a scale from excellent to average to poor. Researchers then translate these rankings into prestige tallies ranging from 0 (low) to 100 (top). The results of occupational surveys tend to remain fairly stable over time. As reflected in Table 11.3, Americans rate most highly those jobs that afford an individual power, require professional skills, and provide high income. Doctors, scientists, lawyers, and some engineers are among the top; garbage collectors, janitors, and shoe shiners at the bottom; schoolteachers, carpenters, farmers, and sales managers in between. But there are some surprises. Americans are not as anti-intellectual as they are sometimes depicted: college professors rank second (even ahead of bankers), and movie actors rank below teachers.[1]

Prestige is a subjective matter, one that is more intangible than tangible. However, since prestige is such an important part of social relations, people give it a more tangible cast through symbolic representations. Titles ("Sir," "Mr. President," "Your Royal Highness," "Doctor," "Professor"), honorary degrees, seats of honor, medals, badges, trophies, and displays of deference are symbolic expressions of prestige.

Corporate life provides countless clues to a person's rank in the prestige hierarchy. A corner office on a top floor, for example, is one sign of success. Bank of America employees know that they have made it when they are given stationery with the bank's logo in gold rather than black ink. The Ford Motor Corporation has a very elaborate system of status classification. Employees are graded on a scale of 1 (clerks and secretaries) to 27 (chairman of the board). Grade 9, the lowest executive level, includes the right to an outside parking place; Grade 13 brings a larger office, windows, plants, an intercom system, and a secretary. Those who reach Grade 16 receive an office with a private lavatory, signed Christmas cards from the chairman, an indoor parking space, and company cars.

ANALYSIS OF SOCIAL STRATIFICATION

In virtually every human society of substantial population, some stratification develops. From the Egyptian pharaohs to the American upper class, from the higher castes in India to the party bureaucrats in socialist countries, some groups of people inevitably end up at the top of the social order, with the rest of the population ranked below. Why does this happen? Two explanations

have been advanced: one that emphasizes functional integration and one that stresses power. Functionalists maintain that stratification serves society's needs and is therefore both necessary and inevitable. Those who hold a power perspective believe that stratification is unnecessary and coercive because it enables certain groups to manipulate the system in their favor. We will first look more closely at the functional and power views of stratification, and then at the efforts of sociologists to bring the two views together.

Although prestige *is a subjective and intangible element of social status, its symbols—like the ornament on the hood of this car or the private jet in the background—are clearly and universally recognized, thanks in part to their constant repetition in print and television advertising. (Gabe Palmer/The Stock Market.)*

---

[1]The occupation of movie actor appeared on an extended scale, and drew a rank of forty-four, compared with eighty-one for a public school teacher (Tumin 1973).

TABLE 11.3   Prestige Ranking of Occupations in the United States, 1983

Highest Ranking Occupations	Score	Lowest Ranking Occupations	Score
Physician	82	Auctioneer	32
College/university professor	78	Bus driver	32
Lawyer	76	Truck driver	32
Dentist	74	Cashier	31
Physicist/astronomer	74	File clerk	30
Bank officer	72	Upholsterer	30
Architect	71	Drill-press operator	29
Aeronautical/astronautical engineer	71	Furniture finisher	29
Psychologist	71	Retail salesperson	29
Airplane pilot	70	Midwife	23
Clergy	69	Gas station attendant	22
Chemist	69	Security guard	22
Electrical engineer	69	Taxi driver	22
Geologist	67	Elevator operator	21
Sociologist	66	Bartender	20
Secondary school teacher	63	Waiter/waitress	20
Mechanical engineer	62	Clothing presser	18
Registered nurse	62	Farm laborer	18
Dental hygienist	61	Household servant	18
Pharmacist	61	Car washer	17
Radiologic technician	61	Freight handler	17
Chiropractor	60	Garbage collector	17
Elementary school teacher	60	Janitor	16
Veterinarian	60	Bellhop	14
Postmaster	58	Shoe shiner	09

Source: Adapted from *General Social Surveys, 1972–1983: Cumulative Codebook* (Chicago: National Opinion Research Center, 1983), pp. 338-349.

The Functional Perspective

One group of sociologists has argued that stratification exists because it serves a functionally positive and important need for society. This view was influentially elaborated by Kingsley Davis and Wilbert E. Moore (1945, 1953) in the *American Sociological Review.* Although their ideas have been modified by later sociologists, Davis and Moore were the first to argue that stratification is both universal and necessary, and that class arrangements of some kind are a feature of every society. Davis and Moore reasoned as follows: If all the positions that have to be filled in a society were equally important and everyone were equally capable of doing these jobs, there would be no need for stratification. But this is not the

case. Some tasks are clearly more essential than others, and some require a great deal more talent and training. As an example, almost any able-bodied person can be taught to dig ditches in a day or two, but it takes years of schooling to become a physician. Medical students must learn how to diagnose and treat innumerable maladies. Then, as interns, they must often work around the clock, sacrificing their sleep and social life. Upon achieving professional status, physicians are still expected to pour considerable time, energy, and compassion into their work. How many people would choose to spend most of their adult years confronting life and death issues if they were not adequately motivated to do so?

The human motivation factor is the key to Davis and Moore's argument. Societies must motivate people to seek socially essential and important positions and to

This business executive might argue that years of hard work and self-sacrifice permitted him to achieve such a high level of success. But will the same degree of struggle and self-sacrifice produce the same results for these Chicano laborers? The complex way in which society distributes its rewards makes it difficult to define what we mean by equality. (Left: Will McIntyre/Photo Researchers; right: James McGoon/Wheeler Pictures.)

perform them conscientiously. The way society does this is by rewarding those who enter challenging fields with more of the things that contribute to sustenance, comfort, diversion, and self-regard. In other words, a society has to have rewards it can use as enticements and some way of distributing those rewards. Otherwise many essential tasks would not get done, and the society itself would start to disintegrate. Social inequality provides this motivational incentive and is consequently both necessary and constructive. Since stratification serves the interests of the society as a whole, most members of a society accept the system and cooperate in preserving the built-in distribution of rewards and opportunities.

It is important to note that the functional perspective is not a justification of stratification; it merely explains why stratification exists. As such, this viewpoint sheds light on why all societies are stratified and why the

stratification systems of industrialized countries tend to resemble one another despite political and economic differences (Wesolowski 1979). One of the major limitations of the functional perspective, however, is that it does not account for the important role of power in generating and maintaining stratification throughout the world.

The Power Perspective

Some of the most vocal critics of the functional view of stratification are those who hold a power perspective (Dahrendorf 1968; Collins 1975; Beteille 1977; Tumin 1953, 1985). Advocates of this viewpoint assert that stratification is "functional" only for some members of

In the medieval world, social stratification was accepted as part of a divine hierarchy. In this scene from a fifteenth-century illuminated manuscript, order and stability emanate from the central figure of the Duke of Berry, presiding over the advisers, servants, and soldiers of his feudal estate. Many sociologists argue that all societies require some degree of social stratification in order to function. (Giraudon/Art Resource.)

society, namely, those with the power to shape the system to their own advantage.

One of the classic arguments in support of the power perspective is that of sociologist Melvin Tumin, who points to the fundamental difficulty of determining what positions are more functionally necessary to society than others. "In the long run," Tumin writes, "some labor force of unskilled workmen is as important and indispensable as *some* labor force of engineers" (1970, p. 380). Tumin also questions Davis and Moore's proposition that only a limited portion of the population has the necessary talents for essential positions. According to Tumin, the stratification system, instead of facilitating the filling of those positions, actually prevents the discovery of talented members of the society because access to education depends on access to wealth. What's more, a stratification system passes on its inequalities from generation to generation because those seeking higher education generally must depend on their parents to pay for it. In addition, one's motivation to succeed is lessened or enhanced according to what one's parents have achieved and can afford. Thus talent is socially constrained.

Tumin also maintains that elite groups tend to restrict access to their privileged position in order to preserve their prestige and power. For example, each year medical schools turn down hundreds of thousands of qualified applicants, thus allowing physicians to protect their incomes by limiting their numbers. In sum, as the British sociologist T. B. Bottomore (1966, p. 11) observes, "It would be a more accurate description of the social class system to say that it operates, largely through the inheritance of property, to ensure that each individual maintains a certain social position, determined by his birth and irrespective of his particular abilities."

Tumin further maintains that, looked at in the long run, the sacrifices that Davis and Moore ascribe to those who train for important positions are *not* true sacrifices. A doctor who must struggle for the first ten years or so of practice to pay for years of training is more than rewarded in the next twenty to thirty years for his or her services.

Tumin and others dispute the idea that the inducements for taking on essential functions must involve access to scarce rewards. Instead, they suggest that the motivation to take on such jobs might be joy in work or pride in social duty and service. Moreover, the person who fills an important position in society enjoys many psychic and spiritual rewards: high prestige, self-development, and access to leisure and freedom denied less privileged persons.

In sum, the power argument is that far from being functional in any positive way, social stratification is dysfunctional. It restricts talent by limiting access to education, which in turn limits the productive capacity of a society. By focusing people's attention on advancing within the hierarchy instead of changing the system, stratification legitimates the status quo, however right or wrong the existing structure might be. Stratification also deprives people at the lower end of the social ladder of the resources necessary to bring about change, and it functions to make the less privileged hostile and suspicious, thereby preventing full social integration. Power analyses draw heavily on the ideas of Karl Marx (1818–1883), whose views of stratification we will now explore.

The Marxist Perspective

As suggested earlier in the chapter, the core of Marx's view of stratification is the assumption that social classes are sharply divided and constantly compete with one another over a limited supply of rewards and resources. Viewed from this perspective, the "winners" in this contest gain a disproportionate share of society's accolades and resolutely undertake to defend and enhance their positions of privilege. As you recall from Chapter 1, Marx depicted capitalist societies as organized to afford some classes power and control over key economic decisions and policies. The classes that are not in a powerful position must adapt themselves to existing arrangements of wealth and power by selling their labor in the marketplace. It is important to note that Marx's analysis was based on his observations of early capitalism in the nineteenth century. Certain aspects of class division may have been more plainly apparent then, before the rise of corporate capitalism. (The large modern corporation, with its widespread stock ownership, was virtually nonexistent in Marx's day.) Nonetheless, modern Marxists still consider class structure to be of central importance to social organization, even though it is more complex (Wright, 1985).

The dominant class in a capitalist society, the capitalists or bourgeoisie, is distinguished from other social classes by its ownership of the means of production, or exercise of control and authority in the workplace (Marx 1867/1976). The other important class, the working class or proletariat, does not own the means of production (most importantly, the factories in which its members work) and must do the bidding of the bourgeoisie. In the Marxist view, class relations inherently involve conflicting interests, with the ruling class having an interest in maintaining the authority structure and the exploited class having an interest in overthrowing it.

Through its ownership of the factories, mines, large farms, and other sources of subsistence, the bourgeoisie strategically positions itself between the proletariat and the means by which the proletariat can earn a living. By gaining mastery of a society's critical resources, the bourgeoisie gains mastery of its people, rendering the masses vulnerable and susceptible to their control. Moreover, by dominating the means of communication, the schools, and other key institutions, the bourgeoisie seeks to socialize the proletariat with opinions and ideas suggestive of the capitalist order so that it cannot easily develop an accurate awareness of its exploited condition. In furtherance of this view, Marx saw the nation-state as an instrument of oppression, religion as a method of diverting and controlling the masses, and the family in its nineteenth-century form as a means of keeping wealth and education in the hands of the few (Marx 1845/1975).

In a famous phrase, Marx said that "the history of all hitherto existing societies is the history of class struggle" (*The Communist Manifesto*, p. 482). This indicates that he viewed classes not as rungs in a hierarchy of status but as powerful collective forces that mobilize human energies to redirect the course of history. Classes are actors on the historic stage, competing, fighting, debating, exploiting, defending, and attacking the society and each other over their respective shares of the wealth and power pie. Marx predicted that as the class of industrial workers swelled, they would become more and more conscious of their exploited condition and of the increasing disparity in wealth between owners and workers. This consciousness would spark class warfare from which the proletariat would emerge victorious. The result would be first a socialist society in which the means of production would be publicly owned under a benevolent dictatorship of the proletariat, and ultimately a classless communist society in which all would be united in a plentiful, cooperative, "full community."

To some extent, the focus on class and class struggle separates Marxist thought from other power perspectives on stratification. Max Weber, as noted earlier, believed that class was only one of many forms of inequality over which people could struggle. Ethnicity, religion, race, and other statuses could easily take priority over class in the minds of even poor workers. Similarly, many contemporary sociologists maintain that conflict is not restricted to relations between classes. They contend that group competition and conflict are an inevitable part of

In contrast to the celebration of an inherent social hierarchy shown in the previous illustration, this twentieth-century urban mural celebrates a classless society organized around and sustained by the common laborer. Both scenes depict idealized concepts of how society ought to divide its work and distribute its rewards. (Roy Morsch/The Stock Market.)

social life, and so reject Marx's idea that class conflict would be eliminated by a proletarian revolution (Dahrendorf 1959; F. Parkin 1979).

Still, an obvious question for Marxist and other power perspectives on stratification is why people have tolerated so much class inequality for so long. Marx felt that capitalism gave workers both the need and the impetus to overthrow the bourgeoisie and establish a socialist society. But so far no such revolution has been successful in the United States or other modern industrial societies. Socialist revolutions that have taken place

transpired in societies that were more agricultural than industrial (Russia, Cuba, China) and the results of these upheavals did not conform to Marx's expectations.

Some sociologists have attempted to explain why the predicted worldwide socialist revolution has failed to occur (Marwick 1980). One explanation is that the considerable growth of the middle class since Marx's time has reduced the polarization between "owning" and "laboring" classes (Giddens 1973; F. Parkin 1979). Moreover, the growing number of intermediate occupations in the workplace has created more opportunity for social mobility among the working class. As we will see in Chapter 15, the traditional working class of manual production workers has declined substantially, while relatively low-paid white-collar and service jobs have grown in number. People who a century ago could only have been employed as manual laborers in factories and on farms can now find work in clerical, sales, and other service positions. In addition, America has long offered some opportunity for social mobility: not a few sons and daughters of working-class people go to college. Even if their social position is not dramatically better than that of their parents or grandparents, it tends to distance their identification with the working class.

Another change that Marx did not anticipate is that workers' lot and pay have improved substantially over the last century. Workers in political democracies have considerable freedom to organize labor unions and to elect leaders who will stand up for their interests. Unionized workers are granted greater protection under the law, and vacations, health plans, and other benefits are now routine. Taken together, these factors help to explain the blunting of sharp edges between workers and owners and suggest why class inequality continues to be tolerated.

Despite their failure to predict future events, Marx's ideas about the relationship between stratification and social conflict are still widely regarded as keen insights. Many power theorists continue to apply Marx's ideas to the changed conditions of today's world. Erik Olin Wright (1981, 1985), for example, has used class-based theories of stratification to analyze the structure of contemporary American society. As part of his attempts to distinguish classes as meaningful groups, he has found growing numbers of people who occupy what he calls "contradictory class positions." These are people whose interests are divided between capitalists and workers. For instance, lower-level managers and foremen are really employees of capitalists, though they often tend to identify with management. By the same token, many proprietors of small businesses (like a corner store) are owners of capital, but their incomes and personal ties to employees link them to the working class. In times of social and economic stability, these people may think of themselves as capitalists. During times of crisis, however, many people in contradictory positions will count themselves among the working class.

Another fruitful area of research for power sociologists is one that Marx himself predicted: the growing internationalization of capitalism. Many experts now believe that the fundamental class division is between the bourgeoisie of rich countries and the proletariat of poor countries (Wallerstein 1979; Lloyd 1982). We will take up this question at greater length in Chapter 22. In any case, Marx's approach to the way capitalism structures stratification is still widely used (Poulantzas 1975).

Functional and Power Views: A Synthesis

Despite sharp differences in the functional and power viewpoints, each has particular value for sociologists in answering different questions (Coser 1965; Lenski 1966). Increasingly, social scientists are seeking to bring the insights of the two views together for a fuller picture of stratification. From a power perspective, the main argument against the functional viewpoint is that it leaves out the important role of power in shaping and maintaining stratification (Beteille 1977). Power, not functional necessity, better answers such questions as who benefits from stratification, who gets assigned to higher and lower positions in the system, and why conflict arises. Conversely, the main argument against a power view is that *all* societies are stratified. There is at least a resemblance among the stratification systems of industrialized countries regardless of whether they are socialist or capitalist (Wesolowski 1979). The exercise of power may help to shape a particular stratification system somewhat, but the pressure of basic social needs appears to be responsible for the system as a whole.

In his evolutionary approach to stratification, sociologist Gerhard Lenski (1966) took a major step toward a workable synthesis of the two perspectives. He noted, on the one hand, that stratification may actually serve a functional need by matching scarce talents with rewards. However, on the other hand, established forms of stratification will tend to persist long after they have ceased to be functional, which supports many of the power claims. Lenski also drew a synthesis between the functional focus on commonly held values and societal stability, and the power focus on divided interests and instability. In his view, society has evolved to reflect both commonly held values and the values of powerful groups. Similarly, stratification simultaneously facilitates some aspects of societal functioning while impeding others.

THE LAND OF OPPORTUNITY: AN EVALUATION

Leonard Stern's father came to this country from Germany several decades ago. When his textile business got into trouble, the elder Stern and a friend decided to import canaries. They were moderately successful, but then their canary business also fell into debt. Meanwhile, Leonard had gone to college and acquired an M.B.A. at record speed. He took over the business in 1959. The younger Stern built the family's Hartz Mountain Corporation into a $150-million-a-year enterprise, and by the time he was thirty-five he had amassed over a half billion dollars (Louis 1973).

This rags to riches success story typifies the American dream. The belief that any person who gets an education, works hard, and takes advantage of opportunities can "get ahead" is central to that dream—and it is one reason why American workers have failed to develop a sharp class consciousness. Another reason is that the difference between incomes of the rich and poor is smaller than in many other countries (see Figure 11.2). However, many Americans have reservations as to whether or not hard work necessarily leads to success. Is this country truly a land of opportunity? Have we moved closer to the ideal of equal opportunity in the last decade? Can we move closer to it?

To answer these questions, we must first determine the degree of social mobility that exists in this country. By **social mobility,** we mean the movement of people from one social position to another. The term **vertical mobility** refers to upward or downward changes in a person's status, as shown in the case of Leonard Stern.

FIGURE 11.2   A Comparative Look at Stratification

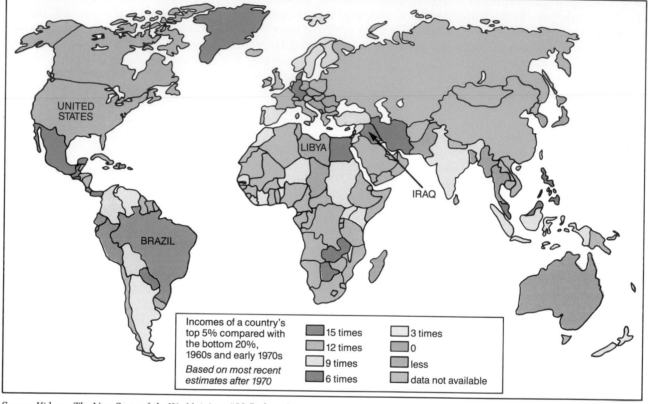

Incomes of a country's top 5% compared with the bottom 20%, 1960s and early 1970s
Based on most recent estimates after 1970

15 times	3 times
12 times	0
9 times	less
6 times	data not available

Source: Kidron, *The New State of the World Atlas*, #38 Rich and Poor People.

Colors on the map indicate how the total income of the richest 5% of people in a country compares with the total received by the poorest 20%. In countries like Brazil or Iraq, stratification is very extreme—the richest 5% receive more than 15 times more than the entire amount received by the poorest 20%. In the U.S. and Libya, by contrast, the incomes of rich and poor are not so far apart.

The term **horizontal mobility** refers to changes in position that do not appreciably alter a person's status, as when a top oil company executive becomes the Secretary of Transportation.

Open and Closed Systems

With regard to social mobility there are two analytically distinct types of stratification systems—open and closed. A truly **open class** system has few impediments to social mobility; positions are awarded on the basis of merit, and rank is tied to individual achievement. Because status depends on what individuals can do by their own effort, it is said to be *achieved* (see Chapter 3). Family origins, race, creed, color, sex, and other *ascribed* characteristics do not matter. Anyone with talent and ambition can advance. Therefore, there is a wide range of status positions, and class lines are blurred. This is not to say that an open society is an equal society. There is a difference between **equality of opportunity** (when the members of a society achieve different standards of living based on their different talents and contributions) and **equality of results** (when all members of a society have the same standard of living). Open systems ideally provide people with an equal chance to succeed. Whether individuals are successful or not depends almost entirely on them, at least in this idealized view. No contemporary society provides true equality of opportunity or equality of results.

A closed or **caste system** is the opposite: Status is ascribed—that is, determined at birth—and people are locked into their parents' social position. In caste systems, ascribed characteristics determine social position, and individuals' opportunities are limited accordingly. Caste lines are clearly defined, and legal and religious sanctions are applied to those who attempt to cross them. The South African apartheid system (which is euphemistically described as "separate development") comes close to exemplifying a true caste system. In South Africa, blacks, Asians, and whites live in separate neighborhoods, attend separate schools, obey separate laws, and endure different punishments. The rigid caste system that existed in India for centuries is illegal today, but strong vestiges of the system remain.

Most societies fall between the two extremes of open and closed stratification systems. In the United States, racism continues to block social mobility for entire groups of people; gender discrimination, too, belies the open system of stratification that Americans pride themselves on.

In evolutionary terms, Gerhard Lenski (1966) has argued that inequality increases with the emergence of a stable agricultural system and with initial industrialization. Often, under these conditions, there is a sizable surplus of goods, and power is concentrated in the hands of a few. But economic inequality declines appreciably as societies continue to industrialize. In advanced industrial societies there is greater equality in the distribution of wealth to the extent that the masses of people acquire and exercise political power. The impetus for this power shift is the rise and continued growth of the middle classes. Socialist countries, Lenski suggests, may eventually reduce economic inequalities still further. Their potential for doing so does not rest with economic redistribution but with dispersing the power that is now concentrated in the hands of a few bureaucrats and party officials.

Social Classes in the United States

The first social scientist to explore in any depth the system of ranking in modern communities was W. Lloyd Warner. His study of "Yankee City" (Newburyport, Massachusetts) yielded a six-class model based on wealth, life style, possessions, and participation in community life and private clubs (Warner et al. 1949). (Note that Warner was using the term *class* in a broader sense

Social mobility has no meaning for these "untouchables" in India, so named because any physical contact with them was considered ritually defiling to members of other Hindu castes. Although this rigid system of social stratification is illegal now in India, the prejudices and injustices of such a system stubbornly persist, as they did in the United States in the century between the abolition of slavery and the Civil Rights movement of the 1950s and 1960s. (Porterfield/ Chickering/Photo Researchers, Inc.)

than Weber.) Warner's six classes broke down as follows: upper-upper (1.4 percent), lower-upper (1.6 percent), upper-middle (10 percent), lower-middle (28 percent), upper-lower (33 percent), and lower-lower (25 percent).

Warner undertook his research prior to World War II. More recently Richard D. Coleman and Lee Rainwater (1978) have investigated the class structure of urban America by sampling residents in Boston and Kansas City. Class emerges from this research largely as a matter of wealth and income, especially as these are translated into a life style based on housing, cars, appliances, and leisure activities. When asked to describe differences between status groups in their communities, the individuals portrayed a many-layered system of social strata, all with rather fuzzy boundaries. However, a rough ranking arrangement emerged:

- *People Who Have "Made It."* The individuals of this level constitute an elite group of wealthy members of the old rich (the Rockefellers), the celebrity rich (television personalities), the anonymous rich (owners of oil wells, shopping centers, and other properties), and the run-of-the-mill rich (well-heeled professionals).

- *People Who Are Doing Very Well.* For the most part this level consists of corporation officers and professional people. They live in large, comfortable homes, belong to country clubs, occasionally vacation abroad, and send their children to prestigious, large state universities or private colleges.

- *People Who Have Achieved the Middle-Class Dream.* Americans of this level enjoy the "good life" but they lack many of the luxuries of those in the higher levels. They are the nation's suburbanites residing in three-bedroom homes with a family-TV room.

- *People Who Have a Comfortable Life.* Although a step removed from those who enjoy the "good life," these individuals nonetheless live a "comfortable" existence in the less fashionable suburbs.

- *People Who Are Just Getting By.* Both husband and wife are typically employed—the husband in a blue-collar job and the wife as a secretary or salesclerk. They rent an apartment or own a small home, but simply "getting by" places a strain on their financial resources.

- *People Who Are Having a Difficult Time.* Unemployment often stalks couples on this level but the husband and wife usually manage to "scrape by." Many single-parent families fall in this category as well. Although these individuals have trouble making ends meet, they are proud that they are not on welfare.

- *People Who Are Poor.* These individuals constitute an "underclass," many of whom are on welfare.

Sociologists recognize that any such system of classes is a device for looking at a stratified society. There are a number of other approaches as well, equally useful in doing analysis. For instance, some practitioners prefer to simplify the division of Americans into upper, middle, and lower classes. Adding more refined occupational or income-based criteria yields a more accurate but also a more unwieldy scheme. And some sociologists find the term *class* too partisan and politically charged. They prefer the more neutral terms *stratum* or *socioeconomic strata.*

Horatio Alger: Myth or Reality?

The stories of the nineteenth-century writer Horatio Alger exemplify the American dream: a poor immigrant boy—like Leonard Stern—works hard, has some luck, and becomes rich. How much truth is there to this tale?

Some sociologists argue that mobility in America has historically been upward. Our labor market has grown dramatically since the turn of the century, with the total number of jobs more than doubling and the number of white-collar jobs skyrocketing. Technology has opened whole new fields, expanding the career opportunities open to technicians, managers, and professionals.

Large scale immigration has also provided an impetus for occupational advancement. An influx of unskilled and semiskilled laborers, such as occurred in this country during the late nineteenth and early twentieth centuries, frees experienced workers to move up the occupational ladder. (For example, an artisan who once did all the work in the shop can hire assistants, expand operations, become a white-collar worker.) The fact that white-collar workers tend to have fewer children than workers in other categories further stimulates upward mobility. Quite simply, white-collar workers do not produce enough children to refill their ranks, which gives individuals from the other groups a chance to move up. Thus changes in the birth rate, improved technology, and migration historically have acted to expand and change the United States labor market.

There is also downward mobility, or descent to a lower social status, as people lose jobs, become disabled, or otherwise fall on hard times (Newman 1988). Loss of social status may also result from changes in the structure of the larger economy. Both individuals and social categories may experience downward mobility when entire industries (like the American automobile industry) face a decline, or when factories and mills are shut down, or when once-valued skills (like glass blowing) are displaced by new technologies (i.e., the manufacture of plastics). A dramatic example of this was the shutdown of the mills of Wisconsin Steel (Bensman and Lynch 1987). The mill closings meant a massive worker layoff and areawide economic decline that forced former mill employees to struggle with unpaid bills, exhausted savings, and lengthy periods of anxiety about the future and economic survival.

Depending on the criteria used to assess social standing, the move from blue-collar to white-collar employment may be only a spurious upward mobility. In traditional class analysis terms, a move from blue-collar factory work to white-collar or service work is considered an upward move. However, many white-collar jobs—including several of those that have increased most rapidly in number—actually offer lower pay and poorer benefits than skilled (especially unionized) blue-collar jobs. So as the laid-off steelworkers gradually retrain in areas like computer programming —a more prestigious, white-collar job—they actually experience downward movement in terms of real pay.

Even though it can be argued that upward mobility in American society tends to outweigh downward mobility, usually only small changes in social mobility occur intergenerationally (i.e., from one generation to another). One way sociologists measure intergenerational mobility is by comparing fathers' and sons' jobs (unfortunately, the available studies are only of men). Using this measure, Peter M. Blau and Otis Dudley Duncan (1967), in a classic study, found that American males as a whole are upwardly mobile, but that most people move only incrementally up the ladder.

David L. Featherman and Robert Hauser (1978), using the same research approach and census data of the male labor force, compared sons' and fathers' occupa-

Dwindling resources and languishing industries have forced our society to look beyond the myth of unlimited upward mobility. Here, hundreds of unemployed steelworkers in a Pennsylvania mill town line up to apply for fifteen jobs. (Hodge/Gamma-Liaison.)

tions in 1962 and 1973. They found in both years that 49 percent of the sons were upwardly mobile, while only 17 percent were downwardly mobile in 1962 and 19 percent in 1973. These findings confirm that upward social mobility is very much a part of the American scene. However, upward social mobility has historically been harder for blacks than for whites. If occupational status is used as a criterion, black fathers have had greater difficulty than white fathers in passing their advantages on to their sons. Fortunately, there are some signs that this pattern may be changing, as more and better jobs have opened up to blacks (Clark 1983).

Sociologists at the University of Michigan's Institute for Social Research have looked at social mobility from an *intragenerational* perspective, which refers to social mobility during an individual's lifetime (Duncan 1982). These researchers have followed the economic fortunes of a large, representative sample of American families since 1967. Each time a family member leaves one household to form another, the new household is added to the sample. The Michigan findings reveal that Americans move up and down the economic ladder with considerable frequency. For instance, only about half of the individuals who in 1971 were living in households with incomes in the bottom fifth were still at the bottom in 1978. Moreover, less than half of the individuals in the top fifth in 1971 had stayed on top. The individuals most affected by these changes were children under age fourteen and their mothers. The divorce or marriage of a woman profoundly influences her fortunes and those of her dependent children (Preston 1984). Divorce has a particularly devastating economic impact, not only because women typically earn less than men do, but also because children usually remain with their mother (see Chapter 16). This research suggests that changes in household composition predict change in economic status better than any of the variables commonly thought to determine success or failure, including intelligence, achievement, motivation, and education.

Featherman's conclusions and those of the Michigan researchers are challenged by Marxist theorists, who are more likely than other sociologists to view class in terms of people's ownership or nonownership of the means of production. For instance, Sidney M. Willhelm (1979, p. 17) claims that mobility and opportunity are under the control of corporate America, which has "transformed great numbers of people from property owners to propertyless individuals." People are not really free to move up or down the scale; instead, they are molded into the type of person who can fill a certain position predetermined by corporate needs. Thus a move from a blue-collar position to a white-collar position is not truly indicative of upward mobility: "That many persons come to shed blue for white collars cannot hide the reality that collars still remain around our necks and, indeed, do what all collars must do: constrain our lives" (pp. 12–13). According to Willhelm, Featherman and many other sociologists make the mistake of emphasiz-

ing life-style in their analysis of what constitutes mobility, whereas the real issue is who controls wealth and production. Willhelm also downplays Featherman's findings of increased intergenerational job mobility among blacks as compared to whites. At most, blacks have been able to achieve occupational stability among their own kind and in the lower-level occupations. Whites have increased their control of the "supposedly superior" white-collar categories.

These differences in defining what constitutes social mobility affect the way sociologists answer the question of whether the United States offers greater opportunities for advancement than do other nations (Tyree et al. 1979; Smith 1981). Many sociologists conclude that the industrialized nations of the world are surprisingly similar in their rates of social mobility (Hope 1982; Grusky and Hauser 1984; Kerckhoff, Campbell, and Winfield-Laird 1985). This conclusion holds for Communist nations as well (Connor 1979). Apparently, rates of social mobility are less a function of political systems and social values than of structural factors associated with technological innovations and industrialization. In most nations the shape of the occupational structure has been shifting from a pyramid (a triangle with most occupations concentrated at the bottom) to an oval (with more occupations concentrated in the middle). Among the factors contributing to this shift in Western nations are the replacement of family-owned enterprises by public corporations, the bureaucratization of corporate life, the recruitment of management personnel from the ranks of college graduates, and the awarding of high positions on the basis of competitive promotions (Lipset 1982).

Status Attainment Processes

Sociologists are interested not only in the larger structures of opportunity and mobility within a society, but also in the factors that underlie individual status transmission and attainment. In their key study, Peter M. Blau and Otis Dudley Duncan (1967) addressed the question of how social origin affects a person's ultimate status and whether factors other than social origin are involved. The researchers developed a measure known as the socioeconomic index that allowed them to compare fathers' educational and occupational attainments with those of their sons. Blau and Duncan concluded that social origin affects ultimate social status primarily by influencing the level of education a person attains. Educational achievement, they believed, was the mechanism by which status is passed from one generation to another.

The Blau and Duncan model of status attainment was amplified by William H. Sewell and his colleagues at the University of Wisconsin (Sewell and Hauser 1976; Hauser et al. 1982, 1983). They followed, at periodic intervals, some 10,000 people who graduated from Wisconsin high schools in 1957. The researchers sought to determine how one's social background influences one's later career and what mechanisms intervene between one's social origins and one's later placement.

The Wisconsin sociologists concluded that educational and occupational attainment are the outcome of two related processes: those that shape a person's status aspirations and those that convert the aspirations into a new status ranking. Practically the entire effect of a family's class position on a child's later attainments is the result of the personal influences that family members bring to bear on the child's status aspirations during adolescence. Parental and teacher encouragement to attend college and the college plans of the adolescent's best friend also influence an adolescent's status aspirations.

From that point on, the impact of the parents' social background becomes inconsequential. The level of a person's schooling then becomes the principal influence. Viewed in this fashion, occupational attainment is shaped by many intervening or mediating links in a chain extending from birth across the life span: Parental status colors the adolescent's aspirations; aspirations contribute to the individual's educational attainment; educational attainment influences the person's first occupational placement; and one's first job affects one's later occupational opportunities (thus, the lower people begin on the occupational status ladder, the higher they have to rise, and the less likely they are to reach the top positions).

The idea that status attainment is based on educational achievement rests on certain assumptions about society—most significantly, that *individual* qualifications are more important than the general labor market. The Blau and Duncan model assumes that a person who gets a good education will also get a good job with good pay. Critics have noted that this is not necessarily the case, particularly for minorities and women, who do not receive the same "return" on their educational investment that white men do. Men and women, blacks and whites also to some extent compete in different labor markets (see Chapter 15). For example, white male blue-collar workers are more often employed in high-paying unionized industries that produce "important" products, such as automobiles; whereas white female blue-collar workers more often work in nonunion plants that produce less valuable products, such as clothing and toys. In addition, other factors not included in the Blau and Duncan model, such as regional differences, also affect status attainment (some regions of the country offer more opportunity than others). Therefore, an understanding of status attainment must take into account the structures of opportunity within which individual achievement can occur.

WHO ARE AMERICA'S POOR?

When the plight of the poor in the United States became a national issue in the 1960s, President Lyndon Johnson responded in 1964 by launching a "war on poverty." The Johnson administration undertook to define poverty in terms of a dollar amount that established a line between the poor and the nonpoor. The poverty line was—and continues to be—based on the minimum amount of money families need to purchase a nutritionally adequate diet, assuming that they spend one-third of their income for food. Defined in this fashion, poverty in the 1960s was concentrated among the elderly, large families, Appalachian whites, white and black rural southerners, and minorities in the cities (Hess 1983).

The years following the war on poverty saw a decline in the number of families officially classed as poor. That decline was reversed in 1978, and in the period between 1978 and 1983 the number of poor rose by 10.8 million, or 44 percent (O'Hare 1986). Although this increase in poverty has been widespread, occurring in many regions of the country and among many racial and ethnic groups, one significant change in the pattern of poverty was evident. Poverty has increased among the young and decreased among the elderly; about 22 percent of those under eighteen are now poor, compared with 14 percent of those over sixty-five (Preston 1984). This is partly the result of cuts in government programs assisting children at the same time that programs assisting the elderly (such as Social Security) have been maintained or expanded. But more complex social changes lie at the root, including changes in the family and wage slowdowns (Levy 1987).

Although the common stereotype of "the poor" is that of black and other minority residents of urban ghettos, typically living in female-headed welfare families, this is a misconception. Actually, the majority of poor people are white. The *rate* of poverty among blacks, however, is higher than it is among whites, so that blacks are disproportionately poor. Moreover, contrary to stereotype, most poor people live in male-headed families, and less than 15 percent reside in inner-city ghettos. And of all poor families, only about 35 percent receive welfare payments (O'Hare 1986), but these are the most visible poor because they are featured in the media. Far-reaching changes in the American economy (from manufacturing to service jobs) have produced a class of people sociologists have called the "new poor" —middle-class or working-class families and young adults who have become poor as a result of job loss or layoff or who simply have never been able to find steady jobs that pay enough to live on. Steelworkers, automobile workers, and other well-paid blue-collar people whose industries have declined, have been laid off and forced to subsist on part-time or minimum-wage jobs if they can find any work at all (Bensman and Lynch 1987). The steady, bread-and-butter paychecks that these individuals could count on are simply no longer available to them—or to their children. This movement of once comfortable persons into poverty (at least for periods of time between jobs) is a significant change in the pattern of indigence in the United States. A related change is the spread of poverty to middle-class neighborhoods and suburbs: one in four poor persons in America now lives in a suburb (O'Hare 1986).

Not only do many kinds of poverty exist, but most poor people, contrary to popular opinion, are not poor for extended periods of time. Studies of the U.S. population over ten-year intervals have found that less than 3 percent of the population is persistently poor (had

This woman and her three children in a Red Cross Shelter in the Bronx fit our stereotype of America's poor, but poverty does not recognize boundaries of race, geography, or even class. The decline of major industries in recent years has led to a growing number of working-class, suburban families living below the poverty line. (Tannenbaum/Sygma.)

an income below the poverty line for eight or more of the ten years). Far more common is the pattern of being poor for one to seven years of the ten-year period (22 percent of the population). Typically, then, *most* poor people move in and out of poverty, some years doing better and other years worse, depending on employment patterns as well as family problems that have an impact on income (divorce, illness, widowhood, and so on) (Duncan 1984). Still, the proportion of the population that lives fairly near the brink—getting along financially, but without enough in reserve to cope with a misfortune —is substantial. In any decade, fully a third of the U.S. population experiences an income decline of 50 percent or more (Duncan 1984). Fortunately, most of these people do not stay poor for long; they find jobs, move in with relatives, remarry, get well, and otherwise come to regain some of their lost income and the status attached to being employed.

How extensive is poverty in the United States? Depending on the yardstick used, poverty in this country is either widespread or negligible. Some have argued that the 35 million or so Americans who are officially below the poverty threshold would not be identified as poor if certain government subsidies were factored into the equation. For example, a 1982 study by the U.S. Census Bureau suggested that the poverty rate would drop from 11 percent to 6.4 percent if noncash governmental benefits were included in income calculations (Smeeding 1982). The study noted that between 1965 and 1980 the value of in-kind transfers—housing subsidies, school lunches, food stamps, Medicare, and Medicaid—rose from $2.2 billion to over $72.5 billion. These in-kind transfers to low-income Americans exceed cash public assistance by more than two to one. Even so, the current definition of poverty includes only money income. By counting the market value of all noncash benefits, for example, the number of elderly below the poverty line would drop from 4.1 million to 1.3 million, a 70 percent reduction produced simply by changing the measurement technique. Hence, some people believe that the extent of poverty in the United States is exaggerated by not including in-kind transfers.

On the other hand, some critics contend that noncash benefits have only a marginal effect on real poverty. They say that the officially defined poverty threshold (about $11,000 for a family of four in 1985, or $916 per month) is unreasonably low, especially in urban areas.

Poverty and Life Chances

The term **life chances** refers to the distribution within a social system of opportunities that affect people's health, survival, and happiness.

Except for those at the absolute bottom of the social hierarchy—the homeless, seen at the beginning of this chapter—most Americans have access to such essentials as food and shelter. But those in the bottom strata have far fewer life chances simply by virtue of their class. Thus the poor are much less likely to reach their first birthday, get an education, be able to afford adequate nutrition, decent housing, and health care, and round out their days in dignity and comfort. And minorities and the poor suffer disadvantages that profoundly affect how they lead their lives. Let us examine the situation in the United States more carefully.

Life Expectancy

In all industrialized nations, the lower one's social class, the greater the risk of death at birth or from occupational hazards, and the shorter one's life span (Gortmaker 1979). The effects of stratification are seen most clearly in occupationally related deaths (such as the miners' black lung disease). But the poor also suffer more from chronic and infectious diseases than the rest of the population, usually because of substandard housing and unsanitary living conditions (see Table 11.4). And when illness does strike, the poor are without the means to pay for the highest quality health care. Moreover, many working-class people put off treatment of health problems in order to stay on the job and bring home the paycheck.

It is hard to specify exactly what role poverty plays in adult mortality because certain behaviors that result in death (such as smoking or reckless driving) are not related to socioeconomic status. However, the effects of poverty on mortality can be seen quite clearly in *infant* mortality rates. Here the hazards of poverty—inadequate housing, poor sanitation, insufficient nutrition, inadequate postnatal medical care—can be crucial. Within the United States the risk of death for infants born into poverty is 50 percent greater than that for other infants (Gortmaker 1979). Among black Americans, the infant mortality rate is more than twice that of whites (National Center for Health Statistics 1987).

TABLE 11.4   General Health by Income

Annual Family Income	Percent of Persons Limited in Activity Due to Chronic Illnesses (1979–80)	Percent of Persons in Fair or Poor Health (1979–80)
Under $3000	27.5	26.5
$3,000–4,999	30.6	26.7
$5,000–6,999	24.5	23.1
$7,000–9,999	20.9	18.6
$10,000–14,999	14.0	12.9
$15,000–24,999	10.0	8.4
$25,000 or more	8.7	6.0

Source: National Center for Health and Statistics, "Health Characteristics According to Family and Personal Income," PHS Series 10, #147, 1982.

Nutrition

The poor spend a much greater proportion of their incomes on food than other Americans do: on the average, 59 percent for families earning less than $5,000 per year, compared with 16 percent for families with incomes of $20,000 to $30,000 per year (U.S. Statistical Abstracts 1988). Often the poor pay more for less: ghetto merchants justify high markups on the grounds that they take high risks working in the area; small local groceries charge high prices and extend credit. The poor not only pay more but also receive poorer quality goods. For instance, chain stores unload day-old bread and other leftovers in low-income neighborhoods.

The low food budgets of the poor usually require that they subsist on the cheapest, most filling commodities available. Millions of Americans (mostly children) live on white rice, spaghetti, macaroni, beans, white bread, and other high carbohydrate foods. When money runs short, many poor people turn to pet food.

From 30 to 50 percent of poor children suffer from protein, iron, and vitamin deficiencies. Malnutrition stunts children's growth and makes them more vulnerable to disease, but that is not all. There is a growing body of evidence to suggest that severe protein deficiency during the first twelve to eighteen months of life causes irreparable damage to the brain and the nervous system. In addition, hungry children are apathetic, lethargic, have short attention spans, and are often irritable and agitated (Winick 1980). In short, hunger interferes with learning and intellectual development.

Housing

Many of the housing units of the poor sections of large American cities are in disrepair; some are condemned and abandoned. Significantly, the poor spend proportionately more of their income on rent than others do—on the average households earning $4,000 or less per year pay about 59 percent of their income for rent, compared with households earning $20,000 to $25,000 per year, which pay about 35 percent (U.S. Bureau of Labor Statistics 1985). These economic pressures are forcing increasing numbers of people to seek housing assistance.

Mental Health

Studies suggest that mental disorders are more common among the lower strata of society than they are among the upper ones (Goodman et al. 1983). Indeed, a classic study conducted in New Haven, Connecticut, during the 1950s found that the ratio of lower-class to upper-class mental patients was a startling 40 to 1 (Hollingshead and Redlich 1958). Similarly, community surveys reveal comparatively higher rates of psychological distress among individuals in the lower than in the upper strata (Kessler and Cleary 1980; Kessler 1982).

Many factors interact to produce the negative relationship between socioeconomic position and psychiatric symptoms and distress. First, people with chronic

Sometimes appearances are not deceiving. One of these pictures suggests prosperity, security, and growth; the other poverty, uncertainty, and decay. But the fresh paint and manicured lawns are merely emblems of a broader horizon in the middle-class community: better health care, more nutritious diet, higher quality education, stronger job market, and even a longer life expectancy. (Left: Michael D. Sullivan; right: Mark Antman/The Image Works.)

mental-health problems often "drift" downward in status or find their upward ascent impeded because their disorder interferes with their gaining or holding many jobs (Eaton 1980). Second, evidence suggests that the lower strata are more exposed to unemployment and other stresses that are known to precipitate emotional difficulties than are people in the upper strata (Myers et al. 1974). And third, their socialization and educational experiences provide them with fewer of the skills and social competencies that are necessary to cope with life's stresses (Kessler and Cleary 1980).

In summary, then, the poor and minorities have far fewer opportunities to enjoy a long, healthy, comfortable, and secure life than do people in higher social strata. That is true not simply because the poor have less income and wealth than others do. The life chances of the poor are also restricted because they lack access to the important resources of power and prestige.

Matters have been complicated over the past fifteen years as the affluence that the United States enjoyed during the two decades following World War II began to decline. Impoverishment of public goods has become a growing concern—air pollution, inner-city decay, health hazards in the workplace, and the decay of mass transit systems. In some areas of American life the actual amounts of goods and services produced has declined. As the economic pie becomes smaller, it is more difficult to find an equitable way of sharing the nation's resources (Magaziner and Reich 1983).

REDUCING INEQUALITY

The Declaration of Independence forthrightly declares as a self-evident truth that "all men are created equal." Yet as our discussion above has shown, inequality is a fact of life in the United States. How do Americans reconcile the dream of social equality with the reality of social inequality? How can the nation's disadvantaged be expected to give their allegiance to a system that provides them with less than their proportionate share of America's wealth?

Part of the answer lies with American conceptions of equality. According to the American dream any poor child can get ahead, just as a rail-splitter named Abe Lincoln could become president. But this promise has been based on the principle of equality of *opportunity*, not equality of *results*. Equality of opportunity aims to

Fact and Fiction about Welfare

Do you agree or disagree with the following statements?

- The eligibility requirements for welfare in this country are far too lenient. A large number of people who could live all right without public assistance are nevertheless receiving it.
- The majority of welfare recipients are shirking the responsibility to earn their own living. They are able-bodied people, but they lack the motivation to work. Instead, they freeload off the government.
- One of the problems with the current welfare system is that it enables recipients to live too well for nothing. Why should people find a job if they have everything they need without working?

The chances are you suspect there is some truth to one or more of these common assumptions. Indeed, many people harbor unfavorable impressions of welfare recipients, as the accompanying graph indicates. Does sociological research substantiate the statements listed above? The answer is a definite no.

First, the Census Bureau's "poverty thresholds," widely used to help establish eligibility for welfare, are hardly what could be called generous. For instance, in 1986 the poverty threshold for a nonfarm family of four was $11,000. These thresholds are partly determined by the U.S. Department of Agriculture estimates of the minimum amount of money needed to keep different-sized families decently fed. But the department's own studies show that only about 10 percent of people spending so little can manage to provide a diet rated as fair or better.

Second, the majority of people on welfare are not shirking the responsibility to earn their own living. Many are either too young or too old to work. (Nearly half of the poor are children under sixteen or people over sixty-five. Hence, a good many of the poor are not even of the appropriate age to be seeking full-time jobs.) As for the able-bodied men that many Americans believe their tax dollars are supporting, they are excluded from most public assistance programs (with the exception of food stamps) no matter how low their incomes are.

Third, individuals do not typically reduce their work effort or quit their jobs in order to get or retain welfare benefits (Pear 1983). For instance, people removed from the welfare rolls by the Reagan administration generally stayed off the rolls and did not leave their jobs in order to qualify for public assistance payments. Further, many of those who lost their jobs and returned to welfare soon found other employment, leaving the welfare rolls once more. Indeed, one factor in the higher unemployment rates of disadvantaged groups is their tendency to turn over jobs more rapidly than the better-off.

Why do so many Americans hold such erroneous views about the welfare system? Part of the reason is their overly idealized image of America as the land of unlimited opportunity. Thirty-two million Americans living in poverty—fully 14 percent of the population—is too discordant a statistic for many people to believe. Consequently, some Americans assume that the majority of those receiving welfare benefits must simply be defrauding the system. Others conclude that those in poverty must somehow "deserve" their fate. The poor must lack motivation and ambition, the argument usually goes. If poverty can be attributed to the shortcomings of individuals, then they do not merit public assistance —"idlers" should not be able to enjoy that for which others work so hard. This rationalization is called blaming the victim, and it is clearly spurious. Willingness to work hard does not guarantee escape from poverty. For instance, a woman with two children, working forty hours a week for fifty-two weeks, at minimum wage, would have an annual income below the poverty threshold, plus the expenses of child care and travel to and from work (Hess 1983). Thus the tendency to blame the victims of poverty for their own plight ignores the fact that poverty is not just an individual matter. It is the result of a system of social ranking that offers those at the bottom society only menial, low-paying jobs or often no jobs at all. Poverty is largely the product of forces beyond the control of its victims—the shift from labor-intensive to capital-

free individuals from discrimination based on race, family, religion, gender, or community, so that they might rise in society according to their own merits. In an order characterized by *distributive justice*, rewards are apportioned in accordance with each individual's contribution to the group (Homans 1974). Those who do more or invest more receive more than those who do less or invest less. This *contributive standard* is rooted in the capitalistic ethic. But if some people become "winners," gaining wealth and high status, others—at least by intensive (particularly from "smokestack" to "high tech") industries, dual labor markets, the flight of the middle classes to the suburbs, banking and real estate practices, extended life expectancies, and changing patterns of family life, especially the rise of single-parent homes (Hess 1983).

"What Is Your Impression of Welfare Recipients?"

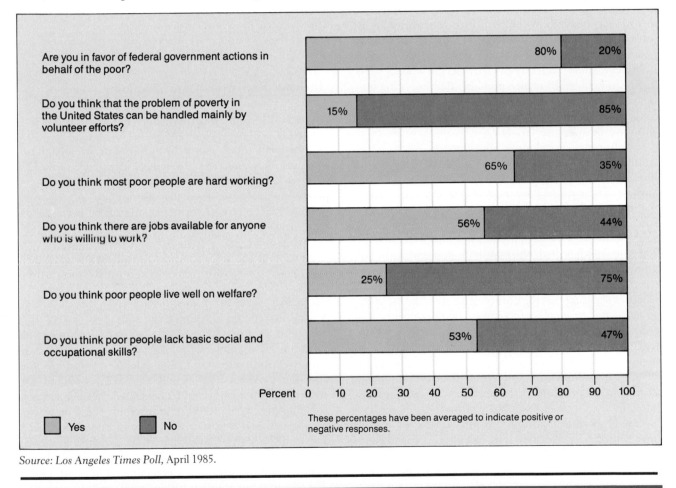

Are you in favor of federal government actions in behalf of the poor?	80% (Yes)	20% (No)
Do you think that the problem of poverty in the United States can be handled mainly by volunteer efforts?	15% (Yes)	85% (No)
Do you think most poor people are hard working?	65% (Yes)	35% (No)
Do you think there are jobs available for anyone who is willing to work?	56% (Yes)	44% (No)
Do you think poor people live well on welfare?	25% (Yes)	75% (No)
Do you think poor people lack basic social and occupational skills?	53% (Yes)	47% (No)

Percent 0 10 20 30 40 50 60 70 80 90 100

☐ Yes ◼ No

These percentages have been averaged to indicate positive or negative responses.

Source: Los Angeles Times Poll, April 1985.

implication—become losers: equality of opportunity produces inequality of results. In fact, given the limited life chances of the poor, minorities, and women, opportunity is *not* equal. "Equality of striving" might be a fairer phrase: all people may aspire to a higher social rung no matter where they start. The American dream has never been one of a classless society in which all individuals enjoy equal wealth, power, and prestige. It is instead a dream of a class society in which people have equal access to the top positions.

The doctrine of equality of opportunity assumes that all men (and recently also women) are created equal. If they are not in fact created equal, it is society's responsibility to make them more equal at the outset so that all people can begin from the same starting line. This argument had provided the rationale for the creation of the nation's public school system and the enactment of compulsory school attendance laws. Nevertheless, Americans have not enjoyed equal opportunities for getting ahead. Chapter 12 details how sexism has handicapped women and Chapter 13 discusses how racism has victimized blacks. President Lyndon B. Johnson, in his June 1965 address at Howard University, noted that much injustice was left untouched by civil rights legislation: "You do not take a person who for years had been hobbled by chains and liberate him, bring him up to the starting line of a race and . . . say, you're free to compete with all the others, and still justly believe that you have been completely fair."

While not abandoning allegiance to the value of competitive success, President Johnson nonetheless alluded to other American values, namely justice and fairness. These values have suggested to some Americans that because the nation had not accorded all its citizens equality of opportunity, it has acquired an obligation to equalize more of the benefits and rewards of the system. They have advocated affirmative action programs for minorities, school busing, and welfare programs financed by taxes on higher-income groups.

Recognizing that the contributive standard associated with the principle of equality of opportunity has produced inequality of results, some Americans have looked to other standards for distributing rewards. One of these is the *needs standard* that is expressed in the slogan of pure communism, "From each according to his ability, to each according to his need." However, this standard does not just apply to communist ideology. Norms of social responsibility within the Western world have historically dictated that people's needs should influence how rewards are distributed. Hence, the sick, the infirm, the elderly, the very young, and others have had a social claim on a portion of a nation's resources.

Another standard for distribution is based on the *equality standard*. This approach has a long history, dating back into antiquity. Many people view a system that allocates its rewards unequally as inherently insensitive and unjust. Instead they favor an arrangement based on the credo, "To each, equally." This type of distributive system is most commonly encountered within families and closely knit in-groups.

The tension in American life between the principle of equality of opportunity and that of equality of results often finds expression in the debate between what is a "right" and what is a "privilege." In general, political conservatives have favored the marketplace as the regulator of need and ambition, whereas political liberals have favored government programs to help the poor, minorities, the handicapped, and women in their struggles to achieve a better life.

Income Redistribution Programs

As our discussion above suggests, the government has undertaken a variety of programs to combat poverty within the United States. In one way or another these programs are intended to reduce inequality through *income redistribution*. The government uses three primary methods to alter the distribution of income: income taxes, transfer payments, and subsidies for goods and services.

Taxes

How does taxation affect distribution of income? The federal income tax is meant to be a **progressive tax**—the more money a person earns, the higher his or her rate of taxation. For example, in 1984 married couples filing joint returns were taxed at a rate of 11 percent for incomes between $3,400 and $5,500, 25 percent for incomes from $24,600 to $29,900, and 50 percent for incomes over $162,400. But some claim that progressive taxation is less effective than it was intended to be. President Reagan's tax bill, passed by Congress in 1981, substantially lowered the progressive tax rates—by 5 percent in 1981 and by 10 percent in 1982 and 1983. The Reagan tax program further weakened the progressive effect of the income tax by extending such "loopholes" as the taxing of capital gains at low rates and depreciation allowances on income-producing property.

The Tax Reform Act of 1986 was aimed at correcting some of these gross inequalities of the tax system. The political appeal of the new tax law comes largely

A good job is more than merely a source of income; it is also a means of breaking the chains of powerlessness and isolation, the indignity of poverty. These Job Corps trainees in Atlanta receive wages, training, job opportunities, and perhaps also the message that the larger society has not abandoned them. (Rob Nelson/ Stock Boston.)

from its sharp drop in the top tax rate on individuals. The benefits of the precipitous rate drop are most pronounced for high-income Americans. But the bill offsets windfalls to the wealthy by sharply limiting the use of tax shelters, eliminating the special low tax rate on capital gains, and reducing various other tax preferences. The new tax law also preserves the deduction on mortgage interest payments, which is a benefit to middle-class homeowners.

Transfer Payments

Another approach to income redistribution involves various transfer payment plans. **Transfer payments** include cash welfare benefits that are designed to raise the income of the poor, the unemployed, the aged, and the blind. Money is transferred from one sector of the economy to another without a corresponding contribution to current production. Over half of all transfer payments are for Social Security; beneficiaries typically receive considerably more over the course of their retirement than they contributed to the system while they worked. The size of a person's Social Security check is determined by his or her prior tax contributions and earnings, not by need. Thus, these recipients are distrib-

uted throughout the income scale and are not concentrated among the lowest income groups.

Workfare

A program that has recently been devised to cope with the problem of "welfare dependency"—people coming to rely on welfare payments rather than employment as their major source of income—is known as workfare. The idea behind workfare is to help welfare recipients become self-supporting by requiring them to enter counseling, training, or educational programs in return for welfare payments. Once a person has found work, the state provides support services (medical benefits, child care) for six months or a year, until the person seems able to carry on independently.

Workfare has been tried in about half the states in the United States, with varying degrees of success. One of the most successful programs has been Massachusetts' Employment and Training Choices, familiarly known as E.T. In E.T., a person receives intensive job counseling, followed by placement in a job that pays approximately $10,000 per year. So far, more than 20,000 Massachusetts residents have successfully moved from welfare to jobs as a result of E.T. In part, this can be tied to the economic boom in Massachusetts, which has meant that many new jobs have opened up. In states with high unemployment rates, such as Michigan, workfare has been less successful, but it is clearly an innovation that finds favor with the American public (Herbers 1987). Congress is considering a major welfare reform proposal which incorporates elements of the workfare idea.

Government Subsidies

Government subsidies of goods and services are closely related to transfer payments, except that they consist of in-kind transfers, not cash benefits. The food stamp program is an example of an in-kind transfer. In 1985, 6,779,000 American families (7.7 percent) received food stamps at some time during the year. Another example is subsidized housing. Of the 29,914,000 families living in rental premises in 1983, 3,234,000 (10.8 percent) resided in subsidized or publicly owned housing. However, not all government subsidies favor lower-income groups. Many state-supported public services, including higher education, highways, airports, and boat facilities, although legally available to all citizens, primarily benefit the affluent classes rather than the disadvantaged ones.

Federal programs have helped to fill basic needs. The beneficiaries of such programs have been primarily the elderly and mothers and their dependent children.

Although such programs have addressed very real needs (and according to critics, have had at best mixed results, perhaps because their benefits seldom get to those who most need them), the 1980s saw increasing recognition that subsidies may have inadvertently helped to maintain a group of 10 million Americans who have come to constitute an "underclass" (Lodge and Glass 1982). Disproportionately black, Hispanic, and young—although by no means exclusively so—its members are more or less permanently unemployed and poor, and pose the problem of long-term welfare dependency. Often left behind in urban ghettos as their working- and middle-class peers leave for more prosperous, safer neighborhoods, members of the underclass find themselves cut off from the world of work, and indeed from the larger society. The predicament of the underclass has been linked on the one hand to the "culture of poverty" in isolated communities, and on the other hand to the effects of declining job opportunities for manual laborers. Most proposals that have been made to deal with these problems stress remedial education, training, and job placement—in fact, the ingredients of the workfare programs that attempt to get people off welfare and into the labor market. How successful work-oriented welfare initiatives are will be seen in the years to come. For now, they offer some opportunity to the poor and unemployed caught in the structural dislocations of the American economy or their own dysfunctional adaptations to them.

SUMMARY

1. Stratification refers to the division of a society into layers (or strata) of people who have unequal amounts of scarce but desirable resources, which affect their life chances and their social standing.
2. Stratification is based on a number of factors, including wealth (what people own), income (what people earn), power (the extent to which a person can compel others to act in a certain way), and prestige (the esteem or respect of the public). In practice, these factors generally reinforce one another.
3. Two general explanations of stratification have been advanced. The functional argument is that stratification exists because societies must entice people into important and difficult jobs by rewarding them more highly than others. By contrast, according to power theorists, the dominant class exercises a monopoly over society's resources and systematically denies opportunities to the poor. The power perspective draws heavily on the ideas of Karl Marx. Marx originated a class-based view of stratification. He focused on class struggle as the means by which class conflict would eventually be eliminated. Increasingly, sociologists are attempting to synthesize the insights of the two perspectives for a fuller understanding of stratification.
4. The American dream of Horatio Alger, the poor boy who becomes rich, is something of a myth. Although Americans as a group are upwardly mobile, most move up only a step or two, and some move downward. Status

at birth plays an important role in determining occupational status later in life. The industrialized nations of the world have surprisingly similar rates of social mobility, but Americans tend to believe that their society offers more opportunity.

5. Equality of opportunity has long been an American goal, though it has never fully existed in practice. Programs promoting this ideal continue to be proposed. Their object is to free individuals from discrimination based on race, family, religion, gender, or community, so that people might rise in society according to their own merits.

6. Most poor people are not persistently poor, but move in and out of poverty as their circumstances change. Most poor people are white, and most live outside urban ghettos. Poverty has recently decreased among the elderly and increased among children born into impoverished families. The "new poor" include those who have become poor as a result of job loss or layoff.

7. Stratification depresses individual well-being and opportunities, with those at the bottom of society at a distinct disadvantage. The lower one's social class, the lower one's life expectancy, the less wholesome the food, and the worse the housing. A poor person is more likely to suffer from mental illness and to suffer chronic health problems.

8. Income redistribution programs include progressive taxes, transfer payments, workfare programs, and government subsidies.

GLOSSARY

Bourgeoisie. The term Marx used to denote the owners of the means of production.

Caste system. A closed system of social inequality in which status is determined at birth, and people are locked into their parents' social position.

Class. The term Marx used to denote the basic groups engaged in social struggle, most particularly the bourgeoisie and proletariat. The term Weber used to refer to people who occupy the same rung on the economic ladder, in income or buying-power terms.

Equality of opportunity. The members of a society may achieve social positions in accordance with their different talents and contributions.

Equality of results. The members of a society enjoy the same standard of living.

Horizontal mobility. A change in a person's position that does not alter the person's rank.

Life chances. The opportunities to realize health, long life, rank, and happiness in a social system.

Open class system. A class system in which there are few obstacles to social mobility; positions are awarded on the basis of merit, and rank is tied to individual achievement.

Prestige. Status resulting from the possession of attributes that are regarded as admirable, and perhaps enviable, by people in a specific social setting.

Progressive tax. A tax rate that increases as a person's income increases; the opposite of a regressive tax.

Proletariat. Marx's term for the propertyless class whose members sell their labor skills to the owners of the means of production.

Social mobility. The movement of people, vertically or horizontally, from one social position to another.

Stratification. The division of a society into layers of people who have unequal amounts of any given scarce reward or resource.

Transfer payments. Cash welfare benefits that are designed to raise the income of the poor, the unemployed, the aged, and the blind.

Vertical mobility. Upward or downward changes in a person's status.

CHAPTER 12
Gender Roles and Inequalities

Edward Pickering, director of the Harvard College Observatory between 1877 and 1919, was one of the first scholars to find a place for women in the science of astronomy. He needed assistants to make long, painstaking calculations of the positions of heavenly bodies based on thousands of photographs taken of the skies through a telescope. He thought this tedious detail work was very well suited to women. Although, in his view, women did not possess very creative intellects, they had the penchant for care and accuracy that would make them perfect for the task. Hiring women had the added advantage of being very cost-effective. For the same amount of money he would have had to pay one man, Pickering could hire three or four women who would be happy to get the work (Rubin 1986).

Some seventy years have passed since Pickering left his post at the Harvard observatory. Since then women have officially entered the field of astronomy and many other sciences. By the mid-1980s they were being awarded about 30 percent of the doctorates in science and engineering. Yet discrimination against women scientists persists. Many people still think of women as better suited to a "caring" profession (nursing, teaching, social work) than to a rigorous science. Employers are sometimes reluctant to offer demanding posts to a woman, for fear that she will give more time to her family than to her job. This is part of the reason that over a third of women with doctorates in science are involuntarily unemployed. When women scientists do land jobs, these are much more apt to be lower paying and less prestigious than the ones offered to men of comparable education and training. Also, compared with men, women scientists have to struggle harder for raises and promotions. As a result, an average salary difference of over $10,000 exists between men and women in science (Rubin 1986).

The unequal distribution of rewards between men and women is part of gender stratification. **Gender stratification** refers to the fact that males and females generally occupy unequal positions in the social hierarchy. In terms of rewards, females typically have lower social standing, with less power, income, wealth, prestige, and personal freedom. Women in America, Europe, Africa, and Asia on average complete fewer years of education, have lower incomes, own less property, and hold fewer positions of power and authority than men do. Gender inequalities even exist in Communist nations, which supposedly aim to eliminate all forms of social stratification (Treiman and Roos 1983). In the Soviet Union, for instance, the occupations in which women are most heavily represented are at the bottom of the pay and status scales (Daniloff 1982; Browning 1987). Seventy-four percent of all Communist party members are male, and men occupy every seat on the all-powerful Politburo and Central Committee. No Soviet woman currently holds a ministerial post or an ambassadorship. Thus, despite Marxist claims about equality and justice for all workers, the Soviet Union is clearly a male-dominated society—a pattern that is found in nearly all industrialized states.

Discrimination against women has appeared in many guises. At the Harvard College Observatory in the 1890s, women's work came very cheaply—at about one-third to one-quarter of a male's salary. Women were also thought to be ideally suited to the uncreative, tedious, detailed calculation work they were hired by the Observatory to do. (Circa 1890 Harvard Observatory.)

Just as women are given different rewards than men, so are they given different tasks and spheres of activities. These tasks and activities that society assigns to each sex are known as **gender roles.** In light of the male gender role, men are the leaders of government and industry, heads of churches, and are dominant in professions such as law and science. In light of the female gender role, women are the centers of the home and family, the caretakers of children, and the ones who nurse the sick. In most societies around the world, the female gender role is not valued as highly as the male gender role.

Related to gender roles are **gender stereotypes,** which are oversimplified but strongly held ideas about the characteristics of males and females (Basow 1986). When Pickering considered women workers careful but unimaginative, he was expressing a gender stereotype. Today people still assume that women in general have less desirable traits than men by the yardstick of their cultures. Women are believed to be dependent, passive, unassertive, and emotional, whereas men are seen as dominant, aggressive, self-reliant, and in control of themselves. In consequence, women are considered better suited to be nurses than hospital administrators, and men are considered better suited to jobs in sales than in child care. The fact that "women's work" is underpaid relative to men's further discourages men from entering these occupations. Sex-based inequalities in pay there-

fore reinforce the lower status given to most of the roles deemed appropriate for women.

One of the fascinating puzzles of social life is why gender roles, stereotypes, and stratification exist at all. What is it about women and men that causes each sex to be viewed so differently and to be assigned such different tasks? The answer cannot be that women lack the mental capabilities of men. From childhood females perform just as well in school and on intelligence tests as males do. Nor can the answer be simply that women, as a matter of tradition, are not trained for positions of leadership, prestige, and power. In our own society, women are now just as likely as men to be trained for certain high-status professions (law and medicine, for instance). Yet once employed in these fields they *still* earn less than their male colleagues, and they are *still* greatly underrepresented in the most prestigious jobs. Table 12.1 shows the occupations that employ the most men, those that employ the most women, and how these numbers have changed from 1970 to 1980.

This chapter provides some insights into the puzzle of gender inequalities. We begin by examining the mental, emotional, and behavioral differences between the sexes. Contrary to what many people think, men and women are not innately different in their interests, abilities, and personality traits. Such differences, if they exist, are demonstrably social creations, and not biologically based. Use of the term *gender* emphasizes this fact.

Whereas sex differences refer to the anatomical distinctions between males and females, **gender** differences refer to all the nonbiological traits that we assign to men and women—everything from different styles of clothing to different norms of appropriate behavior. Sex differences, in other words, are a matter of heredity; gender differences are a matter of what people in a society deem right and appropriate.

After exploring the differences between men and women, we turn to the topic of gender stratification. Despite all the progress women have made in recent years, gender inequalities remain entrenched in both the workplace and politics. One reason some people underestimate the size of these inequalities is that the position of women in society is multidimensional. For instance, the fact that women often make many decisions within the family gives the impression that they exert substantial influence. In the worlds of business and government, however, the voice of women is much weaker. It is the many aspects of women's disadvantaged status that we focus on in this chapter. We also examine the women's movement. How did it begin? What tactics has it used? And what gains has it made? Finally, we explore, from different sociological perspectives, the content of gender roles and how these roles interact with gender stereotypes. Many Americans are currently uncertain about the roles that men and women should play. We discuss both traditional roles and newly emerging ones, and consider points of conflict between the two.

HOW DIFFERENT ARE MEN AND WOMEN?

For centuries people have assumed that innate differences are responsible for the behavior of men and women, that biology decrees different tendencies and personality traits for the two sexes. In our own culture the widespread belief that men are inherently rational and women inherently emotional is just one of many examples of this common point of view. Although there may be some inborn behavioral differences between the sexes, they hardly justify the elaborate gender-role distinctions found in many societies. Far more significant are the social forces that work on people from the moment of birth, helping to encourage conformity to gender roles. Evidence supporting this perspective comes from several sources: psychological and biological research and cross-cultural studies.

Psychological Evidence

Psychologists have studied males and females of all ages to find out just how different they are. Gradually, they have accumulated an enormous body of findings. In their pioneering research, Eleanor Maccoby and Carol Jacklin (1974) reviewed more than 2,000 books and

TABLE 12.1   Percentage of Women in Occupations that Employed the Most Men in 1980 and that Employed the Most Women in 1980

Occupations Employing the Most Men in 1980	1970	1980	Occupations Employing the Most Women in 1980	1970	1980
1. Managers	15.3%	26.9%	1. Secretaries	97.8%	98.8%
2. Heavy truck drivers	1.5	2.3	2. Elementary school teachers	83.9	75.4
3. Janitors and cleaners	13.1	23.4	3. Bookkeepers	80.9	89.7
4. Production supervisors	9.9	15.0	4. Cashiers	84.2	83.5
5. Carpenters	1.1	1.6	5. Office clerks	75.3	82.1
6. Sales supervisors	17.0	28.2	6. Managers	15.3	26.9
7. Laborers	16.5	19.4	7. Waitresses and waiters	90.8	88.0
8. Sales representatives	7.0	14.9	8. Sales workers	70.4	72.7
9. Farmers	4.7	9.8	9. Registered nurses	97.3	95.9
10. Auto mechanics	1.4	1.3	10. Nursing aides	87.0	87.8

Source: National Research Council.

articles on sex differences in motivation, social behavior, and intellectual ability. They concluded that the sexes, on average, do not differ at all in terms of sociability, suggestibility, self-esteem, achievement motivation, rote learning, analytical skills, and responses to auditory and visual stimulation. But males seemed to be more aggressive than females and to perform better on visual-spatial tasks, as well as in mathematics. In contrast, females seemed to be better in verbal abilities. These sex-based differences are small, however. When teams of researchers independently studied the available data on verbal abilities, visual-spatial skills, and mathematical abilities, they concluded that if sex-linked differences in these areas exist, they are quite minimal (Hyde 1981; Sherman 1978; Tavris and Wade 1984).

Why are behavioral differences between the sexes smaller than most people expect? Part of the reason is the wide range of individual variation in the expression of any given trait, with much overlap across the sexes. In fact, there is far greater variation *within* one sex or the other in respect to any characteristic than there is, on average, *between* the sexes (Bleier 1984; Hyde 1984). For instance, there are many men who are good at math, but also some who perform more poorly than the vast majority of women. Similarly, there are many women who do well on verbal tasks, but also some whose language skills are worse than most men's. When researchers summarize this range of variation in terms of averages, the differences between males and females tend to even out.

One behavioral difference between the sexes that is quite reliably present is overall level of aggression (Harris 1987; Wilson 1978). Although, again, there is a wide range of individual variation, men on average tend to exhibit more aggressive tendencies than women. Psychologists have wondered why this is so. Maccoby and Jacklin (1980) have concluded from their review of the research that aggression is a sex difference that transcends culture. Others believe that it is caused by an interaction between biological factors (such as hormones before and after birth) and social influences (such as norms of acceptable behavior). Although scientists continue to debate whether or not aggression is a sex difference that transcends culture, sociologists continue to find evidence that boys are socially encouraged to display aggression while girls are encouraged to inhibit it. Evidence for the importance of social influences comes from the fact that boys and girls do not begin to show differences in their levels of aggression until after

they have had time to learn their culture's expectations about behaviors deemed appropriate for each sex in various situations. Tavris and Wade (1984) are in agreement about the importance of social learning for the display of aggression. These researchers think that many women have the potential to be just as aggressive as men when the norms support female aggression, but that they learn to inhibit aggression in those situations where such behavior would be considered inappropriate.

Biological Evidence

As biological evidence accumulates, it is becoming increasingly clear that biological factors alone are insufficient to produce the behaviors we call masculine and feminine. To understand why, let us review what is known about the genetic and hormonal differences between males and females.

Males and females differ in their **chromosomes,** threadlike structures in each cell of the body that carry within them **genes,** the determiners of hereditary characteristics. Both males and females have twenty-three pairs of chromosomes, all of them identical except one. In female cells, this pair consists of two X chromosomes; in male cells, it consists of an X and a Y chromosome. It is the Y chromosome that prompts an embryo to develop into a male. This it does by triggering the production of male **hormones,** chemical substances that stimulate or inhibit specific physiological processes. If male hormones in large enough quantities are present in an embryo, the individual will go on to develop male reproductive organs. Many researchers think that male hormones also affect the development of an embryo's brain, directing it to become organized in ways that facilitate "male" behavior. Female development, in contrast, requires the absence of male hormones. In fact, all fertilized eggs will undergo female-type development *unless* they are exposed to sufficient amounts of male hormones.

Occasionally, however, something goes wrong during embryonic development, and an intermediate amount of male hormones causes a person to develop a body with both male and female characteristics. At birth the attending physician decides whether the baby is more nearly a boy or a girl. The parents accept this sex identification and raise the child as a boy or a girl

These children do appear to be flouting gender stereotypes. Nevertheless, in general, girls are still encouraged to be nuturing and to inhibit aggression, whereas boys are encouraged to show aggression, to be assertive, and to seize opportunities in the higher-status professions. (Left: Charles Leavitt/The Picture Cube; right: Peter Menzel.)

—whichever they were told. And the child typically grows up to be, in his or her own mind, this assigned sex (Money and Tucker 1975). The ease with which such children become the gender they think they are tells us that biology cannot be the only factor creating masculinity or femininity. Apparently, the label "boy" or "girl" directs the socialization of a child in ways that are critical for developing a gender appropriate self.

Cross-Cultural Evidence

Additional evidence that masculine and feminine characteristics are more than a matter of biology comes from studies of other societies. If gender characteristics were simply a matter of biology, then one would expect to find little cultural variation in gender roles. But that is not the case. What people consider masculine or feminine behavior is actually quite variable. Americans, for instance, typically think of men as naturally tougher than women and better suited to perform the most strenuous physical labor. Not all peoples of the world hold to this distinction, however. The rulers of the African Dahomeyan kingdom employed women as bodyguards because they believed women to be especially fierce fighters. Similarly, Tasmanians assumed that women were perfectly well-suited to the most dangerous hunting tasks, such as swimming out to remote rocks in

the ocean to stalk and club sea otters. In sub-Saharan African countries, women are assigned the arduous tasks of carrying goods to market, hauling firewood, and doing construction on houses. Such differences in people's ideas of what men and women are like and are capable of doing suggest that there are no universal, inborn characteristics of gender as regards skills and general abilities to do various types of work. Instead, gender roles are the result of how societies socialize men and women to behave. Anthropologist Margaret Mead (1935/1963) was one of the first to report on societies whose gender arrangements differ from our own. In an early study of gender roles in three New Guinea tribes—the Arapesh, the Mundugumor, and the Tchambuli—she found evidence of aggression in women, passivity in men, and minimal differences in the roles of men and women.

According to Mead, the mild-mannered Arapesh seemed to expect members of both sexes to be gentle, cooperative, and maternal. In contrast, the neighboring Mundugumor seemed as fierce as the Arapesh seemed gentle. The Mundugumor seemed to apply their aggressive, combative ideal to *both* sexes. Both men and women showed what we might call exaggerated **machismo,** or compulsive masculinity, involving posturing, boasting, and an exploitive attitude (in our society, toward women).

In the third tribe, the Tchambuli, the women were domineering, wore no ornaments, and shaved their heads. They were also the primary food providers. The

This Tchambuli woman of New Guinea is fulfilling her culture's notion of the woman's role—that of hunter and provider. Cross-cultural evidence of wide variation in gender roles undercuts the notion that biology is all-determining. (Agnes Estioko-Griffin and P. Bion Griffin.)

men, on the other hand, were preoccupied with artistic tasks, self-adornment, and gossiping about the women.

Since Mead, anthropologists have documented considerable variation in gender roles from culture to culture, with men and women assuming different rights, obligations, and spheres of influence (Kottak 1987). Cross-culturally, anthropologists have found gender roles to be more equal when women contribute about as much to subsistence as men do (Sanday 1974). Also cross-culturally, as is traditionally the case in the United States, women's rights and duties tend to center more around the home than men's. Nonetheless, cross-cultural evidence suggests that gender roles are highly flexible and reflect environmental and cultural imperatives rather than biological ones.

Taken as a whole, the cross-cultural evidence helps to settle the question of whether gender roles are a "natural" or a social creation. But it leaves open another important question that we have yet to explore. Although gender roles are known to vary, gender stratification appears to be extremely widespread. Why is this so? In many societies, men and women are not just given different roles—they are socially ranked, with men being accorded the greater share of wealth, power, or prestige. These deeply rooted patterns of gender inequality are the topic to which we now turn.

PATTERNS OF GENDER INEQUALITY

There currently is an acute shortage of nurses in the United States. Nineteen eighty-six saw a twofold increase in the number of vacancies on hospital nursing staffs. By mid-1987 the vacancy rate had reached 13.5 percent and was still rising. Fewer and fewer young people are choosing a career in nursing because the pay is relatively low. The basic problem, many think, is that nursing remains the domain of women (only 3 percent of nurses are men), and any profession that is staffed largely by women is undervalued by society (Lewin 1987).

Although by the mid-1980s 16 percent of lawyers in the United States were women, many of those women were encountering discrimination in law offices and the courts. According to Leonard Cavise, a professor at De Paul University College of Law, "A woman lawyer has to fight harder to get respect. She must also put up with sexist habits, like being called honey, or being told by a judge that she should smile more or wear feminine, frilly clothes and not pant suits" (quoted in Blodgett 1986). It is hard, too, for women attorneys to break into the legal establishment, with its male-dominated network and camaraderie. This helps explain why relatively few women lawyers are making it to the very top rungs of their profession (Epstein 1981; Abramson and Franklin 1986).

The problems of women in nursing and law, while in some ways different, echo the same major theme. American women are entering the work force in record numbers, but they still have largely a second-class status in the working world. Although this contradicts the headlines, social research shows that women are still segregated into "female" professions, where the pay is low for the responsibilities undertaken, and the advancement possibilities limited. These professions, such as nursing, secretarial work, and elementary-school teaching, have been dubbed "pink collar ghettoes" (Howe 1977). In other cases, women have been venturing into fields formerly monopolized by men—such as law, science, engineering, and medicine, to mention just a few examples. In such fields, however, women are still struggling to attain an equal footing with men. Even when women have the required talent, education, and credentials, the very best jobs and highest salaries usually fall to males. And employment is not the only area in which gender inequalities exist. Women also have unequal access to power in the political sphere. In view of the fact that women constitute over half the population, they are grossly underrepresented in the executive, legislative, and judicial branches of government. Let us take a closer look at these two areas of gender stratification—in the workplace and in politics.

Gender Stratification in the Workplace

The recent influx of American women into the paid labor force has been called "the single most outstanding phenomenon of this century" (Ginzberg, quoted in Lenz and Myerhoff 1985). Between 1900 and 1985, the proportion of women who worked outside the home rose from 20 percent to 54 percent, almost tripling. It is estimated that by 1990, about 70 percent of working-age women will either have a paid job or be looking for one (Gerson 1985). This statistic signals a dramatic change in the type of woman to be found in the work force. While at the beginning of this century a large proportion of working women were single and childless, today many are both married and have young children at home. In fact, in 1986 over 53 percent of American women with preschoolers had paid jobs.

This steadily increasing flow of women into the labor force has been caused by several factors. Historically, both the Great Depression of the 1930s and World War II did much to draw women into the nation's offices and factories—in the first case because of dire economic need, and in the second case because of a shortage of men in the work force. After the war, women were pushed out of the labor force for a number of years as the soldiers returned home. Then, following this low point in female employment, the participation of women in the labor force began once more to increase. The increase was due partly to economic factors (England and Farkas 1986). For one thing, the number of service-oriented jobs—such as sales clerk, secretary, waitress, or nurse—was increasing rapidly. Since such jobs had traditionally been staffed by women, employers looked for women to fill these openings. Compared with what women had earned in previous decades, these "women's positions" of the 1950s and 1960s were paying better. Women were increasingly attracted to the extra family income, especially when modern technology had made available such an enticing array of new consumer goods. Families wanted to partake of the higher standard of living, and having two wage earners in the home gave them more purchasing power. This was the situation particularly during the high-inflation years of the 1970s when home mortgage payments were beyond the reach

A *shortage of men in the workforce during World War II helped women gain access to jobs traditionally held by men. Women's participation in the war effort is considered an important factor in the breakdown of traditional barriers to women working outside the home. (Culver Pictures.)*

of many families unless both husband and wife worked. Then, too, an upwardly spiraling divorce rate made work outside the home not just a desirable option but an economic necessity for a growing number of women.

At the same time that these economic changes were occurring, attitudes were changing as well. Many women no longer felt that being a full-time homemaker was providing them with an adequate sense of fulfillment and self-worth. With fewer children to care for and more labor-saving appliances at their disposal, many began to feel bored and isolated at home. They hoped that holding a paid job might infuse their lives with more interest and challenge. And this hope, to some extent, proved to be justified. In a set of interviews with women conducted in 1953, 56 percent of all the employed women and 70 percent of those in professional jobs said their work made them feel useful and important (Klein 1984). By the 1960s, the women's liberation movement was bolstering this new point of view. Women began thinking of themselves not just as workers, but as people with long-term occupational or career goals. In this way the self-images of women were putting greater emphasis on independence and self-reliance.

"Women's Work" Today

Still, many career ladders have remained frustratingly difficult for women to climb. Even today women tend to be segregated in jobs that society considers appropriate for women. For instance, in 1980, women made up 96 percent of the sewers and stitchers, 97 percent of the typists and receptionists, 98 percent of the kindergarten teachers, and 99 percent of the secretaries in the labor force (Klein 1984). In contrast, they accounted for less than 10 percent of the engineers, architects, and clergy. Figure 12.1 compares the participation of men and women in the labor force today and projected into the next decade.

What difference does this gender segregation in the work force make? Why does it matter to women that they are channeled into jobs that are different from those being offered to men? The answer is that women's occupations tend to be both lower paying and lower in prestige (Coser 1983). In terms of pay and prestige there is a wide gap between secretaries and corporate executives, between teachers and school superintendents, between sales clerks and sales managers, between nurses and physicians. The first of each pair of occupations in this list is a female-dominated field, the second a male-dominated one. Thus, in virtually every industry in which both men and women work, the women tend to be concentrated at the lower end of the hierarchy while the men tend to monopolize the upper echelons. This pattern is maintained partly because there is little promotion from the lower-paying jobs into the higher-paying ones. An excellent secretary, for instance, might become a supervisor of other secretaries, or she might be offered a secretarial job for a more important executive. But there is little chance she will ever get her feet on the rungs of the managerial ladder particularly without an M.B.A. or other professional credentials required today of anyone who wants to rise to management (Blau and Jusenius 1976). Women are growing in the ranks of doctors, attorneys, business executives, etc., as they become trained in these professions. But even so, women still face obstacles to mobility within organizations dominated by men (Blum and Smith 1988; Kanter 1977, 1983).

And even when we compare *lower*-status male jobs with typical female ones, the men still fare better in terms of compensation. Sewers and stitchers, for example, who are primarily women, earned a median income of $8,632 in 1982. In contrast, carpet installers, who are primarily men, earned a median income of $15,392,

nearly twice as much. Significantly, too, when men work in traditionally female occupations (such as secretaries, nurses, elementary-school teachers), they tend to make more than women.

These inequalities in the work force largely explain the substantial gap in earnings that exists when all male and female wage earners are considered. From 1950 until about 1980, women received only about 60 percent of men's average earnings. This difference began to shrink—especially for younger workers—in the 1980s. By 1986, women between the ages of 25 and 34 were earning 74 percent of what men in this age group earned, while women between the ages of 20 and 24 were earning 86 percent of their male peers' pay (*U.S. Statistical Abstract* 1988). These, however, are still sizable differences in income. And for minority women the picture is much worse. In 1986, black females earned only 88 percent as much as white females, while Hispanic females earned only 83 percent as much. Minority women, in other words, are at a double disadvantage—because of their ethnic background and because of their sex. This fact accounts for the alarming statistic that in 1985, 54 percent of households headed by a black or Hispanic woman have incomes below the poverty line.

Explaining Gender Inequalities on the Job

Human Capital Explanations.   What can explain differences in pay based on gender? One possibility is that women are at a disadvantage when it comes to what economists call human capital. **Human capital** refers to any capabilities people might acquire by making investments in improving their marketability as workers. Attending college, for instance, is an investment in human capital because it gives people knowledge and credentials that make them more desirable to employers. Experience on the job is another form of human capital, as is a network of employment contacts, a strong motivation to achieve, or the ability to organize procedures. According to human capital explanations of gender inequalities in the workplace, a woman's investment in such work-related factors is generally poorer than a man's, so most women end up in lower paying jobs.

Sociologists have found that there is some truth to the human capital theory. One significant way a woman's human capital differs from a man's has to do with how the two sexes are socialized during childhood.

Since 1960, the percentage of women in the labor force has increased greatly. This increase has changed their status in the workplace.

FIGURE 12.1   The Labor Force Participation by Sex, 1960–2000

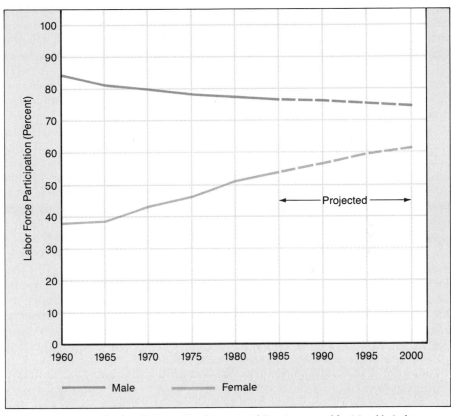

Source: U.S. Bureau of Labor Statistics, *Employment and Earnings,* monthly; *Monthly Labor Review,* September 1987.

Traditionally most girls were taught to develop social skills, as well as skills in homemaking and child care. In contrast, boys were encouraged to excel at physical activities and to be competitive and assertive. These traits, in turn, helped to guide children toward gender-stereotyped jobs. In one study of youngsters between the ages of seven and twelve, well over half the girls planned to be teachers, nurses, homemakers, secretaries, or waitresses, jobs to which only 1 percent of the boys aspired. Similarly, very few of the girls were interested in the jobs that most boys wanted: firefighter, police officer, auto mechanic, construction worker, repairman, or player of some professional sport (Nemerowicz 1979). Since traditional female jobs are much lower paying than traditional male ones, these preferences learned in early childhood tend to perpetuate the gender pay gap.

Whether today's generation of girls is learning different occupational attitudes remains to be seen. One recent study (O'Keefe and Hyde 1983) comparing elementary school boys and girls found evidence of changing preferences and reduced stereotyping among girls. When asked what they wanted to be when they grew up, the 55 boys chose 52 masculine and 3 neutral jobs (the three most popular choices were truck driver, fire fighter, and farmer). But the girls' answers were more diverse. They chose 12 masculine, 14 neutral, and 29 feminine jobs. This reinforces the hypothesis that the presence of many more women in the workforce is making young girls aware of a wider range of occupational choices. Whether this awareness will be reflected in the employment status of today's generation of girls is a question for the future.

Another difference in human capital that helps perpetuate the gender pay gap is the difference between men's and women's years of work experience. In general, women have less work experience than men, and the experience they have tends to be more fragmented because of switches in jobs, absences from work, and periods of part-time employment (England and Farkas 1986). This pattern is due to the fact that many women leave the work force temporarily in order to raise a family. According to estimates, between 25 and 50 percent of the gender gap in pay can be attributed to the resulting differences in job experience (England and Farkas 1986). Of course, as women become more career-oriented, many are postponing or forgoing having children, and others are using professional child care to allow them to return to work soon after they have given birth. This means that the average woman's years of job experience are becoming comparable to a man's. Still, there is a long tradition of defining women as the primary caretakers of children. As a result, a wife is much more apt to quit a job and take care of her child than a husband is to make the same sacrifice for his wife. One possible solution is for more employers to offer paternity leaves to men, such as is mandated by law in Sweden. However, as long as this attitude toward women's role as primary caretakers of children exists, women's work experience will continue to be more fragmented than men's.

Discrimination in Hiring and Promotion. But can differences in human capital alone explain why women, on average, earn less than men? If these differences were the whole story, then women who aspired to "male" occupations and acquired the appropriate training and experience would automatically be paid the same as men. This, however, is not what happens. Women with Masters of Business Administration degrees, for instance, average only 81 percent of their male classmates' salaries, despite having acquired the very same credentials (Gold 1983). Such statistics suggest that women suffer discrimination in the workplace, discrimination that makes it hard for them to land the best-paying jobs.

Discrimination against women can take many forms (England and Farkas 1986). Employers may simply accept gender role stereotypes and assume that women are not strong enough, ambitious enough, or rational enough in their thinking to compete successfully for "male" jobs. Some of these assumptions may be based in part on faulty generalizations. For instance, it is true that women, on average, have less physical strength

than men and less knowledge of machinery. So an employer who is looking for someone, say, to repair heavy equipment might refuse to interview *any* woman, even those who are quite different from the average in regard to the job qualifications.

It is hard to measure how much discrimination impedes women's progress in the workplace, but studies show that discrimination does indeed exist. In one survey, for instance, nearly 900 male managers compared men and women as to characteristics that would help or impair managerial effectiveness (Rosen and Jerdee 1978). Men were judged to be better than women at seeing the big picture and accurately assessing problems, at understanding financial matters and rationally making choices, at setting long-range goals and getting people to work together, and at standing up under fire and keeping calm in emergencies. Compared with women, men were also judged more ambitious, self-reliant, and assertive. Women, in contrast, were deemed to have traits that were not associated with being effective managers. Compared with men, they were deemed to be more emotional, more sensitive to criticism, more timid, and more prone to crying. They were also thought to be less committed to their jobs, more prone to absenteeism and quitting, as well as more inclined to like routine work rather than tasks that present new challenges.

Newer studies have come to somewhat more positive conclusions. For instance, Russell, Rush, and Herd (1988) surveyed university women's expectations of what makes for effective male and female managers. The women in the study basically thought that effective managers of either sex would have essentially similar profiles of leadership. Their study showed more parity between the expectations for male and female managers than did Rosen and Jerdee and thus potentially less reason for discrimination.

In another study, sociologist Anne Statham (1987) questioned 18 men and 22 women managers to explore potential gender differences in management styles. She concluded that men and women have different methods of accomplishing similar goals. One difference she noted is that men managers tend to let employees struggle on their own, believing this is the "best way to manage." Women managers typically show more concern, and may be resented by male subordinates for "standing over their shoulders." Undoubtedly these differences in management styles cause misunderstandings in the workplace. As Statham writes, "We can conclude that perception may not in fact reflect reality, that men and women may be equally effective managers but may not be viewed as such because of certain differences in style or approach" (p. 425). Such findings suggest that sex discrimination based on managerial styles may linger long after more overt forms of discrimination have been outlawed.

The Comparable Worth Debate. How much do differences in human capital contribute to gender inequalities in the workplace and how much of a role does discrimination play? Different researchers give different answers. Those who stress discrimination point out that a pay gap still exists even when male and female jobs of comparable status and worth are compared. How can this gap be explained, these sociologists ask, unless employers are putting a discriminatory ceiling on the amount they are willing to pay for "women's work"?

Researchers have tried to quantify the toll this discrimination takes. They analyze the levels of training, skill, and other qualifications required for different jobs and assign points accordingly. Then they look at men's and women's jobs with the same number of points to see if they pay equally. Most studies show that women's work pays substantially less than comparable men's work. This gap in pay is presumably due solely to discrimination. Some researchers estimate that discrimination accounts for over 70 percent of the total gender pay gap (Gold 1983).

But other researchers argue that it is very hard to measure all the various skills and qualifications needed for different jobs. One may assign an equal value to the skills of both secretary and maintenance carpenter, but these jobs are so different—how can we say with certainty that they are of comparable worth? It may be instead that subtle differences between them make one pay more than the other. It may also be that women are crowded into too few occupations. This would raise the supply of labor for each available female position and depress the wage that it pays.

As to why women usually end up in the lower paying occupations, the same critics contend that it is not largely a matter of their being barred from better jobs because of prejudice. They say that women choose lower-echelon fields for a variety of reasons. One reason is that many women have traditionally thought of their incomes as supplementing the income of their husbands. Given this view, it makes sense to care less about earning the maximum possible and more, depending upon the family's current situation, about finding work that allows flexible movement in and out of the work-force. Lower-echelon jobs offer such flexibility because the work they entail is routine and can be learned with minimal training. A woman can easily quit this type of job when her family life demands it (when her husband gets transferred or a new child is born, for example) and just as easily find another one when family circumstances change (Gold 1983).

But other researchers do not accept these arguments. They say that crowding in women's occupations is no greater than the crowding in men's jobs. Men, after all, are socialized to seek gender-appropriate work as much, if not more, than women (England and Farkas 1986). Nor can it be said that women freely choose to gravitate toward lower paying fields. Gender-role socialization has so instilled in women the concept that they are secondary wage earners that most women are not motivated to pursue higher paying jobs in the same way as men (Gold 1983).

One remedy to the problem of gender inequalities in the workplace would be to revise wages according to comparable worth. Under this arrangement, women would receive the same salaries as men who hold jobs that are different but of comparable value. A secretary, for example, would receive the same pay as a maintenance carpenter or an electrician, both of whom now earn nearly twice as much as the secretary does (Gest 1984). These new valuations would be based on a system that gives points to each occupation for the skill, responsibility, effort, and risk it involves. Such a system, however, is far from being accepted. One reason for the opposition to it is the estimated $150 billion yearly that it would cost employers to raise women's wages to the levels of men's wages for jobs of comparable worth (Lewin 1984). There is no question that the new system would be expensive to implement, but the alternative is to operate under a current system of social injustice.

Gender Stratification in Politics

In 1984 Geraldine Ferraro became the first woman to be nominated for vice president of the United States by a major political party. The publicity that surrounded her selection as a candidate for this high office reminded Americans how much gender inequality still exists in the political arena. The United States probably has more gender stratification in the world of politics than in the world of work.

Statistics on women in politics bear out this generalization. For instance, in the mid-1980s there were only 22 women in the House of Representatives, out of a total 435 members. In the U.S. Senate, female representation was even lower—a mere 2 out of 100, or only 2 percent. There were also only two women in the Reagan cabinet and only one on the Supreme Court. Granted, in state and local politics women have more of a voice. Fifteen percent of state legislators are female and ninety cities with populations over 30,000 have female mayors. But these figures still fall far short of representing equal political participation by women (O'Kelly and Carney 1986).

Attitudes toward women in politics are changing, however. By 1980, 60 percent of American men and 63 percent of American women thought that the two sexes should have equal access to leadership positions in both business and government (Klein 1984). In answer to a question on a 1985 survey, the vast majority of Americans (82 percent) said they would be receptive to having a woman as president of the country if she was the most qualified candidate for the job. This is in sharp contrast to attitudes fifty years ago, when only 34 percent of Americans said they would vote for a woman presidential candidate even if she was highly qualified. Thus, as more and more women enter politics—first at the state and local levels and then at the federal level—they will help to change people's opinions about the appropriateness of women holding public office.

THE WOMEN'S MOVEMENT

Change in people's attitudes toward women in leadership roles would never have proceeded as far as it has without impetus from the women's movement. Organized protest by women on their own behalf is not a new phenomenon. It has been going on in this country since the nineteenth century (Klein 1984). For decades women have been lobbying, picketing, boycotting, and challenging unfair practices in the courts. Often, however, these efforts met with little success. With the exception of women winning the right to vote in 1920, their struggle for equality with men was greeted with opposition, or at best indifference, until quite recently. It was not until large numbers of women developed a sense of shared grievances that their protest politics really began to make inroads.

One turning point came in 1963 with the publication of a book called *The Feminine Mystique*. In it author Betty Friedan described the isolation and discontent that some middle-class housewives across the country had been feeling but had seldom discussed. Friedan put her finger on some of the reasons for these feelings. American women had been trained since childhood to see their personal fulfillment in terms of dedication to a husband and children. But in an era of labor-saving devices time often hung heavy on the full-time housewife's hands, and her creative talents often went unused. The home in the suburbs, supposedly a dream house, began to seem more and more like a prison. Friedan gave voice to this widespread problem, faced by so many women, and in doing so she helped to launch an era of change.

Further catalysts for change came through the mobilization of women who considered themselves **feminists**—people with a strong sense of women's shared experiences and problems and a strong commitment to improving the position of females in society. For instance, in 1966 the National Organization for Women (NOW) was formed. Its aim, according to Betty Friedan, one of its founders, was "to take action to bring women into full participation in the mainstream of American society, *now.*" Two years later, the Women's Equity Action League (WEAL) was formed. Both NOW and WEAL bombarded government with complaints of gender discrimination and proposals for more equal treatment under the law.

The number of bills concerned with women's issues that legislators passed was directly related to the women's protest movement. During the 1960s, when protest was just gaining strength, Congress enacted only ten such pieces of legislation. By the 1970s, however, when women's activism was widespread, over seven times as many laws favorable to women were passed. This amounted to nearly 40 percent of all legislation enacted on behalf of women during the twentieth century (Klein 1984).

A key piece of legislation with which women became concerned in the 1970s was the Equal Rights Amendment to the Constitution, known as the ERA. It stated simply that equality of rights under the law could not be denied on the basis of sex. In March 1972 this amendment, initially proposed almost fifty years before, was approved by Congress and presented to the states for ratification. Within a year, thirty of the necessary thirty-eight states had ratified the amendment and its acceptance seemed imminent. But then support in the state legislatures began to wane. In June 1982, when the

Members of NOW and other groups march for the Equal Rights Amendment in 1978; suffragettes demonstrate for the right to vote in 1920. The struggle for gender equality—like those for racial equality and for economic opportunity—has no clear-cut finish line or permanent victory. It is an ongoing process of education, vigilance, and pressure against ingrained prejudices. (Left: Arthur Grace/Sygma; right: Culver Pictures.)

ratification deadline arrived, the amendment was still three states short of becoming law.

Sociologists have wondered why the ERA failed to be ratified, especially when poll after poll showed that the majority of Americans agreed with its basic principle. A key answer seems to lie in the strategy that opponents of the ERA adopted (Mansbridge 1986). They shifted debate over the amendment away from the abstract issue of equal rights (which most people supported) and onto the possibility that the ERA would prompt fundamental change in women's roles (something that many Americans feared). For instance, there was much concern over whether the ERA would require that women be eligible for combat duty in the armed forces. Most Americans did not believe that men and women were equally suited to this task, nor did they want the sexes gradually to become more similar in this way. Many people who claimed to support the ERA still held many traditional views about women's proper roles in society. When state legislators became concerned that the ERA would change these traditional gender roles, they grew uneasy about the amendment and the drive for ratification faltered.

Public uneasiness about substantive changes in traditional gender roles is reflected in the kind of progress that the women's movement has made to date. While greater opportunities for women in business, government, and the professions have gradually opened up, changes in the domestic sphere have not kept pace. Research shows that women continue to have the major responsibility for household chores whether or not they work outside the home. For instance, a study of women physicians found that 75 percent did all the cooking, shopping, money management, and child care for their families (Collins 1982). Needless to say, such work requires a substantial number of hours each day. In fact, women who hold a paid job of thirty or more hours a week put in an average of nearly five hours a day in routine housework. Significantly, the number of hours a husband spends in household chores does not increase much when his wife takes a job (Pleck 1977). Thus, just because more and more women have jobs outside the home does not mean that traditional views of women's roles are changing rapidly. Women in our society are still considered the centers of home life. They are the ones primarily responsible for maintaining comfortable surroundings and for providing the care and nurturance of the family (di Leonardo 1987). In the following section we will look more closely at the nature of this traditional woman's role.

SOCIOLOGICAL ANALYSIS OF GENDER ROLES

I get up at 6 A.M. and put up coffee and cereal for breakfast and go down to the basement to put clothes in the washing machine. When I come up, I dress Teddy (1½) and put him in his chair. Then I dress Jim (3½) and serve breakfast to him and to my husband and feed Teddy.

After my husband leaves, the day is as follows: breakfast dishes, clean up kitchen. Make beds, clean the apartment. Wipe up bathroom and kitchen floor. Get lunch vegetables ready and put potatoes on to bake for lunch. Dress both children in outdoor clothes. Do my food shopping and stay out with children until 12. Return and undress children, wash them up for lunch, feed Teddy and put him to nap. Make own lunch, wash dishes, straighten up kitchen. Put Jim to rest. Between 1 and 2:30 depending on the day of the week, ironing, thorough cleaning of one room, weekend cooking and baking, etc.; 3 P.M. give children juice or milk, put outdoor clothes on. Out to park; 4:30 back. Give children their baths. Prepare their supper and help put them to bed. Make dinner for husband and myself. After dinner, dishes and cleaning up. After 8 P.M. often more ironing, especially on the days when I cleaned in the afternoon. There is mending to be done; 9 P.M. fall asleep in the living room over a newspaper or listening to the radio. (From Komarovsky 1953, quoted in Hewlett 1986)

Although the above woman's description of her day dates from the 1950s, many contemporary women still perform the very same chores. The only difference is that the modern-day mother of preschool children is apt to hold down a job outside the home as well. In the workplace her duties may be just as tedious and unchallenging as the ones she performs in the house. Perhaps she clerks in a discount store or types in an office. Maybe she helps to make small appliances on an assembly line. Despite the long hours she puts in, her wages are nowhere near enough to support her family. The role of major breadwinner falls to her husband. At night, after putting in a second work shift cooking, cleaning, and caring for the children, she falls asleep watching television instead of listening to the radio.

The degree to which women's role has been subordinate in American society has varied somewhat throughout our history. In colonial times, women had a substantial amount of economic power, partly because they were in short supply but chiefly because they were responsible for producing many of the things the family needed. There was no breadwinner per se, since the work performed by both men and women was essential to survival (Lyon 1986).

The advent of industrialism gradually weakened the economic partnership that had existed between husbands and wives. In an economy based increasingly on

From the corset and bustle of a Victorian matron to the hustle and bustle of a high-powered career, women have made dramatic strides toward economic and political independence. However, without adequate daycare and other services, today's working woman is too often expected to be a "Super-Mom," fulfilling both her career aspirations and her traditional role of child-raiser and homemaker. (Left: Culver Pictures; right: Steven McCurry/Magnum.)

money and wage labor, it was typically the husband whose paycheck supported the family. Long hours of employment outside the home now separated husbands from their families. Because women were the ones who were always at home, they gained greater control over domestic matters. During the Victorian era, segregation of the sexes was almost complete. Women were primarily caretakers of the home and children, except in lower-class families, where the wife's wages were needed.

If anything, modern times intensified this polarity. As jobs required more mobility, fathers were sometimes absent from the family for days at a time, while women stayed home to care for the children and do the housework. The spread of suburbia further served to isolate women from the working world of their husbands. Men in the suburbs often commuted many miles to the central cities, leaving wives alone with the children during most of the day. The woman who described her day at the beginning of this section illustrates this pattern.

The roles expected of American women today are even more demanding, for many women are now both paid employees and centers of the home and family. These dual roles are reflected in the law: We have legislation that removes barriers to women's equality side by side with laws that seek to protect women as if they were still considered the weaker sex. Thus, even though new job opportunities for women are opening up, there remains widespread acceptance of the traditional female gender role (Roger 1984; Mindel and Halbenstein 1981). Granted, the traditional female role varies across social classes and ethnic groups, as does the traditional male role. Black Americans, for instance, have somewhat different expectations about male and female behavior than do Hispanics or Orientals, just as upper-class whites have different views on this subject than do middle- and lower-class whites. Still, there remains a core of traditional shared ideas about the roles appropriate for the two sexes. Let us see what these traditional gender roles have entailed.

The Traditional Female Role

Popular wisdom has traditionally held that all "normal" women want to marry and have children and that whatever other interests they might pursue are secondary to these family roles. Women who do not want to marry

or mothers who do not enjoy being with their children are thought to be unusual or strange. To fill the traditional homemaker role, females have been expected to develop a capacity for warmth, compassion, sensitivity, and caring. Whereas men have generally been raised to be achievement-oriented, women have been raised to be people-oriented and to place great value on cultivating close relationships. The traditional role of wife and mother has also carried with it a dependency on men, especially on the husband. (Taking the husband's name after marriage symbolized this dependency.) Society still considers it perfectly legitimate for a woman to depend entirely on her husband for economic support. Indeed, many a husband still feels that if his wife takes a job it somehow reflects on his masculinity.

The traditional woman's role had a number of benefits. For one thing, in an era of job scarcity, women were not usually obliged to earn a living for their families. Of course, millions of women held jobs out of necessity, but economic support was not a *moral* duty as it generally was for men. To this day, women also have the legal right to claim support from their husbands. In many states, a man is responsible for his wife's debts but she is not responsible for his. In other words, society does not place as much pressure on women to achieve as it does on men. Although a woman may strive to reach the top of her profession, there is less shame for her in failure or in having only moderate success than there is for a man. Women may therefore be less prone than men to the career syndrome, with its almost total devotion to the workplace, often to the exclusion of outside interests. Finally, the female role allows women more emotional freedom than men. Women are permitted to express their doubts and vulnerabilities; they have more outlets for their tension and anxiety; and they have fewer inhibitions about seeking intimacy with others.

But the traditional female role also has its costs. It has denied women full autonomy in most spheres of American life. The dependency taught to girls in childhood often leads to passivity and timidity in later life. (For example, a woman who has not engaged in paid work in ten or fifteen years will think twice before she decides to get out of an unhappy marriage.) In addition, the female role is associated with a higher incidence of certain kinds of emotional problems, such as depression. Perhaps this is partly because homemaking does not provide many rewards for educated women, because housewives feel that theirs is an inferior status, and because the isolation of homemakers leaves much opportunity for brooding—especially when the children have grown up and left home (Gove and Tudor 1973; Rosenfield 1980; Scarf 1980).

Another major way that the traditional female role takes its toll is in the conflicts it presents for career women. Those who temporarily drop out of the job market to devote themselves to their families often suffer setbacks in their careers, while those who compete in the workplace must often forgo having children. Working-class women and women who are single parents often do not have a choice between working and being full-time homemakers; their family depends on the income they earn. Most of these women work in nonprofessional, low-paying jobs, with little expectation of climbing a career ladder. Women who seek to commit themselves to both a career and a family frequently find themselves handicapped by the need to be superwomen who can manage both sets of responsibilities. In contrast, men have been able to pursue both work and a family life much more easily. Indeed, the more successful men are, the more likely they are to marry and have a family. For women the pattern is reversed. Whereas 51 percent of female executives are single, only 4 percent of male executives are. And whereas 61 percent of female executives are childless, this is true of only 3 percent of male executives (Hull 1982). Clearly, the choice between career and family is more stressful and the cost more apparent for women than for men (Rubin 1983).

The Traditional Male Role

The traditional male role is as deeply tied to the family as is the female role, although the connections are not so obvious. First and foremost, a man has traditionally been expected to be a good provider for his wife and children. Americans do not think it odd for a man to sacrifice his leisure hours and even his health to a career. A man's accomplishments and property are often considered indications of his worth as a human being.

The traditional male role also entails a high degree of competitiveness and self-assertion, as well as emotional self-control. Weakness, doubt, and compromise have traditionally been considered unmanly traits. Heterosexual prowess is part of the masculine image, too. Boys and men who show effeminate behavior are greatly stigmatized in our society. Finally, American men are accustomed to being dominant in male-female relationships. When placed in a position that is subordinate to a woman, many feel uncomfortable, even threatened (Mayes 1979).

Along with these pressures, the traditional male role also has many obvious advantages. American men (especially those who are white and middle-class) have access to the pinnacles of institutional power. They have traditionally run the nation's government, churches, corporations, professions, and universities—even its theaters and art galleries. With the notable exceptions of the military draft and some alimony statutes, neither law nor custom has discriminated against or restricted men solely on the basis of their sex. Men have had more opportunities than women to develop their talents and to acquire special skills and knowledge. If a family has only enough income to send one child to college, in all likelihood it will send the son.

But the responsibilities attached to the male role in America can be a source of great anxiety. Being in a position to make decisions is fine for men who are confident about what they are doing, but it promotes much stress in those who are uncertain of themselves. Complicating matters is the fact that men are supposed to maintain an impression of strength and courage at all times. Fear of inadequacy and failure is the dark side of the pressure on men to achieve. Moreover, the emphasis men place on strength, toughness, and superiority can lead them to obsessively test and prove these attributes by engaging in acts of aggression and violence. Equally costly is the competitive syndrome that asks men to consider all other men as either inferiors or rivals. Although men have enshrined the idea of male solidarity, male friendships are not necessarily intimate relationships. And by defining the expression of warmth, tenderness, and sensitivity as weakness, men also limit their relationships with their own children and with women.

The toll of the male role is reflected in physical and mental ill health. Men suffer more heart attacks than women, and their life expectancy is eight years shorter on the average. Men are also more likely to have stress-related illnesses, such as ulcers, asthma, and hypertension. The male suicide rate is triple the female rate, and men are fourteen times as likely to become alcoholics. Finally, more males than females suffer from personality disorders marked by aggression and antisocial behavior (Rosenfield 1980).

The male role, then, although seemingly privileged, is a difficult one to fill, and the "failure" rate is high. In America, as in other industrial societies, few men can hope to achieve the wealth, power, and positions of leadership that social ideals prescribe.

This man may be unaware that he has, all evening long, addressed most of his remarks to the man across the table and cut off the woman to his left several times as she was about to speak. She may expect herself to be "seen and not heard"—she bites her tongue and feigns unflagging interest. (Charles Harbutt/ Archive Pictures.)

Machismo may be a last resort for men who accept the traditional masculine role but cannot live up to it. In an effort to convince other men, women, and above all himself that he is truly all-male, a man uses an exaggerated show of strength and sexual prowess as well as the denigration and often brutalization of women as a front for insecurity, self-doubt, and worldly failure (Aramoni 1972).

Origins of Gender Roles: Functional and Power Perspectives

Sociologists have long wondered about the origins of traditional gender roles. Those who adopt a functional perspective argue that these roles are tied, historically, to the biological fact that women are the ones who bear and nurse children. In eras when reliable birth control and bottle feeding did not exist, the other tasks that women performed in society had to be compatible with their reproductive role. Adjacent activities—such as cooking, weaving—done close to home thus "naturally" clustered around childbearing and child rearing. Similarly, men's lesser involvement with reproductive concerns freed them for other vital undertakings—warfare, hunting—and gave them more mobility. This assigning of warlike duties to men was especially important in times when weapons were rudimentary and combat was often hand-to-hand.

The functional perspective argues that this traditional division of labor by sex has emerged for several significant reasons. One reason is that the two spheres created for men and women are complementary. It is quite efficient to have some members of society raise the children and take care of the home while others are the breadwinners and defenders against enemy attack. These different sets of roles require different sets of competencies—in the first case, caring and sensitivity toward others; in the second, physical strength and competitive strivings. In order to ensure that society will function smoothly, males and females must be socialized for their different spheres. Gradually, then, gender-linked tasks and orientations become socially rooted and set. Henceforth, the idea of separate male and female spheres gets so ingrained in us that we think of this arrangement as natural, even morally right.

But, clearly, pressure for change is mounting and traditional gender roles are starting to break down. Some sociologists argue that we have reached the point where these roles are in some ways *dys*functional. One reason is that the domestic sphere assigned to women has shrunk. As we saw before, now that many women have access to labor-saving goods and services, public education for their children, and can look forward to a life span that

Often the division of labor in the home reinforces gender stereotypes: girls help with the dishes and the cleaning; boys mow the lawn. Today, parents who are themselves struggling with changing roles at home and in the workplace recognize the value of flexible gender training for their children. (John Lei/Stock Boston.)

extends far beyond the age when the young leave home, they find that the traditional female role leaves them with too much time on their hands. In addition, many women are compelled to take jobs because of a rising divorce rate and because of their responsibility, as single mothers, to support their children. Even a large percentage of married women now realize that families need two incomes to maintain an adequate standard of living. Because of all these changes, it is no longer possible to adhere to the traditional division of labor by gender.

Sociologists who adopt a power perspective disagree with the functional interpretation. The power perspective stresses that gender roles involve more than just an efficient division of labor that serves the needs of society. They also involve *domination* of one sex by the other as a reflection of the actual or imputed value of their respective economic contribution. In hunting and gathering societies, for example, where female labor contributes a great deal to subsistence, women are on equal footing with men. Societies that depend on simple hoe agriculture are also quite egalitarian; the tending of small garden plots is compatible with the care of young children, so women in such societies often contribute over half the food-producing labor. The development of plow cultivation, however, makes for radical change. For one thing, the plowing of large fields is often heavy work that does not mesh well with pregnancy and nursing. For another, the use of plows makes farming more efficient

and so reduces the need for agricultural labor. As a result, women in societies that grow food in this manner are often excluded from performing the major food-producing tasks. Most of these cultures are strongly male-dominated and assign women a secondary status (Basow 1986).

The development of plow cultivation had another consequence that affected the status of women. People could now build permanent settlements in a single location. No longer were they required to move periodically when the game or pastureland became depleted. This meant that land could now be *owned* by people: it could become a form of private property. The need to establish indisputable lines of descent became very important, for land that is owned can be passed on from one generation to the next. In response to the need to establish descent there emerged the first true **patriarchies** —societies in which descent is figured through the male line and paternal responsibility becomes a key focus of household and family life. In patriarchies the sexual fidelity of wives is thus essential in order to ensure the legitimacy of children. As a result, the lives of women in these societies become very sexually restricted. It is under such circumstances that truly institutionalized male dominance over women takes root (Basow 1986).

The industrial revolution set the ground for changing the status of men and women in complex ways. As men's work took them out of the home, women took on a more prominent role within it. At the same time, as more and more goods were made in factories by machines, women lost the importance they had once had as the producers of household essentials. Relegated to the tasks of maintaining the household and rearing the children (essential, but formally non-remunerative tasks) women became economically dependent on men. Each sex now specialized in different tasks and man, the provider, and woman, the care-giver, became stock cultural images.

The power perspective also argues that traditional gender roles are maintained because men, who hold most of the formal power in society, try to maintain them. Men find it advantageous to keep women in a sphere that does not threaten or compete with their own. Moreover, the fact that much of the traditional female role involves women providing services for men naturally makes men resistant to changing the status quo. Women, for their part, struggling to redress the balance, have tried in a wide variety of ways to elevate their social position. The result is the classic battle between the sexes that still continues today.

Although the functional and power explanations of gender roles are very different, they are not incompatible. The functional perspective is probably correct in saying that a division of labor between the sexes made a great deal of sense early in human history. But the power explanation is also right in many ways, especially in its emphasis on tension between the sexes and on the fact that male domination of women serves to maintain the dominant male status.

Gender Stereotypes

If one persistent question is how gender roles originate, the other is why they persist and how they are maintained. Gender stereotypes are one important reason. As you read at the beginning of this chapter, gender stereotypes are oversimplified but strongly held ideas about the characteristics of males and females (Basow 1986). They help maintain gender roles by shaping thoughts about the tasks to which men and women are "naturally" suited. For instance, if we think that men are competitive, logical, worldly, and ambitious, we would think them well-suited to be the achievers in society. Similarly, if we think that women are emotional, gentle, tender, and neat, we would think them well-suited to nurturant activities and caretaking roles. Americans do indeed hold gender stereotypes that support the roles traditionally assigned to males and females. When asked to describe the characteristics of the typical man and the typical woman, most people gave answers that made it clear they see men and women as opposites along key dimensions. Men are viewed as being aggressive, independent, objective, dominant, competitive, logical, self-confident, and ambitious, while women are assumed to generally lack these "masculine" traits. Conversely, women are viewed as being tactful, gentle, sensitive to others, neat, quiet, and easily able to express tender feelings, while men are assumed to generally lack these "feminine" characteristics. Research revealing these gender stereotypes was conducted in the early 1970s (Broverman et al. 1972), but more recent studies show that these same stereotypes persist today even among college students at very liberal schools (Ruble 1983; Werner and LaRussa 1985) (see Table 12.2).

TABLE 12.2   Sex-Role Stereotypes

Traits Assigned to Men	Traits Assigned to Women
Favorable adjectives	
frank	poised
industrious	well-mannered
logical	pleasant
ambitious	affectionate
courageous	gentle
aggressive	kind
dominant	warm
self-confident	understanding
independent	sympathetic
forceful	soft-hearted
Unfavorable adjectives	
boastful	submissive
outspoken	fussy
stubborn	fearful
hard-headed	superstitious
reckless	emotional
stern	excitable
opinionated	frivolous
argumentative	shy
prejudiced	snobbish
greedy	touchy

Source: Paul D. Werner and Georgina Williams LaRussa, *Persistence and Change in Sex-Role Stereotypes*, 1985.

Gender roles and gender stereotypes influence one another in both directions. While stereotypes help set our expectations about the tasks men and women should perform, seeing people in these traditional occupations every day reinforces our belief that gender stereotypes are valid. For instance, we think that men are strong and forceful and therefore suited to police work; and when we observe that most police officers are indeed male, we conclude that our gender stereotypes must be right. Similarly, we assume that women are nurturant and tender and therefore suited to child-care work; and when we observe that most child-care workers are indeed female, we conclude that the traits we ascribe to women are warranted. The problem with this reasoning is its circular nature. Because we don't routinely see men and women outside traditional gender roles, we have few opportunities to invalidate our assumptions. Thus, when we do see people performing cross-gender tasks (a male nurse, a female executive), we conclude that, psychologically speaking, they must be exceptions to the rules.

In addition to supporting traditional gender roles, gender stereotypes can actually help to encourage the very behaviors that people assume as natural. For example, if you assume that a little girl is not very self-reliant, you may unwittingly encourage dependence in her by always helping her to do things. Similarly, if you assume that a little boy is active and aggressive, you may actually encourage these characteristics by playing with him in a rough-and-tumble way. Our stereotypes about people can, in short, become self-fulfilling prophecies.

This effect has been demonstrated in experiments. In one study, researchers asked previously unacquainted men and women to get to know one another through a ten-minute phone conversation (Snyder, Tanke, and Berscheid 1977). Beforehand, each man was given a photo of a woman said to be his future "phonemate." In fact, however, the picture was of an entirely different woman—either a conventionally very attractive or a very unattractive one. The men's subsequent behavior was guided by the common stereotypes that beautiful women are poised and outgoing, while homely women are the opposite. Men who thought they were talking with an attractive partner were more friendly, interesting, humorous, and socially adept than men who thought they were talking with an unattractive woman. And, most important, the women responded in kind. Those presumed to be attractive acted friendly and sociable; those presumed to be unattractive acted aloof and withdrawn. Apparently, each took her cue from her partner's behavior. She became the person he expected her to be.

Socialization of Gender Stereotypes and Roles

Our gender stereotypes must, of course, be learned from somewhere, as must our ideas of appropriate gender roles. Three major sources of this gender learning are parents, teachers, and the mass media, including television. So powerful are these agents of gender socialization that people acquire gender expectations at a very early age. In one study, two-year-olds described boys as liking to fight and girls as never fighting. They also said that when boys grow up they mow the lawn, and when girls grow up they clean the house (Kuhn, Nash, and Brucken 1978). Children also learn to differentiate the sexes by psychological traits and income-earning occupations. Let's see how this gender socialization occurs.

The Influence of Parents

Gender-typing and gender-role socialization begin upon birth (Rubin et al. 1974; Paludi and Gullo 1986). Although male and female newborns are indistinguishable except for their genitals, parents (especially fathers) tend to describe them differently. They see their daughters as "weak," "soft," "fine-featured," "awkward," and "delicate," while their sons are "strong," "firm," "large-featured," "well-coordinated," and "hard." Such different perceptions of their children's characteristics set the stage for different behaviors toward boys and girls. For instance, parents decorate the rooms of their sons with animal motifs and provide boys with toy cars and guns, sports equipment, and mechanical playthings. In contrast, they surround their daughters with floral motifs, lace, and ruffles and give them dolls, doll houses, and domestic toys to play with (Rheingold and Cook 1975). Fathers are particularly gender-conscious in their treatment of sons. They tend to be harder on a son than a daughter, even when the child is only one year old. This is because they believe that boys are more active and unruly, and therefore require a firmer disciplinary hand (Snow et al. 1983).

Parents encourage gender-typed behavior in toddlers in more subtle ways as well. When Beverly Fagot (Fagot et al. 1985) conducted an observational study of families with a child aged 13 or 14 months, she found that parents responded differently to a behavior depending on whether it came from a boy or a girl. For instance, parents were more apt to react to boys' physically assertive behaviors than to girls'. They also tended to pay

A male flight attendant? A woman handling the heavy work on an oil rig? Times have changed. But are this man and woman perceived as role models or as exceptions to our ingrained rules about who can do what? (Left: Mark Antman/Stock Boston; right: David E. Kennedy.)

more attention to girls' attempts to communicate with adults than to boys' attempts. When many of these same children were observed in toddler play groups eleven months later, there were gender differences in behavior. Boys were more assertive. Girls talked to their teachers more. In this way, the parents may have subtly perpetuated the stereotype.

When a child reaches the preschool years what were at first casual distinctions about gender-appropriate behavior become explicit lessons. Parents begin to address the child as "Daddy's little girl" or "Mommy's big boy" and they actively discourage (or at least ignore) behavior they consider inappropriate. In some ways the changes required of boys are greater than those required of girls. Boys are expected to outgrow dependency and clinging, whereas this kind of behavior is expected of girls (Bardwick and Douvan 1971). For instance, a mother may begin to ignore a boy's whimpering. If he persists, she may ask him, "Did you ever see your father cry? Do you think Mean Joe Greene cries? Of course not." Gradually boys learn that only girls are permitted to cry. Converse behaviors are frowned upon for girls. For example, a little girl may find that her parents are

genuinely angry when she uses a "nasty" word, but they chuckle if her brother does. The message is clear. Girls are supposed to be pretty, clean, neat, sweet, and popular; boys are supposed to be clever, strong, assertive, fearless, and in control. In addition to instilling these stereotyped ideals, most parents also indoctrinate their children into doing the traditional domestic chores for each sex. Girls are asked to help with cooking and baby-sitting; boys are given yard work and hauling chores (Baker 1984). For most children, striving to live up to these gender expectations is the path of least resistance.

There are signs that parental training may be changing especially by women. Hoffman et al. (1984) found that women treated boys and girls equally in both structured and unstructured play periods. The men in the study did not respond differently to girls and boys during the structured period, but they did talk more with the boys than with the girls during the unstructured one.

In a survey of parents with infants, Michele Paludi and Dominic Gullo (1986) explored the potential effect of gender labels on adults' perceptions of the rate at which children develop. They asked 234 adults of both sexes to indicate on a questionnaire when they thought infants were first able to perform a variety of developmental tasks. One third of those surveyed were asked about "girls," one third about "boys," and one third about just "babies." Contrary to previous research, these investigators found that the gender label had no effect on the adults' ratings.

So far we have focused on the ways that parents may mold and shape their children's behavior in conformity with gender roles. But some researchers maintain that less conscious processes are at work as well. For example, Nancy Chodorow (1978) believes that the traditional division of labor between the sexes is a consequence of women being the primary caretakers of young children. Young girls identify with their mother and so take on many of her traits, including her "feminine" capacity for love, warmth, and nurturance. Young boys, in contrast, are not supposed to identify with their mother, but instead with their father or other adult males. This leads boys to shun the feminine mothering role and turn instead to the impersonal world of work and life outside the home. According to Chodorow, this gender socialization cycle will be repeated generation after generation as long as women are mainly responsible for the emotional nurturance of infants and toddlers.

Chodorow and others see feminine compassion and caring as important elements of society, elements we do not want to lose in our effort to change traditional gender roles (Gilligan 1982). Some argue that rather than trying to make women more like men, we should work toward making both men and women more **androgynous**—that is, more capable of combining the different traits associated with the two genders (Bem 1974, 1975; Tavris and Wade 1984). Androgynous couples, it is said, are more adaptable and more apt to be satisfied with their relationships. They can behave either assertively and independently or compassionately and with nurturance, depending on the demands of the situation (Spence, Deaux, and Helmreich 1985).

The Influence of Schools

Like parents, teachers also indoctrinate children into gender roles, and they, too, seem especially concerned that boys act according to traditional gender expectations. Teachers deny boys the latitude given girls to try out behaviors associated with the opposite sex. Boys who in make-believe play dress up as girls or who like dolls as toys are much more apt to receive a teacher's criticism than are girls who engage in stereotypically masculine

activities (Fagot 1977, 1984). In general, children choosing traditional play styles (boys with transportation toys, hammering, carpentry; girls playing with dolls, dancing, drawing) receive more positive attention from teachers.

Teachers are also quicker to respond to the aggression of boys. In so doing, they inadvertently reward boys with attention when they are disruptive and they communicate to them the expectation that boys have a tendency to fight. At the same time, teachers encourage girls to be dependent by giving them more assistance than they do boys and by paying them more attention when they remain in the teacher's vicinity (Serbin et al. 1973; Fagot 1977).

Children learn gender roles at school in other ways as well. For instance, while 85 percent of elementary-school teachers are women, 79 percent of principals are male (Baker 1984). Repeatedly seeing men in positions of authority over women cannot help but make an impression on children. Underscoring this point, Louis Paradise and Shavaun Wall (1986) found that first-graders attending schools with female principals had less stereotypical views about gender roles than children in schools with male principals. Their findings suggest that the presence of both sexes as models for the role of school principal can have a noticeable positive effect on children's perceptions. In addition, school curricula often reinforce gender roles. Although home economics classes are now open to boys and shop classes to girls, these programs remain largely sex segregated. The same is true of the sports that are played at school. Since the 1970s many schools have tried to combat gender discrimination by organizing coeducational teams. But the "rough" sports (football, ice hockey, wrestling) are still primarily the province of males (see the boxed discussion on the topic of Women in Sports). On the optimistic side, one recent study (Koblinsky and Sugawara 1984) has shown that exposing children to a nonsexist school curriculum may help reduce preferences for sex-typed activities. Preschoolers who participated in a nonsexist program (including photographs, puzzles, block accessories, lotto games, records, and picture books) for a period of six months had less stereotypic attitudes than children in a control group.

In school, children are also exposed to peer influences. Indeed, as more and more American youngsters attend day-care centers and nursery schools, the influence of peers takes on greater significance. Even three-year-olds know "what boys do" and "what girls do," and they exert pressure on one another to conform to these standards. When a child violates gender-role expectations, peers quickly respond: They criticize, complain loudly, and try to stop the deviant's behavior by withdrawing attention or even using physical force. In contrast, when a child acts in gender-stereotyped ways, peers often give encouragement through praise and imitation (Lamb et al. 1980).

The Influence of the Media

Of course, parents and schools are not children's only sources of information on how they are supposed to act. The mass media—TV, radio, magazines, books—are filled with illustrations of traditional gender roles. One study in the early 1970s found that nearly all prize-winning children's books present highly stereotyped and unrealistic images of girls and boys and men and women (Weitzman and Eifler 1972). The ratio of pictures of males to pictures of females was eleven to one; and one-third of the books involved males only. When girls did appear in the children's books, they were nearly always indoors, helping, watching, or loving the book's hero. One set of books, called *Mommies and Daddies*, was not very complimentary to mothers. "Daddies," the author wrote, "know you're big enough and brave enough to do lots of things that mommies think are much too hard." Not one of the books mentioned mothers who work outside the home or showed fathers helping around the house.

A group of researchers (Williams et al. 1987) has recently replicated the 1972 Weitzman study of award-winning books, giving particular attention to the 1980s winners. In contrast to the earlier study, they found that male and female characters are now about equally represented in such books. Furthermore, about one-third of the leading characters are females. In addition, "picture-book" women have begun to move outside the home, but not yet into the labor force. Only one female character among those surveyed worked outside the home, and she was a waitress. These researchers concluded that children's picture books have achieved mixed progress. Female characters are indeed much more visible but still essentially colorless and in line with traditional roles.

Television programs and commercials also reinforce sex-role stereotypes. According to the A. C. Nielsen Company, which specializes in gauging the popularity of TV programs, the television set stays on an average of fifty-three hours a week in homes with preschool children. The average child watches between three and a

half and four hours of TV daily, and half of all twelve-year-olds watch for seven or more hours each day (Nielsen 1985). Television, of course, is filled with examples of traditional gender stereotypes and roles. On children's shows, for instance, there are over twice as many male characters as female ones, and the males are portrayed more favorably. They are typically active, constructive, and rewarded for their actions, whereas the females are deferential and often manipulate others to get their way (Basow 1986; Feldman and Brown 1984). Females are also subordinate on prime-time programs. They are less likely to hold jobs than male characters, and when they do, their occupations are often gender stereotyped (they are the secretaries, nurses, teachers). Male characters, in contrast, are usually the adventurous ones (the detectives, the police officers), and they are over twice as likely as female characters to be competent and self-assured. This stereotyped image of men as competent also occurs in TV commercials (Courtney and Whipple 1983; Downs and Harrison 1985). The knowledgeable, authoritative voice-overs that describe a product's virtues are almost all male.

Does this barrage of gender stereotypes on American TV influence children's thinking? There is evidence that it does. In one study, heavy TV watchers (twenty-five hours or more a week) held more traditional ideas about gender than children who watched ten hours or less a week (Fruch and McGhee 1975). But it seems that the type of TV program watched makes a difference. Children who watch more educational TV than commercial programs tend to have *less* gender stereotyped notions than their peers (Repetti 1984). This may be because educational television is less blatantly sexist in depicting the gender roles. So perhaps, with concerted effort, the mass media could actually be used to help change gender stereotypes.

PERSISTENCE AND CHANGE IN GENDER ROLES

In 1983 *Fortune* magazine surveyed thirty-three of the thirty-four women who graduated in 1973 from the Harvard Business School MBA program. This was the first class in which at least 5 percent of the students were women (Rowan 1983). Ten years after graduation, all but one were working full-time; eighteen had married, and

Women in Sports

Carol Mann, a highly successful professional golfer, knows how hard it is for women to make it in the world of sports. Here is how she describes the obstacles that female athletes encounter, based on her own experience:

> The serious athlete to me is one who is committed to excellence at any level, at any age, in any endeavor, and in either sex. This commitment begins with a dream—a sense of talent and skill and determination to make that dream come true. That sense I call "the burn."
>
> As a male in our society grows up, that burn is rewarded, praised, encouraged, and supported. . . . As a female in our society grows up, the burn is thwarted, barricaded, obstacled, challenged, and condemned. And many women burn out going through all those phases of nonacceptance. (Mann 1984, p. 20)

The widespread practice of discouraging women from excelling at sports has far-reaching consequences. It is not just that entry into a potential career has been made harder, as occurred in Carol Mann's case. It is also that women who are steered away from sports miss an important part of socialization that is available to males.

Team sports teach boys to be assertive and competitive, to cooperate with others and delegate responsibilities, to cultivate leadership potential, and to set goals and strategies while taking calculated risks. These traits are the very ones needed for success in corporate management. Girls who never involve themselves in sports have less of a chance to acquire them. And ironically, even girls who do take up a sport are often at a disadvantage. Because many "female" sports (such as skating, gymnastics, or horseback riding) are not team-oriented, girls miss out on many of the lessons that boys are steeped in.

Legislation is helping to change this pattern. Title IX of the Educational Amendments Act of 1972 prohibited sex discrimination in intercollegiate athletics at schools that receive federal funding. Almost overnight new programs in women's sports sprang up at colleges and universities. Today there are over thirty women's varsity sports in this country, compared with the four or five that existed at most schools in the early seventies. About 15,000 athletic scholarships are now awarded to women each year, compared with none before Title IX was enacted. Women's participation in intercollegiate athletics has grown rapidly, too. In 1972 there were only about 30,000 female college athletes in the

United States; in 1985 there were over 150,000 (Alfano 1985). During the same years, women's professional athletics have also acquired new vitality. For instance, in 1970 the amount of prize money available on the women's tennis circuit was only $200,500. By 1980 this figure had jumped to $9.2 million (Basow 1986).

But participation and prize money are one thing, and performance is another. Are women as well-suited to excelling in sports as men? Women's recent performance records in a wide variety of competitions suggest that the answer is unquestionably yes. In running events, the pace of women's improvements has been particularly impressive. For example, in 1971 the women's world record for running 1,500 meters was off the world record for men by about 20 percent. Just ten years later, in 1981, that performance difference had dropped to less than 10 percent (Jordan 1983). The male-female performance gap in swimming events is now also only 10 percent or less (Doyle 1986). A swimmer who finished the 400-meter freestyle in the same time that won the event for men in the 1964 Olympics would have come in only fifth among women in the 1980 Olympics (Gelman 1981).

Women are at an advantage in long-distance events that require leg stamina and endurance, because

fourteen were mothers. The top earner was making more than $200,000; four others were making at least $100,000; nine were making less than $50,000. Even so, these women were earning less than their male classmates, 35 percent of whom were earning more than $100,000. Much the same picture emerged for the Princeton undergraduate class of 1973, the first to include women. The median salary of the men in the class was $46,000 while the median salary of the women

was only $33,000 (Geist 1983). The Princeton women did not attribute this gap to discrimination. Instead, they attributed it to their having changed jobs to accommodate a spouse or their having taken time off from work to raise children. What they overlooked in giving these explanations was the extent to which traditional gender roles result in subtle discrimination against women by shaping ideas about the duties of a "good" wife and mother.

women's leg muscles are relatively strong and their extra body fat supplies energy for longer periods. These two factors help explain why women have beaten the fastest male round-trip swim of the English Channel by a full three hours. They also help explain why, in long-distance running events, "women tend to do better relative to men the longer the distance gets" (Doyle 1986, p. 49). But women are at a disadvantage when it comes to upper-body strength, a disadvantage that will probably always exist because men have broader shoulders, larger biceps, and longer arms. This means that men will continue to have an edge over women in events that require powerful lifting, pulling, or throwing.

How much have public attitudes toward women in sports changed in recent years? Are women athletes still encountering such strong negative reactions as Carol Mann did? As with such questions relating to other aspects of gender-role change, the answer is mixed. On the one hand, society still tries to reserve certain kinds of sports for men. Most events that involve very aggressive body contact (such as football and boxing) are still largely the province of males. Society prefers to see women in sports that stress grace and beauty (swimming, diving, tennis, and gymnastics, for ex-

Teamwork, grittiness, aggressiveness, and strength . . . Patience, intuition, touch, and grace . . . Female athletes have increasingly demonstrated that they have the "right stuff"—a remarkable potential for achievement in a number of sports. Participation in team sports also gives females a chance to learn the lessons of cooperation, competitiveness, goalsetting, and assertiveness that once only males received. (UPI/Bettmann Newsphotos.)

ample). When females participate in competitions generally considered masculine, they tend to use pastel-colored gear and clothing to avoid being labeled unfeminine (Snyder and Spreitzer 1983). On the other hand, women today have made spectacular strides in athletics, improving on what

the experts predicted of them just a few short years ago. Over and over, female athletes have proven both their psychological and physical resilience and hardiness. Their record has challenged many popular assumptions about the innate capacities and limitations of women in sports.

Trends Among Women

The career paths of both the Harvard and the Princeton women illustrate a persistent trend: Although women have made great strides toward achieving equal opportunities, they are far from being on a totally equal footing with men in the workplace (Strober 1982; Pear 1987). For one thing, the highest ranks in business and government are still not as open to females as they are to males.

Women must struggle hard to obtain what is considered the white, middle-class male's birthright. While a number of women have indeed gained promotions since 1970, women managers remain a small proportion of employed women. In reality, the concentration of most women in subordinate positions, particularly in the clerical work force, persists (Blum and Smith 1988). In addition, many women find it very hard to ignore the expectations that society has regarding their proper place within the family. So women today often assume many of the responsibilities of a traditional wife and mother side by side with the demands of a full-time job. This makes for a substantial amount of role strain and conflict.

Although some see the resistance of men as a major obstacle that is slowing women's further progress toward equality, the picture is actually much more complex. Women themselves have very different views of how best to elevate their position in society. Some women are feminists who are committed to a gender-equal society and economic independence for women. Now that many of the early battles for job opportunities have been won, today's feminists often turn their attention to the new struggles that modern working women face. In particular, they want to help women deal with the dual stresses of career and family. They are therefore working toward such goals as better maternity leave benefits, more quality day-care centers, more flexible work schedules, and more tax deductions for child care (Chavez 1987; Hewlett 1986).

But not all American women are avowed feminists. Some who support feminist goals do not consider themselves a part of the movement. Some others are decidedly antifeminists who think that feminists have brought about destructive change in gender roles. These women prefer a traditional life of marriage and children. Traditionalists fear that women are rapidly losing the protective structures that once enabled them to be full-time homemakers. Sociologist Sylvia Hewlett describes the outlook of traditionalists this way:

> At bottom traditional women see feminists as traitors and fools. They are traitors because they undermine the traditional family-support systems for other women and their children. And they are fools because they do not seem to understand that there is no point in alienating men. Most women want children, and most women have no alternative to marriage if they want decent lives for themselves and their children. Traditionalists see feminists as out of touch with reality. Only elite East Coast "libbers" would be foolish enough to imagine that independence can be found in the labor market, a truth that Nora Ephron discovered in *Heartburn*. "Wives went out into the world free at last, single again and discovered the horrible truth: that they were sellers in a buyer's market and that the major concrete achievement of the woman's movement in the 1970s was the Dutch treat." (Hewlett 1986, pp. 332–333)

But movements are known to generate counter-movements, and during the 1980s American feminism has found itself opposed on a number of fronts. Anti-abortion groups have waged active campaigns. Opponents of the ERA have successfully impeded its ratification by Congress. In sum, feminist and anti-feminist camps have diametrically opposed ideas about what is in women's best interest. This clash of goals and values has significantly slowed the pace at which further social change in gender roles is occurring.

Trends Among Men

Women are not alone in exhibiting signs of confusion and division. Men, too, currently disagree about the future of gender roles. Clyde Franklin (1984) has described four male responses to the changes that have already taken place. "Classical" men cling to traditional gender notions and staunchly resist change. They decry the erosion of male power and prerogatives as women have gained greater equality. To them the only good change would be to turn back the clock to the days when "men were men" and "women were women." Somewhat more progressive than classical men are routine "masculinists." On the surface, they claim to agree with the aims of the women's movement, but their actual behavior shows lingering prejudice. "Anomic" men, in contrast, genuinely accept the concept of sexual equality, yet they remain confused over what the proper roles of men and women should be. Many American males today fall into this category. Out of their confusion they may eventually evolve into what Franklin calls humanists. Humanists actively work to create male and female roles without the traditional gender stereotypes and expectations. Their goal is a society in which most men and women are androgynous—that is, they behave in either "masculine" or "feminine" ways, depending upon the situation.

Supporting such change, however, does not come easily for many men. Joseph Pleck (1983) believes that the complex power relations between the sexes are difficult to undo because of the functions they serve. These functions are especially compelling from the male point of view. For instance, women, according to Pleck, by constituting a large underclass, a group with a status below which most men can never fall, thus provide a status cushion for men. Such an underclass eases the stress experienced by men who lose out in all-male social and economic competition. Women in their traditional roles also provide men with a refuge from the tensions of the competitive male world. The traditional woman is someone in whom a man can confide without fear that his self-revelations will be used against him. Finally, Pleck sees the traditional woman as a means by which men validate their masculinity. The wife who is dependent on her husband and submits to his wishes gives the husband the satisfying feeling that he is a "real" man. With all these functions that traditional gender roles offer them, it is no wonder that many men are slow to accept change in the status quo. As individuals, many men might want to change their behavior, but there are numerous social forces that work against it.

Many men are also poorly informed about the problems that women face. They think of women in traditional terms, as enjoying the support and protection of men. They ask why women would want to change this in some ways privileged status. What they fail to take into account is the fact that today, in addition to being homemakers, the majority of women hold paid jobs, often out of financial necessity. There are also a growing number of women who are postponing marriage, or who marry briefly and then divorce, frequently with children to support. For these women reduction in gender inequalities is not just desirable, it is often a matter of survival. But some men equate a rise in the status of women with a drop in the status of men. They are convinced that whatever social and economic gains women make will necessarily come at the expense of men.

The opposition of some men to gender-role change is reflected in the movement for "men's rights," which started in the late 1970s. Its largest and most well-structured arm is an organization called Free Men, which has members across the country in over thirty-five states. The main goal of Free Men is to change laws it believes discriminate against males, particularly in their roles as husbands and fathers. For instance, Free Men is deeply involved in improving the position of men in regard to alimony laws, child custody, and visitation rights (Doyle 1985). This organization's target is often the feminist woman and her view that females are still the oppressed sex in this country. According to members of Free Men, the pendulum has swung so far in the

If gender equality often means greater economic and political independence for women, for men it may mean liberation from the achievement-oriented workplace—participating more fully in child-rearing and in the nurturing tasks of family life. (Spencer Grant/Photo Researchers, Inc.)

direction of granting women rights that men are often now the unfairly treated ones.

On the opposite side are those men who are working toward the demise of traditional gender roles and distinctions—the men whom Franklin calls humanists. The National Organization of Changing Men (NOCM), formed in 1983, is one arm of this movement. NOCM is committed to full equality and justice for both sexes, including gay and lesbian minorities. As yet its membership is estimated to be only 550 (Franklin 1984). But the very emergence of such an organization attests to the growing awareness that change in male-female relationships depends upon men as well as women.

SUMMARY

1. The system of gender stratification, in which there is an unequal distribution of rewards between men and women, has long existed throughout the world. In terms of rewards, women typically have lower status, and enjoy less income, power, wealth, prestige, and personal freedom. This system also involves gender roles—the different behavior patterns expected of men and women in our society. Related to gender roles are gender stereotypes, oversimplified but strongly held ideas about the essential (or natural) characteristics of males and females.

2. Although genes and hormones determine sex (that is, male or female biology), they do not determine gender (the set of conceptions that people have regarding "masculine" and "feminine" characteristics). Thus we cannot assume that males and females are born with different abilities and temperaments that make them naturally suited for different gender roles.

3. Psychologists have attempted to identify sex differences in personality and ability. Generally, the findings show that sex differences are far smaller than people expect. Moreover, for any particular trait there exists a wide range of variation in its expression among both males and females, and there is considerable overlap between the ranges of the sexes. Thus, on the average, men and women are psychologically very similar, with one exception being their overall level of expressed aggression. Social scientists continue to debate whether the differences in aggression are a matter of biology or of social learning.

4. The considerable variability that social scientists find from one society to another in the behavior patterns of men and women has made them skeptical of claims that biological factors are the primary source of gender ideas and arrangements. Taken as a whole, the cross-cultural evidence supports the view that gender roles are in large part the result of social and environmental forces that encourage conformity to such roles.

5. The number of women in the workforce has increased steadily since the turn of the century due to factors such as World War II, a troubled economy, a high divorce rate, and the Women's Movement. But a pattern of gender inequality on the job continues. Women still tend to be channeled into different occupations from men and to earn less than men do for performing identical jobs. One theory that seeks to explain this phenomenon is the human capital explanation. According to this view, a woman's investment in her work-related credentials is generally poorer than a man's with the result that most women end up in lower-paying jobs.

6. Gender stratification in the political sphere is also very strong in the United States, though there are some signs that attitudes are changing. The trend today shows an increasing number of women in political occupations. Because of their high visibility, these women help to change people's ideas about women in public office.

7. Equal rights for women have been bolstered by feminist movements such as the National Organization for Women (NOW) and the Women's Equity Action League (WEAL). Such organizations have bombarded government with cases of gender discrimination and proposals for more equal treatment under the law. In 1972, the Equal Rights Amendment to the Constitution was approved and presented for ratification by Congress, but, as of today, has still not been passed as law.

8. The degree to which women have been subordinate in American society has varied over time, from the colonial era to the present. The advent of industrialism gradually weakened the economic partnership that had formerly existed between husbands and wives and encouraged a separation of activities. If anything, modern times have intensified this polarity between men as breadwinners and women as caretakers of home and family. The roles expected of American women today are even more demanding, for a majority of women are now both paid employees and centers of home and family.

9. American women were traditionally expected to want marriage and a family and to put the family first; to depend on their husbands, financially and socially; to live vicariously through their husbands and children; to be passive, rather than aggressive and self-assertive; to be attractive, loving, and sympathetic. American men were traditionally expected to be good providers and to be competitive, achieving, self-reliant, and emotionally controlled. Each of these sets of beliefs has involved certain costs and benefits for each of the sexes, and each involves role conflicts.

10. The functional perspective argues that men and women have assumed specified gender roles that are highly complementary and thus ensure that society runs smoothly. The power perspective emphasizes that gender roles involve the domination of one sex over the other—usually, male over female—and reflect the value of economic contributions of men and women.

11. Gender stereotypes support traditional gender roles. They also help to reinforce behaviors that people assume are "natural." Concurrently, gender roles perpetuate gender stereotypes. Gender roles are learned through the process of socialization and are taught to us by teachers, parents, and the media, to name a few. With some effort, it may be possible to use the power of the mass media to help change gender stereotypes.

12. Though the future of gender roles is unclear, the trend today is a slow movement toward equality. Men and women alike are trying, through organizations working toward the demise of traditional gender roles and stereotypes, to close the gender gap.

GLOSSARY

Androgynous. Combining the traits of both male and female.

Chromosomes. Threadlike structures in each cell of the body that carry genes within them.

Feminist. Person with a strong sense of women's shared experiences and problems and a strong commitment to improving the position of females in society.

Gender. Refers to all the nonbiological traits assigned to men and women.

Gender roles. The distinct tasks and activities that society assigns to each sex.

Gender stereotypes. Oversimplified but strongly held ideas about the characteristics of males and females.

Gender stratification. The assigning of men and women to unequal positions in the social hierarchy.

Genes. The determiners of hereditary characteristics.

Hormones. Chemical substances that are produced by the cells and that stimulate or inhibit specific physiological processes.

Human capital. Any capabilities people might acquire by making investments in improving their marketability as workers.

Machismo. Compulsive masculinity, evidenced in posturing, boasting, and an exploitive attitude toward women.

Patriarchy. A society in which the father is the unquestioned head of the family and descent is figured through the male line.

CHAPTER 13
Race and Ethnic Relations

Edmund Perry was a bright and promising young man from Harlem, where his family's roots went back five generations. His family was close, hardworking, God-fearing. In junior high school, Perry tested above the twelfth-grade level in both math and reading. He won a full scholarship to the elite and prestigious Phillips Exeter Academy, a two-centuries-old boarding school in New Hampshire that is a training ground for the best colleges in the nation. Perry spent his junior year in Spain. He graduated from Exeter with honors and a scholarship to Stanford. During the summer between high school and college, he lived at home and earned $175 a week as a messenger for a Wall Street firm. But during that summer, too, Perry mugged a white plainclothes policeman and was shot to death. The policeman was cleared by a grand jury. Nearly two dozen witnesses supported his story. Fifteen hundred people turned up for Edmund Perry's funeral, some to praise this exemplary young man, others to decry the society that had destroyed him.

Another black man killed by violence? Another victim of the system? Another statistic? But Edmund Perry wasn't *supposed* to be another statistic, unless it was a glowing one. He was *supposed* to make it out of the ghetto. He had a strong family behind him, he had ambition and talent, he had the backing of an affirmative-action program, he had scholarships and honors. His death from a street crime surprised many people—but not everyone. One friend of Perry's, a black man who had grown up poor, gone to Yale, and

succeeded in the white business world, said that Perry's death was almost a suicide:

> All this black-white stuff was really grinding him down, and he knew it wasn't going to go away. Yeah, he had gone to Exeter, and yeah, he was going to Stanford, but he was never going to be a member of the club. He was always going to be Eddie Perry, the smart black. Even if he wanted to be different, Harlem wasn't going to let him. That boy was in a box, and he was going to have to deal with that box all the rest of his life. (Anson 1987, p. 45)

It is easy enough to dismiss Perry for putting himself in that box and to argue that with so much social support, he might have seen a way out of it. After all, others have broken through the walls between ethnic and class groups. But that is to underestimate the enormous difficulties that anyone confronts in trying to move between two different social worlds, with their vastly different social structures, values, norms, and opportunities. These different social worlds confer privilege and power on some in vast disproportion to what they give to others. To grow up in a black ghetto is to be gravely *dis*advantaged, to be essentially powerless. When Edmund Perry moved to that other—powerful, privileged, elite—social world, he was, as a black woman said who made the same transition, "in an environment where he was constantly being reminded how powerless he really was. . . . The trouble is, you really aren't a part of your own neighborhood anymore, either"

349

(Anson 1987, p. 39). To be powerless, to be the eternal outsider, to be angry about it, and to act on that anger can be fatal.

The history of race and ethnic relations in this and other countries is that of many people who, like Edmund Perry, feel pulled between separate social worlds. The sense of a divided self is familiar to members of minority groups and to immigrants all over the world. In some cases, minority resistance to separation from the larger society may take forms ranging from suppressed rage to outright rebellion. In other cases, separation is a source of ethnic pride and a sense of community; when this is the case, it may be a basis for coexistence and success.

What makes a minority group in sociological terms? How and why are some groups discriminated against? How do different societies respond to new and alien groups? What is racism? Why does racial and ethnic diversity lead to coexistence in some instances but to bitter inequality in others? In this chapter, we will try to answer these and other questions. In our twentieth-century global village, the answers and solutions to these questions and problems are essential both to the future of American society and to the future of worldwide racial and ethnic relations.

BASIC CONCEPTS

The basic terms and concepts discussed in this chapter are probably very familiar to you. But it is important for a number of reasons to pin down their sociological meanings as precisely as we can.

Minority Groups

Most societies contain **minority groups,** or people whose physical appearance or cultural characteristics mark them as being different from the dominant group *and* subject them to unequal treatment. To sociologists, the term *minority* implies social as opposed to numerical disadvantage. It is entirely possible for a group to be a numerical minority but to dominate others by virtue of power, privilege, and status. White Anglo-Saxon men are a numerical minority in the United States, but they certainly do not have the sociological characteristics of a minority group. It is also entirely possible for a minority group to outnumber the rest of the population but to remain subordinate in power and to have few or none of the social and economic opportunities that give people access to power. In South Africa, for example, non-whites make up 80 percent of the population. Yet they are denied access to wealth, education, income, and other paths to power and equality by the dominant white minority.

In some societies, blacks hold the power, and it is they who discriminate against others. In Uganda, the black government confiscated the property of Indian citizens and expelled them from the country. Blacks in other East African nations, such as Kenya, also resent their Asian minorities. The Japanese, a racially homogeneous society, resent the non-Japanese Asians and Indians who enter Japan to look for work. Minorities of Chinese ancestry living in several nations in Southeast Asia also find themselves the victims of discrimination and prejudice at the hands of other Asians. So do Central American Indians in Mexico, Hungarians in Romania, gypsies in Greece, Armenians in Turkey, aborigines in white Australia. . . . The list could go on and on.

In addition, in many societies, our own included, children (who have virtually no legal rights), the aged, and women (who make up 53 percent of the American population but occupy few positions of power) also have some characteristics of minority groups. Even the idea of the United States as a melting pot of many groups, an idea that on the surface describes a democratic blending, can be seen as the ideology of a dominant group rather than as a description of actual relations between dominant and minority groups.

Thus, minority and dominant groups may reflect patterns of economic and political domination in the power structure of a society. What other factors contribute to the formation of these groups? Primarily, race and ethnicity, and the conflict these social perceptions can engender.

Race and Ethnicity

To all appearances, conflict and competition between ethnic and racial groups are less the exception than the

The theme of a "Rainbow Coalition," introduced in the Rev. Jesse Jackson's 1984 campaign for the Democratic presidential nomination, celebrates both the perceived differences of race and ethnicity and the common humanity underlying such distinctions. Strong identification with a particular racial or ethnic group can be a source of security and self-esteem. (Jean Anderson/The Stock Market.)

rule. Everywhere, race and ethnicity are social facts that significantly affect people's life chances and their relations with members of other groups.

From a biological perspective, a race may seem to be a population that has bred through enough generations to develop distinctive characteristics, which are transmitted genetically. However, the limitations, and even the essential meaninglessness, of this sort of definition soon become apparent. When does a characteristic become distinctive, if there is a great deal of overlap and interbreeding, which of course there is? The biological and physical "facts" are hazy. And in any case, social facts can be very different from biological facts. To sociologists, race is a *social construct*. They study racial differences because people *think* that these differences are significant and act accordingly, because such perceptions have social consequences. Thus, **race** denotes a group of people who perceive themselves and are perceived by others as possessing certain distinctive and hereditary traits. These physical traits, in turn, are assumed to be related to moral, intellectual, and other nonphysical attributes (Van der Berghe 1978). As a result, members of a race tend to think they are different from other groups of people, and other groups tend to treat them as if they were. So a race exists in the perceptions and beliefs of its beholders.

The concept of ethnicity, like that of race, is a social construct. But whereas race is based on the perception of *physical* differences, ethnicity is based on the perception of *cultural* differences. An **ethnic group** is a group of people who perceive themselves and are perceived by others as sharing cultural traits such as language, religion, family customs, and preferences in food. Polish Americans, French Canadians, Jews, Puerto Ricans, and the Navajo are all examples of ethnic groups. The extent to which ethnic group members actually share unique cultural traits is less important than that they and others *believe* that they are ethnically distinct. Thus ethnicity, like race, is a label that people create and apply.

What are the social consequences of these labels? They are, first of all, not necessarily negative. One positive consequence is a sense of "peoplehood" (Gordon 1978), a sense of identification with a relatively small segment of the world's population—those whose ancestry or heritage make them "our own kind." Although we may live and interact with people of other racial and ethnic backgrounds, we continue to feel that they are somehow different. Being different—for example, being black and therefore different from whites—is not just an identity imposed by the other group—say, the whites; it also means participation in a particular cultural tradition, which can reinforce self-esteem. Of course, the consciousness of oneness and the identity that ideas of race and ethnicity provide also can lead to alienation, as it seems to have done for Edmund Perry: If you are not one of "us," then you are one of "them." For Perry, the feelings of identification and of alienation were both strong.

But why is this sense of racial and ethnic identity so compelling? One reason is that it may satisfy an important *psychological* need. As Erich Fromm wrote in 1941:

> This identity with nature, clan, religion, gives the individual security. He belongs to, he is rooted in, a structuralized whole in which he has an unquestionable place. He may suffer from hunger or suppression but he does not suffer from the worst of all pains—complete aloneness and doubt. (Quoted in Isaacs 1975)

This comforting sense of belonging—which Perry, to his private anguish, may have lost—may be one reason that racial and ethnic identities have persisted despite the homogenizing tendencies of modern industrial life.

But a sense of racial and ethnic identity may be compelling for another reason, too—in a sense, a structural reason. Social solidarity with others whom one considers like oneself can serve important economic and political interests. Looked at from the power perspective, for example, the nineteenth-century belief in a superior white race fueled colonial expansion and served as a justification for economic exploitation. Similarly, in the twentieth century, the shared racial consciousness of African blacks did much to unite previously warring tribes in the struggle for independence. From this perspective, then, racial and ethnic bonds can be instrumental in achieving economic and political goals.

Another possible social consequence of race and ethnicity, and of the formation of minority and dominant groupings based on race and ethnicity, is **racism,** the doctrine (or a policy based on the doctrine) that some races are inherently inferior and some inherently superior to others. This doctrine in turn has throughout history served numerous social, political, economic, and personal purposes; when it was backed up by supposed scientific evidence, it often led to tragic results, as we will see in this chapter.

Prejudice and Discrimination

When Edmund Perry was a child, he heard that Martin Luther King, Jr., and the Kennedys had been assassinated, and he told his mother that "white people are the Devil, because they kill the people who are trying to help us." His mother replied that it is wrong to judge people by the color of their skin (Anson 1987, p. 37). Mrs. Perry was giving her son a lesson in *un*learning prejudice. **Prejudice** is a categorical predisposition to like or dislike people for their real or imagined social characteristics. Typically, such characteristics are associated with race, religion, ethnic group, sexual orientation, or even physical disabilities. People can be said to be prejudiced when they are convinced that all members of a group have the same qualities, such as being immoral, violent, and backward (or moral, peace-loving, and brilliant). They cannot see them as individuals and ignore evidence that would refute their convictions. In other words, they perceive everyone in a group in distorted ways, according to their inflexible standard.

Prejudice is a state of mind, but discrimination is actual behavior. **Discrimination** refers to the act of disqualifying or mistreating people on the basis of their group membership. A person who discriminates is not necessarily prejudiced. For example, a black store owner may decide not to hire Jews, not because he himself is prejudiced against Jews, but because he believes that his customers are. But discrimination does tend to create and support prejudice. Conversely, prejudice also tends to create and support discrimination. When minority group members are considered inferior and unsuited to higher-status occupations, discrimination against them seems appropriate. Prejudice and discrimination work together to sustain racial and ethnic stratification. They can be seen as primary components of racism, and are themselves made up of a whole constellation of beliefs and actions.

The distinction between prejudice and discrimination is important. We often hear it said, "You cannot legislate against prejudice." This argument has been advanced by people who say that laws are ineffective for combating racism. What they overlook is that such laws are designed mainly to deter discrimination. Just as laws against murder are designed not to root out people's desire to kill but to prevent them from acting on those desires, so antidiscrimination laws are designed to prevent people from acting in certain ways. On the other hand, it is not unusual for people to bring their attitudes into line with their actions. As legal barriers against discrimination have been erected, people from different racial or ethnic groups have begun to interact in new, unimpeded ways, and many of their prejudices have indeed been undermined.

Institutional Discrimination

At the level of the individual, prejudice and discrimination take place in everyday interactions with others. Discrimination also exists at the institutional level. **Institutional discrimination** refers to the policies and programs that systematically deny opportunities and equal rights to members of particular groups. For example, South Africa's ironclad separation of whites and nonwhites, called **apartheid,** is written into the country's very laws and embedded in its schools and textbooks, politics, land ownership, and housing (see the accompanying box, "South Africa's Apartheid").

The power perspective has contributed a great deal to the sociological analysis of institutional discrimination. As a number of sociologists have stressed, social arrangements in the United States ensure that critical decisions are made, issues defined, and resources allocated in ways that work to the advantage of whites and to the disadvantage of blacks and Hispanics (Allen and Farley 1986; Wilson and Aponte 1985). Take the issue of toxic waste disposal, an issue that would seem to be far removed from racial issues. Toxic waste dumps usually are located in areas where there are predominantly nonwhite residents (Williams 1987). Many sociologists would not be surprised; they would argue that the unequal distribution of power allows dominant groups to endanger the health of the nonwhite minority. In the distribution of both the benefits and costs of production, inequality is perpetuated by the social structure, violating the professed social goals of equal opportunity and social justice (Haar and Fessler 1986).

Again, it is important to recognize that schools, hospitals, factories, banks, and other institutions do not have to be staffed by prejudiced people to create discrimination. Institutional discrimination can very well be—and often is—faceless and impersonal. For instance, employers ordinarily require that the people they hire for certain positions have a certain level of formal education, such as a high school diploma or college degree. When these standards are uniformly applied to all job applicants, people who have not had the opportunity to gain the necessary credentials are excluded. If members of minority groups systematically get less than adequate schooling, they enter the job market educationally handicapped, and they cannot compete with those who have the required test scores, diplomas, degrees, and certificates (McLemore 1983). The recognition of this ingrained discrimination was responsible for Edmund Perry being taken out of the minority-dominated public schools of Harlem (after Perry was singled out for his intellectual promise) and placed on a course that would provide him with the credentials necessary for competing for a higher-status job.

The fact is that institutional discrimination takes many forms. Later on in this chapter, we will discuss attempts to overcome it. Most of these attempts have focused on *desegregating* schools, workplaces, housing, and other areas of life—that is to say, creating laws and customs that are designed to reverse the effects of segregation.

Segregation and Integration

When people from different racial and ethnic groups are physically and socially separated by custom or by law, they are said to be **segregated.** When they are not separated by race or ethnicity, they are said to be **integrated.** Segregation is really a form of institutional discrimination. It serves to maintain prejudice, for it prevents the contact that might disprove stereotypes.

A few strands of barbed wire are the least of the barriers before these black children of South Africa, whose life chances are severely limited by a rigid system of institutional discrimination. (United Nations.)

South Africa's Apartheid

Perhaps nowhere in the world are racial prejudice and discrimination so deeply ingrained in a nation's laws and customs than they are in South Africa. In the view of those who hold power in South Africa, race is an utterly basic division among people, and race determines not only physical but cultural qualities (Thompson 1985). Under South Africa's laws of *apartheid*—literally, "apartness"—all South Africans must be classified by race. That classification determines where they may live, jobs they may hold, schools they can attend, and how they will be governed. The most powerful racial group, the "whites" (those descended from Europeans) make up a numerical minority (15.7 percent of the population). The least powerful groups make up the numerical majority. They are: "Indians" (2.8 percent of the population), the descendants of Indians and Asians; "Coloureds" (9.1 percent), people of mixed descent; and native black "Africans" (72.4 percent). All of these groups are set apart from the whites and discriminated against by South African law (Thompson 1985).

Although those who oppose apartheid revile it as *baasskap* ("domination" in Afrikaans, the language of the white minority), those who support it call it "cooperative coexistence" (Omond 1986). The whites who believe most zealously that apartheid is a *moral* system are the Afrikaners, white descendants of Dutch, German, French, and other northern Europeans who came to South Africa in the 1600s and 1700s. According to the Afrikaners, white Christians are destined by God to remain apart and above all other races. Said one Afrikaner of the ideal of racial apartheid, "The more consistently the policy of apartness could be applied, the greater would be the security for the purity of our blood and the surer our unadulterated European racial survival" (quoted in Thompson 1985, p. 44). There are many South African religious leaders, both black and white, who *oppose* apartheid on moral grounds. And, of course, both sides claim biblical authority.

The earliest European settlers competed with the native Africans for the land and its abundant natural resources. (Beneath the rich soil lie deposits of coal, diamonds, and gold.) White hunting parties, wars, and smallpox killed off many blacks. Then the British arrived in the early 1800s. Seeking economic and political control, they pushed the Dutch settlers inland to rural areas, out of the cities (Omond 1986). By the end of the 1800s, tensions between Afrikaners and the British finally led to the Boer War (1899–1902), in which the Afrikaners were defeated—at least for the moment. South Africa did not become politically independent from Britain until 1961, but it was self-governing long before that, and political power became concentrated again in the hands of the Afrikaner minority. All along, Afrikaner leaders had been advocating apartheid as a tool for resisting British imperialism. In the elections of 1948, there was a victory by the Afrikaners' National Party,

In a segregated society, only certain types of contact between the dominant group and the minority group are allowed. Members of the subordinate group cannot live where those in the dominant group live, they cannot join the same clubs and organizations, and they often cannot use the same public facilities (everything from drinking fountains, public transportation, restaurants, and movie theaters to restrooms, park benches, and beaches). Again, segregation reinforces inequalities in income, power, and prestige. Its most extreme expression is to be found in societies where the dominant group perceives the minority as a threat to the established order, as in South Africa (Berry and Tischler 1978; Forbes 1985).

Where does American society fall? Even though there have been many efforts toward integration of whites and nonwhites, and even though outright segregation is illegal in this country, many aspects of life here continue for all practical purposes to be segregated. For example, minority-dominated public schools in Harlem could be described as segregated; so could the white-dominated prep school Edmund Perry attended. And continued high levels of residential segregation—for blacks, Hispanics, and Asians—have been shown to be closely linked to lower earnings for these three groups (Tienda and Lii 1987). This is not to say that some progress has not been made. Nevertheless, the issue is a complex one.

which meant that apartheid could become the law of the land.

In South Africa today, racial segregation and discrimination are inescapable. Apartheid is ruthlessly enforced by the police power of the state. One of the bulwarks of apartheid is a system of ten "homelands" for blacks that are supposed to eventually become independent states. Four of the homelands have already been granted independence, but no other country in the world recognizes them. Blacks are assigned to homelands and therefore are not considered citizens of South Africa. This policy ensures that black Africans can live and own land only in scattered, squalid, impoverished settlements. The land is so poor and the settlements so underdeveloped that black workers must leave it for jobs in white areas.

Another bulwark of apartheid reviled by its opponents are the separate parliaments for whites, Coloureds, and Indians. Blacks are not represented at all. They conduct their politics in the homelands, where they theoretically have voting and other rights, though critics regard these rights as a sham. Thus, blacks are stripped of their rights and prevented from upsetting the status quo. What the whites fear of course is that, being a numerical majority, blacks in parliament could vote themselves *real* political power. After that, the proponents of apartheid think, would follow such evils as desegregation and majority rule (Wilmot 1987).

Since 1977, and to this day, a series of security laws have allowed the government and police virtually blanket powers to ban, arrest, and hold without trial those (including children, in some cases) who criticize or work against the apartheid system. The government claims it has reformed certain apartheid laws, such as the pass laws (repealed in 1985), which required blacks to carry passbooks stating their places of residence and work. But at the same time the government's emergency powers have been consistently extended. This has meant a large number of arrests, injuries, and deaths, in a nation that is in effect a police state.

Apartheid has made South Africa a pariah among nations. Many of those who oppose apartheid have suggested using economic measures against South Africa in order to undermine the government's power. The proposed measures include divestment by corporations, trade embargoes, economic sanctions, financial support for black businesses, and the like. In 1986 and 1987, more than 100 American companies did leave South Africa. Critics of divestment, however, claim that it will only hurt South African blacks and that selling profitable companies to white South Africans at windfall prices will only make matters worse.

Despite protests, demonstrations of solidarity, and sanctions, apartheid continues. Today in South Africa black unrest is pervasive and many fear the next turn of events. As heavily armed white police stand by, blacks organize, protest, and chant that they *shall* overcome.

WHEN DIFFERENT GROUPS MEET: PATTERNS OF GROUP RELATIONS

Viewed from one perspective, human history has consisted of a long series of contacts between different racial and ethnic groups. Archaeological evidence shows that, long before the dawn of history, human populations were on the move. The migrations of the early Hebrews recounted in the Old Testament were hardly unique (Berry and Tischler 1978). Such contacts were marked by curiosity, conflict, accommodation, and occasionally fusion into new physical and cultural types (Shibutani and Kwan 1965). In this section, we will consider how sociologists have analyzed these basic patterns.

Patterns of Conflict and Domination

When people of different racial and ethnic groups come into contact, they tend to judge others by the standards of their own way of life. As we saw in Chapter 4 ("Culture"), this attitude is known as *ethnocentrism*. When people are strongly ethnocentric (as are the white Afrikaners), they distrust outsiders, seeing them as symbols of strangeness, evil, and danger. To an ethnocentric people, another people's rituals seem sacrilegious, their customs uncivilized, their laws incomprehensible, and their gods pagan. Racism finds fertile soil in the intense glorification of the in-group and loathing of the out-group (Noel 1972; Vander Zanden 1983).

When ethnocentrism is coupled with *intergroup competition* for territory and scarce or desired resources, the results are usually explosive. As mentioned in the box on apartheid, for example, the Afrikaners killed many of the native blacks with whom they were competing for land. Ethnocentrism can fuel and be used to justify competition; the competition can in turn heat up ethnocentrism. The competition for resources, activating prejudice and discrimination, begins to take on racist overtones.

Colonialism: Economic and Political Subjugation

The economic takeover of one nation by another, more powerful nation, and the subsequent political and social domination of the native population is called **colonialism.** When the British settled in South Africa, repealing old Dutch laws, abolishing slavery, establishing a civil service, populating the cities, and dominating the indigenous peoples, they turned South Africa into a British colony. Colonialism often begins when one group of people needs cheap labor (or slave labor), raw materials, and markets to fuel a growing economy. European colonialism, which began in the fifteenth century, is a prime example. Like the British who wanted South

Africa's land and minerals, other colonial powers wanted gold, silver, petroleum, and tin, which were not plentiful in western Europe. From the tropics, they wanted mahogany and teak and crops such as sugar, rubber, cotton, and tobacco. Colonies also provided outlets for surplus capital and strategic military and naval bases. The Dutch first went to Cape Town, for instance, to establish an outpost for sailors who regularly traveled around the African cape on their voyages between Europe and the East. European colonies were established not only in Africa, of course, but in the Middle East, Asia, South America, and the Caribbean.

Early contact with native groups often was limited to a relatively small number of traders. Relations between them and the native populations often were friendly, for the traders seemed to pose no serious threat and expanded the array of available goods. But as trade grew and profitable businesses were established, European governments wanted to make sure that these lucrative trading arrangements would continue indefinitely. Therefore, they declared that these areas of economic holdings were their "colonies." Because they had technological superiority, and because they soon came to dominate most of a colony's resources, the Europeans found that they could maintain their power with a relatively small number of administrators and military people.

Economic uncertainty and unemployment may be partially responsible for the resurgence of a white supremacy movement in the U.S. in recent years. As the emblems and gestures of this group remind us, the twentieth century has witnessed particularly devastating examples of what happens when competition for resources and jobs is linked to ethnocentrism. (Baughman/Sygma.)

Under economic colonialism, the hard and dirty jobs such as janitor, field hand, or garbage collector invariably belong to the natives. This division of labor, plus the mass organization for work in mines and fields, usually results in a system of rigid racial stratification. In South Africa, for example, blacks work the mines, and whites own and manage the mines. Natives seldom can rise above the lowest economic stratum (Lelyveld 1985; Shibutani and Kwan 1965).

Overseas colonialism is perhaps more familiar to us than *internal colonialism*, the colonialism that takes place within a single state. According to sociologist Michael Hechter (1975), internal colonialism typically begins when different parts of a society industrialize at different rates. As a result, two distinct groups are formed, one more advanced than the other, and each economically and spatially segregated from the other. Soon the more advanced group tries to institutionalize its advantages through policies that perpetuate the existing social inequality. Gradually, the dominant, or *core group* takes shape apart from the subordinate, or *peripheral group* (Blauner 1972). The core exploits the periphery economically. The economy of the periphery is little more than a complement to that of the core; often it rests on a single agricultural or mineral export. This economic subjugation is reinforced by political domination (Hechter 1975)

Blacks in the United States have many characteristics of an internally colonized group, even though they are not completely geographically isolated (Clark 1964, 1965; Franklin and Resnik 1973). They are limited as to where they may live, however. And for generations, blacks have been exploited as a source of cheap labor and given primarily menial jobs. Until the middle of this century, voting restrictions denied blacks access to political power, especially in the South. The civil rights movement of the 1950s and 1960s did much to remove the *legal* barriers to black equality. But the United States is not yet a racially integrated society. With few exceptions, there is no easy and fluid mixture of blacks and whites in social cliques, intimate friendships, marriages, or private organizations (Gordon 1964).

Displacement of a Native Population

Economic and political subjugation of a minority group by a more powerful group is not the only pattern of conquest that occurs when different racial and ethnic groups meet. When a weaker group occupies a territory that a stronger group wants, the stronger is likely to displace the weaker. Native populations typically are displaced from areas that are rich in natural resources and whose geography and climate are similar to those of the homeland of the invading group (Lieberson 1961; Van de Berghe 1978). These similarities make permanent settlement attractive to the invaders. As in the early stages of colonialism, early contacts with native populations may be marked by tolerance or friendliness, because the newcomers are few in number. But as their numbers increase, and as more land is taken, conflict between the groups erupts.

Displacement can occur through attrition. Members of the weaker group may die of starvation or disease, as happened in South Africa when the native blacks of Africa died of smallpox while competing with the European settlers for land. Sometimes the displacement takes the form of population transfers: Native peoples are either forcibly expelled from an area or they leave voluntarily because life has become so hard for them. The creation of homelands for South African blacks is a form of population transfer. In extreme cases, a weaker group may be deliberately and ruthlessly exterminated. This is termed genocide.

Attrition, population transfer, and genocide all came into play in the pioneers' handling of Native American groups on the American frontier. The Native Americans did not think of land as a commodity to be bought and sold. Consequently, they did not realize that white occupation of a piece of land meant a monopoly on its use. By the time this became clear, the Native Americans' very survival was threatened. They began to resist white expansion, but by then it was too late. The Native Americans were no match for the endless influx of white settlers with their vastly superior weapons (Spicer 1980).

At first the whites attempted to resolve the conflict by moving the Native Americans west of the Mississippi. For example, in the 1830s the Cherokees, among others, were forced to march from their homelands in Georgia to an arid reservation in Oklahoma. As many as 4,000 Native Americans died on what came to be known as the Trail of Tears. By the early 1840s only a few Native Americans were left in the eastern United States. Later, on the Great Plains, whites destroyed the Native Americans' principal means of survival—the buffalo. Diseases introduced by the white settlers, for which the Native Americans lacked natural immunities, also decimated

Even the myths and legends of Native Americans have come to reflect their displacement from their homelands and the corruption of their cultural heritage by the dominant white culture. Today they are the poorest minority group in America—a legacy so bitter that most Americans prefer to ignore it. (Eve Arnold/ Magnum Photos, Inc.)

either relegated to the lowest rungs of the larger society or placed on poverty-stricken reservations run by the federal government (Brown 1971, 1984).

Unfortunately, similar patterns have been repeated many times, in many places, and under a variety of circumstances. During World War II, for instance, the Soviet Union seized the opportunity to reduce inter-ethnic conflict by expelling "disloyal nationalities"—the Volga Germans, the Chechen-Ingush, the Crimean Tartars, and the Kalmuks—from their homelands. Genocide has also been practiced throughout history. The British settlers in Tasmania hunted the natives there for sheer sport. When the natives fought back, fierce warfare resulted. The British, of course, had the upper hand, and before long only a few hundred Tasmanians remained. These were herded onto a native reserve where the population gradually died out. In our own time the Nazi murder of 6 million Jews is yet another example of annihilation as the "final solution" to ethnic conflict. Thus, sociologists have found that genocide and mass expulsions are not limited to instances of territorial expansion. In general, these occur when the dominant group perceives the threat posed by a minority as too great to be endured, when assimilation of the minority into the dominant group is viewed as impossible or undesirable, and when minority group members are not considered essential sources of labor, knowledge, or skills (Dowty 1987).

Minority Responses to Dominance

How do members of a minority group react to prejudice and discrimination? In what ways and under what circumstances do they attempt to fight back?

Trying to become accepted by the majority is one reaction. Some members of a minority will try to "pass"—change their names, their appearance, and their lives, thus shedding their minority identity. Passing means rejecting one's family and origins, and it may leave a person stranded between two worlds, not entirely accepted by either (as seems to have been true for Edmund Perry). Other minority group members who are unable to pass (because of obvious physical characteristics, for instance) may simply become resigned to their status.

Complete resignation is rare, however. Usually members of an oppressed minority will strike back in some way. When people feel totally powerless to change

large segments of the native populations. Smallpox, for instance, completely annihilated the Missouri Indians. Sometimes whites intentionally left clothing infected with a deadly disease in places where Native Americans were sure to come upon them. The Native Americans, of course, continued to fight back, but this only convinced the white population that the two groups could not live together. A program of mass extermination began. In the end, about two-thirds of the Native American population was wiped out. The survivors were their treatment (because they are greatly outnumbered, lack access to political channels, do not have the weapons for armed rebellion, and so forth), they may retaliate through *covert aggression*. On the surface, they will appear to accept the role the dominant group assigns to them, obeying the etiquette of racism, deferring to members of the dominant group in most interracial contexts. The classic example of this response is Uncle Tom, who smiled, shuffled, and "yes, ma'am"ed his way through Harriet Beecher Stowe's novel *Uncle Tom's Cabin*. But among themselves, minority group members will show their contempt for the majority. They may call them derogatory names (honky, gringo, paleface), laugh at their arrogance and absurdity, and tell stories about how easily they can be duped. Other forms of covert retaliation include loafing or doing shoddy work, feigning illness, stealing tools and work materials or purposely destroying them, and leaving a job at the worst possible time for the employer (Davis 1978).

If members of minority groups believe they have some chance of improving their status by working within the existing system, they will often organize various forms of *political and economic protest*. This is what happened in the United States during the early 1960s. Black leaders felt that by publicizing the injustices they suffered through peaceful demonstrations (sit-ins, boycotts, marches, freedom rides, and the like), they could win civil rights through the legislatures and through the courts. During the summer of 1963, some 1,122 demonstrations were recorded, culminating with the March on Washington. On August 28, 1963, over 200,000 civil rights marchers demonstrated on the Mall between the Washington Monument and the Lincoln Memorial "for jobs and freedom." The wave of demonstrations contributed to the passage of the Civil Rights Act of 1964 a year later. Additional demonstrations, particularly those in Selma, Alabama, in the spring of 1965, convinced Congress to strengthen federal law with the Civil Rights Acts of 1965. During this period, the Reverend Martin Luther King, Jr., served as the leader and the symbol of the civil rights movement.

At other times, however, minority group members believe that there is little hope of improving their lot by working within the system. The dominant group, they feel, is unsympathetic or even hostile toward their cause. Such circumstances are often conducive to *violent protest or outright rebellion*. This is especially true when minority group members believe they have enough strength in numbers to inflict substantial injury on the dominant group, and when they feel that such injury is justified because of past exploitation and oppression (Davis 1978). Sometimes the use of violence is planned in advance as part of a liberation strategy. A number of the slave revolts that took place in the American South before the Civil War are examples of this kind of organized attack on the majority. At other times, however, minority violence is not so specifically goal-directed. It simply flares up spontaneously, often fanned by a particular event or instance of injustice. The violence that broke out in black ghettos across the United States during the late 1960s was of this type, and such incidents still erupt today. More will be said about the causes and consequences of riots in Chapter 21.

Violent resistance, of course, almost always means a loss of life and property for the minority as well as the dominant group. It is usually used only as a last resort. One alternative to violence that a minority may have is to minimize contact with the dominant group, thus limiting degradation and abuse. For example, when anti-Chinese sentiment began to increase in the American West, Chinese families withdrew to cities on the Atlantic and Pacific coasts, shutting themselves off from the hostile society around them (Yuan 1963). At various times since the abolition of slavery, groups of blacks in America have also supported *separatism*; some have even set as their goal the creation of separate black states. Not only does self-segregation provide insulation from aggression and slurs, it also enables members of a minority group to maintain close family ties, to assist one another, to practice their own way of life, and to keep their culture alive. Avoidance of the majority is a two-edged sword, however. While it may give minority group members a sense of solidarity and protection, it may also intensify intergroup prejudice and suspicion and perpetuate discriminatory practices. The line between "we" and "they" becomes all the more heavily drawn.

Patterns of Accommodation

Although conflict and oppression between racial and ethnic groups are pervasive, it is important to recognize that race and ethnic relations can also be characterized by tolerance and accommodation. Sometimes this accommodation follows a period of severe conflict. At other times, there may be no conflict, even initially.

What conditions underlie and promote the various forms of accommodation among members of racial and ethnic groups?

The Melting Pot Concept

One form that interracial and interethnic accommodation can take is for majority and minority to intermarry and for their various customs and values to blend, thus creating a new cultural hybrid. This is what the early-twentieth-century writer Israel Zangwill had in mind when he described America as a melting pot in his popular play concerning the life of a young Russian-Jewish immigrant: "There she lies, the great melting pot—listen! Can't you hear the roaring and bubbling? Ah, what a stirring and seething—Celt and Latin, Slav and Teuton, Greek and Syrian, Black and Yellow—Jew and Gentile" (1909, pp. 198–199). In Zangwill's romantic plot, the poor Jewish boy marries the beautiful Christian girl, all animosities between their families disappear, and the couple lives happily ever after. Such a cultural and biological blending—in which the customs and values of both groups are to some extent preserved—is, of course, possible. It is probably most likely to occur when power among various racial and ethnic groups is relatively equal, when relations among them are more cooperative than competitive, and when ethnocentrism is not strong.

Although the melting pot concept is frequently lauded by politicians, it is not a very accurate description of what actually happened to those who immigrated to the United States. Sociologist Milton Gordon writes:

> There is no reason to suppose that these men [the nation's founding fathers] looked upon their fledgling country as an impartial melting pot for the merging of the various cultures of Europe, or as a new "nation of nations," or as anything but a society in which, with important political modifications, Anglo-Saxon speech and institutional forms would be standard. (Gordon 1978, p. 185)

John Quincy Adams expressed the sentiment in the early nineteenth century:

> To one thing they [immigrants to America] must make up their minds, or they will be disappointed in every expectation of happiness as Americans. They must cast off the European skin, never to resume it. They must look forward to their posterity rather than backward to their ancestors; they must be sure that whatever their own feelings may be, those of their children will cling to the prejudices of this country. (Quoted in Gordon 1978, p. 187)

Contrary to popular opinion, from the earliest days of this country, newcomers were expected to adopt Anglo-Saxon customs and values.

Assimilation

The adoption of prevailing norms and values is part of the process of **assimilation**—the incorporation of a minority group into the culture and social life of the dominant group such that the minority eventually disappears as a separate, identifiable unit. Assimilation is another form that interracial and interethnic accommodation can take.

The sociologist Robert E. Park was one of the first to describe the assimilation process as a cycle of stages through which each new immigrant group to the United States presumably passed (Park 1925). The process begins with the newcomers competing to gain a foothold in their newly adopted nation. But because they do not know the dominant culture, the immigrants can only manage to secure what others do not want—the poorest land, the worst housing, the most menial jobs. As a result, they find themselves scorned and ridiculed, looked down upon by better-established people. Most gravitate to separate ethnic enclaves (often city slums) where they can feel secure and at ease. Eventually, these immigrants, and especially their children and grandchildren, begin to acquire the culture of the dominant group. Their struggle for survival is converted to a struggle for respectability, better living conditions, and higher-paying, more prestigious jobs. This struggle is not an easy one. But gradually more and more members of the ethnic group achieve upward mobility, remnants of their traditional culture fade, and intergroup marriages occur. The result is assimilation.

A look at the racial and ethnic groups that have come to the United States reveals that Park's description applies better to some than to others. The Scottish and Scandinavians, for instance, have been assimilated quite fully, the Italians somewhat less so, and the Puerto Ricans hardly at all. What can explain these differences in the speed and degree to which groups have been absorbed into the larger society?

One factor is simply time; the degree of a group's assimilation obviously depends in part on how long the group has been in a particular place. Most northern European immigrants, for instance, arrived before the turn of the century. In contrast, the influx of immigrants from Puerto Rico has occurred only since World War II, so not surprisingly they are less assimilated. However, the time factor cannot explain all differences in current levels of assimilation. Why, for example, are blacks, who have been here for several hundred years, still excluded from the mainstream of American life? The answer has much to do with a deep ethnocentrism among many Americans of white Anglo-Saxon Protestant heritage. In general, this ethnocentrism has meant that the invitation to participate equally in American society has been offered very selectively. People whose cultural background and physical appearance (particularly skin color) are most similar to those of the dominant group have had by far the easiest time. In addition, the actual size of the minority population may have some bearing on the degree of discrimination and thus on the degree of the minority's assimilation. That is, the larger the minority population, the greater the threat to the dominant group (Lieberson 1980).

Finally, different rates of assimilation are also related to an immigrant group's own *desire* to assimilate. Some ethnic groups have felt more ambivalence than others toward certain aspects of American culture. Many Hispanic Americans, for instance, question the white middle-class custom that parents and their children live apart from other kin (even thousands of miles from parents, siblings, grandparents, aunts, uncles, and cousins). Instead, they value the warmth and security of a large extended family. Such ambivalence toward some of the customs found in the United States could make an immigrant group reluctant to abandon its own cultural ways. We will look at other aspects of assimilation when we consider the history and status of some of the important minority groups in this country.

Pluralism

Because of all these factors, and probably several others, the pattern of racial and ethnic assimilation in the United States has been uneven. In reality, there is considerable cultural and structural **pluralism,** in which each group retains its own language, religion, and customs, and its members tend to interact socially (date,

The "melting pot," pluralism, and ethnic exclusiveness —in what ways is this scene of a saint's day celebration in Brooklyn representative of the experience of ethnic groups in our society? (Katrina Thomas/Photo Researchers, Inc.)

marry, form close friendships) primarily among themselves. Yet all jointly participate in the economic and political systems. A prime example of such an arrangement can be found in Switzerland. There, people of German, French, and Italian heritage preserve their distinct cultural ways while coexisting peacefully and equally. No one group enjoys special privileges or is discriminated against.

Pluralism does not exist to the same degree in the United States, where white Anglo-Saxon Protestant customs and values still predominate. But many members of racial and ethnic groups—from blacks to Italians to

Chinese to Hispanics—do wish to preserve at least some of their cultural identities. People from many ethnic groups do not want to be absorbed totally into the mainstream. Many live within the boundaries of ethnic communities (Farley 1986). Because of this ethnic exclusiveness, both of racial and ethnic groups and of the dominant group, pluralism has been an important part of the American racial and ethnic experience (Lieberson 1980).

WHY DOES IT HAPPEN? EXPLAINING PREJUDICE AND DISCRIMINATION

Why does prejudice exist? Where does racial hatred come from? How can acts as inhumane as genocide and forced expulsion be practiced by so many ordinary human beings? What purposes does discrimination serve? There are a number of ways sociologists analyze possible answers to these questions.

The Psychological Perspective

Suppose a man works five or six days a week in a factory, trying to support his family, but never seems to be able to make ends meet. Given his circumstances, he might blame the well-to-do generally and his employers specifically for failing to pay him an adequate wage. But these people have the power to cut off his income; to oppose them openly could be counterproductive. He might also blame himself for his financial problems, but this is likely to make him uncomfortable. So he looks for another source of blame. Mexican immigrants have begun working in his factory. He does not really know them, but he suspects that they are willing to work for low wages and that many Mexicans are eager to take his job. By a process of twisted logic, he perceives the Mexicans as responsible for his poverty. Soon he is exchanging derogatory stories about them with his cronies and supporting efforts to close the border. Hating Mexicans makes the man and his friends feel a little better.

This psychological portrait of prejudice is based on the **frustration-aggression hypothesis,** which proposes

that people are goal-directed creatures who become angry and hostile when their desires are frustrated. Consequently, they lash out. But at whom do they strike? Presumably, if people do not know who or what is blocking their ambitions or believe the obstacle is too threatening and powerful to attack, they look for some person or group on which to vent their feelings. Frustrated and angry, they often displace their hostility on a substitute target, or a **scapegoat.** Usually, the scapegoat is readily accessible and, conveniently, too weak to retaliate. Remember that even ethnic and racial jokes can be insidious expressions of hostility.

Once they find a group to serve as a scapegoat, people justify their irrational feelings and behavior by "discovering" evidence that the out-group is indeed wicked and inferior. In this way, people can maintain some feeling that they are reasonable and kind. But the catch is that in verbally or physically attacking Mexicans, Jews, blacks, or members of any other group, prejudiced people avoid confronting the true sources of their problems. Consequently, their situation does not change, and frustration and hostility grow. Thus, personal issues can unwittingly take on social significance.

There is another psychological point to be made. Sometimes prejudice and discrimination against a minority can be internalized by the individual minority group members, so that they may believe they in some way must deserve to be victims. In other words, they can feel guilt for their own domination by another "superior" group. This naturally plays directly into the hands of that dominant group and reinforces racism (Allport 1979; Wallace 1976).

The Role of Racial and Ethnic Myths

Another way of analyzing why prejudice and discrimination occur, and often flourish, is to look at the creation and proliferation of powerful racial and ethnic myths. In South Africa, the Afrikaners have created a myth that now pervades the national consciousness: They believe strongly that their ancestors, the Dutch settlers, were the first on the land and so they have absolute rights to it. Even more insidiously, they also have created a myth about their divine origins and God-given obligation to maintain racial purity.

People often justify their cruel and unfair behavior with such myths and belief systems. In India, for example, members of the lowest caste, the untouchables, had, according to religious doctrine, earned their status as social lepers through unworthy deeds in past lives. This belief presumably justified keeping a yawning social distance from these outcasts.

Racism has provided a convenient justification for Europeans' subjugation of other peoples. Sir Harry Johnston, a British colonial administrator and "authority" on Africa, argued that blacks "by nature" were docile and cheerful, quick to forget injustices and cruelties, and always grateful for any kindness (Shibutani and Kwan 1965). According to this view, blacks were simple and childlike and, therefore, biologically suited to be the servants of whites. The same reasoning was used to justify slavery in the southern United States. Harsher views have been used to justify even harsher treatment. Thus, because many settlers believed that Native Americans were savages, little more than wild beasts, the settlers believed that extermination of these people was justified.

Racist views are still common today, although they may take more sophisticated forms. Arthur Jensen, an educational psychologist at the University of California at Berkeley, published a racist article in the *Harvard Educational Review* in 1969. He noted that the average scores for blacks on IQ tests were 10 to 15 points lower than those for whites, and suggested that the reason lay in "genetic factors." Even if genetic factors *were* involved, it is almost impossible to conclude how much these factors actually matter, since socialization, cultural factors, and the whole social context play such enormous parts in education and test making, taking, and grading. Also, since race as a social category cannot be defined in biological terms at all, how can biological (genetic) terms be applied to a discussion of race and race differences? By such criticisms has Jensen's reasoning been discredited, but his work, cloaking age-old racist myths in the rational terms of modern science, caused a great hue and cry at the time. We will return to this controversy in Chapter 17 ("Education").

It bears emphasizing that the stereotypes at the heart of racial and ethnic myths, by nature false or at the very least simplistic, are based on inadequate information about the minority group. As noted already, segregation helps ensure that true knowledge of the "others" will not be gained, so stereotypes cannot easily be corrected. Finally, note too that the media, in news reports, situation comedies, melodramas, and ads, often tend to reinforce stereotypes and maintain the predominant and damaging myths (Lieberson 1982).

The Role of Intergroup Conflict

Psychological perspectives are intriguing, as is the role of myths, but these cannot provide a full explanation for prejudice and discrimination. Why, for example, is one minority group singled out for the most intense bigotry and hatred, when several other subordinate groups, equally powerless to retaliate, would do just as well? And why do myths spring up and proliferate in the first place? One very persuasive explanation is that the intensity of discrimination and the strength of beliefs depend heavily on the level of tension between groups. And the level of tension depends on competing interests between the dominant and the minority groups. When the dominant group perceives a minority group as particularly threatening to its established position, and to its desire for *more* income, power, and prestige, or its opportunities, a great deal of prejudice and discrimination is likely to result. From this perspective, which is basically a power analysis, we can see how social and economic conflict leads to

The fact that whites achieve higher median scores than blacks on standardized educational tests has been used to defend the notion of their genetic superiority. In fact, such scoring discrepancies reflect discrimination in the educational system and cultural biases implicit in the tests themselves. Is her environment or her heredity more likely to set limits on the future that shines so brightly in the eyes of this young spelling champion? (Charles Gupton/The Stock Market.)

prejudice and discrimination, and how prejudice and discrimination are effective means of maintaining conflict (Farley 1987; Newman 1973; Allport 1979). When the British first established themselves in India, for example, they showed little bigotry toward the native population and even encouraged intermarriage. All this changed when the children of the mixed marriages began to outnumber the Europeans and to compete for managerial and administrative jobs. Then, because of competing interests, Indians and "mixed bloods" became the targets of intense discrimination, *justified*, but not necessarily motivated by, the myth of English racial superiority.

Analyses of prejudice and discrimination based on a power perspective ask: Who profits from the conflict, and who loses? The question is central to the power perspective because, in this view, society is seen as a fairly closed system: If one group gains, another must lose—or at least gain less. So according to some sociologists, the dominant group gains from such a conflict and has its interests served by it, whereas the minority group loses. Thus, racial and ethnic prejudice arises from a more or less calculated effort on the part of the elite—say, the owners or the board of a large corporation—to keep large segments of the population at subsistence wages and retain resources for themselves.

From this viewpoint, for example, blacks and immigrant workers form a "reserve labor force." When the economy expands, they can be hired readily; but when the economy contracts, they can be let go just as easily. This often ends up keeping jobs of nonelite white workers pretty much intact. But the whites nevertheless tend to perceive their jobs to be threatened by the availability of other, cheaper labor, so conflict is fostered between these white workers and the reserve black and immigrant workers. While they are fighting it out, the ruling class is enjoying the fruits of the workers' labors. Also, since the workers are in conflict with one another, they are less likely to challenge elitist rule. Thus, this conflict among the workers provides a cushion between the privileged group and the less privileged members of their own race or ethnic group—say, in this case, between white owners and directors, and the lower-class white employees. The conflict between white workers at the low end of the scale and black workers may also explain why, on most tests that measure prejudice, lower-class and working-class whites score higher, on the average, than upper-class whites. It is noteworthy that a study of the Ku Klux Klan showed that the majority of members came from the working and lower-middle classes (Vander Zanden 1960).

We should note that certainly not all these effects that benefit the dominant group and discriminate against the minority are achieved through conscious strategy. Capitalist owners, for example, may start off simply wanting the cheapest labor possible; they are not consciously deciding to reproduce the class structure. But since the result works to their benefit—and since they can make use of the status quo class system without necessarily realizing it—they are likely to continue along the same path.

The Cultural Factor

Some sociologists have stressed, not so much that a dominant group derives benefits from prejudice and discrimination, but that prejudice and discrimination become, in ethnically stratified societies, part of the culture. They are social habits handed down from generation to generation. Children, for example, learn to value their own whiteness or blackness and to avoid or defer to members of different races and ethnic groups, much as they learn their gender identity and sex role. With such early training, it is not surprising that prejudice toward minority groups would seem as natural as love of competition, respect for private property, or any other attitude deeply embedded in American culture. But all these values were once created and consciously taught.

Prejudice remains embedded because in many cases people seldom come in contact with members of the disparaged minority, so they have no chance to have their traditional stereotypes disproven. Even when people do encounter members of a disparaged group, their very prejudice tends to distort their view so that it conforms to their negative preconceptions. They perceive the people of their stereotypes (Lieberson 1982). For instance, traits normally considered virtues can become vices when perceived through a prejudiced eye. The sociologist Robert K. Merton has observed:

Did Lincoln work far into the night? This testifies that he was industrious, resolute, perseverant, and eager to realize his capacities to the full. Do the out-group Jews or Japanese keep these same hours? This only bears witness to their sweatshop mentality, their ruthless undercutting of American standards, their unfair competitive practices. Is the in-group hero frugal, thrifty, and sparing? Then the

FIGURE 13.1   The Vicious Cycle of Prejudice and Discrimination

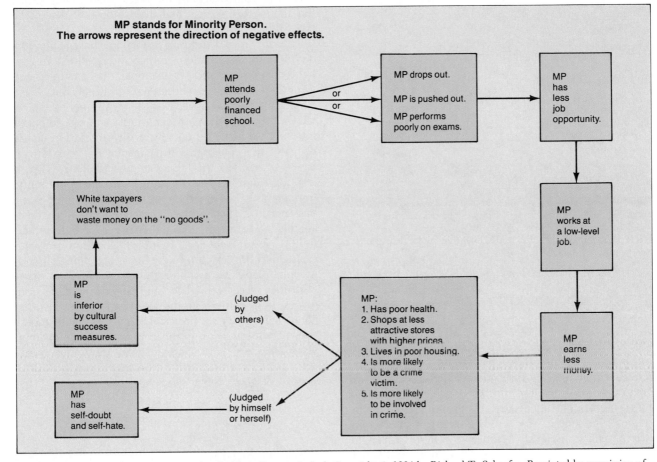

Source: From Richard T. Schaefer, *Racial and Ethnic Groups,* 2nd ed. Copyright © 1984 by Richard T. Schaefer. Reprinted by permission of Little, Brown and Company.

This figure illustrates the vicious cycle that is created by prejudice and discrimination. The outcome of this system—members of minority groups are judged inferior by cultural standards—then becomes the rationale for future discrimination and prejudice.

out-group villain is stingy, miserly and penny-pinching. All honor is due to the in-group Abe for his having been smart, shrewd, and intelligent and, by the same token, all contempt is owing to the out-group Abes for their being sharp, cunning, crafty, and too clever by far. (Merton 1957, p. 428)

In addition, causes and effects tend to become confused. People are adept at using the *consequences* of prejudice and discrimination to prove that their negative evaluation was right. Blacks on average *do* live in poorer houses than whites, they *do* hold lower-paying jobs, and they *do* have fewer years of schooling. But rather than being any justification for prejudice and discrimination, these conditions are the *result* of prejudice and discrimination. Yet whites turn these facts around and use them as evidence that blacks are inferior to whites (see Figure 13.1). Through such illogical reasoning, prejudice can survive even if most people derive little concrete benefit from it.

TABLE 13.1   Racial and Ethnic Categories

White	188,341,000
Black	26,488,000[1]
Hispanics*	14,600,000[2]
American Indian, Eskimo, Aleutian Islanders	1,418,177
Chinese	806,000
Filipino	775,000
Japanese	701,000
Asian-Indian	362,000
Korean	355,000
Vietnamese	262,000
Hawaiian	167,000
Samoan	42,000
Guamanian	32,000

*Due to a peculiarity of the 1980 Census form, many Hispanics were additionally counted in the "white" or "black" categories.
[1]The revised figure for 1985 is 28,151,000.
[2]The revised figure for 1985 is 16,940,000. (Figures for other groups have not been revised since the 1980 Census.)

Source: U.S. Bureau of the Census, Statistical Abstract, 1980, 1987.

Some sociologists would emphasize that culture and structural conditions (such as ethnic or racial stratification, maintained by institutional discrimination) are man-made and therefore ultimately subject to change. The system can be opened up. For example, to lessen or eradicate prejudice, we could confront it directly in schools and consciously teach new values; we could spend more money on education, hire more and better teachers, and offer more places in the schools to minorities. (This topic will be discussed in greater detail in Chapter 17, "Education".) Thus, from this particular perspective, racism may be an embedded cultural habit, but it is not an eternally immutable one.

RACE AND ETHNICITY IN THE UNITED STATES TODAY

One hundred years ago, ethnic and racial relations in this country pitted a host of different European immigrant groups against one another in competition for jobs, education, and political opportunities. All of these groups were in turn actively or passively pitted against Native Americans, and all, including the Native Americans, were pitted against the black population, despite the abolition of slavery and the Union's victory in the Civil War.

Today, most European immigrants have achieved a high level of assimilation, though some still live in very tight-knit communities (for example, the Poles in Chicago or the Finns in the Minnesota Iron Ring). But Native Americans still occupy a very low rung on the social ladder; they form the poorest minority group. And blacks have not yet achieved equality with whites. The major issues of the civil rights struggle of the 1960s remain largely unresolved. And there are new tensions. Hispanics, for example, are the most prominent group of immigrants today, and their influx into the United States has created a good deal of competition between them and black Americans, whom they may soon outnumber. Indeed, Jesse Jackson's "Rainbow Coalition" has addressed just this tension, in the hopes of helping Hispanics and blacks to work together. In addition, many Hispanics face prejudice and discrimination from whites. Immigrants from the Asian nations, on the other hand, have generally been able to achieve educational and economic success in this country more rapidly than blacks, Hispanics, or Native Americans. For a breakdown of the larger racial and ethnic groups in the United States today, see Table 13.1.

Black Americans

The 28.1 million Americans who trace their ancestry back to Africa through three centuries of poverty, exploitation, and violence are this country's largest racial minority: They make up nearly 12 percent of the U.S. population (Pinkney 1987; U.S. Census Abstract 1987). The victories achieved through the civil rights movement, urbanization, political awareness, and some degree of social and economic mobility have made black Americans increasingly a force to be reckoned with. What did they suffer historically, and what is their position today?

Many of the first Africans to come to America came not as slaves but as indentured servants: They were contracted to work for a given number of years, after which they received their freedom. For a time, it seemed as if slavery might not flourish in the new colonies. By the late 1600s, however, nearly all blacks and their descendants had been relegated to perpetual servitude under the law. The reason was primarily economic: Southern planters found slavery very profitable. With the invention of the cotton gin and the consequently enormous increase in cotton production, slavery came to be seen as vital to the prosperity of the South. Before slavery was abolished in 1865, nearly half a million blacks had been brought forcibly to this land, where they were viewed simply as property. They were bought, sold, used, and abused at the will of the white majority. The belief in black inferiority that developed to justify slavery (from a power perspective, to maintain whites' economic dominance) still pervades relations between blacks and whites.

Slavery may have been abolished in 1865, but white terrorism and discrimination were not. **Jim Crow laws** refer to the legal and social barriers erected in the South in the late nineteenth and early twentieth centuries to prevent blacks from voting, using public facilities, and mixing with whites. (Jim Crow was the name of a minstrel entertainer who performed in blackface.) The legal segregation in the South resembled that in South Africa. Periodic lynchings kept blacks "in their place." That place was marked by continued economic exploitation and political exclusion. For example, housing for blacks and whites is still strongly segregated. Sixty percent of blacks and 72 percent of whites live in racially homogeneous neighborhoods; this is a situation that most whites like, but most blacks do not (Freedman 1987). The white exodus from urban centers seems to be increasing de facto residential segregation in the central cities. By **de facto segregation** is meant racial separation that results from unofficial social patterns, as opposed to segregation imposed by law, which is called de jure segregation.

A decisive battle against segregation began in the South in the 1960s: the civil rights struggle, with boycotts and nonviolent demonstrations. Blacks marched, picketed, and sat in at "white only" restaurants. Not long after, blacks began to win civil rights victories in the courts and in Congress. At the same time, they continued to migrate from the South, particularly from the rural South, to northern cities, as they had been doing since the beginning of this century (Pinkney 1987). Northern urban ghettos grew. In a sense, the movement of so much of the black population to northern cities has made black and white relations and civil rights issues of the first importance, not just for the South, but for the country as a whole (Pinkney 1987).

Many blacks today are better educated, better off financially, and have better job prospects than their parents (or even older brothers and sisters) (Farley 1984; Allen and Farley 1986). But they still do not have equality with whites in these areas. Take education, for example. Blacks represent only about 8 percent of the total college population (Pinkney 1987); and 11.1 percent of blacks complete four or more years at college, whereas 20 percent of whites go to college four or more years (U.S. Bureau of the Census 1987). Many black students drop out of college because they are not as well prepared as other students and find the college environment inhospitable. Lack of funding, rising costs, little recruiting among black high schools, and little pressure for affirmative action are also contributing factors. Among blacks, Hispanics, and Asian-Americans, only the last group gained in the percentage enrolled in colleges between 1976 and 1984 (see Figure 13.2; Fiske 1987). Blacks are also likely to attend racially imbalanced schools: predominantly black elementary and secondary schools, and predominantly white colleges. Predominantly black schools tend to offer a lower-quality education than that received by white students, because of inadequate facilities, less trained faculty, lack of money, and other causes (Pinkney 1987).

Economically, many blacks *have* made gains. Increasing numbers of blacks now find themselves in positions of economic authority, in corporations, banks, government offices, executive suites, and other areas. But despite the successes of middle-class blacks, many other blacks remain substantially worse off than whites. Many of the blacks who are hired never make it to positions of authority (Alter 1986). One survey of the nation's 1,000 largest companies turned up only four top executives who were black (Hicks 1987). Generally, a large proportion of employed blacks are in low-paying, low-skill jobs (Pinkney 1987). (Table 13.2 shows that occupational options and job prestige for blacks have been upgraded in the last 40 years but still lag considerably behind the average job status of whites.)

A black worker has a much greater chance of being unemployed—and for a comparatively longer time—than a white worker. The unemployment rate for blacks has run about double that for whites since World War II (Pinkney 1987). In 1985, for example, the total black unemployment rate was over 15 percent, and that for black teenagers, about 40 percent (U.S. Bureau of the

FIGURE 13.2   Minority College Enrollments

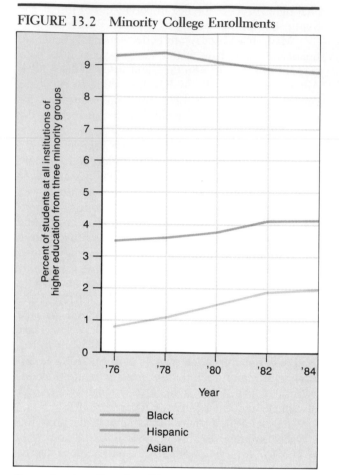

Source: American Council on Education from Federal Education Department.

Black poverty is a consequence of black unemployment and underemployment. In 1985, for instance, the income of 28.7 percent of black families fell below the poverty level, over three times the number of white families classified as poor by the Census Bureau (U.S. Bureau of the Census 1987). The median income of black families has hovered between 56 and 61 percent of white family income. Although black households made up 11 percent of all households in 1984, they held only 8 percent of the combined wealth of blacks and whites (U.S. Bureau of the Census 1987). Since 1980, poverty among blacks has been increasing (Pinkney 1987).

As a result of a small proportion of blacks improving their status but the rest slipping into poverty, blacks themselves have become stratified. Thus, the picture that emerges is of a small black middle class that is gaining in civil rights and in political and economic terms, and developing apart from a much larger group of black poor and underprivileged, the so-called underclass. This **underclass** can be defined as a subgroup with few resources, great despair, and only the dimmest hopes of ever moving from the periphery of society. In some American cities, as many as one-half of the black men are uneducated and unemployed. This poses an enormous problem for this country and its race relations, a problem that will be considered in more detail in the section on the future of American race relations.

Nevertheless, we must point out that over time, urbanization, political awareness, and some social and economic mobility have made black Americans increasingly a force to be reckoned with. Jesse Jackson's campaign for the 1988 Democratic presidential nomination is an excellent case in point. Jackson successfully mobilized black voters. A much higher percentage of eligible blacks registered and voted in the 1988 primaries than was previously true. In New York State, for example, an exit poll showed that 93 percent of the black voters chose Jackson; the same poll showed that 52 percent of the Jackson vote came from first-time primary voters—a very large proportion (*New York Times*, April 21, 1988). In the Deep South, the black vote gave Jackson a substantial lead over opponents (*Southern Exposure*, Spring 1988). Yet Jackson also attracted a substantial number of white voters, particularly among students and higher-income liberals. Indeed, he reversed a traditional racial breakdown in voting: in the past, white voters have not cast votes for blacks, but this time more whites voted for Jackson than blacks voted for all the white candidates combined (*Christian Science Monitor*, March 17, 1988).

Census 1987). In the same year, unemployment among blacks was twice what it had been in 1960 (Freedman 1987). If we count those blacks employed but earning less than the poverty-level income and those working part-time but wanting full-time jobs, we discover the *under*employment rate, which is at least double again the rate of those completely unemployed. In human terms, these figures are staggering, for they depict a group of people who have little hope for a decent living and for whom jobs are a source of frustration rather than satisfaction (Farley 1987).

TABLE 13.2 Occupational Distributions by Race, 1940–1980

Occupation	Black or nonwhite males (%)					White males (%)				
	1940	1950	1960	1970	1980	1940	1950	1960	1970	1980
Professional	1.8	2.2	3.8	7.8	10.7	5.9	7.9	11.4	14.6	16.1
Proprietors, managers, officials	1.3	2.0	3.0	4.7	6.7	10.7	11.7	14.5	15.3	15.3
Clerical	1.1	3.1	5.8	7.4	8.4	7.1	6.8	7.2	7.1	6.2
Sales	1.0	1.1	1.2	1.8	2.7	6.8	7.0	6.5	6.1	6.4
Craftsmen	4.4	7.8	9.5	13.8	17.1	15.7	20.0	19.8	20.7	21.4
Operatives	12.6	21.4	24.3	28.3	23.4	19.0	20.3	19.0	18.6	16.1
Domestic service	2.9	1.0	0.4	0.3	0.2	0.2	0.1	0.1	0.1	<0.1
Other service	12.4	13.5	14.9	12.8	15.8	5.9	5.2	5.6	6.0	7.9
Farmers, farm managers	21.2	13.5	4.8	1.7	0.6	14.1	10.1	6.1	3.6	2.6
Farm laborers	19.9	10.4	9.5	3.9	2.4	7.0	4.2	3.3	1.7	1.5
Non-farm laborers	21.4	24.0	22.8	17.5	12.0	7.6	6.7	6.5	6.2	6.5
Total	100.0	100.0	100.0	100.0	100.0	100.0	100.0	100.0	100.0	100.0
Mean socioeconomic index	16	18	21	27	31	30	33	36	39	40

Source: Allen and Farley 1986, p. 287.

The socioeconomic index at the bottom of each column provides a measurement of comparative job prestige for black and white males. High scores represent high-prestige jobs; low scores, low-prestige positions. As you can see, there are still large differences between the races. Note that in 1980 the average job status of a nonwhite man was comparable to that of a white man forty years earlier. There is a similar pattern for women's jobs.

Hispanic Americans

Spanish-speaking Americans, or Hispanics, are currently the second-largest minority in the United States. The 1980 Census counted 8.7 million Mexicans, 2 million Puerto Ricans, 803,000 Cubans, and 3.1 million "other Spanish." There are many more undocumented Hispanics who live and work in the United States illegally, but no one knows how many. This is one reason that estimating the number of Hispanics in this country is problematical (Exter 1987). But it is clear that Hispanic Americans are the fastest-growing minority in the United States. According to projections, between 1980 and 1990, the Hispanic population will increase by 54 percent, to 22 million. If this rate of increase continues into the next century, Hispanics will replace blacks as the nation's largest minority group (Oxford Analytica 1986). Hispanics are certain to play an increasingly important role in the development of American society.

The Hispanic population is overwhelmingly urban. As of 1980, 80 percent live in metropolitan areas, compared with 75 percent of the population as a whole (U.S. Bureau of the Census 1983). Three out of four

Hispanic immigrants from Mexico live in either California or Texas. About half the number from Puerto Rico live in the New York City area, and 59 percent of Hispanics from Cuba live in Florida (Russell 1983).

As Hispanics migrate to the United States, they compete with blacks for jobs and schooling. In both areas, they seem to be gaining an advantage over blacks, with potentially serious consequences for black progress and advancement (Oxford Analytica 1986). The trends in the migration of Hispanics to the United States are important because many Hispanics are committed to retaining their ethnic distinctiveness. They want to hold on to their language (Spanish), their religion (Roman Catholicism), and a culture that values family ties highly (see Chapter 4, "Culture"). But each group within the Hispanic community also has a unique history and heritage.

Before New England was colonized, the Spanish had settled in what is now the American Southwest. However, it was not until 1848, following wars and conquest, that they and their land became part of the United States. Soon after, English-speaking settlers began edging the Hispanics out: When all else failed, they were "sent back" to Mexico. Except in New Mexico, where Hispanics were able to hold their ground, most withdrew to rural towns and mining camps. When they went into areas dominated by English-speaking settlers to work as migrant laborers, they were housed in segregated camps; when they moved into the big cities, they lived apart from other groups.

Beginning about the turn of the century, a new group of Mexican nationals entered the United States to harvest cotton in east Texas. After each harvest, they would return to Mexico. As the years passed and cotton production expanded into west Texas, agricultural interests in the Southwest became increasingly dependent upon Mexico's vast army of migratory workers. The Mexicans have entered the United States legally under periodic agreements with the Mexican government and illegally by swimming or wading the Rio Grande. In recent years, the smuggling of aliens has become highly organized, with a network reaching from professional smugglers through labor contractors to American growers and manufacturers dependent on cheap labor. Increasingly, the aliens are bypassing the farms and ranches of the Southwest, their traditional sources of employment, for urban jobs elsewhere in the nation's construction, manufacturing, and service industries. Mexican nationals are particularly susceptible to exploitation and abuse because they fear being apprehended and returned to Mexico, or fired. Employers often short-change the alien workers by paying them less than the federal minimum wage, by not providing them with overtime pay, and by short-counting the hours they work.

Population pressures in Mexico and economic opportunities in the United States have encouraged Mexicans to come to this country. Comparable factors have contributed to the migration of Puerto Ricans to the mainland of the United States, particularly to the New York City area. Their influx there is relatively recent. The United States acquired Puerto Rico in 1898, and in 1917 all Puerto Ricans were declared American citizens. Mainland companies began to open branches on the island but were met with violent nationalist resistance. A compromise was reached, granting Puerto Rico aid for modernization and economic development as well as commonwealth status. Most Puerto Ricans did not benefit from economic expansion, however. After World War II, when the airlines introduced lower fares, increasing numbers of Puerto Ricans began leaving their island to seek their fortune in New York.

Behind them lie economic and political instability and severe unemployment; before them lies the prospect of economic exploitation at the lowest rungs of the U.S. workforce. Nevertheless, these Mexicans caught crossing the border will most likely attempt the precarious journey soon again. (Stephanie Maze/ Woodfin Camp & Associates.)

In New York City, Puerto Ricans, one of the nation's poorer groups, suffer acute education and health problems (Schaefer 1984; Hernandez 1983). They have the highest school-dropout rate of all ethnic groups, higher than that of blacks. They also have high mortality rates from drug addiction, alcoholism, accidents, homicides, and diabetes. In city ghettos, Puerto Ricans often are forced to endure double discrimination: discrimination due to their language and due to their color. (The skin color of Puerto Ricans may be black or white or any shade in between, but Puerto Ricans are usually labeled nonwhite.) What makes the Puerto Rican situation unique is that immigration runs two ways: The island is close enough for immigrants to return home, as most do, temporarily or permanently. As a result, most have less incentive than some other groups to learn American ways and English.

Mexican Americans, or Chicanos, live primarily in the Southwest and California, mostly in urban ghettos or as hired workers on farms. Many cross the border into the United States as undocumented aliens, on whom employers depend for low-paying menial work at below-minimum wages. As many as 1 million of these aliens are seized each year by United States federal border guards. Many Mexicans keep trying to cross the border, however, driven by severe poverty and high unemployment in their own country. The United States government did offer an amnesty to illegal immigrants in 1987–1988, but many Chicanos did not take advantage of it, some because of the extensive documentation required, and some because of fear of deportation.

In the United States, Chicanos experience many of the difficulties faced by Puerto Ricans, though a smaller proportion of Chicanos lives below poverty level. Chicanos have maintained a strong cultural identity here. Their civil rights movement has campaigned for better conditions for migrant workers and laborers and bilingual education for their children. Despite the large undocumented population, Chicanos are also beginning to wield more electoral power. Chicano mayors and city council members have been elected in several southwestern cities, most prominently San Antonio (Portes 1985).

In general, like blacks, Hispanics are underrepresented in high-skill, high-income jobs, especially white-collar positions, and they're overrepresented in low-skill, low-paying jobs, although Hispanics have been more likely to be blue-collar or farm employees than blacks. Many young Hispanics enter the job market at a disadvantage. Whether born in this country or elsewhere, many have limited English and little education and feel discriminated against. As the United States has lost jobs in manufacturing, assembling, and related sectors of the economy, many Hispanics (as well as blacks) have lost access to work (Santos 1985). Hispanic median family income languishes at about 70 percent of white family income in the United States (U.S. Bureau of the Census 1987).

Native Americans

Native Americans, the poorest minority group in America, have been the victims of lies, corruption, and abuse for over 100 years. The wars against the Native Americans reached a peak toward the middle of the nineteenth century, when the eastern United States was becoming crowded and the transcontinental railroad made travel easier. During this period, gold was discovered in the Black Hills of South Dakota and on other Native American lands, and adventurers could still make a profit from buffalo hides. Over 500,000 Indians died before the century was over. The 300,000 who survived war, disease, hunger, and bounties ($25 to $100 per scalp in many places) were forced onto inhospitable reservations that were administered by the notoriously corrupt Bureau of Indian Affairs (BIA).

Only 38 percent of the 1.4 million Native Americans live on reservations recognized by state or federal government officials. The remainder are scattered across the United States, nearly 50 percent in urban areas. Forty-eight percent of Native Americans on reservations live below the poverty line, and their unemployment rate exceeds 40 percent. Some 55 percent of those on reservations live in substandard housing, and 70 percent must haul their drinking water a mile or more (frequently drawing it from unsanitary sources). Fifty-eight percent of reservation children drop out of school before completing eighth grade. Thirty-six percent of all Native Americans have a yearly income of $9,999 or less, as compared with only 17 percent of the United States population as a whole. They also have unusually high rates of accidents, homicide, suicide, alcoholism, pneumonia, and diabetes (see Figure 13.3). Overall, they have the highest infant mortality rate and the lowest longevity rate of any American minority group (Hagan 1979; *U.S. News & World Report* 1983).

FIGURE 13.3   The Disadvantaged Circumstances of Native Americans

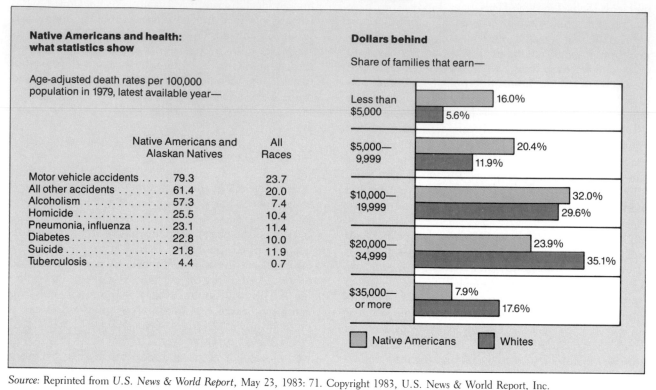

Native Americans and health: what statistics show

Age-adjusted death rates per 100,000 population in 1979, latest available year—

	Native Americans and Alaskan Natives	All Races
Motor vehicle accidents	79.3	23.7
All other accidents	61.4	20.0
Alcoholism	57.3	7.4
Homicide	25.5	10.4
Pneumonia, influenza	23.1	11.4
Diabetes	22.8	10.0
Suicide	21.8	11.9
Tuberculosis	4.4	0.7

Dollars behind

Share of families that earn—

	Native Americans	Whites
Less than $5,000	16.0%	5.6%
$5,000—9,999	20.4%	11.9%
$10,000—19,999	32.0%	29.6%
$20,000—34,999	23.9%	35.1%
$35,000—or more	7.9%	17.6%

Source: Reprinted from *U.S. News & World Report*, May 23, 1983: 71. Copyright 1983, U.S. News & World Report, Inc.

During the early 1970s, as militancy among many black Americans grew, Native Americans also became more insistent in their demands that past wrongs be redressed. Several of their demonstrations—the occupation of Alcatraz Island and the demonstration at Wounded Knee—made national and international headlines. In addition, Native American leaders brought their grievances to the courts. For example, $122.5 million was granted to eight tribes of the Sioux nation in compensation for the United States seizure of the Black Hills of South Dakota. (A treaty that had given the land exclusively to the Sioux was broken when gold was discovered there.) Such suits mark progress in the acknowledgment of the injustices Native Americans have suffered. Again, as with blacks, though there has been some progress, the relations between Native Americans and the dominant group still cannot be described as relations between equals (Cornell 1984).

Asian Americans

There are two major Asian groups that have been in the United States for some time: the Chinese and the Japanese. Since the 1970s, however, large numbers of Koreans, Filipinos, and immigrants from many parts of Southeast Asia have come here to live and work. Some of these groups have been remarkably successful at achieving some degree of equality with whites and/or assimilating into the daily life of America. (For more discussion on immigration, see Chapter 10, "Population.")

In 1987, David Kuo, a Chinese American, won the Westinghouse Science Talent Search, the most prestigious science prize for high-school students. In 1986, his brother had made the finals. In 1985, his other brother made the finals. The frequency of this kind of math and science achievements among Chinese Americans (and other Asian Americans) and Asian Americans' relatively high representation in colleges and universities may fuel the positive prejudice that all Chinese Americans are good at math and science, or that all Asian Americans are academic achievers. But of course these are stereotypes much like any others. So what does the achievement of the Kuo brothers and other Chinese Americans tell us? If we look at the factors underlying the science prizes and academic honors, we may find that, first, Chinese immigrants have tended to come from an affluent, educated stratum of society. In the Kuos' case, the father had been a surgeon and the mother a nurse and teacher in Taiwan. There is a catch here: Neither parent is pursuing this work in the United States; they have taken lower-skill jobs (Quindlen 1987). But their educational values, their cohesiveness as a family, and their emotional support have probably helped the children to grasp the opportunity for upward mobility in this country. They have offered their children the resources to meet their high expectations. Indeed, the success of many Asian Americans, especially the first generation to be raised here, rivals that of Jewish achievers of two and three decades ago.

This is not to say that the Chinese have not encountered prejudice and discrimination, for they certainly have. They began immigrating to the West Coast in the middle of the eighteenth century. Laboring on the railroad, washing, and cooking, they earned a reputation as hard workers. But when the railroad was finished and

unemployment began to rise, white workers turned on the Chinese. The Chinese Exclusion Act of 1882 halted further immigration, and denied Chinese the right to become naturalized citizens or to own land. In most places the Chinese were also denied schooling, jobs, and housing. They withdrew to ethnic enclaves (termed Chinatowns), keeping largely to themselves until anti-Chinese feelings started to subside. In 1943, under the impact of war conditions, the Chinese Exclusion Act was repealed and a quota for Asian immigrants was established. The number was meager, however—only 105 Chinese were permitted to enter this country annually. Finally, in 1965, national origins quotas were abolished, and for the first time Chinese immigrants were treated on a par with other nationalities (Wong 1982). By 1980 there were 894,000 people of Chinese ancestry in the country, an increase of 85.3 percent since 1970 (U.S. Bureau of the Census 1986). Enclaves in four major United States cities—New York City, Los Angeles, San Francisco, and Boston—have absorbed most of this increase, which has come from Taiwan and Hong Kong.

As of 1980, there were 791,000 people of Japanese ancestry in this country (U.S. Bureau of the Census 1986). The Japanese came to America about two decades after the Chinese. They established groceries, flower shops, and other small businesses, and took jobs as truck farmers and laborers in the lumber mills and fish canneries all along the West Coast. But anti-Oriental

While acts of discrimination are often aimed at those who are already too weak, economically or politically, to defend themselves, the 120,000 Japanese interned in "relocation centers" during World War II included many middle-class American citizens. (EKM-Nepenthe.)

sentiments ran high, and in 1924 all immigration from East Asia was halted. Then, during World War II, the Japanese in the United States became victims of racial discrimination in clear violation of their rights. Many people today are still surprised to learn that 120,000 Japanese, including 70,000 American citizens, were rounded up and placed in guarded, barbed-wired camps, or "relocation centers." This action was taken for the ostensible reason of protecting other Americans from the potential misdeeds of Japanese loyal to the enemy, Japan. The vast majority of the interned supported the Allies, but anti-Japanese prejudice had been whipped up by the attack on Pearl Harbor and the Pacific war. During their internment, Japanese families lost an average of $10,000 each (in terms of the 1941 value of the dollar). In late April 1988, the U.S. Senate approved a bill to apologize officially and pay $20,000 in reparations to every living Japanese American who was interned during the war (*New York Times*, April 21, 1988). Many felt that such an act was long overdue and expressed the country's recognition of the great injustice done to these loyal Americans.

American Jews

The first Jews came to North America from Brazil in 1654, but it was not until the 1840s that Jews began arriving in the thousands, fleeing European *pogroms* (periodic massacres of Jews). Today there are more Jews in the United States—about 6 million—than in any other country in the world. (The Soviet Union is second, Israel a close third.) About a third of American Jews live in or around New York City. Since 1970, more than half a million Jews have settled in the United States, the largest proportion coming from Israel and the Soviet Union. Unlike earlier waves of Jewish immigrants from southern and eastern Europe, the most recent arrivals are typically highly educated and skilled.

Urbanites and entrepreneurs throughout much of their past, Jews adapted to America with relative ease. This does not mean that they did not encounter discrimination. Time and again they have been accused of disloyalty, of participation in international conspiracies, of unscrupulous business practices. Traditionally, many corporations, major law firms, banks, and private clubs did not admit Jews (some still do not), and until World War II many universities maintained strict quota systems. Jews prospered nonetheless—in part, by using Old World skills to start businesses (the garment industry, for example), in part, by taking advantage of public education (today 58 percent of Jews hold college degrees as compared with 29 percent of Americans as a whole), and in part, by continuing to some extent to see themselves as the "chosen people," no matter what the circumstances (a doctrine Jews share with Black Muslims). Of course, most Jews are not wealthy, and many are poor, but as a group, Jews have prospered and are strongly represented in business and the professions.

Like other minorities, the American Jewish community has a historic connection with its early roots, traditions, and institutions. It has experienced tension between preserving a cultural heritage and gaining success and acceptance in the larger American society. Jewish identity has been preserved by the family, religion, and the vast network of national and community-based organizations. Simultaneously, anti-Semitism from outside the Jewish community has strengthened in-group feelings and the sense that Jewish survival is at stake. Yet American Jews today confront the new challenge of maintaining their identity in a non-Jewish society where discrimination and prejudice are less pronounced than in the past (Schaefer 1984).

Other White Ethnics

Besides Jews, a diversity of other white ethnic groups make up American society (see Table 13.3). These include Irish, Italians, Poles, and people from other southern and eastern European nations. Many white ethnics are blue-collar workers who work as longshoremen, miners, or mechanics and who own their own homes in communities such as Boston's Charlestown or Cleveland's West Side. Some ethnic groups are concentrated in some regions of the country, as, for example, Italians and Russians in the Northeast and Norwegians and Czechs in the North Central states.

Of course, some of these ethnic groups have been much more accepted and assimilated than others, at least initially. Reasons for this may have to do with prejudice and discrimination against those who were markedly different from dominant WASPs (white Anglo-

TABLE 13.3   White Ethnics, 1980

English	49,598,035
German	49,224,146
Irish	40,165,702
French	12,892,246
Italian	12,183,692
Scottish	10,048,816
Polish	8,228,037
Dutch	6,304,499
Swedish	4,345,392
Norwegian	3,453,839
Russian	2,781,432
Spanish-Hispanic	2,686,680
Czech	1,892,456
Hungarian	1,776,902
Welsh	1,664,598
Danish	1,518,273
Portuguese	1,024,351
Swiss	981,543
Greek	959,856
Austrian	948,558
French-Canadian	780,488
Slovak	776,806
Lithuanian	742,776
Ukrainian	730,056
Finnish	615,872
Canadian	456,212
Belgian	360,277
Yugoslavian	360,174
Romanian	315,258

Source: U.S. Bureau of the Census, *Statistical Abstract*, 1980.

Saxon Protestants) in appearance, religion, and other characteristics. But this explanation goes only so far. Why, for example, were some differences reinforced and others ignored? This may have to do with what was going on socially, politically, and economically, particularly in the labor markets, when the various waves of each immigrant group arrived here. Stanley Lieberson (1981) and other sociologists have recently been focusing on just these aspects of the relative successes of some white ethnic groups compared with others. Richard Polenberg (1980) has argued, however, that though ethnicity among whites may be important, both individually and socially, the actual divisions and differences among the various white ethnic groups matter little in comparison with the differences and the tensions dividing whites from blacks, Hispanics, Asians, and people from the

Third World. Overall, most sociologists agree that white ethnic groups have generally done well in this country, given the passage of time (Sowell 1981).

During the late 1960s, when the country was divided over the war in Vietnam, white ethnics acquired a reputation for being archconservatives; the term *hard hat* became synonymous with *racist* and *hawk*. But this image, like other stereotypes, has proven to be incorrect. In fact, several surveys conducted during the Vietnam War indicated that white ethnics were more likely to be doves and to support integration than WASPs (Greeley 1974).

Recently, a renewed interest in ethnicity has emerged, what some have termed an "ethnic revival." Some Italians, Poles, Czechs, Irish, and others have sought to revitalize their ethnic heritage and identity. The impulse to recapture the ethnic past was heightened by black cultural nationalism and racial polarization accompanying school desegregation. Yet much of the new ethnicity has proven more symbolic than real (Gans 1979; Steinberg 1981). The loss of the mother tongue, the breakup of ethnic enclaves, and the rapid rise of ethnic and religious intermarriage has undercut ethnicity as a significant factor in American life.

Efforts to Eliminate Institutional Discrimination

As noted before, discrimination exists at two levels within society: the institutional and the individual. Discrimination is so thoroughly entrenched in our social institutions that it perpetuates itself, sometimes regardless of whether individuals themselves are prejudiced.

Special measures are needed to eliminate these institutional arrangements. Integration of the schools and affirmative action are among the measures that have been tried in the United States. These are fairly recent steps, taken only when large numbers of people began to protest discrimination and injustice. How well are these measures working?

Desegregation of Education

On May 17, 1954, the Supreme Court ruled, in the landmark *Brown v. Board of Education* decision, that laws requiring racially segregated schools were unconsti-

In 1957, Dorothy Geraldine Counts ignored the jeers of white youths as she went to enroll in a newly desegregated high school in Charlotte, North Carolina. School desegregation has been more successful in the South than in the North, where housing patterns and the number of school districts in and around urban areas have made court-ordered busing a controversial issue. (UPI/Bettmann News Photos.)

tutional. Bitter struggle, violence, and even terror followed the decision. The television news showed frightened black children being ushered into their grammar schools by marshalls, as furious mobs screamed and jeered. But by 1970 the statistics were encouraging: Of the South's 2,702 school districts, 94 percent were estimated by the Justice Department to have been in compliance with the law on school desegregation. By 1987 a new survey showed that the South, where absolute segregation had once been the rule, was more successful at desegregation than the North (Fiske 1987). In northern states, segregated housing patterns and the large number of small school districts (which meant that city-suburban lines had to be crossed in order to integrate) have made desegregation difficult.

The 1987 survey also showed that segregation in our schools is deeply entrenched. Between 1972 and 1984, segregation of black students did not budge. Nearly two-thirds of all black students still go to segregated schools (in which whites make up the minority; in desegregated schools whites make up the majority). Hispanic students, too, attend increasingly segregated schools. Between 1980 and 1984, the number of Hispanic students attending segregated schools actually increased, from 68.1 to 70.6 percent. Only Asian American children, the survey showed, went to integrated schools. As the political scientist who authored the study commented:

> Whatever may be the roots of the "urban underclass," it is certainly true that its children go to schools that are almost totally segregated by race and class and have no viable connection to any paths of mobility in education and employment. (Orfield, quoted in Fiske 1987, p. 24)

The segregation of our schools runs counter to the early American ideal that all children should attend a common school, that by bringing together in the schools children of all races, ethnic backgrounds, religions, and classes, we will create a single and unified nation. European nations have long operated a two-tiered educational system: one set of schools for the elite and one for the masses. Although Americans disavow such a system, we have in effect created a similar arrangement by sorting ourselves into housing patterns that separate people by race and social class and then linking school attendance to neighborhood residence (Coleman 1981).

The courts have devised several remedies for desegregating community schools, including redrawing the boundaries of school districts, relocating schools, and reassigning students. Of all of these remedies, areawide busing to achieve racially balanced schools has been the most controversial and has aroused the greatest tension.

Social scientists hoped that desegregation would improve the academic achievement of black students. After all, research conducted in the 1960s suggested that black children's performance improved as the proportion of white students in a school increased (Coleman 1966). But has this held true? The answer is complicated. Some studies have actually shown that desegregation *negatively* affects black students' achievement (Longshore and Prager 1985). But most studies do show that desegregation improves black students' achievement, though it has little effect on that of white students. What is more, black students' achievement seems to improve most when desegregation begins in the early grades.

But although desegregation may improve minority students' achievement, it does not usually improve relations among racial groups. What ties there are tend to be superficial, even in schools with a strong reputation for integration. The community of New Rochelle, New York, for example, was ordered by the courts to desegregate its schools in 1961. Today the high school is, as its (first black) principal puts it, desegregated but not yet integrated (Rimer 1987). The students tend to be friendly with those of their own race and class, and the friendships that do cross racial lines tend not to cross class lines. As for achievement, although blacks are high achievers, the honors classes and the student government and newspaper staff remain mostly white.

The picture that emerges, then, despite some progress toward desegregation, is still one of largely segregated educational institutions. Where desegregation is achieved, particularly in the early grades, and where schools focus on cooperative learning in small, mixed-race groups, minority achievement does improve, and racial acceptance seems to be fostered (Longshore and Prager 1985). But true integration of the educational system remains a distant ideal.

Affirmative Action

Affirmative action refers to the special consideration and preferential treatment accorded to members of minority groups to remedy past discrimination. Affirmative action programs are designed to remove the institutional barriers to the advancement of minorities and women and to redress historic imbalances. These programs are directed against entrenched institutional practices and, typically, set priorities for the admission of minority-group students to certain schools. Edmund Perry, for example, was sent to Exeter by an affirmative action program called A Better Chance, which places gifted minority students in prep schools (Anson 1987). The programs also set priorities for the hiring of minorities and the establishment of timetables for reaching minority-employment target goals. Critics of affirmative action brand the programs *reverse discrimination*, even reverse racism, and claim that such programs victimize white men.

The legal foundation of affirmative action is the Civil Rights Act of 1964, which is aimed at eliminating discrimination based on race, religion, ethnic origin, or sex. According to its advocates, attacking job and educational discrimination involves more than just eliminating legal barriers, for if we ignore the deficits in skills and credentials minorities and women suffer, little change is likely. Therefore, affirmative action is necessary to eliminate the consequences of past discrimination.

What, more precisely, do affirmative action programs entail? Applied to hiring practices, for example, employers are asked to inventory all employees, and after they have identified areas in which there are proportionately few minorities and women, they are asked to set goals for the employment of members of such groups. Goals are a way of assessing an employer's commitment, but they are not quotas:

> The employer is not compelled to hire unqualified persons or to compromise genuinely valid standards to meet the established goal. If goals are not met, no sanctions are imposed, so long as the contractor can demonstrate that he made good faith efforts to reach them. (U.S. Commission on Civil Rights 1977, p. 6)

One problem is how to monitor and enforce affirmative action programs. The Equal Employment Opportunity Commission (EEOC) is the main government agency assigned this task. One of its most notable successes was a case in which AT&T agreed to set goals for sexual integration of its jobs and to give $38 million in back pay to women it had channeled into low-paying, dead-end jobs. Despite such dramatic cases, however, most complaints to the EEOC languish for years.

Affirmative action has suffered many setbacks since the mid-1960s and the Civil Rights Act. The political mood of the country has grown increasingly conservative, culminating, as some see it, in the two terms of the Reagan presidency. The Reagan administration proved to be actively opposed to affirmative action in all of its forms (Pinkney 1987). One indication was Reagan's firing of members of the Civil Rights Commission who sought enforcement of civil rights laws and his appointment of members opposed to civil rights and affirmative action. It is interesting to note, however, that many state and local governments have held firm in their stated allegiance to affirmative action programs already in place, no matter what the federal government does (Pinkney 1987).

Nevertheless, today affirmative action programs are in a precarious and controversial position. For even when the general idea of affirmative action is supported, there is little agreement as to how to effect it fairly. As Justice Brennan wrote in his opinion on the Alabama Public Safety case:

> It is now well established that government bodies, including courts, may constitutionally employ racial classifications essential to remedy unlawful treatment of racial or ethnic groups subject to discrimination. . . . But although this Court has consistently held that some elevated level of scrutiny is required when a racial or ethnic distinction is made for remedial purposes, it has yet to reach consensus on the appropriate constitutional analysis. (*New York Times*, February 26, 1987)

Some sociologists have suggested that affirmative action programs have helped middle-class blacks, who are able to take advantage of the opportunities the programs offer and are least affected by the accumulated discrimination of the past. But, these sociologists claim, the majority of blacks who make up the poor underclass have not been reached at all (Wilson 1987). William J. Wilson (1987) concludes that the programs are simply not appropriate for the poorer class and have not been directed at that disadvantaged segment of the black population. After all, special graduate-school admission programs favoring blacks will not do anything for those in the ghetto without any hope of obtaining a college degree. This may be one of the problems created by a focus on preferential treatment for groups based primarily on race or ethnicity without regard for the economic and social rankings within these groups. These issues are taken up in the next section.

The Future of Race Relations

We are a nation that upholds an ideal of equality but perpetuates discrimination and prejudice. Given the disparity between our ideal and the reality, how can we assess the status of race relations today? Twenty-five years after the passage of significant civil rights legislation, why do so many nonwhites remain at the bottom of the social hierarchy, locked into a perhaps permanent underclass of poverty, unemployment, and despair? Can this change? What might the future hold?

According to some observers, racial tensions between blacks and whites in this country worsened during the late 1980s. As a black professor remarked, "Where you should see a melting pot, I definitely see polarization" (Freedman 1987, p. 1). This mutual antagonism can be seen in a flare-up such as the incident in December 1986 at Howard Beach, New York, a white, predominantly Italian, middle-class community. A group of white men chased three black men who were walking through the neighborhood and beat them up. When one of the blacks ran onto a highway to escape, he was struck by a car and killed. The police questioned eleven whites and charged and prosecuted three of them, all high school students (Freedman 1987). The majority of both blacks and whites condemned the attack. But it also unleashed pent-up anger among blacks for other brutal assaults over the years. Black leaders insisted that the incident represented the traditional racism of white ethnics in this country. The whites of Howard Beach felt that their entire community should not be condemned for the actions of a few aimless, angry teenagers.

Howard Beach confirmed for many that race relations have been disintegrating and today form one of the primary problems facing the nation. Thus, a number of sociologists argue that the significance of race is *increasing*, especially for middle-class blacks, who, because of school desegregation and affirmative action, come into extended contact with whites (Willie 1979).

Other sociologists have suggested that socioeconomic structural factors, including the stratification of the black population, have become far more central than race itself to the continued deep poverty of the black underclass in the ghetto. The foremost spokesman for this position is William J. Wilson (1978, 1987), particularly in his recent study, *The Truly Disadvantaged: The Inner City, the Underclass, and Public Policy*. Wilson has argued persuasively that the major problems—what he calls the "social dislocations"—of the ghetto underclass are the heavy increases in crime, drug addiction, teenage pregnancy, out-of-wedlock births, female-headed households, dependency on welfare, and joblessness. Defining these problems in terms of race, says Wilson, is simply too easy an answer and actually obscures the real issues. Though its past and present effects are pervasive, racism does not entirely explain why, for example, these dislocations in ghetto life occurred during a period when the broadest antidiscrimination programs to date were put in motion. Rather, it is the economic and demographic shifts in our society that

Did the boldness and clarity of the Civil Rights movement in the 1950s and 1960s spring from the boldness and clarity of the wrongs it addressed? Today, racial discrimination seems to involve a subtler, more complex interaction of economic conditions, demographic changes, and entrenched practices. What strategies are needed to ensure that the march toward true racial equality continues? (Matt Herror/Black Star.)

have heavily affected the ghetto labor market and produced such high rates of long-term unemployment. These shifts include the changeover from a goods-oriented to a services-oriented economy; the movement of industry away from the central city; the split and polarization of the labor market into only low- and high-paying jobs, with little in between; the reductions in the need for unskilled labor; the consequent mismatch between available jobs and the skills of the inner-city residents; the heavy influx of immigrants, particularly Hispanics, which has swollen the ranks of the unskilled and contributed to a population explosion and lower median age among minorities; and finally, the flight of middle-class blacks, with the aid of affirmative action,

from the inner city, which left behind a greater concentration of the poor (Wilson 1987). What Wilson is suggesting is a whole new way of approaching the complex, interrelated problems of the ghetto underclass, as well as the potential reforms needed to address those problems.

Though Wilson's position has been controversial, what does seem clear is that race relations today are a powerful combination of racial prejudice and economic change in our society. The challenge will be to learn how economics and race influence one another—and whether social programs can be designed to improve the life chances of those without decent housing, schools, jobs, or real hope.

SUMMARY

1. Race and ethnic relations are characterized by discrimination and unequal distributions of power, opportunity, and resources or by ethnic pride, assimilation, and success for different social groups.

2. The physical appearance or cultural characteristics of members of minority groups set them apart from members of the dominant group and subject them to unequal treatment. Minority groups reflect patterns of economic and political domination in the structure of a society.

3. Race and ethnicity are social constructs. A race is a population that perceives itself and is perceived by others to have distinctive, physical characteristics. Ethnicity is a social identification based on perceived cultural differences of a group.

4. Social consequences of race and ethnicity include a sense of identity and shared tradition, a sense of alienation from the out-group, social and political solidarity—and racism.

5. Prejudice is a positive or negative attitude toward a group of people for their real or imagined social characteristics. Discrimination is action based on prejudice. Institutional discrimination is the systematic denial of rights and opportunities to a group. It does not necessarily involve prejudiced individuals; it is built into programs and policies. Segregation physically and socially separates groups by race or ethnicity; integration unites them.

6. When different racial and ethnic groups meet, typically either conflict or accommodation results. Patterns of conflict often grow out of a combination of ethnocentrism and competition for resources. Sometimes one group economically and politically subjugates another, as in colonialism, resulting in racial stratification. Internal colonialism is also possible. At other times, the more powerful group displaces the weaker, whether by attrition, population transfer, or genocide.

7. Minorities may react to prejudice and discrimination by trying to become accepted by the dominant group or by engaging in covert aggression, political and economic protest, or violent protest and outright rebellion.

8. Sometimes groups meet with a minimum of conflict, as when they blend, assimilate, or exist in a pluralistic mosaic. Assimilation of a particular group is influenced by time factors, historical and economic contexts, size of the group, similarity to the dominant group, benefits to the dominant group from the other group's minority status, and the minority's own desire to assimilate. The so-called melting pot may be more a figment of political ideology than a reflection of reality. The United States is not really a pluralistic society because white Anglo-Saxon Protestant values and ideals predominate.

9. There are several ways to explain prejudice and discrimination: the psychological need to take frustration out on a scapegoat; the role played by racial and ethnic myths, which serve as a justification for racism; the role played by social and economic conflict, often based on one group's perceived threat from another group and the benefits to be gained or maintained by discrimination (the power perspective); and cultural factors, which maintain prejudice as an embedded, socialized habit.

10. Racial tensions may be worsening in the United States. The largest minority in the United States, blacks, have had to contend with slavery and the myth of black inferiority. Although slavery was abolished in 1865, discrimination continues, despite the victories of the 1960s civil rights movement. There have been improvements for some blacks, but there is not yet equality with whites. The black population is stratified: A black middle class has been growing, but an even larger, very poor underclass, largely confined to urban ghettos, is more isolated and more problem-laden than ever.

11. Hispanics, also disproportionately represented in the urban underclass, make up the second largest minority group in the United States. By the next century, they may be the largest. Hispanics come from many different Latin American societies, but they share a language, religion, and customs that make them a distinctive ethnic group.

12. Native Americans are the poorest minority group in the United States and have suffered all the tragic effects of racism.

13. Asian Americans have been relatively successful in this country. Chinese people have been immigrating into the United States since the mid-1800s and have experienced strong discrimination and exploitation. But strong family emphasis on education and success and relaxed immigration laws have meant that many Chinese Americans could move swiftly into the middle class. Japanese Americans, too, despite prejudice and discrimination, especially during World War II, have as a group succeeded in the United States. Other Asians are arriving in increasing numbers. Jewish Americans rank well above the national average in education and income. Other white ethnics such as Italians, Poles, and Irish are still clustered in many tight-knit city neighborhoods, but they are moving increasingly into the middle class.

14. Attempts to eliminate institutional discrimination in this country have included school desegregation and affirmative action laws and programs. Each has met with some success, and each has stirred up opposition, particularly from the large conservative constituency in the 1980s.

15. Although we are a nation that upholds the ideal of equality, prejudice and institutional discrimination are still pervasive. Some sociologists see race becoming increasingly significant. Others see the isolation of the inner-city underclass and the economic polarization of our society as the central issues. Race relations today must be seen as a system of *power* relations based on race, social status, and economics.

GLOSSARY

Affirmative action. Special consideration and preferential treatment accorded to members of minority groups to remedy past discrimination.

Apartheid. Laws and policies in South Africa that segregate whites and nonwhites at every level of society.

Assimilation. The incorporation of a minority group into the culture and social life of the dominant group such that the minority eventually disappears as a separate, identifiable unit.

Colonialism. The economic takeover of one nation by another, more powerful nation, and the subsequent political and social domination of the native population.

De facto segregation. Racial separation that results from unofficial social patterns, as opposed to segregation imposed by law, or de jure segregation.

De jure segregation. Segregation imposed by law.

Discrimination. Exclusion or exploitation on the basis of group membership.

Ethnic group. A category of people who perceive themselves and are perceived by others as possessing shared cultural traits.

Frustration-aggression hypothesis. The theory that people are goal-directed creatures who become angry and hostile when their desires are frustrated and displace their rage upon a scapegoat.

Institutional discrimination. A structuring of policies and programs so as to systematically deny opportunities and equal rights to members of particular groups.

Integration. The unimpeded interaction and contact between different racial and ethnic groups.

Internal colonialism. The formation of distinct groups within a society, caused by varying degrees of economic opportunity, that are economically and spatially segregated from one another.

Jim Crow laws. The legal and social barriers constructed in the South in the late nineteenth and early twentieth centuries to prevent blacks from voting, using public facilities, and mixing with whites. (Jim Crow was the name of a minstrel character who performed in blackface.)

Minority groups. People who are singled out for unequal treatment in the society in which they live, and who consider themselves to be victims of collective discrimination.

Pluralism. The coexistence of different racial or ethnic groups, each of which retains its own cultural identity and social networks, while participating equally in the economic and political systems.

Prejudice. A categorical predisposition to like or dislike people for their real or imagined social characteristics.

Race. A group of people who believe themselves and whom others believe to be genetically distinct.

Racism. The doctrine that some races are inherently inferior and some inherently superior to others.

Scapegoat. A substitute target on which angry and frustrated individuals displace their hostility.

Segregation. The restricted or prohibited contact between groups that is created by law or custom. Segregation may be ethnic or racial, or based on sex or age.

Underclass. A poverty-stricken subgroup with few resources and few opportunities to improve its status in society.

CHAPTER 14
Politics, the State, and War

I n the mid-1980s, newspapers the world over carried grim stories about acts of terrorism: a truck bomb blew up the American marine barracks in Beirut, killing hundreds of soldiers; the cruise ship *Achille Lauro* was hijacked and an elderly man on board was killed; a TWA plane was hijacked in Athens and a young soldier was murdered. To many people who read or heard about them, these gruesome events seemed to be isolated crimes carried out by madmen. From a sociological point of view, however, these events were neither isolated nor merely the work of a handful of unbalanced and violent people. As one sociologist, Richard E. Rubenstein (1987, p. 51), has noted, "More than five thousand terrorist acts were committed worldwide in the decade of the 1970s, of which approximately 40 percent took place in Western Europe, 25 percent in the urbanized Latin American nations, and 10 percent in the United States."

Terrorism has become so widespread that it is now impossible to dismiss it as the action of a few insane people. In fact, terrorism—the use of violence by small groups of people to accomplish political aims they feel unable to bring about by peaceful, legitimate means —has sociological roots.

Terrorism most often stems from the situation of people who consider themselves a national group but who feel that no *state*, no legitimate and widely recognized autonomous government, represents them. Since all the inhabitable territory of the world is divided into states, which are the main organizational units through which people can exercise political power, people without a state to represent them feel completely powerless and cut off from the world order. To have independence —and even a recognized identity—as a people, those individuals feel that they, too, must have a sovereign state government. Thus terrorism is frequently a tactic of people who find themselves or feel themselves to be stateless. They may seek to overthrow the government of the country in which they live and replace it by one more to their liking, or they may try to secede from the state they inhabit in order to found a new country. Terrorism thus poses a major challenge to an existing state's legitimacy.

It is no accident that many of today's acts of terrorism relate to the political situation in the Middle East. Palestine and the lands around it have been a battleground between two contending groups—Jews and Arabs—for generations. Early in the twentieth century, a movement began among European Jews to settle in Palestine (then a British protectorate) in the hopes of establishing a country of their own. This idea, known as Zionism, was a response to the feelings of statelessness of many Jews. Dispersed throughout many countries in the world, Jews suffered oppression and persecution. Some of the Jews who settled in Palestine became terrorists; they attacked the British regime, blowing up buildings and carrying out other acts of violence. After World War II, when Nazi Germany's efforts to exterminate the Jewish population of Europe were revealed, hundreds of thousands of Jews joined the Zionist movement, seeking a state in Palestine. This plan was supported by the British and other Western governments. When the state of Israel was created, however, thousands of Palestinians joined neighboring Arab countries in denying the legiti-

Terrorism and war, loss and fear, have become part of daily life for the people of once-cosmopolitan Beirut. From a sociological viewpoint, bombings and battles in Lebanon are part of the larger patterns of violence and terrorism that characterize the Middle East today. (Gamma-Liaison.)

macy. Many were seen as security risks and evicted from their homes; all suddenly found themselves "foreigners" in a religious state that excluded them from full rights of citizenship. Some discontented Palestinians turned to guerrilla combat against Israel and others turned to terrorism. A central goal of both peaceful and violent struggle was the creation of an independent Palestinian state. One stateless group—Jews—had gained a state, but this only intensified the desire of stateless Palestinians for a country of their own, on the land of their ancestors.

Terrorism is not, however, confined to the Middle East. American terrorists, ultra left-wing young people in the 1960s and 70s, committed a number of bombings as a protest against the Vietnam War, which they considered to be an undeclared and illegitimate war. Terrorists may also be citizens of an underdeveloped country ruled by a small elite that victimizes peasants and the urban poor (as in the case of Latin American guerrilla movements). Defenders of some ideological position (racial "purity," opposition to abortion, for example) may resort to terrorism as a response to changes

adverse to their position in a pluralist society. Terrorists may also be members of a national or religious group that seeks freedom from the domination of other groups (as Catholics in Northern Ireland or Sikhs in India).

Whatever the motives of those who try to accomplish change by violence, existing governments are likely to label them as terrorists—meaning that they have no legitimacy and few followers. Sometimes, however, history seems to prove that the terrorists' cause was a good and principled one. To the British, the American colonists who threw tea into Boston Harbor before the Revolutionary War were mere terrorists. Today, because a majority of colonists gave their support to this struggle, we revere them as heroes.

In this chapter we discuss the state, a lack of which—as we have seen—is often behind terrorist acts. We discuss how states arise and how they come to be seen as legitimate (or not). More broadly, we consider what power is, how it comes to be contested, and how stable and concentrated it is. Finally, we take up the question of war, or what happens when a contest between two competing states erupts into conflict.

THE CONTEST FOR POWER

Sociologists define **politics** as the social process by which people gain, use, and lose power. And **power,** according to Max Weber's classic definition, is "the probability that one actor within a social relationship will be in a position to carry out his own will despite resistance" (1922/1978, p. 153). Thus, there is an element of politics—of acquiring and using power—in almost all social relationships, not only those that are formally set apart as being about power, such as government, the police, and the military. Parents, for example, seek to maintain power over their children; husbands and wives exercise power over each other; teachers wield power over their students; and business executives use power to run their companies. Hence, politics is an inevitable part of social living, not simply a question of who is running for election or who is occupying public office. In this chapter, however, the focus is on politics in the larger sense, on the specialized institutions of power, especially those linked to government.

Weber's definition of power—the ability to exert control over others despite their resistance—is still widely accepted, but it refers to only one sort of power. Power in Weber's sense is known by sociologists today as **distributive power,** that is, power in relation to that of others. Power in this sense is unequally distributed, and the person or persons with more power will prevail when there is conflict. Sociologists also recognize another kind of power, which is sometimes called **collective** or **enabling power** (Parsons 1960). This is the capacity of people to get things done—to manufacture material goods, for instance. Power in this sense is not distributed among people, but arises out of cooperative effort, a division of labor, and so forth. For example, through a division of labor a factory of workers has the capacity to produce automobiles. Through cooperation, the staff of a hospital can provide patients with the care that they need to get well. Collective power is thus an enhancement of power through cooperation. This collective increase in power through a division of labor happens at the level of the whole society as well. The existence of many different occupations and professions increases the productive, administrative, and even defensive capacity of the whole (Rueschemeyer 1986).

Legitimacy and Authority

When sociologists look at power, they are concerned not only to know how great it is but also whether it is legitimate. **Legitimacy** refers to the extent to which power is recognized as valid and justified by the people in a relationship (and, implicitly, by the society at large). Thus the power of parents over children is generally seen as legitimate (as long as it is not grossly abused), whereas the power of a criminal with a gun is not. Sociologists often refer to legitimate power as **authority,** and note that it is exercised with the social approval of most individuals in a group or society. A simple example should help to illustrate this. We recognize that judges have judicial authority to make decisions on matters of law; whether or not we agree with their decisions, we believe in the judges' right to do so. In contrast, illegitimate power is exercised without such social approval. Such illegitimate power always depends on coercion or the use of force. Berger and Luckman (1966), for example, view **coercive power** as progressing on a continuum from least overtly forceful to most forceful, with persuasion, pressure, and coercion as the major types. Coercive power then could depend on the

use of physical force (a mugging) or on a less overt inducement (such as money), but its goal is to induce people to do something that they may not otherwise want to do. Thus, if coercive power is the ability to control other people's behavior, authority is the right to do so. Coercive power is sometimes used in support of authority, as when police routinely give tickets for speeding and other violations.

Power that is based on authority is usually accepted by those who are subject to it. Power based on coercion, however, tends to be unstable because people submit to it out of fear rather than loyalty and may at some point revolt. In practice, most political systems rest on the exercise of both legitimate authority and coercive power. Few systems are based so completely on force that they do not involve at least an element of consent from the governed. Even dictatorships get some kind of acceptance. But when a political system comes to depend almost exclusively on the use of force, it begins to lose the allegiance of its people, and is liable to experience opposition and even collapse. Such was the precipitous state of affairs in Iran under the late Shah, and in the Philippines under Ferdinand Marcos. Through their continued reliance on force, the authority of these rulers was undermined and their bases of power eventually crumbled. Coercive power may be effective for single acts of submission, but it is not effective in the long run as the primary basis for a government.

People's ideas can differ about the legitimacy of political systems. In the United States we tend to have higher expectations of legitimacy than mere toleration of our political system. As discussed further later in this chapter, Americans hold representative democracy dear as an ideal toward which we strive, not just a system under which we happen to live. But even the American system is not perfectly "democratic." The election of representatives, for example, is actually a compromise of the democratic ideal of direct participation, but this is hardly practical in a large-scale society (Bobbio 1987; Held 1987). The point is that however highly we value democracy, other systems may have legitimacy in the eyes of those who live under them. Other kinds of political authority are recognized. The family is not a democracy, for example, and neither are most churches. In many countries, it is considered legitimate for a political leader to exercise power in the manner of a father or a priest.

As suggested previously, there is no objective basis on which to decide whether a political system is legitimate—legitimacy depends on the consent of the governed. But we may identify weaker and stronger standards of legitimacy. For instance, a government could be considered legitimate unless there is overt, widespread, and public opposition to it. Such a weak notion of legitimacy is particularly characteristic of the functional perspective (Lipset 1981). From a functional viewpoint, as long as people tolerate the political order enough for it to stay in power, then the functional need for legitimacy is fulfilled. In contrast, the power perspective tends toward a much stronger concept of legitimacy (Habermas 1975; Taylor 1985). Power sociologists argue that a system is not legitimate unless the people in it really have the power to make changes if they so desire. Some power theorists would go further and ask whether even institutions that people accept on a day-to-day basis are legitimate if they are not in the people's best interest, and if a visible alternative exists (Connolly 1984).

Legitimacy thus remains an ongoing issue for governments and political leaders. The legitimacy of any political system may fluctuate, depending on events. When a government begins to lose legitimacy, it may come to depend increasingly on the use of force. Such a state of affairs now exists in South Africa, where the government has sought to protect itself by passing harsh "state of emergency" laws, jailing its opponents, and committing other coercive acts. In parliamentary systems, such as that of Great Britain, an election is called when a government is perceived as having lost its legitimacy. In the United States, questions of legitimacy have in recent years been responsible for the retirement of Lyndon Johnson and the resignation of Richard Nixon. Even today, when there is much less of an air of crisis, public confidence in social institutions is not high (Gallup Report 1986). The revelations of the so-called Iran-Contra affair caused the previously high level of confidence in President Reagan to plummet (Harris 1987; Sussman 1988). Revelations that members of the Reagan administration traded arms with Iran for hostages and money, and used the profits from the deal to finance the rebels in Nicaragua raised serious questions about the legitimate conduct of American foreign policy.

When a government is seen as legitimate, people willingly (more or less) submit to its authority. Why do most people accept their leaders and governing institutions? The most influential view of authority is that of Weber, who identified three types of authority: legal/rational, charismatic, and traditional. Each type is characterized by a different base on which legitimate power rests.

Legal/Rational Authority

Legal/rational authority derives from a system of explicit rules or laws that define legitimate uses of power. Authority is vested in offices or positions, not in their temporary occupants. Thus, legal/rational authority is viewed as "a government of laws, not of people." Authority is also limited to "official business." For example, bosses have considerable authority over the way employees spend their working days, but not over how they spend their weekends. Under legal/rational authority, an officeholder can exercise power only within specified limits. People view the officeholder as carrying out his or her responsibilities within the context of a "rational" system defined by rules and regulations.

Charismatic Authority

Charismatic authority is the opposite of legal/rational authority. It derives from exceptional personal qualities that people perceive as a "gift of grace," capabilities that seem superhuman or supernatural. The key to charismatic authority lies in followers' beliefs in the gifts of the leader, not in objective evidence of those beliefs. People follow a charismatic leader out of personal devotion. But Weber (1918/1949, p. 249) observed: "The charismatic leader gains and maintains authority solely by proving his strength in life. If he wants to be a prophet, he must perform miracles; if he wants to be a war lord, he must perform heroic deeds." Because charismatic leaders have unique qualities, successors are not easily found. For this reason, charismatic authority is inherently unstable and does not endure for long. If charismatic authority does not collapse, it is usually routinized into a more traditional or rational/legal form of authority. Examples of charismatic leaders in recent history are Mahatma Gandhi, who led the nonviolent struggle for independence in India, Martin Luther King, Jr., and Malcolm X, black leaders in the United States, and César Chavez, a spokesperson for Mexican-American farm workers.

Traditional Authority

Traditional authority stems from beliefs and practices passed down from generation to generation. In traditional societies people tend to regard the way things have always been done as sacred; kings, queens, chiefs, priests, councils of elders, and the like are part of this

Three types of authority: traditional, charismatic, and legal/rational. Swaziland has a new king, Mswati III, "The Lion," whose family has ruled this small kingdom for generations. Martin Luther King held no public office, but his courage and vision became a source of power and direction for the Civil Rights movement. Margaret Thatcher serves as Britain's prime minister; authority is vested in her office by explicit rules and within specified limits. (Top left: Francois Von Sury/Sygma; bottom left: Dan Budnik/Woodfin Camp & Associates; right: Peter Turnley/Black Star.)

sacred order. Although traditions may limit their authority, such leaders do have some latitude in making decisions. Positions are typically hereditary and people feel a sense of personal loyalty to the occupants.

In practice the three types of authority identified by Weber may overlap. John F. Kennedy, for example, had rational/legal authority by virtue of his election to the presidency; he also had the traditional authority that surrounds the office of the presidency and the power of charisma as well. In any given instance of legitimate power, however, authority often rests primarily on one or another of these three foundations.

THE STATE

Power, as we have seen, is a factor in all human relationships. One of the most distinctive features of modern societies is the extent to which many kinds of power relations are concentrated in a specialized arena. In these societies, certain institutions and organizations specialize in the wielding of power and authority. These include the courts, the police, the legislature, regulatory agencies, the executive branch (the presidency, governors, and so on), and the military. Taken together, and along with other public organizations such as the schools, transportation departments, water and sewer authorities, and so on, these institutions in which autonomous power over a geographical area is concentrated make up what sociologists call the **state**. The state has a monopoly over the legitimate use of force within a given territory. This monopoly depends on the state's acceptance as legitimate by those living within that territory. As we saw at the beginning of this chapter, those who do not accept the state as legitimate are considered by the state as terrorists—or revolutionaries.

The state is not identical with the government. The government is the body of elected and nonelected officials who direct the state at any given period. The state is an abstract entity. Thus, one can in theory be loyal to one's country even while detesting a particular government.

Throughout most of history, abstract states as we know them did not exist. Power was concentrated in people themselves, usually in elders or in heads of families. Tribes or other small groups formed the basic social units. Kinship was the basis of the social order. Personal power and official power were one. Political power was not distinct from personal relationships.

The state as we know it today has come into being largely through a gradual process of ever-greater distinctions being made between private and public—between officials as private persons and officials in their public capacities. The process began with the emergence of chieftains and kings, as political power became more and more specialized. *Kinship* gave way to *kingship*. Eventually, "kingship"—the office of king—came to be understood as something separate from the particular person who held that office at any given time. "The King is dead! Long live the King!" In other words, a king may die, but the office itself continues, occupied by the dead king's heir or other successors (Gluckman 1965; Kantorowicz 1957).

As the state grew and empowered more and more officials, the notion that the authority and rewards of public employment should be distributed on the basis of qualifications rather than on kinship became increasingly accepted (Weber 1922). The public and private spheres grew further and further apart. Today we consider it highly inappropriate for officials to let personal relations influence their actions. Governors, for example, cannot appoint their in-laws to state jobs or treat public funds as their own without risking criminal prosecution. Modern states have grown to unprecedented strength, with an ever-widening gap between public and private life, as we will see in the next section.

The Rise of Modern States and the Origins of Bureaucracy

States as we know them today began to form in Europe around the sixteenth century, and the process of state formation continued through the early nineteenth century. Two major and interrelated forces were behind this process: (1) the expansion and consolidation of territories, and (2) the growth of international commerce. These in turn were linked to other historical trends: the uniting of disconnected principalities through inheritance or royal marriages; the improvement of transportation; wars of conquest; the exploration and colonization of the Americas, Africa, and Asia. Maintaining control over large or far-flung territories became both necessary and possible. In order to secure territorial boundaries, rulers had to be prepared to fight off and stop the empire-building ambitions of rival rulers. This meant that armies had to be assembled and deployed over wide areas. Administering the expanding territories also meant that taxes had to be raised, roads built, and so on. At the same time, merchants and traders were demanding that their goods be protected from marauders and that the safety of their shipping be guaranteed. And this meant that treaties had to be signed and maintained, roads and seas had to be policed, international markets kept open, and domestic peace ensured (Anderson 1974; Hall 1985; Mann 1986).

In order to serve the new territorial and commercial interests, European rulers needed new governmental institutions. The larger the territory and the more complex efficient control over that territory became, the more the European rulers depended upon these institutions. These operated on two basic principles: the strict separation of public obligations from private lives, which we have discussed previously; and the governing of official behavior by formal rules, not by an official's own autonomous decisions. This new class of "public servants" became what we now call a **bureaucracy,** a term coined by Max Weber (1922) to describe rule by formal organizations of public officials. As bureaucracies expanded, two other important characteristics emerged. First, clear hierarchies of power developed within the bureaucracies. And second, the tasks of officials (bureaucrats) became more and more specialized. Thus, the need to administer the newly emerging states created bureaucracies, and bureaucracies continue to be central to the operation of every modern state today (Badie and Birnbaum 1983).

Weber did not intend his term "bureaucracy" to have the pejorative meaning people usually give it today. We often associate bureaucracy with red tape and attention to unreasonably complex rules. For Weber, the advent of bureaucracy, with its division of labor and hierarchy of control, meant that states functioned more efficiently. On the other hand, bureaucracy was inherently both *impersonal* (because of its emphasis on official roles rather than the actual persons who held them) and *formal*, since it was based on the carrying out of specific rules (even to the point of sometimes forgetting the reasons behind them). These characteristics made it easy for a bureaucracy to betray the values on which it had been founded and to appear to value its operating rules in themselves rather than as a means to some human or social end. Nevertheless, Weber saw bureaucracy as an advance because it meant that clear rules and impersonal criteria were being applied to decision making and the appointment of officials, rather than allowing personal whims and connections to dominate.

Since Weber wrote in the 1920s, bureaucracy has grown in importance throughout the world. Indeed, in some countries—the Communist countries in particular—bureaucracy seems almost the basis of the political system (Badie and Birnbaum 1983). Because the state controls most business in these countries, the public bureaucracy is central to economic as well as other areas of life. In the capitalist countries, state bureaucracies have grown as part of the development of "welfare states" (as we see later in this chapter). The growth of very large corporations has also produced significant private bureaucracies. Differing views of how much control the state versus market forces should have over social activity is one of the things that separates Communist and capitalist ideologies and political systems (de Jassay 1985; Lindblom 1977). Nevertheless, both types of systems involve bureaucracies. Bureaucracy has also spread throughout the less-developed countries of the Third World (Thomas and Meyer 1984).

Many sociologists consider the formation of an efficient bureaucracy based on the principles we have discussed (again, they are not talking about the red-tape aspect) to be an essential criterion for economic development (Amsden 1985; Robertson 1984; Rueschemeyer, Skocpol, and Evans 1985). Many Third World countries, for example, have military governments that maintain power by force. But however strong these governments may be in terms of capacity for violence, they generally do not have the benefit of a strong set of state organizations—that is, an efficient bureaucracy. Al-

though these military rulers may have physical control over whether subjects live or die, they cannot extend their power deeply into society, into the daily lives of their subjects, except in terms of fear. Their primary accomplishment is often simply staying in office. A government exists, but not a modern state the way we now define it.

Although personal relationships often continue to play a large role in distributing power and its rewards in many Third World countries, the ideology of a state free from personal domination—one of the principles of a bureaucracy—is widespread. Even in countries in which changes of regime are common, each successive coup is likely to be justified in terms of the corruption of the previous regime. What corruption means, in this context, is largely a failure to conform to the notion of a state in which the public and private realms are separate.

Nationhood and Nationalism

A development related to state formation and the rise of the bureaucracy was the emergence of the idea of nationhood and nationality (Gellner 1983; Breuilly 1985). "State" refers directly to the political institutions established within a given territory—king, president, courts, police, and the like. **Nation** refers primarily to the cultural bonds among a group of people that give them a shared identity. Before the age of state formation, European life had been primarily local. Within a single country, such as France, several languages or dialects might be spoken, and customs might vary greatly from place to place. (This situation is still common in many Third World countries.) Gradually, however, as boundaries were solidified, as transportation between regions grew easier, and as control over large territories that embraced many regions became more centralized and consistent, local differences began to decline. By the end of the eighteenth century, when the United States was born, the idea had become widespread that all the citizens of a single state should share a common culture just as they shared a single government. The growing literacy of the population, the use of printing presses to circulate literature and other documents, and the increasing connections of different districts by trade all contributed to an increasing sense of common identity. Frenchmen came to contrast themselves with Englishmen, rather than with other Frenchmen in the next valley.

Not all Frenchmen really knew each other or necessarily shared a great deal with each other. This was also true in many countries. Thus, to some extent nationhood has always been imaginary, more of an abstract ideal than a reality (Anderson 1983). But that abstract ideal has much to do with personal identity. "Americanness" is a fundamental part of our individual identities, just as being Chinese or Salvadoran is fundamental to those people's identities. We believe that a common identity is based on objective cultural traits, but these traits tend to be quite ambiguous and hard to define (see Chapter 4). Here again we see that nationhood has subjective elements. Cultural identities take their meaning primarily from comparisons with other identities—other nations.

Along with the modern concept of nationhood grew a parallel idea or belief: that all peoples with distinct cultures should have, indeed deserve, their own states (Gellner 1983). This belief, which involves an element of pride in one's own nation, became known as **nationalism** around the end of the eighteenth century (Williams 1976). The rise of nationalism clearly marked a shift in citizens' relation to their state and the power the state wielded. No longer did people identify with and promise loyalty to the interests of a king or emperor. Now they began to identify not only with one another but with broader, truly national power and policies (Morgenthau and Thompson 1985).

The continued discontent of "stateless nations" reveals another important aspect of nationalism: nationalist feelings tend to reinforce any stateless racial, ethnic, or regional group's view that having a state of its own will solve its problems. Think of the Basques in Spain, the Catholics in Northern Ireland, the Jews dispersed through Europe and other areas before Israel was created, and the dispossessed Palestinians today. All these peoples have pressed or are now pressing for their own nation-state. Remember too that nationalism was one of the driving forces behind Hitler's rise to power in Germany. The German-speaking people had never been unified in a single state. Finally, nationalism has proved to be a strong rationale for terrorism because it can unite people of different classes against a clearly defined common enemy (Rubenstein 1987).

The concepts of nation and state are now so closely connected that one hardly exists without the other. The nation-state is the central political unit of the modern world. Almost paradoxically, some nations in the world today were created not only out of a shared culture and nationalist feelings but because the peoples of these nations were in a sense forced to conform to the way the rest of the world was and is organized—according to the nation-state. This happened in Africa, where the invading, empire-building Europeans drew the boundaries of their colonies according to their particular interests —often with little or no respect for tribal cohesiveness or commonalities. In some cases, peoples who had little in common were united in one nation. In other cases, tribes were split up. When independence came to Africa, the colonial boundaries became the new countries' borders. There is no simple way to reverse the situation now, because of the predominance of the nation-state accomplished in the last 300 years (Wolf 1982).

The Modern Welfare State

In the United States and in other relatively rich, industrialized, democratic countries—Canada, New Zealand, Australia, and most of Western Europe—the state has expanded dramatically since the early nineteenth century. The state first began to take on a role in developing transportation and communication systems in the nineteenth and early twentieth centuries, and moved on to become involved with education, health care, and public services. Particularly in the last fifty years, this overall trend has been pronounced in both social democratic (a form of socialism mixed with capitalism under democratic processes) countries such as Austria and Sweden and in capitalist countries such as the United States. This trend, seen throughout the developed world, is one of the primary sociological and political phenomena of our times (Flora and Heidenheimer 1981; Przeworski 1985; Skocpol 1985).

In the United States, we usually trace the development of the broadly expanded state, now known as the **welfare state,** back to Franklin Roosevelt's "New Deal." This set of wide-ranging government programs was instituted in the 1930s to deal with the Great Depression —to boost the debilitated economy, cope with widespread unemployment, and provide for the general welfare of ordinary citizens (hence, the name "welfare state"). However, the Depression did not affect only the United States. Other countries began expanding the role of government at around the same time. The greatest and most influential theorist of government's expanded role was the English economist John Maynard Keynes (Schott 1983). Keynesian theory has provided a basis for

The flag that children salute in their yard represents both a stable set of political institutions and a cultural identity. The stateless Palestinians, on the other hand, fly their flag as a gesture of defiance and militant determination to have their own nation-state. (Left: Rick Brady/Uniphoto; right: A. Tannenbaum/Sygma.)

the enormous growth in government social programs for the poor and unemployed, for peacetime support of the military (including defense research), and for an enlargement of the government work force—in other words, of the bureaucracy.

As the state grew toward becoming the modern welfare state, it took on roles in several major areas. First, it *provided assistance* to people who could not help themselves—for example, the poor and the aged. Second, the government began to provide **collective goods** —goods that cannot easily be bought and sold by individuals because of high costs and the indivisibility of the goods themselves (Olson 1965). Examples of collective goods include national defense, a high level of education, efficient public transport systems, and clean air and water. These cannot be adequately handled by the private economy.

Collective goods can themselves be broken down into several types. *Enabling goods*, for instance, help establish proper conditions for carrying out private activities. The minting of currency by the government, for example, allows us all to buy and sell with some consistency of value. The Federal Reserve System provides for efficient banking. Highway and transportation departments build and maintain roads to enable us to travel and ship goods. State *regulatory activities* oversee the functioning of private activities and protect the public from potential ills. That is, the state regulatory agencies establish licensing criteria and thus ensure that private activities are carried out according to commonly understood rules. The Civil Rights Commission, for example, exists to ensure that all people are treated equally, according to their state-guaranteed civil rights.

The Federal Communications Commission (FCC) ensures, among other things, that the frequency on which a radio station broadcasts has minimum interference.

Some state activities can be seen as both enabling and regulatory. Think of the modern civil (noncriminal) legal system, which enables citizens to sign contracts and go about their daily business assured that their contracts will be enforced and problems redressed. The very complexity of private activities and the frequency of transactions among strangers in our modern world have made an expansion of the state role in these areas necessary.

Today, we can characterize the welfare state by its increasingly prominent part in (1) providing the sorts of services and supports we have just discussed and (2) in managing the economy. The state's control over the economy has enormous repercussions. Some sociologists have pointed out the number of basic contradictions at the heart of the welfare state in a strongly capitalist society (O'Connor 1973; Offe 1984, 1985). A capitalist economy necessarily creates inequalities and economic hardships for those who lose in its competition. Poverty and a very unequal distribution of wealth can become a threat to the legitimacy of both the state and the economic system in a country with acknowledged democratic ideals—that is, citizens may start to question their government's legitimacy. In order to quiet the criticism and avert a crisis, the government begins to spend money on welfare programs. However, if (or when) these programs start to become "too expensive," the middle class may resist footing the bill for helping the poor, and question the state's right to make them do so. Thus, a social crisis may result because the cost of the welfare programs made necessary by the inequalities of capitalism may be higher than the amount the state can raise through taxes (O'Connor 1973).

Through the 1970s and 1980s, there was considerable criticism in the United States of "big government." Indeed, Ronald Reagan was elected twice on a platform that included a reduction of the size of the U.S. government and the extent of its regulatory and social programs (though total government expenditures rose dramatically under Reagan). The Reagan administrations have been somewhat successful in reducing regulatory and relief programs. There have also been heated debates about whom the social programs actually benefit —the poor? the middle class? no one at all? everyone, for different reasons? All of these answers have been offered. Some influential critics, particularly Charles Murray (1984), have claimed that government spending on social programs has increased exorbitantly, perhaps by a factor of twenty from 1950 to 1980, and has been counterproductive. It has reinforced dependency, added to unemployment, and contributed to the rise in single-parent families and the disintegration of family life and values. These arguments have provided important support to the emerging conservative political movement. Liberal social critics, however, have accused Murray and others of implicit racism against blacks and Hispanics, since it is these minorities who are disproportionately helped by welfare programs such as Aid to Families with Dependent Children (AFDC) (Block et al. 1987). In answer to conservative pleas for far less spending on social programs and for business mobilization as the solution to the moral and economic ills of the country, sociologists such as Fred Block, Richard Cloward, Barbara Ehrenreich and Frances Fox Piven (1987) and Michael Harrington (1984) have argued for *new* social programs and an expanded welfare state, based on some challenging principles: a critique of our consumer culture, burial of the "false polarity" of traditional values and permissiveness, the centrality of true material equality, and an emphasis on democratic participation, a topic we consider next.

DEMOCRACY IN AMERICA

The state, as we have seen, is the center of legitimate power in any modern political system. But there are great differences in how states exercise their power and in the role the people play in directing state policies. How do people influence the state? What opportunities do they have for influencing the state and participating in its politics? We will concentrate throughout this section on the democratic state, but we will contrast it to other political systems and the ways in which they answer these same questions.

Democracy and Political Systems

The idea of democracy is very old; it is one of the forms of government described by classical Greek thinkers, such as Plato and Herodotus. The word itself comes from the Greek: *demos*, meaning "the people," and *krátos*, meaning "authority": hence, authority of the people, or government by the people. In a **democratic state,** authority ideally derives from the law, rooted in the consent of the people. Both the rulers and the ruled function according to the principle of *due process*. Democratic politics are based on the belief that power should not be used in capricious or arbitrary ways, and on adherence to the democratic rules of the game—such as the holding of free and open elections, acceptance of the will of the majority, and respect for the right of minorities to work within the system. The government has the power to implement its policies (opposition groups do not succeed in immobilizing the government), but that power is limited. Individuals or parties are granted only temporary authority. Other groups have the right and also the resources—including numbers of people, organizations, knowledge, and private property —to challenge government decisions. The democratic state does not claim exclusive, unquestioning loyalty (Andrain 1975). If the state oversteps the powers people have entrusted to it, the people have a right—even a duty—to oppose it.

These notions of democracy have persisted for centuries. The framers of the U.S. Constitution saw the democratic republic as one of three possible forms of government. The others were the aristocracy and the monarchy. (A republic is a government in which the supreme power rests in the body of its citizens, and which is dependent upon their virtuous participation —primarily a democratic government.) And until the founding—and longevity—of the United States proved otherwise, it was generally believed that democracy was an unstable, inefficient form.

On what social foundations does democracy rest? Or, put another way, what social and economic conditions does democracy require? These questions have been long debated. The notion that democracy rests on the existence of a strong middle class is widely accepted, chiefly because it has been reasoned that any population consisting of only poor and rich could not function cohesively. Many sociologists have argued that capitalism (which is often linked to the rise of the middle class) is the strongest economic basis for democracy (Berger 1987; Schumpeter 1942). The economic freedom on which capitalism rests does seem to correlate with and even foster political freedom. And, in fact, there have been few long-lasting noncapitalist democracies. However, there is no consensus on why this is so. Many scholars argue that in principle political democracy can be combined with economic socialism.

Particularly in this century, with the rise of communist and fascist states, many sociologists worry about the threat democracy faces from its opposite, **totalitarianism,** a form of government in which no opposing opinion, formal or informal, is recognized or tolerated. A totalitarian state differs from a traditional tyranny in degree of effective control. A totalitarian government has the capacity to control far more aspects of people's lives—in other words, its power is much more comprehensive and pervasive. Totalitarian authority typically rests on ideological grounds. Leaders justify their right to rule by claiming that they embody an ideological cause. Power tends to be concentrated in the hands of one ruling party, which is permanently identified with the government: The party and the state are one. The government ideally directs all economic activity. It also seeks to create ideological uniformity by controlling education, the mass media, and the arts and literature. The power of authorities is so great that it may be exercised in capricious and apparently arbitrary ways. The resulting atmosphere of anxiety and insecurity compels citizens to demonstrate active loyalty to the state (Andrain 1975).

The contrasts between these two systems are obvious, and, especially since the Cold War, we are accustomed to think of states as *either* democratic *or* totalitarian. However, many nation-states are neither one nor the other. Most "rulers know," writes the sociologist Barrington Moore (1980, p. 18), "that there are certain bounds to their power beyond which they cannot expect compliance. . . . And to remain rulers, they require [compliant] subjects." Thus, efforts at totalitarianism are seldom as complete as our definition of the term suggests

they might be. Whenever rulers consistently overstep the limits of their authority—when they seek personal gain to the detriment of the social order—they are frequently challenged and even overthrown. The late Shah of Iran is a good example. He amassed an incredible fortune at the expense of society. He misused the state's instruments of violence against Iranian subjects, and he challenged the religious order that mobilized opposition against him until he was driven from power.

In much the same way that totalitarian regimes are seldom completely totalitarian, democratic regimes are

In totalitarianism, party and state are one. In the Soviet Union, the power of authorities is reinforced by required demonstrations of citizen loyalty and homage to the founders of Soviet communism. Here, Marx, Engels, and Lenin watch over a May Day celebration. (A. Keler/Sygma.)

seldom completely democratic. As noted earlier, even the American political system, which is generally considered to be highly democratic, lacks at least some of the elements included in a strict definition of democracy. For example, it is the electoral college that directly elects U.S. presidents, not the citizens themselves. But more practical and important questions than how closely the United States fit the democratic ideal emerge—on what foundation is the American political system based, and how does it function?

Values, Principles, and Rights

Democracy, as we know it in the United States, depends on several basic values. We believe in majority rule, carried out with respect for minorities. We believe also that government must be based on the free consent of the governed and that all citizens are equal and must be treated equally before the law—rich and poor, members of various ethnic, racial, and religious groups, and so on. These values can perhaps best be expressed in the language of "rights" (Dworkin 1977, 1986). In this sense, rights refer to the benefits people can expect from their government as well as the patterns of obligation and respect that they owe one another. The citizens' sense of their rights is a crucial criterion for their judging the legitimacy of their governments.

There are two sorts of democratic rights. Some are known as **civil rights**: those rights people are entitled to by virtue of their citizenship. In the United States, the most famous of these are enshrined in the Bill of Rights, the first ten amendments to the U.S. Constitution, in which all citizens are declared to have the rights to freedom of speech, freedom of assembly, freedom of religion, and the like. There are also **human rights** —those rights that we are all entitled to by virtue of belonging to the human race. The American citizen highlights three of these as the rights to life, liberty, and the pursuit of happiness. American criticisms of nondemocratic states are often focused on human rights violations. Americans deplore both as a government and as individuals the treatment of Soviet Jews, of South African blacks, and leftist opponents of the government of Chile. Sometimes policy decisions are based on, or at least nominally based on, such criticisms. Exactly what constitutes an abuse of human rights is subject to debate. We might argue on the basis of a human right that Soviet Jews should be allowed to emigrate. The Soviets do not see it this way, regarding the right to emigrate as neither a civil nor a human right.

In the same way, many regard the affirmation and extension of rights as a major means of strengthening democracy (Barber 1983). Even in the United States, long struggles and social protest movements have been necessary to ensure that democratic rights were extended to *all* adults. The civil rights movement has fought for equal rights for blacks—for their right to live or even to eat where they wanted, for equal access to educational and professional opportunity, and for voting privileges. The women's movement has sought public recognition that certain civil rights belong equally to both sexes.

Participation in the Democratic Process

One of the most important rights of a citizen of a democratic country is to participate in the political process, since self-rule is central to the very meaning of democracy. How is this to be accomplished? In very small societies *direct democracy* is possible: all citizens assemble to discuss and decide issues. The best example of this form of democracy is the New England town meeting. This was also the theoretical form of government in ancient Athens, but even Athens was too large to include all of its citizens. Only free adult males of independent means could participate in government. Women, slaves, farm and craft workers, and others were excluded. Thus, for practical reasons, participation of citizens in the democratic process is usually accomplished through a *representative democracy*, in which citizens elect officials to make up the government, as in the United States (Bobbio 1987; Held 1987). Even in such political systems, however, there are times when democracy is direct; an example is a statewide (or citywide) referendum in which all state (or city) citizens may vote on a proposed law or regulation.

Traditionally, there have been three major channels for public participation in American representative democracy. Individuals participate through voting; individuals and groups participate through political parties and campaigns; and citizens can also exert influence over their government through organized interest groups and social protest movements. Let us consider the extent and type of participation that actually occur through each of these modes of participation.

Voting Patterns

The American political system is based on mass participation through periodic elections. Ideally, the principle of one person, one vote offsets inequalities of class, sex, and race in our society. But because many Americans fail to vote, the validity of this assumption is questionable. Whereas in Western Europe 80 to 90 percent of the voters regularly turn out for national elections, only 59.9 percent of Americans eligible to vote did so in the 1984 presidential election. And 1984 saw a relatively high turnout. Voter participation in the United States had been declining since 1960 (see Table 14.1). The turnout for off-year (nonpresidential) elections is even lower: In 1982, for example, it was only 48.5 percent.

Polls show that the people who are least likely to exercise their rights to vote are the poorly educated, those with low incomes, and those who are unemployed (Neuman 1986; Piven and Cloward 1988). Table 14.2 shows these patterns in its summary of voter characteristics in 1980 and 1984. In addition, in both years, turnout was higher among whites than among blacks or Hispanics (Bureau of the Census 1986). To the extent that the political preferences of groups of people who are less likely to vote differ from those of other Americans, the views of the first group are not being adequately represented at the ballot box. If America has a government "by the people," it is clearly only by some of them.

Several explanations of low voter turnout in the United States have been proposed. Some political observers have suggested that a majority of Americans feel that their votes do not matter, that things will go on in much the same way whether or not they vote. Recent polls suggest that there may be some truth to this assertion (see Figure 14.1). Surveys also indicate that many people find politics confusing, threatening, or incomprehensible and feel that attempts at understanding or influencing politics would be futile. These people simply tune out political messages of all sorts—including basic information with which the media bombard us. This paints a picture of a fairly uninformed electorate (Neuman 1986). It has also been suggested that elections themselves serve to make people passive, even apathetic or apolitical. With the media and politicians setting the agenda and providing the initiative, people tend to think that politics is "something other people take care of" (Hirschman 1982). Frances Fox Piven and Richard Cloward (1988) also point out that there are institutional barriers to full participation in U.S. elections. For example, voter registration procedures enacted in the

TABLE 14.1   Percent of Voting-Age Population Voting for President

1932	52.4%
1936	56.9
1940	58.9
1944	56.0
1948	51.1
1952	61.9
1956	59.3
1960	63.1
1964	61.8
1968	60.7
1972	55.4
1976	54.4
1980	53.9
1984	59.9

Source: U.S. Bureau of the Census.

late nineteenth and early twentieth centuries—like delays between registration and the opportunity to vote—worked to keep the industrial working class, blacks and poor people from voting. And to the extent members of these groups didn't vote, political parties and leaders paid less attention to them, creating a vicious circle. People are more likely to vote and participate in politics when they feel that their interests are at stake. Hence, youth increased its political involvement in the late 1960s and early 1970s as did the unemployed in the 1982 election (Beck and Jennings 1979; Clymer 1983). People seem to vote their resentments and fears; when there is a dearth of each, people are less likely to vote (Adelman 1980). Actually, there is probably no single or simple reason for the relatively low voter turnout in the United States.

A large voter turnout by itself does not necessarily signal a strong, healthy democracy. Some democracies require people to pay a fine if they do not vote, as in Australia, so that the vast majority of people in those countries vote. Voter turnout in totalitarian nations such as Romania, Albania, and East Germany hovers around 99 percent.

Political Parties

The kinds of choices our electoral system offers are closely related to the nature of American political parties. Traditionally, political activity in the United

TABLE 14.2   Characteristics of the Voting-Age Population, November 1984 and 1980 (Numbers in thousands)

Characteristic	1984			1980		
	Number of persons	Percent registered	Percent voted	Number of persons	Percent registered	Percent voted
Total, 18 years and over	169,963	68.3	59.9	157,085	66.9	59.2
Race and Spanish origin:						
White	146,761	69.6	61.4	137,676	68.4	60.9
Black	18,432	66.3	55.8	16,423	60.0	50.5
Spanish origin	9,471	40.1	32.6	8,210	36.3	29.9
Sex:						
Male	80,327	67.3	59.0	74,082	66.6	59.1
Female	89,636	69.3	60.8	83,003	67.1	59.4
Age:						
18 to 24 years	27,976	51.3	40.8	28,138	49.2	39.9
25 to 44 years	71,023	66.6	58.4	61,285	65.6	58.7
45 to 64 years	44,307	76.6	69.8	43,569	75.8	69.3
65 years and over	26,658	76.9	67.7	24,094	74.6	65.1
Region:						
Northeast	36,868	66.6	59.7	35,500	64.8	58.5
Midwest	42,136	74.6	65.7	41,542	73.8	65.8
South	57,587	66.9	56.8	50,561	64.8	55.6
West	33,372	64.7	58.5	29,483	63.3	57.2
Years of school completed:						
Elementary: 0 to 8 years	20,580	53.4	42.9	22,656	53.0	42.6
High School: 1 to 3 years	22,068	54.9	44.4	22,477	54.6	45.6
4 years	67,807	67.3	58.7	61,165	66.4	58.9
College: 1 to 3 years	30,915	75.7	67.5	26,747	74.4	67.2
4 years or more	28,593	83.8	79.1	24,040	84.3	79.9
Labor force status and class of worker:						
In civilian labor force	111,562	68.4	60.5	101,934	67.4	60.4
Employed	104,173	69.4	61.6	95,041	68.7	61.8
Agriculture	3,132	64.3	55.9	3,015	68.1	60.0
Nonagricultural industries	101,042	69.6	61.8	92,026	68.7	61.9
Private wage and salary workers	77,160	66.7	58.6	69,161	65.1	57.9
Government workers	15,813	82.0	75.9	15,801	82.0	77.0
Self-employed workers	8,068	72.4	65.2	7,063	73.7	67.0
Unemployed	7,389	54.3	44.0	6,893	50.3	41.2
Not in labor force	58,401	68.1	58.9	55,151	65.8	57.0
Family income:						
Under $5,000	7,843	49.8	37.5	8,567	50.4	39.4
$5,000 to $9,999	14,594	56.8	46.2	18,873	58.4	48.8
$10,000 to $14,999	18,131	62.9	53.5	21,746	63.6	54.8
$15,000 to $19,999	15,997	65.5	57.1	18,359	66.8	60.3
$20,000 to $24,999	14,790	68.7	61.1	19,100	73.5	67.2
$25,000 to $34,999	25,322	74.2	67.0	35,427	79.2	73.8
$35,000 and over	35,218	80.7	74.2	35,427	79.2	73.8
Income not reported	8,355	62.9	56.9	9,091	60.2	54.4

Source: U.S. Bureau of the Census, 1986.

FIGURE 14.1   American Beliefs Regarding the Significance of Elections

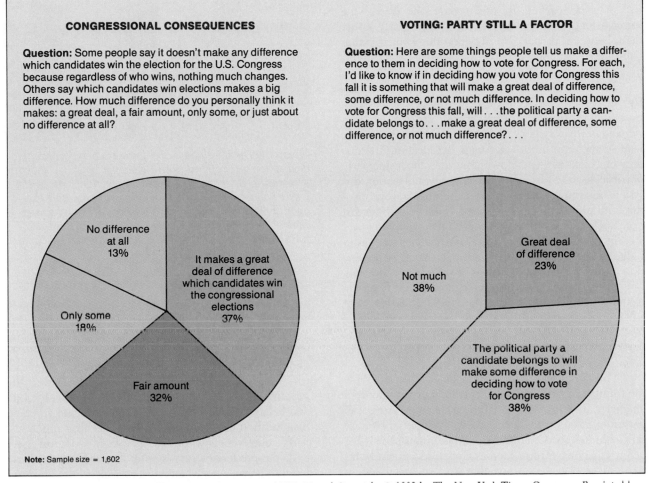

Source: Public Opinion, Vol. 5, No. 6 (December–January 1983): 21 and Copyright © 1982 by The New York Times Company. Reprinted by permission.

States has centered around parties. For most Americans, politics boils down simply to choosing between the Republicans and the Democrats. In 1915 Robert Michels (1915/1949, p. 134) defined a political party as a "society of propaganda and of agitation seeking to acquire power." Although these are not the words contemporary Americans might choose, this definition is essentially correct. A **political party** is a collective group designed for gaining and holding legitimate government power.

Parties perform several crucial functions in large, complex political systems. Ideally, they link the people and the government, transmitting public opinion up to decision and policymakers, thereby converting public opinion into legislation. They mobilize grass-roots support for policy decisions made at the upper level. They also serve as a link between different branches and levels of government (executive and legislative, federal and state) and between official (government) power structures and unofficial (nongovernment) ones. On the practical level, parties play a dominant role in recruiting personnel for elective office (Dowse and Hughes 1972).

Although Americans are accustomed to thinking in terms of two main parties, in some countries there are five or more parties, in others only one (there, the struggle for power takes place within the party rather than between parties). Why does the United States consistently generate two parties, whereas other countries, such as Italy, consistently generate several?

The answer lies largely in the structure of a country's electoral system. In the United States, representatives and other government officials are elected by a *simple-plurality system*. This means that the candidate who secures the most votes wins the election; there is only one clear winner. How many votes the losing party or parties secure is immaterial. As you would expect, this system discourages third parties, because a vote for a minority party is in effect a wasted vote. There is almost no chance that the third-party candidate will win.

In contrast, in *proportional-vote systems* such as in Italy's, a party receives the same percentage or proportion of representatives as it does of votes in the election; how many votes any party receives *does* count. Even if a minority party receives only 10 percent of the votes, it still receives a tenth of the seats in the legislature. Thus, in this kind of electoral system, a vote for a minority-party candidate is not wasted, and the multiparty system is reinforced.

The simple-plurality system determines not only the number of parties in the United States but also their character. To win state and national elections, American parties must embrace diverse kinds of people and a wide range of interests. Differences of opinion must be settled before elections. Critics such as French sociologist Maurice Duverger (1954) argue that the American system forces parties into bland positions and prevents many groups from being represented. Both the Democratic and the Republican parties must lean toward the center and create policies that sound attractive to everyone and offend no one. In other words, the ideology of each of the two major American parties must be considerably broader and often much vaguer than the ideology of any one party in a multiparty system.

Party Loyalty and the Health of the Parties

To what degree does party loyalty determine voting patterns? There are signs that in the United States it is becoming less important and that the parties themselves

Greater hopes for change and for a truer reflection of democracy were offered South Koreans in 1987, shown here voting in that year's national elections. As in the United States, the individual's right to vote and the availability of a real choice of options to vote for are central to bringing the ideals of democracy closer to fulfillment. (Robin Moyer/Gamma-Liaison.)

are generally weakened (Gibson 1985). According to some sociologists, gradual party decay began in the 1960s. As a result, politics have become more candidate-centered and less party-oriented (Price 1986; Salmore and Salmore 1985). The declining influence of parties can be seen not only in elections but also within the government itself; and changes in government structure and behavior in turn influence candidates and voters in *their* relation to parties. First, there has been much less party cohesiveness within the houses of Congress. Second, the president's party's control over Congress is no longer a given; even when it has existed, it has not meant as much as it once did. Thus, the role of parties in shaping public policy has necessarily been reduced. Individual voters too, like the candidates themselves, have seemed to identify less and less with one of the two parties in recent years (Salmore and Salmore 1985).

Many believe that technological advances have contributed to the more marginal role of political parties today. The increasing self-sufficiency of candidates running more personal campaigns has been aided, for example, by computerized direct mail, which can target and reach individual voters. And the media, television in particular, have taken over some of the major functions formerly performed by parties. After all, in news and in ads, a candidate can enter voters' living rooms with her or his message. Television now provides an effective alternative means of informing the electorate about each candidate, a job that once belonged primarily to the parties (Salmore and Salmore 1985). Television and radio news programs now function in part as political talent scouts, and may have an impact not only on who becomes a candidate but also on who wins elections. Newscasters report results of popularity polls and predict winners while votes are still being counted. Both types of information may well be influential. In some cases, newscasters act as self-appointed public defenders, exposing the frailties of candidates and fixing blame for breakdowns in the system. Partly as a result, parties cannot organize and mobilize the electorate as effectively as they once did (Ladd and Hadley 1975; Lipset and Schneider 1983).

Given these trends, it is not surprising that the proportion of voters identifying themselves as independents has increased. Some forecasters have predicted that eventually independents may become an absolute majority (Madron 1979). Indeed, the recent successes of Republican candidates at the national level may be the result of the increased number of independents, and the increased freedom voters feel to cross over from one party to another (Dolbeare and Edelman 1985). This could be an important point, since registered Democrats still outnumber registered Republicans.

There have been criticisms that these trends are not so marked as has been claimed. Some sociologists, including observers who saw party decay earlier, now argue that the parties are "regrouping" and are strengthening themselves once more (Pomper 1980). Others point out that the increase in the number of independents is actually quite modest; those voters who declare themselves independents still tend to vote for one party or the other with nearly as much loyalty as people who classify themselves as Democrats or Republicans. If this is true, observers who have predicted a collapse of the two-party system—and a resulting disaster for American democracy—may find their fears groundless.

Background Factors and Voter Preferences

Another interesting issue concerning party politics is whether and to what degree background factors such as education, socioeconomic status, race, and gender influence or bias voters' party and candidate preferences in any single election. At one time, class and party were seen as closely linked; voters tended to vote the way trusted members of their own social class also voted

—which usually meant consistently voting for "the party." Everybody knew the Republicans were for big business, and that the Democrats were for the underdog. Voting was an exercise in party loyalty, and party loyalty was largely determined by class. How much has this changed, if at all?

There are some indications that background factors are still at least somewhat influential today. Take income, for example. According to two surveys, by the Roper Organization and by the National Opinion Research Center, as income level increases, so does the tendency toward conservative attitudes; at the higher income levels, conservatives considerably outnumber liberals (*Public Opinion*, April/May 1985—see Table 14.3). Occupationally, professionals and managers still exhibit strong support for the Republicans in comparison with lower-status workers (*Public Opinion*, October/November 1985). However, the tendency toward "class voting" has been much debated.

As far as race is concerned, blacks remain overwhelmingly Democratic, even as they move up the economic ladder (*Public Opinion*, October/November, 1985). Blacks have also been underrepresented in Congress and in other political positions. Only in the 1970s did it become common for blacks to become mayors of cities with a predominately black population. Racial prejudice remains a powerful force in American politics, although the 1988 campaign of the Reverend Jesse Jackson for the first time showed the ability of a black candidate to mount a credible presidential campaign. In running second overall in the Democratic primaries, Jackson was able to mobilize a record number of black voters, and gathered a significant number of white votes as well.

Age too—partly as a result of cohort experience (see Chapter 6)—may be linked to party preference. In 1985, for instance, Republicans were generally strong among the young and old, whereas Democrats seemed to appeal most to middle-aged voters.

What about gender, among voters and among candidates? Women are much more likely to be Democrats than to be Republicans and are more likely to be Democrats than men are. The reason that the gender gap may be increasing may have to do with males moving to the right and to the Republican party (Wirls 1986). Men are more likely to respond favorably to "tough" foreign policy and military positions; women are more likely to favor candidates who seem less militaristic and more concerned with domestic welfare issues. Both men's and women's reactions to female candidates are

TABLE 14.3   Income and Political Self-Description

Income	Conservatives minus Liberals	ROPER			NORC			Conservatives minus Liberals
		Liberals	Moderates	Conservatives	Liberals	Moderates	Conservatives	
Less than $10,000	+ 9	27%	37%	36%	29%	40%	32%	+ 3
$10,000–$14,999	+22	22	34	44	25	41	33	+ 8
$15,000–$19,999	+17	23	37	40	22	48	30	+ 8
$20,000–$24,999	+26	20	34	46	23	42	36	+13
$25,000–$34,999	+31	19	32	50	21	45	34	+13
$35,000–$49,999	+25	22	31	47	22	38	41	+19
$50,000 and over	+25	18	39	43	25	26	50	+25

Source: Public Opinion, April/May 1985, p. 37.

This table shows how survey respondents think of themselves politically. Note that, as we would expect, Democrats are far more likely to identify themselves as liberals, and Republicans are far more likely to identify themselves as conservatives.

The Reverend Jesse Jackson's message of hope and determination brought many new voters into the political process. His appeal to those traditionally left out of the process crossed boundaries of race, religion, gender, and economic class, demonstrating both the power of Jackson's "Rainbow Coalition" and his own credibility as a presidential candidate. (John Chiasson/Gamma-Liaison.)

also mixed. At state and local levels, women do not seem significantly more likely than men to vote for female candidates. In national elections, however, there is some evidence that women *are* more likely to favor female candidates. Congresswoman Pat Schroeder's 1988 primary support, for example, came primarily from women. In 1988 as compared with 1958, far more males *and* female Americans (82 percent compared with 52 percent) said they would vote for a female presidential candidate. Southerners, older people, and less educated people claimed very slightly less support for a woman candidate than others did (Gallup 1988).

In terms of educational level, the findings are more difficult to interpret. Some observers point to increased support for Republicans among college graduates since the 1960s. Others point out that regional and other complexities skew such a statement (*Public Opinion,* October/November 1985). It is fairly clear, though, that voters with *less* education still tend toward the Democratic party, partly because of the correlation of educational level with economic class. Many have noted that conservatism and conservative candidates are more likely now to win support on college campuses than was the case in the 1960s and 1970s, when so many students had liberal leanings. However, some surveys have turned up interesting details that alter the picture of a "universal" conservative trend among college students. For instance, the type of school the students attended may have been linked to student preferences in the Reagan-Mondale election in 1984. Mondale tended to be much more popular with students at elite private colleges, predominantly black schools, and a few state universities with liberal traditions. Reagan, on the other hand, was generally more popular at most large state universities and at private colleges with religious or military affiliations (Cook 1985). (See Table 14.4; also compare these findings with studies of different types of schooling in Education, Chapter 17.)

Whether the American party system is well or ill, whether there has been a strong realignment among voters or a "dealignment," are difficult diagnoses to make. One thing is clear: difficulty in the functioning of political parties, far from being a novelty of our times, is one of the conditions that American democracy has confronted from the beginning. The historian Arthur Schlesinger, Jr. (1979), reminds us that American political parties have always been somewhat unmanageable. He points out that over 140 years ago the French writer Alexis de Tocqueville, writing about democracy in the United States, noted that this difficulty stemmed from the dependence of legislators on their constituents:

A representative is never sure of his supporters, and, if they forsake him, he is left without a resource. . . . Thus it is natural that in democratic countries the members of political assemblies should think more of their constituents than of their party. . . . But what ought to be said to gratify constituents is not always what ought to be said in order to serve the party to which representatives profess to belong.

Interest Group Politics

The goals and actions of interest groups and of political parties tend at least to offset one another, if not to be actually antagonistic and opposed. In a sense, interest groups counteract the broad, coalition-building nature of political parties in the United States. One consequence of a weakening of regular party organization is a stronger role for interest groups (Gibson 1985). **Interest groups** are organizations created to influence political

decisions that directly concern their members. They range from business associations (such as the National Association of Manufacturers) to labor unions (including the powerful AFL-CIO coalition), agricultural groups (including the National Milk Producers Association), professional associations (the American Medical Association, the American Bar Association), civil rights groups (The National Association for the Advancement of Colored People), political groups (Americans for Democratic Action, the John Birch Society), and single-issue groups (such as the right-to-life movement). Corporations may form their own lobbies. The most notorious example of this was ITT's attempt to gain a favorable settlement of an antitrust suit by offering to underwrite the 1972 Republican National Convention. Agencies and departments within the government may also lobby, using their resources and spokespeople to influence Congress. For example, members of the Defense Department regularly testify in favor of increased military spending. Foreign governments also maintain lobbies in Washington to look out for their interests.

When Americans are asked by pollsters why they think the American system of government does not work better than it does, they cite by a hefty margin "too much influence on government by special interest groups and lobbies" (Etzioni 1982). Yet special interest groups and lobbies are hardly new to the national scene. They have been present ever since Congress began (Schlesinger 1979). Indeed, private-interest lobbies were never more powerful than in the years following the Civil War. Nor are contemporary single-issue movements—antiabortionists, anti-gun-control groups, antinuclear groups, and environmentalists—a modern innovation. They have also been a part of the political landscape since 1789, raising such issues as the elimination of Freemasonry, the abolition of slavery, the issuance of greenbacks, the free coinage of silver, the restriction of immigration, and the enactment of prohibition.

What is relatively new is the prominence of formal organizations with large advertising budgets and lobbying staff, and well-developed fund-raising programs, dedicated more or less permanently to representing various interests. The more traditional social movement—less formally organized and more dependent on grassroots mobilization—remains significant (see Chapter 21). The influence of formally organized lobbyists and controllers of campaign funds, however, has captured more recent attention.

The House Select Committee on Lobbying Activities estimates that there are at present more than 15,000 lobbyists in Washington—thirty for each member of Congress. More than $3 billion are spent each year trying to influence the actions of government officials. One of the most prominent examples of the success of a special interest group is the National Rifle Association (NRA). Through lobbying and electoral threats from single-issue voters, the NRA gained approval in 1986 for a weakening of the nation's gun-control laws (already among the weakest in the industrialized world). The NRA succeeded in this even though a majority of Americans surveyed and most law enforcement agencies were against weakening the gun-control laws and would actually have preferred stronger laws.

The campaign finance reform laws passed by Congress in the mid-1970s sought to reallocate political power by taking it from the monied interests and dispersing it to the grass roots (Alexander and Haggerty 1981). These measures restricted the role of large contributors, particularly large corporations, labor unions, and special interest groups, by requiring that all direct campaign contributions above $1,000 be reported and by limiting allowable amounts. This was meant to stop secret donors of large amounts of money from demanding favors from, or pressing their influence on, candidates that their money helped to elect. Yet, paradoxically, the laws have served to *increase* the role played by special interests by sanctioning the establishment of *political action committees (PACs)*. A PAC is typically organized by a business, labor, professional, farm, environmental, or issue group to raise money from numerous individuals so that small contributions can be aggregated into large amounts to support the campaign

TABLE 14.4   Divided Academia

	Reagan	Mondale		Reagan	Mondale
"Elite" Private Colleges			*Other State Universities*		
Amherst College (Amherst, Mass.)	25%	75%	University of Florida (Gainesville)	59%	42%
Colby College (Waterville, Maine)	46	54	University of Nebraska (Lincoln)	72	28
Oberlin College (Oberlin, Ohio)	17	83	Oregon State University (Corvallis)	59	41
University of Pennsylvania (Philadelphia)	34	66	Pennsylvania State University (University Park)	64	36
Vanderbilt University (Nashville, Tenn.)	41	59	University of Tennessee (Knoxville)	70	30
Predominantly Black Universities			*Private Colleges with Religious Connection*		
Florida A&M University (Tallahassee)	3	97	Baylor University (Southern Baptist) (Waco, Texas)	89	11
Tennessee State University (Nashville)	4	96	Brigham Young University (Mormon) (Provo, Utah)	95	5
"Liberal" State Universities			Notre Dame University (Roman Catholic) (South Bend, Ind.)	59	41
University of Iowa (Iowa City)	50	50	Oral Roberts University (Evangelical) (Tulsa, Okla.)	92	8
University of Michigan (Ann Arbor)	38	62	*Colleges with Military Tradition*		
University of Oregon (Eugene)	34	66	Air Force Academy (Colorado Springs, Colo.)	85	15
University of Wisconsin (Madison)	38	62	Texas A&M University (College Station)	92	8

Source: 1985 Congressional Quarterly Inc.

of the favored candidate or political party or to lobby Congress directly. PACs are the most rapidly growing source of election finances.

One of the reasons PACs and their contributions have become so important is the high cost of running an election campaign today. For example, according to the Federal Elections Commission, the 1984 elections cost $1.55 billion. Even that figure may be low, because despite the campaign finance reform laws, some campaign expenses need not be reported to the commission (Brownstein and Glen 1986). Some Senate elections in that year cost over $3 million each; a few, such as the hard-fought race in North Carolina between Senator Jesse Helms and former Governor James Hunt, cost several times that amount. State and local campaigns are also quite expensive, though there are wide variations here. PACs are supplying a great deal of all this money. Although at first used primarily by members of the so-called "New Right," today PACs exist in all areas of the political spectrum. Through PACs, church groups, labor unions, corporations, special lobbies such as the National Rifle Association and the Abortion Rights League, and many others collected $228.7 million for the 1984 elections (Brownstein and Glen 1986; Sabato 1984).

Thus, PACs have had a number of consequences, most of which were unanticipated (Alexander and Haggerty 1981). By broadening the financial base for candidates and parties, PACs have taken over some of the functions of the traditional large fund raiser. PACs can organize dinners, cocktail parties, and direct mailings to raise money, and at no cost to the candidates. Simultaneously, PACs have helped wean candidates from dependence on political parties and have weakened political allegiances among elected officials. The result has been the fragmentation of legislative processes and the strengthening of single-issue politics. For the most part, PACs concentrate on a small number of narrowly defined issues in which contributors have a strong interest, often an economic one (Gopian 1984). For example, when a bill to limit hospital costs came before the Senate, the American Medical Association strongly opposed it. Out of the fifty senators whose campaigns had received funds from the AMA, forty-eight opposed the bill (Roeder 1980).

Special interest groups and PACs particularly have acquired a bad reputation. Some researchers doubt that the influence of PACs is nearly as great as has been claimed (Wright 1985), and many social scientists believe that, in general, special interest groups fulfill some

useful functions (Etzioni 1982). For one thing, PACs provide a mechanism for political input that supplements the electoral process. In some cases, PACs have increased the participation of people in the political system by organizing members to campaign for the candidate they support. For another, the various groups operate as a check against one another and create numerous cross-currents in American politics. People are often active in more than one group, so that those with different outlooks may sometimes join forces. For example, in her support of women's rights, a conservative Southern Democrat may find herself aligned with outspoken liberals. The sociologist Seymour M. Lipset (1963) suggests that diverse and conflicting interests, which prevent the formation of solid political blocs, are essential to modern democracies. If interests and affiliations did not overlap, the country might split in half, as the United States did during the Civil War. Hence, multiple loyalties prevent the polarization of society into rigidly hostile groups.

HOW CONCENTRATED AND STABLE IS POWER?

In exploring the American political system, we have found that power is distributed unequally. But how extreme is this inequality? Is power concentrated in the hands of a small minority, or is it broadly shared?

Social scientists have offered several answers to this question. Some claim that power is concentrated in the hands of a select few who dominate and manipulate the many. The most obviously powerful people in America hold public office, but many others, in some cases with power as great or greater than elected officials, are less visible—the heads of giant corporations, behind-the-scenes political power brokers, and others. Many key figures in the power structure operate as leaders of interest groups; others, such as the late Dr. Martin Luther King, stand at the head of protest movements. Still others combine these roles, such as the Reverend Jesse Jackson, who has been simultaneously a leader in protest, the head of an interest group, and a candidate for public office.

Jackson and his supporters clearly have had to struggle against entrenched elites, but many sociologists see their partial success as evidence that the American system is relatively open to all groups. In this view the ideal of power sharing among a plurality of groups is at least largely achieved.

The Marxist View

Before Marx, the political philosophers more or less assumed that social power resided in the state and the military. In contrast, Marx drew attention to the economic roots of power. The people who own the means of production (the factories, the land, and the mines) control the rest of society through their domination of the society's economic activity. They are able to use the force of the state to subdue domestic unrest and to promote their interests in the international sphere.

According to Marx, each historical period is characterized by a predominant mode of production, a way of obtaining a livelihood, such as manufacturing. Each mode of production creates its own power hierarchy, or in Marx's terms, a ruling class and an oppressed class. Under the earliest class system, slavery, the ruling class consisted of slaveowners; and the oppressed class consisted of the slaves. Later, under feudalism, the ruling class was made up of landowners; while the oppressed class was made up of the serfs. Still later, under industrial capitalism, the ruling class is the bourgeoisie (the owners of industry); and the oppressed class is the proletariat (propertyless wage earners). Because the ruling class owns and controls the means of production, it directs not only economic activity but also the institutions shaping the moral and intellectual life of the workers, including law, government, art, literature, science, and philosophy. Thus the ruling class directs all of society's institutions, and in doing so, it ensures its own fortunes and the subjugation of the populace.

Many social scientists have focused their attention on the question of *who* occupies powerful positions and on *how* these individuals are linked with one another in an inner group. However, Marxists argue that it matters little who makes the decisions in a capitalist system. They insist that so long as an economic system is based on private ownership and the concentration of capital, the range of decisions that any politician or any other leader can make is restricted by the requirement that corporations generate profits. Thus when General Motors decides to maximize profits through plant closings in the United States, or through cooperation with foreign companies, the capitalist ordering of affairs dictates that it do so, without regard for the wider social effects.

Marx believed that capitalism, like all previous economic orders, contained the seeds of its own destruction. By this he meant that certain contradictions inherent in a capitalist economy would eventually bring about its overthrow. In particular, the relentless drive of capitalists to maximize profits would progressively worsen the circumstances of the working class, intensify the crippling effects of the business cycle, and deepen international tensions. Ultimately conditions for workers would become so deplorable that the workers would band together and overthrow their exploiters. In short, the downfall of capitalism in Marx's view was inevitable because the system gradually forces its people into abject poverty and degradation, circumstances that eventually become intolerable. This exploitative system, Marx believed, would be replaced by a socialist order that in time would give way to communism, a classless society.

The Power Elite View

Marx's focus on economics and his predictions about the coming of a classless society did not long go unchallenged. Two Italian social philosophers, Vilfredo Pareto (1848–1923) and Gaetano Mosca (1858–1941), saw inequalities of power as inherent in any social order. A classless society was in their view impossible. Pareto (1916/1935) began with the simple observation that some lawyers are sharper, some royal mistresses more influential, and some thieves more successful than others. These are the **elites** of their respective fields—members of that small minority who lead because they are more gifted than other people. The same holds true for society as a whole. Throughout history, small governing elites —individuals distinguished by talent and organization —have ruled the masses by virtue of their social superiority. This, both Pareto and Mosca (1939) believed, was an inevitable pattern—indeed, a desirable one.

Writing in the first decades of the twentieth century, the German economist and sociologist Robert Michels claimed that in *all* organizations, power tends to fall into the hands of a small group of leaders, whatever their goals and ideology. After studying the labor and socialist movements of his time, Michels (1915/1949) concluded that as organizations grow in size and complexity, the need for leadership becomes more and more pressing. Informal decision making in which all members participate becomes impractical. There are too many issues to resolve. Further, the organization must present a united front to the outside world. Leaders chosen for their special talents in administration and public relations gradually take command. In time, these leaders develop a vested interest in maintaining their positions. A combination of admiration and apathy in the rank and file accelerates this concentration of power in the hands of a few. The ruling clique becomes conservative, seeks compromises with its enemies, avoids risk taking, and erects barriers to challenges by opponents—measures designed to protect their positions and advance their fortunes. Nowhere is this process more obvious than it is in successful radical political movements. Revolutions, Michels argues, are little more than the replacement of one elite by another. In Michels' view, "Who says organization says **oligarchy**"—rule by the few. The chain of events Michels portrayed as leading to the concentration of power in the hands of the few has become known as his **iron law of oligarchy.**

Among twentieth-century American sociologists, C. Wright Mills (1959) took the lead in postulating the existence of an American **power elite,** a coalition of military leaders, government officials and business executives that effectively rules the American capitalist society. According to Mills, this small group makes the major decisions that affect the lives of Americans, especially those relating to matters of war and peace. He began with the fact that many people who occupy high positions in government have also held high positions in corporations or the military and seem to move back and forth between these centers of power. America's governing elite, wrote Mills, is "a coalition of generals in the roles of corporation executives, of politicians masquerading as admirals, of corporation executives acting like politicians" (1959, p. 278). Tracing their personal histories, Mills found that by and large these people come from white Anglo-Saxon Protestant, old American backgrounds, attend the same Ivy League schools, belong to the same exclusive clubs, and visit the same resorts. Thus, if the president of an oil company does not know the federal "energy czar" personally, he surely knows someone who knows him (and can place a confidential call, if necessary). Through their social similarities, the power elite's coinciding interests are reinforced, and something like a ruling class emerges.

Mills argued that the different branches of the elite are interlocking. Congress approves billions of dollars in military appropriations every year, dollars that go more or less directly into corporate pockets. Why does Congress make these appropriations? In part for national defense, in part because military contracts create jobs, and in part because business leaders are important campaign contributors. Thus politicians tend to support big business, and business leaders often support politicians. All three sectors—economic, political, and military—have a vested interest in what Mills calls "military capitalism."

Mills believed the trend toward centralization of power would continue unabated. "The top of modern American society is increasingly unified, and often seems willfully coordinated: at the top there has emerged an elite whose power probably exceeds that of any small group of men in world history" (quoted in Olsen 1970, p. 261). Mills (1958:29) summed up his views with these words: "I should contend that men are free to make history, but that some men are indeed much freer than others."

G. William Domhoff (1978; 1983) has attempted to collect evidence for such an elite, although he does not think it is as unified or coordinated as Mills believed. He concludes that half of 1 percent of the United States population controls up to a quarter of the country's wealth and holds a disproportionate number of high-level positions in government and business. Members of "the governing class" attend the same schools, belong to the same clubs and civic associations, and intermarry, producing a tightly knit central circle.

Similarly, the sociologist Michael Useem (1984) says that the primary owners and top managers of America's major corporations constitute an "inner circle." By virtue of their multiple corporate connections, their common social networks, and their commitment to the capitalist system, they share a similar perspective on contemporary political issues and problems. They bring this outlook to bear in government through their participation in top political and decision-making circles and in their direction of key nonprofit organizations and foundations.

The Pluralist View

But in fact are America's political, military, and corporate chieftains all of one mind and do they cooperate with one another? Is not the reverse a more accurate portrayal—that they see one another as rivals? This is the question pluralists ask. They agree with Mills that some people are freer to make history than others and that unorganized individuals (the masses) are relatively powerless. But they do not see a single ruling clique, a power elite at the top of the power structure in this country. Rather, **pluralists** argue that social power is dispersed among a variety of competing interest groups—the oil industry and the coal industry, car manufacturers and ecologists, union and business associations, hunters' lobbies and wildlife foundations, the navy and the air force, and General Motors and Ford. All these groups control resources and activities at different times with varying degrees of success, but no one group is in command. In most cases they can do little more than veto programs that threaten their interests. As the sociologist David Riesman (1951, p. 242) has said, "Today we have substituted for [centralized, mercantile-aristocratic] leadership a series of groups, each of which has struggled for and finally attained a power to stop things conceivably inimical to its interests and, within far narrower limits, to start things" (see also Dahl 1961; Keller 1963; Kornhauser 1961). Economist Lester Thurow (1980) has made this point even more forcefully. He argues that "too much" pluralism may be the reason why we cannot solve some of our major social and economic problems. With many interests competing for a voice in public policy, decision making often becomes hopelessly deadlocked, or legislation is filled with so many compromises that it is totally ineffectual.

In summary, elite theorists such as C. Wright Mills believe that coinciding interests, reinforced by social similarity, bind America's leaders together into a single cohesive power elite. In contrast, pluralists such as David Riesman maintain that diverse, often conflicting, interests preclude united policy or action. Mills argues that members of the power elite settle important questions among themselves, behind closed doors. Riesman disagrees, arguing that fundamental issues are decided through bargaining by and among interested parties, and that the parties who exercise power vary with the issue. (The National Rifle Association, for example, is not interested in farm subsidies or endowments for the arts.) Mills laments the erosion of democracy, the loss of responsible and accountable centers of power, and the alienation of the powerless many. Riesman deplores the dearth of leadership and the lack of direction in American politics.

The sociologist Arnold Rose (1967) concludes that the two sides of this argument are not necessarily mutually exclusive. What exists in our society may be a complex mixture of both. Rose concedes that foreign affairs seem to be dominated by a small group of people who resemble Mill's power elite, but he suggests that the growth of the federal government and the emergence of new pressure groups (such as civil rights organizations) have undercut the power of big business. In his view, there are many power structures in America, not just one, and nationwide decisions are made through a process of bargaining among them (the pluralist view). However, the power structures themselves (political parties, government agencies, legislatures, businesses, and so on) tend to be dominated by oligarchies (the elitist view). In sum, Rose sees the American power structure as a complex plurality of elites.

Other social scientists who have studied the way our policy decisions are actually made have found Rose to be at least partially right. For instance, sociologist J. Allen Whitt (1982) recently investigated the making of a number of key decisions regarding mass transit in California. He found that depending on one's viewpoint and how carefully the evidence is sifted, support for all three theoretical positions might be found. Thus different interest groups (the highway lobby versus central-city businesses, for example) *did* compete with one another to some extent in their positions on public transportation, just as pluralists would predict. And as elite theorists would argue, business leaders *were* highly involved in all of these decisions, and a great deal of cooperation did occur among them. Likewise, as the Marxists would contend, the very need for mass transit *was* in part related to the capitalist quest for ever-increasing profits. Thus Whitt (1979) concludes that an integration of all three approaches may broaden our understanding of policy-making in the United States.

WAR: POLITICS BY ANOTHER NAME

The relationship of war to politics must be placed in the context of legitimacy, a topic discussed at the onset of this chapter. Terrorists fall outside the realm of legitimate politics—until they become heroes and sometimes statesmen, as has often happened. In this way, their earlier career of illegitimate violence is legitimated.

Today, a major aspect of political power has to do with the power to make war and the power to defend against the threat of war. War between modern states may also depend in part on how legitimate the citizens regard their war-making country's claims, which, in turn, depends on their ability to identify with the state and to identify another country or people as the enemy. Before the modern state arose, war was conducted between rulers and their hired henchmen. As the nation-state came into being, a people could see the ambitions, real or imagined, of another state as threats not to the life of their ruler but to their own common way of life. The identification with the state thus gave ordinary people two different and related ideas about legitimacy (Gellner 1983). Threats to the state from without were seen as illegitimate, justifying legitimate force as defense. Similarly, "bad" governments were seen as threats to the state from within, justifying revolution.

With the rise of the modern nation-state, wars have been fought or contemplated for higher and higher stakes—until we reach the point we are at today, when the future of the species and the planet hangs in the balance. Although nuclear war is so different from so-called "traditional" war that to some observers it is an entirely new phenomenon, nevertheless it would still be a war, taken to its most destructive potential. We can still profit from a glance backward at the development of modern war. As Gwynn Dyer has written:

> War is an institution as old, as complicated, and as pervasive as religion or property, and to understand why the unchanging things about it have not changed—why every state in the world constantly prepares for war, no matter what its propaganda says—we have to go back to the beginning of civilization. (1985, p. 3)

Early Warfare

In early human societies—tribes or groups of people organized on the basis of kinship—war was largely a ritual activity. There were few stable territorial boundaries or durable goods over which to fight. Warriors in such circumstances, like those in prestate societies today, may confront each other in episodic skirmishes. But conflicts were usually contained and few people were killed. Friends and relatives often intervened to limit the fighting and to enforce some resolution. A second pattern of early warfare, the feud, involves protracted hostility between two groups. In this pattern, there is a sharp distinction between "us" and "them" over a long

The ritual masks of the Mudmen of New Guinea may have their origin in an actual battle, in which the survivors of a surprise attack hid in a riverbed overnight and then routed their attackers at daybreak because, caked with mud, they appeared to be the ghosts of those already killed. In the episodic warfare of early societies, relatively few people were actually killed—in contrast to modern warfare, which has grown steadily in destructive capability. (Burt Glinn/Magnum.)

period of time that persists even when no fighting is going on. Occasionally conflict erupts: a member of one side is killed, and then a member of the other side is killed in retaliation. All-out war never erupts, but there is never a state of peace, either. Something of this feuding pattern persists in certain modern conflicts, such as that between the Israelis and the Arabs: hostility between the two groups is constant, but it rarely escalates into full-scale war. The Arabs, themselves split up into many factions, have seemed to regard their ongoing struggle with Israel as a feud; they often consider their terrorist acts against Israel as acts of vengeance. Israel, however, is a modern state that is not interested in feuding. It is likely to respond to a car bomb with an air raid, which may strike Arabs as out of proportion to the provocation. This then calls for more acts of Arab vengeance. We can see the U.S. bombing of Libya in the summer of 1986 in the same way: the U.S. response to terrorist acts not only may have been out of proportion but may also have played into the terrorists' hands (Rubenstein 1987).

The Path to Modern War

Modern warfare—in contrast to tribal skirmishes or feuding—began with the development of rich and settled agricultural societies and fortified cities (Dyer 1985). Such societies had governments, boundaries, and wealth enough to tempt others. These three conditions were necessary for the emergence of warfare as a rational, strategic institution: a means to get something of value from the other side. In tribal warfare, "winning" was of little importance, and one faction rarely made an all-out effort to defeat another. By contrast, the wars fought by early states were far more serious. Their goals were generally conquest (expansion of territory), the payment of tribute, or escape from domination by another state. These goals required armies bent on winning.

Wars among early states rarely involved the civilian population directly; the main body of this population formed an almost completely separate society from that of their rulers and armies (Giddens 1985). Wars were fought mostly by hired foot soldiers who met each other in massive battles. While officers directed from chariots or horseback, tightly packed ranks of soldiers armed with spears or swords charged each other.

> The men in the front ranks fought each other for a time, being replaced from behind as they fell, until one side or the other thought it was getting the upper hand. At that point all the ranks united their efforts in a gigantic shove to break the enemy's line decisively, and if they succeeded, they had won. The enemy's formation would crumble, men would turn to flee, and the massacre would begin. The losers would typically suffer casualties of half their force or more—almost all of them killed, for no quarter was given—while the winners lost no more than 5 to 10 percent of their men. (Dyer 1985, p. 37)

Since such battles were usually fought in open plains, civilians were rarely killed in the fighting, although they might be killed or captured (later to be sold into slavery) by rampaging victorious troops.

This basic pattern of warfare continued until the late Middle Ages. Although there were some technological innovations (the replacement of bronze and iron by steel, the growing involvement of navies, the breeding of bigger, sturdier horses for cavalry soldiers), war was recognizably the same kind of man-to-man confrontation between large bodies of armed men (McNeill 1982). The technology and tactics of the era may seem primitive to us today, but warfare in ancient and medieval times was no small-scale endeavor. The three Punic Wars (264–146 B.C.), between Rome and Carthage, can on some levels be likened to total war between modern superpowers. At the height of the conflict, nearly a third of Rome's male citizens were serving in the army, a figure seldom matched in modern wars, and 10 percent of Rome's adult men were killed (Hopkins 1978). When Rome defeated Carthage, the city was completely demolished; salt was ground into the earth so that the very soil would not support life. Carthaginian captives were sold into slavery, and no one lived on the site of the city for a hundred years. Thus, even though the technology of this era was primitive, the result of the warfare was not

Over 21 centuries ago, Rome left defeated Carthage in ruins, thus ending the large-scale, 100-year-old Punic Wars. The utter destruction of Carthage was on a scale that today can be compared to the effect of a bomb dropped on the city. (Editorial Photocolor Archives, Inc./Art Resource.)

much different (except perhaps for the numbers of civilian casualties) from what would have happened if a nuclear bomb had been dropped on Carthage (Dyer 1985).

The Changing Nature of Warfare

To understand how warfare changed its course after the Middle Ages, we must look beyond changes in technology or tactics. States were forming, and the European political world was changing. If, as the Prussian general Karl von Clausewitz once said, "War is the continuation of politics by other means," we must look at the political changes that were taking place at this time.

As we have seen, the most crucial development in the European political world in this era was the rise of national states. Governments became more centralized and exercised tighter control over their territories. Boundaries between these territories became more clearly marked. Politics was becoming a matter of relations between centralized, and increasingly homogeneous, states. This political change meant that when conflict between states became war, it meant large-scale war involving a state's territorial boundaries, economic interests, and national goals.

Growing nationalism was another significant factor. People's increasing sense of being citizens of a particular state meant that they were more willing to fight for their states, even to be conscripted. They saw war as something they had a stake in, since the outcome might mean the destruction of their state and their own distinctive way of life. People's feelings of nationalism also paved the way for internal wars—revolutions—aimed at improving the state. Up to this time, there might have been outbreaks of rebellion, but no true revolution, which depends on the existence of a state, on a government to seize or transform, and people with a sense of common citizenship determined to seize it (Eisenstadt 1978; Goldstone 1985; Skocpol 1979). Revolutions and civil wars have been the most common kind of conflict throughout the modern period. Of the forty wars underway in the early 1980s, for example, only five were between established states; the rest were civil wars (Kegley and Wittkopf 1985). Revolutions are aimed at transforming the *existing* state, keeping essentially the same national boundaries. Secessionist civil wars aim to create a new state from existing state territory, but the extent of that territory is not usually in question.

The Transformation of Combat

At the beginning of the modern era, war was still largely a matter of massive battlefield confrontations. Battles were large and fierce, with many thousands of men killed in a few hours (Strachan 1983). Many of the soldiers were mercenaries (the word *soldier* literally means "hired man") who joined the army because they had no other way of making a living. In such a situation, tight discipline was necessary to keep soldiers from running away or refusing to fight; those who disobeyed orders would be flogged, or even killed.

Gradually, however, armies were transformed from mere collections of hired men into bodies of citizen soldiers. The first great example of this was the mass mobilization of the French in 1793, which turned some 770,000 Frenchmen into soldiers in a matter of months (Dyer 1985). Citizen armies, who had something to fight for in addition to pay, could be deployed differently than in the tightly controlled ranks of mercenary armies. For example, small groups of citizen soldiers could carry out raids on larger armies that occupied their lands, using their superior knowledge of the terrain (and perhaps the support of friendly civilians). This pattern of fighting, known as guerrilla warfare, is characteristic of many wars today. (*Guerrilla* is Spanish for "little war.") Guerrilla warfare works best against a foreign occupying power, a situation in which repeated guerrilla raids can make it increasingly costly and demoralizing for the foreign army to remain in place. (This was roughly the position of the U.S. forces in Vietnam.) Guerrilla fighting also allows small numbers of troops to be scattered throughout a large area, an important factor in defense against an enemy's superior supplies of bombs and missiles.

Not only has the nature of armies changed, weapons have also changed. Starting with the invention of the rifle at the end of the eighteenth century, and continuing with the invention of machine guns, missiles, and bombs, the arsenal has become more lethal and the distance between killer and killed has become much greater. In addition to the development of weapons, methods of supply have also changed dramatically. As recently as the eighteenth century, wars had to be fought primarily between the months of May and October, because this was the only time of year in which there was enough forage in the fields to feed the horses. Feeding the soldiers themselves was also difficult until fairly recently; before the invention of dried, canned, and other kinds of preserved foods, troops often lived off the lands they occupied—much to the dismay of the local

Transformed warfare both echoes and helps create a transformed and perhaps more violent world. Catapults and bows were the chosen weapons of the 13th century; today, our vast and lethal arsenals are controlled from underground command centers, far removed from actual targets. (Top: The Granger Collection; bottom: Diego Goldberg/Sygma.)

peasant farmers. Although in a sense technology has made war easier and more "efficient" to wage, it has also made war far more expensive. Modern armies depend on expensive weapons and material in great quantity, which are used up in battle far more quickly than they can be manufactured at home. This means that any major war becomes a war of domestic production capability. Both world wars, for example, were in part won by the side with superior industrial capacity (McNeill 1982). The winners simply outproduced the losers and ultimately outlasted them in a war of *attrition*—a war in which losses eventually eat up all of one side's resources.

Willingness to Kill: A Problem for Military Socialization

During and after World War II, sociologists began to study the way the
military worked. One of their most
important findings concerned motivation, the source of the will to fight.
Comparably skilled soldiers performed
better or worse, it was found, not so
much in proportion to their national
loyalty or ideology but rather in proportion to the strength of common
feeling and solidarity within the immediate group of people with whom
they fought. Soldiers in a fighting
group might feel even closer than
families, for they not only lived and
worked together but risked their lives
together—and each might save the
lives of others repeatedly. The key to
military motivation, in short, was to
form strong primary groups among the
soldiers (Dyer 1985; Shils and
Janowitz 1948).

Through the twentieth century, and
especially since World War II, the
military has applied social and behavioral science to improve its organization. Basic training, for example, is a
carefully planned sociological and psychological experience designed not
just to impart skills but to change personal identity and enhance loyalty to
the organization and the primary
group. Among the military's challenges
are the need to keep tight discipline
and to ensure obedience to orders; the
fact that army life may involve long,
boring periods of waiting between episodes of action; the abstractness of the

issues for which soldiers are asked to
fight; and the presence of fear. Fear
might seem to be the heart of the
matter, and it *is* important, but the
military surprised itself on that score
during World War II. U.S. Army
Colonel S. L. A. Marshall studied the
impact of the dispersion of soldiers (a
situation in which infantrymen spent
large amounts of time out of sight of
their fellows). He did not find a tendency to flee or a dramatic increase in
cowardice or fear. What he found was
an unwillingness to kill. To his
amazement, he found that only 15
percent of trained infantrymen fired
their guns in battle. They did not
shoot even when their own positions
were under attack and their lives were
in danger. "In the most aggressive infantry companies, under the most intense local pressure, the figure rarely
rose above 25 percent of total strength
from the opening to the close of an
action" (Marshall 1947). Studies repeatedly confirmed Marshall's
findings, and they seemed to be true
for both sides during the war (Dyer
1985).

These studies illustrate people's
basic disinclination to kill. In ordinary
social life, we build up a respect for
human life and a sense of the mo-
mentousness of the act of killing that
does not vanish automatically on the
battlefield. It is in order to overcome
this inhibition that marine corps drill
sergeants now make their recruits

chant about killing, practice brutal
hand-to-hand combat (even though
that is extremely rare for today's military), shoot at apparently live targets,
and learn to place the values of the
marine corps above not only their
own but those identified with civilian
society as well. And it works. The first
generation of recruits trained under
these methods fought in Korea, and
they fired their guns more than three
times as often, on average, as their
predecessors had done in World War
II (Dyer 1985). Basic training has
been redefined still further, but the
idea is the same. It is particularly important in societies, such as the United States, which is highly individualistic and in which civilian life differs
markedly from military life. From the
day recruits enter the Marine Corps
(or any of the three other branches of
military service), experts concentrate
on rebuilding personal identity and
breaking the bonds of ideas that are
appropriate to civilian life but not to
war. One problem in this necessary
process is that neither the military nor
other institutions have yet developed
comparable methods for helping soldiers who have seen intense combat
and killed other people to reenter
everyday society and reassume its patterns of thought. This is one of the
many reasons why returning home
was so hard for so many Vietnam vet-
erans who had imagined that return as
their greatest joy.

Technology, Warfare, and the Military-Industrial Complex

Modern warfare depends greatly on technology, and
preparations for war focus not only on having an army in
readiness but in having huge stockpiles of weapons and

armaments of all kinds. Former President Eisenhower,
the commander of Allied forces in Europe during World
War II, was well aware of the role industrial production
had played in winning the war. But he also issued a
famous warning about the growth of what he called the
"military-industrial complex." What Eisenhower was

worried about was the tendency for the companies that supplied the military to earn unfair profits at taxpayers' expense and the related tendency of these companies to join forces with Pentagon officials to push for the development of ever more expensive weapons systems —regardless of whether they were needed or even whether they worked. That Eisenhower's fears were legitimate ones has been borne out by stories in recent years of staggeringly overpriced hammers (at $500) and coffee pots (at $7,000), as well as hugely expensive larger equipment and parts, all approved for purchase from military contractors. There has also been massive invest-

Those who speak of world peace, of a time when nation-states are superseded by world government and a global sense of community, are often accused of naiveté and innocence. Innocence comes from the Latin in, not, and nocere, to harm. Perhaps such innocence is called for in a world where everyone in every nation lives in the embrace of nuclear destruction. (Top: G. Vandystadt/Photo Researchers, Inc.; bottom: James L. Long/Black Star.)

ment in poorly designed equipment—tanks that aren't waterproof, planes that crash frequently—intended for military use.

Beyond waste and boondoggles, the modern military faces a serious manpower problem, both at the top and the bottom. At the top, each of the branches of the U.S. military has developed a huge bureaucracy, and many of those who are in command have had relatively little combat experience. Advancement within the military bureaucracy depends on the kinds of organizational and political skills that are an advantage within any bureaucracy. At the bottom of the military, at the level of the average recruit, there is a potentially more serious problem: lack of the education and training needed to cope with complex weaponry and organization. As a consultant to the U.S. military has asked:

> What happens when you have an antitank missile which, if it strikes an enemy tank, has a 100 percent probability of disabling or destroying that tank, but in which the system for aiming and firing the missile is really only capable of being used by someone with an IQ of over 100—whereas most of the people in forward combat units in your army have an IQ of about 85 or 90, and the smart ones have a lot of other jobs to do? (quoted in Dyer 1985, p. 193)

This illustrates the extent to which an effective military is tied to the soundness of the society it is trying to defend (McNeill 1982). A modern army needs literate (even computer-literate) soldiers. The military depends on the larger society to deliver the material resources and manpower it needs. In short, war is a matter of social organization.

The Threat of Nuclear War

So far, we have spoken of technological change in warfare and weaponry without mentioning the most important and most terrifying change of all: the development of nuclear weapons. Since atomic bombs were dropped on the Japanese cities of Hiroshima and Nagasaki at the end of World War II, the world has lived with the knowledge that the nature of war has changed. Indeed, the word "war," which brings to mind armies, generals, columns of tanks, and so forth, seems hardly appropriate to describe what might happen in a nuclear catastrophe, when a few world leaders could push buttons that might result in the obliteration of entire nations, continents, or even the entire population of the earth. Clearly, nuclear war could not be fought like conventional war in which each side vies to muster enough force to avoid defeat and weighs prospective gains and losses. In a war between two nations with nuclear arms, both can annihilate one another (Schell 1982). Gains and losses lose all meaning. Some military and other theorists and observers claim that nuclear weapons are not basically different from other weapons and that they could be used to advantage in "surgical strikes" against very specific enemy targets, thus "limiting" the destructiveness of a war with nuclear weapons. However, others argue with logical force that a "limited" nuclear war is really an impossibility (Zuckerman 1983).

The spread of nuclear capability and nuclear weapons to nations beyond those already possessing them; the buildup of new and more "advanced" weapons and weapon systems, like President Reagan's proposed Strategic Defense Initiative, or "Star Wars," which expands the arms race into space; the place of nuclear arms in defense policy; the negotiation of treaties and what is considered negotiable have been at the center of the debate over nuclear weapons and nuclear war. These debates themselves continue to overshadow—as some believe they must—other moral as well as foreign and domestic policy concerns. A broad policy of **deterrence** between the superpowers (the United States and the Soviet Union) has prevailed since the Cold War. This means that each country restrains (at least in theory) the other from a nuclear attack by its power to destroy the other in retaliation—actually, to inflict what are called "unacceptable" losses. (Another name for mutual deterrence is "mutually assured destruction," or MAD.) Proponents of deterrence argue that a buildup of at least equal amounts of weapons on either side promotes peace and deters war. In other words, according to this line of reasoning, the United States must continue to build and stockpile weapons in order never to have to use them. Most observers agree that a policy of deterrence has, in fact, continued to fuel the arms race, in which each superpower tries to gain the upper hand, thus destabilizing any "balance" of nuclear power. As Lord Solly Zuckerman, former chief scientific advisor to the British government, has pointed out:

> By 1962 the buildup of the American nuclear forces and, correspondingly, those of the Soviet Union, had already gone well beyond the rational requirements of any

mutual deterrent threat. Not only did the buildup never stop, it has . . . surpassed any reasonable level. . . .

Ignorance, mutual suspicion, the belief that more destructive power implies greater military security, and the simple difficulty of reducing the momentum which drives an arms race in which thousands are engaged, were the reasons why the two sides did not get together before 1970 to consider how to stop the process. If it is ever negotiated, a curb will still leave enough in both armories to blow the USA, Europe and the USSR apart. . . . Unfortunately, the concept of deterrence has always been too vague for definition in terms of units of destruction. Once the numbers game took over, reason flew out the window. (1983, pp. 47–48)

In the last twenty-five years, while the arms race continued to accelerate, the United States and the Soviet Union were attempting to negotiate various means of arms control, mutually agreed-upon limitations on nuclear weapons, and curbs on their testing and use. For despite the heavy influence of the military-industrial complex both here and abroad, there is fairly constant pressure worldwide for the superpowers to achieve and maintain some sort of arms-control agreement. A number of treaties between the United States and the Soviet Union have actually been signed and to some extent observed, although verification—keeping the other side "honest" and measuring its capability has often proved to be a sticking point. Nevertheless, arms control occupies a central place in U.S.-Soviet relations and 1988 saw each country actually destroying some missiles by agreement. Although worldwide proliferation of nuclear weapons has certainly not been stopped, the United States has had some limited success since the mid-1970s in working toward nonproliferation—that is, in putting diplomatic pressures on potentially nuclear nations to slow down their development of nuclear weapons (Spector 1985). Many observers are concerned that with proliferation, the threat of nuclear terrorism looms larger and larger, especially in the Third World.

Arguments for **disarmament** go beyond those for arms control. Disarmament would mean a considerable reduction in, or even elimination of, the weapons in the world's nuclear arsenals. Those who work for disarmament believe that *all* nuclear weapons by their very existence are unmitigated threats to world peace and security. Continuing to make and stockpile these weapons only makes it more, not less, likely that they will someday be used.

The total elimination of nuclear weapons already in existence may not be a feasible plan in today's world. It may not be possible to turn back the clock and pretend that we know nothing about splitting atoms and building bombs. On the other hand, a halt to the arms race and to the proliferation of nuclear capability may not only be possible, it may be absolutely necessary.

Even though we can regard the threat of nuclear war as an outgrowth of the social and political trends in the modern nation-state, the kind of destructive power nuclear weapons gives us is unprecedented in history. Some hope that in coming to terms with this power we will find war and the nation-state have been made obsolete. States will give way to a world government. But it may be equally likely that nuclear power will, in making the nation-state obsolete, perform the same function for at least a large part of the human race.

At bottom, the problem of war is political, but modern scientific weaponry has turned it from a bearable affliction into a potentially terminal crisis. . . . War and the state were centrally important elements in our strategy for gaining more control over our environment, but they have brought us inescapably to our present dilemma, which involves the potential extinction of the human species. (Dyer 1985, pp. 246, 252)

J. Robert Oppenheimer, the American physicist who supervised the building of the first atom bomb at the Los Alamos, New Mexico, laboratory, reported that when he saw the first test explosion of the bomb in the desert, these words from the *Bhagavad-Gita* went through his mind: "I am become Death, destroyer of worlds."

SUMMARY

1. Politics is the social process by which people gain, use, and lose power. Power is the ability to exert control over others despite their resistance. Power in this sense —distributive power—is unequally distributed. Collective or enabling power is the power of a group to get things done through cooperation and division of labor.

2. Legitimacy is the extent to which power is recognized as valid and acceptable by the participants in a social relationship and implicitly by society at large. Legitimate power is known as authority, which is exercised with the social approval of most individuals in a society. Illegitimate power, on the other hand, is exercised without such social approval and tends to involve force. Most political systems rest on the exercise of both power and legitimate authority. The legitimacy of a political system may fluctuate depending on events.

3. Weber has distinguished three types of authority: legal/rational authority deriving from law, charismatic authority deriving from exceptional personal qualities, and traditional authority deriving from beliefs and practices passed down from generation to generation.

4. The state, an abstract entity, is the sum of the institutions that specialize in wielding power and authority. It includes the courts, police, legislature, the executive branch, the military, regulatory agencies, and other official bodies. Throughout most of history the state did not exist. States arose as rulers sought to expand their territories and commercial interests and sought protection for trade. The modern state is based upon the distinct separation of private and public lives.

5. The administration of increasingly large territories and commercial interests made necessary a class of state employees known as the bureaucracy. The functioning of a bureaucracy depends upon the separation of public and private and a formal set of rules governing official behavior. As bureaucracies themselves expanded, they developed clear hierarchies of power, and the tasks of bureaucrats became increasingly specialized. The formation of an efficient bureaucracy may be essential for a country's economic development.

6. The idea of nationhood and nationality arose as states and bureaucracies took shape. The advent of easy transportation and the centralization of government led to increased communication among previously isolated localities and a sense of common identity and culture. The parallel rise of nationalism toward the end of the 1700s meant that citizens had begun to identify with their state and its power. In our day, nationalism has proved to be a strong rationale for terrorism on the part of stateless peoples.

7. A welfare state is a state that has considerably expanded its functions, in the form of social and governmental programs, to take more responsibility for the welfare of its citizens. In effect, it provides goods and services that are not easily accessible to the individual. These include assistance to the needy, collective goods like national defense, enabling goods, and regulatory activities. The modern welfare state also manages the economy.

8. In a democratic state, authority ideally derives from the consent of the people. A main concern of the democratic state is the protection of human and civil rights, and criticisms of nondemocratic states focus on the violation of these rights. Totalitarian states tolerate no dissenting voices; a single party and the state are one. Authority tends to be concentrated in a few hands.

9. Mass participation in the political process is a key right of citizens of a democratic state. But only around 60 percent of the American electorate votes (less in nonpresidential election years). Political parties —collective groups designed for gaining and holding legitimate government power—may be declining in importance as politics become less party-oriented and more candidate-centered. By contrast, interest groups and political action committees (PACs) seem to be gaining influence in the United States, especially as campaigns grow more expensive, and technology allows candidates to reach voters and supporters directly, without a party's help.

10. U.S. officials are elected through a simple-plurality system: the candidate with the most votes wins. This system reinforces the American two-party structure. In some other Western nations, a proportional-vote or multiparty system prevails: a party receives the same proportion of representatives as votes.

11. Several background factors, such as race, gender, income, and education influence the preference of voters for a particular candidate.

12. Marxists believe that power in American society is lodged in the hands of the capitalists, who dominate and manipulate the workers in pursuit of their own class interests. They also contend that this power distribution is inherently unstable because it generates class conflict that will eventually lead to its downfall. Power elite theorists also believe that power in the United States is monopolized by a relative few, but they maintain that this pattern is self-perpetuating and therefore unlikely to change. Finally, pluralists see power as more broadly dispersed than Marxists and elite theorists do. They also believe that the distribution of power is constantly shifting, as groups compete with one another for influence, and alliances are formed and broken.

13. Warfare in many early societies was usually a ritual

activity, or an ongoing feud. Modern warfare began with the development of settled agricultural societies and fortified states. Early wars were fought by large armies of foot soldiers, often mercenaries, and rarely involved civilians. With the rise of national states, citizen armies developed. These armies identified with and were more willing to fight for their state and their national way of life.

14. Modern warfare depends increasingly on technology and on the productivity of entire states. The military-industrial complex has grown quite large and powerful as a consequence. The military today finds itself challenged to find literate, educated recruits who are well-equipped to handle modern weapons and tasks.

15. Nuclear weapons, which have been stockpiled since the end of World War II, are the single most important —and frightening—tool of war that modern technology has provided. They may make the conventional waging of war meaningless. An arsenal of advanced nuclear weapons is seen by some as providing necessary political leverage and security in a world in which other states have nuclear power as well. This is the belief on which the prevailing policy of mutual deterrence is based. Deterrence is criticized by many who press for disarmament and world peace. Arms control and its negotiation are major aspects of foreign policy today.

GLOSSARY

Authority. Power that is viewed as legitimate and exercised with the social approval of most individuals in a group or society.

Bureaucracy. Formal, rule-governed hierarchical organization of public servants.

Charismatic authority. A type of authority identified by Weber that derives from public recognition of exceptional personal qualities.

Civil rights. Rights to which people are entitled by virtue of their citizenship; examples include freedom of religion, voting rights, and the like.

Coercive power. Power aimed at controlling other people's behavior; can be exercised more or less forcefully.

Collective goods. Goods not easily bought and sold by individuals and provided to citizens by the modern welfare state.

Collective or **enabling power.** The capacity of people to get things done; an enhancement of power that arises out of cooperation and a division of labor.

Democratic state. A state based on political participation by the people.

Deterrence. A policy in which countries with nuclear power restrain (deter) one another from a nuclear attack because of their ability to retaliate and destroy the attacker; also called mutually assured destruction.

Disarmament. Reduction in and eventual elimination of nuclear weapons.

Distributive power. Power in relation to that of others and distributed unequally among people.

Elites. Members of that small minority who lead their respective fields because they are more gifted than other people.

Human rights. Rights to which all are entitled by virtue of belonging to the human race.

Interest groups. Organizations created to influence political decisions directly concerning members.

Iron law of oligarchy. According to Robert Michels, the chain of events that leads to the concentration of power in the hands of the few.

Legal/rational authority. A type of authority identified by Weber that derives from a system of explicit rules defining the legitimate uses of power. It is vested in positions, not in specific individuals.

Legitimacy. The extent to which power is recognized as valid and justified by people in a social relationship and (implicitly) by society at large.

Nation. A group united by shared cultural bonds who usually share a state.

Nationalism. Belief that a people with a distinct culture (i.e., a nation) should have its own state; pride in one's own nation is linked with this belief.

Oligarchy. Rule by the few.

Pluralism. The view that the political power structure is composed of a variety of competing elites and interest groups.

Politics. The social process by which people gain, use, and lose power.

Power. The ability to get people to act in accordance with one's wishes even when they prefer not to do so, according to Weber's definition, "the probability that one actor within a social relationship will be in a position to carry out his own will despite resistance."

Power elite. A coalition of military leaders, government officials, and business executives united by common interests and social affinity. In C. Wright Mills' view, this coalition rules America.

State. An abstract entity, composed of the public organizations in which autonomous power over a specified geographical area is concentrated.

Totalitarianism. A political system in which no opposing opinion or party is tolerated, and in which the government controls many aspects of citizens' lives.

Traditional authority. A type of authority identified by Weber that stems from sacred traditions of loyalty to monarchies, chiefs, and priests.

Welfare state. Broadly expanded state, characteristic of affluent, industrialized countries today, which provides for the welfare of ordinary citizens by assuming responsibilities of local communities and families, such as unemployment compensation, health care, and the like.

CHAPTER 15
The Economy, Business, and Work

The typical American, 1980s-style, wears a Japanese watch, drives a Japanese car, and plays videotapes through a Japanese VCR and watches them on a Japanese TV. A slight exaggeration, perhaps, but one with a nagging element of truth. As manufactured goods from Asian countries—particularly Japan—have increasingly overwhelmed American products in world markets, we have become aware of a major new source of economic competition. First Japan, and now Taiwan, Hong Kong, and South Korea have begun to challenge U.S. dominance of international trade, competing successfully with American manufacturers of cars, televisions, computers, electronic equipment, and the like. Our gross national product, while still the largest in the world, is growing at a slower rate than the economies of many of our Asian competitors. Moreover, we import more goods from Asian countries than we export to them, resulting in a sizeable trade deficit. And Asian countries have moved ahead of the United States in exports to many other parts of the world. Not surprisingly, these and other economic developments will play a vital part in America's future.

Why are Asian entrepreneurs threatening both our world economic leadership and our domestic economic stability? What social factors have enabled Asian countries to make such dramatic gains in their economic competition with us? The noted American economist Lester Thurow (1985) points to a wide range of possible answers, including: (1) cultural differences between Eastern and Western societies, such as a stronger Asian "work ethic"; (2) superior Asian business initiative and organization; and (3) lower wages and generous govern-

ment subsidies for certain Asian industries. Still another significant factor is the changing structure of the world economy, which makes it difficult for any one country to remain dominant for very long in the face of so many competitors.

None of these answers is definitive, of course, but each points to the fact that no matter how the differences between Asian and American economies are explained, we can see that a nation's financial status has a social basis. For example, Japan's success may in part be linked to social homogeneity, a highly competitive educational system, a large proportion of intact families, or any number of other social factors. It is also clear that the state of a country's economy has social consequences. The weakening American economy, for example, has resulted in unemployment, wage "givebacks" and other labor union concessions, an increasing need for two incomes per family, and a host of social problems related to the increasing scarcity of well-paid factory jobs.

The **economy** is the social institution that accomplishes the production and distribution of goods and services within a society. From a sociological viewpoint, the economy is a social system comprising social relations of all kinds and profoundly affecting all aspects of social life. In this chapter, we will consider the major economic systems—capitalism and socialism—and the ideals on which they are based. We will focus on key features of modern capitalism and such important capitalist economic institutions as the corporation and small businesses. Finally, we will examine one of the most basic of all human activities—work—and the organization and meaning of work in the larger economy.

Goods from all over the Mediterranean world filled the shops of this busy commercial street in a 15th-century Italian city-state. Centers of international trade, ruled by wealthy merchant oligarchies, these dynamic city-states provided the context for the social and cultural movement toward secularism and humanism that has become known as the Italian Renaissance. (Art Resource.)

THE ECONOMY AS A SOCIAL SYSTEM: ACTION AND STRUCTURAL PERSPECTIVES

As we listen to economic reports on the evening news ("The Dow Jones average fell ten points today"; "The U.S. economy grew in May for the twenty-second consecutive month"), we may begin to think of the economy as some kind of natural force, like the weather. Both seem hard to predict with any accuracy, much less

to control. But although the economy is affected by certain natural phenomena (like droughts, which may help drive up agricultural prices), it is fundamentally a *social* system. People create economies; people interacting with one another in culturally patterned ways are the source of economic phenomena, from shifts in oil and food prices to the fluctuations of the Dow Jones average.

A particular concern of sociologists is the connection between individuals and larger economic forces: do small-scale economic transactions account for trends, or do larger trends stimulate or depress the economic activities of individuals—or both? One useful approach to questions such as these is to consider the economy from action and structural perspectives.

From an action point of view, the economy can be seen as the accumulation of many individual economic actions. In this sense trends are best explained as the sum of the economic choices of millions of people. For example, the decline of the American automobile industry could be considered a result of consumers' preference for cheaper cars that use less fuel. Since most of the cheap, gasoline-efficient cars on the market until recently were Japanese, Japanese cars were snapped up by eager buyers while U.S. cars sat on the lots unsold. Thus, the problems of the American automobile industry could be traced to several million car buyers' selection of a Toyota or a Honda instead of a Ford or a Pontiac.

The predicament of the car companies can also be seen in a structural context. What structural factors caused Americans to want smaller, cheaper cars? An important one was that the major part of the world's oil supply lay outside the United States, leaving us vulnerable to the price hikes of the OPEC oil cartel. Another was that the growing numbers of two-worker families created a need for second, "commuter" cars. Moreover, it could be argued that the relative lack of public mass transportation in the United States, and of industry-wide requirements that American cars be safe and reliable, were also involved in encouraging the sale of foreign cars.

In fact, both action and structural views have merit and both are needed to help explain economic phenomena. For example, the views together shed light on the October 1987 stock market crash. From an action perspective, there can be no doubt that the crash was caused at least in part by the simultaneous decisions of many individuals and institutional managers to sell their stock. But from a structural perspective, it is easier for the stock market to crash when the bulk of shares are held by a small number of institutional investors and when so many transactions take place by computer.

The essential interrelationships of individual economic activity and larger social forces are captured in the word "market." In traditional terms, a market is a place where people come to buy and sell goods. But today the word "market" is also used to describe the workings of impersonal economic forces: the stock market, the market for new housing or automobiles, and the like. Thus we can speak of the "market" exerting pressure on automobile makers to lower their prices or make more fuel-efficient cars, without ever referring to the specific people who buy (or refuse to buy) automobiles. Nonetheless, the role of individuals in making markets work is obvious—people are the buyers and sellers in the marketplace, as they have been throughout history.

The terms "market" and "marketplace" are also used to characterize global economic relationships. The United States and other industrialized nations must compete in a world market where capital, jobs, and goods flow daily across national boundaries. As our opening example suggests, position in the world marketplace affects a wide range of social matters, such as what

products people buy, whether factories thrive or shut down, whether a society is gaining or losing jobs, and whether a country's standard of living rises or falls. We will now look at the major forms of economic activity in the industrialized nations of the world.

ECONOMIC SYSTEMS AND IDEALS

The Rise of Capitalism

Until the eighteenth century, economic activity took place chiefly at the local level. Farmers grew most of the food for a surrounding region and brought it to the local marketplace to trade with other farmers and residents of small villages. Local craftsmen supplied most of life's other necessities. By the beginning of the nineteenth century, however, local farmers and craftsmen were leaving home and village to become factory workers, a process that continued for many years and signaled the

How is the market doing? Today, that question makes most of us think of some impersonal and disembodied force undulating across computer screens in Wall Street, London, Tokyo. . . . However, the Thai farmer with his floating market of fresh vegetables is engaged in the same essential activity as the Japanese broker with a phone at each ear: both must convince someone to buy what they have to sell. (Below: K. Kurita/Gamma; right: Ron Sanford/Black Star.)

start of dramatic social changes. The coming of the Industrial Revolution, first to England and eventually to the rest of Europe and the New World, brought a vast expansion of manufacturing—most notably of textiles, but also of pots and pans, furniture, shoes, and other goods. With it the idea of "market" expanded—for the market for all these goods extended as far as European ships could carry them. Sugar, cotton, grains, and other foods and natural materials were shipped from rural regions of the world to the increasingly industrialized ones, boosting economic activity and furthering the Industrial Revolution.

As industrialization spread and the European nation-states became richer and more powerful, a new form of economic organization took root. This was capitalism, the most revolutionary approach to the production, distribution, and exchange of goods that the world had ever seen. Indeed, capitalism in its early stages was so dynamic that it was a major impetus for the extension of European exploration, trade and colonization into the rest of the world (Wallerstein 1974, 1980; Frank 1980; Wolf 1982). As Karl Marx and Friedrich Engels described these developments:

> The bourgeoisie cannot exist without constantly revolutionising the instruments of production, and thereby the relations of production, and with them the whole relations of society . . . The need of a constantly expanding market for its products chases the bourgeoisie over the whole surface of the globe. It must nestle somewhere, settle everywhere, establish connexions everywhere. (1976; 1848, p. 451)

Thus the **capitalist market system** is one recognized by friend and foe alike as an extremely dynamic one, a system that has continued to create unprecedented wealth and revolutionized the means of production. Even today, observers of capitalism would agree that Marx's observations about its productive capacity still hold true, despite declining growth rates in some capitalist countries (Berger 1986; Drucker 1986).

All capitalist systems rest on certain ideal assumptions. According to Adam Smith, the author of *Wealth of Nations* and an influential theorist in both sociology and economics (see Chapter 1), a capitalist society is based on three basic principles: private property, the profit motive, and free competition.

In a pure capitalist system all the means of production—from farmlands to oil refineries to factories producing ballpoint pens—are owned by individuals

rather than by the state. Capitalist ideology holds that *private property* is an inalienable, almost sacred right. People in a capitalist society define fulfillment and success largely in terms of the ownership of property. And it is private ownership of the means of production that provides capitalism with its driving force—the *profit motive*.

Capitalist ideology contends that owners of businesses are strongly motivated to maximize profits. As Smith noted, the reason is simple: by increasing profits, entrepreneurs also boost their own wealth and prestige. Thus it is easy to understand why being able to own productive property and earn a profit is highly desirable from the capitalist's viewpoint. But why would society in general endorse the profit motive? The answer is less obvious but, according to Smith and his followers, equally compelling. Capitalist ideology holds that the drive for ever-greater profits ensures that entrepreneurs will produce the goods and services consumers want most and at the lowest possible price. Entrepreneurs who persist in producing things that consumers do not want will soon be driven out of business. And if the cost of producing a certain good is higher than the price that consumers are willing to pay for it, then no profit can be earned and production plans must be reassessed. The result is that capitalists are constantly looking for both new markets to enter and new technology to lower their manufacturing costs. From society's standpoint, therefore, resources are used with the greatest possible efficiency. Hence everyone benefits, not just the entrepreneur. When people are permitted to pursue their self-interest, society achieves its greatest good.

But what is to prevent an enterprising capitalist from charging exorbitant prices in order to maximize profits? Capitalist ideology says that because a capitalist market economy is characterized by *free competition*, no one entrepreneur is able to earn more than a "normal" profit. If one firm's products are overpriced, consumers will simply reject them in favor of similar products produced by other firms. The same competitive forces presumably operate in the market for productive resources. If one firm tries to augment its profits by paying workers less than the going wage, its best employees will find work elsewhere, resulting in the lowering of the quality of the firm's product. In the end, such a firm may be driven out of business, or at least be forced to pay higher wages. The result, of course, is that everyone else benefits. Products are priced fairly, workers are paid fairly, resources are used efficiently, and capitalists earn a normal profit. Or, at least, this is how the system is supposed to work, though in reality monopolies sometimes restrict free competition or other factors may intervene.

Thus, in the very broadest sense, a capitalist is someone who owns money or some other form of wealth and invests it to make a profit. This deliberate pursuit of financial gain is the goal of economic activity. In the words of Max Weber, the primary aim of capitalism is "production for the pursuit of profit and ever renewed profit." By this definition, capitalism has existed in many societies for centuries. Indeed, by this definition farmers who invest in land, seed, and animals and later sell their produce at a profit are as much capitalists as factory owners are. But modern capitalism is a system, not just an individual pursuit. It rests on other assumptions as well: capital accumulation, the creation of wealth, and expansionism. Let's take a closer look at these three crucial features of modern capitalism.

Capital Accumulation

Modern capitalism depends on a particular orientation to money-making activities: the drive to accumulate capital. This means more than just earning a profit: in essence, it means returning a share of the profits to the business, thereby providing an enterprise with a growing supply of capital. In other words, modern capitalists (which nowadays include corporations as well as individuals) are unlikely to spend all their profits on personal consumption. Instead, profit is reinvested in the hope of making still more money in the future.

Max Weber stressed that capitalism's success in generating continual growth depended on two related changes: the separation of the finances of businesses from the personal or household finances of their owners, and the rise of capital accounting. Throughout most of history, little distinction has been made between personal and business expenses. Just as kings ran their kingdoms as extensions of their households, so small farmers or craftsmen did not differentiate between their business accounts and their household ones. If money was needed for food or for new seeds, it came from the same pool of savings. Even very wealthy merchants usually worked this way; it was not until the early modern era that entrepreneurs began to look at business as separate from private life.

Capital accounting, a system that became widespread in the nineteenth century, enables business people to focus on long-term investments rather than day-to-day transactions. In the past, merchants evaluated their businesses simply by comparing their expenses and profits to see whether they had come out ahead. This method, known as current accounting, resembles the way one keeps a checkbook, balancing inflow against outflow. Capital accounting, on the other hand, calls for keeping track of the rate of return on one's whole investment; it considers the size of the initial investment as well as the size of the profit. For example, a capitalist who invests $1 million in new equipment will want to know how much he or she will earn each year as a percentage of that investment. A profit of $50,000 may sound like a lot of money, but it only represents a 5 percent rate of return on the capital invested, or less than an ordinary investor could get on a regular savings account. A modern capitalist would be unlikely to consider this a particularly good rate of return on investment.

As the new system of capital accounting took hold, it encouraged capitalists to compare carefully various possible investments. When considering any venture, the modern capitalist will ask "Is this the best use of my money? Will this investment bring the most gain?" The focus is on a business's growth and earnings, not on a particular product. Accordingly, a contemporary capitalist may choose to change products, to move manufacturing operations overseas (where costs are lower), or even to give up manufacturing altogether in favor of more profitable investments.

The Creation of Wealth

Modern capitalists do not make money simply by exchanging goods that are bought cheap and sold dear—they make money by organizing production in ways that increase the total supply of goods. This is generally done by gathering a group of laborers who, working together and using machinery or other technology, are able to produce more than the same workers could generate alone. For example, five people running power looms can produce far more cloth in a day than can ten weavers working at hand looms. But only the capitalist has enough money to provide power looms (in capitalist terms, an investment). Every additional investment in better machinery increases productivity—that is, allows the same number of workers to produce even more goods—and expands the total supply of goods even more.

This notion—that the capitalist's desire to make ever-increasing profits could create wealth in the form of material goods and social benefits (such as employment) —served as a moral justification for capitalism in the nineteenth century. Before that time, people who professed a desire to amass personal profit were deemed morally tainted by many Christians and others in society. At the dawn of the capitalist era in England, however, the social theorist Bernard de Mandeville summed up the new attitude by declaring that certain "private vices" might become "public goods." In other words, from the point of view of individual morality, it might be considered selfish and greedy to seek wealth aggressively. But if in the course of doing so you created more wealth, not just for yourself but for others, then this should be praised as serving the public good. Thus, the greed for profits that early critics of capitalism had condemned as morally wrong could be seen as ultimately producing social good for all (Dumont 1977; Hirschmann 1977).

Expansion into a Total System

Capitalism is not simply one possible approach to economic activity within a society; where it really takes root, it normally dominates economic organization within its sphere.

Individual capitalists, managers, workers, and others involved in capitalist economies all find their options largely determined by the system as a whole. For example, if most of the firms in a business are constantly improving their products, other firms cannot simply keep making their products the same as always. These firms will not just stagnate or fail to grow, they will go bankrupt. In a capitalist society, competition among different businesses is crucial, and a company that does not move forward will eventually collapse.

Because of capitalism's built-in need to constantly expand production and seek new markets, it tends to

Keeping up with the Joneses on an international scale. In the 1970s, when American automobile manufacturers failed to respond to changing social and economic conditions, the Japanese dramatically expanded U.S. sales of their smaller, more fuel-efficient cars. Does failure to innovate make economic decline inevitable—for a company or for a national economy—in a system that defines success as constant expansion? (J. P. Laffont/Sygma.)

form a more and more all-encompassing or total system. In order for capitalism to take root as a total system, the nature of labor and property had to change. Whereas in the past laborers supplied their own tools and raw materials, with the advent of capitalism labor was separated from the physical means of production. The shoemaker who once provided his own leather and nails and made shoes to order went to work in a shop where the owner provided the raw materials and conditions of employment. From there it was only a short step to factories and other forms of production that require an extensive division of labor—that is, the different aspects of a single craftsman's job are broken down into simpler tasks that can be done by less skilled (and cheaper) workers. In one sense, this change "freed" workers because they could go to work for whoever paid the best wage. But it also meant that workers found themselves with no independent resources, with nothing to sell but their labor.

The same process that separated workers from the means of production also furthered the development of the modern concept of property. Although property rights existed before the eighteenth century, they were generally bound by many restrictions. A feudal lord, or vassal, was entitled to the wealth produced by the peasants who worked his land, but he only "owned" the land on approval from the king or another, more powerful lord. In exchange, the vassal owed certain obligations to the peasants, such as to provide them with enough land to make a living and to protect them from marauders. The modern concept of property rights, on the other hand, specifies that land (and other possessions) can be sold at will and accumulated in much larger parcels than those worked by peasants on the feudal manors. It was this concept of property rights that enabled European colonists to seize land from unsuspecting native populations. In North America, for example, colonists (and the government) repeatedly forced Indians who had no concept of land ownership to treat their hunting and planting grounds as private property and "sell" this land to the settlers.

The transition to the new economic system brought opportunity to some, but left behind those people who lost their customary way of making a living (Thompson 1968; Seldon 1974; Himmelfarb 1983). In strictly economic terms, the major advance of early capitalism was ever-increasing productivity. But as skilled craftsmen came to be replaced by less skilled workers, it became easier for capitalists to think of labor as one of the many raw materials they had to buy. And workers themselves became more interchangeable with each other because their jobs depended less on specialized abilities.

Early capitalists also experimented with new technology and new forms of workplace organization in order to maximize productivity and get more out of capital investments. Some of these innovations, like power-driven looms, simply enabled individual workers to produce more. Others, like the assembly line, increased production efficiency while at the same time setting a common speed at which laborers had to work. Time clocks with punch cards were designed to monitor workers, not to help them produce more. And night shifts were a way of getting more productivity from a fixed investment in machinery and other facilities.

Since the Industrial Revolution began, efforts to increase productivity have been central driving forces of capitalism. These efforts have included the development of new technology, closer supervision of workers, better accounting, and improved transportation (Landes 1965). Though in recent years the provision of services (rather than goods) accounts for much of the economic activity in the industrialized nations, the concern for increasing productivity has remained central (Mandel 1976; Thurow 1985). It has been, for example, the main focus in the debate over how to help American industry gain a better position in competition with Japan.

Socialist Economics

The modern state socialist economy arose in response to some of the abuses and excesses of nineteenth-century industrial capitalism—long hours, low wages, dangerous work conditions, and child labor. Particularly influential were the criticisms raised by the social philosopher Karl Marx. Marx believed that far from promoting the greatest good for society as a whole, capitalism benefits mainly the owners of the means of production, the capitalists. He argued that capitalists were motivated only by the desire to maximize their profits and so had no reason to pay workers more than the minimum needed to keep them at their jobs. And when machines are widely used and few skilled jobs are available, this amount can be extremely low—sometimes only enough to keep the workers and their families alive at the barest subsistence level. Thus the economic freedom that nineteenth-century capitalists extolled was to Marx simply a means of exploiting the workers (the proletariat) to the advantage of the bourgeoisie (the capitalists).

Marx believed that through a long process of self-awareness, discussion, and organization on their own behalf, workers would eventually rise up against the capitalists and wrest control of the means of production. In Marx's vision, capitalism would ultimately be replaced by a classless society. Although he did not describe in detail the economic system that would bring about this egalitarianism, he did propose its basic elements. First, it would be socialistic, meaning that all the means of production would be collectively owned and production would be organized for the benefit of everyone in society, not just individual capitalists. Second, economic decision making would not be left to the vagaries of the market but would be placed in the hands of a central planning board. This board would have the enormous task of determining what goods society would produce and in what quantities, and where and how it would produce them. Marx thought that after an initial transition period, a socialist system would require less and less state control because its citizens would be guided by a desire to cooperate. So far, the rulers of existing socialist societies have not allowed their people the chance to see whether this is possible.

Although Marx thought that socialism would follow capitalism in the most advanced industrial countries, so far the most dramatic (if not necessarily the most successful) experiments with socialist economics have been in poorer countries located on the periphery of the industrial capitalist world. Many of these experiments began with a revolution aimed not just at instituting socialist reform but at the elimination of all inequality —communism. The first modern communist system was established in the Soviet Union after the Bolshevik Revolution of 1917. Many other socialist societies have since emerged, but the U.S.S.R. is still the country that most immediately comes to mind when many Americans think of a socialist state. The Soviet Union, however, does not adhere strictly to the model of a communist economy, just as the United States does not strictly follow the capitalist market model. For example, although virtually all the means of production and capital assets are state-owned in the U.S.S.R., housing is not. About half of all urban homes and almost all rural ones are privately owned. Nor is the market mechanism of supply and demand completely absent in the Soviet Union. For example, a small "capitalist" sector is permitted in which farmers can sell produce in open-air markets; doctors, lawyers, and other professionals can conduct private practices; and people can operate some small-scale business enterprises (dry cleaners, repair shops, restaurants) so long as they do not breach a constitutional ban on private hiring. Moreover, under a law passed in early 1987, the government is proposing joint business ventures in the Soviet Union with up to 49 percent ownership by U.S. companies and other foreign partners. The day may eventually come when there is a

The monolithic economy and the open market. The very architecture of the huge "GUM" Shopping Center on Red Square in Moscow is suggestive of a planned economy rigidly controlled by the state. However, free enterprise does exist on a small scale in the Soviet Union, as in this free-price farmers' market in Samarkand. (Left: M. Bertinetti/Photo Researchers, Inc.; right: George Holton/Photo Researchers, Inc.)

Changes in the Soviet Economy

Since March 1985, when Mikhail Gorbachev came to power in the Soviet Union, much has been written about the reforms he has brought to the Soviet system. *Glasnost* (openness, public disclosure) and *perestroika* (restructuring) have become familiar words to Americans. Although exactly how deep these changes may ultimately go is not yet known, it is clear that the Soviet Union under Gorbachev is in the hands of a more modern and vigorous leader than ever before. Beyond his political reforms, such as relaxing press censorship somewhat, he has instituted a number of economic reforms. These programs, though tentative and small-scale, represent the first attempts by the Soviet Union to become part of a world economy.

The problems of the Russian economy are legendary. One need only think of the kind of anecdotes that reach the West—constant shortages of staple foods (bread one week but no butter; the next week butter but no bread; and long lines for whatever is available), ugly and shoddy clothing, poor-quality cars that cost several years' wages, and so on. And there is truth to these complaints. For example, a Moscow newspaper reported in 1987 that 40 percent of the fires reported in the city during the previous year were caused by faulty TV sets (Sancton 1987). Improving the quality of Soviet goods has been a priority of Gorbachev, not only because he wishes to better the Soviet citizen's standard of living but so that Soviet products can compete in a world economy—thus giving the U.S.S.R. valued hard

currency to buy the sophisticated electronics and other products it needs from abroad to implement further modernization. To encourage the manufacture of better products (and more of them), Gorbachev has tightened the system of inspection, so that faulty goods are rejected. He has increased the powers of factory managers somewhat and asked them to be accountable for their plants' performance. (No longer is it enough to meet a government-determined production quota; goods must be of acceptable quality and delivered on time.) Gorbachev has also introduced the idea that industrial workers who produce more should earn more—a notion previously too capitalistic to be acceptable in the Soviet Union. Among other changes Gorbachev has advocated are a decrease in state subsidies for certain goods (prices of food, clothing, and shelter are now generally set by the government) and less centralized control, streamlining the links between bureaucrats and producers. The long-term goal is increased productivity, a moderate shift away from heavy industry to the production of consumer goods, and modernization of factories by the installation of computers, robots, and other high-tech advances from the West.

To some extent, a model for Gorbachev's plans for the Soviet Union already exists—the economy of China. Since the late 1970s, under the leadership of another vigorous, innovative head of state, Deng Xiaoping, China has achieved a remarkable economic success story. Per-

sonal income has risen sharply, as has farm production; consumer goods are more available than ever before; relaxation of laws forbidding private ventures has spawned millions of small income-producing businesses; and exports have increased dramatically (more than $27 billion in 1985). Although China is still emphatically a socialist society, it has absorbed certain capitalist ideas and practices with good results. The Soviet Union under Gorbachev may be inching in that direction. Already, for example, the reform measures have legalized small-scale service businesses—carpenters, restaurateurs, hairdressers, plumbers, and the like, can now go into business for themselves.

As yet, the free-market mechanisms introduced by Gorbachev are miniscule compared with the massive planned economy of the Soviet Union. Moreover, Gorbachev's proposals for further change have not been warmly welcomed by all sectors of Soviet society. Some powerful political officials see the reforms as a threat to their authority, and some average Soviet citizens are cynical about reforms that as yet seem to suggest that they will be expected to work harder and pay more for goods and services. Nevertheless, there can be no doubt that Gorbachev is determined to push (or perhaps drag) his country forward. Another decade may show changes in the Soviet economy as significant as those in China's. Indeed, China points the way the Soviet Union must go if it is to prosper in a global economy.

McDonald's stretching its yellow arches over some street corner in downtown Moscow.

The move to give more freedom to the marketplace is one of the key elements in Soviet premier Mikhail

Gorbachev's efforts to restructure and reduce the rigidity in the Soviet system. Gorbachev's economic and social reforms, known collectively as *perestroika*, are part of a push for increased productivity and an overall campaign to restore life to a stagnant Soviet economy. While the Soviet system has clearly succeeded remarkably well in some areas, such as military fortification, its economic performance has declined sharply in recent years. Chronic shortages, falls in hard currency earnings, high worker absenteeism, and low worker discipline have become chronic signs of the failing Soviet economy.

Gorbachev's willingness to press ahead with change is part of his policy known as *glasnost*, or *openness*, and bears considerable political risk. But it also recognizes the inability of the centrally controlled economy to satisfy growing consumer demand and at the same time meet the enormous costs of lifetime social benefits and a huge military establishment. In addition, the Soviet economy is still feeling the effects of plummeting oil prices and the Chernobyl nuclear disaster (Trimble 1986).

The proposals of *perestroika* are more far-reaching than any since the ferment of the 1920s, just after the Bolshevik Revolution. Indeed, in its early years the Soviet Union made massive gains in industrialization, though under Stalin and his successors its economy began to stagnate. It remains to be seen whether Gorbachev's reforms will be extensive enough to enable the Soviet Union to realize its hopes of modernization. Few analysts expect the Soviet reform measures even to approach those instituted in China, where workers can be fired, money-losing enterprises can be shut down, and other experiments in redefining socialism are under-way. Instead, Soviet innovations are expected to resemble the incentive systems of East Germany, the most prosperous of the Soviet-bloc nations. So firmly entrenched is the current Soviet system, however, that even limited reforms will mean a difficult adjustment period for officials and citizens alike.

But many observers believe that Gorbachev has more latitude to carry out changes than did Kremlin predecessors Nikita Khrushchev and Aleksei Kosygin in the 1960s and 1970s. One reason for optimism is Gorbachev's success in spurring the economy so far. The basic Soviet economic indicator is material net product, somewhat akin to gross national product in the West. The material product increase of 4.3 percent in the first nine months of 1986 was the best of the decade (Galuszka et al. 1987).

Yet in spite of these deviations from strict socialist philosophy and recent attempts at economic reform, the Soviet Union cannot be said to be embracing capitalism. The Soviets adhere to very different economic values

East may meet West, yet despite Premier Gorbachev's economic reforms, including the proposal for joint business ventures with U.S. companies, Soviet economic values remain very different from ours. (Peter Turnley/Black Star.)

than we do under capitalism. Their **state socialist economy** is based on collective (not private) ownership of the means of production, centralized planning for the collective good (not decentralized planning by individual firms and consumers), and an ultimate vision of a truly classless society (not simply the equality of economic opportunity that we value). Many Americans do not understand the ideological appeal of the Soviet system and believe that military power is the Soviet Union's sole source of strength. However, close observers of the Soviet people note that the communist ideology provides Soviet citizens with a consistent view of history and of world events and shapes their daily lives and outlook (Satter 1983). In sections that follow, we will explore the kinds of economic institutions to which our own capitalist values have given rise. We begin with a look at modern corporate capitalism and the role played by government in our capitalist economy.

MODERN CORPORATE CAPITALISM

The modern American economy is not dominated by individual capitalists or their descendents. For the most part, entrepreneurs like Henry Ford, the Lever brothers, and W. K. Kellogg have passed from the scene. Instead, American business activity is dominated by a few dozen gigantic corporations—oil companies, automobile manufacturers, and various **conglomerates** (giant corporations made up of a cluster of smaller companies, such as United Technologies or International Telephone and Telegraph [ITT]). A **corporation** is an organization created by law that has an ongoing existence and powers and liabilities that are independent from those of its owners and managers. The word "corporation" means literally a "created body": its "owners" are thousands of shareholders (a different group daily as stocks are bought and sold), and its managers are employees hired to run the company. In the United States, a corporation can be created by almost any group of people who sign appropriate papers and register these with the state government. Although some churches, charities, schools, and other professional groups might choose to incorporate, the term is usually associated with business corporations.

One way to understand how American corporations developed is to look at the first large-scale business organizations in the United States, the railroads. According to the business historian Alfred Chandler (1976), the railroad was both the model American corporation and the crucial innovation that made possible the development of other large-scale business enterprises. (Without the transportation links provided by the railroads, which allowed shipment of raw materials and finished goods, business on even a regional scale would have been virtually impossible.) The railroads were themselves the first businesses to pose demands for efficient large-scale organization. First of all, railroads were extraordinarily expensive, so many different investors were needed to provide a pool of capital to build and operate them. Second, since it was inefficient for many small railroads to be run independently of one another, companies had

to work together to coordinate scheduling (and for that matter, even to agree on a common track size). And third, railroads required careful management. It would not do for ticket agents in two cities to sell two different people tickets for the same seat on the same train to Cleveland, for example. Even making sure that trains didn't run in opposite directions on the same track took considerable organization. A central management was needed to delegate authority and to coordinate the activities of many local managers. Railroads thus provided the model for the modern corporation by developing techniques for capitalization (raising money from investors) and by setting up internal management on a very large scale. Railroads were too big to be run as family businesses; they needed managers who would work primarily for salaries, not be owners of the business.

Although the characteristic features of the modern corporation can be seen developing in the prototype of the railroads in the nineteenth century, it is important to note that this was not an inevitable or wholly uncontested process. It required certain social interventions that might not have occurred or might have taken a somewhat different form. Legally, for example, we now treat a corporation as a kind of "artificial person" (Dan-Cohen 1986). Like a person, a corporation can hold property, make contracts, and sue or be sued in a court of law. In the nineteenth century many people opposed these ideas, fearing that such liberties would allow corporations to grow too large, or enable managers to shirk responsibility for their actions, or generally create an unfair system. Another significant action by the American legal system to further the evolution of the corporation was the development of the doctrine of "limited liability" (Ohrnial 1984). What this means is that those who invest in corporations cannot be held responsible for any wrongdoings of the corporation's management or employees. Thus, if you own 100 shares of stock in a pharmaceutical company that markets a new drug that ends up killing people, you cannot be forced to pay damages to the victims or their heirs. Nor are you liable to the company's creditors should it go bankrupt. Your liability is limited to the amount of money you invested in the stock. Limited liability thus protects investors and by so doing enables corporations to raise large sums of capital by selling stock. The concept of limited liability is now part of U.S. business law, but it took more than a century of controversial court decisions to establish it (Friedman 1973; Horowitz 1977). The doctrine is still controversial today, with detractors claiming, among other things, that it compromises a corporation's accountability to the public (Nader, Green, and Seligman 1976).

An examination of the resources controlled by the largest American corporations indicates how enormous many of these organizations have become (see Table 15.1). The annual sales of the thirty largest corporations exceeded $10 billion in 1986. And when these sales falter—as in recent years in the automobile industry —many thousands of employees across the country can be thrown out of work for indefinite periods. The power

of American corporations contrasts strikingly with that of ordinary American citizens: the result is what sociologist James Coleman (1982) has called an "asymmetric society." Large, powerful corporations outlive individual people and can muster resources far beyond those held privately. On the one hand, corporations can accomplish undertakings far beyond the scope of individuals; on the other, corporations can drag out lawsuits from injured individuals for years or decades, knowing that the individuals will sooner or later die or lack the resources to continue the lawsuit.

TABLE 15.1 The *Fortune 500* Top 25 Largest U.S. Industrial Corporations, 1987

Rank		Company	Sales		Profits			Assets	
1987	1986		$ Millions	% Change from 1986	$ Millions	Rank	% Change from 1986	$ Millions	Rank
1	1	General Motors *Detroit*	101,781.9	(1.0)	3,550.9	4	20.6	87,421.9	1
2	2	Exxon *New York*	76,416.0	9.3	4,840.0	2	(9.7)	74,042.0	2
3	3	Ford Motor *Dearborn, MI*	71,643.4	14.2	4,625.2	3	40.8	44,955.7	4
4	4	IBM *Armonk, NY*	54,217.0	5.8	5,258.0	1	9.8	63,668.0	3
5	5	Mobil *New York*	51,223.0	14.2	1,258.0	11	(10.6)	41,140.0	5
6	6	General Electric *Fairfield, CT*	39,315.0	11.7	2,915.0	5	17.0	38,920.0	6
7	8	Texaco *White Plains, NY*	34,372.0	8.7	(4,407.0)	480	–	38,962.0	9
8	7	AT&T *New York*	33,598.0	(1.4)	2,044.0	6	1,370.5	38,426.0	7
9	9	E.I. du Pont de Nemours *Wilmington, DE*	30,468.0	12.2	1,786.0	8	16.1	28,209.0	10
10	11	Chrysler *Highland Park, MI*	26,257.7	16.6	1,289.7	10	(8.1)	19,944.6	15
11	10	Chevron *San Francisco*	26,015.0	6.8	1,007.0	19	40.8	34,465.0	8
12	12	Philip Morris *New York*	22,279.0	7.7	1,842.0	7	24.6	19,145.0	17
13	15	Shell Oil *Houston*	20,852.0	23.9	1,230.0	13	39.3	26,937.0	11
14	13	Amoco *Chicago*	20,174.0	10.4	1,360.0	9	82.1	24,827.0	12
15	17	United Technologies *Hartford*	17,170.2	9.6	591.7	37	713.6	11,928.6	28
16	19	Occidental Petroleum *Los Angeles*	17,096.0	11.4	240.0	95	32.5	16,739.0	20
17	18	Proctor & Gamble *Cincinnati*	17,000.0	10.1	327.0	69	(53.9)	13,715.0	23
18	20	Atlantic Richfield *Los Angeles*	16,281.4	11.6	1,224.3	14	99.0	22,669.9	14
19	14	RJR Nabisco *Atlanta*	15,868.0	(6.6)	1,209.0	15	13.6	16,861.0	19
20	16	Boeing *Seattle*	15,355.0	(6.0)	480.0	46	(27.8)	12,566.0	26
21	21	Tenneco *Houston*	15,075.0	3.6	(218.0)	474	–	18,503.0	18
22	35	BP America *Cleveland*	14,611.0	58.5	564.0	41	–	23,287.0	13
23	22	USX *Pittsburgh*	13,898.0	(0.7)	219.0	106	–	19,557.0	16
24	27	Dow Chemical *Midland, MI*	13,377.0	20.4	1,240.0	12	69.4	14,356.0	22
25	26	Eastman Kodak *Rochester, NY*	13,305.0	15.2	1,178.0	16	215.0	14,451.0	21

Source: Fortune, April 25, 1988, p. D11.

Government Economic Activity

As suggested earlier in the chapter, American capitalism comes closest to the ideal model, but it also differs in important respects. Ideal capitalist theory calls for a minimum of government intervention in business and other areas of economic life. But ever since the Great Depression, when the capitalist system appeared on the verge of total collapse, the general consensus has been that some degree of government economic intervention is essential. As we saw in Chapter 14, the government plays two principal roles in the modern state. It is an "enabler," that is, it provides goods (such as money) and services (such as the civil courts) that make it possible for individuals and businesses to engage in a wide variety of activities and transactions. The government is also a "regulator," protecting businesses from unfair forms of competition, consumers from potentially harmful products, society at large from unfair practices such as discrimination, and so forth. Not only in the United States but throughout the modern world the government has assumed an increasingly prominent role in regulating business activity, managing the money supply, and providing financial support and services to individuals, families, communities, and businesses.

In the United States, the growth of government that led to today's welfare state (see Chapter 14) is commonly traced back to the New Deal programs of President Franklin D. Roosevelt, which represented attempts to boost the economy and soften the social effects of the Great Depression. The most famous theoretical proponent of an expanded role for government, however, was an Englishman, the economist John Maynard Keynes. Keynes' most influential idea was that governments should increase their spending when private economic activity declines. Government spending during hard times (made possible by borrowing if necessary) would both stimulate economic recovery and cushion the effects of unemployment and other social problems. Until the late 1970s, this principle predominated in both academic circles and in government policy throughout the Western world. It provided the basis for a dramatic growth in government social programs, for peacetime military spending, and for a substantial increase in the number of government employees.

A prominent American Keynesian, John Kenneth Galbraith (1978), has argued that permanent big government has become essential, not only because people want the services it provides but because modern business depends on it. Big corporations, according to Galbraith, need a stable environment within which to plan new products and make expensive investments of capital, and only government can maintain this environment. Moreover, government contracts provide long-term guaranteed profits for corporations, making possible extensive research programs, and these in turn result in new inventions that benefit the public. (One such is the non-stick surface Teflon, a by-product of military research.) The modern computer industry has also been supported largely by government contracts from the military and agencies like the Internal Revenue Service, which require computers to manage their enormous record-keeping tasks (Goldstine 1972). In short, the so-called welfare state provides many public benefits besides financial assistance to the poor. The latter, in fact, accounts for a relatively small (5 to 12 percent) proportion of government spending.

In the late 1970s, Keynesian views of the government's role in the economy came under attack. One of Keynes' basic ideas was that although government spending might create **inflation** (an undue increase of a country's money supply), this was a necessary evil, since the same spending would reduce unemployment. But following the OPEC oil price increases in 1973, inflation and unemployment rose to high levels simultaneously. Government initiatives that had worked before failed to solve the problem this time. Moreover, because of both individuals' and corporations' vested interests in government programs, it proved difficult to scale back government spending. The situation seemed to be getting closer to Galbraith's model of a permanent big government, but one unable to solve economic problems either by spending more or spending less.

Of the several explanations for the "stagflation" (inflation combined with declining business activity and rising unemployment) of the 1970s that were proposed, two alternative theories to Keynesian ideas were most prominent. The first, **monetarism,** argued that changes in the money supply determine the direction of a nation's economy; thus control over the money supply is the key to a sound economy. In this view, government should take on minimal economic roles other than ensuring a stable currency; the rest should be left to the free market. Monetarism had a substantial influence on the Federal Reserve Board's decision to keep interest rates high through most of the late 1970s and early 1980s (this is a way of limiting growth in the money supply and fighting inflation). A second alternative theory, called "supply-side" theory, was advanced by politicians, more than academics. Supply-side thinkers (including many powerful people in the Reagan administration) felt that Keynesian thinking was too concerned with assuring that people had money to spend (the "demand side"). In their view, the way to lower prices to consumers is to enable businesses to increase productivity. Accordingly, the supply-side thinkers favored tax cuts designed to free up private wealth for investment in industry (the "supply side"). It is important to note that neither of these economic theories propose the kind of expansion of the welfare state favored by Keynesians. Although government expenditures have doubled during the 1980s (from a total federal budget of $590.9 billion in 1980, to a Reagan administration proposal of $1,015.6 billion in 1987), the largest increases have been in the military and defense budgets. The Reagan administration has effectively curtailed many of the social programs that were supported previously on economic as well as humanitarian grounds. Some Keynesians argue that although Reagan denounced government borrowing, he has actually raised U.S. debt more than any previous president; this may be one source of the relative economic prosperity of the middle 1980s.

BUSINESS INSTITUTIONS IN AMERICA

The Large Corporation

There is no disputing the fact that a small number of large corporations control a disproportionate share of the American economy. In 1982 the top 500 companies accounted for nearly $2.4 trillion in sales, equal to about 78 percent of the gross national product of the United States. Moreover, the largest 808 firms employed 21.6 million people, or one out of every five working Americans. Of these 21.6 million workers, 20 percent were employed in ten firms (*Forbes* 1983). Of the nation's industrial firms, 259 corporations own 65 percent of all corporate assets and account for nearly 70 percent of all profits (U.S. Bureau of the Census 1983). There is no sign that the economic share of the largest corporations is decreasing. In fact, the last several decades have seen a steady trend toward greater and greater concentration of wealth and earnings in the hands of a relatively few firms. The 1980s have seen corporate takeovers of unprecedented size and frequency.

Many American industries are *oligopolies*—industries dominated by only a few very large firms. In the manufacture of products as diverse as automobiles, chewing gum, tennis balls, razor blades, cigarettes, detergents, steel, canned soups, and cameras, the four largest firms are responsible for over 80 percent of total United States output. The effects of this are to reduce competition and to make it hard for a new company to enter one of these businesses. Overall, about 60 percent of manufacturing in this country is oligopolistic. In addition, there are signs that the trend toward increasing concentration is now spreading to the economy's service sector (those firms that provide the public with services rather than tangible goods). The fifty largest banks in the nation employ about a third of all banking personnel, and about half of all those in the insurance industry work for the fifty largest insurance firms (Heilbroner 1976). In short, the trend toward oliogopoly seems likely to continue, at least into the near future.

America's large corporations are very different from the sort of businesses that the founders of capitalist theory had in mind. The most famous of these early theorists, Adam Smith (1776), thought that capitalism would be a system in which individual capitalists operated independently and in which order was brought to the whole economy by what he called the "invisible hand." This invisible hand was his phrase for market pressure, the automatic reward for work, creativity, and risk and the punishment for sloth, conventionality, and excessive caution that would be enforced by market prices.

For the invisible hand to work, however, the individuals in the marketplace had to be more or less equally vulnerable to market forces. In theory, for example, businesses introduce new products (supply), customers make a rational choice of the best product (demand), and its producer thrives accordingly. This stimulates competitors to work harder and come up with better or cheaper competing products. In fact, however, when the marketplace is dominated by a few giant corporations, small producers, however good and innovative their products, are at a great disadvantage. The large corporation has vast resources to produce and promote its products and to *create* demand through sophisticated advertising. Moreover, the large corporation can take advantage of economies of scale, selling its products for less because it manufactures in very large quantities, which makes each product less expensive to assemble. Faced with new competition, it can cut prices on its own product, offer rebates, or launch aggressive promotion—all of which are beyond the resources of a new small business.

When a few corporations provide nearly all of a particular product, those companies are virtually free from the restraints that exist in a competitive market. They can charge as much for the product as consumers will pay before they turn to less desirable substitutes. And through extensive advertising, corporations can often ensure that demand for their product will remain high despite an inflated price tag. In addition, by taking out patents, controlling raw materials, and either convincing the government to suppress competition or colluding with other corporations, oligopolies can prevent new firms from entering the market. They can also buy up other companies—competitors, suppliers, manufacturers of related or different products—and become a conglomerate, thus controlling even more resources and jobs through subsidiaries.

In addition, by deciding when and at what pace to invest, huge corporations determine the rate of growth not only of their own corporations but of related industries as well. For example, decisions by steel companies to maximize short-term cash flow instead of modernizing steel production facilities in this country caused shortages in the 1950s and again in the 1970s (Bensman and Lynch 1987). Our steel mills are outdated in comparison with those of other nations, and we now import much of our steel—which affects employment rates, the price of anything made with steel, and even taxes (because steel is vital in the manufacture of defense equipment).

Large corporations are also free to decide what new technologies to explore through research and development and what innovations will be translated into new products and services. Technology has a profound impact on all aspects of social life (as we will see in Chapter 20). If, for example, Ford and General Motors had put more of their assets into developing more energy-efficient cars during the 1960s and early 1970s, American relations with oil-producing nations and our competition with the Japanese could be very different from what they are today.

Adam Smith's concept of the "invisible hand" of market pressure has given way to the visible logo of the multinational corporation, reaching out worldwide to create new markets for its products. The cola competition is as keen in rural Kenya as anywhere. (John Moss/Photo Researchers, Inc.)

The Global Power of Multinationals

As we noted earlier in this chapter, the domestic economies of many nations are yielding to a global economy. The key players in today's worldwide economic system are the multinational corporations. A **multinational corporation** is a private business firm with operations and subsidiaries in many different countries. Crossing national boundaries to obtain raw materials and to market goods is a tradition that dates back to the Phoenician glass merchants and even earlier. But the actual integration of peoples from all lands into a world economy began with the expansion and conquests of European nations in the fifteenth century. Colonial territories exported spices, coffee, tea, and tobacco to Europe. Later they became suppliers of agricultural and mineral raw materials. However, today's multinational corporations are not simply buying and selling abroad; they are actually *producing* there. For instance, Exxon, the world's largest oil company, operates approximately seventy refineries in thirty-seven countries. In 1986, international business accounted for 72 percent of Exxon's revenues and 74.9 percent of its profits (see Table 15.2).

Not all multinational corporations are American. European and Japanese multinational companies include the mammoth Royal Dutch/Shell Group (oil—Netherlands/United Kingdom), Mitsui (wholesaler—Japan), and the Volkswagen Group (automotive—Germany). Multinational corporations do not consider foreign factories and markets as adjuncts to home operations. Instead, they view the entire world as a single economic system.

Critics charge that multinationals are too big, too rich, and too powerful. It is nearly impossible for many national governments to impose control over such enormous firms. The annual incomes from sales of big oil firms such as Exxon and big auto companies such as General Motors exceed the gross national products of most nations in which they do business. Indeed, the financial resources of major multinational corporations are so large that these companies often can manipulate the economies of the nations in which they operate. For example, should a multinational decide that a country's currency is overvalued or unsafe, they can shift to another country's currency. Or if they believe that a particular nation is politically unsympathetic or unstable, they can take their investments elsewhere. Such decisions have a profound impact on the wealth—and the politics—of nations.

Furthermore, by shifting assets and operations abroad, multinationals are able to avoid government regulations, high taxes, and labor unions. For example, by selling to their own divisions, they can take a loss in countries with high taxes and show a gain in countries with low taxes.

Moreover, global corporations often have a significant impact on the political and social institutions of the countries in which they operate, especially developing nations. For instance, when multinationals become extensively established in a developing country, equality of income distribution frequently declines and overall economic development often lags (Bornschier and Ballmer-Cao 1979; Bornschier and Hoby 1981). The reason has to do with the efforts of multinationals to further their own growth. These giant corporations may use their substantial economic and political influence to keep taxes and wages low and to foster other conditions that increase their profitability (Chase-Dunn 1975). At their most blatant and aggressive, such efforts may involve bribery and other illicit dealings, as well as deliberate attempts to topple unsympathetic regimes. The most highly publicized example of the latter was ITT's spending of $1 million to overthrow Chile's socialist president Salvador Allende. As a result of the embarrassment such disclosures have caused, some multinationals have established specific policies trying to limit their involvement in a host country's politics (U.S. Commission 1978).

But such gestures on the part of multinationals only indicate that a new economic power structure is emerging—one that transcends the political power of nations. Increasingly, the managers of GM, IBM, Pepsico, General Electric, Pfizer, Shell, Volkswagen,

TABLE 15.2   The 10 Largest U.S. Multinationals

1986	Company	Total revenue (millions)	Total operating profit (millions)	Total assets (millions)
1	Exxon	$69,888	$5,219	$69,484
2	Mobil	46,025	1,407	37,233
3	IBM	51,250	4,789	57,814
4	Ford Motor	62,716	3,285	37,933
5	General Motors	102,814	2,945	72,403
6	Texaco	31,613	1,187	34,940
7	Citicorp	23,496	1,058	184,013
8	E.I. du Pont de Nemours	26,907	1,791	26,733
9	Dow Chemical	11,113	1,285	12,242
10	Chevron	24,352	1,055	34,583

Source: Forbes, July 27, 1987, p. 152.

Exxon, and perhaps 100 other global corporations influence the prosperity, balance of payments, and political strength of the countries in which they operate. Yet even so, corporate managers do not have a completely free hand. Workers have organized themselves into labor unions as a counterbalancing force to the growth of mammoth corporations. And governments in Western nations have placed curbs on the unrestricted use of corporate power. However, the emergence of gigantic multinational corporations has provided new dimensions to the exercise of power by organizations pursuing economic gain. This has raised the question of who has control of the corporations.

Who Controls the Corporations?

In the "old days" (the early nineteenth century), individual owners–entrepreneurs ran their own businesses, made all the key decisions, and reaped the profits or suffered the losses of their economic policies. Two of the key features of the modern corporation, however, are shared ownership (through sale of stock) and the separation of ownership and management. The owners do not manage, and the managers do not own (although managers receive substantial salaries and may own some stock). Hence corporate ownership and corporate management are two very different things and make the question of corporate control considerably more complex (Berle and Means 1932; Herman 1981).

In principle, ownership is still the basis for controlling the corporation. But there are several reasons why the power of owners has been greatly reduced. In the first place, ownership is diffuse rather than concentrated; it is based, as previously noted, on shareholdings of stock. Although an individual or family may hold substantial shares in a corporation, most large corporations are owned by thousands of shareholders. Many of these shareholders are not individuals at all, but large institutional investors—mutual, trust, and pension funds (Glasberg and Schwartz 1983). Nowadays, such institutional investors control at least 70 percent of all stock traded.

Another reason why stockholders (even major ones) have limited control is because each owns too few shares to make it worthwhile to take an active role in corporate affairs. If stockholders don't like the way a company is run, they will more likely decide to sell their stock than voice their disapproval in person at the annual stockholders' meeting. Further, owners are unable to exert effective managerial control because they are a widely dispersed group with few social connections. The thousands of people who own stock in IBM would have great difficulty taking direct action in regard to company policy. Moreover, they often lack the technical and legal expertise to make decisions for "their" company. In general, so long as the company makes a profit, the hired managers are free to do what they think best.

Given various limitations on the powers of owners, the question remains: who controls the corporations? Theoretically, top management must answer to the corporation's board of directors, which in turn is responsible to stockholders. Most boards of directors consist of a dozen or so senior managers of the company, prominent businesspeople from other companies, and public figures. The board is charged with protecting the stockholders' interests and, to some extent, the public's interests by overseeing the legalities of operations. But while the board's responsibility to owners is true in theory, it is less true in practice. Top management usually picks members of the board and the board rarely intervenes in management unless a crisis arises (Herman 1981).

Some sociologists take this observation one step further. In his history of American business, Alfred Chandler (1976) comments on the corporation's role in replacing the "invisible hand" of the market with the "visible hand" of the managers. Other writers argue that top managers, board members, and major stockholders form a "capitalist elite" because their interests are largely the same (Mills 1951). This capitalist elite, the argument goes, extends its influence even further by means of **interlocking directorships**—networks of people who serve on the boards of directors of two or more corporations (Mintz and Schwartz 1986; Useem 1980). Figure 15.1 illustrates the interlocking directorate of General Motors and other large firms. According to Michael Useem, these network ties create a feeling of solidarity and common purpose among owners and managers of different corporations. That purpose, Useem holds, is one managers themselves identify as "maximizing the rate of return on capital."

Other researchers, however, find the notion of a corporate capitalist elite to be overstated. Edward Herman (1981), who has conducted detailed research into the operations of corporate boards and their top managers, finds that members of these groups often have opposing interests that keep them from acting as a monolithic entity. To cite one example, financial institutions such as banks may have seats on the board of directors of a company for which they have arranged loans. The banks' representatives are likely to be con-

Who controls the corporation? In principle, ultimate control rests with stockholders, such as those pictured here attending an annual shareholders' meeting. Nevertheless, effective control is concentrated in a handful of top managers and directors, many of whom may also sit in the boardrooms of other corporations. What are the benefits and drawbacks of such a network of power? Who ought to control the corporation? (Left: Catherine Ursillo/Photo Researchers, Inc.; right: Jacques Charlas/Stock, Boston.)

cerned solely with matters of financial security and thus opposed to more risky moves that managers support. In the case of a threatened takeover, financial institutions generally stand to benefit by having the company sold to the highest bidder. The firm's managers, however, stand to lose their jobs in the deal and can be expected to try to block a takeover attempt (Hirsch 1986).

Questions of corporate control affect not only owners and managers, but "ordinary" employees, and the general public. Useem (1984) documents the extent to which top corporate managers band together to promote the common interests of business as a whole. Not only do they give money to political candidates who support their interests, they also take part in lobbying groups and sponsor advertising for their views on a variety of issues—from tax reform to military spending to protection against foreign imports. Top corporate managers frequently serve as cabinet secretaries, advisers to presidents, and directors of charitable concerns. Even within their individual companies, they make decisions that can affect the welfare of thousands of people. They decide whether to use dangerous chemicals in their plants and how much to spend on safety procedures. They decide whether to rebuild factories in the Midwest or move production to the South or to South Korea. No matter what their views on these issues, middle- and lower-level managers cannot challenge the top corporate leaders on whom their careers are completely dependent (Jackall

1988). In all these ways, top corporate managers constitute a controlling group with significant social power inside and outside the corporation.

Small Business

Although American business makes us think of corporate giants like General Motors and IBM, small businesses —defined by the government as any firm with 100 employees or fewer—are a significant part of the economic scene. Fully one-half of the labor force is employed by small businesses (Birch 1982, 1988).

The small business picture is a varied one: it encompasses everything from coffee shops and dry cleaners to doctors' offices, law firms, building contractors, and suppliers of computer software. As this list suggests, small businesses differ greatly in the skills and resources of their owners and in their financial stability. Several factors are common to small businesses, however, and most of them are problems. Lack of capital is almost a defining characteristic of a small business, especially at the beginning. Banks are reluctant to lend money to unproven enterprises, and many entrepreneurs start by using their own savings, often supplemented by loans from family members. Another common problem is vulnerability to fluctuations in the marketplace

FIGURE 15.1   The Interlocking Directorship of General Motors and Other Firms

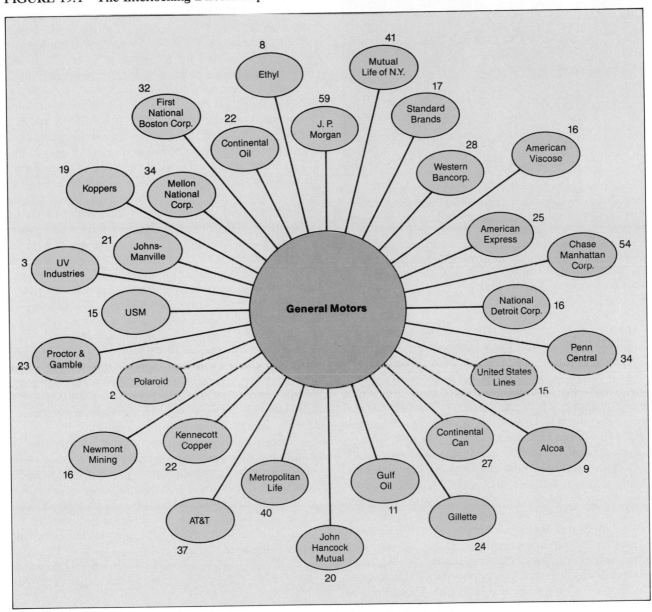

Source: Beth Mintz and Michael Schwartz, "Interlocking directorates and interest group formation," *American Sociological Review*, 46 (December 1981), figure 3, p. 857.

Individuals who sit on the board of directors of General Motors also sit on the boards of directors of 29 other firms. In turn, the members of each of the 29 firms sit on the boards of directors of still other firms. For instance, the people who sit on the board of J. P. Morgan are also linked to the boards of 59 other firms. Through such ties, General Motors is embedded in a network of 728 corporations.

The variety of services offered by small businesses is limited only by the ingenuity of the entrepreneurs who start them and by the appetites of the customers who support them. The owner of this dog-walking business can rest assured that demand for his services will not suddenly run dry. On the other hand, his business is not terribly likely to make him rich. (Chuck Fishman/ Woodfin Camp & Associates.)

(Markusen and Teitz 1985). These may be seasonal (few people want garden equipment in the winter); a result of the business climate (high interest rates or high inflation may eat up profits); tied to problems in specific industries (the market for farm machinery collapsed after farm prices plummeted) or the result of changes in the business's milieu (a business may suffer from a neighborhood's decline as customers move out, or be unable to pay an increased rent if the neighborhood gentrifies).

Even given these problems, hundreds of thousands of businesses are founded each year. Owning one's own little store, or restaurant, or office, seems to fit well with the American ideal of independence. (It also requires the American ideal of hard work; owners of small businesses typically work far more than forty hours a week, and often entire families work long hours. When small businesses succeed, it is often by one of several strategies. One is growth by opening new branches. A food store or a dry cleaner, for example, may open a second or third outlet in a nearby neighborhood. Another strategy is product diversification—a toy store adds a line of children's clothing, or a health-food store begins selling exercise equipment. Another technique is product differentiation, or selling a product or service a little different from what competitors are offering—as when a pizza parlor is the only one in the neighborhood to feature free delivery or to sell kosher pizzas.

An interesting aspect of the small-business picture in the United States is the frequency with which these concerns are owned by members of ethnic minorities, particularly recent immigrants (Aldrich and Auster 1986). For example, in 1976, 25 percent of the Korean families in Los Angeles county were in family-owned small businesses, a proportion three times higher than the rate for the total work force. In New York, a sample of restaurants in 1980 revealed that 60 percent were immigrant-owned (Aldrich and Auster 1986). A number of explanations have been advanced for this phenomenon, among them discrimination against ethnics in the larger economy; special characteristics of immigrants themselves (a Chinese person might know little English but be able to cook Chinese food well and have relatives willing to invest in a restaurant); extended families in certain groups that supply both a pool of funds to start up a business and a pool of low-wage employees to work in it; and residential patterns that simultaneously confine recent immigrants to ethnic neighborhoods and supply them with customers with familiar needs and tastes. Finally, for some ethnic entrepreneurs, self-employment —even behind a lunch counter—is more attractive than a low-paying job in the mainstream economy.

Small businesses of all kinds are born in hope every year, but the mortality rate among them is very high indeed. Over 50 percent fail within two years; 75 percent within five years; and 90 percent within ten years (Aldrich and Auster 1986). Smallness and newness are definite liabilities in the business world.

Small businesses, however, are extremely important to the American economy. Not only do they serve consumers, they generate many more *new* jobs than do large companies (although large companies account for a greater percentage of existing jobs) (Birch 1982, 1988). Table 15.3 compares the percentage of jobs created by small businesses with those spawned by middle-sized and larger companies.

WORK IN AMERICA

Americans talk about their work, from Studs Terkel's *Working: People Talk About What They Do All Day and How They Feel About It* (1972):

I have to be a waitress. How else can I learn about people? How else does the world come to me? I can't go

TABLE 15.3   Percentage of Jobs Created by Size of Firm and Region

Number of Employees in Firm	Percent of Jobs Created				
	Northeast	*North Central*	*South*	*West*	*U.S. Average*
0–20	177.1%	67.2%	53.5%	59.5%	66.9%
21–50	6.5	12.0	11.2	11.6	11.2
51–100	−17.4	5.2	5.5	6.3	4.3
101–500	−33.3	3.1	9.4	9.3	5.2
501+	−32.9	12.4	20.4	13.3	13.3
Total	100.0%	100.0%	100.0%	100.0%	100.0%

Source: M.I.T. Program on Neighborhood and Regional Changes.

to everyone. So they have to come to me. Everyone wants to eat, everyone has hunger. And I serve them. If they've had a bad day, I nurse them, cajole them. Maybe with coffee I give them a little philosophy. They have cocktails, I give them political science.

> Dolores Dante, waitress (p. 294)

I was a kid in 1942 when I got out of art school. I wanted to make a lot of money and become famous. In five years I'll own the world. I'll be in New York driving a Cadillac and owning my own plane. I want gold cuff links and babes and the big house in the country. The whole bit. The American Dream. (Laughs.) That beautiful, ugly, vicious dream that we all, in some way, have. I wanted to be a key man in the industry. Over the years I realized there isn't any key man—that every man, every human is a commodity to be exploited. And destroyed and cast aside. For thirty years I've been a commercial hack.

> Walter Lundquist, commercial artist (p. 525)

All I do now is get up in the morning, go there, and I don't be thinking about that. Like a machine, that's about the only way I can feel.

> Will Robinson, bus driver (p. 201)

I run into people who say how much they admire what I do. It's embarrassing. I don't make any judgments about my work, whether it's great or worthless. It's just what I do best. It's the only job I want to do. I work hard because I have to. I get tired. At four I feel as though I'm ready to die. (Laughs.) I don't feel bad about it. This is my life. I just *am.*

> Pat Zimmerman, alternative school teacher (p. 493)

Karl Marx argued that work is a distinctively human activity. Animals may build and produce—bees, for instance, construct complex and structurally perfect honeycombs and make honey—but they do not work. What distinguishes the worst human architect from the best bee, according to Marx (1867), is that the architect devises a plan and works self-consciously to execute it. Human work thus always involves both a mental and a physical component. In the social organization of work, however, these two are often separated. Since the beginning of the capitalist era especially, some people plan and manage production processes while others do manual labor.

The Meaning of Work

Work is effort aimed at producing a product or service that we usually reward with pay and to which we often attach a moral value. The importance with which we view work can be appreciated if we think of the first question we often ask when we meet someone new: "What do you do?" By this we mean, "What is your job?" not what hobbies you have or how you entertain yourself on weekends and evenings. Work offers a way of defining other people—and ourselves. If the man sitting next to us on the plane says he is a prizefighter, we get one kind of impression; if he tells us he is a psychiatrist, we get quite another. And likewise for any number of different occupations: we have certain assumptions about and expectations of the kind of person who is a sheet-metal worker, a nurse, a physical education teacher, a stockbroker, an astronomer, a dairy farmer, and so on. We see, therefore, that work becomes a highly significant part of our own identity and that of others.

As the above list of occupations suggests, jobs in America differ greatly in pay and skill level, the proportion of mental versus manual effort involved, the extent of autonomy or control, opportunities for advancement, risk of injury, and many other factors. One traditional way of distinguishing jobs has been to call them white-collar (broadly speaking, office work) or blue-collar (factory work or other manual labor). At one time, most of the population consisted of blue-collar workers (including farmers in this group), and white-collar work was reserved for a smaller, educated middle class. This is no longer the case: most working people in America today have white-collar jobs. At the same time, the distinction between white-collar and blue-collar work has lost much of its meaning. Even though white-collar jobs still carry more prestige, many pay no more than (or even less than) skilled factory work. A substantial number of clerical, sales, and semiprofessional jobs (lab technicians, computer programmers) actually offer fairly modest pay and few opportunities for advancement (Calhoun 1981; Piore and Sabel 1985).

While almost every job (or the lack of one) figures into a person's identity, a job in itself can either give pleasure or create (or maintain) frustration. What makes one job satisfying and another dull, unfulfilling, frustrating, even alienating? This is a central question for sociologists studying the nature of work.

First, it appears that even if many people gripe about working, a large majority express favorable opinions about their jobs (Tausky 1984). This is particularly true of those in professional and technical jobs for which substantial training is required: mathematicians, biologists, lawyers, and journalists are among the most satisfied with their jobs, as evidenced by the fact that from 80 to 90 percent of them report that they would choose the same kind of work again. By comparison, only 24 percent of a cross-section of blue-collar workers said that they would choose the same kind of work again (Tausky 1984).

It might be assumed that job satisfaction is higher among professional workers because of the higher pay and prestige that come with their jobs. But although pay and prestige are certainly important aspects of job satisfaction, they are not the only reasons why people express pleasure with their work. Others include the inherent interest of the work itself; the sense that one is doing something worthwhile and contributing to society; the sense that one is supporting oneself and/or one's family and doing what is expected of an adult; the pleasure of developing competence at something and

exercising a skill; and enjoyment of the company of co-workers.

But many people work at jobs that do *not* offer these satisfactions. Many factory jobs, for example, are organized in such a way that they are inherently boring, unchallenging, and isolating, as well as poorly paid and unprestigious. Workers who do the same manual tasks all day, who are pressed to do these tasks as quickly as possible, and who never have the sense of seeing a process from beginning to end are likely to find their jobs dissatisfying. They are likely to feel alienated from their environment, from society as a whole—even from themselves. A job becomes something to endure in order to survive and to obtain the things one really desires.

> Because workers are not involved in the overall decision-making process, because work is not organized in a meaningful way, it becomes increasingly common for workers to treat their jobs as only a necessary evil, as the price they must pay for leisure time and pleasurable activities outside of work. This is one of the reasons that the demands of workers, especially through trade unions, have focused so heavily on pay and other aspects of material security. . . . Workers continue to fight largely for more money because, like management, they are convinced that they cannot find work itself pleasurable, and so must seek all satisfactions in leisure time activities. (Calhoun 1981, p. 288)

The Marxist view of this situation is extremely clear-cut. Its followers argue that the capitalist organization of work makes it intrinsically alienating and dehumanizing. Workers have no control over the production process, work is not organized in any socially unifying way, and work is done for capitalist employers whose goals are opposed to those of workers. Workers must sacrifice their labor—basically, a part of themselves—to enrich the capitalists. For a worker to fulfill her or his own potential in a capitalist society is an impossibility.

People want their work to be meaningful; even at the factory level, they want to be treated like skilled individuals who are performing a valued role, not like robots who mindlessly do what managers tell them to do.

The Social Organization of Work

Traditionally, sociologists have considered the work group to be the most basic unit in the social organization of work (I. Simpson in press). A *work group* is a group of

From mill to factory to assembly line to automated plant, the process of industrialization has meant the increasing subservience of human labor in a workplace where both physical space and the marking of time are shaped and determined by the labor of machines. The structure of work itself can begin to resemble that of a giant machine, with individual workers as mere cogs. (Left: Courtesy General Motors; right: Ethan Hoffman/Archive Pictures.)

people who work together at the same time in the same place—whether the crew of a spacecraft or the kitchen help in a restaurant. Perhaps the most famous research on work groups is the Hawthorne studies, done in the Hawthorne works of the Western Electric Company, near Chicago, between 1924 and 1936. These studies, which were undertaken to identify factors that would increase workers' productivity, yielded a number of important findings, the most famous of which, since known as the Hawthorne effect, was discovered by accident. As researchers looked at the effects of alterations in the working environment, smaller work groups, higher pay, and so on, they found that *any* change in a group's conditions of work increased productivity, at least for a while. Apparently, being part of the study itself made workers feel that management was interested in them, and this increased their output. The Hawthorne studies also revealed that *social* factors, such as the bond between workers, were quite important in motivating people (Tausky 1978). Ever since the Hawthorne studies, sociologists have been aware of the importance of the social context of the workplace.

Of course, most work groups exist within a larger organization of some kind, and the size and type of organization has an important impact on workers' lives on—and off—the job. Most organizations develop shared cultures, and these affect everything from the kind of clothes employees wear (and are expected to wear) to the amount of socializing colleagues do after work. Compare the gray-flannel atmosphere of a Wall Street law firm with the informality of a chain of sporting-goods stores. In some cases, a distinctive corporate culture is actively fostered by management. At IBM, for example, company songs are sung at special celebrations at which employees are given awards and the values of the company are ritually reinforced. Many factors go into giving an organization a particular culture, among them its size, the degree to which it is hierarchical, the number and size of its work groups, its stress on rules and order, and its orientation—scientific, creative, high-finance, or other.

The most important issue for contemporary sociological studies of the organization of work is *control* (R. Simpson 1985). Because the production of goods now involves not one craftsman but hundreds of people functioning much like cogs in a giant machine, considerable planning and coordination are necessary. In most modern work settings coordination is bound up with control, with managers seeking to maximize their own power at the expense of workers. This is characteristic of (though not limited to) capitalist production. As sociologist Richard Edwards has written:

Variety may indeed be the spice of life. The Hawthorne studies investigated how changes in the workplace affected productivity. What measures might have been taken to improve the productivity of this work group at Western Electric's Hawthorne works? (Courtesy of AT&T Archives.)

Coordination occurs in capitalist production as it must inevitably occur in all social production, but it necessarily takes the specific form of top-down coordination, for the exercise of which the top (capitalists) must be able to control the bottom (workers). (1979, p. 17)

In small firms, control is usually *simple control*. This was characteristic of early capitalist enterprise and persists today in small businesses. It is direct and "face-to-face": control is usually exercised by the owner of the company and/or a few top managers. This kind of control can be both arbitrary and harsh; workers question or disobey the managers' wishes at their peril.

As organizations grow and become more complex, simple control becomes impossible. For one thing, there is a limit to the number of workers any one manager can supervise directly; for another, in large organizations workers may be unionized and thus have some protection against arbitrary dismissal or discipline from management. To deal with these situations, management has devised two new styles of control, both of them "structural"—that is, they are built into the work organization itself and are not dependent on close personal supervision. First, there is *technical control*. In a factory, for example, the physical process of labor compels workers to perform their tasks in a certain way within a specific time period. The assembly line is a prime example of technical control, since workers are required to do their jobs—such as attaching the fenders to a car—in just enough time to pass the task on to the next group of workers as they finish *their* appointed tasks. Compulsion is built into the assembly line itself.

In environments such as offices, where technical control is unfeasible, workers are expected to respond to *bureaucratic control* (Edwards 1979). In this case, workers are controlled by a hierarchical system that assigns different rewards to various levels of jobs: one works harder to obtain one's own letterhead stationery, a reserved spot in the company parking lot, the rank that allows access to the "executive" dining room, and so on. In general, bureaucratic control is associated with white-collar jobs, but it should be noted that the advent of office automation now allows office managers to exert some degree of *technical* control. The output of employees who work at computers, for example, can be precisely monitored by management, and the workers can be pressured to work faster just as factory workers can be pressured to tighten more bolts or solder more connections per hour. We will look again at questions of control and its consequences when we focus on technology in the workplace at the end of this section.

Changing Patterns of Work

The American paid labor force has traditionally been dominated by men. For the past 100 years, the proportion of men sixteen and older who work for pay has fluctuated only slightly from a consistent 80 percent. By contrast, the proportion of women in the paid labor force in that same time period has increased from 15 percent to just over 50 percent (Tausky 1984). This striking change in the American work force has significant implications for marriage, family life, the birthrate, and other areas of social life.

Another change that has taken place in patterns of work is the dramatic increase in service occupations, coupled with a sharp drop in agricultural work and a steady decline in employment in manufacturing (see Table 15.4). The growth of the service sector has been so prodigious that some sociologists and economists are calling for a subdivision of the umbrella term *services* into more practical and distinct categories, including perhaps an "information sector" based on the new computer technologies (Jones 1982).

Several social, cultural, and technological factors account for these two major changes. Women first entered the work force in substantial numbers during World War II, when millions of men were taken into the military and women were needed to work in munitions factories and other wartime industries. The changing nature of the family in the 1960s and 1970s—the increase in divorce rates, the development of reliable contraception, the revival of the feminist movement, and the need for a second family income to counter the effects of inflation—brought many women workers, particularly the married ones, into the labor force. Note too that the increase in women workers goes hand-in-

hand with the other major shift in labor patterns—the growing number of service-oriented jobs. These, after all, are the jobs women are most likely to gravitate to (Shank and Getz 1986).

The decline in farm employment is largely a result of mechanization in agriculture, which has enabled individual farmers to cultivate much larger areas of land. Manufacturing jobs have also declined because of technological changes such as the advent of computers and industrial robots (Jones 1982). But we must look at changes in the world economy to account fully for the decline of jobs in the industrial sector. First, the movement of factory production overseas by American firms in search of cheap labor and second, introduction of cheap manufactured goods (cars, shoes, steel, textiles, electronics) from abroad have made very heavy dents in U.S. industrial jobs. From all this results the phenomenon of the dislocated worker, now familiar from newspaper and television accounts: the laid-off steelworker who works at a fast-food restaurant at a fraction of his former pay; the auto worker forced into retirement at fifty whose wife now supports the family (Schwartz and Neilcirk 1983). As a basic trend, the decline in both agricultural and manufacturing jobs is likely to continue.

This trend, by the way, has a significant educational implication: higher and higher minimum credentials are required to enter the work force. Young people need more formal education than ever before to get their first job. The most obvious reason for this is that so many jobs now depend on technical skills like computer programming. But beyond this kind of technical qualification, in almost every job category minimum credentials have been upgraded. Jobs that required no degree at all fifty years ago now call for a high school diploma; other jobs for which a secondary education was once adequate now call for a college degree; and applicants for many professional jobs are expected to have graduate degrees. Since the 1970s, for example, business executive positions have typically required an M.B.A. (Master of Business Administration), a degree extremely rare before World War II.

Of course, just because degrees are required does not mean that workers necessarily *use* their education. Feeling overqualified can easily feed the sense of frustration and alienation that many American workers feel (Carnoy and Levin 1985). Furthermore, the more exacting the job requirements—many minimum wage jobs now call for a high school diploma—the more limited are the job prospects of lower-class youths (Oxford Analytica 1986). The unemployment figures for the

TABLE 15.4 Percentage of the Labor Force in Various Sectors of the U.S. Economy, 1910–1980

Year	Agriculture	Blue Collar Manufacturing	White Collar/ Service Workers
1910	31%	38%	31%
1920	27	40	33
1930	21	40	39
1940	17	40	43
1950	12	41	47
1960	6	41	54
1970	3	37	60
1980	3	30	67
1995*	2	26	71

*Projected.

Source: Data from U.S. Bureau of the Census and U.S. Bureau of Labor Statistics.

underclass, particularly blacks, are already very high. Thus, higher credentials have their own socioeconomic implications. We will look more closely at other aspects of "creeping credentialism" in Chapter 17.

Labor Markets

Basically, labor markets match people and their skills to available jobs. And like jobs, workers have various attributes that make them more or less desirable. Education, manual dexterity, and other abilities are considered legitimate advantages in the labor market, but race, gender, and social-class background, which are not considered legitimate grounds for employment, usually matter as well. Sociologists distinguish two broad labor markets in modern capitalist economies, the primary and the secondary, with most advantaged workers finding employment in the first and most disadvantaged workers in the second (Sabel 1982). The *primary labor market* is that in which workers are employed by stable, successful, usually relatively large firms; these workers have job security, health and retirement benefits, and relatively good incomes. The *secondary labor market* fills in the smaller, less stable niche in the economy, in which demand for products fluctuates. Workers in this market have jobs in fast-food restaurants and small businesses like florists, caterers, and liquor stores, and it is this market that has been creating most new service-sector jobs. Many of the jobs in the secondary labor market are part-time or seasonal. Wages are low and work is unstable, so that workers are likely to be unemployed fairly often—especially during economic recessions—and health care and other benefits are rarely provided. Women, minorities, young people, and the less educated are concentrated in the secondary labor market.

Many secondary-labor-market jobs offer virtually no chance for career advancement, or even stability and the accumulation of seniority—thus we can say there are few real careers in this market, merely job slots. Moreover, these jobs are unlikely to enable workers to acquire a skill that might serve as a springboard to a better job. Workers in this market are apt to remain at or close to a "base" position and wages for as long as they are in the work force. Secondary-labor-market jobs are truly dead-end positions. The "working poor"—people who work full time but fail to earn enough to provide for their basic needs—can usually be found in the secondary labor

market (Levitan and Shapiro 1988). Their ranks have grown by nearly 50% since the 1960s (Simon 1988).

It is interesting to note that in modern Japan, which offers the United States such stiff economic and industrial competition, the segmentation of the labor market into primary and secondary submarkets is very marked, more so than in our own country. In the primary labor market, dominated by the large corporations like Mitsubishi, the stability of the work force is reinforced by "motivating" programs and attitudes (pleasant work spaces, minimal direct supervision, shares in profits, and so on) that foster long-term prospects—and long-term loyalties (Cole 1979). The Japanese corporate model has had a great deal of influence on the structuring of the computer firms in California's famous Silicon Valley where employers provide gymnasiums and elegant lunches in return for employee loyalty (Howard 1985). However, this hands-off management style does not transfer easily out of the high-tech, privileged sector (Piore and Sabel 1985).

What counts as a job skill is defined by the labor market, and the labor market mirrors demand. Jobs are not intrinsically and permanently part of either a primary or secondary labor market. Changes in technology and in the organization of production means that the demand for various skills is always changing, as we've already seen. At any given time, certain skills may be in high demand, as computer programming now is, while other abilities are devalued, as bookkeeping skills have been since the advent of computers.

Professionalization

At the other end of the job spectrum from secondary laborers are the professionals, workers who usually command good salaries and have the prestige and job stability that secondary-labor-market workers lack. This is partly due to the fact that most professionals have educational credentials, licenses, or other forms of certification that limit competition for their jobs. In addition, professions offer considerable autonomy (see also Chapter 19). Professionals such as physicians, lawyers, architects, and so on, tend to be self-employed, with their own offices or partnerships; thus, they are free from supervision by a boss and governed not by hierarchical control but by professional codes of ethics and the desire for a good reputation. However, the proportion of self-employed professionals, including doctors and lawyers, is declining. More and more professionals are

Secondary and primary labor markets. Selling flowers on a street corner in Rome seems romantic, but it is an uncertain and difficult way to make a living. By contrast, workers at a Japanese electric plant enjoy stable jobs, the prospect of advancement, health and retirement benefits, and a strong sense of community. As for romance—or at least its corporate shadow, motivation— they begin their day by lining up and singing a company song. (Above: Catherine Ursillo/Photo Researchers, Inc.; right: © Hiroji Kubota/Magnum.)

working for large, relatively bureaucratic organizations. While relatively privileged compared with most workers, corporate professionals are subjected to some degree of bureaucratic control (Friedson 1985; Powell 1986).

The oldest and most respected professions are, of course, law and medicine. The ministry, in some other countries and historical periods the most elite profession, is less prestigious in the contemporary United States, partly because of the lack of an established church and/or government certification of clergy. (In the United States, anyone can set up shop as a minister.) In recent years, a number of other occupations have sought to organize themselves as professions; some have succeeded fairly well (dentistry, accountancy), and others have done less well (nursing, social work). Because professionals typically enjoy high prestige, pay, and relative autonomy, there is an incentive for more and more groups to try to achieve professional status. Professionalization can also be seen as contributing to the upgrading of minimum schooling credentials throughout our society. Professional organizations and the various licensing and credentialing associations that certify professional standing are likely to continue to expand their role in the regulation of work in the United States (Friedson 1985).

Productivity and Technology

Productivity refers to how much work, time, land, or some other factor of production is required to produce a given output. For example, an acre of land might yield five tons of soybeans or ten tons depending on a farmer's skill, the amount of fertilizer used, the quality of the land, and so on. Similarly, a twenty-acre soybean plot might need the work of several laborers if no farm machinery were available, but only one laborer with a tractor, a harvester, and other machines. In sociology and economics, the main concern is the productivity of labor: how much human work is needed to produce a given amount of goods. Better tools and technology, better work organization (a division of labor, for example), and greater effort are all ways of increasing the productivity of a day's labor.

One of the most important social and economic trends since the Industrial Revolution has been rapid and continuing increases in the productivity of labor. In many ways, this has had beneficial effects for society: it is the basis for the high standard of living we enjoy. But the ways in which productivity has been achieved and maintained have raised some questions. Perhaps the most important is whether the introduction of machinery and the reorganization of the workplace around it—the phenomenon known as **automation**—makes work less satisfying and indeed even less available as machines replace human workers. If so, how can workers be motivated and jobs themselves made more satisfying—and available—without sacrificing today's high productivity levels?

Automation in a Single Industry

We can best see the effects of automation by looking at its impact on a single industry. The textile industry was once dominated by individual craft workers weaving cloth on looms in their homes. In the early nineteenth century, power looms were developed: steam power greatly speeded the workings of the loom, and a single worker's daily output of cloth was multiplied. This technological change brought about a number of social changes as well. The most significant was the movement of work from homes to factories. Power looms were too large and expensive for individual weavers to own and operate, so weaving became an industry, carried on in factories, rather than a craft done at home. Moreover, far fewer weavers were needed to operate the power looms. A single skilled weaver operating a machine might do the work that many weavers had once done. Typically, the weaver would be assisted by unskilled workers—usually children. (One of the scandals of the nineteenth century was the employment of young children in textile mills, often for ten or twelve hours a day for very low wages.) Weavers who had once been independent craftspeople were now factory laborers; their skills at the hand loom were now worth little. Since running a power loom was a simpler skill, new employees could easily be hired and trained to replace malcontents. Thus, as automation in the textile industry increased the productivity of workers, it also qualitatively changed the nature, organizations, and experience of their work—and forced many craftspeople to seek other employment.

A second wave of technological change hit the textile industry shortly after the end of World War II. Synthetic fibers, such as polyester, were produced in highly automated factories; comparatively few workers were needed to prepare these fibers for spinning and weaving. Computers were introduced to monitor and control the process of weaving, further decreasing the need for human workers. What jobs remained were simple and easily learned. When factory owners realized that unskilled foreign workers could fill these jobs as well as Americans (and at a far lower wage), a large part of the textile industry went abroad, mostly to Third World countries (Evans 1981; Rada 1982). In order to compete with foreign suppliers, textile manufacturers still producing in the United States had two choices: to lobby for government protection against imports, which would increase U.S. consumer costs, and/or to automate still further so that they could reduce their own labor requirements, leaving them with fewer jobs to offer Americans. All these trends are actually going on in many industries besides textiles. As the economy becomes more international, and as automation becomes more available and more advanced, job growth in material production has come to a halt. The 1970s and 1980s have seen U.S. jobs in automobiles, shoes, steel, electronics, and other industries decline as companies opened automated plants overseas or cut costs at home.

The Promise and the Cost of Technology

Unquestionably, increases in productivity benefit consumers, allowing them to choose from more products at lower prices. Society benefits, too, from the resultant economic expansion and increased wealth, although, of course, this wealth is not equally distributed: a large part of it goes to capitalist owners and other privileged groups.

But how do we measure what increased productivity means for workers? As we've seen, automation reduces the need for labor, and it can make jobs far less stimulating and satisfying. Traditionally, there have been two schools of sociological thought on this issue. The first, which is allied to a functional view of industrialization, maintains that the better pay of today's workers makes up for their often less attractive jobs. Those who hold this view believe that industrialization serves a need and is technologically determined: it could not have been stopped or slowed in any fundamental way by human choices. Functionalists equate industrialization with progress and maintain that it has paved the way for modern society. Conversely, a second school of thought contends that because industrialization took place under a capitalist system—indeed, because capitalism fueled it—industrialization is necessarily biased against workers and serves the needs of owners. (You'll recognize the power perspective here.)

In this age of increasing automation and computerization, productivity is based not on how hard people

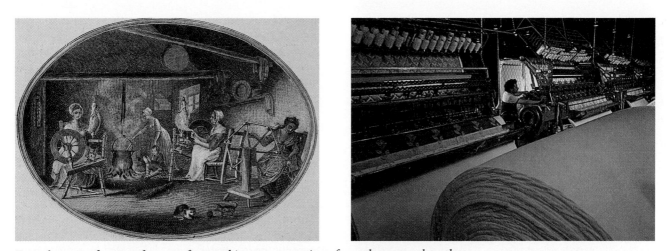

From home to factory, from craftsmanship to automation, from the natural to the synthetic, from a local mill to "made in Hong Kong," from many hands to few to none—the history of the textile industry appears, at least in part, to support the power perspective's contention that industrialization serves the needs of owners at the expense of workers. (Left: The Granger Collection; right: Craig Hammell/The Stock Market.)

work but on the technology they use and the organization or social structure of the workplace. For example, the number of American farmers has declined drastically in the last century while farm productivity has climbed ever upward because of expensive machinery that multiplies efficiency to a remarkable degree. By the same token, in other types of work lack of technological support has meant growth in the number of workers, as for example in the secretarial and clerical fields, at least until recently. Whereas the average factory worker in 1975 had the assistance of more than $50,000 of equipment, the typical office worker had about $2,000 worth. But by 1985 the latter figure had climbed to $5,000 and was increasing rapidly (Forester 1985).

Along with automation and technological advances come shifts in the power structure of the workplace. In large corporations most of the power is held by managers, who seek to maintain this control while at the same time reducing labor costs and increasing productivity and sales. These are the criteria they often use in choosing and implementing technology. Some sociologists believe that in fact it is control—not concern with productivity or profits—that motivates managers to automate the workplace (Noble 1984; Edwards 1979; Braverman 1974). Indeed, most recent sociological research shows that the changes in the nature of work and the workplace that have accompanied increased automation have both reduced workers' required skill levels and autonomy and increased managerial control.

In some cases, technology itself reinforces the dominance of managers. Word processors in offices count typists' keystrokes per minute or hour; computers at phone companies keep track of the amount of time operators spend on calls for assistance. Monitoring of this kind may contribute to higher rates of work-related stress and illness (Howard 1985; Shaiken 1984). This brings us to a long-debated sociological question that has been woven throughout our discussion: Does automation, by reducing worker responsibility and skill levels, reduce the pride and satisfaction workers get from their jobs? The answer, in many cases, is yes. Typesetting provides a good example. Typesetters, when they worked on old-fashioned linotype machines, were responsible for spacing out the letters and words in each line and for hyphenating words accurately between syllables at the end of lines; these workers were proud of their skill and their literacy. Today, most typesetting is done at machinery with simple typewriter keyboards, and only a typist's skill is needed—spacing and dividing of words is automatically done by the machine. In this case, not only has a craft job been "deskilled" or simplified; it has been turned from an occupation of mainly unionized men to one of mainly nonunionized, less skilled women—who of course work for far lower wages.

There are also instances in which a skilled worker initially welcomes the challenge of learning, mastering, and putting to efficient use a new technological tool, such as computerized equipment, only to find himself or herself excluded from official training, from actual programming, and even from control of the on/off switch. The result can be damaged self-esteem and a gnawing sense of dispossession (Howard 1985).

Sociologist David Halle (1984), in a study of New Jersey's highly automated chemical industry, found that the closely supervised, automated work certainly does not make for job satisfaction. One worker told Halle:

> It's hard, brutal work in poor air and bad fumes. There is tremendous heat from the kettles. No brains or talent are required. You blindly follow orders from insecure, unfeeling, insensitive clods. You smash up material with sledgehammers in bad heat like a convict, constantly worried about being caught sneaking a smoke or standing still. It's great to develop muscles and petrify brains. (p. 105)

We should note, however, that some new technologies, such as the computer, have numerous beneficial applications for workers and society: business letters are typed, bookkeeping data are stored, medical tests are performed, industrial machinery is designed, books are printed, scientific experiments are conducted—all with the aid of the computer. Although when they first appeared computers were greeted with a certain amount of "computer phobia" and dread, few people who have grown accustomed to them would gladly go back to the precomputer days (for more on computerization and social change, see Chapter 22). Moreover, computerization and automation in general have not only reduced the drudgery involved in some jobs, they have created new jobs—for computer programmers, systems analysts, repair workers, and so on (Schwartz and Nekirk 1983; Gill 1985). And some sociologists, such as Paul Attewell (1987a,b) have argued that, overall, the trend is for higher skill requirements for the labor force.

Nevertheless, there are those who think it wise to confront the dangers imposed by an apparently benign and national technology. Robert Howard (1985), for example, warns of the vision, advocated by a new breed of corporate managers, of a highly efficient, streamlined, caring, and all-encompassing work environment made possible by technology. Within this vision, the centralized sources of corporate power "disappear behind the opaque impersonality of the machine" (p. 66). Howard is at pains to show that it is not computer technology per se that is dangerous, but the degree of managerial control over workers that it allows at each step of production. Howard notes that, in any case, corporate utopia that meets all social and health needs is not to everyone's taste.

Howard sees the technologically transformed vision of working life as another attempt to cope with the

A future of user-friendliness? Do computers extend or abridge our freedom? Perhaps both. It is difficult to predict whether advantages—the elimination of drudgery, the creation of new jobs, the expansion of skill requirements—will eventually outweigh the dangers—high degrees of managerial control and worker powerlessness, suppression of potential problems, and ultimate subservience to the impersonal machine. (Brownie Harris/The Stock Market.)

problem of work in America. As he writes in *Brave New Workplace:*

The almost desperate search for new paths to economic success—perhaps best symbolized by the recent fascination with "Japanese management"—has made the problem of work less a social issue than a matter of industrial competitiveness and economic survival. And where earlier observers of working life tended to view the corporation as an obstacle to reform, today more and more see it as the primary vehicle for social change.

The allure of the brave new workplace is that it promises a wholesale transformation of working life precisely when we seem to need it the most. . . .

. . . But far from resolving the problems of work, it tends to disguise them, suppress them, and in the process create new problems (as yet unrecognized, let alone understood) even more difficult to address. For this corporate utopia for work denies the essential fact that this new model of the corporation, much like the old, is founded on the systematic denial of influence and control to the large majority of working Americans.

Thus, when technology is linked to the imperatives of corporate control, work often becomes the antithesis to the realm of freedom. (1985, p. 9)

Whether or not the future of the brave new workplace is bankrupt, as Howard claims, sociological questions about work must be asked.

SUMMARY

1. The economy is not a natural phenomenon but a social institution that accomplishes the production and distribution of goods and services. From an action perspective, economic trends arise from individual choices, but from a structural perspective the direction of the economy is influenced by various funds of external forces. Both viewpoints are needed to explain the workings of the market nationally and internationally.

2. Two types of economic arrangements exist today. One of them is capitalism, which rests on privately owned means of production and distribution. Besides private property the other cornerstones of capitalism are the motivation to maximize profits and free competition (access to the market by anyone with the resources to compete). Modern capitalism is also characterized by accumulation of capital (by the reinvestment of profits in business), creation of wealth (by an increase in the supply of goods), and continual expansionism (by its tendency to dominate economic activity in its own setting and to expand into new settings).

3. The other modern economic arrangement is socialism, which rests on public ownership of the means of production and distribution. Public ownership entails centralized planning of all economic activities. But recently many socialist nations, notably the Soviet Union, have experimented with allowing more private economic initiative. Despite this deviation from principles, socialist economies are still largely centrally planned and are committed to broad-based economic equality to eliminate social classes.

4. Capitalism in modern America is dominated by large corporations—legal entities that are owned by stockholders and that have powers and liabilities that are independent from those of its owners and managers. But corporations are both aided and regulated by the government. The U.S. government became more involved in the economy during the Great Depression, in line with the principles of Keynes, who suggested that the government spending programs are needed to control economic swings from unemployment to inflation. The welfare state that resulted has been challenged recently by two alternate theories of government's role—monetarism and supply-side economics.

5. A small number of large corporations control the American economy. Many of those corporations are multinationals, with operations in many different countries and no special interest in any one nation. Multinationals influence both the economic and political life of the countries in which they operate. The stockholders of such large corporations are too diffuse to exert much control over policy, so that decisions affecting both the corporations and the host countries are largely in the hands of corporate managers.

6. Although corporations dominate business in the United States, small businesses also play a role as a significant employer. Small businesses are often owned and operated by recent immigrants. Despite their high rate of failure, small businesses create many more jobs each year than do larger firms.

7. Work is rewarded not only by pay but by the sense of identity it gives to those engaged in it. Today, white-collar workers are more prevalent than blue-collar workers and seem to be more satisfied as well. Both classes of workers are subject to control, or the coordination of their work effort—blue-collar workers by the technical requirements of the production line and white-collar workers by the promise of nonmonetary rewards.

8. Two current work trends in America are the increasing proportion of women in the paid labor force and the decline in farm and factory work and increase in service occupations. Many women (and minorities) work in the secondary labor market, where jobs are part-time or seasonal and offer few career opportunities. The more rewarding and secure primary labor market is reserved for those with academic credentials—requirements that over the years have become inflated. At the high end of this market are the professions such as law and medicine, which offer the best pay, most prestige, and most autonomy.

9. The productivity or output of most workers has been increased by automation—the introduction of machinery and reorganization of the workplace around it. Automation has benefitted consumers by making more products available at lower prices. But it has shrunk the need for workers. Some argue that for remaining workers, it has also decreased job satisfaction by requiring less skill. Others argue that, on the contrary, automation has taken the drudgery out of some work and created new, more interesting jobs. A third view is that automation is not dangerous per se but can pose a threat to worker freedom by allowing managers more control.

GLOSSARY

Automation. The use of machinery to replace human workers and the reorganization of the workplace around it.

Capitalistic market system. An economic system based on private ownership of the means of production and distribution and on free competition among business firms aiming at ever-greater accumulation of capital.

Conglomerate. Giant corporation made up of a cluster of smaller companies.

Corporation. An organization created by law that has an ongoing existence, powers, and liabilities independent from those of its owners and managers.

Economy. The social institution that accomplishes the production and distribution of goods and services within a society.

Inflation. An undue increase of a country's money supply created by government spending.

Interlocking directorship. A network of people who serve on the boards of directors of two or more corporations.

Monetarism. A theory holding that changes in the money supply determine the direction of a nation's economy.

Multinational corporation. A very large and usually diversified corporation that has operations and subsidiaries in many countries.

Productivity. The amount of work, time, and resources required to produce a given output.

State socialist economy. An economic system based on collective ownership of the means of production and the centralization of economic decision making in the hands of the state.

PART FIVE

SOCIAL
INSTITUTIONS

In Chapter 3, a social institution was defined as a set of patterned behaviors and status/role relationships that fulfills basic societal needs by providing essential goods or services. These next four chapters examine (from various theoretical perspectives) key social institutions, how they vary from one culture to another, and how they adapt to changes in our own society.

The family plays a vital role in preparing individuals for successful participation in a social world, but different societies have very different ways of organizing family life. Chapter 16 looks at social interaction in different types of families and explores how changes in our society have given rise to alternatives to the traditional nuclear family.

To the sociologist, education involves much more than the subject matter and skills taught in the classroom. Our society is unique in its emphasis on free universal education, but does our education system really offer equal opportunities to all students? Has busing brought racial equality or integration? What are the effects of tracking students according to tests or teachers' perceptions of their abilities? How much does it matter what college a student attends? Chapter 17 shows education to be shaped by a variety of social forces and to have effects far beyond the classroom and the formal curriculum.

Like family life and education, religion is a subject that involves deeply rooted personal convictions. Sociology provides a context in which to explore the role of religion in society without adherence or offense to a particular set of beliefs. Chapter 18 offers several theoretical perspectives on why religion is such a vital part of virtually all cultures and why people adopt religious beliefs and practices. The text distinguishes between churches, sects, and cults as religious institutions, asks which churches are gaining or losing members today, and looks at the rise of the "electronic church" in our own society.

Most of us think of "health care" and "medical care" as synonymous phrases; our health-care system is one that emphasizes medical intervention and the preeminence of the medical profession. Chapter 19 asks us to look at health care in broader terms: the social factors that influence changing patterns of illness and disease; the sociological dimensions of current health problems such as smoking and AIDS; and the challenges facing a health-care system in which, at present, the quality of care depends on one's ability to pay.

CHAPTER 16
The Family

Allen came home one day and found that his wife had run off with one of his friends. He was left with the house and two children. Allen had known things were shaky in the marriage, but he had not expected this. Suddenly he was left with a number of brewing crises. He had to decide what to tell the children. He had to go to work and arrange for child care. He had to figure out how to do the housework, handle the laundry, and prepare meals. Finally, he had to sort things out for himself. There were many things about his failed marriage he did not understand. Three months later, Allen's wife returned. Her new relationship had fallen apart, and she wanted the children and the house. Allen said no, and they went to court. The judge thought the children were better off staying where they were: Allen won. (Greif 1985, p. 1)

I n 1983, nearly 600,000 fathers as single parents were raising almost a million children under the age of eighteen by themselves (Greif 1985, pp. 4–5). Although the number of mothers who are single parents is still much larger (4.2 million in 1983), the proportion of fathers as single parents is increasing, for several reasons. Sex roles have become less rigid, and career opportunities for women have increased. Many more women are working outside the home. At the same time, men are becoming more involved in the role of father, in both intact and divorced families. Their wives' incomes give married fathers more leisure time to spend with their children. Having reflected on their own childhoods, many men consciously strive to be different from their own fathers, who were preoccupied with work and were distant from their children. Finally, changes in the divorce laws have caused the courts to view men and women as more equal in family responsibilities. Child custody is no longer automatically awarded to the mother.

How do fathers cope as single parents? Do they manage any differently because they are men? Geoffrey Greif's survey of 1,136 single fathers (1985) found that housekeeping was the least of the worries of single fathers. Even if they had rarely shopped for food or for children's clothes, cooked a meal, or done the laundry before their marriages broke up, most single fathers found that once they put their mind to it, housework was manageable.

Caring for small children was also something that the men seemed to master and to enjoy. Most single fathers are pleased about their relationships with their children and happy with their children's progress. The younger their children are, the more competent they feel as fathers—a surprising finding, but perhaps it stems from the fact that small children do not generally question or challenge their fathers' competency in that role.

The most difficult problem for single fathers, Greif found, is in balancing the demands of work and child care. Most single fathers discovered that they had to choose between being successful at work or successful as a parent. They could not play both roles well; one had to suffer. The more children there were to raise, the younger the children, and the younger and less established the father was in his career, the greater were the

453

American society has long regarded child rearing as primarily the mother's realm of expertise. But for fathers who find themselves unexpectedly in the role of single parent, necessity shows the way. Many men adapt quite successfully to the role of primary parent and homemaker, belying gender stereotypes. (Alexander Lowry/ Photo Researchers, Inc.)

the future? As Greif notes, if men were to become more involved fathers, they would not have to defer to their wives in making decisions concerning their children. Having experienced the difficulty of balancing home life and work life, men would become more sensitive to the need for day care, flexible work schedules, and other institutional changes that are considered "women's issues" today. And women would have more options to explore different careers, different relationships with their children, and different relationships with their husband. In short, "there would be more choices for everyone" (1985, p. 165).

In the last decade, the growing numbers of single fathers and single mothers have added to the array of variations in family forms and life styles in America. The goal of this chapter is to examine the role the family plays in society, how different societies organize family life, social interaction within different types of families, and how American families are changing.

problems. Most of the men in the study had to cut back on the time they spent at work; sixty-six changed jobs and forty-three were fired.

For almost all men in the study the realization that they were not earning as much as they had earned before, and that they were not advancing as quickly in their careers as they might have, hurt. When they were married, these men had thought of themselves as workers first and fathers second; now those priorities were reversed. This affected the way they saw themselves as *men*. (Although women face numerous problems when they become single parents, they do not have to cope with this role reversal to the same degree.)

The implications of Greif's study go beyond the observation that fathers make good parents. If men can rear children successfully, then the clichés of separate male and female "realms" may have to be reexamined. The relative ease with which men learn housekeeping and child care suggests that they have always had the capacity to perform these roles, but rarely had the chance. Both men and women have played a part in maintaining traditional gender roles, and both have been wary of losing their realm of exclusive expertise.

The point is that the men in the study changed dramatically because they had to change. If they had not become single fathers, they would most likely never considered reordering their priorities. What potential benefit might this hold for male-female relationships in

THE NATURE OF FAMILY LIFE

What is the family? How do we know who is included in the family and who is not? At first glance these questions seem easy: everybody has an idea of what a family is. Yet when we begin to survey family life across a broad spectrum of the world's cultures, we find many different types of arrangements. In some societies, a man may have several co-wives and many children, all of whom consider themselves members of a single family. In other societies, a couple lives with the wife's relatives; the couple and the children are seen, not as a distinct family, but as part of this larger group. Yet one need not travel to other cultures to find variations in family arrangements. Our own society includes large numbers of single-parent families, unmarried couples living together, married couples with no children, second marriages and stepfamilies, and multigenerational families (not to mention single adults of all ages). To accommodate these variations, the U.S. Census Bureau now defines a **family** as "two or more persons living together and related by blood, marriage, or adoption." But this simple, efficient definition does not do justice to the role families play both in our private lives and in society as a whole.

Why Are Families Essential?

The family in some form is a conspicuous feature of social organization in all societies. Indeed, it is sometimes referred to as the most basic social institution. Why this sense of primacy? The family responds to or relates to some of our most basic needs.

- *The regulation of sexual behavior.* All societies place limits on the sexual behavior of their members and specify who can have sexual relations with whom. For example, every society has an incest taboo that bars sexual relations among certain relatives. Societies differ, however, as to the relatives for whom sexual relations are prohibited. The royal families of ancient Egypt and Hawaii allowed, indeed expected, brothers and sisters to marry (apparently as a means of keeping power and property within the family). By contrast, in traditional Chinese society the incest taboo included all individuals bearing the same clan name, even if they were cousins a thousand times removed.

- *Reproduction.* If a society is to survive from one generation to the next, it must have some arrangement for replacing its members. Since sexual needs can be satisfied without reproduction, societies must motivate people to have children. In traditional Chinese society, ancestor worship provided the incentive: the couple's well-being in the afterlife depended on its having many sons. Sons also provided for the parents in their old age. In the United States, the pressures to become parents are more subtle. Children's achievements have been seen as enhancing their parents' social status, even if the children do not provide their parents with direct financial aid. This is especially true in immigrant communities.

- *Socialization.* Children are society's "raw recruits," as we pointed out in Chapter 5. Their social development depends on acquiring those elements of culture that are necessary for competent participation in social life. Today, as in the past, the family is the primary means of transmitting culture from generation to generation. It serves as the link between the individual and the larger community.

- *Care and protection.* During infancy and early childhood, human beings are unable to fend for themselves. They are totally dependent on others for food, clothing, and shelter. In addition, over the course of their adult lives all individuals experience episodes of illness, disability, and dependency. During these times the family assumes responsibility for care and protection of its members.

- *Social placement.* The social structure of a society is an intricate web of social roles and statuses. Individuals must somehow be placed within these statuses and motivated to play the appropriate roles. Many of our ascribed statuses, including our national, ethnic, racial, religious, class, and community identities, derive from family membership (see Chapter 4). Even in societies such as the United States that stress equality of opportunity and advancement based on merit, the family plays a critical part in facilitating (or limiting) the social mobility of its members (see Chapters 11 and 17).

Perspectives on the Family

Why does the American family have the structure it does? What could explain the fact that throughout most of the modern era, the nuclear family of husband, wife, and children has prevailed, with the man being the primary (in some cases the only) breadwinner? Sociologists have different answers to these questions, depending on whether they emphasize functional integration or power as the answer to the question of what holds society together.

Sociologists who take a functional perspective have argued that this family pattern serves a purpose in industrial societies, where people must often move from one city to another in order to find work (Goode 1963). Given this need for mobility, it is more advantageous for a family to have one primary wage earner who is free to accept employment without having to consider the jobs of other family members. When the husband has the breadwinner role, the wife can devote herself to full-time care of the house and children. This choice is functional not just because it gives the husband job mobility but also because a family that is separated from the emotional support of other kin benefits from having one adult member who serves as the group's emotional "hub." For their part, American children are not usually required to share in many of their mother's homemaking duties. Instead, they are considered "dependents" until they are young adults. This arrangement again makes sense in an industrial society, where people must acquire much formal education in order to become productive workers. Thus, according to a functional perspective, the traditional American family complements both the economic and the educational systems. Because it has evolved to mesh with other parts of society, the American family has the form it does.

But sociologists who take a power perspective see more than this in traditional Western family patterns. They point out that throughout most of modern history, husbands have exercised greater power and authority within the family. Husbands have traditionally had the right to control their wives' property, to make all the major family decisions, and to expect obedience from their wives and children. Viewed from a power perspective, there is nothing particularly functional about these arrangements. Instead, these patterns are a result of the simple fact that men have managed to secure a privileged status in society. Men, because they have amassed an unequal share of social power, have been able to shape family roles to their own advantage (Sprey 1979).

Traditional family roles have been changing in recent decades, with relationships between husbands and wives becoming more egalitarian. From a power perspective, sociologists argue that this trend is in part the result of women entering the labor force in record numbers. Today, 58% percent of married women are engaged in paid employment, and with this greater financial contribution to the family has come a stronger power base. Contemporary wives are in a position to demand equal status with their husbands because they too are wage earners, not just dependents. But sociologists with a functional perspective look upon these changes differently. To them, women's struggle for power is not the only reason why family roles are changing. They contend that the trend toward more egalitarian roles within the family complements the economic trend toward two-career households. The two patterns, in other words, are co-evolving because they "fit" together. Undoubtedly, both the functional and the power perspectives are helpful in explaining changing family roles. The structure of the family reflects both power relations and the tendency for a social institution to mesh with other aspects of society.

Another framework for analyzing family patterns is the second basic sociological question that asks about the relationship between society and individuals. To what extent are family patterns created by individual choices?

To what extent are they the product of external social forces? The action and structure perspectives provide different answers to these important questions.

The rising rate of teenage pregnancy and parenthood is an issue that can be used to illustrate the differences between the action and structural points of view. According to an action perspective, individual choices play a key role when a teenager becomes pregnant. The girl may want to prove her maturity to classmates, to escape from an abusive parent, or to have someone she can love. Whatever the particular reasons, her subjective view of life prompts her to see having a baby as a generally positive event.

A structural perspective would consider an action analysis of this phenomenon to be incomplete. It argues that it is not just individual choices that have given rise to the marked increase in single, teenage mothers. This family pattern is also the result of broader social forces that arise from the social structure. Adolescents who become pregnant and decide to keep their babies are more likely to be poor than middle or upper class, more likely to live in inner cities or rural areas than in suburbs, and more likely to be friendly with other teenage mothers. In short, there is a whole set of social structural factors that shapes the way adolescents look upon pregnancy and parenthood.

Both the action and the structural perspectives offer valuable insights into the reasons behind other family patterns. For example, although people make private choices about when to marry, their choices are influenced by structural forces such as the number of potential partners available in the population. Thus, as recent studies show, women who wish to marry after age forty often have trouble finding marriageable men in their age group because most of the remaining men are either already married or are dating younger women (Gross 1987). Similarly, the decision of how many children to have is partly a personal choice. Yet in making this choice, individuals are influenced by structural trends —such as the steady rise in the age at first marriage. In summary, then, the family can be seen as a social construction shaped by individual action and external forces. A fuller understanding of the family must take into account the variation in the social construction of the family that exists from one society to another. We now highlight some different ways that human beings have for ordering relationships among men, women, and children.

The Wide Variation in Family Form

Like most peoples, we tend to see our own way of organizing social behavior, reproduction, and socialization as the only natural way. It is hard for us to realize (or accept) that other peoples, in other cultures and times, have very different family arrangements. For an example, consider a Nayar girl who lives in Kerala, India (Gòugh 1974). During her adolescence a Nayar girl is encouraged to have several lovers. If she becomes pregnant, one or more of these lovers acknowledges paternity and pays the costs of delivering the baby. Beyond this, however, none of the lovers has any obligations toward the girl or her child. The mother's kin are completely responsible for both care of the child and support of the mother. The Nayar do have a form of marriage, but it is simply a ritual that marks a girl's passage into adulthood; it is not a ceremony that heralds the beginning of a family as we know it. During the ritual marriage, the woman's relatives choose a man to be her husband for three days. Afterward, husband and wife may never see each other again. The mother's brother assumes the male responsibility in rearing her children. The children owe allegiance to the uncle and not to the father. In turn, property and privileged status are transmitted not from father to son but from maternal uncle to nephew. Family life revolves about the brother-sister relationship.

For the Dani of West Irian, Indonesia, the family is not a particularly meaningful unit; in fact, the Dani language lacks a word meaning "family" (Heider 1972). Although the Dani do have a form of marriage (and one man may marry several women), husbands and wives do not necessarily live in the same compounds. For those of us reared in Western cultures, the most striking feature of Dani life is the seeming indifference to sex. Men and women generally sleep in separate quarters. The Dani also observe long periods of ritual sexual abstinence, particularly after the birth of a child. Husbands and wives may abstain from sexual relations for four to five years after a baby is born, and the Dani do not define this abstinence as creating a special hardship (Heider 1972).

The collective communities in Israel, called **kibbutzim,** provide yet another example of a family life style that is different from ours. On many of these collective farms, the activities we associate with family life are performed by the community as a whole. Cooking, laundry, and recreation are all communally

The standard American nuclear family would seem utterly strange to this Dani woman, who lives separately from her husband and whose son will probably move away when he is about ten to live with distant relatives. In fact, there is no word for family *in the Dani language. (Malcolm S. Kirk/Peter Arnold.)*

organized. Men are not responsible for the economic support of their wives; both men and women work for the community and are supported by it. Women are not exclusively responsible for the care of their children; child care is the community's responsibility (Tàlmon-Garber 1962). A biological mother nurses her child during the first eight months of life, but after this time children are cared for by communal nurses in separate children's houses. Since the children's houses are organized into homogeneous age groups, each child grows up with the same group of peers. This group plays an enormously important role in the child's life.

Family form also varies over time. In seventeenth-century England, the ideal working-class family consisted of a dozen or more members (Laslett 1974). A baker's household might have included the baker and his wife, four journeymen (paid employees), two apprentices, two maidservants, and the baker's three or four children. The distinction between work and family life as we know it did not exist in such households; apprentices and servants were considered part of the family, and the baker's children were expected to earn their keep. With the possible exception of the journeymen, all of these individuals worked, ate, and slept under the same roof. Thus we see that the term *family* applies to very different modes of domestic life.

Patterns of Family Organization

Our descriptions of Nayar, Dani, and Israeli kibbutzim practices testify to the great many ways societies have for ordering relationships among men and women. How are we to make sense of these differences? Sociologists and anthropologists have done so by distinguishing among differing patterns of family organization. Let us consider a number of these.

Family Types

In structuring their relationships, a people can assign priority either to marital ties or to blood ties. When priority is given to marital ties, the arrangement is termed a **nuclear family.** The core family consists of the spouses and their offspring; blood relatives are functionally marginal and peripheral. This arrangement is the preferred form of family life in the United States. Normally, during the course of one's life, a person is a member of two different, overlapping nuclear families. The first consists of oneself and one's father, mother, and siblings—**the family of orientation.** The second consists of oneself and one's spouse and children—the **family of procreation.**

When priority is given to blood ties (those between parents and children or between brothers and sisters), the arrangement is termed an **extended family.** The core family in this large network consists of blood relatives, with spouses being functionally more marginal and peripheral. This arrangement is found among the Nayar,

where the role of spouse is virtually nonexistent and family life revolves about the brother-sister relationship. Extended families have continuity across generations in a way the nuclear family does not. The operation of incest taboos makes the nuclear family discontinuous over time. Sons and daughters must secure mates outside the family of orientation, contributing to a break between this nuclear family and the family of procreation.

The people who "count" as part of the family also vary cross-culturally. In our society, children are considered part of both their mother's and father's kin groups, and they may inherit money from both their maternal and paternal grandparents. In other societies, descent is traced only through the male line. When a couple marries, the wife becomes part of the husband's family and the children are considered members of his kin group. In still other societies, descent is traced through the female line only. At marriage, the husband becomes part of the wife's family and their children are considered part of her kin group.

Conventional wisdom holds that extended families are characteristic of traditional, agricultural societies, and nuclear families are characteristic of modern, industrial societies. In reality, the distinction is not so clear-cut. Tamara K. Hareven (1982) studied the relationship between family and work in an industrial setting—the Amoskeag Manufacturing Company of Manchester, New Hampshire, a large textile factory founded in 1838. She learned that the extended family, rather than being disrupted by the new industrial order, became its linchpin. The family was the primary unit for supplying a workforce for factories, the base for community morality and stability, and the socializer of the young. Nor did migration to a new community necessarily break kinship ties. Rather, the factory system reinforced family ties by permitting grown children to find work in the same community and thus remain near their parents and their adult siblings. Sons and daughters became fathers and mothers and later, when their aging parents needed assistance, they became sons and daughters again, frequently taking on filial responsibilities. During the transitional period prior to marriage, young adults often lived in their parental households and worked in the mill. And after they married, it was not uncommon for young adults to continue to live for a time with their spouses in the family home. Thus life in an industrial community offered many opportunities for family interdependence and for overlap among generations within the family.

Rules of Descent

Through the years a good many Americans have taken an interest in their family genealogies, an interest heightened by the television dramatization of Alex Haley's novel, *Roots*. We reckon descent through both our father's and mother's families, a system termed **bilateral descent**. In George Peter Murdock's (1949) survey of some 250 societies, 30 percent of them followed this procedure. Another 42 percent traced their kin only through their father's lineage—**patrilineal descent**—whereas about 20 percent reckoned descent only through their mother's line—**matrilineal descent**. Very often the inheritance of property follows the rules of descent.

Why are egalitarian patterns of authority becoming more common in modern families? The answer, in part, involves women's growing participation in the workforce. As working women have made gains in educational, financial, and professional status, a greater share in the decision-making power in family life has followed. (Mimi Forsyth/Monkmeyer Press.)

Such rules define the family as a social group rather than as simply a biological unit.

Rules of Residence

In nuclear family arrangements, the husband and wife typically take up residence together. Because they come from different families of orientation, one or the other or both must move at marriage. The most prevalent arrangement is **patrilocal**—the married couple lives with or near the husband's family. In a **matrilocal** arrangement, the husband leaves his family and sets up housekeeping with or near his wife's family. Finally, a couple may establish a new or **neolocal residence**. This arrangement is the preferred pattern in the United States.

Types of Authority

In theory three types of authority patterns are possible within the family: power may be vested in males, **patriarchy**; in females, **matriarchy**; or relatively equally, **egalitarian**. Throughout most of history the prevalent pattern has been the patriarchal arrangement, the system found among the ancient Greeks, Romans, and Hebrews. In no society has matriarchy been the norm, despite legends of Amazon women. The authority of women typically varies from family to family, depending upon the personalities of the spouses and the nature of their relationship. And when children are born out of wedlock, when a couple divorces, or when the husband dies or deserts, women gain an autonomous position by default. Egalitarian patterns are becoming more prevalent in modern societies. In 1962, for instance, 66 percent of American women interviewed by University of Michigan researchers said that the major family decisions should be made by the man of the house, but in 1980 only 28 percent felt that way (Klemesrud 1980).

MARRIAGE

Marriage is a socially recognized union between two or more individuals that typically involves sexual and economic rights and duties. It marks the start of a nuclear family or the expansion and continuation of an extended family. In either case, marriage is backed by strong social sanctions. Although we may feel that we are "free" to make our own decisions about whether and whom to marry, there are, in fact, powerful social forces pushing us into marriage and into selection of an "appropriate" partner (Turner and Helms 1988).

Forms of Marriage

One way societies undertake to regulate marriage is through norms that define the range of potential marriage partners available to an individual. **Endogamy** is a rule that requires a person to marry someone from *within* his or her own group—tribe, nationality, religion, race, community, or other social grouping. **Exogamy** is a rule that requires a person to marry someone from *outside* his or her own group. These regulations frequently operate as a circle within a circle. The rule of exogamy bars marriage within a small inner circle, whereas the rule of endogamy stipulates the limits of the outer social circle that the individual is not to exceed. Among the early Hebrews, for instance, incest taboos operated as exogamous norms curtailing marriage among close relatives whereas endogamous norms forbade marriage with non-Jewish outsiders. Within the United States rules of exogamy have extended incest taboos outward roughly to second cousin relationships, whereas rules of endogamy, until loosened in recent decades, served to forbid interracial and in some cases interethnic and interreligious marriages.

Marriage relationships may be structured in four basic ways: **monogamy,** one husband and one wife; **polygyny,** one husband and two or more wives; **polyandry,** one wife and two or more husbands; and **group marriage,** two or more husbands and two or more wives. Although monogamy is found in all societies, only about 20 percent of the 238 societies in Murdock's (1949) cross-cultural sample were strictly monogamous. In contrast, four-fifths of the societies permitted polygyny. But in most of these societies, few married men actually had more than one wife. Typically only economically advantaged men can afford to support more than one family. Thus in China, India, and the Moslem nations, polygyny was usually limited to the wealthy.

Polyandry is quite rare, being found in less than 1 percent of the societies in Murdock's sample. And where it is found, it typically does not allow women free sexual choice of male partners. The most prevalent form of polyandry is fraternal, or the sharing of a spouse by brothers, the practice among the non-Hindu Todas of southern India. Apparently few disputes or jealousies arose among Todas brothers because they did not view women as sexual property. Since the biological father of a child remained unknown, the Todas socially established paternity by a ceremony in which one of the husbands would present a toy bow and arrow to the mother-to-be. It seems that the polyandrous arrangement evolved among the Todas as an adjustment to poverty. Their subsistence being precarious, a man could have a wife and child only by sharing the burden of their support with other men. Further, polyandry kept the birthrate in check. Since a woman could have only one child a year, it did not matter how many sexual partners she had.

Group marriage also appears relatively rarely and then not as the preferred cultural arrangement. It has been reported among the Kaingang of Brazil, the Dieri of Australia, the Chuckchee of Siberia, and the Marquesan Islanders. On occasion it arises out of some combination of polygyny and polyandry or out of the sharing of sexual privileges among couples.

Choosing a Marriage Partner

Americans as a whole believe that the only legitimate reason for getting married (or, indeed, for ending a marriage) is romantic love. We see marriage as a perfect union and like to believe that each of us will meet the perfect partner, marry, and live happily ever after. Our culture idealizes and exalts romance (Luhmann 1986; De Rougemont 1940). It is the theme of most of our popular songs and the subject of many of our movies and television shows. More than that, entire industries in this country depend on romance and sustain its popular imagery. This emphasis on romantic love and personal choice is not universal, however.

Arranged Marriages

When a man and a woman marry, their union binds together many other people as well. Because so many people are involved in the outcome, certain societies have felt it was too risky to leave such an important

To those of us reared with cultural values of individual rights and free choice, being able to marry whomever we choose is considered part of our birthright. In more traditional societies, marriage is usually seen less as an expression of personal choice than an acknowledgement of ties to a larger social group. (Left: David Burnett/ Contact Press Images; right: Ethan Hoffman/Archive Pictures.)

decision to the discretion of the young. In some societies and religious groups (for example, the Jewish Hasidic sect), families may arrange marriages for their offspring, often without consulting the young people themselves. The couple may not meet until their wedding day. In other societies, strict rules govern who an individual may and may not marry, thereby narrowing the pool of eligible partners down to a chosen few. In such societies, kin groups usually exercise "veto" power over the young person's choice of mates.

Although systems of arranged marriages seem unromantic and constraining to those of us raised with values of individualism and free choice, it is possible to understand why such systems develop and flourish. Think of societies in which newlyweds move into the husband's family's household. In such cases, the family has an important stake in the type of woman the son brings home. Will she share the family's ideas about what is good and worthwhile? Will she readily adjust to the family's codes of behavior? Will she pull her weight in the household? If a new wife is to live in her husband's household forever, it is reasonable for the members of that household to have some say about the new addition. Moreover, in societies where the newlyweds live with either the bride's or the groom's family, it makes sense to avoid matches based entirely on romantic love. In such situations an intense emotional attachment could have a

disruptive effect. For instance, if the husband were strongly devoted to his wife, he might ally with her against other household members, thereby imperiling customary family relationships and practices. For these reasons, therefore, people in traditional societies will try to control the additions to the family by arranging marriages for the young.

Subsurface Controls

Although marriages in our own society are seldom formally arranged, they are not the acts of spontaneous love we often think they are. Parents and the rest of society shape children's marriage aspirations from a very early age. This shaping process is often very subtle, however.

Parental choices of neighborhoods and school districts influence the kinds of peers children will have to choose from for playmates and later for dates (Gallup Youth Survey 1985). Such intangibles of family life as the development of a sense of "we" and "they"—of "our kind" and "their kind"—influence young people's ideas concerning whom they will consider attractive. A family's choice of recreational activities and vacation spots and style of celebrating holidays and special occasions will also influence the kinds of potential mates that young people from that family will meet or eventually seek on their own.

These kinds of subsurface controls direct a young person's love interests toward an appropriate pool of eligible mates. And, in fact, the effectiveness of these subtle influences shows up in the marriage statistics. Although religious intermarriage in the United States appears to be increasing, marriages between people of different races and nationalities are relatively rare, particularly among those who belong to the higher strata of the society (Udry 1974). Only when young people have learned what sorts of people their families consider eligible are they encouraged to let the impulses and emotions of romantic love take over.

Romantic Love: Pros and Cons

Sociologically, there are understandable reasons why romantic love has become the accepted basis for marriage in our society (just as there are good reasons why systems of arranged marriages may prevail in more traditional societies). When a man and a woman in the United States marry and set up a new household (as more than 2 million American couples did in 1988), they are relatively independent (at least geographically) of other kin. As a result, they are free to love each other without creating tensions, jealousies, and competition among other household members. Also, since the married couple will depend on each other for a wide range of emotional and physical support, they will be better able to meet each other's needs if they are guided by love rather than by strictly defined rights and obligations. Romantic love also helps weaken the strong emotional ties that bind young people to their own families and enables them to move more comfortably into their own independent world.

But as the basis of marriage, romance has its limitations. In some ways romance is completely antithetical to the daily demands of married life. Romance thrives on mystery, distance, and uncertainty, whereas daily married life is anything but mysterious. When romance fades, all too often the marriage fades with it. Thus, by exalting romance, our society may be simultaneously undermining the very relationships it tries to promote: stable, enduring, child-producing marriages. Marriage is a business partnership as much as a romantic fairy tale; it involves compromises, divisions of labor, specialization, financial arrangements, and communica-

tion systems. To bill marriage as a flower-strewn paradise is to risk its eventual abandonment for a more perfect union.

STRUCTURE AND INTERACTION IN THE AMERICAN FAMILY

In studying family interaction, it is important to distinguish between what people deem ideal and what they practice. Simply because most people label a particular social pattern ideal does not mean that they will follow it. Indeed, the society may operate in ways that preclude their conforming to prevailing norms. Thus, even in a society in which individuals prefer the nuclear family arrangements, factors such as high rate of illegitimacy and divorce, widespread poverty and unemployment, or an unbalanced sex ratio may prevent many people from living in a nuclear unit. The contemporary United States provides a good illustration of this situation.

Polls consistently show that Americans consider the nuclear family ideal (Gallup Youth Survey 1985). But a great diversity of family arrangements prevails: many single people living alone, many childless couples, many single-parent families, many families with two breadwinners, and many cohabiting couples. We consider alternative family forms shortly, but first let us look more closely at the traditional nuclear unit.

Characteristics of the Nuclear Family

What is life within a nuclear family? How does it differ from extended family arrangements? Table 16.1 summarizes the major differences between the modern nuclear family and the traditional extended form. We explore two of these: the isolation of the family and the division of labor. It should be remembered, however, that how closely a family conforms to either pattern is influenced by its ethnic group, class, and place of residence and that new social and sexual patterns are evolving in response to divorce, voluntary nonparenthood, and other factors that we consider later in the chapter.

TABLE 16.1 Traditional Versus Modern in Family Form, Function, and Ideology

Traditional	Modern
1. Kinship is the organizing principle of society.	1. Kinship is separate from the socioeconomic and political spheres.
2. The extended family is the basic unit of residence and domestic functions.	2. The nuclear family is the basic unit of residence and domestic functions.
3. Home and work are fused; the household is the center of production.	3. Home and work are separate; the household is the center of consumption.
4. Low geographic and social mobility; children inherit their parents' statuses and roles.	4. High geographic and social mobility; children achieve their own social positions and roles.
5. High fertility rates and high death rates, especially in infancy.	5. Low, controlled fertility rates and low death rates, especially in infancy.
6. Kin obligations have priority over individual achievement.	6. Kin obligations recede in favor of individual achievement.
7. Duty, tradition, and individual submission to authority and the needs of the family are emphasized.	7. Individual rights, equality, self-realization, and pursuit of happiness are emphasized.
8. Children are seen as economic rather than emotional assets, although the subordination and dependency of children on their parents may continue as long as the parent lives.	8. Great concern with child's development, current adjustment, and future potential; upon attaining adulthood, children make a sharp break with parental authority.
9. Blurring of boundaries between home and larger community; high degree of communal sociability.	9. Sharp line between home and outside world; home is seen as private retreat; greater emphasis on family privacy.

Source: Adapted from Arlene Skolnick, 1973, *The Intimate Environment.* (Boston: Little, Brown), Table 1, p. 97.

Isolation of the Family

In the traditional extended family, as we noted earlier in the chapter, married couples from different generations —and their children, and often other relatives as well— typically live and work together in the same household. By contrast, the nuclear family is isolated: Each new couple sets up a household independent of the parents' homes. In the absence of large numbers of kin living under the same roof, husband and wife must depend on each other almost exclusively for a sense of emotional well-being and comfort. In addition, they must be self-supporting, and they must take care of all household chores (including child care) by themselves. Thus, whereas the traditional family is knitted together and bound to the larger society by kinship relations, the nuclear family centers on the mutual dependence of husband and wife. It is relatively free of other social bonds. Because mutual dependence is so critical to keeping the nuclear family intact, society has institutionalized love—once an almost irrelevant feature of marriage—as the social glue to replace the structural supports that fastened the traditional family to its social surroundings. Paradoxically, the prevalence of love as a primary bond correlates with high divorce rates, since it justifies breaking up a marriage when the couple is no longer in love.

The Division of Labor

In the isolated nuclear family the division of labor between husband and wife is such that either one member must remain home during the child-rearing years or the couple must arrange to pay for child care. In an extended family, other adult relatives typically assist in caring for the children or in performing other important domestic functions. Until recently, the American ideal has been for the husband to earn the money and the wife to maintain the home (although we must remember that between this ideal type and the actual reality, there has always been much disparity).

No matter who is the breadwinner and who raises the children, though, the dependency of husband and wife on each other makes the nuclear family extremely fragile. In traditional extended families, for instance, the death or departure of one member was not likely to have a crippling effect on the family. But when an isolated

In a large, extended family, like the Hispanic group shown here, members can help each other and provide the support needed to raise children. The nuclear family, often isolated from relatives, relies on itself to fulfill all the demands of family life. (Top: Craig Aurness/ West Light; bottom: Susan McCartney/Photo Researchers, Inc.)

nuclear family loses one member (through death, separation, or divorce), the disruption can be enormous. And even if there are no such disruptions, the nuclear family is still destined to undergo great change once the children leave home. Children used to remain subordi-

nate to, and dependent on, their parents for as long as their parents lived; today, children are encouraged to strike out on their own as soon as they reach maturity. Later, when the parents grow old and are less capable of attending to their own needs, the ideal of the nuclear family inhibits them from moving in with their grown children. They must either manage on their own or be turned over to institutions specifically designed to care for the aged. Thus, the isolated nuclear family may not perform many of the functions traditionally assumed by the extended family.

Variations in American Family Patterns

An abiding American myth has been that the vast majority of Americans live in intact nuclear families. Generations of children learned to read from textbooks describing a married couple and their children, living with their dog Spot in their own home behind a white picket fence. In these books, families with different structures and life styles simply did not exist. The message transmitted was that there was only one desirable type of family in American society: a competent working father and a devoted housebound mother, both preferably young, native-born, and middle class, and their two or more well-adjusted children. This image became the American ideal, although it does not reflect the American reality (Figure 16.1). In recent years, however, sociologists have increasingly focused on other family types, recognizing that the isolated nuclear model is now literally reduced to a quarter or less of all American families.

Composite Families

One variation in American family structure is the nuclear family embedded in a network of extended kin (Winch and Blumberg 1968). This family form is typical in many ethnic enclaves in cities. It may consist of three generations of the same family occupying separate apartments in one building or separate single-family houses located near one another in a neighborhood. The fact that the separate related parts of this family stay in close, day-to-day contact classifies it as extended rather than nuclear. Traditionally, immigrants to urban areas in the

United States have made use of this type of extended family. Isolated from the national culture, these immigrants relied on their family bonds for support and identity.

Increases in life expectancy make composite families more of a possibility. Many more people live to see their grandchildren become parents today than did people in the past. This is particularly true in the United States, which has a higher proportion of four-generation families than either Denmark or Great Britain (Streib in Quadagno 1980). But this does not necessarily mean that members of three- and four-generation families are living in the same house or even in the same neighborhoods. Increasingly, third-generation immigrants are moving away from extended family arrangements and are forming nuclear families. This shift may reflect the acculturation of later, American-born generations to the privacy and independence of the isolated nuclear model.

Single-Parent Families

Between 1970 and 1986, the number of single-parent families in the United States grew dramatically, from 3.8 million to nearly 9 million, or about 16 percent of all families. If current trends continue, population experts predict that nearly half of all children born in the 1980s will live in a single-parent household for at least a portion of their childhood. About 70 percent of one-parent households originate through divorce, 10 percent from the death of a spouse, and 20 percent through the birth of a child out of wedlock. Over 90 percent of one-parent families are headed by women. Over 55 percent of families headed by single-parent mothers are living below the official federal poverty line (Current Population Reports, March 1986).

Psychologist Eleanor Maccoby (1978) expresses concern that the rise in single-parent families (especially those headed by women) may pose considerable problems for the welfare and socialization of children. A father, she feels, is more effective at commanding obedience than a mother—his presence, at least, can alter the balance. He can take over child care when the mother is unable to cope for any reason, and he is able to provide important emotional support for his wife and family. In addition, fathers play an important financial role in intact nuclear families. Many single mothers receive no financial help from their ex-husbands, or they receive only irregular child support payments (Cherlin et

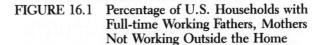

FIGURE 16.1   Percentage of U.S. Households with Full-time Working Fathers, Mothers Not Working Outside the Home

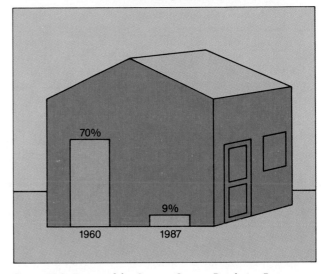

Source: U.S. Bureau of the Census, *Current Population Reports, Population Characteristics,* Series P-20, No. 424, Household and Family, 1987.

al. 1983; Weitzmann 1985). For all these reasons, a single mother may undergo a great deal of stress in trying to cope alone. A single father may also undergo stress, as noted at the start of the chapter. Often the stress comes out in interactions with children. Angry outbursts, lack of affection, poor communication, inconsistent discipline, and irregular meals and bedtimes are indicative of the deterioration of family functioning in the single-parent home. Maccoby (1978, pp. 206–207) concludes that child rearing "is something that many people cannot do adequately as single adults functioning in isolation. Single parents need time off from parenting, they need the company of other adults, they need to have other voices joined with theirs in transmitting values and maturity demands to their children." (See the boxed discussion on Family Structure and Teenage Delinquency.)

Many single parents are also members of minority groups. (Nearly seven out of ten black and Hispanic families are headed by women.) Whatever problems they experience as single parents are compounded by these other social handicaps. Most single parenting in middle-class households is the product of divorce. Research suggests that the difficulties experienced by newly di-

Family Structure and Teenage Delinquency

Sociologists have long known that a high proportion of teenage delinquents come from homes without fathers. This social fact is usually attributed to a combination of factors. Separation and divorce often force a mother and her children into poverty: about half of the poor families in the United States are headed by women. In addition, a high proportion of mother-only households are members of minority groups. The "double whammy" of racial and economic inequality increases the likelihood of teenage delinquency. According to this view, poverty and discrimination are the leading causes of delinquency, and father absence is a minor factor or by-product of these other problems.

A recent study by researchers at the Stanford Center for the Study of Youth Development (Dornbusch et al. 1985) tested this line of reasoning by examining a representative national sample of 7,541 adolescents. Information on each teenager's health history and behavior was obtained from a parent; a separate interview on behavior, attitudes, and beliefs was conducted with the adolescent; and additional data were gathered from school officials and school records. Social class was measured in terms of family income and parental education. Delinquency was measured on a weighted scale in which smoking and disciplinary action at school were assigned 1 point, running away from home and truancy 3 points, and trouble with the law 2 to 4 points (depending on how

many encounters with police the adolescent had had and whether or not he or she had been arrested). A teenager's score could range from 1 to 12 points on this scale.

The Stanford team found that family structure alone accounted for differences in rates of deviance. When they controlled for race and social class, comparing only members of the same groups, the relationship between mother-only households and deviance remained consistent. "With no exceptions, the proportion of deviants among mother-only households is greater than the proportion of deviants among households with two natural parents" (p. 332). The researchers found that the problem was not so much the absence of the adolescent's natural father, but the absence of *another adult*. When a grandparent, another relative, a lover, or a friend lived in the household, rates of adolescent delinquency were lower than in mother-only households (though not as low as in two-parent homes).

Why should this be so? The Stanford team suggests that the structure of the family affects patterns of decision making. Adolescence is a time when young people prepare for the transition out of the home in which they grew up into homes of their own, the transition from dependence to independence. Part of this transition is learning to make decisions for themselves. The Stanford interviews with both parents and adolescents included a set of questions about decisions con-

cerning clothes, money, friends, and curfews. The researchers asked who made such decisions, the parent alone, the youth alone, or the parent and youth together, through discussion and negotiation. Responses were much more likely to fall into the "youth alone" category when the mother headed the household. This suggests that when mothers have no adult support in the home, they are less likely to insist that a teenager follow their orders, less likely to go through the sometimes difficult and time-consuming process of negotiating with an adolescent, and more likely to allow a young person to do as he or she likes. The higher rates of delinquency among teenagers from these families suggest that, on their own, adolescents sometimes make poor decisions.

The researchers conclude "that the raising of adolescents is not a task that can easily be borne by a mother alone" (p. 340). But they add that the presence of another adult, even if that person is not the adolescent's father, adds an important element of control. Nontraditional households can do the job of rearing adolescents almost as well as traditional parents.

Source: Sanford H. Dornbusch, J. Merrill Carlsmith, Steven J. Bushwall, Philip L. Ritter, Herbert Leiderman, Albert H. Hastorf, and Ruth T. Gross (1985). Single parents, extended households, and the control of adolescents. *Child Development, 56,* 326–341.

vorced parents are complicated by the recent disruption of their emotional and social lives (McLanahan 1983).

The long-term impact of single parenthood and socialization of the next generation by one rather than two adults (overwhelmingly the mother) cannot as yet be

assessed but will have to be monitored into the future.

Variation by life cycle and social experience such as divorce is one source of variation for the contemporary American family. Ethnic, racial, and class differences are other important sources of variation.

The Black American Family

The black family in America today is the result of adaptations to unique historical circumstances. The American black family traces its origins back through slavery to West Africa. Historical research suggests that despite active efforts to undermine black family ties under slavery, kin loyalties remained strong. With the ending of slavery, the migration of blacks from plantations to cities after the Civil War, and from the South to the North following World War I, posed new problems of adjustment. Poverty and discrimination made blacks' efforts to establish an urban foothold all the more difficult. Two of the distinctive features of black families —mutual aid among extended kin and dependence on two breadwinners (long before two-breadwinner families became common in the white middle class)—derive from this long period of hardship and adjustment.

Talk of "the" black family obscures the fact that the black subculture (like white society) is stratified, and each class level has its own characteristic family arrangement. Billingsley (1968) suggested that the black community is divided into three classes: a small upper class (10 percent) that stresses family lineage and is politically conservative; a middle class (40 percent) that is concerned with respectability and achievement; and a lower class (50 percent) composed of both stable blue-collar families and poor, multiproblem families.

The typical arrangement in the black middle class is the intact nuclear family. In these families both husband and wife usually are jobholders. The parents place a high value on education and upward mobility, and instill strong success strivings in their children (Willie 1981). In contrast, the bottom rung of the black underclass is characterized by poverty, chronic unemployment and underemployment, marital breakup, and single motherhood. In this segment of the black community extended kin offer material and emotional support to one another. It is also in this group that one finds *matrifocal* (or "mother-focused") households, composed of a mother, her dependent children, one or more of her grown daughters and their children, and perhaps other relatives. The husband-father(s) may be unemployed or absent. The wife-mother serves as the head or center of the family, and the female relatives cooperate in supporting the family and rearing its children. Husbands and boyfriends may contribute to family upkeep, but the women are its mainstay.

Analyses of these arrangements tend to be controversial (Edelman 1987). In the past, some observers saw the absence of intact nuclear families in the black lower class as evidence of family pathology. But this view has been criticized as implying that family pathology was the cause rather than the consequence of poverty. Researchers such as Robert Staples (1978), Herbert Gutman (1977), and others now view matrifocal families as a positive adaptation over time to conditions of chronic poverty. Black men leave their families, not because they do not want to be husbands or fathers, but because the jobs available to them do not pay enough to enable them to act as providers. Rather than face their failure day in and day out, black men move to the outskirts of family life. Nevertheless, by maintaining extensive kin networks, black women hold their families together under harsh circumstances.

This pattern of poverty centered on women and children seems to be continuing in the black underclass today. One signal of this pattern is the rise in teenage motherhood among blacks (Ladner 1986). The fertility rate for sexually active black women between the ages of twenty and twenty-nine years is 1,054 per 1,000, compared to 215 per 1,000 for white women the same age (Tanfer and Horn 1985, p. 17). The rate of motherhood among black teenage women is three times that for white teenagers (Westoff, Calot, and Foster 1983, p. 109). In 1983, 32 percent of sexually active white women between the ages of twenty and twenty-nine became pregnant, compared to 70 percent of comparable black women. Only 14 percent of white women in this age group gave birth out of wedlock, compared to 62 percent of black women. This means that young, unmarried white women who became pregnant often chose to have abortions, whereas black women chose to become mothers. Finally, marriage rates for black women are lower than those for white women: 53 percent of white versus 29 percent of black women in this age group marry within three years of having a child out of wedlock (Tanfer and Horn 1985, p. 17).

By middle-class standards, these statistics may seem to support the claim of an unstable family structure in the black lower class. Seen through the eyes of the black subculture, however, other factors must be taken into account. Greater sexual permissiveness may reflect the absence of a double standard and greater sexual freedom for women, as well as a lower degree of sexual repression. A subcultural pattern of teenage pregnancy takes on a somewhat different character within a tradition of mothers and grandmothers taking in the children of their adolescent daughters. Simply put, unwed black mothers are typically not isolated as parents in the way that unwed white mothers often are; rather, they are members of extended kin networks and matrifocal, multi-generational households.

Many sociologists today hold that the black family should not be seen simply as a departure from white, middle-class family arrangements, but rather as a unique and vital subcultural variation in family form. They point out, however, that economic and educational resources exert a similar impact on white and black families. The more resources a family possesses, the more likely it will exhibit middle-class patterns, including two-parent nuclear families, smaller family size, and sound family planning.

Social Class Differences

Of all the factors that tend to influence the nature of family life, social class is one of the more important. No matter how social class is defined (by income, occupation, or education), it invariably affects the organization of family life. Of course, on the superficial level, this statement is self-evident. A family's resources clearly influence the quality of the food it consumes, the number and kind of leisure activities it enjoys, the amount of space it has to live in, and the schools its

The black American family has a long history of adapting to unique and difficult circumstances. Two of the distinctive features of the black family today—extended kin loyalties and dependence on two breadwinners—reflect this long period of adjustment. (Donna Jernigan/Monkmeyer Press.)

children will attend (see Chapter 11). But beyond these obvious options that money will buy, there are other class differences in family life. We look at differences in demographic factors, early marital stress, and child-rearing practices.

Demographic Factors

Social class influences the number of children born to each family and its members' death rates. Surveys show that families lower in the social hierarchy typically have (and desire) more children than do those higher in the social hierarchy (Gallup 1986). The death rate is substantially higher among lower-class families, which means that people in the lower social strata are likely to die at a younger age than people in higher strata. Of course, the death rate is related to such class variables as health care, nutrition, living conditions, and occupational hazards. In addition, lower-class families are more likely than upper-class ones to be disrupted by illness, desertion, and divorce.

Early Marital Stress

The effects of social class differences on the early years of marital and family life are strikingly portrayed in Lillian Rubin's *Worlds of Pain* (1976). Rubin compared fifty white working-class families with twenty-five white professional middle-class families.

As would be expected, economic problems are an enormous source of stress in working-class families, far more so than in professional middle-class families. Quite young when they marry, the working-class men lack the job experience that allows them to count on a steady income. Typically, they must take low-paying, insecure jobs; layoffs are a common problem. Twenty percent of the working-class families Rubin studied had to rely on welfare at some point in the early years of their marriage. It was a struggle just to pay for food and rent. Speaking of these early years, one working-class wife said:

> I don't know how we survived that period. The first thing that hit us was all those financial problems. *We were dirt poor.* Here I'd gotten married with all those dreams and then I got stuck right away trying to manage on $1.50 an hour—and a lot of days he didn't work very many hours. (Rubin, 1976, p. 71)

The usual pattern was for the wife to become frightened and to get angry at the husband, and for the husband to react defensively: "I couldn't figure out what the hell she wanted from me. I was trying, and I didn't like how things were coming out any better than she did" (p. 77). Rubin points out that men and women in the professional middle class have an economic cushion that allows them to gradually work out the problems of entering adulthood, usually before they get married. Working-class couples, often just teenagers when they marry, find themselves catapulted into adult responsibilities.

One responsibility that working-class couples take on very early is parenthood. In the working-class group Rubin studied, the average time between marriage and the first child was nine months. By contrast, the first child of a professional middle-class couple was born, on the average, three years after marriage. Parenthood posed an enormous economic and emotional burden for working-class parents, who quickly shifted roles "from girl and boy, to wife and husband, to mother and father" (p. 79). The wife gave up her freedom (and her job in most cases), and the husband yielded his place as the center of his wife's affections while simultaneously assuming responsibility for an infant.

Although acknowledging that such adjustment problems are not class-specific, Rubin believes that the pain of the experience is heightened in working-class families. Many working-class men and women had looked upon marriage as a haven from their own deprived childhoods and broken homes. A frustrated construction worker, who had married at eighteen and become a father five months later, told Rubin: "There I was, just a kid myself, and I finally had someone to take care of me. Then suddenly, I had to take care of a kid, and she was too busy with him to take care of me. The whole thing didn't make sense" (p. 84). The economic security enjoyed by professional middle-class couples allows them to keep their wife/husband roles more central, even in the early years of childbearing.

Relationships with in-laws also proved more troublesome for working-class couples. Half of the working-class wives ranked mother-in-law difficulties second only to financial ones. Wives often complained that their husbands paid more attention to their mothers than to them. In contrast, the middle-class families had fewer dealings with their in-laws. Professional middle-class couples generally did not live near their families, and those that did were usually not in daily contact with them. Thus, by minimizing the ties to in-laws, they also minimized the friction. The working-class couples, on the other hand, tended to live near (or even with) their families, and to see them frequently. For instance, grandmothers were very likely to baby-sit for the children while the parents worked. In addition, many of the working-class men still had strong ties to their families because they had moved directly from a dependent role in their parents' homes into marriage. The professional middle-class husbands, in contrast, had made a break with their parents long before marriage, for they had all lived away from home while at college.

Rubin's study does not suggest that the early years of marriage are easy for professional middle-class couples. They too have their share of problems. But most escape the chronic unemployment, marginal incomes, early parenthood, and in-law difficulties that distress many working-class couples. As a result, young professional middle-class couples frequently experience less frustration, conflict, and disillusionment than do their working-class counterparts.

Are Class Differences in Family Life Declining?

Some sixty years ago sociologists Robert and Helen Lynd investigated class differences in Muncie, Indiana. They found marked differences in life style between the working- and business-class families in "Middletown" (their fictitious name for Muncie). The sociologists Theodore Caplow and Bruce Chadwick (1979) decided to explore whether these patterns had changed since 1924, the year of the Lynd investigation. So in 1978 they replicated the Lynds' study in Muncie, and discovered some very interesting trends.

The most striking change was in family work patterns. In 1924 most women in Muncie did not seek work outside the home unless their husbands were unemployed. In fact, many more working-class wives held paid jobs because the rate of unemployment was much higher then for working-class men. By 1978, however, nearly as many business-class wives worked outside the home as did working-class wives. From their responses it seems that women of both classes now tend to seek employment not just because they financially have to, but because they want to.

Caplow and Chadwick also found substantial change in work patterns within the home. Most working-class wives still spent relatively more time on housework than did most business-class wives, but the gap between them had narrowed. Also, paid domestic help is now relatively rare. However, in 1924 roughly 90

Although all couples face an adjustment period during the early years of marriage, working-class families often have economic stresses that professional families do not experience. Adult responsibilities can place overwhelming pressure on young working-class couples, who tend to marry earlier and have children sooner than their professional middle-class counterparts. (Peter Menzel.)

working-class norms of 1924. In still others a new shared norm seemed to be emerging. In short, Caplow and Chadwick found a partial convergence of family life styles among people of different social classes. We should not conclude, however, that all class-related differences will eventually disappear. If nothing else, the income gap between lower- and upper-class families will inevitably ensure that they generally live in different kinds of housing, engage in somewhat different leisure-time activities, and encounter somewhat different kinds of problems related to family life. The Rubin study described earlier shows, for example, that the low income and educational attainment of many working-class newlyweds condemns them to stressful experiences that professional couples usually escape. Caplow and Chadwick's findings do not deny that such differences still exist. But they do suggest that social changes over the last fifty years have significantly reduced the even greater disparities that once existed between working-class and business-class family life styles. Other researchers have found that differences in child-rearing styles are more a function of parental education than of occupational status (Alwin 1984).

percent of business-class families had household help, as compared to 5 percent of the working-class families.

Child-rearing approaches have also tended to converge. In 1924 working-class mothers and fathers spent less time with their children than business-class mothers and fathers did. But in 1978 this difference had disappeared. Differences in educational aspirations for children had also changed dramatically. In 1924 only 31 percent of working-class parents expected their children to complete high school and 23 percent expected them to go on to college (compared with nearly all of business-class parents), while in 1978 a high percentage of both working-class (83 percent) and business-class families (90 percent) expected all their children to receive higher education.

In none of the areas investigated by Caplow and Chadwick did the working- and business-class families grow further apart. In some areas the working class moved toward the business-class norms of 1924, whereas in other areas the business class moved closer to the

Violence in the Family

Although we would like to picture the family as a haven from violent conflict and abuse, this is all too often not the case. The use of physical force is distressingly widespread in American families; in fact, there are few other groups in American society in which violence occurs more frequently (Gelles 1983; Steinmetz and Straus 1974; Lincoln and Straus 1985).

The family is vulnerable to violence for a variety of reasons. For one thing, Americans make a large emotional investment in their family relationships, so the words and actions of family members are seldom viewed dispassionately. As a result, petty family disagreements can easily escalate into conflicts. Add to this the fact that our culture condones violence—in sports and in movies and television programs—physical aggression thus comes to seem less unusual in the family. The isolation of nuclear families also makes violence less visible and less subject to social control. Our strong belief in the sanctity of the family frequently makes police, social workers, and even well-meaning relatives and friends reluctant to intervene lest they be considered to be invading a family's privacy. Finally, and most critically, family violence reflects entrenched cultural attitudes toward those who are its main victims—children, wives, and the elderly.

Child Abuse

Violence in American families takes many forms. One prevalent form that we often overlook is the physical punishment of children. Perhaps 93 percent of all parents spank their children in order to discipline them (Stark and McEvoy 1974). Young children receive the most punishment, but studies reveal that about 50 percent of high-school seniors report experiencing or being threatened with physical punishment. Punishment of children varies from a light tap to a brutal beating, but historically we have granted parents the right to use physical force against their children. A law passed in 1696, for example, called for the death penalty for a child of "sufficient understanding" over the age of sixteen who cursed or struck a parent or who was "stubborn and rebellious" in refusing to obey a parent. From interviews with 2,143 married couples constituting a cross-section of American families, sociologists estimate that parents kick, punch, or bite some 1.7 million children a year, beat 460,000 to 750,000 more, and attack 46,000 with guns or knives (Straus and Gelles 1986; Straus, Gelles, and Steinmetz 1980).

Physical punishment of children that results in injuries requiring medical treatment is now generally considered to be abusive. Most people do not realize, however, that it is the regular use of "ordinary" physical punishment, and the cultural approval it enjoys, that lays the groundwork for child abuse. According to David Gil (1974), "In most incidents of child abuse the caretakers involved are 'normal' individuals exercising their prerogative of disciplining a child whose behavior they find in need of correction." If one adult were to strike another, most people would regard such behavior as abusive.

Most parents use physical punishment in the belief that it will control the aggression in their children and make them obedient. In fact, violence—whether verbal or physical—sets children a poor example. An adult who yells at or slaps a child unwittingly supplies the child with a model for aggression. Studies have found that the frequent use of physical punishment for aggressive acts by a child results in a marked increase in the child's aggression (Walters and Grusec 1977). Perhaps not surprisingly, abusive parents are themselves likely to have been abused when they were children (Gelles 1985; Reed 1975). The pattern of abuse is unwittingly transmitted from parent to child and thus from generation to generation.

How can child abuse be checked? Some sociologists maintain that child abuse can end only when the social conditions that bring it about are alleviated (Gelles 1974, 1985; Gil 1974). In general, researchers find that violence is used as a resource by those who experience stressful situations, such as the loss of a job or divorce or teenage pregnancy, and who feel the need to compensate for their lack of such other resources as money, knowledge, and respect (Wolfe 1985). Moreover, families living in social isolation, without any networks of support, are more at risk for maltreatment of children than are those with extensive social ties (Garbarino and Gilliam 1980). Support groups may therefore offer some remedy. In recent years, Parents Anonymous groups have been formed across the country so that abusive parents can talk about their problems and give each other support and comfort in a group setting. Yet another sort of approach would be simply to make physical punishment of children illegal, as has recently been done in Sweden. By removing the stamp of approval for physical punishment, the propensity to strike a child might be undermined. In the short term, it is important to identify the individual child abusers and to attempt to give them treatment. All 50 states have enacted compulsory reporting laws for child abuse and neglect; and public and private social services have been enlisted to help treat and prevent child abuse (Straus and Gelles 1986).

Wife Abuse

Force or the threat of force between husband and wife is also common in the American family. The study of 2,143 couples revealed that in any one year 1.8 million wives are beaten two or more times a year (Straus and Gelles 1986). Research suggests that child and wife abuse is more prevalent in, although not confined to, families of low socioeconomic status. In part, the higher prevalence of violence in these households is caused by the more stressful situations and conditions that are present. For instance, unemployment or part-time employment of males increases the incidence of family violence. Child abuse also is more prevalent in single-parent than in two-parent families (Gelles 1983; Straus and Gelles 1986).

A husband may use force on his wife for several reasons (Okun 1986). A primary factor derives from the tradition of male superiority that prescribes the husband "should be in control." If he feels he is losing control, he is more likely to strike out. Some men have felt themselves threatened in recent years by the increasing tendency of women to seek equality with men in matters of employment, mobility, decision making, and sexual relations. The tension underlying a relationship may erupt in violence, especially when a spouse is under the influence of alcohol. Complicating matters, Western culture has traditionally approved the use of violence by an aggrieved husband. For instance, for most of recorded history the man who killed an adulterous wife had the law on his side. Moreover, males are socialized in ways that reward them for acting tough. And male folklore and pornography portray females as enjoying aggressive treatment by males. Finally, men are permitted and encouraged to give physical expression to their hostile feelings, whereas women are culturally expected to suppress their anger or to express it in nonphysical forms (taunts, gestures, and arguments).

Elder Abuse

Who would think that the frail, sweet, grandmotherly figure of our national imagination would be subjected to vicious physical violence—by a member of her own family? But such violence, or elder abuse, as it is called, is on the increase in our society, by family members. Karl Pillemer (1986) compared forty-two physically abused elders to forty-two controls. The aim of the study was to determine what makes some older people likely to be abused. One common hypothesis is that elders who are physically impaired and therefore dependent upon family members for feeding, bathing, and other sorts of care are most at risk. According to this view, the elder's frailty and demands cause stress for the abuser, who responds with violence. Pillemer found this hypothesis false. If anything, the abused elders in the study were in better health and more independent than the controls. The critical difference between the two sets of families was that the *abusers* were dependent on the elders for housing, help with household repairs, financial assist-

ance, and transportation. Violence was a response to the abusers still needing one's aging parent, not to the parent's neediness. Pillemer also found that two-thirds of the abusers were described as having mental or emotional problems or as being alcoholics. Finally, abused elders were more likely than the nonabused controls to describe themselves as socially isolated. Whether this was a cause or a consequence of elder abuse is difficult to say. There was no evidence that the abusers had been victims of family violence themselves (the cycle of violence hypothesis). Nor was there evidence that the households of the abused elders were under chronic economic stress. Taken as a whole, this study suggests that the degree to which elderly Americans are at risk of abuse depends primarily on the characteristics of their "caregivers" and their "caregivers'" levels of self-control and frustration.

Divorce

That American society has been successful in promoting marriage as a way of life is clear from American marriage statistics. Nine out of ten people in America get married at least once—and they do it fairly early in life. The median age for first marriages among women is slightly over twenty-three years, and for men it is between twenty-five and twenty-six years (Current Population Reports, March 1986). But what happens to all of those marriages that start out with so much love and so many high hopes? Unfortunately, it is very difficult to know for certain what *does* happen.

To begin, it is difficult to define satisfactorily what constitutes happy and unhappy marriages. And without such a definition, we cannot expect to determine how many of each kind occur. And even if we rely on information that does seem to be measurable—for instance, the number of marriages that end in divorce—the task remains very complicated.

The Difficulty of Measuring Divorce

Measuring the divorce rate would seem to be an easy job. Just count up the number of divorces granted in any one year and compare that statistic with the number of marriages performed in the same year. For example, in 1987, there were 1.2 million divorces and 2.4 million marriages (National Center for Health Statistics 1988), for a divorce rate of nearly 50 percent.

It seems simple, but the wrong things are being compared and, in fact, we are learning nothing about the *rate* of divorce. A valid divorce rate must compare the number of divorces in one year with the *total number of marriages that exist in that year*. Thus when you compare the more than 50 million marriages existing in 1987, with the 1.2 million divorces in that year, the divorce rate turns out to be only about 2 percent.

Many observers compare current divorce statistics with those of an earlier era (413,000 divorces in 1962, roughly a third of the 1987 total) to show that today marriage is passé and that the institution of the family is decaying. But comparing divorce statistics from two eras is tricky. Say we were to compare the rate of divorce today with that in 1920. One problem would be that divorce rates then were unreliable estimates based on records from less than half the states. Moreover, in 1920 there were more inhibitions about getting a divorce: it was costlier, there were fewer grounds on which to sue, and there was greater social condemnation. Finally, life expectancy was considerably shorter then, which meant that some marriages were dissolved by death before they could be dissolved by divorce. So, for various reasons, many couples who stayed married in 1920 would obtain divorces if they lived today. Hence, divorce rates alone are an inaccurate indicator of the health and happiness of family life (Crosby 1980).

Another problem with a general rate of divorce, like our 2 percent figure, is that it reveals nothing about how many marriages do last and for how long. For instance, 19 percent of couples now marrying will end their marriage before the fifth anniversary, 33 percent before the tenth, 40 percent before the fifteenth, 47 percent before the twenty-fifth, and 50 percent before the fiftieth. As these figures reveal, the risk of divorce declines rapidly after the first decade (Weed 1982).

Explaining Divorce Rates

Over the course of recent decades, divorce rates have been going up (see Figure 16.2). The rate rose fairly steadily throughout the 1960s and 1970s, stabilizing somewhat in the early 1980s. The 1986 and 1987 rates are the lowest since 1975. But even so, should current rates persist, the Census Bureau estimates that six out of ten American women now in their thirties will experi-

FIGURE 16.2   Divorce Rate per 1,000 People in the U.S.

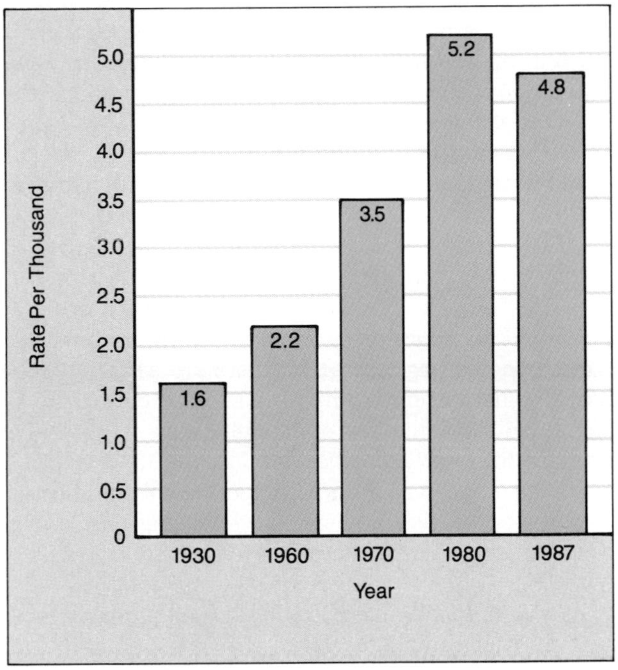

Source: U.S. Department of Commerce, Bureau of the Census.

ence at least one divorce. Social factors have played a major part in this trend, all involving change—in values, in institutions, and in the position of women. The major change in values has involved a shift from a philosophy of self-sacrifice to one that emphasizes individual happiness. The principal reason for getting married today is to satisfy one's personal and psychological needs as these find expression in romantic love. Failure to have these needs met now leads to dissolution of the marriage rather than to an attempt to stay together "for the children's sake." Instead of all divorces being regarded as a sign of personal failure (as in past eras), some divorces today are viewed as "a sign of psychoemotional health, of personal growth, and of the ongoing struggle for personal fulfillment" (Crosby 1980, p. 57). Sociologist Sam Preston (1984) maintains that the rise in divorce reflects increased incentives to divorce and increased willingness "to act on those incentives in a narrowly self-interested way" (p. 445).

Institutions affecting family life have also changed. For instance, most churches now recognize divorce. In addition, the legal apparatus for obtaining divorce has been made less complex; forty-seven states now have some form of no-fault divorce laws, and free legal aid is often available for those unable to afford lawyer fees and court costs (Melville 1983). Finally, the change in the position of women has contributed to increasing divorce rates. Women have become less economically dependent on men, and therefore freer to opt out of marriage.

Who Gets Divorced?

Are some marriages more prone to divorce than others? Certainly, marriages in which there are personal problems, sexual incompatibility, infidelity, excessive drinking, financial difficulties, or difficult in-law relationships are divorce-prone. Less obvious factors also make a marriage prone to divorce. A composite of the findings of sociological studies produces the following profile of a marriage particularly susceptible to divorce:

- The husband and wife live in (and probably grew up in) an urban area.

- They both work, but their incomes are not high.

- They were married early and have not been married long.

- They have a young child.

- The wife has egalitarian attitudes about division of labor in the home and the husband does not.

- Neither husband nor wife has strong religious convictions.

- Both husband and wife are liberal in their attitudes and rather pessimistic about life.

- One or the other has parents who are divorced (Booth and White 1980; Huber and Spitze 1980; Yoder and Nichols 1980).

Of course, none of these factors alone, nor even all of them together, guarantees that a couple will become divorced. But as they accumulate, the statistical likelihood that the marriage will eventually be dissolved increases.

The Personal Costs of Divorce

It is easier to get divorced today than in times past, but it is no less painful. Studies have shown that both men and women suffer significant stress at two key points: before the decision to divorce and at the time of the final separation (Chiriboga and Cutler 1977; Jacobs 1982). Poor health, difficulty in sleeping and working, loneliness, depression, anxiety, lowered self-esteem, and impaired memory are all associated with the divorce process. In their study of 252 men and women currently undergoing a divorce, David A. Chiriboga and Loraine Cutler (1977, p. 104) found that "the whole process of separation is highly traumatic, generally more so than is the stress associated with the marriage from which respondents were seeking to escape." They found that men were more vulnerable to stress than women. At the same time, close to 50 percent of both men and women reported that they felt some relief as a result of having initiated the divorce process.

In financial terms, however, women pay a higher cost for divorce than men do. Indeed, separation and divorce are major factors in the feminization of poverty (see Chapter 12). The impoverishment of divorced women and their children is one of the unintended consequences of a major reform in the divorce laws, which began in California in 1970. Under the old laws, the sole grounds for divorce were charges of misconduct (adultery) or cruelty. As a result, couples seeking divorce were forced to engage in bitter (sometimes exaggerated or even false) accusations, even in situations in which both parties wanted the divorce. The new, no-fault divorce laws eliminated these adversarial procedures, substituting "irreconcilable differences" and "irremedial breakdown" of the marriage as grounds for divorce. Neither party was deemed guilty, and neither party was to be punished.

The new laws made the divorce proceedings themselves more honest and humane, but inadvertently created economic hardship for the woman and the children in her custody. Under no-fault divorce, the couple's household assets are divided equally, but women are awarded child custody in 90 percent of divorce cases. This means that the woman's half of the family's assets must cover both her own and her children's expenses. Furthermore, the average woman earns only about two-thirds of what men earn. As a result, women usually experience a dramatic decrease in standard of living after a divorce; many fall below the poverty line.

The changes in the divorce laws that have helped to create economic hardship for women have had quite the opposite effect for men. According to a major sociological study (Weitzmann 1985), one year after the divorce, the ex-husband's standard of living improved by 42 percent, whereas that of the ex-wife dropped by 73 percent. The new laws require men to pay less in child support and alimony than in the past. This reduction in divorced men's financial obligations, together with higher incomes and other forms of financial security (pensions, insurance policies, health plans), leaves divorced men with more spendable income. Thus the equality promised by the new divorce laws has proved to be illusory because it did not take into account the differences between men's and women's basic economic opportunities and their different financial responsibilities for their children.

Whatever the pain that divorce inflicts, it does not seem to sour people on the institution of marriage. A fourth of the people who get divorced are remarried within the year, and 75 percent remarry within nine years of divorce. About five of every six divorced men and three of every four divorced women marry again. One reason that men are more likely to remarry than women is that men typically marry younger women. When we consider that by age twenty-seven women begin outnumbering men, we can see how middle-aged and older men have a larger pool of potential partners from which to choose than do women (Glick 1984). In sum, although marriage may be difficult to sustain, it is certainly not going out of style.

The Effects of Divorce on Children

The children of a couple planning to divorce share in the pain, especially immediately following the separation. In their study of family breakup, Judith S. Wallerstein and Joan B. Kelly (1980) found that parents rarely prepare their children for the coming crisis, nor do they provide their children with the necessary assurances that they will be cared for. Preoccupied by their personal problems, the parents are often insensitive to their children's anger, fear, feelings of responsibility, or perplexity. When divorce necessitates that the mother go to work,

the child may be placed in unfamiliar child-care arrangements, and both mother and father become substantially less available. In one study of 131 children of divorcing parents, from nursery school age to adolescence, almost all clung to the hope that their parents would somehow be miraculously reconciled (Wallerstein and Kelly 1980). Even five years after their parents' separation, over a third of these children remained intensely unhappy with their new family lives. Many of these children were moderately to severely depressed and lonely, and a substantial number of them were angry much of the time.

At times children, particularly sons, pose management problems for single-parent mothers. Sons can become abusive, demanding, and unaffectionate, and their mothers may respond with depression, low self-esteem, and a badgering type of parenting (Francke, 1983; Hetherington, Cox, and Cox 1977).

But investigation into the effects of divorce on children has also uncovered some more positive facts. First, the passage of time seems to help. Within three years following a divorce, the adjustment of most children, particularly those of well-off parents, improves markedly (Elias 1987). Second, when *both* parents are consistently supportive, understanding, and affectionate, children of divorce adjust much more readily (Clingempeel and Reppucci 1987). One recent researcher has suggested that the adjustment may be easier if the child remains with the parent of the same sex (Peterson and Zill 1986). Moreover, if the custodial parent is relatively secure financially and is making a healthy psychological transition to his or her new social status, the adjustment of the children is usually even better (Lamb 1977a). An important aspect of adjustment seems to be if the child is able to return to a consistent and secure family routine (Peterson and Zill 1986).

All of these findings challenge the popular assumption that divorce is unalterably bad for children. A hostile and conflict-ridden family atmosphere can potentially be just as or more damaging to a child than divorce (Kurdek and Siesky 1980; Zill 1984). On the other hand, it would be wrong to assume that divorce is necessarily good for the children if it is good for the adults involved. Children of divorce can continue to suffer psychological and financial hardships even when their parents are happy (Preston 1984). In short, the effects of divorce on children are very complex and a matter of continuing controversy.

THE CHANGING AMERICAN FAMILY

People today are living longer. They are also marrying later and divorcing more. They are engaging less in casual sex, in part a response to the health risks from acquired immune deficiency syndrome (AIDS) and genital herpes. Couples are deciding to have fewer children than their parents did, and women continue to enter the workforce in record numbers. These changes in mortality, marriage, sexuality, fertility, and employment patterns are having a profound effect on family life. We examine two major areas of change—the increasing diversity in family structure and the changing roles of husband and wife.

Alternative Life Styles and Family Structures

One of the most striking aspects of American life over the past two decades has been the expansion in the available life styles. As individuals move from youth through old age, they often experience a greater range of household arrangements than did earlier generations of Americans. Even so, public opinion polls show that marriage is by far the preferred life style. Only 5 percent favor remaining single and another 3 percent prefer living with someone but not marrying. We now examine some of these alternative arrangements.

Singlehood

In recent times the idea that one must be married in order to be happy has been seriously questioned (Cargan and Melko 1982). However, not too long ago, Americans attached a stigma to the term *spinster*. For instance, a 1957 survey found that 80 percent of Americans believed that a woman must be "sick," "neurotic," or "immoral" to remain unmarried. But by 1978 this proportion had dropped to 25 percent (Yankelovich 1981). Paralleling these changes in attitudes, singlehood among men and women under the age of thirty-five has risen sharply, outpacing the growth of most other household arrangements. The population of single adults in the United States now numbers about 20.6 million, an astounding 90 percent jump in single-person households over the last fifteen years (U.S. Department of Commerce 1985). Even so, only one out of every five households in the United States consists of one person living entirely alone (many of whom are widowed). More than two-thirds of the single adults live with a friend, relative, or "spouse-equivalent."

The rapid increase in singlehood can be attributed to a number of coinciding social and economic trends: the postponement of marriage, the rise in the divorce rate (about a fourth of the adults living alone are separated or divorced), career breakthroughs for women, the easing of salary and credit discrimination against women, and the growing independence of young people from their parents.

Whereas many men and women have simply decided to put off getting married, the recent trends signal that a growing number will remain single throughout their lives. For many people singlehood is a deliberate choice of one life style over another—not necessarily a matter of not having found the right mate. Many people who live alone say that they are wary of marriage and that they value their freedom and independence over whatever advantages married life may have to offer them. In addition, single adults today, especially those in metropolitan areas, can take advantage of a growing singles' subculture. They can live in special apartment complexes, join singles' clubs, go on singles' vacations, take singles' courses, and so on. Single adults have found that as their numbers have risen, so have their status and life style opportunities.

Cohabitation

Although unmarried couples living together still account for only about 6 percent of all cohabiting adults, the practice is on the rise. There were 2.2 million unmarried couple households in 1986—four times the number in 1960 (Current Population Reports, March 1986). In particular, the student movements of the late 1960s and early 1970s brought about a substantial increase in the number of cohabiting college students. It is estimated that during the 1970s about 25 percent of college students lived with a dating partner at some point in their college careers, although the trend may now be reversing on some college campuses. Cohabitating students typically view their relationship as part of the courtship process rather than as a long-term alternative to marriage. Of interest, cohabiting couples are no more likely to get married nor to break up the relationship than are couples who are simply "going together" (Risman et al. 1981). Cohabitation has appealed primarily to young and middle-age adults: Most of the tremendous increase since 1970 has been concentrated among men and women under the age of forty-five (Glick 1984, p. 209).

Changing attitudes toward premarital sexual relations and the increasing availability of easy-to-use, effective, and inexpensive contraception has made cohabitation a more acceptable life style. For instance, the use of birth control is now widely accepted, as is making birth control information available to everyone —including unmarried teenagers. This situation is a far cry from the national attitudes that showed up in a Gallup poll in 1936. In that study, 70 percent of the American people opposed the legalization or distribution of birth control information, even to married people (Wattenberg 1973).

Such enormous changes in attitudes and in sexual behavior make couples feel increasingly free to live with each other before marriage or after a marriage has ended. Adolescents, in particular, are increasingly coming to view marriage "as but one of the relationships in life in which sexual encounter is acceptable. Thus, cohabitation has gained increased acceptance in the views of youth and the urgency for a 'marriage' relationship has lessened" (Walters and Walters 1980, p. 191, Tanfer 1987). The law, too, is beginning to catch up with the unmarried who live together. Live-in companions in some cases now qualify for "palimony."

What types of individuals are likely to adopt the pattern of cohabitation? Using Census Bureau data to compare married couples with unmarried adults living together, Paul C. Glick and Graham P. Spanier (1980) found that young cohabiting couples are likely to be more educated than married couples in general, but cohabiting couples over age thirty-five are more likely to be less educated. Cohabiting couples are also more likely to live in urban areas than in rural areas, and more blacks than whites choose to cohabit. Overall, couples living together are characterized by lower income than married couples. Unemployment is more prevalent among cohabiting men than it is among married men, although it is less prevalent among cohabiting women than it is among married women.

More recent research has questioned whether cohabitors differ from noncohabitors in their feelings of commitment to relationships in general, either marital or nonmarital. Using data from a 1981 survey of Swedish women, a team of sociologists (Bennett, Blanc, and Bloom 1988) looked at the relationship between their premarital cohabitation and subsequent marital stability. They found that the Swedish women who lived with their husbands before marriage were divorced at a significantly higher rate than those who did not cohabit before marriage. They also found higher rates of subsequent marital failure among couples who cohabited before marriage. This bore out their hypothesis that cohabitors as a group feel weaker commitments to the institution of marriage and to relationships in general.

Marriage Without Children

Childless households include those in which a married couple have decided not to have children, those in which the children have grown up and left home, and those headed by a single man or woman with no children present. In 1986, the number of married couple families with no children under 18 present in the home outnumbered those with such children present, 26.3 million versus 24.6 million (Current Population Reports, March 1986).

By 1990 only half of all married couples are expected to have children under age fifteen living at home. When these couples (25 million) are added to the expected number of female- and male-headed households without children living at home (34 million), the total number of households without children (59 million) will constitute about *two-thirds* of the projected number of households in 1990 (Masnick and Bane 1980).

One reason for the increase in childless households is today's longer life span. In 1920 the average American lived fifty-four to fifty-five years. Today, the average man lives about seventy years, and the average woman seventy-eight years. This means that a couple who marries young and stays married can now expect almost fifty years of togetherness, as compared to only about thirty-five years in 1920. Since married life for those who remain married is now longer than ever before, and since children take approximately the same number of years to raise to adulthood, a much smaller proportion of married life now needs to be child-oriented.

The trend toward fewer households with children is accentuated by the fact that over the past twenty-five years women have been gradually marrying later, having children later, and having fewer children. In fact, the proportion of Americans saying that the ideal number of children in a family is two rose from 41 percent in 1972 to 59 percent in 1986, and the proportion of those favoring four or more children declined from 31 percent to 11 percent (Gallup 1986). These are the largest and smallest proportions to express these views since Gallup first started recording the public's preferences in 1936. However, blacks are far more inclined than whites to favor large families, as are older, less educated, and less affluent Americans (Gallup 1986).

While only about 10 percent of women born in 1940 will remain childless, more than 30 percent of those born since 1954 are expected to remain childless. Many factors have contributed to this trend, including the use of effective contraception, the availability of abortion, the two-income household, and changing attitudes toward family life. Women who voluntarily remain childless typically fit the following description: white, living in an urban area, employed, highly educated, not devoutly religious, and separated or divorced. Education has a particularly important role in childbear-

These mothers in their thirties are part of a trend of postponing motherhood in order to pursue educational and career goals. But this greater freedom of choice presents women and their partners with difficult decisions on how and when to fit child rearing into their lives. "Beating the biological clock" involves balancing career objectives against the fact that the longer motherhood is postponed, the less likely it is that a woman will bear children. (Alan Carey/The Image Works.)

ing decisions. Young couples who have a child in their teens or early twenties usually are not able to continue in school. In contrast, women who complete college or graduate school not only postpone childbearing during these years but then further delay it to take a job. The longer parenthood is postponed, the less likely it is that a woman will bear children (Pebley and Bloom 1982).

Those "older" women who do have children may be faced with the demands of dependent children and aging parents when they themselves are middle-aged. This rarely happened in the past. Today, however, a majority of women aged fifty have living mothers, and a substantial minority also have teenage children (Menken 1985, p. 477).

Stepparenthood

In one out of every three marriages one partner has been previously married. Half of those who are remarrying are parents, which creates a stepparent arrangement. If present trends continue, up to 50 percent of all American children will have experienced divorce and remarriage in their families by 1990. Thus the stepfamily is likely to become common.

Most adults approach stepparenthood seeking to create a traditional nuclear family because it is the only model they have. Yet there are very often stepbrothers and stepsisters, stepgrandparents, and in-laws from previous marriages, all of whom present myriad complications. Perhaps not surprisingly, some 44 percent of blended families fail within the first five years (Kargman 1983).

Stepfamilies have special problems (Bohannan and Erickson 1978; Turnbull and Turnbull 1983). Stepparents frequently set unrealistically high expectations for themselves. They often expect to be able to relate to their stepchildren as "real" parents do and to find instantaneous love and acceptance. When their hopes and fantasies go unfulfilled, they feel that there is something wrong with themselves and with the children—contributing to anger, guilt, and low self-esteem. And children who are expected to respond to a stepparent as though the person were the child's natural parent often react with hostility, rebellion, and guilt. And some children worry, "If I love my stepparent, will I betray my real dad (mom)?"

Other problems also abound. Frequently there are financial strains, especially if a man must make child-support payments to another household. Differences in food preferences are common. And discipline typically is a touchy matter for the stepparent. However, family counselors have a number of suggestions that can help families deal with the various stresses. These include moving to a new home, setting and enforcing limits on which both the natural parent and stepparent agree, allowing children an outlet for feelings for the absent natural parent, letting time take its course in forging emotional bonds, and maintaining the primacy of the marital relationship (Turnbull and Turnbull 1983).

The Elderly and the American Family

As we noted earlier, many of the increasing number of childless families in the United States are ones in which the children have grown up and left home. The parents in these households are often nearing retirement age, and many have already retired. In the future the proportion of such older American families is going to increase substantially, as individuals born during the postwar baby boom reach later adulthood. Today, one in nine Americans is sixty-five or older, but between 2010 and 2020 the proportion will be nearly one in six.

What kind of family life can these people expect? Since women will continue to outlive men, at least in the near future, and since women generally select husbands several years their senior, there will be more elderly widows in the year 2000 than there will be elderly widowers. Currently three out of four American men sixty-five or over are married and living with their wives, whereas only one out of three women in this age group is married and living with her husband. It is difficult to say exactly what marriage will be like for these older couples, but some of the current signs are quite positive. Several recent studies suggest that although marital satisfaction often declines after the initial years of marriage, it frequently takes a significant upswing after retirement, when husbands and wives have more time to devote to one another (Rollins and Cannon 1974; Rollins and Feldman 1970). This turnabout may be particularly true for professional or managerial couples, probably because their relatively comfortable incomes allow them to escape the financial insecurity that plagues a large number of working-class retirees. A comfortable income also enables a couple to purchase adequate health care, and good health is strongly associated with marital satisfaction (Beck 1982; Renne 1970).

Grandparenting will also continue to be an important part of the lives of older Americans during the coming decades. The fact that more people are living to become grandparents and that more people including adolescents and adults have living grandparents has generated interest in the phenomenon of grandparenthood. Research shows that grandparents often play an important role in their extended family—as baby-sitters, resources in times of family crisis, caretakers when parents are ill or away, trusted confidants and companions, and suppliers of gifts and financial assistance (Robertson, in Quadagno 1980, p. 291). Because women are traditionally associated with the home and family, and because women live longer, much of this research has focused on grandmothers. One study of 125 grandmothers (Robertson, in Quadagno 1980) found that the majority (80 percent) actively enjoyed their new role in the family. Most women in the study felt that being a grandmother was easier than being a mother; freed from the daily responsibilities of child rearing, they enjoyed their grandchildren more. Indeed, 37 percent said they preferred grandparenting to parenting. A good grandmother was seen as one who loves and enjoys her grandchildren, sets a good example, helps when asked or needed, and does not interfere too much in her grandchildren's lives or parental upbringing. These grandmothers were frequent baby-sitters, and were invited to visit and play with their grandchildren more often than they invited themselves.

In *The New American Grandparent* (1986), the sociologists Andrew Cherlin and Frank Furstenberg suggest that the companionate style of grandparenting—in which the grandparent and grandchild are pals—is increasing. Unlike many parents today, grandparents have ample time to play with their grandchildren, read to them, watch television with them, help them with their homework, and take them to a ball game or Disneyland.

Finally, most older Americans want to maintain relationships with their children and grandchildren while continuing to live as independently as possible.

Changing Roles for Husbands and Wives

With all of these changes in family structure, what has happened to the nuclear family made up of husband, wife, and children? Is it also changing? The answer is a resounding yes.

The Changing Couple

In their study of 300 American couples, Philip Blumstein and Pepper Schwartz (1983) explored constancies and changes in intimate relationships.[1] They found that the roles of husband and wife have undergone substantial revision in recent years (as discussed in Chapter 12). In part, these changes have been prompted by the women's movement, with its stress on equality between the sexes. They have also been prompted by married women entering the labor market in growing numbers. As a result, it is no longer clear how men and women should relate to one another. Later age at first marriage, smaller family size, greater acceptance of cohabitation, more open homosexuality, the increasing numbers of single parents, and the high rates of divorce and remarriage have also affected relationships. No one doubts that contemporary couples are in a state of transition. "But transition to what?" (1983, p. 47).

Contemporary couples have many more choices of life style than were available to couples in the past, but they also have fewer guidelines. As symbolic interactionists point out, the taking on of new roles and the negotiating of new responsibilities is a major task of marriage. In traditional marriages, each partly was automatically assigned certain roles, responsibilities, and privileges. The couple did not have to think about how money would be earned or how the house would be cleaned; a division of labor was taken for granted. Today, as symbolic interactionists remind us, almost every aspect of the couple's relationship—from cooking dinner to initiating sex—is subject to negotiation. Should they live together? Get married? Have children? The answers are no longer automatic. When both spouses are equally involved in earning a living and both derive personal satisfaction from their jobs, work becomes a key domestic issue. What should they do if he is offered a promotion in a city where she cannot find a job in her field? What if she often works evenings and weekends or

---

[1]The study included 120 heterosexual couples, 72 of whom were married and 48 unmarried and living together, 90 lesbian couples, and 90 gay couples.

travels frequently and his job leaves plenty of time for leisure? For many people now in their thirties or forties, the need to make such decisions comes as a surprise. They grew up in a culture that took the rules of marriage as "given"; now, suddenly, in midrelationship (and midlife), they are being forced to make difficult adjustments.

Blumstein and Schwartz suggest that three distinct forms of marriage are evolving, each with its own set of rules and regulations. In traditional marriages, the man works outside the home and exercises unquestioned authority in the home; the wife is a full-time homemaker. For such couples, divorce is unthinkable. The second type, voluntary marriage, lasts only as long as the couple is in love. The couple places a high priority on "happiness" and "compatibility," and realizes that these high expectations make permanence unlikely. Both may draw up a special marriage contract, which is renewable every five years. The third modern variation is trial marriage. Trial marriage is most like traditional marriage, in that the couple looks forward to eventual lifelong commitment. But the couple has not yet made a final decision, and this indecision colors the relationship. Even if the woman intends to become a full-time homemaker, she continues to work during the trial marriage. Such couples generally do not have children (although one or both may have children from a previous marriage).

Someday these different types of marriage may be formalized and accompanied by more "rules" that attempt to provide greater security. At present, however, Blumstein and Schwartz find a good deal of ambivalence in attitudes. The provider role has long been central to men's sense of identity and self-esteem. In addition, although many men want their wives to be financial collaborators, they nonetheless want to remain the key providers. Indeed, the fact that they are no longer automatically seen as heads of their households makes outside achievement all the more important to men. When men were the sole providers, the emphasis was on their occupational opportunities and they expected more homemaking services from their wives. Many men find it difficult to give up these privileges. Increasingly, women as well as men see employment as part of their self-image as well as being essential to the family's financial stability. In exchange for sharing financial responsibilities, women want help with the housekeeping. They also want their needs and desires to be given as much consideration as their husband's.

The question for society, say Blumstein and Schwartz, is how couples can face changing social circumstances and the difficult problems these create, and yet endure and be happy (1983). In the following section we look at some of the problems posed by two-career marriages.

Two-Career Marriages

Marriages in which both husband and wife work have long prevailed among working-class couples, for whom two incomes are often a financial necessity. But the wife's job is usually considered of secondary importance, and she continues to perform most of the household chores. In recent years, however, a new, more egalitarian marital arrangement has been appearing. This is the **two-career marriage**—a marriage in which both partners pursue careers and share family responsibilities. The major difference between dual-career and dual-worker marriages is the wife's level of education, motivation for working, and degree of commitment to her career (Thomas, Albrecht, and White 1984).

In dual-career marriages, both partners must somehow mesh the demands of their jobs with the demands of the family. If they have children, they must arrange for the children to be looked after; they must make sure that necessary domestic tasks get done; and they must also try to set aside time simply to be together. Even with careful coordination, not all problems can be anticipated and avoided. Unlike the 9-to-5 worker, career men and women often have to bring work home, attend unscheduled meetings, or travel (Skinner 1983). The baby-sitter may not show up, and vacation times and work schedules may not coincide. How are these conflicts settled? Most studies (Shenon 1983) show that, as in dual-worker marriages, the wife assumes primary responsibility for housekeeping and child care (see Figure 16.3). In their study of dual-career couples, in which the wife was a professor, lawyer, or physician, Brian F. Pendleton, Margaret M. Poloma, and T. Neal Garland (1980) discovered that the women tend to agree that the mother has primary responsibility for child care, that the burden of household responsibilities rests primarily on the wife, that work is an enjoyable job rather than a lifelong full-time commitment, and that a woman's career history is different from a man's. But most of these women

disagreed with statements that a husband must approve of a wife's employment, that the husband should not be called on to assist in household tasks, and that it was impossible for a married professional woman to combine a full career with family demands.

But household responsibilities and child care are not the only issues for dual-career couples. They must also coordinate their careers and make time for themselves as a couple. One study of thirty-four professional

The changing dynamics of the two-career marriage permit men to play a greater role in aspects of child rearing and family life once assumed to belong exclusively to women. This enhanced sense of partnership often begins with greater participation by fathers in the earliest stages of parenting. (Peter Menzel/Stock, Boston.)

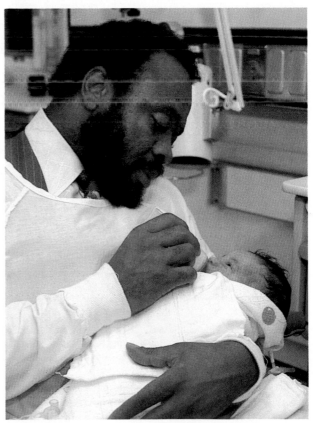

FIGURE 16.3   Time Spent on Housework Among Married Couples

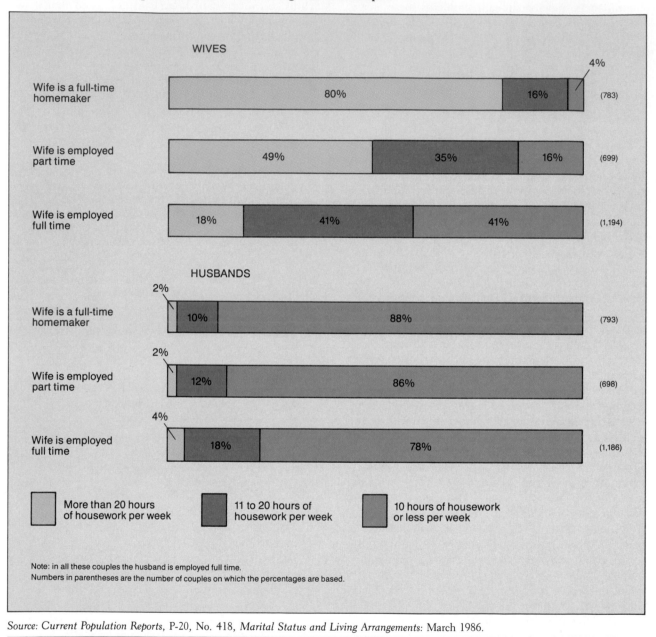

WIVES

Wife is a full-time homemaker — 80% | 16% | 4% (783)

Wife is employed part time — 49% | 35% | 16% (699)

Wife is employed full time — 18% | 41% | 41% (1,194)

HUSBANDS

Wife is a full-time homemaker — 2% | 10% | 88% (793)

Wife is employed part time — 2% | 12% | 86% (698)

Wife is employed full time — 4% | 18% | 78% (1,186)

Legend: More than 20 hours of housework per week | 11 to 20 hours of housework per week | 10 hours of housework or less per week

Note: in all these couples the husband is employed full time.
Numbers in parentheses are the number of couples on which the percentages are based.

Source: Current Population Reports, P-20, No. 418, *Marital Status and Living Arrangements:* March 1986.

couples compared the life styles and patterns of interaction in high-quality and low-quality marriages (Thomas, Albrecht, and White 1984). All of the couples in the study said that two incomes made an important difference in their life styles, and that being able to hire domestic help, go out for dinner, and the like contributed to the quality of their marriages. Conflict over money only arose when the wife earned more than the husband did. In high-quality marriages, the wives had made concessions regarding their careers in order to meet family demands. Most of the women had "broken career lines" because they had taken time off to care for young children. Moreover, most of the women saw their husband's careers as being more important than their own. Problems developed when the husband did not support the wife's career involvement, or when their careers were out of sync. In several low-quality marriages the wife's delayed career was accelerating at the point when her husband was becoming disillusioned and bored with his work—"the Late Bloomer versus Career Burnout Syndrome."

Differences in patterns of interaction also distinguished the high- and low-quality marriages. In low-quality marriages, the husband and wife had different perceptions of the importance of the wife's career and her level of stress. In many of the high-quality marriages, the husband and wife were involved in similar careers (both educators, both researchers, both executives), although not for the same institution or company. Career similarity enhanced understanding. Communication was a problem for all dual-career couples. By the end of the workday, they were "overloaded," too tired to talk. In high-quality marriages the couple made a concerted effort to schedule time alone together. In low-quality marriages the wives were disappointed with the level of "intellectual intimacy." In particular, they felt their husbands showed too little interest in their career-related problems and achievements. Finally, high-quality marriages reported a high degree of "recreational intimacy"; low-quality marriages reported conflict over how to spend precious leisure time. The researchers conclude that most studies of dual-career marriages have put too much emphasis on how couples handle domestic and child-care issues, and too little on career coordination and simply having fun.

Hertz conducted an in-depth study of highly successful two-career couples of the 1980s (1986). These couples were members of a privileged minority whose college diplomas, connections, and income opened many doors to material security and advancement that are not available to most couples. They are able "to have it all" (careers and family) in part because they can afford to hire housekeepers and child caretakers (usually less advantaged female workers). But Hertz sees their success

as a double-edged sword; it enables the couples to hire helpers, but also makes both partners less willing to sacrifice career opportunities to keep the family together. Hertz found that these couples had not set out consciously to create an egalitarian marriage. Rather their career choices and success had caused their attitudes toward family life to change.

Studies of dual-career marriages highlight the uneven nature of change in the family. In their careers, women in these marriages have escaped stereotypes about the female role. Often, their husbands applaud their success. At home, however, both husband and wife still cling to many elements of traditional sex roles (such as the wife's responsibility for housekeeping and the preeminence of the husband's career). For these couples, a truly egalitarian marriage is within sight, but not totally within grasp.

PROSPECTS FOR THE AMERICAN FAMILY

Many innovative family arrangements are attempts to enhance the commitment of marriage while increasing individual freedom and fulfillment. In this way, families are adapting to such broad social trends as delayed marriage, delayed childbearing, greater participation of women in the job market, and a rising rate of divorce. Undoubtedly, the American nuclear family will continue to adapt to such pressures, but how rapid and extensive will these future adaptations be? Opinions are mixed. Some observers feel that the changes in family life in the next two decades will be small compared with those in the last two decades (Glick 1979). Others predict that we shall see more fundamental changes in the American family before the year 2000—further changes in child-rearing practices, in the division of labor between husbands and wives, in methods of coping with two-career households, and in people's general expectations about marriage and family life (Skolnick 1978). Despite these differences, there is agreement that family life is becoming increasingly diverse (Bumpass 1985, pp. 621–622) and in need of normative and institutional supports for social change.

SUMMARY

1. The family is a key element of social organization, charged with regulating sexual behavior, reproduction, socialization, care and protection, and social placement.

2. Sociologists disagree over the question of whether the family patterns in Western societies are functional for society or whether they reflect unequal shares by men and women of social power. They also disagree about whether family patterns are best seen as arising from external structure into which individuals must attempt to fit, or as created by many individual decisions.

3. Patterns of family organization vary between cultures and over time. The two basic family forms are the nuclear family (which emphasizes the marital bond) and the extended family (which stresses blood ties).

4. Views of marriage also vary: Some societies permit marriage to more than one spouse, where others prefer monogamy; some idealize romantic love, where others emphasize extended family obligations.

5. The nuclear family is still the ideal in our society, but the reality of American family life includes many variations. The numbers of single-parent families and families in which both parents work are growing. When people marry, the number of children they have and how they rear their children vary by social class. As a group, black Americans have developed distinctive family patterns.

6. The American family is not conflict-free. When family members do not live up to high ideals, the response is often violence, toward children, spouses, and even aging parents.

7. Divorce is also common. Some marriages are more vulnerable to divorce than others; women may suffer more than men do from a divorce; and children need time to adjust.

8. In recent decades, the American family has changed in a number of ways. Many people are marrying later, having children later, or having fewer children or none at all. These social changes have resulted in diverse household patterns, including single-person households, cohabitation without marriage, childless couples, and stepfamilies.

9. These changes have a direct impact on couples: The rules for marriage and family life are no longer given, but subject to negotiation. In many ways, attitudes and expectations have not kept pace with behavior. Two-career couples are on the cutting edge of these changes.

GLOSSARY

Bilateral descent. The reckoning of descent through both the father's and mother's families.

Egalitarian authority. A pattern in which power within the family is vested equally in males and females.

Endogamy. A rule that requires a person to marry someone from within his or her own group—tribe, nationality, religion, race, community, or other social grouping.

Exogamy. A rule that requires a person to marry someone from outside his or her own group.

Extended family. A household consisting of married couples from different generations, their children, and other relatives; the core family consists of blood relatives, with spouses being functionally marginal and peripheral.

Family. A group of people who are united by ties of marriage, ancestry, or adoption, having the responsibility for rearing children.

Family of orientation. A nuclear family consisting of oneself and one's father, mother, and siblings.

Family of procreation. A nuclear family consisting of oneself and one's spouse and children.

Group marriage. Marriage consisting of two or more husbands and two or more wives.

Kibbutzim. Collective settlements in Israel in which individuals work for, and children are raised by, community nurses and teachers.

Marriage. A socially recognized union between two or more individuals that typically involves sexual and economic rights and duties.

Matriarchy. A pattern in which power within the family is invested in females.

Matrilineal descent. The reckoning of descent through the mother's family only.

Matrilocal residence. An arrangement in which the married couple, upon marriage, sets up housekeeping with or near the wife's family.

Monogamy. Legally prescribed arrangement of one husband and one wife.

Neolocal residence. An arrangement in which the married couple, upon marriage, sets up a new residence.

Nuclear family. A household consisting of husband, wife, and children; blood relatives are functionally marginal and peripheral.

Patriarchy. A pattern in which power within the family is vested in males.

Patrilineal descent. The reckoning of descent through the father's family only.

Patrilocal residence. An arrangement in which the married couple, upon marriage, sets up housekeeping with or near the husband's family.

Polyandry. Marriage consisting of one wife and two or more husbands.

Polygyny. Marriage consisting of one husband and two or more wives.

Two-career marriage. A marriage in which both partners pursue careers outside the home.

CHAPTER 17
Education

I n traditional societies, children learn from their parents and friends, and from religious specialists rather than through formal instruction. Children follow their parents into occupations and other social roles. The girls follow the older women into the roles of farmer or forager, cook, wife, and caretaker of children. The boys follow the men into the roles of husband and fisherman, herder, or hunter. Children learn by watching their elders—skinning a seal, carving a bowl, cooking a stew—and then try out their own skills. Spoken stories and myths are the other major source of knowledge about the culture.

In complex societies, education is carried out largely in formal and specialized institutions, namely schools. *Formal* is perhaps the key term here. Elementary schools, high schools, and colleges are formal organizations that carry out important socialization functions. Socialization, as we know, is the broad, overall process by which individuals acquire those modes of thinking, feeling, and acting that are necessary to participate effectively in society. **Education** is the specific, structured form of socialization in which a culture's knowledge, skills, and values are formally transmitted from one generation to another. Education is not limited to schooling. Schools are simply the major means by which modern education is provided. In other words, just as education is a specialized form of socialization, so schooling is a more specialized form of education. It trains young people for work, introduces them to shared traditions, and prepares them for participation (and often

leadership) in public life. Education is a very conscious, deliberate act: both teacher and student are aware that learning is *expected* to occur.

AMERICAN EDUCATION: GOALS, VALUES, AND DILEMMAS

No modern nation's people believe so deeply in education and schools as those in the United States. By the middle of the 1800s, the United States had pioneered a system of free public schools. Children were expected to attend school not only so that they might advance economically but also so that they might understand the principles of democracy and participate in government affairs. Today education is considered to be so important that all children in the United States are required by law to attend school. Americans still feel that education opens opportunities and allows all individuals to advance in society according to their abilities.

The strong American commitment to the ideal of free and universal public education has had mixed results. Serious problems abound in our schools, and the public perception of these problems has grown more acute in recent years. One problem has been to provide students with basic verbal and arithmetic skills. Schools in the United States turn out too many students who

Education is structured socialization. In traditional societies, children learn through imitation and practice under the supervision of a parent, a religious leader, or the master of a special skill. In our complex society, education is formalized and takes place largely in schools. (Michael Melford/Wheeler Pictures.)

cannot read, write, or calculate well enough to balance a checkbook or follow a road map. Several major studies have produced a disturbing picture: millions of Americans who cannot use written information to function in society or to achieve their personal goals. According to a study supported by the federal government, "Literacy: Profiles of America's Young Adults," as many as one young adult in three may be barely literate (Fiske 1986a).

American education thus can be seen in two ways. On the one hand, ninety-five out of 100 adults can read at a fourth-grade level—the level that educators consider basic literacy. In this respect, the United States is one of the most literate nations on earth. On the other hand, twenty out of those 100 Americans cannot perform at more than an eighth-grade level (Fiske 1986a), and their ability to think abstractly or to solve problems is poor. People who read at that level cannot, for instance, understand what the label on a can of drain cleaner says to do if a child swallows the poison. The 25 million Americans who read at a fourth-grade level cannot make sense of road signs or menus in fast-food restaurants (King and Weaver 1986). In addition, blacks and Hispanics generally score lower in literacy than whites.

What is wrong with the American modern schools and education systems? Why are so many Americans socialized so inadequately? In our modern, fast-moving society, is there too much to teach and learn, and no clear method of organizing that knowledge? Or is that too simple a diagnosis? It does seem paradoxical that our "advanced" society cannot accomplish what traditional societies have managed to achieve. One observer put it this way:

> Given that for approximately 5 million years human societies have managed to rear their young so that almost every one in the society has been able to master the knowledge and skills necessary for survival, why does this not happen in modern societies in schools? . . . Why is it that when we know that the cognitive operations necessary to learn to speak a language are mastered by almost every child by age 5, many of those same children seem unable to learn to read in school, even though the cognitive complexity of learning to read, at least at the early stages, is so much less than that required to learn to speak? (F. Erickson 1977, p. 527)

This paradox points to another question: Are we expecting too much of our schools? Do we, for example, expect our schools to solve major social problems that may actually be beyond their scope? Do we assume that our schools will somehow make democracy—equality, opportunity for all—come true? Perhaps schools are not really equipped for such complex or such sweeping socialization tasks.

We must also ask what values the modern educational system actually functions on and fosters, overall and day to day. We must look at the original goals of schools, both in general and in our country specifically, for Americans have had a very significant role in the history of education. Schools were originally created several thousand years ago to prepare selected individuals to serve as leaders and professionals, although many people were taught by private tutors until the 1800s. However, the system of free public schools that Americans created in the mid-1800s was unprecedented. The system was (and is) supported by taxes and paid for by all citizens, even those who do not have children in the public schools, because education was, and is, believed to improve the lives of everyone throughout the society. In the late 1800s and early 1900s, education by formally certified experts in schools rather than at home came to be required of all American children. (There is a connection here with child labor laws, passed in the early part of this century; as we saw in Chapter 6, mandatory school attendance kept children out of the factories and off the streets.)

What were schools intending to do during this period? First, to teach the "three Rs," basic skills considered necessary for modern democratic life. Schools also trained children from rural backgrounds in the disciplined routines of factory and office work in an increasing industrialized society.

Another major goal, one this country has shared with all other societies undergoing modernization, is the development of a common sense of cohesive nationality. This was particularly important for the United States during the late nineteenth and early twentieth centuries, with its enormous influx of immigrants from all over the world. In school, the children of these immigrants could learn a common fund of knowledge—could learn, in other words, to be American (Violas 1978). It does seem that schools can provide a very important means of knitting people of diverse ethnic background together into a common nation. Our history has proved somewhat successful in this effort. Not least significant is that in school children learn a common language. In China today, for example, attempts are being made to conduct more and more schooling in *putongua* (literally, common people's language), or the language of the whole nation, rather than in the many local dialects.

Generally, the goals of schools are closely tied to a society's economic development, as can be seen from the emphasis on industrialization. The degree of schooling is believed to be an indication of the level of development both in this country and around the world. In the less developed Third World countries, for instance, schooling typically ends with elementary school. This is largely because adolescents form an important pool of labor, particularly in agricultural communities. These young people cannot be spared to go to school; they are needed for work. Also, there are usually not sufficient resources in these countries to support a higher education system.

In the same way, the educational systems of modernized, affluent societies share many underlying goals that are related to economics and age structures. Their general educational methods too are similar and have been described as a kind of military basic training in social terms:

> A modern society is . . . like a modern army, only more so. It provides a very prolonged and fairly thorough training for all its recruits, insisting on certain shared qualifications: literacy, numeracy, basic work habits and social skills. . . . The assumption is that anyone who

has completed the generic training common to the entire population can be re-trained for most other jobs without too much difficulty. (Gellner 1983, p. 28)

Even so, differences in educational values in the various modernized, affluent societies account for some important differences in their educational systems. In the United States, we value providing educational opportunity to all, even at the expense of lowering educational standards. Thus, some 86 percent of Americans finish high school, and about one-third of these graduates enter a four-year college. In Great Britain, by contrast, only about 12 percent of eighteen-year-olds (compared with more than 28 percent in the United States) are eligible to attend a university. British schoolchildren take national examinations that allow only this small group to prepare for a university education. (The same is true in Japan.) British values—sometimes considered "elitist" in comparison with ours—emphasize academic standards above democratic opportunity. British universities generally do have a higher average standard of instruction than ours, but they are available to a smaller segment of the population. When we consider that high school graduates in the United States can also enter two-year colleges and the other forms of adult university education that do not exist in Britain (or elsewhere), the contrast becomes all the more striking.

Thus, when we look at any system of education, including our own, we must analyze the patterns of opportunity and achievement. What are the levels of achievement, and who can reach them? Who among both the educators and the students can—or will—rise to the top, and who can—or will—not? And what do these patterns of achievement reflect about broader social issues such as social class, mobility, ethnic relations, gender roles, and group dynamics?

SOCIAL INTERACTION IN SCHOOL

In his 1970 study of an all-black kindergarten with a black faculty, researcher Ray Rist found that after only eight days of school, the pupils were permanently assigned to three separate worktables based on the teacher's perception of their academic abilities. Table 3, the lowest-ability table, was at the back of the classroom, farthest away from the teacher; Table 2 was in the

As the children progressed through elementary school, the categories and labels stuck. In the first grade, Table 1 students were dubbed the Tigers and were placed in the "high" group; the children from Tables 2 and 3 became Cardinals and Clowns and were given less demanding readers. The IQ scores of the Cardinals and Clowns, however, were not significantly lower than those of the best students, the Tigers. But the Cardinals and Clowns were never really given the chance to catch up.

Judgments about who is bright and who is slow are often made this early in children's school careers and in much the same way as Rist described. Clearly, group assignments and labels based on such judgments and expectations affect children's experience in school: A "slow" group and a "smart" group, whether in terms of whole classes or groupings within classes, have very different classroom experiences. These children are often treated differently by teachers, assigned different tasks, and are expected to move at different paces and to work according to different standards. The group dynamics of a classroom or school, including teacher-student interactions and interactions among student groups—what we might call the sociology of the classroom—are important contributors to patterns of opportunity and achievement in the educational system and, because of the large role that system is expected to play, in our society as a whole.

Expectations Come True: The Self-Fulfilling Prophecy

A traditional though somewhat controversial way to analyze classroom dynamics and their effects is to see them in terms of a phenomenon called the self-fulfilling prophecy. For example, by the time a pupil is categorized as a Clown, as in Rist's study, teachers and other pupils have already formed an idea of how that child will behave in school. Clowns, as the derogatory name suggests, are not expected to do well—and given this expectation, they are quite unlikely to. This is the **self-fulfilling prophecy:** as sociologist Robert K. Merton (1968, p. 447) describes it, an initially *"false* definition of the situation evoking a new behavior which makes the originally false conception true." In other words, an originally incorrect or biased belief is confirmed: treat a student as dumb, and eventually he or she will begin to behave just as you would expect.

Some educational approaches and skills appear to cross all cultural boundaries. However, students in industrialized societies will receive many more years of formal schooling than their peers in traditional cultures. What differences in the rest of society lead to greater emphasis on formal schooling? (Top: Victor Englebert/Photo Researchers, Inc.; bottom: R. Doisneau/Photo Researchers, Inc.)

middle, and Table 1, assigned to the highest-ability pupils, was at the front of the room. Rist discovered that, in fact, the teacher's perceptions of the pupils' abilities were based on socioeconomic criteria: middle-class students were assigned to Table 1, and the less well-off students were assigned to Tables 2 and 3. Not surprisingly, the teacher tended to ignore the students whom she presumed to be slower—and who were at the back of the room. In time, these students disengaged from classroom activities. When "reading readiness" tests were given at the end of the year, the Table 1 children scored highest.

The underlying force behind the self-fulfilling prophecy is labeling (discussed in Chapter 7). When pupils are called Clowns or are recognized by peers as being in "group three" or "the dumb group," they eventually take on this definition as their own and stop trying to do well.

Teachers' attitudes are especially important determinants of pupils' progress. Not only do teachers begin the labeling process by assigning students to different groups in the first few weeks of class; they also act on those initial judgments throughout the school year. Consider the following scene in an elementary school classroom:

> A fourth-grade math teacher writes a half-dozen problems on the board for the class to do. "I think I can pick at least four children who can't do them," she tells the class, and proceeds to call four youngsters to the board to demonstrate, for all to see, how correct the teacher's judgment is. Needless to say, the children fulfill the prophecy. (Silberman 1971, p. 139)

Does the self-fulfilling prophecy really work—do things really happen this way in school? In a famous experiment, Robert Rosenthal and Lenore Jacobson (1968) randomly selected elementary school students and told their teachers that the tests indicated that these students were "bloomers"—children who would spurt ahead academically in the upcoming year. A year later, retesting showed that the IQ scores of these "bloomers" had risen nearly four points higher than the scores of the rest of the student body had. Rosenthal and Jacobson concluded that the teachers' high expectations had affected their interaction with these randomly selected children in a way that helped raise their IQ scores.

Attempts by other experimenters to replicate these findings have had mixed results. One researcher (Brophy 1983) concluded, after reviewing many studies, that only a minority of teachers hold expectations that affect their students' achievements differentially. Most teachers were found to hold *generally accurate* expectations and to be open and flexible about altering their initial expectations. What is more, even when teachers did hold differential expectations, the effects of their expectations on student achievement depended on how each student interpreted and reacted to these expectations. But a number of field studies of actual interaction in classrooms *have* supported Rosenthal and Jacobson's basic premise: Teacher expectations regarding a student's per-

formance can inadvertently be fulfilled, even though there are other influences besides these expectations that temper their effects.

Other field studies (Crano and Mellon 1978; Gouldner 1978; Leacock 1969) have confirmed the strong influence of a child's social class on teacher expectations and have suggested some factors that may contribute to this bias. For example, Eleanor Leacock found that whereas teachers delight in the probing questions and ideas of bright students in middle-class schools, they are annoyed by the same behavior among bright students in lower-class schools. They consider these intelligent but underprivileged students to be smart alecks. But low-income children can also contribute to these sorts of expectations. Often, the values instilled in them by experience and socialization run counter to values honored in school. Boys in particular learn from their homes and neighborhoods to belittle intellectual knowledge and to respect practical skills and "manliness." Their attitudes confirm teachers' stereotypes and set the boys on the road to low achievement.

WHAT SOCIETIES ASK OF SCHOOLS

If we step beyond the classroom, its group dynamics and the expectations and values of teachers, we can focus on the broader expectations our society has for both teachers and students, and the social values that schools attempt to instill as a consequence. In other words, how does the educational system serve societal needs—particularly in the way it groups students, as we have been discussing? How do the different rates and degrees of educational attainment fit in with broad social needs? How do we interpret the way schools socialize students for their particular society?

Since the American Revolution, Americans have believed that public education helps to preserve democracy. Educated citizens, the Founding Fathers believed, would be productive, law-abiding, and slow to embrace monarchs or demagogues. What is more, they felt that education was the key to eliminating poverty and crime —an ideal still widely held today. Are these functions and ideals fulfilled? Are these the actual goals (or the only goals) of education today? As we will see, functional and power theorists have different answers to these questions.

Socialization, Discipline, and the Hidden Curriculum

One clear-cut task of schools is to wean children away from the private world and rules of the family and to socialize them to a public world in which impersonal rules and social status replace personal relations. In school, children learn to accommodate themselves to a hierarchical institution in which power and privileges are distributed impersonally and unequally (Apple 1979; Parsons 1959).

The **hidden curriculum** is the set of unwritten rules of behavior that prepare children for the world outside (Jackson 1968). To advance from grade to grade, to survive academically as well as socially, youngsters must learn to be quiet, to line up, to wait, to act interested even when they are not, to please their teachers without alienating their peers, to come to grips with the inevitability of school—in short, to play the role of student.

Kindergarten is the child's initiation into the student role. In kindergarten activities the children learn to do what the teacher wants, when the teacher wants it done. There is a story time, a nap time, a pickup time—an official routine. Day after day, children are taught behavior and attitudes teachers believe to be essential, and they are drilled in these patterns. As noted earlier, early schooling tends to resemble boot camp: It is "successful" if youngsters learn to follow routines and obey orders without question, even if the orders are trivial.

The teacher is the child's first boss. Learning to accept orders from a boss, to cope with contradictory evaluations, to tolerate frustrations, and to be one among many are the very qualities people need if they are to function effectively on an assembly line or in a large corporation. In effect, the hidden curriculum is designed to mold students into good workers.

Most Americans apparently agree that the hidden curriculum is necessary and desirable. Asked in 1983 by Gallup pollsters what qualities were important in the development of a child, nearly as many adults responded "the ability to get along with others" as "learning to think for oneself." Asked how to improve the overall quality of education, as many people responded "enforce stricter discipline" as "devote more time to teaching basic skills." Indeed, most Americans consider the lack of discipline the biggest problem in our schools (Gallup 1985).

Political and Social Integration

As mentioned at the outset of this chapter, a major function of formal education is to integrate individuals politically and socially into the mainstream culture—to teach students what it means to be American or English or Russian or Chinese. Functional theorists focus on this aspect of socialization, noting that it is both direct (classes in civics, history, and government) and indirect. Classes are conducted and students are evaluated in ways designed to socialize them to their particular culture. In some cultures, the schools teach that the group rather than the individual is central. In these schools, group pressure is mobilized to correct problematical behavior by individuals. For example, in the Soviet Union, students are divided into "links" (groups), and the group may be punished collectively for one individual member's misbehavior (Bronfenbrenner 1970; Daniloff 1983). In contrast, the American school system stresses individuality. Students who are found helping one another solve a math problem during a test are punished for cheating.

Social integration reduces the likelihood that those at the bottom of the social hierarchy will rebel against the system: another function of schooling. This rationale has been offered for public schooling from the revolutionary era to the Great Depression, when school boards were urged to maintain their support for education because it was good insurance against social radicalism. Thus, although public education aims to prepare citizens to participate in a democratic society, it also emphasizes the creation of "good" citizens, that is, citizens who accept the basic rightness of American institutions. Schools try to mold such citizens by emphasizing the merits of the American way of life—our political and economic processes, our form of family life, even our educational system itself.

Historically, Americans have also used the educational system to prescribe values (Tyack and James 1985). For example, in response to the influx of immigrants to this country, the American Legion called for the "Americanization of America" through required courses in civics for students in public schools, and various states required courses in American history, government, citizenship, the Constitution, and patriotism. Some states required that all schools teach in English only. For example, until the late 1960s, Texas law forbade teaching in any language but English. These attitudes—that minority group members must be integrated into the mainstream—persist. In 1986, California passed a law that made English the state's "official language," partly as a reaction to bilingual education programs.

These historical trends, say power theorists, reveal that the social and political integration of students into American society actually means that Americanism is *forced* on students with minority backgrounds. Observations of schools in black and Mexican-American communities and on Native American reservations support this view. For example, approximately one-third of all Native American youngsters attend boarding schools run by the white-dominated Bureau of Indian Affairs. These schools were first instituted in the nineteenth century for the express purpose of separating children from their "savage" parents so that the youngsters might learn to be "Americans." Visits to and from parents are discouraged. The result is that as many as 16,000 Native American children do not go to school at all because their parents refuse to send them away, and every year hundreds more run away from school.

Native Americans are not the only ethnic group whose heritage is ignored or denigrated in schools. Most textbooks still give only brief consideration not just to Native Americans but to Mexican-Americans and black history as well. The assumption in our schools has always been that minorities must be assimilated—for their own good—and that they will not become "Americanized" unless they abandon their different ways. This view defines their cultural ways as inferior and not worth preserving.

But as indicated, other trends are evident. Many schools in the United States have adopted some form of bilingual education. (The 1986 California law on official language was after all part of a backlash against such programs.) Spanish-English is probably the most prevalent combination, because of the numbers of Hispanic immigrants in several parts of the country. But Chinese-English and French (Acadian)-English programs, to name a few, also exist. However, educational researchers have not been able to reach a consensus on how effective bilingual education is in comparison with education conducted primarily in the dominant-culture language.

In the past fifteen to twenty years, largely as a result of the civil rights and women's movements, courses geared to minorities, such as black history, black literature, and women's studies, have been added to school curricula. However, this has happened primarily in higher education, so that the opportunity for all minority students to take advantage of such offerings is necessar-

The "hidden curriculum" is meant to prepare students to take their places in the society at large. As society changes, so do the educational methods. In the past, strict discipline in the classroom readied children for the more rigid structures of the newly industrial society. Recently, the looser structure of some classrooms may reinforce the American ideals of individualism and entrepreneurship in our information age. (Top: Culver Pictures, Inc.; bottom: Nancy J. Pierce/Black Star.)

ily limited. Minority students, who are often from low-income backgrounds and who may be "turned off" by dominant-culture schooling in the elementary and secondary school years, are not as likely as, say, middle-class whites to go on to college.

Navajo students receive instruction in English pronunciation. The heritage of many minority groups has often been ignored or denigrated in favor of dominant white values. Today, there is greater awareness of this "Americanization" tendency. (Tom McHugh/Photo Researchers, Inc.)

Cultural Transmission

Another way to think about social and political integration, as well as the hidden curriculum, is to focus on cultural transmission as a major function of schooling. The transmission of cultural values is an important aspect of socialization. Where Soviet children may see portraits of Lenin or Marx or Gorbachev on their classroom walls, and are taught to think in Marxist-Leninist terms and learn why the Communist system serves them best, American children see portraits of Washington, Jefferson, and Lincoln, pledge allegiance to the flag, sing the "Star-Spangled Banner," learn the virtues of democracy and capitalism, and imbibe the "melting-pot" mentality. Both the American and Soviet school systems, in other words, have their respective ideologies to promote. Despite criticisms that have been leveled in recent years against American schools for ignoring the history and contributions of minorities, and despite minority studies and bilingual education, the American system continues to promote the ideology and value of the dominant culture, at least according to some sociologists, particularly power theorists.

Theorists such as Samuel Bowles and Herbert Gintis (1976) have argued that schools are agencies by which capitalist societies perpetuate in their young people the existing social structures and class relations of the society, based on the society's means of and needs for production. These sociologists have argued that there is a "correspondence principle": the social relations and structures fostered in schools mirror those of the workplace. Thus, the authoritarian structure of the school corresponds to the bureaucratic order of the corporation. The school promotes submissiveness and diligence, characteristics desired by capitalist enterprise. Michael W. Apple (1979, 1982) and other Marxists contend that the cultural dominance of capitalists means that the members of society are saturated with the language, symbols, values, and concepts of a capitalist social order. There is no room in people's consciousness for other language, symbols, values, or concepts. In other words, it looks very much to these theorists as if "Americanism" —here spelled out in the specific terms of dominant culture, "free"-enterprise capitalism—is being forced upon all students, especially minorities.

But from the power perspective, this does not mean that all students are treated equally as they are being "Americanized." The correspondence principle also implies that the schools socialize and reward students from various backgrounds differently, in a way that is consistent with the requirements of their future occupational roles in this culture. Power theorists point out that different schools teach different "status cultures" (a concept of Max Weber's)—that is, they teach the culture that is typical of a certain social status. Thus teachers in middle- and upper-class schools stress proper English, whereas teachers in working-class or slum schools may permit ethnic slang and street grammar in the classroom. Topics brought up for class discussion are also likely to differ, reflecting class differences in leisure-time pursuits, entertainment, and so forth. The result of such differences is that middle-class students will fit more easily into middle- or higher-status positions in society: They will know how to speak and act and will have that important (if intangible) asset, a middle-class "background." Less-advantaged students will often be marked by their speech, manners, and past experiences. They will thus be brought into the "status culture" of the blue-collar worker just as more privileged students will be brought into that of the professional or manager. However, the evidence for this argument is in dispute (Olneck and Bills 1980).

Even if we grant some of the points of the power perspective, it must be noted that cultural transmission does not *only* mean indoctrination. In transmitting cultural values, ways of thinking, and knowledge, schools are also serving another function: they are providing and maintaining a tangible sense of cultural continuity. In other words, schools give us the benefit of sharing in a positive group identity. It is largely for this purpose that schools in the United States teach English and American literature and Western and American history. These disciplines are directly based on another important function of the school: the teaching of basic and complex skills, to which we turn at the end of this section.

Selecting Talent

Another task of educational institutions is to select and screen talent. Ideally, according to functional theory, the school system identifies those students with the particular talents society needs and trains them to fill important leadership positions. But this means that schools must screen out individuals with lesser talents. How does this tally with the American principle that all people are created equal? Schools must give every individual an equal opportunity to display his or her talents; then the right people will be selected for the right jobs, regardless of who they are or where they come from. Providing equal opportunity to each student so

that all able individuals can rise to the top is both a fundamental function and rationale for American public schooling.

Power theorists point out, however, that although during the twentieth century average schooling levels have increased dramatically, the privileged classes have maintained their advantage over the poorer classes in completing more years of school (Mare 1981). There is considerable evidence that equal opportunity is not a reality. As we have seen, low-income students are usually assigned to lower academic groups and/or classes—a placement that is typically permanent. And what is more serious, even those poorer children who later earn high scores on academic aptitude tests are far less likely to go on to college than are more affluent students. Of the brightest 25 percent of the eleventh-grade class, only half of the lowest-income students go to college, whereas almost 90 percent of the more affluent students do. Among the *weakest* students, 26 percent of those from affluent homes go to college, whereas only 6 percent of those from poor homes go (Bowles 1977). Moreover, a relatively high proportion of black and Hispanic youths drop out of school before completing high school (see the box on Dropouts).

Although the rapid growth of community colleges since the 1960s has extended the opportunity to many students who might not otherwise have gone to college, it has also channeled many working-class students into low-status jobs. Students who attend community colleges are more likely than students at four-year colleges to come from families in which parents have only a high school education or less. Many are eager to use the community college as a steppingstone to a four-year institution. But although some make it to senior colleges, community colleges urge many students into vocational programs—a goal that is also supported by business, government, and foundations. Counselors, for example, frequently urge students not to have "unrealistic aspirations," that is, to accept the two-year program as the most they are qualified for. As a result, many students who enter community college with the hope of becoming managers or professionals often end up as technicians or paraprofessionals. In effect, power theorists contend, community colleges are merely the upward extension of the public school tracking system, which acts to keep lower- and working-class students at about the same social level as their parents (Karabel 1977). Marxists argue that these and related patterns show that the purpose of schools in a capitalist society is

The Chronic Problem of High School Dropouts

In a society in which even unskilled jobs require strong educational credentials, the problem of students leaving school before graduation is a serious one—for dropouts themselves, for educators, and for society at large. One estimate is that as many as one in four fifth-graders will never graduate from high school (Mann 1986). The chronic dropout problem endangers a democratic society that relies on an informed citizenry.

Why do students drop out? There is no simple answer to this question. Reasons may include poor teachers and/or a rigid educational bureaucracy, among other possibilities (Mann 1986). But should the dropout rate be considered a problem in itself, or is it really a symptom of other, larger problems?

Who drops out? Why does one student drop out but not another? How does dropping out affect achievement test scores? What happens to dropouts while others their age stay in school? In order to help answer such questions, between 1980 and 1982, the U.S. Department of Education sponsored a longitudinal study of 30,000 American high school students (Ekstrom et al. 1986).

The study showed that dropping out afflicts certain types of students in certain types of schools. For one thing, a student's background is likely to influence the kind of schools and educational processes to which he or she has access. For another thing, particular schools attract students with certain characteristics. A student from a minority or a disadvantaged group is much more likely to drop out than are other students. Although fewer black students of both sexes and fewer white girls are dropping out now than during the last fifteen years, more white

and Hispanic boys are dropping out. Students from single-parent and large families and students from the South and large cities also are more likely than others to drop out. The families of these children are less likely than others to have books or study aids at home or to foster learning. In the end, in other words, it is socially, academically, and economically disadvantaged students who drop out (Ekstrom et al. 1986; Natriello, Pallas, and McDill 1986).

These students usually have suffered years of problems in school. They are likely to go to public school—and dislike it. Often they are late to class or skip it entirely, act up in school, or get suspended—the whole gamut. Not surprisingly, these students generally feel alienated from school and have low self-esteem. In fact, when they are asked why they dropped out, most dropouts say that they left school because they got poor grades and disliked school. Low achievement test scores and no educational plans beyond high school are also typical. Most dropouts have been on vocational or general nonacademic tracks in school; many already have jobs. The more serious problems of adolescence —delinquency, truancy, and pregnancy—also beset this group (Ekstrom et al. 1986).

Sociologists have suggested many specific programs to combat such a complex and stubborn problem. Parents could be taught to show more interest in and to monitor their children's progress in school. Programs to identify potential dropouts at the first signs of discipline problems, poor grades, and poor attendance long before high school have been proposed. So have programs that keep dissatisfied, restless, low-achieving teenagers

in school (Ekstrom et al. 1986).

But reforms have been proposed in the past, and the problem keeps growing—to the level of a national scandal in the eyes of some sociologists. The truth is that no one is quite certain just how many dropouts there really are (school attendance figures are often manipulated to ensure funding, for one thing), nor is anyone certain how effective existing programs are. So schools will first have to develop accurate measurements of how their programs affect "stayers" and dropouts alike (Natriello, Pallas, and McDill 1986). Educator Dale Mann (1986) has argued that to solve the intractable problem of dropouts, society will have to devote more resources than ever before. We may have to think about dropouts, Mann says, as "insoluble problems masquerading as wonderful opportunities."

Dropout Rates for Hispanics, Blacks, and Whites

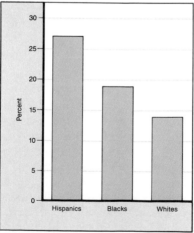

Source: U.S. Census Bureau

not to simply select and train the brightest but to perpetuate class differences and legitimate them with "objective" certificates of educational achievement.

The English sociologist Paul Willis (1977) insists that the effects of the hidden curriculum and similar selection procedures do not just *happen* to students; students' actions are a part of the process. Thus, in school, working-class students are taught a variety of platitudes about how anyone can grow up to be president or prime minister; about how jobs are distributed according to merit, not background; about how those who work hard succeed and those who fail must be lazy. But working-class students realize that the educational establishment represents a middle-class view of the world. Faced with this conflict between the view of the world they are taught and that based on their own experience, working-class students develop a culture of their own. It is, in part, a culture of resistance to and rejection of middle-class views and values. It includes, for example, hostility toward schoolwork and a refusal to accept the school's standards for what constitutes failure and success. In other words, told that they are less valuable to society because they achieve less in school, these working-class students respond by constructing an alternative culture that promotes other values. Thus, they may gain prestige among their peers through being tough, or sexy, or athletic, good drinkers, or quick with a joke. Within their counter-culture they create a more acceptable set of meanings for their own lives. The catch is that by rejecting the values of school, they fail in the eyes of the school, so they cannot gain acceptable educational credentials and therefore end up as members of the same disadvantaged class as their parents. Breaking school rules may make working-class students *feel* more powerful, but the crucial effect is to reinforce their own disadvantaged position.

According to Willis, a structural view can demonstrate that working-class students do less well at school, get lower-status jobs and therefore remain in the working class themselves. What a structural view does not show us is *how* working-class students help to make this happen, how it results from the struggle between them and school authorities, and thereby *"how* and *why* young people take the restricted and often meaningless jobs in ways which seem sensible to them in their familiar world as it is actually lived" (Willis 1977, p. 172). So we need both the action and structure perspectives in order to develop better ideas about how to help working-class children break this vicious cycle.

The Teaching of Skills

We return now to perhaps the most obvious function of schools—to equip individuals with those fundamental social capabilities that are essential for effective participation in modern societies. This task involves teaching basic skills (reading, writing, and arithmetic); developing the ability to think (to apply mental skills to new problems); and providing both general knowledge and specific skills that will be useful in jobs.

Most respondents in a 1985 Gallup poll said that mathematics and English should be required of all high school students. For students who planned to go to college, 91 percent of the respondents would require mathematics, and 88 percent English. In contrast, for students who did not plan to go to college, 85 percent of the respondents would require mathematics, and 81 percent would require English. For students planning on college (but *not* necessarily for others), most respondents would require courses in history and U.S. government, science, and computers. Fewer respondents, but still a majority, would also require business, career education, and foreign language (Gallup 1985).

Although the teaching of basic skills does seem to be the most obvious and necessary function of schools, considerable evidence exists that schools are failing in this all-important role, as we noted at the beginning of the chapter. In 1986, as many as one young adult in three was found to be functionally illiterate; he or she could not read at an eighth-grade level (Fiske 1986a). Functional illiteracy among minority youth is about 40 percent. Few seventeen-year-olds can express their thoughts effectively in writing. Although their spelling and grammar are adequate, they use short, childlike sentences and cannot organize coherent paragraphs (National Commission 1983).

A similar pattern is evident in arithmetic skills. Most young adults can perform basic mathematical operations, but they have trouble using these operations to solve problems. Less than half can figure out the most economical size of a product; only 45 percent can read a federal income tax table; and a mere 1 percent can balance a checkbook (NAEP 1979). Between 1975 and 1980, remedial math courses in public four-year colleges increased by 72 percent and now constitute a fourth of all math courses taught in these institutions (National Commission 1983). Overall, American students seem to have trouble applying the skills and facts that they know to new situations.

Reactions and Reforms

These and other sorts of weaknesses in the schools have angered the public. Through the 1980s, polls have registered frustration with public education; and the need for strong reform has been repeatedly voiced. What have the public and the various commissions appointed to study the situation been saying?

In a 1985 survey, respondents showed concern over (in this order) lack of discipline, drug use, poor curriculum and standards, and the serious difficulty schools face in finding good teachers (Gallup 1985). There is indeed some evidence that many teachers are poorly trained and that schools of education do (and admit they do) admit aspiring teachers who have academic weaknesses (Goodlad 1983; Kerr 1983).

Improving the quality of teachers and teaching has become the central thrust of reform proposals since the public debate over the schools heated up with A *Nation at Risk*, the 1983 report of the National Commission on Excellence in Education. The debate has stayed at the forefront. In 1986 the Carnegie Foundation published a follow-up report called A *Nation Prepared*. This report argued that improving the quality of teachers and thereby increasing American students' intellectual skills was essential in maintaining this country's competitive position in the world.

Recent proposals for improving the quality of teachers include merit pay for teachers and teacher competency testing, which is now required by some states (Johnson 1984; Sedlak 1987). Both reforms are controversial. The unionization of teachers has come up rather consistently; it too has its forceful proponents and opponents. Altering the format of teacher education has also been proposed. The Holmes Group—deans of education and other academic officers from universities across the country—suggested that teachers' undergraduate work should provide a solid liberal arts background and education courses should be restricted to graduate-level training only. Several other task forces and panels have echoed this proposal, to varying degrees (Fiske 1986b). A recently formed National Board for Professional Teaching Standards plans to implement the first nationwide system for certifying teachers (Fiske 1986b).

A factor that may indirectly contribute to lower-quality education is the high rate of violence and crime in the schools. Over 2 million thefts and 200,000 assaults on students and teachers occur in American schools every *month* (National Institute of Education 1978). Some sociologists, however, caution us to look at the picture both more carefully and more broadly. According to Joan McDermott (1983), for example, most crimes in schools are minor assaults and petty thefts. Also, discipline may be too simplistic an answer to change whatever patterns of crime and violence do exist in the schools. McDermott and others have argued that crime and fear of crime in the schools are inseparable from crime and fear of crime outside the schools. High-crime schools tend to be in high-crime neighborhoods. Crime must be eradicated from these neighborhoods if it is to be eradicated in the schools; reform must focus on the larger society. McDermott is basically agreeing with the theorists who claim that schools reflect the structures and values of society. With the public so concerned about discipline, it is possible that once again, teachers and schools are being asked to solve a problem that is too large for them—that of crime, fear, and violence in a complex society.

Education and the Workplace

In summary, we have noted that there are a number of important links and similarities between schools and elements of the larger society, particularly the workplace, which is in one sense or another the end toward which most lives tend. Whether the schools actually prepare us for the work we choose (or find ourselves in) is another recurrent question. Many sociologists, whether functional or power theorists, have considered the school either a preparation for or a reflection of the world of work. An interesting light on the relationship between education and work is shed by a recent study by Martin Carnoy and Henry Levin (1985). They argue that the education-work relation is a great deal more complicated than others have seen it. They point up an important difference between school and the workplace: There is generally greater equality in schools (despite the inequalities that do exist there) than at work. The egalitarian ideals on which our school system was at least partially based have had some actual effects, whether or not schools can or intend to fulfill these ideals completely. In short, "public education both reproduces the unequal hierarchical relations of the nuclear family and capitalist workplace and also presents opportunities for social mobility and the extension of democratic rights" (Carnoy and Levin 1985, p. 76). According to Carnoy and Levin there is an inherent tension between the ideological goals of school and the practical needs of the workplace. On the one hand, there are pressures to make schools serve the democratic purpose of training citizens for political and civic participation. On the other hand, there are pressures to make education serve the needs of capitalist employers and supply a work force according to their requirements. Throughout their history, American schools have responded to both types of pressures, sometimes becoming more oriented toward capitalism and sometimes becoming more democratically oriented. This alternating pattern, say Carnoy and Levin, describes the shifts in American education since revolutionary times. We see elements of this pattern again in the next section, as we consider both the recent broadening of educational opportunity and the discrimination that still remains and contributes to differing levels of attainment within the educational system and in society.

OPPORTUNITIES AND LEVELS OF EDUCATIONAL ATTAINMENT

Since the beginning of this century, the number of people from all socioeconomic levels attending schools has grown dramatically. As Table 17.1 shows, in 1940,

TABLE 17.1   Years of School Completed by Persons Age 25 and Over, by Race: 1940 to 1984

	Year						
	1940	1950	1960	1970	1980	1983	1984
All persons							
Percent not high school graduates							
Total	75.5	65.7	58.9	47.7	33.5	27.9	26.7
With less than 5 years of school	13.7	11.1	8.3	5.5	3.6	3.0	2.8
Percent with 4 years of high school or more							
Total	24.5	34.3	41.1	52.3	66.5	72.1	73.3
College, 4 years or more	4.6	6.2	7.7	10.7	16.2	18.8	19.1
Median school years completed	8.6	9.3	10.6	12.1	12.5	12.6	12.6
Black persons							
Percent not high school graduates							
Total	92.7	87.1	79.9	68.6	48.8	43.2	41.5
With less than 5 years of school	42.0	32.9	23.8	14.6	8.2	7.1	7.0
Percent with 4 years of high school or more							
Total	7.3	12.9	20.1	31.4	51.2	56.8	58.5
College, 4 years or more	1.3	2.1	3.1	4.4	8.4	9.5	10.4
Median school years completed	5.7	6.8	8.0	9.8	12.0	12.2	12.2

Source: U.S. Bureau of the Census, *U.S. Statistical Abstract*, 1985.

75 percent of adults had not finished high school, and the median number of years of school completed was eight. But by 1984, only about 27 percent of adults had not finished high school, and the median number of years of school completed had increased to twelve. More people in our society are graduating from high school and college, and from graduate and professional schools.

Schooling in America is seen as the broad road to opportunity. The cherished American ideal is that if all students are given free, high-quality, public education, they become free to advance as far as their talents will allow them to. However, opportunities within the educational system itself are not necessarily equal. Thus, despite the ideal of equal opportunity, the system is plagued with marked inequalities of attainment. Many people are going *into* the educational system, but they are reaching vastly different levels within it.

A high level of attainment at high-quality schools opens the way to (some would say, nearly guarantees) economic and professional opportunity. A high level of attainment also means credentials, or a kind of educational seal of approval, which is increasingly important in our society. In effect, though, some members of society have a much smaller chance than others of getting a high-quality education. Such credentials are only selectively available. (See the box on Credentialism.) The supposedly broad road to opportunity has many obstacles and roadblocks along the way. So we must ask ourselves, what are these inequalities of attainment and opportunity, what can be done about them, and what is the relation to social structure and inequality in our society in general? Why do credentials matter? And what, after all, does a quality education involve? This has become a crucial question, with the recent and widely publicized heavy criticism of American schools.

Is educational equality a reality? More women and minorities are reaching higher levels of education than ever before. But the young woman in law school probably had more hurdles in her way—gender stereotypes, family expectations—than her white male classmates. Factors other than effort and ability may help determine the limits of the first-grade scholar's enthusiastic reach. (Left: Suzanne Szasz/Photo Researchers, Inc.; right: James McGoon/Wheeler Pictures.)

Credentialism

Sociologist Randall Collins (1979) has argued that the enormous demand for schooling in our society is driven largely by a "cultural market" in which educational credentials are a major resource. He suggests that the real purpose of education is not essentially to satisfy industrial demand or to match economic growth but to maintain the elite's position in society. The educational system is a mechanism by which the elite seeks to perpetuate itself by keeping tight control over who gets what credentials. In other words, educational attainment and credentials are a resource such as gold or oil or coal and are competed for actively.

The result is that in our society today, people need educational credentials to get even the most menial, unskilled jobs. (The term **credentialism** refers to the requirement that an individual hold an educational degree as a condition for employment.) The levels of skills for most jobs have not actually altered much: this is one reason Collins and others claim that credentialism does not reflect real economic and job-market needs. The demand for credentials can mean that people who have the necessary skills but who do not happen to have the credentials have trouble finding work. Whereas a century ago, an immigrant worker might have gotten started by carrying bricks to a more skilled construction worker or by taking a job in a mill that required no formal education, people who want to enter the work force today need at least a high school diploma. The diploma is not so much a sign that people have learned to read, write, and calculate (often, as you've seen, it does not guarantee those skills at all) but a partial guarantee that they have been regular enough in their habits, diligent enough in their work, and bright enough to have graduated from high school. In a mobile society, a diploma also gives an employer a fairly standardized, simple, and quick criterion for judging job applicants.

Whether students go to college may well be the essential discriminator of status in American society today. At one extreme are the doctors and lawyers whose educational credentials give them monopolies over certain kinds of knowledge and skills. Their credentials afford them not only prestige but also valuable economic rewards. But credentialism also creates an underclass among those without a high school or college diploma.

Credentialism even affects which college majors that people follow. The emphasis in college has switched from a liberal arts background, with broad experience in basic courses, to majors in business, technology, or whatever students believe will equip them best for the job market. This view can be a shortsighted one, however, for when a specialized market closes, people with those skills will find themselves out of work. Today, many of those studying the problems in the schools are recommending that would-be teachers concentrate on liberal arts rather than education in their undergraduate work. This should put them in a better position not only to teach basic skills but to provide a broad intellectual perspective and encourage critical thinking—all elements that have been found lacking in what could be seen as today's mentally impoverished students. In the same way, employers may grow weary of workers with business or technical training who have trouble putting a sentence together, thinking creatively, or performing basic arithmetic and who have no fund of general factual knowledge. Would credentialism then remain intact, simply changing its course and following the new fashion? Many say that it would.

Discrimination, Tracking, and IQ

That there are significant differences of attainment by race, socioeconomic class, sex, and other background factors is clear. What type of evidence supports this statement? For example, among students who took SAT tests in 1980 and 1981, the verbal and math scores varied directly with the students' family incomes. Scores were lowest among those from the lowest-income groups and highest among those from the highest-income groups (see Table 17.2). The SAT scores also varied with the students' ethnic background, with whites and Asian– and Pacific–Americans scoring highest, followed by Mexican–Americans and blacks.

College attendance also depends in part on the students' socioeconomic background (Lee 1985). As sociologist James Hearn (1984) has characterized the situation, despite our commitment to equality of opportunity, the socioeconomically rich tend to get richer—that is, go to schools with better intellectual and material

TABLE 17.2   Race, Social Class, and SAT Scores. Results from SAT Test Taken in 1980–1981; Scores Range from 200 to 800

Race	Annual Parental Income							
	Under $6,000	$6,000– $11,999	$12,000– $17,999	$18,000– $23,999	$24,000– $29,999	$30,000– $39,999	$40,000– $49,999	$50,000 and over
Asian–Pacific American								
Percent of test-takers in income group	7.1%	16.8%	17.0%	15.8%	12.3%	14.2%	7.2%	9.7%
Median verbal score	299	331	362	388	409	426	443	455
Median math score	485	494	502	508	519	535	544	563
Total number of respondents: 31,329								
Black								
Percent of test-takers in income group	17.5%	30.9%	20.3%	12.9%	6.9%	6.7%	2.9%	1.8%
Median verbal score	284	302	323	339	352	370	392	414
Median math score	319	331	348	361	377	393	409	433
Total number of respondents: 82,162								
Mexican–American								
Percent of test-takers in income group	8.8%	22.4%	22.5%	18.6%	11.7%	9.8%	3.3%	3.1%
Median verbal score	321	337	357	378	391	397	410	421
Median math score	359	384	403	418	428	442	450	455
Total number of respondents: 15,765								
White								
Percent of test-takers in income group	2.2%	8.5%	14.2%	19.0%	16.2%	18.2%	8.9%	12.8%
Median verbal score	404	412	420	427	436	447	456	461
Median math score	435	446	460	472	486	497	505	509
Total number of respondents: 747,712								

Source: Adapted from the College Entrance Examination Board, the American College Testing Program.

resources—whereas the poor become poorer. The proportions of blacks, Hispanics, and Native Americans in higher education, although somewhat improved, still trail far behind that of whites. Enrollment in graduate schools paints a similar picture: more whites than members of other races, more white men than white women, but more black, Native American, and Hispanic women than men from these groups.

One of the important considerations in looking at unequal patterns of higher education and attainment among different ethnic groups is the tendency for students from lower economic groups to be channeled into lower-status and lower-quality courses of study and educational institutions. How does this happen? Often, this results from what is known as **tracking,** the grouping of students according to their *perceived* abilities and career interests. (Here, power theorists might assert that tracking by ability is the *rationale* used to channel students from lower socioeconomic backgrounds into lower tracks—which can be seen as synonymous with lower-quality education.) Tracking is perhaps the greatest obstacle to equal opportunity in American schools. The tracks that students find themselves on may lead them far along the road to opportunity or straight into a deadend or roadblock.

Students' performance on intelligence tests is one of the most common criterion for assignment to tracks. Even when intelligence test scores are not used for tracking, a student's intelligence quotient (IQ)—the score on a test of mental abilities that is a ratio of mental age to chronological age—can nevertheless affect teachers' expectations about his or her ability (Berk, Bridges, and Shih 1981).

Many people mistakenly believe that IQ tests measure the intellectual capacity with which a person is born. But intelligence is not the same as what intelligence tests *measure*. Although there have been many theories about which factors make up that elusive quality called "intelligence," no one really knows what it is. What is more, intelligence tests measure only a limited range of mental abilities—mainly verbal and mathematical—but little or nothing of a person's creativity, flexibility, street-smartness, insight, ability to learn from context, or skills with people, music, dance, or design. The tests are good at picking up students who are gifted in traditional academic subjects, but they are particularly poor at picking up those—many from minority and underprivileged groups—who already lag behind in the educational system. Students who lack test-taking skills —how to answer questions rapidly and in English, for example—and who lack the cultural frame of reference of the test are penalized.

Intelligence tests measure what people have learned over the years—the effects of environment—as well as certain aspects of their innate mental capacity. Because scores on IQ tests are heavily influenced by environment, it follows that some environments may be more conducive to exceptional performance than others. This is definitely the case. IQ tests are biased in favor of those who come from a middle-class, predominantly white, Western, industrialized culture (the same culture that produced the people who devise and administer the tests). Thus the fact that a young black child does not know many of the words on the vocabulary portion of an IQ test may not mean that this child lacks "intelligence."

It may simply mean that he or she comes from an environment where these words are seldom if ever used.

Educational psychologist Arthur Jensen (1969, 1979) deemphasized such environmental factors when he suggested that inheritance accounts for a large part of the ten- to fifteen-point difference between the average IQ scores of white and black Americans. As we pointed out in Chapter 13, widespread prejudice against blacks makes it impossible to equate the environmental experiences of white and black children, even when their parents' levels of income and education are similar. And more often than not, these factors are *dis*similar. In almost all the studies comparing the IQs of blacks and whites, the black sample has been drawn from a more socially and economically disadvantaged group than the white sample (Joseph 1977). Equally significant, when the average IQ scores of white children from privileged and disadvantaged homes are compared, the differences between them are equal to or even greater than those that exist between white and black youngsters (Hurn 1978).

What, then, can we say about the relationship between heredity and intelligence as measured by IQ tests? At most, genetic heritage helps establish a rather wide range of "intelligence" that a person can potentially manifest. But precisely where within this range the person will actually score is determined largely by environmental factors. This is why the use of IQ tests to discriminate between "inherently" bright and dull students is so unwarranted. Fortunately, the use of such tests for this purpose is now decreasing.

Inequality and the School's Role

What part does the school really play in establishing the patterns of inequality in our lives? What can be done about inequality in American public schools? Over the last several decades public officials have given serious attention to these important questions.

The Coleman Report

As part of the implementation of the Civil Rights Act of 1964, a team of sociologists headed by James Coleman

(1966) was asked to undertake a nationwide study of inequality in the schools. This study eventually included 570,000 students and 60,000 teachers in 4,000 schools. Halfway through the research, Coleman told an interviewer that "the study will show the difference in quality of schools that the average Negro child and the average white child are exposed to. You know yourself that the difference is going to be striking" (quoted in Hodgson 1973, p. 37).

The final results were not at all what Coleman had expected. He found relatively little difference between predominantly black schools and predominantly white ones in expenditure per pupil, building age, library facilities, number of textbooks, teacher characteristics, and class size. Even more surprising, he found that modern buildings, up-to-date texts and curricula, and higher expenditures per pupil had *no discernible effect* on the students' achievement test scores. The government and most educators have always assumed a cause-and-effect relationship between school resources and student performance: The more money spent on pupils, they believed, the better their education would be. Traditionally, equality of opportunity has meant trying to give all children access to the same kinds of educational *inputs* —teachers, facilities, and the like. This approach may be roughly equivalent to giving identical sets of clubs and balls to one person who has never played golf and another person who is an experienced player and pointing them toward the same tee. There is little doubt as to who will win; this initial inequality is part of Coleman's message. Coleman concluded that

> schools bring little influence to bear on a child's achievement that is independent of his [or her] background and general social context. . . . This very lack of independent effect means that the inequalities imposed on children by their home, neighborhood, and peer environment are carried along to become the inequalities with which they confront adult life at the end of school. (Coleman quoted in Silberman 1971, p. 71)

In other words, the schools themselves seemed to have little effect on student achievement, with two exceptions. Coleman did find that teaching quality made a small difference and that low-income blacks who attended middle-class schools performed better than low-income blacks who attended ghetto schools. But mainly Coleman found the family, not the school, to be the major educational institution, even in modern society. Families pass on to their children their socioeconomic status, which strongly affects the children's chances for educational opportunities and achievement. In other words, class is almost all-determining in terms of a child's achievement in his or her education.

The Coleman Report provided a strong rationale for what became known as **compensatory education,** enrichment programs that help students from disadvantaged backgrounds to "catch up" with more privileged students. Coleman argued that to achieve true equality of opportunity, we must create a situation in which each person has an equal chance of achieving a certain outcome. In education, equal opportunity will exist when the average scores of graduates from different schools (not per-pupil expenditures, facilities, and the like) are about the same. In order to achieve this equality, disadvantaged youth need compensatory education to help them compete fairly with other students.

Christopher Jencks and his colleagues in *Inequality* (1972) reinforced Coleman's diagnosis. Jencks agreed that inequality of social class outside school is the determining factor of inequality in school and that the money spent on students in any one school system was immaterial. (Note that Jencks echoes the power perspective here; schools reflect the class structure and opportunities of society.) Jencks argued further that there was nothing the educational system itself could do about this; it could not "fix" social inequality. Reforming the schools would not alter society at large nor ensure opportunity for all, or even just for *more* of the disadvantaged. In answer to the question raised earlier in the chapter—Do we expect too much of schools?—Jencks would say yes. Schools cannot be doctor or miracle worker and cure the ills of society.

Discrimination, Desegregation, and Busing

But before Jencks had published his controversial book, the United States was making efforts to alter the pattern of educational inequality—specifically, the pattern of racial desegregation. This effort began with the Supreme Court's ruling in 1954, *Brown* vs. *the Board of Education,* which undermined the traditional (and up to then, legal) strict segregation of black and white schoolchildren in the South and the virtual segregation in the North, based on residential patterns (Orfield 1983).

Coleman's 1966 study strongly influenced subsequent desegregation processes and plans, particularly his

Family life and socioeconomic status play a major role—the primary role, according to some sociologists—in determining a child's educational opportunities and level of achievement. A child from a poor, illiterate family will need early and special attention in order to compete on an equal footing with this middle-class toddler who is already "reading" with her daddy. (Joel Gordon.)

finding that low-income black children in ghetto schools performed more poorly than low-income blacks did in largely middle-class schools. We have seen that the policy and programs of compensatory education owe a great deal to Coleman. The courts and policymakers also turned to busing to desegregate schools, which, it was hoped, would eventually equalize educational opportunity and break down racial barriers.

Busing has proved a very useful approach (Sheppard 1981). In many cases, no other strategy has proved as effective. The principal cause of lingering segregation in today's school districts is the widespread residential segregation and adherence to the concept of the neighborhood school. Since low-income blacks live in predominantly black neighborhoods, their local schools are also predominantly black. In order to achieve integration, the courts obviously cannot move households, but they *can* move children by busing. As discussed in Chapter 13, court-ordered busing has prompted a massive reduction in public school segregation, especially in the South. Fewer blacks now attend highly segregated schools in the South than in the North (Fiske 1987).

Despite its effectiveness in achieving integration, and despite majority opinions in favor of integration, busing itself has never been popular, particularly among middle-class whites. Not surprisingly, black parents largely *support* busing. Many of those who oppose busing suggest that the tactic frequently backfires. They argue that court-ordered busing encourages white parents to remove their children from urban public schools, either sending them to private schools or moving to a distant suburb not affected by busing. Consequently, busing is said to result in even *more* segregation in city schools as the ratio of white to black students drops sharply. However, most studies show that "white flight" from the cities is a trend that has been going on for decades. Overall, it does not seem to have been hastened by the desegregation of public schools (Daniels 1983; Pettigrew and Green 1976). In one recent national study, Franklin Wilson (1985) found that white flight is a general trend—and that the positive results of desegregation are short-lived. The Wilson study also found that white families generally tried to avoid desegregated school districts, whatever their desegregation history had been.

Clearly, desegregation of the public schools has been somewhat effective, but whether or not it has resulted in better academic performance among minority group students is not entirely clear, as we saw in Chapter 13. Most research does suggest that the academic performance of minority students tends to improve in desegregated schools (Daniels 1983). What kind of effect desegregation has had on society in general is also unclear. Present-day experiences in desegregated schools may very well lay the foundation for less segregation in adult life and among future generations (Daniels 1983). Others have found that desegregation has few long-term positive effects. Jencks's thesis that a policy such as school desegregation cannot alter segregation in society has been neither entirely proved nor disproved.

Do Schools Make a Difference?

In the 1960s and the 1970s, Coleman and Jencks were addressing not only the specific question of racial and ethnic inequality but also the general question, Do schools make a difference? Both reports had a great deal of influence on public opinion and policy decisions during those decades. Even though the Coleman Report, for one, was used to back up both compensatory education and busing, Coleman's conclusion could be—and was—also read in the opposite way: that is, schools make no real difference, as Jencks's conclusion seemed to reinforce even more strongly.

Other studies have challenged both the methods and the conclusions of the Coleman and Jencks research and have suggested instead that there are, first, qualitative differences in schools and second, that, *these* differences do in turn make a difference in student learning and student lives. Some particularly interesting data came from Barbara Heyns (1978), one of Jencks's coauthors on *Inequality*. She found that schools *do* make a difference in learning for all groups, but the difference is most pronounced for the poorest children. The reason why is that better-off children have more opportunities for learning outside of school; this is where socioeconomic status and family background have their biggest effects. Children from affluent groups have a greater opportunity to move ahead *consistently* than disadvantaged students, as a result of the greater stimulation in the affluent children's family and community environment. This is true throughout the year, but the effect is more pronounced during the summer than during the regular school term. Summer vacations make a difference, because in the summer affluent children get more stimulation, instruction, and educational resources—camps, trips, and so on. Other children, who do not have the chance to go to computer camp or Europe fall behind a little more each year. Between the sixth and

twelfth grades, Heyns found, most of the measurable differences in learning took place in the summer. This was strong evidence that schools do make a difference, but that reforming educational programs during the existing school year would not be an adequate way to overcome inequality.

One of the implications of Heyns's research is that schools might learn from the pattern of affluent children's achievement and introduce similar types of stimulation, instruction, and resources into the school curricula. In other words, if schools could improve in these specific ways, they might be able to make even more of a difference. Nevertheless, the problem of reversing the "slippage" that occurs for disadvantaged youth during summers at home would still remain. Providing good summer schools or other effective forms of stimulation for disadvantaged children seems the obvious policy response.

An English group headed by Michael Rutter and his colleagues (1979) found that schools make a difference in the lives of students from various social backgrounds, perhaps more of a difference than Heyns had indicated. Rutter criticized Coleman's study for using crude measures and for never finding out what actually went on inside the schools. (Jencks's study has been criticized on similar grounds.) Rutter also pointed out that cross-sectional surveys such as Coleman's cannot measure changes over time. What we need, then, is a longitudinal study.

In their study, Rutter and his colleagues carefully assessed ten-year-olds in inner-city London schools, measuring their verbal ability, reading achievement, family background, emotional and behavior problems, and the like. They also asked the teachers to report on the children's behavior. Detailed assessments of the quality of the schools were then made, using survey data, classroom observations, and interviews. Finally, this process was repeated four years later to see what changes had occurred in the students. All this careful measurement was designed to assess intake (the character of the students at the start, including social class), process (what the schools did), and outcome (what changes occurred in the students).

What Makes a Quality Education?

Unlike Coleman, Rutter found great differences from school to school—in attendance, behavior, and academic performance. Some schools were clearly "better," that is, their students performed and behaved better than students of similar background and ability did at other schools. What made good schools good was primarily *how teachers taught.* In good schools there was a strong emphasis on academic achievement. Students were given regular homework and their work was carefully checked. The students were expected to master the classwork, to turn in their assignments on time, to use the library, and the like. The students were expected to be responsible. Teachers in good schools had a distinctive style of teaching: They interacted with the whole class, had clear and enforced standards of discipline, and rewarded good work. They made school a comfortable environment for students, decorating their classrooms and urging students to feel free to consult with them about personal problems. Moreover, in good schools, the staff was stable and efficiently organized. Rutter's conclusions have been supported by a study of effective schools in the United States that was conducted by researchers at the Harvard School of Education (Williams et al. 1981).

Providing an interesting and useful angle on the attributes of "good" schools and on the possibility of achieving such a goal, Sara Lightfoot has written:

> The search for "good" schools is elusive and disappointing. . . . [A] more modest orientation towards goodness does not rest on absolute or discrete qualities of excellence and perfection, but on views of institutions that anticipate change, conflict, and imperfection. The search for good schools has often seemed to me to be marked by a standard much like the societal expectations attached to good mothers: enduring qualities of nurturance, kindness, stimulation, and stability. Inevitably, this search finds no winners. No mothers can match these idealized pictures. . . . In many ways, I believe that [a] more generous view should also apply to perceptions of schools. (Lightfoot 1983, pp. 309, 311)

Schools, Lightfoot argues, cannot be measured according to standards of impossible perfection. Flexibility is perhaps the key attribute of a good school.

Public and Private Schools

We have looked at problems that riddle the public schools. If they do not always (or cannot at this point) provide a quality education, can private schools do so? Many affluent parents have turned to private schools in their disappointment with the public school system.

What are the actual differences between the two types of schools?

Coleman and his associates (1987) recently compared students' academic achievement in public and private schools. They found that the average private school is superior to the average public school in many ways. The environment in private schools generally is more disciplined and orderly, and these qualities are probably connected with the schools' success. Private school students generally achieve higher levels of academic performance, even when family background and other factors are held constant. For example, when students from private and public schools were compared, those from private schools were much more likely to enter college than those from public schools. These differences remained even when factors such as academic track, ability, educational aspirations, and socioeconomic class were held constant (Halsey and Heyns 1984). The differences may be attributable to the extra push that a private school staff can afford to give students, and perhaps also to the private schools' focus on college as an important goal for students. The following is a description of elite boarding schools, their curricula, and, by implication, their agenda for their students:

> Boarding school curricula are demanding and students are required to work hard at their studies. Although there is no requirement that they be intellectually curious, part of entitlement to privilege is proving one's merit by mastering a difficult curriculum. The academic skills that boarding school students acquire may help them to get into a select college and master the technical and social intricacies of the business, political, and financial worlds. Being comfortable in the world of ideas and being able to express thoughts in a concise and logical manner are not only the mark of a well-educated person, but are essential skills in the struggle for power today. (Cookson and Persell 1983, p. 30)

But the Coleman group found that, while some private schools are very elite (especially boarding schools), others cater largely to the middle class. And many—especially the Catholic schools and the so-called Christian academies—have many children from working-class families. Even those that do not have elite intellectual standards may offer high levels of order and discipline. Coleman and his colleagues concluded that policies that encourage students to attend private schools (such as tuition tax credits) would increase the proportion of minority and low-income students, and in this way would benefit students from disadvantaged groups.

HIGHER EDUCATION AND AMERICAN SOCIETY

Prior to 1960, only about one person in four went to a four-year college. By 1970, that ratio changed to one person in three and it has remained at that level ever since. Nevertheless, recently there has been sharp criticism of American higher education. Critics point out, as we noted earlier, that blacks, Hispanics, and members of low-income groups are underrepresented among college students (Lee 1985). Is a college education worth the time and money it requires? If so, why? Just what do people get out of college?

The Value of a College Education

A college degree, as we have seen, is an important credential in our society. It is expected to raise the earnings of those who graduate, and it is expected to confer nonmaterial advantages as well—better cognitive abilities, love of learning, respect for personal rights, among others.

Thus, one reason that people go to college is to increase their earning power. Calculated in terms of the purchasing power of 1981 dollars, the added lifetime value of a college degree versus a high school diploma was $329,000 for men and $142,000 for women. In 1983, the median income of a man who had graduated from high school was $17,600, of a woman, $7,400. The median income of a man who had graduated from a four-year college was $28,100, of a woman, $14,600 (see Figure 17.1). The sex differentials are due largely to the number of women not employed for at least part of their adult lives, but also to differences in pay for predominately male and female jobs and for men and women in similar jobs (see Chapter 12).

The kind of college that a student attends may make as much difference to his or her income as whether the student attends college at all. Richard Coleman and Lee Rainwater (1978) divided colleges into three categories. The 15 percent of students who attend the most elite private colleges and universities can expect to earn 85 percent more than those who have not graduated from college. The 45 percent of students who attend the less elite but still selective private colleges and major state universities can expect to earn 52 percent more than

those who have not graduated from college. For the remaining 40 percent of college graduates, a degree will give them no extra income, as compared to a high-school graduate. Many will hold jobs that might be called "white-collar working class," jobs that require college degrees (the degree itself may have little or nothing to do with the actual job) but offer few real opportunities for advancement.

Some bachelor's degrees are no longer worth much financially because of educational "inflation." This means that too many college degrees have been granted for the number of jobs that require a college education. A college degree is a minimum credential for middle-class jobs, much as a high school diploma is a minimum credential for working-class jobs. Through the process of educational upgrading, more jobs that were once done by high school or technical school graduates are now being done by college graduates (Berg 1970; Collins 1979; Rodriguez 1978). Whereas in 1972, college graduates made up only one in seven workers between the ages of twenty-five and sixty-four, in 1982, they made up one in four workers (Ehrenhalt 1983). As a result, many college graduates have had to scramble for any job at all and so are driving taxis, selling shoes, or typing and filing—perhaps temporarily, perhaps permanently. In addition, an economic slowdown that coincided with the last of the baby-boom generation's search for jobs has meant that college graduates in the 1970s faced a tight labor market and found their degrees worth less than they had originally expected. (See also box on Credentialism, p. 501.)

The value of a college education cannot, however, be measured solely on the basis of monetary gains to individuals. Howard Bowen (1977) argues that college significantly improves the quality of people's lives. The studies he cites show that college brings about many desirable changes in the individual—for example, increased cognitive abilities through the acquiring of verbal and mathematical skills, more logical thinking, increased knowledge and intellectual curiosity, and increased interest in and responsiveness to the arts. The research of sociologist Herbert H. Hyman and his associates (1975, 1979) in particular has documented the enduring effects of education. According to Hyman, it increases receptivity to further learning, stimulates the active seeking of new knowledge, encourages respect for civil liberties, and enhances students' emotional and moral development. What is more, students generally *expect* college to provide these nonmaterial benefits.

FIGURE 17.1 Median Income by Education, Male and Female, 1985.

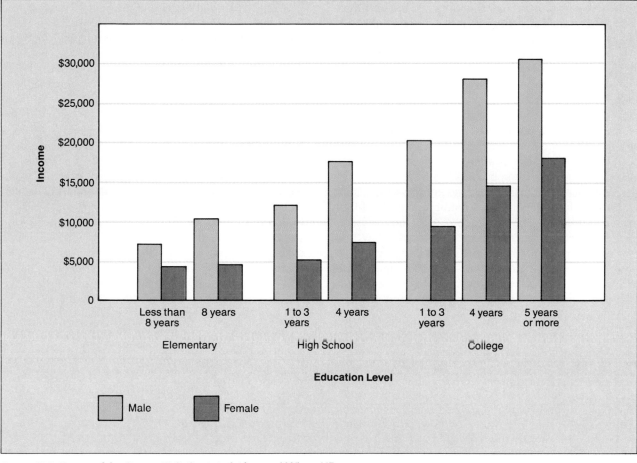

Source: U.S. Bureau of the Census, *U.S. Statistical Abstract*, 1985, p. 447.

Who Are Today's College Students?

Who makes up this ever-growing college population in the United States? What are their backgrounds, their interests and attitudes, and how do they spend their time? What do they expect a college education to do for them after their graduation?

The average age of the college student has increased to almost twenty-two years, partly because older students have been returning to school to improve their job skills, and partly because others have taken time out to decide what they want to do and then returned to college. In

fact, probably the most rapid change in higher education today is taking place in adult education, both degree and nondegree, as colleges, universities, corporations, and other private providers offer literacy training, enrichment courses, and career retraining to adults (Eurich 1985).

Just over half of all students in college are now women (Casale and Lerman 1986). Most college students are white; under 10 percent are black, and about 1 percent each are Native American, Puerto Rican, Asian, or from other minority groups. Thirty percent come from families in which the father has received a high school diploma, and 20 percent come from families in which the fathers have graduated from college. More mothers than fathers—40 percent—have graduated from high school, although slightly fewer mothers than fathers have graduated from college—17 percent (Astin 1987).

What do the students themselves say about their decision to go to college? They offer a number of intellectual, social, and financial reasons for this decision. Seventy-six percent want to go to college so that they will get better jobs than they could get without a degree, and nearly as many—73.5 percent—want, appropriately enough, to learn more. Sixty-one percent want to gain a general education, and 56 percent want to meet new and interesting people (Astin 1987).

Slightly more than half—and more women than men—classify themselves as political middle-of-the-roaders, and about one-fifth each classify themselves as liberal and conservative. A very small percent say that they are far right or far left (Astin 1987). Most college students in the conservative 1980s like and try to emulate their parents' lives, although they want to be even better off financially than their parents (Casale and Lerman

1986). Two-thirds consider themselves moderately religious, and 15 percent consider themselves deeply religious. Nearly all the students polled agreed that relations between the United States and the Soviet Union should be improved, and three-fourths agreed that the U.S. government should give nuclear disarmament high priority. Three-fourths also agreed that a woman should be able to choose whether to have an abortion (Boyer 1987). Eighty-five percent want to get married, preferably in their mid-twenties. Over 90 percent of the women want to work after they are married. Only 15 percent of the men and 6 percent of the women want to be in a marriage where the wife stays at home and the husband works (Casale and Lerman 1986).

Outside of the classroom, many students work. Nearly 30 percent of full-time students and 84 percent of part-time students work 21 hours or more each week. As tuition costs keep rising, the numbers of students who work will most likely rise, too. Students also spend time talking informally to other students, listening to music, reading, playing sports, exercising, and watching television. Many are careful about staying fit and healthy, which is a promising improvement since the 1970s.

"This process of training, by which the intellect, instead of being formed or sacrificed to some particular or accidental purpose, some specific trade or profession, or study or science, is disciplined for its own sake, for the perception of its own proper object, and for its own highest culture, is called Liberal Education." What would John Henry Cardinal Newman, who wrote "The Idea of a University" in 1852, have to say about the typical college curriculum today? (Left: Joe McNally/Wheeler Pictures; right: Jill Cannefax/EKM-Nepenthe.)

FIGURE 17.2   Freshman Goals: Spiritual vs. Financial, 1967–1987

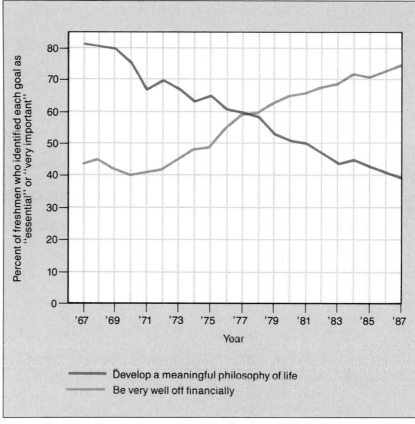

Source: The Higher Education Research Institute, University of California, Los Angeles; Carmody, Diedre, "To Freshman, a Big Goal is Wealth," *New York Times*, January 14, 1988, p. A14.

Today, more students—over 25 percent—plan to major in business than in any other course of study. Next, in order of popularity, are engineering, education, biology, science, psychology, communications, computer science, English, and political science. These fairly recent trends, illustrated in Figure 17.2, may have to do with increased concern among students with making money. The number of students majoring in literature and the humanities may have declined for the same reason: these fields are less specifically related to the current job market or to economic gains. As we mentioned earlier, employers, however, may begin to want stronger backgrounds in English, the humanities, and the natural sciences from college graduates, which could eventually reverse the business-oriented trend.

Once they have finished college, 44 percent of students plan to work full-time, 24 percent to go to graduate school, and 16 percent to work and go to school at the same time (Casale and Lerman 1986). Thirty-eight percent plan to get a bachelor's degree, 31 percent a master's degree, 15.2 percent a doctorate, and 6.2 percent an associate degree (Astin 1987).

Junior and Community Colleges

The overall growth of American education and the increasing proportion of college students are two very important trends. But the actual number of enrollments in four-year colleges has been dropping recently. This is balanced by the trend in two-year college enrollments, which for both full-time and part-time students continue to surge ahead, year after year. In 1981 two-year colleges enrolled 32 percent of undergraduates, up from 27 percent in 1970 (U.S. Census Bureau 1983). The increase may reflect, first, the older age of the average student (more adults taking "extension" courses, for example) and, second, the concern of today's students with receiving more practical and more immediate vocational training (rather than liberal arts/humanities training) from school. In addition, community and junior colleges are providing Americans with a kind of middle ground between high school and a four-year college course.

The first *private junior* colleges in this country were designed to provide students who could not get into four-year schools an opportunity for higher education. The first *public community* colleges were an extension of the local school system and were intended primarily for students who could not get into or who could not afford four-year schools. Today, both junior and community colleges serve several worthwhile functions. They round out education for students who otherwise would leave school after graduating from high school; they prepare students for enrollment in four-year colleges; they train semiprofessionals; and they provide continuing education for adults.

Junior and community colleges usually offer three types of programs: vocational training (in such areas as health services, mechanics, business skills, computer programming, and police training); "transfer" programs (which emphasize academic subjects to help students transfer to four-year colleges); and community education (special-interest courses in civic and cultural affairs and recreational activities). Three out of four students in two-year schools cite getting a better job as their primary reason for attending school (AACJC 1977).

Most community colleges are oriented toward technical or career education. Students who follow such vocational courses are aiming for semiprofessional jobs in science, health, engineering, and various technical fields. (Such workers make up about 35 percent of the American labor force.) The problem with pursuing such jobs in order to attain higher paying, more prestigious jobs is that most have short career ladders. A nurse, teacher's aide, or laboratory technician, for example, may find little opportunity for advancement. Moreover, many community college graduates cannot find jobs in the fields for which they have trained. For example, only 11 percent of science graduates had science-related jobs in 1976 (Pincus 1980). Thus, the community college is often of only limited help to the student who wants to get a better job. Sociologists such as Randall Collins (1971, 1979) point out that in any case, with the exception of a few highly specialized professionals like medicine and engineering, most occupations require little of the kind of skills that schools teach. More often, individuals acquire the necessary skills on the job and not in school. It is, as we saw in the box on Credentialism, the credentials a school can bestow that matter most.

Nevertheless, community colleges do offer their students substantial opportunities. Two years of college may now be as essential in the job market as a high school diploma was twenty years ago. Even though community college students as a group do not experience significant upward mobility, and even though students who enter two-year schools are far less likely than those who enter four-year schools to get a bachelor's degree (Veles 1985), they may be better off than similar students who decided not to go to college at all. And a community college education often provides rewards of considerable personal significance. For example, community college courses can awaken dormant interests and develop latent talents that enrich students' lives immeasurably. And because community college students are more likely to be older, married, and working than are students in four-year college, junior and community colleges have opened up a system of education to a large number of students who are unable to attend four-year colleges and universities. This group also includes minorities; even though minorities are still underrepresented in all types of colleges, the career education and vocational training offered by community colleges *have* helped move blacks upward in the job market, into more people-oriented and data-processing occupations (Kerckhoff and Jackson 1982).

WHAT THE FUTURE HOLDS

American education is undergoing great change. Pessimistic observers call this a time of decline and disorder; optimistic ones consider it adaptation and renewal. Whatever view one takes, change seems inevitable.

Community colleges present opportunities for personal growth and career advancement to many who would not otherwise continue their education. In an era of "education inflation," technical or vocational training from a community college may be more likely to ensure employment than some four-year college degrees. (R. Bossu/Sygma.)

At the very least, changes in the size and composition of our population will affect the shape of American education (see Chapter 10). Elementary school enrollments declined until the middle 1980s, when the "echo boom" children—those born to the post-World War II baby boom generation—reached school age. Now elementary schools are temporarily overcrowded. High school and college enrollments will follow the same pattern: a continual decline (in this case through the 1990s) followed by a resurgence as the "echo boom" students come of age. At the same time a growing number of active and healthy older people, and an increasing number of middle-aged adults forced to train for new careers, will make continuing (or adult) education of even greater importance. Until now, most of those taking advantage of continuing education have been middle-class. But this may change as adult education programs become more widely publicized. Indeed, continuing and adult education is probably *the* growth area for colleges and universities—and sometimes for private businesses and community organizations.

Demographic trends will not be the only factors shaping the course of American education. Equally important will be pressures to improve the quality of our schools and programs and to give students a greater range of choices in the types of institutions they may attend. New stress is being placed on the teaching of "basics."

And many colleges are urging students to take a strong, academically oriented program in high school.

In modern, technologically based societies, knowledge assumes a critical role. The National Commission on Excellence in Education noted in its report, *A Nation at Risk* (1983, pp. 6–7):

> The world is indeed one global village. We live among determined, well-educated, and strongly motivated competitors. We compete with them for international standing and markets, not only with products but also with the ideas of our laboratories and neighborhood workshops. . . . Knowledge, learning, information, and skilled intelligence are the new raw materials of international commerce and are today spreading throughout the world as vigorously as miracle drugs, synthetic fertilizers, and blue jeans did earlier. . . . Learning is the indispensable investment required for success in the "information age" we are entering.

Hence, education has strong ties to other social institutions and plays a critical part in contemporary society. Indeed, we find ourselves increasingly turning to the nation's schools and colleges to provide solutions to personal, social, economic, and political problems that the home and other institutions are having difficulty resolving. Whether schools *can* solve these problems—or to what extent—remains much debated.

SUMMARY

1. In traditional societies, socialization takes place primarily through observation, imitation, rituals, myths, and legends. In affluent societies, education is a formal, structured, and deliberate socialization process that takes place primarily in schools. Americans as a nation have a strong commitment to free universal education, and the creation of our public school system was unprecedented.

2. Within the classroom itself, the group dynamics of teachers and students can play an important role in patterns of opportunity and achievement. Judgments about students' abilities are often made quickly and early in children's school careers. The self-fulfilling prophecy, the subject of much controversy, is an initially incorrect judgment about a student's ability that is eventually confirmed by the student. It seems clear that teachers' expectations can weigh heavily on student behavior, but there are other influences as well, including a child's social status and any antischool values children pick up from families and neighborhoods.

3. The original intentions of American public education were to preserve democracy and better society. The general functions society expects schools to serve today include preparing children for social relations in a public world of hierarchies and inequalities; the transmission of cultural values, which may involve both indoctrination and the fostering of a positive sense of national identity; selection of talent for future social roles; and the teaching of basic and cognitive skills.

4. Both functional and power theorists generally view the tasks of schools as dovetailing into the larger society's requirements. But functional theorists focus on the maintenance of social order and cultural cohesiveness.

5. Power theorists focus primarily on the ways in which schools reflect the class system and its conflicts and preserve the essential inequalities of society. They point out that social integration may mean suppression of class identity; that talent selection often is the rejection of the disadvantaged; that cultural transmission and socialization mean different things depending on social status; and that skills training is often inadequate.

6. The teaching of basic literacy and numeracy skills may be the most obvious school function, but many schools may not be adequately fulfilling this task. Numerous task forces and commissions have confirmed the schools' and students' weaknesses and have proposed reforms aimed at improving the quality of teaching. These include changes in teacher training, better ways of accrediting teachers, merit pay, and unionization.

7. Some theorists describe the history of American education as alternately responsive to egalitarian ideals and to capitalist/workplace requirements.

8. Our educational system is plagued by unequal levels of attainment; these are closely correlated with race, socioeconomic status, and other background factors. The consequences of the attainment inequalities are enormous for society and the individual. A high-quality education leading to a high level of attainment helps ensure economic and professional success. This kind of credential is increasingly important as an end in itself.

9. There is a general tendency for lower-class students to be channeled into lower-status and lower-quality courses and institutions, often by a process known as tracking. Tracking is based on perceived ability, which in turn is traditionally judged according to IQ test results. The tests, however, may be geared to dominant-culture knowledge.

10. The 1966 Coleman Report on inequality in the schools, an outgrowth of the 1964 Civil Rights Act, concluded that the quality and type of school had little or no effect on student achievement; the primary influence was found to be family and social class background. Others, particularly Jencks in the early 1970s, reinforced Coleman's message, maintaining that schools cannot overcome the social inequities students bring with them to the schools. The Coleman Report was originally used as a rationale for both compensatory education for the disadvantaged and busing to achieve integration.

11. The effort to desegregate American schools began with the 1954 Supreme Court *Brown* vs. *Board of Education* decision. Busing has proved to be the most useful approach to desegregation, though it has met with some resistance. The effects of segregation on minority achievements are unclear.

12. More recent studies have criticized the work of Coleman and Jencks and asserted that quality schooling *can* make a difference to student achievement and students' lives. A chief element in quality of education seems to be the methods, stability, and quality of teaching. Flexibility and adaptability may also be of major importance.

13. Private school students on average may get a higher-quality education and achieve higher academic levels than public school students, even when family and other background factors are held constant. However, private schools do not seem to be as elitist as is often supposed.

14. More people are attending college, since a college degree has become such an essential credential for so many jobs. However, there may also be a steady devaluation of this credential because of educational inflation. At this point, a college degree *does* afford people higher incomes. But the kind of college attended may be of equal importance to success.

15. Today's college students are older on average, partly as a result of the recent expansion of adult education. Ethnic and racial minorities are still underrepresented in colleges. The most popular major is business, since a majority of students now claim that their main purpose in attending college is economic and material.

16. Enrollments in junior and community colleges are up, although these schools do not necessarily provide the upward mobility that many expect; they may be a kind of lower-status track in themselves. Nevertheless, the expansion of junior and community colleges does indicate some broadening of opportunities in higher education.

GLOSSARY

Compensatory education. Enrichment programs to help disadvantaged students compete on a more equal basis with privileged students.

Credentialism. The requirement that an individual hold an educational degree as a condition of employment.

Education. The formal, systematic transmission of a culture's skills, knowledge, and values from one generation to the next.

Hidden curriculum. A set of unwritten rules of behavior taught in school that prepare children for academic success and social relations for the world outside school.

Self-fulfilling prophecy. An initially false judgment about a person's ability that eventually evokes behavior appropriate to the judgment; an expectation that comes true.

Tracking. Grouping children according to their scores on aptitude and achievement tests (in effect, according to their *perceived* ability).

CHAPTER 18
Religion

The modern world may not strike you as especially religious. Prayer, worship, sacred rituals consume only a small part of most people's lives. Yet religion remains a vital force for humans everywhere. It has ignited some intense conflicts, pitting Jew against Palestinian in Israel, Muslim against Druze and Christian in Lebanon; Hindu against Sikh and Muslim in India; Protestant against Catholic in Northern Ireland. Religion is also involved in more peaceful political struggles. Adherents of liberation theology have worked for peace and justice in Latin America, and striking workers in Poland have rallied around religious symbols. Religion can even induce people to renounce their current way of life and adopt an entirely new one, as when someone abandons job, family, and friends to join a religious cult. In the Soviet Union, where atheism has been taught for some seventy years, religion still survives. What is this powerful force that underlies so much of human behavior?

Religion is one of the hardest sociological concepts to define. An adequate definition must be broad enough to include the great variety of religions that have existed throughout history, but not so broad that it also encompasses beliefs and practices generally considered nonreligious. The classical definition, and the one that served for many years, was proposed by Émile Durkheim. Durkheim defined religion as a set of beliefs and practices pertaining to sacred things that unite people into a moral community. A key element in this definition is the idea that religion pertains to the sacred. By **sacred**

Durkheim meant that which is set apart from everyday experience and inspires awe and reverence. He contrasted the sacred with the **profane,** that which is mundane and ordinary. The quality of sacredness is not inherent. A community *bestows* sacredness on things. Thus, people can consider almost anything sacred, such as a cross, a lizard, even an oddly shaped stone.

But some sociologists think that Durkheim's definition is overly broad. It can apply to philosophical and other nonreligious outlooks, as well as to religious ones. Rodney Stark and William Bainbridge (1986) argue that religion is better defined as the work of organizations primarily engaged in providing people with the hope of future rewards to compensate for things they greatly desire but have not obtained in life. This hope is based on a set of beliefs in supernatural forces, beings, or places. Stark and Bainbridge's definition is much narrower than Durkheim's. For them, a religion must include a belief in the supernatural, as well as the idea of compensations offered to believers. Nevertheless, this definition incorporates a wide variety of religions, from Christianity, Islam, and other widely held faiths, to the ancestor worship of a remote tribal people or the belief in an afterlife among ancient cave dwellers.

Rather than trying to resolve how best to define the essence of religion, we will approach the question somewhat differently. We will look for resemblances among religions, without looking for any single identifying feature. This is similar to looking for resemblances among family members without identifying any single feature that makes all those members look alike. Some of the elements found in most religions include religious beliefs, symbols, and practices, a community of followers, and a variety of religious experiences. After exploring these elements we will look at religion from the sociological perspectives of function and power, and structure and action. These perspectives help to answer the important questions of why cultures everywhere have some kind of religion and why people adopt the religious beliefs that they do. Next we will consider three different types of religious institutions—church, sect, and cult—and we will explore a number of religious responses to the process of modernization. Finally, we will take a look at religion in the United States today.

THE BASIC ELEMENTS OF RELIGION

Religious Beliefs

Religion is partly a system of beliefs about what is sacred. The Mbuti Pygmies of Africa believe that the forest in which they live is a supernatural being. They personify it as Mother and Father, Life-Giver, and occasionally Death-Giver. The Pygmies' belief is an example of **animism,** or the idea that things in the world (a forest, a tree, an animal, a mountain, or a river, for instance) are imbued with active, animate spirits. In some religions people believe in the existence of ancestral spirits. This is true of the 38 million followers of Shintoism, most of whom are Japanese.

More familiar to Westerners is the religious belief known as **theism,** which is the idea that powerful supernatural beings are involved with events and conditions on earth. *Mono*theists, such as the world's 1.7 billion Christians, 18 million Jews, and 840 million Muslims (Brittanica 1987) believe in a single supernatural being, called God, Yahweh, or Allah. *Poly*theists, in contrast, believe in several deities. Today's 648 million Hindus, most of whom live in India, have a pantheon of many minor gods and five major ones, who are in turn reflections of a higher, more sacred principle of *Brahman,* or "Oneness."

In other religions, beliefs center around a supernatural force rather than a supernatural being. Poly-

Sacredness is not inherent in objects but is conferred on them by a culture's customs and beliefs. The cows that wander busy streets in India are protected and venerated as symbols of the Hindu belief in the unity of all living things. (Benares.) (Van Bucher/Photo Researchers, Inc.)

nesians, for example, believe in a supernatural force called *mana,* which can inhabit objects and people. A canoe that is able to withstand intense storms or a farmer whose crops flourish is said to possess *mana.* This kind of religious belief is most common in preindustrial societies.

Émile Durkheim was one of the first sociologists to propose explanations for the religious beliefs that people develop. He began by studying Australian aboriginal clans, which he believed were the simplest kind of human society and therefore should have elementary forms of religion. A central part of aboriginal religion is the **totem:** an object (usually an animal or plant) that symbolizes both the clan itself and that which the clan considers sacred. Durkheim was intrigued by this dual symbolism of the clan and the sacred. He argued that in worshiping a totem, the aborigines were essentially revering their own society. This insight led Durkheim to the conclusion that religious beliefs stem from people's experiences with the social forces that shape their lives. For instance, a belief in divine creation stems from the fact that we are products of a culture that seems outside us, not of our own making. "We speak a language that we did not make," wrote Durkheim; "we use instruments that we did not invent; we invoke rights that we did not found; a treasury of knowledge is transmitted to each generation that it did not gather itself" (Durkheim 1912/1965, p. 212). This gives rise to the idea that we are fashioned by external forces beyond our control, forces that deserve our awe and devotion. The same idea is embodied in the belief in a creator god.

In addition to beliefs in deities, spirits, or supernatural forces, most religions also incorporate moral principles. Moral principles are beliefs about what is right and wrong, good and bad, proper and improper. They are not just abstract ideas, but prescriptions for behavior. Adherents of the religion are expected to use them as guides in their daily lives (Gellner 1972). In some nontheistic religions (those without ideas of a deity) the moral principles are paramount. Buddhists, for instance, are less concerned with revering the Buddha than they are with achieving the ethical and spiritual ideas that the Buddha set forth in his message of the "four noble truths." Other religions that center around a striving toward moral goals are Confucianism and Taoism, both of which originated in China.

Religious Symbols

Virtually all religions are expressed through symbols, or things that stand for something other than themselves. As we said in Chapter 4, nothing is symbolic in and of itself. People *assign* symbolic meanings and agree among themselves as to what those meanings are.

Words and actions as well as objects can be religious symbols. The Christian Communion ceremony, for example, includes both symbolic acts (drinking wine and eating bread as a symbolic reenactment of the Last Supper) and symbolic things (the wine and bread themselves, which symbolize the blood and body of Christ). Durkheim argued that the use of such religious symbols often involves what he called collective representation: communication from larger social bodies to individuals. Thus, the various symbols employed in a Christian Communion speak from all those who share the Christian faith (including all past generations) to all those who are currently participating in the ceremony.

Religious Practices

The activities of religious people are also shaped by their faith. Consider the Christ Communal Organization (CCO), an outgrowth of the Jesus movement of the 1960s. Its members lead very ascetic lives. They do not use drugs, tobacco, or alcohol, nor do they have extramarital sex. They rise early and pray together before breakfast, and they pray again before beginning work.

Religious symbolism is a complex language of images and gestures. This famous 15th-century painting appears to be a simple domestic portrait of husband and wife, but symbolic elements—the husband's raised hand, the single candle burning in the chandelier, the fruit on the window sill, and in fact virtually every detail in the painting—transform it into a powerful commentary on the sacredness of marriage. (London National Gallery.)

While at work (mostly in agricultural jobs), they sing spirituals together. Each night they gather for evening prayer and Bible study lasting several hours. In their spare time, the members engage in evangelizing; They spread the doctrines of their religion to others (Richardson, Stewart, and Simmonds 1979).

The community prayer, singing, studying, and preaching in which CCO members participate are examples of religious practices. Religious practices are activities that adherents of a religion engage in to express their faith, communicate it to others, seek supernatural guidance or intervention, honor their deities, affirm their sacred beliefs, or simply produce religious experiences. Such practices may be shared or solitary, compulsory or optional, rigidly structured or open to creative innovations. The range of religious practices is enormous. Music, dance, prayer, meditation, feasting, and fasting are just a few of the many activities carried out in the name of religion.

Some religious practices can be classified as **rituals,** or standardized sets of actions used in particular ceremonies or on other specific occasions. Rituals rely on symbols to convey their meaning and to reinforce that meaning for participants. Some rituals are secular rather than religious. For instance, the custom of people standing when a judge enters a courtroom, of witnesses raising their right hand when swearing to tell the truth, and of a jury foreman rising to formally give the verdict are all rituals that lend symbolic respect and gravity to legal proceedings. Religious rituals are usually accorded even greater sanctity. The ritual cleansing with water in a Christian baptism or the ritual reading from the Torah in a Jewish bar mitzvah are solemn acts that convey deep spiritual meaning to participants, also helping to give them a sense of religious community (Douglas 1970; Gluckman 1962; Turner 1970).

People who claim to be followers of a particular religion do not necessarily observe all of that religion's rituals and other practices. Not all professed Christians go to church, for example, and not all who go to church take Communion. One recent survey found that only about 40 percent of Americans report attending religious services weekly, even though many more report some religious affiliation (Princeton Religious Research Center 1986). Regular attendance is greatest among Roman Catholics, followed by Protestants, and then Jews (Gallup Report 1982). In part, these differences reflect the different meanings that the various religious groups attach to attendance at religious services.

Religious Community

As a system of sacred beliefs, rituals, and symbols, religion shapes individuals' lives, but it also has a social character. One of its typical elements is, to use Durkheim's term, **a moral community.** This community is composed of those whose shared beliefs, symbols, practices, and experiences bind them together into a larger social whole. So important is community to the life of a religion that the absence of it is seen as a serious problem. For example, many contemporary clergy are concerned about the spread of TV evangelism partly because it promotes a religion without community. The viewers are not part of any local congregation, nor are they encouraged to identify with a body of believers worldwide. They can connect and disconnect their religious attachments simply by turning their sets on and off.

The scope of a religious community varies with the type of society involved. In a small tribe, religion encompasses everyone and affects every aspect of life. People might seek the guidance of ancestral spirits regarding family matters, and those same spirits would be thought to affect political and economic conditions. In this case, the religious community and society as a whole are virtually one and the same (Calhoun 1980; Evans-Pritchard 1965; Fortes 1969). In larger, more complex societies, by comparison, religion is more compartmentalized; it has institutions of its own, such as a variety of different churches. Each church carves out its own religious community, making it more difficult for religion to foster social unity. The churches tend to be at odds over the kind of community the larger society should build and what share in that community each church should have. This has been a recurring theme in American religious history. Periodically new sects have broken off from established churches and searched for places (often on the Western frontiers) where they could fashion their own ideal communities. The Mormons who settled in Utah are one example. Other American sects have followed a similar pattern (Marty 1984).

Sometimes the idea of religious community is used in more radical ways. For example, during the Middle Ages the Franciscan order of Catholic monks renounced all personal property in favor of a community sharing of possessions. This life style, which was intended as a message to the world about proper Christlike behavior, resulted in conflict with the Church hierarchy. A somewhat similar process has occurred in modern times with the rise of liberation theology. Liberation theology originally referred to a movement of Catholic priests in Brazil and other Latin American countries. The priests pursued economic justice as well as spiritual salvation partly because of a belief that a Christian community is destroyed by too great a gulf between rich and poor. Ministering especially to the poor and landless, these priests founded "base communities," or settlements in which, like early Christians, they emphasized a common struggle against oppression (Gutierrez 1973, 1983). Liberation theology has now spread to many American Christian churches, both Catholic and Protestant (Tabb 1986).

Religious Experiences

The idea of religious community focuses on the collective aspects of religion, on the fact that religious beliefs, symbols, and practices are shared among a group of adherents. But religion also involves individuals who have religious experiences. These experiences are an important way in which followers express their faith (Stark and Bainbridge 1985).

Sometimes religious experiences involve intensified awareness of a supernatural being or power. This may be accompanied by a sense of spiritual cleansing or purification. The so-called born-again experience associated with conversion to fundamentalist Christianity often takes this form (Tipton 1982). Other times religious experiences are ecstatic states that transcend the here and now. Among certain Muslim ascetic groups, for instance, violent whirling, dancing, and shouting are used to reach states of altered consciousness. In other religions drugs may be ritually used to achieve the same goal. Religious experiences also include the feeling of having attained personal contact with a deity. People may even report being given divine revelations. Closely related is a sense of oneness with other people (especially members of one's own religious group) or a strong identity with nature.

The religious experiences that people have are not just a product of their own personal history and psychological makeup. Religious experiences are also partly social phenomena; they are shaped by the expectations of the group to which the people having them belong (Snow and Machalek 1984). For instance, a study of the Jehovah's Witnesses found that new recruits learned to

Public or communal worship is regarded as an essential element of most religions—a means both of strengthening the individual's faith and of affirming a sense of community. Daily life in this Mongolian Lamasery, like that in a Christian monastery, is ordered around periods of communal worship and private meditation. Here, two Lamas blow conch shells to call the community to prayer. (George Holton/Photo Researchers, Inc.)

describe their conversion experiences in ways that conformed to the organization's ideas about what these experiences should entail (Beckford 1978). This is not to say that the new recruits fabricated their stories. They simply filtered what they experienced through the group's expectations about the conversion process. Thus, although each account had individual twists and variations, all incorporated the same major themes of the group.

PERSPECTIVES ON RELIGION

Religion and the Social Order: Function and Power

The remains of flowers found among the skeletons at a Neanderthal burial site, the huge stone slabs at Stonehenge in England, the massive heads carved from

The word religion *comes from Latin* re-, *back, and* ligare, *to bind or fasten. Religion binds one to the past, to the natural world, and to other members of one's society. It also reinforces a sense of mystery about the world and one's place in it. Though their origin and purpose are not fully understood, these monolithic carvings on Easter Island (the island's Polynesian name means "Navel of the World") fill us with an awe that echoes, perhaps, the awe of the builders confronting their world. (Tardos Camesi/The Stock Market.)*

volcanic rock on the slopes of Easter Island in the South Pacific, and the ruins of ancient temples that dot the landscapes of Greece attest to the existence of religion among people across the ages. In fact, there has probably never been a society where religion was altogether absent. From this sociologists infer that religion must be a crucial part of social life. But why is it so crucial? What needs or purposes does it serve?

Those who take a functional perspective argue that religion serves a number of very important purposes for societies and individuals. For one thing, religion tends to promote social solidarity, partly by providing norms that reduce conflict in the community. Precepts like "Love thy neighbor," "Thou shall not steal," and "Turn the other cheek" are more than pious abstractions. They are concrete guidelines for everyday behavior that encourage harmonious interactions. Religion also promotes social solidarity by imposing sanctions against antisocial conduct and offering ways to atone for mistakes. For instance, in the Manus society of the South Pacific, families kept the skull of an ancestor in their homes. The ancestor, referred to as "Sir Ghost," is believed to keep a

careful eye on the behavior of his descendants. If someone transgresses, Sir Ghost may cause a person (not necessarily the offender) to become ill, have poor fishing, or suffer some other misfortune. Thus, the potential intervention of the ancestor functions as a constraint against misbehavior (Pelto and Pelto 1976).

Those who take a functional perspective also point out that religion serves to consecrate major life events. Virtually all religions have ceremonies that mark birth, maturity, marriage, and death. Such ceremonies help individuals interpret these events, while at the same time linking the participants to the larger community. For example, the wedding of Prince Charles of England to Lady Diana Spencer reaffirmed for the British people the values of church and crown. On a smaller scale, every wedding binds a couple and their social group to the laws and values of their community.

Another function that religion can serve is to help immigrants in a society adapt to their new environment. This has occurred in the United States (Greeley 1972a). Churches modeled after those in the immigrants' homelands provided a haven of traditional beliefs and customs that helped to ease the transition to a new way of life. At the same time, religion often provided an ethnic cohesion and discipline that helped some immigrant groups become upwardly mobile. This has been true of Irish Catholics, Polish Catholics, and Jews. In some parts of the United States, these groups have surpassed Methodists, Presbyterians, and Episcopalians in income and wealth (Greeley 1972b, 1976). In the case of Jews, the intellectual and emotional adaptability they have needed for survival as a persecuted minority facilitated their ascent in American society.

Religion also serves to legitimize the established social order by sanctioning the social arrangements that prevail in it. Guy Swanson (1974) showed this in a study of fifty non-Western societies. Just as Durkheim had suggested, each society tended to reflect itself in its religion. For instance, in societies where elders occupied key positions, ancestors were worshiped; and in societies with large inequalities in wealth, religion tended to support a wide gap between rich and poor. In our own society, for example, when television preachers like Rev. Robert Schuller encourage people to fulfill their individual potentials, they are endorsing the American values of ambition and individual opportunity (see Chapter 4). Thus, with some notable exceptions such as Latin American priests who declare the dominant regime to be immoral, religion often serves to reinforce and justify existing social arrangements.

Religious legitimization of the established social order can be seen in what sociologist Robert Bellah (1970) calls national, or civil religion. **Civil religion** is essentially a sanctifying of the nation by associating its history, values, and institutions with God's special favor. One study of civil religion among elementary-school children found that 85 percent believed that America "has been placed on this earth for a special purpose," that it is God's chosen nation, and that its success is a reward for its goodness (Smidt 1980). Most adults also feel that our country was created "under God," and that from God the government derives its ultimate legitimacy. Of course, the American Constitution expressly forbids any ties between the state and *particular* religions. As a result, civil religion involves a very general seeking of blessings from God. God's aid on behalf of the nation is invoked at the opening of Congress, at political party conventions, when officials take their oaths of office, and in political speeches, including every presidential inaugural address but one (Washington's second, which was only two paragraphs long). Civil religion, then, creates links between the sacred and the secular. In so doing, it encourages a willingness to care about and sacrifice for the public good (Bellah and Hammond 1980; Coleman 1983). Civil religion can come in both conservative and liberal forms, and can stress both our freedom to choose and our obligations to each other (Wuthnow 1988).

Sociologists with a functional perspective see religious legitimization of the social order as a positive force that helps to bind society together. Bellah, in fact, has expressed concern that civil religion in America may be declining, for if this is so, he feels that we are losing an important source of social unity (Bellah 1975). Wuthnow (1988) sees struggles between liberal and fundamentalist Christians undermining the effectiveness of civil religion. Sociologists with a power perspective, however, are apt to claim that civil religion achieves the appearance of unity by obscuring differences. They contend that religion serves not the *general* interests of society, but rather the interests of powerful elites.

Karl Marx, for example, believed that religion in capitalist societies was under the domination of those who owned the means of production. He argued that in justifying the power of this ruling class, religion performed the *negative* task of pacifying the exploited working classes. Marx called religion the opium of the people because it lulls workers into complacency by creating a false sense of well-being and discourages them from overthrowing their capitalist oppressors. This is not to say that Marx was blind to the times when religion has supported the underdog. He acknowledged that in previous historical periods, religious ideas were sometimes rallying points for protest by oppressed groups. But Marx maintained that in the capitalist era religion would not serve this role. Instead, members of the working classes would fight for their interests without relying on religion.

Marx was an atheist, and his views on religion were negative in the extreme. Most contemporary sociologists with a power perspective believe that he underestimated the degree to which religion can be involved in struggles for social justice within capitalist societies. For instance, the Reverend Martin Luther King, Jr., and the Southern Christian Leadership Conference appealed to religious ideas and concepts when they spearheaded the civil rights movement in the United States. The notion of Christian brotherhood was central to their cause, and they drew upon biblical stories (such as the Israelites' exodus from Egypt) as "templates" for understanding their own situation and organizing their own resistance (Lincoln 1984; Walzer 1985). Similarly, in several Latin American countries today, many Catholic bishops and priests see their mission as one of defending the poor against exploitive regimes, which they believe may be ready to be forced into accepting change (Hehir 1981; Gutierrez 1983).

These examples show that although religious institutions usually reflect the social structure and values of the dominant group, they may also embody a vision of what life should be like and how people should treat one another. These religious beliefs sometimes serve as an impetus for social change. Thus, the role religion plays in social class struggles depends upon how people decide to *use* religion. Christianity can just as well be a religion of the oppressed as of the oppressor. It is capable of both persuading the underclass to accept their fate, *and* of offering them a basis of resistance. In contemporary South Africa, for instance, Bishop Desmond Tutu and the Reverend Allan Boesak are leaders of religious opposition to the racist apartheid regime. They contend that Christianity considers all people equals before God, and that racial segregation is contrary to Christian ideas of justice. At the same time, however, the white rulers of South Africa have long claimed religious legitimation for apartheid. Each side in this argument believes the Bible to be divinely inspired and points to passages which it claims support its position on relations among people of different races. The political uses to which people put Christian doctrine depend upon their individual interpretations of it.

In Poland, the Solidarity movement and social unrest are motivated by economic factors, but the Catholic faith provides a source of strength and a sense of community for workers in separate industries and cities. Here, a portrait of Polish-born Pope John Paul II hangs above workers as they block a factory gate. (Alain Dejean/Sygma.)

Religion and the Individual: Structure and Action

In addition to asking what roles religion plays in society, sociologists also want to know why people adopt the religious beliefs that they do. Émile Durkheim gave one answer, which we mentioned earlier. He argued that "the idea of society is the soul of religion," meaning that religious beliefs arise from people's experiences with the society they live in. Thus religion, in Durkheim's view,

is the outgrowth of a relatively fixed social structure beyond the individual's making and control. This social structure powerfully shapes behavior, often without the individual's awareness. But action theorists caution that Durkheim's structural view can be overstated. Religion, they say, is also the product of individual activities and choices. It stems from people's efforts to creatively solve the problem of finding meaning in their lives. The process of converting to a new religion nicely illustrates these two contrasting views.

Conversion to a new religion is not a subject of central interest to sociologists with a structural perspective. When it comes to the study of religion, structuralists are more taken up with such concerns as patterns of religious organization, rises and declines in church memberships, and rates of attendance at religious services. Still, structuralists do have something to contribute to the study of religious conversion. They focus on objective factors in people's backgrounds and social contexts that encourage them to adopt a new faith.

One such study was conducted by John Lofland, who became intrigued by widespread conversions to the Unification Church of the Reverend Sun Myung Moon (Lofland and Stark 1965). Moon preached that the end of the world was approaching and that salvation in heaven could be attained by following him. Lofland wondered why people would forsake conventional lives to become full-time disciples of this self-appointed Christ. While Lofland is not an extreme structuralist, he did focus on some broadly structural forces in seeking an explanation. One such force is disruption or strain in the potential convert's life. This could be anything from marital problems to failure in college, prolonged unemployment, or a bad experience with drugs. Other studies tend to confirm the importance of this factor. For instance, in interviews of new converts to an unconventional religious sect, Richardson, Stewart, and Simmonds (1979) found that 54 percent had experienced disruptive events immediately prior to joining the group. Similarly, in a study of the members of a small fundamentalist Baptist church, James Ault (1987) found that all the married couples he interviewed in depth described their marriages prior to conversion as conflict-ridden, disordered, and meaningless.

A second broadly structural force encouraging religious conversion is the formation of social ties to one or more members of the new religion. For many of the converts Lofland studied such ties already existed through friendship or marriage. The same was true among the fundamentalists studied by Ault. All the original members of the church were related to the pastor by blood or marriage. After experiencing a born-again conversion, each worked to bring other relatives into the group.

A third factor encouraging conversion is the severing of old ties with people outside the new religion. The members of the Unification Church, for instance, have some of their greatest successes when they recruit social isolates, people who already have few or no ties to the mainstream community. This makes it easier to build strong social bonds with cult members. Isolation of believers from nonbelievers continues to be important even after conversion is complete. The new members are more likely to stay members if they become dependent on the group for the satisfaction of their emotional and social needs (Lofland and Stark 1965; Stark and Bainbridge 1980; Barker 1987).

So far in discussing social forces that encourage religious conversion we have considered forces that *currently* impinge on people, or forces that have influenced them in the very recent past. Other researchers, however, have looked at social forces in the *childhood* of converts, forces that may have shaped their earliest outlooks in ways that make them susceptible to new religions. For example, in her study of the members of the Unification Church, Eileen Barker (1984, 1987) found that converts tended to have similar childhood backgrounds. For one thing, they tended to come from homes where the parents stressed service, responsibility, and duty, the very values needed to devote oneself to a cult. The converts also tended to have parents who were quite religious, but who had often been raised in different religious traditions (one parent Catholic and the other Protestant, for example). Thus, while religion was emphasized in the home, no one set of religious beliefs and practices was presented as being the right ones. This could prompt enough of a religious open-mindedness in children to make them willing to listen to the gospel of an unconventional faith. Interestingly, too, the childhood families of converts tended to be very close-knit and protective. Perhaps this early family experience promotes a desire to find similarly close-knit social bonds in adulthood, the kind of bonds that exist in the Unification Church.

Identifying the background variables that might encourage a person to abandon the cultural mainstream and join a religious cult is one concern of sociologists who study religion from a structural perspective. This approach is in keeping with the belief that people are shaped by social forces outside themselves, forces over which they have little or no control. But this approach says nothing about the role that people play in interpreting their world and shaping their own realities. Such a focus is the domain of sociologists who take an action perspective.

Action theorists see conversion to a new religion as part of the individual's search for moral meaning in life. During the 1960s, for example, many young adults were disillusioned with the values of conventional American culture, yet disappointed with the limited success the counterculture had had in trying to bring about a fundamental change in these values. A variety of new religious movements appealed to these young people because they saw conversion to them as a way of surviving in the modern world. As sociologist Steven Tipton explains:

> For some youths the social and ideological stability of these [new religious] movements has meant psychological and even physical survival. For many more, membership in alternative religious movements has meant moral survival and a sense of meaning and purpose. . . . (Tipton 1982, p. 30)

From an action perspective, then, conversion to a new religion is not thrust upon people by outside social forces. Instead, conversion is partly a matter of people actively seeking solutions to the problem of finding meaning in their lives (Berger 1969). As such, we cannot fully understand religious conversion without looking at how particular converts interpret their own lives, how they view their relationship to conventional society, and how they experience a new sense of purpose through involvement in an alternative faith. Of course, these are matters of cultural categories as well as individual beliefs (Wuthnow 1987).

Subjective interpretations and understandings continue to be important even after religious conversion takes place. People are not just bound to a new religion by external forces, like bits of iron bound to a magnet. Instead, they also help create their own religious bonds. A good example can be seen among the members of the fundamentalist Baptist church that James Ault (1987) studied. Every day these converts created and recreated their own Christian community. This they did partly through language, especially the terms of address they used. Members typically referred to one another by kinship names ("Brother Jo," "Aunt Kate"), even when they were not actually related by blood or marriage. In this way they symbolically established close, enduring social ties. Members of the Unification Church do much the same thing when they refer to the person who introduced them to the new religion as "Mother" or "Father." They are actively helping cement the very bonds needed to maintain their own conversion (Barker 1987).

Another example of how people can actively maintain their own conversion can be seen in the way the members of the fundamentalist church in Ault's study helped to answer one another's prayers. Every week the pastor would ask the congregation for prayer requests, and members would respond by telling the group what they wanted the Lord to provide them. (Jim might need a job, Alice a little extra grocery money, Barbara some help caring for a sick child, and so forth.) In the weeks that followed, other members of the church would try to provide for these needs through acts of Christian charity and kindness. But rather than attributing this help to themselves, they would attribute it to God's intervention. ("God always works through people," they reasoned.) Thus, by essentially creating their own proof that their religious beliefs were valid, these fundamentalists strengthened their own religious commitment. Here again we see that people are not just passive recipients of religion. Instead, they are also active creators of it.

TYPES OF RELIGIOUS INSTITUTIONS

Most religious communities organize themselves into some type of institution: some set of relatively stable roles, statuses, groups, and values. Religious institutions vary greatly, however, depending on such factors as their size, doctrines, membership, origins, and relations with the rest of society. On the basis of such factors, sociologists recognize church, sect, and cult as the three major forms of religious institutions.

Churches and Sects

The sociologist Ernst Troeltsch (1931) viewed religious institutions as typically falling in the categories of either churches or sects. Table 18.1 lists some of the character-

istics of church and sect according to Troeltsch and his followers. Note that any given religious group need not conform 100 percent to one or the other list of features. These descriptions are merely *ideal types*, which serve as conceptual tools that can be used to measure reality and to make comparisons.

Troeltsch defined the **sect** as a small, exclusive, uncompromising fellowship of people seeking spiritual perfection. Members are voluntary converts, and their lives are largely controlled by the sect. Troeltsch found that sects are usually characterized by asceticism: Their members adopt austere, disciplined life styles. Most are concerned strictly with their own religious doctrines. They see themselves as select groups that have been granted special enlightenment. Often they discourage their members from extensive participation in worldly affairs because they consider the world outside the sect to be decadent, corrupt, and sinful.

As the sect grows, Troeltsch believed, it evolves into a **church,** a large, conservative, universalist religious institution. Its growth increasingly comes from those born into the group, not from conversions. A church is more tolerant than a sect of other religious groups. Because it is large, it tends to acquire a certain amount of social and political power, and more often than not it retains that power by becoming associated with the government or the ruling classes. A church thus accommodates itself to the claims of powerful groups and the dominant institutions, and it tends to support the status quo. The Church of England, the Catholic church in Spain, and the Muslim Shiites in Iran come close to fitting this model.

Although Troeltsch's descriptions offer many valuable insights about church and sect, some sociologists think that his models may lead to confusion over how to classify certain real-life religious institutions. Granted, there are both churches and sects with all the traits in Troeltsch's definitions. But there are also churches with some of the traits of sects, as well as sects with some of the traits of churches. That is why some sociologists prefer to classify religious institutions according to the single dimension of whether the institution accepts or rejects its social environment (Johnson 1962; Stark and Bainbridge 1986). At one end of this continuum is the church that is at one with its social environment; at the other end is the sect that exists in a perpetual state of tension with the larger society. Most religious groups fall somewhere in between these two extremes.

This model has the advantage of emphasizing the dynamics of an organization as it moves up or down the

TABLE 18.1   Church and Sect

Characteristic	Church	Sect
Size	Large	Small
Relationship with other religious groups	Tolerant	Rejects; feels it has sole truth
Wealth	Extensive	Limited
Religious services	Limited congregational participation; formal; intellectual emphasis	Extensive congregational participation; spontaneous; emotional emphasis
Clergy	Specialized; professional	Unspecialized; little training; part-time
Doctrines	Liberal interpretation of Scriptures; emphasis upon this world	Literal interpretation of Scriptures; emphasis upon other world
Membership	By birth or ritual participation; social institution embracing all socially compatible	By conversion; moral community excluding unworthy
Social class of members	Mainly middle class	Mainly lower class
Relationship with secular world	Endorses prevailing culture and social organization	Renounces or opposes prevailing cultural standards; requires strict adherence to biblical standards

Source: Adapted from Lifton Pope. *Millhands and Preachers: A Study of Gastonia.* New Haven, Conn.: Yale University Press, 1942.

scale of tension with its environment. For example, as a sect gains stability and respectability, it begins to coexist more harmoniously with the surrounding society, thus moving more toward the church end of the continuum. This model also highlights national variations in those institutions we call churches. The Catholic church in Ireland, for example, is more churchlike than the Catholic church in the United States because in Ireland the church is more tightly woven into the social fabric. In a similar manner we can say that some churches in the United States are more churchlike than others in this country. The Episcopal church and the Presbyterian church are more churchlike, for instance, than the Jehovah's Witnesses or the Church of the Nazarene.

Cults

Stark and Bainbridge (1985) point out that religious institutions existing in tension with their environment can have very different origins. Some are formed by breaking away from an established church. The founders often claim that they are the authentic, cleansed version of the faith from which they split. Stark and Bainbridge reserve the label *sect* for these schismatic institutions. The Puritans who broke with the Church of England and formed their own religious community are one example of a sect. Other religious institutions in tension with their environment are imported from other cultures or are formed when people create entirely new religious beliefs and practices. These institutions have no prior ties to established religious bodies in the same society. Stark and Bainbridge refer to these more innovative institutions as **cults**. In its early years Christianity was considered a cult. In fact, all the major religions of the world started as cults.

Stark and Bainbridge describe three types of cults, based on how tightly they are organized. *Audience cults* have practically no formal organization. The members are actually consumers of cult doctrines delivered over the airwaves or in books, magazines, and newspaper columns. In *client cults*, the religious leaders offer specific services to those who follow them. Although the leaders are rather well organized, the clients are not. An

These Chasidic Jews in New York City are members of a sect characterized by strict adherence to religious laws and strict observance of ritual practices. Like some Protestant Christian sects—the Amish, for example—the Chasidim choose to limit the degree of their assimilation into American culture in order to preserve their religious and cultural values. (Catherine Ursillo/Photo Researchers, Inc.)

example of a client cult is Scientology, which uses an organized network of staff to dispense cult doctrine to groups of clients. Some client cults evolve into *cult movements* as they become larger and more tightly organized. This happened with transcendental meditation and the Reverend Sun Myung Moon's Unification Church. In the process of becoming larger and better organized, cult movements often generate opposition in their social environment. Cults that permit their members to pursue normal lives and occupations typically arouse less opposition than do cults whose members abandon their normal activities and become full-time converts. Why is the larger community more hostile to cults that consume all their members' energies? Partly because these cults rupture the convert's ties to conventional institutions, including the family.

RELIGION AND MODERNIZATION

The Religious Roots of Modernization

According to Max Weber, the modernization of Western societies was partly a product of religious change effected by the Protestant Reformation. This sweeping change began in the sixteenth century when religious leaders, such as Martin Luther and John Calvin, objected to what they saw as decadence within the Christian church. Luther, for instance, was particularly opposed to the church's practice of granting indulgences. A person could obtain an indulgence by donating money to help finance some church project, such as the building of St. Peter's Cathedral in Rome. In return, the donor would obtain a promise that he would be spared some of the punishment for his or her sins that awaits a person in purgatory. To Luther this practice was a modern corruption of sacred beliefs. How, he asked, could God's grace be traded for money, like a commodity sold at market? In the name of a purer Christianity, Luther and others called for radical reforms in church doctrines. For many, this protest led to a split with the Catholic church; hence the name "Protestant" (other reformers preferred to work within the Catholic church).

Max Weber believed that some of these reforms laid the groundwork for modern capitalism by promoting new attitudes toward work and investment. He began with the observations that capitalism emerged in Christian-dominated Europe, not in Asia or Africa, and that Germany, which was largely Protestant, was more industrialized than the parts of Europe that remained largely Catholic. Weber also noticed that Protestants were more likely than Catholics to be industrial millionnaires. What could explain these patterns, he wondered. To find an answer he examined Protestant beliefs, particularly those of John Calvin (1509–1564) and his followers.

At the heart of Calvinist doctrine is the concept of predestination, the belief that a person's fate after death, whether it be salvation or damnation, is determined at birth. Eternal life, according to Calvinists, is bestowed by God's grace, not by individual merit. Thus, Calvinists could not turn to a priest for intercession with God or find promise of absolution from a church hierarchy. No human efforts, even by members of the clergy, could alter God's plan. Nor could Calvinists hope to learn of God's particular intentions for them; such information was not available to mere humans. These religious beliefs left Calvinists with a profound uncertainty about their future, coupled with a deep sense of isolation. Many responded by trying to prove they had a place among God's chosen few by achieving success in life. This meant hard work, frugality, self-denial, and astute investment for future gain—in short, a kind of worldly asceticism. The Calvinist outlook is captured in such traditional sayings as "Idle hands are the devil's workshop" and "A penny saved is a penny earned." Weber called this outlook the Protestant ethic.

The Protestant ethic, according to Weber, fostered the "spirit" of capitalism; it consisted of ideas and attitudes that encouraged the growth of privately owned businesses. This it did especially by encouraging the owners of the means of production to reinvest their profits rather than spending them all on luxuries (as many earlier aristocrats had done). Calvinists were highly motivated to make this personal sacrifice, for they saw self-denial of material pleasures as the road to business success, and success, in their minds, was tangible proof of God's favor.

Weber's theory that Protestant values laid the groundwork for capitalism and economic modernization has been much debated since he first proposed it over eighty years ago (Marshall 1982). Critics have argued, for example, that the changes Weber described were not confined to Protestants, but affected some Catholics as well. Others argue that religious changes followed capitalist development rather than preparing the way for it. Despite debate and qualifications, Weber's theory is an excellent example of the interplay between religion and the secular world. As religious beliefs were changed in an effort to purify Christianity, those beliefs set in motion forces with the potential to help alter the

economic system. Thus, Weber showed how religious reform and change in the secular spheres of society can go hand in hand.

Religious Responses to Secularization

Once capitalism and other aspects of modern society were established, the new social order started to become **secularized**: It became more concerned with worldly matters and less concerned with spiritual ones (Martin 1978). This secularization has occurred for several reasons. First, modernization has involved the creation and growth of science, which endorses reason and systematic observation as the supreme authorities in our knowledge of the world. As people have come to "believe in" science, to accept its rationalistic outlook, the capacity for faith in the supernatural may have gradually eroded. Second, modern societies are much more heterogeneous than traditional societies, not just in terms of racial and ethnic diversity, but also in terms of religious diversity. With such a large number of religious beliefs to choose from, it is hard to think of any as embodying absolute truth, and so the traditional authority of religion may be eroding further. Finally, the nature of modern life, with its complex machines and rapid pace, is not always compatible with spirituality. If the angels spoke to us all the time, explains sociologist Peter Berger (1979), the business of modern living would probably grind to a halt. A substantial degree of concern with secular matters is essential if we are to keep our modern societies running.

Some have predicted that relentless secularization would eventually spell the end of religion. Secular views and interests would become so predominant that there would be little room left for other worldly concerns. Despite this gloomy prediction, however, religious faith is not disappearing in the modern world. In fact, it remains pervasive and strong, as we noted at the beginning of this chapter. Even in highly industrialized societies, religion is still a powerful force. In one recent survey of Americans, 56 percent said that religion was "very important" in their lives, and 61 percent thought that religion could answer all or most of today's problems (Gallup Report 1985). In another survey, this one of Christians in Minnesota, 71 percent described prayer as "very important," and 88 percent looked to religion to give meaning to their existence (Chittister and Marty

1983). How could religion stay so vital when secularization is a fact of modern life?

The answer is that as secularization occurs it tends to encourage two opposing trends (Stark and Bainbridge 1985). One of these trends is **religious revival:** an effort to restore more traditional, spiritual features to established religions. The other trend is **religious innovation:** an effort to create new religions or to change existing ones to better meet people's current needs. These two trends together counteract the influence of secularization so that the importance of religion remains relatively constant. The nature of religious belief, practice, communities, and experience have all changed, however, in a process of restructuring (Wuthnow 1988).

The processes of religious revival and innovation can best be understood by looking at some examples. In the following sections we will examine the creation of the Mormon religion in the nineteenth century, the emergence of Islamic fundamentalism in Muslim nations today, and the fundamentalist Christian and Jewish revivals in the contemporary United States. When reading about these instances of religious change, notice how modernization and the growing influence of secular institutions (especially government) often help to restructure religion.

Religious Innovation: Creation of the Mormon Faith

The Church of Jesus Christ and Latter-day Saints, better known as Mormonism, was founded in 1830 by Joseph Smith, who claimed to have had a series of sacred visions. The first took place while Smith was still a teenager. Confused by the many modern Christian sects that were all competing for followers, Smith decided to ask God which faith was right. So he went alone to the woods to seek divine guidance. As he described the incident:

> ". . . immediately I was seized upon by some power which entirely overcame me, and had such astonishing influence over me as to bind my tongue so that I could not speak. Thick darkness gathered around me, and it seemed to me for a time as if I were doomed to sudden destruction. . . . just at this moment of great alarm, I saw a pillar of light exactly over my head, above the brightness of the sun, which descended gradually until it fell upon me." (Quoted in Marty 1985, p. 199)

Out of the light there appeared two persons, suspended in the sky and dazzling Smith with their brightness. One identified the other as his "beloved Son" and instructed Smith to listen to what he had to say. Smith boldly asked which of all the sects was right. He was told that all were wrong, that all in fact were corrupt and abominations.

If we take Smith's words at face value, there is no denying that something extraordinary happened in the woods that day. But what meaning should be given to this strange event? A Methodist preacher advised Smith that the event was the work of the devil, who was trying to weaken Christian faith on earth. Others may have told Smith that he had merely hallucinated, that the vision was an illusion, perhaps a sign of mental strain. But Smith interpreted the event as a visitation from God, whose purpose it was to express strong dissatisfaction with modern-day churches. Later, Smith claimed to have had a second vision, in which a messenger of God revealed to him the whereabouts of a sacred text written on golden tablets. According to his account, Smith found the tablets, translated them, and published the *Book of Mormon.* Shortly thereafter, he confirmed his two brothers and three other young men as the first followers of the Mormon faith. Thus the seeds of a new religion were sown.

What is extraordinary about the Mormon faith is not so much its beginnings as a reaction against the increasingly secularized religions of the nineteenth century. This reason for starting a new religion is quite common. What is remarkable about Mormonism is the phenomenal degree to which it has grown since its inception. While most new religions die in almost total obscurity, Mormonism has enjoyed the highest growth rate of any new faith in American history (Stark 1984). By 1840, only ten years after Smith and his five followers declared themselves the first Mormons, membership in the Mormon church had reached about 30,000. Ten years later, in 1850, there were 60,000 Mormons. This doubling of membership took place despite persecution from non-Mormons, a change in leadership following the death of Joseph Smith and a grueling migration across the plains and Rockies to start a new community in Utah. By 1950, there were over a million Mormons, and by 1980, over 4.6 million. This means a growth rate of well over 50 percent for the three intervening decades. Such an impressive growth rate was due in part to the custom of young Mormon men (and increasingly women) volunteering for several years of unpaid missionary work. In 1980 these were 30,000 young Mor-

This 19th-century lithograph depicts Joseph Smith receiving the golden tablets inscribed with the Book of Mormon. The new religion, divinely inspired or not, evidently responded to the needs of its adherents. The rapid growth of Mormonism suggests that Smith's teaching appealed, and continues to appeal, to people dissatisfied with traditional modes of Christian faith and worship. (The Granger Collection.)

mons serving as missionaries around the world, converting other young adults to the Mormon faith. By projecting into the future, we see that there could very likely be over 250 million Mormons in another century (Stark 1984).

Religious Revival: Islamic Fundamentalism

The resurgence of fundamentalist Islam is another good example of a religious response to the modern world.

Since the days of the prophet Muhammad nearly 1400 years ago, Muslims have reasserted their traditional beliefs and practices in times of serious threat from competing social forces. As a result, the Islamic faith has not undergone such widespread secularization as mainstream Christian denominations in the West (Dekmejian 1985).

A recent instance of this periodic Islamic revival occurred during the Iranian revolution. The Iranian people, faced with the problems that accompanied an influx of Western ideas and economic modernization, chose to reaffirm traditional religious authority by actively supporting the Ayatollah Ruhollah Khomeini (Brown 1980; Kedourie 1980; Lewis 1979). Had the modernizing changes brought about by secularization been highly rewarding, they might have been worth the strain of adjustment. But for thousands of Iranians these changes meant dislocation in the cities, unemployment, and a repressive secret police force. Much of the new wealth from oil went to a handful of multimillionaires. The turning point came when Iranians who had supported modernization lost faith in it. This loss of faith was particularly critical for the more than half of all Iranians who were under the age of twenty. Like young people everywhere, they were seeking ideals by which to guide their lives. No longer believing in modernization, they turned to traditional Islam (Lewis 1979a). Their Islamic faith was the one institution that stood squarely against "Western godlessness and paganism."

The mosques of the Muslim sect known as Shiism, which had a long history of blending politics and religion, provided ready-made sanctuaries for meeting and organizing outside the Shah of Iran's control. In these mosques young Iranians heard idealized accounts of the pristine Islam of old, represented by the exiled leader Ayatollah Khomeini. Here plans for a revolution began to take shape, a revolution that would restore the traditions of early Islam.

The revolution that followed was not effected without difficulty, however (Kedourie 1980). Some Iranians found it hard to turn back the clock on the new freedoms they had experienced as a result of modernization. The revolutionaries also faced opposition from other religious sects and from the westernized educated class. Thus, the revolution produced new tensions in Iranian society. Although the balance has tipped in favor of fundamentalist resurgence, the countervailing force of secularization still lies beneath the surface (Rubin 1983; Smith 1984).

Religious Revival: Fundamentalism in America

Muslim societies are far from the only ones to have had fundamentalist revivals. Around the world, secularist trends are countered with a resurgence of traditional religious beliefs and rituals. This pattern can be seen in the United States among both Christians and Jews (Wuthnow 1985, 1988).

In response to a liberalization of beliefs in many of the mainstream Protestant churches, an increasing number of Christians are turning to what they consider the fundamental values of their faith. This fundamentalist revival is taking place both in sects that have spun off from the major churches and in well-established denominations, including Methodists, Presbyterians, and Episcopalians. Participants in this revival who feel a calling to emphasize the teachings of the Scriptures and to bear witness to God's influence on earth are often called **evangelicals.** According to a recent survey, about 22 percent of adult Americans are evangelicals, and that number is rising (Gallup Report 1985).

Although evangelicals are quite a diverse group, they tend to have several traits in common (Gallup Report 1985). For one thing, they accept the absolute authority of the Bible, and many interpret very literally what the Bible says. Most describe themselves as "born-again" Christians: people who have had a significant conversion experience in which they came to accept Jesus as their Lord and Savior. Evangelicals also tend to proselytize; they try to encourage other people to believe as they do. Finally, many evangelicals adopt conservative social values, such as abstinence from alcohol and strict marital fidelity. They say that these demanding standards, coupled with a strong religious commitment, give structure and meaning to their lives in a world that otherwise seems debased and chaotic (Ault 1987).

A revival of traditional religious beliefs and practices is also under way among many American Jews. This is in marked contrast to the trend toward secularization and assimilation that was typical of Jews in the United States until the late 1960s. In the fifties and early sixties the predominant Jewish goal was to gain success and acceptance in modern American society. This involved a good deal of secularization; Jews abandoned some traditional Jewish customs and rituals that did not mesh well with mainstream American culture (Goldscheider 1986). But then a series of events occurred that encouraged a reaffirmation of Jewish identity (Cohen and Fein 1985). For one thing, by the late 1960s, many Jews had achieved considerable economic success and social acceptance, and no longer felt a need to downplay their heritage. At the same time, American society was

Hands raised in prayer a world apart—one pair in the Islamic Kingdom of Saudi Arabia, the other at Oral Roberts University in Tulsa, Oklahoma—remind us that Islam and Christianity share a common sacred tradition. But common heritage has rarely guaranteed trust, understanding, or tolerance between members of different religions or even different sects. (Left: C.J. Collins/ Photo Researchers, Inc.; right: Tom McHugh/Photo Researchers, Inc.)

more tolerant of ethnic diversity. Asserting one's ethnicity had become almost faddish. Then there was Israel's impressive victory during its six-day war with Egypt. This victory reminded Jews around the world of their long struggle for survival. Many Jews responded by reasserting their religious traditions.

This trend can be seen in synagogues throughout the country where some classic Hebrew worship practices have been revived. In some Reform congregations, for instance, the men have resumed the wearing of skullcaps and prayer shawls during services. Orthodox Judaism has found new popularity among younger Jews, as has Jewish education (Gittleson 1984; Loar 1984). Attendance at Jewish schools climbed from 60,000 in 1962 to 110,000 in 1983, despite a decline in Jewish birthrates (Sanoff 1983). We will say more about this reaffirmation of traditional Judaism when we survey mainline American churches later in this chapter.

RELIGION IN THE UNITED STATES TODAY

Unlike societies in which there is only one predominant religion, the United States is characterized by religious pluralism. This means that Americans have dozens of religious denominations to choose from. Today, about 33 percent of the population associate themselves with one of the many liberal or moderate Protestant denominations. These include the Congregationalists, the Unitarians, the Episcopalians, the Presbyterians, the Methodists, and the Lutherans, among others. Another 15 percent of the population are affiliated with conservative Protestant churches, such as the Southern Baptists, the Pentacostals, and the Assemblies of God. Black Protestant groups account for approximately 9 percent of the population, Catholics for 25 percent, and Jews for 2 percent. The remaining 16 or so percent are divided fairly evenly between those who claim some other religious faith and those who have no religious affiliation (Roof and McKinney 1985).

But statistics like these give only a static picture of religion in America today. Religious affiliation is a dynamic process, constantly undergoing change. As one denomination loses followers, another gains in strength. As one sect disappears from the social landscape, a new

one emerges and attracts adherents. One of today's major changes, suggests sociologist Robert Wuthnow (1988), is an overall decline in denominationalism. There is much less competition among Protestant denominations like Baptists and Methodists; Protestant and Catholic leaders are more cooperative. People are more likely to shop among several denominations when they look for a new church in a new community. Among those groups experiencing growth is the Catholic church. Catholic membership has risen substantially in recent years, largely due to a high birthrate among Catholics, as well as to Hispanic immigration. Evangelical Protestant groups have also expanded, often at a faster rate than the population as a whole. In contrast, the more liberal Protestant churches have experienced decline, losing converts, especially younger ones, to the evangelical groups. Similarly, the American Jewish population is not on the rise though attendance at services is up slightly. It has remained small due to a low Jewish birthrate and a high rate of intermarriage. These, of course, are simply the data on changes in church membership. They tell us nothing about any changes taking place in how the people in each religious group feel and think. For this we must look more closely at events occurring in each of the major churches in the United States today.

Trends in Mainline American Churches

Although many Americans have recently sought new avenues of religious expression, for the most part they have not abandoned traditional religion. Instead, they have sought to make the existing churches more responsive to their needs. In the 1980s this has involved both a search for stronger spiritual moorings and an increased activism among church leaders in response to social issues (Gallup Report 1985). Recent developments among American Catholics, Protestants, and Jews illustrate these trends.

Catholics

Over the past twenty years American Catholics have experienced a profound upheaval in their religious lives. In many respects, the reforms instituted by Vatican II marked a turning point for traditional Roman Catholicism in the United States. Vatican II (the Second Vatican Council, held in Rome between 1962 and 1965) eliminated the Latin mass and meatless Fridays, allowed laity to receive Communion wafers in their own hands and to take wine from the chalice, redefined non-Catholics as no longer heretics but separated brothers and sisters, and repudiated anti-Semitism. After Vatican II, the church continued to change. In the United States, a great many Catholics dissented from papal teachings on a number of issues. For instance, more than four-fifths of young-adult Catholics reject their church's teachings on birth control, divorce, and remarriage, and many also do not accept the concept of papal infallibility. Yet they remain solidly Catholic in their fundamental convictions about life, death, and God, and they say they intend to remain in the church, though on their own terms (Greeley 1982).

Other forces of change have also been at work in American Catholicism. In a few generations the descendants of Catholic immigrants have become well-educated, suburban, middle-class Americans. Success, power, and prosperity have increasingly become the lot of the nation's non-Hispanic Catholics. At the same time, there was a sharp falloff in the ranks of priests and nuns. A fifth of all Catholic priests left the ministry, and an even higher proportion of nuns withdrew from religious orders. These changes encouraged lay people to become more involved in parish affairs. Lay Catholics have taken on administrative and liturgical duties once reserved for priests, including the reading of Scripture and the distribution of Communion.

Although officially much has changed for lay Catholics since a generation ago, the role of women in the modern church is a deepening source of tension. Many Catholic women are deeply troubled by rulings from the Vatican (the papal seat in Rome) that call upon them to stay in traditional roles. Pope John Paul II has spoken out strongly against birth control, premarital sex, remarriage, optional celibacy for priests, altar girls, and women's ordination. The result has been a mounting strain between Vatican officials and senior officials in American Catholic churches who suggest different interpretations of God's laws. Nuns, who still outnumber priests by two to one, have taken the lead in the movement to change the role of women in the church. At the same time, they have assumed a wider, bolder role in American society. Thousands of nuns have served as lawyers, lobbyists, and political activists; these roles are sharply different from the teaching and nursing posts they traditionally filled before.

On other social issues, American Catholic bishops have adopted a new, much stronger role of advocating change. The welfare of the poor and concerns about peace and the nuclear arms race are moving to the forefront, overshadowing more traditional church and parish preoccupations (O'Rourke 1983). This new political advocacy first emerged in the spring of 1983 with the publication of a pastoral letter on nuclear weapons. Then, in the fall of 1984, the first draft of a pastoral letter on the U.S. economy was released. It called for efforts to eliminate poverty and unemployment, as well as a policy of increased aid to Third-World nations. Suddenly, the Catholic church seemed to be adopting the role of social conscience and liberal advocate for change that some of the mainline Protestant churches had adopted in the 1960s (Marty 1985).

Protestants

In the mid-1960s mainline Protestant denominations began experiencing a drop in membership. Between 1972 and 1982, membership in the United Methodist Church fell 10 percent; in the Episcopal Church, 15 percent; and in the United Presbyterian Church, 21 percent. During this same period, evangelical Protestant churches were attracting new members in record numbers. Membership in the Southern Baptist Convention rose 20 percent; in the Seventh-Day Adventists, 36 percent; and in the Assemblies of God, 62 percent. Although the declines in the mainline denominations now seem to have bottomed out, the losses experienced were enough to prompt a marked reaction. These denominations began acknowledging the trend toward traditionalism by placing more emphasis on worship, prayer, religious faith, and spirituality. As yet, however, the mainline churches have not rebounded. This is partly due to a low birthrate among their remaining members (Mann 1983).

The renewed stress on traditional faith and worship has also helped to spur the ecumenical movement, which fosters worldwide Christian unity and encourages the merging of Christian churches, especially Protestant ones. In the United States northern and southern Presbyterians voted to merge in 1983, and in 1987 three major Lutheran groups followed suit. The United Church of Christ and the Disciples of Christ are also discussing union. Sociologists have differing opinions on how rapidly denominationalism is declining among Protestant groups (Wuthnow 1988; Roof and McKinney 1985).

All agree, however, that the gap in understanding that separates conservative from liberal Protestant churches is particularly wide (Gallup Report 1985). This can be seen, though, as a contrary force to denominationalism, as, for example, conservative evangelical Christians create organizations and networks which link different Protestant groups and make common causes (for example, in the fight against abortion) between Protestants and Catholics.

Jews

Among Jews, the Orthodox, Conservative, and Reform temples in some respects resemble Protestant denominations (Harrison and Lazerwitz 1982). Orthodox Jews are the most traditional in their beliefs, ethnic loyalties, and religious practices; Reform Jews are the least traditional; and Conservative Jews are intermediate. One of the few issues on which all three groups are similar is in their concern for Israel and world Jewry. Indeed, even Jews who consider themselves nonreligious express deep attachment to and caring for Israel (Cohen 1983).

Many American Jews find that they want something more meaningful in their religious life than passive worship in large, frequently impersonal congregations. They have turned to *havurah*, a movement that aims to make religion more spiritually and personally meaningful (Novak 1981; Sanoff 1983). A *havurah*, a Hebrew word meaning *group*, typically consists of a number of families who meet on a regular basis. Some function as study groups, others emphasize social service activities to help the sick and needy, and still others attempt to personalize and humanize Judaism by getting families together for worship and the celebration of holidays. *Havurahs* also allow greater participation by women in religious services. (Among the three branches of Judaism, the Reform temples ordain most of the women rabbis.)

Like mainline Protestant denominations, many Jewish groups were active in the civil rights movement and other activist causes of the 1960s and 1970s. But increasingly, Jews are looking inward and focusing on religious renewal. Many young Jews are involved in efforts to revitalize religious practices in their synagogues or in campus organizations. Others have found meaning in stricter observance of dietary laws, or in more study of the Torah, Talmud, and modern Jewish scholarship. These efforts are giving American Judaism considerable new vitality.

Can religion preserve time-honored beliefs and rituals and still be responsive to a changing world? Some would say yes. A Christian couple can without embarrassment say grace before a meal in a modern restaurant; a woman can become a rabbi, as Amy Eilberg, the first female Conservative rabbi in America, has proved. (Top: Michael O'Brien/Archive Pictures, Inc.; bottom: Dana Fineman/Sygma.)

Invisible or Private Religion

Although trends in mainline churches are important, they do not tell the whole story of contemporary American religion. Many people who are critical of organized religion are in fact religious. They practice what Thomas Luckmann (1967) has called **invisible** or **private religion,** which refers to the practice of thinking about religion as a subjective, personal experience, not as group doctrine. Studies suggest that this outlook is quite widespread. For instance, in a survey of Christians in Minnesota two-thirds said that people could "reject some church teachings and continue to have a deep Christian faith" (Chittister and Marty 1983, p. 79). For many, this sort of private religion is also invisible because it resides only in the minds of those who believe in it. These people are usually not members of traditional churches. They do not proselytize, nor do they even talk about their religious beliefs except to very close relatives and friends. They tend to keep their faith, worship, and spiritual life to themselves (Hart 1987). The existence of invisible religion helps explain why, although 95 percent of Americans say they believe in God, only 42 percent or less regularly attend religious services (Harris 1987). Even at the peak of church attendance in the United States (in 1958), only 49 percent of adults went to church on a regular basis.

Some theologians are concerned about the pervasiveness of private religion because they fear it can undermine the sense of community that churches offer. Private religion, however, seems the natural product of several powerful forces. Some of these have to do with American ideology and values (Hart 1987). In a democratic society such as ours, which respects freedom of choice, it makes sense to think of religion as a matter of personal preference. Our capitalist market economy tends to reinforce this outlook. We are used to shopping around for products and buying on the basis of personal taste without having to explain our choices to others. This experience may encourage us to think of religion as a similarly personal matter. In addition, the fact that we have access to religious information (through books, magazines, radio, and TV) without having to become connected to any religious organization makes it easy for us to practice religion in whatever way we think best. For all these reasons private religion is apt to remain an important feature of American religious life.

The Electronic Church

One of the factors that facilitates private religion is the "electronic church," by which we mean the broadcasting of religious programs on radio and television. This new vehicle for religious communication fits modern life well. In a transient world, in which people often move to different communities and find it hard to switch from church to church, participation in a worship service is available with the simple turn of a TV dial. Moreover, people can tune in whenever it suits them; they do not have to mesh their busy schedule with that of a formal church group. Finally, although TV evangelism is

disengaged from any particular community, it gives people the illusion of a face-to-face relationship with the performers. In time the viewer may come to see the preacher as a friend, counselor, comforter, and model.

Evangelistic messages on radio and television have a large audience. A 1985 Neilsen poll found that 60 million Americans tune in to at least one of the evangelical programs weekly (*Economist* May 16, 1987). Who are these millions of people who turn to the airwaves for spiritual guidance and comfort? The radio programs, in particular, tend to appeal to the poor and less educated segment of society; these are people who are susceptible to "troubles" and experience a sense of helplessness in coping with them. Age and sex are other significant characteristics. Two-thirds to three-quarters of the audiences are fifty years old or over, and of these roughly two-thirds are women (Hadden and Swann 1981). For some of these people, listening to and watching evangelical programs seems to serve as a substitute for going to church (Gaddy and Pritchard 1985). This is especially true among elderly and socially isolated individuals. For other viewers, however, the evangelical programs complement and reinforce their church-related activities (Jacquet 1985).

Of course, the media preachers do not spread their messages without expecting some return. Much time is devoted to soliciting funds (Horsfield 1985). In addition to asking for donations to support the ministry, viewers are also offered merchandise for sale: calendars, books, magazines, transcripts of sermons, records, religious art, lapel buttons, necklaces, decals, and countless other items. And TV solicitations constitute only half the effort devoted to fund-raising. The other half is in the form of solicitations through computerized mail:

> Like an invisible spirit, the computer allows the prime-time preacher to come down out of the television and listen to you alone, or seem to, and to pray with you, or seem to, and to call you by name when he holds out the collection plate. . . . [The computer] is the thinking machine that plugs in names, thanks Martha or Ray for the $10 contribution, tells John that the Lord will see him through unemployment, and asks Jim one more time if he won't make a special sacrifice for the glory of God. (Hadden and Swann 1981, pp. 104, 107)

Through a combination of all these efforts, evangelical TV programs bring in millions yearly. In 1986 the Reverend Jimmy Swaggart alone took in an estimated $142 million (*Economist* May 16, 1987).

In the mid-1980s, however, the electronic church came under something of a cloud. One of its preachers, the Reverend Jim Bakker, was found to be paying blackmail to a woman with whom he had had a brief affair several years earlier. Bakker was forced to resign from his ministry, which was then discovered to be about $50 million in debt (*Economist* May 16, 1987). Some Americans began to wonder about the integrity of TV evangelists. In one Harris poll at the time, 41 percent of those who watched religious television programs thought that the preachers may do more harm than good, and 54 percent believed that TV evangelists are primarily in the business of raising money. Disillusionment deepened when it was discovered that the Reverend Jimmy Swaggart was also guilty of sexual indiscretions. Thus, the electronic church set to work to restore its somewhat tarnished reputation. For the foreseeable future, however, it will remain a significant part of religion in the United States.

Preachers, like politicians, have discovered how to reach us directly—and profitably—in our living rooms. And sometimes preachers are politicians. (Jeff Jacobson/Archive Pictures, Inc.)

The New Christian Right

In the 1980s, also, fundamentalist Christians abandoned their former aloofness from American politics and became active advocates of conservative policies. The New Christian Right, as the movement has been dubbed by the media, emerged in the context of a broader conservative movement that culminated in the 1980 election of Ronald Reagan. Many forces contributed to the politicization of fundamentalists (Wuthnow 1983, 1988). The presidency of born-again Christian Jimmy Carter increased the public's recognition of evangelicals and gave them more legitimacy. In addition, the Watergate scandal and the Supreme Court's ruling on abortion removed some of the symbolic boundaries between morality and politics. Suddenly, important political issues seemed intertwined with moral questions. Three major organizations arose to facilitate fundamentalist political action. The first, Christian Voice, resulted from the 1979 merger of several antigay, antipornography, and profamily groups on the West Coast. The second, Moral Majority, was founded by the Reverend Jerry Falwell in July 1979; its strength is centered in the South and Southwest. The third, Religious Roundtable, was set up to attract conservative clergy who were not comfortable with either Christian Voice or Moral Majority (Guth 1983).

The New Christian Right does not speak with one voice on current issues. Nonetheless, three ideological themes have pervaded the movement: economic libertarianism, social traditionalism, and militant anticommunism (Himmelstein 1983). The New Right blames economic problems such as inflation, unemployment, high taxes, and high interest rates on government interference. It opposes abortion, school busing, the Equal Rights Amendment, sexual permissiveness, drugs, prohibitions on school prayer, pornography, and gay rights. It also portrays the United States as being engaged in a life-or-death struggle with the Soviet Union and world communism. Organizationally, the New Christian Right has extensive networking, up-to-date methods of computerized fund-raising, targeted lobbying, and mass media publicity. This has helped to make it an important political force of the 1980s (Yinger and Cutler 1984).

While many Americans oppose abortion and gay rights and favor school prayer and traditional roles for women, national polls have shown only limited support for Moral Majority (Shupe and Stacey 1983, 1984). Even conservative and predominantly southern groups like the Southern Baptists are divided in their stance toward Moral Majority. Support comes primarily from ministers at the margins of the Southern Baptist Convention, those with rural backgrounds, modest educations, and the least involvement in the convention (Guth 1983). Survey data further show that support for Moral Majority is strongest among devalued groups seeking to enhance their status within American life (Simpson 1983). Feeling threatened by changing life styles and the mounting secularization of American society, they turn to political action to increase their power and prestige.

The New Christian Right is a social movement, and social movements come and go. Groups and movements that were the center of public attention in the 1970s, such as the Black Panther Party, the Weather Underground, and the Symbionese Liberation Army,

are now virtually forgotten. In the early 1980s, the American Catholic church, with its relatively liberal pastoral letters, spoke out to challenge the conservatism of fundamentalists. How much popular support the Catholic bishops will muster remains to be seen. But regardless of the outcome, they illustrate the dynamic nature of social movements. As one movement rises, countermovements often emerge that can help to change the tenor of thought in a society.

SUMMARY

1. Durkheim defined religion as a set of beliefs and practices pertaining to sacred things that unite people into a moral community. This definition is very broad, capable of being applied to nonreligious philosophies as well as to religions. An alternative approach defines religion as the work of organizations primarily engaged in providing people with the hope of future rewards to compensate for things they greatly desire but have not obtained in life. This hope is based on beliefs in supernatural forces, beings, or places.

2. Regardless of how the general concept of religion is defined, particular religions have certain elements in common. These include religious beliefs, symbols, and practices, as well as a community of followers and a variety of religious experiences.

3. Functional and power perspectives help explain why religion is so widespread. From a functional perspective, religion serves a number of important purposes for societies and individuals. These include promoting social solidarity (through norms that reduce conflict and sanctions against antisocial acts), consecrating major life events, helping immigrants to adapt to a new society, and legitimizing the established social order by sanctioning its social arrangements. However, sociologists with a power perspective see things differently. They say that religion may indeed perform certain functions, but those functions serve the interests of elites, not of society as a whole. For instance, Karl Marx argued that in legitimizing the power of the ruling class, religion pacifies the oppressed workers, lulling them into accepting an exploitive economic system. But, from observation, it can be said that religion is capable of both persuading the deprived and oppressed to accept their fate, and of offering them a basis of resistance. The

political uses to which people put religion depends upon their individual interpretations of it.

4. Structural and action perspectives can help explain why people adopt the religious beliefs that they do. From a structural perspective, commitment to a certain religion is shaped by powerful social forces beyond the individual's making and control. From an action perspective, religious commitment is also the product of people's subjective understandings and individual choices.

5. Sociologists distinguish among three types of religious institutions: church, sect, and cult. A church is a large, conservative religious institution that tends to coexist harmoniously with the larger society. A sect, in contrast, is a small, uncompromising fellowship of people who seek spiritual perfection and tend to reject the larger society. Sects form when people break away from established churches and claim to have adopted a more authentic, purer version of their faith. A cult is like a sect in most respects except its origins. Cults are imported from other cultures or are formed when people create entirely new religious beliefs and practices.

6. Max Weber believed that the rise of modern capitalism had important roots in certain religious ideas of the Protestant Reformation. In particular, the Calvinist concept of predestination encouraged hard work, frugality, and astute investment in order to be successful in life and thus provide proof of God's favor. Weber's theory is a good example of how religious change can promote change in other aspects of society.

7. Modernization has generally been accompanied by secularization, which entails a greater concern with worldly matters than with spiritual ones. But secularization has not spelled the end of religion. Religion remains

a powerful force because of two countervailing trends: religious revival (an effort to restore more traditional, spiritual features to established religions) and religious innovation (an effort to create new religions or to change existing ones to better meet people's needs). The Mormon faith, founded in the United States in 1830, is an example of religious innovation; Islamic fundamentalism in Iran and fundamentalism among Christians and Jews in the United States are examples of contemporary religious revival.

8. Religion in America today is undergoing many changes. The mainline churches are trying to become more responsive to people's needs. This has involved both a greater emphasis on spirituality and an increased activism in regard to certain major social issues. Another change is the growth of invisible, or private religion. These terms refer to the view, held by many, that religion is a subjective, personal experience, not a matter of group doctrine. Private religion is facilitated by the "electronic church," a descriptive term for the broadcasting of religious programs on radio and TV. These programs, which are largely fundamentalist Christian, have huge audiences and raise large sums of money. In the last decade, fundamentalist Christians have abandoned their former aloofness from American politics and become active advocates of ultraconservative policies. The American Catholic church, however, has recently challenged this trend in its pastoral letters on social issues.

GLOSSARY

Animism. The idea that things in the world are imbued with active, animate spirits.

Church. A large, conservative, universalist religious institution that makes few demands on its members and accommodates itself to the larger society (Troeltsch).

Civil religion. Bellah's term for a sanctifying of the nation by associating its history, values, and institutions with God's special favor.

Cult. A religious group that tends to exist in a state of tension with the surrounding culture and that has no prior ties to any established religious body in the larger society (Stark and Bainbridge).

Evangelicals. Christians who feel a calling to emphasize the teachings of the Scriptures and to bear witness to God's influence on earth.

Invisible or private religion. Terms that reflect the view that religion is a subjective, personal experience, and not a matter of group doctrine.

Moral community. A group of people who share religious beliefs, symbols, and practices that bind them together into a social whole.

Profane. That which is mundane and ordinary (Durkheim).

Religion. A set of beliefs and practices pertaining to sacred things that unite people into a moral community (Durkheim). Organizations primarily engaged in providing people with the hope of future rewards to compensate for things they greatly desire but have not obtained in life; this hope is based on a set of beliefs in supernatural forces, beings, or places (Stark and Bainbridge).

Religious innovation. An effort to create new religions or to change existing ones to better meet people's needs.

Religious revival. An effort to restore more traditional, spiritual features to established religions.

Ritual. A standardized set of actions used in a particular ceremony or on some other specific occasion.

Sacred. That which is set apart from everyday experience and inspires awe and reverence (Durkheim).

Sect. A small, exclusive, uncompromising fellowship that makes heavy demands on its members and sets them apart from the larger society (Troeltsch). A religious group formed by breaking away from an established religious body (Stark and Bainbridge).

Secularization. The process by which people and their social institutions become more concerned with worldly matters and less concerned with spiritual ones. Secularization is often associated with modernization.

Theism. The idea that powerful supernatural beings are involved with events and conditions on earth.

Totem. An object, plant, or animal that is worshiped as the mystical ancestor of a society or other social group.

CHAPTER 19
Health Care and Medicine

One February morning in an East Coast city, a twenty-six-year-old Hispanic woman brought her twenty-month-old daughter to a public health-care clinic. According to the mother, the child had falling spells, sometimes vomited, complained of pains in her head, and had "sandy" diarrhea. The fourth-year medical student on duty, alert to the possible meaning of the last symptom, asked the mother, "Does your daughter ever eat paint chips or plaster?" "Oh, yes," the mother replied, "she eats the walls all the time. I can't stop her; she eats them right down to the wood."

After being given a series of tests, the child was diagnosed as having severe lead poisoning and anemia. The paint chips she had eaten had introduced a dangerous level of toxic lead into her body. Although the mother had found her daughter's chewing on plaster an annoyance, she had not considered this to be health-threatening behavior. After all, other children in her neighborhood of deteriorating houses had done the same and seemed all right. Besides, young children seemed to find paint chips and plaster pleasant and sweet-tasting to eat (Light, Phipps, and Sorbello 1982).

As this example indicates, the biochemistry of disease is intertwined with the social, economic, and cultural context of the individual. The child's lead poisoning, which resulted from her eating paint chips and plaster, relates directly to her environment. She lived with her family in rental housing that was built before 1940, when lead-based paint was commonly used as a wall treatment. The landlord who owned the inner-city slum building had allowed it to deteriorate, and the peeling paint could easily be picked from the walls and ingested by a curious toddler. Lead accumulates in the body, where it can attack and damage the central nervous system.

It was a comparatively straightforward matter to admit the child to the hospital and treat her for lead poisoning. But medical treatment alone will not guarantee an end to her health problems. Unless the landlord repairs the walls of the apartment and the mother is instructed about the dangers of eating paint and other nonfood substances, the child will still be in danger of being poisoned.

Disease is a medically diagnosed pathology, and sociologists distinguish it from **illness** (the sense that one feels unwell) and **sickness** (society's acceptance that one is not well, as in an allotted number of "sick days"). Of course, these fine distinctions often overlap. In the case cited above, the girl felt *ill*, was diagnosed as having the *disease* of lead poisoning, and was treated as a *sick* person in a hospital. At times, however, a person may have a disease and not yet feel ill, as in the early stages of cancer or tuberculosis, or feel ill with a headache or upset stomach and yet have no apparent disease. Whatever label we apply to a person's state of health, both the state of health itself and the label are always affected by social factors, among them age, sex, ethnicity, social class, and subculture. Old people and poor people in general are more often sick, for example; blacks have higher rates of hypertension than whites; the Japanese, who eat a low-fat diet, have lower rates of heart disease.

In this chapter we will consider the major patterns of illness and disease and some of the sociological factors that influence them. We will examine the sociological

Living in a culture that equates health care with medical technology, we are apt to recognize only one of these scenes as health-related. In fact, social services like this free meal program are as vital to our health-care system as the most sophisticated intensive care unit. Health is a social issue of which medicine is merely one facet. (Left: Danuta Otfinowski/Archive Pictures Inc.; right: Jan Halaska/Photo Researchers, Inc.)

dimensions of some current health problems, such as hunger, smoking, and AIDS. Finally, we will take a brief look at the American health-care system and the problems it is now facing.

SOCIAL PATTERNS OF DISEASE AND ILLNESS

The leading causes of death in 1900 were pneumonia, influenza, and tuberculosis. Today, these acute diseases rarely cause death; instead, most people die of chronic diseases such as heart and blood-vessel disorders or cancer (see Figure 19.1). Why the change? Antibiotics and similar drugs that can cure infectious diseases did not exist in 1900. Also, standards of living and public health have improved: more people today eat a healthier diet, drink comparatively clean water and milk, and live in environments relatively free of insects, rats, and other vectors of disease. People in generally good health can often fight off acute infections.

Today's diseases reflect certain changes in American society. Because most acute illnesses are no longer life threatening, the majority of people in this country now live long enough to develop what have been called "diseases of civilization." A sedentary life style and a diet high in fats and salt have been linked to the development of heart and vascular disease. Dietary patterns and long exposure to low-level carcinogens (cancer-causing substances) have been linked to certain malignancies. Prosperity and the good life have their medical consequences. In this section, we examine disease and illness as they vary by sex, race, ethnicity, and socioeconomic status.

Differences by Sex and Race

Although some evidence exists that women experience more minor illness than men (Gove and Hughes 1979), women outlive men by an average of more than seven years. No one knows why this is so, but sociologists and others have proposed explanations that take into account differences in life style, diet, activity level, and social circumstances between men and women. Some point to the fact that more men smoke cigarettes, engage in risky behavior (drinking too much, participating in dangerous sports, driving too fast), and until recently men experienced more of the stresses and strains of the workplace and of the breadwinner role. Other analysts maintain that certain genetic factors make women, in a sense,

This figure shows the 11 leading causes of death in 1900 (based on data from states that had death registration) and in 1983, with the latter arranged in descending order of importance. Notice how death from infectious diseases declined, making way for the diseases of old age. Sociologists and physicians have shown that medicine played only a modest role in this historic shift, and its role in postponing death today also seems modest.

FIGURE 19.1 Leading Causes of Death in the United States, 1900 and 1983

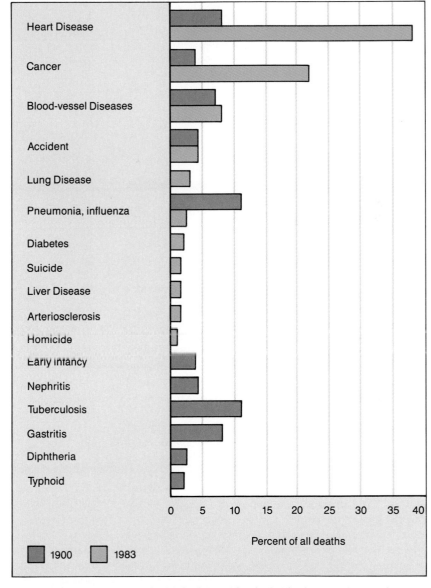

Source: Avedis Donabedian et al., *Medical Care Chartbook,* 8th ed. Ann Arbor, Mich: Health Administration Press, 1986.

physiologically or medically superior to men. Female hormones, for example, seem to play a role in protecting premenopausal women from heart disease, and women seem less prone to high blood pressure than men.

Black people and Hispanics have higher mortality rates than whites. The cancer rate among black men is nearly one and one-half times what it is among white men, and more than double what it is among white women. And black men have twice as many strokes as white men. Blacks and Hispanics are also far more likely to report themselves in "fair" or "poor" health, as opposed to "excellent" or "good" (U.S. Department of Health and Human Services 1986). These racial and ethnic differences point to the role of social factors, such as poverty, in illness. Blacks and Hispanics are on average poorer than whites, and lack of material resources is linked to ill health throughout the world.

Poverty and Health

Poverty means inadequate nourishment, unsanitary, poorly heated housing; fewer trips to the doctor to treat minor illnesses before they become major ones; and more exposure to stress and violence. The frustrations of poverty may, in turn, foster self-destructive behavior such as alcoholism, smoking, drug abuse, and other forms of risk taking that weaken the body's immune system and leave a person more likely to get sick when confronted with an infectious agent.

Although Americans spend more on health care than any other nation in the world, statistically we are not the world's healthiest nation. Our overall infant mortality rate has continued to fall, but it is edging upward again in some areas, particularly in states where reductions in government aid have forced cutbacks in prenatal, maternal, and preventive health services. In cities such as Washington, D.C., with a substantial underclass of poor and disadvantaged families, the infant mortality rates can be higher than in such nations as Jamaica, Cuba, and Costa Rica.

Unfortunately for the poor, poverty and illness often go hand in hand. The poorer you are, the sicker you are likely to become. And the sicker you are, the poorer you are likely to become. Moreover, the poor not only get the diseases of poverty, such as infections and diet-deficiency diseases; they also suffer more from the so-called diseases of affluence—cancer and heart disease. Why? Because their diet is more fatty and they are exposed to more pollutants. And above all, their life is frequently more stressful.

The connection between poverty and poor health is a worldwide phenomenon. Among the countries of the world, there is a strong correlation between a nation's per capita gross national product and such indices of

This impoverished family in rural Maine shows the physical effects of inadequate diets and inferior health care. (Arthur Grace/Stock, Boston.)

health as its infant mortality and life expectancy. In the more developed nations the infant mortality rate is under 20 per 1,000 infants; in the poorest regions it ranges up to half of all infants (most of these deaths are traceable to malnutrition and diarrheal and infectious disorders). Similarly, life expectancy at birth is about seventy-two years in developed countries, but it is only forty-nine in Africa and fifty-one in southern Asia (Mahler 1980).

The pattern of disease in underdeveloped nations differs appreciably from that in developed nations. Infectious, parasitic, and respiratory diseases cause more than 40 percent of the deaths in developing nations. By comparison, they cause about 10 percent of deaths in industrialized countries, where the chief causes of death are heart and vascular diseases and cancer. The most widespread diseases in poorer regions are diarrheal ones transmitted by human fecal contamination of food, water, and soil; only about a third of the people in underdeveloped nations have access to safe water. Parasitic diseases such as malaria and schistosomiasis also tend to be widespread, infecting a quarter of the world's population. Malaria, which is transmitted by mosquitoes, is the most prevalent disease worldwide—around 100 million cases every year—despite the fact that it can be prevented by the routine administration of inexpensive drugs (World Malaria Situation 1987). Schistosomiasis—caused by a snail-borne parasite—infects some 200 million people. Both malaria and schistosomiasis are chronic and debilitating diseases that sap the energy and strength of their victims.

Many underdeveloped countries spend a major portion of their health budgets on establishing medical schools and building hospital complexes. Yet this approach addresses the health problems of only 10 to 15 percent of the population, chiefly members of elites. The resources are used mainly to cure disease with increasingly expensive technology (intensive care units, bypass surgery, "life-support" systems, and whole-body scanners). However, the health needs of the population at large would be better served by an attack on parasitic and infectious agents, programs of preventive medicine, more and better food, and the elimination of contaminated drinking water. Malnutrition and parasitic and infectious diseases continue to be the principal sources of suffering, disability, and death in the poorer nations. Inasmuch as the incidence of most of these conditions can be dramatically reduced at relatively modest cost, the problems they cause are largely preventable.

Currently, four-fifths of the world's population does not have access to *any* permanent form of health care. The public health services of the sixty-seven poorest nations, excluding China, spend less on health care than the richer nations spend on tranquilizers alone. Moreover, richer nations (chiefly, Australia, Canada, West Germany, the United Kingdom, and the United States) are attracting physicians from the poorer ones. Although it costs eight times more to train a physician than to train a medical auxiliary, many poorer countries still continue to emphasize training physicians. If the goal of good health is to be achieved for the great masses of the world's population, existing health-care strategies will have to be vigorously transformed (Mahler 1980, 1981).

Unemployment and Health

Given the relationship between poverty and illness, it is hardly surprising that unemployment should also exert a detrimental effect on health. For many of the approximately 500 million people worldwide who have lost (or who have never had) a job, unemployment means having to do without many of life's necessities. In poor countries, medical care may not be easily accessible even for working people; for those with no income, it is simply unavailable. Moreover, many countries have no "safety net," such as transfer payments or disability benefits, for people who lose their jobs, and unemployment quickly reduces individuals and entire families to destitution. When these countries go into economic decline and unemployment rates rise sharply, as happened in the Latin American nations in the wake of the debt crisis in the mid-1980s, the impact on national health can be enormous (Musgrove 1987).

The effects of unemployment on health extend beyond the suspension or reduction of income. Even in the United States, where workers' compensation and other programs offer some assistance and where many families have two wage earners, researchers have discovered that the experience of unemployment itself can undermine health. One study (Brenner 1987) stirred controversy by showing that the death rate for heart disease increases when unemployment rises. Unemployment has also been linked to anxiety, depression, and abuse of alcohol and tranquilizers (Kessler et al. 1987). These effects still exist when pre-existing illness that may have contributed to job loss are statistically eliminated. Apparently, unemployment statistics can serve as health indicators as well as economic indicators—and reductions in unemployment may yield improvements in health.

SOCIOLOGICAL DIMENSIONS OF SPECIAL HEALTH PROBLEMS

The perception and experience of health and illness vary among social groups. This point can be illustrated by analyzing the physical and social effects of hunger, smoking, and AIDS—three health problems that exact a frightful toll in terms of human suffering and costs to society.

Hunger in the 1980s threatened the health not only of the chronically poor but also of working-class families caught between job lay offs, cutbacks in social programs, and the high cost of living. Here, unemployed steelworkers line up at a food bank in Braddock, Pennsylvania. (UPI/Bettmann Newsphotos.)

Hunger

To most Americans, hunger means a slight feeling of discomfort brought on by dieting or skipping a meal. But to as many as 20 million people in this country (Brown 1987) hunger means chronic misery and impaired health.

In the 1960s, when hunger in America first came to public attention as a social problem, several government programs were instituted to make sure that food was available to the poor. Among these were food stamps, school lunch and breakfast programs, and a Women, Infants, and Children (WIC) program to provide free food to pregnant women, babies, and young children. By the mid-1970s, these programs had made considerable headway in assuring that most Americans had enough to eat (Brown 1987). Beginning in 1981, however, the federal government started to withdraw funds for social programs, forcing several public agencies to close their doors and putting a strain on private efforts to feed the poor. Within five years, churches and social-service agencies were once again being overwhelmed by starving people, who flocked to soup kitchens and food pantries that had been set up in urban centers and in areas of high unemployment. Many of these food-distributing centers reported that they were feeding entire families, not just

the "down and out" men and women who had lined up for free food in the past.

This increase in hunger can also be traced to a surge in unemployment in 1982–1984 and to a tightening of eligibility requirements for virtually every federal assistance program in the early 1980s. What this meant was many of those who lost their jobs were deemed ineligible for unemployment benefits, food stamps, or Medicaid, and their children were unable to qualify for free or subsidized meals at school. During the same period, inflation (especially in the cost of housing) meant that a family hit by unemployment had to stretch its reduced income even further. The result, predictably, was a sharp rise in the numbers of people seeking food from charitable organizations—as well as an increase in the infant mortality rate in eleven states and several urban areas (Brown 1987). Inadequate diets are partly to blame for the latter phenomenon, as poorly nourished mothers give birth to smaller, frailer babies.

Smoking

The Surgeon General of the United States declared in 1982 that cigarette smoking is "the chief, single, avoidable cause of death in our society and the most important public health issue of our time" (Davis 1987). Despite this dramatic statement, and many other warnings that "smoking may be hazardous to your health," millions of Americans continue to smoke and every year substantial numbers of young people adopt the habit. The health consequences are serious indeed: the U.S. Public Health Service estimates that smoking kills 350,000 Americans per year and accounts for about one-sixth of this country's death toll (Davis 1987). Health-care costs for smoking-related diseases, such as lung cancer, emphysema, and heart disease, are massive.

Why do so many people smoke? Part of the answer is found in the fact that cigarettes are America's most heavily advertised consumer product. In 1984, tobacco companies spent $2.1 *billion* on cigarette advertising and promotion. The industry, well aware that antismoking agitation is encouraging many people to kick the habit, has aimed its advertising campaigns at those groups within the population who smoke most or who have shown less inclination to quit smoking: women, blue-collar workers, blacks and Hispanics, and members of the military. For example, cigarettes are heavily advertised in publications that are read primarily by women (*Family Circle*), male laborers (*Popular Mechanics*), blacks (*Ebony*), and service men and women (*Army Times*). Brands with Hispanic-sounding names (Dorado) have been introduced, and billboard ads in Spanish are common in Hispanic neighborhoods. Although the tobacco companies deny slanting their advertising to children and teenagers, they do advertise frequently in magazines with millions of young readers (*TV Guide*, *Sports Illustrated*, *Glamour*, *Cosmopolitan*), and ads often feature attractive young models in poses that suggest that smokers are independent, fun-loving, and sexy.

Tobacco companies also promote cigarettes in less direct ways. Many companies sponsor sporting events (such as the Virginia Slims tennis competition), in part because of the association of sports with health. Sponsoring sports tournaments also permits the companies' products to be mentioned on television and radio, which would otherwise be prohibited by law.

Perhaps more significantly, tobacco companies' massive advertising budgets give them what comes close to veto power over the editorial content of magazines that accept cigarette ads. Any magazine that runs articles on the health risks of smoking, or even gives prominent play to antismoking crusades, is likely to find itself minus millions of dollars of advertising. The result is that "the media's dependence on revenue from cigarette advertising has repeatedly led to suppression of discussion of smoking and health matters" (Warner 1985, p. 385). In 1976, fifteen years after the U.S. Public Health Service issued a report linking smoking to cancer and other diseases, a cover story in *Newsweek* on "What Causes Cancer" failed to mention cigarettes. When a magazine does carry an antismoking article, such as a 1983 issue of *Newsweek* that had a piece on the nonsmokers' rights movement, the tobacco companies pull out all their ads for that issue. (The cigarette companies are usually informed in advance when an "anti" story is to appear.) Angering the tobacco companies can be costly indeed: when the advertising firm Saatchi & Saatchi created an ad for Northwest Airlines in 1988, highlighting the airline's new no-smoking policy, the R. J. Reynolds tobacco company withdrew its entire multimillion-dollar advertising account from the firm. The financial resources at the disposal of the tobacco companies give them considerable power.

Against the tobacco companies stand various "antismoking" forces. These include the Surgeon General, the Public Health Service, medical journals such as the influential *New England Journal of Medicine*, and citizens' groups such as Action on Smoking and Health (ASH). Although antismoking agitation may seem a comparatively recent phenomenon, it is not. Smoking has been attacked since at least 1604, when England's King James I issued a tract against tobacco and imposed high import duties on it (Troyer and Markle 1983). In this country, anticigarette campaigns succeeded in the nineteenth century in banning cigarette sales to minors and, by 1909, in prohibiting cigarette sales altogether in fifteen states. A reaction of sorts seems to have set in around the time of World War I; new efforts to pass anticigarette laws failed, and citizens' groups began to send cigarettes to the troops as an aid to the war effort. (General John J. Pershing was even quoted as saying that tobacco was as necessary to win the war as bullets.) Still, anticigarette forces did not give up; tobacco was viewed by many of the reformers who urged the prohibition of alcohol as almost as great an evil. But it was not until evidence began to accumulate on the health risks of smoking—in the late 1950s—that the modern antismoking movement began.

The antismoking crusade can be seen as a movement to delegitimize smoking: to undermine the tobacco companies' message that smoking is a harmless personal pleasure—something people choose of their own free will and engage in out of the enjoyment it gives. This is the basic content of cigarette ads: smoking is something independent, virile, healthy-looking young adults do for fun. Antismoking forces, on the other hand, maintain that smokers (1) take up cigarettes in their youth as a response to peer pressure and advertising, (2) continue to smoke because the nicotine in tobacco is an addictive drug, and (3) are at much greater risk than nonsmokers of developing a number of life-threatening diseases. These competing definitions of smoking—as a pleasant pastime or as a health-destroying addiction so serious as to constitute our major public-health problem—are at the heart of the battle over cigarettes.

Some evidence suggests that the antismoking campaign is succeeding in changing people's ideas about smoking—if not their behavior. For example, more than 90 percent of the public now accepts the claim that smoking is harmful to health (Troyer and Markle 1983). Even though knowledge of smoking's ill effects is usually shallow (Warner 1985), health-related concerns have probably inspired most of those who have managed to give up cigarettes. Decreases in smoking in recent years have been marked: per capita consumption of cigarettes has declined every year since 1973 (Warner 1985). Of course, tobacco companies have fought back, spending more for advertising and attempting to overcome tobacco's unhealthy image (promoting low-tar and "light" brands; using slogans such as "Alive with pleasure").

But as evidence has accumulated on smoking's dangers even to nonsmokers who must breathe the smoke of others, antismoking ordinances of all kinds have taken effect. For example, the Federal Aviation Administration (FAA) no longer permits smoking on shorter airplane flights, and in a number of cities smoking has been banned in certain public buildings. Again, the tobacco companies have responded, in this case by promoting the idea of "smokers' rights" and challenging the government's authority to ban smoking. Given the millions of people who still smoke and the increasing efforts of the antismoking forces, it seems likely that this conflict will continue for some time. In this case, issues of health and disease are played out in the domains of political and economic power.

Women and Smoking

With the breakdown of social and cultural strictures that once discouraged women from smoking, females have become a primary target of cigarette promotion. Women's smoking habits are worth considering as an example of how smoking can be made to appeal to people and what meaning it can fill in their lives.

In their efforts to appeal to women, tobacco companies have tried to associate smoking with "womanly" qualities, such as femininity, sophistication, sexiness, and fashionableness. They have introduced brands designed to appeal to women—Virginia Slims, Eve, Satin, and Ritz (the last, which bears the logo of Yves Saint Laurent, has been advertised as the first "designer" cigarette). Models in cigarette advertising are beautiful, dressed in the height of fashion, and often pictured in affectionate or provocative poses with men. Another theme in cigarette advertising is thinness. This is apparent even in the cigarettes' names: slims, thins, and lights. ("Keep thin and light" is one brand's slogan.) Cigarette ads are prominent in *Weight Watchers* magazine as well as in fashion and home-oriented periodicals.

Since many women smokers believe that smoking helps curb their appetite—and that stopping smoking will cause them to gain weight—this is a powerful appeal. It may be one reason why smoking has declined significantly more slowly among women than among men in recent years (Davis 1987).

A recent study identified several patterns of smoking among low-income women and offered some reasons why women choose to smoke. Besides noting that smoking was more common among lower-income groups, who are perhaps less well-informed about the health risks involved, the study found that smoking was closely tied to the idea of relaxation, often as part of a coffee break or a few moments of peace and quiet snatched in a day devoted to the care of other members of the family. As one smoker noted, "I think it gives me a break. Having a cigarette is an excuse to stop for five minutes" (Graham 1987, p. 52). The women in the study looked to smoking as their one bit of self-indulgence in budgets that didn't allow for new clothes, makeup, restaurant meals, or other treats. One woman told the researcher, "I try to cut down on cigarettes to save money but cigarettes are my one luxury and at the moment they feel a bit like a necessity" (Graham 1987, p. 55).

Sadly, women's smoking has unfortunate effects that extend beyond the health of the smoker herself. It has long been known that smoking hurts unborn babies; children of smoking mothers are more likely to be premature, of low birth weight, and have other health problems (Graham 1987). "Passive" smoking (breathing the smoke of others) has been linked to a number of respiratory conditions in children, such as asthma, bronchitis, and pneumonia, as well as problems such as stomachaches, ear discharges, and behavioral disorders. In addition, the mother who smokes communicates a powerful message to her children that smoking is acceptable (even enjoyable) adult behavior. Since children of smokers are more likely to become smokers themselves (Graham 1987), maternal smoking helps perpetuate the cigarette habit.

AIDS

Acquired immune deficiency syndrome, commonly known as AIDS, was first identified in the United States in 1981. It has since been declared the nation's "number one health priority" by the Department of Health and Human Services. The condition is caused by a virus that attacks the immune system, rendering it powerless to protect the body from so-called "opportunistic" diseases and infections, such as pneumonia and certain types of cancer. Most researchers believe that the AIDS virus is spread from person to person through sexual activity or exchange of body fluids, or transmitted from an infected mother to her unborn infant. AIDS has spread rapidly among intravenous drug abusers, who pass the virus to one another by sharing infected hypodermic needles.

When the AIDS virus first enters the body, it may remain inactive for months or even years, during which time the infected person may not feel ill, but is capable of transmitting the virus to others. No one knows how the AIDS virus is activated, but once this happens the opportunistic infections begin to take hold, and death usually occurs within two years.

Although most of the first known AIDS victims in this country (about 70 percent) were homosexual men, leading to the stigmatization of AIDS as a "gay disease," there is evidence that the illness is now more prevalent among intravenous drug users, who in turn have transmitted it to heterosexual sex partners and to unborn children. Current estimates of the number of persons infected with the AIDS virus vary from 1 to 2 million; of this number, an estimated 30 percent or more will eventually develop the disease itself (Berk 1987). Since AIDS is a new disease, full of medical and social complexities, no one yet knows exactly how many people—even among those who can be shown to be infected with the AIDS virus—will eventually get sick. But so far, of those who have developed AIDS, no one is known to have recovered.

The AIDS epidemic is a clear illustration of the effects of society on disease and of disease on society. In the United States and other industrialized countries, the spread of the disease has followed particular demographic patterns. In addition, the socially marginal status of most AIDS victims thus far—homosexual men, intravenous drug users and their sex partners, impoverished Haitian immigrants—has given the disease a stigmatizing image. Often AIDS victims, even "innocent" victims such as young hemophiliacs who contracted the virus through the blood products they use to help their blood clot normally, have been treated like pariahs. One family's house was burned to the ground after townspeople learned that three children in the family, all hemophiliacs, were infected with the AIDS virus. This action

is in sharp contrast to the sympathetic social attitudes toward most serious or terminal diseases. Think of fund-raising telethons for muscular dystrophy and door-to-door campaigns for the American Cancer Society. Public attitudes about AIDS range from exaggerated fears (dentists wearing rubber gloves to examine every patient) to outright moral condemnation (religious and political leaders suggesting that AIDS is a punishment for wicked or unnatural behavior).

Just as doctors and other clinicians are still grappling with the medical consequences of AIDS, sociologists are only beginning to understand how AIDS is changing our social landscape. Even at this early point in what many experts fear will be a long epidemic, some AIDS-related social patterns have begun to emerge. The first is a change in sexual behavior and attitudes about sex. Since the AIDS virus is found in the bodily fluids of an infected person, public health officials such as the Surgeon General of the United States, C. Everett Koop, have stressed curbing sexual promiscuity as a way of reducing the risk of getting AIDS. In 1988, a brochure sent by Dr. Koop to every household in the United States summed up "safe" sexual behavior as "(1) Not having sex; (2) Sex with one mutually faithful, uninfected partner" (U.S. Department of Health and Human Services 1988). Evidence suggests that homosexual men, in particular, are now having sex with fewer partners and are avoiding "risky" behavior such as anal intercourse (which enables the AIDS virus to enter the body through tears in the lining of the rectum) (Friedman et al. 1987). And because of the necessity of educating the public about how AIDS is spread, the subject of sex has been given a public forum. Even previously taboo subjects such as condom use (to prevent transmission of the virus during intercourse) and anal sex are now discussed in "family" magazines and on television. AIDS has put a damper on the so-called "sexual revolution" of the 1960s and 1970s, and it has also, unfortunately, erased some of the progress that homosexuals have made toward acceptance in the mainstream of society.

Another consequence of AIDS is the challenge it presents to civil liberties. As fears of AIDS have grown, some politicians and others have suggested that some or even all Americans should be tested for the AIDS virus and that carriers be quarantined. For example, William F. Buckley, the conservative spokesman, has advocated mandatory universal testing for the AIDS virus, with all those who test positive to be tattooed on their forearms and buttocks (Brandt 1986). In 1986, Californians voted on a proposition that would have required a quarantine of all AIDS victims. (The proposition did not pass, but it was supported by a third of the voters.) The state of Illinois now requires that all applicants for a marriage license be tested for AIDS.

Society still has not decided what rights people with AIDS (or the AIDS virus) have. Should they be allowed to continue to work if they are able, or should employers be permitted to fire them? Should they be able to buy health or life insurance, or should insurance companies be allowed to deny them coverage? Should children with AIDS be able to attend public schools, or should school authorities accede to demands that these children be barred from the classroom? Should topics such as condoms and anal intercourse be omitted from sex education curriculums because some parents believe that their children are not ready to learn about these subjects—even if this means incomplete instruction about AIDS? These and many other questions involving the conflict between individual liberties and protection of the public health remain heated matters of debate.

AIDS has also changed our ideas about health and medicine in general. As one researcher has written:

> AIDS has threatened our sense of medical security. After all, the age of transmissible, lethal infections was deemed long past in the Western world. Ours was the age of chronic disease—heart disease and cancers that principally strike late in life. Communicability—epidemics of infectious diseases—had receded in the public memory. Not since the polio epidemics of the 1950s has fear of infection reached such a high pitch as it has in the 1980s (Brandt 1986, pp. 233–234).

While fear of infection remains the chief public concern about AIDS, many observers have expressed uncertainty regarding the ability of our health-care system to cope with the epidemic. Not only has a cure for AIDS remained elusive, those who have gotten sick (and their numbers are increasing) require a considerable amount of care and treatment—much of which the patients themselves are unable to pay for. Cost-benefit discussions inevitably arise: should there be a limit to the amount of money the government spends on the care of AIDS victims, all of whom are likely to die? How much money should the government allocate for research? Spokesmen for homosexual groups have charged that Congress was reluctant to appropriate funds for AIDS research until the virus began infecting considerable

numbers of heterosexuals. As the AIDS virus claims more and more victims, the health-care system will be harder pressed—both practically and financially—to take care of the sick.

AIDS has fostered apprehension about strangers and distrust of people who are members of groups associated with AIDS. This means that inner-city blacks and Hispanics (disproportionately represented among AIDS patients because of intravenous drug use) may experience more prejudice and discrimination (Mays and Cochran 1987). Men who are homosexual, or who display stereotypical homosexual behaviors, may be avoided or shunned. In the words of one writer, "homosexuality itself is feared as if it were a communicable, lethal disease" (Brandt 1986).

In response to the AIDS epidemic, homosexual communities throughout the country have mobilized to extend support and care to AIDS patients. In San Francisco, for example, a number of volunteer organizations—the San Francisco AIDS Foundation, the

For decades, condoms were not mentioned in polite company, and drug stores kept them behind the counter. A shift in cultural attitudes has moved them out to display racks, but it is the deadly fear of AIDS that has led to public advertising like this one in San Francisco where the infection rate is high. AIDS has changed the function and image of condoms to a hygienic device for preventing fatal disease. (Terrence McCarthy/The New York Times.)

Shanti Project, and others—have provided information, medical referrals, help with housing, financial assistance, nursing care, counseling, home-attendant services and hospice care (Arno 1986). Not only have these efforts been of immense help to people with AIDS; they have helped minimize the burden on public institutions. (Patients who can live at home with some help do not have to be hospitalized, for example.) Although drug users and drug treatment agencies have made a few efforts to provide similar services, in general drug users "have had few formal organizations, and their informal organization is not well adapted to dealing with individual behavior change to reduce the risk of AIDS nor to collective action" (Friedman et al. 1987).

Because the AIDS epidemic has developed as a social phenomenon as well as a disease, the response to it has been social as well as medical. In the process, much about our society's underlying values will be revealed.

FUTURE TRENDS: THE COMPRESSION OF MORBIDITY

As we noted at the beginning of this chapter, few people today die of infectious diseases such as influenza or pneumonia. Instead, most deaths are caused by heart disease, cancer, and other chronic "diseases of civilization." Unlike infectious diseases, which strike suddenly and run their course in a matter of weeks or even days, chronic diseases develop slowly and may impair their victims' health for ten or twenty years or more. Often these diseases result from a long period of exposure to a combination of risk factors: smoking, a high-fat diet, lack of exercise, or environmental carcinogens. What would happen if these risk factors were eliminated, or at least sharply reduced? James F. Fries (1983) of the Stanford University School of Medicine has suggested that we may eventually observe a phenomenon he calls the **compression of morbidity**. This means that most people would live long, active lives comparatively free of illness; disease, when it did hit, would be confined to the last few years of life. As Fries puts it, "the 'firm' period of adult vigor is prolonged and the 'infirm' period of disease or senescence is compressed against the natural barrier at the end of life" (1983, p. 409).

The relationship of risk factors and illness can be seen in a hypothetical case that Fries outlines:

> Consider two brothers, one of whom smokes three packages of cigarettes daily while the other smokes one-half package a day. . . . In 1900 perhaps [the heavy-smoking brother] would have encountered pneumonia at age 30 and have died, after a life of 30 years and an illness of three days—premature death, to be sure, but inexpensive (at least in terms of direct medical costs), with relatively little illness burden upon the society, and with a high proportion of vigorous life to sickness. Now, with penicillin, this man survives to begin to develop a cough, wheezing, and shortness of breath at age 40. If he continues to smoke, he will be increasingly short of breath for the remainder of his life. In his fifties he has a heart attack; perhaps, prior to modern management, he might have died at this point. Now his arrythmia is controlled and he goes on to encounter a stroke a few years later, requiring intensive rehabilitation efforts. Throughout, he remains short of breath. Finally, a lung cancer develops and he dies, in a crescendo of chronic disease. . . .
>
> In contrast, the light-smoking brother does not develop symptomatic emphysema until perhaps age 70. The heart attack is postponed a few years, as is the stroke. The lung cancer is postponed all the way out of his lifetime and does not occur. This individual is more vigorous, with a higher quality of life, for a longer period of time, and represents socially a much smaller burden on society. The change in the point of first breathlessness represents, in this commonplace example, as much as thirty years of improved quality of life for the individual without the heavy-smoking habit. (Fries 1983, pp. 409–410)

Thus, compression of morbidity depends on the reduction of risk factors—such as smoking—that might induce chronic disease. But even if no one smoked, or drank too much, or became obese, we are all at risk from environmental pollution. Fumes emanating from smokestacks, automobile exhausts, toxic waste dumps, and nuclear reactors, have been implicated in many cancers, lung diseases, and other illnesses. The workplace, too, contains many hazardous substances, and certain occupations pose particular risk by exposing workers to carcinogens. Researchers at the Harvard School of Public Health find that the rate of leukemia is 78 percent higher among shoe-factory workers than in the population at large. Prostate cancer is 156 percent higher among welders; esophagus cancer 97 percent higher among plumbers; oral cavity and pharynx cancer 152 percent higher among workers in printing trades; and multiple myeloma 186 percent higher among carpenters. Hazardous materials have been implicated in still other occupation-related diseases, including black-lung disease among coal miners and chronic bronchitis and emphysema among textile workers. But all these statistics should not distract us from the fact that pollutants and toxins can be responsibly controlled. This requires a "get-tough" policy with businesses that do not follow environmental and safety regulations.

The goal of "compression of morbidity" is also compromised by opportunistic germs that seize on a slight environmental change (Russell 1983). Toxic shock syndrome is an example of a microbe that adapted itself to a product designed for feminine hygiene—tampons with greater absorbency, which provided a hospitable home for staphylococcus microbes. Similarly, Legionnaire's disease surfaced in 1976 as a puzzling pneumonia epidemic among American Legion conventioneers. The germ had lived harmlessly in soil and water for thousands of years. It found a hospitable new environment in modern plumbing and air-conditioning systems. AIDS, too, has become epidemic by taking advantage of changes in technology and life style. Among these factors are air travel (which seems to have spread the virus from Africa to many parts of the world), anonymous sexual encounters in large cities, needle-sharing among drug users, and the use of blood-clotting factors by hemophiliacs. Without these modern means of transmission, the AIDS virus might have remained confined to a small geographical area.

Obstacles to the compression of morbidity, whether new acute diseases or chronic diseases related to life style, illustrate once again the social nature of disease. Whether people get sick, what illness they contract, and whether they get well again depend on social factors. These may be matters of economics (whether a person can find a job that offers health insurance, or is free of exposure to hazardous substances), politics (whether the government subsidizes tobacco farming and permits the promotion of smoking), or technology (whether a vaccine or an effective new drug is discovered).

Although our health-care system, as we will see below, is designed to treat illness—not to prevent people from getting sick, Fries' concept is characteristic of a new emphasis on wellness that is beginning to take hold.

We now turn to the social aspects of the American health-care system.

HEALTH CARE IN AMERICA

The American health-care system is the nation's second largest industry, accounting for more than a tenth of the gross national product—around $600 billion (Conrad and Schneider 1980; Mechanic 1986). This enormous enterprise employs more than 5 million people: doctors and nurses, of course, but also technicians, therapists, pharmacists, and others working in a variety of settings, from hospitals, social agencies, and schools to nursing homes and hospices.

Two important characteristics distinguish the American system of health care. First, American health care is essentially a system of intervention rather than prevention; the system is oriented toward treating and curing disease rather than preventing it. Thus Americans usually do not come into contact with health-care providers or institutions unless they are sick. Many health-care practitioners in this country are highly trained specialists who use the most advanced technology in providing treatment—if their patients can afford it. And that brings us to the second distinctive quality of the health-care

Most doctors prefer treating the affluent to working in an urban ghetto. Consequently, hospitals in poor urban neighborhoods are often understaffed, and people may have to wait hours to see a doctor. (Barbara Pfeffer/Photo Researchers, Inc.)

Emergency helicopter service is a striking example of our health-care system's reliance on the most advanced technology in providing treatment. In contrast, preventing illness is the goal of this exercise class at a Ford Motor plant; helping employees stay fit and healthy increases their productivity, reduces absenteeism, and results in lower costs for medical care and insurance. (Left: Chris Jones/The Stock Market; right: Michael L. Abramson/Woodfin Camp & Associates.)

system: it is the only modern system besides South Africa's that does not provide comprehensive care for all its citizens.

The American system has three tiers of health care: one for the well-off and well-insured (the middle and upper classes); one for the poor who are eligible for government assistance in the form of Medicaid; and one for the 35–40 million citizens with no insurance (Schwartz 1987). The health care one receives in America depends on one's financial and insurance status—and it may depend as well on where one lives. Doctors, hospitals, high-tech medical facilities, and other sources of care are concentrated in and around large cities, and many residents of rural areas live far from skilled health-care providers.

The American health-care system now faces great challenges. Sharply rising medical costs have led to cost-containment efforts, and these have both changed treatment of patients and threatened the autonomy and authority of physicians. Advocates of expanded access to health care have urged a greater federal role in ensuring that people get the care they need; at the same time, those who administer government programs have been trying to cut costs. Critics have charged that given the chronic nature of most diseases today the entire structure of our health-care system is wrong in that it focuses too

much on heroic cures of acute disease and ignores long-term care and public health measures that might prevent illness in the first place. We will explore some of these problems and challenges in the sections that follow. But first we need to consider briefly how the American health-care system came to be what it is today.

The Development of American Medicine

Doctors occupy a position of such esteem and respect in contemporary American society that it is difficult to believe that this has not always been the case. For most of the nineteenth century, however, a doctor's social position and income were often little better than those of a manual worker.

In colonial America, anyone could become a physician merely by adopting the label. There were no medical schools or medical societies to license or regulate what was a free-for-all trade. Sometimes clergymen tried to provide medical care to their parishioners, and care of a sort was offered by all kinds of laypeople as well. Documents of the time record a doctor who sold "tea, sugar, olives, grapes, anchovies, raisins, and prunes" along with medicinals, and also tell of a woman who "Acts here in the Double Capacity of a Doctoress and Coffee Woman" (Starr 1982, p. 39). Training for medical practice, such as it was, was given by apprenticeship.

Medicine became a full-time vocation in the United States (though still not an established profession) in the early years of the nineteenth century (Conrad and Schneider 1980). Medical schools began to open around the country, and the few doctors who had education and training succeeded in convincing state legislatures to adopt laws regulating the practice of medicine. However, the period of "Jacksonian democracy" (1828–1836) saw most of these regulations repealed as elitist. Throughout the first half of the nineteenth century, a variety of doctors—some trained, some not—practiced different kinds of medicine. Many of the treatments then common date back to the Middle Ages or even earlier: applying leeches to drain blood believed to be excess or tainted, inducing the patient to vomit, and applying hot objects to the skin to produce blisters. Medicines were concocted from roots and herbs (Conrad and Schneider 1980; Starr 1982). In addition to those who called themselves doctors, there were a variety of "specialists": abortionists, midwives, bonesetters, and cancer doctors (Starr 1982). One reason so many of these people found clients at this time was the primitive nature of medical science itself. Effective anesthesia, for example, was unknown, as was the crucial fact that invisible agents—germs—cause many diseases. Even doctors who received medical-school training practiced a kind of medicine that often hurt the patient more than it helped. In such circumstances, the efforts of trained physicians to distinguish themselves from lay herbalists, traveling peddlers of medicine, and other irregular practitioners had only modest success at first.

It was not until the 1920s that scientific advances, coupled with the ascension of the American Medical Association (AMA), the physicians' professional organization, enabled doctors to acquire enough political and social clout to prevail over other people who claimed to be healers (Starr 1982; Burrow 1981; Larson 1977). The widespread acceptance of scientific medicine as superior to traditional attempts at cure put trained physicians in a position to assert that medical education was necessary to produce a legitimate doctor. In essence, medicine began to define itself as a true profession, one that because of its expertise deserved to dominate care of the sick. New laws were passed that set licensing requirements for doctors and made medicine a legally defined monopoly (Conrad and Schneider 1980; Freidson 1970). The AMA also pressed for legislation that limited the kinds of medicine that could be sold to the public directly. Once preparations containing opium, cocaine, and other powerful drugs could be bought by anyone; now a doctor's prescription was needed to obtain such substances (Starr 1982). Physicians also secured the right to set their own fees (before the mid-nineteenth century, some states set legal limits on the amount doctors could charge for their services). Soon after World War I, the medical profession as we know it had begun to appear, although subsequent decades have seen physicians' professional status rise substantially.

Professional Dominance of Medicine

American medicine transformed itself from an occupation into a **profession** by restricting the title "doctor" to those who had substantial medical education and by reserving certain prerogatives, such as prescribing medicine and setting fees for itself. Advanced education and skill distinguish the professional from the lay person and legitimize the professional's claim to certain privileges. Generally, members of a profession determine who may practice it. In the case of medicine, there are a number of hurdles each aspiring doctor must leap: admission to medical school, graduation as an M.D., a passing score on a licensing exam, board certification, and so on. In each of these cases, other doctors decide who succeeds and who does not; even the state licensing exams are prepared by physicians. Moreover, a doctor's clinical performance can in principle be judged only by another doctor, because outsiders are considered unqualified to evaluate medical decisions.

An important distinguishing characteristic of professionals is the autonomy (independence; freedom from the control of others) with which they operate. All professionals—not just physicians—have some degree of autonomy: compare lawyers' or architects' freedom to set up an independent office, choose their own clients, and establish standards for their work, with factory workers' time-clock restrictions and inability to deviate from an assigned task. Of course, certain nonprofessionals enjoy some autonomy in their work—owners of small businesses, homemakers, and self-employed people often work with little or no supervision from others. But physicians enjoy the prestige and financial rewards that go with being viewed as the most important figures in a complex and increasingly technical field.

One measure of physicians' dominance of the health-care system is that doctors alone have the authority to diagnose illness, prescribe and evaluate treatments, and convey information to patients. Seriously ill patients may not be fully informed about what is wrong with them, often on the pretext that they lack the expertise to understand medical information or are so upset by their condition that they will misinterpret any information given. As a result, seriously ill people are often forced to revert to a childlike dependence on their doctors. In recent years, some patients have rejected this position, asserting that they have a right to know about their health status and to participate in their own medical care (see box feature).

The preeminent position of doctors also implies a certain relationship to other health workers. Physicians exist in what sociologist Eliot Freidson (1970) has called a state of organized autonomy: theirs is the dominant profession in the health-care field and is sustained by a number of subservient professionals and semiprofessionals (nurses, physical therapists, pharmacists, and so forth). Clinicians in these "lesser" fields, because they are often reduced to following doctors' orders, may become alienated from their work, like factory workers and others who have little autonomy. It is likely that problems of morale are as important as low pay in the current shortage of nurses, for example. As Freidson has written, "The paraprofessional worker is, then, like the industrial worker, subordinated to the authority of others . . . to the putatively superior knowledge and judgment of professional experts" (1970, pp. 144–145).

Doctors' assumption of their position at the top of the health-care system is the result of a long period of socialization into the practice of medicine. As medical students, interns, and residents, those who train to be doctors internalize the ideals of the profession. Some of these ideals, of course, involve dedication to caring for the sick. But others involve maintaining the prestige of the profession (learning never to criticize another doctor in front of lay people) and accepting the idea that the practice of the profession necessarily involves a high degree of autonomy. Since the work in question is thought so difficult and complicated, it is often assumed that the person who is able to do it must be extraordinarily gifted: accordingly, most young doctors develop notions of professional pride, if not superiority or arrogance

(Freidson 1970). The structure of the profession itself affects the attitudes of doctors and by extension the kind of care they offer to patients.

Medicalization

An important by-product of the growth of medical knowledge and the prestige of the profession, is an increase in the number of conditions thought to be of medical concern. In the not-too-distant past, birth and death usually occurred at home, with family members and friends in attendance or close by. Now most people are born and die in a hospital, surrounded by bright lights and expensive machines. People who were addicted to alcohol or drugs were once considered sinful or lacking in willpower; now they are considered "sick." Problems that used to be accepted as part of life— baldness, wrinkles, overweight, acne, small breasts, lack of sexual responsiveness, anxiety, sleeplessness—are now deemed proper matters for medical intervention. Some criminologists have even defined antisocial behavior as a medical problem—lawbreakers of all kinds, from the shoplifter to the mass murderer, may potentially be labeled "sick." This annexation into the health sphere of many problems once considered nonmedical has been called the medicalization of American society. As Eliot Freidson has written,

> The physician is the ultimate expert on what is health and what illness and on how to attain the former and cure the latter. . . . the world is presently inclined to turn to him for advice on all matters related to health and illness regardless of his competence. Given the highly visible miracles medicine has worked over the past century, the public has even been inclined to ask the profession to deal with problems that are not of the biophysical character for which success was gained from past efforts. What were once recognized as economic, religious, and personal problems have been redefined as illness and have therefore become medical problems. (1970, p. 147)

One obvious result of medicalization has been increased attention to life activities that are relevant to disease (Zola 1972). Since much medical care is directed at treating chronic disease, the patient's habits (patterns of sleeping, eating, working, and playing) may come under the doctor's scrutiny. A modern doctor's "prescription" might be to stop smoking, eat fewer fatty foods, or

Health Care and the Revolt of the Consumer

It is easy to discuss the health-care system and its problems and lose track of the long-suffering object of medical care itself: the patient. Indeed, medical sociologists have jokingly called the passive recipient of medical care a "breathing brick" (Goldsmith 1984). Many people have had the experience of being treated by physicians and other health workers as if they were inanimate objects, or children who must be told what to do in as simplified a manner as possible. Patients who objected to this treatment got responses from their doctors ranging from incomprehension to hostility.

In the late 1960s, a groundswell of protest arose against dehumanized, authoritarian medical care. In the forefront of this movement were feminists who were irate over the treatment of women by male doctors, particularly obstetricians and gynecologists. The 1970s saw the publication of a number of books and articles documenting paternalistic (and even abusive) treatment of women by male physicians. These included doctors who dispensed birth-control pills without informing patients of the risks involved; doctors who performed unnecessary hysterectomies and who (incorrectly) told patients that radical mastectomy was the only appropriate treatment for breast cancer; doctors who delivered babies to suit their convenience, using cesarean section if necessary to hurry things along; and doctors who dismissed women's complaints as "all in their head" and thus missed diagnosing disease (e.g., Corea 1977). Partly in response to such problems, a women's health cooperative in Boston compiled a book called *Our Bodies, Ourselves*, originally published in 1973, which has sold over a million copies in several editions (Ruzek 1978). What the women's health movement was demanding was information from doctors about their medical condition, a voice in choosing their treatment, and respectful treatment as adults rather than paternalism or condescension. These goals have long since transcended the women's movement; doctors are no longer surprised when patients of all ages and philosophies demand a voice in their care.

Such demands on doctors may well begin to influence the kind of care they provide—doctors who offend patients may find themselves with a dwindling number of patients and a shrinking income. There is currently a doctor surplus, and it is almost certain to get worse in the next decade or so (Coddington and Moore 1987). So doctors who want to prosper might have to attune themselves more to patients' needs and concerns.

Another indication of patients' determination to challenge the medical establishment has been a steep increase in malpractice suits in the past decade (Press 1984). This phenomenon is not solely the result of consumer dissatisfaction with the performance of their doctors. American society in general has become more litigious and the number of lawyers available to bring malpractice suits has also increased. But the rise in such suits, starting in the 1970s, certainly reflects a tide of patients angry about medical mistakes—inaccurate diagnosis, failure to perform necessary tests, bungled operations—and ready and willing to sue.

The cost of malpractice insurance has risen markedly in the wake of the increasing number of lawsuits—and this extra cost must be paid by all doctors, good, bad, and mediocre, since almost all doctors carry malpractice insurance. In response to the malpractice threat, doctors are increasingly practicing what is called "defensive medicine": they give a patient every conceivable diagnostic test and call in consultants even when unnecessary to protect themselves from a patient's

begin an exercise program. Going further, physicians may attempt to influence the habits of an entire society —promoting restrictions on smoking, for example.

Medicine's privileged access to certain private and personal aspects of people's lives has expanded as the role of other institutions—particularly the family and the church—has shrunk. Births were once family matters, and now they are usually overseen by doctors and nurses. Indeed, virtually everything relating to birth—sexuality, contraception, infertility, prenatal care—has become a medical matter. Other highly personal concerns that once might have been taken to a member of the clergy or to a respected person within the family—drug or alcohol use, misbehaving children, and emotional disturbances —are now talked over with a doctor.

Another sign of medicalization is the use of medical arguments to help advance causes not immediately or directly connected with medicine (Zola 1972). For example, the noise level of rock music is cited as being damaging to hearing and bad for children's mental health. Environmental pollution is condemned for being ugly and destructive to plants and animals—and charge that they were not careful enough. And some practitioners have simply stopped offering certain services that demand unusually high malpractice premiums, such as delivering babies. The malpractice problem has also added significantly to the cost of medical care. Since the doctors' malpractice insurance costs so much, doctors' fees rise. And "defensive medicine" is expensive: either the patient or the patient's insurer must pay for all the extra tests and consultations.

One final aspect of the consumer revolt against conventional medicine is the self-care movement. People have always treated many of their own medical problems, of course, either with drugstore remedies (everything from corn plasters to laxatives) or with home remedies (chicken soup, an ice pack, a heating pad, a salt-water gargle). And today health-food stores offer self-care methods and products in modern, and perhaps dubious, incarnations, such as books on bee pollen therapy and bottles of vitamins and obscure mineral supplements. Self care also encompasses a large network of self-help groups, some of which deal with problems that are beyond the scope of traditional medical care. Perhaps the oldest such group is Alcoholics Anonymous (founded in

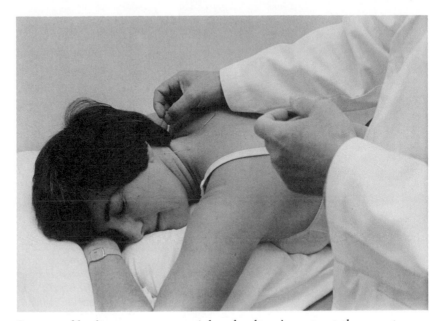

Systems of healing are more a social and cultural construct than most people realize. Acupuncture is a complex, sophisticated system for healing disorders and reducing pain. Yet it was totally ignored by "scientific medicine" until leading American surgeons witnessed such operations as Caesarean-section births with Chinese patients awake and relaxed. (Judy S. Gelles/Stock, Boston.)

1935), and many modern groups have been inspired by AA's organization and philosophy. These groups include Mastectomy, Inc., for women who have had breasts removed; Mended Hearts, for heart attack victims; and Make Today Count, for terminally ill cancer patients.

for causing cancer. One great exploiter of medical rhetoric has been the advertising industry, which successfully markets in the name of health everything from high-fiber cereal to aspirin to low-calorie sweeteners and "lite" beer.

Medicalization also involves a redefinition of social issues. For example, if homeless people are characterized as mentally ill, this obscures the fact that much homelessness is related to unemployment among unskilled workers and a lack of affordable urban housing (Snow et al. 1986). If drug abuse is considered a disease, then why

are users of certain drugs sent to jail instead of being placed in a treatment program? Similarly, if rapists are "sick," perhaps they would benefit more from psychiatric treatment rather than incarceration. As these last two examples suggest, society is uneasy with the distinction between sickness and criminal deviance, since a person who is sick is in large measure relieved of responsibility for his or her actions. Although considering some deviant behavior, such as alcoholism and drug abuse, as illness rather than crime would seem to be compassionate, it raises questions of social control. For example, can

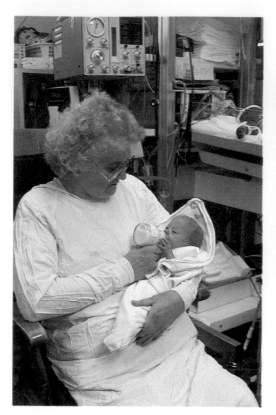

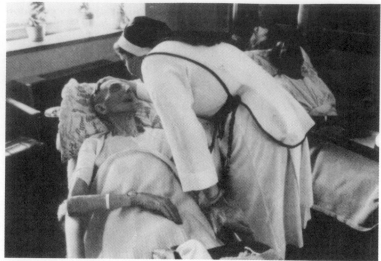

Many women are choosing to give birth at home or in homelike birth centers, attended by nurse-midwives and family members; terminally ill hospice patients choose to die in a homelike setting where the emphasis is on comfort and care rather than prolonging life. The natural-birth and hospice movements offer people alternatives to conventional health-care arrangements. (Left: Will & Deni McIntyre/Photo Researchers, Inc.; above: Abraham Menashe/Photo Researchers, Inc.)

random drug testing of employees be a bad thing, a violation of people's rights, if it is done to protect their health? As medical rhetoric expands to embrace so many human activities, such questions will continue to be debated.

Medicalization has not been without its critics; in a number of ways, both doctors and patients have attempted to remove some aspects of human behavior from the purview of medicine (Fox 1977). Women's health groups have pressed for the demedicalization of the birth process, setting up "birthing centers" and clinics in which babies can be born in a homelike setting and mothers can be spared as much medical intervention as possible (often they are attended only by nurse-midwives). Similarly, patients' advocates have asserted that terminally ill people should be able to die without heroic medical intervention if they wish. In 1980 the medical establishment deleted homosexuality from its official manual of psychiatric disorders, holding that homosexual acts between consenting adults were not "sick." And people with a wide variety of problems—overweight, gambling, spouse abuse—have formed self-help groups to cope

with their problems without turning to medical authority. Although these efforts suggest some uneasiness with the medicalization of society, perhaps even the beginnings of a backlash against it, they seem as yet isolated exceptions to the medicalization trend.

CHALLENGES TO THE HEALTH CARE SYSTEM

Medicalization and professional dominance of the health-care system are signs both of the system's strengths and of its vulnerabilities. In a sense, the system might be called a victim of its own success: its guiding philosophy—vigorous (even heroic) intervention to cure acute disease—has led to an array of extremely expensive high-tech treatments. This intensive, specialized care has without doubt saved lives, but it has caused medical costs to rise so spectacularly that insurers and the government have balked at paying the bills. Pressures have been put on doctors and hospitals to contain costs, and doctors' professional judgments have come under scrutiny. Questions such as, "Is this expensive test needed?" "Does this patient really need to be in the hospital for a week, or can she be discharged in three days?" "Is surgery the best treatment for this patient's condition, or is there a good chance that he will get better without an expensive operation?" herald the beginning of a new era in which doctors are being held accountable for their decisions.

The challenges to the medical status quo affect more than doctors: hospitals, insurers, and patients themselves find their needs and roles changing. In particular, as it becomes apparent that a health-care system based on heroic intervention in acute disease is not well suited to deal with a predominance of patients suffering from chronic diseases, the medical establishment is challenged to respond in a new way to patients' and society's needs.

Revolutionary Changes in Health Care

The late 1970s and the 1980s have seen changes in the health-care system, most of them sparked by the spiraling cost of medical treatment. A visit to a specialist now costs well over $100, state-of-the-art medical tests cost many times that much, and the cost of a hospital stay is well beyond the means of most individuals. The only people who can take full advantage of what medical science has to offer are the very wealthy and those who are insured. Skyrocketing medical costs, however, have been matched by ever-increasing insurance premiums, and those who must foot these bills have looked for a way to cut costs. One strategy, called self-insurance, has been adopted by many employers who pay a large percentage of their employees' insurance premiums. Self-insurance enables companies to keep insurance premiums in a fund under their own management, rather than paying premiums to a profit-making insurance company, such as Blue Cross. Today, a majority of the nation's major employers (particularly the large corporations) have devised self-insurance plans (Goldsmith 1984).

Other cost-saving strategies adopted by employers include:

Putting service contracts out on a competitive-bid basis, that is, offering providers such as hospitals

and health-maintenance organizations the chance to provide care for a large group of employees—if they can do so at a price attractive to the employers.

· Passing on the cost of insurance to employees by raising deductibles and copayments (the percentage of a medical bill the patient must pay).

· Gathering data on fees charged by hospitals and doctors to identify particularly expensive providers and discourage employees from using them.

· Requiring that employees seek second opinions on whether surgery is needed.

· Starting or expanding programs to help employees give up smoking, stop abusing alcohol or drugs, lose weight, control high blood pressure, manage stress, and so forth, thereby reducing the chances that expensive health care will be needed (Leyerle 1984; Light 1988).

The high price of health care poses challenges for government as well as private employers. The costs of Medicare (for the elderly) and Medicaid (for the poor) have risen dramatically since these programs were established in the mid-1960s, causing concern among legislators. To cut costs, lawmakers introduced the Prospective Payment System (PPS), a radically new method of compensating hospitals for patient care. Previously, a hospital submitted a bill for services rendered and Medicare paid it. Under the Prospective Payment System, the hospital receives a fixed payment for the condition being treated. In essence, the government has allocated a certain amount of money for gall bladder removal, another amount for cataract surgery, and so on. Initial reports on PPS suggest that it does indeed reduce Medicare expenditures (Guterman and Dobson 1986). But it also provides an incentive to discharge patients early, because hospitals earn the same amount for a particular service whether they keep a patient for three days or three weeks. Under the old system of reimbursement, hospitals earned more money by providing more services. Under PPS, they earn more by providing fewer services, meaning that Medicare patients with multiple problems may not fare well under PPS. Not surprisingly, many hospitals, squeezed between giving patients the care they need and being paid by Medicare only the amount patients are "supposed" to need, are in financial difficulty (Guterman and Dobson 1986).

Medicaid, originally conceived as a program that would cover medical costs for all poor people, is now available to only about 47 percent of the poor (Davis and Rowland 1983), primarily because both the federal government and many states have tightened Medicaid eligibility requirements. Two-parent families, for example, are usually ineligible for Medicaid, and single adults are rarely covered unless they are elderly or disabled (Davis and Rowland 1983). In many states, people with incomes below the poverty-level do not qualify for Medicaid. Besides reducing the numbers of people eligible for Medicaid, recent cutbacks have also limited benefits and the fees paid to physicians and hospitals (Kern and Windham 1986). What this means is that people who need medical care are not able to obtain it, and public hospitals that are willing to provide care to the poor have been inundated with patients who cannot pay.

Consequences of Change

One of the most significant consequences of changes in the health-care system is an altered balance of power, with those who pay the bills—the government (through Medicare and Medicaid), employers, and insurance companies—chipping away at physicians' absolute power to determine patient care. As one commentator put it, "What has happened . . . [recently] is that economic power so carefully accumulated and nurtured for the better part of five decades has begun to shift from those who provide care to those who pay for it. . . . Increasingly, those who pay for care are demanding economic accountability from those who provide it and are altering many of the historic ground rules" (Goldsmith 1984, p. 453).

Economic accountability is taking a number of forms. The buyers of medical care are beginning to set the prices that doctors can charge. They are monitoring doctors' performance—questioning whether patients need surgery or hospitalization, for example, and once patients are in the hospital questioning what tests they need and how long they should be hospitalized. The old deference to doctors—the assumption that doctors know best and their decisions should not be questioned—is becoming a thing of the past.

The way hospitals work has changed radically too. First, hospitals have found various ways to limit the number of days a patient stays in the hospital (because of the fixed pay per stay). Hospitals now do all the prelimi-

nary tests and paperwork prior to admission. Patients scheduled for some kinds of surgery often are admitted to the hospital early in the morning and have surgery the same day. In addition, some hospitals are designating certain rooms as reduced-rate areas to accommodate patients who need further recuperation but require fewer services than other patients.

Hospitals are also attempting to increase their profits by providing services that meet the special needs

Selling health care at the mall. This free medical screening service is in reality a marketing event—an effective way for a pharmaceutical company, for instance, to promote its products to potential customers. When was the last time you had your blood pressure taken by a trained salesperson? (David Hurn/Magnum Photos.)

of people in the community. "Urgicenters," for example, offer drop-in care in convenient places such as shopping centers, and women's health-care centers and plastic surgery centers target specific populations. Many hospital services, such as X-rays, pharmaceuticals, laboratory tests, and laundry, have been made into separate businesses so that patients can be billed for these items separately at higher rates.

Cost concerns have also led to new forms of health-care delivery. Two of the most notable of these are **health maintenance organizations** (HMOs) and **preferred provider organizations** (PPOs). HMOs, which date back to the nineteenth century, have grown rapidly since the 1970s because they meet their subscribers' medical needs for a fixed price per year. Since HMOs lose money if patients require many expensive treatments in a given year, these plans often offer preventive programs to keep patients healthy. PPOs are groups of doctors who offer specific services to groups of patients (such as all the employees of a company) at discount prices. The organization's clients get a price break, and doctors get a steady stream of patients. A PPO also allows considerable freedom: a patient who doesn't like the doctors in the PPO can go elsewhere, but he or she must pay the difference in fees. Similarly, doctors who see PPO patients can also see non-PPO patients; they are not merely employees of an organization. PPOs come in many forms and sizes. They are organized by doctors, by employers, by insurance companies, and by hospitals that want to expand their range of services to include ambulatory care.

Corporatization and Public Health

As we noted earlier in this chapter, health care is America's second biggest business. It is hardly surprising that in a country as devoted to free enterprise as the United States health care should be a source of entrepreneurship and profit making. Increasingly, the provision of medical services is being taken over by for-profit corporations, and these corporations are being consolidated into even larger corporations—what some have called the "medical-industrial complex" (Relman 1980; Light 1986). This corporatization process has consequences for public health. As one researcher has noted,

As health care becomes a profitable market for corporate investment, health services are treated as commodities —products that are bought and sold in the marketplace like automobiles, hats, iron, or oil. The deciding factor as to whether to provide a service or produce a particular piece of equipment is made according to whether that "product" will sell. The bottom line is marketability and whether the company providing the service will make a profit on its sale. (Levitt 1986, p. 483)

Corporatization is a fairly recent phenomenon in health care. It might be dated from 1968, the year a Nashville doctor and a former executive of Kentucky Fried Chicken formed the Hospital Corporation of America (HCA), an investor-owned for-profit hospital chain (Light 1986). Proponents of for-profit hospitals usually argue that there is nothing wrong with making a profit from health care, and that their hospitals are profitable because they are run more efficiently than nonprofit institutions. Large chains of hospitals do benefit from economies of scale (buying large quantities of supplies at a discount, for example) but nonprofit hospitals have to some extent followed the example of the for-profit hospitals by combining into nonprofit chains to realize the same advantages. There is evidence, however, that for-profit hospitals have nicely positioned themselves in a health-care niche in which sizable profits can be made. In many cases, they have done this by not offering services that lose money, such as obstetrics, and by locating in areas where relatively few poor or uninsured people live. When poor patients arrive in the emergency room of a for-profit hospital, they may be turned away (Light 1986).

Hospitals are not the only profit-making enterprises in the health-care field. In recent years, medical laboratories, kidney dialysis centers, CAT scan units, ambulatory care clinics, nursing homes, and many other enterprises have been organized as corporate ventures. Doctors, too, are becoming more entrepreneurial, incorporating themselves as group practices and investing in expensive medical equipment so that they can perform costly tests and procedures in their offices. And like the hospitals, groups of doctors are establishing freestanding clinics—women's health centers, psychiatric centers, and others. In such an atmosphere, the independent practitioner may find it increasingly hard to compete.

Although health care in America has long had ties to money making, until recently it also embraced an ideal of service to the public. To be sure, not every

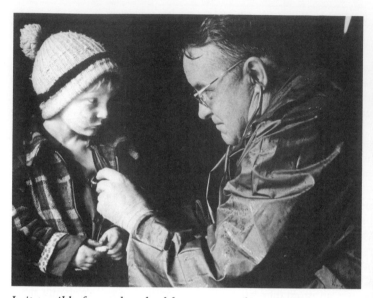

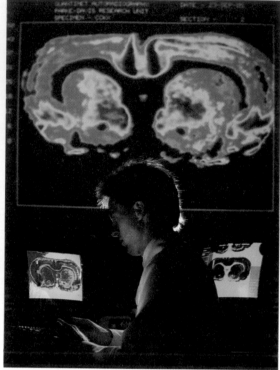

Is it possible for modern health care to combine the dedication and personal touch of the country doctor of old with the technical resources of the "medical industrial complex"? Or is the personal art of healing one of the casualties of our health-care system's success? (Above: Bruce Roberts/Rapho/Photo Researchers, Inc.; right: Ted Horowitz/The Stock Market.)

doctor displayed altruistic impulses, but many did waive or defer fees for patients who could not afford to pay, while charging affluent patients a bit more. The government itself endorsed this ideal in its Medicare and Medicaid programs, which offer poor people health services that are paid for by the taxpayers in the middle and upper classes. As we approach the twenty-first century, however, the goal of comprehensive health care for all Americans remains an elusive one. Institutional buyers—employers and insurance companies—only want to pay for the care their employees or clients receive, and the amount they are willing to pay is shrinking (Goldsmith 1984). Medicare and Medicaid payments have been cut back dramatically, leaving as many as 35–40 million people without medical insurance of *any* kind (Davis and Rowland 1983). Indeed, one illuminating study shows that insured persons receive 90 percent more hospital care than do the uninsured—surely not because they experience 90 percent more serious illness (Davis and Rowland 1983). Uninsured people also receive far less ambulatory care

than the insured, especially preventive care. In the words of researchers who have examined this issue:

> Lack of insurance has three major consequences: it contributes to unnecessary pain, suffering, disability, and even death among the uninsured; it places a financial burden on those uninsured who struggle to pay burdensome medical bills; and it places a financial strain on hospitals, physicians, and other health care providers who attempt to provide care to the uninsured. (Davis and Rowland 1983, p. 523)

In the current atmosphere of cost containment and worries over the federal budget deficit, more and more people are falling through the cracks in the American health-care system. Yet cost containment has illuminated the seriousness of medical poverty, providing additional fuel for the movement to extend health insurance to every man, woman, and child in the United States (Light 1986). Whether such a system is acceptable to the American public over the long term remains to be seen.

SUMMARY

1. Causes of mortality have changed in the past century from acute diseases to chronic diseases, principally heart disease and cancer.

2. Women outlive men, although they report more minor illness. Black people, Hispanics, and the poor have higher mortality rates and a poorer health status in general. Factors contributing to health problems among the poor are inadequate food and housing, less medical care, and more exposure to stress.

3. The connection between wealth and health is worldwide. Poorer countries are still plagued by infectious diseases. Throughout most of the world, people lack access to adequate health care because they or their countries are without the money to pay for it.

4. Unemployment is related to ill health. It deprives people of income to pay for health care and of medical insurance, and the stress connected with not working in itself contributes to health problems.

5. Hunger, first recognized as a social problem in the United States in the mid-1960s, has again emerged as a health issue. Budget cuts and unemployment during the 1980s, combined with a rising cost of living, make many people unable to afford an adequate diet.

6. Smoking is increasingly recognized as a critical public health problem. Although many people have quit, heavy promotion of cigarettes constantly attracts new smokers. Antismoking activists have been partially successful in their efforts to delegitimize smoking.

7. AIDS has brought a number of social consequences in its wake. These include changes in sexual behavior and attitudes about sex, more openness in discussion of taboo topics, stigmatization of homosexuals and other high-risk groups, and challenges to civil liberties. The spread of the AIDS epidemic illustrates the role of social, technological, and political factors in disease.

8. One expert has suggested that if the population's exposure to risk factors can be reduced, there will be a "compression of morbidity": people will live healthy lives and only get seriously ill in old age. At present, however, exposure to risk factors is not easily controlled.

9. The nation's second biggest industry, the American health-care system is one of intervention rather than prevention and one in which care is not universally provided but related to the patient's ability to pay.

10. Medicine slowly emerged as a profession during the nineteenth century. The profession was fragmented until the twentieth century, when scientific advances and vigorous campaigning put science-oriented doctors in a dominant position. Laws and financing further strengthened their power.

11. Physicians enjoy an unusual degree of autonomy in their profession; until recently they have been protected from intervention, competition, and evaluation. The medical profession's preeminence in the health-care field is sustained by a number of subservient professions and occupations.

12. A by-product of the prestige of the medical profession has been the medicalization of society. Many problems once the province of the clergy, the family, or the legal system are now taken to doctors. Medical language is now used in many contexts to lend authority to various proposals and claims. Some critics have sought to redefine aspects of life, such as birth, death, and sexual behavior, as private matters in which medical intervention should be limited.

13. Rising medical costs have led institutional buyers of medical care to a variety of cost-containment measures. This has put limits on both physicians' autonomy and the amount and kind of care patients receive. Cuts in Medicare and Medicaid have constituted a retreat from the goal of providing care for those unable to pay.

14. Health-care institutions have changed in a number of ways as a result of financial pressures. Hospitals offer streamlined procedures and have expanded into profitable sidelines. Health maintenance organizations and preferred provider organizations seek to offer care to groups of people in a less expensive package than conventional care.

15. Medical care has undergone a process of corporatization: it has become a profitable market for corporate investment. For-profit hospitals have expanded, doctors have become entrepreneurs, and all kinds of health-related industries have sprung up as profit-driven enterprises. Increasing emphasis on money making points up the problems of the uninsured: who will offer care if no money is to be made on it? Increasingly, the American health-care system offers first-class care to those who can pay and ignores the needs of those who cannot.

GLOSSARY

Compression of morbidity. A situation in which illness would occupy only the last years of a person's life.

Disease. Medically diagnosed pathology.

Health maintenance organization. A health care organization that provides all of a patient's care for a fixed price per year.

Illness. The personal sense that one is unwell.

Medicalization. Annexation into the medical sphere of many problems once considered nonmedical.

Preferred provider organization. A group of doctors that offers specific services to patients at discount prices.

Profession. An occupation for which one must prepare with advanced education and training in the exercise of a special skill.

Sickness. The social recognition that one is not well.

PART SIX

THE TRANSFORMATION OF SOCIETY

Stability and change have been major themes throughout this text. Ultimately, sociologists seek to understand large, historical patterns of social change (or resistance to change) in order to confront more effectively the challenges of the present. The final three chapters ask you to consider the forces that give rise to fundamental transformations of the social world, such as those which define the modern era.

We live in an era in which developments in science and technology threaten to outstrip our understanding of their social implications. The acquisition and application of scientific knowledge is, in fact, a social process, and Chapter 20 examines the rise of modern science, the social norms by which it operates, its links to advancing technology, and the role of science in the making of public policy.

Think of something you have done as a member of a group that you would not have dared to do alone: what made you do it? Chapter 21 compares functional and power perspectives on collective behavior and discusses such phenomena as hysteria, rumor, and social contagion. We look at the spontaneous aspect and the social organizational patterns of riots. And we examine different views of how social movements arise and develop, focusing on such recent examples as the civil rights and anti-war movements of the 1960s.

Chapter 22 takes up the subject of social change itself. Is social change an evolutionary process for which we can identify both a course and a mechanism? How and why does social change occur? The text explores these and other questions, focusing on the example of computer technology and its effects in the workplace and in society at large. Social change is also a critical issue from a global perspective: the gap between rich and poor nations continues to widen, while the world becomes a smaller and more fragile place to live.

CHAPTER 20
Science and Technology

The work force employs nearly 4 million scientists and engineers, and every year our colleges and universities award over 350,000 more degrees in these fields. This vast army of technical personnel turns out over a billion words of scientific articles annually. At the rate of 250 to 300 words a minute for a solid eight hours a day, readers would take from twenty-five to thirty *years* to absorb this much material! Equally astounding is the rate at which American scientists produce new discoveries and inventions. In the decade of the 1980s, the U.S. Patent Office granted over 60,000 new patents a year on average and received applications for many more. What is the cost of all this research and development? In 1985 the price tag was $107 *billion*. That amounts to almost $500 for every man, woman, and child in the country (Science Indicators 1985).

Without question, science and technology are enormously important in American society. By **science** we mean the systematic pursuit of reliable knowledge about natural phenomena and about the social world. By **technology** we mean the application of knowledge (scientific or otherwise) to the solution of practical problems. The scientific and technological advances of modern times have transformed our lives. Alexander Graham Bell's invention of the telephone, for example, has made long-distance conversation a routine affair. The Wright brothers' experiments in aviation and Henry Ford's mass production of the car have allowed us to take for granted long-distance travel. The development of the atomic bomb has likewise changed our lives, embroiling us in an arms race on which we spend billions of dollars a year. Scientific research into space travel has pushed the frontier of exploration millions of miles beyond our planet.

Because of their far-reaching effects on society and social relationships—and because they require collective efforts—science and technology are *social* phenomena. Exploding the first atomic bomb or sending the first astronauts to the moon involved hundreds, even thousands, of people working together. Contrary to popular belief, major discoveries almost never emerge from the laboratory of an isolated scientist. Rather, individual scientists generally share their findings with the rest of the scientific community. Each member of this community works with and builds on the discoveries of others, constructing a body of knowledge.

American science and technology in the mid-twentieth century has undergone explosive growth (Price 1962). Indeed, science and technology have been growing at an extraordinary pace for the last 300 years. Measured in terms of either workers or number of publications, science and technology have been doubling every fifteen years throughout this period. This means that over the last three centuries, science and technology have increased a *million*fold.

Today we think of ourselves as living in an era of "Big Science"—big in terms of the vast scale that our scientific efforts, achievements, and institutions have reached (Price 1962). In fact, science has grown so big that its rate of increase has had to start leveling off. A

567

What would happen if you suddenly transplanted this 17th-century astronomer from his studio to a modern observatory with its giant infrared telescope? His bewilderment would attest to the fact that scientific knowledge emerges from a particular social and historical context. Flights of inspiration notwithstanding, scientific discovery is a highly social achievement. (Left: Art Resource; right: Prof. R. Gehrz/ Photo Researchers, Inc.)

doubling time of fifteen years cannot go on indefinitely when the rate of population growth is near zero. If it did, every man, woman, and child in the country would be a scientist in another hundred years, and science would account for our entire gross national product! Clearly the end of rapid scientific growth must come at some point, and for America that point seems to be starting now. Thus, the era of Big Science is also an era in which science remains huge and tremendously important but tends not to grow as rapidly as it did in earlier times.

In this chapter we explore the social phenomena of Big Science in America. We begin by asking why science has grown so enormous. What factors have caused it to become such a dominant, highly respected feature of modern societies? We then take a look at the rules of science, the guidelines by which scientists carry out their work. Do these rules strongly mold the behavior of researchers? Or do scientists flexibly interpret them depending on the situation? Next we explore the process of "doing" science, of actually making scientific discoveries and contributing to scientific knowledge. This section emphasizes that science is a highly social undertaking and that scientists actively construct the "truth" as they know it. We then examine the process of technological change and how it too is socially constructed. Finally, we look at the role of scientists and technical experts in making public policy choices.

EXPLAINING THE GROWTH OF SCIENCE

Why has science grown at such an extraordinary pace? What can explain the rapid rise of this social institution? As with so many other sociological puzzles, two basic answers have been offered—one that takes a functional perspective, the other a power view. From a functional perspective, the growth of science is explained by its value to the smooth running of society. Science provides the reliable knowledge needed to control nature and our complex social order. As a result, people are better able to achieve their collective goals, and so science has grown and flourished. From a power perspective, in contrast, the rise of science is explained not in terms of its value to society but its utility to those who control the social order. Powerful groups promote science to enhance their own strength and further their own interests. Science creates a new form of power by which dominant groups can control weaker ones.

Both the functional and the power perspectives offer important insights into the rapid expansion of science during the last 300 years. The explanations they propose are complementary: each adds a dimension of understanding by having a different focus. In the following sections we will explore scientific developments that illustrate the usefulness of both views.

The Functional Perspective

By the early 1970s, the federal Department of Health, Education, and Welfare (HEW) had a major problem on its hands. A large number of programs for the poor, the elderly, the unemployed, and the underprivileged had been enacted in the 1960s. But how many people were eligible to participate in these programs? Was it many more than the number currently receiving benefits? Did the number change often throughout the year as people drifted in and out of jobs? And what was the impact of all these programs? Did they significantly raise the quality of people's lives? Were tax dollars being spent economically? Or were some people receiving assistance illegally from three or four programs without the knowledge of program administrators? HEW officials did not have the tools to answer these questions. The Census Bureau's yearly income survey did not provide the necessary data, and no researchers had addressed this particular topic. The solution seemed to lie in constructing a new survey, one specifically designed to find out about the financial lives of Americans in need of public assistance.

So the Survey of Income and Program Participation was developed. It involves interviews with members of 25,000 households in cities and towns across America. The subjects are asked in detail how much they earn, what savings they have, what property they own, and how much government assistance they get (both cash and noncash benefits, including food stamps, subsidized housing, free health care, and the like). The same people are surveyed every few months for several years. In this way researchers can see not just the current status of low-income households, but also how changes in income and government assistance affect family life among the poor (Hunt 1985).

The Survey of Income and Program Participation illustrates the use of science to solve the problem of obtaining reliable data for government decision making. This problem has existed ever since societies grew so large that rulers could not personally know every member. At first government officials conducted censuses to find out what they needed to know. After the Norman Conquest in 1066, for example, William the Conqueror of England sent census takers throughout his new realm. Their job was to go to every household, count the number of men who could bear arms, and describe and record every piece of taxable land and property. For many generations the census remained the only method of collecting national data. But it was such a huge,

expensive undertaking it could not be done very often. Then, in the 1930s, the Great Depression struck, and policymakers needed to know more about its effects. Fortunately, social researchers were developing a much less costly and time-consuming way of collecting social data—the *sample* survey. By means of statistical theory and scientific tests, they showed that questioning as few as 1,500 people carefully selected from the population could accurately reveal the opinions and preferences of *all* Americans (Hunt 1985). Here, then, a technique of social science, the sample survey, arose because of a demand for more national information. From a functional perspective, much of the growth of science can be explained in a similar way. Science has expanded because it has fulfilled a vital societal need.

Émile Durkheim epitomized the functional perspective on the rise of science. "That [science] was born," wrote Durkheim, "indicates that society needed it" (Durkheim 1925). Durkheim suggested that science grew at an extraordinary pace because the need for scientific data remained urgent. But why does society have this urgent need for science? What function does science serve? Durkheim argued that as societies grow larger and more differentiated (with members from a variety of groups holding diverse beliefs and values), it becomes increasingly difficult for people to agree on what is known. Science solves this dilemma by providing something that people can agree on—knowledge that virtually everyone considers reliable because it is systematically gathered and empirically tested. This knowledge, moreover, can be used to achieve collective goals in a rational, objective manner. With scientific knowledge of nature, for example, people can predict natural phenomena (from the course of a disease to the eruption of a volcano to the depletion of farming soil) and sometimes learn to control them. Similarly, with scientific knowledge of society and social relations, people can anticipate social forces (such as the course of an economic downturn) and take steps to direct these events. Thus, science is a tool for understanding, planning, and control. It allows people to take greater charge of their physical and social worlds. Since science serves these important functions, little wonder that it has expanded into the huge institution it is today.

But some sociologists doubt that a functional perspective can explain entirely the rise of modern science. They argue that science has grown so dramatically partly because it provides a way for certain groups to exercise power over others. These sociologists see science not as something that benefits *all* of society, but as a tool used by dominant groups to impose social order and advance their own interests, often at the expense of the powerless. A stark illustration of this power perspective can be found in what has come to be called the Tuskegee study.

The Power Perspective

In the summer of 1972 an Associated Press reporter released a story that shocked and outraged Americans (described in Jones 1981). For forty years the U.S. Public Health Service, an agency supposedly dedicated to improving the health of our citizens, had allowed nearly 400 black men suffering from syphilis to go without treatment for this potentially deadly disease. (Syphilitic microorganisms can ravage the internal organs, including the heart and brain.) The men lived in and around Tuskegee, Alabama, a poor, rural region of the country where the incidence of syphilis among blacks was unusually high. In the early 1930s the Public Health Service had initiated a free syphilis treatment program in the Tuskegee area, but it had not been very successful. Treatment for syphilis in those days was long, often painful, and even potentially dangerous for it involved drugs that could have harmful side effects. Public Health doctors had trouble convincing syphilitic blacks that the long-term risks of the disease were worse than those of the treatment. When the treatment campaign ended, a few of the doctors involved wanted to salvage something of benefit from their efforts. So they decided to conduct a scientific study of the physical effects of syphilis on *un*treated black males.

Black men in the later stages of the disease were recruited for the study. To gain their cooperation, the doctors falsely led the men to believe they were receiving treatment for syphilis. For years the men were given extensive physical exams, including one that involved a very painful spinal tap. Doctors offered some treatment to keep the subjects interested in the study, but not enough to cure the disease. Sometimes the palliative amounted to nothing more than aspirin and an iron tonic. Even when penicillin, a drug that readily cures syphilis, was discovered in the 1940s, the Public Health Service still did not end its Tuskegee study. The project continued to the very day that the news story broke, and by then most of the syphilitic men were dead. The study did not yield as much as a single piece of new information about the disease.

What could prompt medical researchers to attempt to augment scientific knowledge with a study so blatantly unethical? The answer lies in understanding the interaction between some powerful groups and a very powerless one. One powerful group consisted of the Public Health doctors who initiated the study and pressed for continuing it. They were seeking to enhance their own prestige and influence by becoming scientific researchers, an elite in the medical profession. These doctors legitimated their experiment by conducting it under the auspices of a U.S. government agency. They then sought to avoid any local opposition by enlisting the aid of another powerful group, the white plantation owners in the Tuskegee area. The white planters were persuaded not just to approve of the study but also to give their active cooperation (for instance, by allowing field hands "time off" for physical exams). Their motive was the hope that the study would help lower the incidence of syphilis in their black workers. But their impulse was not purely humanitarian: a high incidence of syphilis among blacks reduced the cheap labor force on which the planters depended. If enough blacks were debilitated by the disease, agricultural wages might be driven up, thus reducing the planters' profits. At the same time, the unspoken fear was that unchecked syphilis among blacks might lead to more syphilis in the white population. So the white planters went along with the Tuskegee study, convinced that it would serve their interests.

On the opposite side in this tragic affair were the powerless black subjects. They were ripe for exploitation for a number of reasons. They were so poor that the offer of a free lunch and a ride in a car was enough to keep them coming in for physical exams. They were so uneducated that they could not assess the truthfulness of what the doctors said. They were so lacking in collective organization that mounting an effective protest was unlikely even if they did see through the deception. And they were such targets of white racism that they were blamed for their own plight. The white doctors reasoned that promiscuity among blacks was the cause of the subjects' suffering, not the fact that treatment was denied them.

In summary, the Tuskegee study represents a confrontation of the powerful against the powerless. It illustrates how science can become a tool that one interest group wields at the expense of another. It also shows the power of science itself, the authority science brings to bear on projects carried out in the name of scientific research. In the Tuskegee study doctors used this authority in an attempt to enhance their own prestige and influence. Here science "grew" (more scientific research was conducted) because powerful groups used science for their own ends. This is not to say that self-aggrandizement is the force behind all scientific expansion. But in the development of any large institution that commands both prestige and money, a struggle to consolidate and exercise power plays an inevitable part.

THE RULES OF SCIENCE

You are invited to play a new game—a game called Truth. To play you must join with others to form a Truth team, which may have up to 100 people. The aim is to collect as many facts about the world as possible and to be able to demonstrate that each fact is correct. You are left to your own devices to determine the best way to carry out these objectives. What do you think would be needed to play the Truth game effectively?

Although there really is no game of Truth, the goals of this fictitious pastime are identical to those of science. Scientists strive to collect information about the physical and social worlds. Their data must be reliable—that is, collectible in such a way as to rule out distorting factors such as personal bias, careless observation, or freak chance occurrences. There are two sociological perspectives on the rules that govern science: a structural viewpoint and an action one. Each sees the rules for playing Truth differently.

The Structural Perspective

From a structural perspective participants in science are far from free to play the "game" in whatever way they wish. Instead, they are constrained by a set of institutionalized norms prescribing appropriate behavior. These norms include not just the methods of organizing experiments, conducting observations, and doing other kinds of research, but also rules that establish the ethos,

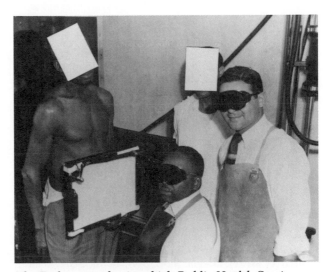

The Tuskegee study, in which Public Health Service doctors studied the progress of syphilis among a group of black men rather than treating them for the disease, was a particularly blatant misuse of scientific power and authority. In many cases, however, the issues are more subtle and deal with everyday realities. What types of scientific research are currently stirring debate in our society? (Center for Disease Control, Atlanta, Ga.)

or fundamental spirit, of science. Such norms are essential, structuralists contend, if the game of Truth is to be played with any degree of success.

The Ethos of Science: Four Basic Norms

Robert K. Merton (1973) has identified four basic norms, which together constitute the ethos of science. He refers to these norms as "institutional imperatives," *institutional* meaning that they are built into the historical structure of science (and are not just passing fads or individual whims), and *imperatives* meaning that they are rules a scientist adopts and abides by in order to maintain good standing in the scientific community. Thus, from Merton's structural perspective, the Truth game has strict rules that are independent of players' wishes and constantly guide participants' behavior. The players, for their part, internalize the rules; they come to consider them both right and essential to their goal of pursuing knowledge.

The first of the four basic norms that make up the ethos of science is what Merton calls "universalism." **Universalism** means that the scientific community will consider the theories and research of *all* of its members, not just a prestigious few who are affiliated with the "best" institutions. Contributions to science are therefore assessed solely on the basis of the evidence that supports them, not on the basis of the particular researcher's background and reputation. Universalism also means that rewards and opportunities (from the acceptance of a paper for publication to the granting of a Nobel Prize) are allocated according to competence and achievement, not according to who one is or who one knows. The opposite of universalism is discrimination —granting acceptance and issuing rewards to people with certain social characteristics (fame, professional influence, an Ivy League affiliation, being male, white, Western European, and so forth). When discrimination is rejected and universalism prevails, all scientists are motivated to work hard at their profession, for they know they will be judged by what they accomplish.

The second of Merton's four basic norms is known as "communalism." **Communalism** means that scientific findings are public (communal) property, not the private property of the researchers who discovered them. Data, in other words, are shared by the entire scientific community. Such widespread sharing of information has many benefits. For one thing, it reduces duplication of effort. It also allows researchers to assess one another's contributions, weed out what is weak, and build upon what is sound. In this way scientific knowledge gradually expands. Individual scientists do, of course, receive recognition for their work. But the act of hoarding scientific data, of deliberately concealing it, directly violates the ethos of science.

A third norm of science, **disinterestedness,** does not indicate that scientists are expected to lack interest in their work or concern about its outcome. It simply means that they should deemphasize personal gain (fame, power, economic rewards) in the pursuit of knowledge. Scientists, in other words, should not use their work mainly for self-aggrandizement. The motive to acquire accurate new knowledge should take priority over personal ambitions. Of course, scientists are not required to eschew recognition, professional awards, and prestigious appointments, but concern for such personal achievements must not supersede a commitment to doing "good" science. A scientist in pursuit of fame and fortune may be tempted to doctor findings in order to win glory.

A fourth norm of science, which Merton terms **organized skepticism,** means that scientists, as a matter of professional procedure, critically evaluate one another's contributions to the field. Scientists, in other words, are professional doubters. They are always questioning the validity of data, the soundness of theories, and the thoroughness of research methods. They are always challenging the logic of an explanation and offering alternatives. They do this not just to be argumentative. They are skeptical because discovering the truth demands that every finding and idea be subjected to rigorous scrutiny and testing before it is tentatively accepted. We say *tentatively* accepted because in science few things are considered absolutely and forever proven. Scientists believe that a healthy skepticism toward all knowledge is the only way to refine and expand our understanding of the world. In this respect science is very different from religion. Religious truths are not subjected to relentless questioning but are accepted on faith. In contrast, the very structure of science is built on doubt. Doubt motivates the quest for hard evidence, which lies at the heart of science.

Although most scientists accept these rules as essential to pursuing truth, science, like other fields, has its unethical practitioners. Deviance from the norms —scientific fraud—is taken quite seriously in the scientific community.

Deviance in Science

By the spring of 1981 research fellows at the Harvard Medical School were more than a little suspicious. John Roland Darsee, one of their young colleagues who did cardiovascular research, had published almost 100 papers and abstracts in only two years (Broad and Wade 1982)! He was thus churning out work for publication at the incredible pace of nearly one piece per week. Pressed by his colleagues, Darsee confessed that he had indeed violated a cardinal rule of scientific ethics: "Thou shall not fake data." But he swore that this was his first offense.

Darsee's mentor, a famous cardiologist and medical researcher who ran the lab where Darsee worked, decided not to ruin Darsee's career by making the fraud public. Darsee was allowed to continue doing research, under the assumption that he would never cheat again. All went well for a few months. But then an official from the National Institutes of Health reported misgivings about some of Darsee's data in a study the NIH was funding. The dean of the Harvard Medical School appointed an investigative committee, which found Darsee guilty of fraud and barred him from participation in NIH research for ten years. Eventually, Darsee was forced to resign.

Unfortunately, the Darsee case is not the only one of its kind. In 1974 William Summerlin, a researcher at the prestigious Sloan-Kettering Institute, admitted to faking evidence of successful skin grafts between genetically different animals. (The fraud was discovered accidentally by a technician who swabbed with alcohol the dark-skin graft on a white-skinned mouse. To his amazement the "graft" wiped away; it had simply been inked on!) Another highly publicized scientific fraud was the skull of Piltdown Man, supposedly found in Piltdown, England, in 1912. At the time, the skull was reported to be between 200,000 and 1 million years old. In the 1950s, however, new archaeological dating techniques and X-ray analyses showed that it was nothing more than a cleverly assembled forgery. It seems that in every decade some such incident of scientific deception comes to light. Are these isolated cases or merely the tip of a huge iceberg of deviance?

Some sociologists argue that scientists today are under enormous pressure to make their findings "look good." Unlike their counterparts in previous centuries, contemporary scientists earn their living by doing research. They may be employed by a publicly or privately funded laboratory, or their tenure on the faculty of a university may depend on gaining a favorable reputation through their published papers. In any case, their salary, standard of living, and the respect of their peers are directly related to how well their work is received. As William Broad and Nicholas Wade write:

If the luminaries of scientific history would on occasion misrepresent their data for the personal vindication of seeing their ideas prevail, the temptations must be all the greater for contemporary scientists. Not only personal justification but also professional rewards depend on winning acceptance for an idea or theory or technique. Often an extra measure of acceptance can be won by minor misrepresentations. "Tidying up" data, making results seem just a little more clear-cut, selecting only the "best" data for publication—all these seemingly excusable adjustments help toward getting an article published, making a name for oneself, being asked to join a journal's

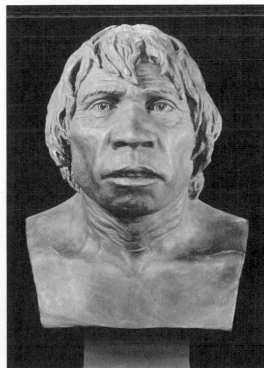

While most scientific fraud involves subtle manipulation of data, the Piltdown Man was an example of outright forgery—a skull "discovered" in Piltdown, England, in 1912 and reported to be hundreds of thousands of years old. New techniques for the analysis and dating of archaeological materials eventually determined that, in fact, the Piltdown Man was not much older than the report of his discovery. (Below and right: Courtesy Department Library Services/American Museum of Natural History.)

editorial board, securing the next government grant, or winning a prestigious prize. (Broad and Wade 1982, pp. 36–37)

But other sociologists feel that estimates of misrepresentation in science are often overstated (Zuckerman 1977). They contend that the professional socialization of scientists strongly inhibits fraud. Graduate students are repeatedly warned that willful distortion of study results is "the worst sin a scientist can commit since such actions threaten to destroy the very heart of the scientific system" (Aronson 1975, p. 115). If this cardinal rule is not internalized enough to deter deviance, the realization that others will be scrutinizing their work keeps most potential forgers in line. The norm of organized skepticism demands that scientists try to replicate interesting new findings. Few researchers would dare to publicize fraudulent data when they know that their colleagues are likely to catch them in their lie. Being caught in an act of fraud in science is no trivial matter. The deviants are subject to the indignation and contempt of their colleagues, as John Darsee was. Severe enough acts of misrepresentation result in expulsion from the profession and the end of the scientist's career.

It is very hard to determine the true extent of fraud in science, for researchers are unlikely to confess such acts even in strictest confidence. According to those with a structural perspective, however, the existence of some misrepresentation doesn't negate the ethical norms of science. These norms are the ideal—the way the Truth game *should* be played. In the structural view the norms are standards that scientists constantly use to guide their own conduct and to judge that of others.

There is another, very different view, however. According to sociologists who take an action perspective, the norms of science do not exist outside their *use* by scientists. Scientists, the action view contends, employ norms to justify or condemn certain actions. In the process the norms are open to a variety of interpretations depending on the particular situation. The action perspective is clearly illustrated in what has come to be called the "Velikovsky affair."

The Action Perspective

In 1950 a physician and psychoanalyst named Immanuel Velikovsky published a book called *Worlds in Collision* that created a furor in the scientific community. Velikovsky pointed out that ancient writings from around the world chronicle a set of great natural catastrophes on earth. For example, the Old Testament's description of how Moses won the release of the Israelites from Egypt tells of a tremendous storm of hail, lightning, and fire; of a thick darkness that enveloped the world for days; and of tidal forces strong enough to part the Red Sea. These catastrophic events, Velikovsky argued, were caused by close encounters between the earth and the planet Venus. Venus, according to Velikovsky, broke off from Jupiter to form a huge, fiery comet that swept past the earth twice in the days of Moses and then collided with Mars, ricocheting off into its current orbit. Velikovsky's dramatic portrait of ancient times captured the public imagination, and his book became a best-seller.

But scientists were not as intrigued by Velikovsky's ideas. They scoffed at his theory and flatly refused to see it as a legitimate possibility worthy of being put to scientific tests. Many launched fierce attacks against Velikovsky without ever having read *Worlds in Collision*; they based their criticism merely on secondhand accounts that appeared in the popular press. Scientists around the nation wrote letters to Velikovsky's publisher threatening not to buy the company's science texts if it continued to sell Velikovsky's work. The editors of scientific journals refused to publish articles by Velikovsky in which he defended himself. The few scientists who dared to say that Velikovsky should be given a fair hearing were ridiculed by their colleagues and some even lost their jobs (Mulkay 1969).

The scientific community's vehement reaction to Velikovsky seemed on the surface to violate several norms of science. Scientists appeared to violate universalism by refusing to give respectful attention to the ideas of someone who at least was a scholar if not a bona fide scientific researcher. They also appeared to violate communalism by trying to block distribution of Velikovsky's book. And they seemed to violate the spirit of organized skepticism by so flatly rejecting the unconventional theory without any effort to test it. What could explain this response by scientists? Were they jointly engaged in a deliberate act of deviance from the norms of science?

Sociologists who take an action perspective point out that the scientists who criticized Velikovsky certainly did not see themselves as deviants from professional norms. They believed that they were acting in a normatively proper manner, that they were right in responding to Velikovsky as they did. They felt justified because they interpreted the norms of science in ways that supported their views.

For instance, Velikovsky's critics considered him an "outsider" to the scientific fields related to his theory (astronomy, astrophysics, geology, archaeology, anthropology). As a result, they thought it legitimate to interpret universalism as inapplicable to Velikovsky (Storer 1977). In addition, the 1950s, when Velikovsky's book was published, was a time when scientists and other intellectuals were under attack from conservatives. Velikovsky's views seemed like just another attempt to discredit the scientific community. So scientists felt they could reasonably exclude Velikovsky's work from the norm of communalism (Storer 1977). Velikovsky's views were also diametrically opposed to established ideas about our solar system's formation. Because Velikovsky challenged these ideas, because his theory simply did not fit within the framework of accepted "truths," scientists deemed it correct to interpret organized skepticism as inapplicable to Velikovsky (Mulkay 1969).

In summary, then, the action perspective sees the rules of the Truth game somewhat differently than the structural perspective. The norms of science do not exist independently of the interpretations scientists give to them. Such interpretations are essential because no norm has a single meaning that applies to all circumstances. People must always analyze the situation at hand and decide how norms pertain to it (Mulkay 1976). In the Velikovsky affair, scientists reconsidered the meaning of universalism, communalism, and organized skepticism, and they concluded that these norms did not apply. In the process they turned what first appeared to be a violation of the ethos of science into a response that they believed was a legitimate defense of scientific "truth." At the same time they *used* the norms as ideology (Mulkay 1976), and in so doing they justified their actions to others and furthered their own interests. From this perspective, the norms of science are not rigid rules imposed on people but highly flexible guidelines that scientists are constantly interpreting and redefining.

EXPLORING THE PROCESS OF "DOING" SCIENCE

The Social Process of Discovery

At the beginning of this chapter we said that science was a social phenomenon partly because it involves many people working collectively and sharing their ideas. The belief that important discoveries come from the laboratories of a dedicated scientist who diligently works alone fits our romantic notions but not reality. This fact surprises many people, for we often hear great scientists described as if they were solitary heroes. For example, James Watson and Francis Crick, the biologists who discovered the structure of DNA (the molecule that carries genetic information), are often portrayed as two brilliant scientists who tinkered with models of DNA in an isolated laboratory room until finally—Eureka!—

James Watson (left) and Francis Crick (right) received a Nobel Prize in 1962 for their deduction of the structure of DNA. The competition among scientists for funding, publication, and acclaim sometimes obscures the fact that science is a collective, methodical enterprise in which many threads of research come together to produce new knowledge. The work of many scientists contributed to Watson and Crick's "discovery" of the double helix of the DNA molecule. (Top: Photo Researchers, Inc.; bottom: Dr. A. Lesk/Photo Researchers, Inc.)

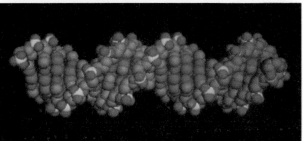

they had the answer to one of biology's greatest puzzles. Nothing could be farther from the truth. Watson and Crick, like all scientists, were part of a collective, worldwide effort to amass factual knowledge. Although they won a Nobel Prize for finally putting the pieces of the DNA puzzle together, they were not responsible for producing those pieces, nor were they alone in the quest for an answer. Many other scientists in Europe and America made critical contributions. The discovery of DNA's structure, in short, was a social achievement, not an individual one. This is true of all scientific findings.

The seventeenth-century philosopher Francis Bacon was one of the first to describe just how social a process scientific discovery is. Let us consider his description, as summarized by Robert Merton (1973), in light of the story of the discovery of the structure of DNA:

1. *Scientific discoveries are built on knowledge that many people provide.* They are the product of a large body of information, accumulated over many years, that serves as a foundation for new understandings. In the case of DNA, a number of different researchers contributed important information. Chemists had determined the various components of DNA (phosphate, sugar, and several nitrogen-containing bases), but they did not know how those components were assembled. The famous American chemist Linus Pauling had a suggestion: he had found that protein molecules are often spiral in shape, and he suspected that DNA might be similar in structure. X-ray diffraction photographs of DNA taken by the Englishman Maurice Wilkins and his assistant Rosalind Franklin showed that this suspicion was probably right. The photos also revealed that the width of a DNA molecule was uniform along its entire length. This finding ruled out many arrangments that would produce an irregular shape. These and other pieces of data allowed Watson and Crick to deduce the correct structure. Thus, without the many clues provided by their colleagues, they would never have solved the mystery.

2. *Scientific discoveries and the knowledge on which they are based require a division of labor and a sharing of information.* Effort would be wasted if all the scientists concerned with a certain problem go about solving it in exactly the same way. It is much more efficient for each person to pursue a somewhat different approach and then to pool their findings. As Bacon wrote: "Men will begin to understand their own strength only when, instead of many of them doing the same things, one

shall take charge of one thing and one of another." In the search for the structure of DNA, scientists adopted this kind of specialization. Some conducted chemical studies to discover DNA's components. Others used X-ray diffraction techniques to get a general sense of DNA's shape. Still others, like Watson and Crick, built physical models to see how the parts of DNA might all fit together. Out of this division of labor came a relatively speedy answer to the puzzle.

3. *Scientific discoveries are facilitated by the use of systematic methods.* Not only do these methods make data collection more reliable, but they also increase the number of researchers who can make significant contributions to science. With established methods to follow, scientists do not have to be geniuses to make valuable discoveries. Even if only of average intelligence they can still be very productive. Bacon likened the methods of science to the tools that a draftsman uses to draw a straight line or a perfect circle. These tools greatly reduce the need for extraordinary talent in the person who uses them. Many people, for example, can be trained in the scientific technique of taking X-ray diffraction photos. Of course, it helps if a researcher using this technique is especially insightful in analyzing the results. With specialization and division of labor, however, all such challenging tasks can be accomplished by the members of a research team.

4. *Scientific discoveries are "the births of time."* In other words, they are the products of a certain era in which the necessary groundwork has been laid. The discovery of DNA's structure could never have occurred in the mid-nineteenth century, the era in which researchers first learned of the molecule's existence. Then, scientists had only scant knowledge of what DNA was composed of; in no way were they ready to explore the arrangement of its parts. The situation was very different in the mid-twentieth century, when scientists had all the pieces of data needed to deduce DNA's structure. Watson and Crick, in fact, were constantly worried that other scientists would beat them to the discovery. They knew the time was ripe for the puzzle to be solved.

5. *Scientific discoveries are apt to be made simultaneously by different researchers.* This assumption follows directly from the one above. If an era is "ripe" for a certain scientific discovery, that discovery probably will be made by more than one person. Realizing this, Watson and Crick hastened to publish the structure of DNA in a scientific journal. If they had delayed even a few months, other researchers might have succeeded in putting all the pieces together and "stealing" the glory.

Scientific Revolutions

The discovery of the structure of DNA was extremely important. It allowed scientists to understand how the information needed to construct a living organism is coded in genes and how that information is transmitted from one generation to the next. It also opened the door for genetic engineering, the process whereby researchers deliberately alter genes and create new forms of life. But as far-reaching as all these developments have been, they do not really constitute a revolution in our way of thinking about heredity. Since the turn of the twentieth century, scientists have believed that hereditary characteristics are determined by discrete entities (what we now call "genes") contained in the sperm of a male and the egg of a female. The discovery that DNA was the molecule that carried genes, Watson and Crick's determination of DNA's structure, and a wealth of later findings about how each gene is coded were all efforts to fill in the gaps of a preexisting picture of how heredity works. Thomas Kuhn (1970) refers to this process of filling in the gaps as "normal science." **Normal science** involves collecting facts and data to substantiate a set of current theories about the world. As such, it consumes most—often all—of many scientists' careers.

Kuhn points out that normal science always proceeds within some **paradigm**—a set of general assumptions about how a certain aspect of the world works. A paradigm serves as a framework that tells researchers what important questions remain unanswered and how these questions might be approached. For example, the paradigm that hereditary traits are the product of discrete entities called genes naturally led to a search to discover what a gene is and how it governs development. Similarly, the paradigm in astronomy that the sun is the center of our solar system, with the planets revolving around it, inevitably led to many questions about our solar system's place in the universe. Contemporary study of human physiology has likewise been framed by the paradigm that a human body is like a highly complex machine. Thus, modern physiologists diligently search for how the human brain is "wired" because they think of the brain as analogous to an electrically driven computer.

In addition to guiding the direction of research, a paradigm also limits its scope. A paradigm defines the world in a certain way, thus eliminating the need for researchers to consider a great many other alternatives. Even more than this, a paradigm creates in scientists a certain mental set—a tendency to see the world as the

paradigm says it is. A paradigm, then, is like a pair of tinted glasses; put them on and the world appears to be a particular color.

Scientific paradigms do change, of course. Before the assumption that discrete entities called genes carry hereditary information, people believed that a mixing of male and female fluids formed a third fluid with the power to generate a new organism. Before the assumption that the sun is at the center of our solar system, people believed that the entire universe revolved around the earth. Before the assumption that the brain is a complex machine that controls behavior, people believed that thoughts and actions were the product of an internal spirit or soul. The replacement of an earlier paradigm constitutes a true **scientific revolution**—a new outlook, radically different from the previous one. If an old paradigm seems ludicrous to you, it is only because, as an educated person, you have been indoctrinated into the scientific paradigms of today. From the perspective of future generations some of our current assumptions about nature may seem equally absurd.

Why does one scientific paradigm replace another? Why do researchers abandon an old way of thinking in favor of an entirely new framework? The answer begins with the appearance of anomalies—findings that contradict the existing paradigm or that significantly deviate from its predictions. For instance, in the mid 1800s Gregor Mendel, an Austrian monk, conducted a series of cross-breeding experiments with peas and showed that inherited traits must be determined by a pair of hereditary units (genes), one of which comes from a female, the other from a male in sexual reproduction. Mendel's experimental findings were published in 1866 but were virtually ignored for the next thirty-four years. They simply did not fit within the nineteenth-century paradigm of biological inheritance. A major anomaly in science often meets this fate. Eventually, however, more and more anomalies may arise—too many to be simply overlooked or awkwardly explained within the existing paradigm. When this happens, the scientific field involved enters a crisis in which it becomes apparent that the old paradigm is inadequate.

The time is now ripe for a new paradigm to emerge, one that can explain all the known facts more successfully. When such a paradigm is finally proposed, it may, at first, be resisted. Charles Darwin's theory of biological evolution elegantly explained the fossil record of the history of life on earth, but many people were still reluctant to accept it. Decades are sometimes needed for

Every sailor knows that a boat's motion is relative to the motions of wind and water, but it was Albert Einstein who applied this idea—that all motion is relative—to the existing paradigm of physics. The result was his General Theory of Relativity, which like previous scientific revolutions, both created a new paradigm and gave us a new way of looking at the world, a world in which "everything is relative." (AP/Wide World Photos.)

a new paradigm to gain widespread favor. When it finally does, another wave of normal science begins. Researchers put on glasses of a different color and see a whole new world with a new set of questions to be answered.

The Social Construction of Scientific Knowledge

Paradigms point to an important fact: what we "know" about the world is not simply a direct reflection of what is "out there" in the environment. Instead, the questions

scientists ask, how they conduct their studies, and how they interpret their findings are all filtered through, and greatly biased by, prevailing assumptions. As a result, scientists do not simply "discover" scientific data, as if they were lying about like pebbles on a beach, waiting to be seen and collected. To put it another way, the knowledge that scientists amass is never a literal reflection of nature as it "really is." Rather, researchers actively *build* a model of natural and social phenomena out of their collective understandings.

The process of constructing scientific knowledge is well illustrated by the way physicists came to believe that elementary particles called quarks are the smallest bits of the nucleus of an atom (Pickering 1984). Quarks are extremely hard to isolate, if they can be isolated at all. Thus, in the 1960s when the quark theory was first proposed, no one had ever seen a quark or gathered any other concrete evidence that such particles existed. Physicists had to work for many years in order to demonstrate quarks. A belief in their existence *preceded* any data to substantiate the quark theory. Physicists, in other words, formed a perception that quarks were real and then interpreted findings to verify this view.

This process is the opposite of most people's conception of how science proceeds. Most people think that scientists conduct experiments to reveal ultimate truths about the world, truths that are out there just waiting to be unveiled. This description, however, oversimplifies the research process. Scientists are not like newspaper reporters who simply "tell the facts." Instead, they are more like journalists who *make* their own stories, who come to believe that a certain event took place (a crime, a scandal, a political blunder) and then look for evidence to substantiate their view. But how does the belief in a certain "truth" arise in the first place? What causes a person to develop a particular perception of reality? For the scientist, as for the journalist, it is a matter of social context—the goals, interests, and values of the community with which the scientist identifies.

One aspect of the social context that encouraged a belief in quarks was the prevailing paradigm that governs work in elementary particle physics. That paradigm assumes that matter is composed of subunits so tiny that the human eye cannot see them. Coming to the conclusion that quarks exist involved applying this basic assumption to the already recognized components of atomic nuclei (the protons, neutron, and so forth). Thus, theoretical physicists hypothesized that the components of nuclei could be divided into even smaller components called quarks. This hypothesis was very much in keeping with their training and experience. In short, the hypothesis "fit" their fundamental view of matter (Pickering 1984).

Another aspect of the social context that encouraged a belief in quarks was a good match between the quark theory and the various resources that elementary particle physicists possessed. These resources included their training and skills as well as their established approaches to exploring the nature of matter. A belief in quarks created many new opportunities to use these resources to good advantage. Researchers could turn their attention to searching for evidence of quarks, and if they found it they would win a handsome payoff in terms of peer recognition and career advancement. A belief in quarks, in other words, "fit" the interests of certain scientists, and so they constructed a quark model.

At the same time, the quark model fit the technological context of its day. Had a quark theory been proposed twenty years earlier, it would have been a virtually unresearchable topic. Scientists then did not have the equipment needed to look for evidence of these minuscule particles. Such studies had to await the development of particle accelerators (devices that produce beams of high-energy atomic particles, which are then subjected to collisions). They also had to await the development of particle detectors (devices that record information about the even smaller atomic particles produced by particle accelerators). Inventing these highly sophisticated pieces of research equipment, and securing the huge sums of money needed to build them, set the stage for physicists to explore the possibility of quarks.

As research on quarks proceeded and data accumulated, new opportunities in turn arose for theoretical physicists. They could elaborate and refine their hypotheses regarding quarks, building even more sophisticated models. Thus, a kind of symbiotic relationship developed between quark researchers and quark theorists. Each group provided the other with both problems to solve and a justification for continuing work in the quark field (Pickering 1984). This made the quark concept a very profitable one.

Of course, not everyone immediately accepted the quark model. Some elementary particle physicists continued to resist it even after empirical evidence in its favor began to mount. Such resistance shows again that establishing scientific truths is not just a matter of passively accepting whatever facts nature presents. In-

stead, scientific truths are actively constructed by scientists to fit their current social contexts.

SOCIETY AND TECHNOLOGY

Caliente was in every way a model American community. Its homes, stores, streets, and parks were attractive and well maintained. Its schools were good; its local government was honest; its citizens were public-spirited and hardworking. Caliente was precisely the kind of community that Americans want to preserve. That is why it was so tragic when the railroads switched to diesel trains during the 1940s. Caliente, you see, was a railroad town. It was built in the desert of the American Southwest for the sole purpose of maintaining the steam-driven locomotives that passed through it daily. The steel boilers of these locomotives were under tremendous

Truth, Beauty, Strangeness, Charm . . . Even the names of quarks seem to acknowledge the social origins of scientific knowledge. At the Fermi National Accelerator Laboratory, electrons, protons, and other subatomic particles are accelerated nearly to the speed of light, traveling in opposite directions round and round through several kilometers of pipes in the circular tunnel shown here. When these particles collide, they disintegrate into such elementary particles as . . . Truth, Beauty, Strangeness, and Charm. (Dan McCoy/Rainbow.)

stress from the high temperature and pressure needed to keep up a head of steam. So every hundred miles they were disconnected from the train, checked for damage, and repaired or replaced. Caliente was one of the "division points" where this work took place. Most of the men of Caliente were employed by the railroad. Those who were not provided the goods and services that the railroad workers needed.

The introduction of diesel trains spelled disaster for Caliente. That, at least, was the opinion of W. F. Cottrell, who published a classic study of the situation in 1951. Diesel locomotives do not require frequent servicing, so some of the former division points, including Caliente, became obsolete. Except for a handful of men offered jobs elsewhere in the railroad system, most of the men of Caliente found themselves out of work. Because of the widespread unemployment, the town's whole economy suffered. Sales in the business district plummeted and many stores closed. Property values fell precipitously, causing many families to lose most of their life savings. To make matters worse, the situation seemed permanent. Try as they might, the residents of Caliente could not attract another large employer to such an isolated part of the country.

Analyzing Technological Change

Cottrell's study of the effects of dieselization on Caliente anticipated some of the central ideas in sociologists' current view of technological change, such as the notion that the rate and direction of change in technology is not determined by the technology itself. Nothing about steam-powered engines necessitated the development of diesel-driven ones. But there were some good social reasons.

In fact, contemporary sociologists see technology and society as inseparable. "Technological systems," writes Thomas Hughes (1987, p. 51), "are both socially constructed and society shaping." By this he means two things. First, the social context determines which inventions will be accepted and how enduring they will be. For example, the invention and acceptance of diesel locomotives were influenced by a number of social factors: profits for the railroads due to reduced labor and repair costs, increased sales for oil companies that produced diesel fuel, and weakened public opposition to

the loss of railroad jobs because of a scarcity of workers during World War II. Hughes' second point is that while technologies are socially constructed, they also shape and change the societies in which they are used. In the case of Caliente, a single shift in technology undermined the community's entire way of life.

How do people interpret a change like dieselization? What meaning do they give to a new technology? Contemporary sociologists argue that the meaning varies depending on who you ask. Dieselization of locomotives may have been "progress" to the average American who appreciated speedier travel, but it was a tragedy to the people of Caliente who lost their means of support. Thus, perceptions of technological success or failure, advancement or decline, lie in the eye of the beholder; they, like technology itself, are social constructions. No new machine or method is *inherently* better than what it replaces. Its desirability and value are a subjective judgment made by the social groups involved. Of course, not everyone agrees on what technology is most advantageous and useful. When marked differences of opinion arise, the preferences of those who wield more power usually prevail. Thus, diesel locomotives replaced steam-driven ones because diesel technology was preferred by some very powerful groups (the railroad companies and oil corporations, for instance)—groups with more power than the residents of Caliente.

The Evolution of Technological Systems

Technologies, such as the diesel engine, do not exist in isolation. They are part of broader technological systems dedicated to solving practical problems. The diesel engine belongs to a technological system that includes machines and equipment (trains, tracks, switching equipment), social organizations for producing and utilizing the engine (factories and national railroad corporations), and the scientific knowledge that made the diesel possible (the physical principles of air compression and ignition). These elements form a "system" because they are inescapably interconnected. Each one needs the others for its existence.

Thomas Hughes (1987) has constructed a model for the evolution of large, modern technological systems. This model recognizes five stages, the first of which is *invention*—the initial creation of a new technology.

Invention can pertain to physical things (the car, the typewriter, the potato peeler) or to social organization (the invention of the corporation or the holding company, for instance). Some inventions are "radical"; they launch a whole new technological system. Other inventions are "conservative"; they further develop existing systems. Independent inventors (as opposed to those employed by organizations) are responsible for a disproportionate share of "radical" inventions, probably because they have little vested interest in maintaining the status quo. Examples of independent inventors and their "radical" inventions include Alexander Graham Bell and the telephone, the Wright brothers and the airplane, and Thomas Edison and the electric light and power system.

The second stage in Hughes's model is *development*, the process whereby an invention is given social, economic, and political features that will help it survive. Many inventors gradually incorporate such features into their products. For instance, Thomas Edison deliberately designed his electric lighting so that it would be economically competitive with gaslights. Similarly, the Wright brothers consciously took into account the physiological traits of pilots when they designed their aircraft. Such efforts help ensure that an invention will be accepted.

Development is typically followed by a stage in which the invention is surrounded by a complex system of manufacturing, sales, and service operations. Sometimes the original inventor takes charge of this process and becomes both an inventor and an entrepreneur. Thomas Edison, for example, was intimately involved in setting up and managing the companies established to support and market his electric lights and power. George Eastman, inventor of the Kodak camera, also played a key role in mass producing and selling his own products. But these men are the exception rather than the rule. Most inventors tend to turn over the manufacturing and marketing of their inventions to people with special expertise in these fields. When this stage in the evolution of a new technology is completed, the invention has become what Hughes calls an *innovation*.

Once an innovation is established, a fourth stage, called *technology transfer*, may begin. It involves modifi-

Both inventor and entrepreneur, Thomas Edison understood that, in order to be more than just a bright idea, his electric light bulb had to offer advantages of economy and convenience over existing gaslights. No matter how ingenious or successful its design, an invention that fails to provide any practical benefit to society will, like Ayres's Aerial Machine of 1885, never get off the ground. (Left: Culver Pictures; right: The Bettmann Archive.)

cation of the new technological system in order to make it suitable for transfer to another time or culture. Thus, Japanese engineers have adapted their cars to suit the needs of American buyers, just as American fast-food chains have adapted their menus to suit the tastes of customers in Japan.

A final stage in Hughes's model is *growth and consolidation*, the process whereby a technological system becomes very large and solidifies its position in society. Examples in modern industrial nations include the technological systems that have developed around the car, the telephone, the airplane, the television, and the computer. Large-scale growth of a technological system is never problem free, however. Sometimes one component of the system develops less quickly than others, and the lagging component produces a bottleneck that must be removed in order not to limit the system's potential. In the nineteenth-century British textile industry, for example, development of weaving equipment would sometimes lag behind that of spinning devices, while at other times the reverse would happen. Inventors tended to concentrate on the lagging component in order to raise the efficiency of the overall system.

Sometimes a problem arises that cannot be solved within the framework of existing technology. For instance, designers knew in the late 1920s that no further refinement of the piston-engine/propeller plane could ever get it to approach the speed of sound. Since both business and the military valued high-speed travel, the time was ripe for the development of a brand new invention, the turbojet engine. Replacing an established technology is not always easy, however. People often have a vested interest in maintaining an existing technological system, both because they have invested time and money in its development and because it affords them a livelihood or profit. Such resistance to change must be overcome if a new round of technological evolution is to begin.

SCIENCE, TECHNOLOGY, AND PUBLIC POLICY

In 1960 the Food and Drug Administration banned the interstate transport and sale of Laetrile, a drug extracted from apricot pits and claimed by some to be an effective treatment for cancer. Most doctors and cancer researchers scoffed at Laetrile, since they considered it a useless substance that held out false hopes to cancer patients and sometimes even duped them into abandoning traditional treatments. But proponents of Laetrile vehemently defended the drug in a series of court cases aimed at lifting the FDA ban. They argued that Laetrile's critics were deliberately suppressing research data on the drug's effectiveness for fear that widespread use of Laetrile would greatly reduce their profits from the use of conventional cancer therapies. In the end Laetrile's proponents managed to legalize the drug in twenty-two states, not because lawmakers there were convinced that Laetrile cures cancer, but because they believed that dying people should have freedom of choice regarding their treatments (Petersen and Markle 1984; Markle and Petersen 1987).

In December 1981 a trial was held in Little Rock, Arkansas, that challenged the constitutionality of a recently passed state law. The law required Arkansas public schools to present a balanced treatment of two views of the earth's origins: "creation science" (which holds that the earth was created suddenly, in its present form, some 6,000 to 20,000 years ago as the Bible describes) and the science of evolution (which argues that the earth and all living things have evolved gradually, through natural processes, over a period of 4 or 5 billion years). At the trial advocates and opponents of the law tried to convince the court that their own view was the only reasonable and scientifically sound one. But the judge ultimately decided in favor of the plaintiffs and prohibited enforcement of the controversial statute (Gieryn, Bevins, and Zehr 1985).

In a society where modern science and technology are ubiquitous, they inevitably become embroiled in public policy decisions (Nelkin 1975, 1982). In the first policy issue described above, the scientific community tried to convince the federal government that an unconventional cancer drug was totally ineffective. In the second policy issue, scientists went on the defensive and tried to persuade the court that creationism was really religion in scientific clothing and therefore had no place in public schools. In the making of countless other public policy choices, scientists and technical experts are asked for opinions. Whenever a nuclear power plant is built, an airport expanded, a new pesticide tested, an offshore oil well drilled, a change in a social welfare program discussed, or whenever any one of hundreds of other policy choices are considered, scientists and technical experts are usually asked to provide data.

But exactly what should we expect of these scientists and experts as they perform this role? Should we view them as rational, unbiased arbiters of public controversies, always able to provide the facts on which sound decisions can be based? The history of public policy making has repeatedly shown that this view is unrealistic. The information that scientists bring to public policy issues is almost never cut and dried. Often it simply adds more fuel to the conflict instead of decisively showing which choices should be made. Why does scientific input add so much complexity to public policy debates? Some reasons are illustrated by the Laetrile and "creation science" cases.

First, in the debate over virtually every public policy issue, scientists and technical experts are mobilized on *both* sides. In other words, no single scientific "truth" unequivocally answers all of the questions raised. Instead, many competing "truths" each claim to be the accurate version. But how can this happen when scientific views are based on factual data? Every scientific field has some gray areas, some topics on which the available data are not completely clear. Adversaries in a public policy debate exploit these gray areas to their own advantage. For instance, in the Laetrile controversy, a few studies suggested that perhaps this drug did have some anticancer effects. Proponents of Laetrile used these studies as "proof" of their position, while opponents stressed that these isolated findings could not be reliably replicated.

In addition, both sides in a policy debate can appeal to science because each side tends to define its subject matter differently. In the creationism controversy, for example, both sides agreed that the public schools should teach science, not religion, but they disagreed strongly on what science is. The creationists defined science simply as a set of theories in support of which one can marshal a variety of "facts," some of which are only hearsay. The evolutionists, in contrast, defined science as a set of rigorous and systematic methods for gathering reliable data and testing the accuracy of theories. With these very different definitions, it is easy to see how the two sides could claim to represent science and yet differ so greatly.

Also, scientific input into public policy issues is almost never cut and dried because emotions and value judgments inevitably are mixed into the presentation of

Pharmaceutical companies spend millions of dollars on research and development and millions more on the manufacture and marketing of drugs. They are therefore likely to resist, as in the case of Laetrile, the introduction of competing drugs or methods of treatment, regardless of their merit. Can you cite examples of a similar resistance to changing technology in other industries? (Hank Morgan/Rainbow.)

technical data. In the Laetrile controversy, for example, establishment doctors and scientists portrayed those who supported Laetrile as generally lacking "good" credentials and the respect of the medical profession. This labeling tactic helped to undermine the credibility of Laetrile supporters. Soon the debate became a kind of "class conflict," with opponents of Laetrile at the top of the prestige scale and proponents at the bottom. Proponents responded by making Laetrile a populist cause. They decried the arrogance of establishment doctors in assuming that the average person lacks the ability to

The word cryogenics *literally means, in Greek, "frostborn." Here, laboratory technicians prepare a human ovum and sperm for cryogenic storage in a nitrogen-filled tank. This is just one of several technologies that seem to have outpaced our understanding of their social implications. What others are there? As the gap widens between science and the ordinary person, who or what will define the means and objectives of scientific growth? (Hank Morgan/Rainbow.)*

make rational choices regarding medical treatment. In their arguments to the courts, the right to use Laetrile became a matter of personal freedom. Thus, proponents bolstered their case by appealing to a deeply ingrained American value.

The creationists, likewise, bolstered their case by arguing that people should have the freedom to consider alternative points of view in science. They were unable to convince the courts, however, that creationism is in fact a science. Scientists who testified that creationism is *not* a science were motivated by more than just a desire to define science as they knew it. They correctly perceived that a victory for the creationists threatened the fundamental authority of all traditional science. Their struggle, then, was partly to protect the privileged position of science in our society.

The complexity of these cases clearly shows that scientific information alone does not resolve public policy issues. Such data inevitably raise questions and are always closely tied to particular researchers' values. But this does not mean that an appeal to science is futile when making public policy choices. Most modern social issues are complex and demand the specialized knowledge of well-trained experts. Without such knowledge we would be reduced to speculation about the effects of a new medical drug or the value of an educational program. Used effectively, moreover, scientific and technical knowledge allows decisions to be more rational and objective than they otherwise might be.

On the other hand, an increased role for technical experts in public policy choices involves risks. As the voice of the expert grows louder and louder, that of the average citizen may be drowned out. If experts become too powerful, that power might be abused, leading to a flood of programs that most people do not want. Finally, science is never value neutral. Scientific facts do not speak for themselves; they are always interpreted by people with likes and dislikes, personal motives and personal interests. As a result, scientific data can be used to legitimate a variety of different positions. When data are selectively presented and skewed to support a particular view, rational decision making may be undermined. Policymakers, therefore, must be aware that scientific and technical data have these limitations.

SUMMARY

1. Science is the systematic pursuit of reliable knowledge about natural phenomena and about the social world. Science has grown tremendously in the past 300 years, judging by the number of people it now employs, the amount of money spent on it, and the number of scientific discoveries, articles, and books. The functional perspective explains this growth as stemming from society's need for reliable knowledge that can be used to predict and control natural and social phenomena. The power perspective, on the contrary, holds that science has grown because it serves the needs of dominant groups to exercise power over others.

2. The rules of science are a set of institutionalized norms that prescribe the methods of data collection and the fundamental ethos, or spirit, of science. According to Robert K. Merton, science has four basic norms: universalism, communalism, disinterestedness, and organized skepticism. Deviance from these norms by scientists who falsify data is considered a serious breach of the scientific community's ideals. But according to sociologists who adopt an action perspective, these norms do not exist independently of the interpretations scientists give to them in use, and no norm has a single meaning that applies to all circumstances.

3. Science is a social process of discovery in that an understanding of any given phenomenon arises through the collective efforts and shared ideas of many scientists. Thomas Kuhn distinguishes two different levels of scientific knowledge. *Normal science* consists of facts and data to substantiate current theories about the world. The theories themselves fall within a *paradigm*—a framework of general assumptions that tell those pursuing normal science what questions to ask. When paradigms change, a *scientific revolution* has occurred. Paradigms point to the fact that scientists actively construct, rather than passively reflect, what are known as *scientific truths*.

4. The application of scientific and other knowledge to the solution of practical problems is called *technology*. Technology changes in response to social needs and in turn helps shape society. According to Thomas Hughes, technological systems evolve in five stages: invention, development, innovation, technology transfer, and growth and consolidation.

5. Scientists play a major role in public policy decisions. Although they provide valuable knowledge on which to judge the effects of possible decisions, their input is never value free. The public and policymakers must be alert to the possible biases that expert opinions reflect.

GLOSSARY

Communalism. A basic norm of science that holds that scientific findings are public property, not the private domain of the researchers who discovered them.

Disinterestedness. A basic norm of science that requires scientists to deemphasize personal gain in the pursuit of knowledge.

Normal science. The process of collecting facts and data to substantiate a set of current theories about the world.

Organized skepticism. A basic norm of science that mandates scientists to critically evaluate one another's contributions to the field.

Paradigm. A set of general assumptions about how a certain aspect of the world works.

Science. The systematic pursuit of reliable knowledge about natural phenomena and the social world.

Scientific revolution. The replacement of a paradigm by a new outlook, radically different from the previous one.

Technology. The application of knowledge (scientific or otherwise) to the solution of a practical problem.

Universalism. A basic norm of science that holds that the theories and research of *all* members of the scientific community—not just a prestigious few—will be reviewed and studied, and awards will be allocated on the basis of merit.

CHAPTER 21

Collective Behavior and Social Movements

To the middle-aged, middle-class residents of American suburbs, the year 1965 was, to say the least, disturbing. American youth, including their own sons and daughters, seemed to have lost all sense of decency. It was most obvious in the youthful fashions of the times (Skolnik 1978). Young women's hemlines rose to mid-thigh level, with paste-on decals of flowers and butterflies decorating bare knees. Long, straight hair hung freely, sometimes down to the waist, and on public streets the bra, that staple of proper feminine clothing, was often conspicuously missing. If young women's attire was shocking to older Americans, the impact of young men's dress was even worse. Their shoulder-length hair worn with headbands, their scraggly beards, bare chests, necklaces, and frayed jeans all symbolized to older, staid Americans a degenerate new generation.

Youthful fashion was not the only thing that disturbed middle-aged and middle-class people. American youth's concept of entertainment seemed decadent in the extreme. In the San Francisco area, novelist Ken Kesey and his band of Merry Pranksters treated the youthful public to a series of drug-centered parties, open to anyone who wanted to drop by. As Todd Gitlin described these events:

> The dozens, then hundreds who caught wind of these occasions were given the purest LSD (still legal in California), and treated to costumes, [body] paint, pulsating colored lights, Prankster movies, barrages of sound and music, weirdly looped tape recorders, assorted instruments, and a flood of amplified talk [over a PA system]. . . . The Pranksters had fantasies of slipping LSD into the public skin with solvents; and eventually, in Watts [a section of Los Angeles], while Kesey himself was on the lam in Mexico from marijuana charges, other Pranksters dispensed Kool-Aid spiked with LSD, didn't notify the novices, and treated one woman's bad trip by having her rant over the PA system to the dazzled, dazed assemblage. (Gitlin 1987, p. 207)

By the end of the sixties, tension had mounted between the youth generation and the establishment. Growing opposition to the war in Vietnam provided an issue around which a variety of young people rallied. Mass protests, which became larger and more emotionally charged, increasingly prompted violent exchanges between police and demonstrators. In August 1968, for instance, thousands of young antiwar protestors traveled to Chicago, where the Democratic National Convention was being held (Albert and Albert 1977). Massing in Chicago's Lincoln Park, they painted antiwar posters, listened to activist speeches, discussed their tactics, and waited. At night Chicago police were ordered to use tear gas to clear the park. Most of the demonstrators ran, but some held their ground and resisted, fighting the police with bottles, sticks, and rocks. As the violence escalated, President Lyndon Johnson called in the National Guard, which descended on the city with tanks and soldiers brandishing rifles with bayonets. In the week that followed, police brutally suppressed antiwar protests in the streets. The suppression became a symbol for the antiwar movement, which the following year staged its biggest demonstration yet: a peace march of half a million people on Washington, D.C.

What can we make of the unusual events that occurred during the 1960s? What insights do sociologists offer to help us understand this decade of defiance, rebellion, protest, and change? Many of the phenomena just described are examples of **collective behavior,** or socially shared, but relatively nonroutine, responses to events, things, or ideas. These nonroutine responses differ (often strikingly) from the more habitual patterns of everyday life in which people follow established social norms (Rose 1982). Collective behavior also tends to involve large numbers of people, who, frequently, do not even know each other. Thus, a clothing fashion that sweeps the country, another type of fad that becomes a national craze, a bizarre rumor that spreads from city to city, a sudden mass hysteria or panic, a riot or other unusual form of crowd action are all incidents of collective behavior.

At times collective behavior is transformed into a **social movement,** "a conscious, collective, organized attempt to bring about or resist large-scale change in the social order by non-institutionalized means" (Wilson 1973, p. 8). Sociologists who take a functional perspective tend to group social movements and collective behavior together. They see both as involving breaks with our social expectations, and both as frequently disrupting the established social order. Sociologists fa-voring a power perspective, however, see things differently. They argue that most social movements are only superficially related to sudden and often irrational phenomena like fads, mass hysteria, and panics. In their view, social movements are the product of rational thought and planning. They represent deliberate efforts to resist or bring about change by a group whose interests are being disregarded by the existing social system, but that lacks the power to change the system through other means than mass protest. Thus, sociologists with a power perspective tend to consider collective behavior and social movements as separate phenomena. We will return to the issue of the nature of social movements later in this chapter.

This chapter begins with a look at two theories of collective behavior, one highlighting social strain as a central cause and the other the mobilization of resources by interested parties. The first of these two theories stems from a functional perspective, the second from a power perspective. We then turn a sociological eye on mass hysteria and rumors, two forms of collective behavior that arise in stressful situations. We also explore a process called **social contagion,** in which a mood or behavior spreads rapidly through an emotionally aroused group of people. Next we look at crowd behavior, especially the behavior of volatile, potentially violent crowds. Why do people in crowds sometimes go on a rampage and do things they would never do when alone? Finally, we turn our attention to social movements and examine different types of movements, including some recent ones.

"By the time we got to Woodstock, we were half a million strong." As the nostalgic lyrics of this popular song of the 1970s suggest, the 1969 Woodstock Music and Art Fair came to epitomize the "flower power" and youthful activism of the sixties' generation. Despite inadequate preparations for so many people, jammed country roads for miles around the festival site, and bad weather, the Woodstock crowd persevered in sharing a joyous and peaceful celebration. (UPI/Bettmann News-photos.)

PERSPECTIVES ON COLLECTIVE BEHAVIOR

Because some forms of collective behavior spring up so suddenly and are so emotionally charged, many people consider them beyond comprehension. For example, many Americans were incredulous at the violence that erupted on the streets of Chicago in the summer of 1968. They watched their TV screens with wonderment and horror as the nightly news showed protesters being brutally beaten by police. But though this event seemed inexplicable to the average person, sociologists have a different view. They argue that incidents of collective behavior do not just occur any time, any place. Powerful preconditions set the stage for them. Neil Smelser has proposed one theory that sets forth these preconditions.

Smelser's Social Strain Theory

According to Smelser (1962), six conditions typically precede an episode of collective behavior: structural conduciveness, social strain, a generalized belief, precipitating events, mobilization of participants, and a breakdown of social control. These conditions occur in sequence, each one creating a social environment that helps make the next one possible. Smelser does not say that collective behavior will always occur when a few or even all of these preconditions are present. But as each one is added on, the likelihood of alternative responses decreases, until eventually some kind of collective behavior becomes virtually inevitable.

Structural Conduciveness

By structural conduciveness Smelser means that certain aspects of social organization facilitate collective action. In 1968, for instance, nationwide TV networks facilitated the publicizing of antiwar views. TV coverage of the Democratic National Convention provided a forum where student activists could voice their opposition to the administration's policies in Vietnam. Of course, such structural conduciveness is very general and in no way necessitates collective behavior. But it does provide a setting that makes possible certain forms of collective action.

Social Strain

Social strain can arise from various sources. It can spring from a sudden disruption of the existing social order, as when a disastrous flood or tornado strikes; or it can come from long-term social change, such as the changes that led to the medieval witch craze (see box, p. 590). Strain can also arise when the culture offers inadequate guidelines for responding to an event or situation, or it can result from persistent and intense value conflicts between different segments of society (incompatible religious groups, hostile economic classes, or widely disparate political camps, for example). This last situation seems to have been at work in Chicago in 1968. The political establishment had embroiled the nation in a foreign conflict that the majority of young people neither understood nor wished to give their lives for. This intense clash of values and interests was a powerful source of social strain.

Generalized Belief

Usually a generalized belief develops to explain the strain that people are experiencing. In 1968 young people with antiwar views had developed the generalized belief that high-ranking public officials were insensitive to the will of the people and were determined to suppress any opposing points of view. This generalized belief served to heighten tension by defining formerly vague ideas, giving them a shared reality. Increasingly, the stage was set for an incident of some kind to surface.

Precipitating Events

Often an episode of collective behavior erupts when something happens to confirm people's generalized belief. In Chicago the precipitating event was the report that Mayor Richard Daley of Chicago, an old-line political boss, refused to grant permits for peaceful antiwar demonstrations. Soon rumors spread throughout the antiwar community. People claimed that Chicago police were training dogs to attack demonstrators and that the mayor had ordered the city's sewers to be prepared as additional jail space. Here was supposed concrete evidence that the political establishment *was* oppressive, and that it would use any measures to stamp out opposition.

The European Witch Craze

In one of the most bizarre and macabre episodes of human history, between 200,000 and 500,000 European women were executed for witchcraft during the fourteenth and fifteenth centuries. When we consider such strange episodes of collective behavior, we might well conclude that they are the work of some malevolent person who has succeeded in stirring people to an irrational frenzy. At times this may be a factor. Yet deeper social forces are generally also at work, which some leaders may seek to exploit and turn to their advantage. According to sociologist Nachman Ben-Yehuda (1980), the European witch craze was not simply an irrational outburst; it was also a response by established institutions and their elites to the social changes taking place at the end of the Middle Ages.

Fomenting the persecutions were the Church and its Inquisition, which had earlier focused its energies on fighting heretics. Why did the medieval Church, particularly its branches in Germany, France, and Switzerland, feel itself threatened? And why did it choose to strike out against "witches," most of whom were apparently ordinary women? To answer these questions, we must consider a number of social, economic, and demographic changes that were occurring in these countries.

First of all, economic development was accelerating and eroding the traditional medieval order. Under feudalism, social and economic life was strictly ordered. From the king and top Church officials down to the most impoverished peasant, each member of society occupied a place. The family was tightly ordered, with a clearly defined role for each member in a structure centered on household production. In the fourteenth century, this structure began to break down. Economic development meant more trade, industry, and urbanization. With the rise of industries, the family began to lose its importance as a productive unit: Manufacturing was increasingly carried on in workshops and factories. The new urban order of cities, factories, and a secular life did not fit into the feudal scheme. As people moved from being peasants to being workers, they lost the security of a life in which their role and tasks were clearly defined. As more single men and women moved into the cities to seek work, women became more visible. Often unable to find jobs as spinners and weavers, many women were reduced to prostitution to eke out a livelihood.

All these changes produced a mood of insecurity and uneasiness. To many, society seemed to be coming apart, particularly as the influence of the Church slipped. To make matters worse, the fourteenth century saw the devastating plague, the Black Death, eventually kill between one-third and one-half of Europe's population. This calamity created a sense of pervasive doom and decline.

The witch craze was a reaction to these developments, an attempt to "counteract and prevent change and to reestablish traditional religious authority. . . . By persecuting witches, this society, led by the Church, attempted to redefine its moral boundaries" (Ben-Yehuda 1980, p.14). Witches served as convenient symbols of all that was wrong. As the position of women changed, they became prime targets for the fears and anxieties that change engenders.

The witch hunts are a dramatic example of the elaborate stratagems to which dominant elites may resort in order to protect their hold on the social order. The witch-hunters' attempts to purify the faith, redefine moral boundaries, and halt the tide of change obviously failed. These desperate efforts at cleansing society represented attempts to forestall the death of institutions by destroying the lives of thousands of individuals.

Although much is understood about the witch hunts of Europe, many questions remain. Why did they occur just when they did—mostly within a 100-year period—and then abruptly cease? Why were women the prime targets and victims? What latent social needs did the persecutions reflect and what were the structural impacts? These questions still await answers.

Mobilization of Participants

When evidence for a cause accumulates, people begin acting on their beliefs—in other words, they mobilize. Mass hysteria breaks out, panic erupts, mobs form, social movements organize, or some other form of collective behavior takes shape. In 1968 this mobilization took the form of a decision by many antiwar activists to go to Chicago and express their views regardless of the consequences.

Breakdown of Social Control

Governing elites often attempt to stop or deflect collective behavior. In so doing they can influence the timing, content, direction, even particular outcomes. The results, however, are not always what the agents of social control intend. Sometimes their efforts backfire completely. In Chicago, Mayor Daley's dispatching of police to clear Lincoln Park and President Johnson's mobilization of the National Guard did not restore order. Instead, they only fueled the protest and violence.

Evaluating Smelser's Theory

Smelser's theory highlights how social strain interacts with a number of other social factors to activate an episode of collective behavior. His view is closely aligned with a functional perspective. It sees collective behavior as a breakdown of the established social order, an event signaling that the normal, harmonious workings of the social system are for some reason out of phase. The start of this disruptive process is some kind of social strain, an unusually stressful situation that taxes people's ability to cope. As a result, established social norms are ignored and collective behavior erupts. Smelser's model has been applied to many different phenomena, from mass hysteria to riots and social movements.

But not all sociologists agree with Smelser. Those who take a power perspective argue that society always has some groups of people who are experiencing strain. Society, they reason, is dominated by elites, who lock out others for their own advantage. The vast majority of people lack wealth and privilege, and many feel deprived to the point of undergoing enormous stress, which is then ready to be activated. Yet such stress does not automatically translate into collective action. What enables some groups who feel they are unfairly treated to act on their own behalf and challenge the social order, while other groups, equally disadvantaged, tend to accept their plight? One answer points to the power to mobilize resources in pursuit of desired goals.

Tilly's Resource Mobilization View

A leading proponent of a power-oriented perspective is sociologist Charles Tilly (1978; 1987). He proposes a set of conditions leading to collective action that are quite different from Smelser's. Tilly's factors include shared interests, organization, mobilization of resources, and opportunity. Let's look again at events in Chicago in the summer of 1968, this time through Tilly's eyes.

Shared Interests

In order for some form of collective action to take place, the people involved must first come to realize that they share certain views of the social world and have common interests. This process involves broadening the outlook that one's personal wants and needs are unique, and coming to see that one's viewpoint is held by many others in similar circumstances. The process also involves recognizing that joining forces would be beneficial, and that if all those with certain shared interests could unite, they might have the power to bring about change. The student demonstrators of the 1960s had a shared interest in ending the Vietnam war. After all, members of their generation were the ones being enlisted to fight.

Organization

But shared interests alone are not enough to bring about collective action. Black slaves in America had shared interests, but incidents of collective action against white rule were extremely rare in the late eighteenth and early nineteenth centuries. One important factor the slaves lacked was organization. Organization strongly affects a group's ability to *act* on its collective interests. The antiwar protesters of the 1960s were quite well organized. Antiwar groups formed on college campuses across the country, each group linked to others by means of an effective communications network. This organizational network was responsible for encouraging thousands of students to go to Chicago in August 1968.

Mobilization of Resources

Mobilization is the process whereby a group gains control of the resources needed for collective action. Those resources may be time, labor, money, equipment, or anything else that can be used to act on shared interests. Thus, mobilization is the turning point that takes a group from passive acceptance of the status quo to an active effort to change or resist the social order. Antiwar protesters reached this turning point well before the summer of 1968. Teach-ins, sit-ins, picketing, and marches against the Vietnam War were becoming increasingly common in the late 1960s. In October 1967, for instance, a large antiwar sit-in was held on the steps of the Pentagon. The ability to stage such massive

The leaders of the antiwar movement were sophisticated organizers, adept at using even playfulness for political ends. At this 1967 sit-in on the steps of the Pentagon, an attempt was made, through chanting and meditation, to levitate the building, headquarters of the U.S. Department of Defense. The Pentagon stayed on the ground, but the antiwar movement got a lift from the heightened media coverage. (Dennis Brack/Black Star.)

demonstrations as occurred on the streets of Chicago testified to a strong mobilization of resources on behalf of the antiwar cause.

Opportunity

Opportunities arise when some aspect of a group's environment changes, affording the group new chances

to act on its interests. In 1968 an opportunity arose for antiwar activists to communicate their views to a major political party and, on nationwide TV, to the rest of the country by demonstrating in Chicago during the Democratic National Convention. This almost irresistible chance for widespread public exposure was the final impetus for a massive episode of collective action. Notice that Tilly uses the term collective *action*, not collective behavior. He thereby emphasizes that such events are the rational, purposeful efforts of a group of people pursuing collective goals.

Evaluating Tilly's Theory

Tilly's resource mobilization perspective helps us to predict when collective action will arise and how widespread it will be. Without organization, a pooling of resources, and the right opportunities, a group, though greatly dissatisfied and stressed, may never instigate collective action on behalf of its shared interests. Of course, Tilly's model is more applicable to some forms of collective behavior than others. Phenomena like fads and fashions, panics, mass hysteria, and rumors do not readily lend themselves to resource mobilization theory. But when it comes to explaining certain crowd actions, demonstrations, and social movements, Tilly's perspective is essential. It prevents us from seeing participation in these events simply as emotional outbursts by people undergoing strain. It also encourages us to view these incidents as, in many ways, deliberate, calculated efforts to bring about desired goals.

MASS HYSTERIA, RUMORS, AND SOCIAL CONTAGION

The Seattle Windshield-Pitting Incident

On March 23, 1954, Seattle newspapers carried the first of several stories about damage to automobile windshields in a town eighty miles to the north of the city. The windshields had small pit marks and bubbles in them, and occasionally tiny, metallic-looking particles were embedded in the glass. The cause of this curious damage was unknown, but police suspected vandals.

Then, on the evening of April 14, the mysterious destructive agent appeared to hit Seattle. During the next two days, nearly 250 people called the Seattle police, reporting windshield damage to over 3,000 cars! By far the most frequently rumored explanation for the epidemic was radioactive fallout from H-bomb tests in the north Pacific. As this rumor swept Seattle, frightened residents desperately tried to devise protective shields. On the evening of April 15, the mayor of Seattle appealed to the governor and to the president for emergency help. But then, as quickly as it had arisen, the mass hysteria died down. Later, a team of experts determined that the pit marks had always been there. People simply had not noticed them before because drivers customarily look *through* their windshields, not *at* them (Medalia and Larsen 1958).

At first glance this case of **mass hysteria,** by which we mean an uncontrollable outburst of fear on a social level, seems to have arisen out of nowhere. Someone in the Seattle area first noticed pits in a windshield, called them to other people's attention, which led to more pits being noticed, until an epidemic was under way and bizarre rumors spread, causing people to panic. Sociologists have found, however, that as bizarre as such incidents seem, they do not simply spring up at random. A theory of collective behavior, such as that of Neil Smelser, can help to pinpoint a number of determining factors that bring them about.

First, structural conduciveness for mass hysteria existed in Seattle. The area was densely populated, with rapid, widespread communication made possible via newspapers and radio. Second, residents were under psychological strain because of their relative proximity to atomic bomb tests. They were anxious about the possible harm to them of nuclear fallout, but did not know how to protect themselves. Third, a generalized belief was fostered by the local press. For several months before the windshield-pitting incident, newspapers had published stories about recent H-bomb tests in the Pacific. "Atomic Energy Commission Discloses Blast Amid Mounting Concern" announced one headline; "Witness Says Hydrogen Test Out of Control" warned another; "Three H-Bomb Victims Face Death" declared a third. Such unnerving reports helped substantiate people's fears. Fourth, a precipitating event took place: the discovery of a few pitted windshields. Since people were in the grip of widespread apprehension over nuclear testing, these discoveries presumably provided concrete evidence that the terrible consequences of nuclear fallout were at hand. The result was the start of mass hysteria.

Rumors

The Seattle windshield-pitting hysteria was spurred both by front-page news coverage of what was regarded as an emergency and by the rapid spread of rumors among the area's residents. A **rumor** is an unverified story that circulates from person to person and is accepted as fact, although its original source may be vague or unknown. Rumors proliferate in tense and ambiguous situations, when people are unable to learn the facts or when, for one reason or another, they distrust the information they receive. Thus, rumors entail a dispersing of information, even though that information is unproven and suspect. Rumors differ from gossip in that in some cases gossip involves known facts. Furthermore, gossip deals with the personal affairs of people whereas rumors typically deal with broader events and issues (Rosnow and Fine 1976).

Rumormongering is not simply a response to idle curiosity. It reflects people's desire to find meaning in events, and thus it represents a form of group problem solving. In Seattle, residents thought the pittings in their windshields were caused by radioactive fallout from H-bomb tests. Although this interpretation turned out to be wrong, it did temporarily solve their problem of finding some reason for the mysterious damage. Similarly, in Chicago in 1968, rumors reached the mayor's office that demonstrators at the convention planned to assassinate the presidential candidates and lace the city's water with LSD (Albert and Albert 1984). Again, these rumors, however farfetched, were a way for people to understand the protestors' determination to come to Chicago.

Competitiveness and secrecy encourage rumors. That is why war and politics give rise to many rumors, as do financial and corporate dealings. The competition and secrecy that surround important exams make college students receptive to rumors. (Indeed, some students have been known to float false information to mislead their unsuspecting peers and give themselves a competitive edge.) In the Soviet Union, where for a long time an authoritarian regime prevented a free flow of reliable information, people relied heavily on word-of-mouth rumors to help make sense of current events (Rosnow and Fine 1976).

Most rumors are born, live, and die within a relatively short time period. After studying the transmission of rumors in the laboratory and in the field, psychologists Gordon W. Allport and Leo Postman (1947) discovered a basic pattern to them. A person hears a story that seems interesting and repeats it—or what is remembered of it—to a friend. Gradually, the original story is reduced to a few essential details that are easy to tell. Allport and Postman call this process **leveling:** "As a rumor travels, it tends to grow shorter, more concise, more easily grasped and told. In successive versions, fewer words are used and fewer details are mentioned" (p. 75). As a result of leveling, certain details gain in importance, and the rumor is *sharpened:* People remember and pass on only part of the original story.

As a rumor circulates, people also tend to alter details to make the story more coherent and more in keeping with their preconceptions. In one of Allport and Postman's experiments, for instance, a story about an ambulance carrying explosives was changed in the retelling to a story about an ambulance carrying medical supplies. The retold version conformed to people's common expectations. Similarly, in the summer of 1968 antiwar activists embellished rumors that the Chicago police would deal harshly with demonstrators (attacking them with dogs, jailing them in sewers) because they *expected* such insensitivity from the political establishment. It conformed to their stereotypes.

Social Contagion

Just as rumors are related to tension and stress, so is social contagion, which, as mentioned before, relates to the relatively rapid and spontaneous spread of a mood or behavior from one individual to another. The hysteria over pitted windshields that spread rapidly through Seattle in 1954 involved social contagion. Researchers have studied many other incidents of this collective process. For example, in 1972, thirty-five women who worked in a university data processing center were stricken with nausea, dizziness, and fainting spells (Stahl and Lebedun 1974). Ten had such severe symptoms that they had to be taken to the infirmary. Rumor spread that the symptoms were caused by an unidentified gas leaking into the data processing workrooms. Investigators closed the building and searched for the mysterious gas, but none could be found. Nor could traces of any toxic gas be located in the victims' bloodstreams. The building was reopened, but the very next day more workers fell ill. Again, the building was closed, and again an extensive search produced no physical cause.

What investigators did find, however, was a clear-cut pattern in the social-psychological backgrounds of the women with the most severe symptoms. They tended to be the ones who were very dissatisfied with their jobs, and job dissatisfaction can be considered an indirect measure of stress. It is equally interesting to note that the spread of severe symptoms followed a social pattern. Women who became the most ill did not work near one another, as would be expected if a toxic gas were the cause. Instead, symptoms spread along friendship networks, regardless of how far away from one another the various friends worked. Such findings are a strong indication that an unwitting incident of social contagion had occurred.

CROWD BEHAVIOR

Types of Crowds

Temporary collections of people who gather around a person or an event and who are conscious of and influenced by one another's presence are called **crowds.** Crowds differ from other social groups primarily in that they are short-lived, only loosely structured, and use conventional areas or buildings for unconventional purposes (Snow, Zurcher, and Peters 1981).

In his classic essay "Collective Behavior," sociologist Herbert Blumer (1939/1951) described four kinds of crowds. One is a **casual crowd,** which forms spontaneously when something attracts the attention of passersby. For instance, when a number of people walking along a city street stop to view a window washer high overhead, they form a casual crowd. The members of such a crowd, writes Blumer, "come and go, giving but temporary attention to the object which has awakened [their] interest . . . and entering into only feeble association with one another" (p. 178).

In contrast, passengers on a plane, shoppers in a store, or the audience at a concert illustrate what Blumer called a conventional crowd. Members of a **conventional crowd** gather for a specific purpose and behave according to established norms. For example, although booing is expected of the crowd at a football game, it is considered quite inappropriate for the crowd at a classical music concert. Relatively little interaction occurs in a conventional crowd. People are pursuing a common goal, but they tend to do so as individuals. Exchanges among such people are usually highly routinized and impersonal.

People at rock festivals, revival meetings, and exuberant carnivals (such as those held at Mardi Gras in New Orleans and Rio de Janeiro) present examples of expressive crowds. The emotionally charged members of **expressive crowds** get carried away by their enthusiasm and intense feelings, behaving in ways they would consider unacceptable in other settings. Expressing their feelings becomes their primary aim. The legendary Woodstock Music and Art Fair, held in New York's Catskill Mountains in August 1969, provides an example of such a crowd. An impressive array of rock stars drew over 300,000 young people to the farm where the festival was held. The mood of the crowd became increasingly joyous, and today the event is remembered perhaps more for this experience and expression of good feeling than for the concert itself.

The emotional tone of an acting crowd is different from that of an expressive crowd. An **acting crowd** is an excited, volatile collection of people who focus on a controversial event that provokes their indignation, anger, and desire to act. Gang members who beat up a youth from another neighborhood who happens to enter their turf or fans at a soccer match who go on a rampage when a referee makes a questionable call are examples of acting crowds. Unlike members of an expressive crowd, who see release of their feelings as an end in itself, members of an acting crowd seek redress of a perceived wrong. When a large acting crowd engages in violence or threatens to do so, it is often referred to as a **mob** (Hoult 1969). Because the social effects of mob action can be far-reaching, we will examine it in some detail.

Mob Action

For centuries mass uprisings and destructive orgies have been the nightmare of people in power. Mob action was common in eighteenth- and nineteenth-century Europe. In town and country, throngs of armed men and women took over markets and warehouses, demanding the rollback of prices and sometimes seizing goods. In England, angry bands of craftspeople burned factories and destroyed the machines that threatened their liveli-

hood. On July 14, 1789, Parisians stormed the ancient Bastille prison in the most famous confrontation of the French Revolution.

Violent crowds have also figured importantly in American history. The nineteenth century was marked by farmers' revolts, miners' rebellions, bloody battles between unions and police, lynchings, and urban riots. The Civil War draft riots of 1863 raged for four days and were probably among the worst riots in this country's

Herbert Blumer's four kinds of crowds serve as helpful models to sensitize us to the complexities of human behavior. Precise lines are hard to draw. Is this street clown's audience in a New York City park a casual or a conventional crowd? At what point do these soccer fans in Rio de Janeiro cease being a conventional crowd and become an acting crowd or a mob? (Top: William Edward Smith/The Stock Market; bottom: Robert Fried/Stock, Boston.)

history. Mob action has also arisen in the twentieth century, such as in the civil disorders of the 1960s. In cities across the country, riots erupted in black ghettos that were so violent that the National Guard was often called in to help restore order.

Why do riots break out? Why do people abandon the routines of daily life and become participants in hostile crowds? One popular explanation is the riffraff theory. It holds that only criminal types participate in riots, and that a hard core of agitators incites violence despite the strong disapproval of area residents. However, the National Advisory Commission on Civil Disorders, appointed by President Johnson, disproved this theory. In the Detroit riots of 1967, for instance, it was found that nearly 40 percent of ghetto residents either participated in the mob action or were bystanders to it. This hardly represents a deviant minority. The Detroit rioters, moreover, were on average better educated, better informed, and more involved in the community than were the nonrioters. And most of the rioters were employed, although they thought their jobs were beneath them. So why, then, did these people become involved in violent mob action? The following account of the Detroit riots (based on the *Report of the National Advisory Commission on Civil Disorders*, 1968) may not fully explain mob violence, but it does provide some insights into its causes.

Profile of the Detroit Riots

In the summer of 1967 black ghettos in twenty-three cities exploded in violence. Civil rights legislation had raised hopes but delivered little in the way of concrete improvements. Many blacks were frustrated and disillusioned. The National Advisory Commission on Civil Disorders found that 70 percent of the rioters believed they deserved better jobs and blamed their problems on racism, not on lack of training, ability, or ambition. In short, ghetto dwellers were subject to substantial social strain. In addition, ghettos are structurally conducive to mass action. Residents live in close proximity to one another, and substandard housing encourages many to spend a great deal of time outdoors, especially during the hot summer months. As a result, the streets are normally filled with people. Such conditions increase the possibility that collective behavior will arise.

Still, when they experience social strain in a conducive social setting, people do not necessarily engage in mob violence. To do so they must usually have developed a generalized belief that they are the victims of great injustice. In the ghetto, stores that tantalize residents with goods they cannot afford and police who harass and sometimes abuse residents are ever-present reminders of white domination. Frustration, anger, and resentment are widespread. All that is needed is a spark to set off an explosion.

That spark occurred on Saturday night, July 22, when the Detroit vice squad conducted gambling raids on five social clubs frequented by blacks. These mass arrests provided a focus for the ghetto dwellers' discontent. By the time police hauled the last of the participants away on Sunday morning, a crowd of 200 had gathered on the street. A bottle hurled from the crowd crashed through the window of the last retreating patrol car. This act triggered other aggressive outbreaks, mobilizing people for more violent action.

By 8:00 A.M. a crowd on 12th Street had grown to 3,000. Finding themselves outnumbered, the police withdrew. For a few hours a carnival mood prevailed, but by noon the police had positioned themselves on surrounding streets. Rumors spread rapidly among the crowd. According to one rumor, a police officer had bayoneted a black person just blocks away. As police reinforcements mounted and more rumors spread, the crowd's mood shifted, so that revelry turned into anger. People began stoning police and setting fire to stores. Firefighters tried to control the blazes, but by 4:30 on Sunday afternoon, they were exhausted and abandoned the area. At this point the mayor proclaimed a curfew and summoned the National Guard.

The number of fires and lootings declined, but reports of snipers increased. The reports had peaked to 534 by Wednesday, July 26. Panic and confusion spread among ghetto residents, and police actions compounded the fright. Police broke into homes on the slightest excuse and arrested anyone found to have a weapon. These frantic efforts to reimpose social control only served to intensify the violence and exacerbate the problem.

Before the end of the week, the police had arrested 7,200 people, and 43 people had been killed (30 or more by police and soldiers, 2 by store owners, and 2 or possibly 3 by rioters). Included among the dead were one National Guardsman, one firefighter, and one police officer (killed accidentally by a fellow officer). Thirty-three of the victims were black, ten white. Property damage was estimated at $22 million.

National Guardsmen patrol a deserted street during the Detroit Riots of 1967. Far from being the work of mindless mobs or a hard core of agitators, the ghetto riots of the 1960s were a spontaneous but purposeful response to unacceptable social and economic conditions. (Dennis Brack/Black Star.)

Researchers found that participants in the ghetto riots of the 1960s sought to benefit from, not overthrow, the American social system (Allen 1970). In short, these collective actions were "spontaneous protests against unfair conditions" (Campbell and Schuman 1968). This violent form of protest proved effective, moreover. As one observer put it: "Reporters and cameramen rushed into ghettos; elected and appointed officials followed behind; sociologists and other scholars arrived shortly after. The President established a riot commission; so did the governors" (Fogelson 1970, p. 146). Thus, the riots brought immediate, if not long-term, results that had not been produced by decades of peaceful protest (Button 1978).

Analyzing Mob Behavior

The consensus regarding the 1960s riots is that these civil disorders were purposeful attempts to voice anger over white oppression and to redress racial injustice. It is significant that in most cases only white-owned ghetto stores were burned and looted. The destruction was not haphazard; it was directed toward specific goals. This view of mob action as relatively rational behavior has not always prevailed. Until quite recently, mobs were seen as little more than unchained beasts, spurred by powerful, violent urges, and with no sense of reason. A chief proponent of this psychological perspective was the Frenchman Gustave Le Bon.

The Psychology of Crowds.   Le Bon (1841–1931) was an aristocrat in an era when the masses of common people were challenging the hereditary ruling class. As far as Le Bon was concerned, the old social system, with its privileges and security for elites like himself, was being threatened by emotionally volatile mobs. Le Bon regarded mobs as purely irrational and destructive, capable of tearing apart the social order. He developed a deep distrust of all political dissent, whether it was in support of parliamentary democracy or socialism. "The age we are about to enter," wrote Le Bon, "will be in truth the *era of crowds.*" He meant this as a dire warning.

In his book *The Psychology of Crowds* (1895/1960), Le Bon argued that involvement in a crowd puts individuals "in possession of a collective mind" that makes them think, feel, and act quite differently than they would if each person were alone. Crowds, Le Bon maintained, gain control over people, much as hypnotists do. Individuals in crowds become highly suggestible; they "will undertake . . . acts with irresistible impetuosity." Waves of emotion sweep through crowds, infecting one person after another, much as a highly contagious disease spreads. The thin veneer of civilization falls away, allowing primitive motivations and antisocial impulses to rise to the surface.

In the 1950s sociologist Herbert Blumer (1939) refined Le Bon's ideas. He traced the social contagion said to occur in crowds to an "exciting event" that creates unrest in a group of people. The people begin milling about, "as if seeking to find or avoid something, but without knowing what it is they are trying to find or avoid" (p. 173). As they search for clues, excited behavior or rhetoric catches their attention. Instead of judging these actions, as they ordinarily would, they respond impulsively and model their own behavior after them. This reaction reinforces the original actors, making them still more excited (what Blumer called the **circular reaction**). As excitement builds, people become more and more inclined to act on their mounting feelings of agitation. In Blumer's view, this tendency explains the social contagion that frequently occurs in crowds.

Emergent Norms and Social Relationships.   Few contemporary sociologists dispute the observation that emotions and behavior sometimes spread through crowds as

Social contagion or an emergent norm? Walking alone, most of us would avoid the puddles. The presence of a crowd appears to have put these impetuous bathers, in Le Bon's words, "in possession of a collective mind." Other sociologists, however, would argue that their unanimity shows some conformity to new social norms. (Peter Menzel.)

if they were contagious. However, most contemporary sociologists believe that Le Bon and Blumer underestimated the organization of crowds and their capacity for rational behavior. It is simplistic, they argue, to view people in crowds as impulsive, unpredictable creatures who can no longer control their own behavior. Sociologists Ralph Turner and Lewis Killian (1972), for example, question the implicit assumption that social conformity no longer operates in a crowd. According to their **emergent norm theory,** people evolve new social norms as they interact in situations lacking firm guidelines for coping. These norms then exert a powerful influence on their behavior.

The new norms evolve through a gradual process of social exploration and testing. One or more people may suggest a course of action (shouting obscenities or hurling bottles, for example). Other suggestions follow. The crowd begins to define the situation, to develop a justification for acts that would in other circumstances seem questionable. In this way new norms may emerge that condone violence and destruction, but still impose some limits on crowd behavior.

The emergence of new norms, Turner and Killian argue, does not mean that members of a crowd come to think and feel as one. Although it may appear to outsiders that a crowd is a unanimous whole, some participants may just be going along to avoid disapproval and ridicule. Thus, unlike Le Bon and Blumer, Turner and Killian believe that crowd unanimity is little more than an illusion. The illusion is created by the fact that crowd members tend to demand at least surface conformity to the new norms that have evolved.

Extending Turner and Killian's ideas, other sociologists have argued that new social relationships also emerge in crowds (Weller and Quarentelli 1973). Consider lynching, a fairly common form of crowd violence in the early American West and, until recent decades, in the South as well. A lynch mob dispenses with conventional norms of trial by jury, rule of law, and execution only by the state, replacing them with the norms of a vigilante trial and punishment by mob consensus. But new social relationships develop, too. Participants, improvising a division of labor, informally designate such roles as prosecutor, witnesses, jury members, and executioners. Crowds, in short, are neither normless nor totally lacking in social organization. Both norms and social relationships always emerge in them, making them much more structured than they seem at first glance.

Mob Behavior as Rational Decision Making. One problem with Turner and Killian's view is that it fails to explain why the new norms that emerge in a crowd are often so extreme. Why do some crowds endorse behaviors strongly condemned under normal circumstances, such as arson, looting, and personal assault? Sociologist Richard Berk (1974) suggests one answer. His explanation draws on rational choice theory. In his view, people do not suspend their rationality simply because they are part of a crowd. They continue to weigh the costs and benefits of possible courses of action. The costs associated with rioting are the risk of personal injury and the likelihood of being arrested. In a crowd that greatly outnumbers police, these risks are relatively small. In contrast, the benefits of mob action may be great for people who are disadvantaged and have many pent-up frustrations. These benefits can be tangible, such as looted merchandise, or intangible, such as social recognition and emotional release. In any case, Berk argues, people in mobs calculate that, given their particular situation, violence will pay off.

Not all sociologists agree that crowd action is indeed this calculated. But the fact that the ghetto riots of the late 1960s did get dissatisfied blacks the renewed attention of white America seems to lend some support to Berk's hypothesis. From the perspective of rioters, violent action may in fact offer some benefits.

SOCIAL MOVEMENTS

So far we have focused on relatively transitory forms of collective behavior. Mass hysteria flares up and quickly dies down; crowds gather and soon disperse; even rioting triggered by deep-seated social injustice typically runs its course over a fairly brief period. But collective action is not always short-lived. At times collectivities of people launch sustained and deliberate efforts to bring about or resist social change. Such efforts are called social movements.

Social movements differ from other kinds of collective behavior not just in terms of their endurance, but also their degree of organization. Norms and roles form in riots and other crowd actions, as Turner and Killian point out. But the structure that is present in these volatile incidents is much more fluid than that found in

social movements. In fact, social movements that have existed for a long time and have grown large and influential often encompass organizations with formal hierarchical structures and formal ties to one another.

This does not mean, however, that social movements are the same as institutionalized efforts to bring about or resist social change. When oil companies lobby Congress to pass tax laws in their favor, or when doctors petition the FDA to speed approval of a new drug, they are not engaged in social movements. Social movements always involve at least some *non*institutionalized means of persuasion, including mass marches and rallies, sit-ins, boycotts, and sometimes even violence, sabotage, and other illegal acts (especially when agents of social control try to suppress them). These tactics go beyond conventional procedures for airing grievances, just as panics, mass hysteria, and riots go beyond conventional ways of coping with stressful situations (Traugott 1978). Why do participants in social movements rely on noninstitutionalized methods? Because they lack the social power to advance their collective interests in solely institutionalized ways (McAdam 1982). In the 1950s and 1960s, for instance, American blacks had to use boycotts, mass demonstrations, and sometimes violent insurrection to make the depth of their discontent known. They simply did not have the power to bring about desired changes through conventional interest-group politics. This is true of participants in other social movements.

Types of Social Movements

Social movements can develop around almost any significant social issue, such as environmental quality, nuclear weapons, women's rights, apartheid in South Africa, drug use, or religious salvation, to name just a few. Given the great variety of social movements, a number of sociologists have tried to classify them. David Aberle (1966) bases his categories of social movements on two criteria: the *type* of change their members seek (either a change in individuals or a change in the social order) and the *amount* of change desired (either partial or total). This approach has yielded four types of movements: alterative, redemptive, reformative, and transformative.

Alterative movements aim to achieve some limited but specific change in individuals. Their participants view human beings as essentially good, but they believe that character flaws or societal pressures can lead people astray. When members of the Women's Christian Temperance Union sought to teach people about the evils of alcohol and discourage them from drinking, they were engaged in an alterative movement.

Redemptive movements also focus on the individual, but they seek total, not partial, change. Participants believe that people must be converted to an entirely different inner state. Most redemptive movements are religious. For example, according to members of the evangelical Christian movement, humans are racked with sin and able to redeem themselves only by accepting the teachings of Christ.

Reformative movements differ from both alterative and redemptive movements in that they seek change in society rather than in individuals. Their aim is partial change since they view the present social order as basically workable. But their members are dissatisfied with policies in one or more areas of social life. Civil rights movements of various kinds (on behalf of racial and ethnic minorities, women, homosexuals, and the like) are examples of reformative movements. These movements aim not to overturn the prevailing social system, but to distribute its benefits more widely.

Moderate change is not the goal of **transformative movements,** which aim at total change in the social order. Transformative movements are true revolutions. The changes they endorse are all-embracing; nothing of the old order is to survive. The Bolshevik movement in Russia in the early twentieth century is one example. Its followers sought a complete overthrow of the traditional ruling class. The results of such movements can be cataclysmic.

Explaining Social Movements

Why does a social movement arise? Under what conditions do people engage in collective action to resist or bring about change? Researchers have proposed two basic answers. One is that social movements arise from social and economic deprivation, a form of social strain. When discontent with existing social arrangements becomes deep and broad enough, people join together and fight back, according to this perspective. Most sociologists, however, see deprivation alone as an insufficient explanation for the rise of a social movement. They contend that discontent is always widespread, and yet full-fledged social movements are relatively infrequent. The reason, they argue, is that discontent must be coupled with the ability to mobilize resources on behalf of a group's collective interests. Without sufficient resources and the organization to use them effectively, even the most aggrieved people cannot launch a social movement. In the following sections we will explore the ways in which deprivation and resource mobilization may both be important.

Social and Economic Deprivation

The most basic form of deprivation is a lack of life's necessities: inadequate food, shelter, and clothing. Such conditions seem likely precursors of revolution, and sometimes they are. The French Revolution, for instance, was preceded by a sharp increase in the price of bread (the highest price in seventy years) due to poor harvests in 1787 and 1788. Workers in the cities and even rural residents faced severe hunger. In 1789 they rebelled.

The argument that revolutionary movements spring up when people cannot satisfy their most fundamental needs was basic to Marx's theory of revolution. Marx held that the ever-increasing use of machinery and factory production would condemn workers to more and more menial tasks, thus continually depressing their wages and feeding their sense of alienation. The economic cycle of boom and bust that characterizes capitalist societies would only aggravate and compound the misery of the working class. Eventually, workers would be cast into a state of such intolerable exploitation that they would organize to overthrow their oppressors (and, unlike earlier economic systems, capitalism would give the working class the social organizational capacity to win its revolutionary struggle).

But not all sociologists agree with the view that progressive impoverishment puts people in a revolutionary frame of mind. Over a hundred years ago the French observer Alexis de Tocqueville (1856) studied economic and social decline in the seventeenth century, which was followed by a period of advancement in the eighteenth century. He concluded that revolutionary movements generally occur *not* when conditions are most hopeless, but after they have begun to improve. During periods of improvement, Tocqueville argued, people begin to realize that abject deprivation is not inevitable. The downtrodden suddenly see that a better life is possible, and they react by reaching for it. "Evils which are patiently endured when they seem inevitable," wrote Tocqueville, "become intolerable once the idea of escape from them is suggested" (p. 214). Sociologists call this gap between people's expectations and their actual conditions **relative deprivation** (Gurr 1970).

Relative deprivation occurs under a variety of circumstances. Tocqueville identified one condition, that of *rising expectations*. It was a sense of rising expectations, some sociologists say, that bred the black protest movement and the ghetto outbreaks of the 1960s (Geschwender 1964; Abeles 1976). The economic prosperity of the 1950s and the early gains of the civil rights movement led blacks to believe that their circumstances would improve substantially in the foreseeable future. But the new civil rights legislation and President Lyndon Johnson's War on Poverty program delivered little. Dreams of a Great Society faded as the United States became increasingly preoccupied with Vietnam. To raise people's expectations that a feast is at hand and then to deliver crumbs is to create a socially explosive situation. Not surprisingly, ghetto riots and the Black Power movement followed.

Sociologist James Davies (1962, 1974) has identified another condition that fosters feelings of relative deprivation: a rise-and-drop, or a J-curve, situation. He bases his observation on an analysis of such events as Dorr's Rebellion in Rhode Island in 1842, the Pullman strike of 1894, the Russian Revolution of 1917, and the Egyptian revolution of 1953. Davies concludes that revolutionary movements are most likely when a prolonged period of economic and social improvement is followed by a drastic reversal in people's fortunes. The first period presumably creates an expectation that things will steadily get better; the second period stimulates a terrible fear that all past progress will suddenly be irretrievably lost. Davies believes that the actual conditions prevailing in the period of reversal are less important than the psychological state they foster. Some people may even be better off objectively than they were before the economic and social downturn began. But they *feel* deprived in relation to their expectations. They feel robbed of what they thought they should receive. Consequently, they experience intense frustration. Figure 21.1 summarizes Davies's theory. It shows that revolutions flare up when the gap between what people expect and what they actually receive suddenly widens.

The ideas of Marx, Tocqueville, and Davies on the role of deprivation in fostering revolution seem on the surface quite different. According to Marx, progressive impoverishment causes rebellion; according to Tocqueville, revolution springs from rising hopes for a better life; and according to Davies, a sharp reversal of improved conditions sets the stage for a popular uprising. Despite their differences, however, a common psychological process underlies all these views. In all cases, people are experiencing intense dissatisfaction over their current share of valuable rewards. It may not be crucial whether that current share is steadily declining, gaining slightly, or taking a temporary downturn. What may be most important is that people *perceive* themselves to be unfairly deprived in relation to other people. (The deprivation may be economic, social, or both.) As a result, they are frustrated and their frustration causes them to launch an organized, often violent demand for change.

In 1894, workers at the Pullman Palace Car factory outside Chicago walked off the job to protest wage cuts. Members of the American Railway Union supported the workers by refusing to handle trains with Pullman cars. Eventually, troops were used to break the strike. The Pullman strike occurred during an era of rapid industrialization, expanding employment, and rising expectations, which intensified the worker's sense of relative deprivation. (The Granger Collection.)

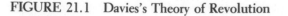

FIGURE 21.1   Davies's Theory of Revolution

This graph illustrates Davies's theory that revolutions are most likely to occur when a period of economic and social progress is succeeded by sharp reversals, fueling fears that all gains will be lost.

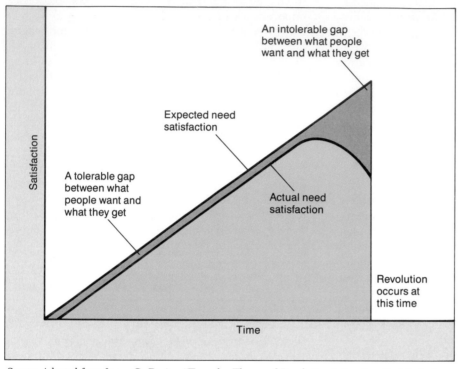

An intolerable gap between what people want and what they get

Expected need satisfaction

A tolerable gap between what people want and what they get

Actual need satisfaction

Revolution occurs at this time

Satisfaction

Time

Source: Adapted from James C. Davies, "Toward a Theory of Revolution." *American Sociological Review*, Vol. 27 (February 1962), Fig. 1, p. 6.

Resource Mobilization

However, most contemporary sociologists argue that perceived deprivation is only one factor precipitating a social movement. To change existing values or norms, they say, people must mobilize resources in support of their cause. Without resources, even the most deprived and frustrated group will not be able to bring about change (Jenkins and Perrow 1977; Snow et al. 1981). Thus, sociologists such as Charles Tilly (1973, 1978), whose theory we outlined at the start of this chapter, argue that social movements occur only when aggrieved groups can mobilize the resources needed to take significant actions to promote their collective interests. Aggrieved groups, in other words, must mobilize the resources to increase their limited power, thereby enabling them to challenge the social arrangements that have been established by those who control society.

The resources capable of being mobilized in support of a social movement include both human skills and tangible assets (Freeman 1979). Among the primary tangible assets are money (which can purchase a variety of other things), channels of mass communication (leaflets, radio, and television, which can publicize a movement's goals), and space to house a movement's headquarters. Human skills include leadership, organizational talent, personal prestige (which is helpful in attracting followers and in gaining social acceptance), and in-depth knowledge about the people or institutions the movement hopes to change. Time to devote to movement activities and commitment to movement causes (meaning willingness to endure risk and inconvenience so that movement goals can be achieved) are also critical. For example, in its early years, the civil rights movement depended heavily on the mobilization of supporters' time and commitment. Students in particular, both black and white, were mobilized for sit-ins, marches, and voter-registration drives. In this way the movement gained a great deal of national attention and sympathy at relatively low cost.

White-student participation in the civil rights movement illustrates another important point. Mobilized resources for a social movement do not always come exclusively from within the aggrieved group. The resources of a disadvantaged minority are often insufficient to launch a successful social movement. Usually, there must be at least some resources from people who do not stand to gain directly from the changes that the movement seeks but who are nevertheless sympathetic to them.

But even with outside help, resource mobilization is never easy. Success depends on a number of factors. One is organization (Tilly 1978; McAdam 1982). For instance, black churches, black colleges, and long-established black groups such as the NAACP (the National Association for the Advancement of Colored People, originally concerned mainly with abolishing lynching) provided an important organizational base for the civil rights movement of the 1950s and 1960s. These organizations made communication, planning, and resource mobilization possible.

The ability to mobilize resources also depends on favorable opportunities in the social environment. For example, it was fortuitous for blacks that the 1950s and 1960s were prosperous economic times. During prosperity people are generally more receptive to improving the conditions of underprivileged groups. Civil rights leaders took advantage of this relatively favorable social climate in timing their demands for change. Similarly, in a study of black protest in American cities during the 1960s, Peter Eisinger (1973) found that protest tended to be greatest in those communities where government officials showed some receptiveness to racial change. The implication is that resource mobilization depends in part on favorable political opportunities.

Still another factor conducive to resource mobilization is what Doug McAdam (1982) calls cognitive (mental) liberation. Cognitive liberation is similar to what Charles Tilly refers to as a sense of shared interests. More specifically, cognitive liberation is a collective perception by members of an aggrieved group that they suffer an unjust situation that could be changed through collective action. Such a collective perception is related to both a favorable opportunity structure (which holds out hope that change is possible) and organization

On the anniversary of the Chernobyl accident, demonstrators in London march to protest the use of nuclear energy—whether in weapons systems or power plants. What theory best explains the rise of such a movement —one that focuses on social strain or one that focuses on the mobilization of resources? (Stuart Franklin/ Magnum Photos.)

(which allows insurgents to share their views). The end result of all these factors is collective action.

But whether or not collective action is successful is another matter. Usually, a social movement owes much of its success to effective leadership. Sociologists have identified several types of leaders, ranging from the "agitator" or "prophet," whose skills at articulating some demand compel public attention, to the "administrator," who puts together the nuts and bolts of an organized campaign (Wilson 1973). Sometimes a single leader exerts several kinds of leadership simultaneously. Martin Luther King, Jr., and Betty Friedan were both influential prophets who voiced the concerns of blacks and women, respectively. In addition, both functioned as administrators. King was spokesperson for the Southern Christian Leadership Conference and Friedan for the National Organization for Women. Such versatile leaders, however, tend to be the exception. More often, a movement develops a division of labor among several leaders with different kinds of skills.

Sociologists John McCarthy and Mayer Zald (1973, 1977) have proposed that many modern-day social movements are largely the creation of outside leadership. They say that a groundswell of discontent among aggrieved individuals is of secondary importance in generating a social movement. Skilled leaders can take weak and ill-defined discontent and broaden its base. For this reason, grass-roots support for some social movements actually comes *after* the movement is under way. For example, the movement to provide federally funded health care for the elderly in the United States did not derive initially from an outcry among senior citizens. Instead, the movement's principal organization, the National Council for Senior Citizens for Health Care through Social Security (NCSC), was staffed primarily by young and middle-aged professionals and funded by the AFL-CIO. Organizers staged rallies across the country and encouraged mass petitioning. Later, when the movement encountered opposition from the American Medical Association, the NCSC began to use its resources to mobilize a large membership base among the elderly. Thus, active support from the aggrieved group was sought *after* the movement was in full swing. Far from involving a popular outcry of discontent, this social movement was professionally planned and directed by outsiders (Rose 1967).

This view of the emergence of social movements is very different from the one that focuses on discontent and protest among members of a deprived group. The social and economic deprivation perspective looks to the internal frustrations and feelings of injustice that spur people to rise up and seek change. The resource mobilization perspective looks mainly to the external conditions that make organized protest possible. Yet the two views are not mutually exclusive. Both provide important insights, and neither is completely adequate by itself. Only by considering both the social forces of discontent *and* the process by which resources are mobilized can we fully understand how social movements arise, develop, and decline. In this regard, sociologist Theda Skocpol has made a notable contribution in her theory of social revolutions.

Theda Skocpol and Social Revolution

Skocpol defines **social revolution** as "rapid, basic transformations of a society's state and class structures . . . accompanied and in part carried through by class-based revolts from below" (1979, p. 4). The simultaneous occurrence of class upheaval and sociopolitical transformation distinguishes a social revolution from a rebellion (which does not result in structural change), from political revolution (which involves no change in social structure), and from such revolutionary processes as industrialization (which involve no change in political structure).

Skocpol explains social revolution by combining aspects of Marxist and resource-mobilization theories. She finds that although underlying class conflict is fundamental to revolution, it is also necessary to consider how the class members are organized and what their resources are. Rather than attempting to create a general theory for all revolutions, she wants to construct a valid explanation for social revolutions in three agrarian states: France at the time of the overthrow of Louis XVI (1789), Russia at the time Czar Nicholas II was deposed (1917), and China at the time the Ch'ing dynasty was ousted (1911).

Based on careful study of these revolutions, Skocpol highlights three factors that tend to be ignored in other theories of revolution. First, revolutions are rarely started intentionally; they generally emerge from crisis situations. Second, revolutions are not purely products of internal forces. International relations and developments (particularly long, drawn-out wars and military defeats) contribute to the emergence of crises and revolutions by undermining old political regimes. Third, states have an existence of their own and are not necessarily dependent on the interests and structure of the dominant class.

Other studies have focused on the economic consequences of revolution. In an examination of the aftermath of the Cuban Revolution, led by Fidel Castro in 1959, Michael Lewis-Beck (1979) finds that in the short run the revolution had positive effects on the Cuban economy, as measured by an increase in the growth of per capita gross national product. However, these positive effects were short-lived. Because of trade difficulties, a scarcity of managers and materials, and administrative errors, the Cuban economy soon began to suffer a decline. Lewis-Beck calls this a "euphoric" pattern: Initial prosperity immediately following the revolution creates a feeling of unequivocal success, but it is not sustained for long. This study, however, looked only at the effects of the Cuban Revolution on the nation's economy. The social changes brought about by the revolution may have been more substantial and more enduring.

Profiles of Some Contemporary Social Movements

We live in an era of protest, judging by the number of recent social movements. The farm workers' movement, the civil rights movement, the antiwar movement, the women's movement, the ecology movement, the antinuclear movement, the gay rights movement, the prison-reform movement, the zero population growth movement, the right-to-life movement, the evangelical Christian movement: All these and others arose or were renewed during the sixties, seventies, and eighties. What can sociologists learn from studying such social movements? Are there similarities in the ways different movements have developed? And what success have recent movements had in the long run? Perhaps the best way to answer these questions is to take an in-depth look at three contemporary social movements: the women's movement, the environmental movement, and the movement against nuclear war.

The Women's Movement

Protest by women predates the 1960s. In the early twentieth century a strong women's movement arose to demand the right to vote. Following this victory, feminist protest waned as women entered a period that has been called the "barren years" (Klein 1984). But even in this time of little mass protest, some activism remained. The women who sustained it were primarily upper-middle-class professionals, and this fact limited their mass appeal. But they kept women's issues alive until social forces set the stage for renewed grass-roots support (Rupp and Taylor 1987).

One of those social forces was the publication in 1963 of Betty Friedan's book *The Feminine Mystique*. In it, Friedan spoke to millions of American women about "the problem that has no name." Trained from childhood to relinquish self-reliance, careers, and personal autonomy and to dedicate their lives to the full-time care of home and children, many women felt dependent, isolated, and unfulfilled. Friedan helped them to identi-

fy the causes of these feelings. She also brought to public attention the private grievances of women who worked outside the home and were trapped in dead-end, low-paying, unchallenging jobs. Thus, women across the country became aware of a shared discontent and the possibility that together they might improve their lives. It was the start of what McAdam calls their cognitive liberation.

But it was not just a book that triggered this new outlook. A number of other factors worked to encourage equal rights for women. One was the black civil rights movement. It stimulated increased awareness of injustice and oppression in a number of groups, including women. Interestingly, women's experiences in the civil rights movement also served as an important catalyst. The thousands of women who worked for the movement were often relegated to routine jobs such as typing, answering phones, and making coffee. As a result, they were forced to confront the contradiction of working in a freedom movement without themselves being free.

Of course, a social movement requires more than a sense of shared injustice. Resource mobilization is also needed. This mobilization is, in turn, facilitated by organization. Especially important were the commissions to investigate the status of women that were established in each of the fifty states in 1963. Sociologist Jo Freeman (1973) argues that the women's movement of the sixties would not have materialized without the communications network that these commissions provided. They brought together large numbers of knowledgeable and politically active women and gave them channels for discussing common problems and planning collective solutions. Thus, although the position of women in the 1960s was the same as it had been for decades, something critical had changed. "What changed," writes Freeman, "was the organizational situation. It was not until a communications network developed between like-minded people beyond local boundaries that the movement could emerge and develop past the point of occasional, spontaneous uprising" (1973, p. 804).

Organizational structure was furthered in June 1966 when a small group of women attending the Third National Conference of Commissions on the Status of Women met in Betty Friedan's hotel room and founded the National Organization for Women (NOW). With Friedan as president, NOW began to attract women in the professions, labor, government, and the communications industry. NOW received a major impetus in 1969 when the national media began to carry news stories on women's liberation. Through its national board and 800 or more local chapters, NOW has used legal suits, lobbying, demonstrations, boycotts, and other methods to press for such goals as educational reform; nonstereotyped portrayal of women in the media; repeal of laws outlawing abortion; lesbian rights; enhanced roles for women in religion, politics, and sports; and passage of the Equal Rights Amendment (ERA). In addition, a number of other organizations of professional women have been formed, such as WEAL (Women's Equity Action League), which focuses on legal questions, and the NWPC (National Women's Political Caucus), which focuses on electing more women to public office.

Simultaneously, at the grass-roots level, many younger women also began organizing. These women rejected hierarchical, highly structured organizations, believing that they inevitably stifled those at the bottom. Instead, they created egalitarian women's groups. These groups sought not only to increase opportunities for women, but also to change the structure of human relationships and roles. Many of the groups emphasized consciousness-raising: Through sharing ideas and experiences, members attempted to identify their previously unconscious attitudes and behaviors in dealing with both males and females. This new awareness, they hoped, would help to change their attitudes and behaviors, fostering a more egalitarian society. In addition, these groups undertook a variety of local educational and service projects. They established women's centers, abortion-counseling clinics, centers for rape victims and battered wives, feminist bookstores and publications, and day-care facilities.

By the 1970s the women's movement had made substantial progress in expanding female career opportunities. Barriers and inequalities still remained, but women were entering fields once considered the domain of men and their salaries were rising. The entry of many women into full-time professional jobs, however, raised a new issue that had to do with the problem of how to manage both career commitments and family roles. This problem prompted women activists to seek some new objectives, including affordable day care, paid pregnancy and parenting leaves, more flexible work hours, and job sharing between husband and wife (Klein 1984). Such objectives continue to be important today.

But a major new obstacle, in the form of a countermovement, has slowed the progress of the women's movement. A **countermovement** is a social movement that forms to resist a movement already under way. The antifeminist countermovement emerged to fight passage of the ERA. As discussed in Chapter 12, the leaders of this countermovement blamed feminists for a variety of social changes (from no-fault divorce laws to legal abortion) that they saw as threats to family stability. To them, the ERA represented the final assault on the traditional roles of wife and mother. To block its ratification, they formed countermovement groups, such as Humanitarians Opposed to Degrading Our Girls (HOTDOG) in Utah, Protect Our Women (POW) in Wisconsin, and Women Who Want to Be Women (WWW) in Texas (Marshall 1985). Leading the counter-

Both the civil rights movement and the women's movement have been effective at mobilizing grass-roots support and producing fundamental social change. The values, objectives, and methods of these two movements often overlap—a fact embodied in the slogan on this woman's T-shirt, which echoes the words of Martin Luther King's famous speech at the Lincoln Memorial in 1967: "I have a dream . . . " (Jean-Louis Atlan/ Sygma.)

movement at the national level was antifeminist activist Phyllis Schlafly, who organized several thousand women in a campaign called STOP-ERA. All these efforts proved successful. The strong initial momentum in favor of the ERA slowed dramatically after 1973 and came to a halt by 1977. Between 1977 and the deadline for ratification, in 1982, not a single additional state voted to approve the amendment.

Today the battle lines between the women's movement and the antifeminist countermovement are clearly drawn. On one side are mostly younger, better-educated, professionally employed women who want to extend the gains women made during the sixties and seventies. On the other side are primarily older, less educated women, who are often full-time homemakers with strong religious beliefs (Deutchman and Prince-Embury 1981; Mueller and Dimieri 1982; Burris 1983). With the ERA defeated, these antifeminists have set new goals, such as rescinding legalized abortion and affirmative-action programs for women. Members of NOW and other women's movement organizations are forced to devote much of their time, energy, and money defending against attacks (Chavez 1987). Will either side be defeated in the near future? Probably not. Members of both sides are strongly committed to their objectives and are able to mobilize resources on their behalf. Most likely this struggle between movement and counter-movement will continue into the 1990s (Hewlett 1986).

The Environmental Movement

Somewhat in the way Friedan's *The Feminine Mystique* gave rise to the women's movement, so did Rachel Carson's book *Silent Spring* (1962) give a powerful impetus to the forming of the environmental movement. The book describes a future in which the indiscriminate use of pesticides will "still the songs of birds and the leaping fish in the streams." Carson's warning led President John F. Kennedy to direct federal agencies to take a close look at the issue. The book also prompted a spate of local and state laws for regulating the use of pesticides; it began a groundswell of support that led to the creation of the Environmental Protection Agency (EPA); and it generally helped to make ecology a popular cause (McDowell 1982).

Why was Carson's book needed to ignite a social movement when millions of Americans already lived in smog-ridden cities and had watched industrial pollutants

accumulate in many lakes and rivers? The answer is that most people did not realize the extent of the ecological damage. Carson masterfully pulled together a large number of facts, the sum total of which showed that we were gradually destroying the environment, to the point of threatening our own survival. She made clear that even invisible pollutants can have devastating effects on human health and welfare, and she also exposed some of the vested interests in the business and scientific communities that were knowingly engaged in environmental degradation. The exposé aroused public anger and indignation. Concerned experts, media commentators, and other authors took up the cause, and the shared discontent needed for a social movement was born.

But resource mobilization was needed, too. As with the women's movement, mobilization to defend the environment was also facilitated by movement members' prior experience in other movements, especially the civil rights movement. Young people who had taken part in civil rights campaigns could apply the skills they had acquired to the present compelling cause. From the civil rights movement they had learned techniques for mass participation, including how to conduct sit-ins, marches, and demonstrations, and how to picket, distribute leaflets, and stage media events. These techniques, which had been refined during the movement to stop the Vietnam War, were easily transferred to ecological concerns (Schnaiberg 1973). At the same time, the communications networks established by the civil rights and peace movements could be employed to spread information about the environment.

A quarter-century after Carson's book ushered in an era of environmentalism, we see some encouraging signs. The air in twenty major American cities is measurably cleaner than it was before the passage of the Clean Air Act of 1970. Fish now swim in rivers and lakes that several years ago were devoid of life. In 1987 the EPA agreed to burn all the dioxin-contaminated soil taken from the Love Canal area in Niagara Falls, New York, a residential section formerly used as a chemical dump. Environmentalists hope that this $30 million project will spur the cleanup of other contaminated sites across the country, and public opinion seems to be on their side. According to a 1983 New York Times/CBS News poll, 58 percent of Americans agreed that "protecting the environment is so important that requirements and standards cannot be too high, and continuing environmental improvements must be made, regardless of cost" (Shabecoff 1983). This mass-based support for

The role of collective behavior in the rise of social movements ought not to obscure the importance of individual responsibility. The environmental movement operates on a field of confrontation as large and complex as the earth itself, but the movement's success ultimately depends on the sum of our individual actions—not merely our "non-routine responses" to environmental causes, but what we take from and add to the environment by our daily actions. (Ted Spiegel/ Black Star.)

environmentalism is reflected in the growing political power and activism of such organizations as the Sierra Club and the Wilderness Society.

In spite of this evident progress, the United States still confronts major problems in cleaning up the environment. Air pollution standards in areas affecting 50 million people have not been met. The exhausts of midwestern industries and automobiles reach the Northeast as acid rain, which kills wildlife and destroys property. Pollution of the water supply by cancer-causing chemicals continues (Taylor 1983; Beck 1983). Although aboveground toxic waste sites also pose health hazards, only 3 percent of them are slated for cleanup (Beck 1983). The potential danger of radiation leaks from nuclear power plants were made all too real with the explosion of the Chernobyl plant in the Soviet Union in 1986; eventually 24,000 Soviet citizens may die of cancer as a result of exposure to radiation (Diamond 1986).

The environmental movement faced a major challenge during the 1980s when President Reagan's secretary of the interior freed large amounts of public land for oil, gas, and coal exploration; relaxed federal restrictions on strip mining; and otherwise gave the impression that he favored business over environmental interests. The EPA's budget was also cut, and it handled fewer cases against polluters. Enforcement of environmental standards was increasingly left to the states and became more lax. Environmental groups, however, staunchly fought this trend and have succeeded in having federal legislation introduced on air pollutants, acid rain, and pesticides (Shabecoff 1987).

In some ways the views and strategies of environmentalists are changing. Many are now coming to believe that cooperation with industry is essential. One environmental advocate who is working toward this goal is actor Robert Redford. His Institute for Resource Management in Sundance, Utah, sponsors conferences at which business executives can meet with leading conservationists to seek mutually agreeable solutions. At the same time, recognition that environmental management is a global problem has become more widespread. Acid rain caused by factories in the American Midwest falls on Canada as well as New England; radiation released from Chernobyl affects people throughout eastern Europe. Since cooperation among nations is essential, the environmental movement has become increasingly international. Finally, environmentalists today feel a pressing need to educate the public about environmental problems. Many believe that traditional capitalistic values of production, economic progress, and material success pose a major obstacle to their goals (Pirages and Ehrlich 1974). Studies show that acceptance of these values is related to lack of concern for environmental issues (Dunlap and Van Liere 1984). What is needed, environmentalists contend, are new values that stress limited growth and an effort to live in harmony with nature (Gray 1985).

The Movement Against Nuclear War

Though the possibility of nuclear power-plant accidents is frightening, the prospect of nuclear conflagration is even more terrifying. Consequently, a strong movement against nuclear war has arisen in recent years. During the 1980s the numbers of Americans enlisted in the campaign to end the nuclear arms race has steadily grown. Thousands of groups have sprung up, producing a loosely linked and diverse movement. Some, such as the War Resisters League, Women Strike for Peace, and the National Committee for a Sane Nuclear Policy (SANE), are longtime fixtures of the American peace movement. But most of the groups in this movement are relatively new.

Why did the movement take off in the 1980s when nuclear weapons have been proliferating since the 1950s? Probably because as the United States entered the 1980s, the rhetoric and policies of the Reagan administration focused public attention on issues surrounding national defense. President Reagan proposed a substantial increase in defense spending; the deployment of MX, Trident 2, and Pershing missiles; and the development of a new generation of weapons (the Strategic Defense Initiative, dubbed Star Wars). Many Democratic party leaders rallied their constituencies in opposition to these costly programs, as well as to the accompanying cuts in social welfare budgets. Dramatic anti-nuclear demonstrations in Western Europe provided cogent examples for Americans to follow. The widespread participation of church leaders also fueled the movement. America's Roman Catholic bishops, for example, came out firmly in favor of a bilateral nuclear freeze by the United States and the Soviet Union and forthrightly condemned nuclear war as immoral. Thus, church groups, as well as women's groups and civic organizations, provided a structure that helped to organize opposition to the arms race.

But despite the sizable number of people who have committed themselves to the movement against nuclear war, not all Americans are certain about what stance to take on disarmament. A review of American opinion on nuclear weapons and war reveals that this uncertainty goes back four decades (Ladd 1982). On the one hand, many Americans believe that a nuclear war would kill millions, and they want to contain its destructive potential. On the other hand, many distrust the Soviets and believe they should not be allowed to gain a military advantage. Thus, Americans seem ambivalent about nuclear arms. They feel that the United States must be militarily strong, but they fear the threat inherent in larger and larger arsenals of nuclear weapons.

As might be expected, supporters and opponents of a freeze on nuclear weapons tend to differ in their degree of suspiciousness toward the Soviet Union (Feshbach and White 1986). Opponents are more hostile and distrustful than supporters. They believe that it would be foolish for the United States to agree to a bilateral freeze. They also feel that Americans who support a nuclear freeze are not patriotic. Thus, if members of the movement against nuclear war wish to strengthen their grass-roots support, they will probably have to demonstrate that their goals are in keeping with both patriotism and national security. Emphasizing only the horrors of nuclear war will do little to win over those who currently oppose arms agreements with the Soviet Union.

Sisters and brothers in arms, citizens of the Soviet Union and the United States march together in the Russian city of Novgorod to promote world peace and protest their countries' nuclear arsenals. Perhaps the complex equations of mutual deterrence that embroil the experts can be simplified by the goodwill of ordinary people. (Sygma.)

SUMMARY

1. Collective behavior refers to socially shared, but relatively nonroutine responses to events, things, or ideas. These nonroutine responses differ from the more habitual patterns of everyday life in which people primarily follow established social norms. Some examples of collective behavior include panics, riots, mass hysteria, fashions, fads, rumors, and exuberant crowds.

2. Although incidents of collective behavior often appear to erupt suddenly and for no apparent reason, sociologists have found that certain preconditions make their occurrence much more likely. According to sociologist Neil Smelser, these preconditions include structural conduciveness, social strain, a generalized belief, precipitating events, mobilization of participants, and a breakdown of social control. According to sociologist Charles Tilly a different set of factors are most important: shared interests, organization, mobilization of resources, and opportunity. Smelser's theory is associated with a functional perspective, Tilly's with a power perspective. Each is more useful for explaining some types of collective behavior than others.

3. Mass hysteria and rumors are both related to tense, ambiguous situations, in which people are experiencing substantial social strain. The rumors that grow out of these situations provide people with explanations for what they are experiencing. Mass hysteria also involves social contagion, a process in which a mood or behavior rapidly and unintentionally spreads from one individual to another.

4. Crowds are temporary collections of people, gathered around a person or event, who are conscious of and influenced by one another's presence. Crowds are also short-lived and loosely structured. Sociologist Herbert Blumer has identified four kinds of crowds, each formed under distinct circumstances, each for its own purpose. These are the casual crowd, the conventional crowd, the expressive crowd, and the acting crowd. The actions of violent, unruly crowds have been important in human history. A recent example in the United States was the series of riots that occurred in major cities in the summer of 1967. In analyzing these disturbances, sociologists have focused on both the social strains that ghetto residents were experiencing and their deliberate use of rioting to try to effect social change.

5. A number of different theorists have characterized the nature of crowd behavior. The French aristocrat Gustave Le Bon, writing in the eighteenth century, argued that a crowd possesses a collective mind, which makes people act differently than they would if they were alone or in small groups. The twentieth-century sociologist Herbert Blumer has refined Le Bon's ideas, focusing especially on the social contagion that occurs in crowds. In contrast, Ralph Turner and Lewis Killian argue that crowds are much more structured than Le Bon and Blumer maintain. They say that crowds evolve new social norms, to which crowd participants then tend to conform. Finally, Richard Berk contends that the extreme behavior that often occurs in crowds results from people weighing the costs and benefits of their actions, and making conscious choices.

6. A social movement is a deliberate, organized attempt to resist or bring about relatively large-scale social change through noninstitutionalized means. The tactics of participants include mass demonstrations, boycotts, and sometimes violence and sabotage. David Aberle has identified four categories of social movements, based on the type and amount of change the members seek. These are alterative, redemptive, reformative, and transformative movements.

7. Underlying the emergence of a social movement are both social and economic deprivation and resource mobilization. Theoreticians have differed in their assessment of the role of deprivation in fostering demands for change. Marx thought that progressive impoverishment leads to rebellion; Tocqueville believed that rising hopes precede a revolution; and James Davies postulates that a sharp reversal of improved conditions makes for a popular uprising. The common denominator in all three views is that the people who launch an organized, often violent demand for change perceive themselves to be unfairly deprived in relation to other people.

8. The resources that can be mobilized in support of a social movement include human skills and tangible assets. Human skills include leadership ability, organizational talent, personal prestige, and in-depth knowledge about the people or institutions under siege. Among the main tangible assets are money, channels of mass communication, and the space to house a movement's headquarters. It is also important to note that mobilized resources for a social movement do not always come exclusively from within the aggrieved group; the resources of a disadvantaged minority are often not

enough. (In fact, sociologists John McCarthy and Mayer Zald claim that many modern-day social movements were created by outside leadership.) Successful mobilization of resources also depends on favorable opportunities in the social environment as well as what Doug McAdams calls cognitive liberation. This latter concept refers to a group's collective perception that they suffer an unjust situation that could be changed through collective action.

9. Sociologist Theda Skocpol studied the French Revolution, the Russian Revolution, and the revolution in China in 1911, and she came up with three factors that are usually ignored in other theories of revolution. She points out that revolutions are rarely begun intentionally; they usually grow up out of crisis situations. In addition, revolutions are not simply the products of internal forces; they are influenced by international relations and developments. Finally, states have an existence of their own, independent of the interests and structure of the dominant class.

10. Recent decades have been replete with social movements, and many of these movements demonstrate the characteristics we have discussed in this chapter. For example, the women's movement grew out of the discontent of women shut out from full participation in society; but without leaders and organization, this discontent would not have produced a movement. The environmental movement and the movement against nuclear war arose from concern about the human race's very survival; both movements mobilize resources through organizational techniques that the leaders learned in previous mass movements, such as the civil rights movement and the movement to stop the Vietnam War.

GLOSSARY

Acting crowd. Blumer's term for an excited, volatile collection of people who are focused on a controversial event that provokes their indignation, anger, and desire to act.

Alterative movement. Aberle's term for a social movement that aims at limited but specific change in individuals.

Casual crowd. Blumer's term for a spontaneous gathering whose members give temporary attention to an object or event and then go their separate ways.

Circular reaction. Blumer's term for the tendency of people in crowds to impulsively copy someone else's unusual behavior, thereby encouraging the original actor to continue it.

Collective behavior. Socially shared, but relatively non-routine, responses to events, things, or ideas.

Conventional crowd. Blumer's term for people who gather for a specific purpose and behave according to established norms.

Countermovement. A social movement that forms to resist a movement already under way.

Crowd. A temporary collection of people who are gathered around some person or event and are conscious of and influenced by one another.

Emergent norm theory. The principle that crowds develop new norms in order to define an ambiguous situation.

Expressive crowd. Blumer's term for a crowd whose members express feelings and behave in ways they would not consider acceptable in other settings.

Leveling. What happens in the process of transmitting rumors: A complex story is reduced to a few simple, easy-to-tell details.

Mass hysteria. An uncontrollable outburst of fear on a social level.

Mob. A large crowd whose members are emotionally aroused and are engaged in, or threaten to engage in, violent action.

Redemptive movement. Aberle's term for a social movement that aims at total change in individuals.

Reformative movement. Aberle's term for a social movement that aims at partial change in the social order.

Relative deprivation. The gap between people's expectations and their actual conditions.

Rumor. An unverified story that circulates from person to person and is accepted as fact, although its original source may be vague or unknown.

Social contagion. The relatively rapid and unintentional spread of a mood or behavior from one individual to another.

Social movement. A deliberate, organized effort to bring about or resist large-scale change through noninstitutionalized means.

Social revolution. According to Skocpol's definition, a rapid and basic transformation of a society's state and social class structures.

Transformative movement. Aberle's term for a social movement that aims at total change in the social order.

CHAPTER 22
Sociology and Social Change

I n 1987 Americans had good reason to celebrate the two hundredth anniversary of the United States Constitution. That document not only created an entirely new form of government but it also stood the test of time over a period of enormous social change. In the sweltering summer of 1787, 55 delegates from each of the rebellious North American colonies but one (Rhode Island) met in Philadelphia to construct their national government. Despite the heat, the delegates worked behind closed doors and windows to maintain their discussions under total secrecy. The delegates had no difficulty in agreeing that the new country would have no king or established church and that elected representatives would write the new nation's laws. But much debate and compromise were necessary before they could agree on the precise nature of the government. In its final form the document produced at the convention called for dividing power between a national government and the states, balancing power among the three branches of the national government, and giving the ultimate power to the voters (who at the time included only white male property owners and excluded all blacks and women).

At the time of the creation of the United States Constitution in 1787, written constitutions had only been used to revise and formalize procedures for countries already in existence. The United States Constitution was the first set of written rules to guide the affairs of a new country. The disparate colonies that had previously made up Britain's New World empire had united in rebellion against British rule. They objected to specific British colonial policies and they shared a distaste for monarchy and aristocracy in general. The social and economic conditions in the New World, which fostered individual initiative and an independent spirit, were at odds with the very idea of colonial rule. The colonists found that their affairs were managed best by those who lived and worked in their midst, not by a king and Parliament who were 3,000 miles across the sea.

The United States was not only a new country but in several respects it was a new society as well. First, it was a settler society (Lipset 1979; McMichael 1984). Colonists severed their ties with established older communities in the mother country and formed new communities, often with new customs and habits. The settlers had not come to the New World simply to make their fortune and return home, as many Spaniards and Frenchmen had previously done. Moreover, many of the settlers were motivated by collective ideals, such as the freedom to worship. These ideals fostered a strong sense of community.

American society was also new in the sense that it was a capitalist society. After the Revolution American businessmen did not have to contend with a "feudal" order in which nobles controlled economic rights and restricted business activities, nor was the average white citizen tied by birth to an agrarian occupation, or even to a specific farm. The Americans at the time of the Constitution were fiercely independent, many of them owned their own property, and they pursued their occupations, whether on the farm or in business, in individualistic ways. Instead of grouping themselves around a central village, the new Americans often lived spread out on their individual farms. In pushing westward into new territory, they often could rely only on their families or on very small communities.

Perhaps because of all the ways in which it was new, American society did not have much use for the traditional European ways of ordering affairs. Indeed, many Americans had come to the new country in order to establish a different way of doing things. Benjamin Franklin and Thomas Jefferson, along with some of the other founders, thought of building a new society in much the same way that they thought of experiments in the natural and physical sciences, which were also new in their day. They liked to think of their country as an "experiment in liberty" (Osborn 1978).

The new Americans were an unusually independent breed, but the creation of the United States was not simply the result of the idiosyncratic features of its people. Instead, American society developed as part of a long historical process of social change that also led to the emergence of many other "modern societies." From medieval times onward, society came to be unified on a much larger scale as communications and transportation improved, cities grew, labor became more specialized,

government became more centralized, and trade brought far-flung countries in contact with one another.

The world and the United States have continued to change. Americans now live in ways the framers of the Constitution never dreamed of. Thomas Jefferson had envisaged a society in which most people worked as farmers or craftspeople and lived in small communities. Today, most Americans live in cities and work either in industrial or service jobs, not on the farm. The American economy, the world's largest, is dominated by a few hundred corporations, each richer than the whole country at its founding. Americans make daily use of computers, telephones, automobiles, and jet airplanes. Today we can hear sermons on television rather than in church.

The study of the processes of social change is an important part of sociology. We have seen how researchers study a variety of changes in different areas of social life. Until now, this text has focused on short-term changes that affect our daily lives, such as the prevalence of divorce and the growing number of white-collar crimes.

In this chapter we look at the ways in which sociologists have tried to make sense of large patterns of social change, the ones that bring about fundamental, enduring transformations, such as the shift from feudal

When the leaders of the former British colonies in North America gathered in Philadelphia in 1787, the constitution they drafted reflected a long process of social change in European culture, as well as new social conditions arising from the colonial experience. And, of course, transformations have continued in American society. Thus the United States Constitution marked both a culmination and a beginning, a key step in an ongoing process of social change. (The Granger Collection.)

agrarian societies to capitalist industrial ones. We examine the major theoretical perspectives on social change and then look closely at one contemporary social change with long-term consequences—the use of computers. At the end we ask what the era called "modernity" has been like and whether similar patterns of change lie in store for societies throughout the world.

THEORETICAL PERSPECTIVES ON SOCIAL CHANGE

Social change refers to basic alterations, over time, in the behavior patterns, culture, and structure of a society. Clearly, this is a broad definition, but not all changes are social changes. For instance, the socialization we experience as children profoundly affects our personal lives, but it generally does not alter the basic organization of the family or larger society and, therefore, is not social change. On the other hand, the creation of communal child-care centers in Israeli kibbutzim, where the young are housed, fed, and taught, constitutes a major social change. The child is socialized in a way that differs from traditional socialization within the family.

Social change occurs in all aspects of the social order. It affects both our everyday patterns of social interaction, as can be seen in the kibbutz experience, and the larger structures of our social institutions. Consider, for example, how the organization of work has transformed our occupational structure. Today, some observers believe, we are entering a new phase in human history, the restructuring of America from an industrial to an information society. Just as the steam engine transformed agricultural society, the computer is seen as transforming the American industrial society. One result of this change is the loss of manufacturing jobs to automation and the increase of jobs in the service sector and in managing information.

Two questions are of concern to many sociologists today: Is there an overall explanation of social change, and does social change in general follow a discernible course? Connected with these concerns is the question of whether the course of social change is an evolutionary process. In this section we look at the perspectives of the classical founders, Marx, Weber, and Durkheim, as well as the views of more contemporary theorists on these matters. We conclude with a discussion of innovation and diffusion, the ways in which specific social changes take place.

THE CLASSICAL THEORISTS

Karl Marx

In earlier chapters we saw that Marx's perspective on society emphasized relations of power and conflict. Those in a position of power—those who own the means of production in a capitalistic society—are locked in conflict with those whom they dominate, the workers who sell their labor in the marketplace. The interest of the owners lies in maintaining their authority and control over economic decisions, whereas the interest of the workers lies in overthrowing that class in order to reap the profits of their labor more fully. Marx's views of social change focus on the process of struggle, but this struggle is of two kinds.

The first kind of struggle is common to all people: overcoming the limits of nature and existing technology. For example, in a hunting and gathering society, the availability of animals and fruits in the surrounding area sets a "natural" limit on that society's population and standard of living. But if the members of that society "invent" agriculture, their numbers can increase and they can live better (as Plato would have it, "Necessity is the mother of invention"). Marx believed that at every stage in the Industrial Revolution, advances in productive capacity radically altered what were believed to be natural limits and established the basis for social change.

According to Marx, advances in production almost always change social organization. A factory is a social organization of relationships among people as surely as it is a technical organization of relationships among machines (Marx 1976/1867). As industry became more complex, it became more and more socially organized until today we have a large-scale division of labor, huge factories, and elaborate financial institutions.

The problem with this scheme of things, in Marx's view, was that at the same time that the production processes were becoming more socially organized and cooperative than before, the ownership of the means of production was being concentrated in the hands of a relatively small elite class. This development set the scene for the second kind of struggle Marx described—

the struggle between classes for control of the production process and, by extension, for control of social life (Marx and Engels 1976 [1848]). For Marx, class struggle was not just an economic battle but a political struggle to shape the whole of social organization. To Marxists, there are strong links between economic struggles and political struggles of all kinds—involving age, gender, race, and so on (Poulantzas 1974; Vogel 1983).

Whereas the first struggle (the overcoming of limits by means of advances in production) provides the basis for social change, the second struggle (the one that pits one class against another) shapes the course that social change will take. Advances in production make new forms of social organization possible, but relations of power determine how such advances will be used and whether social organization will be fundamentally changed. Old elites whose power is based on old ways of production may be overthrown by new elites who have control over new means of production. The class struggle determines which elites will dominate and how much freedom they will have. Thus kings and feudal lords had to be overthrown by early revolutions to make the growth of modern capitalism possible. Marx envisioned that the working classes in capitalist society would, in turn, revolt against the capitalist owners in order to first create a socialist society in which the workers would dominate and then a new kind of classless society—communism—in which the state would "wither away."

Max Weber

Max Weber looked at many of the same historical issues as did Marx but drew different conclusions. Weber argued that no single factor could explain all the major social changes of history. In Weber's view a culture's many different ideas and beliefs—not just its material means of production—played an important role in bringing about social change. In fact, although Weber acknowledged advances in productive capacity, he considered it impossible to say whether those advances constituted "progress." "Progress" is a subjective idea, a value judgment. For example, from the point of view of many church leaders, industrialization did not constitute "progress" at all because it reduced their social role and threatened aspects of traditional morality and community life.

Weber did not identify a single factor as being responsible for major social changes, but he did point out at least one important cumulative *pattern* in historical change, which he labeled *rationalization*. As we saw in Chapter 1, **rationalization** is the tendency to base action on a logical assessment of effects. For example, a young woman who chooses a college based on its ability to prepare her for a desired profession is making a rational choice; if she were to choose a college simply because her parents and grandparents went there, she would be following a tradition. Weber believed that almost all societies of the world have been basically governed by tradition. Occasionally a charismatic leader rose to challenge the established authorities, but eventually tradition took over under new leadership, perhaps with some new ideas mixed in (see Chapter 14). Weber found only one great exception to the predominance of tradition, the rise of modern Western societies.

Weber attributed this exception to the Protestant Reformation in the West. Various charismatic leaders disrupted traditional patterns of religious authority with rational, disciplined world views, and their ideas spread beyond religious bounds. For example, the Protestant religious groups that sought refuge in the New World helped set into motion the events that led to the creation of the United States, the world's first large-scale democracy and the first to separate church and state. Weber also noted the close connection between the Protestant work ethic, with its stress on hard work and discipline, and the rise of modern capitalism (see Chapter 18).

The most significant feature of the upheavals of the Protestant Reformation, in Weber's view, was that they did not lead back toward a new traditionalism. Tradition was replaced in Western Europe (and its colonies), by a more rational outlook on life, government, and the economy. This rational approach to action set the course for social change: increasingly bureaucratic states, increasingly specialized work tasks, and more rules and regulations to bring order to an increasingly complex society. Capitalist economies have become more rationalized, with large corporations, "scientific" management techniques, computer systems, and the like. Few companies today, for example, would rely on a hunch when deciding whether to introduce a new product. Instead they conduct scientific market research. Similarly, government has become increasingly rationalized, creating what Weber called bureaucracy—government by officials and formal rules. The idea of bureaucracy was to create an efficient division of administrative tasks (although anyone who has had to deal with bureaucratic "red tape" could be forgiven for doubting whether this is true). Officials are expected to follow formal rules and procedures, not instincts or intuition or personal whims (see Chapter 14). Even private life has become more rationalized; we now structure our activities by the clock rather than by the more natural rhythms of night and day and the seasons (Young 1988). Life choices are no longer largely predetermined, but are made after a careful calculation of costs and benefits.

For Weber, the pervasive theme of all modernity, all social change, is rationalization. And rationalization is spreading beyond the boundaries of the Western societies with modernization.

Émile Durkheim

Émile Durkheim's (1893) views on social change center on his concept of social solidarity, the way in which people are knit together in society. As we saw in Chapter 1, mechanical solidarity binds people who are alike, those who live in simple societies and share similar values and activities. Organic solidarity is the glue that binds people who are different from one another but who need to find a way to live together in complex modern societies. The main mechanism by which they do so, according to Durkheim, is **division of labor,** the specialization of the economic tasks of workers. People in primitive societies grow their own food, make their own clothes, build their own houses; people in modern societies rely on others to do each of these things. Modern societies therefore make people highly interdependent.

Durkheim believed that the conditions of modern life actually bound people more tightly in organic solidarity than the primitive conditions of simple societies bound their members in mechanical solidarity. For example, if one part of a tribe decided to move away, life would probably not change much for those who were left behind. But if one part of the United States were to break away, the secession would disrupt the whole country a great deal. In modern societies many institutions work for the whole society. We all depend on wheat from the Middle West, fruit from California and the South, government in Washington, D.C., corporate leadership in New York, and so on.

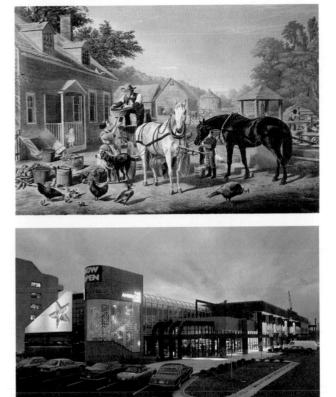

Émile Durkheim stressed the importance of the division of labor in changing the structure of society. This lithograph from the mid-1800s shows a family farmer preparing for market. He would trade only a limited range of goods; food, clothing, and other necessities were produced at home. Today, we depend on a vast network of specialized jobs and services to deliver the necessities of life. Department stores, like the one in the photo, market a wide range of goods from all over the world, not just from nearby farms and craftsmen. (Top: The Granger Collection; bottom: Stacy Pick/Stock, Boston.)

Durkheim worried that individualism and rapid social change might blind people to their interdependence. When society changes rapidly—for better or worse—people tend to lose their bearings, to become unsure of what social rules apply, and to lose connections to support groups. Durkheim (1897) described such conditions as anomie, a state of disrupted, problematic, or diminished meaning (see Chapter 2).

Despite the problems that may be brought on by social change, Durkheim thought a society's journey from mechanical solidarity to organic solidarity was generally one of evolutionary improvement. The capacity for material production was enhanced. Even culture was improved by the substitution of science for mythology. Individuals had a wider choice of actions than in primitive societies, as well as greater opportunities for creativity and distinctive development.

Thus far we have been considering Durkheim's views on the *course* of social change (from mechanical to organic solidarity), but he also had ideas on the mechanism that produced the change. Durkheim argued that pattern-breaking social change, which created modernity, was brought about primarily by an increase in the **dynamic density** of social interaction. The term refers to the frequency and impact of interactions among members of the population. The division of labor, the multiplication of different jobs in society, new technologies of communication and transportation—all combined to increase dynamic density and to bring about the new form of social integration Durkheim called organic solidarity.

The Three Theorists Compared

To summarize the views of the classical theorists on social change, we can say that Marx thought that advances in production, which resulted from human triumphs over natural limits, made social change possible, whereas the results of struggles between the classes shaped the course of social change. Weber believed that no single factor brought about social change, but stressed the importance of cultural beliefs and ideas in addition to advances in productive capacity. Weber saw the course of modern social change as being set by increasing rationalization in all aspects of life. Durkheim explained social change as the outcome of the increase in dynamic density of personal interactions, and the course of social change as proceeding from mechanical to organic solidarity. In each case we have considered where the theorist thought change came from and what its overall course was. These two questions are central to the biggest debate in the study of social change, that is, whether social change should be seen as a process of evolution.

THE QUESTION OF EVOLUTION

The question of evolutionary social change really involves two questions: Is there a cumulative course of historical change, and is there a general mechanism of social change? Many sociologists who came after the founding theorists would argue that there *is* an identifiable course of social change, generally proceeding from simpler to more complex forms. But this argument does not in itself make them evolutionists, in the sense that Darwin was an evolutionist in his biological theory. The test of an evolutionary theory is that it recognizes a *mechanism* that produces change. For Darwin that mechanism is the process of natural selection, by which characteristics that give a species advantages in its environment persist and get reproduced in the offspring. Natural selection, then, describes those characteristics that make organisms most suited to their environments, but says nothing about where the evolutionary process is going. When the environment changes, characteristics that were once advantages may become disadvantages (Mayr 1988).

Sociologists have come up with at least three answers to the question of whether there is—or even should be—a theory of *social* evolution. The first answer, which corresponds to Max Weber's theory, holds that no theory of social evolution is needed, only a set of limited generalizations about the course of social change (Ragin and Zaret 1980). According to this view, we may sometimes identify patterns in large-scale social change occurring in many societies, in different aspects of social life, and over a long period of time. Rationalization is an example of such a pattern. But the causes of this pattern may be multiple and may in fact change from time to time. Not only is there no single underlying mechanism that ties all of social change together but there is no single direction in which historical processes are headed. We tend to see the course of history as leading to where we are, or think we are going, but history could reverse itself or head in a new direction.

The second answer also denies the need for a theory of social evolution, but holds that the pattern of large-scale social change is more fixed and inevitable than the theorists of the first group would acknowledge. The theorists in the second group argue that history has a course or direction, though they recognize no mechanism of change.

Those who take a cyclical perspective, for example, believe that history moves in cycles that are neither cumulative nor progressive. Every society, then, has a natural life cycle: birth, adolescence, maturation, decay, and eventual death, followed by the birth of some new social order. A graph of the history of societies would thus show a continual series of waves, rising and falling, rising again and falling again.

Perhaps the most famous exponent of the idea that just as Western culture could rise to the pinnacle of civilization, so too could it fall, was Oswald Spengler. In his widely read book *The Decline of the West* (1926–1928), Spengler argued that all cultures are destined to follow a course of growth and decay in much the same ways as do individuals. In its youth a society is most creative and most idealistic. As it matures, society becomes less flexible, more materialistic, and more prone to decay in the form of war and social disintegra-

A key question sociologists ask is whether social change is organized into an evolutionary process. For many who think it is, modern societies with their new technologies represent an evolutionary advance over earlier ones. Others would argue that while social change produces great differences between societies, these differences cannot be clearly evaluated as more or less advanced. Is the skyscraper, for example, an evolutionary advance over the Egyptian pyramid or the Chinese imperial palace? (Clockwise from bottom left: Peter Menzel/Stock, Boston; Dick Durrance II/Woodfin Camp & Associates; R. Ian Lloyd/The Stock Market.)

tion. Spengler was convinced that Western society had reached its "golden years" and was on the decline. Few contemporary sociologists share Spengler's pessimism, in part because his theories tend to be more poetic than scientific, appealing to a cosmic destiny rather than observable causes.

Arnold Toynbee (1946), a British historian, has offered a more optimistic cyclical theory of change. Central to his theory are the concepts of "challenge and response": the measure of a civilization's success is found in its responses to specific challenges posed by its physical and social environment. All civilizations, in his view, rise and fall according to their ability to meet these challenges, although later civilizations have the benefit of learning from the mistakes of civilizations before them.

Not all approaches to social change that see a course to history hold that the course is cyclical. Some, such as Talcott Parsons (1977), suggest that societies grow and change in patterned ways and the changes they experience tend toward progress or development. Like the cyclical theorists, however, these theorists offer no explanation of the mechanism by which the changes take place. The cyclical theorists do not explain why societies become rigid, nor does Parsons explain why social changes tend to be progressive.

The third answer that sociologists have is that there is indeed a theory of social evolution and the theory accounts for both the course of social change and its mechanism. The first sociologist to offer such a theory was Herbert Spencer (1820–1903). Spencer (1896/1974) drew elaborate parallels between the development and evolution of biological organisms and the development and evolution of human societies. Just as a human being develops from a relatively undifferentiated embryo to a complex, highly differentiated adult, so society undergoes structural change from simple homogeneous forms (e.g., tribes) to organizations of great complexity (e.g., nation-states). The mechanism of change, according to Spencer, is the need to adapt to a constantly changing environment. Like Darwin, Spencer saw adaptation as a struggle for existence in a world of competition and scarcity. Only the "fittest" social forms survive.[1] As

---

[1]Unlike Darwin, however, Spencer's ideas on the source of variation focused on the adaptation of individual organisms to their environment rather than on random variation. Spencer's view is associated with the biologist Lamarck and has been discarded by modern biologists. Nevertheless, some argue that Spencer's view may still apply in human social evolution because of the special role of learning.

humans adjust to their surrounding conditions, including their social arrangements, they develop new habits and traits; those traits that help them survive get genetically passed on and influence the way subsequent generations create their social forms. Thus, individuals and their social arrangements are constantly modified in reciprocal fashion through succeeding generations (Haines 1988).

A leading contemporary evolutionary theorist is Gerhard Lenski. He too sees direct parallels with biological evolution, but he recognizes a cultural as well as a genetic heritage in every human society. Human societies, in interacting with their natural and social world, develop characteristics that enable them to cope and grow. These characteristics get encoded in the society's information system, just as a plant or animal species' record of experience in an environment gets encoded in its genes (Lenski and Lenski 1987).

Lenski believes that to grow in size, complexity, wealth, or power a society has to make advances in what he calls "subsistence technology." This term refers to the information a society uses to give its members the energy they need to sustain their activities. The more information used, the more energy there is; the more energy, the more a society can do. Advances in technology stimulate further advances, leading to further growth. Thus the process of societal development, once set in motion, tends to be self-sustaining. The society that does not make advances in technology will not grow and in the long run will not survive. Lenski recognizes other factors that can limit a society's growth, such as its physical environment, beliefs, and values. These can produce obstacles or resistance to innovation and social change. Lenski's theory is a prime example of the structural/functional perspective; he focuses to a far lesser extent on social action or power struggles.

INNOVATION AND DIFFUSION

No matter what sociologists might think about an overall theory of social change, they are all likely to be concerned with the ways in which specific social changes take place. Basically, two processes are involved: **innovation**, the creation and institutionalization of new social practices or structures, and **diffusion**, the spread of innovative patterns from one social setting to another.

A Roman cart wheel, an 18th-century mill wheel, and a trimming wheel at a modern paper manufacturing plant. . . . Though the wheel first appeared thousands of years ago in Mesopotamia, succeeding ages and societies, including our own, have continued the process of innovation by which an invention becomes a useful tool. (Clockwise from top left: Art Resource; Gabe Palmer/The Stock Market; John Blaustein/ Woodfin Camp & Associates.)

Forms of Innovation

Innovation is, in fact, a two-step process. It can begin with a **discovery,** when some natural phenomenon is first brought to people's attention, or with an **invention,** when someone devises a new way of doing things. But whether we are talking about a new natural phenomenon or a new machine, innovation is not complete until a second step is taken: people must decide to put the new discovery or invention to use. For example, long ago people discovered the natural phenomenon that round objects roll and they invented the wheel. But the invented wheel had no great value until people made use of it for transportation. The second step—using the new

discovery or invention—does not necessarily follow closely on the first step. For example, some new agricultural techniques were invented in the late Middle Ages, but were not put into practice until the seventeenth and eighteenth centuries. Only then did population pressures create the need for using the new techniques to increase food production. Moreover, new uses can continually be found for old inventions. The invention of the wheel took place thousands of years ago but we are still finding new ways to use it. Social change can take place through innovation in **technology,** knowledge applied in practical ways to the material aspects of life, as well as through innovation in the realm of ideas, or cultural values.

Technological Innovation

We tend to think that technology is a fairly recent development in history. But technological innovation leading to social change has gone on from the beginning of human history. Even such a relatively simple invention as the stirrup, which allowed the rider of a horse to stay firmly seated in the saddle, produced a major social change. This medieval innovation led to a completely new form of attack—mounted shock combat—in which a rapidly moving warrior could slash and jab at his opponent without fear of tumbling unchivalrously to the ground. This new mode of fighting, in turn, made novel demands on soldiering. No longer could a freeman simply take up arms and declare himself fit for battle. The new technique of mounted combat required many years of training, not to mention the great expense of horses, attendants, and equipment. Thus, a whole new social aristocracy was born—the knightly class—and with it a new set of social patterns attuned to the needs of a mounted warrior's way of life. "Few inventions have been so simple as the stirrup," writes Lynn White, Jr. (1962, p. 38), "but few have had so catalytic an influence on history."

In our own times several technological changes have had equally profound effects. Consider the automobile. On a personal level it has had an enormous impact on our everyday patterns of social life. It has allowed us great mobility in visiting friends and relatives, participating in community organizations, engaging in sports and other leisure-time pursuits, and even dating and courtship. In considering society as a whole, the vast influence of the automobile is also apparent. The car has encouraged the development of many major industries, in addition to car manufacturing, shipping, and marketing—supplying materials to auto makers, seeing that their products are cared for and serviced, producing the fuels to run automobiles, and providing the roads they drive on. In this way, the automobile directly or indirectly employs many millions of American workers. The car has greatly affected our settlement patterns as well. Without the car, it is unlikely that today's sprawling suburbs would have evolved as they have. Accompanying these changes in residence patterns are other transformations. For instance, the car has promoted great change in retail distribution: the small, main-street merchants are being replaced by huge shopping malls located on the outskirts of town. The car, in short, has virtually revolutionized the American way of life.

As this example of the car's social impact illustrates, most technological innovations involve not only the creation of a new physical object but also a managerial and support system to control and exploit that product (Brooks 1980). The car has brought with it a vast economic, social, and political complex: assembly lines, service stations, oil companies and refineries, automobile insurance, highways and highway lobbyists, driving laws, and the police, courts, and bureaucracies to enforce them. Similarly, elaborate support systems have grown up around all our major technological developments—from atomic weapons to spacecraft to television to techniques of modern brain surgery.

Cultural Innovation

What is the effect of innovative ideas or values on social change? As we saw at the beginning of this chapter, a new idea of how to organize a government based on a written constitution resulted in the formation of a new nation, a nation that has been at the forefront of social change ever since. And as we saw earlier, the seventeenth-century ideals of hard work, frugality, and self-denial that were part of the Protestant ethic established behavior patterns that were consistent with the requirements of modern industrial capitalism.

New ideas that are in step with the values of a society can facilitate social change, but sometimes for one reason or another a society is not receptive to new ideas or even actively resists them. For example, giving women the right to vote was not uniformly welcomed. Female suffrage had been proposed in the United States as a reform as early as 1848, when American feminist leaders conducted their first women's rights convention. But for the next seventy years, both men and women raised vocal opposition to the idea, and some suffragists were even imprisoned for their demonstrations on behalf of their proposal. Not until 1920, when the Nineteenth Amendment to the Constitution was finally ratified, were proponents of women's right to vote able to overcome the traditionalists' fear that admission of women to political life would undermine the family.

There are many examples of similar resistance to change in our own era. Though the Supreme Court declared in 1954 that segregated schools were a violation of blacks' constitutional rights, battles over integrating school systems are still taking place. The argument against school desegregation has taken various forms over the past thirty-five years. At first, opponents argued that the regulation of education was a state right, not a national responsibility, the federal government had no right to declare state-mandated segregation laws illegal. As whites began to leave the inner cities for the suburbs, and schools became increasingly segregated because of housing patterns rather than specific laws, the argument shifted to support for "neighborhood schools." Opponents of school desegregation then argued against the practice of busing students to distant sites to attain racial balance. Behind both arguments, however, lay the traditional belief that close association of blacks and whites is undesirable.

Thus, new ideas and values can be readily absorbed by the society that is ready for them, but they may be temporarily or permanently resisted by a society whose traditional values and ways of doing things clash with the new ideas and practices. Sometimes it is necessary to wait for cultural values to catch up with the technological and cultural innovations.

Diffusion

Anything that is invented and put into practice in one area of society can be spread throughout the society or introduced into other societies. The process by which this is accomplished is called *diffusion* because it entails the gradual dissemination of technological and cultural innovations. Soldiers, colonial administrators, missionaries, migrants, traders, visiting scholars and artists, exchange students, tourists—all are potential agents of diffusion. We can see the results of diffusion even in something as all-American as the United States Constitution. It was written in English, a language borrowed from England, using an alphabet that came to us from ancient Phoenicia by way of the Greeks and Romans. The various sections of the document are denoted by Roman and Arabic numerals. It was printed by means of a process invented in Germany; the paper it was printed on was derived from an invention of the ancient Egyptians. Finally, many of the political ideas incorporated in that constitution were cultural legacies of French and English philosophers.

The extent to which diffusion actually occurs will vary. At one extreme, contact between societies may result in a cultural "takeover." For example, the Dutch colonials transformed Indonesian society from a group of subsistence horticulturists who lived in small, egalitarian villages into a competitive, stratified society oriented toward the world market (Plog, Jolly, and Bates 1976). At the other extreme, contact may prompt people to withdraw and cling to their traditions. Although the Sumu Indians of Nicaragua have been trading with neighboring groups for centuries, until recently they shut their doors when strangers entered their villages, kept their ways secret, and married only among themselves.

Between these two extremes are numerous examples of societies borrowing foreign traits selectively. For instance, Marco Polo introduced his Italian countrymen to the long, thin, round noodles eaten by the Chinese. They soon became popular in Italy, where they were called spaghetti. Italian immigrants later brought spaghetti to America. Similarly, the Incas of Peru discovered quinine and passed it along to their Spanish conquerors, who then shared it with other Europeans, who in turn used it in Africa to offset malaria attacks. (Thus, were it not for the Incas, Europeans might never have colonized Africa.)

Although material objects and technology spread more readily than do systems of beliefs and values or forms of social organization, these too may widely diffuse. Examples are the missionary religions, Buddhism, Christianity, and Islam. The Napoleonic Code, the basis for law in France and all its former colonies, was adopted by many other societies, including the state of Louisiana.

Sometimes in the process of being diffused, a cultural idea or technology is modified to suit the needs of the society adopting it. For instance, the Haitians wove together myths and rituals from Catholicism and West African religions into a new religio-magical system, voodoo. This process of modification can even mean that the original trait gets totally transformed.

The processes of innovation and diffusion, then, are basic to almost all social change. We offer an example of this in our in-depth look at the computer revolution.

In Depth: Computers and Social Change

Computer technology had to begin with an invention, and the credit for that invention goes to a nineteenth-century British mathematician named Charles Babbage.

Satellite communications have sped up the pace of cultural and technological diffusion, as evidenced by this cable television receiving antenna on the island nation of Barbados in the Carribean. Sometimes the process of diffusion and modification can lead to startling practices: here is one way to get better mileage from your camel! (Left: Robert Knowles/Photo Researchers, Inc.; below: Robert Azzi/Woodfin Camp & Associates.)

Here's how Babbage himself describes the origins of his invention:

> One evening I was sitting in the rooms of the Analytical Society at Cambridge, my head leaning forward on the table in a kind of dreamy mood, with a Table of logarithms lying open before me. Another member, coming into the room, and seeing me half asleep, called out, "Well, Babbage, what are you dreaming about?" to which I replied, "I am thinking that all these Tables (pointing to the logarithms) might be calculated by machinery." (Quoted in Goldstine 1972, p. 11)

The year was around 1812, and Babbage devoted the next sixty years of his life to developing computing machinery. He realized that for any task that could be subdivided and routinized, there was a potential for automating it. His conception of an "Analytical Machine" using digital computation was more than a century in advance of its time; it was to receive instructions and variable data from the insertion of punched cards, working on the same principle as a player piano. Unfortunately, the prototypes of Babbage's invention were cumbersome, clanking affairs. They were never put to use, partly because the production technology of his day was too primitive to make an efficient model and partly because the technology level of the day did not require going beyond what people could calculate by hand.

Real practical developments in computer technology did not come about until the next century. In the 1930s, scientists again began to think about digital computation on a machine. By then some other inventions—for example, vacuum tube technology and electronic counters—made it possible to put together practical working models. By that time, also, the needs for a computer were clearly in place. The army was particularly interested in developing a machine to calculate the trajectories of shells, and the federal government needed an efficient system of record keeping, especially in the Bureau of the Census and in the Internal Revenue Service. The first fully electronic digital computer built by a commercial manufacturer was Sperry's UNIVAC (Universal Automatic Computer), installed at the Bureau of the Census in 1951. These early computers were huge machines that filled entire rooms and depended on large, fragile vacuum tubes to process the punched-in information.

Further innovation in computer technology came about through miniaturization of component parts

(Braun and McDonald 1978). Vacuum tubes were replaced by semiconductor transistors which themselves got smaller and smaller and at the same time more and more powerful through the invention of integrated circuits. When a way was found to mass produce these integrated circuits using silicon, a cheap, effective semiconducting substance, the computer industry took off. In 1957 the average single silicon transistor cost $17.81; today a $2 silicon chip may have the equivalent of thousands of transistors incorporated in its integrated circuits (Noyce 1979; Forester 1988). With the advent of inexpensive, powerful, "user friendly" microcomputers in the 1980s, computers entered the homes of millions of Americans.

Range of Uses

The wide-ranging impact of the computer was well expressed by President Ronald Reagan in a speech he gave to students in the Soviet Union in May 1988:

> It's been called the technological or information revolution. And as its emblem, one might take the tiny silicon chip no bigger than a fingerprint. One of these chips has more computing power than a roomful of old-style computers. These microcomputers today aid the design of everything from houses to cars to spacecraft. They even design better and faster computers. They can translate English into Russian, or enable the blind to read, or help Michael Jackson produce on one synthesizer the sounds of a whole orchestra. (*New York Times*, June 1, 1988, p. A12)

Hardly any area of our lives today remains untouched by computers, but in what follows, we consider some of the most important of these: industry, offices, education, research, military technology, and communications.

Industry

Some industries use computers in the full range of their production processes. For example, in the automobile industry, computers guide robots in welding bodies; operate paint sprayers; and grind tools, dies, and parts to precise tolerances (Gunn 1982; Noble 1984). Not only do computers operate machinery, they also process crucial information. Supervisors enter production and quality-control data into computer systems. Automobile dealers place orders on computers, which then calculate what parts are necessary and what plants those parts should be shipped to. Computers even keep track of how many cars need which color paint, which size engine, what kind of tires, and so on. Thus, both skilled and unskilled industrial workers are finding their job requirements reduced by the use of computers. The process of computerization is really an extension of the division of labor. As Babbage discovered, once a task is broken into several parts, it is easier for it to be automated.

Offices

Twenty-five years ago the typical office consisted of executives dictating to secretaries, secretaries typing up the dictation and making copies, file clerks placing folders into huge metal file cabinets, and mailboys delivering interoffice mail throughout the day. Then, when the computer industry began to explode in the

1970s, the predictions of the "office of the future" envisioned a fully automated office:

> . . . a paperless, push-button, electronic world where high finance meets high technology in a triumph of white-collar productivity. In the office of the future, company execs will send personal memos to employees 10,000 miles away with the touch of a button and instantly extract vital data for a board meeting from the company's electronic files. They will browse electronically through video calendars and tickler [sales prospect] files to schedule meetings with subordinates or check on overdue reports. And they will chat simultaneously with division chiefs in Pocatello, Auckland, and Buenos Aires via a televised conference at company headquarters. (Immel 1985, p. 313)

The technology for such fully automated offices is now in place, but centralized electronic systems have not been installed at the pace or on the scale many had predicted. Some companies are unwilling to make the

From the vacuum tube to the transistor to the silicon chip . . . The powerful, portable microcomputer that fits on this young woman's lap bears no apparent relation to its cumbersome ancestor, ENIAC, the first working electronic computer, developed during the 1940s by engineers at the University of Pennsylvania in cooperation with the U.S. military. Here, one of ENIAC's inventors adjusts dials on a control panel of the room-sized computer. (Left: UPI/Bettmann Newsphotos; below: Mike Mazzaschi/Stock, Boston.)

necessary huge investment because they fear the system they buy will soon become obsolete; other companies, overwhelmed by the options available to them, put off making any decision (a condition described as "paralysis by analysis"). Many observers think that the automated business machine manufacturers overestimated the amount of change that offices need to make (or are ready to make) at this time. Another problem is the confusion caused by disparate office products. Every office machine manufacturer builds to its own design and standards, so that many office products are incompatible with one another (Immel 1985; *Business Week* 1985).

In companies that have put off installing a centralized computer system, many managers have brought personal computers to their desktops. The inexpensive, portable, easy-to-use microcomputers have permitted these executives to do their own word processing, data processing, and electronic mailing. But the corporations still have the problem of getting the desktop units to work together and to link up with a central data base. With the proliferation of personal computers, as one executive has noted, "our concern was 10 guys might sit in their offices solving the same problem" (*Business Week* 1985, p. 331). Moreover, maintaining the desktop units involves hidden costs, such as purchasing printers, additional memory, software programs and the like. For these reasons some company analysts foresee an increased need for the institution of large centralized systems. Another scenario calls for giving personal computers a double use by keeping them as autonomous units but also linking them to a central mainframe computer. This will permit a user to extract certain data from the mainframe's memory, make alterations on the microcomputer, and then return the data to the mainframe for computation. The time the data are being processed only by the microcomputer is time that is saved—usually at considerable financial benefit—on the mainframe. Communication networks linking computers are among the most active areas of development at present.

Education

At one time some people thought that computers would revolutionize education through computer-assisted instruction. This revolution did not come to pass. For one thing, equipping a school with all the computer terminals needed to provide that kind of instruction was very expensive; for another, educators discovered that computers did not have the warmth and flexibility of flesh-and-blood teachers.

As the cost of computers has come down, more schools have been able to purchase more computers, allowing their students access to a computer for a certain number of periods a week. Most of the available computer programs, however, offer only drill and practice, rather than creative participation. Elementary school students learn to write and do mathematics with the help of computers. High school and college students use the computers for word processing or to help them get the information they need. Computers can search library catalogs in minutes for references that it would take the students hours to find on their own. Increasing numbers of libraries are providing computer work stations for their patrons to use. According to one New York City librarian, in the future much of the information that libraries contain will be "machine readable" (Markoff 1988).

Many educators believe that "computer literacy" —familiarity with the way computers work and how to use them—will be essential for most jobs by early in the next century. For this reason many people today are concerned that children of poor families who attend schools that cannot afford computers will be severely disadvantaged when they try to become part of the job market.

Research

The use of computers is vital to research carried on in all the sciences—natural and social. Astronomy, for example, depends on the computerized calculations of radio waves and light emissions to determine the location, movement, mass and other characteristics of "black holes" and distant "invisible" stellar objects. In the social sciences, research dealing with large populations (such as those measured by the census) would be impossible without the aid of computers. Not only do the computers count, they also help scientists construct models to simulate various natural or social processes.

Military Technology

The military, which was one of the first customers for computers, continues to be an important user. For example, the Strategic Air Command requires a huge and complex computer program to deal with numerous contingencies and chains of events. Variables of climate must be related to shifts in the functioning of equipment and normal air traffic patterns; these data must be correlated with information regarding enemy, ally, and domestic military operations. For every conceivable combination of data, the mainframe computer must have a definite procedure.

The Defense Department is spending $1 billion to build one of the world's largest supercomputer complexes that can simulate various nuclear war scenarios. These calculations will be used to assess the value of different parts of the proposed Strategic Defense Initiative (also known as "Star Wars"). On a smaller scale, modern tanks are computer-driven and equipped with small computers to scan the environment in order to detect possible threats. Modern military planes have highly sophisticated computer systems; their pilots are more like computer technicians than the aerial acrobats of old who "flew by the seat of their pants." The military also uses computers to keep records on personnel, logistics, and the procurement and shipment of supplies and weapons.

Communications

Computers are used in a vast number of applications in the area of communications (Calhoun 1986). The telephone industry uses computers in switching and in such former personal services as directory assistance. Many home computer users communicate by means of electronic bulletin boards and networking with hundreds or thousands of other computer users on a variety of subjects, from politics to computer games. Business and professional people use networks to keep in touch with each other. Some corporations hold entire conferences by computer. Many people now **telecommute**—that is, they work at home with a computerized telephone hookup to an office. Such computer activities as word processing, report writing, filing information, and calculating statistical data can be performed at home because it matters little whether the link between the computer and the visual display terminal is 40 feet, 40 miles, or 4,000 miles away. Computers can also be used at home to pay bills, make bank transactions, order groceries, and perform a growing number of other tasks.

THE SOCIAL ASPECTS OF COMPUTER USE

The computer era has come upon us so suddenly and is so rapidly changing that it is difficult to assess its social impact on individuals and on society in general. Some social scientists believe that the short-term effects of computers have thus so far not been as pervasive and dramatic as had been forecast. Change for most individuals has been modest, and most organizations have not greatly shifted their standard operating procedures. Generally, computer technology has been made to adapt to existing practices, and only a few major immediate transformations have taken place (Danziger 1985).

One area of debate among social scientists is whether the use of computers isolates individuals or creates more interaction with other people. An argument can be made that programmers, systems analysts, organizational decision makers, data-entry staff, and even clients of the organization are being drawn together in one complex "web of computing" (Kling and Scacchi 1982). On the other hand, an argument can also be made for the "antisocial" effect of computer use. Time spent with a computer does reduce time spent with other individuals, and studies show that instead of increasing workers' free time, computers engage their users in an increasing amount of work time. Moreover, individuals who are given the choice of interacting with computing systems or humans are more likely to choose the former. That choice can be seen in those who prefer playing a computer game to throwing a frisbee with friends, people who prefer to go to automated tellers than to human tellers in banks, and people who use electronic mail rather than the telephone at the office (Danziger 1985).

Another matter of debate is whether computers are more likely to increase or decrease the hierarchical nature of organizations and their centralization of power and information (King and Kraemer 1987). Some experts believe that the computerized access to information that is available to all employees in an office has a leveling effect on organizational hierarchy, since it is no longer as easy for an elite group to filter down information selectively (Naisbitt 1982; *Christian Science Monitor*, June 6, 1988, p. 1). Others, however, do not find the existing organizational hierarchy altered by computerization but rather see the power of the dominant elite enhanced by having centralized control of the source of information (Sterling 1986). Still, the extensive use of microcomputers as independent, unmonitored systems might have the effect of undercutting the ability of an elite group to control information (Danziger 1985). Thus far, however, research on computers in professional use (for example, by doctors or lawyers) shows little tendency for this last possibility to be realized; there is too much social power stacked against it (Calhoun and Copp 1988).

Public Concerns

Privacy

The growing use of computers to collect data and to handle information raises the issue of individual privacy and the confidentiality of personal data. Increasingly, the Social Security number is becoming a "single identifying" number for keeping track of people and developing individual "data images" of them. For instance, credit bureaus and local police departments have come to rely increasingly on centralized computers as sources of information. The growing numbers of items that are computerized combined with the multiplying links among computer data bases make possible the construction of complete electronic profiles of people —including where they travel, what they eat, what their life styles are, what medicines they take, and with whom they speak. Many civil libertarians fear the "big brother" potential for electronic snooping, which can endanger individual freedom in democratic societies.

Another problem is how to make data banks secure from intrusion by outsiders, who might use the information inappropriately or even alter or falsify the stored information there. Individuals also must be able to verify the accuracy of the data about themselves. Some credit reporting services and government agencies use data from sources over which people have no control and which are frequently inaccurate (Burnham 1983; Landon 1986; Rule et al. 1980). An individual named Terry Dean Rogan can testify to the damaging consequences of inaccurate data. His birth certificate had been stolen by a criminal, which caused Rogan's name to be entered in the FBI's computerized data base. Law enforcement agencies across the nation have access to this data bank. As a result, Rogan was arrested five times between 1982 and 1984 for crimes he did not commit (Markoff 1988).

Computers have become powerful catalysts of social change, in part because they have changed the nature of work in so many different kinds of workplaces. Here, an auto mechanic tunes a car's engine with the aid of a diagnostic computer. (Michael L. Abramson/Woodfin Camp & Associates.)

Jobs

High technology, particularly the application of electronics to industry, communications, medicine, and other spheres of life, is transforming the job market (see Chapter 15). The number of jobs available in manufacturing is down, whereas the number of jobs in the service sector, especially those related to managing information, is up (Cetron 1983; Lyon 1988). This has resulted in dislocations and disruptions for many individuals, communities, and regions (Webster and Robins 1986). According to some views, however, whether these changes are alarming or encouraging depends on whether one looks at the short-term or long-term effects.

In the short run, the loss of jobs and the "deskilling" of jobs as a result of automation are devastating for workers, particularly in manufacturing. Some experts predict that by the year 2000, factory robots will be doing what 7 million human beings were doing in 1980. At the same time office automation is likely to sharply reduce white-collar jobs, particularly clerical and stenographic jobs. Computers already handle much of the "paper shuffling" between individuals and organizations. Paychecks are typically prepared by computers. Banking has also computerized many of its operations. In the local supermarket, electronic scanners read and record product/price codes and produce a printed bill for the customer and inventory data for the store.

Another problem is that whereas highly skilled high-tech jobs are challenging and well paid, the vast majority of jobs are mind-dulling, menial, and poorly paid. Many offices and home offices are now more like "electronic sweatshops" (Andrew 1983; Garson 1988). Jobs involving technology that is simple and repetitive can readily be exported to nations where wages are low. The loss of unskilled and semiskilled jobs to overseas nations makes it even more difficult for American industry to absorb unemployed workers and a growing labor force.

Those who take the long-term view argue that automation can gradually improve the competitive position of the United States in international trade, thereby forestalling the migration of jobs overseas. Also, by lowering the prices of goods so that people can afford more of them, technology will eventually increase total production, creating more jobs among suppliers. This perspective gives the out-of-work factory mechanic the dubious assurance that twenty or thirty years in the future, the rise in productivity through automation will pay off in the possibility of a job.

In short, computerization has eliminated many jobs and taken the skill out of others; it has created some new jobs, but not as many as it has destroyed. The question is whether the new wealth that computers help create will be spent or invested in ways that indirectly lead to the creation of other new jobs, and whether these jobs will be as good as those that have been eliminated (Francis 1986).

Technological Leadership

Diffusion has made computer technology a worldwide commodity, and the United States is feeling the pinch of

While many contemporary composers and musicians employ computers, concert pianists probably do not need to worry about being replaced by performers like Wabot-2, a musical robot at Waseda University. However, in some highly automated industries, computer-driven robots (which are not usually modelled after a human being) are already calling the tune. (Ethan Hoffman/Archive Pictures, Inc.)

global competition, especially from Japan and other Asian countries who have an expertise in electronics. Many people, who are concerned that the United States will fall permanently behind in technological and industrial leadership, are calling for increased funding for computer research (Feigenbaum and McCorduck 1983). The problem is a real one but not one that is susceptible to easy solution. With technological development occurring on a global scale, any one country will be hard-pressed to stay on top for very long. Such changes have led some observers to postulate the development of a postindustrial society in the United States (see feature).

THEORIES OF DEVELOPMENT

The discussion of social change in this chapter has largely focused on Western societies. But what of the rest of the nations—the so-called Third World, constituting two-thirds of the world's population—that have not shared equally in the fruits of economic development?

The Postindustrial Society

The prominent sociologist Daniel Bell (1973, 1980) believes that we have already entered the postindustrial age. Whereas the development of the machine was the central force in industrial society, in postindustrial society, the central force is the organization of theoretical knowledge. Energy production, fueled by capital and labor, drove industrial society; information production, fueled by technology, drives the postindustrial society. Economic growth was the goal of the industrial age; advancement of theoretical knowledge is the new goal. The class structure of postindustrial society (or the "information society") is based on access to information and control of decision making rather than on ownership of property. The emblem of the new information society is the university, which another sociologist views as occupying the same place as the great capitalist enterprises once did (Touraine 1971).

Bell envisions a society that is made more humane by its reliance on technical efficiency. Social arrangements will be based on expert, scientific knowledge and technical planning. Because their material needs will be met beyond the basic level, people will be able to turn their attention to improving quality of life, as measured by services and amenities. The dominant theme of Bell's work is how much more rationally the postindustrial society can be run in contrast to the hurly-burly of early capitalism.

Bell's views are not universally accepted. Some critics argue that industry has not been replaced; it is still extremely important. The reason the

United States has fewer industrial production jobs is that it is relying increasingly on *imported* industrial goods. In other words, we have simply looked for labor elsewhere rather than doing without labor altogether by shutting down industry or relying on automation. Indeed, some social scientists would argue that employers have systematically pursued a policy of "de-industrializing" the United States by investing in overseas plants, a trend they see as threatening our collective economic well-being as well as the jobs of specific workers at home (Bluestone and Harrison 1982).

Still other critics argue that Bell is not asking the most important question. It should not be "Are we becoming postindustrial?" but "Are we becoming *postcapitalist*?" The term *industrial society* does not make the important distinction between capitalism and socialism. These critics suggest that we are still very much a capitalist society and that Bell fails to consider the powerful vested interests that would oppose his vision of the future. Nor, according to these critics, does Bell give enough attention to how much the same capitalist pressures that drove industrial organization also drive the activities through which knowledge is created and used, such as research and development (Giddens 1987; Kumar 1980).

Another criticism of Bell's scenario is that he fails to consider politics, the major means people have for influencing social change; political ideology is not usually the most rational basis of decision making. Finally, critics point out the dubious empirical

evidence for some of Bell's claims (Badham 1984). For example, soon after Bell's book was published, much of the growth in the sector of government-supported human services was halted or reversed, especially by the Reagan administration. Bell's prediction of the predominance of the information sector in postindustrial society is very much a matter of debate, though consumer services like restaurant work have grown dramatically.

Even if Bell's idea of information technology as the basis of a postindustrial society is misconceived, might we still think of high technology as a new industrial revolution, on the order of the industrial revolution of the late eighteenth and early nineteenth centuries? That is, indeed, the view of a number of critics, but at least one group of social scientists would disagree. They believe the effect of the new technology is an "intensification of old tendencies" rather than a new beginning. The new technology will have to be put to work to alleviate old problems, such as the exploitative use and dwindling supply of energy sources, instead of leading to an era in which work becomes largely unnecessary. In their view "the problems we shall face will be not wholly new ones, but those with which we are familiar, though perhaps intensified and extended. There is likely, for example, to be a progression away from blue-collar jobs to white-collar or service occupations, but these could well take on more of the character that factory work has had in the past, if the tendency is not resisted". (Rosenbrock et al. 1985)

Although the first world of capitalist countries and the second world of eastern bloc Communist countries are far along the path of industrialization, urbanization, and increasingly complex social organization, the Third World lags. Will the less developed countries gradually catch up or will they fall farther behind?

This issue is an important one not just for citizens of the poor countries but for those of rich ones as well. Our world has become increasingly interdependent; we buy electronic products from South Korea, copper from Zambia, oil from the Arab peninsula, and coffee from South America. The United States depends on other countries for more than just material goods and raw materials; it needs them to cooperate in the pursuit of world peace as well. Joint efforts are necessary to control terrorism, restrict the spread of nuclear weapons, and settle disputes through diplomacy rather than weapons. On several levels, what happens in the Third World is of some importance to all of us. In what follows we consider three major sociological viewpoints on the course of change in the Third World and consider the prospects for that area of the world today.

Modernization Theories

In the 1950s many sociologists and economists were convinced that most of the poor countries of the world were simply "underdeveloped." In their view, these countries would eventually experience industrial revolutions like those of Europe and North America. The problem was that certain preconditions for social change that the classical theorists had stressed were missing in those countries. The nations were thought to lack the self-discipline, devotion to hard work, and willingness to save that Weber attributed to the Protestant Ethic and other processes of rationalization. These countries lacked the complex division of labor that Durkheim associated with organic solidarity. Above all, they lacked the material means of production and the social organization of production that Marx emphasized. Analysts thus proposed **modernization theories,** which focused attention on how to provide the social, cultural, and material conditions needed for the underdeveloped countries to begin an economic "take-off" (Rostow 1952). These theories have tended to identify progress with becoming more like the West.

Partly as a result of the modernization theorists' recommendations, relatively rich Western nations offered aid to poor countries; schooling was provided, roads and factories were built, and government ministries were reorganized. Some improvements resulted

from this and some modernization theorists continued to focus on these improvements (Inkeles and Smith 1980). But unfortunately, the expected modernization in the image of Western-style development failed to occur in most (if not all) of the Third World nations. Moreover, a number of those countries suffered damaging civil wars, military takeovers, and other repressions of freedom as a consequence of their rising expectations. Why did these well-intended plans fail? The dependency theorists have provided some answers.

Dependency Theory

Critics of modernization theories (e.g., Frank 1967) propose as an alternative **dependency theory** which holds that the Third World countries, especially those in Latin America, did not "take off" precisely because they were so dependent on the capitalistic countries. The best entrepreneurs in such countries as Brazil and Argentina were working as agents of American and European companies instead of acting as capitalists on their own. The political leaders in these countries primarily acted as intermediaries between their own countries and the governments of the rich nations who gave them aid. The aid itself often made things worse in the local economies. Technological aid called for dependence on foreign supplies, such as machine parts and computer systems, to be paid for with scarce U.S. dollars. Often the technology came without the information and training required to run it. When the technology took hold, it frequently put local workers out of work; for example, a new shoe factory built with foreign aid might provide jobs for some, but at the same time it put traditional shoemakers out of work. Financial problems arose when the foreign aid came in the form of loans. When the economy of the poorer countries did not modernize as planned, the countries had trouble paying back these loans. The richer countries induced their banks to loan still more money, which has led to the current international loan crisis.

Dependency had political repercussions as well. The leaders of the United States and other rich nations tended to help the countries they considered friendly (which, in the case of the United States, generally meant "anti-Communist"). This resulted in the support of a number of unattractive military dictatorships. These governments were often as attentive to their foreign benefactors as they were to the wishes and needs of their own people, an attitude that made democracy—one of the supposed elements of modernization—hard to develop (Evans 1980).

While the dependency theorists pinpointed the weaknesses of modernization theories, they themselves have been subject to criticism, primarily for failing to specify what policies will work best to promote development. At one time many dependency theorists favored socialist governments to bring about modernization. Socialist governments have arguably performed better than capitalist-oriented governments in such areas as improving health care and education, but they have not done significantly better in overall economic development. The reason may be that development in a modern world depends on external trade, which is played by capitalist rules. Some modernization theorists also point out that whereas material factors may not be sufficient for modernization, certain of these factors are at least crucial; for example, roads and communications still matter, dependency or no dependency (Rostow 1980).

World Systems Theory

Yet another theory draws on dependency theory but takes it even further. Basically it holds that the poorer nations have little chance to ever follow in the footsteps of the richer nations because the rich nations are already so far ahead. The American sociologist Immanuel Wallerstein (1974, 1979, 1980) developed this idea in the 1970s as a central conclusion of his **world systems theory**. His analysis focuses on capitalist countries and their relationships to the non-Communist countries of the world, since he believes the Communist nations have largely opted out of the economic network that enmeshes the rest of the world.

Wallerstein divides the nations of the world into three categories. The *core* group consists of the world's powerful industrial economies, which now include the United States, most Western European countries, and Japan. The core nations provide the management and much of the essential machinery for the production of the world's goods, and they also reap most of the profits.

Outside the core the vast majority of the world's nations are a part of the *periphery*. The peripheral nations consist of the many countries limited to subsistence agriculture, which are overwhelmingly dependent on foreign aid or able to participate in the world system only on terms set by the core countries. Such countries include Chad, Botswana, Peru, and Guatemala. Very loosely knit into the world system, these countries supply raw materials and buy small amounts of manufactured goods in return.

Between the core and the periphery lies a *semiperiphery* of countries moving up or down in the system. These nations are still partly able to determine their own economic well-being while being actively involved in the world system. South Korea provides a good example of a semiperipheral country on the rise as it finds a receptive world market for its manufactured goods. The success of South Korea typifies the so-called newly industrialized countries of Asia. So does its problem; as the South Korean economy heats up, its citizens grow restive and demand more of the democratic and welfare characteristics of the core countries. South Koreans, today, for example, are demanding higher wages, shorter workweeks, and union protection, and are resisting the authoritarian measures the government institutes to hold back domestic consumption in favor of investment. Britain might also be seen as a semiperipheral nation today. Its economy has declined so far that it seems to have fallen out of the core group, although in political terms it is still very much a part of the Western power structure.

By means of his three-tier world system theory, Wallerstein is suggesting that we can no longer view modernizing nations as isolated units undergoing a largely *intra*national process. Modernization must be seen as an *inter*national phenomenon, with the development of any particular nation basically determined by its role in the world system. The limits of that system are defined by capitalist trade, an area in which the core nations had a major head start. These nations can set the terms of this trade because they control the currency system, the shipping system, and the markets; they are in a position to trade high-priced manufactured goods for raw materials, agricultural products, and low-priced industrial products. The problems of the peripheral nations are compounded when they compete in producing the same sorts of goods, such as sugar or rubber, which only serves to drive down the world prices for these commodities.

WORLDS APART

> Year by year the world becomes more sharply divided into two. On the one hand there are the advanced, industrial, developed, mature economies. And then there are the rest—developing, less developed, underdeveloped, undeveloped, pre-industrial or backward. The precise shade of euphemistic description is unimportant; for the basic division is, of course, one between Rich and Poor. (Donaldson 1986, p. 11)

This was not always the case. Less than 150 years ago the preindustrial economies held 74 percent of the world's population and 72 percent of the world's income. But by 1960 their population share was 65 percent and their income share a mere 22 percent. If the poorer countries continue to grow in output per year at their present rate, they will take 191 years to reach the *present* American level. By then, of course, the American economy will have grown at an even faster rate (Donaldson 1986).

What has caused this great gap? For one thing, the modernized rich nations had the luxury of developing over centuries, without the interference of more advanced countries setting the rules for modernization. Consider, by contrast, the plight of the developing nations. As colonies, most of them were the prey of colonial powers, who manipulated the conditions of trade to serve their own purposes. In some cases the colonial powers actually destroyed local production to create a market for their own manufactured goods; Britain, for example, destroyed the textile industry in India in the last century. Colonial America was also subjected to trade restraints that favored the mother country, but the independent-minded American settlers were able to overthrow their colonial ruler while time was still left to get into the capitalistic race.

At the same time that the developing nations have been futilely trying to compete in what might be called a "fixed game," they have been bombarded with images of Western-style affluence (Harrison 1981). As Peter Donaldson notes, "no longer do the poor remain in blissful (or even miserable) ignorance of what is going on elsewhere. The cinema, radio and other mass media have opened the eyes of the poor two-thirds of the world to the levels of affluence achieved elsewhere. Increasing-

ly, they will demand their share of it. This is the so-called 'revolution of rising expectations'" (1986, p. 16). Another problem in the developing nations is a consequence of population pressures; many poor nations have grown beyond the capacity of the land to support them, not just in foodstuffs but in firewood and clean water as well. Finally, not only are the poor people of the world largely discontented and needy but they are also often neglected or exploited by their own corrupt government leaders and administrators.

Marx would not be surprised that contemporary Third World countries are breeding grounds of revolution and civil war. The ideologies may vary widely, from fundamentalist Islam to nationalism to Communism, but the conflict is basically the same—between those who have and those who have not. Nicaragua, Argentina, Chile, Brazil, Panama, Guatemala, Cuba, San Salvador, Iran, Lebanon, Libya, Uganda, Kenya, Ethiopia, Sudan, Zambia, Mozambique, Vietnam, Cambodia, Laos, India, Sri Lanka—all have experienced (or are still undergoing) violent upheavals in their social and political organizations. The common thread is the desperation of people who have little reason to believe that the existing system will ever help them. This frustration has spread beyond national boundaries in alarming ways in the form of international terrorism.

It is a sad irony that in a world growing ever smaller and more unified through technological advances in communications and transportation, nations are being pulled apart from one another economically, politically, and socially. Absorbed in our own "lifeworld"—our everyday experience and network of relationships—we find it difficult to take in, much less analyze, the dimensions of the social ills manifested in the large-scale "system world," the term used by German sociologist Jurgen Habermas (1984, 1988) to describe the global system of indirect relationships of markets, technology, governments, and mass media. In time, perhaps, the world's citizens will turn their collective attention to the needs of this huge, diverse, system world and find a way to harmonize their interests and to channel social change in beneficial ways. There is, after all, a precedent for such collective action. Just over 200 years ago a revolutionary document, the United States Constitution, was the catalyst that enabled a sprawling region of divergent social and economic interests to unite and modernize as one strong nation.

SUMMARY

1. Social change refers to basic alterations, over time, in the behavior patterns, culture, and structure of society. Sociologists are interested in seeking explanations of social change and determining whether social change follows a discernible course.

2. The classical theorists emphasized the study of social change. Marx thought that advances in production made social change possible, whereas the results of struggles between the classes shaped the course of change. Weber identified no single causal factor, but saw a pattern of social change in the growing rationalization of all aspects of life. Durkheim saw social change as the outcome of an increase in dynamic density of personal interactions, which caused a society to move from mechanical solidarity to organic solidarity.

3. Sociologists today are engaged in a debate over whether social change can be seen as a process of evolution. Evolutionary theory must postulate a mechanism of change, not just a course of development. There are three main viewpoints in this debate. The first holds that no theory of social evolution is possible, since there is neither a course nor mechanism of social change, though it is possible to make a set of limited generalizations about social change. The second viewpoint finds a definite course to social change (either cyclical or progressive) but specifies no mechanism for such change. The third viewpoint holds that a theory of social evolution is possible; these theorists identify a mechanism of social change and find that the course of social change is progressive and cumulative.

4. Social change takes place through innovation, the discovery or invention and putting into practice of new ways of doing things, and through diffusion, the spread of innovative patterns from one social setting to another.

5. Computer technology represents an innovation that has brought about social change in the last few decades. Computers have entered almost every area of our lives and have transformed the organization of work. Computers have important uses in education, research, military technology, and communications as well.

6. Assessing the social impact of computers is difficult because the computer era is both ongoing and constantly changing. The effect on personal interaction is not clear.

Whereas computer use has resulted in a "web of computing" among users, time spent with a machine is time spent away from other individuals. Some sociologists think computers in the workplace have a leveling effect on an organization's hierarchy, but others think existing hierarchies are strengthened by the centralized control of the source of information.

7. Computers are cause for public concern in several respects. First, they have the potential for compromising individual privacy and the confidentiality of personal data. Second, computerization in the workplace has resulted in the loss of many jobs, and many of these jobs that have been created are menial and low-paid. Third, if the United States does not invest heavily in computer research, it may fall permanently behind other countries in technological and industrial leadership.

8. A vast majority of the world's nations—known as the Third World—are currently engaged in the struggle to develop economically. The modernization theorists of the 1950s held that the Third World countries could experience an economic take-off if the industrialized nations provided them with the necessary social, cultural, and material conditions for social change. As it turned out, large amounts of foreign aid did not have this intended effect. The dependency theorists attributed this failure to the fact that foreign aid made the developing nations too dependent on the capitalist countries. Wallerstein's world systems theory holds that the poorer nations have little chance of ever following in the footsteps of the richer nations, which are already too far ahead on the path. Wallerstein views economic development as international, rather than intranational: the development of any particular nation is basically determined by its role in a world system defined by capitalist trade.

9. The gap between rich and poor nations is widening. The frustration that accompanies being discontented, needy, and exploited has made the Third World a breeding ground of revolution and civil war. The collective attention of all countries is needed to halt the trend of nations being pulled ever farther apart in a world growing ever smaller and more unified through technological advances.

GLOSSARY

Cyclical perspective. The belief that history moves in cycles that are neither cumulative nor progressive.

Dependency theory. A critique of modernization theories that holds that Third World countries were not becoming more economically developed because they were so dependent on capitalist countries.

Diffusion. The spread of innovative patterns from one social setting to another.

Discovery. A new natural phenomenon that is brought to people's attention.

Division of labor. The specialization of the economic tasks of workers.

Dynamic density. The frequency and impact of interactions among members of the population; a cause of social change postulated by Émile Durkheim.

Innovation. The creation and institutionalization of new social practices or structures.

Invention. A new way of doing things.

Modernization theories. A related set of sociological and economic views adopted in the 1950s that focused attention on how to provide the social, cultural, and material conditions needed for the underdeveloped countries to begin an economic take-off.

Rationalization. The tendency to base action on a logical assessment of effects.

Social change. Basic alterations, over time, in the behavior patterns, culture, and structure of society.

Technology. Knowledge applied in practical ways to the material aspects of life.

Telecommute. Work at home with a computerized hookup to a central office.

World systems theory. Wallerstein's theory that holds that a nation's development is determined by its place in a world system that is defined by capitalist trade; Wallerstein divides the world into core nations, peripheral nations, and semiperipheral nations.

References

AACJC (American Association of Community and Junior Colleges). 1977. "Students in Two-Year Colleges" (May). [17]

Abadinsky, Howard. 1981. *Organized Crime*. Boston: Allyn and Bacon. [7]

Abeles, Ronald P. 1976. "Relative Deprivation, Rising Expectations, and Black Militancy." *Journal of Social Issues* 32:119–137. [21]

Abercrombie, Nicholas, Stephen Hill, and Brian Turner. 1986. *Sovereign Individuals of Capitalism*. Oxford, England: Basil Blackwell. [4]

Aberle, David. 1966. *The Peyote Religion Among the Navaho*. Chicago: Aldine. [21]

Abramson, Jill, and Barbara Franklin. 1986. *Where They Are Now: The Story of the Women of Harvard Law 1974*. New York: Doubleday. [12]

Adelman, Kenneth L. 1980. "Non-voting: A Sign of Decay or Health?" *Wall Street Journal* (October 15):20. [14]

Adler, Peter, and Patricia A. Adler. 1985. "From idealism to pragmatic detachment: The academic performance of college athletes." *Sociology of Education* 58:241–250. [5]

Akers, Ronald K., Marvin D. Krohn, Lonn Lanza-Kaduce, and Marcia Radosevich. 1979. "Social Learning and Deviant Behavior: A Specific Test of a General Theory." *American Sociological Review* 44 (August):636–655. [7]

Albert, Judith Clavir, and Stewart Edward Albert. 1984. *The Sixties Papers: Documents of a Rebellious Decade*. New York: Praeger. [21]

Aldous, Joan. 1978. *Family Careers: Developmental Change in Families*. New York: Wiley. [6]

Aldrich, Howard, and Ellen R. Auster. 1986. "Even Dwarfs Started Small: Liabilities of Age and Size and Their Strategic Implications." *Research in Organizational Behavior* 8:165–198. [15]

Aldrich, Howard E., and Jeffrey Pfeffer. 1976. "Environments of Organizations," pp. 79–105. Palo Alto, CA: Annual Reviews. [8]

Alexander, Herbert E., and Brian Haggerty. 1981. *The Federal Election Campaign Act*. Citizens Research Foundation. Los Angeles: University of Southern California. [14]

Alexander, Jeffrey (ed.). 1988. *Durkheimian Sociology*. New York: Columbia University Press. [1]

Alfano, Peter. 1987. "Women's Sports in the '80s: Women Finding Signs of Problems Amid the Progress." *New York Times* (section 5):1, 6. [12]

Allen, Irving L. 1984. "The Ideology of Dense Neighborhood Redevelopment." In J. J. Palen and B. London (eds.), *Gentrification, Displacement, and Neighborhood Revitalization*. Albany: SUNY. [9]

Allen, Vernon L. 1970. "Toward Understanding Riots: Some Perspectives." *Journal of Social Issues* 26 (Winter):1–18. [21]

Allen, Walter R., and Reynolds Farley. 1986. "The Shifting Social and Economic Tides of Black America, 1950–1980." *American Review of Sociology* 12:277–306. [13]

Allport, Gordon. 1958/1979. *The Nature of Prejudice*. Garden City, NY: Doubleday. [13]

Allport, Gordon W., and Leo Postman. 1947. *The Psychology of Rumor*. New York: Holt. [21]

Alter, Jonathan. 1986. "No Room at the Top." *Newsweek* (December 1):79–80. [13]

Alwin, D. 1984. "Trends in Parental Socialization Values: Detroit 1958–1983." *American Journal of Sociology* 90 (2):359–382. [16]

Amsden, A. 1985. "The State and Taiwan's Economic Development." In P. B. Evans, D. Rueschemeyer, and T. Skocpol (eds.), *Bringing the State Back In*, pp. 107–168. New York: Cambridge University Press. [14]

Anderson, Benedict. 1983. *Imagined Communities*. New York: Schocken. [14]

Anderson, Elijah. 1978. *A Place on the Corner*. Chicago: University of Chicago Press. [3]

Anderson, P. 1974. *Lineages of the Absolutist State*. Chicago: University of Chicago Press. [14]

Andrain, Charles F. 1975. *Political Life and Social Change: An Introduction to Political Science* (2nd ed.). Belmont, CA: Duxbury. [14]

Andrew, A. M. 1983. *Artificial Intelligence*. Turnbridge Wells, Kent: Abacus Press. [22]

Andrews, Lori B. 1984. "Exhibit A: Language." *Psychology Today* (February):28–33. [4]

Anson, Robert Sam. 1987. "Best Intentions." *New York Times Magazine* (May 11):31–46. [13]

Apple, Michael W. 1982. *Education and Power: Reproduction and Contradiction in Education*. London, England: Routledge & Kegan Paul. [17]

Apple, Michael W. 1979. *Ideology and Curriculum*. London, England: Routledge & Kegan Paul. [17]

Applebombe, Peter. 1987. "1,000 New Inmates a Week Jam Too Few Cells." *New York Times* (March 7). [7]

Aramoni, Aniceto. 1972. "Machismo." *Psychology Today* 5 (January):69–72. [12]

Arensberg, Conrad M., and Arthur H. Niehoff. 1964. *Introducing Social Change*. Chicago: Aldine. [4]

Arenson, Karen W. 1983. "Management's Ranks Grow." *New York Times* (April 14):31. [8]

Ariès, Philippe. 1962. *Centuries of Childhood*. R. Baldick (trans.). New York: Random House. [6]

Arno, Peter S. 1986. "The Non-Profit Sector's Response to the AIDS Epidemic: Community-Based Services in San Francisco." *American Journal of Public Health* 76 (11):1325–1330. [19]

Aronson, Elliot, and J. Merrill Carlsmith. 1968. "Experimentation in Social Psychology." In G. Linzey and E. Aronson (eds.), *The Handbook of Social Psychology* (vol. 2, 2nd ed.). Reading, MA: Addison-Wesley. [2]

Aronson, Elliot, and J. Mills. 1959. "The Effect of Severity on Liking for a Group." *Journal of Abnormal and Social Psychology* 59:177–181. [2]

Aronson, L. 1975. "The Case of the Midwife Toad." *Behavior Genetics* 5 (2):115–125. [20]

Astin, Alexander. 1987. *The American Freshman: National Norms for Entering College Freshmen*. Washington, D.C.: Office of Research, American Council on Education.

Astin, Alexander W. 1983. *The American Freshman: National Norms for Fall 1983*. Los Angeles: Cooperative Institutional Research Program, Graduate School of Education, University of California. [4]

Ault, James. 1987. "Family and Fundamentalism: The Shawmut Valley Baptist Church." In J. Obelkevich, L. Roper, and R. Samuel (eds.), *Disciplines of Faith: Studies in Religion, Politics and Patriarchy*. London, England: Routledge & Kegan Paul. [18]

Bachman, Jerald, et al. 1978. *Adolescence to Adulthood: Change and Stability in the Lives of Young Men*. Ann Arbor, MI: Institute for Social Research. [5]

Badham, Richard. 1984. "The Sociology of Industrial and Post-Industrial Societies." *Current Sociology* 34 (1):1–94. [22]

Badie, Bertrand, and Pierre Birnbaum. 1983. *The Sociology of the State*. Chicago: University of Chicago Press. [14]

Baker, P. 1984. "Age Differences and Age Changes in the Division of Labor by Sex: Reanalysis of White and Brinherhoff." *Social Forces* 62:808–814. [12]

Bales, Robert F., and Fred L. Strodtbeck. 1951. "Phases in Group Problem Solving." *Journal of Abnormal and Social Psychology* 46:485–495. [8]

Barash, David P. 1977. *Sociobiology and Behavior*. New York: Elsevier. [4]

Barber, Benjamin. 1983. *Strong Democracy*. Berkeley: University of California Press. [14]

Bardwick, Judith M., and Elizabeth Douvan. 1971. "Ambivalence: The Socialization of Women." In V. Gornick and B. K. Moran (eds.), *Women in Sexist Society*. New York: Basic Books. [12]

Barker, Eileen. 1987. "Being A Moonie: Identity with an Unorthodox Orthodoxy." In J. Obelkevich, L. Roper, and R. Samuel (eds.), *Disciplines of Faith: Studies in Religion, Politics, and Patriarchy*. London, England: Routledge & Kegan Paul. [18]

Barker, Eileen. 1984. *The Making of a Moonie: Brainwashing or Choice?* Oxford, England: Basil Blackwell. [18]

Basow, Susan A. 1986. *Gender Stereotypes*. Pacific Grove, CA: Brooks/Cole. [12]

Beaulac, Willard L. 1981. "The Latin American Church: Marxist Inroads." *National Review* (April 17):422–423. [18]

Beck, Melinda. 1983a. "The Toxic-Waste Crisis." *Newsweek* (March 7):20–24. [21]

Beck, Melinda. 1983b. "The Bitter Politics of Acid Rain." *Newsweek* (April 25):36–37. [21]

Beck, Paul A., and M. Kent Jennings. 1979. "Political Periods and Political Participation." *The American Political Science Review* 73:737–750. [14]

Beck, Scott H. 1982. "Adjustment to and Satisfaction with Retirement." *Journal of Gerontology* 37:616–624. [16]

Becker, Ernest. 1973. *The Denial of Death*. New York: Free Press. [6]

Becker, Gary S. 1976. *An Economic Approach to Human Behavior*. Chicago: University of Chicago Press. [1]

Becker, Howard. 1986. *Doing Things Together*. Evanston, IL: Northwestern University Press. [4]

Becker, Howard. 1984. *Art Worlds*. Berkeley: University of California Press. [4]

Becker, Howard S. 1963. *Outsiders: Studies in the Sociology of Deviance*. New York: Free Press. [7]

Beckford, J. A. 1978. "Accounting for Conversion." *British Journal of Sociology* 29:249–262. [18]

Bell, Daniel. 1980. *The Winding Passage: Essays and Sociological Journeys, 1960–1980*. Cambridge, MA: Abt Bks. [22]

Bell, Daniel. 1979. "The Social Framework of the Information Society." In M. Dertouzos and J. Moses (eds.), *The Computer Age: A Twenty-Year View*, pp. 163–211. Cambridge, MA: MIT Press. [22]

Bell, Daniel. 1973. *The Coming of the Post-Industrial Society*. New York: Basic Books. [22]

Bellah, Robert N. 1975. *The Broken Covenant*. New York: Seabury Press. [18]

Bellah, Robert N., and Phillip E. Hammond. 1980. *Varieties of Civil Religion*. New York: Harper & Row. [18]

Bellah, Robert N., Richard Madsen, William M. Sullivan, Ann Swidler, and Steven M. Tipton. 1985. *Habits of the Heart: Individualism and Commitment in American Life*. New York: Harper & Row. [4]

Bem, S. L. 1975. "Sex-Role Adaptability: One Consequence of Psychological Androgyny." *Journal of Personality and Social Psychology* 31:634–643. [12]

Bem, S. L. 1974. "The Measurement of Psychological Androgyny." *Journal of Consulting and Clinical Psychology* 42:155–162. [12]

Beniger, James R. 1986. *The Control Revolution: Technological and Economic Origins of the Information Society*. Cambridge, MA: Harvard University Press. [1, 22]

Bennett, Neil G., Ann Klimas Blanc, and David E. Bloo. 1988. "Commitment and the Modern Union: Assessing the Link Between Premarital Cohabitation and Subsequent Marital Stability." *American Sociological Review* 53:127–138. [16]

Bensman, David, and Roberta Lynch. 1987. *Rusted Dreams*. New York: McGraw-Hill. [11]

Bentham, Jeremy. 1798/1970. *An Introduction to the Principals of Morals and Legislation*. London, England: Methuen. [1]

Ben-Yehuda, Nachman. 1985. *Deviance and Moral Boundaries: Witchcraft, the Occult, Science Fiction, Deviant Sciences and Scientists*. Chicago: University of Chicago Press. [7]

Ben-Yehuda, Nachman. 1980. "The European Witch Craze of the 14th to 17th Centuries: A Sociologist's Perspective." *American Journal of Sociology* 86 (1). [21]

Berg, Ivar. 1970. *Education and Jobs: The Great Training Robbery*. New York: Praeger. [17]

Berger, Peter L. 1987. *50 Propositions about Capitalism*. New York: Basic Books. [14]

Berger, Peter L. 1986. *The Capitalist Revolution*. New York: Basic Books. [15]

Berger, Peter L. 1979. *The Heretical Imperative: Contemporary Possibilities of Religious Affirmation*. Garden City, NY: Doubleday/ Anchor. [18]

Berger, Peter L. 1963. *Invitation to Sociology*. New York: Doubleday. [3]

Berger, Peter L., and Brigitte Berger. 1979. "Becoming a Member of Society." In P. Rose (ed.), *Socialization and the Life Cycle*. New York: St. Martin's Press. [5]

Berger, Peter L., and Thomas Luckmann. 1967. *The Social Construction of Reality*. New York: Doubleday. [1]

Berger, Peter, and Thomas Luckmann. 1966. *Social Construction of Reality: A Treatise in the Sociology of Knowledge*. New York: Doubleday. [14]

Berk, Richard A. 1987. "Anticipating the Social Consequences of AIDS: A Position Paper." *The American Sociologist* (Fall):211–241. [19]

Berk, Richard A., William P. Bridges, and Anthony Shih. 1981. "Does IQ Really Matter? A Study of the Use of IQ Scores for the Tracking of the Mentally Retarded." *American Sociological Review* 46:58–71. [17]

Berle, Adolph A., Jr., and Gardiner C. Means. 1932/1968. *The Modern Corporation and Private Property* (rev. ed.). New York: Harcourt, Brace and World. [15]

Bernardi, B. 1955. "The Age-System of the Masai." *Annali Lateranensi* 18:257–318. [6]

Bernstein, Basil. 1981. "Codes, Modalities, and the Process of Cultural Reproduction: A Model." *Language in Society* 10:327–363. [5]

Bernstein, Basil. 1977. *Class, Codes, and Control* (vol. 3, rev. ed.). London, England: Routledge & Kegan Paul. [5]

Bernstein, Basil. 1971. *Class, Codes, and Control* (vol. 1). London, England: Routledge & Kegan Paul. [5]

Berry, Brian J. L., and John D. Kasarda. 1977. *Contemporary Urban Ecology*. New York: Macmillan. [9]

Beteille, Andre. 1977. *Inequality Among Men*. New York: Oxford University Press. [11]

Bettleheim, Bruno. 1987. "The Importance of Play." *The Atlantic Monthly* (March):35–46. [5]

Billingsley, Andrew. 1968. *Black Families in White America*. Englewood Cliffs, NJ: Prentice Hall. [16]

Bingham, Richard D., Ray E. Green, and Sammis B. White. 1987. *The Homeless in Contemporary Society*. Beverly Hills, CA: Sage. [11]

Blau, Francine, and Carol Jusenius. 1976. "Economists' Approaches to Sex Segregation in the Labor Market: An Appraisal." In M. Blaxall and B. Reagan (eds.), *Women in the Workplace: The Implications of the Occupational Segregation*, pp. 181–199. Chicago: University of Chicago Press. [12]

Blau, Judith R., and Peter M. Blau. 1982. "The Cost of Inequality: Metropolitan Structure and Violent Crime." *American Sociological Review* 47:114–129. [7]

Blau, Peter M. 1987. "Microprocess and Macrostructures." In K. S. Cook (ed.), *Social Exchange Theory*, ch. 4. San Francisco, CA: Sage. [3]

Blau, Peter M. 1963/1986. *Exchange and Power in Social Life*. New Brunswick, NJ: Transaction Books. [1, 3]

Blau, Peter M. 1977. *Inequality and Heterogeneity: A Primitive Theory of Social Structure*. New York: Free Press. [3]

Blau, Peter M., and Otis Dudley Duncan. 1967. *The American Occupational Structure*. New York: Wiley. [11]

Blau, Peter M., and Marshall W. Meyer. 1987. *Bureaucracy in Modern Society* (3rd ed.). New York: Random House. [8]

Blau, Peter M., and Joseph E. Schwartz. 1983. *Cross-Cutting Social Circles: Testing a Macrostructural Theory of Intergroup Relations*. New York: Academic Press. [3]

Bleier, Ruth. 1984. *Science and Gender*. New York: Pergamon Press. [12]

Block, Fred, Richard A. Cloward, Barbara Ehrenreich, and Frances Fox Piven. 1987. *The Mean Season: The Attack on the Welfare State*. New York: Pantheon. [14]

Blodgett, Nancy. 1986. "'I Don't Think that Ladies Should be Lawyers,'" *ABA Journal* (December 1):48–53. [12]

Bluestone, Barry, and Bennet Harrison. 1982. *The Deindustrialization of America*. New York: Basic Books. [22]

Blum, Linda, and Vicki Smith. 1988. "Women's Mobility in the Corporation: A Critique of the Politics of Optimism." *Signs* 13 (3):528–545. [12]

Blumenthal, Albert. 1932. *Small-Town Stuff*. Chicago: University of Chicago Press. [9]

Blumer, Herbert. 1986. *Symbolic Interactionism: Perspective and Method*. Berkeley: University of California Press. [1]

Blumer, Herbert. 1968. "Fashion." In *International Encyclopedia of the Social Sciences* (2nd ed.). New York: Macmillan. [4]

Blumer, Herbert. 1939/1951. "Collective Behavior." In A. M. Lee (ed.), *New Outline of the Principles of Sociology*. New York: Barnes & Noble. [21]

Blumstein, Philip, and Pepper Schwartz. 1983. *American Couples: Money, Work, Sex*. New York: Simon and Schuster. [16]

Bobbio, Norberto. 1987. *The Future of Democracy: A Defense of the Rules of the Game*. R. Bellamy (ed.). Minneapolis: University of Minnesota Press. [14]

Bock, Kenneth. 1980. *Human Nature and History: A Response to Sociobiology*. New York: Columbia University Press. [4]

Boffey, Philip M. 1983. "Panel of Experts Challenges Gloomy Forecast for 2000." *New York Times* (May 30):9. [10]

Bogue, Donald. 1985. *The Population of the United States: Historical Trends and Future Projections*. New York: Free Press. [10]

Bohannan, Paul, and Rosemary Erickson. 1978. "Stepping In." *Psychology Today* 11(January):11+. [16]

Booth, Alan, and Lynn White. 1980. "Thinking About Divorce." *Journal of Marriage and the Family* 42 (3):605–616. [16]

Borden, Anthony. 1986. "G.M. Comes to Spring Hill." *The Nation* (June 21):852–854. [9]

Bornschier, Volker, and Thanh-Huyen Ballmer-Cao. 1979. "Income Inequality: A Cross-National Study of the Relationships Between MNC-Penetration, Dimensions of the Power Structure and Income Distribution." *American Sociological Review* 44 (June):487–506. [15]

Bornschier, Volker, and Jean-Pierre Hoby. 1981. "Economic Policy and Multinational Corporations in Development: The Measurable Impacts in Cross-National Perspective." *Social Problems* 28:363–377. [15]

Bottomore, T. B. 1966. *Classes in Modern Society*. New York: Pantheon. [11]

Bourdieu, Pierre. 1987. *Choses Dites*. Paris: Edition de Minuit. [11]

Bourdieu, Pierre. 1984. *Distinction: A Social Critique of the Judgment of Taste*. R. Nice (trans.). Cambridge, MA: Harvard University Press. [1, 11]

Bourdieu, Pierre. 1977. *Outline of a Theory of Practice*. R. Nice (trans.). New York: Cambridge University Press. [1, 4]

Bowen, Howard R. 1977. *Investment in Learning: The Individual and Social Values of Higher Education*. San Francisco: Jossey-Bass. [17]

Bowlby, John. 1973. *Separation: Anxiety and Anger*. New York: Basic Books. [5]

Bowles, Samuel. 1977. "Unequal Education and the Reproduction of the Social Division of Labor." In J. Karabel and A. H. Halsey (eds.), *Power and Ideology in Education*. New York: Oxford University Press. [17]

Bowles, Samuel, and Herbert Gintis. 1976. *Schooling and Capitalist America*. New York: Basic Books. [17]

Boyer, Ernest L. 1987. *College: The Undergraduate Experience in America*. New York: Harper & Row. [17]

Boyte, Harry. 1986. *Community is Possible*. New York: Harper & Row. [4]

Brain, R. 1976. *Friends and Lovers*. New York: Basic Books. [1]

Brandt, Allan M. 1986. "AIDS: From Social History to Social Policy." *Law, Medicine and Health Care* 14 (5–6):231–242. [19]

Braun, Ernest, and Stuart MacDonald. 1978. *Revolution in Miniature*. Cambridge, England: Cambridge University Press. [22]

Braverman, Harry. 1974. *Labor and Monopoly Capital: The Degradation of Work in the Twentieth Century*. New York: Monthly Review Press. [15]

Brenner, Harvey M. 1987a. "Economic Change, Alcohol Consumption and Health Disease Mortality in Nine Industrialized Countries." *Social Science and Medicine* 25 (2):119–132. [19]

Brenner, Harvey M. 1987b. "Economic Instability, Unemployment Rates, Behavioral Risks, and Mortality Rates in Scotland, 1952–1983." *International Journal of Health Services* 17 (3):475–487. [19]

Bretherton, Inge. 1984. "Representing the Social World in Symbolic Play: Reality and Fantasy." In I. Bretherton (ed.), *Symbolic Play: The Development of Social Understanding*. New York: Academic Press. [5]

Breuilly, John. 1985. *Nationalism and the State*. Chicago: University of Chicago Press. [14]

Brewton, Berry, and Henry L. Tischler. 1978. *Race and Ethnic Relations*. Boston: Houghton Mifflin. [13]

Bridges, William P., and Wayne J. Villemez. 1986. "Informal Hiring and Income in the Labor Market." *American Sociological Review* 51:574–582. [3]

Britannica Book of the Year, 1987. 1988. Chicago: Encyclopaedia Britannica. [18]

Broad, William, and Nicholas Wade. 1982. *Betrayers of the Truth*. New York: Simon and Schuster. [20]

Brodsly, David. 1981. *LA Freeway*. Berkeley: University of California Press. [9]

Bronfenbrenner, Urie. 1970. *Two Worlds of Childhood*. New York: Russell Sage Foundation. [17]

Bronson, Gail, and Robert Morese. 1983. "How the Boss's Paycheck Weathered Recession." *U.S. News & World Report* (May 30):59–61. [11]

Brooks, Harvey. 1980. "Technology, Evaluation, and Purpose." *Daedalus* 109 (1):65–81. [1, 22]

Brophy, Jere E. 1983. "Research on the Self-Fulfilling Prophecy and Teacher Expectations." *Journal of Educational Psychology* 75 (5):631–661. [17]

Broverman, I. K., S. R. Vogel, D. M. Broverman, F. E. Clarkson, P. S. Rosenkrantz. 1972. "Sex-Role Stereotypes: A Current Appraisal." *Journal of Social Issues* 28:59–78. [12]

Brown, Dee. 1971/1984. *Bury My Heart At Wounded Knee*. New York: Doubleday. [13]

Brown, J. Larry. 1987. "Hunger in the U.S." *Scientific American* 256 (2):37+. [19]

Brown, Jane D., and Kenneth Campbell. 1986. "Race and Gender in Music Videos: The Same Beat But a Different Drummer." *Journal of Communication* 36 (Winter):94–106. [2]

Brown, L. Carl. 1980. "Ayatollahs and Abracadabra." *Princeton Alumni Weekly* (October 6):22–28. [18]

Brown, Lester R. (ed.). 1987. *State of the World: A Worldwatch Institute Report on Progress Toward a Sustainable Society*. New York: W. W. Norton. [10]

Brown, Roger. 1986. *Social Psychology* (2nd ed.). New York: Free Press. [13]

Brownstein, Ronald, and Maxwell Glen. 1986. "Money in the Shadows." *National Journal* (March 15):632–637. [14]

Brubaker, Rogers. 1984. *The Limits of Rationality*. London, England: George, Allen and Unwin. [1]

Bumpass, Larry. 1984. "Some Characteristics of Children's Second Families." *American Journal of Sociology* 90 (3):608–623. [16]

Burch, David. 1987. *Overseas Aid and the Transfer of Technology: The Political Economy of Agricultural Mechanization in the Third World*. London, England: Gower. [15]

Burdman, Geri. 1986. *Healthful Aging*. Englewood Cliffs, NJ: Prentice Hall. [6]

Burnham, David. 1983. *The Rise of the Computer State*. New York: Random House. [22]

Burridge, Kenelm O. L. 1957. "A Tangu Game." *Man* 57:88–89. [4]

Burris, Val. 1983. "Who Opposed the ERA? An Analysis of the Social Bases of Antifeminism." *Social Science Quarterly* 64:305–317. [21]

Burrow, James G. 1971. *Organized Medicine in the Progressive Era: The Move Toward Monopoly*. Baltimore, MD: The Johns Hopkins University Press. [19]

Burt, Ronald S. 1987. "The Principles and Promise of Network Theory." Unpublished conference material, Columbia University, New York. [3]

Burt, Ronald S. 1983. *Corporate Profits and Cooptation*. New York: Academic Press. [3]

Burt, Ronald S. 1982. *Toward a Structural Theory of Action*. New York: Academic Press. [3]

Burton, L. M. 1987. "Early and On-Time Grandmotherhood in Multigenerational Black Families." Unpublished doctoral dissertation, University of Southern California, Los Angeles. [6]

Burton, L. M., and V. L. Bengston. 1985. "Black Grandmothers: Issues of Timing and Continuity of Roles." In V. L. Bengston and J. F. Robertson (eds.), *Grandparenthood*, pp. 61–77. Beverly Hills, CA: Sage. [6]

Business Week. 1985. "Personal Computers Invade Offices." In T. Forester (ed.), *The Information Technology Revolution*, pp. 322–333. Cambridge, MA: MIT Press. [22]

Butler, Robert N. 1975. *Why Survive: Being Old in America*. New York: Harper & Row. [6]

Button, James W. 1978. *Black Violence*. Princeton, NJ: Princeton University Press. [21]

Cain, Mead. 1985. "Fertility as an Adjustment to Risk." In A. S. Rossi (ed.), *Gender and the Life Course*. New York: Aldine. [10]

Calhoun, Craig. 1986. "Computer Technology, Large-Scale Social Integration, and the Local Community." *Urban Affairs Quarterly* 22:329–349. [22]

Calhoun, Craig. 1981. "The Political Economy of Work." In S. G. McNall (ed.), *Political Economy: Critique of American Society*. Glenview, IL: Scott, Foresman. [15]

Calhoun, Craig. 1980. "The Authority of Ancestors." *Man* 5 (2):304–319. [18]

Calhoun, Craig, and Martha Copp. 1988. "Computerization in Legal Work: How Much Does New Technology Change Professional Practice?" *Research in the Sociology of Work* 4:233–259. [22]

Calhoun, Craig, and Henryk Hiller. 1988. "Coping with Insidious Injuries: The Case of Johns-Mansville Corporation and Asbestos Exposure." *Social Problems* 35 (2):162–181. [7]

Campbell, A., and H. Schuman. 1968. "Racial Attitudes in Fifteen American Cities." In *Supplementary Studies for the National Advisory Commission on Civil Disorders*. Washington, DC: U.S. Government Printing Office. [21]

Canino, Ian A., Brian F. Earley, and Lloyd H. Rogler. 1980. *The Puerto Rican Child in New York City: Stress and Mental Health*. New York: Fordham University Hispanic Research Center. [4]

Cantril, Hadley, with Hazel Gaudet and Herta Herzog. 1947. "Invasion from Mars." Princeton, NJ: Princeton University Press. [21]

Caplow, Theodore. 1969. *Two Against One: Coalition in Triads*. Englewood Cliffs, NJ: Prentice Hall. [8]

Caplow, Theodore, and Bruce A. Chadwick. 1979. "Inequality and Life-Styles in Middletown, 1920–1978." *Social Science Quarterly* 60 (3):367–386. [16]

Cargan, Leonard, and Matthew Melko. 1982. *Singles: Myths and Realities*. Beverly Hills, CA: Sage. [16]

Carmody, Deirdre. 1988. "To Freshman, A Big Goal is Wealth." *New York Times* (January 14):A14. [17]

Carnoy, Martin, and Henry M. Levin. 1985. *Schooling and Work in the Democratic State*. Stanford, CA: Stanford University Press. [15, 17]

Carson, Rachel. 1962. *Silent Spring*. Boston: Houghton Mifflin. [21]

Casale, Anthony M., and Philip Lerman. 1986. *USA Today: Tracking Tomorrow's Trends*. Kansas City, MO: Andrews, McMeel & Parker. [17]

Cater, Douglass, and Stephen Strickland. 1975. *TV Violence and the Child: The Evolution and Fate of the Surgeon General's Report*. New York: Russell Sage Foundation. [5]

Centers for Disease Control. 1987. *Morbidity and Mortality Weekly Report* 36 (January 16):1–11. [10]

Cetron, Marvin J. 1983. "Jobs with a Future." In H. F. Didsbury, Jr.

(ed.), *The World of Work*. Bethesda, MD: World Future Society. [22]

Chambers, D. S. 1970. *The Imperial Age of Venice*. New York: Harcourt Brace Jovanovich. [9]

Chandler, Alfred. 1976. *The Visible Hand*. Cambridge, MA: Harvard University Press. [15]

Chandler, Alfred D., Jr. 1962. *Strategy and Structure: Chapters in the History of the Industrial Enterprise*. Cambridge, MA: MIT Press. [8]

Chase-Dunn, Christopher. 1975. "The Effects of International Economic Dependence on Development and Inequality: A Cross-National Study." *American Sociological Review* 40 (December):720–738. [15]

Chassin, Laurie, Clark C. Presson, Steven J. Sherman, Eric Corty, and Richard W. Olshavsky. 1984. "Predicting the Onset of Smoking in Adolescence." *Journal of Applied Social Psychology* 14 (3):224–243. [7]

Chavez, Lydia. 1987. "Women's Movement, Its Ideals Accepted, Faces Subtler Issues." *New York Times* (July 17). [12, 21]

Chen, Pi-Chao. 1984. "Birth Planning and Fertility Transition." *The Annals of the American Academy of Political and Social Science* 476 (November):128. [10]

Cherlin, Andrew, and Frank Furstenberg. 1986. *The New Grandparent: A Place in the Family, a Life Apart*. New York: Basic Books. [16]

Cherlin, Andrew, J. Griffith, and J. McCarthy. 1983. "A Note on Maritally-Disrupted Men's Reports of Child Support in the June 1980 Current Population Survey." *Demography* 20:358–390. [16]

Childe, V. Gordon. 1952. *Man Makes Himself*. New York: New American Library. [9]

Children's Defense Fund. 1987. *The State of the World's Children*. New York: Oxford University Press. [10]

Chiriboga, David A., and Loraine Cutler. 1977. "Stress Responses Among Divorcing Men and Women." *Journal of Divorce* 1 (2):95–106. [16]

Chittister, Joan D., and Martin E. Marty. 1983. *Faith & Ferment*. Minneapolis: Augsburg Publishing House. [18]

Chodorow, Nancy. 1978. *The Reproduction of Mothering: Psychoanalysis and the Sociology of Gender*. Berkeley: University of California Press. [12]

Choldin, Harvey M. 1978. "Urban Density and Pathology." *Annual Review of Sociology* 4:91–113. [9]

Christian Science Monitor. 1988. (June 6):1. [22]

Circirelli, Victor G. 1980. "A Comparison of College Women's Feelings Toward Their Siblings and Parents." *Journal of Marriage and the Family* 42:111–118. [5]

Clark, David. 1985. *Post-Industrial America: A Geographical Perspective*. New York: Methuen. [1, 10]

Clark, Kenneth B. 1965. *Dark Ghetto*. New York: Harper & Row. [13]

Clark, Kenneth B. 1964. *Youth in the Ghetto*. New York: Haryou Associates. [13]

Clark, Reginald M. 1983. *Family Life and School Achievement: Why Poor Black Children Succeed or Fail*. Chicago: University of Chicago Press. [11]

Clinard, Marshall B., and Peter C. Yeager. 1980. *Corporate Crime*. New York: Free Press. [7]

Clingempeel, W. Glenn, and N. Dickon Reppucci. 1982. "Joint Custody after Divorce: Major Issues and Goals for Research." *Psychological Bulletin* 9L:102–127. [16]

Clymer, Adam. 1983. "Jobless Were More Likely to Vote in '82 Than in Previous Off Years." *New York Times* (April 18):1, 8a. [14]

Coddington, Dean C., and Keith D. Moore. 1987. *Market-Driven Strategies in Health Care*. San Francisco: Jossey-Bass. [19]

Cohen, Steven M. 1983. *Attitudes of American Jews Toward Israel and Israelis*. New York: Institute on American Jewish-Israeli Relations. [18]

Cohen, Steven M., and Leonard J. Fein. 1985. "From Integration to Survival: American Jewish Anxieties in Transition." AAPSS *Annals* 480 (July):75–88. [18]

Cole, Charles L. 1977. "Cohabitation in Social Context." In R. W. Libby and R. N. Whitehurst (eds.), *Marriage and Alternatives: Exploring Intimate Relationships*. Glenview, IL: Scott, Foresman. [16]

Cole, R. 1979. *Work, Mobility and Participation: A Comparative Study of American and Japanese Industry*. Berkeley: University of California Press. [15]

Coleman, James. 1982. *The Asymmetric Society*. New York: Syracuse University Press. [15]

Coleman, James S. 1987. *Public and Private High School: The Impact of Communities*. New York: Basic Books. [17]

Coleman, James S. 1981. "The Role of Incentives in School Desegregation." In A. Yarmolinsky, L. Liebman, and C. Schelling (eds.), *Race and Schooling in the City*. Cambridge, MA: Harvard University Press. [13]

Coleman, James S. 1971. In C. E. Silberman (ed.), *Crisis in the Classroom*, p. 71. New York: Vintage. [17]

Coleman, James S. 1966a. *Equality of Educational Opportunity*. Washington, DC: U.S. Government Printing Office. [13]

Coleman, James S. 1966b. "Equal Schools or Equal Students?" *The Public Interest* 4 (Summer):70–75. [17]

Coleman, James S. 1961. *The Adolescent Society*. New York: Free Press. [6]

Coleman, John A. 1983. "The Christian as Citizen." *Commonweal* CX:457–462. [18]

Coleman, Richard, and Lee Rainwater. 1978. *Social Standing in America: New Dimensions of Class*. New York: Basic Books. [11, 17]

Collins, Glenn. 1987. "As the Nation Grays, A Might Advocate Flexes Its Muscles." *New York Times* (April 2):B1, C7. [6]

Collins, Glenn. 1982. "Unforeseen Business Barriers for Women." *New York Times* (May 31):18. [12]

Collins, Randall. 1985. *Three Sociological Traditions*. New York: Oxford University Press. [3]

Collins, Randall. 1979. *The Credential Society*. New York: Academic Press. [17]

Collins, Randall. 1975. *Conflict Sociology*. New York: Academic Press. [1, 11]

Collins, Randall. 1971. "Functional and Conflict Theories of Educational Stratification." *American Sociological Review* 36 (December):1002–1018. [17]

Conger, J. J., and A. C. Peterson. 1984. *Adolescence and Youth* (3rd ed.). New York: Harper & Row. [6]

Connolly, William. 1984. "The Dilemma of Legitimacy." In W. Connolly and S. Lukes (eds.), *Legitimacy and the State*, pp. 122–149. New York: New York University Press. [14]

Connor, Walter D. 1979. *Socialism, Politics, and Equality*. New York: Columbia University Press. [11]

Conrad, Peter, and Joseph Schneider. 1980. *Deviance and Medical-*
ization: From Badness to Sickness. St. Louis, MO: C. V. Mosby. [19]

Cook, Rhodes. 1985. "Divided Academia: No Republican Monolith." *Congressional Quarterly* (November 23):2424. [14]

Cookson, Peter W., Jr., and Carolina Hodges Persell. 1983. *Preparing for Power: America's Elite Boarding Schools*. New York: Basic Books. [17]

Cooley, Charles H. 1964. *Human Nature and the Social Order*. New York: Schocken. [5]

Cooley, Charles H. 1956. *Social Organization: A Study of the Larger Mind*. Peoria, IL: Free Press. [5]

Cooley, Charles H. 1909/1929. *Social Organization*. New York: Charles Scribner's. [8]

Cordes, Colleen. 1985. "Officials Overload Roles of Culture, Self-Motivation in Family Planning." *APA Monitor* (May):14–16. [10]

Corea, Gena. 1985. *The Hidden Malpractice: How American Medicine Mistreats Women* (rev. ed.). New York: Harper & Row. [19]

Cornell, Stephen. 1984. "Crisis and response in Indian-white relations: 1960–1984." *Social Problems* 32 (1):44–59. [13]

Corrections Year Book. 1986. Washington, DC: Bureau of Justice. [7]

Corsaro, William A. 1985. *Friendship and Peer Culture in the Early Years*. Norwood, NJ: Ablex. [2]

Cortés, Carlos E. 1980. "Mexicans." In S. Thernstrom (ed.), *Harvard Encyclopedia of American Ethnic Groups*. Cambridge, MA: Harvard University Press. [4]

Coser, Lewis. 1965. *The Function of Social Change*. Peoria, IL: Free Press. [11]

Coser, Lewis A. 1974. *Greedy Institutions: Patterns of Undivided Commitment*. New York: Free Press. [8]

Coser, Rose Laub. 1983. "Where Have All the Women Gone?" In L. Richardson and V. Taylor (eds.), *Feminist Frontiers*. Reading, MA: Addison-Wesley. [12]

Cottrell, W. F. 1951. "Death by Dieselization: A Case Study in the Reaction to Technological Change." *American Sociological Review* 16:358–365. [20]

Cramer, James C. 1980. "Fertility and Female Employment: Problems of Causal Direction." *American Sociological Review* 45:167–190. [10]

Crano, William D., and Phyllis M. Mellon. 1978. "Causal Influence of Teachers' Expectations on Children's Academic Performance: A Cross-Legged Panel Analysis." *Journal of Educational Psychology* 70:39–49. [17]

Crittenden, Ann. 1981. "Demand Outpaces World Food Supply." *New York Times* (August 16):1, 12. [10]

Crosby, John F. 1980. "A Critique of Divorce Statistics and Their Interpretation." *Family Relations* 29 (January):51–58. [16]

Current Population Reports. 1987. *Household and Family Characteristics: March 1986* (Series P-20, No. 419). [16]

Currie, Elliott. 1985. *Confronting Crime: An American Challenge*. New York: Pantheon. [7]

Curtiss, Susan. 1977. *Genie: A Psycholinguistic Study of a Modern-Day "Wild-Child."* New York: Academic Press. [5]

Dahl, Robert. 1961. *Who Governs?* New Haven, CT: Yale University Press. [14]

Dahrendorf, Ralf. 1968. "On the Origin of Inequality Among Men."

In *Essays in the Theory of Society*. London, England: Routledge & Kegan Paul. [11]

Dahrendorf, Ralf. 1959. *Class and Conflict in Industrial Society*. Stanford, CA: Stanford University Press. [11]

Dan-Cohen, M. 1986. *Rights, Persons and Organizations*. Berkeley: University of California Press. [15]

Daniels, Lee A. 1983. "In Defense of Busing." *New York Times Magazine* (April 17):34–37+. [17]

Daniloff, Nicholas. 1983. "Are Soviet Schools as Good as They Look?" *U.S. News & World Report* (March 28):33–34. [17]

Daniloff, Nicholas. 1982. "For Russia's Women, Worst of Both Worlds." *U.S. News & World Report* (June 28):53–54. [12]

Danziger, James N. 1985. "Social Science and the Social Impacts of Computer Technology." *Social Science Quarterly* 66 (1):3–21. [22]

Davies, James. 1974. "The J-Curve and Power Struggle Theories of Collective Violence." *American Sociological Review* 39:607–619. [21]

Davies, James C. 1962. "Toward a Theory of Revolution." *American Sociological Review* 27:5–19. [21]

Davies, Mark, and Denise B. Kandel. 1981. "Parental and Peer Influence on Adolescents' Educational Plans: Some Further Evidence." *American Journal of Sociology* 87:363–387. [5]

Davis, F. James. 1978. *Minority-Dominant Relations*. Arlington Heights, IL: AHM. [13]

Davis, Fred. 1968. "Professional Socialization as Subjective Experience: The Process of Doctrinal Conversion Among Student Nurses." In H. S. Becker et al. (eds.), *Institutions and the Person*. Chicago: Aldine. [5]

Davis, Karen, and Diane Rowland. 1983. "Uninsured and Underserved: Inequities in Health Care in the United States." *Milbank Memorial Fund Quarterly/Health and Society* 61 (2):149–176. [19]

Davis, Kingsley. 1955. "The Origin and Growth of Urbanization in the World." *American Journal of Sociology* 60:429–437. [9]

Davis, Kingsley. 1949. *Human Society*. New York: Macmillan. [5]

Davis, Kingsley, and Wilbert E. Moore. 1945. "Some Principles of Stratification." *American Sociological Review* 10(April):242–249. [11]

Davis, Ronald M. 1987. "Current Trends in Cigarette Advertising and Marketing." *New England Journal of Medicine* 316 (12):725–747. [19]

de Jassay, Anthony. 1985. *The State*. Oxford, England: Basil Blackwell. [14]

de Rougemont, Denis. 1940/1983. *Love in the Western World*. Princeton, NJ: Princeton University Press. [16]

de Solla Price, Derek J. 1962. *Little Science, Big Science*. New York: Columbia University Press. [20]

de Tocqueville, Alexis. 1835/1961. *Democracy in America*. H. Reeves (trans.). New York: Schocken. [4, 18]

de Tocqueville, Alexis. 1856. *The Old Regime and the French Revolution*. J. Bonner (trans.). New York: Harper & Row. [21]

Dekmejian, R. Hrair. 1985. "Fundamentalist Islam: Theories, Typologies and Trends." *Middle East Review* (Summer):28–33. [18]

Deutchman, Iva E., and Sandra Prince-Embury. 1981. "Political Ideology of Pro- and Anti-ERA Women." *Women and Politics* 1:39–55. [21]

Diamond, Stuart. 1986. "Two Experts Foresee Deaths of 24,000 Tied to Chernobyl." *New York Times* (August 27):A1, A6. [21]

DiLeonardo, Micaela. 1987. "The Female World of Cards and Holidays: Women, Families, and the Work of Kinship." *Signs* 12:440–453. [12]

Dolbeare, Kenneth M., and Murray J. Edelman. 1985. *American Politics* (5th ed.). Lexington, MA: D. C. Heath. [14]

Domhoff, G. William. 1983. *Who Rules America Now?* Englewood Cliffs, NJ: Prentice Hall. [11, 14]

Domhoff, G. William. 1978. *The Powers That Be*. New York: Random House. [14]

Donabedian, Avedis. 1987. *Medical Care Chartbook* (8th ed.). Ann Arbor, MI: Health Administration Press. [19]

Donaldson, Peter. 1986. *Worlds Apart: The Economic Gulf Between Nations*. London, England: Penguin. [10, 22]

Dornbusch, Sanford M., J. Merrill Carlsmith, Steven J. Bushwall, Philip L. Ritter, Herbert Leiderman, Albert H. Hastorf, and Ruth T. Gross. 1985. "Single Parents, Extended Households, and the Control of Adolescents." *Child Development* 56:326–341. [16]

Douglas, Jack D. 1967. *The Social Meaning of Suicide*. Princeton, NJ: Princeton University Press. [2]

Douglas, M. 1970. *Purity and Danger*. New York: Penguin. [18]

Dowse, Robert E., and John A. Hughes. 1972. *Political Science*. New York: Wiley. [14]

Drucker, Peter. 1986. *The Unseen Revolution: How Pension Fund Socialism Came to America*. New York: Harper & Row. [15]

Drucker, Peter F. 1983. "Squeezing the Firm's Midriff Bulge." *Wall Street Journal* (March 25):14. [8]

Duberman, Martin. 1973. *Black Mountain: An Exploration in Community*. New York: Anchor Books. [8]

Dumont, Louis. 1977. *From Mandeville to Marx: The Genesis and Triumph of Economic Ideology*. Chicago: University of Chicago Press. [15]

Duncan, Greg J. 1982. "Who Gets Ahead? And Who Gets Left Behind?" *American Demographics* 4 (July–August):38–41. [11]

Duncan, Greg J., et al. 1984. *Years of Poverty, Years of Plenty: The Changing Economic Fortunes of American Workers and Their Families*. Ann Arbor, MI: Institute for Social Research. [11]

Dunlop, Riley E., and Ken D. Van Liere. 1984. *Environmental Concern: A Bibliography of Empirical Studies and Brief Appraisal of the Literature*. Monticello, IL: Vance Bibliographies. [21]

Dupuy, R. Ernest, and Trevor N. Dupuy. 1986. *The Encyclopedia of Military History from 3500 B.C. to the Present* (2nd rev. ed.). New York: Harper & Row. [8]

Durkheim, Émile. 1893/1985. *The Division of Labor in Society*. New York: Free Press. [22]

Durkheim, Émile. 1893/1985. *The Division of Labor in Society*. New York: Free Press. [1]

Durkheim, Émile. 1895/1982. *Rules of Sociological Method*. New York: Free Press. [1]

Durkheim, Émile. 1925/1973. *Moral Education*. New York: Free Press. [20]

Durkheim, Émile. 1912/1965. *The Elementary Forms of Religious Life*. J. W. Swain (trans.). New York: Free Press. [1, 18]

Durkheim, Émile. 1897/1951. *Suicide: A Study of Sociology*. J. A. Spaulding and G. Simpson (trans.). New York: Free Press. [2]

Duverger, Maurice. 1954. *Political Parties*. B. North and R. North (trans.). New York: Wiley. [14]

Dworkin, Ronald. 1986. *Law's Empire*. Cambridge, MA: Harvard University Press. [14]

Dworkin, Ronald. 1977. *Taking Rights Seriously*. Cambridge, MA: Harvard University Press. [14]

Dyer, Gwynn. 1985. *War*. New York: Crown Books. [14]

Easterbrooks, M. Ann, and Wendy A. Goldberg. 1984. "Toddler Development in the Family: Impact of Father Involvement and Parenting Characteristics." *Child Development* 55:740–752. [5]

Eastman, C. M. 1975. *Aspects of Language and Culture*. San Francisco: Chandler and Sharp. [4]

Eaton, William W. 1980. "A Formal Theory of Selection for Schizophrenia." *American Journal of Sociology* 86:149–158. [11]

Eberstadt, Nick (ed.). 1980. *Fertility Decline in the Less Developed Countries*. New York: Praeger. [10]

Edelman, Marian Wright. 1987. *Families in Peril*. Cambridge, MA: Harvard University Press. [16]

Edwards, Richard. 1979. *Contested Terrain: The Transformation of the Workplace in the Twentieth Century*. New York: Basic Books. [15]

Ehrenhalt, Samuel M. 1983. "What Lies Ahead for College Graduates?" *American Demographics* 5 (September):29–33. [17]

Eisenstadt, S. N. 1978. *Revolution and the Transformation of Societies*. New York: Free Press. [14]

Eisenstein, Elizabeth. 1979. *The Printing Press as an Agent of Change* (2 vols.). New York: Cambridge University Press. [4]

Eisinger, Peter K. 1973. "The Conditions of Protest Behavior in American Cities." *The American Political Science Review* 67 (1):11–28. [21]

Eisslin, M. 1982. *The Age of Television*. New York: Freeman Press. [4]

Ekstrom, Ruth B., Margaret E. Goertz, Judith M. Pollack, and Donald A. Rock. 1986. "Who Drops Out of High School and Why? Findings From a National Study." *Teachers College Record* 87 (3):356–373. [17]

Elder, Glen H., Jr. 1987. "Families and Lives: Some Developments in Life-Course Studies." *Journal of Family History* 12 (1–2):170–199. [6]

Elder, Glen H., Jr. 1978. "Approaches to Social Change and the Family." *American Journal of Sociology* 84 (suppl.):170–199. [6]

Elder, Glen H., Jr., A. Caspi, and L. M. Burton. 1986. "Adolescent Transitions in Developmental Perspective: Historical and Sociological Insights." In M. Gunnar (ed.), *Minnesota Symposia on Child Psychiatry* (vol. 21). Hillsdale, NJ: Erlbaum. [6]

Elias, Marilyn. 1986. "Divorce Is Easier on Well-Off Kids." *USA Today* (September 9):1A. [16]

Elkin, Frederick, and Gerald Handel. 1984. *The Child and Society: The Process of Socialization* (4th ed.). New York: Random House. [5]

Ember, Carol R., and Melvin Ember. 1977. *Anthropology* (2nd ed.). Englewood Cliffs, NJ: Prentice Hall. [4]

England, Paula, and George Farkas. 1986. *Households, Employment, and Gender*. New York: Aldine. [12]

Entwisle, Barbara, and William M. Mason. 1985. "Multilevel Effects of Socioeconomic Development and Family Planning Programs on Children Ever Born." *American Journal of Sociology* 91:616–649. [10]

Enzer, Selwyn, Richard Drobnick, and Steven Alter. 1978. "World Food Prospects: The Next 20 Years." *The Futurist* 12 (October):283–288. [10]

Epstein, Cynthia Fuchs. 1981. *Women in Law*. New York: Basic Books. [12]

Erickson, F. 1984. "School Literacy, Reasoning and Civility: An Anthropologist's Perspective." *Review of Educational Research* 54 (4):525–546. [17]

Eriksen, E., and W. Yancey. 1980. *Class, Sector and Income Determination*. Unpublished manuscript, Temple University, Philadelphia. [3]

Erikson, Erik. 1968. *Identity, Youth and Crisis*. New York: W. W. Norton. [6]

Erikson, Erik. 1950. *Childhood and Society*. New York: W. W. Norton. [6]

Ermann, M. David, and Richard J. Ludman. 1982. *Corporate Deviance*. New York: Holt, Rinehart and Winston. [7]

Etzioni, Amitai. 1982. "Making Interest Groups Work for the Public." *Public Opinion* 5 (August–September):52–55. [14]

Etzioni, Amitai. 1961. *A Comparative Analysis of Complex Organizations*. New York: Free Press. [5]

Eurich, N. 1985. *The Corporate Classroom*. New York: The Carnegie Foundation for the Advancement of Teaching. [17]

Evans, Christopher R. 1981. *The Micro Millenium*. New York: Viking Press. [15, 22]

Evans, L. B. 1981. "Industrial Uses of the Microprocessor." In T. Forester (ed.), *The Microelectronics Revolution*, pp. 138–151. Cambridge, MA: MIT Press. [15]

Evans-Pritchard, E. E. 1965. *Theories of Primitive Religion*. London, England: Oxford University Press. [18]

Exter, Thomas. 1987. "How Many Hispanics?" *American Demographics* (May):36–39. [13]

Fagot, Beverly I. 1984. "Teacher and Peer Reactions to Boys' and Girls' Play Styles." *Sex Roles* 11 (7/8):691–702. [12]

Fagot, Beverly I. 1978. "The Influence of Sex of Child on Parental Reactions to Toddler Children." *Child Development* 49:459–465. [12]

Fagot, Beverly I. 1977. "Consequences of Moderate Cross-Gender Behavior in Preschool Children." *Child Development* 48:902–907. [12]

Fagot, Beverly I., Richard Hagan, Mary Driver Leinbach, and Sandra Kronsberg. 1985. "Differential Reactions to Assertive and Communicative Acts of Toddler Boys and Girls." *Child Development* 56:1499–1505. [12]

Falsey, Barbara, and Barbara Heyns. 1984. "The College Channel: Private and Public Schools Reconsidered." *Sociology of Education* 57 (April):111–122. [17]

Farley, John. 1987. "Segregation in 1980: How Segregated Are America's Metropolitan Areas?" In G. A. Tobin (ed.), *Divided Neighborhoods*. Newbury Park, CA: Sage. [13]

Farley, John. 1986. "Segregated City, Segregated Suburbs: To What Extent Are They Products of Black-White Socioeconomic Differences?" *Urban Geography* 7:180–187. [13]

Farley, Reynolds. 1984. *Blacks and Whites: Narrowing the Gap?* Cambridge, MA: Harvard University Press. [13]

Feagin, Joe R. 1985. "The Global Context of Metropolitan Growth: Houston and the Oil Industry." *American Journal of Sociology* 90 (6):1204–1227. [9]

Featherman, David L., and Robert Hauser. 1978. *Opportunity and Change*. New York: Academic Press. [11]

Feigenbaum, Edward A., and Pamela McCorduck. 1983. *The Fifth Generation: Artificial Intelligence and Japan's Computer Challenge to the World*. Reading, MA: Addison-Wesley. [22]

Feshbach, S. 1976. "The Role of Fantasy in the Response to Television." *Journal of Social Issues* 32:71–85. [5]

Feshbach, Seymour, and Michael J. White. 1986. "Individual Differences in Attitudes towards Nuclear Arms Policies: Some Psychological and Social Policy Considerations." *Journal of Peace Research* 23 (2):129–139. [21]

Festinger, L., S. Schacter, and K. Black. 1950. *Social Pressures in Informal Groups: A Study of Human Factors in Housing*. Stanford, CA: Stanford University Press. [3]

Fine, Gary Alan. 1987. *With the Boys: Little League Baseball and Preadolescent Culture*. Chicago: University of Chicago Press. [5]

Fischer, Claude S. 1982. *To Dwell Among Friends: Personal Networks in Town and City*. Chicago: University of Chicago Press. [9]

Fiske, Edward B. 1987a. "Enrollment of Minorities in Colleges Stagnating." *New York Times* (April 19):1. [13]

Fiske, Edward B. 1987b. "Integration Lags at Public Schools." *New York Times* (July 26):1. [13]

Fiske, Edward B. 1986a. "Literacy in America: Beyond the Basics." *New York Times* (September 26):A15. [17]

Fiske, Edward B. 1986b. "Teacher Quality Becomes Top School Issue." *New York Times* (October 17):B1, B2. [17]

Fitzpatrick, Joseph P. 1971. *Puerto Rican Americans: The Meaning of Migration to the Mainland*. Englewood Cliffs, NJ: Prentice Hall. [4]

Flora, Peter, and Arnold J. Heidenheimer (eds.). 1981. *The Development of Welfare States in Europe and America*. New Brunswick, NJ: Transaction Books. [14]

Fogelson, Robert M. 1970. "Violence and Grievances: Reflections on the 1960s Riots." *Journal of Social Issues* 26 (Winter):141–163. [21]

Foner, Anne. 1986. *Aging and Old Age: New Perspectives*. Englewood Cliffs, NJ: Prentice Hall. [6]

Foner, A., and H. Kertzer. 1978. "Transitions Over the Life Course: Lessons from Age Set Societies." *American Sociological Review*. [6]

Forer, Lucille K. 1976. *The Birth Order Factor—How Your Personality Is Influenced by Your Place in the Family*. New York: David McKay. [5]

Forester, T. (ed.). 1985. *The Information Technology Revolution*. Cambridge, MA: MIT Press. [15]

Forester, Tom. 1988. *High Tech Society*. Cambridge, MA: MIT Press. [22]

Fortes, Meyer. 1969. *Kinship and the Social Order*. Chicago: Aldine. [18]

Fox, Renee C. 1977. "The Medicalization and Demedicalization of American Society." *Daedalus* (Winter). [19]

Fox, Robin. 1970. "The Cultural Animal." *Encounters* 35 (July):31–42. [4]

Francis, Arthur. 1986. *New Technology at Work*. Oxford, England: Oxford University Press. [22]

Francke, Linda Bird. 1983. "The Sons of Divorce." *New York Times Magazine* (May 22):40+. [16]

Frank, A. Gunder. 1978. *World Accumulation, 1492–1789*. New York: Monthly Review Press. [15]

Frank, Andre Gunder. 1967. *Capitalism and Underdevelopment in Latin America*. New York: Monthly Review Press. [22]

Franklin, Clyde W. 1984. *The Changing Definition of Masculinity*. New York: Plenum Press. [12]

Franklin, Raymond S., and Solomon Resnik. 1973. *The Political Economy of Racism*. New York: Holt, Rinehart and Winston. [13]

Freedman, Samuel G. 1987. "New York race tension is rising despite gains." *New York Times* (January 9):1. [13]

Freeman, J. 1982. "Organizational Life Cycles and Natural Selection Processes." In B. M. Staw and L. L. Cummings (eds.), *Research in Organizational Behavior*. Greenwich, CT: JAI Press. [8]

Freeman, Jo. 1979. "Resource Mobilization and Strategy." In M. N. Zald and J. D. McCarthy (eds.), *The Dynamics of Social Movements*. Cambridge, MA: Winthrop. [21]

Freeman, Jo. 1973. "The Origins of the Women's Liberation Movement." *American Journal of Sociology* 78:792–811. [21]

Freeman, John, and Michael T. Hannan. 1983. "Niche Width and the Dynamics of Organizational Populations." *American Journal of Sociology* 88 (6). [8]

Freeman, John H., Glenn R. Carroll, and Michael T. Hannan. 1983. "The Liability of Newness: Age Dependence in Organizational Death Rates." *American Sociological Review* 48:692–710. [8]

Freud, Sigmund. 1930/1962. *Civilization and Its Discontents*. J. Strachey (ed. and trans.). New York: W. W. Norton. [5]

Freud, Sigmund. 1920/1953. "Beyond the Pleasure Principle." In J. Strachey (ed. and trans.), *The Standard Edition of the Complete Psychological Works of Sigmund Freud* (vol. 18). London, England: Hogarth Press. [5]

Freud, Sigmund. 1923/1947. *The Ego and the Id*. London, England: Hogarth Press. [5]

Freudenburg, William R. 1984. "Boomtown's Youth: The Differential Impacts of Rapid Community Growth on Adolescents and Adults." *American Sociological Review* 49 (October):697–705. [9]

Friedan, Betty. 1963. *The Feminine Mystique*. New York: W. W. Norton. [12, 21]

Friedman, L. 1973. *A History of American Law*. New York: Simon and Schuster. [15]

Friedman, Samuel R., Don C. Des Jarlais, Jo L. Sotheran, Jonathan Garber, Henry Cohen, and Donald Smith. 1987. "AIDS and Self-Organization Among Intravenous Drug Users." *The International Journal of the Addictions* 22 (3):201–219. [19]

Friedson, Eliot. 1985. *The Power of Profession*. Chicago: University of Chicago Press. [15]

Friedson, Eliot. 1970. *Professional Dominance: The Social Structure of Medical Care*. New York: Atherton Press. [19]

Fries, James F. 1983. "The Compression of Morbidity." *Milbank Memorial Fund Quarterly/Health and Society* 61 (3):397–419. [19]

Fruch, Terry, and Paul E. McGhee. 1975. "Traditional Sex Role Development and Amount of Time Spent Watching Television." *Developmental Psychology* 11 (1):109. [12]

Fuguitt, Glenn V. 1985. "The Nonmetropolitan Population Turnaround." *Annual Review of Sociology* 11:259–280. [9]

Furstenberg, Frank F., Jr. 1984. "The New Extended Family: The Experience of Parents and Children After Remarriage." Paper presented to the Changing Family Conference XIII: The Blended Family, University of Iowa, Iowa City. [6]

Furstenberg, Frank F., Jr. 1976. *Unplanned Parenthood*. New York: Free Press. [6]

Furstenberg, Frank F., Jr., J. Brooks-Gunn, and S. P. Morgan. 1987. *Adolescent Mothers in Later Life*. New York: Cambridge University Press. [6]

Gaddy, Gary D., and David Pritchard. 1985. "When Watching Religious TV Is Like Attending Church." *Journal of Communication* (Winter):123–131. [18]

Gaensbauer, Theodore, and Susan Hiatt. 1984. *The Psychobiology of Affective Development*. New York: Erlbaum. [5]

Galbraith, John Kenneth. 1987. *Economics in Perspective: A Critical History*. Boston: Houghton Mifflin. [15]

Galbraith, John Kenneth. 1978. *The New Industrial State* (3rd ed.). Boston: Houghton Mifflin. [15]

Gallup, Alec M. 1985. *The 17th Annual Gallup Poll of the Public's Attitudes Toward the Public Schools* (Report No. 240, September). [17]

Gallup, George. 1988. *The Gallup Poll: Public Opinion 1987*. Wilmington, DE: Scholarly Resources. pp. 192–194. [14]

Gallup, George. 1987. *The Gallup Poll: Public Opinion 1986*. Wilmington, DE: Scholarly Resources. [16]

Gallup, George. 1986. *The Gallup Poll: Public Opinion 1985*. Wilmington, DE: Scholarly Resources. [10]

Gallup, George. 1983. *The Gallup Poll: Public Opinion 1982*. Wilmington, DE: Scholarly Resources. [6]

Gallup Report. 1986. *Political, Social and Economic Trends* (Report No. 253, October). [14]

Gallup Report. 1985. *Fifty Years of Gallup Surveys on Religion*. (Report No. 236, May). [18]

Gallup Report. 1982. *Religion in America* (Report Nos. 201–202, June–July). [18]

Galuszka, Peter, Bill Javetski, John Pearson, and Rose Brady. 1987. "Gorbachev Has Planted the Seeds, But Will They Grow?" *Business Week* (February 2):44–45. [15]

Gans, Herbert J. 1979. "Symbolic Ethnicity: The Future of Ethnic Groups and Cultures in America." *Ethnic and Racial Studies* 2:1–20. [13]

Gans, Herbert J. 1962. *The Urban Villagers*. New York: Free Press. [9]

Garbarino, James, and Gwen Gilliam. 1980. *Understanding Abusive Families*. Lexington, MA: Lexington Books. [16]

Garfinkel, Harold. 1967. *Studies in Ethnomethodology*. Englewood Cliffs, NJ: Prentice Hall. [3]

Garson, Barbara. 1988. *The Electronic Sweatshop*. New York: Simon and Schuster. [22]

Geertz, Clifford. 1973. *The Interpretation of Culture*. New York: Basic Books. [4]

Gellerman, Saul W. 1986. "Why Good Managers Make Bad Ethical Choices." *Harvard Business Review* (July–August):85–90. [7]

Gelles, Richard. 1985. "Family Violence." *Annual Review of Sociology* 11:347–367. [16]

Gelles, Richard J. 1983. "Violence in the Family." In D. H. Olson and B. C. Miller (eds.), *Family Studies Review Yearbook* (vol. 1). Beverly Hills, CA: Sage. [16]

Gelles, Richard J. 1974. "Child Abuse as Psychopathology: A Sociological Critique and Reformulation." In S. K. Steinmetz and M. A. Straus (eds.), *Violence in the Family*. New York: Harper & Row. [16]

Gellner, Ernest. 1983. *Nations and Nationalism*. Oxford, England: Basil Blackwell. [14, 17]

Gellner, Ernest. 1975. *Legitimation of Belief*. New York: Cambridge University Press. [18]

Gellner, Ernest. 1972. *Legitimation of Belief*. London, England: Weidenfeld and Nicholson. [18]

Gelman, E. 1981. "In Sports, 'Lions vs. Tigers.'" *Newsweek* (May 18):75. [12]

George, Katherine. 1968. "The Civilized West Looks at Primitive Africa: 1400–1800." In A. Dundes (ed.), *Every Man His Way: Readings in Cultural Anthropology*. Englewood Cliffs, NJ: Prentice Hall. [4]

Gerson, Kathleen. 1985. *Hard Choices*. Berkeley: University of California Press. [12]

Geschwender, James A. 1964. "Social Structure and the Negro Revolt: An Examination of Some Hypotheses." *Social Forces* 43:248–256. [21]

Gest, Ted. 1984. "Battle of the Sexes over 'Comparable Worth.'" *U.S. News & World Report* (February 20):73–74. [12]

Gibson, J. L. 1985. "Whither the Local Parties? A Cross-sectional and Longitudinal Analysis of the Strength of Party Organization." *American Journal of Political Science*. [14]

Giddens, Anthony. 1987. *Sociology: A Brief but Critical Introduction* (2nd ed.). San Diego, CA: Harcourt Brace Jovanovich. [22]

Giddens, Anthony. 1985a. *The Constitution of Society: Outline of the Theory of Structuration*. Berkeley: University of California Press. [1]

Giddens, Anthony. 1985b. *The National State and Violence*. Berkeley: University of California Press. [14]

Giddens, Anthony. 1973. *The Class Structure of the Advanced Societies*. New York: Cambridge University Press. [11]

Gieryn, Thomas F., George M. Bevins, and Stephen C. Zehr. 1985. "Professionalization of American Scientists: Public Science in the Creation/Evolution on Trial." *American Sociological Review* 50 (June):392–409. [20]

Gil, David G. 1974. "Helping Parents and Protecting Children." In S. K. Steinmetz and M. A. Straus (eds.), *Violence in the Family*. New York: Harper & Row. [16]

Gill, Colin. 1985. *Work, Unemployment and the New Technology*. Cambridge, England: Polity Press. [15]

Gilligan, C. 1982. *In a Different Voice: Psychological Theory and Women's Development*. Cambridge, MA: Harvard University Press. [12]

Gitlin, Todd. 1987. *The Sixties: Years of Hope, Days of Rage*. New York: Bantam Books. [21]

Gittleson, Natalie. 1984. "American Jews Rediscover Orthodoxy." *New York Times Magazine* (September 10). [18]

Glasberg, Davita S., and Michael Schwartz. 1983. "Ownership and Control of Corporations." *Annual Review of Sociology* 9:311–322. [15]

Glick, Paul C. 1984. "How American Families Are Changing." *American Demographics* 6 (January):21–25. [16]

Glick, Paul C. 1979. "The Future of the American Family." *Current Population Reports Special Studies* (Series P-23, No. 78). Washington, DC: U.S. Government Printing Office. [16]

Glick, Paul C., and Graham P. Spanier. 1980. "Married and Unmarried Cohabitation in the United States." *Journal of Marriage and the Family* 48 (1):19–30. [16]

Gluckman, Max. 1962a. "Les Rites de Passage." In M. Gluckman (ed.), *Essays on the Ritual of Social Relations*. Manchester, England: University of Manchester Press. [6]

Gluckman, Max. (ed.). 1962b. *Essays on the Ritual of Social Relations*. Manchester, England: Manchester University Press. [18]

Gluckman, Max. 1965. *Politics, Law and Ritual in Tribal Society*. New York: New American Library. [14]

Goffman, Erving. 1974. *Frame Analysis: An Essay on the Organization of Experience*. Cambridge, MA: Harvard University Press. [3]

Goffman, Erving. 1959. *Presentation of the Self in Everyday Life*. New York: Doubleday. [3]

Gold, Michael Evan. 1983. *A Dialogue on Comparable Worth*. New York: ILR Press. [12]

Golding, William. 1954. *Lord of the Flies*. New York: Coward-McCann. [8]

Goldscheider, Calvin. 1986. *Jewish Continuity and Change: Emerging Patterns in America*. Bloomington: Indiana University Press. [18]

Goldsmith, Jeff. 1984. "Death of a Paradigm." *Health Affairs* 3 (3):5–19. [19]

Goldstine, Herman H. 1972. *The Computer from Pascal to Von Neumann*. Princeton, NJ: Princeton University Press. [15, 22]

Goldstone, Jack (ed.). 1985. *Revolutions*. San Diego, CA: Harcourt Brace Jovanovich. [14]

Goleman, Daniel. 1986. "Major Personality Study Finds That Traits are Mostly Inherited." *New York Times* (December 2):C1, C2. [5]

Goleman, Daniel. 1985. "Spacing of Siblings Strongly Linked to Success in Life." *New York Times* (May 28):C1, C4. [5]

Goleman, Daniel. 1984. "Order Found in the Development of Emotions." *New York Times* (June 19):C1, C8. [5]

Goode, William J. 1978. *The Celebration of Heroes: Prestige as a Control System*. Berkeley: University of California Press. [11]

Goode, William J. 1967. "The Protection of the Inept." *American Sociological Review* 32 (February):5–19. [8]

Goode, William J. 1963. "The Role of the Family in Industrialization." In *Social Problems of Development* (vol. 7). The U.S. Papers Prepared for the UN Conference on the Application of Science and Technology for the Benefit of the Less Developed Areas. Washington, DC: U.S. Government Printing Office. [16]

Goode, William J. 1960. "A Theory of Role Strain." *American Sociological Review* 25:483–496. [3]

Goodlad, John I. 1983. *A Place Called School: Prospects for the Future*. New York: McGraw-Hill. [17]

Goodman, Ann B., Carole Siegel, Thomas J. Craig, and Shang P. Lin. 1983. "The Relationship between Socioeconomic Class and Prevalence of Schizophrenia, Alcoholism, and Affective Disorders Treated by Inpatient Care in a Suburban Area." *American Journal of Psychiatry* 140:166–170. [14]

Gopian, J. D. 1984. "What Makes PACs Tick?" *American Journal of Political Science* 28 (2):259–281. [14]

Gordon, David M. 1984. "Capitalist Development and the History of American Cities." In W. K. Tabb and L. Sawers (eds.), *Marxism and the Metropolis* (2nd ed.). New York: Oxford University Press. [9]

Gordon, Milton M. 1978. *Human Nature, Class and Ethnicity*. New York: Oxford University Press. [13]

Gordon, Milton M. 1964. *Assimilation in American Life*. New York: Oxford University Press. [4]

Gordon, Susan. 1978. *Lonely in America*. New York: Oxford University Press. [10]

Gortmaker, Steven L. 1979. "Poverty and Infant Mortality in the U.S." *American Sociological Review* 44 (April):280–297. [10, 11]

Gough, E. Kathleen. 1974. "Nayar: Central Kerala." In D. Schneider and E. K. Gough (eds.), *Matrilineal Kinship*. Berkeley: University of California Press. [16]

Gouldner, Alvin. 1980. *The Two Marxisms: Contradictions and Anomalies in the Development of Theory*. New York: Oxford University Press. [1]

Gouldner, Helen, with the assistance of Mary Symons Strong. 1978. *Teacher's Pets, Troublemakers and Nobodies*. Westport, CT: Greenwood Press. [17]

Gove, Walter R., and Michael Hughes. 1979. "Possible Causes of the Apparent Sex Differences in Physical Health: An Empirical Investigation." *American Sociological Review* 44 (February):126–146. [19]

Gove, Walter R., and Jeannette F. Tudor. 1973. "Adult Sex Roles and Mental Illness." In J. Huber (ed.), *Changing Women in a Changing Society*. Chicago: University of Chicago Press. [12]

Graham, Hilary. 1987. "Women's Smoking and Family Health." *Social Science and Medicine* 25 (1):47–56. [19]

Granovetter, Mark S. 1984. "The Strength of Weak Ties: A Network Theory Revisited." In R. Collins (ed.), *Sociological Theory 1983*, ch. 7. San Francisco, CA: Jossey-Bass. [3]

Granovetter, Mark S. 1974. *Getting a Job: A Study of Contacts and Careers*. Cambridge, MA: Harvard University Press. [3]

Granovetter, Mark S. 1973. "The Strength of Weak Ties." *American Journal of Sociology* 78 (6):1360–1381. [3]

Gray, David. 1985. *Ecological Beliefs and Behaviors*. Westport, CT: Greenwood Press. [21]

Gray, Herman. 1986. "Television and the New Black Man: Black Male Images in Prime-Time Situation Comedy." *Media, Culture and Society* (vol. 8):223–242. [4]

Greeley, Andrew M. 1982. "Going Their Own Way." *New York Times Magazine* (October 10):28–29+. [18]

Greeley, Andrew M. 1974. "Political Attitudes Among White Ethnics." In C. H. Anderson (ed.), *Sociological Essays and Research*. Homewood, IL: Dorsey. [13]

Greeley, Andrew M. 1972a. *The Denominational Society*. Glenview, IL: Scott, Foresman. [18]

Greeley, Andrew M. 1972b. *Unsecular Man: The Persistence of Religion*. New York: Schocken Books. [18]

Green, Marshall, and Robert A. Fearey. 1978. *World Population: Silent Explosion*. Washington, DC: U.S. Department of State. [10]

Greif, Geoffrey L. 1985. *Single Fathers*. Lexington, MA: D. C. Heath. [16]

Griswold, Wendy. 1988. "Formulaic Fiction: The Author as Agent of Elective Affinity." *Comparative Social Research* (vol. 11). [4]

Griswold, Wendy. 1987. "The Fabrication of Meaning: Literary Interpretation in the United States, Great Britain, and the West Indies." *American Journal of Sociology* 92 (5):1077–1117. [4]

Gross, Jane. 1987. "Single Women: Coping with a Void." *New York Times* (April 28):A1, B2. [16]

Grusky, David, and Robert M. Hauser. 1984. "Comparative Social Mobility Revisited: Models of Convergence and Divergence in 16 Countries." *American Sociological Review* 49:19–38. [11]

Gumperz, John J. (ed.). 1982. *Language and Social Identity*. New York: Cambridge University Press. [4]

Gunn, Thomas. 1982. "The Mechanization of Design and Manufacturing." *Scientific American* 247 (3):115–130. [22]

Gurr, Ted Robert. 1970. *Why Men Rebel*. Princeton, NJ: Princeton University Press. [21]

Guterman, Stuart, and Allen Dobson. 1986. "Impact of Medicare Prospective Payment for Hospitals." *Health Care Financing Review* 7 (3):97–114. [19]

Guth, James L. 1983. "The New Christian Right." In R. C. Liebman and R. Wuthnow (eds.), *The New Christian Right*. New York: Aldine. [18]

Gutierrez, G. 1983. *The Power of the Poor in History*. Mary Knoll, NY: Orbis. [18]

Gutierrez, G. 1973. *A Theory of Liberation*. Mary Knoll, NY: Orbis. [18]

Gutman, Herbert. 1977. *Black Family in Slavery and Freedom*. New York: Random House. [16]

Haar, Charles M., and Daniel William Fessler. 1986. *The Wrong Side of the Tracks*. New York: Simon and Schuster. [13]

Habermas, Jurgen. 1987. *The Philosophical Discourse of Modernity: Twelve Lectures*. Cambridge, MA: MIT Press. [15, 22]

Habermas, Jurgen. 1984. *The Theory of Communicative Action (vol. 1)*. Boston: Beacon Press. [22]

Hadden, Jeffrey K., and Charles E. Swann. 1981. *Prime Time Preachers: The Rising Power of Televangelism*. Reading, MA: Addison-Wesley. [18]

Hagan, William Thomas. 1979. *American Indians* (rev. ed.). Chicago: University of Chicago Press. [13]

Haines, Valerie. 1988. "Is Spencer's Theory an Evolutionary Theory?" *American Journal of Sociology* 93 (5):1200–1223. [22]

Hall, G. Stanley. 1905/1981. *Adolescence: Its Psychology and Its Relations to Physiology, Anthropology, Sociology, Sex, Crime, Religion, and Education* (2 vols.). Norwood, PA: Telegraph Books. [6]

Hall, John A. 1985. *Powers and Liberties*. Berkeley: University of California Press. [14]

Hall, Richard H. 1982. *Organizations: Structure and Process* (3rd ed.). Englewood Cliffs, NJ: Prentice Hall. [8]

Hall, Richard H. 1963–1964. "The Concept of Bureaucracy: An Empirical Assessment." *American Journal of Sociology* 69:32–40. [8]

Halle, David. 1984. *America's Working Man: Work, Home and Politics Among Blue-Collar Property Owners*. Chicago: University of Chicago Press. [15]

Hallin, Daniel C. 1986. "We Keep America on Top of the World." In T. Gitlin (ed.), *Watching Television*, pp. 9–41. New York: Pantheon. [4]

Hannan, Michael T., and John Freeman. 1977. "The Population Ecology of Organizations." *American Journal of Sociology* 82 (5):929–964. [8]

Hanson, Sandra L. 1983. "A Family Life-Cycle Approach to the Socioeconomic Attainment of Working Women." *Journal of Marriage and the Family* 45 (2):323–338. [6]

Hare, A. Paul. 1976. *Handbook of Small Group Research* (2nd ed.). New York: Free Press. [8]

Hareven, Tamara K. 1982. *Family Time and Industrial Time*. New York: Cambridge University Press. [16]

Harrington, Michael. 1984. *The New American Poverty*. New York: Penguin. [14]

Harris, Chauncy D., and Edward L. Ullman. 1957. "The Nature of Cities." In P. K. Hatt and A. J. Reiss, Jr. (ed.), *Cities and Societies*. Peoria, IL: Free Press. [9]

Harris, Chauncy D., and Edward L. Ullman. 1945. "The Nature of Cities." *Annals of the American Academy of Political and Social Science* 242 (November):12. [9]

Harris, Louis. 1987. *Inside America*. New York: Vintage. [14, 18]

Harris, Louis. 1981. *Aging in the Eighties: America in Transition*. Washington, DC: National Council on Aging. [6]

Harris, Marvin. 1987. *Cultural Anthropology* (2nd ed.). New York: Harper & Row. [12]

Harris, Marvin. 1980. *Cultural Materialism: The Struggle for a Science of Culture*. New York: Vintage. [4]

Harrison, Michael I., and Bernard Lazerwitz. 1982. "Do Denominations Matter?" *American Journal of Sociology* 88:356–377. [18]

Harrison, Paul. 1984. *Inside the Third World* (2nd rev. ed.). New York: Penguin. [10]

Hart, Stephen. 1987. "Privatization in American Religion and Society." *Sociological Analysis* 47 (4):319–334. [18]

Hauser, Philip M. 1981. "The Census of 1980." *Scientific American* 245 (November):53–61. [10]

Hauser, Robert M., Archibald O. Haller, David Mechanic, and Taissa S. Hauser (eds.). 1982. *Social Structure and Behavior*. New York: Academic Press. [11]

Hauser, Robert M., Shu-Ling Tsai, and William H. Sewell. 1983. "A Model of Stratification with Response Error in Social and Psychological Variables." *Sociology of Education* 56:20–46. [11]

Hawley, Amos H. 1971. *Urban Society: An Ecological Approach*. New York: Ronald Press. [9]

Hearn, James C. 1984. "The Relative Roles of Academic, Ascribed, and Socioeconomic Characteristics in College Destinations." *Sociology of Education* 57 (January):22–30. [17]

Hechter, Michael. 1975. *International Colonialism*. Berkeley: University of California Press. [13]

Hehir, J. Bryan. 1981. "The Bishops Speak on El Salvador." *Commonweal* (April 10):199, 223. [18]

Heider, Fritz. 1958. *The Psychology of Interpersonal Relations*. New York: Wiley. [8]

Heider, Karl G. 1972. *The Dani of West Irian*. Andover, MD: Warner Modular. [16]

Heilbroner, Robert L. 1976. *Business Civilization in Decline*. New York: W. W. Norton. [15]

Held, David. 1987. *Models of Democracy*. Stanford, CA: Stanford University Press. [14]

Helson, Ravenna and Geraldine Moore. 1987. "Personality Change in Women from College to Midlife." *Journal of Personality and Social Psychology* 53:126–186. [6]

Hennig, Margaret, and Anne Jardim. 1977. *The Managerial Woman*. Garden City, NY: Anchor Press/Doubleday. [12]

Herbers, John. 1987. "Job Training Efforts in Massachusetts and Michigan Move Poor Off Welfare." *New York Times* (March 30):A14. [11]

Herbers, John. 1983. "Large Cities and Suburbs Giving Way to the Sprawl of Small Urban Areas." *New York Times* (July 8): 1. [9]

Herman, Edward. 1981. *Corporate Control, Corporate Power*. New York: Cambridge University Press. [15]

Hertz, Rosanna. 1986. *More Equal than Others: Women and Men in Dual-Career Marriages.* Berkeley: University of California Press. [16]

Hess, Beth B. 1983. "New Faces of Poverty." *American Demographics* 5 (May):26–31. [11]

Hetherington, E. Mavis, Martha Cox, and Roger Cox. 1977. "Divorced Fathers." *Psychology Today* 10 (April):42–46. [16]

Hewlett, Sylvia Ann. 1986. *A Lesser Life.* New York: William Morrow. [12, 21]

Heyns, Barbara. 1978. *Summer Learning.* New York: Academic Press. [17]

Hicks, Jonathan P. 1987. "A Black's Climb to the Executive Suite." *New York Times* (May 22):D1, D 4. [13]

Himmelfarb, Gertrude. 1983. *The Idea of Poverty.* New York: Knopf. [15]

Himmelstein, Jerome L. 1983. "The New Right." In R. C. Liebman and R. Wuthnow (eds.), *The New Christian Right.* New York: Aldine. [18]

Hirsch, Paul. 1986. "From Ambushes to Golden Parachutes: Corporate Takeovers as an Instance of Cultural Framing and Institutional Integration." *American Journal of Sociology* 91 (January):800–837. [7, 15]

Hirsch, Paul M. 1971. "Processing Fads and Fashions: An Organization-Set Analysis of Cultural Industry Systems." *American Journal of Sociology* 77 (4):639–659. [4]

Hirschman, Albert. 1982. *Shifting Involvements.* Princeton, NJ: Princeton University Press. [14]

Hirschman, Albert O. 1977. *The Passions and the Interests: Political Arguments for Capitalism Before Its Triumph.* Princeton, NJ: Princeton University Press. [15]

Hirschman, Charles, and Morrison G. Wong. 1986. "Socioeconomic Gains of Asian-Americans, Blacks, and Hispanics: 1960–1976." *American Journal of Sociology* 90 (3):584–607. [13]

Hirschman, Robert S., Howard Leventhal, and Kathleen Glynn. 1984. "The Development of Smoking Behavior: Conceptualization and Supportive Cross-Sectional Survey Data." *Journal of Applied Psychology* 14 (3):184–206. [7]

Hodge, Robert, and David Tripp. 1986. *Children and Television: A Semiotic Approach.* Cambridge, England: Polity Press. [5]

Hodgson, Godfrey. 1973. "Do Schools Make a Difference?" *Atlantic Monthly* 213 (March):35–46. [17]

Hodson, Randy. 1984. "Companies, Industries, and the Measurement of Economic Segmentation." *American Sociological Review* 49:335–348. [3]

Hoffman, Charles D., Sandra Eiko Tsuneyashi, Marilyn Ebina, and Heather Fite. 1984. "A Comparison of Adult Males' and Females' Interactions with Girls and Boys." *Sex Roles* 11 (9/10):799–811. [12]

Hogan, Dennis P., and Nan Marie Astone. 1986. "The Transition to Adulthood." *Annual Review of Sociology* 12:109–130. [6]

Holden, Constance. 1986. "A Revisionist Look at Population Growth." *Science* 231:1493–1494. [10]

Hollingshead, August, and Frederick Redlich. 1958. *Social Class and Mental Illness.* New York: Wiley. [11]

Homans, George C. 1974. *Social Behavior: Its Elementary Forms* (rev. ed.). New York: Harcourt Brace Jovanovich. [3, 11]

Hoover, E. M., and R. Vernon. 1959. *Anatomy of a Metropolis.* Cambridge, MA: Harvard University Press. [9]

Hope, Keith. 1982. "Vertical and Nonvertical Class Mobility in Three Countries." *American Sociological Review* 47:99–113. [11]

Hope, Marjorie, and James Young. 1986. *The Faces of Homelessness.* Lexington, MA: Lexington Books. [11]

Hopkins, K. 1978. *Conquerors and Slaves: Sociological Studies in Roman History.* New York: Cambridge University Press. [14]

Horkheimer, M. 1982. "The End of Reason." In A. Arrato and E. Gebhardt (eds.), *The Essential Frankfurt School Reader,* p. 28. New York: Continuum. [4]

Horn, Jack C., and Jeff Meer. 1987. "The Vintage Years." *Psychology Today* 21 (5):76–90. [6]

Horowitz, Morris. 1977. *Entry-Level Health Occupations: Development and Future.* Baltimore, MD: The Johns Hopkins University Press. [15]

Horsfield, Peter G. 1985. "Evangelism by Mail: Letters from the Broadcasters." *Journal of Communication* (Winter):89–97. [18]

Hostetler, John A. 1980. *Amish Society* (3rd ed.). Baltimore, MD: The Johns Hopkins University Press. [8]

Hoult, Thomas Ford. 1969. *A Dictionary of Modern Sociology.* Totowa, NJ: Littlefield, Adams. [21]

House, J., and G. Kasper. 1981. "Politeness Markers in English and German." In F. Coulmas (ed.), *Conversational Routine: Explorations in Standardized Communication Situations and Prepatterned Speech,* pp. 157–185. The Hague: Mouton. [4]

Howard, Michael. 1961. *The Franco-Prussian War.* New York: Collier. [8]

Howard, Robert. 1985. *Brave New Workplace.* New York: Viking. [15]

Howe, Louise Knapp. 1977. *Pink Collar Workers.* New York: Putnam. [12]

Hoyt, Homer. 1943. "The Structure of American Cities in the Post-War Era." *American Journal of Sociology* 48 (January):475–492. [9]

Huber, Joan, and Glenna Spitze. 1980. "Considering Divorce: An Expansion of Becker's Theory of Marital Instability." *American Journal of Sociology* 86 (1).75–89. [16]

Hughes, Robert. 1987. *The Fatal Shore.* New York: Knopf. [7]

Hughes, Thomas P. 1987. "The Evolution of Large Technological Systems." In W. Bijker, T. P. Hughes, and T. Pinch (eds.), *The Social Construction of Technological Systems,* pp. 51–81. Cambridge, MA: MIT Press. [20]

Hull, Jennifer Bingham. 1982. "Female Bosses Say Biggest Barriers Are Insecurity and 'Being a Woman.'" *Wall Street Journal* (November 2):29. [12]

Hunt, Morton. 1985. *Profiles of Social Research.* New York: Russell Sage Foundation. [2, 20]

Hunter, Albert. 1978. "Persistence of Local Sentiments in Mass Society." In D. Street et al. (eds.), *Handbook of Contemporary Urban Life,* pp. 134–156. San Francisco: Jossey-Bass. [9]

Hurn, Christopher J. 1978. *The Limits and Possibilities of Schooling: An Introduction to the Sociology of Education.* Boston: Allyn and Bacon. [17]

Hyde, Janet S. 1984. "How Large Are Gender Differences in Aggression? A Developmental Meta-Analysis." *Developmental Psychology* 20:722–736. [12]

Hyde, Janet S. 1981. "How Large Are Cognitive Gender Differences?" *American Psychologist* 36:892–901. [12]

Hyman, Herbert H., and Charles R. Wright. 1979. *Education's Lasting Influence on Values.* Chicago: University of Chicago Press. [17]

Hyman, Herbert H., Charles R. Wright, and John Shelton Reed. 1975. *The Enduring Effects of Education.* Chicago: University of Chicago Press. [17]

Ianni, Francis. 1972. *A Family Business: Kinship and Social Control in Organized Crime*. New York: Russell Sage Foundation. [7]

Immel, A. Richard. 1985. "The Automated Office: Myth vs. Reality." In T. Forester (ed.), *The Information Technology Revolution*, pp. 312–321. Cambridge, MA: MIT Press. [22]

Inglis, B. 1972. *Poverty and the Industrial Revolution*. London, England: Panther. [10]

Inkeles, Alex, and David Smith. 1974. *Becoming Modern: Individual Change in Six Developing Countries*. Cambridge, MA: Harvard University Press. [22]

Isaacs, Harold R. 1975. *Idols of the Tribe: Group Identity and Political Change*. New York: Harper & Row. [13]

Jackall, Robert. 1988. *Moral Mazes: The World of Corporate Managers*. New York: Oxford University Press. [15]

Jackson, Philip W. 1968. *Life in Classrooms*. New York: Holt, Rinehart and Winston. [17]

Jacobs, John W. 1982. "The Effect of Divorce on Fathers: An Overview of the Literature." *American Journal of Psychiatry* 139:1235–1241. [16]

Jacquet, C. M. (ed.). 1986. *Yearbook of the American and Canadian Churches, 1985*. Nashville: Abingdon Press. [18]

Janis, Irving L. 1972. *Victims of Groupthink: A Psychological Study of Foreign-Policy Decisions and Fiascos*. Boston: Houghton Mifflin. [8]

Janowitz, Morris. 1978. *The Last Half-Century: Societal Change and Politics in America*. Chicago: University of Chicago Press. [7]

Jencks, Christopher. 1972. *Inequality: A Reassessment of the Effect of Family and Schooling in America*. New York: Basic Books. [17]

Jenkins, J. Craig, and Charles Perrow. 1977. "Insurgency of the Powerless: Farm Worker Movements (1946–1972)." *American Sociological Review* 42:249–268. [21]

Jensen, Arthur. 1979. *Bias in Mental Testing*. New York: Free Press. [17]

Jensen, Arthur. 1969. "How Much Can We Boost IQ and Scholastic Achievement?" *Harvard Educational Review* 39:273–314. [13, 17]

Jiao, Shulan, Guiping Ji, and Qicheng Jing (C. C. Ching). 1986. "Comparative Study of Behavioral Qualities of Only Children and Sibling Children." *Child Development* 57:357–361. [5]

Johnson, Barbara A., and Jonathan H. Turner. 1984. "A Formalization and Reformalization of Anomie Theory." *South African Journal of Sociology* 15 (4):151–158. [7]

Johnson, Benton. 1963. "On Church and Sect." *American Sociological Review* 28:539–549. [18]

Johnson, Dirk. 1987. "The View from the Poorest U.S. Suburb." *New York Times* (April 30):A18. [9]

Johnson, Susan Moore. 1984. "Merit Pay for Teachers: A Poor Prescription for Reform." *Harvard Educational Review* 54 (2):175–185. [17]

Jones, Barry. 1982. *Sleepers, Wake!: Technology and the Future of Work*. Melbourne, Australia: Oxford University Press. [15]

Jones, James H. 1981. *Bad Blood: The Tuskegee Syphilis Experiment*. New York: Free Press. [20]

Jones, Landon Y. 1980. *Great Expectations: America and the Baby Boom Generation*. New York: Coward, McCann & Geoghegan. [6]

Jones, M. C. 1965. "Psychological Correlates of Somatic Development." *Child Development* 36:899–911. [5]

Jordan, Nick. 1983. "You've Run a Long Way, Baby." *Psychology Today* (June):79. [12]

Joseph, Andre. 1985. *Intelligence, IQ and Race—When, How, and Why They Became Associated*. San Francisco: R & E Research Associates. [17]

Kagan, Jerome. 1984. *The Nature of the Child*. New York: Basic Books. [5]

Kamin, Leon J. 1986. "Is Crime in the Genes? The Answer May Depend on Who Chooses What Evidence." *Scientific American* (February):22–27. [7]

Kane, Penny. 1987. *The Second Billion: Population and Family Planning in China*. New York: Penguin. [10]

Kanter, Rosabeth Moss. 1983. *The Changemasters: Innovation and Entrepreneurship in the American Corporation*. New York: Simon and Schuster. [12]

Kanter, Rosabeth Moss. 1977. *Men and Women of the Corporation*. New York: Basic Books. [12]

Kanter, Rosabeth Moss. 1972. *Commitment and Community: Communes and Utopias in Sociological Perspective*. Cambridge, MA: Harvard University Press. [8]

Karabel, Jerome. 1977. "Community Colleges and Social Stratification: Submerged Class Conflict in American Higher Education." In J. Karabel and A. H. Halsey (eds.), *Power and Ideology in Education*. New York: Oxford University Press. [17]

Kargman, Marie Witkin. 1983. "Stepchild Support Obligations of Stepparents." *Family Relations* 32:231–238. [16]

Kaufman, Sharon R. 1986. *The Ageless Self: Sources of Meaning in Late Life*. Madison, WI: The University of Wisconsin Press. [6]

Kedourie, Elie. 1980. "Islam Resurgent." *Britannica Book of the Year, 1980*. Chicago: Encyclopedia Britannica. [18]

Kegley, Charles W., and Eugene R. Wittkopf. 1985. *World Politics* (2nd ed.). New York: St. Martin's Press. [14]

Keller, Suzanne. 1963. *Beyond the Ruling Class: Strategic Elites in Modern Society*. New York: Random House. [14]

Kelley, Allen. 1986. "The Birth Dearth: The Economic Consequences." *Public Opinion* 8 (December/January):14–17+. [10]

Kelly, Gail P. 1986. "Coping with America: Refugees from Vietnam, Cambodia, and Laos in the 1970s and 1980s." AAPSS *Annals* 487 (September):138–149. [10]

Kelly, Joan B., and Judith S. Wallerstein. 1976. "The Effects of Parental Divorce: Experiences of the Child in Early Latency." *American Journal of Orthopsychiatry* 46:20–32. [16]

Kephart, William M. 1982. *Extraordinary Groups: The Sociology of Unconventional Life-Styles*. New York: St. Martin's Press. [8]

Kerckhoff, Alan, Richard T. Campbell, and Idee Winfield-Lourd. 1985. "Social Mobility in Great Britain and the United States." *American Journal of Sociology* 91:281–308. [11]

Kerckhoff, Alan C., and Robert A. Jackson. 1982. "Types of Education and the Occupational Attainments of Young Men." *Social Forces* 61:24–45. [17]

Kern, Rosemary Gibson, and Susan R. Windham, with Paula Griswold. 1986. *Medicaid and Other Experiments in State Health Policy*. Washington, DC: American Enterprise Institute for Public Policy Research. [19]

Kerr, Donna. 1983. "Teaching Competence and Teacher Education in the United States." *Teachers College Record* 81:525–552. [17]

Kerr, Peter. 1987. "Drug Smugglers: New Breed of Ethnic Gangs." *New York Times* (March 21):A1, 31. [7]

Kessen, William (ed.). 1975. *Children in China*. New Haven, CT: Yale University Press. [5]

Kessler, Ronald C. 1982. "A Disaggregation of the Relationship Between Socioeconomic Status and Psychological Distress." *American Sociological Review* 47:752–764. [11]

Kessler, Ronald C., and Paul D. Cleary. 1980. "Social Class and Psychological Distress." *American Sociological Review* 45:463–478. [11]

Kessler, Ronald C., James S. House, J. Blake Turner. 1987. "Unemployment and Health in a Community Sample." *Journal of Health and Social Behavior* 28 (March):51–59. [19]

Kett, Joseph F. 1977. *Rites of Passage: Adolescence in America 1790 to the Present*. New York: Basic Books. [6]

Keyfitz, Nathan. 1981. "Statistics, Law and Census Reporting." *Society* (January–February):5–12. [10]

Kidron, Michael, and Ronald Segal. 1987. *The New State of the World Atlas* (rev. ed.). New York: Simon & Schuster. [11]

King, John Leslie, and Kenneth L. Kraemer. 1987. *The Dynamics of Computing*. New York: Columbia University Press. [22]

King, Wayne, and Warren Weaver, Jr. 1986. "Briefing: Alarming Words." *New York Times* (October 8):B10. [17]

Klein, Ethel. 1984. *Gender Politics: From Consciousness to Mass Politics*. Cambridge, MA: Harvard University Press. [12, 21]

Klemesrud, Judy. 1980. "A Wife's Role in Big Decisions." *New York Times* (November 13):68. [16]

Kling, R., and W. Scacchi. 1982. "The Web of Computing: Computer Technology as Social Organization." *Advances in Computers* 21:1–90. [22]

Knight, Robin. 1983. "Another Deadly Famine Stalks Black Africa." *U.S. News & World Report* (August 22):27. [10]

Koblinsky, Sally A., and Alan I. Sugawara. 1984. "Nonsexist Curricula, Sex of Teacher, and Children's Sex-Role Learning." *Sex Roles* 10 (5/6):357–367. [12]

Kohn, Melvin L. 1981. "Personality, Occupation, and Social Stratification: A Frame of Reference." In D. J. Treiman and R. V. Robinson (eds.), *Research in Social Stratification and Mobility: A Research Annual* (vol. 1):276–297. Greenwich, CT: JAI Press. [5]

Kohn, Melvin L. 1976. "Occupational Structure and Alienation." *American Journal of Sociology* 82 (July):111–130. [5]

Kohn, Melvin L. 1959. "Social Class and Parental Values." *American Journal of Sociology* 64 (January):337–351. [5]

Kohn, Melvin L., and Carmi Schooler. 1983. *Work and Personality: An Inquiry into the Impact of Social Stratification*. Norwood, NJ: Ablex. [5]

Kohn, Melvin L., and Carmi Schooler. 1978. "The Reciprocal Effects of the Substantive Complexities of Work and Intellectual Flexibility: A Longitudinal Assessment." *American Journal of Sociology* 84 (July):24–52. [5]

Kornhauser, William. 1961. "'Power Elite' or 'Veto Groups'?" In S. M. Lipset and L. Lowenthal (eds.), *Cultural and Social Character*. Peoria, IL: Free Press. [14]

Kottak, Conrad Phillip. 1987. *Anthropology* (4th ed.). New York: Random House. [12]

Krohn, Marvin D., William F. Skinner, James L. Massey, and Ronald L. Akers. 1985. "Social Learning Theory and Adolescent Cigarette Smoking: A Longitudinal Study." *Social Problems* 32 (5):455–471. [7]

Krosnick, Jon A., and Charles M. Judd. 1982. "Transition in Social Influence at Adolescence: Who Induces Cigarette Smoking?" *Developmental Psychology* 18:359–368. [5]

Kübler-Ross, Elisabeth. 1969. *On Death and Dying*. New York: Macmillan. [6]

Kuhn, Thomas S. 1970. *The Structure of Scientific Revolutions*. Chicago: University of Chicago Press. [20]

Kumar, Krishan. 1978. *Prophecy and Progress: The Sociology of Industrial and Post-Industrial Society*. London, England: Allen Lane. [22]

Kurdek, Lawrence A., and Albert E. Siesky. 1980. "Children's Perception of Their Parents' Divorce." *Journal of Divorce* 3 (Summer):339–378. [16]

Lacayo, Richard. 1987. "Considering the Alternatives." *Time* (February 2):60–61. [7]

Ladd, Everett Carl. 1982. "The Freeze Framework." *Public Opinion* 5 (August–September):20, 41. [21]

Ladd, Everett Carl, Jr., and Charles D. Hadley. 1975. *Transformation of the American Party System*. New York: W. W. Norton. [14]

Ladner, Joyce A. 1986. "Teenage Pregnancy: The Implications for Black Americans." In J. D. Williams (ed.), *The State of Black America*, pp. 65–84. New York: National Urban League. [16]

Lamb, Michael E. 1977. "The Effect of Divorce on Children's Personality Development." *Journal of Divorce* 1 (Winter):163–174a. [16]

Lamb, Michael E., M. Ann Easterbrooks, and George W. Holden. 1980. "Reinforcement and Punishment among Preschoolers: Characteristics, Effects, and Correlates." *Child Development* 51:1230–1236. [12]

Landes, David S. 1969. *The Unbound Prometheus: Technological Change and Industrial Development in Western Europe from 1750 to the Present*. Cambridge, England: Cambridge University Press. [15]

Landon, Kenneth. 1986. *Dossier Society*. New York: Columbia University Press. [22]

Langlois, J. H., and C. Stephen. 1977. "The Effects of Physical Attractiveness and Ethnicity on Children's Behavioral Attributes and Peer Preferences." *Child Development* 48:1694–1698. [5]

Langlois, Simon. 1977. "Les Reseaux Personnels et la Diffusion des Informations sur les Emplois." *Recherches Sociographiques* 2:213–245. [3]

Larson, Magali Sarfalti. 1977. *The Rise of Professionalism: A Sociological Analysis*. Berkeley: University of California Press. [19]

Laslett, Peter. 1974. *Household and Family in the Past Time*. New York: Cambridge University Press. [16]

Latané, B., K. Williams, and S. Harkins. 1979. "Many Hands Make Light the Work: The Causes and Consequences of Social Loafing." *Journal of Social Psychology* 37:822–832. [2]

Laumann, Edward O., and David Knoke. 1986. "Social Network Theory." In S. Lindenberg et al. (eds.), *Approaches to Social Theory*, pp. 83–104. New York: Russell Sage Foundation. [3]

Laumann, Edward O., and Franz U. Pappi. 1976. *Networks of Collective Action: A Perspective on Community Influence Systems*. New York: Academic Press. [3]

Leacock, Eleanor. 1969. *Teaching and Learning in City Schools*. New York: Basic Books. [17]

Leahy, Robert L. 1983. "Development of Self and the Problems of Social Cognition: Identity Formation and Depression." In L. Wheeler and P. Shaver (eds.), *Review of Personality and Social Psychology* (vol. 4). Beverly Hills, CA: Sage. [5]

Leahy, Robert L., and Stephen R. Shirk. 1985. "Social Cognition and the Development of Self." In R. L. Leahy (ed.), *The Development of Self*. New York: Academic Press. [5]

Le Bon, Gustave. 1895/1960. *The Crowd: A Study of the Popular Mind*. New York: Viking. [21]

Lee, Richard B. 1979. *The Kung San: Men, Women and Work in a Foraging Society*. New York: Cambridge University Press. [3]

Lee, Valerie. 1985. *Access to Higher Education: The Experience of Blacks, Hispanics, and Low Socio-Economic Status Whites*. Washington, DC: American Council on Education, Division of Policy Analysis and Research. [17]

LeGates, Richard T., and Chester Hartman. 1986. "The Anatomy of Displacement in the United States." In N. Smith and P. Williams (eds.), *Gentrification of the City*. Winchester, MA: Allen and Unwin. [9]

Leiss, W., S. Kline, and S. Jhelly. 1986. *Social Communication in Advertising: Persons, Products, and Images of Well-Being*. Toronto: Methuen. [4]

Lelyveld, J. 1985. *Move Your Shadow: South Africa, Black and White*. New York: Times Books. [13]

Lenski, Gerhard E. 1966. *Power and Privilege: A Theory of Social Stratification*. New York: McGraw-Hill. [11]

Lenski, Gerhard, and Jean Lenski. 1987. *Human Societies: An Introduction to Macrosociology* (5th ed.). New York: McGraw-Hill. [22]

Lenski, Gerhard, and Jean Lenski. 1982. *Human Societies: An Introduction to Macrosociology* (4th ed.). New York: McGraw-Hill. [3]

Lenz, Elinor, and Barbara Myerhoff. 1985. *The Feminization of America*. Los Angeles: Jeremy P. Tarcher. [12]

Levinson, Daniel J. 1978. *The Seasons of a Man's Life*. New York: Knopf. [6]

Levinson, S. C. 1983. *Pragmatics*. New York: Cambridge University Press. [4]

Levitan, Sar A., and Isaac Shapiro. 1988. *Working But Poor: America's Contradiction*. Baltimore, MD: The Johns Hopkins University Press. [15]

Levitt, Jane. 1986. "The Corporation of Health Care." In S. Jonas (ed.), *Health Care Delivery in the United States*. New York: Springer. [19]

Levy, Frank. 1987. *Dollar and Dreams: The Changing American Income Distribution*. New York: Russell Sage Foundation. [11]

Lewin, Tamar. 1987. "Sudden Nurse Shortage Threatens Hospital Care." *New York Times* (July 7):A1, A19. [12]

Lewin, Tamar. 1984. "A New Push to Raise Women's Pay." *New York Times* (January 1):F1–F15. [12]

Lewis, Flora. 1979a. "Basis of the New Moslem Fervor Seen as Rejection of Alien Values." First article in a series: "Upsurge in Islam." *New York Times* (December 28):A1, A6. [18]

Lewis, Flora. 1979b. "Students and the Young Leading Moslem Fundamentalist Revival." Second article in a series: "Upsurge in Islam." *New York Times* (December 29):A1, A4. [18]

Lewis-Beck, Michael S. 1979. "Some Economic Effects of Revolution

Models, Measurement and the Cuban Evidence." *American Journal of Sociology* 84 (March):1127–1149. [21]

Leyerle, Betty. 1984. *Moving and Shaking American Medicine: The Structure of a Socioeconomic Transformation*. Westport, CT: Greenwood Press. [19]

Lieberson, Jonathan. 1986. "Too Many People?" *New York Review* (June 26):36–42. [10]

Lieberson, Stanley. 1980. *A Piece of the Pie: Black and White Immigrants Since 1880*. Berkeley: University of California Press. [13]

Lieberson, Stanley. 1963. *Ethnic Patterns in American Cities*. New York: Free Press of Glencoe. [13]

Lieberson, Stanley. 1961. "A Societal Theory of Race Relations." *American Sociological Review* 26:902–910. [13]

Liebow, Elliot. 1967. *Tally's Corner: A Study of Negro Streetcorner Men*. Boston: Little, Brown. [3]

Light, Donald W. 1988. "Social Control and the American Health Care System." In H. E. Freeman and S. Levine (eds.), *Handbook of Medical Sociology* (4th ed.). Englewood Cliffs, NJ: Prentice Hall. [19]

Light, Donald W. 1986. "Corporate Medicine for Profit." *Scientific American* 255 (6):38–45. [19]

Light, Donald W. 1980. *Becoming Psychiatrists: The Professional Transformation of Self*. New York: W. W. Norton. [5]

Light, Donald W., Etienne Phipps, and Alfred Sorbello. 1982. "Dilemma of Comprehensive Care." *The New Physician* 31 (5):39–40. [19]

Light, Ivan. 1986. "Ethnicity and Business Enterprise." In M. M. Stolarick and M. Friedman (eds.), *Making It in America: The Role of Ethnicity in Education, Business Enterprise and Work Choices*, pp. 13–42. Lewisburg, PA: Bucknell University Press. [3]

Lightfoot, Sara Lawrence. 1983. *The Good High School: Portraits of Character and Culture*. New York: Basic Books. [17]

Lin, Nan, Walter M. Ensel, and John C. Vaugh. 1981. "Social Resources and Strength of Ties: Structural Factors in Occupational Status Attainment." *American Sociological Review* 46:393–405. [3]

Lincoln, Alan Jay, and Murray A. Straus. 1985. *Crime and the Family*. Springfield, IL: Charles C. Thomas. [16]

Lincoln, C. E. 1984. *Race, Religion, and the Continuing American Dilemma*. New York: Hill and Wang. [18]

Lindblom, C. 1977. *Politics and Markets*. New York: Basic Books. [14]

Linton, Ralph. 1947. *The Study of Man*. New York: Appleton-Century-Crofts. [3, 4]

Lipset, Seymour M., and William Schneider. 1983. *The Confidence Gap*. New York: Free Press. [14]

Lipset, Seymour Martin. 1982. "Social Mobility in Industrial Societies." *Public Opinion* 5 (June–July):41–44. [11]

Lipset, Seymour Martin. 1979. *The First New Nation: The United States in Comparative and Historical Perspective*. New York: W. W. Norton. [22]

Lipset, Seymour Martin. 1963. *Political Man*. New York: Doubleday/Anchor. [14]

Lloyd, Peter. 1982. *A Third World Proletariat?* London, England: George, Allen and Unwin. [11]

Loar, R. Michael. 1984. "National Trends in Jewish Ethnicity: A Test of the Polarization Hypothesis." *Journal for the Scientific Study of Religion* 23 (June):140–154. [18]

Lofland, John, and Rodney Stark. 1965. "Becoming a World Saver: A

Theory of Conversion to a Deviant Perspective." *American Sociological Review* 30.865–875. [18]

Logan, Charles H. 1985. "Incarceration, Inc.: The Privitization of Prisons." Paper presented at the Society for Study of Social Problems annual meeting, Washington, DC, August 23–26. [7]

Lomnitz, Larissa Adler. 1977. *Networks and Marginality: Life in a Mexican Shantytown*. New York: Academic Press. [3]

Longshore, Douglas, and Jeffrey Prager. 1985. "The impact of school desegregation: A situational analysis." *Annual Review of Sociology* 11:75–91. [13]

Lorence, Jon, and Jeylan T. Mortimer. 1985. "Job Involvement Through the Life Course: A Panel Study of Three Age Groups." *American Sociological Review* 50:618–638. [5]

Louis, Arthur M. 1973. "The New Rich of the Seventies." *Fortune* 88 (September):170–175. [11]

Lowenthal, Marjorie F., Majda Thurnher, and David Chiriboga. 1975. *Four Stages of Life*. San Francisco: Jossey-Bass. [6]

Luckmann, Thomas. 1967. *The Invisible Religion*. New York: Macmillan. [18]

Lucy, John. 1988. "Grammatical Categories and Cognitive Processes: An Historical, Theoretical, and Empirical Re-Evaluation of the Linguistic Relativity Hypothesis." Unpublished Ph.D. dissertation, University of Chicago. [4]

Luhmann, Niklas. 1986. *Love as Passion*. Cambridge, MA: Harvard University Press. [1, 16]

Lyon, David. 1988. *The Information Society: Facts and Fantasies*. Cambridge, England: Polity Press. [22]

Lyon, Eleanor. 1986. "The Economics of Gender." In F. Boudreau, R. Sennett, and M. Wilson (eds.), *Sex Roles and Social Patterns*. New York: Praeger. [12]

Maccoby, Eleanor E. 1978. "Current Changes in the Family and Their Impact upon the Socialization of Children." In J. M. Yinger and S. J. Cutler (eds.), *Major Social Issues*. New York: Free Press. [16]

Maccoby, Eleanor E., and Carol N. Jacklin. 1980. "Sex Differences in Aggression: A Rejoinder and Reprise." *Child Development* 51:964–980. [12]

Maccoby, Eleanor E., and Carol N. Jacklin. 1974. *The Psychology of Sex Differences*. Stanford, CA: Stanford University Press. [12]

Macpherson, C. B. 1974. *The Theory of Possessive Individualism*. New York: Cambridge University Press. [4]

Madron, Thomas William. 1979. "Political Parties in the 1980s." *The Futurist* 12 (6):465–475. [14]

Magaziner, Ira C., and Robert Reich. 1983. *Minding America's Business*. New York: Vintage. [11]

Mahler, Halfdan. 1981. "The Meaning of 'Health for All by the Year 2000.'" *World Health Forum* 2:5–22. [19]

Mahler, Halfdan. 1980. "People." *Scientific American* 243 (September):67–77. [19]

Mann, Carol. 1984. "Sacrificing a Social Life for Sport." *Women's Sports* (September):20. [12]

Mann, Dale. 1986. "Can We Help Dropouts: Thinking About the Undoable." *Teachers College Record* 87 (3):307–323. [17]

Mann, James. 1983. "Protestants Shift from Issues to Prayer." *U.S. News & World Report* (April 4):36–38. [18]

Mann, James. 1980. "Old-Time Religion on the Offensive." *U.S. News & World Report* (April 7):40–42. [18]

Mann, Michael. 1986. *The Sources of Social Power* (vol. 1). New York: Cambridge University Press. [14]

Mansbridge, Jane J. 1986. *Why We Lost the ERA*. Chicago: University of Chicago Press. [12]

Mare, Robert D. 1981. "Change and Stability in Educational Stratification." *American Sociological Review* 46:72–87. [17]

Marger, Martin N. 1981. *Elites and Masses*. New York: D. Van Nostrand. [11]

Markle, Gerald E., and James C. Petersen. 1987. "Resolution of the Laetrile Controversy: Past Attempts and Future Prospects." In H. T. Engelhardt, Jr., and A. L. Caplan (eds.), *Scientific Controversies*, pp. 315–332. Cambridge, England: Cambridge University Press. [20]

Markoff, John. 1988. "Wider Threat to Privacy Seen as Computer Memories Grow." *New York Times* (June 1):A1, C10. [22]

Markusen, Ann. 1985. *Profit Cycles, Oligopoly & Regional Development*. Cambridge, MA: MIT Press. [15]

Marsden, Peter V., and Jeanne S. Hurlbert. 1986. "Social Resources and Mobility Outcomes: A Replication and Extension." Unpublished paper. (A prior version of this paper was presented at the Fifth Sunbelt Social Network Conference, February 1985.) [3]

Marshall, S. L. 1947. *Men Against Fire*. New York: William Morrow. [14]

Marshall, Susan E. 1985. "Ladies Against Women: Mobilization Dilemmas of Anti-Feminist Movements." *Social Problems* 32 (4):348–362. [21]

Martin, David. 1978. *A General Theory of Secularization*. New York: Harper & Row. [18]

Marty, Martin E. 1985. "Transpositions: American Religion in the 1980s." *AAPSS Annals* 480 (July):11–23. [18]

Marty, Martin E. 1984. *Pilgrims in Their Own Land: 500 Years of Religion in America*. New York: Penguin. [18]

Marwick, Arthur. 1980. *Class: Image and Reality in Britain, France and the USA Since 1930*. New York: Oxford University Press. [11]

Marx, Gary. 1987. "The New Surveillance." *Technological Review* 88:42–48. [22]

Marx, Karl. 1852/1979. "The Eighteenth Brumaire of Louis Bonaparte." In *Collected Works* (vol. 11):99–197. London, England: Lawrence and Wishart. [11]

Marx, Karl. 1867/1976. *Capital* (vol. 1). B. Fowkes (trans.). Harmondsworth, England: Penguin. [11]

Marx, Karl. 1845/1975. "The Holy Family." In R. Dixon and C. Dult (trans.), *Collected Works* (vol. 4). London, England: Lawrence and Wishart. [11]

Marx, Karl, and Friedrich Engels. 1848/1976. "Manifesto of the Communist Party." In *Collected Works* (vol. 6). London, England: Lawrence and Wishart. [22]

Marx, Karl, and Friedrich Engels. 1848/1967. *Communist Manifesto*. New York: Pantheon. [15]

Masnick, George, and Mary Jo Bane. 1980. "The Nation's Families, 1960–1990." Cambridge, MA: Joint Center for Urban Studies of MIT and Harvard University. [16]

Massey, Douglas S. 1981. "Dimensions of the New Immigration to the United States and the Prospects for Assimilation." *Annual Review of Sociology* 7:57–85. [10]

Mayes, Sharon S. 1979. "Women in Positions of Authority: A Case

Study of Changing Sex Roles." *Journal of Women in Culture and Society* 4 (3):556–568. [12]

Mayhew, Bruce H. 1980. "Structuralism versus Individualism: Part 1, Shadowboxing in the Dark." *Social Forces* 59 (December):335–375. [3]

Mayr, Ernest. 1988. *Toward a New Philosophy of Biology: Observations of an Evolutionist.* Cambridge, MA: Belknap Press of Harvard University Press. [22]

Mays, Vickie M., and Susan D. Cochran. 1987. "Acquired Immunodeficiency Syndrome and Black Americans: Special Psychosocial Issues." *Public Health Reports* 102 (2):224–231. [19]

McAdam, Doug. 1982. *Political Process and the Development of Black Insurgency.* Chicago: University of Chicago Press. [21]

McCarthy, John D., and Mayer N. Zald. 1977. "Resource Mobilization and Social Movements: A Partial Theory." *American Journal of Sociology* 82:1212–1241. [21]

McCarthy, John D., and Mayer N. Zald. 1973. *The Trend of Social Movements in America.* Morristown, NJ: General Learning Press. [21]

McDermott, Joan. 1983. "Crime in the Schools and the Community: Offenders, Victims, and Fearful Youths." *Crime and Deliquency* 29:270–282. [17]

McDowell, Edwin. 1982. "'Silent Spring,' 20 Years a Milestone." *New York Times* (September 27):C16. [21]

McKeon, Nancy. 1985. "Consuming Passions." *New York* (May 13):62–68. [9]

McLanahan, Sara S. 1983. "Family Structure and Stress: A Longitudinal Comparison of Two-Parent and Female-Headed Families." *Journal of Marriage and the Family* 45:347–357. [16]

McLemore, S. Dale. 1983. *Racial and Ethnic Relations in America* (2nd ed.). Boston: Allyn and Bacon. [13]

McMichael, Philip. 1984. *Settlers and the Agrarian Question.* Cambridge, England: Cambridge University Press. [22]

McNeill, William H. 1982. *The Pursuit of Power.* Chicago: University of Chicago Press. [14]

Mead, George Herbert. 1934. *Mind, Self and Society.* Chicago: University of Chicago Press. [1, 5]

Mead, Margaret. 1935/1963. *Sex and Temperament in Three Primitive Societies.* New York: William Morrow. [12]

Mechanic, David. 1986. *From Advocacy to Allocation: The Evolving American Health Care System.* New York: Free Press. [19]

Medalia, Nehum Z., and Otto N. Larson. 1958. "Diffusion and Belief in a Collective Delusion: The Seattle Windshield Pitting Epidemic." *American Sociological Review* 23:221–232. [21]

Melville, Keith. 1980. *Marriage and Family Today.* New York: Random House. [16]

Menken, Jane. 1985. "Age and Fertility—How Late Can You Wait?" *Demography* 22 (4):469–483. [16]

Merton, Robert K. 1973a. "The Normative Structure of Science." In R. K. Merton (ed.), *The Sociology of Science.* pp. 267–278. Chicago: University of Chicago Press. [20]

Merton, Robert K. 1973b. "Singletons and Multiples in Science." In R. K. Merton (ed.), *The Sociology of Science.* Chicago: University of Chicago Press. [20]

Merton, Robert. 1968a. *Social Theory and Social Structure.* New York: Free Press. [3, 8]

Merton, Robert K. 1968b. "Social Problems and Social Theory." In R. Merton and R. Nisbet (eds.), *Contemporary Social Problems,* p. 447. New York: Harcourt, Brace and World. [17]

Meyrowitz, J. 1985. *No Sense of Place: The Impact of Electronic Media on Social Behavior.* New York: Oxford University Press. [4]

Michels, Robert. 1915/1949. *First Lectures in Political Science.* A. de Grazia (trans.). Minneapolis: University of Minnesota Press. [14]

Milgram, Stanley. 1970. "The Experience of Living in Cities." *Science* 167 (March 13):1461–1468. [9]

Mills, C. Wright. 1959/1970. *The Sociological Imagination.* New York: Pelican. [1]

Mills, C. Wright. 1959. *The Power Elite.* New York: Oxford University Press. [14]

Mills, C. Wright. 1958. "The Structure of Power in American Society." *British Journal of Sociology* 9 (March):29–41. [14]

Mintz, Beth, and Michael Schwartz. 1981. "Interlocking Directorates and Interest Group Formation." *American Sociological Review* 46:851–869. [15]

Mitchell, J. Clyde. 1969. *Social Networks in Urban Situations.* Manchester, England: Manchester University Press. [3]

Mitroff, Ian, Richard Mason, and Vincent Barbara. 1983. *The 1980 Census: Policymaking Amid Turbulence.* Lexington, MA: Lexington Books. [10]

Molotch, Harvey. 1976. "The City as a Growth Machine: Toward a Political Economy of Place." *American Journal of Sociology* 82 (2):309–332. [9]

Molotsky, Irvin. 1988. "Senate Approves Bill for Japanese Americans." *New York Times* (April 21):A1, A23. [13]

Money, John, and Patricia Tucker. 1975. *Sexual Signatures: On Being a Man or a Woman.* Boston: Little, Brown. [12]

Moore, Barrington, Jr. 1979. *Injustice: The Social Bases of Obedience and Revolt.* White Plains, NY: M. E. Sharpe. [14]

Morgan, Michael. 1982. "Television and Adolescents' Sex Role Stereotypes: A Longitudinal Study." *Journal of Personality and Social Psychology* 43 (5):947–955. [12]

Morgenthau, Hans J., and Kenneth W. Thompson. 1985. *Politics Among Nations* (6th rev. ed). New York: Knopf. [1]

Morrisroe, Patricia. 1985. "The New Class." *New York* (May 13):34–39. [9]

Mortimer, Jeylan T., Jon Lorence, and Donald S. Kumka. 1986. *Work, Family, and Personality: Transition to Adulthood.* Norwood, NJ: Ablex. [5]

Mortimer, Jeylan T., and Roberta G. Simmons. 1978. "Adult Socialization." In R. H. Turner, J. Coleman, and R. C. Fox (eds.), *Annual Review of Sociology* (vol. 4). Palo Alto, CA: Annual Reviews. [5]

Mosca, Gaetano. 1939. *The Ruling Class.* New York: McGraw-Hill. [14]

Mueller, Carol, and Thomas Dimieri. 1982. "The Structure of Belief Systems among Contending ERA Activists." *Social Forces* 60:657–675. [21]

Mulkay, Michael J. 1976. "Norms and Ideology in Science." *Social Science Information* 15 (4/5):637–656. [20]

Mulkay, Michael J. 1969. "Some Aspects of Cultural Growth in the Natural Sciences." *Social Research* 36 (1):22–52. [20]

Murdock, George Peter. 1949. *Social Structure.* New York: Macmillan. [16]

Murdock, George Peter. 1945. "The Common Denominator of Cultures." In R. Linton (ed.), *The Science of Man in World Crisis.* New York: Columbia University Press. [4]

Murray, Charles. 1984. *Losing Ground: American Social Policy, 1950–80.* New York: Basic Books. [14]

Musgrove, Philip. 1987. "The Economic Crisis and Its Impact on Health and Health Care in Latin America and the Caribbean." *International Journal of Health Services* 17 (3):411–441. [19]

Myers, Jerome K., Jacob J. Lindenthal, and Max P. Pepper. 1974. "Social Class, Life Events and Psychiatric Symptoms: A Longitudinal Study." In B. P. and B. S. Dohrenwend (eds.), *Stressful Life Events*. New York: Wiley. [11]

Myrdal, Gunnar. 1973. "How Scientific are the Social Sciences?" *Bulletin of Atomic Scientists* 29 (January):31–37. [2]

Nader, Ralph, M. Green, and J. Seligman. 1976. *Taming the Giant Corporation*. New York: W. W. Norton. [15]

NAEP (National Assessment of Educational Progress). 1979. *Changes in Mathematical Achievement, 1973–1978*. Denver: Educational Commission of the States. [17]

Nash, Nathaniel C. 1987. "Call Mounts for Curbs on Markets." *New York Times* (February 14):33, 37. [7]

National Center for Health Statistics. 1988. *Monthly Vital Statistics Report: Births, Marriages, Divorces and Deaths for 1987* 36 (March). [16]

National Center for Health Statistics. 1987. *Morbidity and Mortality Weekly Report* 36 (January 16):1–12. [11]

National Commission on Excellence in Education. 1983. *A Nation at Risk*. Washington, DC: U.S. Government Printing Office. [17]

National Institute of Education. 1978. "Violent Schools—Safe Schools." Washington, DC: U.S. Department of Health, Education and Welfare. [17]

National Institute of Mental Health. 1982. *Television and Behavior: Ten Years of Scientific Progress and Implications for the Eighties* (vols. 1 and 2). Washington, DC: U.S. Government Printing Office. [5]

Natriello, Gary, Aaron M. Pallas, Edward L. McDill. 1986. "Taking Stock: Renewing Our Research Agenda on the Causes and Consequences of Dropping Out." *Teachers College Review* 87 (3):430–440. [17]

Nelkin, Dorothy. 1982. "Controversy as a Political Challenge." In B. Barnes and D. Edge (eds.), *Science in Context*, pp. 276–280. Cambridge, MA: MIT Press. [20]

Nelkin, Dorothy. 1975. "The Political Impact of Technical Expertise." *Social Studies of Science* 5:35–54. [20]

Nemerowicz, Gloria Morris. 1984. *Children's Perception of Gender and Work Roles*. New York: Praeger. [12]

Neugarten, Bernice L., and Dail A. Neugarten. 1987. "The Changing Meanings of Age." *Psychology Today* 21 (5):29–33. [6]

Neuman, W. Russell. 1986. *The Paradox of Mass Politics: Knowledge and Opinion in the American Electorate*. Cambridge, MA: Harvard University Press. [14]

New York Times. 1988. "Reagan's remarks to students" (June 1):A12. [22]

Newman, William M. 1973. *American Pluralism: A Study of Minority Groups and Social Theory*. New York: Harper & Row. [13]

Nisbet, Robert, and Robert G. Perrin. 1977. *The Social Bond* (2nd ed.). New York: Knopf. [3]

Noble, David F. 1984. *Forces of Production*. New York: Knopf. [15, 22]

Noel, Donald L. (ed.). 1972. *The Origins of American Slavery and Racism*. Columbus, OH: Charles E. Merrill. [13]

Novak, William. 1981. "From Somerville to Savannah . . . and Los Angeles . . . and Dayton." *Moment* 6 (January–February).17–24. [18]

Noyce, Robert N. 1979. "Hardware Prospects and Limitations." In M. L. Dertouzos and J. Moses (eds.), *The Computer Age: A Twenty-Year View*, pp. 321–337. Cambridge, MA: MIT Press. [22]

O'Connor, James. 1973. *The Fiscal Crisis of the State*. New York: St. Martin's Press. [14]

O'Hare, William. 1986. "The Eight Myths of Poverty." *American Demographics* 8 (May):22–25. [11]

O'Keefe, Eileen S. C., and Janet Shibley Hyde. 1983. "The Development of Occupational Sex-Role Stereotypes: The Effects of Gender Stability and Age." *Sex-Roles* 9 (4):481–492. [12]

O'Kelly, R., and P. Carney. 1986. *Women and Men in Society*. Belmont, CA: Wadsworth. [12]

O'Rourke, David K. 1983. "Revolution and Alienation in the American Church." *Commonweal* CX:76–79. [18]

Offe, Claus. 1985. *Disorganized Capitalism: Contemporary Transformations of Work and Politics*. J. Keane (trans.). Cambridge, MA: MIT Press. [14]

Offe, Claus. 1984. *Contradictions of the Welfare State*. J. Keane (ed.). Cambridge, MA: MIT Press. [14]

Ohrnial, T. (ed.). 1984. *Limited Liability and the Corporation*. London, England: Croom Helm. [15]

Okun, Lewis. 1986. *Woman Abuse*. Albany: State University of New York Press. [16]

Ole Saitoti, Tepilit, and Carol Beckwith. 1980. *Masai*. New York: Harry N. Abrams. [6]

Olneck, Michael R., and David B. Bills. 1980. "What Makes Sammy Run? An Empirical Assessment of the Bowles-Gintis Correspondence Theory." *American Journal of Education* 89:27–61. [17]

Olsen, Marvin (ed.). 1970. *Power in Societies*. New York: Macmillan. [14]

Olson, M. 1965. *The Theory of Collective Goods*. Cambridge, MA: Harvard University Press. [14]

Omond, Roger. 1986. *The Apartheid Handbook*. London, England: Penguin. [13]

Opie, Iona, and Peter Opie. 1959. *The Lore and Language of Schoolchildren*. Oxford, England: Oxford University Press. [5]

Orfield, Gary. 1983. *Public School Desegregation in the United States, 1968–1980*. Washington, DC: Joint Center for Political Studies. [17]

Orwell, George. 1933/1972. *Down and Out in Paris and London*. San Diego, CA: Harcourt Brace Jovanovich. [3]

Osborn, Ronald E. 1978. *Experiment in Liberty*. St. Louis, MO: Bethany Press. [22]

Osofsky, Gilbert. 1966. *The Making of a Ghetto*. New York: Harper & Row. [9]

Oxford Analytica. 1986. *America in Perspective: Major Trends in the United States Through the 1990s*. Boston: Houghton Mifflin. [4, 10, 13]

Page, Benjamin I. 1983. *Who Gets What from Government*. Berkeley: University of California Press. [11]

Palen, J. John. 1986. *The Urban World* (3rd ed.). New York: McGraw-Hill. [9]

Paludi, Michele A., and Dominic F. Gullo. 1986. "The Effect of Sex Labels on Adults' Knowledge of Infant Development." *Sex Roles* 16 (1/2):19–30. [12]

Paradiso, Louis V., and Shauvan M. Wall. 1986. "Children's Perceptions of Male and Female Principals and Teachers." *Sex Roles* 14 (1/2):1–7. [12]

Pareto, Vilfredo. 1916/1935. *The Mind and Society.* A. Bongiorno and A. Livingston (trans.). New York: Harcourt Brace Jovanovich. [14]

Park, Robert E., Ernest W. Burgess, and Roderick D. McKenzie (eds.). 1925. *The City.* Chicago: University of Chicago Press. [9, 13]

Parkin, Frank. 1976. *Marxism and Class Theory: A Bourgeois Critique.* New York: Columbia University Press. [1, 11]

Parkin, Frank. 1971. *Class Inequality and Political Order: Social Stratification in Capitalist and Communist Societies.* New York: Praeger. [11]

Parkinson, C. Northcote. 1957. *Parkinson's Law.* Boston: Houghton Mifflin. [8]

Parsons, Talcott. 1977. *The Evolution of Societies.* Englewood Cliffs, NJ: Prentice Hall. [22]

Parsons, Talcott. 1960. *Structure and Process in Modern Societies.* New York: Free Press. [14]

Parsons, Talcott. 1959. "The Social Class as a Social System: Some of Its Functions in American Society." *Harvard Educational Review* 29 (Fall):297–318. [5, 17]

Pear, Robert. 1987. "Women Reduce Lag in Earnings but Disparities with Men Remain." *New York Times* (September 4). [12]

Pear, Robert. 1986. "6.2 Billion World Population Foretold by 2000." *New York Times* (December 22):A7. [10]

Pear, Robert. 1983. "Administration Balks at Cost of Amnesty for Illegal Aliens." *New York Times* (April 30):8. [10]

Pebley, Anne R., and David E. Bloom. 1982. "Childless Americans." *American Demographics* 4 (January):18–21. [16]

Pendleton, Brian F., Margaret M. Poloma, and T. Neal Garland. 1980. "Scales for Investigation of the Dual Career Family." *Journal of Marriage and the Family* 42 (2):269–275. [16]

Pescosolido, Bernice A., and Robert Mendelsohn. 1986. "Social Causation or Social Construction of Suicide? An Investigation into the Social Organization of Official Rates." *American Sociological Review* 51:80–101. [2]

Peter, Laurence F., and Raymond Hull. 1969. *The Peter Principle.* New York: William Morrow. [8]

Petersen, James C., and Gerald E. Markle. 1984. "The Laetrile Controversy." In D. Nelkin (ed.), *Controversy: Politics of Technical Decisions* (2nd ed.), pp. 175–195. Beverly Hills: Sage. [20]

Peterson, Ivan. 1986. "People Moving Back to Cities, U.S. Study Says." *New York Times* (April 13):1, 12. [10]

Peterson, James L., and Nicholas Zill. 1986. "Marital Disruption, Parent-Child Relationships, and Behavior Problems in Children." *Journal of Marriage and the Family* 48:295–307. [16]

Peterson, Richard A. 1979. "Revitalizing the Culture Concept." *Annual Review of Sociology* 5:137–166. [4]

Peterson, William. 1975. *Population* (3rd ed.). New York: Macmillan. [10]

Peterson, William. 1960. "The Demographic Transition in the Netherlands." *American Sociological Review* 25:334–347. [10]

Pettigrew, Thomas F., and Robert L. Green. 1976. "School Desegregation in Large Cities: A Critique of the Coleman 'White Flight' Thesis." *Harvard Educational Review* 46:1–53. [17]

Phillips, David P. 1986. "The Found Experiment: A New Technique for Assessing the Impact of Mass Media Violence on Real-World Aggressive Behavior." In G. Comstock (ed.), *Public Communication and Behavior* (vol. 1). San Diego, CA: Academic Press. [2]

Phillips, David P. 1974. "The Influence of Suggestion on Suicide: Substantive and Theoretical Implications of the Werther Effect." *American Sociological Review* 39:340–354. [2]

Phillips, David P., and Lundie L. Carstensen. 1986. "Clustering of Teenage Suicides After Television and News Stories About Suicide." *New England Journal of Medicine* 315 (September 11):685–689. [2]

Pickering, Andrew. 1984. *Constructing Quarks: A Sociological History of Particle Physics.* Chicago: University of Chicago Press. [20]

Pillemer, Karl A. 1986. "Risk Factors in Elder Abuse: Results From a Case-Control Study." In K. A. Pillemer and R. S. Wolf (eds.), *Elder Abuse: Conflict in the Family,* pp. 239–263. Dover, MA: Auburn House. [16]

Pincus, Fred L. 1980. "The False Promises of Community Colleges: Class Conflict and Vocational Education." *Harvard Educational Review* 50 (August):332–361. [17]

Pinkney, Alphonse. 1987. *Black Americans* (3rd ed.). Englewood Cliffs, NJ: Prentice Hall. [13]

Piore, M., and Charles Sabel. 1985. *The Second Industrial Divide.* New York: Basic Books. [3]

Pirages, Dennis, and Paul R. Ehrlich. 1974. *Ark II: Social Responses to Environmental Imperatives.* San Francisco, CA: W. H. Freeman. [21]

Pleck, Joseph. 1983. "Men's Power with Women, Other Men, and Society: A Men's Movement Analysis." In L. Richardson and V. Taylor (eds.), *Feminist Frontiers.* Reading, MA: Addison-Wesley. [12]

Pleck, Joseph. 1977. "The work-family role system." *Social Problems* 24:417–427. [12]

Plog, Fred, Clifford J. Jolly, and Daniel G. Bates. 1976. *Anthropology: Decisions, Adaptation, and Evolution.* New York: Knopf. [22]

Polenberg, Richard. 1980. *One Nation Divisible.* New York: Viking. [13]

Pomper, Gerald. 1980. *Party Renewal in America.* New York: Praeger. [14]

Portes, Alejandro. 1985. *Latin Journey: Cuban and Mexican Immigrants in the United States.* Berkeley, CA: University of California Press. [13]

Postman, Neil. 1986. *Amusing Ourselves to Death.* New York: Penguin. [4]

Postman, Neil. 1979. *Teaching as a Conserving Activity.* New York: Delacorte. [5]

Poulantzas, Nicos. 1975. *Classes in Contemporary Capitalism.* London, England: New Left Books. [11]

Poulantzas, Nicos. 1974. *Political Power and Social Classes.* London, England: New Left Books. [22]

Powell, Michael J. 1985. "Developments in the Regulations of Lawyers: Competing Segments, and Market, Client, and Government Controls." *Social Forces* 64 (2):281–305. [15]

Powers, Charles. 1981. "Role Imposition and Role Improvisation: Some Theoretical Principles." *The Economic and Social Review* 12:287–299. [3]

Press, Irwin. 1984. "The Predisposition to File Claims: The Patient's Perspective." *Law, Medicine and Health Care* 12 (2):53–62. [19]

Preston, Samuel F. 1984. "Children and the Elderly: Divergent Paths for America's Dependents." *Demography* 21 (4):435–457. [6, 16]

Price, David. 1986. *Bringing Back the Parties.* Washington, DC: Congressional Quarterly. [14]

Princeton Religious Research Center. 1986. *Emerging Trends* (September). [18]

Przeworski, Adam. 1985. *Capitalism and Social Democracy.* New York: Cambridge University Press. [14]

Quadagno, Jill. 1986. "Aging." In G. Ritzer (ed.), *Social Problems* (2nd ed.). New York: Random House. [6]

Quadango, Jill. 1980. *Aging, the Individual, and Society.* New York: St. Martin's Press. [16]

Quindlen, Anna. 1987. "The drive to excel." *New York Times Magazine* (February 22):32. [13]

Rada, J. 1982. "A Third World Perspective." In G. Friedrichs and A. Schaff (eds.), *Microelectronics and Society: For Better or For Worse*, pp. 213–242. Oxford, England: Pergamon Press. [15]

Ragin, Charles, and David Zaret. 1983. "Theory and Methods in Comparative Research: Two Strategies." *Social Forces* 61:731–754. [22]

Reed, Judith. 1975. "Working with Abusive Parents." *Children Today* 4 (3):6–9. [16]

Reinhold, Robert. 1986. "Surge in Bogus Papers Predicted in Wake of Change in Alien Law." *New York Times* (October 20):A1, 24. [7]

Reisman, David. 1961. *The Lonely Crowd.* New Haven, CT: Yale University Press. [4]

"Religion in America." 1987. *The Economist* 303 (7498):23–28. [18]

Relman, Arnold S. 1980. "The New Medical-Industrial Complex." *The New England Journal of Medicine* 303:963–970. [19]

Renne, Karen S. 1970. "Correlates of Dissatisfaction in Marriage." *Journal of Marriage and the Family* 32 (1):54–67. [16]

Repetti, Rena L. 1984. "Determinants of Children's Sex Stereotyping: Parental Sex-Role Traits and Television Viewing." *Personality and Social Psychology Bulletin* 10:456–468. [12]

Report of the National Advisory Commission on Civil Disorders. 1968. Washington, DC: U.S. Government Printing Office. [21]

Rheingold, Harriet L., and Kay V. Cook. 1975. "The Contents of Boys' and Girls' Rooms as an Index of Parents' Behavior." *Child Development* 46:459–463. [12]

Richardson, James T., Mary White Stewart, and Robert B. Simmonds. 1979. *Organized Miracles: A Study of a Contemporary, Youth, Communal, Fundamentalist Organization.* New Brunswick, NJ: Transaction Books. [18]

Riesman, David, with Nathan Glazer and Reuel Denney. 1951. *The Lonely Crowd.* New Haven, CT: Yale University Press. [14]

Riley, John W., Jr. 1983. "Dying and the Meaning of Death: Sociological Inquiries." *Annual Review of Sociology* 9:191–216. [6]

Riley, Matilda W. 1987. "On the Significance of Age in Sociology." *American Sociological Review* 52 (February):1–14. [6]

Riley, Matilda W., and Anne Foner. 1968. *Aging and Society Vol. I: An Inventory of Research Findings.* New York: Russell Sage Foundation. [6]

Rimer, Sara. 1987. "At 2 schools, stubborn racial divisions." *New York Times* (March 30):1. [13]

Rindfuss, Ronald R., Larry Bumpass, and Craig St. John. 1980. "Education and Fertility: Implications for the Roles Women Occupy." *American Sociological Review* 45:431–447. [10]

Rindfuss, Ronald R., S. Phillip Morgan, and G. Swicegood. 1988. *First Births in America: Changes in the Timing of Parenthood.* Berkeley: University of California Press. [10]

Rindfuss, Ronald R., C. Gray Swicegood, and Rachel A. Rosenfeld. 1987. "Disorder in the Life Course: How Common and Does It Matter?" *American Sociological Review* 52:785–801. [6]

Risman, Barbara J., Charles T. Hill, Zick Rubin, and Letitia A. Peplau. 1981. "Living Together in College: Implications for Courtship." *Journal of Marriage and the Family* 43:77–83. [16]

Rist, Ray C. 1970. "Student Social Class and Teacher Expectations: The Self-Fulfilling Prophecy in Ghetto Education." *Harvard Educational Review* 40. [17]

Robertson, A. F. 1984. *People and the State: An Anthropology of Planned Development.* New York: Cambridge University Press. [14]

Robertson, Thomas S. 1980. "Television Advertising and Parent-Child Relations." In R. P. Adler et al. (eds.), *The Effects of Television Advertising on Children.* Lexington, MA: Lexington Books. [5]

Robey, Bryant. 1987. "Locking Up Heaven's Door." *American Demographics* 55:24–29. [10]

Robins, Kevin, and Frank Webster. 1985. "Higher education, high tech, high rhetoric." *Radical Science* 18:36–57. [22]

Rodriquez, Orlando. 1978. "Occupational Shifts and Educational Upgrading in the American Labor Force Between 1950 and 1970." *Sociology of Education* 51 (January):55–67. [17]

Roeder, Edward (ed.). 1986. *PACs Americana: The Directory of Political Action Committees and Their Interests* (2nd ed.). Washington, DC: Sunshine Services. [14]

Roethlisberger, F. J., and William J. Dickson (with the assistance and collaboration of H. A. Wright). 1961. *Management and the Worker.* Cambridge, MA: Harvard University Press. [8]

Rogers, E. M. 1986. *Communications Technology: The New Media in Society.* New York: Free Press. [4]

Rohatyn, Felix. 1987. "The Blight on Wall Street." *New York Review of Books* 34 (4):21–23. [7]

Rollins, Boyd C., and Kenneth L. Cannon. 1974. "Marital Satisfaction over the Family Life Cycle: A Reevaluation." *Journal of Marriage and the Family* 36 (2):271–283. [16]

Roof, Wade Clark, and William McKinney. 1985. "Denominational America and the New Religious Pluralism." *AAPSS Annals* 480 (July):24–39. [18]

Ropp, Theodore. 1959. *War in the Modern World.* Durham, NC: Duke University Press. [8]

Rose, Arnold M. 1967. *The Power Structure.* New York: Oxford University Press. [14, 21]

Rose, Gerry B. 1982. *Outbreaks.* New York: Free Press. [21]

Rose, Stephen J. 1986. *The American Profile Poster.* New York: Pantheon. [10]

Rosen, B., and T. Jerdee. 1978. "Perceived Sex Differences in Managerially Relevant Characteristics." *Sex Roles* 4:837–843. [12]

Rosenbaum, David E. 1977. "The Myths of Welfare." *New York Times* (May 22):3. [1]

Rosenbrock, H., et al. 1985. "A New Industrial Revolution?" In T. Forester (ed.), *The Information Technology Revolution*, pp. 635–647. Cambridge, MA: MIT Press. [22]

Rosenfeld, Anne, and Elizabeth Stark. 1987. "The Prime of Our Lives." *Psychology Today* (May):62–72. [6]

Rosenfield, Sarah. 1980. "Sex Differences in Depression: Do Women Always Have Higher Rates?" *Journal of Health and Social Behavior* 21 (1):33–42. [12]

Rosenthal, Robert, and Lenore Jacobson. 1968. *Pygmalion in the Classroom: Teacher Expectation and Pupils' Intellectual Development.* New York: Holt, Rinehart and Winston. [17]

Rosnow, Ralph L., and Gary Alan Fine. 1976. *Rumor and Gossip: The Social Psychology of Hearsay.* New York: Elsevier. [21]

Rosow, Irving. 1978. "What is a Cohort and Why?" *Human Development* 12:65–75. [6]

Rostow, Walt Whitman. 1980. *The World Economy: History and Prospect.* Austin: University of Texas Press. [22]

Rostow, Walt Whitman. 1952. *The Process of Economic Growth.* New York: W. W. Norton. [22]

Roth, Guenther, and Wolfgang Schlucter. 1979. *Max Weber's Theory of History.* Berkeley: University of California Press. [1]

Rothman, Stanley, and S. Robert Lichter. 1982. "The Nuclear Debate: Scientists, the Media and the Public." *Public Opinion* 5 (August–September):47–52. [21]

Rowdon, Maurice. 1970. *The Silver Age of Venice.* New York: Praeger. [9]

Rubenstein, Richard E. 1987. *Alchemist of Revolution: Terrorism in the Modern World.* New York: Basic Books. [14]

Rubin, Barry. 1983. "Iran's year of turmoil." *Current History* (January):28–31. [18]

Rubin, J. Z., F. J. Provenzano, and Z. Luria. 1974. "The Eye of the Beholder: Parents' Views on Sex of Newborns." *American Journal of Orthopsychiatry* 44:512–519. [12]

Rubin, K. H. 1980. "Fantasy Play: Its Role in the Development of Social Skills and Social Cognition." In K. H. Rubin (ed.), *Child's Play.* San Francisco, CA: Jossey-Bass. [5]

Rubin, Lillian. 1976. "Changing Expectations: New Sources of Strain." In *Worlds of Pain: Life in the Working-Class Family.* New York: Basic Books. [12]

Rubin, Lillian B. 1980. "Women of a Certain Age." *Society* 17 (March–April):68–76. [12]

Rubin, Lillian Breslow. 1976. *Worlds of Pain: Life in the Working-Class Family.* New York: Basic Books. [12, 16]

Rubin, Vera. 1986. "Women's Work." *Science 86* (July/August):58–65. [12]

Rubin, Z. 1980. *Children's Friendships.* Cambridge, MA: Harvard University Press. [5]

Ruble, Thomas L. 1983. "Sex Stereotypes: Issues of Change in the 1970s." *Sex Roles* 9 (3):397–402. [12]

Rueschemeyer, D., and P. B. Evans. 1985. "The State and Economic Transformation: Toward an Analysis of the Conditions Underlying Effective Intervention." In P. B. Evans, D. Rueschemeyer, and T. Skocpol (eds.), *Bringing the State Back In*, pp. 78–106. New York: Cambridge University Press. [14]

Rueschemeyer, Dietrich. 1986. *Power and the Division of Labor.* Stanford, CA: Stanford University Press. [14]

Rule, James, Douglas McAdam, Linda Stearns, and David Uglow. 1980. *The Politics of Privacy.* New York: Elsevier. [22]

Rupp, Leila J., and Verta Taylor. 1987. *Survival in the Doldrums: The American Women's Rights Movement, 1945 to the 1960s.* New York: Oxford University Press. [21]

Russell, Cheryl. 1983. "The News about Hispanics." *American Demographics* 5 (March):15–25. [13]

Russell, Cristine. 1983. "Infectious Diseases Rage On." *Washington Post* (April 28):E1. [19]

Russell, George. 1986a. "The Fall of a Wall Street Superstar." *Time* (November 24):71–72. [7]

Russell, George. 1986b. "Going After the Crooks." *Time* (December 1):48–56. [7]

Russell, Joyce E. A., Michael C. Rush, and Ann M. Herd. 1988. "An Exploration of Women's Expectations of Effective Male and Female Leadership." *Sex Roles* 18 (5/6):279–287. [12]

Rutter, Michael, et al. 1979. *Fifteen Thousand Hours.* Cambridge, MA: Harvard University Press. [17]

Ruzek, Sheryl Burt. 1978. *The Women's Health Movement: Feminist Alternatives to Medical Control.* New York: Praeger. [19]

Sabato, L. J. 1984. *PAC Power.* New York: W. W. Norton. [14]

Sabel, Charles. 1982. *Work and Politics: The Division of Labor in Industry.* Cambridge, England: Cambridge University Press. [15]

Sahlins, Marshall. 1981. *The Use and Abuse of Biology.* Ann Arbor: University of Michigan Press. [4]

Salmore, Stephen A., and Barbara G. Salmore. 1985. *Candidates, Parties, and Campaigns: Electoral Policies in America.* Washington: CQ Press. [14]

Sanday, P. R. 1974. "Female Status in the Public Domain." In M. Z. Rosaldo and L. Lampere (eds.), *Woman, Culture, and Society*, pp. 189–206. Stanford, CA: Stanford University Press. [12]

Sanoff, Alvin P. 1983. "Jews Find New Solace in the Old Traditions." *U.S. News & World Report* (April 4):43–44. [18]

Santos, Richard. 1985. *Hispanic Youth.* New York: Praeger. [13]

Sapir, Edward. 1949. *Selected Writings in Language, Culture, and Personality.* Berkeley: University of California Press. [4]

Satter, David. 1983. "Soviet Threat Is One of Ideas More than Arms." *Wall Street Journal* (May 23):22. [15]

Scarf, Maggie. 1972. "He and She: The Sex Hormones and Behavior." *New York Times Magazine* (May 7). [12]

Scarr, Sandra, and K. McCartney. 1983. "How People Make Their Own Environments: A Theory of Genotype-Environment Effects." *Child Development* 54:424–435. [5]

Schaefer, Richard T. 1984. *Racial and Ethnic Groups* (2nd ed.). Boston: Little, Brown. [13]

Schell, Jonathan. 1982. *The Fate of the Earth.* New York: Knopf. [14]

Scherer, Klaus R., and Howard Giles (eds.). 1979. *Social Markers in Speech.* New York: Cambridge University Press. [4]

Schiller, Bradley R. 1986. *The Economics of Poverty and Discrimination.* Englewood Cliffs, NJ: Prentice Hall. [1]

Schiller, Bradley R. 1981. "Welfare: Reforming Our Expectations." *The Public Interest* 62:55–65. [1]

Schlesinger, Arthur, Jr. 1979. "Crisis of the Party System." *Wall Street Journal* (May 10):22. [14]

Schlossberg, Nancy K. 1987. "Taking the Mystery Out of Change." *Psychology Today* (May):74–75. [6]

Schnaiberg, Allan. 1973. "Politics, Participation, and Pollution: The 'Environmental Movement.'" In J. Watson and D. E. Carns (eds.), *Cities in Change: Studies on the Urban Condition.* Boston: Allyn and Bacon. [21]

Schott, K. 1983. "The Rise of Keynesian Economics." In D. Held, J. Anderson, B. Gieben, S. Hall, L. Harris, P. Lewis, N. Parker, and B. Turok (eds.), *States and Society,* pp. 338–362. New York: New York University Press. [14]

Schudson, Michael. 1984. *Advertising: The Uneasy Persuasion.* New York: Basic Books. [4]

Schuman, Howard, and Stanley Presser. 1981. *Questions and Answers in Attitude Surveys.* New York: Academic Press. [2]

Schumpeter, Joseph A. 1942. *Capitalism, Socialism, and Democracy.* New York: Harper & Row. [14]

Schutz, Alfred, and Thomas Luckmann. 1973. *Structures of the Life World.* London, England: Heinemann Educational Books. [1]

Schwartz, Gail Garfield, and William Neikirk. 1983. *The Work Revolution.* New York: Rawson Associates. [15]

Schwartz, Howard (ed.). 1987. *Dominant Issues in Medical Sociology.* New York: Random House. [19]

Schwirian, Kent P. 1983. "Models of Neighborhood Change." *Annual Review of Sociology* 9:83–102. [9]

Science Indicators. 1985. Washington, DC: National Science Board. [20]

Scott, W. Richard. 1981. *Organizations: Rational, Natural, and Open Systems.* Englewood Cliffs, NJ: Prentice Hall. [8]

Scrimshaw, Nevim S., and Lance Taylor. 1980. "Food." *Scientific American* 243 (September):78–88. [10]

Secord, Paul F., and Carl W. Backman. 1974. *Social Psychology* (2nd ed.). New York: McGraw-Hill. [8]

Sedlak, Michael W. 1987. "Tomorrow's Teachers: The Essential Arguments of the Holmes Group Report." *Teachers College Record* 88 (6):315–326. [17]

Selim, Robert. 1980. "The 1980s: A Decade of Hunger?" *The Futurist* 14 (April):29–38. [10]

Selznick, Philip. 1949. *TVA and the Grass Roots: A Study of Politics and Organizations.* Berkeley: University of California Press. [8]

Serbin, Lisa A., K. Daniel O'Leary, Ronald N. Kent, and Illene J. Tonick. 1973. "A Comparison of Teacher Response to the Preacademic and Problem Behavior of Boys and Girls." *Child Development* 44:796–804. [12]

Sewell, William H., and Robert M. Hauser. 1976. "Causes and Consequences of Higher Education: Models of the Status Attainment Process." In W. H. Sewell and R. M. Hauser (eds.), *Schooling and Achievement in American Society.* New York: Academic Press. [11]

Shabecoff, Philip. 1987. "Congress Again Confronts Hazards of Killer Chemicals." *New York Times* (October 11):E5. [21]

Shabecoff, Philip. 1983. "Politics and the E.P.A. Crisis: Environment Emerges as a Mainstream Issue." *New York Times* (April 29):13. [21]

Shank, Susan E., and Patricia M. Getz. 1986. "Employment and Unemployment: Developments in 1985." *Monthly Labor Review* 109 (2):3–12. [15]

Shenon, Philip. 1983. "What's New with Dual-Career Couples." *New York Times* (March 6):F29. [16]

Sheppard, Nathaniel, Jr. 1981. "Schools Ending Chapter in U.S. Desegregation Saga." *New York Times* (June 10):A28. [17]

Sherman, Barry L., and Joseph R. Dominick. 1986. "Violence and Sex in Music Videos: TV and Rock and Roll." *Journal of Communication* 36 (Winter):79–93. [2]

Sherman, Julia. 1978. *Sex-Related Cognitive Differences.* Springfield, IL: Charles C. Thomas. [12]

Shibutani, Tamotsu, and Kian M. Kwan. 1965. *Ethnic Stratification: A Comparative Approach.* New York: Macmillan. [13]

Shils, Edward A., and Morris Janowitz. 1948. "Cohesion and Disintegration in the German Wehrmacht in World War II." *Public Opinion Quarterly* 21:281–315. [14]

Shupe, Anson, and William A. Stacey. 1984. "Public and Clergy Sentiments Toward the Moral Majority: Evidence from the Dallas-Fort Worth Metroplex." In D. G. Bromley and A. Shupe (eds.), *New Christian Politics.* Macon, GA: Mercer University Press. [18]

Silberman, Charles E. 1971. *Crisis in the Classroom.* New York: Random House. [5, 17]

Silverstein, Michael. 1976. "Shifters, Linguistic Categories, and Cultural Description." In K. H. Basso and H. A. Selby (eds.), *Meaning in Anthropology,* pp. 11–55. Albuquerque: University of New Mexico Press. [4]

Simmel, Georg. 1950a. *The Sociology of Georg Simmel.* K. W. Wolff (ed. and trans.). New York: Free Press. [8]

Simmel, Georg. 1950b. "The Metropolis and Mental Life." In K. Wolff (ed.), *The Sociology of Georg Simmel,* pp. 409–424. New York: Free Press. [9]

Simon, Jacqueline. 1988. "Workers' State." *The Nation* (September 19):187–188. [15]

Simon, Julian L. 1981. *The Ultimate Resource.* Princeton, NJ: Princeton University Press. [10]

Simon, Julian L., and Herman Kahn. 1984. *The Resourceful Earth: A Response to Global 2000.* New York: Basil Blackwell. [10]

Simpson, Ida Harper. 1979. *From Student to Nurse: A Longitudinal Study of Socialization.* New York: Cambridge University Press. [5]

Simpson, John H. 1983. "Moral Issues and Status Politics." In R. C. Liebman and R. Wuthnow (eds.), *The New Christian Right.* New York: Aldine. [18]

Simpson, R. 1985. "Social Control of Occupations and Work." *Annual Review of Sociology* 11:415–436. Palo Alto, CA: Annual Reviews. [15]

Singer, Dorothy G. 1983. "A Time to Reexamine the Role of Television in Our Lives." *American Psychologist* 38:815–816. [5]

Singer, Jerome L., and Dorothy G. Singer. 1981. *Television, Imagination, and Aggression: A Study of Preschoolers.* Hillsdale, NJ: Erlbaum. [5]

Sjoberg, Gideon. 1960. *The Preindustrial City: Past and Present.* Peoria, IL: Free Press. [9]

Skinner, Denise A. 1983. "Dual-Career Family Stress and Coping." In D. H. Olson and B. C. Miller (eds.), *Family Studies Review Yearbook* (vol. 1). Beverly Hills: Sage. [16]

Skocpol, Theda. 1985. "Bringing the State Back In: Strategies of Analysis in Current Research." In P. B. Evans, D. Rueschemeyer, and T. Skocpol (eds.), *Bringing the State Back In,* pp. 3–43. New York: Cambridge University Press. [14]

Skocpol, Theda. 1979. *States and Social Revolutions: A Comparative*

Analysis of France, Russia, and China. New York: Cambridge University Press. [**2, 14, 21**]

Skolnick, Arlene S. 1978. *The Intimate Environment: Exploring Marriage and the Family.* Boston: Little, Brown. [**16**]

Skolnick, Jerome H., and David H. Bayley. 1986. *The New Blue Line: Police Innovation in Six American Cities.* New York: Free Press. [**7**]

Skolnik, Peter. 1978. *Fads.* Toronto: Fitzhenry & Whiteside. [**21**]

Slater, Philip E. 1976. *The Pursuit of Loneliness: American Culture at the Breaking Point* (rev. ed.). Boston: Beacon Press. [**4**]

Smeeding, Timothy M. 1982. *Alternative Methods for Valuing Selected In-Kind Transfer Benefits and Measuring Their Effect on Poverty* (U.S. Bureau of the Census, Technical Paper No. 50). Washington, DC: U.S. Government Printing Office. [**11**]

Smelser, Neil J. 1962. *Theory of Collective Behavior.* New York: Free Press. [**21**]

Smidt, Corwin. 1980. "Civil Religious Orientations Among Elementary School Children." *Sociological Analysis* 41:24–40. [**18**]

Smith, Adam. 1776/1976. *The Wealth of Nations.* Chicago: University of Chicago Press. [**1, 15**]

Smith, Kevin B. 1981. "Class Structure and Intergenerational Mobility from a Marxian Perspective." *The Sociological Quarterly* 22:385–401. [**11**]

Smith, James P., and Ward, Michael P. 1984. *Women's Wages and Work in the Twentieth Century.* R-3119-NICHD. Santa Monica: Rand. [**12**]

Smith, Simon E. 1981. "San Salvador: A Chronicle of Intimidation." *America* (March 28):250–251. [**18**]

Smith, Terrence. 1984. "Iran: Five Years of Fanaticism." *New York Times Magazine* (February 12):21–32. [**18**]

Snow, David A., Susan G. Baker, Leon Anderson, and Michael Martin. 1986. "The Myth of Pervasive Mental Illness Among the Homeless." *Social Problems* 33 (5):45. [**19**]

Snow, David A., and Richard Machalek. 1984. "The Sociology of Conversion." *Annual Review of Sociology* 10:167–190. [**18**]

Snow, David A., Louis A. Zurcher, Jr., and Robert Peters. 1981. "Victory Celebrations as Theater: A Dramaturgical Approach to Crowd Behavior." *Symbolic Interaction* 4 (1). [**21**]

Snow, Margaret E., Carol Nagy Jacklin, and Eleanor E. Maccoby. 1981. "Birth-Order Differences in Peer Sociability at Thirty-Three Months." *Child Development* 52:589–595. [**5**]

Snow, Margaret Ellis, Carol Nagy Jacklin, and Eleanor E. Maccoby. 1983. "Sex-of-Child Differences in Father-Child Interactions at One Year of Age." *Child Development* 54:227–232. [**12**]

Snyder, E., and E. Spreitzer. 1986. *Social Aspects of Sport* (2nd ed.). Englewood Cliffs, NJ: Prentice Hall. [**12**]

Snyder, M., E. D. Tanke, and E. Berscheid. 1977. "Social Perception and Interpersonal Behavior: On the Self-Fulfilling Nature of Social Stereotypes." *Journal of Personality and Social Psychology* 35:656–666. [**12**]

Sobel, Dava. 1980. "Siblings: Studies Find Rivalry, Dependency Revive in Adulthood." *New York Times* (October 28):C1. [**5**]

Sowell, Thomas. 1981. *Ethnic America: A History.* New York: Basic Books. [**13**]

Spector, Leonard S. 1985. *The New Nuclear Nations.* New York: Vintage. [**14**]

Spence, J. T., K. Deaux, and R. L. Helmreich. 1985. "Sex Roles in Contemporary American Society." In G. Lindsey and E.

Aronson (eds.), *Handbook of Social Psychology* (3rd ed.). Reading, MA: Addison-Wesley. [**12**]

Spencer, Herbert. 1974. *The Evolution of Society: Selections from Herbert Spencer's "Principles of Sociology."* Robert L. Carniero (ed.). Chicago: University of Chicago Press. [**22**]

Spengler, Oswald. 1918/1922/1962. *The Decline of the West.* New York: Knopf. [**22**]

Spicer, Edward H. 1980. "American Indians." In S. Thernstrom (ed.), *Harvard Encyclopedia of American Ethnic Groups.* Cambridge, MA: Harvard University Press. [**13**]

Spitz, R. D. 1951. "The Psychogenic Diseases of Infancy: An Attempt at Their Etiological Classification." *Psychoanalytic Study of the Child* 6:255–275. [**5**]

Sprey, Jetse. 1979. "Conflict Theory and the Study of Marriage and the Family." In W. R. Burr, R. Hill, F. I. Nye, and I. L. Reiss (eds.), *Contemporary Theories About the Family* (vol. 2). New York: Free Press. [**16**]

Stack, Carol. 1975. *All Our Kin: Strategies for Survival in a Black Community.* New York: Harper & Row. [**3**]

Stahl, Sidney and Marty Lebedum. 1974. "Mystery Gas: An Analysis of Mass Hysteria." *Journal of Health and Social Behavior.* 15:44–50. [**21**]

Stahura, John M. 1986. "Suburban Development, Black Suburbanization and the Civil Rights Movement Since World War II." *American Sociological Review* 51 (February):131–144. [**9**]

Staples, Robert. 1978. *The Black Family* (2nd ed.). New York: Wadsworth. [**16**]

Stark, Rodney. 1984. "The Rise of a New World Faith." *Review of Religious Research* 26 (1). [**18**]

Stark, Rodney, and William Sims Bainbridge. 1985. *The Future of Religion: Secularization, Revival and Cult Formation.* Berkeley: University of California Press. [**18**]

Stark, Rodney, and William Sims Bainbridge. 1979. "Of Churches, Sects, and Cults: Preliminary Concepts for a Theory of Religious Movements." *Journal for the Scientific Study of Religion* 18:117–133. [**18**]

Stark, Rodney, and James McEvoy III. 1974. "Middle Class Violence." In S. K. Steinmetz and M. A. Straus (eds.), *Violence in the Family.* New York: Harper & Row. [**16**]

Starr, Paul. 1982. *The Social Transformation of American Medicine.* New York: Basic Books. [**19**]

Statham, Anne. 1987. "The Gender Model Revisited: Differences in the Management Styles of Men and Women." *Sex Roles* 16 (7/8):409–429. [**12**]

Steinberg, Stephan. 1981. *The Ethnic Myth: Race, Ethnicity, and Class in America.* New York: Atheneum. [**13**]

Steiner, Rodney. 1981. *Los Angeles: The Centrifugal City.* Dubuque, IA: Kendall-Hunt. [**9**]

Steinmetz, Suzanne K., and Murray A. Straus (eds.). 1974. *Violence in the Family.* New York: Harper & Row. [**16**]

Stephan, Cookie White, and Judy Corder. 1985. "The Effects of Dual-Career Families on Adolescents' Sex-Role Attitudes, Work and Family Plans, and Choices of Important Others." *Journal of Marriage and the Family* (November):921–929. [**12**]

Sterling, Theodore. 1986. "Computers and Democracy." *The Information Society.* [**22**]

Sterngold, James. 1987. "With Key Executives' Arrest, Wall Street Faces Challenge." *New York Times* (February):A1, 38. [**7**]

Stockwell, Edward G., and H. Theodore Groat. 1984. *World Population: An Introduction to Demography*. New York: Franklin Watts. [10]

Storer, Norman W. 1977. "The Sociological Context of the Velikovsky Controversy." In D. Goldsmith (ed.), *Scientists Confront Velikovsky*, pp. 29–39. Ithaca: Cornell University Press. [20]

Strachan, Hew. 1983. *European Armies and the Conduct of War*. London, England: George, Allen and Unwin. [14]

Straus, Murray A., and Richard J. Gelles. 1986. "Societal Change and Change in Family Violence from 1975 to 1985 as Revealed by Two National Surveys." *Journal of Marriage and the Family* 48 (August):465–479. [16]

Straus, Murray A., Richard J. Gelles, and Suzanne K. Steinmetz. 1980. *Behind Closed Doors: Violence in the American Family*. Garden City, NY: Doubleday. [16]

Strober, Myra. 1982. "The MBA: Same Passport to Success for Women and Men?" In P. Wallace (ed.), *Women in the Workplace*. Boston: Auburn House. [12]

Sullivan, Harry Stack. 1953. *The Interpersonal Theory of Psychiatry*. New York: W. W. Norton. [5]

Sullivan, Scott. 1986. "Europe's Population Bomb." *Newsweek* (December 15):52. [10]

Summers, Gene F., and Kristi Branch. 1984. "Economic Development and Community Social Change." *Annual Review of Sociology* 10:141–166. [9]

Sussman, Barry. 1988. *What Americans Really Think and Why Our Politicians Pay No Attention*. New York: Pantheon. [14]

Suttles, Gerald D. 1968. *The Social Order of the Slum*. Chicago: University of Chicago Press. [9]

Swanson, Guy E. 1974. *The Birth of the Gods*. Ann Arbor: University of Michigan Press. [18]

Tabb, William. 1986. *Churches in Struggle: Liberation Theology and Social Change in North America*. New York: Monthly Review Press. [18]

Talmon-Garber, Y. 1962. "Social Change and Family Structure." *International Social Science Journal* 14 (3):468–487. [16]

Tanfer, Koray, and Marjorie C. Horn. 1985. "Contraceptive Use, Pregnancy and Fertility Patterns Among Single American Women in Their 20's." *Family Planning Perspectives* 17 (1):10–19. [16]

Tausky, Curt. 1984. *Work and Society: An Introduction to Industrial Sociology*. Itasca, IL: F. E. Peacock. [15]

Tausky, Curt. 1978. *Work Organizations: Major Theoretical Perspectives* (2nd ed.). Itasca, IL: F. E. Peacock. [15]

Tavris, Carol, and Carole Wade. 1984. *The Longest War: Sex Difference in Perspective* (2nd ed.). San Diego: Harcourt Brace Jovanovich. [12]

Taylor, Charles. 1985. "Legitimation Crisis?" In *Philosophy and the Sciences of Man*. New York: Cambridge University Press. [14]

Taylor, M. Susan, and Janet A. Sniezek. 1984. "The College Recruitment Interview: Topical Content and Applicant Reactions." *Journal of Occupational Psychology* 57:157–168. [3]

Taylor, Ronald A. 1983. "Cleaner Air and Water." *U.S. News & World Report* (February 28):27–28. [21]

Temerlin, Maurice K. 1975. *Lucy: Growing Up Human*. Palo Alto, CA: Science and Behavior Books. [5]

Terkel, Studs. 1972. *Working: People Talk About What They Do All Day and How They Feel About It*. New York: Pantheon. [15]

Thomas, A., and S. Chess. 1980. *The Dynamics of Psychosocial Development*. New York: Bruner & Mazel. [5]

Thomas, A., and S. Chess. 1977. *Temperament and Development*. New York: Bruner & Mazel. [5]

Thomas, A., S. Chess, and H. G. Birch. 1968. *Temperament and Behavior Disorders in Children*. New York: New York University Press. [5]

Thomas, G. M., and J. Meyer. 1984. "The Expansion of the State." *Annual Review of Sociology* 10:461–482. [14]

Thomas, William I., and Dorothy Swaine Thomas. 1928. *The Child in America*. New York: Knopf. [3]

Thomlinson, Ralph. 1976. *Population Dynamics* (2nd ed.). New York: Random House. [10]

Thompson, E. P. 1968. *The Making of the English Working Class*. Harmondsworth, England: Penguin. [10, 15]

Thompson, Leonard. 1985. *The Political Mythology of Apartheid*. New Haven, CT: Yale University Press. [13]

Thurow, Lester. 1985. *The Management Challenge: Japanese Views*. Cambridge, MA: MIT Press. [15]

Thurow, Lester C. 1980. *The Zero-Sum Society*. New York: Basic Books. [14]

Tieger, Todd. 1980. "On the Biological Basis of Sex Differences in Aggression." *Child Development* 51:943–963. [12]

Tienda, Marta, and Ding-Tzann Lii. 1987. "Minority Concentration and Earnings Inequality: Blacks, Hispanics, and Asians Compared." *American Journal of Sociology* 93 (July):141–165. [13]

Tilly, Charles. 1978. *From Mobilization to Revolution*. Reading, MA: Addison-Wesley. [21]

Tilly, Charles. 1973. "Revolutions and Collective Violence." In F. I. Greenstein and N. W. Polsby (eds.), *Handbook of Political Science*. Reading, MA: Addison-Wesley. [21]

Tipton, Steven M. 1982. *Getting Saved from the Sixties: Moral Meaning in Conversion and Cultural Change*. Berkeley: University of California Press. [18]

Touraine, Alain. 1971. *The Post-Industrial Society*. New York: Random House. [22]

Toynbee, Arnold. 1946. *A Study of History*. New York: Oxford University Press. [22]

Traugott, Mark. 1978. "Reconceiving Social Movements." *Social Problems* 26:38–49. [21]

Treiman, Donald J., and Patricia A. Roos. 1983. "Sex and Earnings in Industrial Society: A Nine-Nation Comparison." *American Journal of Sociology* 89 (3):612–650. [12]

Trimble, Jeff. 1986. "Earning a Fast Ruble." *U.S. News & World Report* (November 24):36–37. [15]

Troeltsch, Ernst. 1931. *The Social Teaching of the Christian Churches*. New York: Macmillan. [18]

Troll, Lillian E., and Vern Bengtson. 1982. "Intergenerational Relations Through the Life Span." In B. B. Wolman (ed.), *Handbook of Developmental Psychology*. Englewood Cliffs, NJ: Prentice Hall. [5]

Troyer, Ronald J., and Gerald E. Markle. 1983. *Cigarettes: The Battle over Smoking*. New Brunswick, NJ: Rutgers University Press. [19]

Tumin, Melvin M. 1985. *Social Stratification* (2nd ed.). Englewood Cliffs, NJ: Prentice Hall. [11]

Tumin, Melvin M. 1973. *Patterns of Society.* Boston: Little, Brown. [11]

Tumin, Melvin M. (ed.). 1970. *Readings on Social Stratification.* Englewood Cliffs, NJ: Prentice Hall. [11]

Tumin, Melvin M. 1953. "Some Principles of Stratification: A Critical Analysis." *American Sociological Review* 18 (August):387–393. [11]

Turnbull, Sharon K., and James M. Turnbull. 1983. "To Dream the Impossible Dream: An Agenda for Discussion with Stepparents." *Family Relations* 32:227–230. [16]

Turner, Jeffrey S., and Donald B. Helms. 1988. *Marriage and Family.* New York: Harcourt Brace Jovanovich. [16]

Turner, Jonathan. 1981. "Returning to Social Physics: Illustrations from the Work of George Herbert Mead." *Current Perspectives in Social Theory* 2:187–208. [5]

Turner, Ralph H., and Lewis M. Killian. 1972. *Collective Behavior* (2nd ed.). Englewood Cliffs, NJ: Prentice Hall. [21]

Turner, Victor W. 1970. *The Ritual Process.* Chicago: Aldine. [4, 6, 18]

Tyack, David B., and Thomas James. 1985. "Moral Majorities and the School Curriculum: Historical Perspectives on the Legalization of Virtue." *Teachers College Record* 86 (4):513–537. [17]

Tyree, Andrea, Moshe Semyonou, and Robert W. Hodges. 1979. "Gaps and Glissandos: Inequality, Economic Development, and Social Mobility in 24 Countries." *American Sociological Review* 44 (June):410–424. [11]

U.N. Commission on Transnational Corporations. 1978. "Transnational Corporations in World Development: A Re-examination." Fourth session. New York (May 15–26). [15]

U.S. Bureau of the Census. 1987. *Statistical Abstract of the United States: 1988.* Washington, DC: U.S. Government Printing Office. [11]

U.S. Bureau of the Census. 1986. *Statistical Abstract of the United States: 1987.* Washington, DC: U.S. Government Printing Office. [10]

U.S. Bureau of the Census. 1985. *Statistical Abstract of the United States: 1986.* Washington, DC: U.S. Government Printing Office. [6, 14]

U.S. Bureau of the Census. 1983a. *Statistical Abstract of the United States: 1984.* Washington, DC: U.S. Government Printing Office. [15]

U.S. Bureau of the Census. 1983b. News Release (June 30). [16, 17]

U.S. Bureau of the Census. 1980. *Current Population Reports* (Series P-20, No. 349). "Marital Status and Living Arrangements: March 1979." Washington, DC: U.S. Government Printing Office. [16]

U.S. Commission on Civil Rights. 1977. Statement on Affirmative Action, for Equal Employment Opportunities. *Clearinghouse Publication* 54. Washington, DC: U.S. Government Printing Office. [13]

U.S. Department of Health and Human Services. 1988. "Understanding AIDS." Washington, DC: U.S. Government Printing Office. [19]

Udry, J. Richard. 1974. *The Social Context of Marriage* (3rd ed.). New York: Harper Colophon. [16]

Udy, Stanley H., Jr. 1959. "'Bureaucracy' and 'Rationality' in Weber's Organizational Theory: An Empirical Study." *American Sociological Review* 24 (December):791–795. [8]

Useem, Michael. 1984. *The Inner Circle: Large Corporations and the Rise of Business Political Activity in the U.S. and U.K.* New York: Oxford University Press. [14, 15]

Useem, Michael. 1980. "Corporations and the Corporate Elite." *Annual Review of Sociology* 6:41–77. [15]

Vaillant, George. 1977. *Adaptation to Life.* Boston: Little, Brown. [6]

Van Creveld, Martin. 1985. *Command in War.* Cambridge, MA: Harvard University Press. [8]

Van den Berghe, Pierre. 1978. *Race and Racism: A Comparative Perspective* (2nd ed.). New York: Wiley. [13]

Van Gennep, Arnold. 1961. *Rites of Passage.* M. B. Vizedon and G. L. Caffee (trans.). Chicago: University of Chicago Press. [6]

Van Maanen, John. 1976. "Breaking-in: Socialization to Work." In R. Dubin (ed.), *Handbook of Work, Organization and Society.* Indianapolis, IN: Bobbs-Merrill. [5]

Vander Zanden, James W. 1960. "The Klan Revival." *American Journal of Sociology* 65 (5):456–462. [13]

Velez, William. 1985. "Finishing College: The Effects of College Type." *Sociology of Education* 58 (July):191–200. [17]

Vert Willie, Charles. 1979. *The Caste and Class Controversy.* Bayside, NY: General Hall. [13]

Violas, P. C. 1978. *The Training of the Urban Working Classes: A History of Twentieth Century American Education.* Chicago: Rand-McNally. [17]

Vogel, Ezra F. 1979. *Japan as Number One: Lessons for America.* Cambridge, MA: Harvard University Press. [22]

Waite, L. J. 1980. "Working Wives and the Family Life Cycle." *American Journal of Sociology* 86:272–294. [6]

Wallace, James. 1983. "Nuclear Freeze Crusade." *U.S. News & World Report* (April 25):18–21. [21]

Wallace, Michelle. 1976. *Black Macho and the Myth of the Superwoman.* New York: Doubleday. [13]

Wallace, Walter L., and James E. Conyers. 1976. *Black Elected Officials: A Study of Black Americans Holding Governmental Office.* New York: Russell Sage Foundation. [13]

Wallerstein, Immanuel. 1974/1980. *The Modern World System* (vols. 1 and 2). New York: Academic Press. [15, 22]

Wallerstein, Immanuel. 1979. *The Capitalist World Economy.* New York: Academic Press. [22]

Wallerstein, Judith S., and Joan B. Kelly. 1980a. "California's Children of Divorce." *Psychology Today* 13 (8):67–76. [16]

Wallerstein, Judith S., and Joan Berlin Kelly. 1980b. *Surviving the Breakup: How Children and Parents Cope with Divorce.* New York: Basic Books. [16]

Walsh, Doris L. 1987. "What Women Want." *American Demographics* 8 (June):60. [10]

Walters, Gary C., and Joan E. Grusec. 1977. *Punishment.* San Francisco: W. H. Freeman. [16]

Walters, James, and Lynda Henley Walters. 1980. "Trends Affecting Adolescent Views of Sexuality, Employment, Marriage, and Child Rearing." *Family Relations* 29 (2):191–198. [16]

Walzer, Michael. 1985. *Exodus.* New York: Basic Books. [18]

Warner, Kenneth E. 1985. "Cigarette Advertising and Media Coverage of Smoking and Health." *New England Journal of Medicine* 312 (6):384–388. [19]

Warner, Sam Bass, Jr. 1972. *The Urban Wilderness.* New York: Harper & Row. [9]

Warner, Sam Bass, Jr. 1962. *Streetcar Suburbs: The Process of Growth in Boston, 1870–1900.* Cambridge, MA: Harvard and MIT Press. [9]

Warner, W. Lloyd, Paul S. Lunt, Marchia Meeker, and Kenneth Eels. 1949. *Social Class in America.* Chicago: Science Research. [11]

Watson, John B. 1925/1970. *Behaviorism.* New York: W. W. Norton. [5]

Wattenberg, Ben. 1987. *The Birth Dearth.* New York: Pharos Books. [10]

Wattenberg, Ben J. 1973. "A Family Survey: Is the Family Really in Trouble?" *Better Homes and Gardens* 51 (March):2, 30, 31, 33. [16]

Weber, Max. 1922/1968. *Economy and Society.* E. Fischoff et al. (trans.). New York: Bedminster Press. [1, 11, 14]

Weber, Max. 1904/1949. *The Protestant Ethic and the Spirit of Capitalism.* New York: Charles Scribner's. [1]

Weber, Max. 1918/1949. *From Max Weber: Essays in Sociology* (2nd ed.). H. H. Gerth and C. W. Mills (trans.). New York: Oxford University Press. [14]

Webster, Frank, and Kevin Robins. 1986. *Information Technology: A Luddite Analysis.* Norwood, NJ: Ablex. [22]

Weed, James A. 1982. "Divorce: Americans' Style." *American Demographics* 4 (March):13–17. [16]

Weinberg, Martin S., and Colin J. Williams. 1975. "Gay Baths and the Social Organization of Impersonal Sex." *Social Problems* 23 (2):124–136. [2]

Weitzman, Lenore. 1985. *The Divorce Revolution: The Unexpected Consequences for Women and Children in America.* New York: Free Press. [16]

Weitzman, Leonore J., and Deborah Eifler. 1972. "Sex Role Socialization in Picture Books for Preschool Children." *American Journal of Sociology* 77 (May):1125–1144. [12]

Weller, Jack M., and E. L. Quarantelli. 1973. "Neglected Characteristics of Collective Behavior." *American Journal of Sociology* 79 (November):665–685. [21]

Wellman, Barry. 1983. "Network Analysis: Some Basic Principles." In R. Collins (ed.), *Sociological Theory*, pp. 115–200. San Francisco, CA: Jossey-Bass. [3]

Werlin, Herbert H. 1983. "Oh, Calcutta: The Challenge of Urban Misery." *Development International* (March/April). [9]

Werner, Paul D., and Georgina Williams LaRussa. 1985. "Persistence and Change in Sex-Role Stereotypes." *Sex Roles* 12 (9/10):1089–1100. [12]

Wesolowski, W. 1979. *Classes, Strata and Power.* London, England: Routledge & Kegan Paul. [11]

Westoff, Charles F., G. Calot, and M. Foster. 1983. "Teenage Fertility in Developing Nations: 1971–1980." *Family Planning Perspectives* 15 (3):105–114. [16]

Wheeler, Stanton. 1966. "The Structure of Formally Organized Socialization Settings." In O. G. Brim and S. Wheeler (eds.), *Socialization After Childhood.* New York: Wiley. [5]

White, Burton L., Barbara T. Kaban, and Jane S. Attanucci. 1979. *The Origins of Human Competence.* Lexington, MA: D. C. Heath. [5]

White, Lynn, Jr. 1962. *Medieval Technology and Social Change.* New York: Oxford University Press. [22]

Whitt, J. Allen. 1982. *Urban Elites and Mass Transportation: The Dialectics of Power.* Princeton, NJ: Princeton University Press. [14]

Whitt, J. Allen. 1979. "Toward a Class Dialectical Model of Power: An Empirical Assessment of Three Competing Models of Political Power." *American Sociological Review* 44 (February):81–100. [14]

Whorf, Benjamin L. 1956. *Language, Thought, and Reality.* Cambridge, MA: MIT Press. [4]

Wiley, Norbert. 1979. "Notes on Self Genesis: From Me to We to I." *Studies in Symbolic Interaction* 2:87–105. [5]

Wilford, John Noble. 1981. "9 Percent of Everyone Who Ever Lived Is Alive Now." *New York Times* (October 6):13, 14. [10]

Willhelm, Sidney M. 1979. "Opportunities Are Diminishing . . ." *Society* 16 (3):5, 12–17. [11]

Williams, D. A., J. Huck, C. Ma, and S. Monroe. 1981. "Why Public Schools Fail." *Newsweek* (April 20):62–73. [17]

Williams, J. Allen, Jr., Joetta A. Vernon, Martha C. Williams, and Karen Malecha. 1987. "Sex Role Socialization in Picture Books: An Update." *Social Science Quarterly* 68 (March):148–156. [12]

Williams, Lena. 1987. "Race bias found in location of toxic dumps." *New York Times* (April 16):A20. [13]

Williams, Monci Jo. 1986. "What's Legal—And What's Not." *Fortune* (December 22):36. [7]

Williams, Raymond. 1982. *The Sociology of Culture.* New York: Schocken. [1, 4]

Williams, Raymond. 1976. *Keywords: A Vocabulary of Culture and Society.* London, England: Fontana. [14]

Williams, Robin. 1970. *American Society* (3rd ed.). New York: Knopf. [4]

Willie, Charles V. 1981a. *The Ivory and Ebony Towers: Race Relations and Higher Education.* Lexington, MA: Lexington Books. [16]

Willie, Charles V. 1981b. *A New Look at Black Families* (2nd ed.). Dix Hills, NY: General Hall. [16]

Willie, Charles V. 1979. *Caste and Class Controversy.* Bayside, NY: General Hall. [13]

Wills, Kendall J. 1983. "Losing the Salary Game." *New York Times* (February 20):27. [12]

Wilmot, James G., and Andre du Pisanie. 1987. "End of a new deal." In J. G. Wilmot (ed.), *The State of Apartheid.* Boulder, CO: Lynne Rienner. [13]

Wilson, Barbara Foley, and Kathryn A. London. 1987. "Going to the Chapel." *American Demographics* (December):26–31. [16]

Wilson, Edward O. 1978. *On Human Nature.* Cambridge, MA: Harvard University Press. [4, 12]

Wilson, Franklin. 1985. "The Impact of School Desegregation Programs on White Public-School Enrollment, 1968–1976." *Sociology of Education* 58 (July):137–153. [17]

Wilson, James Q. 1985. *Thinking About Crime* (rev. ed.). New York: Basic Books. [7]

Wilson, James Q., and Richard Herrnstein. 1985. *Crime and Human Nature.* New York: Simon and Schuster. [7]

Wilson, John. 1973. *Introduction to Social Movements.* New York: Basic Books. [21]

Wilson, William Julius. 1987. *The Truly Disadvantaged: The Inner City, The Underclass, and Public Policy.* Chicago: University of Chicago Press. [13]

Wilson, William Julius. 1978. *The Declining Significance of Race: Blacks and Changing American Institutions.* Chicago: University of Chicago Press. [13]

Wilson, William Julius, and R. Aponte. 1985. "Urban Poverty." *Annual Review of Sociology* 11:231–258. [13]

Winch, Robert F., and Rae Lesser Blumberg. 1968. "Societal Complexity and Familiar Organization." In R. F. Winch and G. B. Spanier (eds.), *Selected Studies in Marriage and the Family* (3rd ed.). New York: Holt, Rinehart and Winston. [16]

Winick, Myron. 1980. "Nutrition and Brain Development." *Natural History* 89 (12):6–13. [11]

Winn, Marie. 1985. *The Plug-in Drug: Television, Children and the Family.* New York: Penguin. [5]

Winn, Marie. 1983. *Children Without Childhood.* New York: Pantheon. [6]

Wirls, D. 1986. "Reinterpreting the Gender Gap." *Public Opinion Quarterly* 50:316–330. [14]

Wirth, Louis. 1938. "Urbanism as a Way of Life." *American Journal of Sociology* 44:1–24. [9]

Wolf, Eric. 1982. *Europe and the People Without History.* Berkeley: University of California Press. [14, 15]

Wolfe, David A. 1985. "Child Abusive Parents: An Empirical Review and Analysis." *Psychological Bulletin* 97:462–482. [16]

Wolfgang, Marvin E. 1979. *Prisons: Present and Possible.* Lexington, MA: Lexington Books. [7]

Wong, Bernard P. 1982. *Chinatown: Economic Adaptation and Ethnic Identity of the Chinese.* New York: Holt, Rinehart and Winston. [13]

World Bank. 1985. *World Development Report 1987.* New York: Oxford University Press. [10]

Wright, Erik Olin. 1985. *Classes.* London, England: New Left Books. [11]

Wright, Erik Olin. 1981. *Class, Crisis and the State.* London, England: New Left Books. [11]

Wright, J. R. 1985. "PACs, Contributions and Roll Calls: An Organizational Perspective." *The American Political Science Review* 79 (2):400–414. [14]

Wright, James D., and Sonia R. Wright. 1976. "Social Class and Parental Values for Children." *American Sociological Review* 41 (June):527–548. [16]

Wrong, Dennis H. 1977. *Population and Society.* New York: Random House. [10]

Wrong, Dennis H. 1961. "The Oversocialized Conception of Man in Modern Sociology." *American Sociological Review* 26:183–193. [5]

Wuthnow, Robert. 1988. *The Restructuring of American Religion.* Princeton, NJ: Princeton University Press. [18]

Wuthnow, Robert. 1987. *Culture and the Moral Order.* Berkeley: University of California Press. [18]

Wuthnow, Robert. 1985. "The Growth of Religious Reform Movements." AAPSS *Annals* 480 (July):106–116. [18]

Yankelovich, Daniel. 1981. "New Rules in American Life." *Psychology Today* 15 (April):35–91. [16]

Yankey, David. 1985. *Demography: The Study of Human Population.* New York: St. Martin's Press. [10]

Yoder, Jan D., and Robert C. Nichols. 1980. "A Life Perspective Comparison of Married and Divorced Persons." *Journal of Marriage and the Family* 42 (2):413–419. [16]

Young, Michael D. 1988. *The Metronomic Society: Natural Rhythms and Human Timetables.* Cambridge, MA: Harvard University Press. [15, 22]

Yuan, D. Y. 1963. "Voluntary Segregation: A Study of New York Chinatown." *Phylon* 24 (Fall):255–265. [13]

Zangwill, Israel. 1909. *The Melting Pot.* New York: Jewish Publishing Society of America. [13]

Zey-Ferrell, Mary. 1981. "Criticisms of the Dominant Perspective on Organizations." *Sociological Quarterly* 22:181–205. [8]

Zill, Nicholas. 1984. National Survey Conducted by Child Trends, Inc., Washington, DC (1984). Reported by Marilyn Adams. "Kids Aren't Broken by the Break-Up." *USA Today* (December 20):5D. [16]

Zola, Irving Kenneth. 1972. "Medicine as an Institution of Social Control." *Sociological Review* 20 (November):487–504. [19]

Zucker, Lynne G., and Carolyn Rosenstein. 1981. "Taxonomies of Institutional Structure: Dual Economy Revisited." *American Sociological Review* 46:869–884. [3]

Zuckerman, Harriet. 1977. "Deviant Behavior and Social Control in Science." In E. Sagarin (ed.), *Deviance and Social Change*, pp. 87–138. Beverly Hills: Sage. [20]

Zuckerman, Harriet. 1972. "Interviewing an Ultra-Elite." *Public Opinion Quarterly* 36:159–175. [2]

Zuckerman, Solly. 1983. *Nuclear Illusion and Reality.* New York: Vintage. [14]

Zukin, Sharon. 1987. "Gentrification: Culture and Capital in the Urban Core." *Annual Review of Sociology* 13:129–147. [9]

GLOSSARY

Achieved status, 76
Acting crowd, 611
Action perspective, 24
Adaptation model, 226
Affirmative action, 381
Age grading, 165
Ageism, 165
Age structure, 165
Aggregate, 226
Agrarian societies, 76
Alterative movement, 611
Altruistic suicide, 48
Androgynous, 347
Animism, 539
Anomic suicide, 48
Anomie, 24, 48
Anticipatory socialization, 134
Apartheid, 381
Ascribed status, 76
Assimilation, 381
Authority, 416
Automation, 450

Bilateral descent, 484
Birth cohort, 165
Bourgeoisie, 317
Bureaucracy, 226, 416

Capitalistic market system, 450
Capitalists, 24
Caste system, 317

Census, 286
Charisma, 226
Charismatic authority, 416
Chromosomes, 347
Church, 539
Circular reaction, 611
City, 254
Civil religion, 539
Civil rights, 416
Class, 317
Class consciousness, 24
Closed response, 48
Coercive power, 416
Collective behavior, 611
Collective goods, 416
Collective power, 416
Collectivist organization, 227
Colonialism, 381
Communalism, 585
Community, 254
Compensatory education, 515
Compression of morbidity, 564
Concentric zone model, 254
Conformity, 198
Conglomerate, 450
Consolidated Metropolitan Statistical Area (CMSA), 254
Content analysis, 48
Conventional crowd, 611
Co-optation, 227
Corporate crime, 198
Corporation, 450
Correlation, 48
Correlation coefficient, 48

NAME INDEX

SUBJECT INDEX

National Organization for Women (NOW), 330, 331, 605–6, 607
National Organization of Changing Men (NOCM), 345
National Rifle Association, 402
National Women's Political Caucus (NWPC), 606
Nation at Risk, A, 498, 513
Nationhood and nationalism, 389–90, 409, 489
Nation Prepared, A, 498
Native Americans, 357–58, 371–72, 493
Native population, displacement of, 357–58
Natural selection, 94, 95, 618
Nature and nurture, debate over, 109–12
Nayar, the, 457, 458
Nazi murder of Jews, 358
Needs standard, 314
Neighborhood change, ecological processes and, 246–47
Neighborhood life-cycle model, 247
Neolocal residence, 459
Network analysis, 66–71
Networks, 65–71, 235
New American Grandparent, The (Cherlin and Furstenberg), 479
New Blue Line, The (Skolnick & Bayley), 194
New Christian Right, 537–38
New Deal programs, 431
New England Journal of Medicine, 547
Newsweek, 546
New York City, 229–30, 231, 246–47
New York Times, 34–35, 102, 181
Nineteenth Amendment, 622
"Nixon syndrome," 173
Nobel prize recipients, interviewing, 40
Nodes, 71
No-fault divorce laws, 474–75
Nonmaterial culture, 81
Nonparticipant observation, 44
Normal science, 577
Norms, 82–84
  conformity to group, 205–6
  cultural transmission, 176–77
  defined, 82
  emergent norm theory, 598–99
  ethos of science, 571–72, 574, 575
  group, 203
  reciprocity, 64–65
  values vs., 83–84
  see also Deviance
Nuclear family, 458, 462–64, 467
Nuclear war, 407, 413–14
  movement against, 609
Nurture and nature, debate over, 109–12
Nutrition, poverty and, 310

Objectivity, 36–37
Observation, field, 43–44

Occupation. *See* Work
Occupational socialization, 132–33
Office use of computers, 626–27
Old age, 154–64
Old Order Amish, 211–14
Oligarchy, 405
Oligopolies, 432
On Death and Dying (Kübler-Ross), 164
OPEC oil price increases (1973), 431
Open class system, 302
Open response, 40
Operational definition, 29
Opportunities
  collective behavior and, 592
  educational attainment and, 499–507
  equality of, 302–3, 311–14
Opportunity structure, 46
Opposition, techniques for reducing, 218
Organic solidarity, 18, 618
Organization(s), 201–2, 215–24
  bureaucracy, 218–23
  collective behavior and, 591
  collectivist, 223–24
  computers and, 628–29
  family, 458–59
  formal, techniques of, 201, 215–18
  hierarchy in, 219, 628–29
  see also Groups
Organized autonomy, 555
Organized crime, 188–89
Organized skepticism norm of science, 572, 574
Orientation, family of, 458
Other-representations, 119
Our Bodies, Ourselves, 556
Out-groups, 208
Overcrowding in cities, 242
Overload, psychic, 232
Overpopulation, problems of, 272–75
Overt participant observation, 43
Owners, corporate crimes against, 190
Ownership, corporate, 435

Palestinians, 383–84
Paradigm, 577
Parents and parenthood
  early marital stress and, 469
  single, 453–54, 465–66, 475
  socialization by, 123–24, 338–40, 455
  stepparenthood, 478–79
  teenage, 150–51, 456, 467
  see also Family
Parents Anonymous, 471
Parkinson's law, 222–23
Participant observation, 43, 44
Participation in democratic process, 394–403

ABOUT THE AUTHORS

Donald Light is Professor of Sociology at Rutgers University and Professor of Social and Behavioral Medicine in the Department of Psychiatry at the University of Medicine and Dentistry of New Jersey, School of Osteopathic Medicine. Born and raised in Massachusetts, Professor Light went to college at Stanford and completed his graduate work in sociology at the University of Chicago and Brandeis University. Along the way, he helped to implement President Kennedy's Equal Employment Opportunity Program for minority workers and became increasingly interested in the field of education and health. He is now conducting research on the sociological changes taking place in the American health-care system.

Professor Light's first appointment was to the faculty of Princeton where he taught the introductory course in sociology as well as courses in education, deviance, and the professions. It was there he met and became friends with Suzanne Keller and subsequently developed the first edition of this text. He has published a well-known study of medical training entitled *Becoming Psychiatrists: The Professional Transformation of Self* (Norton 1980). His latest book, *Political Values and Health Care*, is published by the M.I.T. Press. He is the author of numerous articles, which have appeared in *The American Journal of Sociology*, *The Journal of Health and Social Behavior*, *The Administrative Science Quarterly*, *Daedalus*, and *The New England Journal of Medicine*.

Suzanne Keller is currently Professor of Sociology at Princeton University, where she has served as Chairperson of the Department of Sociology. She was born in Vienna, Austria, and came to the United States as a child. After college she spent several years in Europe, mainly in Paris and Munich, where she worked as a survey analyst and translator. She received a Ph.D. in sociology from Columbia University in 1953. In 1957, she became an Assistant Professor at Brandeis University, where she taught courses in social theory, stratification, and the sociology of religion. A Fulbright Lectureship in 1963 at the Athens Center of Ekistics marked the beginning of her interest in architecture and community planning. At the completion of her Fulbright in 1965, Professor Keller joined the Center, where she remained until 1967. That year she came to Princeton University as a Visiting Professor, and in 1968 she was the first woman to be appointed to a tenured Professorship there. She has held several elective offices in the American Sociological Association, including that of Vice-President, and most recently as President of the Eastern Sociological Society.

At Princeton, Suzanne Keller teaches courses on contemporary elites, comparative family systems, theories of gender, and social psychiatry. The author of numerous articles and several books, Suzanne Keller helped launch the program in Women's Studies at Princeton. She is currently completing a book on the creation of community and embarking on a study of contemporary elites. A consultant to many universities, corporations, and government agencies, both here and abroad, Professor Keller has received a number of fellowships and honors, including a Guggenheim Award. Her interests in teaching, writing, and world-wide travel still leave her time to smell the flowers.

Craig Calhoun is Associate Professor of Sociology and Director of the Program in Social Theory and Cross Cultural Studies at the University of North Carolina at Chapel Hill. He received his doctorate from Oxford University after previous study at Southern California, Columbia, and Manchester Universities. His main specialties are sociological theory and comparative historical sociology. Calhoun has done research on a range of topics from education and political action through kinship and community organization to social and economic change and the social impact of computers. He has edited two books and is the author of numerous journal articles and of *The Question of Class Struggle: Popular Protest in Industrializing England*. Currently the editor of *Comparative Social Research*, Calhoun has also served as Chair of the American Sociological Association's Section on Comparative Historical Sociology. His current research focuses on transformations in the social foundations for public discourse, and changes in tort law and other means for coping with occupational and product-related injuries.

A NOTE ON THE TYPE

This book is set in Electra, a typeface designed by W.A. Dwiggins. This face cannot be classified as either modern or old-style. It is not based on any historical model, nor does it echo any particular period or style. It avoids the extreme contrasts between thick and thin elements that mark most modern faces, and attempts to give a feeling of fluidity, power, and speed.